# BASILEUS

History of the Byzantine Emperors 284–1453

WESTON BARNES

authorHOUSE®

*AuthorHouse™*
*1663 Liberty Drive*
*Bloomington, IN 47403*
*www.authorhouse.com*
*Phone: 1 (800) 839-8640*

*Published by AuthorHouse  02/22/2019*

*ISBN: 978-1-5462-5920-6 (sc)*
*ISBN: 978-1-5462-5919-0 (hc)*
*ISBN: 978-1-5462-5918-3 (e)*

*Library of Congress Control Number: 2018910599*

*Print information available on the last page.*

This is dedicated to my mother, Marla Graham Barnes – an Empress in her own right.

# ABBREVIATION KEY

(CSHB) *Corpus Scriptorum Historiae Byzantinae*

(CFHB) *Corpus Frontium Historiæ Byzantinae*

(CSEL) *Corpus Scriptorum Ecclesiasticorum Latinorum*

(AB) *Absolute Monarchs* by John Julius Norwich

(APO) *Byzantium: the Apogee* by John Julius Norwich

(DAF) *Byzantium: The Decline and Fall* by John Julius Norwich

(EC) *Byzantium: The Early Centuries* by John Julius Norwich

(AHV) *A History of Venice* by John Julius Norwich

(MS) *The Middle Sea: A History of the Mediterranean* by John Julius Norwich

(WIP) *Women in Purple: Rulers of Medieval Byzantium* by Judith Herrin

(BAIA) *Byzantium and Its Armies* by Warren Treadgold

(LRE-I) *History of the Later Roman Empire from the Death of Theodosius to the Death of Justinian, vol. I* by J.B. Bury

(LRE-II) *History of the Later Roman Empire from the Death of Theodosius to the Death of Justinian, vol. II* by J.B. Bury

(AI-II) *A History of the Later Roman Empire from Arcadius to Irene (395 to 800 A.D.), vol. II* by J.B. Bury

(ERE-I) *A History of the Eastern Roman Empire, from the Fall of Irene to the Accession of Basil I, A.D. 800- 867* by J.B. Bury

(CAJ) *The Cambridge Companion to the Age of Justinian* ed. by Michael Maas

(OHB) *The Oxford History of Byzantium* ed. by Cyril Mango

(BYZ) *Byzantium: an Introduction to East Roman Civilization* ed. by Norman H. Baynes & H. St. L B. Moss

(AWC) *Byzantium: A World Civilization* ed. by Angiliki E. Laiou & Henry Maguire

# Contents

Empire of Late Antiquity.................................................................xv

## I. LATE ANTIQUITY........................................................... 1

Diocletian (284-305)...........................................................2
Maximian (285-305).............................................................2
Galerius (305-311) ............................................................3

### CONSTANTINIAN DYNASTY

Constantine I 'The Great' (305-324) ....................................... 14
Constantine II (337-340).....................................................26
Constans I (337-350).........................................................26
Constantius II (337-361) ....................................................26
Julian The Apostate (360-363).............................................. 31
Jovian (363-364) ............................................................ 38

### VALENTINIAN-THEODOSIAN DYNASTY

Valentinian I (364-375) ..................................................... 38
Valens (364-378) ............................................................ 38
Valentinian II (382-392) .................................................... 44
Gratian (375-379) ........................................................... 44
Theodosius I 'The Great' (379-395)........................................ 47
Arcadius (395-408) .......................................................... 57
Theodosius II 'The Calligrapher' (408-450) ..... 62
Marcian (450-457)........................................................... 71

## LEONID DYNASTY

Leo I 'The Thracian' (457-474) .................................................. 77
Leo II (474) ............................................................................ 77
Zeno (474-491) ...................................................................... 83
Basiliscus (475-476) ............................................................... 83
Anastasius I 'Diocorus' (491-518) ........................................... 90

## JUSTINIANIC DYNASTY

Justin I (518-527) .................................................................. 99
Justinian I (327-365) ........................................................... 104
Theodora (527-548) ............................................................ 122
Justin II 'The Younger' (565-578) ........................................ 129
Tiberius II Constantine (578-582) ....................................... 129
Maurice Tiberius (582-602) ................................................. 138
Phocas 'The Tyrant' (602-610) ............................................. 148

# II. THE FIRST BYZANTINE AGE............154

## HERACLIAD DYNASTY

Heraclius (610-641) ............................................................. 155
Constans II Heraclius 'The Bearded' (641-668) .................... 171
Constantine III Heraclius (641) ........................................... 171
Heraclonas (641) ................................................................. 171
Constantine IV (668-685) .................................................... 182
Justinian II 'The Slit-Nosed' (685-695, 705-711) ................. 189
Leontius (Leo) (695-698) ..................................................... 205
Tiberius III Apsimar (698-705) ............................................ 205
Philippicus Bardanes (711-713) ........................................... 209
Anastasius II Artemius (713-715) ......................................... 209
Theodosius III 'The Reluctant' (715-717) ............................. 209

## ISAURIAN DYNASTY

Leo III 'The Isaurian' (717-741) .......................................... 215
Constantine V 'Copronymus' (741-775) .............................. 228
Leo IV 'The Khazar' (775-780) ............................................ 243

Constantine VI 'The Blinded' (780-797) ...................................248

## (END OF ISAURIANS)

Irene 'The Athenian' (797-802) ...................................254
Nicephorus I 'The General Logothete' (802-811) ...................................269
Stauracius (811) ...................................270
Michael I Rhangabe (811-813)...................................281
Leo V 'The Armenian' (813-820) ...................................286

## AMORIAN DYNASTY

Michael II 'The Amorian' (820-829) ...................................296
Theophilus (829-842)...................................306
Michael III 'The Drunkard' (842-867) ...................................321

# III. HIGH BYZANTIUM...................................338

## MACEDONIAN DYNASTY

**Basil I 'The Macedonian'** (867-886)...................................339
Leo Vi 'The Wise' (886-912)...................................355
Alexander III (912-913)...................................355
Romanus I Lecapenus (920-944)...................................375
Constantine VII 'Porphyrogenitus' (913-959) ...................................394
Romanus II (959-963) ...................................410
Nicephorus II Phocas (963-969)...................................417
John I Tzimisces (969-976) ...................................431
Basil II 'The Bulgar-Slayer' (976-1025)...................................443
Constantine VIII (1025-1028) ...................................465

## (END OF MACEDONIANS)

Romanus III Argyrus (1028-1034)...................................469
Michael IV 'The Paphlagonian' (1034-1041)... ...................................474
Michael V 'The Caulker' (1041-1042)...................................483
Theodora & Zoe (1042) ...................................483
Constantine IX Monomachus (1042-1055)...................................490

Theodora (1055-1056)............................................................490
Michael VI Bringas 'The Old' (1056-1057)............................503
Isaac I Comnenus (1057-1059) ............................................508

## DUCAS DYNASTY

Constantine X Ducas (1059-1067) ......................................... 514
Eudocia Macrembolitissa (1067) ........................................... 519
Romanus IV Diogenes (1068-1071) ....................................... 519
Michael VII Ducas 'Parapinaces' (1071-1078)........................530
Nicephorus III Botaneiates (1078-1081)................................538

## COMNENIAN DYNASTY

Alexius I Comnenus (1081-1118) ..........................................542
John II Comnenus 'The Beautiful' (1118-1143) .......................570
Manuel I Comnenus (1143-1180) ..........................................584
Alexius II Comnenus (1180-1183)..........................................609
Andronicus I Comnenus 'The Terrible' (1183-1185)................609

## ANGELUS DYNASTY

Isaac II Angelus (1185-1195, 1203-1204).............................. 621
Alexius III Angelus Comnenus 'Bamabacariotus' (1195-1203) ..............633
Alexius IV Angelus (1203-1204)............................................633
Alexius V Ducas 'Murtzuphlus' (1204) ..................................644

## IV: AN EMPIRE DIVIDED ................................................653

## LASCARID DYNASTY

Theodore I Lascaris (1208-1222) ...........................................655
John III Ducas Vatatzes (1222-1254)......................................665
Theodore II Lascaris (1254-1258)...........................................679
John IV Lascaris (1258-1260)..................................................680

# PALEOLOGAN DYNASTY

Michael VIII Paleologus (1259-1282) ................................................687

Andronicus II Paleologus 'The Elder' (1282-1328) ...............................703

Michael IX Paleologus (1293-1320)....................................................703

Andronicus III Paleologus 'The Younger' (1328-1341) .........................720

John V Paleologus (1341-1376, 1379-1391) .......................................730

John VI Cantacuzenus (1346-1354) ..................................................748

Andronicus IV Paleologus (1376-1379) .............................................763

John VII Paleologus (1390)...............................................................763

Manuel II Paleologus (1391-1425) ....................................................773

John VIII Paleologus (1425-1448).....................................................790

Constantine XI Paleologus Dragases (1448-1453)...............................805


Conclusions ....................................................................................823

Bibliography ...................................................................................833

Appendix 1 - Genealogies.................................................................853

Appendix 2 - Rulers Of The Byzantine Era .........................................869

# EMPIRE OF LATE ANTIQUITY

The failure of the pagan Roman Empire to maintain cohesion before massive barbarian invasions and internal turmoil after 476 CE was stemmed somewhat by the reforms of the emperor Diocletian (284-305), beginning a new era under the radical changes of his dynamic successor, Constantine I (305-337). The Classical Roman Empire and its pagan culture, however, failed to fade entirely by 330 CE at the advent of Constantine's Christian Roman Empire, but instead assimilated in a way wherein it survived under separating forms. Ecclesiastical authority would show to take precedence over secular authority less than a century later when Theodosius I (379-395) was, without precedence, excommunicated by Ambrose, Bishop of Milan. The *Basileus* made obeisance and penance to the Bishop to be forgiven for was done after he slaughtered the entire male population, like a Roman tyrant, of the Greek city of Melitene in 381 to legitimize his own imperial force.

Classical culture would suffer a shameful, but not total, defeat by religious zeal when the Library of Alexandria was burned by Egyptian Christians under the same ruler. Riots would break to burn universities and mercilessly slaughter learned people, scientists, and mathematicians of every ethnicity and both genders. Active canon law sat in judgment over civil law, espousing new Christian values in legislation, as seen later when Justinian I (521-565) closed the 1,000-year-old Platonic school of Athens. The examples go on and on over the fact that the origins of the Christian Byzantine Empire of a newly emerging medieval Europe developed from more dramatic changes when compared to the more fledgling West and its slower transitions.

Yet, the political separation of Western and Eastern Rome allowed the East to culminate into Byzantium, a civilization as unique as Anglicanism, Islam, or even that of the Tartars. Accelerating this separation included cultural views on Christianity, openly defying the Western Catholic doctrine with Chalcedonian Orthodoxy. Moreover, Byzantium was a Greek Empire in spoken language, traditional culture, and intellectual values of philosophy, literature, and the sciences. State-centralized military organizations of Eastern Rome turned to the innovative and unique jurisdictions of the *Theme*, ruled by the nobility through changing the legal classes and the law itself. Unfortunately, this also made, over time, centralization difficult and internal war easier as well as the East deteriorating Byzantium into West-dominated feudalism. In its ecclesiastical definition, Byzantium's art sought to glorify the images (*eikons*) artistically just as secular portraits would be assembled by glass and ceramic tile work, but in an inferior manner of style. Byzantine secular leadership also had a unique shape as a source in the military, legal, political, and ecumenical centers as the center of these secular influences were the towering institution of the Emperor and his authority.

The Byzantine Empire's origin as the eastern half of the Roman Empire was already marking itself out as a new Rome from its start. It was the product of a redistricting of Roman authority under Emperor Diocletian due to dramatic and imperative changes brought about by barbarian invasions and the rise of a 'Galician' Empire centered in Gaul (modern France) defying containment. In the aftermath of a five-decade period of political and military turmoil (235-284) where twenty-two emperors with an average span of an emperor's rule was around four years, these invasions mostly caused Diocletian to create the Tetrarchy – a rule of four rulers (one ruling *Augusti* East and West, two minor *Caesari* East and West under the *Augusti*) ruling Rome and Illyricum in the Balkans from Diocletian's villa at Split in his native Illyricum.[1]

This proved to be a difficult policy to administer as the successors of the abdicated Diocletian and his counterparts Galerius, Constantine, and Maximian plunged central Europe into civil war until Constantine won through the power of a divine vision of the Invincible Cross at the Battle of the Milvian Bridge in 311 CE. This monumental event in the history of Christianity and Western Civilization comes from the *Church History* of the Greek historian Eusebius. Though he never converted from his paganism to Christianity until his deathbed, Constantine I allowed unprecedented tolerance of Christian educators, administrators, and philanthropists. With the guidance of his mother, St. Helena, Rome would now have an Eastern throne with a future involving Christianity to be a Western movement beyond displacement. In fact, we will see the obviousness of how the advent of Byzantium, the beginning of

---

[1] Scarre, Chris. *Chronicle of the Roman Emperors,* New York, NY: Thames and Hudson, 2012, 204.

Christianity in the Empire, and Medieval monarchism came together at one juncture. Mainly this is due to the faith in Christ as one ruler of the Church and one ruler for the World; this would be the signature of Constantine and the some ninety emperors following him.

## A NEW ROME

On May 11, 330 CE, the city of Constantinople was founded, named for a combined Greek and Latin title of Constantine and his City. This capital of Empire was founded at the ancient village of Byzantion founded in the seventh century BCE, mentioned in the histories of Alexander of Macedonia as a quaint iron-producing community. In such histories from Greek historians like Plutarch (45-120 CE) and Arrian (92-175 CE), the city had natural defenses in three directions of shore-less seas and an easily defensible western quadrant. It was a triumph of the military engineering of the Byzantines to create a pair of impassable walls, the Constantinian and the Theodosian, remaining impenetrable until the inventions of gunpowder and cannon in the fifteenth century.

Until the fourteenth century and its subjugation by the Seljuk Turks, this 'Queen of All Cities' would be the capital of all Eastern Imperial business, never moving its center as the capital would in the West between Rome, Ravenna, and Avignon. This city on the European Bosporus separating Turkey from the Balkan Peninsula was a major sea trade route from the Sea of Marmora between Eastern Europe and Western Asia to the Dardanelles, its peninsula earning it the moniker of the 'Golden Horn.' It would dominate the Greek economic holdings fought for in the Trojan War a millennium before as another symbol of Greek dominance over the Eastern Mediterranean and its Oriental inhabitants. Over the span of 1,100 years, Constantinople would see major architectural marvels in its churches, estates, palaces, public meeting spaces, and baths as Ancient Rome had. The notoriously unruly Roman Senate in the East was demoted to the puppetry of the legal classes of privilege as the competing families of military commanders under the Emperor would hold the real power on the throne, pacifying a millennium of divisive administrations.

The Eastern court would further adopt more Oriental values in dress, language, court etiquette, and other peculiarities in spite of, or borrowing from, neighbors such as the Sassanid Persians, the Abbasid Caliphs, and ideas stemming from Islamic and Hebraic spirituality. This has, over time, given the impression of an 'oriental' culture in Byzantium contrasting with the founding

Greco-Roman, and there are attributes in Byzantine traditions that support these distinctions. Obeisance to absolute monarchy, Eastern mystical religion as its base for worship steeped in personal salvation and an Afterlife, even the lavish uses of conspicuous luxuries as a form of superior quality to the ruling class are among those very distinctions. Also, the uses of valuable metals, precious woods, and lustrous jewels with superior craftsmanship and design also epitomize the icons and bindings of bibles to show the esteem given to Christ, the Virgin, and Scripture. Changes and new traditions abounded with the evolution of Byzantine culture and within the past half-century, Byzantine scholarship would also undergo its own evolution.

Adding to this last concept, academic questions fill journals on understanding all we may exhaustively know about our subject. When the Turks in 1453 entered Constantinople, any Byzantine who was asked replied that they were 'Romaioi' (Romans). Why? These were Greek Orthodox Christians far removed by time to be called an 'ancient' people. Modern scholars ask why this appreciation for the link between Byzantine and Roman identities failed distinction during the time. Of course, it does not matter if we do not consider them Romans when the fact remains they called *themselves* Romans and saw these traditional connections. That is why, to these medieval Greeks, tradition won out over time.[2] The continuity of this civilization had not as shaky a foundation as it was in the West. The Byzantine identity was from an Eastern Roman identity that stood legally, politically, and culturally for 1,100 years of historical change. The rise of Islam, Turkish incursions, Slavic hostility, Church schism – none of these could take away the right of these Byzantines to be called Romans.[3] The last of these emperors, Constantine XI Dragases, remarked to his soldiers in his final speech on the day of the city's fall: "Hurl your javelins and arrows against them…so that they know that they are fighting…with the descendants of the Greeks and Romans.'[4]

---

[2] Kaldelis, Anthony. "Why Don't We Believe the Byzantines When They Say They Are Romans?" Paper presented at *The Thirty-Fifth Annual Byzantine Studies Conference.* (Sarasota, FL: Florida State University, November, 2009.)

[3] The term 'Byzantine' was only discovered to describe this unique civilization in the nineteenth century; before then, historians classified as an expanded strain of the Western emperors ending in 476 CE.

[4] George (Phrantzes) Sphrantzes. *The Fall of the Byzantine Empire: A Chronicle of George Sphrantzes, 1401-1472*, trans. by Marios Phillipides. Amherst, MA: Amherst University Press, 1980.

## AN EMPIRE REDISCOVERED

The accomplishments signified by the emperors and empresses include the incomparable architectural wonders of the Church of the Hagia Sophia (now the Great Mosque of Istanbul), the Hippodrome, the Walls of Theodosius, or the Church of the Theotokos. Byzantine ecumenical decisions on Christ's nature are still in belief in the twenty-first century Eastern Churches of Greece, Bulgaria, Serbia, and Russia. Artistically and literarily, handbooks on court administration and etiquette juxtaposed inspiration for artistic wonders such as the mosaics of San Vitale and the beautiful frescoes of the Paleologan Renaissance. Their contributions to Greek intellectuals sponsored by the Crown and various Universities to literature and learning were vital in fueling that of the Western European Renaissance thanks to such scholars as the Patriarch-turned-Cardinal Basileos Bessarion.

Byzantine society and their imperial likenesses grace statuary, mosaics, fresco paintings, lead seals of office, and coin engravings, yet their culture and even scholarship once carried stigma from Enlightenment moralists to Soviet atheists. In the seminal history of George Ostrogorsky,[5] *History of the Byzantine State,* a stand was made that the Byzantine Empire (and thus, its rulers) no longer needed justification, and the history of its own historical thought reads adventurously through the Renaissance where Greek knowledge traveled west and Latinists went after it from the east over four centuries to the court of Louis XIV, the German Romantics, and Russo-Slavic Orthodoxy in Stalin's regime.

These rulers did not merely sit upon thrones of absolute power as the one-dimensional, stony-eyed depictions in countless textbooks, art books, and the wooden and gold icons would suggest. Their responsibilities included legislation above the Senate, being the *only* supreme judge over legal interpretation, creating *edictum* with the power of law through executive decision, and being keepers of the *oikmemnos,* or the defense of the faith.[6] Even like the U.S. Presidents, they were the sole commanders-in-chief whether or not they had ever personally fought in battle. Even despite this, Byzantium had a separate cultural life that transcended mere political events and evaluations  Their only small reprieves

---

[5]  Ostrogorsky, George. *History of the Byzantine State, 2ᵈʰ edition.* New Brunswick, NJ: Rutgers University Press, 1968, 1-21.

[6]  *ibid.,* 31.

were in that of their Caesars that held full authority in leading armies, issuing laws, and easing administrative burdens off of the *Basilii*.[7]

The military culture of Byzantium was unique and almost without peer; the Byzantine commander and his army were lauded as having '…cool headedness under duress, caution in the face of the enemy, and a thorough understanding of tactics, operations, and logistics. As compared with the blunt tactics of leaders in neighboring societies, the Byzantine generals acted more like surgeons than butchers with measured gains and a clear appreciation for the delicate instrument of the army in their hands.'[8] However, most historians iterate that it was the strength of Byzantine leadership that decided favorably on its fate, not military arms[9] striving to be masters of diplomacy and peace. Byzantium was also a fount of Greek culture with dedicated artists in tile and iconography, poetry, history, science, and philosophy. It benefited from the marriage of a Greek culture and Roman law, also having a rich pageantry of cultural heritages borrowed from neighboring Persian and Muslim practices. Byzantium itself was not merely the gilded hall of intrigue, insane zealotry, backstabbing, choking incense, shifty obese eunuchs, or dreary and mad-eyed monks the modern imagination and moralists like Edward Gibbon describe, despite being invaluable sources. A new imagination of Byzantine society has arisen, of everyday people, habits and cultures, sitting besides stunning *tromp l'oeil* as rich as anything envisaged in the epic of Western Rome seen on television and the movies of the 1950's and 60's.

Of course with all rulers of complex societies and interests, there are the questions of scandal and decision that haunt the historical mind as well. Why did Constantine I hesitate to convert until his death? Did Theodora have a secret son she had tortured and murdered in order to hide her checkered past? What happened to the technical marvels with which Theophilus entertained guests? Why did the Roman Church never truly forgive Constantinople? There are also the horror stories: when Constantine VI was blinded by his own mother Irene almost to the point of death, Basil II blinding and mutilating over ten thousand Bulgars to show his power, or Nicephorus I's skull becoming the drinking vessel of a Bulgar Khan. On top of these are the many nicknames

---

[7] Brownworth, Lars. *Lost to the West: the Forgotten Byzantine Empire that Rescued Western Civilization*. New York, NY: Three Rivers Press, 2009, 4.

[8] Decker, Michael J. *The Byzantine Art of War*. Yardley, PA: Westholme Publishing, 2013, 50.

[9] Barker, David. *Manuel II Paleologus (1350-1425): A Study in Byzantine Statesmanship*. New Brunswick, NJ: Rutgers University Press, 1969.

these Imperial masters received: Constantine V 'Name of Dung,' Justinian II 'Slit-Nosed,' John II 'the Beautiful,' and Andronicus I 'the Terrible.' The Calligraphers and lawgivers, the Greats, the Tyrants, these were all part of the Byzantine imperial pageant.

However, it was certainly not without violence and raw ambition; in the book *The Walking Drum* by Louis L'Amour, the clairvoyant Western protagonist foretold the horrendous torture and death of Andronicus I Comnenus to take place in 1185, reportedly the worst in all of history. All Andronicus did after being told this revelation to respond was to ask if he had been emperor at the time, and when told yes, Andronicus responding tantamount to 'then it was worth it', simply walking away.[10] This scene captures the will of some men to gain the throne at any risk for its power, station, and consequence as the head of the Eastern Empire, its people, army, and Church, no matter the cost. These only add psychological insight into these Byzantine rulers who could will themselves into absolute power and what goals they achieved in which to do it.

This book, if anything, is a tribute to a rich cultural heritage seen through the lives of its rulers. Each name signifies new developments on the world stage in a great city on the Bosporus, and their time line sees these names partnered with great achievements and momentous events in history. This is a civilization whose armies defended Christendom from dominating Muslim adversaries until Western Europe could modernize itself against them. Their Civil Law Code is still recognizable as the modern law code in European countries until Napoleon, and is seen in the codes made beyond the nineteenth century. As Louisiana state law is said to have come mainly from the Napoleonic Code, founded by the Justinianic Code, Byzantine law can be said to have come to America fifteen hundred years later than its creation. Byzantine art, paintings, and mosaics are considered some of the most alluring and pious on Western records as its cultures of Classical learning were being the building blocks of the new ideas of modern Europe. Orphanages and hospitals as we now know them were a hallmark and invention of Byzantine charitable institutions brought west by the West's knightly orders such as St. John. Everywhere influence and implications of the Byzantine Empire exist and it is the epic of its secular leaders we read of here that hallmark them.

---

[10] L'Amour, Louis. *The Walking Drum*. New York, NY: Bantam Books, 1984, 380.

# I. LATE ANTIQUITY

The Empire at this time was solidifying in the East (Egypt, Asia Minor, Illyricum, Pannonia, and Greece) due to constant barbarian threats and a new Persian Empire in West Asia that caused tension not seen in the region since before Alexander the Great. This sacrificed the West as the traditional center of Roman activity and would, over centuries, allow Germanic tribal armies in Gaul, Britain, and eventually Spain to become the *de facto* rulers and exploit weaknesses to superior invading armies. The West became exhausted in its morale and internal corruption led to a fatal lack of confidence in leadership, resulting in a diminished quality in administration with an authority Romans could not trust. Even the invincibility of the city of Rome was dashed by attacks and it faced sacks by Goths and Vandals not seen in 700 years of unbreached peace. A capital at Ravenna would become necessary under Theodosius I 'the Great' just so an urban military position could be defensible enough against the tribal armies. In 410, Rome would face its first fall since the fourth century BCE to invasion by the Ostro- (Eastern) goths.

An East needing defense against the spillage of eastern tribes and Persian soldiers would require a new capital that a sitting emperor could best evaluate the situation and possibly prepare for the inevitable. At one time a periphery ripe for rebellion and the Parthian and Pontine containment, Constantinople would now be a forefront of Roman administrative and military affairs. But, with this new phenomena came influences given by the Greek and Oriental East as well. Emperors would wear Persian silk togas and robes unheard of eras before while the polyglot linguistic culture of the East would become common in all but the most official of documents (to be in Latin only until the 6th century). Eastern religion would become a major issue in ways not thought of in a Western Rome: the numerous Pagan mystery religions of ancient times would battle for the Roman soul with the teachings and mysteries of Christ, the Virgin, the Resurrection, and the miracles of one faith strong enough to finally conquer old ways.

An army whose nature conquered the world centuries ago had to adapt. Instead of light armor and endless infantry, heavy army and plate needed to suffice and cavalry would be the predominant use of force to match that of the Sassanid Persian and barbarian tribal military forces. New tactics would later solidify after Justinian, but its roots would come in the form of decentralized generalship, redistricting, and a slew of warrior emperors that crossed almost every ethnic line. This inability to adapt in the West would lead to their fall to barbarians who had learned to master such tactics. It would become the mainstay indefinitely with the coming of the master horseman and cavalry tactics of the Ghassanids and Arabs conquering with the force of the wind to spread to the East in the name of the Prophet Mohammed and the Word of the Koran.

The evolution of the Empire and its Emperors to a Byzantine culture distinctive of Roman will be seen in this section of the book. With Rome's fall and the rise of the East, Byzantium would be free to change itself into an Oriental culture on par with its eastern allies, neighbors, and even enemies. Christianity would challenge itself in its methods to worship, but would be regarded and made as compatible in everyday life in an Orthodox East every much as that in a Trinitarian, Medieval West. This was not in spite of, but because: 'The true ruler of the Empire was Christ himself. It was his word, as manifested in the Gospels, that provided the ultimate authority; His Cross was carried at the front of military processions; His image, crowned with the imperial diadem, was imprinted on coins; it was His name, "The Lord Jesus Christ Our Master," that laws were promulgated…Everything was dedicated to the service of God.'[11]

The climax would even be a loss of the West to the barbarians known for conquering it by an emperor not even known for leaving the capital. The City of Constantine would rise to rival all other cities in Europe and Asia for centuries and hold dear the type of cosmopolitan culture the West could not re-discover until modern times.

## DIOCLETIAN
(284-305)

## MAXIMIAN
(285-305)

---

[11] Sherrard, Philip. *Great Ages of Man, A History of the World's Cultures: Byzantium*, ed. by Maitland A. Edey & Time-Life Books. New York, NY: Time Incorporated, 1966, 80.

# GALERIUS
(305-311)

Despite the controversy by Christian writers such as Eusebius (263-339 CE) and Lactantius (250-325 CE), Diocletian was a traditional Roman with radical ideas who treated the Empire as a responsibility through the crisis of keeping its unity. According to the semi-anonymous sources of the *Historia Augustae* from the fourth century CE, Diocles, a domestic cavalry officer (*protectors domestici*), took the office of emperor from the end of a half-century time of turmoil where the former Emperor, Carinus, having died, was being prostrated as being alive by an intermediate courtier controlling the armies, only being discovered fighting Persia in Nicomedia. It could not be a better allegory that Diocletian took control from misrule and courtier-driven anarchy in rule a fragmented Rome, the emperor literally being a puppet. Since 20 November, 284, until his abdication in 305, he was a savior to public order, a bane of Christianity, an oppressive dictator, and a vigilant general against barbarian and rebellion alike.

Born in Illyricum on December 22, 245, the son of a freedman scribe, Gaius Aurelius Valerius Diocletianus (Diocles) had a liking for numbers and accounting that would later serve him in economic administration. Though his origins were in Asia Minor, the name Diocles does have a connotation of questionably Greek origin.[12] Though he was a symbol of Roman power and admiration, and the adopter of the name 'Jovius' (derivative of the Roman king of gods Jove), his life was dedicated to prefer the Greek East where he ruled the so-called 'Rule of Four' from his impressive palace in Salona (modern Split on the Adriatic coast in Croatia). He had a religious fervor for Greek deities such as Zeus and Hercules (as well as the Roman translations Jove and Heracles), of which he defended in the Christian persecutions of 297-304. The Latin West was given to his co-ruler, Maximian, who ascended in 286 and was given the title 'Herculius'. But even then, Diocletian's executive legislation were understood to be final when applied to the West as well as the East. Two of his seemingly few concessions to Western Romanism in his personal life was his change of the Greek name Diocles to the Latin Diocletian. Following this was his mytho-religious appellation upon his colleague Maximian, though this would not become a tradition among the Pagan or Christian rulers anteceding them.

---

[12] Treadgold, Warren. *History of the Byzantine State and Society.* Stanford, CA: Stanford University Press, 1997, 13-14.

Practically from his first day, Diocletian began a series of administrative, military, and economic reforms that would become the framework of the later Byzantine East. The incomparable size of the Roman Empire (possibly rivaling in square mileage the Achaemenid Persian Empire (existing from the sixth to third centuries BCE) needed new leadership to handle an unwieldy bureaucracy from only one capital city. It reached from modern Scotland (Britannia south of the lands of the Pictish tribes) to Egypt and Syria, to western Turkey (Asia Minor) and the Balkans to Portugal (Lusitania). To combat this, Diocletian imposed the joint rule of Rome between Maximian in the Roman capital to his own Nicomedian palace in the East. He quickly adopted Maximian as a 'son' (a tongue-in-cheek proposition as Maximian was only five years his adoptive father's junior) to create the dual *Augusti* of the Empire's two halves. And when this became insufficient, the emperor created the office of *Caesar* to act as successors to the two Emperors. For this, his choices were Maximian Galerius and Lavius Valerius Constantius (I) Chlorus. It was a well-regarded opinion that the four hardly trusted each other and the future Emperor and son of Constantius, Constantine, was kept as a hostage in Diocletian's court to curb his father's ambitions.

The two Roman Empire's halves were divided into provinces (*dioces*) where the emperor changed all military administrative posts to purely civil ones (*vicari*), increasing the bureaucracy, each of the four ruling with their own Prefects. And when new provinces were added such as when Armenia and Iberia in Asia Minor was claimed from the Persian King Narseh, the East adopted them as separate provinces. Since this era, the Eastern Empire and the Byzantines would rely on strategic depth and linear defense as a bulwark to the East.[13] The eastern provinces included Asiana (western and southern Anatolia), Pontica (northern and eastern Anatolia), East (Syria and Egypt), all of which Diocletian commanded. Galerius ruled the Pannonias (northern Illyricum), the Moesias (southern Illyricum and Greece), and Thrace. These administrations would later be the support system for the Church and the Themes of the seventh century.

When the two Persian provinces were incorporated, it raised the number of eastern provinces from twelve to fourteen, demonstrating that the East was growing faster than the West, subtly laying foundations for the Byzantine east.[14] Italy and the West, it was decided, were to become practically inferior compared

---

[13] Decker, 51.
[14] Ostrogorsky, 35.

to the East. Maximian was designated to rule the Italian, Latin African, the two Gaullic, British, and Spanish provinces through the Prefects he had appointed. The East, however, had the advantages over the West with Illyrica's higher population, the Egyptian grain trade, and jurisdiction over the *annoniae* (government-controlled bread doles) to the two Romes. Unfortunately, the expanded bureaucracy also allowed for higher rates of embezzlement and political corruption, a trend that would be strife in all subsequent Byzantine centuries.

A further impending problem was that after Diocletian's reign would end, the succession of the four would lack stability and break almost as fast as it was cemented. An old problem of the Empire since the Julio-Claudians in the first century CE was maintaining stable successions and policies over the change of time. These considerations were included in the dynamic Diocletianic reforms, a result being the need for the person of the emperor needing a new style and image with his people. Diocletian lived in an earlier era of military leaders becoming rulers moderated by assassination (as Voltaire described) only to allow for a repeating cycle a short time later. This instability was something Diocletian would wish to avoid with a ceremonial change in order to rehabilitate the institution of the Emperor and its executive duties.

Superhuman statuary would become a norm, (Constantine once had a 40 ft. Colossus built from 312-315 whose head and foot still exist in the *Piazza Capitoliani*) with rhetoric and ceremony as well, emphasizing the divine favor of the emperor and his succession to be indoctrinated. The emperor's image and presence were the most important, taking from an Oriental heritage; from trends from the Sassanid Persian court,[15] he, according to Eutropius (d. 399 CE) in his *Brief History*, wore "...clothes and shoes decorated with gems whereas previously the Emperor's insignia composed only the purple robe and the rest of his dress was ordinary." Religion was his political policy as the sacrosanct person of the emperor would be removed from all society, a living god among men, where acts of revolt were impiety and assassination sacrilege.[16]

He also held a more private court and appeared less in public, adding a mystery and awe to such an industrious, yet still present, ruler. Above all was the now mandated prostration before him, instead of a mere greeting and salute,

---

[15] Ensslin, Wilhelm. 'The Emperor and Imperial Administration.' *Byzantium: An Introduction to East Roman Civilization,* ed. by Norman H. Baynes & St. L. B. Moss. Oxford, UK: Oxford University Press, 1969. 268-307.

[16] Brownworth, 6.

such prostration being a practice early Greeks considered 'groveling like a dog at a barbarian's feet'. The use of the Byzantine tradition offering *proskynesis* to the emperor (and eventually, Patriarchs), likely originated here as a Persian-born tradition would also appear in Caliphate and Sultanate courts,[17] characterized by a four-legged bow with the forehead touching the ground until the ruler bid you to rise, it became a mainstay of Oriental court presentation as described by Alexander A. Vasiliev (1867-1953). It is certain that Constantine I, Diocletian's successor, would institute the wearing of an imperial diadem that had Oriental origins.[18] Also, the unofficial 'tradition' of Byzantium's household servant and eunuch policymakers and generals appeared. The 'Grand Chamberlain' of later eras would become the power behind the throne, which perhaps began with Diocletian's *magister officiorum* who kept records, organized personal security and ran the Emperor's plans of civil bureaucracy.[19] Time would show that this office would only breed intrigue and rebellion in the imperial palaces. Most importantly, he replaced the Praetorians with personal guards to prevent the 'fractiousness, insubordination, and regicide' from affecting the future.[20]

Despite his separating civil and military provincial administration, Diocletian managed within three years of increasing the army from around 400,000 troops to 600,000.[21] There was necessity in this increase mainly to handle internal rebellion and barbarian incursion. Besides Persia, there were barbarian threats in Germany, a Berber 'confederation' in North Africa, and Sarmatians on the Danube. In Britain, a rival claimant, Marcus Aurelius Carausius, gathered an army to lay claim to the West, building fortifications on the Saxon shore which also supported his heading east as well. In summer of 293, the general Allectus was killed at Farnham by Constantius and Britain was restored after a decade of separation.

The finances of the empire were grave at the time of Diocletian's succession. The coinage was at an all time low of debasement, taxation was inefficient and mismanaged, and the standard of paying troops was based on private largesse that soon ran out; the army was eventually paid 7,500 silver *denarii* with

---

[17] Vasiliev, Alexander A. *History of the Byzantine Empire, 324-1453*, 2nd Edition. Madison, WI: University of Wisconsin Press. 1952, 62.

[18] Bury, James Bagnell. *History of the Later Roman Empire from the Death of Theodosius I to the Death of Justinian, vol. I*. New York, NY: Dover Publications. 1958, 10.

[19] Ostrogorsky, 37-38.

[20] Decker, 67.

[21] Treadgold, 19.

scattered bonuses and holiday pay.[22] Diocletian attempted to restore the gold *solidus* standard, but the drop in the purity of the coins made stable gold prices rare, and in reality, a new silver standard (*argentum*) was put into effect. The inflation of the debased silver even made necessary a copper coin in specie, the *billon*. Diocletian attempted to hold back price inflation by imposing his main economic reform, the Edict on Maximum Prices, that fixed prices on grain, beer, meat, wool and silk clothing, shoes, wages, freight, and other goods usually bartered.[23] Unfortunately, the coinage issue was never made totally resolved by the end of Diocletian's reign as financially, land assessments and holdings would mean nothing over time with massive inflation.

Despite this despotic, yet impractical trend in assessments, more success was made in taxation reform. A census of 293-296 tabulated the livestock, wealth, and even army recruits of the entire Empire in an assessment of *indictio*. Mostly, taxation benefited the military as Diocletian would pull his weight over the West when collecting taxes for army conscription. Taxation would be separate from the wholesale earnings of provinces and companies, 'heads' (*capitum*), and the micro-managing of individual property earnings, or, 'yokes' (*jugum*). This system had a sense of fairness to it socially; taxation was standardized by ability to pay a maximum: uniform rates on the head of each household took less from lower-class citizens and the higher amounts from the richest landowners. This seems to be a way in controlling the landed (*latifundiae*) gentry and their incomes with capital gains, redirecting it to the central authority in the Empire.

More importantly of note, it leads to decisions reminiscent of the later feudal economy of the Middle Ages to develop, East and West, a centralizing effect for the monarch. As the farming class could simply defect to provinces with lower tax bases, Imperial laws were made that tied these farmers to the land by the census to combat tax sheltering – in essence creating the ancestors of the feudal system of vassalage, a 'tying' to the land. This would be a Byzantine model for centuries thereafter, marking it for distinction as a 'Medieval' Empire over the Classical model. The villages and estates bordering the periphery of the Empire was obligated to provide annual surpluses of agricultural product based on its population, or buy out of it themselves.[24]

Diocletian attempted, as well, to undermine corrupting religious influence

---

[22] Decker, 89.
[23] Treadgold, 16.
[24] Decker, 84.

from a more stable and traditional Rome. The fastest-growing 'cult' at the time was Christianity, its pacifist nature always upsetting the enrollment of viable soldiers. The act of disqualification by thumb-cutting, for example, allowed army exemption as no thumb meant a shield could not be held for duty. Severe penalties, eventually death, were given to those attempting this as a mark of cowardice and state defiance. But, what good could it do to those persecutors when the Christians believed in eternal peace for those so martyred? This question loomed largest for the faithful in 297 and 298 when it was made law that all soldiers regularly sacrificed to the pagan gods upon pain of death. In fact, this was made difficult by the rites having to be re-performed numerously because Christian genuflections made to protect Christian souls during these rites insulted the state gods.

The old rumors abounded of Christian vices: infant sacrifice, cannibalism, sex orgies, even plots against the state. When harmony was made more routine in the Empire, Diocletian attacked Christians in earnest, setting aside any tolerance. It all boiled to its worst head in February 303, when Diocletian's palace at Nicomedia burned down and all Christian clergy were ordered arrested and imprisoned across the Empire. Just as in Nero's time, the Christians were scapegoated and numerous martyrs were made by the Romans as they were burned, boiled, and fed to lions as the legends of the Persecutions relate, as these stories and more involved, mostly, the *Caesar*, Galerius. In April of 304, all Christians were ordered to give sacrifice to the Roman gods upon pain of death.[25] However, these actions as well had far-reaching consequences with less efficacy. These atrocities and persecutions would, of course, only inspire Christianity in their present and future by holding on to their past. It must have been with certain satisfaction that Helena, mother of the emperor Constantine I saw Christianity re-instated by her son when it was an impossibility mere decades before.

Realizing his health was failing, on May 1, 305, Diocletian decided to willingly abdicate his throne, a first in Roman imperial history. Upon a pact that had been pledged in 285, Maximian begrudgingly did so as well in the western capital of Milan, allowing Galerius and Constantius I to be the new *Augusti* in the Empire. Diocletian would retire to his luxurious palace in Salona to raise cabbages, and after a spectacularly full and dramatic career on the throne, Diocletian was believed through with politics until, in 308, he attended a convention in Carnuntem and was offered the throne again. He refused,

---

[25] Scarre, 202.

politely joking if his cabbages at Salonae could be seen, no one would ever again judge [Imperial rule] a tempting prospect. A greedy usurper, Maximian Daia, later expelled Diocletian's family from Split in the anarchy of succession, so, in December of 311, the retired emperor was said to have starved himself to death in protest.

It is not easy evaluating such a career as Diocletian's. He had so many practical ideas, but after his generation, they would seem to crumble before new problems and changes. His press is, no doubt, an interesting dichotomy: a pagan savior of '. . .exceptional character . . .' (Which was most likely a quote by the Pagan historian Zosimus in his *New History*) on one side, monster and tyrant on the opposing side of Christianity by authors such as Eusebius. He did seek peace and unity in a fragmented Empire, bringing order from chaos, but his price was high. He effectively strengthened Roman frontier and interior fighting against barbarian and usurper alike. But, when it came to his own religious desires, he broke the code of tolerance and ease other emperors adopted and attacked fellow Romans because of their Christianity with the easy excuse that they had forfeited their Roman identity by accepting this strange faith.

The fourth century CE was a time of Eastern cultism and fragmented religious fervor, but the Christians were considered a threat that had to be eradicated in theory and in person. What would mar his legacy more was the meeting of his overt and over-the-top violence with Christian dissent that was actually benign and fraught with unfounded allegations. These were not religious wars and insurrections that would pepper Byzantine history later, but an extermination and assimilation: kill the Christian, but save the Roman. Diocletian made wise decisions for the Romans and it shows in his effectiveness on the throne, but, what appears as Roman ingenuity through pragmatism is revealed later as palaces on clouds. His innovations of imperial Tetrarchy were not doomed to failure, but they still failed before Diocletian's death. His persecutions only doomed pagan domination over a mere 'cult' in his eyes, strengthening the church.[26] He was a brilliant, but tragic, ruler in the end.

Much less is known about Diocletian's western confederate Maximian besides his Imperial title, the bestowed 'Herculius', and his description by some as Diocletian's 'old drinking buddy.'[27] He was no mirror image of his Eastern

---

[26] Treadgold, 25.

[27] Brownworth, 3.

*Augustus*; his territories were inferior, he was railroaded by Eastern edicts, and powerless before a pledge to abdicate in 305. He was an ally and military friend of the actual emperor that seemed could have been anyone. When it was said he wished to ascend his son Maxentius to the role of the western *Caesar,* it coolly went unrecognized. He would then choose his praetorian son-in-law Julius Constantius Chlorus on March 1, 293, whose son would actually be sent to Nicomedia. But despite this seeming captivity of Chlorus' son, chroniclers usually contend they had a trusting relationship.[28]

Marcus Aurelius Valerius Maximinianus was the son of proletariat shopkeepers and was probably the product of a lifelong military career, born around 250 in Sirmium, being only five years Diocletian's junior upon his 285 accession as co-ruler of the Empire. He was a fellow soldier on the Mesopotamian border with Diocletian, thus his humble origins of becoming co-ruler of the known world from obscurity. He was given the name 'Herculius' for propaganda reasons – he was the heroic and evil-fighting Heracles to Diocletian's 'father-like' Jove. Of course this was all allegorical as Maximian could not be seen as the son of a man his age (although he was legally adopted in April, 286); Diocletian was the Father of the Empire, as Maximian was its warrior demigod.

Warrior he was in defending the Gallic frontier in 286 from robber-tribes, the Danube frontier from the Alamanni with Diocletian in 288, and fighting the pretender Carausius's British navy in 289, all with moderate success. In 297, he quelled the Berber 'Quinquegentiani' in North Africa and in the Christian persecutions, he took his part in defending paganism with the *Caesar* Galerius. He abdicated, supposedly without question, in May 305 as his co-ruler did and that should have ended that. But, by 306, unstable power transitions had the Italian armies flocking to Maximian's leadership in Milan and Maximian attempted to rule again, this time with his son Maxentius as successor as previously intended. Later, in November 308, a peace conference was held at Carnuntum and it was decided Maximian would be in the care of Constantine, son of Constantius. In April, 310, to supposedly offset more instability, Constantine less than scrupulously compelled him to commit suicide and allow the rise of Licinius as Constantine's co-ruler in Italy.

Maximian seems like a footnote and puppet when viewed from afar. Though he accepted Diocletian's authority over him, the theory of any 'shared power' in the Empire is laughable. He was a courageous, willing, and successful

---

[28] Scarre, 204.

general protecting the borders of his Western Empire when it was needed, however. It is just unfortunate, though inevitable, that the lure of power just had to be called and the type of confusion over succession and authority Diocletian tried to avoid would take place between six men in a matter of five years - it seemed the 'Time of Troubles' Diocletian had ended in 284 was returning. This bad hand dealt to Maximian, through poor power decisions in the Roman power game, lead to his ultimate demise as it had to so many before.

Son-in-law and former Praetorian Prefect under Diocletian, Galerius Valerius Maximinianus's origins and much of his past is scarcely recorded,[29] though he may have been born in 260 near Serdica. He was *Caesar* of the East from 285 until his succession as *Augustus* in 305. He also had built, in Grecian Thessalonica, a great palace now compared to the architectural triumphs of the Pantheon of Rome and the future Hagia Sophia of Constantinople. After a slow start, his military career was a marvel of successes in various corners of the East. During the wars of 297 with the Sassanian Persian King Narseh I, Galerius fought the Persians in Charrae by Callinicum and again in Armenia using Danubian forces. And although Charrae was a sound Roman victory, the rest of the war for Galerius resulted in priming him for the military adventures resulting from the battles of succession that would arise. Though he lacked his predecessor's vision, his victory was the fuel for the claims that Galerius was as accomplished a superior warrior and administrator than Diocletian was.[30]

Upon his succession in 305, he had a hand in choosing the next *Caesar* of both East and West. His choice for the East was his own son-in-law Maximinus Daia and in the West a personal friend, Severus II, would rule under the ascended Constantius I, though the latter was in perilously ill health. It is to be noted that neither were blood relatives of the *Augusti* and that those who were, Maxentius and Constantine, would only seize power by force. In the West, Constantius's death (his moniker Chlorus or 'the Pale' might suggest a diagnosis of leukemia[31]) led to the claim that Constantine was awarded *Caesar* on his father's deathbed, with enthusiastic approval from the army, but without the approval of Galerius.

Support for Severus and Galerius in Italy was made unstable enough,

---

[29]  Even in Scarre, a reliable source on such details as dates and names.
[30]  Treadgold, 28.
[31]  Scarre, 208.

a tax structure for households not in rural areas was created as well as his heavy-handed persecution tactics (called 'Acts of Pilate') alienating the strong religious community in Italy. Though Constantine was given the purple, it did not take much for rebellion to re-emerge as Maximin's son, Maxentius, led a revolt in Rome in 306 with Praetorian support (perhaps being the reason of Constantine's disbanding of the Guard). Without eastern recognition, he made himself *Augustus* in October of 307, and took control of Italy, Sicily, Corsica, Sardinia, Egypt, and North Africa, formerly Severus's domains. Severus himself was caught, imprisoned and forced to commit suicide after failed tax policies and a military endeavor against his co-rulers ended in ruin.

These operations were getting out of hand after Maximian attempted to seize the West and was ousted by Constantine. Here, a dangerous game of civil war and fragmentation was being played. We see the failures of the Tetrarchy system, not in that one ruler would still control the Empire as Constantine or Theodosius later would, but in that too many men of the purple would challenge each other and the Romes would burn with '. . .plotting and campaigning against each other, continuing without intermission.' And as Eusebius continues, '...no one could look for anything but an enemy attack every day'.[32] The Carnuntem peace conference was then called on the lower Danube in 308, where Constantine brought Maximian and Maxentius, all *Augusti* and *Caesari* were participated. Diocletian was brought into attendance to consult on matters (probably arbitrating or advising as a wise and trusted man, or as a 'neutral party' needing a voice in the proceedings).

As a result, Maxentius and Maximian kept position in a constitutional conflict, and a Praetorian Prefect and friend of Galerius, Licinius, was made western *Augustus* with Constantine as his *Caesar*; Galerius and Maximinus Daia would remain as they were. The weakness of the Tetrarchy's constitution should not escape notice as the provinces of the Empire could be cut up like a cake served to petty and greedy purple-bearers. The best example so far is Maximin and Maxentius keeping Italy and North Africa as well as the rest of the West in Licinius/Constantine's domain. Galerius would keep Illyricum and Daia, Egypt, and Syria. In a matter of two decades, a simple co-ruler situation had grown to four, and now because of military and legal complications, *six* men ruled the Roman Empire in an inane 'Sextarchy'. Diocletian's system had gone from safety net to a nearing failure in a matter of a few years.

---

[32] Eusebius, *Ecclesiastical History*, trans. by G.A. Williamson. New York, NY: Penguin Publishing. 1989, 16.

Something that set Galerius apart, with Maximian later following his example, from his other colleagues was his ardent positions against the Christians. He was Diocletian's most apt student in the persecutions and would continue this bloody swathe across Europe, as he was said to have 'intensified the butchery of Christians by axing, roasting, and mutilation,'[33] only to ironically strengthen Christianity's strong cause in the process. Between him and Maximius, Galerius tortured and killed 1,500 Christians in ten years, being an average of 150 martyrs per year, [34] yet, undoubtedly, the more Christians killed, the more veneration the faith seemed to earn from the survivors to other Christians! And this statement from Gibbon and the Church historians must speak of how well-reported, recorded, or publicized each individual execution probably was. It was not difficult finding them as he kept up the laws of the Pagan state sacrifices during the censuses and the taking of offices both civil and military.

Galerius was noted as being a 'textbook tyrant' for his appetites, zeal, and policies by modern detractors as well as Christian apologists. Galerius is even the one who convinced Diocletian in 302 to begin a widespread anti-Christian campaign in the Empire. His records of a cancerous growth in 310 and subsequent death in spring of 311 was seen by Christians, and perhaps himself,[35] as a punishment by God. A pestilent growth would eat at his bowels and teem with worms, giving a sickening stench that doctors abhorred, with years of flab decomposing, and having these doctors said to have neglected their duties, they were unmercifully executed by the tyrannous ruler: these are the researched accounts of Eusebius in his *Church History*. Even Galerius must have feared divine retribution, as he immediately rescinded all anti-Christian laws and edicts, restoring their property, and even asking for divine mercy and the prayers of the persecuted from an agonizingly pained deathbed decree. However, this may have been propaganda by men such as Eusebius as Maxentius did most of the revocations and Galerius did not seek conversion.

Galerius was a true furtherance of Diocletian, in economy, religion, administration, and military accomplishments; however, he was still a sign that time was not treating the Empire well. Diocletian fought off barbarians and usurpers, but Galerius found himself fighting and even capitulating to

---

[33] Montefiore, Simon Sebag. *Jerusalem: The Biography.* New York, NY: Vintage Books. 2011. 147.

[34] Gibbon, Edward. *The History of the Decline and Fall of the Roman Empire, vol. I-III,* ed. by J. B. Bury. New York, NY: The Heritage Press. 1946, 452.

[35] Treadgold, 30.

usurper successors to the throne and Diocletian's precautions would never have allowed that to happen. Exiting the scene as he did, his legacy would be religious intolerance, oppression, political weakness, and mixed amounts of mercy. Still, despite this, he maintained his interests well regarding invasion and rebellion in the turmoil the West embodied. The constitutional failings were not his fault, either; the flaws inherent in such a system made its nullification inevitable until a strong ruler could see it dismantled completely from what it originally was. After his death, Maxentius would immediately move on Asia Minor and Nicomedia to cancel Galerius's taxation and convince the citizens to forget his administration.

## CONSTANTINE I 'THE GREAT'
### (305-324)

It was Constantine, son of Constantius Chlorus, that would be the dynamic leader who shaped a new civilization from an old one, needing change in adversity. He not only brought sole rule back to Rome, he kept it going as well as it had in earlier pagan times with good administration and a dedication to unity in *all* types of its citizens. With the influence of his mother Helena and a shrewd political sense, Constantine created a new administration through the early Christian Church that was dedicated to philanthropy, urban conversion, and a place in the military, built on a belief in salvation of the soul and the Afterlife. By recognizing a strong unity and hierarchy in the Christian faith, he was able to change the Empire forever. It would take time and energy to realize this as, in 312, the Empire's Christian population would only reach from five to ten percent.[36]

He is also noted as the founder of the city of Constantinople and the Byzantine Empire itself on May 11, 330 AD. From the seaside of the City, well-guarded by nature, he and dozens of subsequent rulers would decide the fate of millions in variations of nationalities, ethnicities, and faiths, but above all that of Christianity. But as with all of those responsible for such achievements were the complexities of a character with the mind of a rough soldier, a holy visionary, and a murderous autocrat at the pinnacle of human supremacy with his shoulder-length hair (longer hair being the style in Oriental rulers), brilliant bracelets, and bejeweled robes.[37] He was the sort that would both engage

---

[36] Brown, Peter. *Poverty and Leadership in the Later Roman Empire: The Menahem Stern Jerusalem Lectures.* Hanover, NH: University of New England. 2002, 17.
[37] Montefiore, 151.

enthusiastically in power's pageantry and spectacle, and also the debates of the Pagan philosophers and Christian Bishops.

Born on February 27, 272, in the Dacian city of Naissus, he was the son of the Praetorian Constantius I Chlorus (later *Caesar* and *Augustus*) and his Christianized wife, Helena, yet it is recorded how Constantine's earlier years was spent as a hostage of Diocletian in Nicomedia.[38] Whether this was a source of resentment towards Diocletian is unclear, but whether it was or not, Constantine shadowed the Eastern *Augustus* in politics and administration as he would use this in a superlative manner in later decades. He had, after all, eight consulships and four tribunal titles during his twenty-year reign. His physical strength was well respected by his young peers and the nickname 'Bullneck' was given to him. He began a military education by witnessing Galerius and his Egyptian wars of 297-298 and he had gained his enemies early: there are 'legends' told of Galerius's plans of assassination, wherein Constantine fled, killing all the horses behind him to stymie any pursuit by his enemies.

This period, however, begins the issues of his political and military career in the hotbed of the Tetrarchy's 'anarchy' as Constantine feared for his life on being passed over for the Caesarship of the West as he fled Rome.[39] This may indicate that Galerius saw Constantine as a threat of *rebellion* and not inheritance. The Western army approved highly of Constantius and if Constantine wanted to question Nicomedia's authority, he may have been successful. What may have honed such authority was his Pictish victory in 305, earning him the name 'Britannicus Maximus'. A year later, his father administrated from modern York in Britainnia, where he would later die on July 25, 306. These facts may have smoothed the way of the western acceptance of being granted *Augustus* from his dying father, likely making the story of the deathbed entitlement, despite Severus's account, true. Unfortunately, this presents the first of the Tetrarchy's constitutional crises: Galerius Augustus never recognized Constantine as *Augustus*, but only as a *Caesar*, under Severus II.

Severus's fate definitely intertwined with the young *Caesar*'s when the Maxentius revolt of 307 saw him self-anointing as *Augustus* when Severus's army fled to Maxentius. When Galerius recognized Constantine as Augustus out of need, Maxentius capitulated and Severus was hunted to Ravenna, shamed into abdication, and executed at Tres Tabernae near Rome on September 16,

---

[38] Norwich, John Julius. *Byzantium: the Early Centuries*. New York, NY: Alfred A. Knopf Publishing. 1997, 34.

[39] *ibid.*, 37.

307. Constantine, however, would cloud issues with Galerius by marrying Maxentius's daughter that year. This would prove another shrewd tactic by the *Augustus* because Maxentius and his family with the armies he commanded against Galerius were stalled, and a new and united Western dynasty was founded. Galerius, raising an army to invade Italy over this event was as about as successful as Severus, and perhaps Constantine knew this or threw all his worth into one cast of the die and was rewarded for it, a practice in which he would excel.

After the rebellions were quelled, Galerius adamantly called a peace conference to decide Imperial leadership in 308 at Carnuntum. Constantine was allowed to remain *Augustus* of the West, but without Maximin's or Maxentius's control, they would control North Africa and Italy. In 309, he would then declare himself *Augustus* on October 28, and again the following April, falsely claiming that Constantine had died.[40] This preposterous move was his last as Constantine would send his troops to arrest him and the Emperor would force suicide on his duplicitous father-in-law. It was this act in 310, however, that led to one of the most decisive battles and events of religious experience in all of Western history.

Upon the death of Galerius, Constantine would challenge Maximian Daia and the vengeful Maxentius for dominion over sole rule of the Empire. After victories at Verona, Modena, Aquilea, and Turin in Italy, Constantine in 312 saw a decisive battle at the Milvian Bridge over the Roman Tiber in a defense of the city by Maxentius. Crossing the Alps with an army of 40,000, Constantine descended on Italy. It would be as historically decisive as the outcome of the Greco-Persian War of the fifth century BCE or Caesar at Pharsalus in the first century BCE in deciding the course of all Western civilization.

Maxentius was tolerant of the Pope and even pulled down temples of Jove and Venus in Northern Italy, still having some Christian support in Rome, nevertheless being still a professed pagan. However, though his mother Helena was a Christian by 312, Constantine worshiped the Eastern sun-deity Sol Invictus (the Unconquerable Sun). Yet, this is what helped bring the army together under Constantine as the common religions of the soldiers were Eastern mystery deities. Mithra, (of Persian descent), Helios (the Sun of Apollo), Serapis (the Greco-Egyptian serpent of fertility), Malagbel of Emessa (Elagabal in Latin, or Heliogabalus in Greek), Belleharmon of Phoenicia (Baal Hammon), Benefal, and Maravat in Danube provinces, all somewhat misspelled

---

[40] Scarre, 209.

to represent some of these faiths of the army.[41] This came about from what the Pagan historian Zosimus (460-520 CE) calls it a 'barbarization' of the army, though it was necessary in a decade of endless warfare and depopulation as a result.

In the midst of this battle on October 28, Constantine is said to have had a miraculous and divine vision. Eusebius describes from the emperor '...a most marvelous sign appeared to him from heaven, the account of which it might have been difficult to receive with credit had it come from any other person. But since the victorious Emperor himself long afterwards declared to the writer of this history when he was honored with his acquaintance and society, and confirmed his statement by an oath, who could hesitate to accredit the relation, especially since the testimony of hindsight has established its truth? He said that about midday, when the sun was beginning to decline, he saw with his own eyes the trophy of a cross of light in the heavens, above the sun, and bearing the inscription Conquer by This (Hoc Vince). At this sight he himself was struck with amazement and his whole army also.'[42]

However, Lactantius, as a Christian, in his *De Mortibus Persecutorum* would say it was a dream the night before the battle and not a vision during the battle;[43] even the visions are argued over: was this cross a chi and rho (P, X) or was it a +, an equilateral cross, he saw? What certainly helped the battle were the bolts of the bridge giving way by the strain of the many soldiers with most of Maxentius's troops falling into the Tiber. As they crowned and crushed each other in the fray to reach the Roman bank from the pass, Maxentius also died as a result.

If this vision is somewhat true, it refreshed the vigor of Constantine's army with the glory of divine intervention. Most likely, this was a sort of pep talk that spoke to the Greek troops (chi and rho being Greek letters and the origin of the name 'Christ' in Latin Roman vocabulary) and the Eastern religious whose faith came about from Oriental divine dreams, visions, symbolism like

[41] MacMullen, Ramsey. *Constantine.* New York, NY: The Dial Press. 1969, 68. For a better background on the Pagan religions and Christianity of this time, see: Burckhardt, Jacob. *The Age of Constantine the Great,* 2nd ed., trans. by Moses Hadas. Berkeley and Los Angeles, CA: University of California Press. 1949, 1983.

[42] Eusebius. 'Life of Constantine'. *'A Select Library of Nicene and Post-Nicene Fathers of the Christian Church, vol. I: Eusebius'.* trans. By E.C. Richardson; ed. by H. Wace & P. Schaff. Oxford, UK: Parker & Co., 1890.

[43] Lactantius. *De Mortibus Persecutorum.* Oxford, UK: Clarendon Press, trans. by J.L. Creed, 1984.

a 'cross' embossed on a shield, and direct support or punishment from the deity. The Pagan Maxentius lost because God's favor was with Constantine and the influence of his Christian mother. Constantine entered Rome victoriously, he somewhat changing forever; the Empire, too, would change for it.

However, many modern scholars agree that this was yet another strategic and shrewd manipulation of fact and propaganda by a master of the art, though news of divine favor emboldening an army was as old as religion and warfare themselves. It would have been a cynical and calculating scheme to gather his polyglot army under one banner only intimated divinely to the soldier-emperor, and most likely was inspired by the wily and inventive character of Constantine. His mother must have given him advice and perhaps coercion to choose the Christian banner because he would remain a Pagan until his deathbed conversion in 326. Whether it is clear or not, Christianity would later prove to provide sound administrative purposes to the urban sectors of the Empire.

Like the Church titles would suggest, provincial government remained in diocese under the watch of *episcopuloi* (soon, Bishops). These would also become Church offices that handled daily administration, especially amongst the separate classes of the urban sectors of the Empire. The Bishop's Court (*Episcopalism Audientia*) was a body given power to oversee the welfare of the urban poor that proved to be a major step in Christian administration.[44] Bread doles for the poor (*annonae*) would, in a matter of thirty years, increase from 214 tons in the Empire in 332 to over 3,000 tons by 363. Allotments to the poor were side by side with doles given to govern and administer cities in the Empire, paying soldiers and ensuring the role of ecclesiastical offices doubling as that of the laity. Except for the few years of the last Pagan emperor, Pagan religious practice would shrink in the cities and be kept the province of rural (*pagani*) areas and their traditional circles.

This would, eventually, charge an explosion of Christian sentiment in the Empire among the urban poor and retired veteran status soldiers of the cities. However, there is much evidence how the Christian Emperor was becoming almost as intolerant as Diocletian was in the opposite direction, ostracizing parts of his own populace over faith. By 324, sacred prostitution, religious orgies, and similar sexual 'immorality' were outlawed and transgressors were ordered burned alive, and all pagan sacrifices were made illegal and their temple wealth was confiscated. The tradition, founded from Oriental religion, of the

---

[44] Brown, 67.

gladiatorial shows would be replaced (at least in Constantinople) by the more acceptable chariot races and crucifixions were abolished indefinitely.

Oddly, much of this prostitution was in response more to paying the tax of the *chrysargyron,* an unpopular urban gold and silver tax that caused 'great beating of breasts . . .weeping and screaming' from the observance of Eastern fertility cults. Eutropius had no reservations in thinking these laws and taxes 'most of them superfluous and a few severe'. A more vainglorious, anti-Pagan view of the Emperor would have his court Bishops claiming the divine presence paradise and that he was a thirteenth apostle of Christ to have an honorary burial among them after 326. He would turn this ecclesiastical authority over to questions of doctrine and the nature of Christ himself. The difficulty would be in balancing a unifying religious leadership beyond the Bishops with dividing interests and details in Christ's nature.[45]

By 325, the heresies of Donatism and Arianism, alive since 321, had plagued the early Church. Basically, they believed Christ had only one nature, of Godhead with no human basis or 'enfleshment' of the Holy Spirit. The Trinitarian creed believed in a separation of God, Christ, and the Holy Spirit; Christ was of a 'similar substance' to the Father (*homoiousos*), said the Trinity, as a created and separate entity of the Father, but the believers of the heretic Arian claimed it was ridiculous God should suffer like a man would on the cross. Thus, he was (*homoousos*), or 'same substance' (the two words being the origin of the phrase 'the difference of one iota') and co-eternal with God. To simplify this, Constantine called for a total convocation, or a Council, of the Empire's Bishops at the city of Nicaea on the Bosporus.

Here at the Council, Arianism was considered a heresy to be forbidden and the 323 excommunication of the Bishop Arius stood. Likewise, in a 327 Council in Egypt, the Bishop-historian Eusebius, not surprisingly, upheld Nicaea's decisions, but in reality, it was a firm belief that these arguments would not die away. It was Constantine's desires of unity in the Empire that kept away ideas of religious violence on a large scale. He is even considered quite neutral in the case, standing on the Empire's side wherein both parties were participants. So these were the roots of the divisive Byzantine tradition of Imperial Church Councils over heresies in the teachings and nature of the divine, an unintended consequence of Constantine's vision for the faith unifying Rome and Constantinople. It was Constantine who would say how 'sedition in the Church of God . . .is [something] I am more opposed to than

---

[45] Brownworth, 15.

anything else.' These were the kinds of words that would echo almost seventeen centuries of religious-inspired bloodshed.

These issues would even be the subject of the literary culture such as the *vicennelia* of 324, inspired by Constantine's rule by Publius Otatianus Porphyrius (233-305 CE). This poet uses Virgil and Horace's styles to praise the emperor in twenty odes. On the cover of a vermillion-inked text was a 'ship of state' with the chi rho as its sail. This stands as an impenetrable ode to Constantine and his East's accomplishments over twenty years. Architecturally, he presented Rome with a Triumphal Arc near the Colosseum and several churches, some lasting today such as the Church of St. John Lateral from the ruins of a first-century cavalry barrack,[46] and a church at Santa Costanza. Included were baths and a basilica started by Maxentius, now Constantine's basilica with a colossal statue of the emperor replacing one of Maxentius's. Though it was followed by a harsh expulsion of the Jewish inhabitants, Constantine's plans for Aelia Capitolina, the ancient city of Jerusalem as a New Jerusalem was meant to succeed as the new Golden Dome of the Rock was made to surpass the Holy Mount and demonstrate Christ's victory over the Jewish God.[47] Constantine definitely showed a streak of anti-Semitism in diverting glory from Jerusalem's Jewish holy sites to the new Christian ones, including Helena's discoveries of the holy relics.

She was a true mistress of propaganda and this is shown by the discoveries of these relics in places throughout the East. Besides Constantine's self-granted titles of 'Greatest' after the Milvian Bridge and 'Victor' after Constantinople's founding, there was the first Christian pilgrimage ever made by his mother, Helena. She built hospitals and hostels and the Church of the Nativity in Bethlehem was commemorated over the site of Christ's birth. At Golgotha in Jerusalem, she discovered the True Cross of the Crucifixion on the site of a Temple to Venus built by Hadrian, and it is here, over Christ's empty grave was built the Holy Church of the Sepulcher.[48]

On the topic of succession, by 311, the Empire stood as Constantine and Maximin Daia in the East and Licinius as Galerius's chosen successor. Daia's days were numbered with Galerius dead and the Eastern Augustus seeking sole rule of the East. As Licinius's western army (approved by Constantine) neared

---

[46] Norwich, John Julius. *Absolute Monarchs: A History of the Papacy.* New York, NY: Random House Publishing. 2011, 16. It was once the donation of the Roman aristocratic family of the Lateranni.

[47] Montefiore, 155-156.

[48] Brownworth, 16.

his palace, Maximin Daia took poison and died painfully in June of that year. To cement the West and East, Licinius married Constantine's sister at Milan. Licinius was a lukewarm supporter of Constantine and was only tolerated until it was necessary. Schism between the two was only a matter of time by 313. Between then and 315, Licinius would win laurels defending the Danube and southern Armenia from encroaching barbarians and although a persecuting pagan, he returned Christian property to their rightful places.

So it was hardly a surprise that in 315, Constantine sought to break a western dynasty as Diocletian did by offering his brother-in-law Bassianus as Western *Caesar* instead of the anticipated son of the *Augustus*, Licinianus. When refused, Constantine invaded Licinius's Pannonian dioces for support. He succeeded as always in the Battle of Cibalae in Serdica in March of 317, defeating Licinius's armies and granting '*Imperator*' status to the chief general Valens. Christianity was another hot-button for the two when the Egyptian Bishop Peter of Alexandria went into hiding to be replaced by Melitius, setting off the 'Melitian Schism' between the supporters of the two and a Synod was called for. Along with this and the Arian Controversy, Licinius showed his impatience by expelling his Christian troops (unwisely dividing the army) and ending tax exemptions to all clergy.

In 323, Constantine crossed Licinius's last line in the sand by personally defending Western territories from Goths and Sarmatians. In high protest, Licinius gathered troops and marched east for Nicomedia. An unsuccessful route at Hadrianopolis on July 3, 324 caused Licinius to flee to Byzantion, where he was defeated in a naval battle to Constantine's son, Crispus, then fleeing to Chrysopolis across the Bosporus. Finally, he surrendered to Constantine in 324 and was imprisoned and executed for his sedition a few months later. The emperor would also, by now, take note of how this city and its isthmus would make a stronger defensive military position than Nicomedia or Thessalonica had been.[49] Not as dramatic a vision against Maxentius, but just as historic as another victory led to the founding of the City.

Yet, the converted population of the Empire would see the infamy from Constantine's will in the middle era of his reign, marring the Christian ideal of his perfection. Severe taxes and draconian laws, pagan intolerance and bloodshed, neutrality in Christ's nature as the Church tore itself apart, and now an infighting war of aggression would take its toll on the Emperor. Even a family sex scandal in 326 between Crispus and his stepmother, an affair worthy

---

[49] Treadgold, 39.

of an ancient Greek tragedy, led to a possible assassination attempt and the executions of both put Constantine's reputation in peril. But, at the discovery of the well-defended Byzantium in 324, this is where his destiny would truly take shape and Byzantium's story would truly begin.

Diocletian had been a roamer and whatever city he was in at the time was his capital, traveling around the East with his entire court.[50] Yet, such a capital had been thought of before by Constantine; the Emperor considered using the plains of Troy in western Asia Minor itself as its foundation. A symbol of Greek pride and conquest would have been appropriate over Troy's defeat, but, the city on the Marmara offered more and a chance for a new symbol to emerge. Constantinople – the 'City of Constantine' was a Greek verbal transplant by a life-long Latin speaker. And indeed, the City was a subtle blend of the old Greek Classicism and the new Christian Empire. It began in 328 with the first milestone planted, or the *milion*. When it was officially founded on Monday May 11, 330, the emperor christened it by appointing his son Constantius to be his *Caesar* and successor the same day.

But, like Rome, it was not built in a day; Zosimus notes the city which would become the largest in Christendom started at a mere eight kilometers (five miles) squared.[51] It would only start with four arches, two senate houses, harbors of an inlet easily protected and regulated by a chain, a stadium, baths and an aqueduct by Constantine's death who was also known as a 'cheerful giver' of Christian Churches.[52] The plans were well known, however, that it was to be grander than Nicomedia or any other eastern city. In fact, the city was not a mere backwater never touched by the Empire; in the third-century, the emperor Septimius Severus I (193-211 CE) had its walls strengthened against Danubian invasion in the early third century and it was Constantine's wish to strengthen them more. In the days before Alexander the Great, it traded well in northern furs, woods, and amber, eastern spices and flax, papyrus, and oils from the Mediterranean.[53] To populate such a place, Constantine encouraged wealthy western patrons, both Christian and Pagan, to settle there.

Within the city, the Mese, or the magnificent forum begun by Septimius Severus, was completed. Constantine even added eastern pagan monuments

---

[50] Brownworth, 20. Mostly, though he stayed near Nicomedia, visiting Rome only once in his life.

[51] Scarre, 208.

[52] Brown, 26.

[53] Herrin, Judith. *Byzantium: the Surprising Life of a Medieval Empire*. Princeton, NJ: Princeton University Press. 2007, 5.

such as the 'Serpent Column' taken as a trophy when the Persians of King Narseh were defeated at Plataea. Ancient landmarks included an obelisk from Karnak which was taken from an Egyptian triumph[54] in 10 CE by Augustus Caesar and made by Tutmosis III (1481-1425BCE), and one of the city's classical features before Constantine was the 'Maiden's Tower' where the mythical Leander swam to his love, Hero. A golden statue of Apollo was re-carved to resemble Constantine, crowned with golden rays found to be containing the Nails of the Crucifixion. Buried under the column of the statue by Constantine's priests and astrologers was the Sacred Cloak of Athena, the ax Noah used to build the Ark, and the Baskets of the Fishes and Loaves.[55]

Of course, these were juxtaposed with holy churches and relics: The Church of St. Irene was built in the city, housing a piece of the True Cross in a universal orb held in the hand of Constantine's giant statue, an invaluable holy relic from the Crucifixion donated by the Imperial mother, Helena. Even the Empress Constantina used the city's coffers to donate restoration to the Nativity of Bethlehem and the Olive Groves of the Holy Ascension along with places in Tyre and Antioch.[56] Unfortunately, Classical learning would decline over time as this city was not the library and academic centers such as Pergamum, Alexandria, or Antioch. In the end, the Christian City would lose touch altogether from its Classical and eastern roots.[57] The Column of Constantine would also stand until today, restored by the Ottoman Sultan Mustafa II Ghazi in 1701. Now, though, it is a haunting reminder of Byzantium's triumph by Islamic culture such as Istanbul is today.

Another more unintentional goal achieved was the return of the city-state mentality of ancient Greece. There is a difference in what the Emperors would do for their Empire versus the City. And due to the rise of Christianity in urban centers, Bishops, administrators, clergy, all would represent and be identified by their cities and not dioces for their sacred duties. The rural areas outside a city were always the realm of the Pagans that shunned cosmopolitan life for that and other reasons. So, for many centuries, that would be the difference between the thinking of peasants versus urbanites. To be added, most peasants found it safer to live in the rural areas outside the city, but still were protected by the city walls if space were available alongside the cemeteries mostly put there. They

---

[54] Norwich, (EC), 65.

[55] Brownworth, 23.

[56] Eusebius, *Life of Constantine*.

[57] Norwich, (EC), 63.

would mostly be identified with the 'suburban' Romans of the middle and noble classes. Senators and peasants alike were enticed to the City with a new sense of social mobility little seen in the West.[58]

Modern historians would also point out, dispelling myths of the city's unconquerable geographic location that the City was in the heart of its own enemies. 'Sarmatians on the lower Danube . . .Ostrogoths north of the Black Sea and . . .the Persians, whose great Sassanian Empire by now extended from the former Roman provinces of Armenia and Mesopotamia as far as the Hindu Kush.' As well as military consequences, trade would be in the hands of these barbarians, each a stake covered by Persian and Gothic authorities. Only the Mediterranean around Armenia proper, Syria, and Asia Minor would have the least amount of enemies, all based on Herrin's trade research of the region. Elsewhere in the economy was the emperor's policy on the Empire's coinage. The taxes of the *chrysagyron* were paid in the new gold *solidus* (*nomisma* in Greek), which he changed to seventy-three coins per pound from Diocletian's sixty. Also, Constantine split his household budget (*comes rei privatae*) from the official largesse given to public funds and sacred donations (*comes sacrarum largitionem*).[59] This would cut down, at least, embezzlement in the Imperial Grand Palace otherwise enjoyed by certain eunuch administrators (*cubicularii*).

All of these eastern improvements and the official moving of the capital from the West cost Rome dearly. It was now decided that the West was to remain inferior and a second-class region in the Empire. Though Constantine would still visit it (once), there was no *Augustus* or *Caesar* to reign in Rome or Ravenna. The Empire would return to the time before the Tetrarchy, with the East now the central authority and the West to be plagued by certain amounts of neglect, fortunate that the West had no eastern Goth or barbarian tribes, and no Persians rushing its gates for the moment. It was not perfect, but it was the best situation the reality of the times for which to hope. Caution internally was still a goal with the Praetorians disbanded by Constantine, so the imperial secret police, the *agens in rebus,* were developed as informers on corruption and sedition. One way to achieve this was by giving them the courier-ship of the postal roads, traveling and spying with another purpose for sensitive missions and vital embassies.[60]

Constantine's last adventure was attempts at Christianizing Persia by

---

[58] Brownworth, 21.
[59] Treadgold, 40.
[60] Decker, 144.

penetrating Armenia and enthroning a nephew, Hannibalianus, as its 'King of Kings' and the 'King of Pontus' who then married his cousin, the emperor's daughter. This was a method of diminishing the power of the title *Caesar* to heighten his own son's authority and this Persian conversion and Roman-Oriental autocracy ran out of steam quickly as Constantine fell ill in 337 when he traveled to Helenopolis to be treated in their hot springs. He converted to Christianity officially, at last, in white robes and died on Whit Sunday (May 22) of that year, seven years and eleven days after founding his masterpiece of a legacy.[61]

The most important fact about his death was his deathbed baptism and conversion. Why then? Edward Gibbon gives the best answer, although from the point of view from a biased theist, 'The sacrament of baptism was supposed to contain a full and absolute expiation of sin; and the soul was instantly restored to its original purity, and entitled to the promise of eternal salvation. Among the proselytes of Christianity, there were many who judged it imprudent to precipitate a salutary rite, which could not be repeated; to throw away an inestimable privilege, which could never be recovered.'

Was this another cynical explanation, perhaps, of Constantine's practicality over authenticity? Maybe, but a grain of truth lies in the belief of salvation and purity to wipe away decades of slaughter, Imperial vices, and compromise. He believed in the power of Christianity on earth, with his army, his City, his religious policies, and their interpretations, so the power in the Afterlife is not such a high step. The timing was something duplicated time and again to clean the soul before it could be besmirched again. Even Voltaire was baptized in such a manner (though he is not to be compared to the 'thirteenth apostle'). Constantine was buried in Rome, to the dismay of his Constantinopolitan subjects who buried their dead, in the center of the symbolic twelve coffins of the apostles in 337.

The Age of Constantine or of any such man is usually a myth, relating the will and vision of one man only shaping society and millions of lives and their consciences. If this were true, no pagans would exist, Rome would have capitulated its status with no grumbling, and the divisions in the Church was his doing in personality. All of this, of course, is false, yet, if Constantine were a product of his times instead, the picture would be more realistic. Eastern cult-like, as well as Christian, zeal caused violence and unwillingness to compromise in emperors long before and after Constantine. The East was a force militarily

---

[61] MacMullen, 224.

and economically in Diocletian's day at the latest. And the idea of a 'City of Godly Paradise' was inevitable when conversions were multiplied in all classes of the cities. Even the *Life* written about him by Aurelius Victor[62] stood also as a funeral oration in the annals of Christianity. Constantine's real innovation was raising Christians to the positions of provincial administration and the *Illustrious* class of legal status that included a Christianized Senate; it was one act that allowed a domino effect of change leading to a new era in Western civilization. His greatest accomplishment was the subsequent dynasties and cultures that would survive him as the Byzantine achievement for over a thousand years.

## CONSTANTINE II
### (337-340)

## CONSTANS I
### (337-350)

## CONSTANTIUS II
### (337-361)

As the Christian Empire would began to flourish as Pagan conservatives such as Zosimus declared that this was the true end of Roman values, disfavor by the gods, and a 'true ruin of Roman affairs.'[63] With the source of the establishment in the Empire now dwindling, it was a necessity that a strong continuity of policy and the constant energy of an emperor maintain order to avoid more civil conflict. Yet some degree of conflict seemed inevitable as all three sons of Constantine were 'born into the luxury of the palace, served by attendants and surrounded since birth by the cloying ceremonies of royalty. Educated by swarms of tutors, flattered by the attentions of courtesans, they had little time to develop brotherly bonds, and this led to a troubled family dynamic to say the least.'[64]

---

[62] Aurelius Victor. *Liber de Caesaribus,* trans. by H. W. Bird. Liverpool, UK: Liverpool University Press. 1994.

[63] Kaegi, Walter. *Byzantium and the Decline of Rome.* Princeton, NJ: Princeton University Press. 1968, 232. A thorough evaluation of Zosimus and his views are outlined in all discussions on Constantine I.

[64] Brownworth, 28.

The eldest living son of Constantine upon his death, Constantine II, would become the *Augustus* of the East on September 9, 337. In reality, the three remaining sons of Constantine – Constantine, Constantius, and Constans, would rule the Empire in a state of semi-independence until 350. This marks the death of the Tetrarchy, wherein now, it would stay mainly free of abdications, peace conferences, and with or without blood or marital relation or by merit. Now, the Constantinian dynasty of three was the norm with titles of *Augustus* or *Caesar* given by a consolidation of hereditary power by Constantine.

Constantine II was born in February, 317 when his older brother, Crispus, was fourteen. This means he was about nine when his brother was executed for conspiracy against the emperor and so, he was made *Caesar* of the East. Upon his father's death, he was passed over in succession of the East for his brother Constantius and would be *Augustus* of northern Italy, Spain, Gaul, and Britain. Although the Praetorian historian Sextus Aurelius Victor gives a good account, not enough is said about this young ruler who died three years later. Upon Constantine's death, a scrap of parchment was (conveniently for the three sons) found, implicating the three brothers' uncles, Julius Constantius and Dalmatius, with poisoning him. So, these two possible claimants and probable sources of rebellion and their sons were executed by the Praetorians. As things evened out, the last brother, Hannibalianus, was killed as well, freeing the East for Constantius. The three sons also agreed with the Patriarchs of Constantinople Paul and Eusebius to uphold the Nicene Creed of 324. Constantine II proved capable in administration as well as he would collect 80,000 pounds of grain from Egypt, enough to feed 240,000 inhabitants of Constantinople.[65]

Constantine II had played a respectable part in his father's military career beginning with the Sarmatian raids of 332, where the *Caesar* killed around 100,000 of the enemy and captured the Gothic King.[66] Perhaps purely for dynastic reasons to unite the Empire under one command, Constantine invaded his brother Constans's western holdings south of Rome. He was defeated and killed in battle at Aquileia in spring of 340. This would mark the first true dynastic battle and death of an imperial brother by his brother, which was to be another unfortunate trend in Byzantium. New problems had arisen when official authority was given to multiple siblings in one Empire, and ambition with personal slights over territory would be the death of civil stability. An

---

[65] Treadgold, 45.
[66] MacMullen, 146-147.

advantage of the purely Eastern Empire being the dismantling of this aspect of the *Augustus/Caesar* relationship (despite the crises in successions).

The youngest of Constantine's heirs, Constans I, was born in 323 and made *Caesar* on the Saturnalia of December 25, 333. He was given the provinces of southern Italy, Macedonia, Thrace, the Danube, and North Africa at nine years old. But, with the defeat of the over-reaching Constantine II by his forces, he later progressed to gaining all of the western territories as *Augustus* at the age of seventeen. He was to keep the cities of Rome and Ravenna, but in 339, gave up this claim to his brother Constantius for military support against Constantine. His prospects were thought to be furthered by a marriage to the daughter of the Christian Cretan family of the Ablablii who was known for their Praetorian and numerous Italian vicariate posts. Unfortunately, these Cretan resources were distanced when she ended up marrying the Persian King, Shapur II.

Aurelius Victor (320-390 CE), however, recounts Constans I's character as a base one as his defeated brother was 'a minister of unspeakable depravity and a leader in avarice and contempt for his soldiers' in his *Book of the Caesars*. So he was the first Christian emperor to follow in the ranks of those emperors that at too young an age gained the absolute rule of (at least half) a world Empire: Caligula, Nero, and Elagabalus. It is then no surprise when he neglected the Danube, taking debauched pleasure with his own German prisoners[67]. Avarice may also mean certain meanness in paying his troops, leading to greater dissatisfaction. In January of 350, at a hunting expedition for a banquet at Augustodunum, a pagan officer named Magnetius attacked the party, succeeding in assassinating the Augustus. Donning the purple as emperor for two years, the assassin gained the entire western territories but Illyricum as the scene of another self-crowning general; he was later found and killed by the usurper's troops. Decidedly, Constans I was spoiled and selfish, whose reign was only extended by his brother's defeat, further proving the decay of the Constantinian legacy.

Constantius II was the 'middle child of the remaining heirs', but won the sweetest prize: control over the administrative and economic center of

---

[67] Norwich, (*EC*), 82.

the Empire and its capital in the East. Because such incongruity between the placements of heirs on the throne, it led to much western resentment and political violence. However, the fact only Constantius arrived for his father's funeral may hint at a closer personal relationship between father and younger son, or at least a respect for tradition. Constantius was of a very serious and sober character in demeanor, perhaps it was this fact that decided the issue.[68] He was a better choice as the eastern violence was well contained, helping make Constantius rule the longest and most prosperous of the heirs to continue the line.

Born on August 3, 317, he was another infant during the fiascos of Crispus and Licinius. He joined a consulate title in 326, even appearing in parades his father could not attend in Rome, with a triumph of elephants marked with the traditional (but by now ironic) 'SPQR.'[69] Becoming *Caesar* of the East in 324, he would later marry a daughter of his doomed uncle Julius Constantius. In 335, the nineteen-year-old would begin his long military career against the Persians of Shapur II, whose brother the emperor had killed in battle. To solidify his policy on this cause, Constantius would move to Antioch, closer to the Eastern front to boost morale and lead more expeditions. By 345, Constantius would take advantage of uprisings in the Hindu Kush, winning victories in the upper Tigris and the Persian front itself in Thrace, until a treaty was made with the King. One consequence from this defeat would be the retaliatory persecution of Persian Christians by Shapur at Sangaree in 348.

The 350's were most kind to the sole Emperor, having taken care of the pretender Magnesius in September 351 in Pannoniar Mursa, and in 356 and 357 receiving for Constantinople the bones of Sts. Timothy, Luke, and Andrew.[70] In another act of preserving the faith of the Nicenes and Arian 'Consubstantualists', he championed these causes with Bishopric Councils at Antioch, Seleucia, and Arminium, deposing the Patriarch Paul to confirm Eusebius to the office. Unfortunately, this clouded the issue of what imperial policy of Christ's nature was and with no clear answer, Constantius was doomed to be seen as neutral as his father had been by the clergy. When riots resulted by his Nicene subjects, they had to be suppressed and the grain dole was halved as penalty. Constantius (and Constans as well), proved to be determined Christians when it came to the zeal of fighting what was described as 'superstition and Paganism,'[71] and

---

[68] Treadgold, 52.

[69] MacMullen, 218.

[70] Herrin, 10.

[71] Gregoire, Henri. 'The Byzantine Church.' *Byzantium: An Introduction to East Roman Civilization,* ed. by N.H. Baynes and H. St. L. B. Ross. Oxford, UK: Oxford

this would be an ardent policy of the two in the 340's. To top it all, Constantius would christen the first Church of the Holy Wisdom (*Hagia Sophia*) to 'house the mystery of the Holy Communion,[72] and surpass the splendor and piety of the imperial Church of St. Irene of Blacharnae in Constantinople.

In the late 350's, Constantius would retire back to Constantinople to settle domestic affairs. He had already over the years filled the coffers by confiscating rebel property and using supplemental taxes. He would extend this in 359 by persecuting Pagan rituals and temples as his father had done. He would also obfuscate and entangle the works of the declining senatorial powers by packing a Senate of 300 to around 2,000 members[73] to include provincial governors, vicars, and other such office holders. The matter of the succession, of course, was the most important focus and the executing of threatening relatives including his cousin, the *Caesar* Gallus, in 349, who was infamously known for the inept and sickening slaughter of Galilean Jewish rebels in Jerusalem.[74] In autumn of 355, his remaining nephew, Julian, was sent to administer the Gallic provinces under the title of western *Caesar*. Still, Constantius would attempt sabotage him by sending as reinforcements 360 men who knew, supposedly, how to pray rather than fight.

Constantius would resent his nephew's youth and popularity until his death in 361, but he had very little choice than to accept him as blood was the only loyalty left to him. Perhaps he sensed trouble ahead given Julian's Greek philosophical and Pagan style of education, despite his Christianity, and also by his growing popularity among the troops when Constantius's prowess was ebbing. When he did attempt to diminish Julian's military and administrative powers, a loyal Western army declared him *Augustus* in 360. Constantius attempted to suppress this unrecognized elevation with Roman troops from Mesopotamia, but fell ill in Cilicia and died in the village of Mopsucrene on November 3, 361.[75] Despite his fever, it was said he was the picture of health, but poison was actually not suggested at the time.[76]

Constantius II had serious challenges in his reign from the start in 337. Constantine's seemingly favored son enjoyed fraternal loss, rebellion, and growing barbarian activity until his reign's later years. Also, irreconcilable

---

University Press, 1969, 86-135.

[72] Brownworth, 84.

[73] Treadgold, 58.

[74] Montefiore, 157.

[75] According to Gibbon, however, it was November 30 as opposed to modern estimates.

[76] Norwich, (*EC*), 90.

differences in the Church marred the Constantinian dream of unity under one ruler and a healthy process of succession. His domestic policies promoted centralized authority by weakening the Senate and reforming the vicarages, governorship, and prefectures as a result. However, he also grew economically on the misfortunes of taxpayers and enemies of the state, real or imagined.

To further fuel these sentiments of tyranny, he used his father's method of a secret police force, the *agens in rebus,* who infiltrated all of the noble courts, ruling bodies, and even the cities themselves. These informers (*curiositi*) would grow in centuries to come and by the fifth century, 1,200 were found in the Eastern half of the Empire,[77] also having an abysmal reputation for paranoia, viciousness, and intrigue, keeping stately manors and even marrying into noble houses. These were Pagan or Christian agents who spied on their own kind to be oppressed by tyrants by informing and aiding in these persecutions.

But, those later years seem shadowed darkly by self-doubt as Constantius feared any favored competence in Julian who was loved by the Gallic regions more than Constantius seemed to have been with his own Eastern forces. He was like an old father who no one paid attention to because of the hope of a fresh, prodigal son. His detestation, unfortunately, went unheard, dying with his worst fear realized – Julian's imminent rise to the throne. Though not as illustrious as his father, he was a competent ruler loyal to his God (if not his Church) and his State in the manners in which he believed was best for others. But, once again, his story would pale to the legends of the last Pagan Emperor.

## JULIAN THE APOSTATE
### (360-363 CE)

Raised in worlds both Classical and Christian, the imperial anomaly of Julian the Apostate is a fascinating example of power and will against a changing society. Spurning imperial tradition of over half a century, his authority was absolute, used in upsetting the old order with a will not to compromise his values. He began his life as a quiet and serious scholar who preferred a studious exile and had no resentment for his family nor any aspirations for the throne. He fell into old patterns of persecuting 'the other' in the Empire and had ambitions later thought to be over-reaching his actual abilities (even by his seminal historian Ammianus Marcellinus (330-400 CE). But he had potential for an enlightened return to Classical education and values, both philosophical and aesthetic.

---

[77] Ostrogorsky, 37.

It is for his turning back on a Christian upbringing and by persecuting Christian historians as the Apostate, a byword associated with blasphemy and immorality today. He was a lover of Neo-Platonist philosophy in which he facilitated, opening new schools and academic chairs in the University of Constantinople with the new anti-Christian ethic of the *Misopogon* ('Beard-Hater') where Christ and Constantine were selected above all others as having harmed the Empire. Partially an astute snob among barbarians, he would keep the traditional haughtiness of the Greco-Roman by finding vile, for example, the beer of the Rhine Germans he commanded. He said it all when he said that he only recognized the god of wine, Dionysus, smelling of nectar as beer smelled of goat.[78]

Born on April 7, 331, at Constantinople and taken to Basilia as an Asia Minor Greek, he was the son of the executed traitor against Constantine, Julian Constantius I, as his early years included living in the shadows of his father's accusations. His brother Gallus was sent to Constantius's court while Julian studied Classicism and Christian texts in Pergamum, Ephesus, Antioch, and Athens in Neo-Platonism under Pagan teachers such as Libanius. Why did he prefer paganism so strongly? Was it a personal choice in the values of the ancients that a certain ideal of Roman and Greek manliness found Christianity weaker and impious? Marcellinus's comments and praise for his more 'manly' virtues may support this,[79] perhaps being an act of defiance against a Christian family such as Constantius's branch causing him to want radical change in what Christian Rome held dear. The question of why this occurred has challenged and inspired many scholars contemporary and modern, such as the Cappadocian Church Father, Gregory of Nazianzus (329-390 CE).[80]

He had an electric personality that charmed the West's army and most of the East, though he was also known for his shyness and an awkward intellectualism. But, typically Christians such as the Nicene St. Gregory Nazianus described him as having . . . 'no sound character. . .' in a disjointed neck, the way he walks and a wild, darting eye.[81] His brother Gallus, the former Praetorian Prefect,

---

[78] Brownworth, 30n.

[79] Ammianus Marcellinus. *The Later Roman Empire (AD 354-378)*, trans. by W. Hamilton and A. Wallace-Hadrill. New York, NY: Penguin Publishing. 1986, 88.

[80] Bowersock, Glen Warren. *Julian the Apostate.* Cambridge, MA: Harvard University Press. 1978.

[81] Gregory of Nazianzus, St. 'Selected Orations and Letters'. *Nicene and Post-Nicene Fathers, I-VII*, trans. by C. G. Browne and J. E. Swallow. Oxford, UK: Oxford University Press. 1900.

more by tradition than trust, had been made *Caesar* by Constantius. Before 355, however, Gallus had been executed for crimes of cruelty against members of Constantius's court. Infamous tales of the cruelty by Gallus were already surfacing: a love of gladiatorial games (which was much more pagan than Christian), neglect of regions by famine, and execution of the entire Antiochene Senate, among others.[82] The execution of his brother did not bode well for Julian's future, as he was the only heir left to Constantius, and at the same time, a potential threat.

Julian had been, since late 355, *Caesar* of the West and commander of the Rhine auxiliaries in Paris as well as frontier defense of the Danube by the Alamanni tribes. Wisely, Julian remained in the West and in his army's company after Gallus's execution, gaining acclaim for his leadership qualities in the face of Constantius's failings. In fear for his life did he return to Constantinople, first visiting the site of Troy,[83] only to be made *Caesar* of the East. In 359, his popularity rose as he, with an army of 13,000, defeated 30,000 Alammani in a major Gallic campaign east of the Rhine at Strausborg with only 247 Roman casualties against 6,000 barbarians.[84] When it ended in 360, a grateful army proclaimed him the western *Augustus* and draped him in purple. The next year, Constantius was dead and Julian ascended to the emperor in Constantinople. It was here that Julian's most notorious histories are told as the role of the true Apostate.

One of his first acts centered on cleaning house in the administration: at Chalcedon, he assembled a tribunal to try members of Constantius's household, court, and military for abuses of power. There is a question of bias as these Christians appointed by the previous Emperor were suspected as possible *agens in rebus,* wherein those found guilty were buried alive – a cruel practice with roots in Classical history. In an ironic twist, Julian was guilty as well by the time of his death in packing his household in a complex structure of grants to 'a thousand cooks . . .barbers . . .and butlers . . .There was a swarm of lackeys, the eunuchs were more in number than flies around the flocks of spring . . .'[85] citing the words of Libanius (314-394 CE).

This court was every bit as decorous and sumptuous as Constantius's with jeweled robes and ostentatious extravagance that would naturally include

[82] Marcellinus, 50-53.
[83] Brownworth, 29.
[84] Norwich, (*EC*), 86.
[85] Libanius. *Selected Works, 2nd ed,* trans. by A. F. Norman. Cambridge, MA: Loeb Classical Library, XVIII, Harvard University Press. 1969, 1976, 130.

corruption in Julian's presence; Julian would only wear simple robes and only call himself 'first citizen' as Augustus had done.[86] What was worse was the erosion of the virtues of Classical Roman manliness and honor in exchange for rampant materialism with its eunuchs and clouds of incense. Christianity was destroying all of Rome's best attributes by its virtues of meekness, forgiveness, and pacifism that defied, especially, the possibility of a Persian war. Was the only difference religious conviction? It doesn't seem so, but absolute power has always invited flatterers and majordomos, it only mattering on how the emperor receives them.

His actions do speak on this, however, as he is known for his abstention to luxury, purging his court and his numerous administrative posts throughout the Empire of corrupt courtiers. Though his household was large, his attitude toward administrators demonstrates a willingness to practice honest government. Of course, he was just as severe with religious authority; he dismissed the clergy from civil government and teaching positions, also recalling Constantine I's old faith of Sol Invictus along with the former Greco-Roman pantheons. It is surprising that a student of Classical Greek culture would choose an eastern Oriental deity as well as the Greek, but it is to be remembered that he was instructed in eastern cities such as Antioch where such cults were numerous.

Here also, he showed a commendable restraint in the treatment of Christians as he ordered no radical *purges*, per say, as Diocletian had, and even punished justly with a respect to fair trials between Pagans and Christians[87]. He detested persecutions and showed promise of a reign not built on bloodshed (religiously). A riot in 362, at Alexandria, over Christian-Pagan reaction to an arrest and execution of a certain officer angered the emperor, though he used leniency on the guilty parties. He did, however, begin to lose popularity when he rebuilt the Temple of Jerusalem on July 19, therefore favoring the requests of the Jews citing prophecies of the Roman Sybilline Books over a prophecy supposedly made by Christ, inciting both Pagans and Christians.

The statues of Hadrian and Antoninus Pius erected within the Temple were removed, considered a blasphemy by the state religion, and synagogues were built by Jews from all over the East.[88] It is written that Julian did so at the whim of a candid conversation with one Jew and that he planned to rebuild the Temple for the 'One Most High God'. This did not contradict Greek Paganism

---

[86] Brownworth, 32.

[87] Marcellinus, 240.

[88] Montefiore, 157-158.

as the God seen as Yaweh by the Jews was well known to be seen as Zeus by the Greeks. Politically, it was a boon to gain approval by the Jews of Babylon for his trek to conquer Persia. This was another blow against Christianity as this city was a new Israel for them given by the prophet Daniel and Christ as the quiet persecution of Christians continued. When arson destroyed the Temple of Apollo at Antioch during the emperor's presence, it caused the city's Christians to be blamed and many were executed, as the city's cathedral was then closed.[89] Other Christians had no choice but to apostatize in order to fit into the emperor's new Empire; restraint was a virtue with him, but tolerance was not in Julian's plan.

But one of his most important policies in his reign was that of the Persians; it was almost certain that the Christianity Constantine fought for would be buried by the victory of a Pagan emperor against the Sassanids.[90] In order to restore his reputation, Julian played at being Alexander to restore the Empire's faith in paganism, as the likeness of Alexander the Great in art propaganda was a hallmark of the Constantinian line.[91] Though Constantius II wished to demure himself from unnecessary conflict, Julian did not detour in what could only be described as naked adventurism. His virtues in pacifying Christian resentment failed when two martyrs refused to remove Christian symbols from the banners of barbarian tribes were beheaded. This was no auspicious start to this campaign and the religious rifts in the Empire threatened the unity of the army the Empire had. The army was paid well enough with the standard five *solidi* and a pound of silver,[92] just a little over the pay scale given at least two centuries later, but this would not regain the lost morale later found in the troops.

Julian wished to attack in a two-pronged assault, splitting the army. Julian's troops would ride east along that of the Euphrates and the other half, led by a general Procopius, would gain Armenian support before riding the Tigris. The target was the Persian capital of Ctesiphon; Julian entered 'Assyria' and took the city of Pirisabora, sacking Maozamalcha as Marcellinus elaborates. At Ctesiphon, unfortunately, the Roman fleet was burned by Julian[93] as the two

---

[89] Treadgold, 60.

[90] Decker, 11.

[91] MacMullen, 66.

[92] Decker, 90.

[93] Out of pure necessity as it would not fit down the Tigris as he intended to meet with Procopius's legions; Treadgold, 61, notes the expedition was seemingly a failure before forces were met with Persia. This may be due to Julian's dividing his forces.

main forces met at the city's walls. On March 5, Julian set for Ctesiphon and on May 29 defeated a Persian army with 2,500 casualties with a mere 70 Romans. Nearing the Persian capital, his forces of 23,000 were slowly succumbing to hunger and thirst and retreat was called on June 16. It was then that tragedy later struck on June 26, 363, as the emperor was fatally struck from behind by the spear through the liver by an Arab assassin.

Of course, the identity of the actual assassin is conjectural and academic; the probable assassin was either: 1) a Persian, 2) a barbarian camp-follower, 3) a Saracen (nomadic Arab soldier hired for either side), or 4) one of Julian's soldiers 'fed up with his campaign'.[94] It is a matter of Syriac translation in some texts from Libanius using the Hellenized word (taienos) for the Syriac for Saracen (tayyaye).[95] Pagans say it was the missile of a zealous Christian Roman soldier, though this seems only propagandistic. Ephraem of Nisibis was said to after the battle find Julian's corpse among the dead outside the city walls.[96] What was most important was that it was now headless, the army roused in panic, fleeing through the deserts of Mesopotamia with no order or preparation against Persian pursuers.

This story is reminiscent of another failed eastern expedition some 700 or 800 years before. The mercenary Greeks under the historian Xenephon writes of a failed mission to re-instate a deposed Persian King, Cyrus. When Cyrus was struck down more than halfway, there was no point in continuing east, so the Greeks fled west through Ionia. It was a relentless race against the Persian general Tissaphernes to the finish, which they eventually reached in Greece. Now, the Romans of the defeated Julian would face the same ordeal of desperate escape, seeing the passing over of the imperial title twice before refuge was possible.

What's to be said about the soaring and then burning star of the Apostate, Julian? His reign and personality were as complex as Constantius, or perhaps Constantine, also open to much interpretation. He had well-written histories from Marcellinus, although he is notorious for his adulation of Julian's works and intentions. However, Julian always seemed sincere in his actions and chose a more austere life he might have studied in a more Stoic Greek education. He was a competent general of the West and loved by the army, but his weaknesses were in underestimating the Persian East, paying the ultimate price. The

---

[94] Bowersock, 117.

[95] Libanius, *Orat.* XXIV.

[96] Bowersock, 10.

rumors of a Christian assassin may even be a sign of army misgivings, though he seemed successful until the Persian capital.

The fact he was the *last* Pagan emperor may have meant that along with being the last of the Constantinian dynasty, and childless, a new era was beginning in Christian sensibilities as being the center of the Empire. Constantinople would only have Christian emperors with Christian civic virtues and an ecclesiastic policy (the age of Caesaropapism) until paganism was irreparably vanquished and a learning of Pagan culture lost in a 'Dark Age'. He captured the imaginations with his exploits with such historians as Nazianzus who noted him as a serpent and Anti-Christ and twentieth-century writers such as Gore Vidal evaluating his humanity and convictions. Renaissance writers portray him as a tragic hero, Enlightenment rationalists as a man of philosophy and reason, and the Romantics as a courageous rebel.[97] Those that could offset Christian faith with Classic objectivity or reason saw the numerous facets on the jewel that was this complicated man's life.

With the end of Julian's reign, cut so short, the first Byzantine dynasty ended on a Persian battlefield. Now, New Rome and the Empire would see a new dynasty in the Valentinians, as the Roman army fled the chaos of Ctesiphon, facing a desperate situation for which Julian was, unfortunately, responsible. The later results were invective by Pagans, a rising power in the eastern tribes, and a controversial crusade against Classical Paganism in which Julian would have seen him despair. In a contradiction which would also define his reign, he was a lover and adherent of the law, sitting among the senators as Augustus had done.[98] His policy was that he was not above the laws of Rome, yet this was heavy-handed, spurned in the case of Christianity, demonstrating classic tyranny. After Julian, any adherence to the ancient institution of the Senate and the Pagan respect of their words would never be repeated under a Christian Empire.

Culturally, Julian allowed a new era of letters to form based on the educational policies of his great-uncle and his love of libraries, building one that had 250,000 volumes by 476 CE. He represented the rhetoric that was countering Christian apologetic in his *Contra Galilaeos*[99] and the 17,000 word *Hymn to Cybele* written in a single night.[100] On his coinage is his youthful and

---

[97] Norwich, (*EC*), 99.

[98] Brownworth, 32f.

[99] Mango, Cyril. 'The Revival of Learning.' Chap. 8 of *The Oxford History of Byzantium*, ed. by Cyril Mango. Oxford, UK: Oxford University Press. 2002, 224.

[100] Norwich, 94.

bearded profile in Classical style in transverse by the Pagan (but Oriental) Egyptian symbol Apis the Bull.[101] The prolific writer and Antiochene, Libanius, used these measures to create his sixty-four orations, 1,544 letters, and fifty-one declamations as he chaired the college of rhetoric at Antioch's university.

Most of all was his *Misopogon* ('Beard-Hater'), an infamous invective mocking the Chi and Kappa of Christ and Constantine, railing on the absurdities of the Antiochene Christians, it also shows the spirit of ingratitude Antioch felt towards Julian as an emperor of benevolence.[102] Christianity had for half a century been the mainstay of religious faith in a new and improved Empire of the fourth century and a re-establishment of civil administration in which Romans could believe. Had he lived, the uphill climb of bringing Rome back to the age of Diocletian would never have stopped in his life, perhaps, and a strong heir would be needed to be in place to continue his vision. Ironically, such an heir could not be as duplicitous with Paganism as his father was with Constantius II and Christianity.

# JOVIAN
## (363-364)

# VALENTINIAN I
## (364-375)

# VALENS
## (364-378)

Along the eastern bank of the river Tigris the remaining army of Julian marched. They had no emperor nor any Roman city that might aid them, as the Persians were surely aware. They kept to harassing the Romans as they fled towards Corduba. In desperation, a senior signatory who had made a limited distinction at Maozamelcha was raised to the purple to find a way home west. The few cries of *'Jovianus!'* were thought to be *'Julianus!'* in the hopes the emperor recovered. When the mistake was found out, supposedly the grief over their monarch was enough that none cared to correct it. This was after the title was offered to the commander Salutius who was a moderate Pagan, but his denial of the responsibility of leading left the Christian Jovianus, son

---

[101] Mango, 'Revival', 228.
[102] Bowersock, 104.

of a reputed Count Varronianus.[103] These lamentations were certainly felt by Marcellinus who might have exaggerated the 'tears', though Julian's death was still tragic as he could always rouse the loyalty of his armies. Jovian's reign was brief and anti-climactic; he seemed only the better of a bad situation.

Ammianus Marcellinus exclaimed how ten battles should have proceeded rather than lose one fortress Julian had acquired. This may be so, but it was not the time to use demoralized men, marshaled by an Augustus no one could have faith in, and defend these places against a fresh Persian defense; catastrophe would have resulted. At least a trip to the capital to refresh the troops and plan the next step was called for. Through a hundred miles of desert the troops marched from Hatra to Nisibis on the Tigris (his general Procopius was to bury Julian, maybe even become successor). Eventually, they did make it to Antioch, where Athanasius of Alexandria met him, celebrating a Christian emperor. In Ancyra on January 1, 364, Jovian took the consulship with his infant son, Varronianus, effectively giving him lone rule. Just afterward, Ammianus writes, a tribune named Valentinian brought the news that his succession was accepted by the Gallic army. Though it was cited as a 'shameful peace,' the negotiations with Shapur II for safe passage could not be countered; Rome lost the regions of the Tigris, Arzanene, Moxoene, Zabdicene, Rehimene, Corduene, Nisibis, Singara, and fifteen more forts.[104]

But during his stay in Dadastana between Ancyra and Nicaea, in February of 364, Jovian died. Gibbon proclaims poison mushrooms (like Claudius Caesar), but Marcellinus outlines the three rumors of the cause: of carbon monoxide being generated from burning charcoal overnight, of the fumes of fresh wall plaster in his sleep, and of indigestion from overeating.[105] Bizarre but natural deaths, murder was not considered, but it is a likely way to die not arriving at the capital with an infant heir. If it was not murder, it was a bad omen that came true for the Empire and incompetence to boot on behalf of the appointed household on staff. A panic had surfaced at that time wherein two tribunes were lynched by the army for a fraud concerning Julian's actual demise. Jovian seemed to have lacked personality or distinctness, but very little time was spent before he died (whether accident or assassination) to judge his actions

---

[103] Bowersock, 118.
[104] Marcellinus, 304.
[105] *Ibid.*, 311.

as an Augustus. After all, in the past, generals from the army without previous scandal and no dynastic opposition had done well for the Empire.

With Julian and Jovian gone in less than a few years, any future of stability in Rome and Constantinople looked bleak. Once again, choices from the army would prevail with some dynastic ambition. The return to the capital with a carefully selected Augustus would set the armies and subjects of Constantinople at better ease as strong military leadership would be needed if the Persian East broke their truce. It would come as a relief to some and a disappointment in others that the new Emperor was a stalwart Christian and an anti-intellectual who cared little for Classical learning. But, an Emperor selected by the army alone saw a return to the time when favoritism by the few put a commander on the throne, hoping he was a good administrator. Of course, Pagan historians would seek to undermine him, as Ammianus Marcellinus wrote of his cruel streak, feeding prisoners to two she-bears he kept as pets. On March 1, leaving Nicomedia, it was conveniently suggested that his brother Valens become Caesar, supposedly to Valentinian's surprise,[106] and it would be done after the return to Constantinople on March 28.

Born in southern Pannonia in the years 321 and 328 (respectively), Valentinian and Valens were sons of Gratianus Major, a peasant commander under Constantius. Their father was appointed Comes of Africa in the late 320's, but was forced to retire over embezzlement charges. Valentinian joined the army and was made a Protector Domesticus and Comes of Britain. He fought first at Mursa Major and then at Mons Selecus against the usurper Magnentius as John Zonaras (1075-1130)[107] and Eutropius[108] both report. It was after this that their father's property in Africa was confiscated by Constantius by showing the usurping emperor hospitality in his home. But what choice might he have had? He had no armies such as Magnentius did, no Praetorian protection, and assassinating him might have cost him, and maybe his sons, their lives. In Gaul under Constantius, he was ostracized in the army over allowing the king of the

---

[106] Marcellinus, 317, Valentinian could be a cunning officer and might have very well manipulated the scene; he had a close bond with Valens and making him heir could not have been far from his mind.

[107] Johannes Zonaras. *Annals,* ed. by Buttner-Wobst, CSHB. 1897.

[108] Eutropius. *Breviarium ad Urbae Conditium,* trans. by F. Ruehl and ed. by J.S. Watson. 1890.

Alemanni tribe, Chnodomarius, to escape after the tribe sacked Lyon. Under Julian, he was present when the armies of Gaul made him Augustus, but may have ostracized himself by refusing to paganize in later years, remaining a Nicene Christian, yet he was still tribune by his accession in 364.

When the armies proclaimed him emperor, upon their insistence, Valentinian's first act was agreeing to make his brother, Valens, co-Augustus of Syria, Anatolia, and Pannonia as his domain as Valentinian took the remaining North and East; Valens would also have armies of the East, the Emperor's presence, and Thrace, totaling 60,000 men.[109] Although he held a great command, he was untested in serious battle with only a few years in the imperial armies Scholae to his credit at just thirty-five years old. The courts they held were made of Pannonian favorites, excluding the traditional aristocratic families known for flattery and suspicion of the military command. When he returned west, Valentinian resumed war against the Alemanni in the Upper Rhine.

In 375, Valens was to show how weak the grip of the Valentinian dynastic claims actually was. As he fought the Persians who had now re-taken Armenia, Julian's former general, the spurned Procopius, proclaimed himself emperor at Constantinople. When this was put down, Valentinian headed east to fight the Quadi and Sarmatians, where during a speech he died of an apoplectic stroke on November 17, 377. His son Gratian would take his western throne and his other son, Valentinian, would be Caesar of the East though they were children next to their seasoned father; yet, the childless Valens had no choice but to accept. In 376, events in the East would take place that would permanently change the West. The Huns first appear in the history of the Ostrogoths, as the tribes of the Tervingi and Greuthungi from the Black Sea region under the King Emaric fled west and asked Valens for sanctuary in Thrace in exchange for a use in the armies of the East. Another tribe already held an undefeated, but exhausted, settlement in modern Transylvania. Valentinian's relations with the barbarians were cautious, but he encouraged Romanization with legal protection of marriage between Roman soldier and Goth civilian (*de nuptiis gentilium*) in edicts found in Theodosian Code 3.14.1.[110]

---

[109] Treadgold, 63.

[110] Sivan, Hagith S. 'Why Not Marry A Barbarian? Marital Frontier in Late Antiquity (the Example of *CTh* 3.14.1)'. Chap. 11 of *Shifting Frontiers in Late Antiquity*, ed.

Valens was an odd choice as co-emperor, given a pot belly, squinty eyes, and 'bandy' legs – described him as nothing short of grotesque.[111] By 377, Roman mal-administration had shown its true colors as lack of food and other necessities were felt by the Gothic refugees as the authorities neglected their duties out of want for themselves. This was so because of corruption and inability to gather civilian supplies in short amounts of time in regard to military need. The Goths organized and rebelled against the Roman garrison at Marianople in Lower Moesia and Syria, the Comes Lupericinus being defeated by a concerted army of Ostrogoths and Thracian Visigoths with the migrating Huns. A year later, Valens himself led armies north to the fields of Marianople (Adrianople) to disperse the barbarians in a historically doomed campaign.

There, around 20,000 Goths[112] created an impenetrable center around the women and children of the settlement and routed the Romans, killing an entire fourth of the Roman army including Valens himself on August 9. A Roman surge of cavalry and infantry used their numbers to march headlong towards a Gothic defensive of covered wagons; they were unexpectedly flanked from the west by Gothic calvary equipped with the stirrup, an innovation unknown to the Romans. At that point, Gothic infantry attacked their northern flank and enveloped the Roman infantry. Poor administration left the Romans badly-equipped with no professional training or discipline – they were easily outmatched. The Goths were not planning any rebellion or even a battle, but Valentinian's insistent policies of 365-6 that the Goth nation was dangerous was a platform he made about the Alamanni to gain political popularity through fear of the enemy,[113] pushing Constantinople to foolish measures. Valens's arrogance and underestimation of the Goths were only accentuated when he refused to wait for the reinforcements of his western *Caesar* Gratian – a vain and costly maneuver.

Upon reflection of Adrianople, this battle is considered the turning point in the history of Late Antiquity as the inevitable signed death warrant of the

---

Ralph W. Mathisen and Hagith S. Sivan, 136-145. Brookfield, VT: Variorum/Ashgate Publishing. 1996, 137.

[111] Norwich, (*EC*), 104.

[112] Penrose, Jane. *Rome and Her Enemies: An Empire Created and Destroyed by War.* New York, NY: Osprey Publishing, (2005), 238-9. This estimate was said to be more accurate than the 200,000 cited by contemporaries.

[113] Drinkwater, John F. 'The "Germanic Threat on the Rhine Frontier": A Romano-Gallic Artefact?' Chap. 2 of *Shifting Frontiers in Late Antiquity,* ed. by Ralph W. Mathisen and Hagith S. Sivan, 20-30. Aldershot, Hampshire: Variorum Publishing. 1996, 25.

Empire and was the military equivalent of a crumbling state and army as at Yarmuk, Manzikert, Recroi, Borodino, and Tet. Never had a defeat such implicit value in this period. The argument of Adrianople's importance comes from the fact that it was soon after that the Goths grew bolder in their frontier territories and the Huns came west to an Empire unready for their tactics that eventually spelled Rome's demise. Yet, Rome's fall would be ninety-eight years afterward and the other two events were mutually exclusive of an inevitable fall. The Goths barbarized the Roman army and it was the mismanagement of subsequent emperors that caused the last fall of 476. It was not simply Rome versus the Gothic hordes and the hordes would win, it was the weak succession of a Ricimer and a mismanaging Romulus Augustulus to militarized Oadacer that let Rome fall. Rome fell to a practice centuries old where the armies ruled the Empire rather than the Roman government. This, therefore, despite what traditionally said, did not come from Adrianople or anything else happening in 378.

What did happen in 378 was bad enough, but by 382, with both emperors dead and the only ones to rule in their stead were the nineteen-year-old Gratian in the West and the seventeen-year-old Valentinian in the East which caused great doubt as to their youth. Administratively, both Augusti sought tax and office reform and in the Senate, Decurion class officers could be appointed if they had land requirements enough to have sons take over councils. They could also take ecclesiastical office and independent tax collection officers and tax courts on complaints and appeals were created under the two. This did seem to halt tax increase under Valens and he would later, in 375, half the amount of tax obligations. Also, the wealth of the pagan temples and heretical Arians was, again, confiscated. These actions against the Arians were applauded by Nicene Bishops such as Basil of Cappadocian Caeserea in the face of Arian radical Eunomius of Cyzicus who went as far to say that Christ had **no** substance (*aousos*) like that of the Father.[114]

Valens's religious policy would be rife with persecution as he showed anti-Arianism by re-exiling the Bishops banished by Constantius, but Julian had tolerated where Valentinian was known for further persecuting them. This was a definite statement, how a missed opportunity to reconcile Arians and Nicene Christians existed. On top of this, he showed a certain superstition when a diviner claimed his successor would have a name beginning with T-H-E-O-D. In a rage at this bad omen, or to keep this a secret from any prospective claimants, Valens executed the soothsayer along with a courtier named Theodore. Harking

---

[114] Treadgold, 65.

back to Pagan tyrants, it would stand as an omen supporting superstition that the Empire would succeed to Theodosius I. Valens's xenophobia and instability were setting in as he even had the Armenian king assassinated when he proved disloyal. Despite this, the new regime of teenage emperors in an Empire now in crisis was not encouraging and the new changes were met with high skepticism.

# VALENTINIAN II
## (382-392)

# GRATIAN
## (375-379)

Two child emperors were now in control of the largest Empire in the known world when bad precedents of this kind were exemplified by Gaius Caligula, Nero, and Constans I as any others who did. Under Roman law, they needed no regents; they were male heirs who were of age to inherit their halves of the Empire. Strong empresses, advisers, anyone would be needed to aid the new Augusti now that a Gothic incursion east to the capital would be imminent. If Constantinople fell, what would happen in the West? The Empire was always surrounded by barbarian enemies from out and would-be rulers and usurpers from within. But now, the legendary Huns were crossing into Roman lands, savagely de-settling the Eurasian lands Goths and Alan tribes had originated, closer to the lands where Adrianople took place.[115]

Gratian was co-emperor with this father in the West, beginning in 367, and was born on April 18, 359, in Sirmium. He ascended at a critical period in the Empire and, of course, his younger brother was less mature, being more interested in shooting game preserve beasts than actual rule. Gratian was described, however, by Marcellinus as possessing competence and warlike virtue, but when his armies successfully routed the Leutensis of the Rhine, he was said to be running away. Gratian almost married the daughter of Constantius II, but was overruled by an official, a clear demonstration of the Augustus's weaknesses at court, and she was smuggled to Sirmium; she was recovered and the wedding took place as he ascended.

The Goths, Huns, and Alans underestimated the Eastern Romans by assaulting Constantinople in 387; they lacked any navy that could attack from the east and north, and breaching the walls Constantine built would never have

---

[115] Marcellinus, 412.

been successful. They took cities such as Philippopolis and some in Serdica and Macedonia, but a contingent of Saracens summoned by Roman pay savagely defeated the eastern forces (Ammianus said their leader savagely drank Goth blood from their slit throats) and for the time being, the City was safe.

On January 1, 379, Gratian rose to co-Augustus with his brother Valentinian II. Challenges would plague the West after his brother's death in 379, as the Spanish-born Comes of Britain, Theodosius, was made Augustus. This relationship was not even strained when Gratian had Theodosius the Elder executed as his son remained publically neutral.[116] In 382, Theodosius would settle a peace amongst the barbarian tribes of East and West. By 383, however, the inexperienced emperor had moved away from the Roman army by preferring and awarding the Alan contingencies in the ranks. When a certain officer, Maximus, in Britain proclaimed himself emperor of the West, Gratian met him in Gaul with his forces. Unfortunately, his Moorish cavalry defected to Maximus and they defeated the Romans and Gratian fled to Lyons.

The barbarians were crafty in somewhat gaining Gratian's trust and invited him to a peace banquet. In 380, he had settled a peace in Sirmium (under an ill Theodosius's guidance), a peace with the Thracian Greuthungi and Trevingi. After the 382 peace, however, a civil war of tribes had broken out in the West and these rebels met with Maximus, wherein Gratian was assassinated in Paris at the banquet on August 25, 383 at twenty-four years old. He was able in battle, but not an illustrious sort with the patterns of a jaded prince. His best decision, indeed, may have been giving power to the elder Theodosius, an experienced general twice his age. Gratian also was the last emperor of Rome to bear the title 'Pontifex Maximus'[117] ('Bridge Builder'), a title afterwards held by the Popes, divesting himself on the insistence of the Milanese Bishop Ambrose (337-397 CE), a strong advisor to Gratian and Theodosius. This was a title meant to 'bridge' the realms of man and the gods in Pagan Rome which offended the Church and Gratian would be the last temporal ruler to have it. It would be revived in 590 by Pope Gregory I to signify it as 'pontiff', or 'chief priest of Christianity'.[118] On his suggestion in Ambrose's Letters and *Epistulae*,[119]

[116] Norwich, (*EC*), 108.
[117] Ostrogorsky, 47f.
[118] Brownworth, 45f.
[119] Ambrose, Saint. 'Opera'. *CSEL, vol.* 73. 1964.

Gratian confiscated the earnings of the Vestal Virgins and an oppressor of Pagan temples and worship.[120]

Valentinian II was born in 361 to the Emperor Valentinian I and his second wife, Justina, also having a sister, Galla, that Theodosius I would later marry. In 365, he was elevated to Caesar of the West, but was only four years old at the time. After lack of success in maintaining peaceful resolutions with the western barbarians, in an unprecedented event, his brother Gratian transferred the eastern throne from Valentinian to Theodosius in 379 after Valentinian and his mother fled to him at Thessalonica. Like his brother, therefore, they were actually puppets to Theodosius and the Frankish warlord Arbogast was only beholden to the senior Emperor over Valentinian's court at Vienne.

As for Arbogast and the Franks, the alliance deteriorated when the Franks would not allow Valentinian's forces from Gaul to enter Italy and put down a rebellion. This rebellion was from a teacher of rhetoric named Eugenius that disaffected Italian troops made Augustus in favor over a young boy hundreds of miles away, Arbogast also supporting the usurper choice and emperor over Valentinian. The next details are heavily contended by two superior historians of the time over what was considered the truth. In May, 392, Valentinian II was found hanging in his Vienne residence as Arbogast swore it was suicide, but the obvious case was agreed upon by Eunapius (b. 346 CE) and Zosimus that Arbogast simply had the boy killed as he had outlived his usefulness.

Either way, the result would be a lone emperor, military veteran, and radical Christian fanatic that opened the way for western Church intervention in any state affair, the first step in the world empire of the Church sought after throughout the Middle Ages and centuries beyond. But, with two child Emperors dead and a new dynasty shaping itself in Roman affairs, the figure of Theodosius the Great would not succumb to barbarian guile. A hammer against Paganism, barbarians of both sides of the Cross would not expect nor receive the weaknesses of the imperial purple of the past.

---

[120] McMullen, Ramsay. *Christianizing the Roman Empire, A. D. 100-400.* New Haven, CT: Yale University Press. 1984.

# THEODOSIUS I 'THE GREAT'
## (379-395)

At this particular time of crisis, a dynamic figure of strong character and focused complexity was needed on the throne of the Empire, and it got it. After Gratian confirmed him as co-emperor and died childless, the responsibility would go to the appointed eastern *Augustus*, Theodosius, almost by default. Technically a member of the family himself (by marrying the sister of Valentinian II, his claim was legitimized), this would result in a new dynasty of *Augusti* and *Caesari* for another few generations. As with Diocletian and Constantine, his rule was invariably a hydra in nature carrying the burdens of military, administrative, and religious duty, most of which would be 'successfully' challenged by the Church. This precedent would result in a new religious culture where the word of the ecclesiastical world could supersede the temporal. He would also be the last to rule a single Empire, east and west, but his succeeding sons and the dynasty would be strong for almost a century.

The Theodosians were nobles from Galatea near Gaul and Spain, also a region of strong Nicene Christian and anti-Arian faith, more so, commentators claim, than the Italian senatorial class.[121] Indeed, the strength of Theodosius's faith and deeds would earn him sainthood in the Orthodox Church. He was born on January 11, 347 in his native Galatea in the ancient Roman province Lusitannia, now modern Portugal. He received as good an education as a wealthy Christian family could, understanding a good handling of Greek and, perhaps in irony, some Classical learning. His twenties were spent in Britain with his father, including suppressing a violent rebellion during the Valentinian crisis. In 376, however, Theodosius the Elder would be executed in this political chaos and his illustrious young son would temporarily be retired from public life. However, in 379, a good reputation from his post in Britain would induce Gratian to appoint Theodosius as the eastern Augustus in his own stead on January 19. His policy of peace treaties with the superior arms of the Gothic tribes in the West would then earn him favor to his subjects by 382. Valens would appoint him as Prefect of Illyrium, Macedonia, and Dacia in 379 and as a fortunate consequence, he did not fight in Adrianople where his benefactor died.[122]

In the 380's, Theodosius would spend most of his time in the West,

---

[121] Williams, Stephen and Gerard Friell. *Theodosius: The Empire at Bay.* New Haven, CT: Yale University Press. 1994, 23.

[122] Treadgold, 69.

containing various rebellions. In 383, a rebellion by the usurper, Maximus, who eliminated Gratian at a state dinner to discuss peace, would break out in Gaul and be appeased by recognition as Caesar by the emperor. As a precaution, Theodosius had already appointed Gratian as Prefect of Illyricum and Pannonia, a true demotion, before his assassination. In 387, Maximus would invade Italy and the unprepared royal family would flee to Theodosius in Thessalonica. Theodosius would march west to suppress Maximus and a year later, he would defeat Maximus twice in Pannonia and finally in Italy. To effectively keep his dynastic plans safe, he entrusted his son Arcadius under the protection of the Eastern Prefect, Tatius.

Later that year, Theodosius would make the Frankish king Arbogast his 'Master of Soldiers' (*magister militium*), though this would give him all but nominal power in the West, beyond the Augustus Valentinian II, of whom he was considered a 'regent'. This first use of the title would be a boon and a disaster for the Empire as it would split Rome into military and political spheres, allowing barbarians to eventually disband the latter with the former. But for a future military Emperor such as Theodosius, this would not be a serious issue as he would collectively handle both spheres without being overshadowed, it being an effective reform for the army. However, in 392, Valentinian II would be dead and Arbogast would be a main suspect to most of the Empire as a murderer. He joined with the usurper Eugenius in 394, and Theodosius fought them in Gaul at the decisive battle at Frigidus. After a strong turn-over, the Emperor would be victorious, Eugenius would be dead, and Arbogast along with his general Flavianus, would fall on their swords.

This was the principle and prime example of the hazards of 'barbarizing' the Roman military command would cause; this was mostly hindsight, however, as the Emperor was at first applauded and eulogized for choosing Gothic troops and officers so 'the barbarians may bleed each other out.'[123] Though in such a crisis, choice would be limited; barbarian allies with higher ambitions in an imperial career would cause unrest and state financial deficits in hiring soldiers until the last time it was to be done in the West in 476. But, the major problem would be in knowing just what barbarian general or king to trust as an Arbogast would attempt to seize power by any means. Lars Brownworth is quick to condemn the Later Empire by means of barbarization in that although immigration had been a source of strength of the empire with emperors originating from Britain and Africa, these foreigners would never

---

[123] Decker, 164.

abandon their language or customs. They would grow more powerful in the government and bring about the Dark Ages, concluding that, 'Though he had no way of knowing it at the time, Theodosius had signed the death warrant of the Roman West.'[124]

Perhaps this administrative undermining was causing the Empire to slip more than the singular loss at Adrianople. An opposite side of the scale is the Goth Magister Flavius Stilicho, a German veteran of the Persian frontier and the emperor's 'Master of the Stables.' He proved to be loyal to a fault to the house of Theodosius, making the Magister system work, before becoming another tragic victim to court intrigues by suspicious royal relatives. But before the Emperor's death in 395, his title would include the unique moniker *Utriusque* ('both'),[125] denoting a universal military position in the West and East. The only limitation was the fact no barbarian could become Emperor (at this point), but this would only induce more puppeteering by regency and assassination to gain a *de facto* chance to rule.

Theodosius was an able administrator. Like many Emperors before them, he employed the detested *agens in rebus* that Constantine and Constantius II had founded. He was seen as congenial and patient, a diplomat in a crisis unprecedented since Diocletian; he was well-known for his placation of his 'allies' (*foederati*) more ably than Constantine I or his heirs were. This allowed him to add barbarian forces to the Roman army to counter enemy barbarians, including the 20,000 Goths of the half-Vandal Stilicho and his commander Alaric at Trieste on September 5, 394.[126] It was most fortunate that the death of Persian King Shapur II and the reigns of Ardashir II and Shapur III left Persia in peaceful times, at least if it only for any urgent need for introspected administration, for fifty years (known as the *Pentekontaetia*).

As a born westerner, it can easily be seen why a military emperor would have more success with western barbarian tribes anyway. Nonetheless, a massive recruiting of soldiers was a strong policy through most of his reign. From Constantinople, he ordered a re-organization of noble troops (hedging a purely professional army) into five numerous units of around 21,000; two of each went to the Court (*in praesenti*), the others to the 'Orient', Thrace, and Illyricum.[127] These kinds of numbers denote the need for smaller sortie troops rather than

---

[124] Brownworth, 43.
[125] Williams and Friell, 132.
[126] Norwich, (*EC*), 115.
[127] Ensslin, 295.

the larger and more decisive battle troops. Tax restructuring, conscription, and compulsory service were common measures and as in Diocletian's time, severe penalties were meted out for pacifists who cut off their own thumbs as to not carry a shield.[128]

He had even married his daughter Galla Placidia to the ill-fated rebel Maximus who misinterpreted this union as a legitimacy in trying to take the throne. In 390, he ordered the same policies between Decurions and their councils as the Constantinian dynasty had, despite it being a great strain on their resources. They did receive higher ranks and privileges for their service, but still at the cost of being tax collectors, which was an unenviable task for local authorities in such a crisis for the peasantry. This year also hallmarked an unprecedented event in imperial history as Theodosius moved the western imperial capital from Rome to Milan for it defensible position in being surrounded by swampland; this became his center in the West diplomatically and militarily.

But his most affecting, famous, and at the same time infamous, policies were those of retaining the dominance of the Nicene Creed and the Church. He would not be baptized until death (as his father had), but before, his ardent Christian faith (which Spanish Romans were especially noted for) would not be suppressed by circumstance. Simple acts such as appropriating the statue of Athena from Lindos was one thing (at least temples and statues were officially considered public buildings and works of art), but another was his massive bans on Paganism: cancelling the historic Olympic Games, suppressing the Delphic Oracle, snuffing the eternal Vestal flame of Rome, dismissing the Virgins dedicated there. In the East was the closing and destruction of many temples in Syria, Pannonia, Illyricum, Egypt, and other sites throughout the Empire. He forbade the worship of Jupiter, Magna Mater, and Pater Liberi and his theocracy facilitated the riots of Christian zeal against the Emperor's wishes, burning of the precious Library of Alexandria and many of its priceless antiquities and manuscripts in 394. In 391, pagans were outlawed in Rome and Egypt; a year later, he did the same to all private and public pagan worship in the Empire.[129] Some customs still survived until 692, however, such as vintners invoking Dionysus and using grapes and bears to tell the future.[130]

Pagans were denied civil rights such as the right to assemble, given to

---

[128] Treadgold, 70.

[129] Norwich, (EC), 118.

[130] Brownworth, 46f.

the Nicene Christians; in the Theodosian Code (XVI, 1, 2)[131] were the exact words of the author's grandfather that Arians, as non-Orthodoxists were 'mad and insane' and had no right to call their heretical churches meeting places of faith.[132] This last vicious act would be a regretful and irreversible event to the rest of history. But, not so oddly, he had a respect for *secular* Pagan antiquities; in the Hippodrome he placed the obelisk of Ramses II (1279-1213BCE) from Karnak, created in 1440 BCE, in 10 BCE. For the City itself, he ordered a new Forum, a weather vane to be used as a public clock such as at the Tower of Winds in Athens,[133], and a commemorative statue of himself on a Column. And of course, some pre-Christian traditions were static in East Roman life[134] as the sagacity and rhetoric of philosophers were still more sought after than the Church Fathers and monks. Popular entertainment was the best example as the idea of mollifying Rome with 'bread and circuses' was catered to by the favorite sport of chariot-racing. This would be of greater value when the gladiatorial games were made illegal in 408 across the Empire by Emperor Honorius for Christian reasons. Despite clerical disapproval, theaters still proliferated with dancing girls, nude pantomiming, Pagan mythological themes, and re-enactments. These clerics had more success closing the gymnasiums where men competed in sports nude and homosexuality was more a norm and a temptation.

His most submissive feat to Christianity was his excommunication and capitulation to St. Ambrose of Milan, also being a strong anti-Arian. Ambrose and the emperor had a strong relationship before his coronation as a confessor and collaborator in faith. Ambrose secular experience as a diplomat to the Goths that killed Gratian, as well as Eugenius, and aided the propping of Maximus as a commander. He had grand attitudes for Theodosius proclaiming him in his obituary of the Emperor, *De Obitu Theodosii* as '. . .a pious emperor, a merciful emperor, a faithful emperor, concerning whom the Scripture has spoken...What is more illustrious than the faith of an emperor whom sovereignty does not exalt, pride does not elevate, but piety bows down?'[135]

Yet, it was tainted at one time by disapproval. In 389, a small rebellion broke out in Thessalonica and the captain of the imperial garrison was murdered,

---

[131]  Theodosius II. *The Theodosian Code,* ed. by T. Mommsen and P. Meyer, trans. by C. Pharr. Princeton, NJ: Princeton University Press.

[132]  Vasiliev, 80.

[133]  Herrin, 13.

[134]  Treadgold, 125.

[135]  Ambrose, Saint. 'De Obitu Theodosii'. *CSEL.* Vienna, Austria. 1964.

upon his hearing of this, Theodosius flew into another of his passionate rages. Ambrose, perhaps present at the court, attempted to temper his anger, but to no avail as 7,000 citizens were ordered trapped within the Hippodrome of the city and massacred to a man. This barbarity reached all ears, an act of cruelty worthy of an oriental tyrant from Milan, to a horrified Bishop Ambrose. As the emperor attempted to enter the Church in the city, Ambrose dramatically refused him entry at the doors and informed Theodosius he faced excommunication for his crimes in Thessalonica.

Theodosius was the first emperor to receive communion years before death (and not on his deathbed) so he had submitted before the Bishop as to ignore spiritual peace was to endanger his soul.[136] He was made to submit publicly and ask for penance and absolution from the Bishop, which he did with the pressure coming from the Church. Ambrose then forgave the Emperor and allowed him entry again into the Church to receive the body and blood of Christ. It was considered a first, true act of religious Medievalism - now Christ would rule Rome and not Caesar.

There would in almost every century of the Empire's existence argument over if the emperor was merely a temporal leader or, as divinely appointed, a symbol of Christ in the Empire. *Christiomimesis*, the Imitation of Christ, was a constant motif of Byzantine art and a topic of the emperor as *sacerdos* and *saeculum*. Yet, it was the public and loyal nobles that would wish to exalt the emperor in life and death. Years after Theodosius and Ambrose, Christ and Emperor would be equals in ruling Earth and Heaven, deifying the Emperor *de iure, de facto*. This transcendent and mystical atmosphere had the divinizing effect in its ritual and ceremony, supplying the *de iure*. This would even be a main topic of interest in the administrative guidelines of the future tenth-century Emperor, Constantine VII Porphyrogenitus.

If this is a rule, Theodosius I definitely proved his dominion over the Empire's *sacerdos* as creator and judge of imperial ecclesiastical councils. At the Church of St. Irene, Theodosius and Ambrose both being fanatically devout anti-Arians, would call the Second Council of Constantinople of 150 bishops in 381, demanding the eastern bishops accept the Nicene Creed and permanently condemn Arianism. But, many Constantinopolitans voiced an acceptance of the Orthodox Patriarch Gregory of Nazianus, successor of Basil of Caesarea as an Arian and one of Theodosius's greatest adversaries. Unfortunately, Theodosius was in no position to take a hard-line stance on Arians as in the

---

[136] Brownworth, 44.

West Arianism was the majority professed faith of the barbarians with whom he treated. Only outside the Roman Empire would the emperor accept Arianism where he had less control and a need for their cooperation.

The wars would end the issue until 381, where a council was called at Constantinople, and where the Nicene Creed was made the official creed of Christianity as faith and as organized religion, all else being heresy to be rooted out. The figure of Christ and the Holy Spirit were both divine and part of the 'Godhead', a single figure where the three parts of Father, Son, and Holy Ghost were all part in a 'Trinity'. Here, Trinitarianism was first officially applied as the foundation of Catholic and Nicene Christianity, a practice held dear to this day. All not accepting this were called 'Macedonians' named for the Arian Bishop Macedonius (these were the heretics worded by Theodosius *demente vesanesque* – 'demented and insane'). And materialistically, any not accepting this new creed were to give up their Churches to Constantinople's investiture.

Not surprisingly, the Patriarch of Constantinople was to be one Nectarius, not Gregory, and it was also now that the Pope allowed the City to be known as the New Rome. It was also an auspicious time in the Church of the West as Damasus I, as Pope, was consolidating spiritual and temporal power in Rome. Though relations between Rome and Constantinople were still deteriorating, Damasus would make certain and official the claim by St. Matthew of Christ's investiture of Rome in light of the Council and adopt the Vulgate translation of the Bible created by the Egyptian monk now known as St. Jerome (347-420 CE).[137]

However, the City's own reaction was one of tolerance among the moderate Constantinopolitans who only opposed the duality of Christ simply by arguing matters outside Arianism.[138] Also, enacting the law on Arian Church forfeiture would face less opposition due to a lack of Arianism in Constantinople. Perhaps Gregory was accepted by eastern barbarian inhabitants of the City such as Ostrogoths, Visigoths, and maybe Alemanni or Huns, resulting in a middle ground between two said evaluations of the Empire's reactions. However the Nicene and Arian Creeds, just like Christianity and Paganism, would have no middle ground.

It was a new era when the visiting Gregory of Nyssa describes, 'Every slave and artisan is a profound theologian. Ask one to change some silver and he instead explains how the Son differs from the Father. Ask another what the

---

[137] Norwich, *(AM)*, 48.
[138] Treadgold, 72-73.

price of a loaf of bread and he replies the Son is inferior to the Father. Ask a third if the bath is ready and he tells you that the Son is created out of nothingness.' In a return to Roman religious values seen under Constantius II, Paganism would be further in its death throes as ritual sacrifice would become an illegal practice, starting with the purposes of divination. The temples that were not allowed re-built would join the Arian churches that had the same fate. Since the end of Julian's reign, twenty years before, Paganism would face its worse opposition.

The emperor saw death coming quickly over a bout of dropsy in his western capital of Milan and he made his preparations for the Empire's future. His succession in the East with Arcadius and in the West with a younger son, Honorius, Theodosius also entitled Stilicho and received the last rites from Ambrose as he died on January 17, 395. His body remained at the Palace until February 26 where Ambrose said Mass and the body was then taken to and buried in the Church of the Holy Apostles in Constantinople[139] where Constantine was buried a half-decade before. Zosimus would mistakenly put the words of religious ambiguity in Theodosius's mouth as one of his last acts. He writes of how a meeting of the Senate was to be called to discuss a question: '...should the worship of Christ or Jupiter be the state religion?' Christ was said to win out and a Bishop was called for the last rites. Zosimus then intimates that, 'Not one answered his summons, nor chose to abandon those ancestral rites handed down since the foundation of the City [Rome]. By observing those rites they had possessed a City that was unconquered for twelve hundred years, and they could not imagine what might befall if they now changed their religion.'

None of this took place, however: If Zosimus truly understood Theodosius's character, the Pagan historian would never question if the emperor would change Christianity in Rome, East or West. He would have been appalled at such a meeting of the Senate. Also, how could no Senator have dismissed Christianity in the legal constitution? Why wasn't one self-respecting Christian (or at least self-serving) noble or Senator not been in attendance to the emperor? That would have been instant hostility to the establishment of Church and State and none of his heirs would have approved.

Zosimus was notorious with his hostility to Theodosius as a devout Pagan in a Christian Empire in his *Novum Historium* written around the Emperor's time. According to his observances, Theodosius had a love of lavish entertainments and after his first wife's death, a weakness for beautiful women that his daughter Galla would exploit to take on marriage in June of 388 with

---

[139] Norwich, (EC), 116.

a war in Macedonia as a result.[140] Zosimus voices allegations of Theodosius hastening the deterioration of the Empire through licentiousness, folly, 'filthy conduct', gluttony, corruption, selling public offices, and weakening the army with foreign mercenaries.[141] But, all other sources never mention any vice of his except extreme temper and a violent zealotry, so posterity might judge Zosimus's scandals as sour grapes at a world in which he could not adapt.

Theodosius spent twenty years holding together an Empire threatening to fall apart. Barbarians flowed in from all sides that only appeasement could offer due to a weak military; after the Persian invasions in 386, only one-fifth of Armenia would be Roman. The Bishops of the Churches were divided over Christ's nature and threatened the maintenance of the Empire's cities with a divided populace. Theodosius was a stalwart and decisive figure that brought a kind of unity that even handled interior menaces such as Eugenius and Arbogast. At his death, the younger heirs of Valentinian were dead, but he offered two new young Augusti under strong female regents and influences such as Galla Placidia and her sister-in-law Eudoxia. In the end, the Empire was in a better place than left by Valens, if only by a small margin.

But, more importantly, the religious character of Europe for almost 2,000 years was decided by this dedicated character. He asserted the Christian faith in a way not seen before and not seen for years to come. Any idea of another apostate Augustus was burnt away by the fire of the zealot, in the fiery language of the ecumenical, and the conflagrations swallowing temples and art existing for centuries. Unfortunately, within the next two decades, in 410, the year the Theodosian dynasty of Emperors would die out, the Eternal City of Rome would also burn.

But in a wider context, the East was militarily beginning their 'Byzantinization'; around this era to the time of Justinian, it was probably on Theodosius's insistence that the army be restructured. St. Jerome provides a clear picture of hierarchy[142] from the Magister Militarum and the regional mobile armies down to the Dux and the frontier forces equating to the Legate/ Prefect and the legionary command exclusively superior to the Tribune and the regimental command. Heavier and more organized mobile and garrison infantry were seen in the eastern Mediterranean basin. Illyricum had 17,500 while neighboring Thrace had 24,500. This was despite that the adult male

---

[140]  *Norwich, (EC)*, 111f.
[141]  Kaegi, 122-123.
[142]  Decker, 69, (Fig. 3.1).

population of the Empire in the military would drop from twenty-five percent in Diocletian's time to fifteen percent for another century as discipline suffered.[143] The Imperial Presence in Constantinople had a combined force of 42,000 mobile troops.

The Egyptian and Nile region would have over 60,000 troops garrisoned and the Armenia–to-Palestine region would total 90,000. Dacia and Moesia would garrison over 43,000. Combined this approximates around 280,000 troops mobile and garrisoned in the nineteen divisions of the Roman East.[144] This heavy militarizing of the Eastern Empire was solid ground for the changes coming in the next three centuries to the East when future emperors would combine civil and military authorities in 662. Theodosius saw an accumulation of soldiers rise over the West by 395 and this would constitute the Roman army beyond the fall of 476. As for the numbers of Visigoths, Ostrogoths, and other invaders by the years 406 to 407, they counted in the hundreds of thousands, though it is rightfully believed the commentator Eunapius may have miscalculated.[145]

As opposed to Constantine, Theodosius, ultimately, was only 'the Great' when it came to triumphing Christianity (although he waited until February, 380, to be baptized). He did restore some peace under his 'allied' policies, but lost territory as well to Persia and the Goths. But, his success was growing by 395 and a longer life would have earned him an even better place in the annals of Byzantine history. As for his care of the people, he showed Christian mercy in allowing thirty days for the condemned or exiled to settle his worldly affairs, including leaving behind some wealth for his children who would be free from account of the parents' crime. As for the peasant, farmers who sold product to the government would not do so for any lower than the open market was allowing.[146] As harsh a master as he was with his faith, he showed a penchant for fairness, seemingly, to those left on Earth. Finally, his savagery before Classical and Pagan learning, as a zealous anti-Julianist, was still an unforgettable crime to history and the extent of its harmful effects may never be fully known in today's culture of Classicism and Hellenic study.

---

[143] Treadgold, 112.

[144] Treadgold, Warren. *Byzantium and Its Army: 284-1081*. Stanford, CA: Stanford University Press. 1998, 48.

[145] Bury, J. B. *History of the Later Roman Empire: From the Death of Theodosius I to the Death of Justinian, vol. I*. New York, NY: Dover Publications. 1958, 104-105.

[146] Norwich, (*EC*), 117.

# ARCADIUS
## (395-408)

Now, the two Roman capitals were divided and would remain forever so; Theodosius's elder son Arcadius ruled the East since 395 and his younger brother, Honorius, from the West starting from 393. Again, two more Emperors were now the *Augusti* of the Empire being only eighteen and sixteen, despite what the ascension of Theodosius had designed to eliminate as a liability with the sons of Valentinian I. This could have spelled disaster for Rome as it did after Constantine's and Valentinian's deaths with foreign generals as regents and weak puppets on the throne. Once again, the hereditary method of succession showed to be inadequate at another important juncture in Rome's history. But, looking at these two, can it be that the situations they were exposed to with the Church, the barbarians, and the army beyond their control deciding the fate of two princes who were to manage an Empire?

Another question develops concerning the fall of Rome in 410 and 476: Was it the further barbarization of the western armies that led to such calamities that the witness and writer St. Augustine would see as signs of God's wrath, or was there another answer to be later considered? Diocletian had an answer perhaps sufficient when saying that the new Oriental culture of the court he provided included restricted access to the Emperor; he once decried this as something easily abused by flatterers and illusions when in the rule of the weak and inexperienced.[147] This drives to the heart of the matter as the story of Arcadius as Emperor was more the story of these barbarian generals and their accomplishments as the boy Emperor's youth and unpreparedness was the main catalyst for such bold moves for the Goths, Vandals, and Huns. The worst of these foreign menaces were the Huns, notoriously known for their efficiency and savagery in taking Caucasia, Armenia, and Syria in only one year.

Arcadius was born in his father's native Andalusia at Galatea in 377, the son of Theodosius with his first wife, Aelia Flaccila. As he had an absolutely non-intimidating presence and appearance, many doubted he could be Theodosius's son; he was 'small, dark and swarthy, slow in speech and movement, with heavy-lidded eyes that always appeared that he was in sleep.'[148] Arcadius's popularity would wane as the number and strength of Gothic and Vandal influence in the 'regency' of his reign would increase; many catastrophic events in Arcadius's

---

[147]  Bury, (*LRE-I*), 116.
[148]  Norwich, (*EC*), 121.

time occurring to be seen as God's disfavor with him. The Church History of Philostargius (368-439 CE) would include earthquakes, droughts, solar eclipses that showed the stars at daytime, and even the landing of a cone-shaped meteor.[149] As he lacked the motivation and authority to act independently, the Christian orator Synesius of Cyrene (373-414 CE) would describe him generally as spineless as an 'inert jellyfish.'[150]

When Theodosius died, Arcadius and his half-brother Honorius were left in the care and guidance of Flavius Stilicho, Magister of Soldiers, one barbarian who would at least act in the pairs' best interests. This effectively made Stilicho master of the Empire as well as the leader of the decisive role of the army in Rome. Despite this, however, the *Augusti* were residing in the capitals of Constantinople and Milan as Arcadius was succumbing to the influence of the Eastern Prefect Rufinus with Stilicho in the West. Though now of age in 395, Arcadius did not have the wit and will of his father and Rufinus had the powers of the Augustus in theory; he was made *Praepositus Sacri Cubiculi* (Super-intendant of the Sacred Bedchamber) responsible for Palace meals, the cushions at table, and wardrobe. Though a seemingly odd office to wield power, but still controlling the daily workings of the Palace, he could control access to the Emperor (as Diocletian feared as a flatterer), the Senate, the generals and even the City – a future custom throughout the history of Byzantium.

Opposed to him was the wife of Arcadius, Aelia Eudoxia, a strong personality in her husband's rule and years beyond Rufinus as the daughter of a Frankish general, Bauto. Upon Theodosius's death in 395, the new emperor married Eudoxia at the insistence of a court advisor, the eunuch Eutropius, severing the hopes for a tie to Rufinus by dynasty, the eunuch making a play to weaken his barbarian adversary. To add insult to Rufinus's well-deserved plight, Zosimus gleefully relates how on her wedding day, Eutropius's officials in gold plate, ceremonial soldiers, and a throng of curious and optimistic subjects all came to 'fetch' her to her bridegroom, though it is doubtful this happened.[151]

Meanwhile, the difficulties against the Eastern Prefect were compounded by the influx of eastern barbarians as Visigoths and Huns threatened to pour into the East. The Vandal king Alaric was summarily appeased by Rufinus to settle in Thessaly by bribery, although he later revolted on April 27, 395, seizing Athens, Corinth, and the Peloponnesus. As a response, Eutropius cultivated the

---

[149] Kaegi, 167.
[150] Treadgold, 135.
[151] Norwich, (*EC*), 121.

armies of Thrace, the East, and Illyricum into five separate commands south-east to cover ground.[152] A desperate Rufinus demanded Stilicho send troops east, as another army under another barbarian, Gainas, marched to the City. Unfortunately, Gainas decided to assassinate Rufinus on the spot on November 27 as he also was supposedly expecting to become co-emperor with Arcadius.[153] Whether this was the work of a scheming, desperate Stilicho is speculative, but Arcadius then found himself guarded by Eutropius as Alaric plundered the Peloponnese for the second time in two years.

Eutropius welcomed Gainas's troops with the five commands he had re-organized throughout the East and ignored Stilicho, speaking against the concerted plot against Rufinus, with whom he appeared to side. In 397, Stilicho was himself fighting the African Visigoths of Gildo, who was the former Count of Africa attempting to split West and East by supplying Africa to Arcadius instead of Honorius to upset the delicate balance in the map of the Empire.[154] After victory, Stilicho settled the barbarians in Epirus near Greece, out of Africa, and was appointed Magister of Soldiers for Illyricum to spread his influence east. The able Eutropius, meanwhile, was facing decisions in two spheres of influence; first, he appointed the brilliant preacher John Chrysostum (349-407), or (Golden-Tongued), as Patriarch in 398 who was a renowned Christian apologist, orator, and anti-Arian. At the same time, his armies were failing against the Huns now invading the East, so the eunuch appeared at the head of an army and drove them back to Armenia in 399. He was made consul the same year, beginning precedents to the Byzantine eunuchs whose infirmities disallowed succession to the throne directly, but, allow these 'beardless men' to suit the posts administrative and military in the Arab Caliphates.[155]

A turnover was in the works for Gainas, who defected to the Phrygian Visigoths that invaded Anatolia. As far as Eutropius appearing in failure before Arcadias's court (though it is not recorded he did anything himself), fleeing to Chrysostum for sanctuary, he only alienated Eudoxia, just before his subsequent execution. The Eastern Prefect Aurelian took over as Arcadius's adviser as the Gothic nation of Gainas now allied against the Romans. The foreign 'mercenary' armies of Goths once used by East Rome were overthrowing key administrators with their advantages over the under-recruited Romans. The

---

[152] Treadgold, 81.
[153] Norwich, (EC), 127.
[154] Bury, (LRE-I), 121.
[155] Herrin, 61.

barbarization and fall of Rome was, more or less, under way as Constantinople's resentment exploded in a plot against the 7,000 Gothic inhabitants, trapped by a mob at the Gates and massacred by the citizens. Gainas was made Master of the Armies of the Emperor's Presence in early 400, but was eventually defeated that year by the Visigoth Fravitta, and the Hunnic King Uldric sent to Arcadius Gainas's head as a trophy on December 23.

Finally, in 401, Chrysostum urged Arcadius to send Alaric and his Goths west from Illyricum and when Fravitta protested, playing the dangerous power game in Arcadius and Eudocia's court, he was executed on John's orders. John Crysostum had high favor with Eudoxia, and in being engaged in an affair, with certainty, has reputed to have been the real father of Arcadius's heir, Theodosius II.[156] Meanwhile, Gothic King Alaric had headed straight to Theodosius's capital at Milan to settle in the West with his Goths. In 402, Stilicho chased him back to Illyricum from Milan and settled the West's capital at Ravenna on the Adriatic, naturally protected by the sea which the Goths had yet to master. The changing of the western capital in one century only spells the desperation of its military, relying on geographic considerations alone, and quickly abandoning the city of Rome itself to desperate vulnerability.

In 404, the controversial Patriarch John Chrysostum was exiled by Arcadius after riots in the City commenced concerning the Nicene-Arian Creed controversy. In 403, such an example was an Egyptian monk who was appointed to be the Patriarch of Alexandria, Theophilus, was the center of such religious crisis and chaos in Constantinople, being summarily executed. Religious anarchy over the Nature of Christ was again spreading as Chrysostum was a Nicene and the Patriarch of the key city of Alexandria who contested this was an Arian. This further widened schisms in the West against Pope Innocent I, a man of impeccable integrity and morality, first to use the title of 'Pope' and to Latinize the canons, going so far as to declare only he could call Synods and Councils in the West, not the Emperor.[157] So, it was now a combination of religious division, court intrigue, and self-interest by the growing barbarism of any office they could receive that was allowing the West to rapidly disintegrate.

In that same year of 404, Eudoxia died during a miscarriage, such a tragedy allowing any opportunist to pick up the mantle of *de facto* Emperor of the East, as the idiotic Honorius was still western ruler until 410. For the rest of Arcadius's reign until his death on May 1, 408, he was now dominated by

---

[156] Treadgold, 85.
[157] Norwich, *(AM)*, 21-22.

the Praetorian Prefect Anthemius, who would appoint the Patriarch Atticus in 406, ruling the City, Church, and State in conjunction. Anthemius, in his ruthlessness, had Chrysostum deposed so harshly he died shortly after from his treatment in Pontus in 407. One positive note in this stark corruption, as the first had been torched by Chrysostum's followers in a revolt, was the erection of a new Church of Saint Sophia improving upon Constantius II's, one not to be improved upon until Justinian I. Upon his death of a fever, Arcadius's seven-year-old son Theodosius would rise to the eastern throne. Yet as he was another child-Emperor and another set of regents and opportunistic courtiers would invariably follow to exploit him, first of all Anthemius. The Empire could only hope this would turn out well as the cycle of history had barely taken a breath of respite before it was repeating again.

Not much can be said on Arcadius's personal rule as he had no personality except as a weakling who was easily controlled and stifled by family and allies. But it is said as he ruled the East in the first truly divided Empire, he was the first 'Byzantine' emperor. The Empire made clear resentment at the use of barbarian commanders in charge of the government, especially when Rufinus died. The poet Claudius Claudianus (370-404 CE) would write an epic poem regarding him as a caricature of violence and too sinful a man to enter Hell, thus the judge of the dead Rhadymanthus lowers him into a pit far from Tartarus.[158] The military victories and defeats, religious harmony and controversy, all were the works of mostly eunuchs and barbarians. Can Arcadius be written off as just a facilitator of Rome's deterioration or a non-entity? Of course he could, but as the linchpin between a long-lasting barbarian presence at Court and as a father of one of the Empire's greatest reformers, even his timidity before Rufinus, Eutropius, and Stilicho had its place.

To Arcadius's credit, however, came decorative building projects lasting for centuries, starting in 395 with the magnificent marble portrait of the emperor's head in the Forum of Theodosius, still his foremost portrait. In 403, right in the Forum named for him in Constantinople as it depicts numerous historical scenes, including the 400 revolt of Gainas[159] and the prophetic reliefs about Arthurian 'Savior Emperors' by future Emperor Leo VI 'the Wise'[160] is the Column of Arcadius. Based on the Roman Columns of Trajan and Marcus

---

[158] Bury, (*LRE-I*), 113.

[159] *ibid.*, 135.

[160] Reinert, Stephen W. 'Fragmentation (1204-1453)'. Chap. 10 of *The Oxford History of Byzantium*, ed. by Cyril Mango. Oxford, UK: Oxford University Press, 248-283. 2002, 283.

Aurelius and sketched in detail in 1574, now only the pedestal remains of it in the city of Istanbul. Arcadius was also the subject of *De Regno* ('Oration on Kingship') by Syenius of Cyrene, Bishop of Ptolemais, where the Empire, upon the 'razor's edge', needed the 'Assistance of God and the Emperor to crush the danger which had been troubling the Roman Empire for a long time.'[161]

## THEODOSIUS II 'THE CALLIGRAPHER'
### (408-450)

The infusion of barbarian tribes of all kinds: Ostrogoths, Visigoths, Huns, and Franks put the entire Empire under siege in a crisis worse now than in the reign of the first Theodosius. Barely restrained resentment, lust to conquer and dominate, the Arian faith going unrecognized, and revenge for wrongs real or imagined inflicted by arrogant Romans all were motivation for any barbarian ruler. In 410, the Vandal Alaric would find it in Rome and it would explode in a raid of violence, bloodshed, and abomination upon which Saint Augustine of Hippo (354-430 CE)'s Platonic history *City of God* would be based. In Constantinople, a child-Emperor promised no relief to these difficulties and no easterner was assured who wasn't outright controlling him. But, over the years, with western degradation to barbarians and the Huns led by the rising king, Attila, this internal strife would be met by the mind of what would be a great lawgiver.

Theodosius II was born to Arcadius and the Frankish princess Eudoxia (bestowing him with a half-barbarian heritage) on April 10, 401. The young Theodosius was the youngest ever to be a Roman co-ruler until then at less than a year old when crowned Augustus on January 10, 402. His whole life was given to an extensive Pagan-Hellenic education in the liberal arts, including from the literary circle of Troilus of Constantinople, a friend of his regent[162] and later, in 425, his program when the University at Constantinople would offer more Greek, than Latin, linguistics. His first procession was expert in Roman pomp and ceremony, trimmed with gold and purple banners with regiments bearing lit candles including the court and Senate wearing white as if blanketed in snow, his father behind him as he brimmed with pride.[163] He also showed

---

[161] Kaegi, 152.

[162] Bury, (*EC*), 213.

[163] Hussey, J.M. *The Byzantine World.* New York, NY: Harper & Row Publications. (1961), 133.

a certain worldliness even in his leisure, as he had introduced the royal game of polo from Persia and erected grounds in the Great Palace to be restored for centuries to come.[164]

His parents having both died by 408, his guardian was the Eastern Praetorian Anthemius who, under the Augustus's name in 413, constructed the famed Theodosian Walls around the landward ends of the isthmus of Constantinople to remain until 1453 with the advent of gunpowder and canonry warfare. The genius of its engineering mechanics for defense was the use of limestone to caulk the stones holding it in place.[165] As it hardened, the limestone had elasticity that carried pressure and settlement; along with this development was the ninety-one fortresses intermittently lining these six layers of wall. For it to be competently taken by an enemy siege each of these fortresses would need each clearing and every layer breached.

Great faith was put in the Walls and their fortifications against the Huns, yet as an occurring earthquake that temporarily destroyed of at least fifty-eight of its towers to leave a large and tremendous breach was seen as divine displeasure 'aggravated by a superstitious fear'.[166] The Praetorian Prefect Constantine would then build a moat surrounding the outer wall and terraced defenses between the two walls.[167] In 416, Theodosius II would ascend to the purple, but still under Anthemius's guidance, and his domineering influence of his sister, Pulcheria. Theodosius would then marry Athenais-Eudocia on June 7, 421, a noblewoman of Athenian origin and Pagan belief. Her mother was a sophist that educated her daughter in rhetoric and literature and in an age where women were seen and recorded in histories as 'vicious whores or serene saints', she was seen as a women of exquisite looks and artistic ability.[168]

He was known to have a gentle and merciful disposition, demonstrative in his character arises when observed that he had certain aversions to enforcing the death penalty, while he was held complicit in ordering a failed assassination attempt on the intractable Attila the Hun at Edecon.[169] In 440, he was further tested by an accusation that his wife deceived him in an affair with the Magister

---

[164] Brownworth, 162.

[165] Engineering an Empire. The Byzantines. Season: 1, Episode: 11. Directed by: Rebecca Ratliffe and Mark Cannon. Written by: Rebecca Ratliffe. History Channel: 2/25/2006.

[166] Gibbon, 1071.

[167] Vasiliev, 103.

[168] Montefiore, 161.

[169] Gibbon, 1075.

of Offices, Paulinus.[170] There was said to be little danger, given Theodosius's more pacifist attitude, that Rome might become a military dictatorship. But at the same time, the emperor spent decades using the law to unite the aristocracy and bureaucracy into an entity with a 'confident sense of its own identity', able to 'correct long-standing problems' and foster a sort of absolutism domestically.[171]

In 409, the Romans would defeat the Huns under their king, Uldin, and return them East in chains as a Persian expedition incited the Augusta Pulcheria's Christianity (implemented on July 4, 414), in 421-422, against the Sassanids under King Bahram after the death of his strong ally Yezdegerd I.[172] Until then, the Persians were regarded as allied protectors of the Caucasian mountain passes against the Huns and Thracian troops who were sent east to Persia as Ostrogoth settlers in Pannonia and Thrace. In the West, developments were still changing between Roman and Gothic relations resulting in desperate measures as, in 401, Alaric and his armies invaded and settled in north Italy. In December of 406, they began heavy invasions in southern Gaul and by 409 tensions rose between the hapless emperor Honorius and the Vandal King Alaric who were now in Milan.

Despite a vastly inferior position, Roman pride made Honorius defiant to Alaric, although he was forced to bribe him at Christmas with 5,000 pounds of gold, 30,000 pieces of silver, 4,000 silk tunics, 3,000 scarlet hides, and 3,000 pounds of pepper. A representative, one Jovius, attempted to placate the Goths with Honorius's position, injudiciously reading a response from the emperor flat refusing further tribute.[173] It enraged the Goths further and they prepared for war, a siege starting that year in which, Zosimus would describe, the horrifying privations of food the city of Rome and its citizens would suffer. Before this,

---

[170] Norwich, (EC), 149-150. In what is most likely a parable, the story tells that the empress received the gift of a Phrygian apple from Theodosius and gave it to Paulinus, innocently, as a gift. The emperor found out and when confronting Eudoxia, she lied and said she ate it. Furiously, the emperor took this to mean she also lied about having an affair with the Magister as the apple was a symbol of romantic, even forbidden, love in Roman culture. She and Paulinus escaped execution by shaming Theodosius publicly about his scandal and she was banished, swearing on her deathbed after Theodosius's death that she was innocent.

[171] Harries, Jill. *Law & Empire in Late Antiquity*. Cambridge, UK: University of Cambridge Press. 1999, 42.

[172] In Bury, (LRE-I), 212f., it is noted the Persian King stood as a regent for the infant Theodosius.

[173] Norwich, (EC), 134-135.

Alaric spent time usurping Venetia and Dalmatia before 410, when the Goths breached the Salarian Gate and plundered Rome from the Pincian Hill, they proceeded to killing and enslaving the men, women, and children and burning numerous buildings. But Augustine especially notes how the Arian barbarians left churches and those people inside them alone despite Arian and Nicene differences. This was clear justification for Augustine that this was the work of a God punishing vice and heresy to protect his Church.

When in 421, Honorius's Western Caesar Constantius III was killed in battle, his widow Galla Placidia fleeing to Anthemius's court with their infant son, Valentinian. On August 26, 423, Honorius died and Theodosius II was sole emperor for one year while in Dalmatia[174] as the barbarians attempted to raise a puppet, John, to the western throne at Ravenna. In response, an army led by the Alan Aribandus and his son, Aspar led 60,000 Huns[175] west to support Valentinian III in May 425 after his ascension as Caesar in 424. Later, Valentinian would wed Theodosius's daughter, his cousin Eudoxia, to solidify the dynasty. In 422, after the Persian war, the Magister Helio faced the Hun King Rua for Thrace and Dacia. They were treated with the Romans for supposedly a century with an annual 'stipend of 25,000 *nomismata,* or roughly 350 pounds of gold, wherein any Roman who resisted was crucified.[176] This is yet another ignominious but necessary practice of the Byzantines and barbarians – buying them off for temporary periods of time, if not sending 'tribute' to enemy armies.

After years of reforms in the East, barbarian troubles re-emerged in the West in 431 when the Vandal tribes of North Africa invaded Roman territory. Honorius's widow, Galla Placidia, would apply for help from her imperial nephew in the East and an army under the general Aspar responded and cleared Italy. It was here Valentinian fell ill at Thessalonica and his sister, Honoria, being in the purple with no more male issue, became Augusta. This is not unprecedented as regents in the past had been awarded the title in emergency

---

[174] Bury, (*LRE-I*), 221f.

[175] *ibid.,* 224. In 426, gold coinage would also represent the union of the two *Augusti* with each engraved on the obverse of the *nomisma,* to be issued in Constantinople. On October 29, 437, coins bearing Theodosius's portrait, on the transverse, commemorated Valentinian's marriage representing Theodosius joining the hands of his daughter and the western Augustus. The message was Theodosius being the officiator above his son-in-law, holding the seat of the East Empire's dominance over the West.

[176] Gibbon, 1055.

situations. The Roman general Aetius gave the Huns largess again to return east. In 434, Ariobindus was awarded the East's Consulship of the Emperor.

But, when king Ruga died in 439, he was succeeded by the ferocious Bleda and the East failed to raise the troops needed to aid the West without Aspar. Bleda demanded the return of Hun refugees, an increased tribute of 50,400 *nomismata*,[177] and a promise no treaties or alliances would be made against the Huns. The Romans, made timid by circumstances, agreed. As for the Vandals, that year they took Carthage in Africa and prepared naval advances against Sicily. In 441, a western force, including a naval fleet of 1,100[178] was sent to contain the Vandals under the Gothic general, Ariobindus, despite Aspar's absence to fight more Hunnic invasions in the East.

From here, the Huns attacked Dacia and assassinated the Thracian Magister whose province they then attacked, demanding a new tribute of 151,200 *nomismata* with an additional lump payment of 432,000 to be paid up front! The Romans had given the Huns an inch in their tribute, but now Bleda took a mile. In this prosperous time for the Huns, Bleda was assassinated by his brother who took the army – Attila, the 'Scourge of God.' In one year, he increased the demanded bribes by Rome from 350 to 700 pounds of gold, still crucifying prisoners not ransomed eight *nomismata* a head.

Attila was described as an ugly barbarian with 'a large head, a swarthy complexion, small deep-seated eyes, a flat nose, a few hairs in place of a beard, broad shoulders, and a short, square body',[179] including a nervous and disproportionate energy. In 442, he would divide his contingents between a main force in the West and raiding-style in the East until the Romans withheld tribute in protest. The eastern barbarians would have enough to worry about with Attila's forces in Thrace defeating the Goths under Arnegisclus and his devastation of the Danube. A treaty with the Persians that year regulated the incursions of the *Ephthalite,* or 'White Huns' would broker a truce and a promise not to build new fortifications on the border region. However, Attila would defeat Aspar in the Hellespont and receive his tribute with back payments as he appeared finished it was here when Attila decided to handle the West.

Meanwhile, the remaining Hun forces devastated Thrace without settling and took Anatolia; it was around this time that the Isaurians of the general Zeno from the Caucasus would ally with the Romans and cut off this Hun

---

[177] Treadgold, 93.
[178] Kaegi, 29.
[179] Gibbon, 1056.

terror from the mountains in the East. Chrysaphius, the eunuch and former general-in-command of Constantinople also having internal problems as well as from Zeno, was now made Master of Soldiers in the East. These Isaurians were one of the progressively most loyal tribes to fight for New Rome and would be given more stability in the ranks in 466 under the emperor Leo I as the West crumbled. Chrysaphilus was able against the Huns, but an unsuccessful assassination attempt on Attila humiliated his efforts. Furthering his troubles, Theodosius's sister, Pulcheria, was Chrysaphilus's enemy at court as well, and was stronger than Zeno. Theodosius was a definite ally of Chrysaphilus, but the eunuch's future would become bleak when Theodosius would fatally injure himself falling from a horse on July 28, 450, while hunting.

Earlier that same year, Galla Placidia, daughter of Theodosius I and formidable power-playing mother of Valentinian III, died. As her son was much under her influence, Valentinian was a weak predecessor and would only survive until an assassination in 455. It is here the last of the western Augusti dynasties would rule; from then on would be a series of brief successions only delaying an inevitable fall unless another figure such as Stilicho or Theodosius I would appear, but unfortunately, one would not. Therefore, bickering Senators, barbarian puppets, ineffectual officers, and finally a child emperor would, in twenty years see Rome ruled by a Gothic King and a new era in Western Civilization began.

As for Theodosius II, his death saw Eastern Rome in a greater crisis than he had seen it through Anthemius's eyes. However, as he left it, it was one more educated in Classical learning and ancient Roman law than it had in centuries. Founded in Constantine's era, Theodosius re-organized[180] the laws, finishing on February 7, 425 at the University at Constantinople in wishing to rival the learning that could be obtained at Athens (where his daughter studied) or Alexandria. Two other intentions may have been to Christianize legal educations in the way his ecclesiastic-minded wife would enjoy. Simultaneously, she completed the 'Hellenizing movement' of Eastern Roman culture[181] as Greek chairs were favored over Latin chairs totaling thirty-one tax-exempt professors. These chairs ranged in study from these twenty-one Greek and ten Latin grammarians and philologists, three rhetoricians, one chair of philosophy, and two for law.[182]

---

[180] Vasiliev, 100. There is a misconception that the emperor actually *founded* the school when he really just improved it.

[181] Bury, (*LRE-I*), 228.

[182] *ibid.*, 232.

Along with his magnificent walls, law would be Theodosius II's legacy in Byzantine history, and his contributions would be unrivaled for a century. It was the tradition of over a millennium that the Roman law be based on a civil system, even in criminal claims outside state prosecution. Theodosius commissioned a panel of jurists to combine and update the *Codex Gregorianus* of the year 300 and the *Codex Hermogenianus* dating from 296 to 324. In March 428, work began on these law codes, written in Diocletian's time since the Emperor Hadrian one century-and-a-half before (117-138 CE) to create the *Codex Theodosianus*. The motive of doing so was to help eliminate mistakes in judicial rulings due to lack of reference. In practice, however, the Code's creation divided the legal standing in the Empire by allowing eastern edicts and legal decisions to be excluded from that of the West,[183] further widening the schism of the Empire legally and administratively. Added was the corrections to three main difficulties in standardizing legal practice:

1) Special courts were set up for specific matters and persons (wherein some court officials did not even have legal training).
2) Bishops were granted judicial powers (obfuscating secular and sacred legal opinion).
3) A variety of appeals procedure developed side by side (a threat of *ad hoc* procedure).

And it was within the idealistic framework of Theodosius II that a ruler needs to be governed too, by the rule of law, as he said: '. . .for our authority depends on the authority of law, and in fact the subordination of sovereignty to the law is a greater thing than the imperial law itself.'[184]

In 425, an explosion of legal training and rehabilitating of the profession was the result of imperial orders to equip Athens, Alexandria, Constantinople, and Berytus (Beirut) with the most up-to-date legal learning centers in the Empire. Before this, there also existed schools in Carthage and Caesarea as well, but the West was bereft of these legal revolutions and would suffer for it. Despite Constantinople's best efforts, incidentally, it was Beirut that would have the most prestigious law school throughout Byzantine history. By late 437, the Code was completed by sixteen compilers and inaugurated on February 15, 438, made of sixteen books, or *Tituli* ('Titles') with the addition of *Novellae*

---

[183] Ostrogorsky, 56.
[184] Ensslin, 276.

('Novels') or all edicts made post-Code with 2,500 edited texts, officiated by the Senate on December 23.

The Emperor stated that its purpose was to be a rational 'teacher of life . . .[on] what to be observed and what to be avoided', a maxim which has been compared to Chinese Confucianism in philosophy.[185] Starting with this Code, a cornerstone was made in the international law and modernization of Gothic government, founding the *Lex Romana Visigothorum* ('Roman Law of the Visigoths') whose influence was also felt in the laws of King Alaric II in the sixth century and the Salic Laws of Emperor Charlemagne in the ninth century.[186]

After the same day in 439, no legal matter, opinion, or decision was allowed to be made outside of the Code. The Theodosian Code also included legal opinions put into *Sententiae*, or the force of law, of jurists such as Ulpian, Papanian, Paulus, Modestinus, and Gaius, a few which would reappear in the Justinianic Code a century later. These five, in particular, preserved the *ius vetus* ('Classical Literature') that purified and standardized the language and, therefore, all other such jurists outside the five were considered void.[187] It also strengthened the connotation of the Emperor and the law as the name of each constitution given has the credit of the ruler who made it, so it made itself known as a tool of the emperor as supreme lawgiver. It has been called the top example of administrative and constitutional law in the Later Roman Dominate period. But as for Theodosius, he started to show weaknesses in his authority, as explained by the ninth-century historian Theophanes (758-817) that by Chrysaphilus's time, he was signing documents without even reading them.

In religious matters, controversy spread anew and a favorite of a resentful Emperor would be successfully persecuted. The Emperor was on the side of the Patriarch Nestorius who claimed as the Virgin only begat Christ the Man, she was the Mother of the Son and not the Mother of God, beginning the Nestorian heresy of the Nicene Creed. Pulcheria did not agree Nestorius and Cyril of Alexandria accused him of separating divine and human natures against the theory of Monophysitism ('One-Nature').[188] This was technically not true, because this only divided the assets of Christ and not his person. Nestorius convinced Theodosius, but the Empress and the imperial house, however, were now divided.

---

[185] Harries, 2.
[186] Vasiliev, 100.
[187] *ibid.* pg. 143.
[188] Vasiliev, 99.

The Pope condemned Nestorius in 431 for defying the miracle of the Virgin for Christ had the dual natures of God and Man.[189] An Ecumenical Council was set in Ephesus in the Church of the *Theotokos* ('Mother of God') on June 22, 431. Augustine of Hippo, a Nicene and an elite logician of Christian theology, was invited, but he died the same year in North Africa as more Vandals besieged Rome. At Ephesus in 449, the Eastern Bishops Diodorus and Eutychius favored Nestorianism and condemned Cyril against Pope Leo the Great's wishes.[190] But, in 433, the emperor proved his power over the ecumenical welfare of Eastern Rome when he converted to the Nicene Creed and banished Nestorius to Arabian Petra and then Libya where he died in Upper Egypt. But, of course, despite condemnation, the tradition of Christian martyrdom disavowing the wills of persecutors against the creed of the martyr would not end Nestorianism in the hearts of his true believers. Oddly enough, a Nestorian Church taking the Mother of Christ, and not God, as its creed was established in the Pagan tolerance of Sassanid Persia.[191]

Also at this time, Judaism in the Empire would suffer disenfranchisement and persecution, mainly in 425 when Theodosius executed Gamaliel VI, Judaic Patriarch of Jerusalem, for erecting synagogues and abolishing the Patriarchate title and position in Jerusalem forever.[192] As Judaism would still be legal in Rome, its practices were seriously curtailed by the laws against public observance and the building of new synagogues.[193] This hurt Judaism in the Middle Ages; it saw the end of the line of Judaic Patriarchs in the Empire and further pushed them and their beliefs to the periphery. The royal house had previously shown sympathy for the Jews as, in 438, the Augusta Eudoxia relaxed the laws against Jews and Pagans in Jerusalem, as she herself had once been a Pagan. This charity would eventually be broken by the synagogue-burning havoc of Barsoma of Nisibis. In Pagan lands such as Persia, it must be examined the goodwill that Theodosians and the Sassanids had and the religion's effect by this; in 404, King Yezdegerd I was made a regent of the emperor, separated from Byzantine-style intrigues at Court. Persia was outraged by the peaceful acceptance of the charge and he was called an 'Apostate', 'the Wicked', even a persecutor of the Magi priests of Persia, though this was untrue.[194] In 409 and

---

[189]  Norwich, (*EC*), 147.

[190]  Treadgold, 96.

[191]  *ibid.*, 92.

[192]  Montefiore, 61-62.

[193]  Treadgold, 122.

[194]  Vasiliev, 96-97.

410, a Nestorian Church at Seleucian Ctesiphon was made possible by what was known as Yezdegerd's 'Edict of Milan' of the Assyrian Church.

Reactions to religious instabilities saw the rise in numbers of the 'hermits' (descended from the Greek for 'wilderness') who with hair shirts, practicing 'celibate simplicity' and self-flagellation multiplied in Syria and Egypt, St. Jerome being the best example. Biographies (*hagiographies*) were written on them by churchmen and secular historians; women were even said to have entered monastic life, disguised as eunuchs, and having bastard children with the monks and clergy.[195]

In his freak accident, Theodosius died without an heir and Rome once again faced a crisis with a new Augustus in which to adapt. Another military emperor was more than likely to succeed as the barbarian situation looked its worst in centuries. As the West deteriorated beyond repair, the East was looking stronger in administration and education. The Byzantium of tomorrow would find foundation in these decades and prove that a successful Roman Empire could survive the tests and changes of this unstable century thousands of miles from the Tiber.

# MARCIAN
## (450-457)

In 450, with Theodosius suddenly dying, Pulcheria chose for her next husband an officer of distinction known as Marcian, who first had the intrepid eunuch Chrysaphius executed upon his coronation on August 25. The reason for this particular choice by Pulcheria seems unknown, although Theodosius supposedly approved the union from his deathbed and blessed it before dying, as the historian Count (*Comes*) Marcellinus (d. 534) claims. Marcian had been Aspar's aide-de-camp and a soldier of good standing, an attribute essential in the next few years when Attila the Hun's forces would lay Western Europe to waste and stability was further needed when Valentinian III was murdered without an heir. Edward Gibbon claimed Marcian was a man of character due to the fact he was chosen to restore and re-invigorate an empire, which had almost been dissolved by the weaknesses of its former two monarchs.

This saving of the Theodosian line by a marriage of convenience was Marcian's only purpose; his first wife forced to take a religious vow of chastity. This shows the deteriorated character of the throne as a general in purple was

---

[195] Montefiore, 162.

the only basic requirement to lead Rome politically and militarily. But, the dowager Empress was growing too old to produce an heir. An interesting note on Roman pride has recently been made to remind us that the Romans, despite the obvious realities of their times, never felt in this period as though they were ruled by the Germans. Illusory as this was, Roman supremacy in all of Europe was seen as the standard. Before and after the ascendancy of the Vandal King Gainas, these barbarians were seen only as military officers more or less loyal to a Roman Emperor with a Roman government.[196]

Born in 392 to a minor soldier in Thrace, Flavius Marcianus was stationed near Philippopolis as a Tribune in the Sassanid Persian Wars of 421-422. Notably remembered in the annals of the sixth century, Procopius of Caesarea in his *Vandal Wars* goes on to say how in 433-434, Marcian was a prisoner of the Vandal King Gaiseric. The king received an omen of Marcian's illustrious future, freeing him on oath he never take arms against the Vandals.[197] He seems to have kept this promise, though this may be due to the brevity of his rule and his preoccupation with the Huns. Among such reasons, including his origins, Valentinian held resentment against Marcian over this incident, supposedly, but it seemed to come to nothing.

He immediately stopped paying tribute to the Huns, effectively declaring war on Attila's forces by making use of another barbarian Western Magister of Soldiers, Aetius. To accrue capital for the military operations, he regulated tax arrears and kept internal peace by restricting expenses, raising taxes, and eliminating the *follis* tax on senatorial private property. His administration was responsible for garnering the Roman state a surplus of 7,800,000 *nomismata*, despite an annual budget of the same amount by his death in 457. With a standing army of over 1,400,000, stabilized bread doles, and the pay of an expanded bureaucracy despite a three-hundred percent increase in Hunnic tribute, this showed truly effective economic policy.[198]

The secret to Marcian's balancing of the budget after massive defense spending was not, however, by directly increasing taxation. It was accomplished by the elimination of financial corruption and efficient disbursement of government funds. He suspended indefinitely numerous taxes, including the *follis* of seven pounds of gold from the senatorial class, and in a 450 Novel

---

[196] Treadgold, 100.

[197] Kaegi, 27.

[198] Treadgold, (*BAIA*), 193-195. The increase in two years time went from 50,000 to 150,504 *nomismata*.

abolished tax arrears,[199] also limiting the City Praetorship to senators only, thus halting the venal sale of administrative offices. As for the urban lower classes, he took a conservative view fiscally by re-allocating doles directly to the people and implementing needed public works projects such as aqueducts. Probably, these included responses to the new developments taking place in the bureaucracy wherein officials were earning gold cash payments from the fisc instead of food and kind, which Diocletian instituted to curb corruption.[200] These descriptions of Marcian's policy seem to disenfranchise the lower and middle classes, but the loyalty of the senators as military commanders was of a higher priority in the times of crisis concerning the Goths, Vandals, and Huns.

Yet, in the East, barbarians had made easy fragmentation as only an estimated ten to twenty percent of the East remained purely Greek or Roman. The peasant classes brought up most of the tax burden as military spending demand increased (making seventy percent of the entire state budget). Coupled with these increases were the landowner tax burden, resulting in higher rents for peasants. The senatorial class only paid fifteen percent of the tax burden, but could not have collectively owned and operated more than five percent of Eastern territory.[201] This inequality in land and cash between the rich and poor would only expand until a norm was created where rural rich and poor would only exist, and only the reform of the benefice of Emperors would effect change in favor for the poor upon their whims when paying them proper attention.

Also of note in Marcian's reign are statistics that an almost nine percent drop in population occurred in the Empire since 284 CE with an Eastern imperial population of 16,000,000 due to the unpredictable frontier shifts of barbarian settlement. Only Antioch, Constantinople, and Alexandria were cities with a population in the 100,000's and mostly populated towns were inhabited with only 10,000 or lower people in 457.[202] Constantinople was known for its wealth and metropolitan character in future centuries, but it was a slow process from the crisis of Late Antiquity to the prosperity enjoyed in the truly Greek Empire. Socially, however, a Novel of 454 augmented the edicts of Constantine I which had barred socioeconomic class barriers in marriage between senators and poor women with no status (*humilis*) as long as they were free. This would be vitally important in the sixth century for the Emperor Justinian due to his marriage

---

[199]  Bury (*LRE-I*), 237.
[200]  Treadgold, 116.
[201]  *ibid.*, 114.
[202]  ibid., 137-138.

to the reformed actress and prostitute, Theodora, and was further instituted in the Justinianic Code.

Quite early in Marcian's seven-year reign, enough to make it obvious he had been waiting to address such issues from the background, an ecumenical problem would arise in 451 in the form of the Monophysite controversy and the consequences of the Fourth Ecumenical Council. The events and crises of the time would best be captured by Michael the Syrian, Bishop of Antioch from 1166 to 1199, in his Monophysite *Chronicle,* placing the schisms on Marcian and his Bishops.[203] The nature of Christ's perfect divinity in flesh and spirit between the Monophysites versus Pope Leo I, that Christ's natures were separately human and divine were the dispute. Leo had already agreed to the Chalcedonian 'Dyophisite' single nature in his *Tome.* Leo would, however, make a play at Church primacy by declaring the Roman Bishop as supreme to the other Bishops of the four Churches in Canon 28 of the Creed, but equality between the two Romes were still inferred. Also included was reserved status of deciding the Bishopric appointments of the peripheral Black Sea provinces of the Pontus, Asia, and Illyrian Thrace. Though inhabited by tribal peoples for now (even Pagans) in future centuries, this would have long ranging effects on the Churches of southern Russia and the Balkans.[204]

The Council of Bishops met at Chalcedon across the Bosporus from Constantinople on October 8, 451, in a *Synodos Endemousa* uniting the Roman and Constantinopolitan Patriarchates. By its end on November 1, they refuted the Council of Ephesus of 449, the so-called 'Robber Council', denouncing Nestorianism as ignoring Christ's humanity, condemning the Nestorian Bishop Dioscorus of Alexandria and his followers. The anti-Monophysite creed would now be known as the Chalcedonean Creed and this schism would include a set of Coptic and Egyptian Christian resistances to Byzantine rule until the seventh century.[205] Beginning also this year was a strict ban on Pagan worship, extending the June 8-9, 423, decrees on the 'accursed sacrifice to demons' whose punishment included confiscation and death, but also included reform measures penalizing judges, who did not impose his edicts on Pagans, fifty pounds of gold.[206]

This Fourth Council of Constantinople was also important politically in the districts of the five main Bishoprics of Christendom: Rome (the

[203] Michael the Syrian. *Chronique de Michel le Syrien,* trans. by J.B. Chabot. 1924.
[204] Vasiliev, 106.
[205] Ostrogorsky, 60.
[206] Kaegi, 61.

Western diocese), Constantinople (Illyricum), Alexandria (Egypt), Jerusalem (Palestine), and Antioch (the East). This would divide the Empire into the religious diocese that would later define the Byzantines in their Orthodox belief. These four Churches, bishoprics, and Patriarchates would use their creeds to decide matters of faith and the socioeconomic structures of these cities through capital administration both secular and sacred. The Monophysite Creed was more efficacious than Arianism or Nestorianism, would last longer, and would reach the throne itself, eventually from centers such as Egypt and Syria. They would be the ones to say the decline of the Church leading to Rome's fall would begin with Marcian and this Council.[207] Added to this gridlock was the compromising views of the moderates known as the 'Hesitants' and their middling views of the Third 'Robber' Council and the Fourth that Christ had a single nature *and* a duality at once.[208]

In 452, Attila began his greatest campaign against the Empire yet as he invaded Italy and the forces of the general Aetius under Valentinian III. Concordia, Altino, Padua, Vicenza, Verona, Brescia, Bergamo, Pavia, Milan, and Veneto would be taken, the last of these cities named put to the torch.[209] Diplomacy and embassies got nowhere as Attila would already see himself conquering Rome as the threat of the Huns culminated at the Battle of Chalons in 452 against Aetius's troops and those sent west by Marcian. It was one of the most decisive battles in Western history with a Roman victory, rebuffing the 'invincibility' of the Hunnish King. Marcian's own victories against Attila were commemorated in a Column in Constantinople, still standing today in Istanbul's Faith District, once bearing his statue, refurbished in 1675 and again in 1908. Later that year, on the wedding night of a barbarian princess given to Attlia, he died mysteriously of a nosebleed in his sleep; of course, the possibility of murder is nothing to be discounted and a subject of historical debate in the 20th century, at least.[210]

In 453, the former empress Pulcheria would die leaving her possessions to the poor and two Churches of the Virgin in the City,[211] any influence she had once in handling her family being stopped. Consequently, with Aspar's influence over Marcian now unchallenged, the Theodosian manipulation by

---

[207] Kaegi, 253.

[208] Treadgold, 99.

[209] Norwich, (*EC*), 158.

[210] Babcock, Michael A. *The Night Attila Died: Solving the Murder of Attila the Hun* New York, NY: Berkeley Books, 2005.

[211] Bury, (*LRE-I*), 238. The *Theotokos Chalkprateia and the Theotokos Hodegetria.*

the Arian German generals returned to the norm. On March 16, Valentinian III in the West would be assassinated after the unwise and unpopular choice of executing the war hero Magister Aetius, Gibbon calling it a 'tyrant's death.' Valentinian had many humiliations as an emperor despite his longevity, one of which was the secret marriage proposal in 451 his daughter, Honoria, offered to Attila by his sister. A ring was sent east, but was found out by the Emperor, put a stop to, and she was given a bribe of land for her obedience.[212]

The West lay open to robber emperors and puppets as the East would be ruled by Marcian alone, with no heir. On June 2, 455, Rome would be sacked by the Vandals of northern Italy with two weeks of uninhibited plundering until the 16th, taking prisoner Eudoxia, Valentinian's widow. Silver and gold ornaments of the temples, synagogues, and churches were pilfered and half of the copper roof of the Temple of Jupiter Capitolinus, erected centuries before, was stripped. In July, 455, the Emperor would need to be officiated in Gaul instead of the ravaged capital of the West.

In October, 456, the barbarian general Avitus would be abducted while the German leader Ricimer would keep both sides of the Empire playing against the other for some time (yet another disadvantage of an unwieldy, divided Rome). Ricimer would be 'deposed' by the Roman general Flavius Julius Valerius Majorian, a puppet to other German leaders including Ricimer himself, on the Western throne in 457. In the face of this, the final tragedy struck the Theodosian line as its last male heir, Marcian, died on January 27, 457 of a gangrenous infection inflicted during a seven-mile pilgrimage, as he gave gifts to all on the way,[213] being buried in the Church of Holy Apostles, next to Pulcheria.

On reflection, Marcian's reign was moderately successful internally: frugal, loyal, and protective of his Roman faith (he and Pulcheria were hailed as a second Constantine and Helena at the end of Chalcedon), Marcian handled domestic matters well. In the face of the Huns, whose empire stretched from the Balkans to the Danube, seriously threatening Gaul, Italy, and the gates of Rome itself, he stood what ground he could and ably prepared the East, aiding the West when needed. Of course, Attila's early death was a sigh of relief to the Empire even as death followed him in both halves of the Empire with an empress, emperor, and a Magister of Soldiers dying in two years' span.

---

[212] Norwich, (EC), 157. This was first recounted as fact by the sixth-century Byzantine-Syrian historian John Malalas in Migne's 97th volume of the *Patrologia Graeca*.
[213] Babcock, 280.

Marcian's rule was apparently unspectacular in scope, however, as dramas would take place in the West concerning the Huns with Marcian making no appearance at Chalons. However, the match of Pulcheria and Aspar in his reign would ultimately suggest the power games played throughout the later Theodosians. This is a fact that would obfuscate any talents Marcian may have possessed or exhibited by 453, such posturing would be commonplace. Now, the East would need more generals to clean up after the Huns and regulate the power vacuum created as a result. The Huns would recede, but the struggles for territories by Goths and Vandals would return to their former glory in Atilla's aftermath. This would come from the wily machinations of Aspar's need for another play-king.

## LEO I 'THE THRACIAN'
(457-474)

## LEO II
(474)

Western Rome was now in a downward spiral, perhaps at this point irreversible, due to its barbarian figureheads and weak Roman Emperors. The inability to keep a stable and competent senator or general on the throne was a short-term advantage to the Goths who nonetheless held *de facto* power, but this concept held also a fatal flaw. In the long-term, one Goth leader such as Oadacer in 476 or Theodoric decades later would take the succession by force upon the death of a puppeteer such as Ricimer leaving only a weak heir, such as his son Romulus Augustulus. This would theoretically lead to a possible mirror effect in its traditional capital In the East, exemplified by a threat made by the aspirations of Aspar and the as yet to be determined nature of the succeeding Augustus, Leo. The outcome could have conceivably threatened all forms of Roman rule forever if the Thracian could be cleared out as a mere mouthpiece as Augustulus would be. Fortunately for the future of Eastern Rome, Leo I would disappoint the Alan general, and yet most Byzantine scholarship would not take his bravery too into account, some historians even only granting him a footnote.[214]

Leo was born in 401 in Dacia to an orthodox Thracian family and was a Comes in the Roman army to become a Tribune of the Matriarii and Aspar's

---

[214] Ostrogorsky, 61f. It only mentions Leo was the first Emperor crowned by a Patriarch of Constantinople.

Domesticus. He was nominated by Marcian's son-in-law the Praetorian Prefect, but being an Arian and an opponent of Aspar, he could only play the role of king-maker and Leo, thus, was chosen.[215] To please his armies, Leo, upon succession by a reluctant Senate, gave five *nomismata* to each 'shield', an act recorded centuries later by the studious emperor Constantine VII Porphyrogenitus. He had lacked any formal education, yet was said nonetheless to possess '. . .a full measure of good, sound common sense and – equally important – a mind of his own.'[216] Within the Church of the Holy Wisdom, Anatolios, the Patriarch who crowned the emperor on February 7, 457, did so independent of the Roman see who was only to be succeeded shortly after by a Patriarch known as Timothy 'the Cat', an Arian Monophysite, allied to Aspar co-religiously. Leo, changing his spots to a stringent Chalcedonian, called a Council of Bishops almost immediately in 460 and had Timothy deposed, to the would-be puppeteer's dismay, on heretical grounds.

As he was crowned before Timothy, however, his coronation was not invalidated and Leo remained secure in his rule with the Eastern Church as an ally in Constantinople against the Monophysite Aspar. This was the first of many concessions of an early Byzantine tradition in the face of barbarism; the significance of this simple coronation stems from how the Papacy was no longer 'essential to the legal institution of the Emperor.' The *Augusti* would personally crown the Empresses and choose successors, Caesars, and co-Augusti on their own independent basis, as even the Patriarch of the ceremony was considered his 'master's servant on his own commission.'[217]

On December 28, 457, Ricimer's Master of the Armies, Majorian, was made *Augustus* of Rome, but in another act of defiance Leo would only recognize him as a *Caesar* due to having not been consulted despite Leo's coronation having no Western consent![218] A few years later, an insulted Majorian still would recognize Leo as a concession to facilitate a military alliance against the looming Vandal threat in North Africa. As for barbarization of the Eastern army, Leo chose better allies from the start of his reign, one of Leo's most passionate ambitions being to clear the Germans from the top military posts to be replaced by the Isaurians, choosing one type of barbarian for another, whom

---

[215] Bury, (*LRE-I*), 314.
[216] Norwich, (*EC*), 164.
[217] Ensslin, 270.
[218] Kaegi, 31.

he had been impressed with from their place south of Iconium and Lystra on the Calycadnus River.[219]

Aspar, in 457, was made Magister of Soldiers in the West 'ruling' with a control tighter than perhaps any other such barbarian in Roman memory, allying with Theodoric Strabo in the East. But, in 459, Leo again showed the intentions of his rule by refusing to pay tribute to a minority tribe of Ostrogoths living in Pannonia after betrothing his daughter Ariadne to Aspar's son Patricius, who was made Caesar in the East. These Ostrogoths were Aspar's allies, so he saw this as an ultimatum directly challenging his policies outside the Church, but when these Ostrogoths invaded the East in retaliation, they were paid a higher punitive cost of 21,600 *nomismata*. Leo further separated himself from Aspar nonetheless. As his ally, he chose the strong and loyal (and non-Germanic) Isaurians, the tribe most loyal in Theodosius II's armies, making them his own personal troops and bodyguard in 466.

This foundation was made by an Isaurian known as Terrasicossida Rousoumbladeotes (Hellenized as 'Zeno Tarasius')[220] who uncovered a plot of treason against Persia by Aspar's son Ardabur, resulting in his reluctant dismissal as Aspar's general. Zeno would take his place to found the Excubitors, 300 soldiers serving as the emperor's main bodyguard with ten Domestics, the *Scribons,* who outclassed the superior numbers of 3,500 elite troops of the Scholae. Zeno's position was made the strongest over Aspar by marrying Leo's daughter Ariadne over the betrothal of his son Patricius and Aspar would even unsuccessfully try to assassinate Zeno in 469. Disaster, however, for Leo's army would shortly arrive a year later at what was one of the greatest naval defeats in Byzantine history. A fleet of 1,100 vessels and 100,000 men[221] valued at 7,000,000 *nomismata* was sent by Leo and Ricimer to wrest Africa from Vandal control under its king Gaiseric, who had sacked Rome in the 439. John of Lydus (b. 490), a sixth-century contemporary of Procopius is said to have exaggerated in claiming 65,000 pounds of gold and 700,000 of silver were expended.[222]

Though some historians disagree,[223] perhaps the most accurate and trusted

---

[219] Norwich, (*EC*), 164.

[220] Norwich and Bury agree on this name, but other scholars have shortened it to Taurasius. Brownworth argues 400,000 men were sent 60.

[221] Norwich, (*EC*), 166.

[222] Kaegi, 45.

[223] Gibbon, 1130.

source on the invasion was the sixth-century historian Procopius of Caesaerea[224] who says over 9,000,000 *nomismata* were spent considering western troops sent, but he failed to take into account the 300,000 oarsmen used as field soldiers.[225] Count Marcellinus of Dalmatia as the Roman force's general failed miserably before as the Vandals took Sicily, strengthening Carthage's position. This exhausted Constantinople's coffers and also put Rome in a precarious position, destroying the myth it was the superior sea power force as it had been since the third century BCE (especially with Carthage).

Worse yet, Aspar's prowess was fatally questioned as he failed in 468 to keep the Persians from taking the protectorate of Lazica. Everywhere, the Roman military seemed to fail on its borders as in 470, when another failed expedition led by the able general Basiliscus, was sent and Vandal King Gaiseric mercifully offered peace with the emperor. In 559, John of Lydus wrote on all of this as a following to Zosimus's tradition that oracles and the old gods decided fate, as supposedly, the army ignored warning signs by taking the Prefecture of Egypt from one Cyrus using the Latin language over that of the traditional and ancient Greek.[226]

In 469, Leo's daughter gave birth to a son and heir named Leo, and in the same year Zeno was given command of Thrace and made consul. This was now a desperate situation for Aspar whose usefulness and future in the empire looked outlived. He would throw it all on one toss and led a rebellion in the imperial Army of Thrace, also demanding a tie in succession to Leo with his second daughter, Leontia. Leo agreed to side with his guardsmen with a watchful eye, naming Zeno his Master of Soldiers. Leo did not have long to wait for reprieve from the Alan general, for in 470, the Thracian magister Anagast sent proof of Ardabur's part in the revolt as well as a palace revolt involving the Isaurian guardsmen.

Aspar and Ardabur fled to Chalcedon to escape rioting Constantinopolitans favoring Leo more than the Alans, Leo convincing them to appear in 471 to a peace settlement where he had them assassinated. This act of slaughter he perpetrated by palace eunuchs, earning the Emperor the appellation of *Makelles* ('The Butcher')[227] tainting his legitimacy and place in history mainly by his

---

[224] Procopius of Caesarea. *History of the Wars, IV Bks,* trans. by H. B. Dewing. The Loeb Classical Library, Cambridge, MA: Harvard University Press. 1958. Bk. III.6.1.

[225] Treadgold, *(BAIA),* 190.

[226] John of Lydus. *De Magistratibus Populi Romani Libri,* ed. by R. Wuensch. Leipzig, Ger. (1903). 132.

[227] Norwich, *(EC),* 168.

detractors. Worse was on September 2, 465, when a fire in Constantinople devastated the City's Acropolis, the Senate House, the Nymphaeum, the Tarsus Forum, and the Church of St. Thomas to the Harbor of Julian.[228] Malignant demons and succubi would thereafter be blamed for the conflagration, but it still fell on Leo's head.

The assassination of Aspar set off invasions of the Alan's allied Ostrogoths throughout Greece and Leo was forced to settle a peace granting Strabo Thrace and the rest of the Ostrogoths Macedonia. Strabo would be made Magister of the Emperor's Presence from a very safe distance outside the City as Zeno was fortunately re-instated as Leo's Master of the Isaurian troops but, in the West, matters were different. The Emperor Anthemius and Ricimer could not reach settlements with their German invaders and Anthemius would die in battle in August, 472. Ricimer's nephew Gundobad would take his place, but Leo would see this as an opportunity to detach barbarism from western rule by giving the throne to the general Nepos Dalmatia. He then rode into Rome, drove out Gundobad and made a Roman general Orestes his *Caesar*.

Zeno was passed over as *Caesar* by Leo, perhaps because he thought the Isaurian unbecoming for such a position. What if it led, perhaps in the Emperor's mind, to a new barbarization of the Empire founded in a new tribe trusted to guard the Emperor, something he would finally think about since Zeno's ascension? What if a mass migration of Isaurians west upset the balance against the Goths and tribes in the East? Either way, on February 3, 474, Leo I would die of dysentery and later that year, his seven-year-old grandson and heir, Leo II, would also die of disease in October, placing the heavy responsibilities of the Empire upon the shoulders of the grieving father of Leo II, Zeno. He now had the task of keeping the newly, but barely, Romanized Western and Eastern governments free from Gothic and Vandal barbarian control.

Leo I did much to maintain control in the face of invasion, internal intrigue, and a military catastrophe in Vandal Africa. He also gave contribution to the spirit of the Empire by defending against the specter of Monophysitism, also bringing the bridle and veil of the Mother of God (*Theotokos*) to the Church at Blacharnae in the City to be counted as relics like the True Cross of St. Helena. Conveniently, discovering holy relics would happen whenever the faith of an emperor was challenged or threatened. In 469, he would also build a monastery in Anaplus at the place of Daniel the Syrian, penitent of St. Simon the Stylite. The Stylites, or 'pillar-saints' were penitent hermits who sat upon

---

[228] Bury, (*LRE-I*), 322.

raised columns for years on end to contemplate God and his spiritual kingdom. Such sacrifice of the world would be paid for by donations and charities of food and water as these men inspired others to mimic their sacrifices and example of rejecting the world.[229]

As for the ecumenical sphere, it was a war of wills between the Chalcedonians and Monophysites. This battle would once again see the Church shaken to its very foundations as Monophysitism's survival over the next century would call into question what legitimacy any Ecumenical Council really had. Chalcedonians were painted by Monophysites as corrupt and the Chalcedonians were considered radicals without cohesion as a hierarchical Church order. Besides this, if one Council's mood and results could change the outcome of past Councils, then, were such Councils invalid? If Monophysitism or Nestorianism denied Christ's humanity and Chalcedonianism said they were, implicitly, both part of the divine nature, how did this differ from Nicaea's decision that Christ's whole was part of the father and co-eternal in the Godhead? If Mary was truly the Mother of God and not Christ, why was she not part of the Trinity? These questions would reverberate in continuous Councils to the remaining years in Byzantine history, creating more schisms than ever healing and it was the Council of Chalcedonian in 451 that began this legacy the most since Nicaea.

Yet, more of this legacy included the persecution and zeal to eliminate Paganism in the Empire; along with his western imperial counterpart, Anthemius, Leo I began a new legislative program against Pagan worship.[230] A promulgation that appeared later in Justinian's Code (1.11.8) was put thus by the Emperor, signifying the unabashed differences of class and the imperial privilege: 'If anyone distinguished by a rank or office, he shall be punished by loss of his office and rank and also proscription of their property. However, persons of private status or the humble order after physical torture shall be condemned to perpetual exile or labor in the mines.'

Leo I was still a refreshing change of pace from his predecessors as being unafraid of ruling alone and without instruction by barbarians only ambitious for power such as Aspar. He even dared to reach out to the West and give this incentive for Roman rule to Nepos and Orestes. In most actions, he was

---

[229] Delehaye, Hippolyte. 'Byzantine Monasticism.' Chap. V of *Byzantium: an Introduction to East Roman Civilization,* ed. by N.H. Baynes and H.St.L.B. Moss. Oxford, UK: Oxford University Press, 136-165. 1969, 145.
[230] Kaegi, 61.

not bound to the traditions of barbarian participation. Militarily, he showed weaknesses in his defeat by the Vandals, but most of them were attributable to generals-in-command such as Aspar. However, his wise dependency on a more objective mountain tribe, not yet embroiled in endless politics such as the barbarian nations and confederations of Ostrogoths, would strengthen his legacy and find a trustworthy and successful dynasty in Zeno and his successors.

But, here the Western drama climaxes, for in the next reign Rome will fall to its new Gothic overlords in 476 and the seat of the *Augusti* would never be recovered after 500 years of existence. From here on, no Emperor would rule until the ninth century (and he would be Frankish) and no Emperor will be truly Roman ever again. Soon, a Western age of kingship and manor serfdom would characterize the civilization of the West and the East would be shaped by a half-millennium of different traditions. As for the true foundation of a Greek Empire, traditionally this was around 565 CE with the death of the arguably last Eastern Roman Emperor, Justinian I. There is no denying, however, a Hellenized Roman government would rule until then in the East and desperately hold what place it could in the West.

# ZENO
## (474-491)

# BASILISCUS
## (475-476)

The Eastern Empire still suffered limited stability when compared to the West; Leo had died a relatively successful monarch and there is even contention if he should be known as 'the Great' by modern historians.[231] He did die a popular emperor for standing his ground on ending barbarian corruption in the Palace against Aspar. Zeno, however, was not popular as he was an example of a barbarian general being given the throne, the typical policy Leo and the East were attempting to avoid. Historians intimate how Zeno was unloved by the Greek xenophobia against Isaurians, Zeno being described as physically and morally horrid, and also a coward.[232]

All detractors aside, he was an ironic choice to succeed Leo I and would have to prove the wisdom of his predecessor. He re-organized the security to

---

[231] Vasiliev, 105.

[232] Bury, (*LRE-I*), 390.

be held in the Palace with a foreign guard as another controversial move; he relied mainly on Isaurian Excubitors in his bodyguard, further demoting the Scholae of Constantinople to parade-ground troops and novelty guards for sale to the rich.[233] But, with a 130,000 pound depletion of gold in the treasury due to the African campaign[234] and serious defects in the eastern military system, he showed strong enough to at least weather the chaos of Rome's fall.

Zeno (for the Greek Zenonopolis) was born in Taurasis in Isaurian Rusumblada in 425, the son of the Isaurian Roman commander Tarasicodissa Rusumbladatiodes (also surnamed Zeno) and his wife Lallis. The Isaurians hailed from the Anatolian mountains of Taurus. He was raised Chalcedonian Orthodox, which put him in a favored place in the army and, eventually, the throne for he was not banned from the purple as being a barbarian as was a former custom since Pagan times. His father's fame and own accomplishments would earn him the co-consulship in 468 with Leo the Thracian. In 474, Zeno ascended to the throne, Leo's heir dying in childhood, on November 27.

The Isaurians themselves, however, were seen as absolute chaff to the Greco-Roman culture and society, brash and arrogant, strutting through Constantinople above the Greeks. As they were divided by bloody civil wars within their own tribes, the phenomenon was Rome's 'relief from German pressure [as] the suffering Empire had taken the Isaurian antidote. This worked, but it was an overpowering dose and the Empire was correspondingly affected.'[235] Even Zeno grew cautious of the Isaurians' rising power in the army and as revolts multiplied in the Isaurian mountain regions between tribes, the emperor's decision resulted in the majority of Isaurian fortifications to be eliminated.[236] In 479, riots broke out over Zeno's supposed 'lethargy and softness' on religious and military policies of disengaging the barbarians and appeasing them.[237] The result was a natural fostering of a lack of military confidence in the emperor, who now seemed to shun conflict almost as much as a victim of the Vandal debacle did.

Plot after plot marked a reign that did not start auspiciously as, in 474, his mother-in-law's brother Basiliscus, who led the Vandal excursion, gained usurpation of the title of Emperor for almost two years. Rumors abounded how

---

[233] Treadgold, *(BAIA)*, 92. As stated in the *Codex Justinianus* (XII.35.17), all recruiting was under the central government's jurisdiction.

[234] Ostrogorsky, 61.

[235] *ibid.*, 63.

[236] Vasiliev, 107-108.

[237] Kaegi, 50.

Basiliscus was a traitor who allowed bribery by Gaiseric to betray the armada of Africa, despite a lack of proof, it stands likely a rumor of Roman arrogance bred from denial that the fleet could have been defeated in an unmitigated conflict. When Aspar was murdered, his furious ally in Africa, Gaiseric, pushed the advantage he carried and the retired Basiliscus was recalled from Propontis to arms. His hideous in-law, Verina, convinced Zeno during the races at the Hippodrome that an uprising of the people and the Senate had taken place in the City and being averse and somewhat ignorant to cosmopolitan life, he demurred. Basiliscus's armies took the region as Zeno fled to Chalcedon, allowing Basiliscus – an unpopular[238] Monophysite - to be crowned at the Hebdemon as emperor on January 9, 475, to reign for twenty months. After showing cowardice in battle and attempting to abolish the Patriarchate over one disapproving Patriarch, the general Illus approached Zeno to return. After Basiliscus's brief reign, Illus took the City and, promising the Patriarch no blood would be spilled, Basiliscus was thrown into a cistern to starve to death.[239]

The Patriarch of Alexandria, a Monophysite known as Timothy Aelurus 'the Weasel (or Cat)' had been returned to the court to offset the Constantinopolitan Patriarch Acacius and his passing of anti-Chalcedonian edicts. It was the outcry of those in the region, especially the rousing words of David the Stylite, that caused him to revoke these edicts. As if by divine providence, Classical civilization suffered as a fire broke out in 476 that destroyed the treasured Pagan library of Julian the Apostate, the *Basilike*, which held 120,000 Classical works.[240] Also, from across the Empire, statues of gods in Samos, Lindos and Cnidus were destroyed in the Palace of the Laurus,[241] all seen as more signs of divine acts against heresy, though not Paganism.

To top off the adversarial contempt Zeno felt for his family was his nephew Armatus, who was a foppish officer claimed to be more a Paris (a selfish pleasure seeker) than a Pyrrhus (dedicated civil servant). Zeno gave alarm to the Magister Theodoric Strabos as he feared the rightful place of the Ostrogoths at the head of Western government who had sacked Rome, the general Oadacer, who fled Strabos's counter-strike. The time was just right as Orestes the Pannonian had died the year before and the last recognized emperor Romulus Augustulus, pompously named for both Rome's first king

---

[238] Brownworth, 61.

[239] *ibid.*, 63. A bloodless death at least.

[240] Bury, (*LRE-I*), 94. This included a famed 120-foot scroll written in gold letters of Homer's works written on the intestine of a serpent.

[241] Norwich, (*EC*), 170.

and first emperor, abdicated on September 4, 476, fleeing to Britannia.[242] Oadacer technically destroyed the Western Roman government, but it would be Theodoric who created the system that would kill Leo I's dream of Roman revitalization in 488.

It was now obvious that Roman unity with the Goths was beyond repair and that two distinct halves existed in the Empire[243] and, possibly, two independent states in all of Europe as a whole. Odaocer set up a Germanic monarchical system of tribal organization and aristocracy under a type of combination of the Roman Code and Common law practices. The tragedy of Rome's fall marked in Western history a turning point for the continent all could have been avoided had the Romans kept away barbarians, not from the battlefield, but from the court and from behind the throne.

It was administrative corruption and shortsightedness that allowed the Goths and other tribes to keep power in the dual role of generals saving a threatened Rome and controllers of puppets on a weak throne. Zeno's contribution was ignoring financial administration and by letting replacement corps lapse in the West, a decline set between 395 and 499,[244] allowing the Goths to go west with the emperor's blessing. Another example was the submission of peace with Gaiseric in 474, wherein crimes of raiding Byzantine ports and the seizure of slave and provision ships by Vandals in Leo's time were indemnified and open marketing between the two would commence with Carthage.[245] Gold from the East flooded the West as a result from this trade and the shifting Gothic populations redistributed this wealth, endangering the known security of Eastern Roman investments. Acts of charity once saw such gold given in Jerusalem as well as the Roman, Egyptian, Antiochene, Thebiad, and Palestinian Churches by donations from St. Melania the Younger with a total of 45,000 *nomismata* to fight Western heresy and Paganism, which would now be sacrificed to the West's interests.

But, with Roman recruitment so low due to population deflation by the recent Vandal, Gothic, Alan, and Hunnic incursions in the fifth century, it must be remembered that it is easier said than done to stand up to superior barbarian hordes and their influence in Roman society. Especially so when tribal leaders as Roman generals promised peace settlements with such tribes. So, does this

---

[242] Sarcastically pronounced as 'Little Disgrace' by contemporaries. Brownworth, 64f.

[243] Kaegi, 56-57.

[244] Jones, A.H.M. *The Later Roman Empire, 284-602: A Social, Economic, and Administrative Survey.* Oxford, UK: Oxford University Press. 1964. 680-682.

[245] Kaegi, 250.

argument eat its own tail, as these barbarians were both Rome's solutions and its problems, and was Rome's fall somewhat inevitable as these barbarian tribes became stronger? The nature of this question is the one that has baffled and divided historians since 476 to Gibbon's time to today: Why did Rome fall? With the legal system, trade and artisan-ship or the Roman highways, and a Latin-speaking emperor in a legitimate Eastern Rome, the Empire did not immediately feel broken from this relevant event and its citizens would agree.[246]

Eastern Rome would return to the times of the Constantinians of sole rule, of one true Church, and now the relative ease of ruling a more manageable land mass and population, diverse as it was. This was what the Constantinople of Zeno would later become, as much as we know it today – the Byzantine Empire. Zeno facilitated with tacit approval some of Theodoric's reasons for the West's takeover, first by losing command for not joining against Basiliscus and then, in 477, a refusal to return to service, pressing Zeno to send his Magister Theodoric Amal and his Thracian Ostrogoths after him. Amal met with Strabo at Adrianople and Zeno was prepared to fight both, but managed to appease Strabo with his original Roman service and title. As Zeno must have suspected would be a consequence, Amal felt slighted, sacking Rhodope, Epirus, and Macedonia before his final defeat at Illyricum.

After surviving failed revolutions by distant relatives such as Marcian[247] and Illus (who was butchered at the Kathisma), Zeno kept his place on the throne.[248] But, the last vestige of a purely Roman western government had already been thwarted by the assassination of the exiled Nepos in Dalmatia in 481. When, in 483, Illus's soldiers were brought to heel, this reversal in Amal's alliance won back Zeno's favor and his old position as well when a rival claim as Emperor, Leontius, attempted revolt by gaining the support of the Monophysite Patriarch Calendion of Antioch to crown him.

But it was yet another barbarian general, John the Scythian, who put down Leontius's revolt. Finally, Zeno wished to do something about the unrecognized

---

[246] Brownworth, 64.

[247] Marcian, who even had the Armenians and the Persian King Piroz promising him aid until the Ephthalite Huns destroyed Piroz and his armies at Antioch in January of 484. Bury, (*LRE-I*), 397.

[248] This was mostly on the insistence of Leo's empress, Verina, and Zeno's wife, Ariadne, plotting against him since Basiliscus's revolt and also attended Illus's doomed rival court of 484 after rescue from a monastery. Illus would be defeated and Verina would die in Papirius, besieged by Zeno until 488, to be 'mourned by none.' Norwich, (*EC*), 177.

upstart Odoacer who had overthrown Strabo, and in 487, he unsuccessfully sent a force of Rugians to invade north Italy. So, in a daring and decisive move, he invited Theodoric a year later to overthrow Odoacer and rule in his name as *Rex* ('King'), which had not been used in Rome since 509 BCE, the end to a destroyed legal succession in the West. Theodoric gladly accepted and the ancient Roman State and its magnificent Western Empire ended its 1,200-year era and in 488,[249] and thousands of imperial *foederati* were sent west – men, women, and children, to settle in Ostrogothic Italy.

Another legacy Zeno created was his conciliatory internal religious policy mirroring Marcian's one of passivity: letting Eastern divisions of Christianity affect the West involving native Romans, settling their barbarians, their faiths in Christ's nature, and the supremacy of the Papacy and the Patriarchate. They all shared an 'eastern' imprint and the decline of Rome did not change this environment[250] as tensions between Chalcedonians and Monophysites were as bad as ever, dividing the Church, the citizenry, and the bishoprics of the Empire. It was not long before Monophysite Bishops condemned the Council of 451 and the *Tome* of Leo that officiated its policies. Chalcedonians, on the other hand, wanted the heretical *Encyclical* of Basiliscus revoked on the grounds of its Monophysite defense. Zeno sought to placate both in 482 with the aid of the Patriarch Acacius through a letter noted as the *Henotikon,* or the Act of Union. This was a 'letter' sent to the Egyptian Church of Alexandria[251] over its election of a Monophysite Patriarch, Peter 'the Hoarse.'

It rejected Arianism and sought to validate each of the Three Ecumenical Councils in harmony, containing intentionally ambiguous language condemning Eutyches and Monophysitism, yet not endorsing Chalcedon. It did, for all purposes, condemn the *Tome* of Leo I on grounds of its encroachment in eastern investitures of Bishoprics. Described as 'evasive and purposefully rather obscure'[252] it was seemingly created in an attempt to placate the moderate Hesitant Monophysites[253] with political double-talk, not even giving an answer to the question of Christ's one or two natures. It did, however, endorse the Emperor's full role in deciding these matters in an unquestionable manner on doctrine, not as true 'Caesaropapism', but as a final judge in the cohesion of the civil unrest and argumentation over these subjects cause. It still, however,

---

[249] Hussey, 15.
[250] Kaegi, 226.
[251] Bury, (*LRE-I*), 403.
[252] Vasiliev, 115.
[253] Treadgold, 161.

went to support the necessity of Emperor and Patriarch in the still surviving Roman East.

Its intention was in promoting peacekeeping between the Christian factions, but was ultimately cheap and weak in doctrine, loaded with pandering. When Constantinople's token Patriarch Peter *Mongus* ('the Fuller') accepted Zeno's edict, it furthered divide between extreme Chalcedonians and Monophysites. Also, in the West, it succeeded in condemning Pope Felix III in the Acacian heresy. In the future, when subsequent emperors would try the same measures, the sacred part of the Empire would balk under a platitude of compromises in doctrine such as the Act of Union as the emperor passing it was considered a fraud. Evagrius (345-399 CE), in his *Historia Ecclesiastica,* evaluates the firm stance on the single nature of God as figurehead and Man,[254] but the Council of Chalcedon would be conveniently unmentioned except for anathematizing dissent.[255] This implicitly ignored the question of the union of Christ's divinity and humanity and the issue lost much intrinsic value. Truthfully, the five eastern dioces would never truly get along because of the diverse ideas of their people interpreting Christ or in understanding him. Chalcedon would lose Churches to Monophysitism still existing today in the Copts of Egypt, to surviving Islam, as well as to the Nestorians of Syria, Armenia, and Georgia.[256]

Furthermore, a pragmatic aspect over legitimacy and power politics were at work, along which dioces could get more followers and funds over the others and rival even Constantinople's Patriarchy. Sufficed to say, the Act of Union was a failure and taking only two or three opinions, one of which unintentionally was the imperial one. It even incited a pretext for the rebellious Illus from a very Monophysite Antioch to plan his attacks on Zeno. Furthermore, the practices of Italian Kings eliminating Roman Emperors over the See of Rome had begun, thus the creation of the Medieval Papacy where ancient Christian precedent had no meaning.[257] The *Henotikon* would even spark schisms and divisions that would last in Christianity until the fifteenth century.

Most shocking of all was the rise in Pagan activity in the East and the public assertions of writers of how Christianity's divisions were threatening to break the East apart. Zacharias of Mylitene, a Syrian Pagan writer (465-536? CE), remarked how the 'promises' of 'oracles' were soon to be fulfilled and

---

[254] Evagrius Scholasticus. *Historia Ecclesiastica, vol. III, 14,* ed. by J. Bidez and J. Parmentier. London, UK. 1898, 113.

[255] Vasiliev, 108.

[256] Norwich, *(AM),* 24.

[257] Norwich, *(EC),* 174.

'the cult of the pagans'[258] would be the primary faith upon the success of Illus and Leontius's revolts as late as 484. Indeed, with the Zoroastrian Persians of Azerbaijan and flexible Armenians as main allies, their toleration might have let Paganism gain in strength, but the revolt's failure and the defeat of the allies by the White Huns stamped out this possibility. Also, a lack of cohesion and clear leadership in this Pagan movement kept effective change from occurring on a macro level.[259]

The end of Zeno's reign was approaching, apparent to few including the emperor, having no secure succession for the throne. One of his sons, Zeno the Younger, would die of dysentery after a life of debauchery and his brother Longinus would die of a venal disease after a similar life. On April 9, 491, Zeno died from an epileptic seizure and it was said by modern historians it was from dysentery like his son, Zeno,[260] and as no other signs of epilepsy were supposedly found in the sources, so the inclination towards a death by dysentery is the more likely.

Zeno had more difficulties in the East than Leo did, but the West was handled more ably as Oadacer ended West Rome's systematic and Theodoric put it on terms of which Zeno from the start approved. But, he is seen as an ineffective monarch, not as illustrious as Leo or the future Emperor Anastasius would be with the military and the policies of barbarian rule, and the failure of the Act of Union did more harm to the Church and his reputation than good. Especially when the omission of the Pope would create a thirty-year schism. And thwarting Basiliscus was more an act Basiliscus himself perpetrated rather than Zeno. But, the Emperor consolidated the Eastern Empire in its new, semi-permanent form by cutting what was by then the dead weight of the West and recognizing the right to a peaceful settlement with the Ostrogoths and Germans.

## ANASTASIUS I 'DIOCORUS'
(491-518)

The East Empire's future was not to be written off as economic starvation and military impotence as had been the legacies of the past few decades. What

---

[258] Zacharias of Milytene. *Vie de Severe*, ed. by M.A. Kugener. Trans. by Patrilogia Orientalis, III, 1. Paris, France. 1903, 40.

[259] Kaegi, 96.

[260] Treadgold, 164.

damage would it take to wipe away the Eastern government such as Western Rome had been? Would its government survive the barbarian settlements with which they were surrounded, and now suffered, until a major invasion with what Oadacer had done to the West occurred? Or would it be the dwindling incomes of taxation and huge bribes and tributes to appease tribal kings that would cause an economic toppling and allow another Gothic King to seize a throne without public confidence?

The answers to these questions were taken up by Zeno's successor, Anastasius I; this shrewd and patient monarch pulled Byzantium from its depression and bleak morale with his lasting financial reforms and brought the Eastern Empire into a brief 'Golden Age' secured by his strong administration. Yet, Byzantium was still just an unseen future as it is today familiar only to Late Antiquarians as the era lacked, in this time of one New Roman Empire, a unique culture and definition. In fact, a political climate of reunion with the West still existed as some in the East would not give up hope on a reversal of the Goths' fortune. In 512, the grammarian Priscian (fl. 500) praised the holy virtues of the emperor and his peoples' love for him, while making it clear he should not forget the West as he improved the East.[261]

Anastasius I was born in 430 in Illyria to Pompeius, a noble of Dyrrachium and his wife Anastasia Constantina, who was of Albanian heritage,[262] Pompeius later becoming a brilliant financial civil servant in Constantinople. He was born an Arian, but would later choose the Chalcedonian creed on his mother's behalf to ascend to the purple and give the Empire an Orthodox emperor. Anastasius had a distinct feature as he was *hektachromia,* born with one dark eye and one blue, earning him the moniker 'Two-Pupiled' (*Dicorus*). As a highly trusted palace official under Zeno, he wed Ariadne, Zeno's widow and Leo I's daughter, to ascend in becoming Augustus. To please his electors and promise a new reign of justice and reason over harsher times, he suppressed the practice in his court of execution and mutilation. Other reforms, however, made him unpopular with the City, forbidding animal hunts and cruelty in the Hippodrome and nocturnal feasts rightly known for their 'beautiful dancing' and their excessive licentiousness.[263] His temperance in justice and moral conviction as a leader is reminiscent of Marcus Aurelius of the second century, who also was considered unpopular and unworthy by Rome for similar acts of enlightenment.

---

[261] Kaegi, 210-211.

[262] Vasiliev, 614.

[263] Norwich, (*EC*), 183.

A note on his policy of the fallen West was that Anastasius prudently kept patiently cool-headed and did not try any military adventures or recovery operations of Roman or Western territory, perhaps seeing it as appeasing to Theodoric, being something upon which Zeno agreed. Indeed, Theodoric eloquently sought to justify his situation by legitimizing his use of Rome. In a letter he wrote through the senator Cassiodorus (485-585 CE), he stated to the Emperor that his 'royalty is an imitation of yours, modeled on a good purpose, a copy of the only empire, and in so as we follow you do we excel all other nations.'[264] At face value, the Roman *Rex* seeks to imitate a great tradition with him as a willing 'servant' to the traditions of the original Empire. Yet, underlying this is the sentiment that he is not a mere servant of Constantinople or Anastasius, to be a puppet as so many others. He has a moral right to rule the West, if only to create order within it to bring it to a new glory under the Gothic throne.

Anastasius was publicly described by a Magister of Soldiers on the ceremony of his succession on April 11, 491, and in the Kathisma before the people how he was 'no slave of money, and free from every human vice.' One of his first acts was the recall and annulment of over 1,400 pounds of gold going to the 100,000 Isaurian and Roman nobles patronized by Zeno; to divide the Isaurian population, many of their number were re-settled in Thrace closer to the Emperor's reach,[265] and away from each others'. Another of his priorities was in the City's defense by first improving the new stretches of the Long Wall supplemented in 412, under Arcadius. He added much to the original Constantinian structure, raising it eleven km (just under seven miles) high and stretching it sixty-five km (over forty miles) around the Golden Horn of the Bosporus. This primarily acted as a natural defense of the Sea of Marmara, separating Constantinople from Chalcedon and the far south western Black Sea region.[266]

Oddly, as barbarian armies once approached within forty miles of the Walls had proven, modern historians say these improvements were ultimately a failure as the Theodosian Walls were still superior. At the time, it was considered a heavy contribution to the region's defense; Evagrius noted that it made Constantinople on the Bosporus at the Thracian boundary more an island

---

[264] Cassiodorus, *Variae, vol. I.1.3: Theodoric in Italy,* trans. by John Moorhead. Oxford, UK. 1992, 44.

[265] Bury, (*LRE-I*), 333-334.

[266] Herrin, 14.

than a peninsula.[267] In 506, to defend against Persian hostility, Anastasius built a fort at Dara opposing Persian Nisibis successfully renaming this fortified city 'Anastasiopolis'. These innovations in frontier fortifications were made possible by the addition of 'scientifically built' *castellae* by Justinian I. But, Anastasius I began these programs to bar roads from the enemy and defiles in mountain regions (*chleisoura*), man strategic points, and to guard the countryside.[268]

The first major difficulty in maintaining order did not come from outside Constantinople but from within, as the two *demes* of Blues and Greens were fighting for control of the City streets with Anastasius caught in the middle. The Blues and Greens were factions originating from the supporters of the competing chariot racers of the Hippodrome, representing the two classes in Rome making the competition more fierce. Gibbon unwisely dismisses these factions as such,[269] recalling its leisure in the times of Caligula and Nero, but more than just sports rivalry were at the root of this opposition as it was also a case of class warfare and socioeconomic politics. It is noted that the Blues were the faction of the aristocracy, the nobility, the wealthy, and the entitled and it was wise for upward stratifying officials to take note and change sides if necessary to suit their faction.

Circus factions had a culture within society with particular tastes in dress and manner such as sports fans do today. In their own fashion, 'they grew their beards and mustaches long in the Persian manner; they copied the wild nomads of the steppes by letting their hair grow down long in the back like a mane, cutting it short in the front. They wore capes and trousers in the barbarian fashion, and a tunic gathered rather tight at the wrists with billowing sleeves and exaggeratedly broad shoulders.'[270] The origin of such gaudy fashion in Roman society is unclear, but it made them distinct and recognizable, no one questioning their tastes lest a fight (or even a riot) break out.

The Greens were the faction of the 'people' of the City, the mercantile middle classes, the industrial, the civil service,[271] the lowest statuses and it is theorized they were a city militia.[272] The passion of this crowd could be dangerously powerful in the City and even sway the course of imperial

---

[267] Evagrius, vol. III, no. 38, 136.

[268] Diehl, 48-49.

[269] Gibbon, 1260-1260.

[270] Angold, Michael. *Byzantium: The Bridge from Antiquity to the Middle Ages.* London, UK: Phoenix Press. 2001, 19.

[271] Norwich, (*EC*), 185.

[272] Ostrogorsky, 66.

successions should they choose to do so by brute force alone. The best known example was the faction-driven Nika Revolt under Justinian I's reign to replace him in the 530's as such drastic measures were attempted in 512, decades after the Chalcedonian general Vitalian bid over Anastasius's unfortunate Monophysitism tenancies. Again, in 512, Chalcedonian Blues and Greens tried re-storing the conservative Theodosian line with the general Areobindus, who turned it down.

Both factions resented Anastasius's ascension by his infamous unpopularity and preferred his brother-in-law, Longinus. They rioted, dragging statues of the emperor and his court through the streets,[273] but Anastasius wasn't afraid to face this militarily. After Longinus and his Isaurians were blamed for the affair, Longinus was tonsured to an Egyptian monastery and the Emperor expelled the Isaurian soldiers from the City. This had many dangerous implications with the importance of the Isaurians in the imperial army and bodyguard, being set aflame when the Isaurians in Anatolia revolted and moved to march on Constantinople in 492. The commanders John the Scythian and John the Hunchback led armies that drove them back to Isauria. Anastasius remedied the situation by carefully melding Germans and other barbarians in the thinned ranks of the Isaurian contingents as the Anatolian Isaurians would temporarily retreat.

It was such developments that induced the Wall extensions of the City and the army reorganization to include the arrival of the Hunnic-Bulgar tribes who invaded Thrace in 493, killing its Master of Soldiers. Eastern tribes were now making new settlements and military alliances with both the emperor and his enemies. Along with the White Huns (the Ephthalites) were the Bulgars of the north and the Slavs who, since the first Gothic invasions. They were said by the historian Theophylact Simocotta (580-630 CE) to be the tribe known as the Getae,[274] who would raid Macedonia, Epirus, Thessaly, and Thermopylae.

Along with these incursions, a Green revolt broke out against the monarchy in Antioch. In 502, the desperate Persians, under King Khavad, invaded Syria and Thrace to raise funds, paying off the White Huns whom the Persians had been bound by treaty to keep from Byzantine territory to begin with. Khavad also demanded tribute from East Rome for such protection, but Anastasius refused and the Persians took Armenia, Theodosiopolis, Martyropolis, and Amida in 503. The failure of Illus to take the throne from Zeno now doomed

---

[273] Treadgold, 167.
[274] Bury, (LRE-I), 434-436.

Persia to the Epthalites as it was no doubt seen by Constantinople as a successful check to Persian power. At Anastasiopolis, Anastasius built larger and more centralized fortifications on the Persian border where still today walls, granaries, and cisterns still stand.[275]

Anastasius seized a brilliant opportunity to bring the armies into an unprecedented superiority in the East by raising 52,000 soldiers to push back Persia. He was known to be one of the first emperors to pay cash wages that were adjustable to a living wage by allowing each soldier an *annona* for provisions as well as a modest fifteen to twenty *nomismata* pay for soldiers.[276] But as Valens taught history, superior arms and funds meant nothing next to bad management as the Byzantines were in defeat, and the result was Anastasius was forced to pay 39,600 *nomismata* in tribute to Persia a year.[277] Anastasius also managed to rebuild cities and lower taxes in Mesopotamia, a sign of economic recovery as taxes were never lowered when needed most in Byzantium. In 505, he successfully re-fortified the Persian borders at Anastasiopolis as state funds were fueling the Persian wars, as well as on the Danube, the results of an amazing reform policy on the Empire's finances and be Anastasius's most remembered legacy.

With the able financial administration of Marinus and John in their illustrious year of 498, the monetary policy would improve with the use of the stable copper coin, the *follis*. This was tied to the stable money policy of Diocletian's golden *nomismata* at a ratio of 210:1 as this not only strengthened the gold standard, it allowed stability in value to the least amount of purchases down to the peasant classes. This stability in coinage than led to better tax reform in the Empire as gold coinage would be a norm on transactions, making possible smoother trade, transportation, and less corruption in tax collection. Coins were better for accountability than paper receipts and fluctuating silver/copper values. The military eventually caught on to the practice and stopped the free issue of soldier rations and horse to be bought and sold using the gold coin standard.[278] Anastasius then abolished the trade quinquennial tax, earning him popularity in business circles. Business and trade proved to be stable and

---

[275] Sarris, Peter. 'The Eastern Roman Empire from Constantine to Heraclius (506-641).' Chap. 1 of *The Oxford History of Byzantium*, ed. by Cyril Mango. Oxford, UK: Oxford University Press, 19-70. 2009, 47.

[276] Treadgold, *(BAIA)*, 152-156. A full evaluation of this trend in pay scale is covered by Jones, 670.

[277] *ibid.*, 192.

[278] *ibid.*, 179.

wide-ranging in the East in areas such as Cilicia, Palestine, Syria, Asia Minor, and Gaza as commodities such as olive oil, wine, vegetables, bacon, and wheat were imported into Constantinople under the *annonae*.[279]

Yet, despite the system's best efforts, corruption and embezzlement could not be eliminated, so to curb this the emperor issued the title of Vindex Civitatis (Defender of the City) who validated tax collections. This aimed to excise extorting collectors by the Praetorian Prefect who he was beholden to and supervised the collection by the city councils. It increased tax revenues by way of tax farming and reduced corruption (although the highest levels still could do so unannounced).[280] Anastasius even made up lost revenues with his own private properties (which was probably lucrative) and by returning donatives to the army. Also, with the *annona* largess also in gold, the *coemptio*, or compulsory sale of commodities at a low fixed rate by the government, was abolished.

The tax on receipts, the Diocletianic *chrysagyron*, was also abolished, relieving the poor class and gaining much popularity with the Emperor,[281] as all of these reforms eclipsed the religious and military policies that would work to harm his reputation. Although Diocletian's tax bases were abolished, the new *chrysoteleia* was instituted as a land tax that ended all tax payments in kind for cash. As he used government agents to break up the jurisdictions of the town corporations (*curiae*), individual land owners were responsible for their own payments at a 'surcharge' (*epibole*), which had been a Ptolemaic Egyptian practice. Furthermore, peasants with thirty years settlement of land were given hereditary status without being tied to the land.[282]

This could not be accomplished without a type of independent prosperity, such as imperial population increase possible due to less intrusive barbarian incursions and better economic conditions outside government intervention and control.[283] It is with these policies that the Empire, upon Anastasius's death, Procopius says, he had a surplus of 23,000,000 *nomismata* or 120,000 pounds of gold (exactly the amount lost in the Vandal War of 468). Calculated, this averaged the coin to be a relatively impressive seventy-two percent gold. Byzantium had finally recovered from the failed and costly expenditures of Leo I. But, the success behind Anastasius's reform was on the currency, adjusting

---

[279] *Mango, Marlia Mundell. 'Commerce.'* Inset in *The Oxford History of Byzantium*, ed. by Cyril Mango. Oxford, UK: Oxford University Press, 163-168. 2002, 167.

[280] Treadgold, 167-168.

[281] Bury, (*LRE-I*), 441.

[282] Vasiliev, 113.

[283] Treadgold, 172.

it soundly to other metallic coins and standardizing it as tax income from all classes. The best results of reform were seen in the timely and organized cash payment of troops and recruits, increasing the numbers of each in light of the wars on northern, eastern, and possible danger in western, fronts.

Much more controversial a topic was his religious policy as a reigning Monophysite in a Chalcedonian City, which may be a troubling result of putting a somewhat hastily forced convert on the throne as Anastasius's mother had done. Anastasius's Arian upbringing led to a restless relationship with the Patriarch of Constantinople, Euphemius. So, in 496 Anastasius had a Council called with Peter, the Patriarch of Alexandria, a fellow Monophysite which won him the Egyptian Copts and the Syrians. One of the things that effected opinion of the emperor's rule was his acceptance of the pandering *Henotikon*, deposing Euphemius on an absurd charge of raising a rebellion with the Isaurians and anathematizing both Chalcedon and the contemptible *Tome* of Leo I. Also, the emperor was brokering an independent peace with Pope Gelasius II to heal the Acacian Schism, and in Peter's place was put Macedonius who refused to sign Zeno's *Henotikon*. By his discrete worship of Chalcedon, Macedonius sat as Antioch and Jerusalem were made Chalcedonian with the *Henotikon* in 498 resulting in being a catalyst for the chariot factions having rioted that year.

Anastasius's policy and the religious controversies themselves would bleed down to the very prayers a congregation were to speak. At the end of the blessing during Mass was the *trisagion*, 'Holy God, Holy and Mighty, Holy and Immortal *who was crucified for us.*' These were words anathema to the Monophysites finding it an absurdity that God could be crucified as a man could be. This caused the circus factions to revolt in the City for the Emperor's nephew Pompeius to be on the throne, but Anastasius convinced them with a clever play of reverse psychology by 'abdicating' in the Kathisma.

Some 80,000 Constantinopolitans were softened by his humility and he was re-acclaimed, but as soon as this was over, imperial guards were brought in to massacre them,[284] a brutal, but necessary, tactic in dealing with the mob as to who was to remain emperor. Also around this time, more factional chaos ensued in the Palace's Chapel of the Archangel where screaming matches led to anarchy between Chalcedonian and Monophysite Constantinopolitans during a liturgy at Mass on Sunday, November 4, 512. It is these irreconcilable attitudes and zealous dogmas that proved how Monophysite ecclesiastical

---

[284] Angold, 18.

policy was merely a blind alley.[285] Obviously, some saw this as the limits of what a Chalcedonian Empire could take and a general, Vitalian, rebelled that year for a Council. No major Councils reached any viable conclusion until 519 when an actual Chalcedonian was on the throne. The East would be divided into major cities and provinces such as Alexandria, Tyre, Phoenicia, and rebellious Thrace where Monophysites their defense of the corruptible *Henetikon* existed between the Chalcedonians.[286]

In 515, the empress Ariadne died and on July 8, 518, Anastasius joined her dying at age eighty in the Palace, intending one of his nephews Probus, Pompeius, or Hypatius, to succeed him. Anastasius put down Vitalian's rebels and made peace with a force of 80,000 soldiers by the Thracian Master of Soldiers. After defeating 60,000 Romans, he captured the Emperor's nephew Hypatius, who was ransomed for 9,000 pounds of gold. Considering the decayed look of the army under Leo thirty years earlier, it is clear a vast improvement was made in assessing manpower and finances for such an army.

But that was the excellence of Anastasius's policies, they made use of the strengths New Rome had to build new reforms on that reality. Based on a functional gold standard and coin exchange, Anastasius I was able to lift taxes for trade and industry, easing economic tensions domestically and for the Empire's neighbors. He also issued officers and founded local bodies that overlooked the existing taxation, as in his questionable popularity, his successes as an administrator were beyond reproach. What modern historians value most was a sense of *clarity* in vision of the dogmas of the Church and not toleration or social factors to which Zeno catered. The old *romanitas* – 'what it is to be Roman' was ebbing as the imperial West was fading and cohesion and the strength of conviction for the Church by the Palace which sought to identify this seemed weaker than ever.[287]

But, in his zeal for order on his terms, he persecuted Chalcedonians their faith as being a 'radical' Monophysite, only adding more confusion in the roads constructed between differing points of view. This also only instigated civil unrest as generals rebelled for their interpretations of Christ and the circus factions could find one more thing to fight about. But, it must be remembered that those Alexandrians and Antiochenes who fought Anastasius were also enjoying his tax policies and the new wealth in which the Empire found itself.

---

[285] Ostrogorsky, 68.

[286] Bury, (*LRE-I*), 441.

[287] Angold, 20.

In this time of wealth and possibility, a new era was beginning as an old concept was dying; Anastasius wasted little time in showing his equal status with the powerful Theodoric and made the Frankish King Clovis a legal viceroy of Gaul and an 'honorary consul.'[288] The last emperors of this Late Antique period were on the horizon to restore one last unified Roman Empire with one emperor who created a Code of Roman Law with lasting Christian principles. When this time passed, the roots of a Byzantine culture will bear fruit and the fate of the Middle Ages over all of Eastern Europe would take shape.

# JUSTIN I
## (518-527)

It is not easy saying a lot about Justin without Justinian; Justin I seemed more as a puppet for his illustrious nephew when looking at the circumstances. The Empire was in better order financially than it had ever been, yet its social and ecumenical state was in an uproar. Justin's place was in mostly fixing his predecessors' mistakes and ushering in a new post-Leonid dynasty. In 518, when a Roman embassy came to discuss the Acacian Schism, they were warmly received at port by Justinian. It was with Justin, however, who they met with to end the division and erase Anastasius's and Zeno's names from the diptychs of the councils.[289] But even if his early career shows he asserted his authority, as time went on he was seen to be in Justinian's shadow nevertheless.

This may actually bring a question of why he was given the throne over his illustrious nephew. Perhaps he was a *transition* Emperor, just around until Justinian could be better groomed? Perhaps Justinian sought a kind of legitimacy in his foundation by using his senior, moderate uncle was the way? And perhaps Justin knew his own limitations and saw his family as the only thing he could trust? Whatever the reason, Justin made himself emperor, but barely remained one when his nephew was recalled from Illyrium early in his reign. His heir was nicely groomed and educated in the best Classical traditions and intellectualism that only the climate of Constantinople could seem to offer.

Justin I was born from Illyrian peasant stock on February 2, 452, in Macedonia to a Thracian family near Naissus in the village of Tauresium, where it would also be claimed that he and his next two successors were descended

---

[288] Vasiliev, 111.

[289] Norwich, (EC), 191.

from Albanian Slavonic descent.[290] It is argued by others such as James Bagnell Bury (1861-1927) that he was born in a Dardanian village, Bederiana, which was the reason for his native Latin language.[291] He was considered handsome in his seventies with curly, gray hair and a well-formed nose, as said by John Malalas (491-578 CE). His was a proverbial 'rags to riches story' as he fled the barbarian invasions as a young man with no money or prospects, seeking shelter in Constantinople by 472 at age twenty.[292] He then went where almost anyone who was in such a position went, the army. He fought in Persia and Isauria and against Vitalian, where he earned senatorial rank. He rose through the ranks to become Anastasius's commander of the Excubitors, where legend says a vision of the word R E G N U M under his pillow showed him that Justin's ascension was God's will. Such legends demonstrate that the Emperor's real reasons for choosing Justin seem obscure to the general public.

But, the Excubitors and the Master of Offices both favored him or his nephew as emperor, but Justinian wisely turned down the throne to his uncle. The Blues would refuse any Monophysite candidate, throwing Anastasius's nephews out of the question. So, Justin was eventually raised on the shield of the army (a custom beginning in Late Antiquity) and his ascension was proclaimed outside the Kathisma and the Ivory Gate with his name withheld to avoid more contention. He was accepted into the purple on July 9, 518, in the Triklinos of the Nineteen *Akkubita* and Malalas writes how he guaranteed a largess of five *nomismata* in silver to the troops.[293] Most notably about him upon ascension was the fact he was the first Latin-speaking Emperor of a Hellenizing Eastern Rome since Theodosius the Great, preserving some western heritage on the throne.[294]

By 518, Justin trusted the largess to be given to the army to the eunuch Amantias, at one time a rival for the throne, endowing him with a large amount of gold to pay his armies. But with the 'peasant cunning' John Julius Norwich (1929-2018) attributes him, he pocketed it and told his army to stand their ground against Amantius. Another notorious setback was his illiteracy, as he required a stencil until his death to sign his name[295] on documents all to be

---

[290]  Vasiliev, 129.

[291]  Bury, J.B. *History of the Later Roman Empire from the Death of Theodosius to the Death of Justinian, vol. II.* New York, NY: Dover Publications, Inc. 1958, 18.

[292]  Brownworth, 67.

[293]  Bury, (*LRE-II*), 16-17.

[294]  Treadgold, 174.

[295]  Procopius of Caeserea, *The Secret History,* trans. by G. A. Williamson. New York, NY: Penguin Publishing. 1966, 69.

overseen by Justinian. This meant nothing the emperor did would escape his notice and all the language of said documents could be directed to his interests.

In March, 518, Justin's dependence on his nephew allowed Justinian to broker negotiations with the papal embassy of Pope Hormisdas. Upon his succession, he met with the Pope in Constantinople and the breach of Acacius was healed (at least on parchment) between East and West as Monophysites fled the City once again. The Antiochene Patriarch Severus even fled to Alexandria along with the Monophysite Patriarch Timothy III. The *Henotikon* was again condemned and the ecumenical tug-of-war in Byzantium's culture pulled towards Chalcedonianism once again.

This also pleased the once-rebellious general Vitalian, Justin's enemy in battle, as now it was he who swore his loyalty and was made Consul in 520. Naturally, the resourceful Justinian was jealous and he assassinated Vitalian, stabbing him seventeen times.[296] Taking his place as Consul in 521, rising to *nobilissimus* status, Justinian quite quickly became the heir apparent and power behind the throne. He then began breaking convention by marrying the dynamic theater performer, concubine, and ex-prostitute Theodora as introduced to him by the ballet star of the stage, Macedonia.[297] The conservative financing of Anastasius was further defied as Justin would spend 3,700 pounds of gold on decoration, stage machinery, and largess. Another affront to his predecessor's decency saw him host public animal hunts of at least twenty lions and thirty panthers among other beasts.[298] Justin would always attempt to buy the people's attention away from his nephew the way Gaius Caligula did over Tiberius.[299]

Justin I expanded both the eastern imperial borders and Christianity by accepting in 522 Persian Lazica's offer to Romanize and Christianize the area. This caused major unrest with Persia, Mesopotamia, and Syria which was invaded to the Arabian Strait of Bab el-Mandab. The Jewish king of Yemen would then massacre rebelling Christians and Justin acted fast to retaliate. By 525, Ethiopia (Abyssinia) had subjugated and Christianized the Yemeni government, increasing Byzantine trade to India and the Red Sea, thus securing a more lasting goodwill and economy.[300] Whatever Justinian's role was, he

---

[296] Bury, (*LRE-II*), 21.

[297] Brownworth, 71.

[298] Norwich, (*EC*), 189.

[299] After Tiberius Caesar's death in 37 CE, his nephew Gaius Caligula spent his entire surplus of around 3,000,000 gold pieces, plus 1,000,000 more, into serious debt to entertainments and gifts. Justin was not so ostentatious, but his tactics were the same.

[300] Treadgold, 177.

would benefit greatly from this eastern access. The Persians themselves had been beset by the White Huns of the north and in Justin's reign, these 'Antae' would become the Slavic Bulgar tribes Procopius would write of in his *Wars*.[301]

But in 523, relations with the West became a gathering storm. Talk in the court was arising that Justin planned a reconquest of Italy from Theodoric in an effort to dissolve his legal rule. As this arrangement was made under Zeno it might, on speculation, be a reason for this sentiment as Justin would try to undo anything the author of the *Henotikon* would accomplish. Justinian tactically threw in more western chaos by urging an independent Vandal state which the king, Hilderic, eagerly accepted. Now Italy's east and south, important military and trade centers, worked against the Vandal King.

Africa would be a preserve of the Roman authority with its military marvels of Byzantine engineers creating strong points of cities and forts, resulting in a road system to serve commerce and effective patrol and defense.[302] Without access or protection from Hilderic, many of the Gothic senatorial class were later tried for treason including the executed philosopher Boethius (477-524 CE), author of the classic *Consolations of Philosophy* written in his prison cell. Along with it all, Hilderic imprisoned his predecessor's queen, Theodoric's sister Amalasuntha. Shockingly, it has been found that Hilderic minted his gold coinage in North Africa bearing Justin's portrait!

In 525, Pope John was in negotiations with Constantinople for correcting the Arian menace, but in 526, however, the ardent Arian Theodoric would depose John for a new and more agreeable Pope in Felix IV. This lost a lot of steam when Theodoric soon died on August 30 and his heirs were his wife Amalasuntha and a young, pleasure-loving son, Athalaric, himself in a few years to die of 'venality'. This was an undeserved legacy to Theodoric, harsh and stubborn, but a reformer of the civil service that rivaled the East and a preserver of Classical culture in the arts and architecture. Included with this claim was the 200-ton mausoleum he built in Ravenna, one of the greatest engineering feats of the Middle Ages marking Theodoric as the dominant monarch until Charlemagne three centuries later.[303] There were rumors that Justinian would attempt to marry Amalasuntha himself and destroy the Gothic western

---

[301] Obolensky, Dimitri. *The Byzantine Commonwealth: Eastern Europe, 500-1453.* New York, NY: Praeger Publishers. 1971, 44.

[302] Decker, 140.

[303] Norwich, (CE), 180.

monarchy legally for Byzantine rule, but as he was married to Theodora, her will made this impossible.

Visigothic Iberia would soon follow Lazica's example of Christianization, but strange bedfellows would make the Iberian King a Persian vassal and a major eastern incursion led by Khavad was launched. The capable and illustrious eunuch Sittas and a legendary commander named Belisarius forced them back, taking the hotly contested Persian Armenia and Mesopotamia. All the while, it is to be remembered, Justinian was watching them closely and perhaps planning his ambitions east and westwards. Justinian's control was made complete by the superseding of a law forbidding the senatorial class from marrying actresses. But her own strength, dedication to religious reform, and active champion of the Blues made this law moot in Justinian's case. Who, after all, would deny the brilliant leader of what was to be the Byzantine Empire? Even Anastasius's family begrudgingly accepted, knowing the way the tide may turn.

Due to an ulcer and infection in his foot from an old arrow wound, on August 1, 527, the overshadowed Emperor Justin died, completing Justinian's ambitions. This, anyway, was a moot point as Justinian had been crowned months earlier on April 4 by a Patriarchy and court expecting Justin's death to be sooner than later. Justin I did set right the wrongs and disunity in the Chalcedonian East and West cleaved by Anastasus. But divisions remained on the eastern borders and in an unquiet Italy. As would also be proven, the Blues and Greens would rise again to tear civic order apart in the City and put a puppet on the throne. But at least the Empire was going into capable hands. Justin's power behind the throne was energetic, resilient, and resourceful with an excellent court, especially his Empress. Justinian and Theodora had eventful and astonishing lives (they will be treated separately as co-rulers of Byzantium). Their legacy would endure to shape Byzantium until its eventual fall.

It should be noted that now, especially after the sixth century, the ascension of humble origins and the lower class to the imperial station was now more than a possibility as several instances in future generations would see such a phenomenon become a practice. Armenian and Macedonian peasants, Greek centurions, as well as Isaurian artisans – all would share in the purple. The French philosopher and historian Montesquieu (1689-1755)[304] would describe it in his *Considerations sur le Causes de la Grandeur des Romains et de Leur Decadence* (chap. 21) that "Everyone had the stuff of an emperor in him." Though the purple could be a curse to end in bloodshed, it had an ironic sense

---

[304] Diehl, 127.

of democracy in the Middle Ages unseen in all other such Empires East or West where all strata could transcend restrictions on the throne. Whether by talent, popularity, or by the ambitions of others to pose these men as puppets: "Fortune having chosen emperors from every walk of life, no man was too low of birth or too slender merit to cherish hopes."

# JUSTINIAN I
## (327-365)

The Eastern Roman Empire in the mid-sixth century was in an upswing of undeniable prosperity and financial resources, a disciplined and well-paid military, and a return to traditional Chalcedonian values in the Church. It was with relative ease that Justinian took over the throne from his uncle, his Justinian's programs and policies having already been in place as they had been going long into Justin's reign. In fact, he probably curried jealousy from Justin for his education and popularity. The result would be the zenith of the first 300 years of the Empire's existence, with unprecedented administration, trade, legal reform, and periphery zones to the West.

Justinian I was born Flavius Petrus Sabbatius Iustinianus in 482 in Justin's Illyrian city of Tauresium,[305] the son of peasants as obscure as his uncle's. Upon Justin's ascension, he was called to Constantinople to serve his uncle as Master of Domestics to ascend at forty-five, a man totally opposite from his uncle, upon succeeding. Justinian had much more Classical education and literacy, speaking both Greek and Latin. He gained experience in state affairs his uncle did not representing the Crown for military, foreign, and even papal envoys. He even defied all convention by marrying a Monophysite theater dancer after his forbidding grandmother, Euphemia, died. Both uncle and nephew did have an amount of military experiences in Persia and Thrace as Justinian's military policies and ambitions are some of his most known qualities.

The freshest perspectives on Justinian's foreign policy is one of the emperor seeing himself as a liberator of the true Romans from the barbarian peoples in the Eastern Rome as well as Western Rome, seen by him as his mission to mirror the harmony of Heaven upon earth. The independent barbarian kingdoms of Europe had existed long enough and it was time they return to a unified and enlightened Roman fold. As conceited and chauvinistic a view as it was, Justinian's vision was one in which the very presence of the Byzantine

---

[305] Upon ascension, the Emperor would rename this city Justiniana Prima.

retinues would assure that the city of Rome would throw open its gates in gratitude. But it is true that, even in Justin's time, those oppressed by barbarian tyranny would see Constantinople as a better ally and 'emissaries flocked to the capital.'[306]

In January 532, a real test came in the form of the Nika Revolt between the Greens and Blues that resulted in one of the rare coalitions of *prasino-venetoi* ('Green-Blues') that decided new emperors.[307] It started with the hangings of a Green and a Blue for murder. The ropes broke and the two survived. Both factions then seized opportunity and began a riot of '*Nika!*' ('Victory!'). The two suspects were spirited away to Chalcedon across the Marmara and the factions would then gather to overthrow Justinian for his extradition of the two.[308] Justinian, General Belisarius, John the Cappadocian, Theodora, and others were besieged in the Palace's estates of the Kathisma as the rioters in the Hippodrome demanded the ascension of Justinian's nephew, Hypatius, on Sunday the 18th. Arrangements were made for the court to be secreted away out of the City by sea, but Theodora refused to flee. She gave a rousing account (see below) on how those wearing the purple should conduct themselves: preparing to die for their honor. So, a revitalized emperor sent Belisarius to slip away and gather his troops outside the Hippodrome.

Meanwhile, fiasco and anarchy were the order of the City, especially when the convicts of the prisons were freed to do as they could in storming the streets. Fire was set to the Praetorian Prefecture on Friday the 16th, the Senate House, the Baths of Zeuxippus and Alexander, and the Churches of St. Sophia and St. Irene;[309] hospitals were burnt to the ground with the patients still inside and nothing seemed spared or sacred. It was here Belisarius and an Armenian eunuch, Narses, marched thousands of troops in the Hippodrome, Belisarius inside and Narses outside to catch those who would be fleeing. Procopius of Caeserea (500-554 CE), Belisarius's secretary and Justinian's best historian, claimed this was an atrocity where over 30,000 Byzantines were slaughtered. Perhaps Justinian realized that if a cruelty is to be done by a monarch, it is best

---

[306] Brownworth, 69-71.

[307] Bury, (*LRE-II*), 41.

[308] For the best evaluations on factions and chariot sport culture and their imprint on Constantinopolitan politics by mob rule, see Cameron Alan. *Circus Factions.* Oxford, UK: Oxford University Press. 1976. It includes the notes made by Procopius on their dress and manners.

[309] Norwich, (*EC*), 198.

to take harsh measures in one swoop, rather than draw it out over time and have the people suffer a series of small ones.

This is what the Emperor did and to great effect as there were no more factional riots of importance in Justinian's reign. So, after the armies were finished, Justinian and Theodora entered in full imperial dignity and were praised by the City. Hypatius, an unfortunate victim of mob passions, was executed as a potential threat. Nineteen senators had been executed and mutilated by the mobs and the rest of the nobility were unmercifully taxed to cover the damages. An important note was that this powerlessness of the nobility in the future would deplete the advantage of the petty barbarian kingdoms of the East, tying the nobility to the capital and emperor with peasants soon tied to these lands.[310] The social mobility and prosperity of the Empire would always depend on the Emperor's ability to use his resources in tying the periphery of the Empire to Constantinople as its financial source.

Before civil disorder was arrested in Constantinople, in 529, an army was sent to the kingdom of the Bosporus in Crimea to settle when the Christianized king was overthrown, just as Justin had done with the Yemeni Jews. In 530, the Persian King Khavad would battle for Armenia and Mesopotamia with Belisarius until the King's death and ascension of Khosru I Anushirvan ('Of the Immortal Soul') on September 13, 531, a powerful and ruthless monarch with whom Justinian would always spar. As the emperor officially made clear his military intentions in 532, Procopius, as a witness, was to note that Belisarius and his forces took the news with dread.[311]

But, Belisarius would win at Daras with Hun cavalry after five years of hostility and the Persians would retreat to Armenia, concluding the Endless Peace of 532. Justinian then made a peace with the Arab kingdom of the Ghassanids in the region to be allied with Byzantine command. In like fashion, the rival Lakhmid tribes allied with Persia in an uneasy balance of Arab power. Belisarius would go on to show the courageous and inventiveness great generals showed using expanded Calvary, foot, and the rising use and profitability of the horse archer, mimicking Hunnish methods.[312]

The outlines of Justinian's army of five types of soldier were basically[313]:

---

[310] Brownworth, 81.
[311] Decker, 182.
[312] ibid., 122.
[313] Bury, (LRE-II), 76-77.

1) The Comatitenses were the regular Roman commissioned officer from Illyricum, Thrace, and Isauria also commonly known in the Greek as Stratiotai.

2) The Limitanei were similar troops guarding the borders of the state.

3) The Foederati were the troops consisting of Calvary. By Justinian's time they were the most valuable part of the army, once an exclusive knight class they were nationalized into a division for common enlistment.

4) The barbarians and various other tribesman making up divisions of potpourri of treaties, territories and annual subsidies with the Empire, the Allies.

5) Privately-retained troops, usually, mercenaries, hired by the commanders themselves to match numbers in the armies. In Belisarius's campaigns, they grew to as much as 7,000.

Though it is mostly the estimation that is questionable, the East Roman reserves in the western regions were somewhere around 150,000.[314] This matches the figures of the historian Agathias (536-582 CE), and some even calculate 300,000 to 350,000, but this over-exaggeration may have been used to falsely show Justinian's 'mal-administration' when his armies averaged around 15 to 30,000.[315] African records of the Limitanei survive to allow a representation of the general pay scale of one region in several, wherein constant taxation was needed to balance it. Officers such as the Dux made 1,582 *solidi* annually, cavalry officers were at thirty-three, infantry centurions at twenty, and the rank and file infantry and cavalry were set at five and nine, respectively.[316]

Though it was Justinian's intention to take the glory for himself, the conquered lands such as Africa had populations welcoming Belisarius as a deliverer[317] and Italy would prove no different. In 533, Belisarius was sent west to Sicily with 18,000 soldiers, his wife Antonina, and his secretary Procopius.

---

[314] Treadgold, *(BAIA)*, 63.

[315] Lee, A.D. 'The Empire at War.' Chap. 5 of *The Cambridge Companion to the Age of Justinian*, ed. by Michael Maas. Cambridge, UK: Cambridge University Press, 113-133.2005, 118.

[316] Morrison, Cecile and Jean-Claude Cheynet. 'Prices and Wages in the Byzantine World.' *The Economic History of Byzantium: From the Seventh Through the Fifteenth Century*, ed. by Angeliki E. Laiou and Charalampos Bouras. Washington DC: Dumbarton Oaks Research Library and Collections. 2002, 864.

[317] Brownworth, 87.

Here, he made amends and tempered Amalasuntha's fears of a renewed Vandal invasion on the African coast. A failed attempt would mean a breakout against Ostrogothic lands in retaliation, as Italy was an ally of Constantinople. A lack of preparation is what won the victory for the Byzantines and their 600 Hun mercenaries as a revolt broke in Carthage placing Gelimer on the throne as king. While a revolt broke out in Sardinia at Tripolitania, as Procopius says, at the secret correspondence of Justinian to the Sardinian government, the Vandal fleet was diverted. Some 120 ships and 5,000 men were sent there when the revolt already placed them separated from Carthage.

Concerted by a chance-taking John the Cappadocian, the Byzantine fleet of 900 *Dromoi* survived a surprise attack at Carthage and defeated the Vandal armies at the coastal island of Ad Decimum. Belisarius returned to the City triumphant in 534, the Vandal monarch in tow. Gelimer was treated as a prisoner of Rome, marched through Constantinople to the Hippodrome with Justinian and Theodora in the Kathisma. Drawn before the feet of the populace, he saw the trophies of the past such as the silver menorah of Jerusalem taken by the Roman Emperor Titus in 71 CE, solid gold thrones, and jewel-encrusted chariots. Gelimer is said to have quoted from Ecclesiastes 1:2 that 'Vanity, vanity, all is vanity.'

But, there would be a number of police action warfare against the Moorish Berber tribes until 548 and in 535, trouble would brew in Italy. As Amalasuntha and her husband were deposed and murdered, the new regime refused to open their harbors to Justinian, so Belisarius was sent west to fight the first of the Gothic Wars of Italy. So far, the West's re-conquest of the Emperor was merely reactionary or recovery battles against hostile forces existing before Justinian's intervention. This wasn't the opinion of Procopius in his eyewitness accounts of his *Wars*: 'When the emperor Justinian considered the situation was as favorable as possible, both domestically and in his affairs with Persia, he turned his attention to affairs in North Africa. But when he reveled this to his officials that he was assembling an army against the Vandals and Gelimer, most of them were unhappy about it and regarded it as a mistake, recalling the expeditions of the emperor Leo and the disaster of Basiliscus and remembering how many troops had perished and how much money the state lost.'

Immediately, with his entourage and remaining men, Belisarius took the Neapolitan coast from the Goths, which was a serious blow to their morale.[318] The Goths blamed it on the incompetence and corruption of the general

---

[318] Norwich, (*EC*), 226.

Theodahad, who was hunted and killed on the spot. Belisarius continued north to Rome against the capable Gothic general Witiges, to be made the king of the Italian Goths in 536. Witiges still had the sea port of Ostia and the Roman supply of corn from Egypt as his plan was to besiege Rome at the Vias Salaria and Flaminia and starve Belisarius and his garrison of 4,000 out. Bury and Norwich describe a very lean and dark time for the Eternal City following this plan. Yet, Witigis did commit an error relieving Rome by traveling to Ravenna for a Council of war.

A papal controversy also found its way in the mix. Pope Silverius was a Monophysite sympathizer and allied with the Arian Witiges. Belisarius saw this as treason, deposing Silverius and ascending Virgilius to the throne. In 537, the general John brought supplies, provisions, and 5,600 more men to Rome. The year 538 was spent shoring up against Witiges as Ravenna was taken. 7,000 more Byzantines arrived, now led by the skillful Narses as Belisarius's co-general. This proved to be ill judgment by Justinian as this is what brought his envy to a head by 540 as Narses ignored Belisarius's orders in taking Milan and Genoa, resulting in Narses's recall. The Goths and Romans seemed destined to repel each other anyway as their differing on religion added up with the Romans' ancient contempt of the Goths' culture in their taste in music, their ridiculous trousers, and an overabundance in hair grease.[319]

By the end of 540, a besieged Witiges at Ravenna sued for peace to Belisarius who held Italy south of the Po River. Justinian demanded half the treasury of Ravenna and the lands south of the Po. Belisarius was not satisfied by this and held his peace when Witiges offered him the Roman throne for his loyalty over the Emperor's. Under Belisarius's false agreement to this (he would never betray Justinian in the future as well), he was given Ravenna. This led to the Western re-conquest of Justinian, won by subtlety with a minimal cost of the troops' blood. Unfortunately that year, a Persian invasion of Syria would demand both the emperor's and general's attention.

Khosru I was the first to breach the Endless Peace made in spring of 532 by taking Syria in 540. He then entered Mesopotamia and took the fort of Daras (Anastasiapolis), demanding half a ton in silver and the city of Antioch. On his victorious return to Ctesiphon, he built a city based on Antioc named Rumia (Rome in the Persian), but Procopius chronicles it as named for the King of Kings as Cosro-Antioch after the Greek name for Khosru as Chosroes. In 541, Belisarius and his armies would arrive in Mesopotamia to regain territory in

---

[319] Brownworth, 90f.

what was the Second Persian War. Another incursion that hampered the West was the Bulgarians in the Danube in 540. They spilled east into Greece taking Illyricum, Macedonia, and into the Hellespont.

Justinian had already fortified Petra and the city of Lazica when Khosru demanded a higher tribute of 3,600,000 *nomismata* a year with a further 36,000 for 542, sacking Antioch under the commander Buzes. He then led his force to reclaim Lazica to convince the White Huns to invade Byzantium. Belisarius immediately assembled an Army of the East and obfuscated Persian control by passing Nisibis to take Sisaurana and had the allied Ghassanids invade all over the Tigris coast. Ctesiphon might have been a goal, but the general received word his absent wife, the Empress, and their adopted son were conspiring against (at least making him a cuckold). This made his Emperor doubt him, but Byzantium kept Khosru occupied.

In Italy, the Ostrogothic fortresses left by the Po were taken and the Gothic king, Hildebrad, was murdered by a usurping king, Totila. With the East under an uneasy halt for the time being, in 547, Belisarius went west again to Italy, as Totila retook Rome for the barbarians. Belisarius spent his time there retaking Ravenna on the Po, returning quite wealthy from Italy in 551. This worried Justinian into a paranoia of being overthrown by this popular and rich uber-general and he began to favor a new commander-in-chief for the West in his nephew, Germanus. Germanus had already shown mettle in negotiating the settlement and annexation of Antioch to the emperor as Belisarius fought west, although Byzantium would surrender it later at the next Persian front. Persia would also continue extorting Byzantium and Syria. Perhaps the idea of a nephew, rather than Belisarius, securing the West on the throne for Justinian's family appealed to him more. But, his plans were frustrated as Germanus died of fever in Serdica before setting foot in the West.

In 549, Justinian had commissioned a column and bronze statue on top of the Belisarius in Persian dress, which is now lost, and retired him in a sumptuous, if not well deserved, palace.[320] Yet, the emperor had made up his mind and now the shrewd and experienced diplomat Narses the eunuch was the only general Justinian trusted with Sittas being killed in the East by the Persian general Buzes, giving Narses 35,000 soldiers landing in Italy in 552. As they traveled north up the Flaminian Way outside Rome, Totila attempted to play for time as he was planning an ambush. Narses waited out Totila and his forces advanced on the Goths and Gepids who then fled the battlefield. Totila himself

---

[320] Brownworth, 108.

was wounded in the assault and died a few days later at Caprae. Forces were soon being strained to feed the western front to the point that Justinian broke the taboo of allowing slaves to be enrolled in the army, usually as substitutes in conscription.[321]

Narses's last military siege in the Gothic War was at Cumae against the Franks that guarded Totila's massive treasury. The last obstacle to the Italian re-conquest was Justinian's to enjoy for thirteen years, though Visigothic Spain would be beyond his reach. David Olster in Mathisen & Svian's anthology on changing frontiers in the period recognize that this concept of a 'Roman Universalism' was the work of Justinian's *oikoumene*. This power was as the religious leader of the Empire to cohabit the secular Roman and the sacred Christian 'Universalism' that defined the Middle Ages. Ironically, Justinian's overspread budget could not pay all of the costs of the re-conquest and his ambitions were still somewhat unsatisfied.[322] He was still forced to cut drastically, at times, the military budget and his bloody reign in men saw the Empire holding 500,000 soldiers cut dramatically down to 150,000 by the end of the Gothic Wars.[323]

Justinian's reign saw many years of hardship fought on two large and fortified fronts; but, again, no emperor ever earned the title 'the Great' for combat alone. As the ancient Romans surpassed all previous civilizations in founding a legal science to complement their legal system, Justinian's greatest works were done for Byzantium in its administration and incomparable collection of laws. The laws as they stood before were a 1,000-year-old jumble of contradictory precedent, special exemptions, and conflicting interpretations with no fixed place in which to consult.[324] In April, 529, Justinian commissioned his 'famously corrupt' and Pagan legal adviser Tribonian (500-547 CE) to follow in the footsteps of Theodosius II and create a comprehensive legal code for the laws between 438 and the 530's for his magistrates. This revitalized the law schools in Constantinople, Antioch, and Alexandria, but it was Berytus (Beirut) that once more became the most preeminent. Justinian was already promulgating imperial laws on Christian values, prosecuting homosexual practices and disenfranchising religious sects such as the Samaritans and the Manicheans.[325]

---

[321] Decker, 84.

[322] Treadgold, 213.

[323] Brownworth, 111.

[324] *ibid.*, 74-75.

[325] Treadgold, 180.

The code was made of three complementary parts creating the *Corpus Iuris Civilis* or Body of the Civil Law. First was the *Constitutiones* (Constitutions) in twelve books organizing 4,562 laws commissioned by ten men an entire year, whose laws were attributed to all the emperors still in practice from Theodosius II up to the current times. These laws were inviolate and were open to little interpretation, nullifying all past codes as Theodosius II had done to Hadrian's. These laws were also tools in re-organizing provinces to draw power to the center of Constantinople and out of local, and even international, leaders. Later added, in 534, was the *Quinquaginta Decisiones* ('Fifty Decisions') written, but not officially codified or separated, from the Code. This was created in order to rectify certain legal obscurities and controversies in past texts to satisfy what was called the 'perfection' of the laws by the emperor who felt nothing created by him should be left imperfect.[326]

For example, in 533 in Berytus or as Justinian calls by the ancient name of 'Phoenicia', it was the 'eminent' man in Constantinople that was responsible for maintaining the ordinances of the Code in the region. In the city of Berytus, it was the *vir clarissimus* (Man of the Higher Legal Order) who did these duties as governors of the provinces in conjunction with the professors of law. This was done from 533-536 in the form of appointed titles and imperial Edicts found in a book called the *Novels* which were the Edicts and Constitutions made during the Code's creation, therefore, temporarily omitted from the Code. These were written in Greek only as the rest of the Body was written in Latin, Greek being used for popular and local convenience.

Next was the *Digest, or Pandects,* of Roman law in fifty volumes. This was a casebook of legal decisions and theory created by the jurists Ulpian (170-223 CE), Paulus (fl. 3rd cent. CE), Modestinus (fl. 250), and Gaius (110-179 CE) around the Hadrian's era (117-138 CE). These covered all of the Roman civil background including ordinances, inheritances, manumission (slave freedom), theft, rapine, and murder. It covered fifty-three books and close to 1,000,000 words. Any interpretation beyond the work was forbidden, thus ending the common laws of regions and tribes. It takes the form of legal discussions and conversations between the four jurists. Even this book identified the Emperor

---

[326] Humfrees, Caroline. 'Law and Legal Practice in the Age of Justinian.' Chap. 7 of *The Cambridge Companion to the Age of Justinian*, ed. by Michael Maas. Cambridge, UK: Cambridge University Press, 161-184. 2005, 165-166. This aspect demonstrates a sort of narcissism and 'completion anxiety' in the Emperor's notoriously ambitious search for a re-founding of Roman universal power.

as an institution where all founts to the stratified major cases to that of the lowest private citizen.[327]

Finally, there were the *Institutes* of Gaius, a textbook of the law completed on December 30, 533, to accompany the Digest under the jurists Theophilus (fl. 533) and Dorotheus (d. 542).[328] It covered the civil laws of Persons, Things, Commerce, and Obligations in its four books. It was an elementary framework based on rational legal science and warned against *ad hoc* law[329] and outdated tradition by being a combination of the Code and Digests into a basic understanding of legal issues. Tribonian would include in the Code how Justinian was *nomos empsychos* ('law incarnate'), forever creating precedent that the constitution of the emperor (and his Constitutions) were always legally binding as Gaius's work justified and finished the Body. Altogether, these three works made the *Codex Justinianus* and provided a complete legal education for its students in the Empire. It would even go west and grace the law codes of the Goths combined with their own traditional laws. This is what is meant by Gibbon's rare lack of cynicism in view of Justinian's achievements when he points out that they are 'studiously transfused into the domestic institutions of Europe, and the laws of Justinian still command the respect or obedience of independent nations.'

In 535, Justinian I would tighten his grip on the new bureaucracy by stopping the sale of provincial governorship; they would now be the central government's preserve. It emptied the treasury, but made it up in decreased embezzlement by officials. This is especially seen in the *suffragia*, the taxation privilege governors had to collect on whatever funds they wanted on any grounds; now governors lived only on salaries.[330] To further curb this corruption, he raised these salaries and cut down unnecessary bureaucratic offices, even at the senatorial and bishopric levels. The army was re-organized to fit the cash payment system in the treasury with John the Cappadocian (490-548 CE) who, with the implementation of the Code, discovered a trove of new taxes and levies

---

[327] '*Quod principi placuit, legis habet vigorem*' ('What the Emperor pleases has the force of law'). Justinian. *The Digest of Roman Law: Theft, Rapine, Damage, and Insult*, ed. by C. F. Kolbert. New York, NY: Penguin Publishing. 1979, 17.

[328] Tellegen-Couperus, Olga. *A Short Introduction of Roman Law*. New York, NY: Routledge Publishers. 1993, 144.

[329] Justinian would still implement such laws in conscripting slaves in his Western campaign.

[330] Bury, (*LRE-II*), 335.

he could administer from the wealthy.[331] The Comitatenses of his elite troop were made a soldier class consisting of the lower class and rank soldiers below the noble and knightly military tiers. He eased tax burdens when possible such as abolishing the postal tax system on heavy transport goods for businesses.[332] For the government to capitalize fully on arms for the war effort, monopolies of factories and warehouses were instrumented. Provisions were made and legislation in the Code (C J 85.2) forbade external manufacture and trade.[333]

These could only be possible, however, with a workable economic system of trade and taxation fluidly filling and distributing from the state coffers. The silk trade, enjoyed mostly by the richest class and the imperial household, was a monopoly of trade by the Persians. Fleets in the Indian Ocean cut off the common merchants from China.[334] The Byzantines did not even understand the realities of production, believing silk was spun from Chinese mulberry trees. Procopius tells in his *Gothic Wars* how Justinian remedied this situation by sending spies, possibly Christian monks, to the Far East to China to learn their secrets. They returned in 552 with silkworms and eggs with the news that they propagated and spun the silk as they ate from the mulberry trees. They smuggled samples to Justinian and he home grew a silk monopoly cutting off the Persians from factories in Constantinople, Berytus, Tyre, and Antioch.[335] With such innovation, Justinian turned Byzantium into a center of Mediterranean commerce, especially after freeing the markets of Italy and North Africa[336] by conquest. It was also the hub for the Sassanids that traded with China, India, and Ceylon (Sri Lanka) in spices, wines, ceramics, as well as silks.

---

[331] Treadgold, 179-180. As Brownworth notes, 'he was a charmless, uneducated man who managed to streamline the tax system, close loopholes, and attacked corruption with a dog-like tenacity. The fact that he used torture to correct shirkers seemed not to bother Justinian in the least', pg. 74.

[332] Treadgold, *(BAIA)*, 185.

[333] Decker, 95. This included the Ballistarii, light land artillery and the torsion onager, valuable siege equipment since ancient Roman times, 124-125.

[334] Ostrogorsky, 74.

[335] Vasiliev, 168.

[336] In most territories such as North Africa, these was treated as a 'piggyback' economy to enrich the estate class with its vast agrarian territories, and after the Vandal War in Africa, low success of resistance. As it later periods, this threatened central administration. Haldon, John. 'Economy and Administration: How Did the Empire Work?' Chap. 2 of *The Cambridge Companion to the Age of Justinian,* ed. by Michael Maas. Cambridge, UK: Cambridge University Press, 28-59. 2005, 39.

Constant and vigilant taxation policies were kept in line as it was needed to constantly support both the bureaucracy and the army in action. The Praetorian Prefect John the Cappadocian was the clever tax administrator that handled the imperial coffers – sometimes at sword point door-to-door. His main revenue was the collections of lands inherited by neighbors over confiscation or foreclosure. This method and others were ways John deflated the nobles who rivaled Justinian economically or publicly. Another was the *aerikon*, the tax on tall buildings, something used since Cato the Censor's day, yielding the state 3,000 pounds of gold annually.[337] Most of these municipal proceeds went into non-liquid warehouses known as *Commerciarelli* where armor and equipment were stored to benefit the army, especially after 545 when cash stopped being used as pay.[338]

But the military was the main concern of the tax apparatus; they were obviously paid well enough for their numbers, loyalty, and victories in the West. John the Cappadocian would soon lose popularity for his mischief, especially with the low-grade bread he cut corners on started giving western troops food poisoning. But it must be remembered, these senators had always been hostile to Justinian, so unscrupulous measures in time of need were expected, even from Theodora's tax agent Peter Barsymes (fl. 540-565 CE), who was an opponent of John's. Beginning in 534, Justinian's annual salary totals for infantry and cavalry, officer and soldier, was over 10,000 *nomismata* and in 545 was abolished due to the budget. The emperor then used a civil militia-style system of paying in supplies and soldiers took extra jobs to make the difference when five *nomismata* was a poor amount to feed a family.[339]

Another set of major investments were in the City itself as described in Procopius's *Buildings* going on to praise Justinian in his building of aqueducts and irrigation, draining marshlands, restoring buildings, and building the Churches of St. Sergius and St. Bacchus. In 537, Justinian began his work on the Church of the Hagia Sophia which had not been done since the burning of the Nika revolt five years before. Justinian employed two brilliant architects known as Anthemius of Tralles (474-558 CE) and Isidore of Miletus (fl. 6th cent. CE) to re-finish the dome with diffused light built in apertures to catch the sun. Supporting it was the Byzantine arc style as well as columns and apses that

---

[337] Bury, (*LRE-II*), 350. Bury calls it a 'novelty tax.'

[338] Haldon, John. *Byzantium in the Seventh Century: The Transformation of a Culture.* Cambridge, UK: University of Cambridge Press. 1990, 238-244.

[339] Treadgold, (*BAIA*), 150-151.

carried the load in their structure where the entire interior space could be seen from all seven of its openings, unlike in Western churches.[340] Over 10,000 men worked for five years, ten months, and four days to its completion with Egyptian gold, Ephesian porphyry, Greek marble, Syrian precious stones, and columns from the old, Pagan Roman Temple of the Sun where Constantine sacrificed.

The interior space itself rose 107 feet high and spanned an impressive four acres, decorated with gold crosses, a fifty-foot *iconastasis* depicting Mary, Jesus, and the saints, scroll work with monograms of Justinian and Theodora, and relics from Noah, the Nativity, and the Passion. Its greatest achievement was its dome, completing the Church to 180 feet as the dome itself held a diameter of 100 feet.[341] Brunelleschi (1377-1446)'s Renaissance complement of the Cathedral of Florence, in 1418, would later copy the use of arches and the pedapentia, the rounded triangle, to hold his Dome. It fell in the 530's, but Isidore's nephew of the same name raised the dome twenty-one feet, allowing sideways pressure to curve down and the dome holds its place to this day, mainly with the engineering genius of Anthemius. It was opulently decorated with painted marbles of flowers and trees, mosaics of the saints, and Christ which rightly induced Justinian to whisper to posterity, 'Solomon, I have surpassed thee.'

Along this in the accomplishments in the arts of the period was the work down to Ravenna's Church of San Vitale. This famous mosaic scene of Justinian, Theodora, Belisarius, John the Cappadocian, Antonina, Narses and the rest of the court was a new innovation of situating the Emperor with Christ above the mosaic, blessing the apex of the ceiling.[342] More Christian themes were seen in art as in the Angel Michael in the relief of St. Apollonius Nuovo where he wears Classical robes, but transcends space and uses a more Oriental theme as the Angel whose feet never touch ground.[343] This represents the mixture of Grecian beauty and the new Oriental Christian 'other-worldliness' of representations taken by saints, angels, the Virgin, and Christ. The result would grow to become the classical icon period of revered images defining Eastern Christian worship

---

[340] Brownworth, 85f.

[341] Bury, (*LRE-II*), 50.

[342] Angold, 36.

[343] Rice, David Talbot. *Art of the Byzantine Era*, 2nd ed. New York, NY: Thames and Hudson. 1985, 48-49. Photo: *The Archangel Michael*. Trustees of the British Museum. The British Museum: London, UK.

in everyday life.[344] Elsewhere culturally, to further promote the triumph of Christianity there were problems as Justinian came down hard on the 'Hellenic impiety'[345] of Pagan classical education, including closing the revered thousand-year-old Platonic School of Athens in 529.

His work to the facades and structures of churches were much more successful than his policies to conciliate those opinions inside the churches. The Monophysite controversy was as strong as ever, especially since it still divided the Church and was also the creed of the reformed empress Theodora before her marriage to Justinian as a convert of Severus of Antioch.[346] It threatened to break up the provinces of Syria and Egypt into separate and warring religious communities. Worse still, Monophysitism found a champion and true believer that traveled and consecrated the Copts and Syrians in Jacob Baradaeus (500-578 CE), a wandering Monophysite that captured the attention and implicit support of Theodora. He called for change in doctrine towards a better conciliation, without compromise, than the neutral dogmas that had been offered in the past.

In 518, the newly inducted junior ruler Justinian met with a Scythian monk who offered the designs for what would be the decisions for contemporary Chalcedonianism. This stance was revitalized in 532 with the publication of Leontius of Jerusalem's *Against the Monophysites* that suggested the idea of *'hypostasis'*. This descriptive idea held that Christ had a concrete human nature *melded* with the divine such as hot metals can combine in a foundry or as a sponge soaks water. The next year, an Edict of Unions was created by Justin I as the new creed that 'one of the Trinity suffered.'[347] In 537, however, wounds were torn afresh and growing gulfs dividing faith undermined Justinian's authority when the Palestinian monk Zoilus held the Monophysite cause from the deposed Patriarch Theodosius of Alexandria and his leadership in these communities blossomed. This cut a clear boundary between what was Chalcedonian and what was Monophysite in Eastern Rome and in 544,

---

[344] Vikan, Gary. 'Byzantine Art.' Chap. 6 of *Byzantium: A World Civilization*. Ed. by Angeliki E. Laiou and Henry Maguire. Washington, DC: Dumbarton Oaks, 81-118. 1992, 84-85.

[345] Bury, (*LRE-II*), 357.

[346] Browning, Robert. *Justinian & Theodora*. New York, NY: Thames and Hudson. 1987, 40.

[347] Gray, Patrick T.R. 'The Legacy of Chalcedon: Christological Problems and Their Significance.' Chap. 9 of *The Cambridge Companion to the Age of Justinian*, ed. by Michael Maas. Cambridge, UK: Cambridge University Press, 215-238. 2005, 231.

Justinian used his authority to issue a condemnation of three Bishops from the Council of Chalcedon: Theodoret of Cyrrhus, Ibas of Edessa (both Nestorians), and Nestorius's teacher himself, Theodore of Mopsuestia.

These condemnations of the three bishopric creeds were known as the Edict of the Three Chapters, and as can be expected, if it worked to mollify Monophysites, it failed to do so with Chalcedonians. In 548, Rome condemned the Chapters (under strained circumstances), defending Chalcedonianism to Patriarch Menas, even if this hardly ended the debate.[348] This led, ultimately, to the Fifth Ecumenical Council on May 5, 553, held in St. Sophia, wherein the Chapters were officially condemned, resulting in only mixed results. What is mainly important to note here is that it was Justinian's use of *Imperium* to affect Church doctrine with his own judgment and counsel.[349] It is doubtful the emperor was a cynical politico using what he did not believe in, but doctrine was always used as a tool to attempt containment the Empire under one authority.

The worst condemnation of the decisions of Justinian over the Three Chapters was the Western Church. Although raised to the Papal throne by Justinian and Belisarius in 537 during the Italian-Gothic War, Vigilus refused to condemn the Chapters, this blow to Nestorians also being a boon to Monophysites. An exasperated Justinian invoked his authority of Emperor of the West by sending guards to seize the Pope, as they did on November 22, 545, and bring him to the City. Arriving in January, 547, he refused to submit right to Justinian's face, but the notoriously formidable Theodora was a different story, and the Monophysite Empress wore him down. Vigilius, still verbally upholding his Chalcedonianism, did indeed publish the *Iudicatum* in 548, effectively condemning the Chapters. His submission harmed the Church before secular authority and its cause of Western Christendom[350] even after his revoking of the condemnation after Theodora's death with the *Constitutum*. After eight more years of dispute, a broken Vigilius left for Rome, falling ill at Syracuse and dying in 555, yet he still did so damning the Three Chapters and Justinian.

Terminology was the most abused of all, it seems, as those who were anti-Chalcedonians, but it also believed in the two natures of Christ were considered *Dyaphysites* and the 'tritheists' of Chalcedonianism were considered Miaphysites. By Justinian's death in 565, the doctrine of *aphthartodocetism*

---

[348]  Bury, (*LRE-II*), 386.
[349]  Ostrogorsky, 78.
[350]  Norwich, (*AM*), 36-38.

was developed. In an ill-advised move to concilate Eastern and Western Chalcedonians rejecting pre-Nestorian theology, the emperor officiated that as Christ's body was incapable of sin and, therefore, two natures worked *as one*. This hardly moved Monophysites to acceptance and Justinian's death left the matter unresolved. This doctrine was just another way that brought two forces naturally opposed together in Christian belief, similarly like the nature of the body and soul of Christ, upon which they could not agree. The outrageous nature of *apthartodocetism* compared to the doctrines brought forth in the past has even suggested a touch of senility on Justinian's part in 565![351]

The year 544 saw another turn for the worst in the Empire, as if God was condemning the heresies of the Councils in the coming of the bubonic plague. Coming supposedly east from Egypt, this plague killed around 300,000 people, from 10,000 to 16,000 daily, depopulating areas and lowering birth rates for generations statistically.[352] Fields went fallow and businesses went unsupervised as sudden death took the proprietors, claiming thousands more in Persia and seriously undermining the Monophysite Patriarchy and Church as its Bishops died.[353] Most of what we know of this phenomenon was recorded by the historian Procopius, who based his scholarship on the scientific method of the historian Thucydides (460-395BCE), commenting on the plague of the fifth century BCE in his *Peloponnisian Wars*.

By careful examination and rational analysis (through Classical reasoning) he noted it began with fever symptoms, a violet complexion, black buboes on the joints, and eventual death in a matter of days to hours from infection. It began in the city of Pelusium in 540 and came from traveling ships that would, naturally, include rats. Of course, the rats were not the cause of the disease, though they were generally carriers of *Xenopsylla Cheopsis,* a species of the common flea and the source of the virus's spread in populations, until its fast mortality rate killed itself out over time, stopping human infection.[354] It spread to the imperial Palace, infecting Justinian almost to an early death in 545, but both he and the Empress survived it. This plague was a problem until its

---

[351] Treadgold, 214.

[352] Norwich, (*EC*), 233.

[353] Treadgold, 197.

[354] Rosen, William *Justinian's Flea: Plague, Empire, and the Birth of Europe.* New York, NY: Viking Publishing. 2007, 187-188. This accelerated outbreak lead to a record population drop for the period and is thus theorized to have allowed Western Europe to rise in population and influence.

eventual decline in 558, halting the growing population and the new prosperity benefiting the Justinian's Empire.

Procopius is also important to history as Justinian's main detractor as in his *Anecdota,* or 'Secret History', he told of the underhanded skills of John the Cappadocian and Tribonian as well as the vicious nature of his lord Belisarius's wife, Antonina. Most importantly, however, is his treatment of Justinian and Theodora; Justinian was a 'Lord of Demons'[355] whose head could actually detatch unnaturally from his body. He was a tyrant who all the fear of the Empire was centered upon as well as a dangerous mal-administrator in finances when it came to the people and the army. Of course, all of this was published posthumously after Justinian's death as, 'It is not possible to record in a fitting manner events while the actors in them were still alive. It would have been impossible to escape the attentions of the swarms of spies, or avoid being detected and perishing most miserably.'[356]

This volume seems most likely because of Theodora's checkered past and Justinian's treatment and paranoia of Belisarius's fame. The emperor would later strip the successful general of all of his wealth, honors, and exile him from the City. Procopius, as Belisarius's personal secretary witnessed all of this and after praising the Emperor's accomplishments in other works, he let his hostilities explode in one of the most scandalous works in history. Edward Gibbon was especially trusting in the events (minus the supernatural) of Justinian's reign stating it must be true due to its probability and improbability. But, in recent times, the criticism due to Procopius names him as grossly biased and ignorant of true events.

Definitions of Justinian's reign commonly include 'a new era'. Though his reconquest would not last, he monopolized the silk trade (no one from then on was allowed to wear purple silk or shoes), and his legal code would have no rival save the Ten Commandments in their efficacy. Yet, Justinian was not intending a new era, but a return and perfection of the old. He has been called 'the last Roman emperor' for this reason due to his distinctly Roman Code to his Greco-Latin linguistics to the Classical 'Homeric' and Alexandrian battle tactics of Belisarius which Procopius also describes.[357] This means he had the

---

[355] Procopius of Caeserea, 194.

[356] *ibid.,* 37.

[357] Baker, G.P. *Justinian: The Last Roman Emperor.* New York, NY: Cooper Square Press. 2002, 286.

presence of mind to seize the opportunities of a historic transformation in his society to play both parts with such ease.

One example was the Code, outlining Roman tradition since Pagan times, but recognizing the ultimatum of God's word in deciding the fate of his more 'sinful' subjects[358] (homosexuals, heretics, pagans, and 'seducers'[359]), pederasts were also castrated, virginity protected, and child prostitution condemned. But the truth was, like Valentinian I and Theodosius I, he was a bright star that could not shine past his death on November 14, 565. The legacy he created militarily, diplomatically, and judiciously all reverted in the wake of his successors until radical change occurred in the Emperor Heraclius's innovations a century later. But, the Code refused to be a cold and mechanical instrument of legislation; it was designed to organically fit to all situations for the Empire's far future with Christian guidance and its 'greater humaneness, particularly regarding laws concerning the family.'[360]

Religiously, he sought to reconcile Chalcedonian and Monophysite in a harmonious idea that it was more important what Christ worked *for* in his natures rather than what that nature specifically was, as outrageous as this would seem to pre-modern sensibilities. It was also a matter of keeping Emperor and Patriarch reconciled, even as Justinian re-enacted the Kiss of Peace by Christ before St. Sophia after the liturgy.[361] His principle of aphthartodocetism was the best of a bad situation and a small, if ignored, legacy in Christian doctrine. In the end, Justinian had to be more than a Roman emperor; he had to be both Greek and Roman to preserve Byzantium's past and adapt it to a changing world of Oriental and Eastern synthesis.

Only by autocratic rule as in an Eastern court could the use of imperial power found in ancient Roman institutions be utilized in Constantinople and its world. All of this was due to a massive and perpetually energetic Justinian who was 'perhaps the most hardworking man in the Empire',[362] the Emperor that Never Slept and even his detractors noted his impeccable and sober temperance, resembling an ascetic. In the thirteenth epic poem of the *Divine Comedy*, Justinian, as representative of the Roman Empire – despite

---

[358] Treadgold, 180.

[359] Sherrard, 21. The seducers and their willing victims were executed and if a chaperone allowed it, molten lead was poured down their throats.

[360] Ostrogorsky, 74.

[361] Angold, 24.

[362] Bury, (*LRE-II*), 24.

the bloodshed and his betrayal of allies – earns a place in Paradise.[363] Posterity throughout the centuries holds him in the highest regard despite his faults, a quality of the supposed existence of the historical 'great men.'

But, Justinian could not handle these immense responsibilities of a world Empire and its implications on his own. He had a brilliant general in Belisarius and a wily John the Cappadocian who managed to raise the funds needed for his emperor however he did so. His legal expert, Tribonian, put Justinian's name above the lawmakers Solon, Lycurgus, and Hammurabi. But most of all was who some, especially Procopius, considered the power behind the throne. The Empress Theodora's life reads like a Hollywood movie or an epic poem of Christian redemption from the dregs peasants could not suffer to the most powerful woman in the known world. No one could have more influence over this man of a supposed 'great age', or the realm he ruled (barring himself) as did his complicated wife.

## THEODORA
### (527-548)

No Empress in Byzantium's history could prove to be as proficient and have a most stable influence than Theodora, wife of Justinian I. Her adaptability and range in ideas, as great as her husband's, with her indomitable will to be feared by her opponents has shown her strengths as an exceptional ruler. Her experience in the seedy parts of the 'real' world of Constantinople set her apart at court and demonstrated to her the importance of living and dying as a noble bearer of the purple. She was a woman of complexity and contradiction, but her actions spoke louder than her past and helped bring Eastern Rome to the world's stage as a lasting philanthropic state. Along with this is a legacy even now in popular culture as a dynamic figure in the field of women's history, rehabilitated from her former position as a villain by moralists and detractors, in such works as Stella Duffy's dual fictional historical biographies: *Theodora: Actress, Empress, Whore* (2010), and, *The Purple Shroud* (2012).

Throughout the eighteenth and nineteenth centuries, however, her persona in popular culture was one of a decadent tyrant like the Emperors Caligula or Elagabalus (203-222 CE). The works of Edward Gibbon, who created the greatest achievement of Byzantine history in the English language, espoused the values of eighteenth-century enlightenment that blinded him to misjudging

---

[363] Hussey, 22.

and misrepresenting Byzantium.[364] It has been an almost awesome challenge sifting truth from fiction, what deserves to be trusted from what should not. Though not the perfect monarch cleansed by (Monophysite) Christianity and not without a certain vicious pettiness and favoritism, her complexities have made her a woman as respected as Eleanor of Aquitaine, Queen Elizabeth I, and other such Medieval reformers of strong character, known for her being 'a woman of exceptional brain and courage.'[365]

She was known for her exquisite beauty[366] with a timelessness that benefitted much eastern and western Christian art and ornamentation. She had an antique Greek quality to her, artistically and otherwise, whose styles were reminiscent of the mythical Medea, Dido, and Antigone, 'her presence is oneiric and hieratic: dreamlike and formally stylized.[367] On the famed mosaic of St. Vitale in Ravenna, the Empress is wreathed by a halo of gold around her diadem of pearls and she holds a golden chalice in offering to the altar, as some say it was filled with gold while others say it was a dark space symbolizing her early death.[368] Surrounded by her courtiers and favorites, including her equally infamous niece, Antonina, and her daughter, Joannina, she is cloaked in a purple chlamys about herself. On the hem of this imperial garment is the Three Magi traveling to offer their gifts to the infant Christ as the ultimate symbol of humble charity.[369]

She was born in Constantinople around 500 CE, the daughter of an actress and a bear tamer named Acacius, inhabiting the Hippodrome to oversee animal spectacles for the City. When her father was killed in an accident, Theodora, her mother, and her sisters resorted to begging for alms from the Blues and Greens of the Hippodrome. The Greens were obstinate, though they shared the same social class, so the Blues took the opportunity to show up the other faction and accepted Theodora's family with their own charity. It was since then that Theodora associated herself with the aristocratic Blues and not the Greens that her former social status would usually imply. Her tarnished social status

---

[364] Bridge, Anthony. *Theodora: Portrait of a Byzantine Landscape*. Chicago, IL: Academy Chicago Publishers. 1978, vii.

[365] Bury, (*LRE-II*), 30.

[366] Much is said on her pallid skin complemented with vivacious eyes, a fit figure, delicate and regular by Gibbon, 1259.

[367] Cesaretti, Paolo. *Theodora: Empress of Byzantium*. Chicago, IL: MacGowan Publishing and Vendome Press. 2004, 350-351.

[368] Herrin, 67.

[369] Angold, 36.

growing up was a main issue in her development as she was a dancer, actress, entertainer, and prostitute.

It would not have mattered if she was a prostitute in reality or not, being an actress, she was expected to be one due to the expectations of a social class of performers, below peasantry in contempt, equal to that of slaves. But, she took many men to her side for money to help support her family, eventually being taken to Alexandria as an official's kept concubine. Procopius spends page after page detailing her exploits as someone who acted as a boy to the men in her bed,[370] making lewd jokes to entertain them, and use of all of her three 'appetures' at once to satisfy them. Her onstage act was especially notorious where she would cover her breasts with grain and allow geese to feed themselves right off of her nude body. This was a 'burlesque of the myth of Jupiter and Leda' it is explained, harrowing the blend of pornographic and mythical culture on the Byzantine stage.[371] She was cast as someone who would do anything for her pleasure and that of her numerous clients, merchants, and Senators of the City alike. Though she lacked real talent in the flute or legitimate dancing, her slapstick comedies and pantomimes made her quite popular.[372]

Of course, Procopius cannot be taken very seriously in the estimations of his *Secret History*. Anthony Kaldellis of the University of Ohio and specialist in Early Byzantine literature outlines how the *Secret History* is a narrative without genre in form and structure. It fails to be a true history due to its complete lack of objectivity and subtext. The best evidence for this is not so much his treatment of Theodora, but his own master, General Belisarius and his wife, Antonina, who was also Theodora's niece by her older sister, Comito. These parables detail his own fears of a *gyniokratia*, ('rule of women') over cuckholded men such as in the *Lysistrata* of the comic Aristophanes. Certainly, classic Greek misogyny can be found in Procopius's style when he speaks of the fallen women Theodora sets up nunneries and charitable houses for during her reign. Nevertheless, Procopius's writings were, a true boon to the Classical style of Attic Greek prose and a standard in contemporary Byzantine linguistics and scholarship.

By 520, her reputation was well known and she managed to become the concubine of a certain Hecebolus, governor of Pentapolis around Cyrene in North Africa. Now she was traveling south to a better life outside the

---

[370] Procopius of Caeserea, 83.
[371] Browning, 39.
[372] Herrin, 26.

Hippodrome and semi-respectability in society. She went first to Alexandria in Egypt, where it is possible, though not recorded, she began to understand more of the Monophysitism she would adopt for her faith. In 521, she was cast out by Hecebolus for a different woman, and Theodora sought refuge in the caverns of Egypt in the tutelage of the Monophysite nature of Christ through the city's Patriarch, Timothy.

She was also introduced to the exiled Antiochene Patriarch, Severus where the legend here goes that he taught her etiquette and the ways of respectable, even noble, women in exchange of her becoming his operative in Constantinople. She was no Virgin Mary born again, but she did become a changed woman in that she never prostituted or was seen on stage again. Even Procopius was forced to admit how she was never unfaithful to her husband like her niece would be to Belisarius; now she was a converted and baptized Christian with a purpose towards Monophysitism.[373] The Monophysite chronicles of John of Ephesus (507-586 CE) would sentimentally remark how she was a 'Christ-loving woman...the most Christian Empress sent by God in difficult times to protect the persecuted.'[374]

This is how she returned to Constantinople before meeting Justin's heir apparent. If, indeed, Theodora was as notorious as she was in her days on the stage, it is unlikely that Justinian had never somehow heard of her or her reputation. But, either way, Justinian fell in love with her and she wooed him successfully. One impediment, however, was the old wife of Anastasius I, Euphemia as she disapproved of the union and stressed to the emperor the laws restraining such a union becoming a marriage. She, however, died in 524 and the laws were changed while the couple defied almost all marriage conventions allowable as Theodora was not inspected by bust, waist, or feet as such brides had to be[375] and she received no symbolic golden apple as a favor from her 'choosing' husband and was married in 525. One thing that made this possible was Justinian's reputation and status with Justin and his control of him behind the throne. When Justin died in 527, Justinian and Theodora both

---

[373] In Gibbon, XL it is made clear that Theodora's Monophytism cost her much in the Church's eyes; she had an illegitimate son, and in a footnote, Gibbon tells of how St. Sabas refused to bless him at the cost of being a heretic 'worse than Anastasius (I) himself.'

[374] John of Ephesus. 'Commentarii de Beatis Orientalibus' *Patralogia Orientalis*, XVIII, ed. by W.J. van Douan and J.P.N. Land. Amsterdam, UP: Verhandelingen de Koninklijke Akademie van Wetenschappen. 1889, 114, 247.

[375] Sherrard, 79.

were crowned in the Church of St. Irene as the rulers of the Byzantine Empire and the Emperor would award his consort fifty pounds of gold, the Palace of Hormisdas, and allow her old looming quarters to become a Church of St. Panteelemon.[376]

It was not long before work and agendas by the empress was pressed on Justinian. When he was creating the *Novels* of his Code of Roman Law in 535, she advised whole new legislation based on more advanced possibilities for the legal status of women in the Empire. Women would now equally inherit their sons property, wives' dowries would revert to their own property on their husbands' deaths, and slave status on the children of female slaves was enhanced to their favor (some of these prostitutes were barely ten years old). The most connected to her personal life's experiences was the expulsion of pimping and the exile of brothel-keepers as now retribution on the worst aspects of the City's prostitution trade would be hers completely.

In 532, however, a test unlike any other would plague the stability of this new regime as the Nika Revolts destroyed an important part of the City and threatened to depose and even destroy the new regime on behalf of the mob passions of the Blues and Greens. It was here that Justinian considered fleeing for his and his court's life to Chalcedon across the Bosporus, but Theodora refused. In an awesome speech given before Justinian, Belisarius, John the Cappadocian, Tribonian, and Procopius, the Empress made her opinion clear: 'My lords, the present occasion is too serious to allow me to follow the convention that a woman should not speak in a man's council. Those whose interests are threatened by extreme danger should think only of the wisest course of action, not of conventions. Now in my opinion, in the present crisis if ever, flight is not the right course, even if it should bring us safety. It is impossible for a man, once he has been born into the world, not to die; but for one who has reigned it is intolerable to be exiled. May I never be deprived of this purple robe, and may I never see the day when those who meet me do not call me "Empress." If you wish to save yourself Lord [Justinian], there is no difficulty. Over there is the sea, and there too are the ships. Yet reflect for a moment whether, when you have escaped to a place of security, you will not prefer death to such safety. I agree with an old saying that the purple is a fair winding-sheet.'[377]

---

[376] Bury, (*LRE-II*), 30-31.

[377] Procopius of Caesarea, *Persian Wars*, 35-37. This is said to be a misquote by Theodora or Procopius of the ancient Tyrant of Syracuse, Dionysius the Elder (432-367 BCE), who said that 'Tyranny makes the best shroud', Brownworth, 80f.

Her stunned audience agreed to stay and Belisarius was ordered on the spot by Justinian to make an assault on the rioters and their imperial choice, Hypatius, using imperial troops. They triumphed with tens of thousands dead, and the imperial couple, decked out in their finest raiment returned calm to the Hippodrome from their balcony of the Kathisma. It had unequivocally been Theodora's courage in the direst circumstances that was responsible for Justinian and her both to continue a long and successful reign together.

Yet, Theodora did have a dangerously petty and vengeful side as well-known by the imperial court. In 534, when Queen Amalasuntha of the Roman Goths died, it was supposedly she who influenced Justinian to have it done through her ambassador to Theodahad. It is contended this was out of spite for what she felt was a political rival for Justinian's favor when his options were to destroy the Gothic queen or set aside Theodora to wed her and inherit the West. Also, in 541, with Antonina, she orchestrated the fall of her odious rival John the Cappadocian, finding her opportunity in the words of John's daughter, Euphemia. On these charges of treason whose evidence her spies received, John was disgraced, robbed of all property, and tonsured in a monastery for life in Cyzicus on the Marmara. It had been well known Theodora disliked the Cappadocian and saw him as a threat to her policies. Justinian would now be seen as the one controlled as he controlled Justin and by a will and cunning greater than his own.

Her most remembered work, unfortunately, was in the character assassination of the general Belisarius. After his victories in Africa, Persia, and Italy as well, gaining the applause and Triumph he deserved, she sowed seeds of caution in the emperor's mind that would germinate after her own death. He saw his call for larger armies as a ruse to gain military power against Justinian, especially after he deceitfully took the crown of Italy. In November 562, a plot against the Emperor implicated numerous well-known citizens including the general, and after confiscating his wealth and honors to exile him, he finally executed him a few months before he himself died in 565.

It is conjectural that Theodora's word in Justinian's ear put in motion the mistrust and misgiving to appear fifteen years after her death, probably not at all likely as the emperor grew more paranoid as the years passed after his wife's death. But her hatred of Belisarius was as well known as her hatred for the Cappadocian, so the fact she tried to distance himself from the emperor and used her niece to emasculate and spy on the general in Italy is more realistic. The real truth seems to be that Theodora was psychologically projecting her own insecurities on Belisarius: 'Convinced that Belisarius was as politically-minded as she herself was, she had poisoned her husband's mind against the one man who could have accomplished his dreams of conquest.'[378]

By spring of 548, she saw her life endangered by stomach cancer, and with an entourage of the Praetorian Prefect, treasurers, counts, and 4,000 attendants, she made her way to the healing springs of Pythia. After this treatment, she toured Bithynia and gave 'liberal alms' to the churches, monasteries, hospitals, and even the roads.[379] Her death on June 28 was a great tragedy to the Roman people, especially her devoted husband; now half of his rule had died with Theodora. At her funeral, senators, priests, patriarchs, and the exiled former Monophysite Bishop of Constantinople were present. It happened in the presence of Antonina and Belisarius, and their daughter, Joannina, on a return trip from Italy after the Easter Day diplomatic triumph in 537 for Orthodoxy against Pope Vigilius concerning the Three Chapters. She was consecrated in a tomb built at the Church of the Holy Apostles, which was completed in 550. It was later that the Orthodox Church made her and Justinian saints to the Church for all the accomplishments, even though both never left Monophysitism.

Until the later twentieth century, Theodora was treated as some luxurious Queen of Whores, Procopius noting how she enjoyed hours of luxurious bathing each day and the use of cosmetics.[380] She was made a saint of Orthodox Christianity until the 1683 resurfacing of the *Anekdota* by a Vatican priest under Pope Innocent XI. Since then, she has been a pariah in a strange and stalwartly western culture; this was not just limited to the page, but the stage as well as in 1884 Paris, Victorien Sardou (1831-1908) published a scandalous and Decadent portrayal of the Empress starring the irreverent actress Sarah Bernhardt (1844-1923). Sardou insisted on an 'archeological authenticity' and 'archaeological reconstitution' of Theodora's image and scholar Elena N. Boeck writes this was the justification for the play of 'Oriental savagery and unbridled lust' of Theodora as queen. Accurately, she used her influence to establish charitable houses for such women and abolishing child slavery. Byzantium, it is said, tolerated the evils of slavery and poverty and women had no recourse when this was exploited by the sexual whims of men.[381]

Procopius would spin tales in his *Secret History* that blurred the line of fact and rumor. It is true the pair were to be addressed as Lord and Lady, an arrogant

---

[378] Brownworth, 108.

[379] Gibbon, 1259.

[380] Procopius, 114.

[381] Bridge, 95.

practice, but there is also the fact she supposedly tortured and murdered a secret son has been countered by the literature of other sources, such as St. Sabas. She is also said to have had a handy abattoir under the Palace, quite unconfirmed, to practice torture and execution on criminals and whosoever she saw fit. It might be true she enjoyed her luxuries: food, wine, bathing, and daily siestas, but the 'bloodlust' and severity at court to please her must be exaggerations. Reading Procopius, you can still detect a misogyny Classical Greece fostered in its students and dogmatic bias towards Belisarius by whom Theodora was threatened. However, some criticism is due as she did weaken the treasury by dismissing the Cappadocian, harmed Church unity with the Monophysite antics of Jacob Baradeus, and spoiled by jealousy foreign policy with her hostile actions towards the Goths and Queen Amalasuntha.[382] Her jealous streaks and displeasure justified some of Procopius's charges of maladministration.

Pushing much of history aside, and looking at the latter part of the past century, we see a realistic woman of redemption and intelligence despite, not due to, her traumatic upbringing. Her conversion is story enough for a juxtaposition of Mary Magdalene's journeys with an emperor liturgically commiserate of divinity by ritual and Roman political culture and she even secretly converted Justinian to Monophysitism. Though she was vicious and intolerant of her enemies, nonetheless, her charisma and courage was as strong as any man's at the court as the Nika Revolt demonstrated and she could not quite be a role model. She is a fascinating woman of the Middle Ages next to the queens and saints that also defined unexpected gender roles in the era. When she did leave Justinian, he was half of what he was and never quite recovered, never marrying again despite dying with no heir except for his lackluster nephew, Justin. With both gone, however, the levy that was Justinian's legacy would begin its breakdown and the flood changed East Rome to Byzantium in a mere generation.

## JUSTIN II 'THE YOUNGER'
### (565-578)

## TIBERIUS II CONSTANTINE
### (578-582)

Despite a revival of success in the decades before Justinian's death, the latter part of 565 was actually a time that needed caution and perspective in the

---

[382] Treadgold, 205.

Empire. It had broadened itself in a nice amount of time, but those who did so were now gone: Justinian and Theodora, Belisarius, and John the Cappadocian. It should have been considered that expanding too fast could have had backlashing consequences, something Justin II and his successors would see first hand. As Justinian was energetic and industrious, Justin was reckless and could not handle the pressures of crisis once again arising in the Empire. He proudly believed the fortitude of his uncle would keep the Empire together and had faith he was the one with the will to do it, and he was right on the former, but his opinion that he was the only one capable of doing so was mere naiveté. It was aptly described how upon Justinian's death, 'the winds were loosed from prison, the disintegrating elements began to operate with full force, and the artificial system collapsed.'[383]

Born in 520 to Justinian's sister Vigilantia and her husband, Dulcissimus, he lived in his uncle's court and grew up in Constantinople, being appointed emperor from Justinian's deathbed by his only witness, Callimachus. He was brought before the Senate and crowned by the Patriarch John on November 15, 565, his ascension being received by an Avar ambassador and a Latin poem by the court poet, Corripus. Unfortunately, these same Avars would not get much support from Justin for many years as they would later raid Thrace, spurning a settlement truce in Pannonia in 562. Nonetheless, attempting to mirror his uncle's glory, he would grace the Great Palace with a new throne room in the Chrysotriklinos. Financially, he cancelled tax arrears accrued since 560, despite reports there was little left in the treasury to handle with Justinian's adventures. Despite these events, he reinstated the 535 laws prohibiting office sales, although Evagrius describes him as trafficking in ecclesiastical offices. He also had a reputation for avarice, remitting tax arrears on ship cargoes in his first *Novel* of 566, enriching the treasury at what appeared to be the expense of commerce. Also imposing new taxes on wine and bread,[384] these loaves were now known to Constantinople as 'political' or 'civil' loaves.

Domestically he was acceptable, as the court poet Corripus (fl. 6th cent. CE) wrote of an Avar envoy sent in Justin's first days, where the splendor and luxury of the court made it seem that 'the Palace was another Heaven (*Et credunt aliud Romana palatial coelem*),'[385] but it was in the realm of foreign and military

---

[383] Bury, J. B. *A History of the Later Roman Empire: From Arcadius to Irene (395 A. D. to 800 A. D., vol. II.)*. New York, NY: Elibron Classics. 2005, 67.

[384] Bury, (*AI-II*), 78.

[385] Obolensky, 49.

affairs he was awkward and weak. This was demonstrated by abandoning his uncle's conciliatory religious doctrines, stopping the Avar subsidies, and dangerously risking their hostility. This stoppage was later nullified, likely, by Justin's neutrality in the Gepid slaughter by the combined armies of the needed Avars and Lombard tribes. But, the Avars' refreshed hostilities had projected a war with Byzantium from the formerly Ostrogothic Danube and the Byzantines elected the Lombards to aid them. Headed by the Excubitor Tiberius against Albion, the Avar king, the Lombards prevailed and Justin settled them in north Italy. Not understanding the ramifications, Justin had just dismissed the aged general Narses from Italy and the Lombards had captured Liguria and Pavia by 569.

In 571, the eastern frontier borders of the Empire exploded starting with multiple Avar incursions and, in Africa, the Moors after fifteen years of stability, rose up and killed the Prefect Theodore under King Gelmur. They would later defeat two more Master of Soldiers for the Empire in Africa and the region looked to be successfully slipping away. Later in the year, the Italian Lombards had spread south from Pavia to Spoleto so easily in fact that legend hails the eunuch Narses gave it to them to spite the pernicious Justin for his dismissal.[386] The last Spanish Byzantine vestiges were taken by the Visigoth Leovigild, also strategically taking Asidona and Cordova on the Mediterranean. By 577, the Western Goths were settled completely in modern Tuscany and prepared to invade north and east in Italy. Everywhere, Justinian's western legacy was crumbling under a new regime of weak military leadership by his nephew.

Justin II, meanwhile, was in Eurasia burning bridges: he refused to pay the arrears Persia had annually received, suddenly dismissing all of Khosru's diplomats, and siding with a rebellious Armenia. East Rome also aided the invaders from the northern steppes that attacked Persia, known as the Turks. Already, Justin secured an alliance with the Sogdian Turks for a commercial partnership in the silk trade from China to eastern Persia and Antioch.[387] In 572, the Armenians rose up and killed the Persian governor and Justin made his cousin, Marcian, Master of Soldiers in the East, expelling the Persians from the Armenian city of Arzanene. Marcian then invaded, in 573, Mesopotamia, taking Nisibis, however, they were recalled in the wake of a huge Persian expedition headed west. The Persians, now unopposed as the Romans had fled Armenia and invaded Syria, taking Apamea and the vital fort city of Dara

---

[386] Norwich, (*EC*), 568f.
[387] Obolensky, 167.

on the border with over 292,000 captives. Of the captives, 2,000 of them were Christian virgins set apart for the Turkish King who then drowned and martyred themselves in the rivers, rather than lose their virtue.[388]

A commander known as Tiberius, in the meantime, was given control of the army and reserves by Justin's wife, Sophia. As he was mentally breaking down to the pressures of state, Justin was despondently contemplating suicide. Theophanes the Confessor described the event, 'after having learned of [the capture of Anastasiopolis], Justin in consternation of the greatness of the disaster, was plunged into a deranged state and begged Hormisdas to make peace.' Now, Tiberius had to repair the problems of Justin's 'arrogance and parsimony leading to disaster.'[389] As an outbreak of plague passed over in 574, Tiberius was named Caesar by Justin. Sophia acting on behalf of the Emperor as well, paid the Persians a 45,000 *nomismata* indemnity for a year's truce after the emperor had closed all of the shops in the City in his mental breakdown.[390]

Another factor was the battle of Monophysitism, in which Justin II was not successful, all going badly after the band-aid doctrine of aphthartodocetism was basically being ignored. The Monophysites now called the Chalcedonians true Tritheists, believers in three gods as set in the Trinity, therefore three persons instead of three natures as the Trinitarians of the Catholic Church would. This took farther the Monophysite conclusion that Chalcedoniasm was a belief in two natures and two persons. In 566, the Chalcedonian Patriarch Theodosius died and was replaced by John Scholasticus. In 567, a conference was called for Chalcedonians, Monophysites, and the ineluctable Jacob Baradeus. It is here that Justin laid down a plan all present could agree on and, despite the grumbling of Syrian monks, Baradeus and the rest sought a compromise.

But, not surprisingly, Bishops all across the Empire denounced this as adverse Chalcedonianism and Monophysitism, so, finally forced to choose a side, Justin 're-outlawed' all Monophysitism and hostilities reached their boiling point. Though this 'third-rail' policy of compromise was doomed to fail perhaps from the start, at least something was done to please a believer like Jacob Baradeus. They would both die in 578, Justin doing so on October 4, at fifty-eight years of age, with a deeply troubled mind. A few days before,

---

[388] So says John of Ephesus using this as Christian romanticizing despite the early Christian views of Augustine that life was preferable to forced impurity in his *Ecclesiastical History*, VI, i.

[389] Treadgold, 223.

[390] Vasiliev, 170.

Justin adopted the trustworthy and capable Tiberius as his successor as Constantinople was witnessing his deteriorated state.

Artistically, Justin II's reign was less than Justinian's as well, as he did not possess the adequate funds to the arts his uncle had. But, it must be noted how, though not ideally an art piece, there was a miraculous relic brought to the City in 574 associated with his reign. From Cappadocian Kamoulianai came an icon of Christ that was one of many made *acheiropoietos* ('unmade by human hands'), thus, having a directly divine origin. It would later be made as a war banner leading East Romans in battle against the Zoroastrian Sassanid Persians.[391] Along with this was the commission of a silver cross, now at the Vatican Library, bearing the portraits of Justin and Sophia and supposedly containing within the center a piece of the True Cross.

Justin's death and ceremonial burial is well chronicled in the Coptic Corripus's *Euloigy* as Corripus was a favorite poet of the Emperor's court and a Chalcedonian. He lamented the hemorrhaging strength of Roman virtue and its loss before the arms of the barbaric Avars and Gepids, alluding this to the loss of virtue being the loss of Justin, yet this seems misplaced. It was Justin's impracticality and hubris that led to these events. Yet, was it this weakness of the legacy, or the unrealistic goals of maintaining Justinian's achievements that led to this? For example, were his wishes to goad war with Persia an attempt to prove himself superior to his uncle? It is mostly certain another Justinian would have kept up this legacy, yet a continuous line of Justinians would never be found. The two factors making the difference were that the imperial power was no longer absolute; even his wife, while ambitious, lacked the will and genius of Theodora. At the same time the bonds which linked the outer provinces with the center, and therefore with each other, were loose. Judicial, ecclesiastical, and administrative posts and regulations were relaxed or made more locally autonomous, such as a law in 568 separating these powers in administrative appointments.[392]

This was also true of Diocletian, Constantine and Theodosius; no great Byzantine achievements would survive more than one or two generations. This progressive/regressive cycle is mostly based on social factors, such as the prosperity of Justinian based on constant flow of cash in and out of the treasury. But, when that was diminished in the later years, and Justin had much less state income, it showed Justinian's methods were more on the spot than

---

[391] Angold, 28.
[392] Bury, (*AI-II*), 73-76.

planned and it also did not hurt having a ruthless tax collector like John the Cappadocian. But, Justin II had no ingenuity or skills in administrating these and other aspects as the pressure was more than he could handle.

This was likely the case with Constans I, Arcadius, and others like him, and that is why barbarians stepped in to do this as it tore Rome apart, eventually. Perhaps East Rome's saving grace was the fact a Roman commander stepped in for Justin when direly needed. Tiberius II had problems exterior to the state, but also showed some poor judgment as well. However, a continuous Byzantine administration of the situation kept things in check better than another barbarian general with more ambition than sense.

With the last of Justinian's line gone, a member of Justin's professional staff became Emperor at the behest of Justin's wife. He was the leader of the Excubitors, the emperor's royal guard, meaning he at least, like Justin I, did apply his military skills and organization to solve his problems. That is what Constantinople needed, a smart administrator to galvanize the bureaucracy as well as the battlefield prowess to prepare against the Persian and barbarian backlashes Justin's bad diplomacy brought about. Yet, Justin was an able administrator, nonetheless, and while Tiberius II was the best military provider, bureaucratic skill was something he lacked.[393] This doubling of imperial administration in state and war in the decade after Justinian's death would require a certain balance.

Tiberius was a Thracian born in 535, in 552 he became acquainted with Justin as the notarius to the Constantinopolitan Patriarch Eutychius. He was made *Comes Excubitorum* in 565 after Justinian's death, and joined Justin as consul in 566. In 569, he became Justin's Master of Soldiers throughout the Eastern Empire, setting him to task against the Avars. Justin demanded the Avars return hostages seized from the region and sent Tiberius to collect, but, in 571, Tiberius was soundly defeated escaping only with his life. In subsequent negotiations the Avar envoys were attacked by local highwaymen and Tiberius was sent to clear them out and return stolen goods (there could be a question if this was a set up, but neither Justin nor Tiberius were really that clever), this putting the Romans in a better position with the tribe.

In 574, Justin suffered a breakdown after elevating Tiberius to the rank of Caesar, entitling him under Sophia's trust, to take over responsibilities as

---

[393] Treadgold, 223.

Augustus. He wasted no time gaining popularity by offering large donatives and using the treasury to build fortifications and strengthening old ones, even abolishing some of Justin's taxes. In 575, he made a peace with Persia for 90,000 *nomismata* over three years and used the time rebuilding the Armies of the East led by Baduarius. A year later, the Lomabrd king and his successor were murdered in a coup and Tiberius saw this a time of confusion in which to strike, but he was mistaken in his timing as the Lombards continued their encroachment of North Italy, killing Baduarius in battle.

At their moment of weakness, Khosru struck Armenia once again, where the truce with Persia did not extend. Tiberius sent troops east to Sebastea and Meteline and Germanus's son, Justinian, commanded the troops taking back Armenian territory and sacking the Persians at Atropatene. But, in 577 the Persians retook Armenia and Justinian died, leaving the armies without able military leadership once again. That year, an estimated 100,000 Slavs[394] were settled forcibly into Illyricum and Thrace, but were contained by Tiberius's succeeding Comes Excubitorum, Maurice. This talented field operator recruited the aid of the *Foederati* to the eastern armies, increasing their numbers by fifty percent.

In the City, the Caesar handled the Monophysite recursion after the Patriarch John's death by replacing him with his old friend, the tolerant Eutychius, denouncing once again aphthartdocetism. He tried to reform the bureaucracy by widening the power bases of the Senate and the *demes*, now resurfacing and replenishing after the Nika Riot. Handling the Lomabard situation by bribing them 200,000 *nomismata,* he manipulated the Lombard nobles to hold off on electing a new king. When the Slavs invaded Illyricum again, Tiberius brought in his Avar allies from across the Danube to quell the situation as his lofty title of Master Militium was an expensive, but seemingly effective, one.

The Persians broke their truce early and invaded Mesopotamia in 578, where Maurice drove them back by taking Arazene, then incurring farther inside Aphumon and Singara. Maurice's victories eastward was said to have upset Khosru I to his death in 589, thus, securing East Rome's place in Armenia. In 578, Justin died, leaving Tiberius to become emperor (he then took the name 'Constantine' as he also was the second Tiberius to reign since 14 CE). Sophia entreated Eutychius to marry Tiberius to herself, but Tiberius would not leave his wife, frustrating Sophia's dynastic plans and furthering the heirless empress

---

[394] Norwich, (*EC*), 271.

from the throne. His wife was then accepted by the circus factions who argued, typically, over her royal name being 'Anastasia' (Blues) and 'Helena' (Green); the Blues won out and the Augusta Anastasia was crowned.[395]Tiberius II started out as a popular monarch because of Maurice's successes in Persia and his own laurels, as well. His liberal use of funds was apparent with the excise of 7,200 pounds of gold in 578, also remitting taxes twenty-five percent over four years and rescinding the bread tax of his predecessor. He is also said to donate large sums to professors, silversmiths, bakers, and other professions,[396] although this was probably to endear him to the artisan and professional classes rather than honor their contributions. He was not known as a patron of the liberal arts, crafts, or architecture beyond the capacity of buying the loyalty of the professions.

Tiberius sent 800 pounds of gold to the Asian soldiers[397] and money and troops to Ravenna, pacifying the Lombards. In Spain, creating an alliance, the son of king Leovigild, Hermenegild, converted to Orthodoxy from Arianism and agreed to aid Tiberius. Furthermore, in Africa, the Master of Soldiers in the West killed the Moorish king Garmul, once again securing Africa for the Empire. Tiberius II's reign was unfortunately less dimensional than others, so mostly military exploits fill his achievements over that of more pressing subjects when many other similar warrior-Emperors would rise in such times and in the Empire's near future.

The filling up of the eastern armies left the Balkans undermanned, so in 579, the Avars extorted money from Tiberius to keep it from invasion. Peace was also denied by the new Persian King Hormuz IV who would not free Dara for Iberia, Armenia, or Arazmene. Worse, the Emperor's 50,000 soldiers needed pay and Tiberius's costly expenses made that impossible, mutiny notwithstanding; he kept 'accessional' donatives stable at nine *nomismata* in gold when the earlier centuries used five *nomismata* and one pound of silver per capita.[398] The next year, Maurice decided to invade Persian territory as he burned a path down the Tigris and Euphrates through Mesopotamia, almost

---

[395] Bury, (*AI-II*), 79.

[396] *ibid.*, 81.

[397] John of Ephesus, *iii*, 11.

[398] Treadgold, (*BAIA*), 145; Haldon, John. *Byzantine Praetorians: An Administrative, Institutional, and Social Survey of the Opsikian and the tagmata, c.580-900*, R. Habelt. Series: vol. 3, *Poiklia Byzantina*. 1984, 121. Haldon also clarifies that in the officer corps of the Scholae, these higher ranks were paid the same in such donatives as ordinary soldiers.

reaching Ctesiphon. But, a Persian army marched on the army's right, forcing a tactical retreat from the region; this was on behalf of the Ghassanids, the Empire's Arab allies responsible for cordoning major offensives across the rivers. But, despite decades of negotiating for alliance with Justinian, a betrayal by the Ghassanid Arab king with Persia weakened this position for the Roman frontiers from the north.

Two years later, the Persians still not pacified, Tiberius decided to pay subsidies and keep the merchant's peace with Persia, while the King ceded the region of Sirmium. Unfortunately, in the Peloponnese, Slavic armies were invading, taking Athens. The Persians did receive a sound defeat at Constantina and gave up Anastasiopolis, but this critical opportunity to secure the border could still not be taken by Maurice. He was making speed to Constantinople for the emperor was near death, August 15 of that year, as he had eaten bad mulberries, and was suffering a bad 'consumption.'

Tiberius was dying and leaving no heir, giving him little choice but to elect his best generals at the time, Maurice, and Justinian's grand-nephew Germanus as co-Caesars. The idea was to restore the dual monarchy of East and West in the Roman Mediterranean kingdoms as it was in 395. Unfortunately, before he died, he scrapped the idea, perhaps because the East's situation was looking somewhat dire and no pay could come to the West's troops from the treasury. So, he then named Maurice the successor as Augustus and died a day later on August 13, 582, in the Palace of the Hebdemon in Constantinople.

Tiberius II Constantine did what he could with the bad situation he was given while on the throne. The treasury had little surplus, mainly due to large indemnities and bribes to neighbors quickly dried up the finances of the Empire and at a critical juncture. The West was slipping away slowly to the Avars, Lombards, and other Gothic tribes. Tiberius successfully mollified them for a time as the Moors were driven from African rule (though without the Crown's support), but all of this would prove to be temporary. Without hard cash, supplies, or resources, soldiers went unpaid and rebellion would naturally stir throughout the Empire. Persia and the eastern tribes would get unruly and extortions unpaid left regions open to invasion without impunity. Only a capable soldier-emperor could make a stand to keep Byzantium together at least in the East, and they would get just that in Tiberius's outstanding successor. Thus, the dying emperor's last words to Maurice were to be in his funeral oration: 'Make your reign my finest epitath.'[399]

---

[399] Bury, (AI-II), 82.

The most noted of the historians of this period was Evagrius Scholasticus, a Syrian Orthodox lawyer with high distinctions from Tiberius and Maurice of Quaestor and Praefect, respectively. His history mainly focused on the period of 431 to 593 CE, stopping at the reign of Maurice; he was mainly considered as an authoritative secular source.[400] His style of history was a Christian refutation of the fourth-century Pagan historian, Zosimus (doing as Eusebius had done), to discredit the Pagans of East Rome who still existed by 582. He sought to refute Paganism and any irrelevance felt by ecclesiasticism for it by citing the mistakes of Roman Pagan and heretical Emperors from the Divine Julius to Zeno.[401] His stance on Tiberius was, like the opinions of John of Ephesus, that the military debacles were of course the displeasure of God at the existence of Pagans in the Empire. Implicitly and even unintentionally, he judged that Tiberius II Constantine should have constructed a new persecution, as if the Empire had time and resources for that!

## MAURICE TIBERIUS
### (582-602)

It was obvious, since his succession in 582, that Maurice was the most capable and successful general since Belisarius, though at a smaller scale. Through the painful period of the final separation from the West, the barbarian threats plaguing the East were held in check by Maurice's military skill. With a depleted treasury, soldiers on the verge of rebellion, and even the return of the internal chaos of the *demes,* Maurice would show ability with an expert grasp of warfare. This would result in one of the greatest works of Byzantine literature on military planning, the *Strategikon.* Its result would ultimately be the transition of the civil authority to the military and the creation of the lasting system of the Thematic military districts.[402] What we know of his genius (and faults) come from Theophylactus Simocatta ('Long Cat-Nose'), an Egyptian East Roman who was born in Maurice's reign and wrote of the years 582 until the reign of the future Emperor Heraclius, fighting the Persian enemy, ending with his death in 630. He praised Maurice's love of education and the arts, a proven rarity for military Emperors that his successor would disgracefully neglect.

---

[400] Ostrogorsky, 24.

[401] Kaegi, 218-222.

[402] Diehl, Charles. 'L'Origene du Regime des Themes'. *Etudes Byzantines* 3rd ed. Paris, France. 1888, 1905, 2010, 277.

Though this brilliance was barely rivaled, however, his civil policies almost destroyed the internal workings of both the army, and the Empire, financially. His need to be popular among his troops barred him from making lasting reforms necessary to uphold a treasury squandered by the precedent of Tiberius's gifts made few options available; he is seen to have believed it was better to have no reserve for an emergency than have an emergency.[403] Maurice was seen by his people as avaricious and stingy to a fault, with a 'diseased appetite for gold'[404] that ultimately went to his war efforts when actually carried at all. It was unfortunate that those who judged him could not properly understand his position, only to react more violently than they had with Justinian.

Maurice was born in 539 in an obscure village called Arabissus in Cappadocia and he may have been of Armenian heritage, but the issue is not truly clear; the historian Evagrius Scholasticus believes an origin of an ancient West Roman family. He began in Constantinople as a notarius to the Comes Excuboritum of Tiberius's court and later his imperial successor in 574. Maurice would then marry Tiberius's daughter, Constantina, having a son, Theodosius, on August 4 of the same year. He is said to have been honest, upright, yet resolved to the point of rigidity,[405] a problem that would cost him his family and life, yet negate the assessments of greed made by his detractors. Upon his succession on the 13th of August, 582, Maurice would need thoughtful programs in which to deal with economic forces as the treasury was nearly empty and foreign challenges rose all around East Rome's frontiers.

This started in 582, negotiating a peace with Persia and John Mystocon ('the Moustached') from Armenia was chosen as his Master of Soldiers to keep the territory of Aphumon, but his grip started to slip when in spring 583, when the Avars re-appeared. They demanded 100,000 *nomismata* in subsidy, resulting in Maurice blithely refusing, only to recant when the Slavs crossed the Danube from Sirmium taking Singidunum, Viminacium and pushing to Anchialus at the Black Sea. Concerning the West, Maurice played a dynastic game to quell the Lombards. When in 584, the Visigothic leader Hermenigild took possession, his predecessor's wife and son fled to Spain. Ingund, the former queen, was the sister of the Frankish King Childebert II, whom Maurice used to fight the Lombards by withdrawing support from Hermenigild and paying a 50,000 *nomismata* subsidy to Childebert as inducement to attack Lombardy,

---

[403] Treadgold, *(BAIA)*, 206.

[404] Bury, *(AI-II)*, 84.

[405] Treadgold, 227-228.

though it is likely Childebert had his sights on Italy more so than wishing to aid Maurice. In the Balkans, soldiers needed by the Magister to offset the Slavs would from the East, but John Mystocon would fail at Persian negotiations and be replaced with Philippicus, who would train these Balkan soldiers against Persia. Philippicus would raid Mesopotamia and re-take Arzanene, but by 585, these soldiers were sent west to handle the Balkans under the victor at the Long Walls, Comentiolus.

The Avars were sent from Thrace with a victory north of Adrianople and the Franks this year would again raid the Lomabards in Italy, but this time the Lombard King Autharic was ready and defeated them. The Exarch of Ravenna, the first of this title found in the innovations of the eras military administration in the documented sources,[406] saw no victory in sight and agreed to a three-year truce with the Lombard King. Although John had invaded Persian Mesopotamia in spring 584, Persia used this lull in eastern defenses to go on an offensive and King Hormuzd's forces swept the area, just after Philippicus won at Dara, and the Tigris region in spring 586. The Avars, however, would break the truce and raid south of the Danube to Dobujka, and in further crisis, plague-ridden Slavs would infect and invade Thessalonica.

Maurice's reaction to almost losing the Balkans altogether happened in 587 when Comentiolus was sent to repel the Avars, only succeeding in getting him pushed back to the Black Sea. The situation was saved by the deposed John Mystocon and troops from Armenia, causing the Avars to flee back to Sirmium. Of course, this did nothing to improve the situation in re-capturing Arzamene, which remained Persian, but, beyond the invaders, the worst enemy plaguing East Rome was its poverty. Pay, supplies, and other amenities ran short with a stagnant depletion of the treasury and economic downturn, resulting in a twenty-five percent reduction in pay announced on Easter, 588. This pay decrease from thirty to twenty-two-and-one-half *nomismata* lowered the amount of *annonae* as well, but this was perceived as acceptable terms with the standard of living for soldiers of the period.[407]

The first revolts hit primarily in Mesopotamia where portraits of Maurice were destroyed and a general, Priscus, was actually caused to flee for his life from his own soldiers at Monocartum. They called for the election of a Phoenician duke, Germanus, to take Priscus's place of command. Oddly, Germanus had success against the Persians, driving them from Constantina and Martyropolis.

---

[406]  Ostrogorsky, 80.
[407]  Treadgold, *(BAIA)*, 144.

He even sent loot to the emperor as good faith, demonstrating that a local military officer could provide, through minor border victories without theft, to the distant City, this being the crux of his popularity. A broken Priscus returned to Constantinople and Maurice gave him command of the army against the Avars. Soon after, Avars invaded Thrace and besieged Priscus at the city of Tzurulum as Maurice would pay them 57,600 *nomismata* in ransom.

The Persian situation in Iberia was the crucible of formidable changes. When the Persian general Bahram failed to raid Atropene against Byzantine forces, King Hormuzd humiliated him by sending him a dress to wear. Bahram immediately stormed from Iberia to Ctesiphon in 590 and forced out Hormuzd for his own son, Khosru II. But soon after his succession, he tried to rebel against his father, only to fail, fleeing to Constantinople for aid against Bahram, who now ruled alone.

Maurice now faced a choice concerning Persia: Khosru promised Dara, Martyropolis, and parts of Armenia to the emperor for his help. Bahram promised this and Nisibis across the border from Dara in return for his faction, which Patriarch John IV 'the Faster' supported. However, Maurice had a broader vision in that a young legitimate Persian monarch, owing everything to Constantinople for a long life, would be better in the long run, and he chose Khosru. In spring 591, Maurice sent the army of the East under Narses to restore Khosru II and retook the city of Dara as well as Nisibis, gaining the territory in Bahram's offer at the King's own expense. At Atropatene, Narses and Khosru met to march on Ctesiphon and Bahram fled the city, leading his forces at Lake Urmia where he was defeated. Persia and East Rome would enjoy peace for Maurice's reign, quelling Armenian revolts and winning a part for Christianity as Chalcedonianism won out in the Armenian Church.

Maurice's Chalcedonian dedication was seen in two main events in Orthodox Christian record: First, it was he who placed the icon of Christ over the Chalke Gate which served as the entrance into the City. It is important to note how this was a sign of Christ blessing the City and those who entered it, as if entering the true City of God. Second, he also instated a holy day for the City, the Feast of the Dormition of the Virgin[408]; along with this was Maurice's new symbol for a Roman victory among the armies as the Mother of God, a Chalcedonian symbol honoring one true Chalcedonian Church and one true Empire.

Despite this, or to compensate for it, Maurice held moderate and temperate attitudes towards the Christological problems in the Church, persecuting little

---

[408] Angold, 43.

to none, but currying the disfavor of the uncompromising Pope Gregory I 'the Great', in Rome since 590. Two years before, John the Faster preceded himself as 'Ecumenical' to infer supremacy and universality above all of the other prelates and Churches – including Rome, another division of the East and West unappreciated by Gregory.[409] Not only was the Patriarch doing so, but it was Gregory that was taking in and caring for, in Rome, the refugees of the Lombard War being at odds with Romanus, Exarch of Ravenna. In Iberia, Maurice would win a victory for Chalcedonianism that spread to Armenia, somewhat displacing the Monophysite Church that had split from the Patriarchy.[410]

At the same time, however, problems would be caused by East Rome under-manning the military; first, the Avars drove east in 590 to displace Maurice to Anchialus. Meanwhile, both Syria and Italy were ravaged by plague and Italy needed reinforcements when the Exarch Romanus was stopped just at Lombard Pavia. The road leading from Ravenna to Rome would be taken by the Lombards from Benevento to Speleto, uniting the Lombard kingdom and Pope Gregory I contacted Romanus to make peace, only receiving refusal from the Exarch.

Also, the Balkans were seething as the Slavs and Avars remained in Illyricum and Thrace as the reinstated Priscus decided, in autumn of 593, the best strategy was to take out the barbarian root at the Danube, later winning victories over the Slavs beyond the river region. Lack of funds would induce Maurice to order the troops not to winter from their campaign and live off the land with little support from the City. Priscus, however, would have no choice but to countermand the order and winter at Odessus on the Black Sea, surrounded by soldiers nearing revolt. An undermined Maurice would then recall Priscus and replace him with his own brother, Peter, as commander of the Balkan army while the Slavs would use this opportunity to reclaim all of their Danubian territories. In fact, between the year 602 and the ninth century when the 'Dark Age' ended, not a single city north of Serdica is mentioned in documents nor remains a product of Roman nomenclature, but of the Slavic.[411] This would contribute to the death of Old Romanism and the rise of the polyglot Medieval civilization of Byzantium.

To satisfy an undernourished, under-armed, and underpaid army Maurice promised, in exchange for the pay reductions, a return to receiving supplies and

---

[409] Norwich, *(AM)*, 43-44.
[410] Treadgold, 232.
[411] Obolensky, 20.

uniforms issues in kind that predated the cash payments to receive arms and provisions,[412] where veterans could get stipends, and that benefits of service in the army for soldiers slain in duty would remain in-family to receive pay. This destroyed a cash system of almost 300 years, but Maurice had little choice, relying on a pragmatic method that would last centuries. The army, however, would accept no reductions or compromises and Peter paid them even more wages than before for their service. Resenting his brother's capitulation to what would have been clear mutiny, Maurice finally re-instated Priscus in 595. The Avars were in a weakened position compared to East Rome, however, and tried a diversionary tactic of raiding Sirmium. The tactic in Sirmium failed, and Priscus still pushed to the Danube and cleared the area. The Avar Khan, facing direct Roman incursion, then invaded Dalmatia and the Slavs were finally displaced from Illyrium.

Roman victories would be won in Africa and Italy until Avar resurgence began in autumn of 597 when the Khan gathered a large and concentrated force that displaced Priscus from the Black Sea region again and threw off the general Comentiolus. The Avars entrenched themselves at Druzipara to plan a siege on Constantinople. Maurice would gather his Excubitors and both the Blues and Greens, but not much was done after the Avars caught the plague. The plague burned from Mesopotamia to Italy straining the Empire's budgets, but ravaging worse the Avars, who sued for peace for only a raise in tribute from 100,000 to 120,000 *nomismata* to return to Sirmium and Maurice gratefully paid this off.

But, in the summer of 599, Maurice won another gamble by invading the convalescing Avars at Sirmium. With Comentiolus in the rear at Singdunum, Priscus won major victories and took no less than 17,000 prisoners. It is one of Maurice's strongest stances that gained him unpopularity that he refused the ransom of 12,000 of these hostages who were summarily executed as they were probably deserters.[413] Maurice had pacified the Slavs of Thrace and the Balkans for the rest of his reign as he did in Persia in 595. The Khan released the prisoners in good faith and sued for no peace nor tribute as the armies in Italy were ready to fight the Lombards, but the treasury was not ready and that region was quietly left alone. The Exarch of Ravenna, Callinicus, made a two-year treaty with the Lombards. The reconquest of Justinian would now die a whimpering death to the numerous barbarian tribes who were now partitioning it.

---

[412] Treadgold, (BAIA), 19.
[413] Bury, (AI-II), 86-87.

Later that year, a major chariot faction riot broke out in Constantinople, burning the Praetorian Prefecture of the East with 900 Blues under Cosmas and 1,500 Greens under Sergius. They had been summoned by Maurice to negotiate the formation of the militia guard for Constantinople against the encroachments of the rebelling general Phocas's troops. As there was never middle ground with the factions, the emperor ended up supporting the Greens as they were the majority; an example of the 'mob' democracy that took control when the autocracy was in jeopardy. His relations with the factions had been seriously strained over new taxes and other legislation to the point lyric satire poetry over his illegitimate children were shouted at him from the Hippodrome at races.[414]

A typically unruly day at the chariot races, however, turned into an all-out coup and promising to be a day of slaughter. The demes watched over the Walls of Theodosius, but knowing little loyalty to the rightful emperor, they were instrumental in allowing Phocas access to the City in 602 with the majority Greens being the first faction to defect.[415] As the usurpers neared the Palace on November 22, Maurice, his family, and the Praetorian Prefect Constantine Lardys, fled across the Sea of Marmara in disguise to the Church of St. Antomonos the Martyr in the Bay of Nicomedia. Crippled by gout in his legs[416], Maurice remained at the Marmara with his family under the protection of Lardys and the Persian King's armies.

Maurice survived as long as he had due to the developed military style that came from organization, discipline, and experience to be outlined in his handbook the *Strategikon* ('Book of the General'). It specifies in scope the micro-management of the conduct of the general himself: "to those he deals with the general should appear calm and untroubled; his food and clothing should be plain and simple; his entourage should not be elaborate and ostentatious; he should be tireless and painstaking in attending to his duties, not slack or careless; care and persistence shall easily carry him through the most difficult situations. If he shows no concern for a problem, that problem shall carry no concern for him."[417]

---

[414] Marshall, F.H. and John Mavrogordato. 'Byzantine Literature.' Chap. 8 of *Byzantium: an Introduction to East Roman Civilization*, ed. by N.H. Baynes and H. St. L.B. Moss. Oxford, UK: Oxford University Press, 221-251. 1969, 249.

[415] Norwich, (*EC*), 277.

[416] Theophylact of Simocotta. *History, bk. viii*, ed. by C. de Boor & P. Wirth. Leipzig, Germany. 1972, 9.

[417] Maurice. *Strategikon: Handbook of Byzantine Military Strategy*, trans. by George T. Dennis. Philadelphia, PA: University of Pennsylvania Press. 1984, 9.

Despite the poetry of these descriptions, they are superficial and Maurice's writings have been criticized for not including more detailed qualities of a good general in tactical and strategic leadership.[418] But this is a small flaw in relation to the invaluable advice of the 145 instructions and maxims to be consulted to suit the style of a general and his situations in the best manner possible. It stresses for him a code of conduct based on principles founded for the Romans a millennia ago and differentiates between elite (*epilekta*), such as the bucellarii, foederati, and the optimates ('best men'), and non-elite or 'weaker' troops (*hypodeestera*).[419] This countered such former claims by commentators as Procopius, who in the *Wars* claims Classical formations should not risk itself with innovation.

In a wider scope is the conduct and battlefield organization of the Tagma formations as well as those who served the army by 'pick axe and shovel as well as sword and spear'.[420] These are broken up into the pentarchies of five soldiers, dekarchies of ten soldiers, and the hekontarchies of one 100 soldiers. Byzantine armies at the time averaged from 10,000 to 30,000 troops according to the statistics of the previous two centuries. Also included are flank and center maneuvers and fortification specifications. Together, this made the handbook Byzantine generals would consult and base improvements upon for almost a millennium ahead. New concepts in defending the soldiers were included in these reforms; among the 6,000 troops in each Tagma force, over twenty percent were dressed in chain mail cuirasses of 48,000 metal rings designed for the heavy Calvary (*cataphractoi*).[421]

Foot and horse soldiers were not the only necessities to Maurice's model of an army. In Book XII of the *Strategikon,* from about thirty to fifty percent of the infantry must be composed of archers, an improvement on the conservative advice of the outdated ancient Roman militarist author Vegetius.[422] It also introduced the necessities of the non-combatants in each unit including the military bureaucracy in surgeons and doctors, cape bearers for the tribunes, trumpeters, quartermasters, heralds, and NCO drill sergeants. Included were the improvements on the posts mentioned in the *Notitia Dignitatum,* the leading

---

[418] Decker, 41.

[419] Ensslin, 297.

[420] Dennis, vii.

[421] Decker, 107-108.

[422] *ibid.,* 151. This would include the use of the *solenaricn,* an ancestor of the crossbow, created by Frankish influence in the Crusades. This dart-projectile device for battle would be a prominent piece of artillery until the tenth century.

military handbook from Theodosius II to Justinian, for disciplinary officers, chiefs of staff, secretaries, clerks, and billet officers.[423]

Its practicality was impressive, even serving terminology in the three languages of Greek, Latin, and Germanic to find common roots in the execution of maneuvers in a changing army,[424] although Maurice preferred an exclusively Roman army. Emperor Leo VI (886-912 CE), faced with new Slavic tribes and the power of the Arabs would use this handbook in the creation of his own *Tactical Constitutions*.[425] In practice, his only real error was in not taking advantage of eastern and Slavic reserves and relying too much on a thoroughly Roman army that was unprepared for Slavic warfare. In a demonstration of Roman practical flexibility, most of these defensive tactics included in equipment was attuned to the experiences of foreign battles with the Persians and the nomadic Avars.[426]

In winter 602, the campaign season was ending with the Romans under the Magister Peter wishing to cross Slavic territory past the Danube. Once again, the treasury disallowed formal quartering and the troops were told to live off the land; angry at this repetition, they demanded Peter disobey the Emperor's orders as Priscus had done. Peter bravely refused and the troops rebelled against him and named a general, Phocas, as their new leader. Peter fled to Constantinople where a famine had led to plague and unrest in the City. The army followed and demanded that Maurice's son, Theodosius, take the throne, but on refusing, they next tried Theodosius's father-in-law, the *Caesar* Germanus, who fled for sanctuary in Saint Sophia.

This mob without a candidate broke out in a riot with only the Excubitors, the Blues, and the Greens to protect the Emperor. Maurice fled the City east to Bithynia, asking Persia for help. Germanus, returning to return civic order, tried to fill the throne but the Greens did not accept him and they raised Phocas instead. Eventually, Maurice and his entire family were mercilessly killed by Phocas on November 22, 602. It has been said to have been an event as 'a wave of indiscriminate slaughter' wherein the senatorial class (once Maurice's allies)

---

[423] Treadgold, *(BAIA)*, 88-91.

[424] Bury, *(AI-II)*, 172f adds to this as Theophylact speaks of a new 'Romaic' language in describing the *bandum*, another word meaning 'army'. 'Romaic' was a colloquial, yet not Hellenized, form of Latin in use with the army and Maurice's literature. This became independent to the historian as he was not even aware the Latin *rex* was Latin at all!

[425] Dennis, *xiii*.

[426] Decker, 113.

responded with conspiracies only leading to further executions.[427] Though attempts had been made in the East before, Maurice's end marked the first time an Eastern Roman Emperor was successfully displaced.

It is always an ironic case when such a superior soldier and general as Maurice is deposed because of his armies, but Maurice refused to pay attention to the needs of the treasury before his armies rebelled. The beginning of the Byzantine holding of the West resulted from this more than any barbarian incursion: in North Italy, the Danube, the Mediterranean, until the Balkans were lost, all except for Moorish Africa and Egypt. His only real allies from the Empire's interior was with the aristocratic and senatorial class who reveled in his inattention to the decentralization of imperial power back in their hands; Maurice's actions and support were mainly supplied by these men.[428] Unfortunately, it was superficial as they only wanted to limit their sovereign's power and was conditional upon not being the targets of militant hostility, not lifting much of a finger against Phocas's momentum.

Even so, he lived up to the claims that his reign was half as long as Justinian's and his statesmanship answered the essential core of the Empire.[429] This was because of the Persian diplomatic situation and the creation of the Italian and African Exarchates,[430] expanding the bases of dukes (*duces*) and governors (*cometei*). The Exarchs themselves upheld the judicial, financial, as well as the ecumenical duties of the throne, including the spread of Caesaropapism to the Empire's further reaches.[431] Maurice invigorated what would be a Byzantine world order over the old Roman, leading amazing conquests and victories as a general and even showed a love for literature, poetry, and history,[432] but this could not be reconciled or even complemented with the need for administration. This problem would continue under his usurping successor and in sporadic patterns throughout Byzantine history.

---

[427] Ostrogorsky, 83.

[428] Bury, (*AI-II*), 93.

[429] Hussey, 23.

[430] These Exarchs basically being viceroys of the highest authority answerable to none but the Emperor himself, categorizing him as a 'wise and far-seeing statesman', Norwich, (*EC*), 278.

[431] Vasiliev, 275.

[432] Bury, 182.

# PHOCAS 'THE TYRANT'
## (602-610)

Whether it was because of the timing, his brutality upon succeeding, or because of the popularity of his predecessor, historians and Byzantines alike have marked Phocas as an unjust tyrant and his eight-year rein as a travesty. He is called a 'sadistic and depraved monster[433]' and the historian Theophylactus Simocotta calls him the 'impudent centaur',[434] to others, he was 'a Cyclops', an 'incompetent rebel[435]' and his contemporaries do not say much better. If Maurice's reign was what was good in Eastern Rome and the coming times, Phocas was its opposite. Ecumenically, he betrayed Chalcedonianism by asserting Roman Papal authority as supreme over Christianity, culminating in Pope Boniface III's decree that Rome was St. Peter's Apostolic Church above all the other Churches in Christendom, even in over Egypt and West Asia. It also made Phocas a hero in Rome where the only erection of his reign still stands in the Forum: a Pillar of Triumph dedicated to the Tyrant.[436] His cruelty was beyond doubt as he first slaughtered Maurice's five children before the defeated Emperor's eyes so his punishment would be more severe before his death, and then Phocas '[displayed] their heads in the Camp of the Tribunal for a number of days.[437]'

There is little record on his life before 600 except that he was a Greek-Thracian centurion born around 557 to a 'simple military family.'[438] In 598, when the Avars demanded a ransom for their prisoners, Phocas was sent with a delegation to Constantinople to deliberate and was struck and humiliated by members of the court for his audacity. Whether it is true or not, this was a message by history to show a reason for such ferocity and bloodlust against an Augustus the City appreciated and he was so unlike. After a brutal entrance into the Theodosian Walls by the Green faction, he was proclaimed Emperor on August 23, 602. He was said to have appeared as ugly on the outside as he was within; thick red hair with a uni-brow, his face defying the ancient imperial custom of facial perfection, being maligned by a scar that crimsoned when he

---

[433] Norwich, (EC), 277.

[434] Theophylactus Simocatta, *History*, VIII, vi-xii.

[435] Herrin, 32.

[436] Ostrogorsky, 84.

[437] Theophanes. *The Chronicles: Anni Mundi 6095-6305 (A.D. 602-813)*, ed. by Harry Turtledove. (Philadelphia, PA: University of Pennsylvania Press), 1982, 1.

[438] Treadgold, 236.

was angered. Such angering was a regular occurrence and he was the one who introduced the galley, the rack, and the infamous mutilations and blinding in Byzantine 'justice.'[439]

Phocas, as a military brute, also carried with him a lack and contempt of education and closed the university Maurice had organized as afterwards 'all culture suffered[440]' until his successor Heraclius revived all of these institutions. In 610, eight years after Maurice's assassination, Theophylactus Simocotta would eulogize the learning once found in the City, 'Let theater and platform and freedom of speech mourn with me', calling Phocas 'a father of murder.'[441] Any hand in the state he had was seemingly rebuffed, despite some correspondence said to exist with the Pope according to western historians such as Isidore of Seville (560-636 CE) and Paul the Deacon (720-799 CE), no letters or laws seem to have survived him.[442]

Some of Phocas's first acts were the execution and displaying of Maurice and his family, executing the City commander Comentiolus, and the Praetorian Prefect Constantine Lardys. To show moderation, he appeased the troops by sparing Germanus and making Philippicus Comes of the Excubitors. In December of 602, however, he still had to produce largess for the troops[443] as civil war would begin in 603 with the attempt by Maurice's widow (who was apparently spared for her gender) and her three daughters from the Palace of the Leo to place Germanus on the throne.

Despite the recruitment of and some devastation by the Greens, Phocas won out and tonsured Constantina (one of Maurice's daughters), Germanus, and Philippicus, and in yet another move to legitimate with the past era, naming Priscus Comes of the Excubitors. This attempt failed and many foreign rulers and some generals who did not find Phocas's claim legitimate included the Persian King Khosru II and the Magister of the East, Narses. Narses claimed to be in touch with the son of Maurice, Theodosius, who was rumored to have successfully hidden from Phocas. But, despite Khosru and Narses's union, the Armies of the East mostly stayed loyal under Germanus, as commander of Dara, who was made a rival Magister of the East. Germanus attempted to take

---

[439] Based on the observations of the chronicler George Cedrenus. Norwich, (EC), 279.

[440] Buckler, Georgia. 'Byzantine Education' Chap. 7 of Byzantium: An Introduction to East Roman Civilization, ed. by N.H. Baynes and H. St. L.3. Moss. Oxford, UK: Oxford University Press, 200-220. 1969, 216.

[441] Theophylactus, bk. viii, 12.

[442] Bury, (AI-II), 197.

[443] Theophanes, 2.

Narses at Edessa, but the Persians appeared first, crushing the city with war elephants,[444] defeating the armies, killing Germanus, and laying siege to Dara.

In 604, seeing such imminent danger and after making a hasty peace with the Avars for the Balkans, Phocas collected another Eastern army from Western troops under the eunuch Leontius. Some Slavs took this opportunity of the West's weakness and diversion to enter Thessalonica in spite of this treaty. The Persians, galvanized by their victories, defeated the Constantinopolitans again, killing all who were not prisoners near Dara. A furious emperor recalled and this time imprisoned the commander, Leontius; Narses remained as solid as smoke to capture, with a boy who the soldiers thought was Theodosius, the 'real' son of Maurice. Now the purge to create a united order under Phocas was underway and the result was bitter anarchy.

More dangers faced the crumbling base of the Tyrant with Constantina and Germanus now reappearing to displace Phocas. This time, officers of the inner circle were involved: Theodore, the Praetorian Prefect, Athanasius, also Comes of the sacred largess, and the general Romanus, in June of 605. He tortured and killed the officers, cutting off their hands and feet, beating them mercilessly with leather straps and beheading them; Constantina and Germanus were captured, and when Narses finally surrendered to Phocas's nephew Domentiolus, he was burned at the stake. Persia would now prove a deflated ally with no Narses to guide them (though he was considered a tyrant himself that 'caused Persian children to shiver at his name'[445]) and a dubious claimant in a false Theodosius was all that remained. When the pretender died, Khosru ran out of impetus, destroying Dara instead of capturing it, then settling to raid Mesopotamia and Syria. But, it must be remembered, as Theophylact says that Khosru II was very insincere in his entreaties, Phocas was not the cause of at least the Persian Wars as it was clearly embroiled in the reign of Maurice.[446]

In 607, Phocas married a patrician named Priscus to his daughter and horse races were held in the Hippodrome; the factions, however, put the bride and groom on portraits equal to the emperor. In a fit of hostile and childish rage, Phocas had the factions' leaders brought to the *stama* in public view, stripped naked, and nearly executed. When the crowd and court shouted and pleaded that this portraiture was the normal custom, which a low-born usurping soldier would not know, only then did Phocas rescind the executions that day. Despite

---

[444] Theophanes, 6-7.
[445] Norwich, (EC), 280.
[446] Bury, (AI-II), 198.

Domentiolus's efforts, East Roman Armenia was recaptured by Persia in 607 and the Eastern armies were defeated at Dara. In Constantinople, Phocas's grip was slipping further with civil unrest and another plot of assassination was hatched by Theodore, Praetorian Prefect of the East. Phocas caught him and beat him to death with rawhide strips. In 608, plague returned and the Persian commanders Shahrvaraz and Shahin invaded Byzantine Mesopotamia and Armenia and famine was a result in the Empire.

Matters were made worse for Phocas with the rebelling African Exarch Heraclius cutting off the main grain supply. With a sizable navy, Heraclius fought back the Roman fleet and took control of the Egyptian Exarch in the summer, giving him advantage over the ancient 'breadbasket' of the West. By his side were the energetic officers, his son Heraclius the Younger and his nephew Nicetas as Alexandria and Lower Egypt were then taken. Now a difficult situation faced Phocas: although the governor of Syria was available to be sent to Africa, it was discovered in 609 that manpower was being stretched dangerously thin when facing a Persian threat. Shahin invaded Cappadocia, making his way west to Caesarea and finally Chalcedon right across the Bosporus to the capital.

The same year, after months of covering and losing ground, Heraclius the Younger drove the loyalist general Bonosus from Africa. With these forces, he made his way to Constantinople from the West. In the capital itself, chaos was in charge as fear of not just losing an emperor, but the Empire itself set in as Jews were lynching Christians; the Blues and Greens were fighting small civil wars in Thessalonica, Syria, and Anatolia. Phocas, rather than taking any control, turned to drinking as the relentless crowd and demes jeered at his drunkenness, weakness, and disability at rule crying 'You have drunk again of the cup; you have lost your sense', so, typically, he had them punished.[447] Only tyranny, public disorder, and total chaos were ruling in Constantinople and the Eastern Empire.

The rebels took the Hellespont, Crete, and Sicily preparing a large fleet by Heraclius the Younger to finally sail to Constantinople. This became easy when the Greens betrayed Phocas and gave the rebels safe passage from the harbor. In a quick succession of events, Bonosus and Domentiolus were lynched, more deme infighting occurred despite seizing the City from within, and Priscus hailed the victorious Heraclius as emperor. Phocas was then brought before Heraclius, upbraided for his conduct, beheaded, and dismembered ('as

---

[447] Treadgold, 241.

a carcass fit for hounds' said John of Antioch) for eight miserable years of conflict and mismanagement, and his body burned in the Bovis (Ox) Forum between the Golden Gate and Hagia Sophia on October 5, 610. His statue in the Hippodrome was toppled and burnt as a *damnation memoriae*[448] reserved for the memories of the worst emperors, although one portrait was said to have escaped the flames.[449] Heraclius had already been consecrated on October 3, as Phocas was imprisoned in the Palace's Church of St. Stephen led with his own mystical icon of the Virgin, crafted by angels and not men.[450]

A famous interview was said to have transpired between Phocas and Heraclius before the former's execution, as reported by John of Antioch. This remained as a parable to caution those like Heraclius who claimed they were more qualified to rule than tyrants. One translated version of the two-line conversation goes thus, 'Is it thus', said Heraclius, 'that you have governed the Empire?' 'Will you', Phocas said with unexpected spirit, 'govern it any better?'[451] What question could be put so simply, yet have such implications for the next 850 years of Byzantine rule? Its meaning is pivotal when considering those emperors that rose to the challenge, surpassed it, and those who woefully failed it, letting the Empire slip into anarchy.

In another thoughtful source, the *Spuria Athanasiana,* it is asked of God why a monster such as Phocas was allowed the throne and the reply was, 'Because I could not find anyone worse.'[452] This was likely a tableau of God's punishment on the Empire for its myriad sins, but the tyrant Phocas punished for eight years the Empire with incompetence before the City resulting in civil war among his people. However, to shed some light, Phocas was the first of his kind (though not the last): a usurper with an unprecedented lack of any legitimacy to be emperor. Yet, when asked the question why follow a Phocas, a Julian, or any such heretical emperors in the future, the answer came from Romans 13: 1-4 'the powers that be are ordained by God',[453] so God's will alone raises emperors and allows their usurpation. In the end, he had no army left, just Excubitors and the untrustworthy circus factions. It was all the better a popular and stronger general take his place on the throne and usher in a truly stronger Byzantine civilization.

---

[448]  Ostrogorsky, 85.

[449]  Gibbon, 1529f.

[450]  Bury, (*AI-II*), 205-206.

[451]  Norwich, (*EC*), 285.

[452]  Hussey, 87.

[453]  Mango, 14.

The end of Late Antiquity saw a weakened and bankrupting Empire beset East and West by barbarians with stronger forces and budgets threatening at any time to topple East Rome as they had done so in West Rome. Drastic measures, ingenuity, change, and not a small amount of good luck would see it through. By adapting to a more Greek and Medieval society, Byzantium would pacify regions, strengthen armies and administrations, even finding a way to do it on a budget considerably less than the emperor Justinian's. Once done, the Empire's safe existence of 17,000,000 inhabitants under Phocas, (1,000,000 more than under Maurice[454]) would remain the culture of the East itself for centuries.

Another trend in Byzantine administration would be shown in Maurice's innovation of the Exarchy; now, centralized governments appeared in local spheres of the districts, and with absolute military power, Exarchs would now war with each other as in Africa and Egypt. Just as in the Palace of Constantinople, central authority was easily challenged and changed after the loss of one man and although he was a savior to the Empire, Heraclius was an example that an Exarch can conquer his neighbors and the throne itself with minimal effort – and it set dangerous precedents for what would be the decentralization of the Empire.

---

[454] Treadgold, 278.

# II. The First Byzantine Age

The first three centuries of Eastern Rome saw a separation from the West, seeming inevitable and permanent. Slow, but constant, change was the new norm under this first phase of Late Antiquity. But it ended eventually to make way for the painful birth of a purely Byzantine Empire mostly free from Classical and West Roman character. A new military structure called for a feudal society of peasant and Duke over the partitioned provinces of the Empire centered in its capital in Anatolia. Also, events outside the Empire would change it forever with the rise of Islam and the new Arab civilizations while resisting the civilizations of the Slavic once-'barbarians' creating rival Empires. The West would also heal from division coalescing around a German Empire and a united Church restoring order, yet it was Byzantium that was aptly described as a state 'whose state conception is Roman, whose language and culture is Greek, whose faith is Christian.'[455]

But of course, it was the Christianity of the Orthodox kind that was this signature of Byzantine civilization and the maintenance of the four remaining Churches by their Patriarchs based on their beliefs in Christ's nature was its character. Although this led to constant division and argumentation in the Empire, it was no more than the heresies in the West that plagued and divided their end of Europe later in its development. It was a faith that Byzantium's people were dedicated to and was commemorated in its art and liturgy. Finally, it was a Greek Empire; the language, the geography, the culture all had Greek, if not Hellenistic, roots but would see a culture-transforming 'renaissance' in Homer, Plato, and other Classical works and Christian thought.

The emperors of this period understood this and let the West be its own entity for the most part and if wealth were not going westwards, the lavish Eastern trade of Byzantium would still be a constant. They now were forced to

---

[455] Ostrogorsky, 96.

be concerned with maintaining Christianity in an East by a rising and powerful Islam. But it is agreed that this period in Byzantium was its Dark Age, with achievements towered over by Justinian's traveling in a new and Medieval direction. Only a surge of imperial victories would bring Byzantium to its true golden age around 900 CE. As a fixed center of a network of Slavic, Arab, Baltic, Frankish, and Papal interests, economically and territorally at this time, the proverb rang true that 'he who rules in Constantinople rules the world.'

# HERACLIUS
## (610-641)

Now we come to the Medievalization of the Eastern Empire, Byzantium as its own society, and the emperor that is awarded with the reputation of making it possible. It is vital to note how this had been a time of transition solidifying after three centuries. The key element in this is the definition of Late Antiquity as a system of 'boundaries' and 'frontiers' that shifted continuously after 200 CE.[456] Heraclius was partially responsible for these boundaries settling for the Middle Ages as well as his main opposition, the Umayyad Caliphate of the Prophet Mohammed. This is why the eleventh-century historian William of Tyre (1130-1186) remarks on how Heraclius was the originator of the Crusades in the East. Yet when he began his reign, he held little military experience, no disciplined or veteran troops, and no money to pay what troops he had. This is why Heraclius sought a source of military income not attempted before, in the Church.[457]

Before the twentieth century, however, Heraclius was regarded as an obscure subject in Medieval biography[458]; and as for art, exceptions only existed as in the frescoes of Piero Della Francesca (1416-1492) citing Heraclius's Persian victory in 628.[459] A city in Venetia was named for him, as Heraclea, and a colossal statue of him was cited in Barletta in the thirteenth century.[460] Unfortunately, due to his preoccupations militarily. his reign culturally seems to begin the decline later described as the 'Dark Ages' of Byzantine education

---

[456] Brown, Peter. *The World of Late Antiquity*. London, UK. 1971, 19.

[457] Brownworth, 121.

[458] 'Heraclius is almost lost to our eyes and to those of the Byzantine historians.' Gibbon, 1542.

[459] Kaegi, Walter. *Heraclius, Emperor of Byzantium*. Cambridge, UK: Cambridge University Press. 2003, 4.

[460] Bury, (*AI-II*), 273f.

and literature; there not even existed a reading public that could be identified with such a definition.[461]

By overthrowing Phocas, he gained the responsibility of ruling a turbulent Empire; burdensome financial trouble, typical dead-end Christological controversies, and a broad scaled war with the Persian Empire followed by the unstoppable Umayyad Caliphate. But, with remarkable resiliency, he administrated a cohesive imperial order rivaling Diocletian's and Justinian's reforms with provincial organization. He made the Balkans stable under the Slavs and pulled Byzantium from a crisis threatening its very foundations and survival. With military and state in such concert, the East, shining brighter than ever, would bring Byzantium to Western Europe's envy. Theophanes would give Heraclius at one point super-human status by proclaiming in battle how he 'struggling alone against such a multitude: he spurns their blows like an anvil.'[462] Another historian, George of Pisidia (580-634 CE), in his epic poems, described him as a 'gleaming sun . . . a Phoebus who purifies all the world with his purifying command.'[463]

The son of the rebelling African Exarch, Heraclius, Heraclius the Younger was born in Cappadocia in 575, and described as a handsome and clean-shaven man of pale skin, fine yellow hair, and grey eyes. His military career under his father reached its pinnacle in the successful rebellions against the usurper-emperor Phocas, taking the crown on Christmas Day of 612, given officially by the Patriarch Sergius in high ceremony. He began raising funds by extorting loans, taxes, and reparations from Phocas's supporters and even scandalized the Church by marrying his own brother's daughter when his wife died.[464] Until more modern scholars illuminated Heraclius's life, he was seen as obscure by historians and, consequently, questions were common on how he spent his years from 610 until around 620 and why he lapsed after the Persians fell. It has been said his 'sensibility was more than his intellect and his intellect more than his will.'[465] These myths have been cleared by historians such as Walter Kaegi of Chicago, demonstrating Heraclius's true nature of decisiveness and good judgment.

---

[461] Treadgold, 395.

[462] Theophanes, 21.

[463] George of Pisidia. *The Persian Expedition, Poemi I: Panegyrici Epici,* ed. by A. Pertusi. Ettal, Italy. 1960, 3.7-3.10.

[464] Norwich, (*EC*), 288. Bury describes it as *aimomizia* ('incestuous') and she, and of course not he, was treated as an unclean pariah.

[465] Bury, (*AI-II*), pg. 208.

Almost from the start, Heraclius was troubled by wars inherited in the East from the Emperor Maurice, starting with the Sassanids. Khosru II and Heraclius were at great odds, not just politically, but even on cultural and religious grounds. Khosru, who saw no attributes of Maurice in Heraclius, was noted as saying to Byzantine diplomats how 'I will have no mercy on you until you renounce him who was crucified and worship the sun' in 618, recorded by Theophanes. He further commented on Heraclius's belief in God failing to deliver Caeserea, Jerusalem, and Alexandria as a 'vile and insensate slave' only stopping to ask if he must conquer Constantinople too to prove his superiority.[466]

What peace could be settled between the two peoples when such hatred ruled for either side? Persia held Mesopotamia, Armenia, Syria and other former Byzantine holdings. It would be perfectly ironic later when the Arabs would take all of this when Persia fell, but in Heraclius's early reign, the objective was to wrest land from Khosru. In 612, the emperor recalled Philippicus from his monastery to replace the general Priscus. He strengthened the military ties in his family by marrying his son Constantine to his brother Nicetas's daughter, Gregoria, benefitting all concerned with dynastic security. Along with the Patriarch John 'the Almsgiver' (Sergius), the bonds between these men against the rule of Phocas meant a strong base in Heraclius's political ties. Heraclius's main entourage of military and civil leaders, Sophronius, Germanus, and John were raised to sainthood by the Church, catching the admiration of the holy men of Jerusalem and Alexandria.[467]

The year 614 was a disaster for Heraclius who would nearly lose to Persia, Mesopotamia, Syria, Palestine, and Cilicia killing as many as 90,000.[468] Another 60,000[469] would be the amount of Christians killed in Palestine by the native Jews siding with tolerant Persia, sparking a 'crusade' to free Jerusalem from the Jewish mob.[470] In May, the 'Jewish Terror', Nehemiah II, led an insurrection against Christians on behalf of the Persian Shahvaraz, 'The Royal Boar', where tens of thousands of Christians were converted or murdered. The relics at Jerusalem, The Lance, the Sponge, and the True Cross were sent to the Persian Queen's church in Ctesiphon.[471]

---

[466] Norwich, (EC), pg. 284.

[467] Treadgold, 390.

[468] Theophanes, 11.

[469] Vasiliev, 195. This included the Patriarch Zacharias and the True Cross kept there, taken to Ctesiphon.

[470] Bury, (AI-II), 214.

[471] Montefiore, 170.

From the West, Avars would take the northern cities of Serdica, Salona and Naissus and, taking advantage, the Slavs in the south would invade Thessalonica, Illyricum, and Thrace. Even the Visigoths were restoring to themselves Byzantine Spain and, in the end, only Africa, Egypt, and Anatolia could totally be claimed as Byzantine. In 616, Shahin invaded Anatolia and the Byzantine envoys to Ctesiphon were imprisoned and allowed to die. Shahvaraz next invaded Egypt and spent years there subjugating it under the nose and helpless defenses of Nicetas.

Faith in Christ became a political venue in Egypt and Palestine as the *Basileus* made hasty concessions to recognize the rites of Monophysitism in order to gain alliance against the Slavs, especially when plague threatened the grain dole after Heraclius expelled the anarchic Jews from Jerusalem.[472] Faith in Heraclius was growing dim, and in 619, the Exarch of Ravenna, Eleutherius, unsuccessfully laid claim as *Basileus* to his soldiers, who then murdered him. The same year, Persia courted Alexandria by upholding a Monophysite Church there and the Patriarch John fled to Cyprus and Persia more or less finished their conquest of Egypt in 620, conquering the Christian Coptic Church. The Persians and Avars were by then closing in on Constantinople by taking Taurus in Anatolia. Fortunately, Slavic sea power could easily be checked by the Byzantine navy and the City Walls made land conquest nearly unthinkable, but, however, Heraclius's unpopularity and prospects were still a liability.

But, it was in these circumstances that Heraclius shined as a genius in strategic military administration, pouring over guides of strategy and logistics, especially the *Strategikon* of his predecessor, Maurice. Heraclius was noted as explaining, 'To learn from one's enemy has always been the desire of all true statesmen.'[473] His Tagma or Thema (derived from a definition of headquarters or army command[474]) or 'Theme' system entailed dividing the imperial provinces in Asia Minor into the Opsikions of Anatolia (*Anatolian*) and Armenia (*Armenikon*), and the naval *Carabisiani* on the southern coast. These jurisdictions would be run by both a civil Proconsul authority and a General (*Strategos*) who ran the military staff, administration, and had supreme power in the Theme. The end of Classical administration would see the Praetorian

---

[472] Treadgold, 292.

[473] Vasiliev, 228-229. Taken from E. Stein's *Byzantinisch-Neugriechische Jahrbucher*, *vol. I*. 1920, 84-85. In his work on Justin II, he comments on how 'Heraclius's seed has marvelously grown.'

[474] Decker, 74.

Prefect office be dismissed as 'an anachronistic decoration.'[475] These changes would then be added to the Balkans in the midst of the Slav/Avar situation as a perfect litmus test by the Heraclius.

Economically, changes would be seen between the public largess, especially in the spheres of Church and State funds, now starved by Phocas. The *Comitiva Sacrarum Largitionum* and the *Comitiva Rerum Privatarum* were two government departments of finance that were in need of major reform and a weeding-out of bureaucracy. So, Heraclius transferred the sources of these funds to his *Sacellium*, or keepers of the imperial Privy Purse, centralizing Church and State largess away from the provincial and dioces governments. These new boards of finance were run by officers of the chancery known as the Logothetes (*tou stratiokou, tou genikou, tou idikou*),[476] offices which made the Praetorian Prefecture even more obsolete. The *Logothete* would then evolve to a post of the Master of Offices (*Magister Officiorum*) that would become the chief ministerial position in the Empire. The Sacellium were run by the Sacellerium, perhaps the greatest innovation of the period, suggesting Heraclius's achievements were better discussed in financial and not military terms.[477]

Another financial measure in Heraclius's army was halving the rate of pay to soldiers in 616 from five gold coins to two-and-a-half, or from four to two *annonae*, resulting in less circulation and a reduction in soldiers found in payrolls.[478] He succeeded where Maurice failed in 594, however, by replacing the customary gold coinage in pay with the silver *hexagram* coin and even bronze coins instead of issuing kind on the inflated price of the cloak, mantle, shirt, belt, and boots that made the army uniform.[479] This necessity also cost the civilian officials of the court as well. But, these measures allowed the Persian Wars of 624-631 to successfully occur in the Eastern Empire. They also made possible productive ends to rebellions, as in Italy, where the Exarch

---

[475] Unfortunately, as no ancient source or Heraclius ever mentions this, nor is there explanation why its use would work against Persia, but not the Arabs, many now agree that it was Heraclius's son, Constans II, who instigated these changes. Treadgold, (*BAIA*), 23.

[476] Ostrogorsky, 99.

[477] Kaegi, *Heraclius*, 302.

[478] Treadgold, (*BAIA*), 118. This was a terrible living wage, considering the unskilled laborers made one-half of a *nomisma* more.

[479] Jones, 624-625. Boots and belts having been inflated, since 301, from one-tenth to upwards of one-quarter *nomismata* by Maurice's time.

was murdered in Naples by John of Conza. Eleutherius appeared there with the overdue pay the soldiers asked for, and the troops were mollified as John of Conza was executed legally by his government, rather than by his soldiers.

Another official change in the imperial structure was the use of Greek as a state language, which was difficult as even in educated circles as few men were bilingual from proper Latin.[480] All official documents, future codes, ecumenical decisions, and language of the court were to be in a more colloquial, post-Attic, or Byzantine (or what was to become Middle, or Medieval) Greek. Also, as historically, the terms for the Roman Emperor since the first century BC were 'Imperator' and 'Augustus' and the Greek 'Autokrator', although this was only a rougher translation of 'autocrat'. Creating a new terminology with the changing Greek language of the court, these would be replaced by the older *Basileus* (derived from King)[481] on par with the title of the Great King, as no Roman equivalent existed, never to be confused with a subordinate style. In a truly Byzantine move by Sergius, Heraclius and the *Basilii* were made *isoapostolos*, 'Equals of the Apostles', and the Anointed by God to rule the Empire. The *Basileus* was now *Archeireus Basileus* ('King and Priest as One') as was said of Justinian.[482] Now it was permanent as an official policy of the new Medieval Greek Empire that the Latin language, even in educated circles, would be a rarely known, let alone used as a subject.[483]

These were the major reforms started by 621, when Heraclius combined the Anatolian and Thracian armies to meet his envelopment upon the imperial enemies, resulting in a force of around 50,000 men. Appeasing by necessity the encroaching Avars with a tribute, he turned to western Anatolia where Shahvaraz was invading. Heraclius began in Cappadocia and the Persians prepared for him at the Cilician Gates separating Asia Minor and Syria, but Heraclius in a cunning move made to flank Shahvaraz from Armenia. Displacing the Persian army where the Byzantines defeated them, they ran at the Persians from Anatolia using feigned assaults, taking many prisoners. Many Persians were said to have ran like 'wild goats' being hunted up the crags of Asia Minor.[484]

It was at this time that the Avars broke a truce made in spring 622 and

---

[480] Brownworth, 127.

[481] Norwich, (*EC*), 311. Such titles of absolutism had not been used since before the Roman occupations of the second century BCE.

[482] Diehl, 29.

[483] Ostrogorsky, 106.

[484] Bury, (*AI-II*), 230.

invaded southern Thrace and, in 623, as Heraclius met with the Avar Khan in Constantinople he was ambushed and almost abducted. Thereafter, the Avars demanded a 200,000 *nomismata* tribute and it was here Heraclius began infamously 'borrowing' Church property of all kinds to melt down into coins. A year later, he departed for the East again, leaving his son, Constantine, in the cadre of Sergius and the Master of Offices, and set out for Dara in Byzantine Armenia. Heraclius made successful stands at Dvin, the capital of Persian Armenia, as well as Persian Atropatene, and its capital of Ganzaca under Shahvaraz's 40,000 men, taking Khosru's summer quarters south in the Zagros Mountains with at least 50,000 prisoners taken that winter when Khosru responded.

After another successful raid wherein the Byzantines defeated armies outnumbering them and humiliatingly seizing the wives and goods of the Satraps in 624, Mesopotamia was open to peace with the Byzantines and a chance for a favorable truce with the Persians. After a wintering in Albania, Heraclius gathered a mercenary force of local Christian tribesmen as well as from the provinces of Iberia, Lazica, and Abasgia offering the Byzantines proficient scouts. In spring 625, Persian forces under Shahin, Shahvaraz, and Shahraplakan were gathered against the Byzantines. Heraclius, with 40,000 Turk horseman,[485] made a stand at Sunium in Persian Armenia, defeating both Shahin's and Shahraplakan's armies, then leaving for Atropatene.

Though he had yet to succeed in allying with the Avars and Croats, in 619 he did find support in the Caucasus Balkans with the Siberian Otigur Huns under Khovar, and this supplemented the emperor's Albanian troops with baptism and Roman citizenship with a coveted Patrician status.[486] Having lost his Albanians, however, to homesickness and perhaps a fear for Albania from Persia, Heraclius marched to Armenia to Lake Van. Here he learned that Shahin had set out with an army to besiege Constantinople. Heraclius rode through Armenia to await them in Cappadocia and at the City, Heraclius opted to defend it himself with a third of his forces as the general Theodore was to travel west with another third and defeated the Persians in Anatolia where Shahin was killed. It was said by now, Khosru II was turning into a new Xerxes when he had Shahin's corpse flogged in his presence, described as a sort of *Kaiserwahnsinn* ('the lunacy of a mad king'). Now, he was alienating himself from his nobles and the army, leading to divisions that led to further advantage for Heraclius.

---

485 Montefiore, 172.

486 Obolensky, 62.

A siege of a united Persian/Avar front now gathered at Constantinople and the emperor seriously considered moving to hold court at Carthage to plan, but the loss of the Crown Jewels in a freak storm caused him to reconsider.[487] Heraclius managed to counter this with 40,000 Khazars from the Khan 'Zeibel'. The chaotic Avars raided the rich suburbs by the walls and cut of the aqueducts and the City's largest water source, capturing some 270,000 people there.[488] The Avars and Slavs did this from the west as Shahvaraz and his forces were ready to cross from Chalcedon in the east by June of 626. This crossing was luckily defeated by the Byzantine navy in the Bosporus, sinking transports and killing thousands of Persians and Avars. The Royal Boar even considered setting up another false peace conference to murder the emperor. But, at the meeting, Shahvaraz got wind from an intercepted transmission from Heraclius that Khosru was ordering his execution and the general then focused himself on the King and made a secret alliance with the Byzantines. When the Avars' supplies ran out and wintering was needed, an Avar rebellion to overthrow the Khan was under way, ending the siege with an Avar retreat back to the West.

Earlier, through Heraclius's diplomatic skills, the Avars were contained mostly in the Balkans and southern Peloponnese. Whether it was due to this diplomacy to the Danubian Slavs or not, a new homeland to these Slavic groups was unofficially created known as Sclavinia. The inhabitants of this region, the Sclavenoi, would later be invaders to the Heraclian dynasty past its end in 711 CE. This was the major Slavonization of the Greek coast that would remain until the Balkans of today. In efforts to combat the Avar south, Heraclius, around 626, received the aid of the 'White Croats', a new tribe of Slavs in Byzantine history settling north of the Carpathian Mountains.[489] From there, they were imperial allies Christianized by the Orthodox Church and untroubled before the wars of the 'White Serbs' of the Carpathians. It was these alliances, as well as with other Turkish tribes, that the 'scales were tipped' against Persia and reversals occurred across the Empire to Ctesiphon.[490] This would be a favorite subject, in the tenth century, for the emperor Constantine VII Porphyrogenitus in his histories, as the origins of the rise of the Slavic nations in his own times.[491]

---

[487] Bury, (AI-II), 219.

[488] ibid., pg. 223. An exorbitant number, but Heracleans and Selymbrians were also gathered there in celebration to the emperor and many must have volunteered.

[489] Obolensky, 59-60.

[490] Decker, 137.

[491] Constantine VII Porphyrogenitus. *De Administrando Imperio,* ed. by Gyula Moravcsik and trans. by Romilly J.H. Jenkins. Washington DC: Dumbarton Oaks

In the summer of 627, the Byzantine armies met Heraclius in his headquarters at Trebizond in northern Armenia, where he fought and killed the general Shahraplakan, with his new allies the Khazars and Georgians. By a short time later, he was leading over 100,000 Greeks, Lazicans, Iberians, and Khazars of the Crimea who would become the mighty Bulgarians of future centuries.[492] They overcame the attempts of defense from the Persian general Rahzad and raided Persian Armenia and Atropatene into Assyria.

There, he won a decisive battle with 3,000 men at the ancient capital of Nineveh on Sunday December 12,[493] killing Rhazad and advancing to Khosru's palace at Dastagerd, where he had already fled to Ctesiphon. Gold and silver, seventy or eighty tons of precious aloe wood, sugar, spices, silks and carpets, tigers, and other exotic animals would all be procured from Dasagerd and 50,000 prisoners were freed. Shortly after, he had the holy city and birthplace of the Persian prophet Zarathustra (628-551BCE), Thebarmes, burned to the ground in retaliation for the riots and destruction of Jerusalem.[494] Destroying to ashes the holiest Temple to a deity represented by fire gave new meaning to 'fighting fire with fire'. At Ctesiphon, Heraclius sued for peace, but with King, refusing Heraclius, went on a campaign taking the King's palaces and the city of Beklal across the Torna River, where he challenged three Persian commanders to personal duels, winning them all.[495]

Khosru's government faced a crisis as Heraclius was making for the capital of Ctesiphon on pontoon bridges across the seas.[496] This was only prevented by seasonal floods in the area that rebuffed the Byzantines back to Atropatene. Khosru's son, Khavad, was resentful of his father's rigidity against a peace with Constantinople and his father's mad fits, the final straw being when he called for a rebellion.[497] Khosru was overthrown and brought to the 'House of Darkness', where his son was butchered before him, and he was executed by Khavad II and his armies 'by archery' (basically a medieval firing squad). After this display of appalling Oriental cruelty, the new King appealed for a peace settlement. Heraclius made concessions of Syrian and Egyptian territories for

---

Center for Byzantine Studies. 1967, 147-161.

[492] Obolensky, 172.

[493] Theophanes, 24.

[494] Bury, (AI-II), 230.

[495] Montefiore, 172.

[496] Treadgold noted Heraclius had a strange 'hydrophobia' and these bridges were common rather to sailing, 305.

[497] Brownworth, 126f.

the remaining general Shahvaraz as agreement was reached with a new ally in Ctesiphon. It had seemed like the divisive and destructive times of Khosru II and Maurice were being rebuilt.

But when Khavad died of the plague that had ravaged Egypt, the young King Ardashir III ascended and a separate peace was made between Heraclius and Shahvaraz. They met at Arabissus in Cappadocia and agreed Shahvaraz would restore Egypt and Syria in return for Mesopotamia south of Amida and a claim to the Persian throne. So, on March 21, 630, Heraclius brought the True Cross back to Jerusalem through the Golden Gate, where Byzantines believed Christ was said to have entered on Palm Sunday,[498] and Shahvaraz became King as a firm Byzantine ally. But, in 631, a palace restoration saw Khosru's daughter Boran to the throne, only as a puppet in a male-dominated culture such as Persia's, to retaliate against the Byzantines. Heraclius then saw his chance and advanced into Mesopotamia, easily winning victory when Boran died the same year, causing more confusion in Ctesiphon. After a century, the Sassanid-Roman Persian Wars were over.

In 629, it even became obvious how Heraclius was vying for hearts and minds in the East; in Armenia, a change in appearance with more facial hair on his coinage after this year relates an Eastern custom dating to the Parthian period before the Sassanid dynasty. A connection with the Armenian Bagratuni dynasty and that of the Heraclids was what made possible Armenian pressure to end the war through rebellion. This was commemorated with coinage of the time with Heraclius wearing a Parthian handlebar mustache[499] when Heraclius was notoriously clean-shaven. Yet, it was this time the destiny of West Asia and the major religions of the world to this day began in 622, with monumental events taking place in Arabia.

It was here that the Prophet Mohammed made the first Hegira to Mecca 320 kilometers (198 miles), from June 21 to July 2, and received the revelation that he was the true Prophet of God and he would write of the revelations of the Archangel Gabriel, presented to him, in the Koran. Mohammed, starting in 628, would show his education by writing letters to the emperor about converting

---

[498] Montefiore, 173. Truthfully, this was the Gate the Jews believed the True Messiah would enter Jerusalem on the Day of Judgement. The Byzantines thought this the Beautiful Gate, where the apostles performed miracles.

[499] DowlingSoka, Joel. 'Herakleios' Handlebar: Contextualizing a Change in Imperial Imagery' (Paper presented at the The Twenty-Eighth Annual Byzantine Studies Conference) Colombus, OH: The Ohio State University, Oct. 4-6, 2002).

to this new faith,[500] a system unwisely ignored by the busy Heraclius. As the Umayyad Caliphate, would traverse in conquest in Arabia, Heraclius ignored it as more Arab tribal wars like those in the past and the pleas to convert by denying Christ was unthinkable. The birth of *Islam* ('Submission') and the passion of its faithful believers would write a new and bloody chapter in the history of Byzantium in the seventh century.

If Heraclius had died in 629 at the height of the Empire's glory, returning the True Cross to Jerusalem and recovering the Holy Lance and Sponge present at the Crucifixion, his legacy would have been unimpeachable. But the last twelve years of his reign, those years in wars with the Arabs of the Umayyad Caliphate, brought only, '...disappointment, disillusionment, and ultimately, dishonor.'[501] But no Byzantine ruler could have done much better (as Phocas would have said) against such an onslaught. To Heraclius's credit as a legend among his own people, it is said a gift of mystic prophecy allowed him in a dream to see 'someone' (probably Mohammed or 'Abu Bakr) was delivered to the Sassanid King and induced to invade Persia, according to the Arab historian Mohammed ibn Jarir al-Tabari (838-923 CE).[502]

The first Muslim Arab to invade the East was Mohammed's father-in-law, Abu Bakr, the first Caliph (*Kalifat Rasul Allah* – 'Successor to the Messenger of God').[503] In 632, he began to spread the Koran's word to Syria and Mesopotamia before his death that year, rivaling the Persian government claiming as now they ruled as heathens and atheists. The next year, in autumn, Bakr's 24,000 men took Palestine and in 634, Gaza and Sinai, killing its commander. Heraclius, from Edessa, sent his officer, Theodore, and the Army of the East to recover the territories. The general Khalid ibn al-Walid met Theodore at the border between Palestine and Gaza and defeated his forces.

By 635, the Arabs had taken Syrian Damascus and Emesa as Heraclius responded by making his financial officer, Theodore, the sacellarius. With a Byzantine force of 40,000 (the Muslim historian Ahmed ibn-Yahya ibn-Jaril al-Baradhuri (806-892 CE) in his *Conquest of the Lands* would say 200,000 Greeks, Syrians, and Armenians were dispatched as 70,000 fought and were 'routed and slaughtered' by 24,000 Arabs),[504] the Arabs were expelled from

---

[500]  Bury, (*AI-II*), 261.

[501]  Norwich, (*EC*), 310.

[502]  Kaegi, *Heraclius*, 124.

[503]  Montefiore, 180f.

[504]  Al-Baladhuri, Ahmad ibn-Yahya ibn-Jabril. 'Conquest of the Land's *Readings in Medieval Historiography*, ed. by Speros Vryonis Jr. Boston, MA: Houghton Mifflin,

the Syrian cities. After a skirmishing defeat against the Arabs at Emesa, the Byzantine commander Baianes caught up to the Arabs at Yarmuk. Here, one of the worst losses in Byzantine record – such as Adrianople or Manzikert – occurred due to the tactical errors of the local command. At this point, Syria was unrecoverable to Byzantine hands and it was proven warfare against the Arabs should not be decisive or put on one major battlefield as with Persia.[505]

Egypt was also in danger, and the emperor sent his personal armies to reinforce the garrisons as the rest returned to do the same in Anatolia. The Armies of the East withdrew when Heraclius returned to Constantinople in 636, taking with him the True Cross, to protect it from the Muslims in Jerusalem. Throughout Jerusalem and the Empire, Islam was being met with tolerance and sympathy from the Monophysites, fellow Semites seeing the same way on monotheism.[506] At this point, Heraclius was grayed and balding with a pronounced stoop stricken with dropsy, his health declining during the continuing spread of Islam in the East. In the desperation of physical and emotional collapse, in 618, he considered moving the capital to Carthage, his home territory and only the intervention of the Patriarch Sergius disallowed this. By now, however, Heraclius was fleeing to Constantinople to the Palace of Hieria across the Bosporus.

Although the campaign began with Heraclius playing David against the Goliath of the Umayyads, a prime piece of psychological warfare,[507] the Byzantine reversals provided the opposite effect. It was thought God was taking retribution for Heraclius's sins with these defeats, lost territory, children of his who had died or been crippled, and a plot in 637 perpetrated by a barbarian bastard son, Athalaric. It got worse that year as Damascus was retaken, Antioch and Berorea next to fall. Then, the new Caliph, 'Umar, conquered Mesopotamia and the Persian capital of Ctesiphon, spelling the doom of the Persian government in Syria (and later, its very existence). In 638, to preserve what he could, the Patriarch of Jerusalem surrendered this holy city and the Muslims made their first occupation there. Confusion filled the throne, weakened slightly by the Persian War, by these Arab camel cavalries, some as small as 1,000 men. Succeeding perhaps at the speed of a few small, yet strategic, raids, they managed to bring the Byzantine legions to their knees.[508]

---

343-364. 1968, 354-355.
[505] Decker, 141.
[506] Brownworth, 130.
[507] Decker, 134.
[508] Montefiore, 181.

The Byzantine governor of Osrhoene, John, made a separate peace of 100,000 *nomismata* to the Arabs, but the infuriated Heraclius recalled and exiled him, forbidding future payments. The only restraint to total Arab hegemony in Syria and Egypt was a plague that had broken out later that year, but in 639, the Arabs would take Mesopotamia at Dara and begin the full invasion of Egypt. The region and the Nile area was easy for the commander 'Amr ibn al-'As to take as the garrisons were demoralized and stricken from the plague since the previous year. Worse still, the Egyptian collaborators aided the Arabs to depose the Chalcedonian Patriarch Cyrus and his persecutions by the emperor's new ecumenical policy.

The last resistance of the Nile happened at Egyptian Babylon, where Theodore and the Patriarch Cyrus defended against 'Amr's 15,000-strong armies in the summer of 640. After a Byzantine defeat, the Patriarch would attempt a peace settlement of 200,000 *nomismata* a year to 'Amr, given Heraclius's approval. But the stubborn emperor angrily rejected it, as he did with all the offers to placate the Caliphate, exiling Cyrus. The Arabs then took Babylon and poured into Alexandria, finishing their conquest of Egypt and Palestine as this would be completed with the taking of Caesarea. By the Basileus's death a year later, the Byzantine army would stand at 109,000 soldiers with 21,800 cavalry (estimated at 20 percent) with an annual military budget of 3,707,000 *nomismata,* less than half of Justinian's in 565, and only dropping past the Heraclian dynasty to estimates in 775.[509]

More defeats for Heraclius came from the ecumenical side of the Empire, unbalanced in Egypt, as 30,000 Greek 'Melchite' Christians co-habited a land of five or six million Coptic Monophysites.[510] In 617, Heraclius began another conciliatory campaign in the Empire by expelling Jews from Jerusalem to settle Monophysite Christians there. But, Heraclius's greatest contribution which had moderate success was Monoenergism. Monoenergism, or Monothelitism, accepted Chalcedon's two natures of Christ with the addition that they had a common and 'single' energy, or more accurately, of motivation (*energeia*)[511] acting as the will for Christ's acts on Earth to serve God, sacrifice, and perform miracles. Unfortunately by 638, the cycle of Eastern religious divisions aiding the undivided Persian cause would only repeat itself in the Arab spread of Islam.[512]

---

[509] Treadgold, *(BAIA),* 196.

[510] Bury, *(AI-II),* 249.

[511] Treadgold, 300.

[512] Ostrogorsky, 109.

Monothelitism only emboldened the Jacobites and Theodosiani, the main Monophysite sects, to claim Chalcedonianism has surrendered, incensing the opposition.[513] In 631, the Antiochene Patriarch Athanasius accepted the doctrine and so did Cyrus, Heraclius's ill-fated choice as Alexandrian Patriarch. At a Council in 633, the Egyptian Church agreed on paper to Monoenergism and the Eastern Church had a successful, but brief, peace. Monoenergism did have its ambiguities, but that was nothing abnormal in light of these policies wishing to placate both Chalcedonians and Monophysites at once. Pope Honorius, however, would not accept these issues and stated Christ had one non-contradictory will making Monoenergism moot in the Western Church; the Pope condemned it in 634 and the emperor complied in defeat, but the Orthodox Church and its Patriarchs would not bow down to Rome. That same year, it was shredded by a Palestinian monk, Sophronius, whose skill at sophistry allowed the Mesopotamians to express 'dyotheletism' – two wills.[514]

In 638, the Constantinopolitan Patriach Sergius would outline the Church's position in the *Ecthesis* ('Exposition of Faith'). It offered a less ambiguous alternative to Monoenergism known as Monothelitism: Christ would have two natures and there would be no more discussions on energies, Christ had one will (*Theghema*), and have language more conducive to the Pope. After Sergius's death in 638, the new Patriarch Pyrrhus accepted the *Ecthesis* in-council. It failed to impress subsequent Popes and Monophysites, however, and met strong opposition in Egypt. When Pope John IV condemned the *Ecthesis*, Heraclius abandoned it and died of his continued illnesses of dropsy on February 11, 641.[515] It was an agonizing death that was attributed to divine punishment for an incestuous marriage; out of nine children his wife bore him, all but three died or were deformed.[516]

For three days, Heraclius lay in an onyx sarcophagus to be buried in the Church of the Holy Apostles, thronged by lines of procession to view the brilliant strategist and beloved monarch, and tragic figure that was Heraclius. But one last insult awaited the monarch that the Avar Khan, the Pope, the Persians, Monophysites, the Caliphate, and all their armies had already inflicted: his succeeding and eldest son, Constans would break in his tomb and steal the

[513] Theophanes, 32.
[514] Bury, (*AI-II*), 251.
[515] Although, Treadgold says it was January and Theophanes, in March; Theophanes was using a different calendar and many discrepancies on dates surface. This date was taken from Ostrogorsky, 112.
[516] Ostrogorsky, pg. 110.

diadem[517] off of his head three months later.[518] It was a bitter and undeserved end to the dignity and fleeting glory of the first true Emperor of Byzantium.

A notable mention concerning Heraclius as a ruler came from the poet, panegyrist, and historian George of Pisidia. Writing near the end of the seventh century, he created the epic poem of the emperor's achievements in the *Heracliad*, the *Persian Expedition* (of 623), and the *Avaric Wars*. His fourth was the *Hexameron*, or 'Six Days' comparing the six campaigns of Heraclius with the six days of Creation.[519] His faith was also of note as he wrote a poem against Severus's heresies, the Resurrection, the Vanity of Life, and on the Martyr Anastasius. Though mostly works of literary skill, they stand as historical testaments to Heraclius's reign; it was he who first described the emperor as a 'crusader' championing Christendom, riding into battle in a panoply of pure gold, with a shield of 120 plates.[520]

There seem to have been, at times, two Heraclii, the administrative genius that could appease his armies with funds and create a defensive military bureaucracy quite reminiscent to western feudalism with his Dukes and Counts. Then there is the other side, with military failures and heavy territorial losses to a new and highly energetic enemy force; no Byzantine emperor experienced such a turnover of success to failure in one reign. If anything, it showed how the Persian enemy was so weak in their positions and not, perhaps, that the Byzantines were so great in theirs. A noted French Orientalist, J. P. Mignes, said how the Nile fell due to poor quality in the army, losing despite high expectations.[521] This was due to large landholders abusing their own military districts and administrative disruptions became the result and it was these exact reasons the Theme system would later be needed to curb these municipal nightmares.[522] The 630's were fated to be the doom of the legacy of Heraclius's prowess, but Byzantium and Hellenism was not without its influence on a new and developing Arab culture.

Islam was originated from the teachings of Mohammed in the Koran as the Word of God ('Allah') and, therefore, binding and authoritative (Koran XXX, V V). In it is hailed Alexander the Great as the 'apostle of Hellenism' and

---

[517] Which was valued at seventy pounds of gold by the historian Nicephorus. Bury, (*AI-II*), 285f.

[518] Norwich, (*EC*), 311.

[519] Bury, (*AI-II*), 256.

[520] Gibbon, 1547.

[521] Vasiliev, 210.

[522] Ostrogorsky, 110-111.

Byzantium as those who would fight the fire-worshiping, Pagan Persians in the East. This strengthened the position of the Empire as a 'World Civilization'[523] whose culture was nurtured in the attitudes of Islam towards Philosophy, Logic, Medicine and Science.[524] Ancient texts transcribed into Arabic from the original Greek brought this Hellenistic foundation in education in philosophical works by Aristotle and Plato, the medical texts by Galen and Hippocrates, and contributions by Christian Arabs and even Pagans such as Mohammed ibn-Ishaq ibn-Yasar ibn-Khiyar (704-768 CE) and Ai-Sabi Thabit ibn-Qurra al-Harrani (836-901 CE). Theophrastus (371-287BCE), Euclid (d. 285BCE), Porphry (233-305 CE), Proclus (410-485 BCE), and numerous authors from all over Greece and Asia Minor bridged the vast gulf of ethnicity, faith, and language between Byzantium and the Umayyads. Victory was seen as inevitable as in the Koran (XXX, I), the triumphs and overturns of Heraclius were documented in a section on 'The Greeks' and their 628 victory.[525]

The Arabs were even seeking a cultural synthesis in their political legitimization in numerous ways, including gold coins resembling the Sassanid coins of Yezdegird III and ones that resembled the Heraclian Byzantine *solidi*.[526] On coins that represented the emperor with the True Cross on the opposite side, the Arab Caliph who drew the Sword of Islam and the Cross being his spear on the other side was alternately displayed. This effected how people saw these new world leaders in commerce and everyday life when coins depicting only Muslim characters and the lack of 'graven images' were distributed.[527] Yet, taken as a diversion from Greek Christianity, Islam was the chance for the disunited Ghassanid tribes in Arabia to achieve much needed 'high social and moral reform, which a new religion would naturally cover; there was a higher possibility of higher civilization and a more advanced form of political existence.'[528]

---

[523] Ostrogorsky, 27-29.

[524] Shahid, Irfan. 'Byzantium and the Islamic World.' Chap. 4 of *Byzantium: A World Civilization,* ed. by Angeliki E. Laiou & Henry Maguire. Washington DC: Dumbarton Oaks Research Library and Collections, 49-60. 1992, 50-54.

[525] Vasiliev, 197.

[526] Marinescu, Constantin A. 'Transformations: Classical Objects and their Reuse in Late Antiquity.' Chap. 18 of in *Shifting Frontiers in Late Antiquity,* ed. by Hagith S. Sivan and Ralph W. Mathisen. Aldershot, Hampshire, UK: Variorum/Ashgate Publishing Company, 285-298. 1996, 292-293.

[527] Hoyland, Robert. 'The Rise of Islam'. Chap. 4 of *The Oxford History of Byzantium,* ed. by Cyril Mango. Oxford, UK: Oxford University Press, 121-129. 2002, 127.

[528] Bury, (*AI-II*), 258.

So, it is the best thing possible, perhaps, that Heraclius's greatest legacy were the amazing reforms he submitted in the sterling 620's. Byzantium proper would survive with a cordon of strong, central Dukedoms around the coasts of Anatolia and Thrace. In years to come, they could be seen all over Eastern Europe as Byzantium would later expand to the Black Sea. Heraclius was given a bad situation with the Arab Caliphate, but Byzantium would survive where Persia would perish and still become Europe's Eastern champion versus Islam. But, on the horizon was a series of wars to prove that the Caliph was not through with the *Sahib al-Rum*, or 'Emperor of Rome'.

## CONSTANS II HERACLIUS 'THE BEARDED'
(641-668)

## CONSTANTINE III HERACLIUS
(641)

## HERACLONAS
(641)

A troubled Byzantium was all that remained in 641, perhaps more troubled than it had been forty years before when Phocas ruled. Constantine III Heraclius ascended on January 11, and would only last three months, doling the army 2,016,000 *nomismata*,[529] appointing a commander Magister of the East and Armenia, and having a disastrous campaign to regain Egypt, just before dying of tuberculosis on April 23. Though always a consideration, historians do not believe Constantine was poisoned as he spent so long in the Palace of Chalcedon, unless it was slow acting,[530] which would make little sense. Heraclius's next son with the controversial and 'incestuous' Martina, Heraclonas, succeeded his sickly brother as the 'middle child'. He had been born in 615 and was crowned co-Emperor in 638, also attending his father as a general in the Syrian campaigns.[531] Martina, as empress, unfortunately, lacked sufficient military support and was easily deposed by the armies under the Magister of Offices, Valentine.

---

[529] Treadgold (*BAIA*), 145.
[530] Bury, (*AI-II*), 283f.
[531] Nicephorus of Constantinople. *Short History,* ed. by Cyril Mango. Washington, DC: *CFHB.* 1990.

The people might have had a connection with Martina, as one witness was said to have seen her shout to her people that she was a mother of emperors, though their lords still held precedence.[532] In a famous method of Byzantine humiliation, Martina's tongue was cut out and Heraclonas's nose slit in half, deformed to exclude them from the succession after a six-month reign. Valentine and the armies then raised Heraclius, son of Constantine III, to become Constans II. While only eleven years old at the time, he showed the keen mind his grandfather had and a determination to rise above the control of senators and interests that would consume other rulers – especially in establishing the Themes, or, 'emplacements' along the Imperial coasts.

Yet he bravely and shrewdly, upon his succession, assembled the senators and nobles in 642 and decried the crimes of his stepmother and the unclean examples upon which were perpetrated by Heraclius, Constantine III, and Heraclonas. He concluded this *apologia* with the typical promise set by Theophanes: 'Therefore, I call upon you to be advisers and judges of the common welfare of our subjects.[533]' Without really emphasizing, Constans II had declared that the Senate had an important place in this new era; his intentions were granting only indirect control of imperial power and that their place was seeking the harmony of the subjects, not to obstruct the *Basileus*'s powers. Also, it made implicit claims that Constantine was murdered by his stepmother and that Heraclonas and Martina had 'deprived his excellent hopes' due to envy. This demonstrated the character between the Byzantine institutions of the *Basileus* and a wise, but inferior, Senate known for centuries from experience and history. Although many generals would do so in the future, no Senate ever openly rebelled against an *Basileus*, and understanding this Constans reinstated the loyalty oaths of the army in 645.[534]

Tradition sets down that Constans II, known for his long and luxurious beard (*Pogonatus*), was a failure of an emperor: impious, indecisive ecumenically, and a deserter of the City of Constantinople for the 'Roman' West. But modern historians relate how Constans attempted to conciliate his grandfather's policies and military policy proving that the suspicion of misinterpretation, sabotage, or treason by officers, and ecclesiastical authorities were to blame, causing

---

[532] Bury, (*AI-II*), 282.

[533] Theophanes, 41.

[534] Bury, (*AI-II*), 287.

much of the enmity against Constans.[535] Many Semitic and Arabic historical interpretations also neglect events in his policies and his major blunder was a lack of effective military defense in Africa from his position of the West. His departure for Italy may even have been an attempt to show his personality in the army's presence, such as Heraclius had done, and not to be seen as a man of 'brooding melancholy . . .son of a consumptive weakling . . .a self-willed daredevil . . . [whom] fell to an impractical ideal.'[536]

Though modern historians have rectified this in advancing imperial Byzantine biography for the period, for centuries the 'Dark Age' had only limited knowledge of these subjects between the *Basilii* Maurice to Alexius I (582-1081), excluding Basil II (976-1025), existed.[537] Even his name was a controversy, being the Heraclius of his father as Nicephorus of Constantinople (758-828 CE) always believed, or the coins of the period naming him, Constantine IV. What we now know of his name being Constans (after the son of the first Constantine as Heraclius was sometimes called) came from Theophanes, the most trusted and complete chronicler of the time.[538]

Seen either way, Constans II made mistakes and fared little better than his grandfather did before the Muslim tide. What was important here was the officiating of his grandfather's Thematic administrative system in Thrace and Anatolia. Added here would be Armenia and the districts of the Drungaries (ruled by a *Droungoi*) and Turmarchs (*Tourmarchai*), the latter commanded by

---

[535] Kaegi, Walter. 'Re-interpreting Constans II (641-668).' (Presented at *The Twenty-Ninth Annual Byzantine Studies Conference*, Lewiston, ME: Bates College, Oct. 16-19, 2003). In Kaegi's 'Re-conceptualizing Byzantine's Eastern Frontiers in the Seventh Century' Chap. 6 of *Shifting Frontiers in Late Antiquity*, ed. by Ralph W. Mathisen and Hagith S. Sivan, Aldershot, Hampshire, UK: Ashgate/Varorium Publishing, 83-92. 1996, 84, Kaegi relates the vital need to consult contemporary Arabic sources such as Abu Said al-Basri (642-748 CE), al-Bahadhuri, Abu Qasim Abd ar-Raman bin-Abdullah Abd al- Hakam bin A' Yan al-Qu'ashri al Masri (803-871 CE), al-Tabari, Lut ibn-Yahya ibn-Said ibn-Mikhnaf al Khufi (d. 774 CE), and Agapius of Membij (d. 942 CE) to fully understand Constans's actions.

[536] Ostrogorsky, 144.

[537] Gibbon, 1605-1606. According to Bury, (*AI-II*), 281, three historians who lived a century later: Theophanes, Nicephorus, and John Malalas were all that could be learned from.

[538] Bury, 285f.

soldiers known as Turmae (*Tourmai*).[539] This spread to Samos in the south and was centered in Ancyra in Anatolia.

All of these changes were instituted in the late 650's until 662. By 668, the Themes would include the Opsikian (Obsequium) in northwest Anatolia, and the Exarchates of Africa, Italy, and the coasts from Greece to Crete to Cyprus. This achievement would be credited to Heraclius, but it was Constans's administration that saw wide developments of the idea. Although Constans is given credit for his organization, in truth, the Thematic system was organic and a result of military necessity, not the fiat of a single *Basileus*.[540] It is a precursor to the political-military 'revolution' of the seventeenth century that nationalized armed forces away from feudalism to absolutism.

What Constans also developed was land grants to the soldiers of the new Themes; this would become (only in a *de facto* manner) the controversial pronoia that would bind and sever ties between emperor and state in centuries to come. In exchange for military service, the state provided land that could be inherited directly (as well as any post in military service) for a fifty percent pay cut and a severance on supplies and equipment. Cavalry soldiers would receive minimums of four pounds of gold annually and the 4,000 soldiers used as marines in the Carabisian Theme would receive two pounds. It is noted that land was more common a commodity as little to no evidence of gold, silver, or even bronze coinage have been excavated from Constans's last decade as emperor.[541] This saved a good amount of cash in gold for the coffers to create solid buffers against enemies in all directions for Thrace, Armenia, Anatolia, and Greece, and one-fifth of Anatolia's impressively-sized arable land was reserved for Themes. Funds would prove difficult to get, nonetheless, as state warehouses were now falling under private contractors.

Heraclius Constans II was born on November 7, 630, to the *Basileus* Heraclius Constantine and Gregoria, daughter of Heraclius's brother and cousin, Nicetas. When Martina was no longer an option for a regent, Constans was seen over by the patronage of Patriarch Paul II. However, as he controlled the armies without opposition from the throne, Valentine still counted as leading the Empire. In autumn 642, he showed a lack in enthusiasm in

---

[539] Treadgold, 316. It is held that these were emergency measures against the Western, Syrian, and Egyptian regions' deteriorating into absolute rebellion; the first Themes created were a buffer between imperial center and border.

[540] Bury, (*AI-II*), 341.

[541] Hendy, Michael. *Studies in the Byzantine Monetary Economy, c. 300-1450.* Cambridge, UK: Cambridge University Press. 1985, 640-645.

dispelling Alexandria of 'Amr and his Arab armies to which the Patriarch Cyrus compromised the City by paying tribute. That did not stop Valentine from seating himself within the dynasty by marrying his daughter to the new child emperor, then gathering the Eastern armies to head to Armenia. 'Amr took the opportunity to oust the Byzantines, who fled to Cyprus, as the Arabs taking Libya as well. Valentine would try to claim the throne twice by 644, when his second attempt was halted by Paul II and his faction; Valentine would then be lynched that autumn, giving Constans an unimpeded rule. Constans always showed mistrust in his surviving brothers and although his son became co-emperor in 654, he would have his brother Theodosius murdered six years later.

In the East, the situation was not better as the Muslim general of the Syrian army, Mu'awiyah, approached Constantinople by way of Amorium. The Arabs had renamed Atropatene, the former Persian province Azerbaijan, and invaded Armenia only to be defeated by Theodore Rshtuni, the Armenian ruler. In Jerusalem, the generals were told by the inhabitant Jews that they could not raise a mosque with the Christian crosses still in places, so the 'Christ-haters pulled down many crosses'[542] as if an ominous and unintentional pre-cursor to the Crusades. Italy also suffered when in 644 the Exarch Isaac was killed by the Lombards who took Liguria. That autumn, Constans would make Theodore head of the Eastern armies and the thirteen-year-old emperor now ruled Byzantium alone. All of his trust he put in Armenia – the Armenian generals, the Armenian King Rshtuni, and Armenian Prefects, so he could then focus on Egypt.

Entering Alexandria was not difficult – the Arabs levied heavier taxes and had no real liking of Monophysites – and the Byzantine general Manuel settled in ease when the Caliph named a new governor over 'Amr. But, this ease allowed him to grow slack and unprepared when 15,000 Arabs under a later reinstated 'Amr drove him from the city across the sea. This unlikely threat to Byzantine naval superiority would only grow as Mu'awiyah would go from Cilicia to a fleet taking the African Exarchate, Gregory, Constans's rebellious cousin, and another fleet would raid Cyprus in 648. But, luckily, the Muslims did not approach Africa, whose armies they defeated, and the Cypriot Arab fleet of 1,700 vessels were driven off by the Byzantines as well. This was because Gennadius, a candidate made for Exarch of Africa by the African Church, was able to buy the Arabs out of the region with 330,000 *nomismata*. Gennadius secured

---

[542] Theophanes, pg. 42-43. This marked a true threat to Byzantine sea power only returned by Greek Fire decades later.

himself as the Exarch when a Constantinopolitan monk named Maximus made trouble domestically by convincing the staunchly Chalcedonian Africans that Constans's beliefs were Monothelitist and ambiguous.

By 651, the Arabs had finished the last of the Persian Empire to now concentrate its forces on Byzantium and spread the Islamic Empire. A year later, the once adamant Rshtuni ceded Armenian control to Mu'awiyah, and in response, Constans personally led the Eastern armies to Armenia to recover the area. Mu'awiyah captured Cilicia in the meantime and the commander of the Thracian Armies revolted, but Constans still managed to recover Armenia back to Rshtuni, under the guidance of the Byzantine commander, Maurianus, using the Roman tactic of occupation for the region's safety. Constans also brought order to Italy with a new Exarch, Theodore Calliopas, who arrested Pope Martin I for conspiracy against the Crown in 650 and was taken to Constantinople, where he was stripped of his vestments and kept in chains.[543] The Pope would be exiled to the Crimea where he died in 653; his strife was a reflection of the abject poverty of this region where bread was scarce to the pontiff and would be a breeding ground for the military tensions of the Khazars over the next century.[544]

In 654, a full-scale invasion of the Empire came from the East under Mu'awiyah as naval fleets were sent to Cyprus and Crete, his forces taking Rhodes. It is there that he looted, supposedly, and disassembled the Colossus of Rhodes, Wonder of the Ancient World, sculpted in 304 BCE by Chares of Lindos (fl. 285BCE),[545] and sold it to a Jewish merchants scrap to be hauled away using 900 camels. The source of this was Theophanes, who erroneously claimed the Arabs destroyed the Colossus, when in fact it fell to an earthquake in 225 BCE.[546] The taking of Rhodes was a disastrous loss to Byzantium, and only by disguising himself as a common soldier was Constans able to escape the carnage. Mu'awiyah also took Ancyra, Theodosiopolis, Trebizond, and Armenia sending Maurianus to the Caucasus as Rshtuni was sent to Damascus to die in captivity.

In 655, Mu'awiyah invaded Cappadocia with the fleet on the southern Anatolian coast, but Constans out-thought his adversary by sailing with a fleet in advance, only to still suffer heavy defeat in Caria, sending him back

---

[543] Norwich, (AM), 52.

[544] Obolensky, 170.

[545] Norwich, (CE), 315.

[546] Bury, (AI-II), 290f. An unfortunate consequence of the Dark Age when such errors could be confused for fact.

to Constantinople. Mu'awiyah did fail at Cappadocian Caesarea, but it was a small victory for the outmatched Byzantines; fortunately for Byzantium, the Umayyad Caliphate was overthrown and the Sultan Uthman was murdered while studying the Koran, to be replaced by Ali. Thus, even a state based on faith and the Book must give way to power politics and bloodshed. Mu'awiyah as a member of the Umayyud royal family began a campaign to reclaim the throne with his Syrian forces, and Byzantium would be granted time to recoup and take a breath in 656.

The next few years would be spent perfecting his Theme system in relative peace as the Arab Civil War accomplished two advantages: it occupied the Caliph's time and resources, and reluctantly forced him into a treaty of 3,000 *nomismata*, fifty thoroughbred Arab horse, and fifty Byzantine captives all daily. This quickly filled the coffers and allowed other prosperity in manpower and the policy of kind over cash to be included in the Empire. In 661, the usurper Ali was killed and the Ummayyads returned to the throne in Damascus. They immediately began preparations for the capital and North Africa, but this did not deter Constans from his next policy of moving to Italy to hold the imperial government in the West as his son Constantine would in the East. In the Balkans, for the first time with the scant and sketchy sources given, the Slavs of the Sklavenoi began to appear as being raided by Constans II in 658.[547] The Sklavenoi as a people, nation, and then subjects under Byzantium would have an important role in the next century.

He was the first Eastern emperor to visit Rome since before the fall in 476, intending to make war to straighten out Sclavonia and the Lombards, as well as North Africa. But this made him unpopular in the East as he was seen as a defeatist before the Muslim war effort, and a deserter to Eastern Orthodoxy and the Patriarchs by accepting terms with the Pope, Vitalian, to settle. A few modern historians still go so far as to name it an 'alienation' of the Church and Empire as 'a sign of fragmentation...in the face of Muslim advance.'[548] After a presentation in Rome lasting twelve days as an honored guest by the Pope and bestowing on the Altar of St. Peter's a gold *pallium* ('cloth'),[549] he traveled down

---

[547] Ostrogorsky, 117.

[548] Angold, 48.

[549] Herrin, 92. Though not speculated, this may have been a symbolic gesture of the *Basileus*'s submission to the Roman Church over Constantinople, as Constans and his successors would intend to adopt the Roman See as their own figurehead as the Western emperors had done. His intention appears to have been to mimic Diocletian's Tetrarchy and perhaps another Reconquest.

the coast of Naples and settled in Syracuse, a bulwark between Sicily and North Africa. It is fundamentally noted in the *Liber Pontificalis* how he raised funds by, once again, the unpopular means of levying taxes, confiscating plate, and even stripping the bronze ornaments and roof off of the Church of St. Mary's *ad martyrs*.[550]

He did succeed in stabilizing the Lombards, winning a brief campaign and exacting tribute from their Duke; but his occupations among the civilian Sicilians has been described as 'a living nightmare.' In order to meet the tax needs to fight the Lombards, husbands were sold into slavery, wives into prostitution, and children separated from parents.[551] Although it might be hyperbole adjudicated by his numerous detractors, it put him in a definite category of a tyrant in Sicilian history and no one wept over his failed mission to move the capital west. This hyper-taxation in the Empire was strained by circumstance, however, when the wholesale confiscations of clerical and lay properties were averted as the religious enemies Constans made with doctrinal neutrality and the execution of Maximus made this dangerous ground.[552]

North Africa had to be brought to heel when the Caliph bribed the African Exarchate, Gennadius, to rebel in 665. In less than a year, Constans defeated the rebellious Saracens in Africa and kept a safe vigil on the territory from nearby Syracuse. The Armeniac Theme was then threatened in 665 through 668 wherein imperial territory was breached to become Arabic quarters. One defensive victory occurred in 667 when Yezid, son of Muwiyah, settled a garrison of 5,000 Sklavenoi Slavs in Chalcedon before returning to Syria,[553] all of whom were casualties in a subsequent Byzantine raid. Constans's son, from Constantinople, sent an army under Nicephorus the Patrician to route a weak mob, only to submit when their commander died in a riding accident. Though the Themes were growing and decentralizing power as well as imperial autonomy, Constantine was seen as the victor of an oppressive force and his popularity in the army grew.

Yet, he would not see his father's ambitions in Syracuse be realized, especially since the religious controversies kept diplomacy from allowing the imperial family from moving to their stations in Italy.[554] His army of 20,000 was defeated by the Lombards, causing his future as Western Roman Emperor

---

[550] Treadgold, 319.
[551] Norwich, (*CE*), 322.
[552] Treadgold, (*BAIA*), 172.
[553] Theophanes, 50.
[554] Herrin, 97.

to appear grim. Another motivation for Constans's move may have been more idealistic as it has been noted Western historians merely referred to these 'Romans' as 'Greeks.' Perhaps it is a suitable question that, if Constans was also trying to return the Eastern Empire's identity as the successors of the ancient Romans rather than be noted as the 'Greeks' merely for geographical or cultural reasons?

It was fortuitous, then, for the dissenting westerners on September 15, 668, that the *Basileus* that had faced many humiliations in the East between Muslims and Church fragmentation met an equally humiliating end. Constans was struck down in the bath house of Daphne with a soap dish by a servant named Andrew, son of a Troilus; this was quietly orchestrated by a Count Mizizius on behalf of, somewhat superficially, the Byzantine people. The real humiliations came from the unpopularity he received in his life: religious ambiguity and fierce cruelty to his brother[555] branding him to historians as a 'new Cain',[556] as well as respected defenders of the faith from what seemed a submission to Pope Vigilius in Rome. Christianity faced extinction everywhere in the East, as in 643, when the Caliph ordered the destruction of any present and future Christian temples in Jerusalem. Constans's inability to keep the Church together with ecumenical doctrine puts him in a long list of emperors that could say the same.

His claim to neutrality was his *Type* ('Edict') of 649, which issued Monotheletism and a number of topics on Christ's natures were no longer to be discussed. Yet, despite this stance, his tone was imperious and devoid of bigotry,[557] showing restless energy and devotion to this cause as he did all other subjects of the Empire as toleration was his intention over lethargy. Pope Eugenius I showed indifference to this trite entreaty[558] and it was further undermined by the doomed Chalcedonian Maximus the Confessor who unwisely claimed the *Basileus* was a 'laymen' with no right to raise questions or opinions in the matters of the Church.[559]

Maximus was summarily divested of his heretical tongue and one hand (a

---

[555] He had him executed in 660, on trumped charges as a strategic political move, despite stories by historian John Cedrenus he had delusional nightmares, apparitions of Theodosius, approaching Constans with a chalice of blood offering, 'Drink, o brother.' Bury, (*AI-II*), 298.

[556] Ostrogorsky, 121.

[557] Bury, (*AI-II*), 292-293.

[558] Treadgold, 313.

[559] Ostrogorsky, 120.

common punishment for heresy) while all of his associates were condemned, exiled, tortured, and executed by Constans, including the Anastasius brothers. As Maximus's main disciples,[560] they were complicit in Pope Martin I's support of a usurper for the throne who had been arrested on June 15. In a bloody campaign, all were arrested and executed, including the Western Exarch, Gregory, only emboldening the tenacious West, who made Maximus and Martin martyred saints of the Western Church.

The *Type* permitted the removal of the heretical *Ecthesis* of Heraclius, but was a document no better lauded than the *Henoticon* of Zeno. It only silenced, by law, the question of the Single Will from discussion and doled several punishments if it were broached for different classes:

1) Monks and clerics were excommunicated.
2) Army personnel and civil servants would be deprived of rank.
3) Property was confiscated from Senators.
4) Private individuals (though this is not clarified economically) were flogged and banished.[561]

It also did nothing to alleviate the tensions between Orthodoxy and Monotheletism, nor did it satisfy in most ways any one side alone. Constans's desperate attempt to disallow internal disintegration over faith, in the face of critical external threats in the Empire, only deepened tensions and justified the detractors of his edicts. In October of 649, in the Church of St. Savior in the Lateran Palace of Rome, it was condemned by 105 bishops, not for doctrinal reasons, but for the political motives against the Patriarch Sergius who faced excommunication. Pope Martin would damn them as the 'Impious *Ecthesis*' (*impiissima* Ecthesis) and the 'vicious Typus' (*scelerosus Typus*) and condemn those associated with heresy.[562] This failure to unite Churches in a time of severe military crisis only added to the idea of Constans's incompetence as a leader. His reign would end in the uprising of the Opsikion Theme in the East

---

[560] Theophanes, 50. By naming them 'Orthodox' reformers, it is implicit that they were detractors of, among other things, the *Edict* and this was also set as an example to religious dissension. Not only was this too severe a penalty in relation to Constans's above penalties for crossing the document, but it gained him the explosive enmity of the Church.

[561] Nowich, (*EC*), 317.

[562] Vasiliev, 223.

under its Count, Mizizius. The remaining question was if his teenage son could find suitable support against the threat.

Constans II was vilified by contemporaries for his cruelties against his brother, Theodosius, against Maximus the Confessor, and for his bland, centrist, and heretical opinions. But, as many modern commentators believe, this was slanderous sensationalism written by unenlightened men. Rather than cruel and unimaginative, he had amazing quality in various areas and had ambitions beyond the sensibility of his reforms in the army and protests from the administration. It is better to say: 'Constans grew up a stern and inflexible man, with decided opinions on policy and administration, resolved to act independently and not afraid of innovation, surprisingly free from religious bigotry in a bigoted age, an unusually strong and capable ruler . . .opposed to the tendencies of his age . . .in ecclesiastical color.'[563] His only real crime was the impracticality of trying to remove the scepter from the so-called 'daughter' of Constantinople and return it to the 'mother', Rome.

The numerous Arab historians who wrote on him used his defeats and flight from the East as a pretext to defame him, and Byzantium in general. Yet, his only apparent mistake was trying to keep up a two-front war in Africa without really securing Armenia and Syria. With the fifty percent pay decrease for the soldiery he decreed, he kept military spending low at 2,027,000 *nomismata* without touching the bureaucracy's budget of 500,000.[564] Included in his accomplishments, met by the Theme system, was the infusion of key regions with free peasants upon whom the Empire at the time owed to its later revival and prosperity.[565] The militarization of society in the lower class of soldiery was also prosperous as the 288 *nomismata* of annual pay could buy 144 acres of farmland for six families, tenants, and work hands all under obligation to provide cavalry food, fodder, uniforms, and horse.[566] It would take good fortune to keep the East in order and fortunately this came with military development and a small series of popular and able rulers being on the throne.

---

[563]  Bury, (AI-II), 303-305.

[564]  Treadgold, (BAIA), 196.

[565]  Jenkins, Romilly. *Byzantium: The Imperial Centuries, AD 610-1071*. Toronto, Can: University of Toronto Press and the Medieval Academy of America. 1987, 39. Once again the credit owed to the *Basileus* had been ignored and obfuscated by contemporary historians.

[566]  Treadgold, 381.

# CONSTANTINE IV
## (668-685)

It was in Constans's successor that Byzantium would be presented with as an even more gifted and intelligent ruler. His reputation of excellence and decisiveness won him acclaim with the army, who protected him against the usurpation of Mizizius in the Opsikian. [567] Soon after, he would sail to a stabilized Sicilian/North African region to personally execute his father's assassin, consolidating a complete victory over Mizizius and his rebellion. Ahead for Constantine was a brief era of success against encroaching Muslim forces and the respect of the army and navy earning what would induce all neighboring enemies to capitulate to the Byzantines. His decisiveness would even garner satisfaction from the Western Church and reclaim the reputation as the main power of the East in the West. In a time of unrest, where territories and borders of the Empire were constantly threatened to be seized by the Arabs, Slavs, and Lombards, there was a culture wherein the imperial authority of the *oikemene* was threatened[568] and Constantine was all too aware of it – to him, absolute authority must be the priority.

He was born to a nineteen-year-old Constans II in 652 and was made Caesar, as his eldest son, in 654. It must be noted that there is confusion and perhaps Constantine was to be 'The Bearded' instead of his father, but coinage from the era depicting Constans II leads to the contrary. For 662 to 668, he controlled the Eastern government and army in place of his father, then in Syracuse. Upon his succession in 668, Constantine took charge against the Muslim front; in 670, the African Saracens began land and sea operations against the Empire. This is as they built the town of al-Qayrawan ('The Caravan') to establish a permanent Arab presence independent of Byzantium. They met strong opposition from the Byzantines as a sign of Constans's abilities in the West and in the East Caliph Mu'awiyah was building resources at Cyzicus by the Marmara as a base of operations, raiding the trade of the sea passages. This made an easy center of naval operations against Constantinople from the captured Caribisian Theme as a definite target.

In 672, these tensions came to a head as three fleets of Arab ships were sent

---

[567] Mizizius had fatally overestimated Byzantium's distrust in Constans and soon found himself in great opposition as a usurper; it is likely Constantine galvanized such opposition with his popularity. Treadgold, 322.

[568] Olster, 98.

to conquer the City from the eastern sea of the Bosporus. But, it was here that the Arabs met their greatest opposition yet; a chemical engineer from Syria, Callinicus of Heliopolis (b. 673), fleeing from his home city rather than leaving by choice,[569] who had been refining from the explosive petroleum compounds of the region a napalm-like mixture. Its recipe was a state secret and is lost today as it was in the eleventh-century in Byzantium. However, a speculative recipe has supposedly come from the obscure historian Marcus Graecus from his *Liber Ignius*: 'Take pure sulphur, tartar, sarocolla (Persian gum), pitch, dissolved nitre, petroleum, and pine resin; boil these ingredients together; saturate tow with the concoction and set fire to it. The conflagration will spread and can only be extinguished by vinegar, urine, or sand.'[570]

The methods of extinguishing the fire may suggest that the ammonium found in vinegar and urine may cause a neutralizing effect with the substance by chemically balancing its ph levels, an important clue in experimentation with reproducing the compound. Its effects were marvelous to the Byzantine navy; it was a liquid fire that did not vaporize on ignition and arced downward onto low-riding galleys most effectively.[571] It also burned when spread and could survive douses of water; it was said by witnesses to have burned *on the waters* of the sea and could not be extinguished. This would become known as the famous 'Greek Fire' also known as 'Romaioi' and 'Marine Fire' (*pur thelassion*).[572]

Equal with this innovation was the technology of administering the chemical, the *siphonophore* system, a hydraulic pump and siphon hose that sprayed streams of the chemical upon the enemy. It also showed diversity in later centuries as a fuel for clay-pot grenades and trebuchet fodder in records as later as Anna Comnena's in the early twelfth-century. Manuals on war by the tenth-century *Basileus*, Nicephorus II Phocas, have even produced the possibility of a mobile land transport of Greek Fire resembling the first flamethrower in history.[573] These destructive elements were the reason why, in the mid-eleventh century, clerics and Patriarchs plead for the banning of the creation and use of Greek Fire in all war.[574]

---

[569] Porphyrogenitus, 227.

[570] Norwich, (*EC*), 323. Bury also speculates how the design of such a galley came from the simpler 'fire-ships' of Gaiseric in the sixth century and when Proclus used 'sulphur-machines' against Vitalian.

[571] Decker, 222-224.

[572] Bury, (*AI-II*), 310.

[573] Decker, 226.

[574] Haldon, John. *Warfare, State, and Society in the Byzantine World 565-1204*, part of the series *Warfare and Society*. New York, NY: Routledge Publishing. 1999.

Although the exact recipe is sketchy in any surviving documentation, Byzantine military historians such as John Haldon have experimented with the hose to result in a working apparatus reaching arcs of fifteen meters (fifty feet). Theophanes accounts the successful and frightful destruction the liquid Fire presented to a stunned and intimidated Khagan of the Avars sending a 'loving delegation' with gifts to beg Constantine for a peace.[575] Meanwhile, the Arab offensive was presumably disastrous given this use of weaponry as the eastern ports and walls of the City remained unbreached.

But this did not stop later fleets in 674 to terrorize the Marmara to Thrace, attempting to breach Constantinople at the Procleanesian port of Caesarium, but this, again, met a devastating defeat for the once-invincible Muslims in 673. In that year also, Byzantine victories were inducing a Christian sect-turned-tribe, known as the Arab word 'Mardaites' ('iron clubs'[576]) of Mount Amanus and Lebanon, to rebel and complicate the Arabs' positions. Another Arab expedition to Cyzicus to winter there resulted in meeting a surprise attack by generals Florus, Kyprianos, and Petronas, killing 30,000 Arabs.[577] The Arabs were facing defeat on numerous fronts and the toll was taken since 672, when the Egyptian and Rhodian coasts were taken as the Arabs attempted to grow food on the island[578] which was either one of two dangerous signs of either a long entrenchment or a permanent settlement.

With Constantine also successful in the Balkans, Mu'awiyah sued for peace in 679 and promised fifty horses, fifty slaves, and 3,000 pounds (216,000 *nomismata*) annually. Unfortunately, the Caliph was dead a year later and this issued problems under his son, Yazid, as civil war over succession erupted in the Caliphate in 682. What made matters worse for the struggling Caliph was an unsuccessful raid of Constantinople in summer, 677, to the Greek Fire that massively burned and drowned most of his army, limping back east by autumn. It was a victory honorably compared by historians to the Basileus Leo III in 718 and Charles Martel's victory over the Muslims at Poitiers in 732.[579] The invincibility of the Byzantine navy was restored as all over the Eastern Themes and territories, Arab fleets were turned, raided, and sunk by storms.

In 680, however, Constantine IV succumbed, to his father's paranoid tenancies, deposing his brothers as traitors, but, it may have been justified as

---

[575] Vasiliev, 215.
[576] Bury, (*AI-II*), 312. The Byzantines knew them as *Apelatai*.
[577] Theophanes, 53.
[578] Treadgold, 325.
[579] Ostrogorsky, 125.

his crowned brothers Heraclius and Tiberius were being seen as equals with Constantine. The Senate agreed and was for an unprecedented 'tri-rule' for the Empire,[580] although it was decidedly unwise and unconstitutional to the lone ruler as the Chosen of Christ. Perhaps in a religious fervor concerning the Ecumenical Council occurring at the time, the soldiers of the Anatolic Theme in Chrysopolis, a critical post against the eastern invaders, called for a 'Trinity' of *Basilii*[581]: three emperors for three natures of the Chalcedonian creed that Constantine IV was champion of at the Council.

This strange, but not unexpected, demand might have been a play for the Theme to weaken and divide imperial power, also strengthening the position of the Theme itself. The emperor made a purge in the City and hanged many of these Trinity supporters in the Sykai district and the matter was simply closed. Constantine had his brothers deposed, and later during the Council had their legitimacy cancelled by slitting their noses in the cruel Byzantine manner. This would mark the emperor as a ruler not without a bit of tyranny, like Constans, in his rule of the City and Empire. But a compromise of the external borders had to be made, and a semi-independent 'barbarian' state would come to exist in the northeastern frontiers in 680-681 at a time when the Slavs of Thessalonica were the target of a program of 'Byzantinization' and absorption.[582]

Though there would be this strife in Constantinople, the Slav lands in the West were settled under Byzantine recognition of a Bulgarian/Slavic state in Sclavonia at the Danube and Thessalonica, said to have a taste for 'aggression, piracy, and plunder' since its conception in 615. [583] In 676, the Slav Perbundus seized Thessalonica, only to be defeated and executed by Constantine.

---

[580] Ostrogorsky, 28. Some of these claims were legitimized in 670 with the issuing of coins bearing the three as equals as sons of Constans. This was commissioned and unchallenged for ten years by Constantine himself after he had his brothers crowned co-*Basilii*. Furthermore, mosaic art in Ravenna show a mural of Constantine and his two brothers as one entity as well as Justinian, Constantine's son, in an imitation of the success of Justinian I's court. Treadgold, 324.

[581] Theophanes, 51. Bury points out on (*AI-II*), 309f, that Theophanes was mistaken in his sequencing of events as the slitting of the brothers' noses was done secretly in the Palace. He demonstrates by the use of a German historian, Friedrich Christoph Schlosser (1776-1861).

[582] Obolensky, Dmitri. 'Byzantium and the Slavic World.' Chap. 3 of *Byzantium: A World Civilization*, ed. by Angeliki E. Laiou and Henry Maguire. Washington, DC: Dumbarton Oaks Research Library and Collection, 37-48. 1992, 38.

[583] Jenkins, 45.

Unfortunately, capitalizing Lombards used this distraction to displace the Calabrians west from their current settlement at Italy's 'toe'. In 679, the battle lines were drawn, says Theophanes, in Sklavonia, between the Danube and the Rivers of Pruth and Seret north of the Danube. They also held the mountain passes south leading to the Black Sea where they could receive communication with their allies, the eastern Bulgars. This 'foul, unclean tribe' was also Pagan[584] so they were seen as true enemies of the 'Romans' as well as being non-believers.

In 681, a massive force of Bulgars under the Khan Asparuch invaded the Thracian theme, threatening the Byzantines and Slavs there. Constantine mustered a force of tens of thousands from all five Themes and routed the Bulgar garrisons, besieging them north of the Danube. Asparuch settled for peace from the emperor south of the Danube and Constantine offered a modest tribute to the Bulgars. This was important, as this was seen as an official recognition of an independent and presumably permanent territory for the Bulgars in Thessalonica, bordering Sclavonia in the Balkans. Eventually, Sclavonia would be racially assimilated in the Bulgar tribes and those who entered the Empire peacefully from Sirmium without fleeing south were greeted well by the emperor and settled in Thrace which was operated as a new Theme.[585]

Later, more developments in Slav-Byzantine relations manifested itself in the settling of the Avars in Thrace under their chieftain, Kuver. This was due to a defeat of the Byzantines in Thrace when the emperor needed to leave on account of an attack of gout; the Greeks thought they had been set to retreat by absence of the Basileus, and were said to be defeated in a panic. Constantine had left with simple enough instructions as to his intentions to hold the line, but the blame is placed on the low quality of his staff.[586]

Slavic aggression appeared in the West as the Bulgars settled in Varna and Drobudja in 681 and could not be removed, so Constantine made a peace to this 'Onogur' tribe of Bulgars. This settlement did fulfill a need of a Bulgar bulwark in Thrace more able to protect the capital than the Opsikian. This is another credit to Constantine for his foresight in diplomacy with emerging

---

[584] Theophanes, pg. 55-56. It is an interesting choice of words not repeated in any other description of a tribe in the *Chronographia*; perhaps it was their outdated Paganism or purely barbarian roots that earned them this revulsion. As Theophanes's time was still plagued by powerful Bulgar tribes, that would cost a *Basileus* his life in 811, the presence of ethnic hatred is possible.

[585] Treadgold, 329.

[586] Jenkins, 46.

Slavdom. In a similar note, the Bulgar and Slavic ethnicities were separate genetically, but the Byzantine conquests and re-settlements would meld the two together, almost eliminating any Turkish or Steppe origins the Bulgars had, [587] and uniting them into one people that would only strengthen their resolve for independence from the Empire.

With these successful reconciliations with his neighbors and enemies, matters of faith arose again and Constantine was forced to call for a Sixth Ecumenical Council (or the Third Council of Constantinople). The goal being to reconcile Eastern and Western bishops over Monotheletism in an effort to pacify the Church as the West pacified by its arms, Constantine set aside all warlike activity until his death to accomplish this.[588] Bishops from Palermo, Rheggio, and Porto were called to Constantinople as well as papal envoys at the imperial palace. They met in the lavish *Trullo* Dome in November, 680, joining 289 Bishops and 174 other delegates from the sides of Chalcedonianism and Monotheletism.

The delegation included the Bishop of Alexandria and the Chalcedonian Patriarch of Antioch Marcianus, still in exile from the city in Syria. It was supposedly the *Basileus*'s intention (at least at first) to allow the Church alone the say on decisions on the question, and he suggested the Papal Curia send another delegation of three of their deputies, twelve Bishops, and one monk from each of the four Greek cloisters. By the proceedings of Easter, 680, representatives from the Franks, Lombards, Dalmatian Slavs, and even the Anglo-Saxons of Briton, attended as if to inaugurate a truly Universal Council from all over Christendom.[589] From here, the Churches offered their texts from Marcian's Council of 451 and the troublesome policies of conciliation beginning under Heraclius and his Patriarchs.

Why would Christ have one will? Was it within his power to be divine upon the Cross or human when his miracles were performed? What of the suffering that was his sacrifice before God during the Crucifixion – was this a ridiculous

---

[587] Beckwith, Christopher J. *Empires of the Silk Road: A History of Central Eurasia from the Bronze Age to the Present*. Princeton, NJ: Princeton University Press. 2009, 117-118. The Bulgars of the Volga River were assimilated in a looser dialect of language from the Western Turkic peoples.

[588] Theophanes, 57. This included Mt. Athos, wherein in the *Basileus*'s records, the first use of the *excusia* of the monastery from taxation and certain regulation put down in the imperial law codes; these communities were the precursors of the western model of monasticism in the Medieval era, Vasiliev, 571.

[589] Bury, (*AI-II*), 314-315.

contradiction of God being murdered? These questions were slung like arrows before the Monotheletists who claimed if Christ had one energy from God, one body, and was the one True Son, he must have one will combining the human and divine. An unusually high number of eighteen sessions in the Council lasted from November 7, 680, to September 16, 681.[590] Then, an exhausted Constantine finished the matter with his proclamation using the dual natured tome of the pro-Orthodox Pope, Agathon. It was Constantine's intention to delegate that Christ had one '*hypostasis*' of two natures and energies for the Salvation of Man, forbidding the absurdities of Monophysitism and Monotheletism.

Superstition and non-reason by then had gripped the proceedings as a Monothelete named Polychronius attempted to re-animate a corpse as Christ had done, using the Monothelist documents; it failed and he became a heretic of a now indefensible doctrine. Two things resulted from this parable: that the literal-mindedness by these dogmas of the simple folk would believe in terrestrial miracles of the celestial, and the 289 wisest men of the Church came to conclusion from mountebank antics and demonstrated a sorely lacking intellectual spirit of the century.[591] Another long-lasting issue was the presentation of the condemnation of the Pope Honorius as a heretic, evidence to later call into question the infallibility of the Pope brought up in the Vatican Council of 1869-1870.[592]

Constantine and Agathon stalwartly upheld Chalcedonianism and the two wills and natures in Christ that felt the suffering, was miraculously resurrected, and ascended to the Father without opposition. This was a *hypostasis* of the two wills working together in order to save mankind; of course the Chalcedonians took to this hard-lined approach and honored him as the 'Light of the World, the new Constantine the Great, a new Marcian, a new Justinian, and the Destroyer of Heretics.' Now Monotheletism and Monophysitism would never recover or be bargained over as long as Constantine IV ruled the Empire and its Church in Constantinople. In a political context, Constantine had little reason to uphold the *Type*, anyway, as the heretical Armenian and Syrian garrisons had left him. Also, his Western subjects and clerics rejected it venomously and Constantine wished to keep his needed support against Lombardy.[593] It was

---

[590]  Ostrogorsky, 127.
[591]  Jenkins, 50.
[592]  Bury, (*AI-II*), 318.
[593]  Treadgold, 327-328.

still self-defeating and a hindrance in unity as 'a Monophysite who accepted it would still be a Monophysite.'[594]

With this concluded, Constantine still faced opposition from the Caliphate as, by 684, Yazid the son of Mu'awiyah was Caliph and faced a civil war over the throne. In his position, he offered a peace in 685 with Constantine of 365 slaves, 365 horses, and 365,000 *nomismata* paid annually to Constantinople. The tone of the people in Constantinople, however, was depressed with an impending doom whenever the Arabs were at an advantage; in March of 673, a rainbow appeared in the sky, a symbol of hope since the Flood of Noah, causing 'men to shiver' as a sign of the end of the world![595] Always seeking pacifist diplomacy over war, Constantine found Yazid's terms acceptable and balance in the Byzantine East was restored for the present. But now, this mattered little as Constantine was dying of dysentery and his accomplished life ended on September, 14, 685.

Although he capitulated to the Slavs, he brought a harmony and stability in Byzantium ably by both war and peace that would mark an indelible legacy. Byzantine sea power was restored with new military technologies from ingenuity within the Empire, defending the very walls of Constantinople. A heavy hand was at the helm of Orthodox Christianity, and it would prove almost fatal to heresy in the three Patriarchies, with Constantine in the lead. Constantine was a firm and convicted believer in the sole rule of the Empire as a mystic covenant (*mystikon homologion*) with the Divine despite all of the lost territories the Empire suffered. And it was still an Empire, led by a City of God, where the Savior makes his home. It was a time of marvels not seen for generations, promising a bright future, if the same caution and good sense ruled from the throne after Constantine's reign.

## JUSTINIAN II 'THE SLIT-NOSED'
### (685-695, 705-711)

In yet another time that needed caution, Byzantium received in 685 a *Basileus* more like Justin II than Justinian, in that he tried to fill bigger shoes than he could wear, when the times were not at propitious as the ones making this more possible. He was arrogant, self-glorifying, and careless as he was also the first of only two Roman *Basilii* to lose his throne *twice*. He has been heralded as a 'typical' Byzantine emperor of cruelty, religious confusion, and martial

---

[594] Jenkins, 47.

[595] Theophanes, 52.

hubris before Islam, basically, 'dishonored by the vices of a boy, of whom not the smallest community would have chosen him as a local magistrate.'[596]

He did, however, deliver a broad program of mass settlement of Slavic peoples in the Empire to diffuse tensions, raise revenues, and strengthen the military by as many as 250,000 people.[597] This mass ethnic and cultural diffusion at the periphery of imperial territory, West and East, would begin the process of what the next century would label the 'Slavonization' of the Byzantine Empire. Historically, as with many other Dark Age *Basilii*, light has only recently been shed on Justinian II as a ruler beyond the atrocities he inflicted on his own people; this is emphasized as, before the last forty to fifty years, little had been written on him.[598]

Here, also, we see an interesting character, rich with the decisive ease of his father, if not the timing; he was said, in a rare admission of the times, to be a 'gifted ruler' with the talents for rule of the Heraclian line.[599] And he successfully defied and overthrew Roman convention by being only one of two recognized *Basilii* to rule after a penalty of mutilation meant to illegitimate them from the throne.[600] There is uncertainty whether his nose was 'slit' in half or removed altogether and would later be replaced by a golden prosthetic, needing to look as perfect and 'godlike' as he could to recover from a type of the imperial emasculation such a penalty reflected.[601] Nevertheless, the name *Rhinotmetus*, or 'Slit-Nose', demonstrated his boldness and ambition to rule regardless of cost to his life.

He was born to Constantine IV and the Empress Anastasia in 669 and Constantine Porphyrogenitus would refer Justinian as having a Cypriote heritage, perhaps from his mother as the Heracliads were Carthaginians. In 681, after the fall of his uncles, he was made his father's heir and *Caesar* at twelve years old; in 685, he was another in his line to take the throne at a young age at barely sixteen. As has been said of Rome, *Basilii* made too young were always a gamble in Byzantium, making uncertain the wisdom of Constantine's decision.

---

[596] Gibbon, 1613.

[597] Jenkins, 52.

[598] Vasiliev, 193.

[599] Ostrogorsky, 129.

[600] The other was the blinded Isaac II Angelus, who ruled from 1185-1195 and 1203-1204.

[601] Bailey, Penny. "Losing Face? The Symbolism of Facial Mutilation." *Wellcome Trust Foundation.* November 12, 2012. https://blog.wellcome.ac.uk/2012/11/22/losing-face-the-symbolism-of-facial-mutilation/

In 686, Justinian and Byzantium renewed treaties with the Caliph 'Abd al-Malik by invading Arab territory in the Caucasus Mountains in Albania.

The Magistrianos (descended somewhat from the infamous *agens in rebus*)[602] Paul travelled east and secured the terms of the new treaties. This gave much needed respite and capital to Constantinople as well as predominance in Armenia and Iberia. Justinian promised the Caliph to recall the Mardaites causing trouble from the Gaza region and settle most of them in the Carabisian Theme. From Hellas and Corinth, they made perfect oarsmen, restructuring the northern Byzantine navy, as for defensive measures, Justinian also saw to the fortification of the City (at least the acropolis of the Augustean Palace) with walls as in a sort of 'kremlin.'[603]

As to the cause of such measures, the Bulgars and Slavs of Thessalonica were regrouping near Constantinople and the Anatolian themes were ordered to fall back to Thrace and combine with local troops. As the Bulgars shored up in Sklavonia, settlement peoples also rebelled elsewhere as 12,000 Mardaites[604] required capture in despoiling the Arab lands protected by treaty, and in 688, Justinian routed these Bulgars and drove them out to their southern holdings. In Cyprus, he then began a program of Armenio-Caucasians in the collaboration of creating Eastern buffer states, which was not only feasible, but advisable.[605] Greek-speaking Slavs were exempt from compulsory military service and, in future times, blissfully ignored as resources during the Iconoclast era.

This further enriched the army with an additional 30,000 troops given special land grants in the Farm Law enacted by the *Basileus*; in fact, documents from Feburary 17, 687, name them the new class of the *stratiotai*. These were the new Slav peasants under Byzantine authority found in each Theme and Exarchy of the Empire Justinian used to fulfill the military and economic needs of the region.[606] They farmed private land subject to inheritance of the family as in the traditional Land Laws of previous centuries. Neutralizing the Arab frontier zone with a negotiation of shared revenue seemed to free the emperor to pay attention to the Balkans. However, this act was hotly criticized as compromise and the success of his resettlement policy seems debatable.[607]

---

[602] Theophanes, 61f.

[603] Herrin, 29.

[604] Known as the 'rebels', 'apostates', and 'bandits' whom, Theophanes accounts, created a 'brass wall' in Asia Minor against Islamic incursion. Vasiliev, 215.

[605] Jenkins, 51.

[606] Ostrogorsky, 133.

[607] Angold, 51.

With his armies increased one-third by a decisively professionalizing force in the army,[608] in 689 the emperor raided Arab territory in the former Mardaite lands in Mount Lebanon and Amarnus. During this time more civil strife was hitting the Caliphate guarding Mesopotamia from the Alids. Negotiations were struck whereby 'Abd al-Malik agreed to hold hostilities back from Byzantine Armeina, Iberia, and Cyprus if the emperor would accept 1,000 *nomismata* weekly instead of daily, and Justinian upheld this treaty for the next two years while the Caliph expelled the Alids. By 691, he had moved a great amount of Cypriotes to Cyzicus to repopulate the region. There, he founded there the city of Justinianopolis in imitation of his namesake and competitor, Justinian I, who founded the Bishopric of Justiniana Prima. Yet, Justinian could not compete with Malik in building as he surpassed the *Basileus* in Jerusalem by building the magnificent Dome of the Rock on the site of the Jewish Temple in 692. This measure was to allow the Byzantine and Jewish faiths of the Holy City that its real confession as City of God was to be Islam, it mosaics, ironically, made by the craftsmen lent by Justinian II.[609]

A year later, the 20,000 taken from Sklavonia were assembled to invade the Caliphate, but al-Malik struck first using the broken treaty as his banner. It is said this was over Malik's tribute to the *Basileus* being engraved in the Arab way and not the Greek, honoring Christ; it was a flimsy pretext as the weight in gold was correct.[610] Even with the Caliph's assurance that the proper amount of weight of the gold required was met, Justinian refused, mistakenly assuming Abd al-Malik was only motivated by fear. The Arabs managed to successfully bribe two-thirds of the Sklavenoi with their 7,000 cavalry[611] and Justinian's army was defeated. After, the *Basileus* ordered a brutal retribution: the remaining 10,000 Sklavenoi, along with their women and children, were to be massacred as a lesson from Justinian.[612] The Anatolic Strategos Leontius was also imprisoned for martial incompetence (Leontius would not forget this affront).

---

[608] Treadgold, *(BAIA)*, 26.

[609] Montefiore, 191.

[610] Theophanes, 63.

[611] Bury, *(AI-II)*, 322f.

[612] Although, the economic historian Oikonomides in his review of the silk trade claims many were sold as slaves to the privatized *commercii* warehouses to any bidder. Oikonomides, Nicolas. 'Silk Trade and Production in Byzantium from the Sixth to the Ninth Century: The Seals of Kommerciarikoi.'*Dumbarton Oaks Papers, 40.* Washington, DC: Dumbarton Oaks Research Library and Collection. 1986, 33-53.

In 693, Justinian gathered what he termed as a 'supernumerary army' of 30,000,[613] combined with thematic cavalry to face off with Arabs travelling to Sebastopolis. The Arabs refuted all charges made by the *Basileus* and claimed God would be their judge and avenger in the matter. Theophanes defended Justinian in the matter, saying as treaties were broken, but only after a large amount of 'imperial guilt and indiscretion'. The Caliph disregarded all treaties by assaulting Cilicia and its Byzantine garrisons and in 695, Justinian was preparing an expedition to Armenian Hexapolis to create a base in opposing their raids on the Caliph. He released Leontius and his allies after a three-year imprisonment and made him the Strategos of the Theme of Hellas. This would prove to be the final error of Justinian's first run as *Basileus*.[614] Leontius tricked the Praetorians to allow them passage into their barracks and, with Leontius incapacitating them, opened the prisons of a mob quickly developed that would seek revenge on the *Basileus*.

Before he could leave Constantinople, Leontius and a large mob captured Justinian and dragged him to the Hippodrome, with the consent of the Patriarch, where Callinicus and Leontius seized the diadem of the emperor, denouncing Justinian. Justinian's frantic energy in war and the religious sphere only made his losses and defeats more notable, unmasking his inadequacies and labeling him an incompetent tyrant, with too much tolerance of civilian massacres. Before the crowds, Justinian's nose was slit, or probably removed, and his tongue was supposedly slit as well, though he still managed to speak clearly enough to communicate.[615] The curse (*anaskaphe*) of "Let Justinian's bones be exhumed"[616] rang out loud which was an insult hurled at a living emperor. He was then banished to the backwaters of the Chersonese by the Black Sea to live his days among a backwards people and economy of corn, fish, salt, hides, and oil[617] – likely a barter economy.

This was *Rhinokopia*, the removal of the nose for the purposes of excluding

---

[613] Bury, (*AI-II*), 321.

[614] Although it is believed the emperor questionably intended to have the 'people of Constantinople starting with the Patriarch' massacred by the army, this could have been confused for Cherson.

[615] Vasiliev, 194. This was probably to punishment the 'perjury' or lies betraying the Empire to his detractors. The slitting of his tongue is less emphasized, although it is part of the judgment put down in historical fiction; Turtletaub, H. N. *Justinian*. New York, NY: Tom Doherty Associates, Inc. Copyrighted under Henry Turtledove. 1998.

[616] Theophanes, 67.

[617] Bury, (*AI-II*), 357.

political claimants from the Byzantine throne. It had been used before the Heraclids by Phocas and after this, but its most studied case was with Justinian II, mainly because he overcame this status in 705. Experts clarify this as the Hippodrome itself being a symbol of punishment and humiliation being made spectacle against condemned criminals, notably the mutilated.[618] This would also be used by Justinian II when he reclaimed the throne against his former usurpers, Leontius and Apsimar. It came down to the "surplus power" of the ruler denigrated to the "lack of power" of the condemned, thus, a symbolic means of public spectacle to the ends of the ruler utilizing it.

Symbolism was a mainstay throughout Justinian's reign as the mutilation of the nose was a symbol used as punishment decades later under Leo III for sexual offenses, although it becomes more of a rarity over time, especially in the sources.[619] The reason behind this was important for its use in denouncing monarchs and claimants as it was not a punishment for *their* sexual offenses, but for the disorder and asymmetry the Greek world found abhorrent in their culture since early times. Gelina Tirninac from the University of Chicago equates this symbolism with disease, as lust was a sickness, and therefore, the unclean had to be cast out.

Furthermore, as nasal mutilation was a punishment for adultery in numerous medieval cultures, it was the symbol of similar betrayal Justinian showed the Empire that the removal of the nose would represent.[620] So it is placed beside the hand removed to punish theft, eyes (*glossotomia*[621])for sacrilege, castration for bestiality, and tongue for perjury, all included in the law codes issued by subsequent *Basilii*. These studies thus suggest and stress the importance of this punishment in lieu of execution as a humiliation and infliction of a sociopolitical ailment to be kept from the throne. So it was under such conditions that Justinian was now banished to the Chersonese under the authority of the Khazar Khan, Tervel.

---

[618] Tirnanic, Galina. 'The Mutilated Nose: *Rhinokopia* as A Visual Mark of Sexual Offense.' Presented at the *Twenty-Ninth Annual Byzantine Studies Conference*, (Lewiston, ME: October 4-6, 2003). Washington, DC: Dumbarton Oaks Research Library and Collections. Maximus the Confessor and other heretics were blinded as the eyes were clearly seen to be 'the windows of the soul', so heresy was seen as a betrayal of the soul.

[619] Norwich, (*EC*), 339.

[620] Bailey, 'Losing Face?'

[621] Bury, (*AI-II*), 329.

During these years, Justinian was treated with some niceties by the Khan for his pedigree and despite his circumstances. He offered his daughter, Chikak, around 703,[622] to the deposed emperor who took the name Theodora upon marriage in another imitation of Justinian I, all according to Constantine VII in his histories of the *Administrando*. He was not a prisoner in the strictest sense and had freedom to move about in public, gathering a kind of following among the populace. The situation was that neither Justinian nor the Khan considered this banishment permanent as Justinian's fighting spirit always knew he would lead some armies west to reclaim the throne. He lived in a monastery under the care of an Abbot Cyrus, who coached him and encouraged his hopes of re-conquest,[623] seeing opportunity for advancement when Justinian returned to Constantinople. Tervel also understood this and invested his interests to aid an *Basileus* that would be in a position of gratitude to the Bulgars of the Black Sea. So, Justinian awaited his moment of opportunity, finally arriving when the government slackened without Justinian allowing Africa to be overrun by the Saracens.[624]

It did not come, however, when Leontius was deposed and humiliated by the naval commander Apsimar to become Tiberius III in 698. However, the issue was pressed when, in 705, Apsimar called for the Bulgar Khan to hand over Justinian to Byzantine authorities, also sending the assassins Papatzun and Balgitzin, governor of Bosporus to end the last of the Heraclians. But, Justinian got the upper hand and strangled them both with a cord as he considered this, 'the axe . . .and the rack as the only instruments of royalty.'[625] Justinian and Theodora were living in Phanagoria at the Strait of Kertch when this transpired. Receiving word of this beforehand, Justinian fled, leaving a pregnant Theodora behind him who fled to the Doros Mountains asking Tervel for asylum. An army acting for Apsimar marched east, but Justinian and Tervel circumvented them and sped to Constantinople in a last chance gamble for the throne. It is said the *Basileus*-to-be arrogantly defied those who asked for clemency during the frightful storms that hit the fleet by claiming that he spared any of his enemies, 'may God drown me!'[626] Things were already dire for Apsimar as his armies deserted him and he fled to Sozopolis in Thrace for protection.

---

[622] *Bury, (AI-II)*, 360f.

[623] Head, Constance. *Justinian II of Byzantium*. Madison, WI: University of Wisconsin Press. 1972, 100-101.

[624] Porphyrogenitus, 95.

[625] Gibbon, 1615.

[626] Theophanes, 71-72.

Justinian, seeing his chance, was said to have entered the capital through an abandoned sewer pipe, entrenching his position in the Palace of the Blachernae. Arriving in the City with armed guards, he was welcomed back to the throne as a stabilizing force and a legitimate ruler wrongly usurped. Apsimar was found and returned to the City, and a ceremony of humiliation once again occurred as the imprisoned Leontius and Apsimar were brought to the Hippodrome. Apsimar's nose was removed as Leontius's had been and Justinian personally trod on the necks of the cowed prisoners, symbolically treading on the 'lion' (Leontius) and the 'basilisk' (a play on Apsimar's name) as was said in Psalms 91:13. It must be remembered, despite his tyranny and popularity, he was still the rightful, legal emperor and his mutilation was forgotten in light of military success in the City by a people desperate for leadership.

A number of officers loyal to Leontius or Apsimar were hung on the Hippodrome's walls for their roles in the usurpers' court and the Patriarch Callinicus who crowned them was blinded and executed for his impiety. Then, the usurpers were summarily beheaded in the Kynegion right below the Kathisma (the *Basileus*'s box) during planned chariot races to let all know the rightful ruler brooked no more resistance. He then made his Bulgarian father-in-law Caesar in a flash of unconventionality, though this may have been until his heir in Cherson was available. He would once again receive the acclamation of Constantinople in the Palace under the mosaic of Christ on the apse of the Golden Hall.[627]

He then wastefully sent a fleet to retrieve his wife that was destroyed and sank by storms; after this, he sent one man to bring her from the Chersonese, the Cubicularium Theophylactes, being all that was needed. Then upon returning to the throne was to be the 'punishment' of the Slavs of the Cherson region. This petty revenge was the first of a series of attacks and battles there that would prove that though the Bulgars were finished with Justinian, Justinian was not finished with the Crimean Bulgars. But, his attention was needed elsewhere as his Bulgarian war was turned back and his army needed re-direction.

In 707, the Caliph Ab'd Malik died leaving his son, al-Walid, the new ruler, and problems immediately re-surfaced with the Caliphate. His father had imposed a heavy tax on the Christians (*Haratch*), Walid also converting the 'holy catholic' Church of Damascus into a mosque and making an edict that

---

[627] Herrin, 171.

no more state accounts would be in Greek, but in Arabic. Theophanes notes it was an oddity for financial records due to the fact, although they were brilliant mathematicians that had mastered the zero, the Arabs could not express the values of one, two, three, the Greek *tria,* eight-and-one-half, three-fourths, or a fraction with a denominator of three.[628] The *Basileus* focused more on the Slavs and slaughtered the Armenian nobles, taking in a two-pronged attack the city of Tyana in Cappadocia. In another overturn, balancing territories, the commander Maslamah then defeated Byzantine outposts and armies in Amorium and Isauria.

In 710, the indignant nobles of Cherson rebelled against the emperor for his attempts at naval invasion and a fleet under Stephen the Patrician was called. Stephen defeated the rebels, but more harsh autumn storms wrecked his fleets returning west and the Chersonese took the opportunity of allying with the neighboring Khazars. In 711, Justinian sent the General Logothete George to negotiate with the Khazars, but they killed George and claimed an Armenian named Philippicus Bardanes as emperor. This infuriated Justinian and he set up an expedition under Marus to head to the tumultuous Black Sea; his orders including the razing of the Cherson to the ground and the massacre of all of its inhabitants. He enlisted artisans, senators, guild leaders, confiscated fishing boats, convoys, sailing vessels, and triremes as basically a diverse and well-organized naval force.[629] The atrocity at Cherson was done; the soldiers roasted men on spits and tied others to stones and cast them into the sea. All men and women were slaughtered and the children were only spared to be sold into a miserable life of slavery to Greeks, Slavs, or Arabs.

As they were returning, storms met the ships in October and 73,000 murderous sailors were reported lost,[630] though this tragedy did not phase the coldly entitled Justinian II. He next received renewed Arab attacks in the East. He called for 3,000 Bulgar reinforcements from Tervel and organized the Opsician and Thracian Themes to Sinope as a base. From here he could provide aid to Lazica, Cilicia, and Armenia to oppose the Arabs, then turning his navies against the Chersonese. But, this would become a land race afterwards to Constantinople between the *Basileus* and Bardanes to gain the throne. Justinian just made it to Chalcedon when Bardanes's forces burst into the City and,

---

[628]  Theophanes, 73, and Bury, *(AI-II)*, 362f.

[629]  Bury, *(AI-II)*, 363.

[630]  Theophanes, 75-77.

although the family of Justinian wore amulets to protect themselves, they were burned at the stake in the Mese along with the court officials.

The Spatharios John 'the Ostrich' dragged Justinian's six-year-old-son, Tiberius, kicking and screaming from the sanctuary in St. Irene of Blacharnae where wood from the True Cross was, to be served up to be butchered by troops as the child's throat was cut 'like a lamb'. It was over for Justinian when Bardanes convinced Justinian's soldiers into betraying him and the *Basileus* was beheaded by his own men. His head was sent as far as Ravenna and Rome to demonstrate his execution had happened. Bardanes, his usurper, then went on a rampage in the City, killing Spatharios's families, such as one Helias, humiliating his wife into marrying their Indian cook, chaotic slaughter ruling once more.

Justinian II's second fall appears to have been due to his unswerving attention to the Cherson and punishing his place of exile as a reminder of his humiliations, like a paranoid fixation at times, and he ignored the Arabs that insatiably ate up Byzantine territories east of Anatolia. It might have been forgiven if Justinian had conquered Cherson unquestionably and gotten back on track, but offsets and setbacks only narrowed his focus on the unnecessary target. Things got out of hand quickly and a third usurper gained acceptance from a fickle Constantinople, tired of Justinian's returning to excesses and atrocity, using the emperor's own troops to deal with him and all of Byzantium had enough of Justinian II. But it is important to go over his domestic policies in understanding the complicated details behind the reasons Justinian curried such low favor. He strove to be another Justinian I in this regard, but numerous shortcomings and liberties taken in a Byzantium which was not set for a 'Golden Age' only belied his arrogance and numerous bad choices as ruler. It must be noted that one who loses the throne twice is not really to be forgiven.

Financially, he seemed to have been emulating Justinian I once again as his costly wars with the Slavs were handled by a specific group of tax-farming officials in his court led by Theodotos and the sacullarius, Stephen the Persian. They employed the less than reputable methods of collecting levies John the Cappadocian had used.[631] Stephen would scheme tax arrears to confiscate property and even torture landowners by fire to seize their assets, daring, it is said, to have whipped the *Basileus*'s mother, Anastasia, like a child![632] Far from being enough to make others forgive his methods by his other accomplishments,

---

[631] Head, 89.
[632] Theophanes, 65.

the misjudgments in character of those he appointed only demonized Justinian further in his peoples' (and historians') eyes.

But one of the more important of his legislation – and subsequent sources of complaint from the senatorial class– was the Imperial Farm Law, or Justinian's Law. First, it saw the official death of the Diocletianic *capitio-iugatio* that was still in use,[633] now poll taxes were now levied separate from land taxes. This severed the binding obligation of the farmers from their land and encouraged the free-moving peasant paying imperial taxes. It also insured freedom from a master (*kurioi*) as independent farmers (*georgoi*) and private ownership of property, cattle, and product. This was an original legislative idea that gave primacy to individuals' title to personal property.[634]

More effectively, the Farm Law taxed the villager as an individual and not the village as a whole as had been done before.[635] The new status of the 'free' peasant was tied only to a community of freehold lots divided by borders of natural forests and pasture lands. Three advantages of the system included a simpler taxation structure based on a broader area, independent food production for their Thematic armies, and the ease of the commune as a singular, taxable unit.[636] It also allayed the treasury's needs to pay mercenary soldiers, fostering a sense of patriotism in local troops. This, however, became a strain on the peasants who were used to a more communal ownership of resources, especially upon the foreigners of Thessalonica not used to such strictures. It was this that caused 20,000 Slavs to desert the Empire to fight with the Arabs in 691, incurring the wrath of Justinian to massacre thousands of families as retribution. Other such cruel laws abounded, such as the loss of a hand for burning a barn or blinding for robbing a granary.

He also allowed for the immunities of the *exkeusia* on the churches and monasteries of the Empire. This was an exemption from taxation for the churches and an edict that the *salina,* or money entrusted individually would go towards the expenses of the church itself and its clergy.[637] His first promulgation of this kind came from 688 upon the finances of the Church of St. Demetrius. This demonstrates, among other acts, the religious piety of Justinian II as was also shown in the matters of his religious policies. Although they can be said to

---

[633]  Ostrogorsky, 137.

[634]  *ibid.*, 135. The movements of peasants could be accounted for in the numbers of fields that subsequently went fallow or needed de-forestation.

[635]  Norwich, (*EC*), 330.

[636]  Jenkins, 53.

[637]  Vasiliev, 572.

be misguided attempts of adding to his 'glory', they showed an attempt to place the *Basileus* as a role in submissiveness to Christ as his agent on earth.

In one of Justinian's modern biographies, it is summed up that: 'although they could not be worshiped as divinities, they [the *Basilii*] played the full role of God's deputy on earth.'[638] Yet, he still, in 695, demolished a Church of the Mother of God in the City and forced the Patriarch Callinicus to bless the fountain (*phiale*) he replaced the site with, invoking the 'Glory to God the long-suffering of all times: now and forever, eons upon eons, Amen.'[639] The Church itself was rebuilt in non-native Petrin, demonstrating Justinian's piety still had a streak of his arrogance.

Justinian, like his namesake, did attempt a superficial program of buildings, beginning with a reception hall (*trikilinios*) in 694.[640] Running east to west, it was now joined by a gallery, the *Triklinos Lausiakos* to the larger *Chrusotriklinios*. By the Byzantine era, the *triklinios* had evolved from referring to a dining hall as the ancient Western Romans used it.[641] As these Romans lay on couches to eat their meals, the Greeks never emulated this, eating upon benches or chairs at elevated tables. The Triklinos centered, however, on the Palace itself and not public consumption as Churches and other such buildings were, showing again the *Basileus* missed the mark on what past emperors had done to gain glory and popularity with infrastructure.

To achieve a triumph for Orthodoxy his predecessors could not, in 691 Justinian called a General (but not Ecumenical) Council of Bishops to Constantinople. It did not focus on the Christological issues of the past, but was rather a discussion of guidelines in the day-to-day operations of both Churches. As it lacked the official capacities of the Fifth and Sixth Councils called by Justinian I in 553 and Constantine IV in 680, it was, therefore, known as the Fifth-Sixth Council, or *Quinisext*. Unfortunately, it was flawed from its very concept as it fostered an entirely anti-Latin bias in its 211 attending Bishops, only ostracizing them and setting back Church diplomacy. It served as an assembly of mostly Eastern Bishops gathered to discuss the concerns of the Eastern Churches with no regard or experience to daily Western practices. Also in attendance was Pope Sergius I, one of the last pontiffs of Rome ever to come to Constantinople.[642]

---

[638] Head, 5.
[639] Theophanes, 66.
[640] *ibid.*, 65.
[641] Bury, (*AI-II*), 325-326.
[642] Vasiliev, 225.

It met in the *Trullo*, the Domed Hall, of the imperial Palace, therefore being known as the Council of Truollo owing more to the informality of the Quinisext as it could not be a Council of Constantinople. In the Synod, 102 Canons of Church law were reviewed and prescribed by Justinian II's faction, mostly forbidding certain breaches of Christian conduct.[643] Those presented included, along with deposing some certain clerics:

Canon 3: Second marriages for the clergy were forbidden and the priesthood excluded those married to a widow, prostitute, or slave.

Canon 11: No priest may consult a Jewish physician or bathe in company with a Jew (publicly).[644]

Canon 24: Clergy was banned from attending races or the theater. If attending a wedding with these events present, the priest must excuse himself.

Canon 36: The See of Rome would have primacy over Constantinople in Christendom[645] (This concession was said to be the work of the majority of Greek Bishops in Rome and the military influence of the Exarch of Ravenna).

Canon 39: The Archbishop of Cyzicus shall appoint the 'President', John, in Cyprus as the new city of Justinianopolis shall be the Bishopric seat of the Hellespont to be overseen by John.[646]

Canon 42: Hermits dressed in black with long hair visiting laymen must cut their hair short in the cities and must join a monastery; transgression will mean banishment into the desert.

Canon 50: Playing dice – whether by clergy or laymen – was punishable by excommunication from the Church.

Canon 61: Those who consulted fortune-tellers, used animals to deceive 'the simple', or sold lucky, or magical, charms and amulets were to pay six years of penance.

Canon 62: The festivals of Bota (Pan) and Brumalia (Bacchus) were condemned as well as the traditional practices of wearing masks, whether comic or tragic, dancing, transvestitism honoring Pagan gods, and invoking Bacchus in the grape festivals.

---

[643] All below, except for those otherwise cited were found in Norwich, (*EC*), 331-332.

[644] Jewish practice in the legislation included illegality in eating blood or an animal killed by strangulation, which was said to be rejected. Bury, (*AI-II*), 327f.

[645] Bury, (*AI-II*), 366.

[646] Porphyrogenitus, 224-225. This is one of the few recorded ecumenical-lay administrative laws of the Sixth Synod.

Canon 65: Dancing under the new moon and around bonfires, nude or otherwise, was forbidden.

Canon 79: Christmas presents were forbidden.

Canon 82: Christ was always to be portrayed in Human form as the Son of God rather than the earlier versions where he is anthropomorphized as the Lamb of God.[647]

Canon 91: Doctors and performers of abortions were to be condemned as murderers.

Canon 96: Those who curled their hair provocatively or seductively were to be banned from the Church (a bit subjective as curled hair and beards were a notable Greek trait).

Canon 100: No forms of art portraying lewd material wherein lascivious feeling may be aroused were allowed.

Also, the heathen festivals of the New Year Kalends and that of March 1 were banned from celebration. Pope Sergius agreed to 102 of these Canons, but would not compromise on the issues of clergy marriage and condemning the fasting on Saturdays during Lent; it also lessened the Papal powers considerably. Where once Justinian prostrated himself before the Pope, he now angrily – and precipitously – demanded his arrest. The Exarchs refused and were chased to the Pope's very quarters by an angry mob, but the matter was soon forgotten when Sergius hurriedly left for Rome.

It is also notable that in his second reign, he outlawed second marriages (except his own, of course). Any citizen joined in such a union as of January 15, 686, was enslaved to the State and faced canonical condemnation and excommunication. Any clergy caught in a marriage conducted after their ordination would not partake of the sacred liturgy or rise in any way in the Church hierarchy until they have clearly 'been released from their unlawful cohabitation.' Another debacle was the result of the Eastern and Western Churches attempting conciliation on matters to which they would never yield. Another policy of Justinian's melding ecclesiastical and secular were the changes he made to the printing of the *nomisma*. For centuries, most coins depicted the emperor on one side as the head and the tail was a depiction of the symmetrical Byzantine cross.

Now, Justinian demanded the transverse be a bust of Christ with such acclamation as the 'King of Kings' and the emperor as the 'Servant of Christ', next to 'Long Life', and 'PAX'; these were propaganda titles that implied the

---

[647] Herrin, 95.

rule of the *oikemene* as the civilized world was to be Christian and Roman – including the Islamic East.[648] But others claim this was not just representations of religious or political propaganda, but mass dissemination of the emperor's power and his subjugation and piety to Christ as 'spiritual' ruler of Byzantium. Other studies suggest that Justinian was negating the idea of the emperor's cult as the understanding of Byzantine rule and one more rooted in Christ's power as a temporal and spiritual ruler.[649] Modern historians support these dynamic claims that this ecumenical policy was a 'realizing that a *Basileus* – a Christian ruler – should rule through the church rather than his own account. It was a caesaropapist program: it envisaged a new Israel ruled by a new David.'[650]

Two types of these coin images occurred, one was with the bearded and long-haired Christ before the Crucifixion and secondly, one familiar to makers of icon mosaics, with a younger and curly-haired Christ, thus, artistic principles were also infused in the nature of constructing these coins.[651] As noted above, however, Justinian would even taint this achievement with arrogance and folly. The idea of the Caliph, Ab'd al-Malik, descended from the Prophet, putting Christ on his gold *dinari* would have been absurd, yet Justinian balked when it did not happen. He saw this as a danger to his prestige by infusing this capital in the treasury and circulation, so he used it as a pretext for dishonoring the treaty he had made.

Justinian II attempted to touch all the diversities of life in the Empire: financial, moral, ecclesiastical, and in militarization – his introduction of militarism in civilian society. He made policy in each one as he hoped Justinian I would have, but most failed with disastrous consequences or popular dissent. It lost him his throne and his nose at one point and did nothing to teach him any caution from his reinstatement period of 705-711. He was still a shameful anti-climax of the Heraclian line as a usurper would be, such as Phocas, creating upheaval in the royal line for their own ambitions.

Yet, Justinian II's story is a rich one, described to be suitable of a 'picaresque novel',[652] he definitely was a unique figure in the Middle Ages, let alone Byzantium. Though he lacked a certain caution, Justinian II was courageous

---

[648] Angold, 57-58.

[649] Byrda, Greg. 'Justinian's Numismatics Program: Coins That Say What They Mean and Mean What They Say.' Presented at *The Thirty-Sixth Annual Byzantine Studies Conference*. October 7-9, 2010. (Philadelphia, PA: The University of Pennsylvania).

[650] Angold, 54.

[651] Herrin, 96.

[652] Jenkins, 58.

in re-seizing the City of Constantinople and the Empire. He never let the humiliation before his people and his deformation become a hindrance to his unquenchable ambition and energy. He defied numerous conventions of his time with some success as some future Byzantine coins would continue to honor Christ on the reverse side after Iconoclasm, and defy exile by reclaiming the City from abandoned entrances, though none would give a Bulgar Khan the title of *Caesar*.

Justinian II is, ultimately, a worthy profile to study and his narrative should be appreciated as a legend of Byzantium and a cautionary tale as a ruler of ability devolved into a man of 'almost morbidly perverse cruelty, who brought about himself a tragic end.'[653] His harshness after 705 was attributed to the realities and humiliations of his *rhinokopia* and those hostile sources overlook his more responsible and rational decisions.[654] It is to be added that Justinian led a continent life and, although Theophanes refers to him as an adulterer, this was due to his second marriage. Apparently, he was never described as a sensualist or one who defied conventional sexuality as it is told he inherited the virtues of the Heraclian line.[655]

Thus, with the death of Justinian II, the Heraclian line ended. What can this teach us in the context of Byzantine history? Imperial lines have checkered patterns of success within them? Indeed, it is a revolution in the cycle of time from brilliant beginnings to contemptuous ends. Heraclius proved Byzantium was capable of evolution when necessary to defend itself from drastic external forces. Internally, it was more complicated, as emperors such as Constans II fell to these forces and could not adapt well enough for unity. Constantine IV was as great an addition to this line as Heraclius, but like him, left an operational Empire to an heir that would see inconstancy and defeat rule Byzantium. What about these changes by the *Basilii* and their impact on Byzantines for the unknown future? With the reforms in land grants, military organization and cultural relations with new foreign powers, Byzantium grew as a culture external to the imperial marks on its society. It learned to operate an identity and society that differed from the external and could, naturally, survive it.

Justinian II's reign showed the cold brutality of his people as well as what the murders of Tiberius or Nero (37-68 CE) would prove that this would fuel the fires of the ideas that Byzantium itself was cruel for cruelty's sake, with an

---

[653] Ostrogorsky, 145.
[654] Head, 156.
[655] Bury, (*AI-II*), 363.

Oriental horror of decline. Worse still, the next twenty years after Justinian's exile was one noted as a period of anarchy, a miniature version of the instability between the Severi and Diocletian in Rome (145-284 CE). In that span, seven emperors, including Justinian, would sit on the throne and mismanage the Empire with incompetence and inexperience. But, new challenges always arise and a new one would threaten Byzantium from within based on the transmission of Hebraic and Muslim cultures in Christian ideas as a severe and bloody division in the Church. A new line of *Basilii* would learn the lessons of holding on to crumbling unity in a society quite well from what would be the lowest points in the Byzantine Dark Age.

# LEONTIUS (LEO)[656]
## (695-698)

# TIBERIUS III APSIMAR
## (698-705)

If any amount of time showed how fragile the throne could be, it was the period between 695 and 731. With Justinian, the rightful heir, in the Cherson, Byzantium was now ruled by the former Strategos of the Anatolic who served under Constantine IV. After displeasing Justinian in the war against the Arabs, losing at Sebastiopolis, Leontius was imprisoned in 692 to be later freed to rule the Hellenic Theme outside Thrace. In 695, under the guidance of the Blues,[657] he gathered the forces to overthrow a scheming *Basileus* and take the throne after slitting the monarch's nose as a token, supposedly, to have taken false pity on his predecessor's life. But, it was the fact only military power held Leontius in place through his control of the Anatolic Themes.[658]

The inconstancy of the throne, thus, originated from the outcome of military ventures, the abilities to reimburse troops, or even rival generals and leaders within the other Themes who believed that they had the same rights to end an imperial career as their predecessor had. Leontius was a stark contrast

---

[656] Although crowned by the *Basilia* Verina at Tarsus and the Patriarch Callinicus at St. Sophia, Leontius has never been on the imperial rolls and has never been addressed as Leo; his reign was considered inconsequential enough that his reign and Apsimar's are best associated together. Bury, (*AI-II*), 352-353.

[657] Ostrogorsky, 140. Justinian II, of course, had been a Green.

[658] Treadgold, 337.

from his successor, Apsimar, who would be seen as more popular with the Green factions, opposing Leontius for the sake of jeering the Blues, whose successes would earn him 'a distinguished place on the roll of Byzantine emperors.'[659]

Leontius was an Isaurian from the Albanian Caucasus region and the first year of his reign (September 695-August 696) has been described as 'maintaining a policy of peace in all respects.'[660] He was deemed to use caution where Justinian did not and was slower to react to Arab incursions on the border perhaps by having more front line experience. But the Arabs would soon take a mile rather than the inches they had taken in 696 when Caliph Ab'd al-Malik made threatening expansion into Byzantine Africa. A year later, the commander Hassan ibn al-Nu'man took Carthage for the final time and permanently abolished the Exarchate, said to be the only event of distinction in Leontius's reign.[661] That autumn, the fleets of the Carabisian Theme sailed west and freed Carthage from the Arabs who were battling the local Moorish tribes. A turnover again occurred in 698 when Arabs under Hassan expelled John the Patrician and the Byzantine forces from the city, and Africa altogether, fleeing to the island of Crete to recoup.

But the navy feared Leontius's wrath as they feared Justinian's, or they tired of his 'peace policies' as the enemy cared nothing for diplomacy, and responded in the like manner of the former Hellenic commander. They proclaimed one of their own, a Gothic-descended Armenian[662] named Apsimar, as emperor from his position as the Drungarion captain of the Cibyrrhaeots.[663] He was also given the Roman name Tiberius, after the successful Constantine of 578, who was seen as a symbol of successful rule who 'suffered no calamaties'[664]; the rebellious fleet then prepared their voyage around Anatolia to Constantinople the following summer. Fortunately for Apsimar, the factions of troops in Constantinople were in a state of internal strife; Leontius controlled the Anatolic districts, but ultimately held little legitimacy over the throne. Jealous rivals in the remaining Asiatic districts of Constantinople banded together and made an effective force against the throne.[665]

Leontius was in a vulnerable position at the time as the plague had returned

---

[659] Norwich, (EC), 334.

[660] Theophanes, 67.

[661] Jenkins, 58.

[662] Vasiliev, 194.

[663] Here in Theophanes, 68f., Turtledove likens the position to that of an army colonel.

[664] Treadgold, 338.

[665] Bury, (AI-II), 385.

to the City and weakened the state as it was the people and, due to peace agreements with the Caliph, Leontius's troops and remaining fleets were in Cyprus. With this as the situation, occupying the eastern Bosporus, Apsimar was given the keys to the Gates at the Blacharnae district of the city on an oath of the 'holy table', seizing the *Basileus*'s court.[666] He paraded Leontius through the Hippodrome and publicly slit his nose and tongue and threw him in the Monastery of Delmatos. Leontius ruled less than two years and could not keep the trust of his armies in defeat, not realizing his own weak position, just as Phocas had done. It is said as he strolled the port of the City to his ship to sail to Hellas, he said he was but 'a victim adorned for sacrifice and an inevitable death would lead in his footsteps', but he was assured by his advisors Paulus the Astronomer and Gregory of Cappadocia that he would still gain the purple; this story meaning that both would become true.[667]

Tiberius III Apsimar began his reign in a way that had been done for decades – he planned a military raid on the Arabs, this time in Persia. His organizations of the Eastern armies were effective due to strong ties he had to the Cibryaiot troops of Corcyra and Attalia, where he had fielded Mardaites.[668] He entrusted to his brother Heraclius the four Anatolian Themes and sent him on a southern campaign and in spring of 699, Heraclius invaded Syria, taking Antioch and Samasota before a victorious return to Constantinople. But in the next year, the Caliph sent his son to Armenia in a hard-hitting campaign that met little resistance from the Empire's forces. The Arabs took the once-tentative border city of Dara (Anastasiopolis) and Hexapolis as well as the eastern Euphrates. The Armenian inhabitants wasted no time in submitting themselves before the Caliph, especially when Byzantium could not be depended upon at the time, and especially as the Cilician governor had wished to shudder off Byzantine suzerainty a few years before.

It was also in 699 that Tiberius contributed to the organization of the Western Themes, dividing the Sicilian and Italian territories, founding a new Theme of Sardinia which appeared in the records of 700.[669] These new Themes, as they were distant, surrounded by foreign tribes, and weakly organized, were

---

[666] Bury, (*AI-II*), 354.
[667] Gibbon, 1613.
[668] Bury, (*AI-II*), 350f.
[669] Treadgold, (*BAIA*), 26.

composed of Sardinia, Corsica, the Balearic Isles, the sparse remains of the African Exarchate, and the vulnerable Exarchate of Italy, all joined without increasing the amount of troops therein. Further defense came from the *Basileus*'s brother Heraclius, made Master of the Anatolics, to attack the Arab lands from Syria into Carthage.[670]

In 701, the Romans reached Samasota and Apsimar's successful response to Arab threats in Persia cost 200,000 men in the Arab armies, supposedly.[671] But in 702, the Armenians saw a chance to revolt and asked the Byzantine *Basileus* for soldiers, which would be posted in the Fourth Armenia. The Arab commander 'Abdullah based a good post of operations in Cilicia by subjugating Mopsuestia. A slow spread of Armenian re-conquest continued up to 705 as Heraclius had success over 10,000 Arab soldiers, killed or captured, and killed another 12,000 a year later, yet still could not stop Armenia from falling into 'Abdullah's hands.

At this time in 705, Justinian II and the Bulgar Khan Tervel, was fleeing the Chersonese when Apsimar demanded the former emperor's arrest. Heraclius led an army to retrieve the fugitives; Justinian bypassed and escaped him making for Constantinople, where he made a stand of a three day siege at the Walls. As a precaution, Apsimar fled to Sozopolis in Thrace, but a faithless army bound him and turned him over to the reigning Justinian in the capital. It appeared Apsimar had overstayed his welcome as emperor, despite his successes in the East, due to a lack of preparedness.[672]

In a fit of zeal to prove his dominance, on February 15, 706, Justinian recalled Leontius and drove both defeated monarchs through the streets where they were pelted with manure and offal by the citizens. Reaching the Hippodrome, Justinian stood on their necks in victory, slitting Apsimar's nose and tongue and then executing each one. Apsimar ruled six years, longer than any military usurper since Phocas, but these years were filled with strife. No public works or reforms were attributed to him, just weak military resistance and victories over the Arabs, as usual, built on mud. The Arabs were the Hydra of Byzantium; where once you defeat them in one place, more appear to take back the victory as containing them was an exhausting task. It is little wonder that Tiberius III, like his maimed predecessor, was turned upon by the Byzantine army and the mob of the City, being jeered at and humiliated

---

[670] Treadgold, 339.

[671] Theophanes, 69-70.

[672] The guards at their posts were said to be asleep, Norwich, (*EC*), 337.

in the Hippodrome. Justinian did show mercy towards Theodosius, Tiberius's son and forced him into the Church who, following his father's good example, would rise to be Bishop of Ephesus and a strong opponent to Iconoclasm at the Council of 754.[673]

Yet, Justinian would face defeat by another usurping general who ruled by force rather than doing something more clever, such as being the regent of the six-year-old Tiberius, son of Justinian. A Tiberius IV would have brought legitimacy, somewhat, back to the Heraclian line, but a hostile presence replaced him instead and Byzantium would face more chaos from Constantinople. From the dust of the conflict would come the successfully stable Leo III, but it is said Tiberius III Apsimar had the potential to gain Leo's victories without plunging Byzantium into religious anarchy, but he stands alone in such estimation.[674] Nevertheless, the fear of a vacant throne caused a panic in the army and the Senate and the years of the so-called 'accidental rulers'[675] occurred in 711 as the treacherous Eastern enemies only grew stronger in the face of Byzantine weakness.

## PHILIPPICUS BARDANES
(711-713)

## ANASTASIUS II ARTEMIUS
(713-715)

## THEODOSIUS III 'THE RELUCTANT'
(715-717)

It was by the hand of his Chersonese countrymen against Justinian who demanded their massacre that brought the Armenian Vardan to the throne. For the sake of propriety, he was granted the Roman name Philippicus and the Hellenized form of Vardan – 'Bardanes', an example of a mixture of Roman and Greek traditions.[676] A race to the City was what decided his rise to the throne, and a betraying army offering him Justinian II's head for clemency bought him the legitimacy in the Byzantine world (including the slaughter of

---

[673] Ostrogorsky, 172.

[674] Jenkins, 58.

[675] Vasiliev, 194.

[676] Bury, (AI-II), pg. 343-344.

Justinian's child). But, he took an opportunity as he saw it and the cruelties of the embittered Justinian were too much for the Byzantines who witnessed from their capital. Yet, ironically, cruelty begot cruelty and Justinian's severed head was taken as a prize, being sent to the West to Rome and Ravenna while Justinian's corpse was dumped in the Marmara. So, a third usurper held the throne and again, it was anyone's guess how long he could keep it and if he deserved to.

Phillippicus Bardanes was born in Pergamum, the son of an Armenian-born patrician named Nicephorus. Theophanes relates how, in 702, Philippicus was exiled to Cephalania due to a dream the Basileus, Tiberius III Apsimar, had of an 'eagle shading his head.'[677] This omen symbolically meant Philippicus would one day be *Basileus*. As an official in exile in the Cherson, he rose to power through the Green party with his fellow Monotheletists. It did not start auspiciously; throughout his two-year reign, Arabs took Cilicia and the Eastern Euphrates once more, pushing borders to the Antitaurus to Anatolia. Despite his efforts, Bardanes's Armenian troops could not save the Armeniac Theme from falling to the commander Maslamah, and the Bulgars took the opportunity to raid Thrace near the City.

Due, supposedly, to Bardanes's heretical beliefs and alleged adultery, the aggrieved Italians executed all of the Byzantine officers and agents in Rome,[678] which was a clear indication that the West might turn hostile. The debacle of the Arab campaign made the time ripe for more rebellion from within the ranks of the army, and the Opsikian Count George Buraphus made a play from Thrace. The opportunity came when the emperor entered the Baths of Zeuxippus on horseback, doling food and musical instruments for a vainglorious banquet. The treasury had been recovering as, under Justinian II, it had been filled with 'the fruits of cruelty and rapine.'[679] On Buraphes's orders, officers entered the Palace at Constantinople and, ironically, found the hedonistic and pleasure-loving emperor napping. On Saturday, June 3, 713, Whit Sunday Eve, he was awakened, seized, and then blinded by the troops in the tiring-room (*ornatorion*) of the Green party charioteers, guaranteeing no return to the throne.[680]

Besides military defeats and incompetence, something else that isolated Bardanes was his beliefs in Monothelitism and more breakdowns

---

[677] Theophanes, pg. 69.
[678] Treadgold, 343.
[679] Gibbon, 1617. According to Theophanes, 79, it was the Sabbath of the Pentecost.
[680] Norwich, (*EC*), 348.

in Western diplomacy through ineffective policy. He sought to annul the Chalcedonian policies of the Sixth Council in 712, wherein Armenia had found Monophysitism heretical. He also deposed the Patriarch Cyrus and tried to re-instate Monothelitism as Eastern doctrine under the heretical John with his supporters, the Bishop of Cyzicus, Germanos, the Deacon of the Church, Elpidios, Nicholas the Quaestor, and Antiochus the Cartphylax.[681] He even defaced any visual representations that showed the Sixth Council ever existed, including inscriptions placed on the Milion Gate of the Palace; in its place were put portraits of the Monothelitist Patriarch Sergius with Philippicus.[682]

This was an ill-fated time for such needless controversy and Bardanes lost much support from the Orthodox Byzantines. In all, he was simply counted off as 'the least impressive usurper to date[683]' and as a hedonist as well as an unnecessary gadfly to the Church, he denied the unity the Empire desperately wanted. After his deposing, he was denied by Rome, deprived of impressions on coins, and his name purged from church services, prayers, deeds, and documents, negating an entire two years of administration. Once done, the *Liber Pontificalis* says how Rome commissioned portraits of all six of the ecumenical councils to be hung perpetually in St. Peter's. One of Bardanes's successor's most important acts to regain the Church was deposing the Monotheletist John as Patriarch on August 11, 715.

For these crimes against the fitness of the state and its affairs, Cyrus was blinded by the Opsikian Count who was ready to ascend himself to the throne. But, in the unpredictable, complex game of Byzantine politics, it was the tax-gathering head of the chancery, the Protosecretarius Artemius, who struck first, blinding Buraphus and ascending as Anastasius II in honor of the administrator who had saved Byzantium in another dire time. This was mostly by the machinations of the Senate and civil bureaucracy who needed strength in their faction. Buraphus and Bardanes were both tonsured and sent to a monastery in Constantinople. On Whit Sunday, June 4, 716, Anastasius II Artemius was crowned in St. Sophia. He was destined to be a ruler who in

---

[681]  Theophanes, 78.

[682]  Ostrogorsky, 153.

[683]  Treadgold, Warren. 'The Struggle For Survival (641-780)'. Chap. 5 of *The Oxford History of Byzantium,* ed. by Cyril Mango. Oxford, UK: Oxford University Press, 129-152. 2002, 137.

trouble 'displayed...the virtues of both peace and war' but with an extinguished dynasty, obedience was overthrown and change only bred new revolutions.[684]

Visual representations of this *Basileus* are scarce, but do exist, on coinage and even lead seals found from the *kommerkiarioi* of the Armeniac region.[685] The new emperor sought to heal the rifts caused by Bardanes, first restoring the Sixth Council, then destroying all portraits of Philippicus and his heretical Patriarch Sergius. Anastasius II mostly turned his attentions to the growing Arab problem in the East and in 714 he began sending emissaries to negotiate with the Caliph. He rehabilitated numerous fortifications in Anatolia and completed Constantinople's Sea Walls at the news that the Caliph planned another raid on the City. He had also built biremes and triremes, fitting the City Walls with *ballistae* and catapults, also to 'regenerate the military power of the Empire' by strengthening the Cavalry regiments.[686]

Furthermore, after shoring the granaries, any family that could not survive three years on their own foodstuffs were ordered out of the City so a long siege could outlast famine,[687] which was probably not very popular with the lower classes. While the Arabs outfitted armies for invasion, the Bulgars remained hostile since the death of their ally, Justinian II, and sought revenge with armies going as far south through Thrace as Constantinople. The Khan Terval himself was said to have led a force that surprised a wedding party crossing the Bosporus and massacred them all, stealing their silver plate.[688]

Unfortunately, it is vital to remember that despite a loyal and adequate navy, Anastasius held no moral authority over the troops and a lesser emperor would have seen all preparations shatter.[689] In 715, a large Arab force was gathering supplies in the Carabisian Theme under the commander Sulayman, so Anastasius sent the Opsikian Theme armies, led by the General Logothete John the Deacon, to surprise them. But the Opsikians were hostile due to George Buraphus's humiliations and rebelled on their base of operations, the island of Rhodes. They killed John and, by chance, proclaimed a mediocre tax-collector *Basileus* as Theodosius III at Adramyttium, who was said to carry a certain respectability if not inoffensiveness and 'who at least carried an imperial

---

[684] Gibbon, 1617.

[685] Herrin, plate 8.

[686] Bury, (*AI-II*), 370.

[687] Herrin, 15.

[688] Bury, (*AI-II*), 368.

[689] Jenkins, 61. Of course the example of a 'lesser' emperor was the placid Theodosius III.

name'.[690] They then crossed to Constantinople, entering the Blacharnean Gate where they raided the City, killing all inhabitants in their path.

Anastasius II appeared at the Opsikians in Nicaea to appease the hostile forces when their troops gathered for a naval attack on Constantinople to raise Theodosius. But here, Anastasius did what was best for the well-being of his Empire's internal stability by abdicating in 715 and tonsuring himself as a monk in Thessalonica in exchange for safe passage and immunity. Anatolia and Armenia,[691] however, were not accepting of the Opsikian's choice in Theodosius who called for a stronger military emperor over a bureaucrat with no practical knowledge of Arab warfare. Unfortunately, in exile, Artemius would overplay his hand by gathering a conspiracy composed of Sisinnius, a Bulgarian diplomat, Isoes the Count of the dangerous Opsikian, Xylinites the Master of Offices, Anthrax who commissioned the fortifications, Theocistus the Protosecretarius, and the Bishop of Thessalonica. The Bulgars, however, saw the popularity of Leo the Syrian and betrayed Anastasius at Heraclea. So, the conspirators were executed or mutilated and Artemius himself was executed in the Kynegion sometime in 719.[692]

His successor was known as 'the Reluctant' due to his trepidation of being *Basileus* which at the time was known as a target of hostility, possible mutilation, or death. When made aware of his nomination, he fled to the mountains, but was returned to the City by sword-point by his own troops.[693] Nonetheless, he also faced the Arab threat by naming as Anatolic Strategos the Syrian, Leo. He and his Isaurian troops managed to bar Maslamah from entering and taking Amorium in 716, but when the Arabs then captured Sardis and Pergamum, Leo knew a state of emergency had to be in effect and marched on Constantinople for the throne. Theophanes tells a strange story here of wizardry and atrocity wherein the Pergamum soldiers were caught sacrificing an unborn fetus to a cooking pot and dipping their sleeves in the mess; and it was this abomination that cost them the city in God's judgment.[694] This would stand as another

---

[690] Bury, (*AI-II*), 372.

[691] Treadgold, (*OHB*), 138. Perhaps this was also over Bardanes and his failed Monotheletist policies.

[692] Bury, (*AI-II*), 408-409.

[693] Norwich, (*EC*), 349.

[694] Theophanes, 85.

example of Theophanes's desperate superstition, heresy, and blasphemy justifying a loss before an invading force.

In Nicomedia across the Bosporus, Leo abducted Theodosius's officials and family without harming them and moved them to Chrysopolis to negotiate with the emperor. Theodosius gladly abdicated and tonsured himself (where he reportedly 'made a better monk than emperor') in March, 717 and the Syrian returned to the City as the emperor Leo III. Theodosius was actually known for a peace settlement with the Bulgars, wherein Thrace from Maritsa to Adrianople was now Bulgarian territory with annual tributes of silks and gold[695] with negotiations for refugees and prisoners. The knowledge that such a treaty existed is due to a passing notation by Theophanes as he wrote about events with Bulgaria in 812 where scarlet hides and goods equaling 100 pounds of gold in value were included.[696] The critical consequences of Theodosius III's treaty were basically three-fold[697]:

1) It created a territorial border running from northern Thrace between Philippopolis and Adrianople, holding the ports of Mesembria and Anchialus to Bulgar military intervention.

2) With these ports under *de facto* control by the Bulgars, a new commercialism of manufactured goods and the vital Thracian corn industry in the Black Sea, beginning in 716, flowed from Bulgarian Thrace to Constantinople through modern Belgrade.

3) Turkic and Slavic Boyar aristocracy had a prime position for their hostilities with the Empire's center from Thrace to the Danube. Over time, a homeland for the Bulgars would develop with an independent culture, economy, and government.

This was a necessary move on Theodosius's part, but demonstrated the strength of Khazar and Bulgar power in the northern regions with their effect on Byzantine diplomacy. Theodosius's days as a monk were peaceful and on his tomb is marked the lone word *eugieia* ('Health') to demonstrate his confidence in philosophy and religion and, supposedly, a reputation among

---

[695] Runciman, Steven. 'Byzantium and the Slavs.' Chap. 13 of *Byzantium: An Introduction to the Eastern Roman Empire*, ed. by N.H. Baynes and H. St. L. B. Moss. Oxford, UK: Oxford University Press, 338-368. 1969, 342.

[696] Theophanes, 176.

[697] Obolensky, 65-66.

the native Ephesians for miracles.[698] In 729, he became Bishop of Ephesus and attended the Council of Heira until vanishing from records after 754.[699] So with Theodosius's abdication, after two decades, there had been seven revolutions, mostly bloody and cruel. Byzantium breathed a sigh of relief when this ended and a new dynasty rose to the throne in the form of the Isaurians (717-802 CE). A weight was lifted from the Empire's shoulders as stability against the Arabs was achieved, only to be compounded by religious controversy, just under the surface.

## LEO III 'THE ISAURIAN'[700]
### (717-741)

Now the Empire would be ruled by another of those *Basilii* whose significance would lie beside that of Heraclius's or Justinian I's. His quarter-century reign would see enormous developments in diplomatic relations and ethnic diversity in the Empire, due mainly to his fluent grasp of Arabic as well as Greek. His very name also marks the return of the specialized troops of Caucasian Saurian not used since the *Basileus* Zeno in the fifth century. He had little legitimacy when compared to the Heracliads, but won appeal with his victories, strategies, and his personal presence on the field of battle, which was sort of a lost art among the *Basilii*. The result was an era of external peace not seen for generations, when 'the Byzantine world was left deeply traumatized'[701] by the advent of Islam. Yet, plagued by horrendous internal strife through religious controversy, rebuking Rome and Pope Gregory II, to attempt a cultural diffusion with Judaism and Islam unheard of beforehand. Leo's radical views, however, place him in a new order of statesman for his time and posterity; his modern judges claim such orders as 'orthodox or catholic, freethinkers, nationalist or a socialist.'[702]

---

[698] Gibbon, 1617.

[699] Khazhdan, Alexander. *The Oxford Dictionary of Byzantium*. Oxford, UK: Oxford University Press. 1991.

[700] Although Theophanes says otherwise, the discovery of his roots in Germanicea earned him a Syrian identity by twentieth-century historians and the title 'Leo the Syrian.' The confusion came from a forced re-settlement to Thrace his family endured under Justinian II. He was still the first Syrian *Basileus*, and would have been the second *Basileus* from Isauria proper.

[701] Brownworth, 137.

[702] Jenkins, 68.

His true origins as being from Syria, homeland of the Antiochene Monophysites and Monotheletists, would already promise a heretical flavor to his span with the Orthodox Church. However, Leo sought reforms from reason and the need to stamp out superstition surrounding 'miraculous' icons and other idolatrous worship; it was something getting out of hand as it was even stated how icons served as actual godparents at the christening of infants![703] Finally, though he pacified his borders, Leo laid the groundwork for major internal divisions not to disappear altogether for over a century. An impressively preserved, or invented, conversation between the Arabs of Sulayman the General, the Caliph, and the Saracen troops was written in the *Chronographia* to demonstrate how the Arabs promoted Leo's ascension, inducing the Byzantine Amorians to do the same.[704]

Leo was the son of poor artisans[705] born in 685 in the town of Germanicea, originally named Conon,[706] but his family was relocated to Thracian Mesembria in 705 by Justinian II. It was his ingenuity that brought him to the attention of the late Heraclian court as, once upon meeting Justinian II in his second reign, he offered him a gift of 500 sheep, and the grateful *Basileus* made him a Spatharios and friend from then on. With a supposed 'courage, cool headedness and duplicity'[707] he served as a diplomat to the Armenians, Arabs, Alans, and their neighbors the Asbagians with 3,000 *nomismata* used to restore Phasis in Lazica. But Justinian betrayed Leo and sent troops to take back the money, offering the Alans 6,000 *nomismata* for the Isaurian.[708]

His kinship to barbarian peoples began early, fortunately, and some Alan allies rescued him in an escape. He joined the service of Justinian II's army from Thrace, afterwards, and was part of Terval's 100,000 cavalry contingent and later, he was made the Strategos of the Anatolic Theme under Anastasius II. In 717, seeing such chaos in the Empire, he allied with the Armeniac Strategos Artavasdus by a political marriage of their children. Together, they deposed Theodosius III and in a rare act of grace among the deposed, peacefully turned away Theodosius and his family unharmed, keeping their word to do so. Then on March 25, 717, Leo III was crowned *Basileus* by the Patriarch and three years later would award his infant son, Constantine, as co-*Basileus*.

---

[703] Norwich, (AHV), 12.

[704] Theophanes, 82-85.

[705] Diehl, 127.

[706] Gibbon, 1618.

[707] Jenkins, 62.

[708] Theophanes, 85-86.

No sooner had Leo's ascendency taken place than a major Arab force under the Caliph 'Umar II presented itself by land and sea against the city of Constantinople. In July 717, Maslamah led 120,000 troops from the Anatolian Theme to Thrace, as a navy of 1,800 ships sailed the Bosporus. But in repetition of the events a half-century ago, Greek fire put the navy to flight followed by terrible starvation facing the Arabs that could not breach the City Walls by siege. Theophanes accentuates this event by portraying the Arabs as cannibals eating cakes from their own bodily waste![709] Nevertheless, the Patriarch and the West had no faith in Leo and Sergius had another claimant, Tiberius IV, crowned.

Arab reserves from Nicomedia did little good against the Sea Walls' defenses as well and Byzantine forces killed thousands of men, forcing Maslamah to flee on August 15, 718, the Feast of the Dormition (*Koimesis*) of the Virgin, or the Western Catholic Feast of the Assumption.[710] Straggling Arabs were taken prisoner, killed by Bulgars, and even killed in volcanic attacks in the Aegean. It was a disaster for 'Umar and, it being such a costly expenditure, this was why peace lasted under Leo as the Caliph's army bled insufferably. Insult to injury was added as Leo sent a fleet to sack Arab Laodicea in Syria. On September 1, a fleet of another 1,800 ships[711] docked around the Golden Horn on the Asian bank from Galata to Kleidon. After a brief battle against the Byzantines' Greek Fire, the defeated Arabs retreated to the Bay of Sosthenios. In retaliation, Umar forbade all wine (which was in Communion) in the Caliphate, forced Islamic conversion on the Christians, relieving taxes from converts, but killing those who refused.[712]

Another diplomatic strength Leo possessed was with the favor he held with the Bulgar nations. This was achieved in the ways of transmission in Bulgarian culture with the Byzantine in a 'barbarian' style, gaining Slav loyalty. In 719, when Anastasius II attempted a return to the throne with a promise of 360,000 *nomismata* to the Khagan Terval,[713] it was Leo that convinced the Bulgar armies assisting the former emperor to desert him and thwart the revolution. Anastasius was executed along a number of officials, military officers, and City Guards that aided the coup from inside the City. Much of this goodwill was also due to the loyal efforts of Leo's grateful son-in-law Artavasdus of the Armeniac. Indeed, the entire Isaurian reign would benefit from the diplomatic advantages of blood ties

---

[709] Norwich, *(EC)*, 152.

[710] Herrin, 16. Byzantium created the service first to commemorate the victory as the powers of the Virgin were given credit for Leo's defensive organization.

[711] Theophanes, 88.

[712] *ibid.*, 91.

[713] Treadgold, *(BAIA)*, 189.

to the Slavonic nations. This started early with the marriage of Leo's offspring to Artavasdus's house. In 733, as Constantine, Leo's son and heir, wed the Khagan princess 'Irene', the ceremony was conducted with her wearing the Khagar *tzitzikion* – the national dress of the Khagars.[714] Leo also induced the Bulgars to war with the Arabs at Nicomedia where 22,000 Arabs were killed and such developments made for closer allies for the Byzantines against the Arab threat.

Umar's harsh admonishments of Christians did not deter the Greeks as more defeats awaited the Caliph Yazid II from 720 to 722, with small gains in Armenia being countered with further defeat in Isauria, Yazid only gaining ground in reclaiming the city of Camachum. In 722, Leo encouraged an Arab-Khazar war in Armenia, but found funds for it limited due to condemnation for it by Pope Gregory II from Rome. This was only the start of the long and bitter feud with Rome over the controversies of Christian worship in the two halves of Europe. In 723, Frankish diplomats under King Pepin the Short were considered by the Byzantines as '*kristatai*' or 'those with hair down their backs', unfortunately, the fact Theophanes reports the Byzantines likened them to long-haired swine demonstrated the frustrations of diplomacy between the West Germans and Byzantium that would exist.[715] Over the next few years, a failed attempt by Ravenna to settle Rome would occur and the Khazars would also fail defending Cyprus in 725 and Caesaerea a year later from Muslim incursion in Bithynian Nicaea with 100,000 Arabs.[716]

In 727, the indignant Westerners who found icon-smashing repugnant,[717] assassinated the Exarch of Ravenna and elected local military leaders from garrisons to act as Dux, a certain Orso of Heraclea leading the 'lagoon communities' of Venetia to become the first of 117 Doges of Venice. During this time, Leo would re-organize the maritime Themes. The Carabisian theme's capital at the Aegean was moved to southern Anatolia under the more closely watched Drungus of the Cibyrraeots, expanding the Cibyrrhaeotic Theme by absorbing the Caribisian[718] with a capital at Attalia. At this time, East and West, there remained fourteen Byzantine Themes besides Attalia:[719]

---

[714] Obolensky, 173.

[715] Theophanes, 94.

[716] *ibid.*, 97. Such a siege could only be defeated by low provisions, hunger, possibly disease.

[717] Norwich, (HV), 12-13.

[718] By 732, Caribisia had been sub-divided by units, some independent without the authority of either a Drungarios or Strategos. Ostrogorsky, 158.

[719] Bury, (AI-II), 350-351.

1)Opsikian   2)Anatolic   3)Thracian   4)Armenian   5)Cibyraiot
6)Bucellarian   7) Coloneia   8)Sicily   9)Macedonia   10)Pelopennesian
Hellas[720]   11)Thrace   12)Aegean   13)Exarchate of Italy   14)Cherson

By 730, stability would return to the Empire that had not been enjoyed in over 30 years, but in the West, the Christian nations and the Church were allying to keep Byzantium out of Italy, culminating later in a separate Western Empire in 800.[721] Leo did have some claim over these contested Calabrian regions on the Saracen border due to the linguistic and cultural interests of the ancient 'Magna Graecia', and this supported his claims on these regions in 732.[722] This did not totally quiet the Arabs as they, after 733, would continue raiding Anatolia and, after winning the Khazar War in Armenia, now turned into a full invasion of the Khanate by the Arabs. To affirm military finances, Leo increased the capitation tax and re-directed three-and-a-half talents of gold from the Orthodox churches, also making a census of male babies in the Empire 'as Pharaoh had done once to the Hebrews.'[723]

By 737, the Khan was completely defeated by the Caliph and forced to convert to Islam from his former Paganism, reluctantly raiding Byzantine Thrace thereafter. But for years after, Caliphate expansion in the Empire was halted at all borders by Byzantine forces and the *Basileus*'s presence. A decisive victory for Leo was won at Phrygian Acroinon in 738, as 22,000 Arabs were killed in the Anatolic Theme. Also that year, the Lombard king Liutprand and the Pope lost Ravenna for the Byzantines and set the boundaries of the Lombard kingdom. In May, 740, 90,000 Arabs under Suleiman attacked Romania which was surrounded by 10,000 light troops from different parts of Asia, 20,000 Calvary from Akoinos, and 60,000 men from Cappadocia. Leo and his son Constantine joined the battle and only 6,800[724] Arabs supposedly survived, fleeing to Syria with Suleiman, while in Africa the Arabs met resistance and were defeated. A Turkish national hero and martyr to the Holy Wars of Islam died in the battle, Abdallah al-Battal, who would ascend to be Said Battal Ghazi, a 'champion of Mohammedism' now buried south of old Dorylaeum.[725]

---

[720] Arguably two separate Turmachies as Adriatic Epirus also was.

[721] Hussey, 102.

[722] Jenkins, 67.

[723] Theophanes, 101.

[724] Theophanes, 103. All numbers are Theophanes's and they are not really disputed by modern historians.

[725] Vasiliev, 238.

On June 14, 741, Leo died of dropsy and was succeeded by his son and this latter part of Leo's reign would require deep analysis into the energetic and relentless legal and religious reforms enacted by the *Basileus*. The former would bind the Byzantines and the Slavs in ways new and dynamic than before; the latter, however, would divide the Eastern Church and ostracize Rome totally from Constantinople with policies 'barbarously' originated in the faiths of infidels throughout the Empire, combined with perverted Holy Scripture. A firestorm of violence would arise for another century over these developments in the honoring of Christ, the Virgin, and the Saints. Yet, it is the spirit of Christian humanity that induced the law code of Leo III to be given to the Byzantine State. This was a time in human history where natural disasters were, of course, seen as divine anger over Constantine's new policy for the destruction of icons from which the creation by the Orthodox was revered, also with the fact some Christians denied Iconoclasm. This rare superstition on Leo's belief demonstrates the tensions between educated rationality and the mystical sensibility of Iconodulism ('icon-loving') that guaranteed spreading illiteracy, remedial skills, and the fact clergy alone could interpret Scripture, theology, and the lives of saints.[726] It was a battle of not merely souls, but the intellectual mind of the Empire itself.

Set for the publication date of March of 726, the new Code entitled fully: 'A Compendium selection ('Ecloga') of the Laws Made by the Wise Emperors Leo and Constantine, from the Institutes and the Digest and the Codex and the Novels of the Great Justinian; and an Improvement Thereof in the Direction of Humanity (*eis to philanthropoteron*), Edited in the Month of March of the Ninth Indication in the Year of the World 6248,' attempting to make the language and styles of the Justinianic Code more accessible to contemporary Byzantine authorities, it created a practical handbook to the Empire's lawyers, although Latin was a dying language for diplomats to use in the East and Greek translations were common. It is important how Leo would christen this work as being with 'greater humanity' and 'with a view of improvement' over previous Romano-Byzantine law. Another goal was to curb the rampant corruption of the practices of the officials by, for one thing, having the salaries of judges and Quaestors fixed by and paid for by the state in Patrimonies (*sacellerion*).[727] Seventeen of its titles cover civil and criminal law, marriage and dowries, wills and ward-ships, slave law, and properties.

---

[726] Treadgold, 396-397.

[727] Bury, (*AI-II*), 414-17.

They also included stricter divorce laws, wherein divorce may only legally occur in instances of impotence, female adultery, libels that endanger the spouse's life, and leprosy. Concubinage was made into polygamy (defying Justinian I's decrees), and marriage of cousins up to the seventh degree were forbidden along with marriage to Jews and heretics. The content was mainly legal applications that basically emphasized the Christian character of the Code. Only one title dealt with criminal aspects and punishment, and these punishments were typical of the Empire's penalty by mutilation: tearing out the tongue, severing the hand or nose, blinding, and even the shaving of or burning off the hair from the head.[728]

Its Biblical interpretation was prevalent in its laws on homosexuality (Romans 1:24-32), punishable by death and verses relating to the mutilation of the body as penalty of a crime (Matthew 5:29-30 and Mark 9: 43-48).[729] Though the number of mutilation penalty increases, and improves on capital crimes under Justinian such as in the *Ecloga* (17.29),[730] this is so to achieve the goal of lesser instances of the death penalty, imposing a 'deeper penetration of Christian ethics partly to a coarsening of morals under Oriental influence.'[731] But, morals aside, the borderland emergencies of ceaseless warfare made the sophisticated standards of Justinian's time almost impossible, so this endeavor was abandoned for a Code of smaller, and more practical, government.[732]

Three other legislative documents were enacted by Leo besides the *Ecloga*, the Agricultural Code (*Nomos Georgikos*) or 'Farmer's Law', the Military Code or 'Soldier's Law', and the Rhodian Sea Law or 'Maritime Law' (*Nomos Nautikos*). The Rural Code emphasized and continued the Farmer's Law of Justinian II in instituting communal villages, personal ownership of property, and the abolishing to certain serfdom servitude for the common farmer (especially the Slavic). Its main goal, however, was to initiate the creation of a policing force that could regulate the peasantry and enact the Law.[733] The Maritime Law was the law of commercial navigation and property rights, and an important example was the equity allowed in case of the jettisoning of goods wherein in

---

[728] Ostrogorsky, 159.

[729] Treadgold, (*OHB*), 139.

[730] Treadgold, (*BAIA*), No. 176 notes that seducers of virgins were penalized with fines. As the line of the classes was drawn at two pounds of gold as their net worth, 'rich' soldiers were fined one pound and 'poor' were fined half their property.

[731] Ostrogorsky, 160.

[732] Treadgold, 386.

[733] Bury, (*AI-II*), 418f.

case of no fault, the cost is divided between the ship travelers, captain, and the freight owner.[734]

The Soldiers' Law was a new military discipline enacted by Leo, as a disciplined and experienced army official. They included the enactment of penalties for mutiny, disobedience, desertion (burning at the stake or crucifixion), and even adultery by soldiers (dismissal from service). Soldiers were meant to be honorable in conduct and professional as any career of agriculture, merchant, or as an agent of any other professions were forbidden.[735] All of these reforms were also the attempts of Leo to strengthen Themes under their Strategi by regulating his soldiers' conduct and discipline. Of course, as the priorities of the Empire changed, military leadership far outweighed the presence of the civil bureaucracy by the eighth century. Over two centuries, the numbers of these officials decreased from 2,500 to 600 and the 1,500 provincial administrators were now replaced by a limited number of generals and military leaders. On top of all, the titles bestowed were mere prestige over power and all were now at the favor of the *Basileus*.[736]

This legislation under Leo would need completion under the rule of his son Constantine V. The effect of the laws were especially prevalent with the Bulgars and Slavs who all published or absorbed law codes with the *Ecloga* and the Three Laws. A tight influence with Roman law and the Empire was the result and norm until at least the twelfth or thirteenth centuries directly. Slavic and Russian law afterwards were influenced by Justinian and Leo because of the *Ecloga*. Maximum ease in the diplomatic relations of these regions with Byzantium was very clear and another triumph for Slavic relations for Leo III. But the religious character of Leo would condemn some of his work in later centuries, such as in the opinions of Basil I, founder of the Macedonian Dynasty (867-886 CE), expressing this Code would be marked as the 'annulment of good law'. Leo's controversies with Orthodoxy would prove to be a blemish on his reign to some, but has been described as one of rationalism in a superstitious age comparable to the English Puritans of the seventeenth century.[737]

Theories abound as to why he turned to such a radical stance; reports of a volcanic eruption in 726 and a series of earthquakes that demonstrated to

---

[734] An interesting rational cause of responsibility concerning the example of jettisoning freight in an emergency is actually found in the writings of Aristotle.

[735] Bury, (*AI-II*), 421f.

[736] Treadgold, 384.

[737] Bury, (*AI-II*), 429.

Leo God's anger at an unforeseen reason exist as a cause.[738] Iconoclast means 'a smashing of the idols' in Greek, and that is just what it advocated in the eighth century, the end of veneration for Christian iconography and visual representation throughout Byzantium with a goal of providing a 'Christian faith striving for pure spirituality.'[739] The origins of this idea supposedly stems from three influences:

First, in the *Basileus*'s case, would be Eastern Monophysitism and the Paulician sect of Germanicea known for a contempt for 'Mariolatry,' or the undeserved reverence of the Virgin. As a true believer in the single nature of Christ, to represent the human nature of the Son was an affront to the Father, for Christ's divinity is not something that can truly be represented physically as this divinity is spiritual and invisible. Venerating the icon itself is the result, and therefore Christ, the Virgin, and all other icons are wholly expelled in their worship. His goals exemplified the contradictions and conflicts of a changing society between 'the remains of Greco-Roman culture of the Aegean and the religious instincts of the Syro-Semetic Orient.'[740]

Another influence in iconoclastic thought was, ironically given its constant persecutions, Judaism. In the legends for which Byzantine history is sometimes known, it is said two Jews approached the young Conon (Leo) predicting his ascension, but begged him to banish idolatry and its abuses from the Empire.[741] As is said in the Old Testament, even creating graven images of divinity breaks the First Commandment, and this includes Christian images, as represented in Deuteronomy 5: 9, outright condemning the practice of 'falling down and worshiping images'.[742] The idea was to infuse Old Testament values on the Empire and Church in the face of degenerating universal Christendom to pose as a 'new Israel' against Islam.[743]

This had contradictions in Leo's case due to certain policies and actions; among them was the forced conversion of Jews he orchestrated and his firm belief in a Christian doctrine based on the nature of the Son of God. This would appear that Leo was honoring the Father before the Son, but Scripture in any form was taken quite seriously in Byzantium. This is ironic as Leo attempted in

[738] Theophanes, 97.

[739] Ostrogorsky, 161.

[740] Jenkins, 66.

[741] Bury, (*AI-II*), 430f.

[742] Karlin-Hayter, Patricia. 'Iconoclasm.' Chap. 6 of *Oxford History of Byzantium*, ed. by Cyril Mango. Oxford, UK: Oxford University Press. 153-168. 2002, 157.

[743] Angold, 71.

722 and 723 to force conversion on the Jews, but some were said to have 'washed off their baptism and defiled their faith'. A day was then set where many Jews sealed themselves in their temples and synagogues and incinerated themselves with the buildings,[744] a new Masada prepared for the new Romans of the East.

Finally, was the influence of Islam; in 754, Orthodox theologians would call Leo III 'inclined to Mohammedism'.[745] Records indicate that Leo made more concessions to Constantinopolitan Muslims than Jews by the building of a mosque in the City. This probably marks another development in Leo's policy of transmitting cultures in the Empire to suit foreign peoples; he would thus be also known as 'the Saracen-Minded' (*Sarakhenopron*).[746] Though this was mainly a practice with the Slavs, Leo had respect for Islam's forbidding all images of Allah or the Prophet. It fit in a Judaeo-Christian tradition of honoring the One True God as faceless and without clear attributes, which was also another foundation of the Judaic tradition. But, this idea of Muslim influence had its detraction as well as Patriarchs against Leo's policies exclaimed how the Muslims condemned veneration of objects, but knelt before the sacred Ka'ba – a stone in the middle of Mecca![747] This, however, also worked as a bridge between cultures as the Caliphs would allow Orthodox Patriarchs in Antioch, Jerusalem, and Alexandria and be known as the 'Melchites', derived from the Arabic word for 'Emperor.'[748]

And Iconoclasm had its defenders: the two main Churchmen who agreed with the *Basileus*'s condemnation were of the Opsikian Theme, Constantine of Nacolea and Thomas of Claudiopolis. Of course, however, Leo influenced other Bishops to remove their icons as well. Iconoclasms's main detractors in this early period were John the Damascene (676-749 CE) who wrote the *Treatises Against Those Who Deprecated the Holy Image*. John's practical argument was that, as matter was made divine by the Incarnation in Christ and the Virgin as Mother of God, icons can exhibit 'sanctified matter . . . made not by nature, but by grace and divine power',[749] especially in those miraculous icons made by divine hands, all imbued with the Holy Spirit. Included was the Constantinopolitan Patriarch, Germanus, whom Leo would depose in favor

---

[744] Theophanes, 93.

[745] Vasiliev, (*BYZ*), 317.

[746] The poet Akrites would write of him as the 'Twice-Born the Frontiersman' with rumor of kinship between Leo's family and the Arabs of Upper Syria. Jenkins, 65.

[747] Angold, 72-73.

[748] Treadgold, 392.

[749] Angold, 75-76.

of the Iconoclast, Anastasius. For the most part, Iconoclasm was a polarizing conflict in the early Isaurian period among Byzantium because more outbreaks of religious rebellions and 'civil war' was not something the Empire needed in this time of relative peace.

The controversies started early in Leo's reign as in 726, when volcanic eruptions east of Thera were blamed by Leo as being God's anger against venerating the icons. Abruptly, he had the image of Christ at the Chalke, which protected the City for centuries, torn down before a shocked populace, then forbidding the practice of parading on the City Walls during combat the Image of the *Hodegetria* ('She Who Shows the Way') to bless the soldiers. It was even thought this icon of the Virgin was destroyed by Artavasdus, Leo's son in-law, which only lowered domestic morale. After that, more regulations came down such as the outlawing of personal icons of the saints carried by citizens.

These edicts would bleed into the question of universal education and the secular as Leo fought those mystics such as Pope Gregory II who had claimed that icons aided the illiterate in understanding Christ better than they could in the books.[750] Iconoclasm was igniting revolts all over Byzantine Italy, so Leo confiscated the annual Church income of Iconodule Calabria and Sicily, as well as much of the Balkans, directing them to the City. Thus, began the slow process of estrangement between West and East only to end in Schism in the eleventh century.[751]

These citizens were also armed with scurrilous and trumped-up charges that Leo had burned Iconodule universities down and had the faculties burned at the stake. In fact, Leo only curbed liberal education to stem idolatry by dismissing the Iconodule Ecumenical Doctor, or *Didaskalos*, and his twelve men from their posts, then using them as court intellectuals specialized in art and theology.[752] Education was already at a low with the destroying and discarding of religious texts the Quinisext outlawed a century earlier; this period was only saved by the fact that sixth-century texts were still found in more literate eras after the infamous Dark Age.[753]

In 727, which was the first time in imperial history it happened, Leo faced

---

[750] Angold, 100.

[751] Norwich, *(AM)*, 52.

[752] Bury, *(AI-II)*, 433. Leo tried to alloy his views with the educated leaders of the universities, but conservativeness won out over radicalism and Leo was caught up as an opponent of enlightenment. Along such prejudices Iconoclasm has unfairly been a scapegoat as the reason behind the Dark Age of the eighth century.

[753] Treadgold, *(OHB)*, 149.

an attempt of deposition for religious reasons when the Count of the Hellenic Theme colluding with the Caribisian Theme gathered a naval fleet to take Constantinople and declare an officer, Cosmas, as *Basileus*. Unfortunately for him, they failed to learn the lessons of the Arabs of 718 and were devastated by Greek Fire, the first time it was turned on Christians. In response to this, Leo reorganized the Caribisian Theme with the Cibyrrhaeot to dilute the independent strength of the former. The armies were decidedly motivated by greed for the imperial power and not religious zeal, but the allegation of Iconoclasm as a cause had high importance in the struggle.

In 729, Leo began putting pressure on the Iconophile Patriarch Germanus to convert against the icons. Theophanes, a traditional Iconophile, remarks how, like King Herod and John the Baptist, Leo threatened Germanus with deposition if he did not submit. On Saturday January 7, 730, Leo held an unofficial 'Silentium' or Council of his own court and factions condemning the practices of carrying, possessing, and in any way venerating icons and images of the Saints, Apostles, the Virgin, and especially Christ himself, along with intercessory prayer.[754] It went further to say **any** representations of living beings for religious purposes were included.[755]

The Holy Cross, however was exempt, if not the representation of a crucifix, and it was deemed likely one had replaced the Virgin of the Chalke Gate which was formerly cast down.[756] It was seen, by the emperor whose duty it was to uphold, three creeds: 1) all laid down in Scripture, 2) the seven holy Synods, and 3) the Roman laws.[757] If the barriers of the three need to be crossed for the spiritual good of Byzantium, then so be it. Patriarch Germanus was too offended to attend this meeting, who was then claimed as non-ecumenical, so it was here that Leo instated Anastasius on January 22 as the Iconoclast Patriarch of Constantinople. Oddly, silence from the 'Catholic' parties were said to have shown a reverence for Leo's administrative abilities and mannerisms at court,[758] but could not have been very pleased by the consecration of such a foul heresy.

For such reasons, this succeeded in outraging Rome and the Churches all over Western Europe. In 731, the new Pope Gregory III held a local Synod among the Sicilian and Calabrian Themes, promulgating that Iconoclasm was a heresy and condemning Leo for it. This was exacerbated from years before

---

[754] Jenkins, 82.

[755] Ostrogorsky, 162f.

[756] Angold, 73.

[757] Bury, (*AI-II*), 415.

[758] Gibbon, 1618.

when Gregory II condemned this new heresy. In retaliation, Leo exempted the Western Themes from Papal authority and drew a line in the sand that would permanently be the Empire's westernmost boundary. It was here that the Carolingians, Lombards, and Italians would grow closer to the Pope against Byzantium and begin to shape the development of a 'Western' Empire to rule universal Christendom.[759] Ravenna and its Exarch, Eutychius, was forced to concede to Gregory for its Iconophilism and intractable military position as the Schism of Byzantium and Rome were building strong foundation.

At around 8 a.m. on Wednesday, October 26, 740, an earthquake hit Constantinople and Iconoclasm was blamed for it. The statue of Constantine the Great at the Attalid Gate fell, the Arcadian monument on the Column of Xeropholos and the statue of Theodosius the Great on the Golden Gate did as well, all image-worshippers; buildings in Bithynian Nicomedia, Prainetos, Nicaea, and Thrace were also devastated.[760] Leo enacted a fair one-twelfth surcharge tax for repairs (which became exploited permanently), but this earthquake would be the last tragedy in Leo's life as he died the following year, leaving the matter of the Iconoclasts to his Iconoclast son, Constantine. But Leo's reign was considered successful for its diplomacy, its victory over the Caliph, and its opportunities of foreign trade in the East.

Furthermore, Leo introduced into the circulation of the currency a new silver coin to replace the *hexagram*. This *miliaresion* was one-twelfth the rate of the *nomisma* and equalled 288 copper *folles,* yet gold was now rare among commerce as it alone paid the army and copper coins were more abundant as the money economy became a military, and not public, matter.[761] The silver coin was modeled after the equally stable Arab *dirham,* matching it as a stable element in the economy. Still, however, the *annonae* was on the decline as harsh penalties by law were proscribed to those who stole arms from soldiers (*Ecloga,* 16.2.1, 17.10) and arms as inherited property were closely inspected.[762] In 740, it was also customary to give the officials of the Walls two of these silver coins annually.

Leo's military prowess earned him the reputation as a new Mithridates VI,[763] who conquered the Pontus (Black Sea) in 89-63BCE and historians further likened his struggles to the Greco-Persian Wars of 480-479BCE. At

---

[759] Hussey, 32.
[760] Theophanes, 103-104.
[761] Treadgold, (*OHB*), 149.
[762] Treadgold, (*BAIA*), 181.
[763] Vasiliev, 236.

the same time, he was defamed as a 'lion belching fiery sulphur from an angry heart' when he was declaiming icons as idolatry to be vehemently destroyed by St. Stephen the Younger. It seems as though no Byzantine ruler can escape the dualism of praise and blame by his (or her) very people. In his zeal to inspire pure spirituality among the Empire, he isolated his beliefs from the traditions of centuries and alienated many of the forces that made his reign as *Basileus* possible. At least his motives were pure, and Biblical parallels likened Leo by his defenders as an Isaiah and a Moses, leading his people to a new Promised Land.[764]

Leo the Syrian (as well as his son) has been accurately depicted as 'great emperors, violent, autocratic, passionate, hard, but also great generals that broke the force of Islam.'[765] Any way his reign is viewed, Leo III changed the Empire with his acceptance of Slavic, and even Arabic, norms in Constantinople that suggested a tolerance for their ways, encouraging a kind of peace in the foreign regions of Byzantium and the East. He also, unknowingly, facilitated breaks from the West that would culminate in the West's creation of a new secular Empire to protect Christendom from the Saracens and the Moors around the Mediterranean. A separate thousand-year Empire would take shape because of these breakdowns in relations. But as for the present, in 741 in the Empire, the battle was between Greek and Greek even more so than the battles with Slavs and Saracens as Iconoclasm found a new imperial champion.

## CONSTANTINE V 'COPRONYMUS'
### (741-775)

Constantine V's very start in life was seen as a bad omen – as he was christened, barely six months old, on Christmas Day 718, he defecated in the font at his baptism. This was the origin of his moniker *Copronymus* ('Name of Dung'). Nevertheless, he was brought before the Senate and hailed as Leo's successor, but if one were to read Theophanes on his damnation of Iconoclasm, such a moniker would also not be a surprise, but a 'future great evil.'[766] He has been unjustly slandered by almost all contemporary and latter-century historians, and even artists, but there is silence in other matters such as his moderation in spending despite a 'worldliness' his father lacked. This was even

---

[764] Angold, 94.

[765] Diehl, 11.

[766] Theophanes, 92.

a time of luxury when silk garments, golden shoes, and the imperial display of the Persian tiara and 'state robe' (*skaramangion*) were considered extravagant by the Patriarchs.[767]

There is also no foundation to the outrageous claims of homosexuality (he was married three times) and unbridled lust 'despite sex or species', extracting an 'unnatural delight in the objects most offensive to human sense'[768] in the icons. Shocking allegations of 'wizardry' with blood sacrifices using dung and urine, demon-summoning, and effeminacy[769] ran rampant in his histories to condemn the non-conventional Christian. In truth, how would he find the time to be so licentious when he was such an energetic man with wide vision with lasting plans for the defense of the Empire? It is true how his military organization system of the Tagma was the foundation for the Byzantine army in the Medieval era.[770] Fortunately, as well, was the abundance of the Anatolian plateaus in food, horse, and provisions; its small town actually worked in Constantine's favor as Euchaita and Chonae were in these areas[771] as they proved easier to defend.

Constantine V boldly followed his father's conviction against the veneration of icons, but as his father was harsher, Constantine is said to be more subtle in his expressions. His court was noted as lively and frivolous with praise for secular art, unlike the Puritans to which his father was compared, though he was not as austere in his private life.[772] There is no mistake to think, though, that his reign was not bloody and violent within, as well as without, the Empire. Respecting his accomplishments, but damning his character, was Theophanes and a martyred Bishop with intimate knowledge of the persecutions and their subsequent Council in Stephen the Younger, whose *Life* was clearly documented, as he was sainted by Orthodoxy. However, the Patriarch Nicephorus leaves the scene as a chronicler in 768, just before the Avar Wars of Charlemagne in 796.[773] Constantine V made a sterner war against monasticism than did his father to regain reasonable worship in the Empire as well as economic reasons as monasteries were producing more wealth than secular Byzantine agencies.

---

[767]  Bury, (*AI-II*), 531.

[768]  Gibbon, 1619.

[769]  Theophanes, 105. Probably seen as a terrible crime due to an emperor needing a more masculine image to lead his own troops.

[770]  Haldon, *Byzantine Praetorians*, 191-195.

[771]  Treadgold, 406-407.

[772]  Bury, (*AI-II*), 429.

[773]  *ibid.*, 450f.

These isolated, chaste, unworldly masses in their cloisters presented what was the 'most radical elements of Medieval Christendom.'[774]

Ironically, as he depended on them to secure the northern frontiers, Constantine's toleration of the heretical Paulicians inhabiting the region would decide much of the fate of the future Bulgarian Church. As Armenians, Syrians, and Thracians settled in Thrace in 757, they were able to compete with the Latin and Greek communities upholding their Dualist Paulician creed and settle monasteries with their fortresses. [775] In the *Life of Saint Stephen the Younger,* written in 808 and based on the events written by the Deacon of Hagia Sophia in 767, it chronicles where and how the Crimean and 'Gothian' settlers in the Bosporus strengthened Byzantine influence through monastic communities and missionary position in the steppes.[776] These monastic settlers had been Byzantine orders bankrupted and exiled by Constantine and were, unwittingly, made a choice place for Orthodoxy in the Black Sea.

He was born to the emperor Leo III and his Augusta, Maria, in July, 718. On Easter, 720, he was made co-emperor with his father Leo. He grew to be a capable addition to his father's army and won many of the victories with him against the Arabs. Before this, at the age of fourteen, he was married to the daughter of the Khazar Khan, Tzitzak, who was Hellenized as Irene. At age twenty-two, he took the crown when his father died and faced, almost at once, his first true challengers. Artavasdus, Constantine's father-in-law, icon-lover,[777] and Logothete, took the capital when Constantine and his Magister Theophanes Monotes ('One-Ear') left for Arab negotiations in Bithynia. A trap was set at Doryleum by Artavasdus and the defeated retinue fled to Amorium for the time being. Constantine, in 732, tried to solicit Artavasdus to send his own sons to visit the *Basileus* as a family greeting, but was really attempting to keep them as hostages to maintain peace,[778] but the ruse did not work on Artavasdus.

Artavasdus solidified his position among the City with false news of the childless Constantine's death at Doryleum, spreading confusion and, perhaps, panic. The Patriarch Anastasius, meanwhile, crowned Artavasdus as *Basileus*

---

[774] Bury, (AI-II), 460.

[775] Obolensky, 120.

[776] Stephen the Younger. Vita S. Stephani Juniorus. *Patrologae Cursus Completus, Series Graeca, vol. 100,* ed. by J. P. Migne. Paris, France. 1936, 1120.

[777] For purely political reasons to overwhelm the Isaurian factions, he did not 'explicitly' condemn icons. Treadgold, 357.

[778] Theophanes, 105.

and the usurper began his two-year reign, and once in position, he restored icons to gain balance in the City. Constantine, while in Amorium, gathered the forces of the Anatolic and Thracian Themes and camped at the Bosporus until winter. He, that 'devil' and 'evil prince', was said to have forced faction and Iconoclasm there to the point children were made to murder their idolatrous parents.[779] In 742, a civil war was officially declared when Artavasdus invaded the Thracian and Anatolic Themes with the Opsikian to oppose the rightful emperor. Constantine defeated his rival's son, Nicephorus, in the Armeniac and crossed the Bosporus as his opponent's Thracian general, Sisinnius, crossed the Hellespont from the south-west.

Constantine besieged Constantinople for a year and his loyal Cibyrrheot soldiers foiled any attempts of Artavasdus to gain relief supplies and food. On November 2, 743, the City starving for months due to the prices of olives and wine reaching horribly inflated heights, Constantine assaulted the City and entered it with no opposition by way of the Charsianesian Gate to the Golden Gate from his camp at St. Mamas. Despite this loyalty, private residences were sacked and many citizens had hands and feet cut off, or were blinded. Artavasdus and Anastasius both were led through the Hippodrome where Constantine blinded them with Artavasdus's two sons as the traitors they indeed were. Forty days later, Sisinnius was blinded as well. Luck was with Constantine afterward as another Arab civil war between the Umayyads and the Abbasids had broken out, giving the Empire an external respite. Wisely, Constantine was not lax in the two years this was occurring and used the time to shrewdly reorganize his armies and Themes.

The Opsikian Theme was deemed a dangerous region, as it had been the center of rebellion and usurpation for generations. Constantine put a stop to this by dividing it and creating the Tagmata, a private 'regiment' of Opsikian and Thracian soldiers that served the emperor directly, composed of 18,000 men in six divisions, decreasing over fourty-four percent of the Thematic forces. This core of professional, loyal, and disciplined cavalry units would prove to be far superior to the provincial Themes.[780] Most important were the cavalry regiments that accompanied the emperor in battle, the Scholae and the Excubitors of the Bosporus, each being 4,000 soldiers. Next was the *Vigila,* or Watch, former patrol units better used as a City Guard – the need for which was a lesson Constantine learned with the Artavasdus affair. By 775, it is noted

---

[779] Theophanes, 108-109.
[780] Decker, 24.

how Anatolia was consolidated as an unbreakable bulwark against Islam with around 50,000 soldiers in its Themes. It was fortunate, and not accidental, that the wealthiest part in land, agriculture, and resources in the Empire was seldom raided.[781]

These 4,000 men were joined by the 2,000 infantry of the Wall and the 2,000 of the Numera. The remaining 2,000 were not technically soldiers, but the Optimates (to be kept weaker) – baggage and horse carriers, responsible for transport and logistics.[782] These units constituted a better way of centralizing military and administrative power for the *Basileus*, making it clear that any overthrows against him by usurpers were going to be more difficult. Furthermore, it set up a bulwark against the Thracian Slavs where Artavasdus originated as the emperor as well as when they lost trust in them altogether. A sign of the successes in military finances was the lowering of the state budget, in 775, despite added costs to bodyguard pay (seventy-two *nomismata* annually resulting in 38,000 total) and oarsman (five *nomismata* to a total of 116,000), at 1,900,000 *nomismata*. These figures demonstrate definite growth in the ratio of pay and manpower over the inflated budget of Constans II in 668 at 2,000,000 *nomismata*.[783]

Another important policy was the resettlement of Christians from the Arab-held lands to Thrace. In 743, Constantine began these steps, taking Germanicea and Sozopetra. Unfortunately, as Byzantium was invading Syria, another invader returned to appear in Italy to strike the East: the bubonic plague. Constantine had soundly defeated a rebellious Byzantine fleet expertly at Alexandria in 747, using the Cibyrrheot to destroy 997 ships in a fleet of 1,000 during this time of sickness.[784] But, from the years 745 to 747, plague swept Italy, Greece, the Cycladic Islands, and arrived in Constantinople in full force, as it was sea-borne by sailing vessels, to affect, especially, trade and commerce.[785]

Under-population from the fever threatened the City in 748 when the plague finally subsided, inducing Constantine to settle more Christians from Greece to fill the Constantinopolitan streets. Constantine VII in his work

---

[781] Treadgold, 376-377. Based on a map of Thematic organization in Anatolia around 775.

[782] Treadgold, *(BAIA)*, 74f.

[783] *ibid.,* 196.

[784] Theophanes, 113.

[785] Jenkins, 69. Now it is known bubonic plague is transmitted by fleas transported port to port by trade ships, thereby, any prolific trade was helping the contagion.

*On Themes* summed up that Constantine V 'slavonized' the Peloponnesus as the plague spread through 'the entire universe.' He meant it cynically and in a bitter tone, but this was an action that had little to no alternative for the Grecian population. Furthermore, there is the evidence of Iconoclasm among the Greek population in Thessalonica where its Archbishop, Peter, honored the Thessalonian patron St. Demetrius to Anastius, Peter's successor, honoring on both sides only the perfectly symmetrical Byzantine Holy Cross.[786] How could this not affect the validity of documents in those times of uncertainty and change, from Iconoclast to Iconocdule Church officials, anywhere in the Empire?

A year later, the Arab civil war made a turning point that would eventually put it to a close. In Mesopotamia, the Abbasid Abu'l-'Abbas crowned himself as the Caliph al-Saffah and began consolidating his rule in the Caliphate. Seeing his 'Pax Constantinus' threatened, Constantine's response was to take the fortified city of Melitene, one Greek territory, settling its Christians in Thrace. But these victories and Constantine's astute attention came at the expense of the West: the Lombard King Aistulf seized Ravenna and repudiated any Byzantine representatives sent there. A line had been drawn and the Italians let it be known that Byzantine territory would only include Sicily and small places such as Venetia with the support of the Franks and the Pope Zacharias. It was final when the Lombards were overthrown and its Kingdom dispelled by the Frankish King Pepin, and his sons Charles and Carloman, whose legal action of 'the Donation of Pepin' by the Pope infuriated Constantine, who would ultimately do nothing and lend no aid to save Aistulf.[787] It was ultimately judged that 'No ruler in Byzantium had ever shown so little concern for the maintenance of the imperial authority in Italy.'[788]

This was one of the last slips of the West from Eastern control. The dream of Justinian and his successors was long dead, as seizures of patrimonies and the alienation of the Pope, due to Iconoclastic heresy, was seen as a betrayal to the West.[789] The decision had to be made and Constantine chose the East as the future hope of the Byzantine Empire and its legacy. If the West faded away as a consequence, Constantine would have little choice but to accept it, but, at least, other successors would not give up so easily and this included the hope

[786] Treadgold, 362.

[787] Norwich, *(AM)*, 54-55.

[788] Ostrogorsky, 169.

[789] Gregoire, *(BYZ)*, 121.

of the ultimate marriage in the Empire: an *Basilia* of Byzantium and the leader of a new state of the Holy Roman Empire.

Constantine's decided lethargy in Western affairs (coupled with his Iconoclasm) gave the Papacy ample room to use German allies to expel Byzantine authority altogether. In 754, Constantine prepared debate of Christological issues on iconography in a Council. Pope Stephen II, meanwhile, met with the Frankish King Pepin at Ponthium on January 6, the Feast of the Epiphany, and that seemed to end this debate with Byzantium over authority. This axiom of diplomacy between the two Cities was complete and a turning point in Western civilization.[790] Due to these clearly divided opinions and the neglect of the Western Themes by Constantine in favor of Eastern interests, and growing amount of civil unrest, by 773, the Sicilian Theme captured by Justinian in 559 suffered a devastating 90 percent loss.[791] This meeting of 338 Bishops, without a Pope, was known as the 'headless Synod' presided not by a Patriarch of Constantinople, but the Bishop of Ephesus. This was the Iconoclast, gelded son of Tiberius II, Theodosius, serving after Patriarch Anastasius's death in 753.[792]

In 755, the *Basileus* began an earnest invasion of the Arab territories by seizing Camachum and Theodosiopolis in Armenia, Christians, once again being resettled in Thrace. This resettling to Thrace may have been a program of filling his personal Tagmata army by introducing Greek ethnicity through habitation with the Slavs living there, even the heretical, Iconophile, and Dualist Paulicians in 757. It is in the re-organization around this year that the office of the *Postal Logothete* (*logothetes tou dromou*) officially appears in documents, an evolution of the dissolved office of the Praetorian Prefect of the East.[793] This demonstrates Constantine's motives as being secular in filling a sparsely populated region such as Thrace with Christian Slavs. His identity as the Byzantine representative of Slavism by marriage to a Khazan princess may have warranted this.

The Bulgars of the region were riled by Constantine's policy and responded with an assault in 757 where the *Basileus*'s methods would include dividing the interests of the Slavic and Bulgar aristocracy. The Bulgars were also known for an implacable savagery that was fueled by the need for their own territories

---

[790]  Herrin, 68.
[791]  Treadgold, *(BAIA)*, 74.
[792]  Ostrogorsky, 172.
[793]  Bury, *(AI-II)*, 471.

and peace became just a fragile resentment. By 758, war with the Sklavenoi in Macedonia and Thessaly was a result, and they were brought to heel without Bulgar assistance. Yet, despite such developments, the Arabs shared the most notable ethnic diversity in Byzantium as Constantine's court was based on talent and merit, rather than privilege or race. The Abbasids enjoyed great favor due to this trend and the Arab population in Constantinople expanded as Muslims were given privileges equal to Byzantines.[794]

In 756, the commander Selim had entered Cappadocia with 80,000 men[795] and the next year, he made a quick peace with the Caliph after skirmishing in Cilicia in exchange for Byzantine prisoners, so he could consider entering Europe and invading the restless Bulgars. In 759, he conquered the Bulgar Khanate west of Thrace and routed the Danube area at Marcellae, stopping only to retreat at a defeat at Bergaba. A truce was then called for as the Abbasid Caliph invaded the Armeniac Theme and killed its Strategos in battle. In 762, the Bulgars hanged those who made this truce and went on an offensive on the Empire; these Bulgars fled to the Optimates in Thrace and Constantine prepared an army of 9,000 Tagmata on June 15, 763, to invade the Black Sea with 800 warships and 20,000 Slav allies.

Constantine defeated the Bulgars there and the Bulgars assassinated their Khan, Teletz, by Vinekh (Sabinos), briefly leading his tribes when the former Khan had lost favor. When Vinekh attempted peace with Byzantium, the Bulgars blamed him for enslavement by the Romans; he was deposed for Umar (Paganos) and the fleeing Khan joined Constantine in raiding the Bulgar lands in 765. The following June, he gathered another land and sea expedition to attack Anchialus, but July storms wrecked the fleets and the depleted army from the north coast of the Black Sea returned to Constantinople, in defeat for the first time under Constantine V. The next few years were harsh for the *Basileus* as he discovered a plot against him and the Iconoclast difficulties were exploding due to his continuous assault on monasticism in Byzantium. Idolatrous monks and nuns alike faced merciless persecution and humiliations in the Hippodrome.

The Arab threat resurfaced in 770 in the sacking of Anatolia and the deportation of the local populations in retaliation for Constantine's re-settlements. More disappointment faced Constantine in 772, as the Caliph Mansur entered the Cibyrrhaeot Theme at Sycae, prompting Constantine

---

[794] Jenkins, 70.
[795] Theophanes, 119.

to call for a levy of the Anatolics, Armeniacs, and the new Theme of the Bucellarian to counter this. The Byzantines met a costly defeat and the Caliph allowed no truce to be created with the emperor. In 774, renewed hostilities with the Danubian Bulgars occurred, resulting in a large naval force of 2,000 ships carrying Tagmatic cavalry and soldiers arriving as Constantine reached farther east Russian Varna.

A Slav land army opposed the Tagmata as well as a navy carrying the first Russians officially cited as enemy combatants.[796] A desperate peace was offered by the Slavs, but Constantine kept a vigil over Thrace for signs of Slavic deceit. The Bulgar Khan Telerig was later discovered to have been deporting, in secret, the Christian Slavs in Thrace who had been settled by Constantine years earlier. In summer, 775, another force of 12,000 cavalrymen was sent east, but storms in Mesembria ruined the fleet and Constantine was forced to retreat. Telerig then played a careful game and used peaceful overtures to discover who in his kingdom who were Byzantine spies and those he found were executed, inducing him to send a 12,000 man retinue to seize Berzitia in response.

Constantine was gathering another force when a fever struck him and he was '...given to an unquenchable fire while still alive.'[797] At Arcadiopolis, boils appeared, covering his legs, and he died on his way back to Constantinople on a warship traveling from Selymbria to the fort of Strongylon on September 14, 775. Like the current emperors of the era, most of his reign was spent engaging in hostile wars with neighboring Slavs and Muslims with around 1.7 percent of the Empire's population of 7,000,000 as the combined armed forces.[798] His success was mixed; he protected his borders well, but outright invasions of the Arab lands were costly and caused injury to Byzantium's pride of place in Europe. But, what historians such as Theophanes most passionately write about are his 'wicked deeds', like the Pagan Diocletian, in handling Christianity without icons.

The Seventh Ecumenical Council of 754 was the most notable of Constantine V Copronymous's actions as a secular and a religious leader. He went further than his father when instead of merely repudiating the images, he sought to outlaw them as heresy and purge all Iconodules in the Empire. Yet, the issue itself, long established before the emperor's policies, was a complex

---

[796] Finlay, George. *History of Greece, BC 146 to AD 1864, vol. II,* ed. by H. F. Tozer. 1877, 87.

[797] Theophanes, 135.

[798] Treadgold, *(BAIA)*, 162.

issue of intellectual and superstitious Christological arguments supported by a millennium's worth of research. In the *Symposium* of Plato, though beautiful images are stated as transitory, they are a necessary part to predicate the beauty of the invisible soul. John of Damascus would incorporate this philosophy into the Incarnation of Christ in this argument as icons were necessary to contain the beauty of the images to ensure the sanctity of their meaning; as Christ was materialized as holy, so to should the images of Him.[799]

The most ambitious leap for Iconoclasm was the Church Council the *Basileus* convened to have Iconophilia branded as a heresy by the Church, punishable by blinding as all heresies were. With the blinded heretic, Patriarch Anastasius, having died the year before, the Council was held at the Chalcedonian Palace at Heira without a Patriach, Papal representation, or even the Eastern Bishops of Jerusalem, Antioch, and Alexandria, all three of which were iconodules. Even the 338 presiding Bishops and the Bishop of Ephesus at the Council contemptuously denied Iconoclasm, the Council lasting from February 10 to August 8 of that year, in the Church of the Blachernae. The Second Commandment on graven images interpreted by the fourth-century Bishop Epiphanus of Salamis was failing. But it was the Bishop, Theodosius Apsimar, the castrated son of an Iconophile *Basileus*, who reached the best solution theologically.

The representation of Christ, confused between Man and God, was Monophysitism, but one depicting Christ and God as one was also Nestorianism, a heresy of the fourth-century saying Christ was of the same 'nature' as God the Father. The dual image of Christ was declared unknowable and *aperigraptus* ('uncircumscribable')[800] as a hidden Lord reminiscent of Hebrew testaments of God; either the natures were somehow confused or separated by idol veneration.[801] So Iconophilia was voted a heresy with the Iconophiles former Patriarch Germanus, and especially John the Damascene, being condemned by the Council. The Bishops even agreed to raise the *Basileus*'s choice of Patriarch, Constantine of Syllaeum, on August 29. This gave the emperor a greater ecumenical grasp of the Orthodox Church in Byzantium proving the 'imitator of Christ' knew best, granting Iconoclasm a practical legitimacy foremost in Church policy.

This spurred Constantine to personally write at least thirteen treatises

---

[799] Jenkins, 85-88.
[800] Norwich, (*EC*), 361.
[801] Angold, 91.

and 'two historically significant . . . theological . . . orations'[802] on policies and recorded views of his theology in the *Peuseis* ('Enqueries'), presenting that the Cross was the only true symbol to Christians known for its blessings, curing, and exorcizing of demons.[803] In these works he interpreted how only in the Eucharist was the physical representation of Christ present and how the believer who ate it was endowed with the virtues of Christ as *the believer* was in God's image.[804] This was all based on a letter written by Eusebius of Caeserea in Constantine the Great's time. Ostrogorsky analyzes it as 'neo-platonic sense' concerning the intellectual attitudes that it was idea, not form, that allowed Salvation. The cults of the Virgin and *Theotokos* were outlawed and saints like Peter were only to be referred to as 'Peter the Apostle.'[805] Everywhere, radical changes would seed hatred for the *Basileus* by some as well as adulation by the torn citizens of Byzantium.

It should be mentioned that the banning of icons also cut the throat of many artists making a living as icon makers. After the last Council, the only artists allowed were the ones honoring secular art as ornamental decoration, nature motifs, imperial portraiture, theatrical scenes, battles, hunting scenes, and chariot-racing glorifying Constantine on his stage in the Hippodrome.[806] The defacing of precious works of art included the covering of portraits of Christ's life in the Church of St. Mary's in the Blacharnae by landscape portraits.[807] In the Council of 754, it was remarked how the icon, in the *Definitions* written by Constantine V himself, was 'common and worthless, as the painter who made it.' Elsewhere, Christians in Muslim countries railed against the Iconoclasts and it was the Coptic Christian monasteries in Egypt, far beyond imperial borders, making some of the best iconography of the century.[808]

It is described at the time how that, 'Because the Catholic Church of us Christians stands in the middle between Judaism and Paganism, she walks the new path of piety and worship . . . without acknowledging the bloody sacrifice . . . of Judaism; despising also the entire practice of making and worshiping idols, of which abominable art paganism is the leader and inventor.'[809] Yet Constantine

---

[802] Ostrogorsky, 151.
[803] Herrin, 109-110.
[804] Angold, 78.
[805] Norwich, (*EC*), 360.
[806] Ostrogorsky, 173.
[807] Norwich, (*EC*), 359.
[808] Brownworth, 144f.
[809] Herrin, 110.

was not warring against art itself, merely religious art, and its style was certainly needed to replace the emptiness of the removed icons in palaces, churches, public buildings, and the everyday life of the Empire. Even churches as buildings were not exempt from debasement as one would be converted by Constantine into an arms factory and depot.[810]

Elsewhere in culture could be found applications in the countless allegories found in Medieval literature. John 'the Silent' of St. Sabbas (454-558 CE) oddly created a blend of Indian Bhuddism and Christianity in his *Barlaam and Josephat* with his main character mimicking the life of the Bhudda. It was meant to comment on the human duality of world and spirit, with the wicked facing a grotesque eternity worthy of the horrific and demonic images of the sixteenth-century artist, Albrecht Durer(1471-1528)[811] as a dragon awaiting to devour the sinning spirit tempted by the sweet 'honey' of worldliness. The prolific writer John of Damascus rightfully interprets this allegory with the dragon as the 'belly of hell.'[812] Even loose talk was a danger as the *Basileus* balked at the term *Theotokos*, even when used as a slip of the tongue, as when a monk who had tripped cursed it as a Nestorian. As a fascinating study in linguistic culture of this era, the term 'Saint' was taboo and the Churches of these Saints were called 'the Fortys [Martyrs], the 'Theodora's', or the 'George's'.[813]

A more clarified idea has been noted that the imposition of Iconoclasm to an unwilling Church and public is a remnant of supporting the imperial cult with the remembrance that the emperor was the only Imitator of the Savior while icons inconveniently obscured this image. Imperial portraits, safely under secular protection of images, were encouraged by the Iconoclast emperors and aspired to rise above the authority of the Bishops representing Christ. This included the monastic abbots and monks who imitated Christ to aspire to sainthood, according to leading scholars of the Controversy.[814]

However, the Iconophiles still fought the emperor, as on November 20, 765, an abbot known as Stephen the Protomatyr, from Mount Auxentius in Chalcedon, decried Iconoclasm and the Council of 754, consequently torn to pieces and lynched by angry mobs and the Patriarch. They did not understand, however, that executing martyrs of a cause like Iconophilia only strengthened

---

[810]  Decker, 96.

[811]  Bury, (*AI-II*), 533.

[812]  John of Damascus. 'Orations'. *Patrologia Graeca, 161 vol. III*, ed. by J.P. Migne. Paris, France. 1866, 976.

[813]  Jenkins, 86.

[814]  Treadgold, 388.

the effort as Christian persecutions did in the old Pagan Western Empire, and Stephen was only sainted. Stephen's followers were also executed and a new persecution was made by the *Basileus*. It happened in the Hippodrome, demonstrating the new popular appeal to Iconoclasm with the citizens and army as public memory to commemorate Constantine Copronymus after his death. The Hippodrome, in its long and bloody tradition and history, was, by now, an official ritualistic venue for public humiliations and punishment that the emperors would use to please their supporters.[815]

Anti-monasticism also played a relevant part in Constantine's plan, even as it lacked any biblical basis, yet some monks were believed to have possessed special spiritual powers like the icons.[816] The monastic clergy were forced to take Iconoclastic oaths as their monasteries were known for their iconic artistry. Monks and nuns were forced to marry and hold hands as spouses upon pain of blinding to the jeers of the masses at the Hippodrome.[817] An unfortunate backlash of this persecution would be the decrease in the state of rural education in the Empire as monasteries were closed one after another for displeasing the emperor with their beliefs.[818]

Worse came to worse as an assassination plot by Constantine Podopagurus the Logothete, and his brother Strategius, was uncovered in August of 766. In collusion with Podopagurus was the Strategi of Sicily and Thrace, the Tagma of the Excubitors, the Opsikian Theme, and even the Patriarch of Constantinople himself, all being jailed.[819] He ordered a hundred strikes with an ox-hide to whip the Prefect, Procopius. The pressures of paranoia only accelerated Constantine's mistrust as Iconophilism was thought to be more and more a sedition against the government. He had a special contempt for the monks of the Empire that defied him from their cloisters; these ascetics were seen by the emperor to be 'mainstays of superstition and mental degradation',[820] despite their piety.

Constantine V confiscated monastic property and the gold and silver vestments thereof, burning monastic libraries, which were never to be replaced, and the aforementioned forcing of marriages upon monks and nuns upon pain of blinding or exile upon refusal. The traditional growing of the beard by the

---

[815] Angold, 81.

[816] *ibid.*, 83.

[817] Treadgold, 363-365.

[818] Brownworth, 146.

[819] Theophanes, 126.

[820] Bury, (*AI-II*), 428.

monastics was desecrated as the *Basileus* and his enforcer, Lachandracon, covered them in beeswax and oil, burning the beards off the monks' faces.[821] Constantine congratulated Lachandracon as a 'man after my own heart',[822] words God himself spoke to King David for exemplary conduct in honoring Him; now it being a facetious statement to demonstrate Theophanes's outrage in his history. Of course, no laymen were allowed to take any refuge in monasticism or 'the cowl' and he even desecrated the graves and dumped into the sea the bodies of saints and martyrs.

By 772, no monasteries remained in the Thracian Theme, but some of the capital raised was put to good use reducing food prices in the Empire and renewing the Aqueducts of Valens within the City. From the Pontus to Greece, 1,000 builders, 200 plasterers, 500 Grecian tile makers, 5,000 Thracian workmen and 200 potters made this so.[823] To relieve the hoarding of gold inflating the currency economy, gold coins were freely given to the people on Easter Sunday, 769, at his third wife's coronation and again later at the betrothal and marriage ceremonies of his son and heir Leo to his bride Irene as future Augusta. Furthermore, new coins were minted in denominations between one-third and one-half of a *nomisma* in 769.[824]

Constantine's reign, however, saw abundance in agricultural product that overwhelmed the rural economy with low prices and cash payments, but the inability to pay taxes based on these prices decreased for farmers. Bronze and silver was freely used in the markets and eventually, soldiers' pay in gold circulated until gold was more common in private purchasing,[825] this trend demonstrating urban prosperity at the expense of the rural communities. Chinese silks and Indian spices proliferated well in city markets, but the increasing danger of land routes to barbarians and Muslims made travel less frequent and these interior regions reverted to barter economies and militarized rural areas. More than ever, this trend blurred the lines between military and civil authority which would give rise to the soldier-*Basilii* and usurpation.[826]

In 743, before Constantine's taking of the City, inflation was everywhere: two gallons of barley was at twelve *nomismata*, a *modius* (an imperial 'peck', or two gallons) of pulse for nineteen, one of millet or lupine went for eight. Five

---

[821] Norwich, (*EC*), 362.

[822] Theophanes, 133.

[823] *ibid.*, 128.

[824] Theophanes, 131.

[825] Bury, (*AI-II*), 458f.

[826] Brownworth, 146.

pounds of olives and a *xestes* (or one pint) went for one-half of a *nomisma*[827] all at a time when the economy still worked and depended on silver and copper coins. But, when Constantine began restricting gold coinage, deflation finally spread and as the cost of living decreased, food productions increased. As arable land was gained, the food cultivation from 718 to 800 in Thrace doubled and tripled.[828] Of course, as the farmer throughout history only makes a living on the climbing rates in price for their product, they were at a loss with an increasing treasury and cash tax payments where product was even substituted for cash, as today. These events led to 'scandalously' low prices in product in order to adequately pay taxes.[829] Another serious factor in stemming trade was the *commercii,* which held virtual monopolies over goods such as silks, gold, and slaves (still legal in Muslim territories), who worked on one-eighth of all trade duties (increased from one-tenth around Contans II's time).[830] These warehouses discouraged much trade and choked the market in ways the emperor could not handle.

But the damage was done to his legacy when Iconoclasm was finally purged altogether from Byzantium in the ninth century. In the *Syndikion,* read at Easter to commemorate the emperors, the names of Leo III and Constantine V were condemned as heretics.[831] This long list of heretical names is still repeated by the Orthodox clergy the first Sunday of Lent. After his death and the restoration of the icons, Constantine's body was punitively removed from the Church of Holy Apostles. A symbol of the dual nature of Constantine's reign in the spiritual and worldly affairs of the Empire, paradoxically, was the prayers of ordinary citizens in the City to Constantine to expel Bulgars in the ninth century. But Constantine left the Northern Balkans in a favorable position not seen since the emperor Maurice.[832] He far outstripped his father's efforts and improved greatly upon his policies of a stable Bulgar region.

And another legacy was his completion and application of the legal code his father started in 726, the *Ecloga,* whose biblical teachings in social context originated from the prophet Isaiah. It stood as an epitome of *philanthropia,* the love of the *Basileus* for his subjects with the love of Christ he was instructing to the Empire in his codes; in them, Man's law and God's law could be one.

---

[827] Theophanes, 110.

[828] Jenkins, 72.

[829] Treadgold, (*BAIA*), 185.

[830] Treadgold, 409-410.

[831] Herrin, 112.

[832] Obolensky, 66-67.

Constantine was more energetic than his father and accomplished more, leaving a strong position in Eastern Europe to his son with the hope that he would ban icons, observing God's laws. Strong challenges still awaited the Isaurians in Iconodulism and monastic radicalism, and Mosaic Law would not be enough to be used as effective weapons, so, Christology would have to be employed.[833] Ostrogorsky concludes adamantly that had Constantine not died as and when he did, Byzantine religion would have irrevocably transformed.

As Constantine's daughter by his third wife, Anthusa, took the veil (with her mother's support and to her father's embarrassment) and founded perhaps 'the first orphan asylum established in the Christian world,'[834] she venerated holy pictures. She was named for a miraculous nun of the monastery of the Maintineion who was tortured by Iconoclasts by having burns from red-hot icons.[835] Conspiracies against Iconoclasm would eventually reach within the Palace and choke their heretical enemy from within. Despite this, Constantine V valued his army and they remained loyal. At Christmas, a feast for 204 high officers (except the Optimates) was held in the Hall of the Nineteen Couches along with twelve dignitaries, and twelve paupers for charity's sake.[836]

## LEO IV 'THE KHAZAR'
### (775-780)

The son of Constantine V and his barbarian bride, Irene, Leo IV has been known as 'the Khazar' due to his mixed lineage as the first emperor of that ethnicity. This fact is a reminder just how the Empire had changed in 500 years when non-Romans were considered illegitimate and not accepted as emperors. Less can be said of Leo, unlike his father and grandfather, due to the scarcity of resources on his contributions of only five years of rule - rather brief for an Isaurian. He is mainly overshadowed by his illustrious Athenian *Basilia*, Irene, who for thirty years predominated in the domestic affairs in the Empire compensating for a weak husband and son.

Born on January 25, 748, Leo was 'born in the purple' (*Porphyrogenitus*), a title given to rulers born of a legitimate passage from father to son as a concept

---

[833] Jenkins, 86.

[834] Bury, (*AI-II*), 458f.

[835] Angold, 82.

[836] Treadgold, (*BAIA*), 102-103. In fact, this was held on one of the twelve days of Christmas, a dignitary and a pauper invited for every day.

made sacred by the machinations of Constantine V. It specifically refers to a birthing room in the Great Palace carved from purple stone and decorated in purple silks dyed by the mullex shellfish. It was a symbolic assurance of the heir apparent in the Palace and a Medieval device of excluding the outside aristocracy, Senate, and officer class from dynastic affairs.[837] From 750 until the Empire's end, the purple-born would be a singular qualification to imperial rule and Leo IV was the first offspring of this phenomenon.

He was crowned *Basileus* at twenty-five years old on September 14, 775, yet, his reign began awkwardly as his two brothers, Nicephorus and Christopher, were hastily made co-*Caesari*. Also, Leo's religious alliances were thrown into question, attempting moderation between Iconoclasm and Iconodulism in his Empire. Like his father and brothers, Leo was an Iconoclast, but tensions were already strained since the start of his reign by marrying a powerful and resourceful Athenian Iconophile. Leo considered this and shrewdly made maneuvers that assured him conciliation with his army and bureaucracy to foster the balance of secular spheres over that of the ecumenical. The presence of the legal inheritance of primogeniture, a pillar of the Common Law ironically, stipulated that as he was heir supreme over the other sons of Constantine, Leo would gain the estate of 2,000,000 pounds sterling.[838] This greed and envy of place motivated the brothers into enmity and rebellion more than anything. Although primogeniture's innovation was growing in Europe, it was new and fragile in Byzantium as loyalty oaths from the army and their explicit approval would have been unnecessary.[839] Therefore, some Western and Medieval concepts were slow at this time to be a standard in Byzantium, proving it more an Oriental Empire existing outside Western influence for, at least, a few more centuries.

In 776, Leo 'encouraged' the Tagmata and Thematic troops to consider who would make the best heir to Leo's throne.[840] Naturally, they co-operated with the crowning of Constantine, Leo's infant son, as the heir apparent, this act being treated as the 'popular will' of the City. What was gained from Leo was an honest and direct answer to the troops present on Palm Sunday: 'He is my only son, and I am afraid to do so, lest humanity's fate befall me. Because he would

---

[837] Herrin, 185-186.

[838] Gibbon, 1620. Calculated to over 77,000 pounds of gold.

[839] Ostrogorsky, 176-177.

[840] Treadgold, 367. This argues Leo had more ambition than if this Tagmata and the Athenians forced his hand.

be so young, you would kill him and choose someone else.'[841] Constantine was still urged by the masses to succeed, so Leo exploited the momentum of the people's will and received oaths made on the True Cross, by all present, to defend Constantine's hereditary rights over that of his brothers on April 24, Easter Sunday.

Obviously feeling threatened by this, in May, Nicephorus and Christopher plotted an assassination of Leo, but failed and were incarcerated. A *Silentium* of the court was quickly convened over the princely brothers' fate. Leo spent no time lost in his decisions as he humiliated them in the Hippodrome, tonsuring them and their faction as monks and banishing them to the Chersonese. No executions were meted and mutilations were inflicted, meaning Leo truly appeared to favor a reign of moderation in the Empire. The ultimatum that tonsuring was used as a punishment suggested the tolerance for the future Leo had for monastic institutions and his willingness to fill their ranks with the punished.[842] That same year, Leo made a raid on Arab territory, recovering Samasota on the Euphrates, instigating a need for retaliation, as the Caliphate raided Ancyra.

In 777, Bulgarian relations were improving as the exiled Khan Telerig fled to seek sanctuary in Constantinople for his past loyalties. Leo graciously accepted him, baptizing him, making him a Roman Patrician, and even making blood ties as he married him to a cousin of his wife, Irene.[843] In spring of 778, Leo made a preemptive strike in the East using his father's Strategos of Thrace, Michael Lachandracon. After stopping a Syrian rebellion with 100,000 soldiers, he took Germanicea, defeating the five emirs and 2,000 Arabs there. Settling the Syrian Christians in Thrace, Leo continued the Isaurian policy of populating Thrace with loyal Christians to keep up the boundaries against the Slavs. In 779, he entrenched himself in Adata and wisely took defensive positions through a strategy of attrition.[844] The Caliph Mahdi sent troops to the Opsikian Theme under the commander Hasan in response to the Byzantine victory at Adata. Leo managed to hold off these forces with 3,000 men to burn Arab supplies until they retreated, running out of provisions.[845]

---

[841] Theophanes, 136.

[842] Bury, (AI-II), 477f.

[843] The Athenian people, being Iconoclasts, fought for Leo to place an Athenian princess on the throne beside the emperor in hopes that his religious policy may one day be challenged. Gibbon, 1621.

[844] Treadgold, 369.

[845] Theophanes, 138.

Religiously, Leo IV's tolerance reached the decimated monastic communities as monks were now being bestowed Bishoprics. Constantine V's vivid imagination and paranoia had insisted that the cloistered within were 'unmentionables' preaching the doctrine of Hell and were depraved 'slaves of sexual lust.'[846] Either they fled the persecutions to escape the deportations Copronymous insisted upon them, or be shamed in the Hippodrome for entertainment. Another price for the Empire's military stability was the suffering of culture and education outside City walls as the peasantry and other rural dependants were denied the only education they could receive from the monasteries. Such ignorance and division would perpetuate the Byzantine 'Dark Age' of their early period.

Leo's Icocnoclast policies were deemed very moderate, and in five years only one incident involving Iconodualism resulted in major consequences for Leo's reign and reputation. However, there was a severity to it as it involved the closest members of his court and household; in early summer of 780, Leo caught the officials Theophanes,[847] Strategeos, Jacob, and Papias under orders by his *Basilia* Irene, smuggling icons into the Palace. This was seen as a subversion of high degree exacerbated by the scandal of icons in the imperial presence. Although he appointed an Iconophile Patriarch, Nicetas, on February 7, Leo made an example in the middle week of Lent by parading all the male conspirators in the Mese, publically beating, tonsuring, and imprisoning them in the Praitorian, Theophanes dying from his injuries. This bitter act in 780 has been notified and remarked by Theophanes the Confessor and others to be his only real action persecuting heretics.[848] Furthermore, as a male heir already existed, Leo banished Irene from his bed and it stayed that way until his death later that year.

On September 8, 780, in a greedy fit of love for precious stones, Leo IV seized the crown bestowed to the treasury of Saint Sophia by Heraclius (not the one interred by Constans II). Upon placing it on his head, 'hot coals' fell from the crown and a fever of boils hit the emperor who would die that day.[849] It seems a strange story and, theoretically, as the crown was considered one crafted by divinity, Leo's intent was to mock what he saw as superstitious Iconodulism by wearing it. A question that may be posed is did Irene have anything to do with his true death? His death was considered to be mysterious

---

[846] Jenkins, 91.

[847] Named as a Confessor and martyred by Orthodoxy, but not the historian of the *Chronicle*.

[848] Ostrogorsky, 175.

[849] Theophanes, 139-140.

circumstances and the fierce reputation of the Augusta was one where nothing stood in her way as a ruler of Byzantium, even her own son. It is not impossible to say he was poisoned or some advantage was taken when Leo was in a natural state of illness.[850] Nevertheless, with Leo's death, Irene's place became secured indefinitely over her susceptible son than her surprisingly stalwart husband might have been.

Stalwart did he seem before the Arab threat on his boundaries and Themes, as well as a shrewd politician for weaving at least an illusion of popular will among his officials and armies. This was seen in the dynastic matters such as Constantine's rise as heir and the punishment of Leo's brothers for treason. His reign was brief, but had promise for a *Basileus* that knew moderation was a virtue after fifty years of Iconoclastic oppression and suffering. This suited some of the needs of a Constantinople of 100,000 inhabitants and a shrinking range of cities quickly pouring towards the coasts of Anatolia and Thrace, guarding against enemies on the periphery of the Empire.[851]

He made veneration and the Adoration of the Virgin sacred to the point that he was said to have protected the Blessed Virgin from 'ribald and blasphemous disrespect' and hailed as the 'Friend to the Mother of God'[852] and with his death the first era of Iconoclasm in Byzantium was in its death throes. What he did not really count on was the determination of his wife and her uncompromising Iconophilism. Whether she was responsible for his death or not, her entire record of rule was one of ambition and merciless efficiency. The historian and monk Theophanes the Confessor was a member of Leo's army at one time in a corps of 'Stratores' and was later awarded the higher rank of Spathori. But, he took the cowl sometime before the Nicaean Council of Constantine V, defiantly riding an ass and wearing a hair shirt. He gave his large fortune handsomely to the poor, until his relatives complained and Leo threatened his eyes if he persisted in his 'irrational worldliness.'[353] After Leo IV's death, he gave to charitable institutions and even built monasteries, writing his *Chronicle* around 813 or 814 until his death in Samothrace in 818.[854]

---

[850] Norwich, (*EC*), 366, claimed it was 'probably tuberculosis' and that he was physically, as well as morally, a weak man. Jenkins, 90, postulates he probably dying from it his entire reign, answering the questions of this physical impairment.

[851] Treadgold, 404. Based on a map of small urban centers also recognized in 787 at Nicaea.

[852] Jenkins, 91.

[853] Bury, (*AI-II*), 524-525.

[854] Theophanes, ix.

## CONSTANTINE VI 'THE BLINDED'
(780-797)

Leo and Irene's son was not an able administrator or a military commander, and he was seen even more an appendage to his mother than Leo was. To have the length of any record he possesses, it is only because he lived so long alongside the Empress. He was feckless and unfortunate to have crossed his mother too many times as it cost him his throne and his eyes. His only significance was in demonstrating how the army and court disliked the notion of a woman alone having the throne of Byzantium; to them a eunuch might as well have been *Basileus*! He was applauded on one thing: he was just as responsible as Irene for returning the icons back to the Church and the Empire, being as tolerant as his mother and despite the father he barely knew. But, as with many things, this was not due to the independent moderation of Constantine, but the towering will and manipulation of his mother. It does not help him that his reputation is for being blinded and thought to be dead; decades later, an Iconodule Slav known as Thomas would claim to be him on the borderlands, knowing no idea of Constantine's fate.[855]

He was born on January 17, 771 in the Purple Chamber, as was his father, a true *Porphyrogenitus* prince. He was only nine years old when his father died on September 8, 780, his mother and the army who took Leo's oath of protection doing their best to fulfill their obligations. A plot was ferreted out against him resulting in the Logothete Gregory, Bardas a general of the Armeniac, the Cubicularium Constantine, and the Drungarius, Theophylactus Rhangabe, being beaten and tonsured.[856] So too were the remaining relatives of Leo tonsured and made priests to, later, serve the Festival of Christ's Birth and Irene would then present her little son as emperor, wearing his father's crown studded in pearls. He would not be well-educated, lacking the spirit or sense to rule, but was said to have been stifled by his mother, wearing him down for her ambitions with 'vices she had nourished and secrets actions which she had advised.'[857]

As developments in the West were favoring the Frankish King Charles over the Pope, the *Basilia*, in 782, sent envoys west to appropriate a marriage alliance between Constantine and Charlemagne's daughter Rotrude (Hellenized as Erythro, or 'red'). A scribe, Elissaios, remained to tutor the coarse, Frankish

---

[855] Jenkins, 76.
[856] Theophanes, 140.
[857] Gibbon, 1622.

princess in Byzantine custom and with a Classical education. As Theophanes describes it, however, the Byzantines were not referred to as 'Romans' as the Germans would become, nor 'Hellenes' with its Pagan flavor. Instead he uses the new term of 'Greek' (*Ton Graikon*) which made the Empire stand out as thoroughly Christian and distinct from the West's conceits at using the term 'Roman.'[858]

In January, 785, Irene called a Council of Bishops and made Tarasios Patriarch over the deposed Paul, who was not as adamant on icon veneration as Irene was, forced to resign on the 31st of August (though he was still an Iconophile). Success was easy in this Council as its main purpose was to restore icons in the Empire, as Constantine and Irene were hailed a new Constantine and Helena by all present. As he was only fourteen at the time, Constantine was only a figurehead of imperial-ecumenical power and a rubber stamp for Irene in the proceedings to add legitimacy. By now rumors were abounding, however, that Constantine was showing undertones of Iconoclast sympathy as Leo had, and his place at the Council was only one to avoid civil war at the stern insistence of Irene.[859] In 786, however, the image of their unity, real or otherwise, waxed strong as the imperial mother and son made goodwill tours and appearances in the Empire as far as Berroea at the ends of Bulgar territory.[860]

In the year 787, Constantine and Irene convened the unfinished Seventh Ecumenical Council Constantine V had begun. Held in the Palace of the Magnaura, it answered the vital ecclesiastical question of the eighth century concerning the icons. Irene, being an Athenian Iconodule, had raised her son to oppose the heresy since the death of his father. This act married the concepts of Greco-Latin and Oriental mysticism[861] while denying the former's attitudes of reason over superstition as Leo III had attempted to blend. Misfortune also erupted, however, as King Charlemagne refused the alliance of his daughter and Constantine over his acceptance of Iconoclasm. John the Sacerellios and an army were sent west, but they were defeated by the Franks. Meanwhile, Irene sent her trusted adviser Stauracius and a courtier, Theophanos, to find a suitable bride to save face in desperation. The daughter of a respected patrician leader of the Armeniac – Maria of Amnia – was chosen against Constantine's wishes, as he claimed that he was still betrothed to Rotrud, but the two were wed on November 12, 788.[862]

---

[858]  Theophanes, 141f.

[859]  Jenkins, 99.

[860]  Herrin, 132.

[861]  Norwich, (*EC*), 371.

[862]  Theophanes, 147-148.

Irene's control over her son was seen as total and transparent in character; Theophanes relates how the devil deceived her as she was 'a woman (and power hungry)' thus could have no entitlements to have higher station on the throne, directly or through Constantine, in the practice of ruling the Empire. Constantine saw this, but his filial loyalty and inexperience directed him toward the powerful court eunuch, Stauracius, as he believed the adviser was controlling his mother. In late 789, Constantine orchestrated a plot with the magistrate Peter and the Patricians Damianos and Kamoulianos to seize and imprison Stauracius in Sicily.

In February, 790, as Constantine and Irene went to St. Mamas, this coup was to be set in motion, but unfortunately, Stauracius caught wind and executed countermeasures to see Constantine destroyed in Irene's eyes. The *Basileus's* men were beaten and tonsured in Sicily and the Patrician leaders were put under house-arrest as Damianos was tonsured and sent to Apollonias. Irene also beat and rejected her son and imprisoned him indefinitely, making the armies and the Themes proclaim an oath that "As long as you live, you will not accept my son's ruling." As well as this, in all documents and inscriptions, Irene's name would take precedence over Constantine's[863] as Irene's theft of the throne was a *fait accompli.*

However, the Armeniacs refused this oath and rebelled in Constantine's name. The Drungary of the Watch, Alexius Musele, was sent to respond, but he was overpowered and imprisoned when the Armeniac's chosen leader, Nicephorus, claimed to be Basileus. Soon, emboldened Anatolic Themes resisted Irene and she was forced to release her son from captivity. In October, 790, Constantine VI set up an oath that the Armeniacs would always support him and Irene, for the time being, lacking the leverage to oppose it, and by the time he was twenty, he was 'strong, competent, and saw he had no power.'[864] The nineteen-year-old ruler, however, lacked the savvy to rule and the will to depose his mother, recalling her in January 792 from Eleutherios were she had been exiled on a stipend. His main supporters were Michael Lachandracon and the new commander, Alexius Moseles, that December finally having Stauracius tonsured in Sicily as a not so subtle checkmate.

Something that would have cemented Constantine's position with the army that had first bolstered him was a military campaign ending in a fine

---

[863] But in Norwich, (*EC*), 372, it was understood the oath against Constantine's supremacy caused the attempt of displacing Irene and did not happen after it.
[864] Theophanes, 148.

Byzantine victory. Shortly after the Armeniac affair, in April 791, the Bulgars under Kardam were attacked by the army at the fortress of Probaton (meaning 'Sheep') at the St. George River. It ended in a strange draw as both armies retreated for fear of battling after nightfall. The following July, a disastrous defeat met Constantine at Marcellae on the 20th as Kardam took prisoners, baggage, and horses, Constantine losing important generals in his army faction including Lachandracon and an astronomer that assured Constantine a victory![865] Before this even happened, a shameful peace and exploitative tribute to the Abbasid Caliph of Baghdad, Harun al-Rashid (763-809 CE), was given as the Arabs attacked the southeastern provinces near Syria. Constantine's military passivity was souring his image before his supposed friends, allies, and enemies.

Returning with nothing, the Armeniac Theme immediately went back on their word and attempted to again raise Nicephorus as *Basileus*. Constantine slit his nose, as well as those of Nicephorus's brothers, and in a jarring state of paranoia he blinded Alexius Moseles as well. Upon hearing this, the Armeniacs rebelled against their imperial officers and won a victory over Constantine's forces in November, 792. Further punishing the Armeniac prisoners, on June 24, he imprinted on their faces with black ink, "Armeniac Conspirator", riding them through the Blacharnae Gate. This inner conflict proved unwise as Harun's Arabs used the opportunity to invade the Armeniac and the Anatolic Themes from Syria.

In a series of further poor decisions considering his weak foothold in the Palace, he repudiated his wife Maria of Amnia, whom he had always objected to, and tonsured her at St. Mamas on January 3, 795, in order to marry the low-born *cubicularia*, Theodote, who would present him with a son and heir.[866] This was a shocking turn of events to Irene, Patriarch Tarasius, and Byzantium in general. How may a Christian Roman *Basileus* divorce his wife for a servant? It defied all spiritual convention and the canon law forbidding the sundering of what God brought together, something the Imitator of Christ should never do. Constantine was even bound by the Gospel of Mark (10-11) against adultery by the Studite monks who proclaimed the emperor was not above any law.[867] Irene slandered her son's choice using her friends the monks Plato of Saccudium

---

[865] Theophanes, 151.

[866] Norwich, (*EC*), 374. He would die at about six months of natural causes; Irene's detractors, of course, accused her of poisoning him.

[867] Jenkins, 100.

and his nephew Theodore. It was declaimed by the Patriarch as the Moechian (from the Greek *moichea* – 'adultery') Controversy. Yet why would Constantine VI do this? Is the answer psychological, where, an *Basileus* feeling devoid of emotion would latch onto whoever he felt a connection with, one he did not feel from a wife or mother, even if it was with a servant? Or was this self-destructive rebellion against his powerless position as Irene's son and not the true *Basileus* of Byzantium?

Whatever the case, Irene attempted to save the situation by marrying Constantine next to the daughter of the pious Philaretos the Merciful, a Paphlogonian noble noted for his charity to the Church. This interesting event came from a Khazar custom of election and vote made by nobles over which of a panel of princesses and candidates would be chosen. These contests were naturally rigged, and the practice was abandoned altogether by 900 CE,[868] holding reminiscence to the bride auctions of the ancient days of Babylon. Constantine would later expiate himself, however, on May 8, by rehabilitating a place called Anousan. Remitting the dues of their trade fair of 100 pounds of gold, he appeased St. John in a Church of the Evangelist for its thanksgiving celebration at Ephesus. Merchant fairs commonly made use of religious festivals and celebrations to capitalize on the trade of icons and precious artifacts to pilgrims.[869] This was clearly a boon, perhaps, to Iconodulism as supporting its markets as well as expiation. Freed from Irene, he could still use an able mind saw the opportunity.

In 796, the monks Plato and Theodore rebuked the communion of the Patriarch of Constantinople, Tarasius, who supported Maria's tonsure and Theodote's crowning. Inflamed, Constantine beat them, imprisoned them in the Chapel of Gabriel the Archangel and eventually exiled them to Thessalonica. Irene must not have brooked too much resentment against her son as she still accompanied him to the hot baths at Prusa in September. Perhaps, as Theophanes thought, the monks overstepped some bounds and lost their 'shield' in the *Basileus*.[870]

Disaster for Constantine VI extended to 797 as another campaign against the Arabs met a great defeat in Anatolia. With 20,000 light infantry Constantine marched, not knowing a plot was already being put against him in the Palace. Irene's supporters bribed the Arab sentries and brought false reports

---

[868] Jenkins, 98.

[869] Herrin, 148.

[870] Theophanes, 153.

to Constantine that the Arabs had fled. Dejected, and again without victory, Constantine returned to Constantinople, which by now was probably quite tired of the *Basileus*'s losses and incompetence. On Friday, July 17, imperial guards moved against the *Basileus*, but he escaped to Pylae by warship and fled to the Anatolic Theme for military support, quickly being shown as having no talent for command or the courage of a soldier.[871]

The armies, however, not impressed by Irene, still claimed allegiance to Constantine, the greater of the evils at this point; Irene grew concerned by this and called for a meeting at Eleutherios. She intended to send Bishops to Constantine to gain a safe passage to another exile for her apparent role in this plot against her son. Seeing this, her faction became nervous and seized Constantine as he was at prayer, sending him to the City. At 3 p.m. on Tuesday, August 15, Constantine VI was taken to the Purple Chamber where he had been born and was blinded, on Irene's orders. For seventeen days thereafter, an eclipse darkened the Empire and it was thought to mean that the darkness was the sun shoring up over the emperor's blindness.[872]

The *Basilia* assured the City he had healed, but the injuries were enough that Theophanes said that he died at twenty-six, ruling ten years with Irene, who would now had sole power. Gibbon, however, claims that Constantine survived and was exiled, debunking the myth of any murder, while recounting the wedding of his daughter Euphrosyne to the later emperor Michael II.[873] It is generally agreed he died around 805 at age thirty-five as a monk. Why blind him in the first place? Irene lacked military power, but was strong enough to imprison her son when the army turned against him. Now, however, Irene's plans would backfire as the army and populace would make the legitimate young *Basileus* a folk hero after he was once a prisoner overnight[874] since Irene was exiled and those sentiments hardly diminished.

Also, the Moechian Affair would not be enough to mitigate his total elimination from the throne; after all, Constantine V was married three times without obstruction and with a divided Church, although his military prowess had been a factor. The answer may have been religious as Constantine was accused of Iconoclast leanings that might see the light of day with the emperor's growing independence. After 797, this would destroy the throne's credibility

---

[871] Jenkins, 98.

[872] Theophanes, 155.

[873] Gibbon, 1623. Theophanes supposedly 'killed' Constantine in his history to further defame Irene.

[874] Brownworth, 149.

and lead to more divisiveness and civil war. He was seen not as just an obstacle to Irene's supremacy, but someone who would cast the Empire back into 'darkness and sin' who needed removal.[875]

Could Constantine have survived without Irene? He had the army's favor and his father's oaths, but constant military ineptitude would definitely threaten that arrangement. He was young and a long reign would have meant much dissatisfaction if his character could not change. As time would show, the nobles' and armies' qualms with Irene was mostly of her being a woman and not that she blinded 'the rightful heir.' Compared to the less fortunate Agrippina, mother of Nero, she had a stepson to consider putting on the throne over her willful son. Irene did not have this alternative, and, therefore, the line could only be held together by her own ascension. Constantine VI was the last male heir in the Isaurian line and his death only promised an abrupt end if Irene chose to marry anyone. The choice she did make was one intolerable to Byzantium as it was a grand insult to the East Romans' authority in a male-dominated, and Christian, Europe. It was further burdened with a threatened sexuality, Charlemagne and the old Salic Law of the Franks binding him,[876] and the new, emerging Empire of the Romans in the West, blessed by the ostracized Church.

## IRENE 'THE ATHENIAN'
### (797-802)

'On earth, the crime of Irene was left five years unpunished; her reign was crowned with external splendor; and, if she could silence the voice of conscience, she neither heard nor regarded the reproaches of mankind. The Roman world bowed to the government of a woman, and, as she moved through the streets of Constantinople, the reins of four milk-white steeds were held by as many patricians . . .But these patricians were for the most part eunuchs . . .Raised, enriched, entrusted with the first dignities of Empire, they basely conspired against their benefactress . . .'[877]

Such descriptions of the Empress Irene's ambitions and beauty are filled with mixed praise and contradiction. The Empire in the twenty years after the death of Leo IV, of whom she never agreed to his ill acceptance of icons,

---

[875] Jenkins, 101-102.

[876] Norwich, (EC), 378.

[877] Gibbon, 1623.

was largely dominated by the *Basilia* in matters diplomatic, ecumenical, and military. Meanwhile, her son Constantine was her mouthpiece to a populace not at all prepared to take orders from a woman to disregard a sitting *Basileus*. She refused the situations of past and even future empresses, let alone those from 695-716, who were seen as petty regents to 'play little role in politics.'[878] Her name meant 'Peace' from the Greek, but irony and history laughs at this fact as this was the last type of description one would rightfully use towards her years on the throne.

She was ambitious, clever, and an outstanding figure in imperial history for her relations with the West in a time when their faith in Byzantium was at an all time low. Diplomatically speaking, she brought the role of Kings to prominence in Byzantine relations more than the relations of the Papacy, strengthening secular power in a secular and headless Europe using its elaborate and mystifying court ritual amazingly described in Nicephorus's *Short History*.[879] Yet, a new consequence of her foreign policy was a lack of protection for the Thematic system that would dissipate not by foreign arms, but internal economic imbalance and social revolution.[880]

She was alleged to have inadvertently killed her son by mutilation in 797, of which it was said she felt profound guilt sapping her energy and her will.[881] Whether such presumptions are true, however, her problems in sole rule came from upsetting the traditions of male authority and the misdirection by eunuch advisers on the throne as well as her methods to gain power. What gained her strength were the allies she made in championing Orthodoxy and the restoration of icons in the Empire. But her enemies, though on the periphery, were stronger than she and the last Isaurian ruler would face deposition and exile until an early death in 803. She successfully exerted her will as a lawgiver,[882] changing her identity as a man to do it, and later periods would prove that these laws survived. Also, a problem occurs in understanding the influences of mother and father on Constantine, who practiced his mother's Orthodoxy, but secretly wished to restore the Iconoclasm of his absent father. Even Irene's views on the matter are mitigated by the historians and her supposed lack of proof he venerated such icons and held an indifferent opinion – the Orthodox view was

---

[878] Bury, (*AI-II*), 480f.
[879] Herrin, Judith. *Women in Purple: Rulers of Medieval Byzantium*. London, UK: Phoenix Press. 2001, 51.
[880] Jenkins, 65.
[881] Brownworth, 150.
[882] Vasiliev, 235.

still a strong one and she may have used this theological stance for political means.[883]

Questions and evidence pile up when one considers the representations depicted in the images in the evolution of her imperial coinage. On the early *nomisma*, after Leo IV's death, the obverse depicts Irene and her son and on the reverse, following the laws of Iconoclasm, the Isaurians Leo III, Constantine V, and Leo IV together. After the Council of 787, the copper *follis* depicts Irene on one side and Constantine on the other, a clear message of the regent and son joining in an equal status on the throne. Finally, after 797, when Irene ruled alone, the *nomisma,* somewhat unconventionally, shows Irene on both sides.[884] An odd omission was any sort of Christian imagery except for the Cross on the imperial regalia. Why fight for Orthodoxy and be its champion after eighty years of opposition, finally having the last word in the eighth century and ignore Christ being carved on coins before Leo III? Was this all a growing vanity of Irene's to plead for legitimacy? All three coins could be seen as a testament to the indifference a ruler may have felt over the issue of icon veneration.

Not much is known of Irene before her coming to Constantinople in October, 769, from her native Athens in the Helladic Theme. She was born around 752 and on November 1, 769, Irene entered the City in a curtainless litter to be seen by her people, described as a devastatingly attractive orphan from Athens, two days later being betrothed to the Caesar Leo in the Pharos by the Patriarch. On December 17, she was married and crowned *Augustus* and *Basilissa,* receiving the crowns in the city of Daphne to the oratory of St. Stephen (713-764 CE). It is claimed how her father (dead upon these events, according to Theophanes) was from the noble stock of the Sarandapechys family and surnamed *Tesserandepechys* ('Forty Pieces, Forty Cubits') indicating an epithet of tall ancestors, shedding some light on a mysterious entrance into history as no particular reason has ever been given for why she was selected as *Basilia.*

She was, however, raised by her (probably maternal) uncle, Constantine, and Sarandapechys is the surname she often bore.[885] She faced persecutions for her native Thessalonican Iconophilism with her husband in 779, and knew she needed her son to balance her position with the army if they were to stay loyal; only a the rightful heir – a man – would do to lead the army legitimately.

---

[883]  Herrin, (*WIP*), 85.

[884]  *ibid., (WIP),* plate 1, a-c

[885]  *ibid.,* 55.

Constantine was a Porphyrogenitus after all, a title of legitimacy no one denied and throughout the Middle Ages no other institutions of succession after four dynasties were as 'such a neat and compelling device.'[886] She even gained success in convincing both the Greens and Blues to accept her son as *Basileus* in the Hippodrome. When Leo died in 780, his son was only nine years old and Irene would champion Iconodualism as his mother and *Basilia* of Byzantium, described as a new age of optimism for the throne.

To settle the issues of the court, she chose the wily eunuch and Postal Logothete, Stauracius, and in 781, he was put to use on the battlefield. When the Sicilian army of the Byzantine general Elpidios rebelled in 782, Elpidios sent his son and the Abbasid Caliph Harun al-Rashid ('the Just') to Anatolia, heading an astounding (and oddly precise, according to Treadgold) 95,793 men. Irene fielded palace eunuchs loyal to her to head the army which was more an accepted practice than allowing a woman any direct command, even from Constantinople. As castration was illegal under Islamic law, eunuchs were only slaves in al-Rashid's Baghdad and eunuchs on the battlefield were captured to increase Arabic manpower in entire populations of enslaved men.[887] Rashid was trapped at Sangarius offering a truce, but the greedy and disloyal commander Elpidios betrayed Stauracius after numerous Italian defeats by Irene's general Theodore and a defeat was followed by a shameful peace of 160,000 *nomismata* annually.[888] Elpidios and his duke Nicephorus stayed in Africa and the Caliph proclaimed Elpidios *Basileus*, dressing him in royal raiment.[889]

Fortunately for the eunuch commander Stauracius, the Thessalonicans and Sklaveni were easier to deal with as in 783 when Irene could count on a large tribute to the treasury from the tribes and military spoils. A goodwill tour was then made to Thrace in May taking 'tools and musical instruments', denoting a mission of peace, to the city of Beroa, renamed Irenopolis. However non-military such a procession of the rightful ruler was before the army, these pageants were traditional symbols that peace (as a rare commodity) was restored and it was always welcomed by the populace.[890] Here, her dynastic preparations were clarified as she intended to create monuments to herself over her son.

---

[886] Herrin, 191.

[887] Bobrick, Benson. *The Caliph's Splendor: Islam and the West in the Golden Age of Baghdad.* New York, NY: Simon & Schuster. 2012, 121.

[888] Vasiliev, 238. This came out to around 70,000 to 90,000 *dinars* in semiannual installments, the numbers indicating superiority in the Byzantine gold piece.

[889] Theophanes, 141.

[890] Herrin, *(WIP)*, 81-82.

Yet, Constantine passively accepted this with no forethought to the future and his inexperience cost him observation that his mother probably claimed more power than he. She reached Philippopolis in the far end of western Thrace and concluded diplomatic relations, extending the northern Empire to boundaries that had not been seen for thirty years.

Trouble in the region would not diminish as Irene prepared Christianity with its Eighth, and final, Ecumenical Council, held in the winter of 786 as the Caliph assaulted Adata in Thrace and stonewalled the eastern Patriarchs from crossing this territory. Furthermore, the Strategos of the Armeniac, Nicephorus, destroyed Adata to expel the Arabs. Pope Hadrian, meanwhile, was getting letters from Irene and Constantine (*divilis sacris*) and pleas from Byzantine priests to convoke a Council over Iconoclasm. Included were the writings of Tarasius sent to the Patriarchates of Antioch, Alexandria, and Jerusalem, denouncing heresy and calling for a Council as well.[891] Support even existed from a fourth-century (pre-Islamic) Council of Elvira in Spain, disallowing pictures (*picturas*) in the churches, 'that the walls shall have no images of that which is revered and worshiped' (*ne quod colituret adoratur in parietibus depingatur*).[892]

Irene was attempting to heal internal breaches by suppressing Iconoclasm using their opponents; her major weapons were used refuting Constantine V's *Definitions of Faith* with the agreements she had with her ally, the Patriarch Tarasius.[893] In spring of 787, Irene and Constantine VI led troops in Thrace to stem the invasions of the Slavs and Bulgars in time to return to the capital to have her son lead the Council. Tarasius was an excellent choice as an ally and a Patriarch even though the conservative spiritually-trained opposed him, he also being a 'cultivated layman with sound theological training and clear political judgment.'[894]

In 788, Irene lost much of her success as a military commander by losing battles and territories in the Empire's eastern and western frontiers. Much of this was to replace the Empire's best generals with like-minded Iconodules, crippling military effectiveness and loyalty to be correspondingly weak.[895] Rashid surprised Byzantine armies in the Anatolic at the Cilician Gates and opportunistic Bulgars took armies at the Strymon River. Meanwhile, the

---

[891] Bury, (*AI-II*), 495.
[892] Vasiliev, 254.
[893] Herrin, 86.
[894] Ostrogorsky, 177.
[895] Brownworth, 149.

Franks were occupying Benevento in Italy and an army was sent by Irene to recover the principality, and after defeating this force, the Franks settled a peace with the *Basilia*. With this finally under control, Irene focused on creating a lasting bulwark of troops in western Thrace to protect the boundaries from the Bulgars. As previous *Basileus* had done, she created a new Theme in the region and called it Macedonia.

In 789, the favorable relations with the Franks was seriously threatened by the Lombards in Sicily. As the Empire had made a treaty they could not break with Lombardy, they sided with them against Charlemagne's troops and the general Theodore, so successful before, was destroyed by the Franks. The commanding Sacellarios John was captured by the Franks and executed along with the advising former Lombard monarch, Theodotos. Though this debacle transpired, scholars report that this had little bearing on Charlemagne's decision to terminate the betrothal of his daughter to Constantine.[896] In fact, given the generous offer of marriage to Irene twenty years later, the Frankish King and Byzantium must have healed any wounds between them. Charlemagne had earned his position in the Christian world by absorbing Bavaria and Christianizing Saxony, expanding territory further east into the Slavic lands, destroying the Avar kingdoms, and annexing Lomabrdy.[897]

Domestic affairs turned against her in 790 as her son attempted to oust the eunuch Stauracius from 'influencing' his mother. This failed, but ended up as a debacle for Irene as the Thematic armies made clear their intentions of accepting Constantine as Byzantium's ruler over Irene. The result was a ponderous type of stalemate: Constantine lacked the strength of character or support by the court to depose his mother as the armies, needed for her defense of the boundaries, would not allow the emperor himself to be deposed. Even if seen as a tyrant, it is undeniable that Irene cared for her people and improved social services during this period. Something on her side in the debate were the numerous churches and nunneries she also erected cemeteries for wayward strangers (*xenotaphia*), dining halls (*triklinous*) for the Palace bakeries, hostels to be dedicated to the *Basilia* (*xenon ta Eirenes*), soup kitchens for the elderly (*gerotropheia*), and retirement homes. This stream of philanthropy to demonstrate the institution of Christian charity and generosity for her people was also made possible by easing and eliminating certain taxes (*phoron bare exekopsen*).[898]

---

[896] Theophanes, 147-148.

[897] Ostrogorsky, 183.

[898] Herrin, 104.

For seven more years, this stalemate would be tested with Constantine's defeat at Marcellae in 792 and his humiliating defeat before the rebellious Armeniac armies with his uncle Nicephorus soon after. Irene faced humiliation as the political marriage to Charlemagne's daughter was defaulted and her reckless son divorcing and tonsuring his wife for a Paphlagonian commoner in 795. By 797, Irene was ready to depose her son as the fickle army was turning away from Constantine's disastrous rule. As it is questioned whether her dedication to icon veneration was genuine, she would not see the hard work of 787 wasted in the time of her son's sole rule. She had noted a tendency or two throughout his life that he preferred his father's Iconoclasm; Charlemagne abhorred images unlike the Papacy, and the character of this Frank would easily crush the weak Constantine when he would travel east to fight the Slavs. Politically, it was anathema to her supremacy and the Empire's independence; morally, her son was a dangerous heretic who would lead the Empire again into 'darkness and sin.'[899] So, she seized her chance to upset the stalemate and attempted abduction, but was repudiated, predictably, from some of the armies of the more loyal Themes.

Fearful allies to Irene captured the *Basileus*, brought him to Constantinople, and on the orders of the *Basileus* and her court, blinded him in the Purple Chamber where he was, in myth, dead hours later, when in fact this death did not occur, as it was only an invention of Theophanes's. Finally, Irene asserted herself beyond doubt that she controlled the throne; she was said to show no remorse or guilt over her son as she planned to wed a German Emperor that would surpass in impact 'Antony and Cleopatra.'[900] In the West, it was seen as a travesty as the wily and corrupt Pope Leo III, a Greek Sicilian, snubbed Irene thereafter, including bestowing the keys to the holy sites to Charlemagne only.[901]

She had never been a real mother to him, Constantine being raised by nursemaids and tutors, but the blinding of Constantine was not too auspicious in the East as the Empire's future was in a vulnerable state, especially as succession was now questioned by commanders such as Nicephorus. For the next five years, she would rule but have no respect from her people; 'she had lost her humanity' as maternal bonds had been severed with the all classes of the Byzantines as it had with her own son.[902] It was said that by the reasoning of

---

[899] Jenkins, 102.

[900] Bobrick, 125.

[901] Wilson, Derek. *Charlemagne: A Biography*. New York, NY: Vintage Books. 2005, 80.

[902] Brownworth, 150.

Irene's detractors that her rule was no better than a eunuch's as she was a woman and, therefore, lacked any validity. The West went slightly farther as no woman could inherit independent property and, therefore, the Throne of the Roman Empire was altogether vacant, officially[903]. This degradation and depravity in Constantinople was proof that the Roman Empire had fallen far to the West.

In desperation, Irene documented on coins and official papers herself as a *Basileus* – a man's title, in quelling such infamies. She was as a new Hatsepshut (1507-1458BCE), the widowed Egyptian queen, who had declared herself Pharaoh two millennia earlier, a desperate move that had worked for the best. Irene also used this practice to affirm her rule and perhaps better the Empire, but her (alleged) guilt over her son and outrages from the Themes hampered such a move and it seemed disingenuous. She surrounded herself, naturally, with eunuchs who could not marry her and usurp the throne: Stauracius, Plato, Theodore, and the Patrician, Aetius.

Another serious and powerful threat to the union was Harun al-Rashid in Baghdad; he wanted a weak Byzantium to keep their presence out of Muslim Palestine. He saw opportunity in the mutual aggression between the Abbasids and Charlemagne against the Spanish Umayyids as such alliances stood. By 797, Charlemagne had sent Frankish envoys and a Jewish interpreter to Rashid's court, and the large tributes the empress paid had 'calibrated the relationship' between the two rulers as Byzantium's vassalage to the Caliph.[904] In the end, the inability of Irene to field or lead armies, the disagreements with the Popes over icon veneration, and the loss of prestige over the coronation of a 'Holy Roman Emperor' in Germany hit hard. Finally, the challenge of the powerful eunuchs of Irene's court discouraged the Frankish King long enough for rebellion and revolution by a male ruler to make the point of any union moot.[905]

Exacerbating events, some economic downturns also made Irene unpopular and her answer was re-distributing wealth as a temporary fix and remitting taxes and other fees to monasteries that remained the corner-stone of her political support.[906] She tried settling the matter with some temporary reliefs such as bribery as a method of distributing wealth to the citizens of Constantinople. On Easter Sunday, 799, Irene appeared from the Church of the Holy Apostles in a golden chariot drawn by generals and city officials, but

---

[903] Norwich, *(AM)*, 56.

[904] Bobrick, 139-140.

[905] *ibid.*, 145-146.

[906] Ostrogorsky, 181-182.

no policy worked long-term and she faced hostile criticisms for it. Furthermore was the rescinding of the *commercia* tax on customs and duties in March of 800 in Constantinople, Abydos, and Heira, also forgiving municipal taxes in the City.[907] The commercial tax policy was a problem for the businessmen and officials who depended on it for transporting imports and exports. This unwise decision led to loss of valuable revenue and was a virtual nightmare for the region's commercial economy. To gain a popularity that she already had in monasteries by returning icons to the monks, she eased considerably the duties and taxes they had to pay, especially for the Studites of Constantinople who practiced strict discipline in Christian education.[908]

In 798, more holes in the administration became visible as Rashid raided Thrace all the way to Ephesus and Malagina in the Opsikian. Although Irene sent ambassadors to the general Abu Malik to sue for peace, it would not last due to a court conspiracy. Another debilitating peace reviving the tribute of 782 was reached with Irene and the conspirators would free the exiled brothers of her dead husband, Leo IV, in an attempt to seize power. They failed, and the Empress imprisoned them in Therpeia in October where Aetius promised them safe passage, but betrayed them to the authorities.[909] Irene blinded the brothers and they were then exiled again to Irene's native Athens. As Irene felt defenseless against al-Rashid's onslaught, she turned internally to alleviate the suffering of the Asia Minor Byzantines, which is why she created the Theme of Macedonia to allow a buffer between the City and the Arabs.[910]

Due to an illness Irene suffered in 799, the ruthless eunuchs Stauracius and Aetius showed their lack of character by seeking succession before Irene's fate was even decided. Foolishly, or naively, they saw it as a precedence that a woman could rule, so why not a eunuch? Tradition was obviously declining as a new kind of chaos was becoming a norm on the throne. So, in March of 799, they conspired with the Theme of Hellas and the Belzetia Sklavenoi ruler, Akameros, to put the remaining sons of Constantine V on the throne. Theophanes also said that the Scholarii and the Excubitores were involved.[911] Irene was quick to act and called a Silentium in the Triklinos of Justinian II, but

---

[907] Theophanes, 157. This was the infamous allowance wherein one-tenth to one-eighth of profits increased for the warehouses and they made a monopoly that choked free trade.

[908] Treadgold, 423.

[909] Theophanes, 156.

[910] Herrin, 115.

[911] Theophanes, 157.

before this went further, Stauracius died of illness before the coup could come through and this last affront by the eunuch to Greece, though unintentional, left the conspirators' plans fragmented. On June 3, Aetius attempted to gain control, but his native Cappadocia revolted against him and he faltered to act against the throne. Though she caught the sons of her former father-in-law and blinded them, Irene remained threatened by her Strategos of the Anatolics.

But the biggest blow for Byzantium would take place not in the lands of the Caliph or the Bulgars. It would not be rebellious commanders and eunuchs threatening imperial boundaries or within Constantinople. In 800, such a blow to imperial prestige would come from the West as Pope Leo III decided Byzantine Roman civilization was weakened, decadent, and an absentee landlord not vested in Western interests. After consideration, the Byzantines had failed politically, in doctrine, and militarily; a westerner with all of these qualities in their favor ruling the West was a natural choice.[912]

He recognized the successful and loyal Charles 'the Great' of the Frankish kingdoms as a new Emperor of Rome who could protect the West from its own turmoil with Muslim Moors in Africa and Spain. Amazing theories, once again, appear in Irene's biographies that paint her as a master chess player in the game with the West. An 1893 paper by J. B. Bury dares to suggest Irene was behind the coronation of Charlemagne in her plans for a dynastic tie to the West.[913] The two rulers had means and opportunity, they had relatively good relations with the other, and the new powers emanating from the Frankish King-made-Emperor could not but protect Byzantium from the Slavs and the dominating Abbasids. This is probably a fairy tale, but it demonstrates the ambitions of the *Basilia* concerning the West and a reputation for subtlety and the possible slyness of her character. Charles was anointed and crowned by the Pope at the Christmas celebrations of 800. Byzantium was to be cut off and a 'Holy Roman Empire' blessed by the Church and his representing Christ's rule of the world would be legitimate; Charlemagne's name was to be included on the rolls of the Roman emperors after Irene's. Real fear for the Byzantine throne's future was felt by the stunned court.

Charlemagne, however, had no desire to displace Irene militarily[914] or otherwise, and in fact, he saw great opportunity in this unique situation. It

---

[912] Norwich, (*EC*), 379.
[913] Vasiliev, 269f; Bury, J. B. 'Charles the Great and Irene.' *Hermathena, VIII.* 1893, 17-37.
[914] Wilson, 96.

was clear, however, he brooked no submission to be equals with the Byzantine *Basilia* or a joint authority; though she had ruled three years longer than he at the time, he never referred to her as a 'senior emperor.'[915] His own ambitions were tied into one crown: his own, as he saw as there was one God in heaven, one supreme ruler would rule wherein all dissenters to this idea were blasphemers and imposters.[916] He likely saw that, if he married Irene with the Pope's blessing, his offspring could run in the line of emperors of Byzantium from Constantinople as well as his capital of Aachen and by default would he be Emperor as no *Basileus* sat in Constantinople.

An interesting passage in a Western source by Agobard of Lyons (779-840 CE), *Kolner Notiz* ('The Notes from Cologne') reports that Byzantine envoys in Frankish Sicily supposedly offered to give the Eastern Empire to Charlemagne personally, on Irene's orders.[917] This could have increased the military situation in Francia over the encroaching Khazars, the Abbasid Caliphate, and the steppe Turks fleeing the Chinese Empire's T'ang dynasty.[918] The possibilities of such a union might have been endless for the two Romes and Medieval history might have been very different, it all being a matter of West dominating East, or East, one day, dominating West. As for the Byzantines themselves, though they were revolted by her and her rule, there was little question to her legitimacy, and as they knew nothing of the Salic Law, Constantinople would not be seized by some barbarian and illiterate pretender.

Charlemagne made his intentions known by 802 and Irene seemed eager to accept the offer. At his coronation, he wore the red slippers and golden tunic (*skaramangion*) of the Byzantine imperial ceremony. He even began the tradition of the anointment of the body and soul by holy oils in the form of 'Unction' joining himself to Christ. This particular ceremony was adopted by Leo III, but only in the consecration of Bishops and prelates.[919] But despite all efforts, the Byzantines considered themselves the only Romans and saw the Western Franks as upstart, coarse barbarians with no legitimacy. His military presence, though, was very real, so the nobles of the Eastern Empire scrambled to find a suitable Greek emperor whether Irene approved or not. Also, as ambitious and lofty an idea as such political unions were, detractors used more

---

[915] Herrin, 123.

[916] Norwich, (*EC*), 380.

[917] Herrin, 117. Sicily was a choice location as it had status as a Greco-Latin neutralized zone to meet the Franks and discuss measures of security and peace on the island.

[918] Wilson, 69.

[919] Herrin, 123-124.

practicality in saying that ill-assorted marriages to such polarized cultures and opposition lacked a permanent duration and ended in 'a speedy divorce.'[920] It was never meant to be; the two rulers never even met in person.

The feared and influential Strategos of the Armeniac and Opsikian Themes, Aetius, made a claim for his non-eunuch brother Leo as General of Thrace and Macedonia and as geography was on their side and they made haste to take advantage. It was his 'frequent speeches' that disallowed the Eastern and Western marriage, considering himself by now 'co-ruler' with his brother, displacing Irene.[921] But within the City, the Domestic of the Scholae, Nicetas, opposed Aetius in favor of himself, but the decider of Byzantium's succession was the General Logothete, Nicephorus. In a palace revolt on Monday, October 31, 802, at 4 a.m., Irene was deposed by the Tryphillioi of Nicephorus, Aetius, and his brother Leo whom all 'acted as Judas had at the Last Supper', tonsuring the Empress to a nunnery she had founded, where she sat at a spinning wheel until she died on August 9, 803, on Lesbos.[922]

Her lasting legacy was in the Iconophilism she represented and in also ending the first period of Iconoclasm at the Seventh Council of the Church in 786-7. The monk Theodore the Studite (759-826 CE) wished to make her an Orthodox saint for these actions, but she was never canonized and only myths exist in the Western sources saying she was. Nevertheless, with her son, she effected real change and diplomatic peace with the restoration, and this is why she is considered the 'pious Irene' to Theophanes. It was, indeed, Theodore the Studite that Irene wisely depended on to gain revenue for the Council from the monasteries and the farms of surrounding areas.

Monasticism, however, was going through radical changes itself in a rift tearing at the Orthodox party from within. On one side were the elder conservatives that had lived through the persecution of secular authorities against icons and their way of life; the Studites were the most ardent on this position. However, as religious authorities were breaking down, the next generation under Irene trusted secular authority and preferred them. This was led by laymen giving religious posts, such as simony, like the Patriarch Tarasius.[923]

Theodore the Studite was also the nephew of the eunuch Plato of

---

[920]  Bury, (AI-II), 490.

[921]  Theophanes, 158. At least Charlemagne never ever mentioned displacing her.

[922]  ibid., 159. The Confessor adds a heart-felt speech wherein she confessed her avarice to be 'the only Emperor of Emperors and Lord of Lords.'

[923]  Jenkins, 95-96.

Saccudium and one of Irene's greatest supporters, due to her intentions in the Council. It was with his monastic designs that Theodore would also lead the administrative and educational aspects of Byzantium. This would sharpen the bureaucracy's efficiency and secular learning in the Empire. In 786, Irene called a Council of the Eastern and Western Bishops to end Iconoclasm. This was the final such Council the Empire would have and Pope Hadrian's representatives, those of Antioch and Alexandria, were present on August 31, 786, in the Church of the Holy Apostles. As it was to begin, the Iconoclast Excubitores, Scholarii, and imperial guard stormed the Church and ended the congregation by spear point, forcing them back to their lodgings unharmed, but greatly dishonored. A stunned Irene could do nothing and she realized her predecessor's policies must have been stronger in her people than she had first thought.

The prelates stayed almost a year until work began on a new Council in May of 787 where, in the sixth session, she called for a distinction between the Iconodulist *proskynisos* ('Honor') and *latreia* ('worship') meant for God alone.[924] Icons were indelible parts of worship, but not at all to be its fixation: 'For the more continuously these are seen by means of pictorial representation, the more their beholders are led to remember and to love the originals, and to give them respect and honorable obeisance: not that we should worship them with the true worship which is appropriate only for the Divine . . .'[925] Then Irene called for a Second Council in Nicaea on September 24, where, in the city Constantine I had ruled on the fate of the Orthodox faith, in its Church of St. Sophia on October 11, 350 Bishops convened safely to discuss doctrine using Biblical and Patristic literature favoring iconography. Wisely, nothing new or radical was introduced; just the return of icons and the condemnation of the Iconoclast Patriarchs Anastasius, Constantine, and Nicetas by the newly elected Patriarch Tarasius.

Some trouble brewed as voiced opposition against Iconoclasts included charges of 'selling church perferments' (simony), and Tarasius took notice to them.[926] On October 23, the last session was convened in Magnaura and in November, the Bishops, the *Basileus* Constantine VI (hailed as a new Constantine the Great), and the *Basilia* Irene (a new Helena) entered Constantinople. Officiating by document, Irene and Constantine concluded perhaps the most successful and smoothly-run Council of the Church in the

---

[924] Herrin, 111.
[925] Jenkins, 95
[926] *ibid.,* 97.

400-year history wherein such Councils had been held. Now, thanks to this settlement of the issue of Iconoclasm, the Church and bureaucracy could recover themselves to restore proper education and administration with even a reserve in the treasury to facilitate.[927] The future success of the Empire's peak centuries started with this development.

Due to the Triumph of 787, iconic art was restored and entered a new period, the Arabic swirls of secular art being replaced in the Hippodrome scenes said to be 'satanic.'[928] Among the most notable were the Crucifixion scenes portraying the divine suffering of Christ, an ironic combination of Iconophile and Iconoclast imagery as Crosses were allowed to be used by the Isaurians. Now in the Metropolitan Museum of New York, this depiction includes fourteen saints, Mary Theotokos, and the apostle John before the crucified Christ.[929] Written on it is John 19:26-7 'Behold thy mother, behold thy son', a strong reminder of the rule of the imperial mother and son shadowing the reign of Mother and Son over the spiritual realm. Such concentration on Good Friday supposedly came from new liturgical poetry (*conduce*) and its use in Studite monasteries as well as the Churches of St. John the Baptist and the Virgin of the Spring, built by Justinian I for its waters' miraculous cures.

However, after 787, icons were to be carefully treated to displace error in their veneration; St. Nicolas, for example, was required to sport a black beard in all representation in order that he was correctly identified. Likenesses was an issue in this iconic art as a growing trend of abstraction frontal poses with gold backgrounds, such as St. Demetrius's in Thessalonica, was growing and continued into the thirteenth century as the Church encouraged more realistic portraits. The icons of St. Catherine on Mt. Sinai during the Justinianic era and the Late Roman periods in Egypt were examples of this naturalistic style.[930] Christ, in the abstract style, would once again watch over all who entered the City by an erected mosaic provided by the generous *Basilia*.[931] In architecture, Irene built a Chapel for St. Nikolas and Churches for Sts. Euphemia, Anastasius the Persian, and Eustatius, plus a Monastery of Euphrosyne t*a Libadia*. Business industry also showed improvement as the silk workshops (*ergodosia*) provided trade to the West; even the death shroud of Charlemagne, made in 815, was

---

[927] Treadgold, 424.

[928] Karlin-Hayter, (*OHB*), 162.

[929] Herrin, plate 4.

[930] Mango, Cyril. 'Iconoclasm.' Chap. 6 Of the *Oxford History of Byzantium,* ed. by Cyril Mango. Oxford, UK: Oxford University Press, 151-162. 2002, 152.

[931] Herrin, 90-105.

of Byzantine origin, depicting the German Emperor in a (secular) charioteer scene. Localized and private bakeries (*lamia*) were patronized by Irene to provide employment as well as bread to smaller areas.

Irene also learned from her experiences before and during the throne and it shows in the legislation and *novellae* she enacted in the penal code during her sole and supreme rule. The first such legislation concerned the oaths taken by soldiers, citizens, and all other facets in the Empire. Aside from the first oath excluding her son, they were to be directed solely on Christ instead of the throne, and these oaths were further designed to be more difficult for them to be circumvented. Traditionally, this would be seen as an Orthodox move as Iconoclasts such as Copronymous found its secular use offensive.

It can easily be concluded that the Moechian Affair her son inflicted on the dignity of the throne later induced Irene to produce laws such as that of third marriages being forbidden and seen – in order to maximize the penalty – as bestiality, which was punishable by death in Leviticus. It is again overlooked that the defender of the Empire against the Infidel, Constantine V, had three marriages and no one dared to balk against this. But, Constantine VI did not share his grandfather's other attributes being also seen as a heretic and a tyrant to Irene. Such odious measures would by forbidden by the Civil Law and even upheld by the Orthodox Church in which she was almost consecrated as a saint.

Irene's successes occur mostly when associated as being a regent for her son as the legitimate Basileus, although no one begrudged Irene blinding Constantine when there seemed no alternative. Byzantium was basically concerned with icons and adultery issues over their *Basilia*'s cruelty, yet she tried to fill the throne itself, and all unraveled in just a few years. This was primarily due to her being a woman and the infamous Greek misogyny ruling custom for thousands of years made the imperative that she find a man to handle the Empire's affairs. As well as this, Pope Leo III was shocked and disgusted by Constantine's blinding and considered her coronation void and the throne vacant after 797.[932] It was galling that a daughter of the sinful Eve even attempt to undertake a semi-divine presence on an imperial throne designed for the Imitator of Christ.

Overlooking the Greek nobles for the Holy Roman Empire was ambitious, but unfeasible; Westerners detested the idea as much as Byzantines did and the road was blocked by ambition from the Ducal class in the Eastern Empire.

---

[932] 'It is not for nothing that the adjective "Byzantine" has come to signify the mixture of the complex and the sinister.' Wilson, 75.

She was said to be despised by her people and certain unpopularity with her weaknesses and her actions seemed very probable; selfish, yet, pragmatic, she only showed the West a degraded state of penury.[933] This is a great exaggeration, but the state of affairs could not have looked too attractive to the West as the German Emperor's notorious will, mostly by choice, did not outdo that of the Pope's. Skepticism surrounds Irene's actions at every turn by historians who give Pope Leo all the credit in being a 'subtle, intriguing character' but with 'selfish ambition', 'implacable resentment', and 'unnatural cruelty.' In truth, she was a narcissist and sociopath, using her son as a pawn; evidence supposedly exists that accuse the *Basilia* of 'encouraging' the unlawful second marriage to only inflame the monks to rally by her side and complete her the dominance of their favors.[934]

Had she married the odious Aetius's more respectable brother, Nicephorus the Logothete, all might conceivably had been well and she would still have kept some legitimate power. But her desire to rule in the East married to a husband bound far away to the West was too strong and it cost her a twenty-two-year legacy on the throne. No other *Basilia* would attempt such a bold move as being a *Basileus* again. But, that legacy saw with finality the end of the old Roman order. Octavian Augustus's days were long gone with one undisputed ruler on the throne, especially a woman, and this was the last time in Christendom one would exist.[935]

Literature and legend would be kinder to Harun al-Rashid and Charlemagne, and in such culture, no Byzantine ruler of this era, with except the limited scandals of Irene, would ever dominate Western imagination.[936] Ambitious women such as Zoe or Theodora in subsequent centuries ruled from the regency and this is how power was developed for imperial women in the Greek Empire. It was ancient Roman custom that regents have influence in practice with their imperial children such as the ancient Empresses Livia, Agrippina, or Galla Placidia. The mothers and regents of future *Basilii* Constantine VII, Basil II, Constantine VIII and others exerted more than enough dominance to have effective policies. Irene spent her last months in a nunnery learning this lesson all too well.

## NICEPHORUS I 'THE GENERAL LOGOTHETE'
### (802-811)

[933] Norwich, (*EC*), 380-381.
[934] Jenkins, 100.
[935] Brownworth, 154.
[936] Magdalino, 171.

# STAURACIUS
(811)

As a virtual rush of nobles and interested parties ran to fill a vacant throne in Constantinople, it was a Palace financial officer, Nicephorus, who succeeded in the end winning the crown. It was time for, possibly, a fresh dynasty to replace the one ending in 797 and one beginning a new era of Iconophilism that would banish the heresy of Leo the Isaurian and Copronymous from the Church. Monasteries looked forward to re-investiture, a revitalized industry in artisan icons, and a belief Church property would be thought to be inviolate. But, the efficient and centralizing force of Nicephorus would see a domination of the Church and religious communities under Constantinople to finance risky wars against the expanding Bulgars.

Meanwhile, Nicephorus's piety and energy still won him the acceptance of the imperial officials and clergy.[937] Although a glorious new age of domestic financial reform was enacted by the *Basileus*, the pride of the Empire would be tarnished forever as a travesty unheard of in almost 500 years bolstered the reputation of the northern Slavs. Spoiling his name further was the invectives of Theophanes, resentful of his status as a usurper in ousting Irene, although his military, administrative, and financial improvements are noted as worthy achievements.'[938] Yet, more conservative modern historians such as Bury notes how has he was a 'wicked rebel' against the Empire.

Nicephorus ('Bringer of Victory') was born in 760 in Seleucia Sidera and came from an Arabic background of the Jaballah clan of Ghassanid nobility,[939] a valid claim of many 'Oriental' historians, mainly al-Tabari. He rose in the imperial bureaucracy to the highest financial post, that of the General Logothete. He was made *Basileus* on October 31, 802, gaining the acceptance of Irene by approaching in the humble black sandals of the commoner,[940] making his adolescent son Stauracius his co-*Basileus* in 803. He was an advocate for icons (Byzantium would almost have nothing different) and was approved, anointed, and crowned by Patriarch Tarasius. Still, his treatment of Irene by traditional historians was seen as one of a monster, one of 'hypocrisy, ingratitude and

---

[937] Treadgold, 424.
[938] Herrin, *(WIP)*, 147.
[939] Vasiliev, 312.
[940] Theophanes, 159.

avarice; his want of virtue was not redeemed by his superior talents nor want of talents by pleasing qualifications.'[941]

One of his first intentions was to settle the so-called *Pax Nucifera* with Charlemagne before the year's end to placate the Western emperor who lost the chance at the Byzantine throne. Although Nicephorus intended goodwill, he still disregarded Charlemagne's standing as an equal and balked at his Iconoclast Synod sent eastward to Irene. This was of small importance to Charlemagne, relatively as he still made no effort to besiege Constantinople. Mostly Charles worried about the containment of the Slavs to the Peloponnesian lands out of Frankish territory and Nicephorus was seen as, on par, an equal Roman *Basileus* in the East.[942] Relations would only see a marked improvement in 812 after Nicephorus's death. Settling his ascendancy in Byzantium, the *Basileus* relieved the rival Aetius of his commands over the Anatolic and Opsikian Themes. The Anatolic would be entrusted to a Thracian general, Bardanes Turcus; regretfully, a year later, Turcus rebelled and proclaimed himself *Basileus* interceding on behalf of the deposed Irene.[943] When she died that year, however, Turcus's rebellion ran out of steam and he surrendered to being tonsured as a monk over execution.

On the Eastern front of the Abbasid Caliphate, from 803 to 804, Harun al-Rashid would formally greet the new monarch with a reminder he too had duties to fulfill to the Caliphate. Predictably, Nicephorus sternly reminded Harun that Roman pride would never bow to such demands: 'Nicephorus, King of Rum, to Harun, King of the Arabs: The queen who ruled before me treated you as a rook while she assumed the posture of a pawn. She paid you tribute to which, by right, you should have paid to her. This was but a woman's weakness. When you have read my letter, return the money you took and ransom yourself out of the trouble you are in. If you do not, the matter will be settled by the sword.'[944] The Caliph wasted no time proving his point by invading imperial territory with, supposedly 300,000 men, taking the forts from Tyana to Ancyra, almost capturing Nicephorus in Phrygia.[945] George of Amastris was sent to offer a 30,000 *nomismata* annual tribute from the *Basileus*; Harun also demanded

---

[941]  Gibbon, 1623.

[942]  Wilson, 96-99.

[943]  Treadgold, 425.

[944]  Bobrick, 180.

[945]  Theophanes, 162.

the cowed *Basileus* and his son both pay a head tax of three *nomismata* apiece. Nicephorus's capitulation to such terms were said to surprise even al-Rashid.[946]

But, the year 805 would also see victory for Nicephorus and his son Stauracius as they raided the Peloponnese and the Sklaveni in Greece to make up for their Arabic defeats. The Thematic army of Hellas retrieved the West from the Slavs as the Armeniacs took the city of Melitene. Nicephorus won a major victory at Patras in the Corinthian Gulf,[947] separating the families of the enemy from their property as spoils in the Church of St. Andrew. A historically successful Byzantine ploy against the Sklaveni has always been to assault the families of the absent armies. The Anatolics then closed in on Cilicia and conquered Tarsus, birthplace of the Greek apostle Paul. Cyprus would then rebel against Arab dominion and join the Empire for annexation as did the Peloponnese, expanding the Greek region.

In 806, Byzantium would lose important strategic ground as the Venetian and Dalmatian dukes would defect to Charlemagne, never being recognized as Western Emperor by Nicephorus I. Caught up in this loss, Rashid invaded Cappadocia and took two fortified cities using 135,000 men; naturally a truce of tribute was made to the Caliph by Nicephorus, amounting to 36,000 *nomismata* and an insulting capita tax of three *nomismata*.[948] The Caliph would be placated at present and the emperor furthered an expedition in 807 with naval fleets to assert authority in Venetia and Dalmatia. He reached a settlement and took Serdica to put down a rebellion in the Peloponnese by Slavs influenced by the Arabs of the amicable North African Ablaghid dynasty. Since 800, the Abbasid provinces west of Africa had been neglected by Baghdad to the point a rival Caliphate rose to manage the government from Tunis. As they were armed with a powerful fleet, these western Arabs, when added to the Spanish and Calabrian Arabs, made matters worse for the Greek and Italian holdings of the Empire.[949]

On December 20, 807, Stauracius was married to a cousin of Irene, Theophano, who also was from Athens. Theophano had an engagement to another man, but was forced to marry Nicephorus's son, perhaps in a vain attempt to reconcile the Isaurians. It was not a match that harbored well for the Empire, as snickers were certainly traded at the news Nicephorus spent his son's wedding night with his two new daughter-in-laws along with his son's

---

[946] Herrin, *(WIP)*, 148.

[947] Porphyrogenitus, 231.

[948] Theophanes, 163-164.

[949] Vasiliev, 278.

wife, being made a laughing-stock by the City. This scandalous allegation of Nicephorus's appetite vilified him further in Theophanes's account and it is assuredly true that the choice of empress for his son was purely political.[950] The next February, a clerical plot was instigated with the Quaestor Arsaber in the City to displace the scandalized *Basileus*. Nicephorus punished these men with beatings, confiscation, and a tonsuring for the unfortunate Arsaber in Bithynia.

Much time was spent thereafter on radical new economic reforms by the *Basileus* that caused dissension in ecclesiastical circles concerning taxation. In 808, the Studite monks, led by their founder Theodore and heading 700 monks, rebelled and instigated a plot against the throne using disenfranchised civil servants and clergy. Nicephorus foiled this and tore open a new wound in the Moechian Controversy started by Constantine VI over communion with the right Patriarchs. He demanded Theodore take communion from the Patriarch Nicephorus who succeeded Tarasius in 806. The monk refused twice and the *Basileus* held a brief Synod, exiling the first Studite in January, 809.

Simultaneously, Slav expansionism reached a new height as Krum became the Khan of the Bulgars; in a show of his strength, he united the Danubian and the Carpathian Slavs of Pannonia and Transylvania.[951] Later, in 809, they successfully defeated a 6,000 man barrack at the Strymon, stealing off with a war chest of 1,100 pounds of gold and killing numerous officers, laying waste to the re-taken Serdica. Nicephorus led armies three days' march from Constantinople to Pliska, Krum's capital, and defeated Bulgar forces there. Nicephorus is said to have been gripped by madness, a mental breakdown, resulting wherein women and children were not saved in the city's destruction; disturbing tales are further recounted that babies were thrown in threshing machines.[952] At Serdica, his barely paid men refused to partake in the reconstruction of the city and returned to Constantinople. By this time, the army was approximately 200,000 troops of a force composed of 68,000 Thematic, 90,000 Tagmatic, and 34,000 Marine troops (oarsmen), centered mainly in Anatolia and Armenia, but with an efficient spread of soldiers throughout the border areas.[953]

Western territories were threatened as the Franks aided the Venetian and Dalmatian rebels in defying Byzantine authority. Nicephorus responded by sending a surge of population into the Peloponnese for military preparation

---

[950] Herrin, (WIP), 134.

[951] Norwich, John Julius. *Byzantium: The Apogee.* New York, NY: Alfred A. Knopf. 1997, 7.

[952] *Norwich, (APO),* 8.

[953] Treadgold, (BAIA), 67.

set for the Adriatic shores. For half a year, Thracians and Anatolian families were migrated to new homes in the Balkans. The Themes of this region were re-organized as Hellas was divided into the Peloponnesus and Hellenic Themes including Attica, Boetia, and Phocis. A new garrison of marines called the Mardaites of the West was organized and a new central army was strengthened by the creation of the Tagma of the Hicanti, mostly made from the sons of other officers in the Helladic units to synthesize the main and provincial forces.[954]

In 810, it would also become clear that the Chersonese-Cyprus region was definitely outside the effective scope of the central government of Constantinople.[955] From there, Nicephorus's intentions would include the Christianizing of the Helladic and Peloponnesian Bulgars, traditionally Pagan. The army was increased by 10,000 men as Greece would revert from a Slavonic region to one Greek in language and ethnicity. The period of Peloponnesian Sklavonia was now at an end. However, by this time, a new and revolutionary 'civilizing' process given to the underdeveloped Slavs by the Greeks settled in the region.[956]

A new beginning was made in the West as the Cephalonian fleets reached Dalmatia and Venetia in 810 and a new Venetian Duke was installed by the *Basileus*. The city government would be moved to a more defensible island where the city would now be westernized into the name of Venice. From then until the early Renaissance, Byzantine and Venetian affairs would be inextricably linked in trade, arms, and culture, even after the fatal year of 1453. Venice would be the last link of Byzantium to a forgetful and modernizing West. Under the *Pax Nucifera,* Venice would reach a Commonwealth status allowing Italian politics not to encroach on the city the feudal system, the Lombard and Tuscan communal governments, and the feuds of the Guelphs and Ghibellines.[957] Another groundbreaking event occurred when Charlemagne destroyed the Avar kingdoms, freeing more of the Danube.

This strengthened the Frankish position against the Byzantines, made all the more dangerous when Krum, a resourceful and formidable man, was made their Chieftain. Nicephorus would later have to create a barrier on the eastern boundary of the region including cities like the vulnerable city of Serdica as well as Philippopolis, Delvetia, Adrianople, and Mesembria on the Gulf of Burgas in 809. This shrewd defense tactic protected the Thracian and Macedonian

---

[954] Treadgold, *(BAIA),* 28.
[955] Jenkins, 121.
[956] Magdalino, *(OHB),* 172.
[957] Norwich, *(HV),* 24-25.

regions for the Empire. The Peloponnesian front was guarded by Thessalonica, Athens, Corinth, Monemvasia, and the battle-hardened city of Patras. Although it would become more fragile in coming centuries due to Turkish incursion, Nicephorus's recovery of Patras was a victory for Byzantine authority in the southern Balkans.[958]

The next year, Arabs sacked the Armeniac Theme and destroyed Euchaita; Nicephorus blamed this defeat on the Armeniac Strategos Leo 'the Armenian' and had him banished on the first Saturday of Lent in February.[959] Considering Nicephorus's next move, this perhaps saved his life. Turning west, with a disturbing boldness and with little regard for caution, Nicephorus planned an all out campaign subduing the Bulgars in 811. One of the largest armies in all of Byzantine history was called on and they marched on the Bulgarian capital from Serdica, the *Basileus* ceremoniously exiting by the Golden Gate of Constantinople in May. Krum attempted to reason with the Basileus and sued for peace, but was rebuffed twice as he arrogantly wished the Bulgars' kingdom to be despoiled.

But, unexpected aid came for the Bulgars in Byzantios from a traitor from Marcellae that offered Krum the imperial regalia and 100 pounds of gold. Desperate, the Tsar gambled with an ambush of log palisades in the Pass of Verbose and for two days, the Byzantine army was trapped after being fooled by Nicephorus's palpatations to avoid panic. But in his actual estimation of the situation, the *Basileus* despaired claiming, 'Even if we grew wings, no-one could hope to escape ruin.'[960] On the night of Saturday, July 26, 811, Krum stormed the palisades and a humiliating slaughter of the fruit of the Byzantine military resulted.

The Domestic of the Excubitors, the Drungary of the Watch, the Strategi of the Anatolics and Thrace were among the victims and the Strategos of the Hicanati was taken prisoner. One of the dead was the *Basileus* himself, as Nicephorus's body had been recovered by the enemy. Compounding the tragedy was the capture by Krum of vital Byzantine ballistics and siege engines, including the towering *helepoleis*. Thirty-six siphons of Greek Fire were also recovered to improve the military quality of Krum's navy along with all the gold and silver Nicephorus took.[961] This was the beginning of the decline of the navy's superiority in arms; in a matter of years, the Fire would fall into Bulgar and Slav hands and, eventually, into that of the Caliphate as a new type

---

[958] Obolensky, 75.

[959] Had this not happened, Leo might have died on the campaign and the history of the Empire would have played much differently.

[960] Theophanes, 171.

[961] *ibid.*, 177-178.

of warfare would begin. The death of an emperor in battle was an outrage not seen since Valens at Adrianople in 378; Krum gloried in it and removed Nicephorus's head, first impaling it on a wooden stake for all to see for ridicule, afterwards boiling it to the skull and mounting it in silver.[962] This made for the Khan a drinking cup that he used to ceremoniously bond with his nobles, the Boyars, by sharing wine. With the Persians and Goths these actions strengthen an enemy with pure resolve.

The *Basileus*'s son Stauracius barely escaped, but did so at the cost of being crippled for life. By the time he returned to Constantinople, Theophanes reports that he was 'bleeding violently and excessively in his urine and the blood was dried on his legs and thighs when he came to Byzantium by litter', also bitterly rebuking his wife, Theophano, as a conspirator with members of his court.[963] Showing a weak and low character, he dishonorably won favor with the armies by jeering at and criticizing his father's lack of military skill.[964] Only a month later he was preparing to blind his sister Procopia's husband Michael Rhangabe in a fit of paranoia, when the Domestic Stephen and the court ousted him from the throne on the early morning of Friday October 1, 811, and ascended Rhangabe to the purple as Michael I.

Stauracius had always been jealous of his brother-in-law's abilities and it is said how he intended to let Procopia handle affairs in the City in the *Basileus*'s absence rather than Michael, a ridiculous idea considering the unpopularity of Irene fresh in the minds of the court.[965] Reluctantly, Stauracius resigned himself to the monastic life through a relative known as Symeon, where he would die of his grievous wounds on January 11, 812. The insincere Patriarch, Nicephorus, claimed this was due to his ill health and not a plot, but an endlessly bitter Stauracius did not believe him and parted with the embittered words, 'You will not find him a better friend than myself.'[966] Thus, two emperors died horrible, humiliating deaths due to military hubris and a lust for conquest, avoiding all offers of peace.

---

[962] Norwich, (*APO*), 9.
[963] Theophanes, 172.
[964] Bury, (*ERE-I*), 9.
[965] Jenkins, 126.
[966] Theophanes, 173.

Though he was shamed and made a trophy of in the wake of disaster, Nicephorus I had a certain genius for finances with ruthless efficiency, putting into effect economic processes that would result in prosperity in the long term for the Empire. His major obstacles were his depleting of the rural economy by Harun's aggression and the starvation of the urban economy due to Irene's remissions on resident and capitation taxes, as well as duties in Western exports.[967] It was necessary that the army be showed preference to those landed estates not in service, and Nicephorus demonstrated this with such measures as land re-allotment to the soldiers stationed in these provinces. If provincial estates were not generating enough production to support the soldiers garrisoned there, they were re-located to other imperial lands, in trade for their former land, now extended to the troops.[968]

Though amazingly stable, this reform really had no innovations, just a refurbishment of making checks to balance economic institutions and systems. The Farm Law of Justinian II and its communal system of allelegyon (allelegguon), or 'Mutual Warrant', invoking the shifting of tax burdens onto the rich to appropriate the poor was such an example.[969] But, such implemented policies would bankroll the 'golden age' in Byzantium as the very apex of its eleven centuries existence in history. In September 806, Nicephorus called for a new census in the Empire to revise the tax assessments not made since 733. Unfortunately, as with all censuses since that of Octavian Augustus, it was reviled and cursed as ten 'vexations' by contemporaries,[970] yet better evaluated by modern historians[971]:

1) A levee of troops from the provinces were called to assemble an army in Sklavonia and it is said to have been a collection of prisoners and heretics, so demoralized that many committed suicide. Their orders were to take Hellas for Asia Minor.

2) A census of the Empire was enacted so even the poorest farmers could build a citizen army, and the higher status of farmers paid the remainder of the eighteen-and-one-half-percent *nomismata* tax to equip recruits. In this phenomenon, throughout the Middle Period, this enrichment of the poor by disarming the rich was considered a 'private' economy.

---

[967] Jenkins, 117.
[968] Treadgold, *(BAIA)*, 127.
[969] Vasiliev, 348.
[970] Theophanes, 167-168.
[971] Jenkins, 119-120.

3) New tax assessments resulted in an increase and a further addition of two *keratia* (eight-and-one-third percent *nomismata*) for clerk's fees paid by the individual taxpayer.

4) The remission of all Irene's benefices and tax exemptions; although vilified by Theophanes, it was commonly agreed to in modern works[972] that this was a progressive step in relaxing a serious choke hold on the tax economy.

5) All poll-taxes (hearth-taxes) on charitable institutions, monasteries, orphanages, poorhouses, etc. would necessarily inflate as much as 100 percent. Thematic generals were surveyed and new anti-evasion laws on taxes were put into effect as private treasure troves and war chests were confiscated. A result was a still further division between such military commanders and the civil bureaucracy.

6) On inspection, wine-jars whose contents were twenty-years old or less were taxed. This twenty-year mark would go back into Irene and Constantine's reign, thus farming the taxes formerly remitted and ignored by the *Basilia*.

7) A 'death duty' was instituted, where inheritances of parents who had died in the last twenty years were taxed and to be paid by the inheritors. In the same bend, house slaves who had originally come from the city of Abydos (as a major customs center) and the Dodekanese region were taxed two *nomismata* per capita.

8) All sailors and citizens who made a living by the sea around Asia Minor was given compulsory land to farm so they could be taxed, using these landholders as Thematic troops for the region.

9) All the ship masters of the City, on top of the usual duties and taxes of their commercial ventures, were 'loaned' twelve pounds of gold with an interest rate of four *keratia* per *nomisma*, or 16.67 percent, a seriously higher rate when the former deflated rate went somewhere between 4.17 and six percent.[973] This endeavor was implemented in order that the state could have a monopoly on all loans, enriching the Treasury with interest and devaluing private loaners (including clergy and monasteries).

---

[972] Including Theophanes's translator, Turtledove, 167f.
[973] Herrin, 50.

These were the first effective revisions to the tax systems since 733 under Leo the Isaurian[974] as households, lands, slaves, livestock, and past tax payments were appraised. Though they were harsh and a form of usury, as a sin against God, these were painful, yet necessary, measures to re-align the wheels on the state financial machinery and bring money back to the Treasury, state financing once being Nicephorus's domain. And it was effective in supplying funds to a military pressed Empire to repel Harun al-Rushid and the emerging Bulgars of the north, but blowback, however, was still inevitable.

Naturally, these reforms infuriated and ostracized Nicephorus from the clergy and monastic orders Irene had allied with, and he was even constantly demonized as being 'a new Ahab more insatiable than Phalaris or Midas' tyrannizing the people for gold.[975] Ostracization of the newly recruited Thematic troops and their commanders caused frustrations that led to rebellions not seen on a scale since that of Philippicus Bardanes. On Thursday October 1, 810, an assassin in monastic garb even attempted a crude attempt on the *Basileus*'s life with a sword, wounding two guards.

Theophanes reported that clergy were used as slaves and that the gold and silver eating utensils of some of the monasteries (though a little ostentatious) were to be distributed to the state. Furthermore, he surrounded himself with heretical Paulicians (perhaps from Thrace, where Paulician Slavs were allies) and delighted in Pagan oracles, rites, and even supposedly sacrificing a bull before heretics from Phrygia. Theophanes even absurdly claims that Nicephorus was an Iconoclast when it was common knowledge he was as for iconic veneration as Irene had been! This charge is denied by historians as toleration for heretics politically, not for the atheism he has supposedly been labeled as supporting.[976]

His unpopularity only grew from events on April 12, 805, as he raised Nicephorus to the Patriarchy of the City when Tarasius died. A presence of clergy and 700 monks met to complain how an unworthy civil servant was basically plucked from an office desk and given the highest spiritual seat in Constantinople and Orthodoxy. The *Basileus* preferred administrators and trusted secularist officeholders as he wished to run the Empire as a like-minded financial bureaucrat would, short of paying military debts against the Bulgars. He demonstrated the input and output of luxury goods in relation

---

[974] Treadgold, 427.

[975] Theophanes, 169-170.

[976] Jenkins, 118.

to his powerful and wealthy neighbor, Harun al-Rashid. In order to salve the humiliation he received in 808, the two monarchs would exchange diamond-encrusted belts of gold, rare silk garments of great size, medicinal drugs, opium (*tiryak*), pastries, dates, raisins, and perfumes.

The Byzantines, in return, sent hundreds of silk garments, twelve hawks, four hounds, three thoroughbred horses, and 50,000 *dirhams*.[977] If Hermann Zotenberg's (1836-1894) romance of the *Arabian Nights* is to be believed, Constantinople sent fifty of the fairest virgins from Greece and fifty of the fairest boys of Rum, sent bedecked in gold jewelry and the typical Byzantine great silk robes embroidered lavishly with pictures by needlepoint, to al-Rashid. Interpreted from the English in 1706, the culture of the Byzantines, their eunuchs, their sensuality, and lavish wealth was ingrained in the character of modern consciousness, especially to future historical minds such as Edward Gibbon who scandalously decried it as immorality and inevitable moral decline.

Nicephorus I had great ambitions of expansion in his reign. Had he the option, Hellenizing the Bulgar kingdoms of Krum while reaching to Western European Byzantine holdings would have been his greatest accomplishment. He created a massive army which was paid for by his relentless and lucrative tax revenue reforms. Also, creating a peasant military service also helped as they did manage a number of victories in the Bulgar lands. Theophanes taints all of this with stories of cruelty and robbery to gain gold through typical, godless avarice, yet it is true Nicephorus was rash and underestimated his enemy in the end. He was an inept soldier, lacking experience in military administration as he was never anything else than financial bureaucrat at his succession in 802. Norwich also reminds us that he intended and could have had a dynasty as the Isaurians did if not for the proliferation of the Bulgars. Ineffectiveness against these peoples would be a norm under his ill-fated son's successor, Michael I Rhangabe.

Yet, Krum was not the only ruler in the West that the Byzantines were interested in; it is suggested that Nicephorus used this conflict and even the ones with the Studites as 'test cases' of his authority.[978] The new Holy Roman Emperor could make a lucrative ally against the Slavs if diplomacy had been successful. Nicephorus was as stubborn as he was greedy and missed an opportunity that would have saved him trouble in handling Venetia and Dalmatia by recognizing Charlemagne. It would take a certain amount of

---

[977] Bobrick, 181-182.
[978] Jenkins, 125.

foresight to arrange this possibility into a kind of reality. The first few steps, despite any outcome, were crucial and it would be Rhangabe that extended this olive branch to the imperial garland.

A note on the *Chronicles* of Theophanes ending at Nicephorus's time: it is agreed by modern and some Medieval historians as fact that Theophanes stopped here and an anonymous source used his name as a 'Continuer', Theophanes Continuatus (*Oi Meta Theophanen*). This history from July 26, 811, to that of 813 in the reign of Leo V the Armenian has thus been identified as being written by an anonymous author in a short work known as the *Diegesis*. But, the author of the translation used by the author will be referred to as Theophanes until its end in August of 813 where the chapters concluded with Leo V. These were unfortunate by-products of the 'Dark Ages', where sources were scarce and the bias of its historians was the only account that exists.

# MICHAEL I RHANGABE[979]
## (811-813)

If it was true that Nicephorus I was so inexperienced in war that the army dishonored him after his death, then it is definitely true that Michael I was worse as being far more ignorant in military affairs without Nicephorus's talents as an administrator in the Empire. He was mild-mannered, congenial, and handsome with a black, curly beard also being in the prime of his life,[980] but this only masked his blandness and indecision. The *Basileus* would be a puppet for the more ambitious figures behind the throne – his mother-in-law, the deceitful *Basilia* Theophano (former wife of Stauracius), and his wife, Procopia. They would make the greater decisions of the Empire as he mostly busied himself with Christian philanthropy.[981]

But even they could not handle the degeneracy of the previous two reigns as a strong Bulgar army headed south with the Byzantine armies being unprepared and led by a weak emperor. Stronger and more able generals than Rhangabe saw the crisis after several Bulgar defeats, and the *Basileus's* bodyguard would oust Michael I after two years of dangerously mismanaged rule. Ironically, his

---

[979] Now, in the ninth century, we first see the Byzantine surname directly connected to a *Basileus*. Ostrogorsky, 197f.

[980] Bury, (*ERE-I*), 12.

[981] Herrin, (*WIP*), 249.

mildness might have made him a father of his country had it been a peaceful age, but his ruin was in his resisting of his armies and dangerous enemies.[982]

Michael Rhangabe was born into a noble military family in the Peloponnesian region in 770 and his father, Theophylact, was Drungarius of the Aegean during the Isaurian dynasty. Michael would later take the non-military role of a *Curopalates* ('He Who Takes Care of the Palace') and wear the red belt and robe of the courtier with Nicephorus, marrying his daughter, Procopia. He was never made Stauracius's Caesar for his survival in Plisken was seen as a threat to the crippled Stauracius who tried to have him blinded, only to be overthrown by his own armies on October 2, 811, when Rhangabe was given the purple. He had broad support in the Church (he was a pious Iconophile) as well as the civil service, even freeing Leo the Armenian after a year's imprisonment and re-consecrating Theodore as Abbot of the Studites,[983] winning him more support. It is said the Senate instigated this, but future portraits of the event, especially in the works of the Late Period historian John Skylitzes (1040-1101), clearly demonstrate that it was the army that did this by supporting him and his son, Theophylact, on their shields. This scene of ascension by the army is on a twelfth-century manuscript found now in the Biblioteca Nacional in Madrid.

Unfortunately, these promising horizons were threatened by an old practice that blinded all Byzantine institutions with short-term gratification and made any *Basileus* who did so show their superficial natures: he bought his popularity with more largess. His wife lavished gifts and bribes on the Senate that appointed him, giving a charitable bonus of five pounds of gold to the widows of the soldiers who had died at Marcellai with Nicephorus when being crowned Augusta on October 12. Michael gave a secured bribe of fifty pounds to the Patriarch of Constantinople, Nicephorus, for his support and another twenty-five to the clergy, starting a ninth-century trend that *Basilii* donate 100 pounds of gold to the Church of St. Sophia upon their coronation.[984] He lavished the Church with gold ornaments and jewels, wrapping the icons in imperial purple cloth in gestures of generosity. The grumbling and angry Themes such

---

[982] Gibbon, 1624. A larger factor in his overthrow was, supposedly, Procopia. She was branded a licentious 'Semiramis' (9th cent. BCE) visiting the Roman camps for trysts with the soldiers. But, looking past Gibbon's misogyny, her presence might have meant to inspire the armies with a symbol of the 'Mother of her Country' that did gain her praise in the camps.

[983] Treadgold, 429-430.

[984] Bury, (*ERE-I*), 9-10.

as the Opsikian or Thracian were simply mollified temporarily with more bribes. With further enrichment on all levels of society at the Treasury's modest expense, he had no trouble having his son, Theophylact, crowned co-emperor on Christmas Day, 811.[985]

About this time, the Peloponnesian and Helladic Themes were finally incorporated by the will of a Strategos named Sclerus, who finally finished Nicephorus's designs in the region.[986] As Michael gave large sums to the armies and his supporters, Krum acted on his own momentum by penetrating Thrace and Delvetus in 812. In August, 811, Leo the Armenian had already driven out an enemy army killing 2,000 Bulgars, taking horses and weapons,[987] yet he could not later stem Krum in Macedonia and Thrace. People fled south from Thrace as others attempted to put the blinded and elderly sons of Constantine V on the throne, but Michael spent more funds buying them off. Thracian soldiers mutinied and deserted, leaving the paths to Constantinople almost wide open, but Krum offered to sue for a desperately needed peace by embassies carrying purple-dyed skins and captives worth 100 pounds of gold; included were promises of respect for Byzantine public affairs in Mesembria.[988]

Michael's confidantes, Theodore the Studite and Leo of the Anatolic Theme, persuaded him away from the agreement as Bulgars were also deserting to convert to Christianity,[989] manipulating him with the quoting of John 6:37, 'He that cometh to me I will not cast out.' After refusal by the *Basileus* for peace, Krum bitterly massacred Mesembria, killing all devout Christians on the bloody day of November 5, 812. A particular shame felt by Michael was his failure to properly defend the City with the navies in a state of total disrepair as the naval vessels of Krum, a land power, were supposed to be inferior. Furthermore, Rhangabe made no communication with it in terms of supplies as the missives of ammunition and food, easily sent, were neglected.[990] In early 813, the Roman troops were at Versinica to attack a superior Bulgar force, but Michael hesitated for an entire month, probably fearing another massacre as at Marcellai.

When he did move, it was from behind his army in a show of cowardice,

---

[985] Theophanes, 174.

[986] Jenkins, 122.

[987] Also, Byzantium lost Palestine and much of the East under the growth of the new Caliph, Mohammed, in Baghdad.

[988] Theophanes, 176.

[989] Treadgold, 431.

[990] Norwich, (*APO*), 14.

afterward an exasperated Leo the Armenian called a halt to his 'disgusted' army, calling a mutiny as the *Basileus* withdrew to Constantinople. Once he arrived, riots broke out over their lack of a protective force from the Bulgars as prayers from inhabitants at the grave of Constantine V for a resurrection filled the air, though it was said he had to be returned from Hell among the demons. Leo was then proclaimed *Basileus* with the traditional show of humility denying the crown as Michael abdicated without argument.[991] But, almost prophetically, Leo's most faithful ally, his General of the Armeniacs, would caution him that he should not have raised a hand to his 'fellow-father' regarding Leo's being godfather to Theophylact.[992] Michael I Rhangabe was then tonsured under the name of Athanasius in the Monastery of Prote where many deposed rulers had gone to 'atone for their sins' with an annual stipend.[993] His two sons were castrated and sent there as well and since this did not disallow them from rising to high Church offices, the prince Theophylact would rise high to a Bishopric later in the century.

Though his veneration of icons gained him disapproval and resistance from the army of Iconoclast Armenians and other such provinces, Michael I Rhangabe was dedicated to his cause supported by the Studites and the Patriarchate. Despite glaring inadequacies, Iconodule historians such as Theophanes and Theocistus (d. 855) praise him for his Orthodoxy and resistance to his previous rulers, even in taking the oaths of allegiance.[994] He had re-instated Joseph of Cathara, who had fought Constantine VI in the Moechian Affair, only to show the pliancy he had before his ministers. The Pope demonstrated this by defrocking him again at the insistence of the powerful Studites and their repeal of the Synodal decree of 809.[995] The *Basileus* also perpetrated a persecution of the dualist Paulicians who saw the Old Testament God as evil, terrorizing the 'Jewish' practices of the Phrygian Athingans with such zeal that Theodore appealed to Rhangabe to show relative mercy.[996] It is another negative effect

---

[991] Theophanes, 180. From Michael anyway; of course, Procopia objected profusely but was outvoted by the Patriarch who asked only for safe passage for Michael and his family. Jenkins, 129, suggests at Leo's coronation, he felt 'the pricks and stings of innumerable thorns', probably as he promised himself to Orthodoxy, he was an Armenian Iconoclast.

[992] Bury, (*ERE-I*), 22.

[993] *ibid.*, 15.

[994] *ibid.* 9.

[995] Ostrogorsky, 197-198.

[996] Treadgold, 429-430.

that Michael's persecution of those Iconoclasts left in the City was basically what perpetrated the riots of 813 and his dethronement. These rioters were the 'generally vulgar' actors, brothel keepers, beggars, disbanded City militia, and disenfranchised estate-holders reduced to penury and begging in the streets, who were now becoming starving mobs.[997]

A hermit was caught insulting an icon of the Virgin Mary and was branded a 'wizard', losing his blaspheming tongue. The *Basileus*'s reasoning was said to be Biblical as Peter and Paul killed and called for execution upon those lying and committing bodily sins, so why spare the impure and heretical in spirit who followed with demons, as 'Michael cut down not a few of these heretics?'[998] These were the base in adultery and whoring, licentiousness and greed, opposing all of which the Bible said, also berating those in monastic garb. It is clear that Michael's policies and his reign seemed an unmitigated disaster, as the only thing he was stingy upon was the defense budget. Yet, one beacon stands out in a troublesome reign in the form of relations with Emperor Charlemagne in the West.[999]

In 812, before Krum's incursions in Byzantium, a peace not attempted since Irene's negotiations was made wherein the two Empires formally and officially recognized one another as Western and Eastern Romans. After 811 saw Venice's restoration by Charlemagne, Francia was met by a Bishop and two Greek envoys from the East. Sources then say the diplomats were taken to Charlemagne's capital of Aachen and in a Catholic cathedral (probably vacant of any icons), the *Imperatorum eum et Basileum Apellantes*[1000] were recognized. In 809, Nicephorus had refused to send a Synodica through the Patriarchy to the Western Emperor and another concession by Michael was to restore this in a letter sent to Pope Leo III.

But it must be remembered that this was a disproportionate balance of wills between two monarchs. Michael's apprehensions about the imminent Arab and Bulgar threats probably led to great rashness in his decision. If his wife and mother-in-law directed him (which was likely), this was probably for an approximate reason. The problem with this peace was how fragile it was realistically as functioning diplomacy, especially when a stronger and more forceful Byzantine *Basileus* would have fought Charles over precedence

---

[997]  Jenkins, 132-133.

[998]  Theophanes, 174-175.

[999]  Norwich, (*APO*), 13.

[1000]  Jenkins, 127

between East and West. Future rulers with better positions to argue points over would battle with this question and the prosperity of the East of the tenth century would make this easier. 'The disintegration of the Carolingian Empire and the renewed vigor of Byzantium did, however, make it possible for later rulers of Constantinople to ignore the recognition given to the Western Empire in 812.'[1001] Long after the death of both *Basilii*, this fight over Roman identity and supremacy would lead to a Schism of four hundred years, just as the decline of Byzantium was beginning.

## LEO V 'THE ARMENIAN'
### (813-820)

At last, the Empire would see the man of action and experience it needed against the Bulgars and Caliphate armies that Rhangabe could never provide. Leo V would return Constantinople and Byzantium to a state of preparedness and success not seen since Constantine V, wherein not even the Bulgar threat at the Golden Gate would succeed in penetrating the Walls of Theodosius. And although much of Leo's victories over Krum was attributed to the death of the Khan in 814, Leo's charisma with the Byzantine army and Themes cemented a loyalty lasting for years. Gaining the armies' trust was mostly accomplished with the rejection of icons that the armies of far-bordered provinces favored. Traditionally, Armenians were ardent Iconoclasts, yet Leo succumbed to the need for unity and chose icons instead. What also threatened cohesion in his beliefs was his uneducated status in all theological matters, the Civil Laws, and letters, only knowing best the military discipline that terrorized the innocent and guilty alike.[1002]

Not to be swayed by the advisers of Michael's day, Leo begrudgingly brought Iconoclasm back to the Church and attempted to condemn and erase three decades of stability starting with the Second Council of Nicaea in 787. Yet, in a typical ambiguity found in the *Basileus*'s religious character, J. B. Bury makes it clear he should not be considered anything but 'strictly orthodox.'[1003] During these years, punishments for desecrating icons, tearing up embroideries of Christ or the Virgin to shreds, trampling wooden images, or smearing ordure on them did not exist. The result of the Council of 787 was nothing more than

---

[1001] Ostrogorsky, 199.
[1002] Gibbon, 1625.
[1003] Bury, (*ERE-I*), 21.

the restoration of 'dead figures' and 'lifeless icons', a product of the 'female simplicity' of the *Basilia* Irene.[1004] The ninth century would be haunted by the schism and heresy that the start of the eighth century had seen, but Leo was shrewd in his manners and energetic in getting things done. He intentionally hedged on pledging to Iconodulism and kept a tie with Rhangabe by the ancient Roman tactic of giving him his wife as a concubine in secret as it is aptly noted how, '. . .he had few principles, but many talents.'[1005] These talents, however, were what Byzantium needed to utilize in facing the crises of the Empire, externally and internally.

Leo V was born to a Patrician family of Armenia under the name Bardas in 775 and Theophanes Continuatus would even strongly hint at an 'Assyrian' (Syrian) background in Leo's family. His family had desperately fled their homeland under the economic fiasco of the *Basilia* Irene, living as dispossessed landowners, when they were chased off to Thrace by the Arabs in Armenia. Few words are said on his physical appearance save that he had a curly beard, a short build, and an unusually loud voice. Characteristically, he possessed 'boundless energy, intelligence, and not a small amount of guile.[1006] But, rising in the armies, he was made an officer under the Anatolic Strategos Bardanes Turcas in 802 furthering their relations by Leo marrying one of the daughters. Later choosing imperial loyalty over his mentor, Leo was called to action by Nicephorus I to battle against him when Turcos rebelled and would gain his office with Turcos's defeat.

Some mysticism did surround Leo's future as it was once noted that in 803, at Philomelion, a hermit known for his clairvoyance regarded that Turcos would never wear the crown. However, upon approaching Leo and two other men, the hermit said two would wear the crown and the third would nearly do so. One of the two men was the future *Basileus* from Amoria, to be Michael II, and the other the successful general known as Thomas the Slav, who would never be so. This reminded some historians of the meeting of Banquo and the three Weird Sisters in *Macbeth,* but this is merely an odd, but entertaining, anecdote that may have crossed two literary eras.

As a commander, Nicephorus I would show his incautious and fickle nature by soon exiling Leo for suffering defeats against the Arabs. This was reversed after Pliska, and he returned to his re-instated station at the court. He also had

---

[1004] Vasiliev, 284.

[1005] Treadgold, 431.

[1006] Norwich, (*APO*), 21-22.

a close relationship with Michael Rhangabe as a friend, although Michael's wife Barca would become a mistress of Leo's, and perhaps Michael with Leo's wife. In truth, Leo ruled the soldiers as Michael's hesitations made him an unfit military leader, and eventually being exasperated by this, Leo fled Michael's service, displacing him as emperor. On October 11, 813, Leo was crowned *Basileus*, beginning a reign promising strong arms against the Bulgars. His steps towards a policy of personal defense at all times came in the new guard known as the *Hetaireia* ('Companions'), composed of around 1,200 barbarian mercenaries and old confederates that joined him on campaign and guarded the Palace.[1007] He learned the lessons of Rhangabe's deposition well, but it would still not be enough to stop his own years later.

His first test as *Basileus* was not long in coming: six days after his coronation, Krum appeared at the Walls of Constantinople from Adrianople to finally besiege the City. Seen as a new tyrant of the East, as a Sennacherib (740-681BCE), destroyer of Judah, Krum demanded his spear be put atop the City's walls as a sign of capitulation, of a Bulgarian triumph.[1008] Leo attempted negotiations, but took the opportunity to try and assassinate the Khan to throw the forces into chaos as was done to Nicephorus in 811. The delegate put his hands to his face as an insulting gesture and a signal for the assassins to ride in and kill Krum. Unfortunately, Krum recognized the signal in time and escaped with a serious, but not fatal, injury at the hands of Byzantine darts.[1009]

In Krum's outrage, the suburbs of the nobles and middle class faced devastation, running a path to southern Thrace just beyond the territories of Constantinople before he would retreat. In the city of St. Mamas, he ran amok and captured its bronze lion, bear, and water-spouting dragon statues, and the marbles in the Hippodrome,[1010] committing a systematic destruction of palaces, churches, houses, men, and beasts.[1011] After a capturing of 40,000 prisoners,

---

[1007] Decker, 79. In a strange twist, the name of *Hetaireia* had different connotations of 'companions' in Pagan times as these were known as the upper-class prostitutes of the time. Something Beckwith explains is that as a practice of most Eastern bodyguards, except the Byzantines, existed personal bodyguards of Oriental leaders that dined, drank, bathed and were Spartan-like lovers with them, being true 'companions'. This assured these chieftains that this guard would do anything to protect him. As Leo was an Easterner, could this have had consideration in the composition of his *Hetaireia*?

[1008] Theophanes, 186.

[1009] Norwich, (*APO*), 18-19.

[1010] Theophanes, 187.

[1011] Jenkins, 131.

Krum withdrew the siege and returned to Adrianople. Constantinople itself prepared for an epic siege outfitted with battering rams, scaling ladders, catapults, burning firebrands, boulders on the walls, 1,000 iron-bound wagons, and 1,000 oxen for the haul. Unfortunately, the West was compromised as Charlemagne had just died months before and his son in Francia, Louis II 'the Pious', was unsympathetic[1012] to Byzantine interests.

Krum was not finished with Byzantium, however, and what he saw as a great opportunity for his forces, the Khan sacked Arcadiopolis and Thrace once more to outfit a second siege on the Byzantine capital in 814. Fortunately for Leo and his subjects, Krum died of a sudden brain aneurism and his impetus was undermined by the quick successions and overthrows of two Khans within a year. Had he lived, Krum would most likely have carved a great Bulgar Empire to rival the Greeks and Arabs and what he accomplished in life was enough to make already a fine legacy. When the Khanate settled in 815, the Khan Omurtag raided Thrace capturing prisoners and executing all Christians. By spring of 816, Leo the Armenian would meet them at the ruins of Mesembria. Leo's wily nature allowed for a successful feign of retreat before the Bulgars, only to turn about-face and win in a massive ambush in a fitting retaliation for Nicephorus I near Pliska.

Leo V followed this by raiding the Khanate provinces in retaliation for Thrace and Omurtag was forced into a thirty-year peace, renewable at ten-year intervals. The Byzantines recovered the imperial parts of northern Thrace abandoned by the Khan. Thrace was then divided into two halves under the Greeks and Bulgars. Omurtag held on from the Balkan Mountains to the 'Great Wall' between Adrianople and Philippopolis which was a lasting fortification still somewhat traceable to this day, supposedly.[1013]

In the West, Leo took an offensive against the Saracens of the north Egyptian coast in 817. As a result, the port city of Canachum was recovered, which had been lost since the reign of Constantine VI. Leo even implored aid from Pope Paschal I and the Western Emperor Louis the Pious, but only in arming him against the Iconophiles. Of course, concerning the Church and the new West, this aid could only be the kind Constantinople would expect, the Slavic tribes and Byzantines not interesting Rome as much as unity with the German Emperor. But a new threat was on the horizon as the Viking tribes

---

[1012] Norwich, (APO), 20.

[1013] Bury, J.B. 'The Bulgarian Treaty of 814 A.D. and the Great Fence of Thrace.' *English Historical Review, XXV,* 276-87. 1910; Vasiliev, 282.

known as the Rus were now settling north of Thrace by way of the Don and Dneiper rivers, arriving to attack northern Anatolia in 818.

In desperation, a new re-organizing of the Thematic armies was enacted by Leo dividing the Armeniac Theme into two Turmae provinces with independent armies and navies. In the Western Empire was created the new Theme of Paphlagonia and in the East was created the Ducate of Chaldia. He then successfully handled the Rus and sent them back to their territories as his good fortune and skill in battle won him much popularity (from Iconoclasts, mostly). The Patriarch of Constantinople, Nicephorus, also marshaled armies to oppose the bureaucratic party Leo had collected,[1014] and the culture of quiet animosity between army and state would add a new chapter to its history.

In 820, trouble surfaced from within the Palace when the Logothete of the Drome discovered a plot against the emperor by his Phrygian Domestic of the Excubitors Michael the Amorian, the brother-in-law of Leo's first wife. But timing was everything, as it was Christmas Eve, the *Basilia* Theodosia convinced Leo to stay Michael's execution of being burned alive in the Palace's furnace until after the Christmas celebrations. During the time of Michael's imprisonment as Leo held the key to Michael's tower prison around his neck, he was said to have suffered nightmares and insomnia that night over his guilt.[1015] Unfortunately, this allowed rebellious soldiers (fellow Iconoclasts giving in to necessity) to release Michael secretly. As Leo V the Armenian was conducting the choir at the Matins in the Palace the next morning, his assassins disguising themselves as choristers, brutally cut him down and severed his head in triumph on December 25, 820.

Michael had little trouble gaining the throne, castrating Leo's sons and tonsuring his unfortunate widowed *Basilia*, his unintentional savior, having some mercy for them as he allotted them a portion of Leo's property. They were then exiled to Prince's Island on the Marmara as other relatives of the *Basileus* were also assassinated; as the brutality of Leo V's murder held no regard of Christian sanctity of neither time nor place was a testament to the desperation and attitude of the Byzantine establishment. Michael's scandalous success made clear that ambition held nothing sacred and assassination was a great moderator of the throne of the Imitator of Christ in this period of time. The only comfort was the heroic pose struck by Leo at his assassination, attempting to defend himself with a ceremonial cross, or incense burner, to fight off the

---

[1014] Treadgold, 433.

[1015] Bury, (*ERE-I*), 24-25.

assailants. He held his own until one attacker severed his right arm,[1016] and afterwards, to further humiliate the deposed monarch, Leo was thrown into a sewer[1017] to condemn and profane his memory.

Though his military successes were undisputed, he was still demonized as the restorer of heresy and tyranny by intermittently forbidding the veneration and presence of icons. In 816, he was known to begin the ninth-century trend of sending Christian missionaries to cement peace with the Pagan Bulgars using the liturgy,[1018] to which the Bulgars would eventually convert. It was not particularly well known that Leo was an Armenian Iconoclast when he was crowned in 813, but the necessity of a powerful army general won out in the debate. His hypocrisies and compromises did not go unnoticed and for it he was cleverly known by his opposing Patriarch and like-minded monks as the painfully-punned 'Chame-Leon.'[1019]

When he made his ten-year-old son, Symbatius, his co-emperor in 813, he renamed him Constantine which gave his detractors ample opportunity to rename them as a revived 'Leo III and Constantine V.' Coins of the period show this young Constantine, young and beardless, on the reverse of a typically Iconoclast coin bearing Leo.[1020] Despite this, Leo met little opposition in calling a General Synod on Easter of 814 to once again expel icons from the Byzantine Church. This was a preparation of the *Basileus* to call a full Council on the subject with the classically-learned monk John the Grammarian and Antony, Bishop of Pamphylian Syllaeum. The Patriarch only participated in autumn of 814 when Leo demanded his presence in the Synod's commission.

In this Synod, Leo was quite vocal about his Iconoclast opinions, but using only old views, vague meaningless phrases, and imitations of past gatherings[1021] with no Christological justifications whatsoever. Such descriptions come to us from the Scriptor Incertus (814-912? CE), an anonymous historian known for his chronicles between Leo V and Leo VI. He saw from history that his destiny and the security of Leo V's line lay in the refusal of icons: 'You see that

---

[1016] Gibbon, 1626.

[1017] Bury, (*ERE-I*), 25.

[1018] Shepard, Johnathan. 'Spreading the Word: Byzantine Missions.' Chap. 9 of *The Oxford History of Byzantium, ed.* by Cyril Mango. Oxford, UK: Oxford University Press, 230-247. 2002, 232.

[1019] *ibid.*, 27.

[1020] Bury (ERE-I), 21.

[1021] Ostrogorsky, 202-203. These were noted as pale recycling of the *Acta* of Constantine V in 754.

all emperors who had accepted images and worshiped them died either in exile or in battle. Only those who had not adored images died a natural death while they still bore their imperial rank...I want to follow their example and destroy images, so that, after my long life and the life of my son are over, our rule shall continue until the fourth or fifth generations.'[1022]

Only two fragments of this history now exist; one fragment has been in the Vatican Library since the thirteenth century, covering the Chronicle of the 811 Slav campaign of Nicephorus I. It is known as the Dujcev Fragment as it was discovered and published by I. Dujcev in 1936. The other in the Bibliotheque Nacional in Paris dealing with the reigns of Michael I Rhangabe and Leo V (811-820). Byzantinist Henri Gregoire (1881-1964) has hypothesized after the examination of writing styles that Incertus could be a continuation of the work of John Malalas from the sixth century.[1023]

It is true, historically, that Iconoclast *Basilii* were mostly successes, but this was mainly because of the military control in which they held against foreign enemies with the Isaurians being the main model. In this case, Leo was forced to use political realism in unifying his armies to handle the same set of crises, as the past century had proven, that Iconodule eras only produced 'weakness and some signal disasters.'[1024] It was an old argument, but still compelling when you consider how people believed in divine intervention in everyday events. However, Leo would prove the futility of such a claim as he was assassinated and his line was deposed. And again it was asked by Byzantium why Orthodoxy venerates icons when Scripture does not support it, inducing the Patriarch Nicephorus to defend the many practices and beliefs beyond written authority.[1025]

Leo acted first by removing the icon of Christ over the Bronze Gate of the City, the traditional symbol in which he used to usher a new era. These were to him heresies, daring not to call them idols as these idols represented different 'degrees of evil.' He did, however, stage events, as when images in public would be pelted with stones and mud, ambiguously appearing to stop the desecration

---

[1022]  Vasiliev, 284.

[1023]  Browning, Robert. 'Notes on the "Scriptor Incertus de Leone Armenio"'. *Byzantion*, 35 Louvain, Brussels, Belgium: Peeters Publishing. 1965, 389-411.

[1024]  Bury, (ERE-I), 27. This was exemplified with the degradation of Irene and her son, although Irene's worst attribute was not in incompetency, but in being a woman in the eyes of the Greeks. Propaganda of the Studite Sabbatius during Leo's time dredged up more images of the Theodosia as a 'Leopardess' and a 'Bacchant.'

[1025]  Norwich, (APO), 23.

short of destruction 'lest the soldiery dishonor it.'[1026] He sent mixed signals as well, such as when he made an obeisance to a Nativity on Christmas of 814 in St. Sophia, but refusing to do so on a New Year occasion on January 6, 815. On Easter Sunday, April 1, 815, Leo adapted his new 'Definition' (*Horos*) and the Patriarch Nicephorus was forced to abdicate in exile to the abbey of St. Theodore the Martyr on the Bosphorus. There he favored as a replacement an Iconoclast with connections to the third wife of Constantine V, Theodotus Melissenus, who re-affirmed the 754 Council of Heira condemning icons.

Even the *Basilia* Maria, a granddaughter of the Irene the Athenian, developed followings for the *Basileus* during this debate while following her family's Iconodule traditions. The Studites carried out a campaign of underground letters and correspondences to add cohesion to the Orthodox community after the deposition of 815. Maria knew of this 'secret circle' to sustain Iconophilism, though there are no sources that she had taken an active role.[1027] Any dissenters were, of course, persecuted, executed, and silenced including the outspoken Bishop, Theodore of Studius. Theodore's strong faction worked in secrecy until 820 when they were supposedly responsible for the successful plot against the *Basileus* on December 25.

The Studion was also known for his expressive stance on the actual role of the emperor in the spiritual affairs of the state. Theodore had said that 'Ecclesiastical matters are the province of the priest and [Church] doctors and to the Emperor belong the administration of external affairs. The former alone have the right to make decisions touching faith and dogma; your duty is to obey them and not usurp their place.'[1028] This statement define and sets out to eliminate caesaropapism, the idea that *Basilii* were the religious and temporal leader in one and indivisible. Other *Basilii* used Councils to settle arguments in faith such as Dualism, but only the Iconoclasts used Councils to create new policies that had not existed, as Leo III and Constantine V had done. Yet, Leo was no theologian and never pretended to be one, in order to stand up before a Council he needed theological evidence from some source and the researching abilities to accomplish this. He did so in the form of committees composed of the City's most learned Iconoclasts and their talents in June, 814.[1029]

During this time, a brief resurgence of Classical and secular learning was

---

[1026] Jenkins, 134-135.

[1027] Herrin, (WIP), 153.

[1028] Diehl, 168.

[1029] Jenkins, 133.

occurring throughout the Empire, started by the same committees of research that Leo had assembled secretly in the Palace to justify Iconoclasm in Patristic literature.[1030] John Morochazmanius, or John the Grammarian (d. 867), as religious adviser to Leo V, added a heavily intellectual slant to Iconoclasm in his *Florilegium* ('Anthology'). Centuries beforehand, any secular education was usually the preserve of a few select noble families in the Empire, but the ninth century saw a wider demand for texts of learning for the lower classes. George of Choiroboskos, archivist of St. Sophia, was another such intellectual who published treatises on history and grammar later in the century. And in the 840's, Leo the Mathematician (790-869 CE), a cousin of the Grammarian and Bishop of Thessalonica, compiled vast knowledge of the sciences, travelling east from Andros.[1031]

Leo V instigated, situated from the Caliphate court at Baghdad, a revival of Classical Greek science using his manuscripts and notes, translating and outlining the *Elements* of Euclid and the *Syntaxis* of Ptolemy. Much of these works were recovered and translated to Syriac by the Arab philosopher-scientist Hunain ibn-Ishaq. This revival even traveled west to Italy as the Vatican published Greek works of science (such as the *Almagest,* the Latinized Ptolemy). It was firmly established that this revival won the East on points of Classical heritage and education over the West.[1032] Though this scientific revival began in Leo V's time, its height was in the 830's and 840's and was especially patronized by Michael II's son, Theophilus. Leo V used this as an opportunity to collect Patristic Greek manuscripts that would aid his Iconoclast ambitions. Some of these manuscripts were even held in Arab territories such as Syrian Damascus and Alexandria. It was with these arguments he collected that made possible the persistent badgering of Leo that wore the Patriarch Nicephorus down to attend his new Council.[1033]

Industrially and economically, Leo attempted outreach with the Western Empire in hopes of being motivated to send troops to pacify the Bulgars and the Caliph. The same Louis II 'the Pious' that denied the Eastern *Basileus* so much had a wife, Judith, who was ensconced in, and had a healthy supply of, Byzantine silks. Constant production of this silk was sent bolt by bolt to meet the Empire's need to dominate the market as the West still knew nothing of the

---

[1030] Mango, Cyril. 'The Revival of Learning,' 220.

[1031] Angold, 88-89.

[1032] Jenkins, 136.

[1033] Treadgold, 432.

Chinese silkworm and the myth of the mulberry. Silks were gifts to princes and ambassadors that could not be duplicated, showing the power of any monarch as exporting was so rigorous and prioritized that the women of the Great Palace went without new garments in their quarters.[1034] In the more desperate situation with the icon-painting profession, Leo allowed these painters to retire to Greece to continue their work, and his successor, Michael II, was said to be even more tolerant of them.[1035]

Leo V was not too different from the Isaurian rulers as a devoted Iconoclast and a competent military commander putting back together the Empire broken by Krum's ruthlessness into a state of stability. He also had some visions of an honest government with severe criminal punishments and a policy of appointing judges and officials above the vice of bribery.[1036] He was an ingenious man though, considering his false front at peace with Krum, though a bit Machiavellian, his entreaties only being products of Krum's sudden death. His own death was nothing inevitable or justified as it was cold-blooded murder, not unlike Maurice's. His assassins were Iconoclasts such as he and their only motives boiled down to 'personal treachery and naked treason.'[1037] But Leo V's conviction favoring a strong and secure Byzantium was matched only by his mask of conviction for Iconoclasm to appease his armies and to achieve this security. The defeats in Rhangabe's time shook the military system's foundations and the need for unity in the army prepared the way for policy change and an Iconoclastic revival.[1038]

That is why confusion and ambiguity as to his faith surrounds his reign. First, no persecutions touched silent worship of both types, yet Patriarchs and Iconodules were also said to be forbidden from practicing in public and private. Next, at Christmas Mass in 814, he bowed before the Nativity to quell all speculation in St. Sophia, yet on the Epiphany of 815 two weeks later, those present reported no such act of obeisance by the emperor had ever existed.[1039] Such was the hypocrisy of a religion divided! Many of the Iconoclast emperors were from outside Anatolia: Leo III was Isaurian, Leo V was an Armenian, the new Iconoclast Basileus, Michael II, was Phrygian. The point here is that it was

---

[1034] Herrin, 164.

[1035] Norwich, (APO), 39.

[1036] Bury, (ERE-I), pg. 22.

[1037] Jenkins, 138. Michael still feared his monarch and was said to have hid under his bed as Leo approached, recognizable to Michael by the red shoes he wore.

[1038] Ostrogorsky, 200.

[1039] Norwich, (APO), 24.

foreign origin and influence over the throne in coming years that had transmitted with differing cultures such as the Arabic and Slavic types that disenfranchised iconic worship. Orthodox Iconophilism would not return until after the new dynasty of the Amorians that would start in 820 and it is only here that more domestic Byzantine elements on the throne would bring back true Orthodoxy.

# MICHAEL II 'THE AMORIAN'
## (820-829)

Due to his speech impediment, Michael II is called the 'Lisper' (*Traulos*)[1040] and the 'Stammerer' (*Psellos*)[1041] all at once by historians. His brutal entry into the Byzantine imperial office was not something overlooked by witnesses and peers regarding the murder of Leo the Armenian. What was more, as Leo could be persuaded to show mercy on Christmas Day, Michael took advantage and won his throne with little opposition. Yet this only encouraged dissent and outrage in his people, later exploding into one of the most turbulent periods of civil war in imperial history. It could not be described as anything than an origin to the purple by 'ignoble vices,'[1042] coupled by a supine nature while the territories would shrink, haunting his legacy. By now it was proven that *Basilii* from the Bithynian or Black Sea regions were not coincidentally Iconoclasts as opposed to the Greek Peloponnesian region,[1043] and this backwater area had been known for habits of denying representations and damning such Iconodule or reformist *Basilii*.

Omens are noted as occurring just before Leo's assassination when he stood before, on another Christmas Eve, a mural of a lion being slain between the letters of *Chi* and *Phi*, represented as Christmas (*Christous e gennesis*) and the Epiphany (*Phota*) in January. These dates between 820 and 821 were when Leo was struck down as the lion was[1044] as seen as a sign from the Divine that such events would occur, realizing only too late by the more superstitious. Michael had a certain energy and common sense that, although imitative, made possible a lack of instability and fear in the religious policy that Leo

---

[1040] Porphyrogenitus, 95.

[1041] Norwich, (*APO*), 27f. It is not to be confused with the later historian of the eleventh century, Michael Psellus (Psellos), who never had such an impediment and was a noted orator.

[1042] Gibbon, 1626.

[1043] Vasiliev, 254.

[1044] Norwich, (*APO*), 28.

had faced.[1045] A far more charismatic (and perhaps more deserving *Basileus*) commander was known as Thomas the Slav of Gaziura entering the scene as opponent to the Amorian. As he was a co-conspirator to Leo's assassination and Michael's soldier-confidant, he did not simply rise to rebel by chance. The 'anti-Amorian' faction even crowned Thomas as a rival *Basileus* at Antioch (despite his maimed leg as usually a disqualification to the throne) by the Caliph, enjoying his own appointed Patriarch and court which demonstrated even a certain charisma and urbanity.[1046]

This situation with Thomas the Slav reached deeply into Byzantine society politically, religiously, and socially, consuming the resources, legitimacy, and character of Michael II's reign. Economically, Thomas became a folk hero of justice against poverty by gutting taxation, excises, and the political abuse of the bureaucracy against the peasantry of the Empire. These three aspects were mainly as followed:[1047]

1) As he gathered a large army of multi-ethnic groups, mostly originating from the Balkan and Caucasus, it was demonstrated how Michael II's main threat was the loss of this area. Thomas's impetus also induced the Abbasid Caliph Mamun to ally with Michael's deserting forces.

2) Many fringe supporters adhered to Thomas and as Constantine VI's fate was never truly revealed, especially far in the East, Thomas claimed to be the deposed monarch. His show of Orthodoxy and icon-veneration won the population that rejected Iconoclasm.

3) Class struggles exploded in those divided areas that Thomas kept as his policy of supporting the peasantry to mass rebellions against landholders as oppressors. Imperial aid to this area was cut off and ignored, only enriching Thomas's cause.

The number of peasant rebellions against landowners along with the violence of the civil wars were characterized by Continuatis as 'some bursting cataract of the Nile flooding out the earth, not with water, but with blood.' His reputation as a commander gained him armies of every ethnic region imaginable – Georgian, Slav, Persian, Arab, Armenian,[1048] Isaurian – as well as

[1045] Ostrogorsky, 203.

[1046] Bury, (*ERE-I*), 38-39.

[1047] Vasiliev, 274-275.

[1048] A split of Armenian interests existed as Michael also had a strong Armenian backing from his Iconoclast religious policy. Certain Armenian families of the Black

Greek and the ideologically Iconoclast Paulicians. The strategy of which the above phenomena by Thomas's hand supported the successes he enjoyed until his final military defeat. Yet, Thomas was more cynical than the Iconoclasts, such as Constantine V, who showed conviction despite pragmatic concerns. Thomas appeared to have conceived that one argument was as good as another and professed his faith as practicality dictated.[1049] When in Michael's court, he was as Iconoclast as his *Basileus* and the army, yet when he was with Constantine VI, he just wore a different cloak for public support, all of which being compelling evidence that Iconoclasm was decaying.

Michael II's strenuous campaigns against Thomas, though ultimately successful, only worked to exhaust the army, leaving it vulnerable to the enemies of the eastern regions. It is little wonder that Constantine VII in his evaluation of Michael II a century later considered him a major setback that allowed the Adriatic and Balkan Slavs to arm themselves against the Empire. Compounding this concern was the fact that the navy had been seriously and irreparably neglected since the Umayyad civil wars due to disuse. The Byzantine naval forces resembled a hollow shell that waited to be crushed from above. Domestically, most situations were ably handled by the Amorian's wife, Euphrosyne, who met with the Senate through their wives, daughters, sisters, and others to plan receptions, raising funds and donations, awarding titles, and positions to female nobles.[1050] She was nothing less than a well-matched and dynamic 'First Lady' for Michael that brought etiquette to a *Basileus* known for his roughness.

Michael the Amorian was born in Anatolian Phryigia in 770 into a peasant family who received land grants from Justinian's Law. His origins were somewhat tainted with heresy as his patrons in Phrygia were the Cappadocian Athingans, the accursed 'Judaic' Iconoclast sect of Christianity, Michael also being a noted Iconoclast as well. It has, however, been likely and reasonable that he had Jewish blood,[1051] although he was identified as Christian. This 'rumor' even threatened somewhat the succession according to the historian Michael the Syrian (1126-1199), as a son of the *Basileus* and Euphronyse was secretly killed![1052] This was merely scandal as it must be remembered that the *Basilia*

---

Sea trade industry made up the court in Constantinople, and made a described from within a 'mafia' of Iconoclasm. Herrin, *(WIP)*, 188.

[1049] Jenkins, 76.

[1050] Herrin, *(WIP)*, 163.

[1051] Jenkins, 141.

[1052] Michael the Syrian. *The Chronicles.*

was never accused of Jewish heritage, only Michael, so killing a son of his and putting another on the throne seems a bit ludicrous. The whole province itself, in the central Anatolic region, has the reputation and consistency of a visitor being, 'among heretics, Hebrews, and half-Hellenized Phrygians.'[1053]

He joined the army and on his rise befriended both Leo the Armenian and Thomas the Slav. He was sparsely educated, illiterate, and could not commonly write the six letters in his own Greek name. But his military credentials gained him popularity as Justin I's had, despite such limitations. He was a member of Leo's officer corps and was made the Aide-to-the-Tent in his later campaigns. His reputation has been projected in depictions showing, made in the fourteenth century, that the murdered Leo was taken honorably from the Church as Michael is simultaneously crowned with dignity in manuscript portraits of the historian John Scylitzes, held now in Madrid.[1054]

When a plot was discovered in 820 by Hexaboulos the Logothete,[1055] Michael was imprisoned and was to be executed in a cruel manner by the emperor. On December 25, Michael was rescued and a few co-conspirators ruthlessly killed Leo V in front of the congregation attending the St. Sophia Christmas liturgies; he was even wearing the chains of his imprisonment as he ascended the throne. So also began a new dynasty to last most of the century under Michael II, the Phrygian, or more commonly, Amorian Dynasty. Despite his origins as a soldier, he was the favored candidate of the bureaucracy and not the army. The army preferred, of course, the co-conspirator Thomas the Slav as a more capable general and benefactor. His favor by the government officials was the pedestal of propaganda Thomas used to gain peasant support. Claiming, logically, as the government was corrupt and the government favored Michael, Michael must be corrupt and unfit to rule. This line of thought gained Thomas three years opposing the *Basileus* and nearly usurping the throne.

On Whit Sunday of 821, Michael made his seventeen-year-old son Theophilus co-*Basileus* as war broke out on the peripheral regions of the Paphlagonian, Bucellarian, and Cibyrrhaeot Themes, all of whom openly supported Thomas. Support was given to Thomas also because, oddly, he claimed to be the long-lost Constantine VI whose own fate was covered up by his mother, Irene. It was generally thought by the subjects of the outer

---

[1053] Vasiliev, 272.

[1054] Ostrogorsky, 204-205, fig. 35.

[1055] Hexabulos and Michael both proved their political flexibility when the former became an adviser to Michael as *Basileus* in later years, Bury, (*ERE-I*), 47. The Lisper was proving to be as ambiguous, and even contradictory, in policy as Leo was.

territories that Constantine had been tonsured without being maimed. Michael shored the closer Themes of the Optimates, Opsikians, Thracians, Armeniacs, and Chaldians as his ranks. To gain support, Michael recalled exiled Iconophile Bishops back to their dioces and offered the Patriarchy back to the now aged and exhausted Nicephorus, who declined. Although Michael was a tolerant and dubious Iconoclast in a time when Iconoclasm was 'lukewarm',[1056] he used moderation in his policies, but still appointed an Iconoclast Patriarch of Constantinople.

After driving out the Arabs of the Byzantine-held Themes of the East, Thomas took Theodosiopolis and made a peace with the Caliph Mamun to crown him *Basileus* at the Orthodox Bishopric of Antioch. Mamun even allowed this would-be ruler to recruit and field Christians from Armenia and Syria. After this, it was time for a siege on Constantinople and along with his border allies were the Themes of Greece and even far-off Sicily. He took advantage of Michael's naval weaknesses by assembling a fleet under Gregory Pterotus, leading a land army through Thessalonica, Macedonia, and Thrace, outnumbering the *Basileus*'s Thematic armies considerably. In December of 821, a massive invasion of 80,000 soldiers set to march on Constantinople.

In actions taken to continue the succession, on Whit Sunday, a 'bride show' was held for the seventeen-year-old son of the *Basileus*, Theophilus, who chose the Paphlagonian Theodora on the day of his ascension as co-*Basileus*. This was critical because after the death of Michael's first wife, Thekla, early in his reign, he vowed never to again marry. Such an action was unacceptable as an *Basilia* was needed to supervise court activities and accompany the *Basileus* to court ceremonies, palace rituals, and religious services, when necessary.[1057] Because of Michael's humble origins, a wife of imperial connection was necessary. So, Theophilus was then free, having imperial entitlement, to marry someone with a different background.

How vital Michael II's origins, or that of any emperor, would be to his legacy comes from the sneering insults of the Continuator of Theophanes: 'Michael was well versed in his own pursuits...he could tell if a litter of pigs were healthy and strong...how to stand up well to a kicking horse...and donkey. He was an excellent judge of a mule [and] distinguish the speed and stamina of a war-horse and which of your cows and sheep would be best for breeding or supplying

---

[1056] Treadgold, 434.
[1057] Herrin, *(WIP)*, 155-156.

milk . . .and on these he prided himself to no small degree.'[1058] Contempt and stigma would always be always the hazard of a peasant-ruler going back to Justin I in 512.

But the Walls of Constantinople at the Blacharnae quarter of the City where Thomas chose to invade put an end to Thomas's offensive, as his officers even tried to desert the following spring. On the Walls, the young prince Theophilus would walk in procession bearing the True Cross and the raiments of Christ to embolden the weary defenders.[1059] In the summer of 822, another fleet was raised from the Western Themes of Hellas, and the Peloponnese was destroyed by the *Basileus's* Greek Fire. Unfortunately for Michael, offensives were not an option as he was still entrenched in the City with inferior troops and ships that could not hold their own in open warfare. But, Michael did have one tactic left: reaching out to his Bulgar allies and forcing Thomas to submit to an invasion by the Khan, Omurtag.

Thomas's resources became strained fighting the Khan, though he showed great ability in doing so, and his disillusioned fleets surrendered to the Bulgars. In March, 823, Omurtag and his forces travelled from Mt. Haemus in Thrace to the plains of Kuduktos by Heraclea, winning a critical land victory against Thomas. In May, Michael seized the opportunity using the Opsikians and Armeniacs, and attacked the Slav's army routing it at the Diabasis by the Melas Rivers. Thomas returned to Arcadiopolis where by October of that year, the armies were forced to eat the rotting corpses of their own horses during the City's siege by Michael's forces.[1060] By then, it was said that the soldiers' ambitions for Thomas had cooled and they tired of shedding the blood of fellow Christians and kinsmen. Eventually, they retired to Constantinople to face the odds on 'Michael's clemency.'[1061]

By the war's end in the spring of 824, Arcadiopolis was successfully breached by the Amorian and Thomas was captured and publicly humiliated, his neck under the emperor's foot. Thomas's fate was to have his hands and feet cut off, the Slav defiantly sprinkling the City with his own blood, put on a mule's back to the Hippodrome,[1062] and to be impaled on a stake before the Walls he had once besieged. The emperor's next move was salvaging the remnants of a

---

[1058] Theophanes Continuatus. *Chronographia vol. I,* ed. by I. Bekker Leipzig, Germany. 1883, 43-44.

[1059] Bury, (*ERE-I*), 42.

[1060] Norwich, (*APO*), 35.

[1061] Bury, (*ERE-I*), 45.

[1062] Gibbon, 1626-1627.

broken Empire and trying to return it to a functioning state as his forces were close to ruin by three years of constant warfare, class rebellion, and internal strife.

Michael II released the opposing partisans in good faith and spread the word that Thomas was a rebel and a fraud by pretending to be a deposed emperor. To further show he had legitimacy with the throne over Thomas or even Leo, he married Euphrosyne, the daughter of Constantine VI, to commiserate his reign with legitimacy, military success, and Iconoclasm.[1063] Although this briefly associated Michael and the Amorian emperors with the success and Iconoclasm of the Isaurians, it did not make him a true Isaurian himself and the dynasty had been obsolete and dead since 797 anyway.

Irene was discounted in Roman law that no dynasty could be continued through the princess of the Empire without a prince or emperor to inherit property. The last of the Isaurian male heirs died years before if they were not blinded or tonsured. Perhaps the only Isaurian trait Michael had was the non-superstitious, rational attitude to icon veneration Leo III possessed, despite his Iconoclasm. Despite this, however, he still consulted 'soothsayers' and 'prophecies and omens' in his decisions, which was said to have originated from his Athingian upbringing.[1064] Though limited, some prestige remained in the army when it sacked Sozopetra a year later and bribed the Caliphate armies moving to retaliate, though this would be a compromise on the principle of using military action.

But by 826, the Byzantine military's cracks started to surface when a costly rebellion broke out in Sicily and the Emir of Qayrawan captured North Africa, taking Byzantine Syracuse as well. On June 14, 827, a fleet of 100 ships carrying 700 cavalry and 10,000 foot soldiers was outfitted to retrieve Syracuse, but this was averted when trouble occurred in the east Mediterranean.[1065] Finally, in 828, the issue was settled when Spanish Moor freebooters from Alexandria assaulted and settled on both the Greek isle of Crete and the Cyclades Islands south of Greece founding the moat-entrenched (handak) city of Chandax, or Candia, on the island.

From here and Sicily, offensives were made to capture Calabria and Apulia by the Straits of Messina and even to the Dalmatian coast of the Danube. This was just the beginning for the centuries-long tragedy of invasions and

---

[1063] Treadgold, 435.

[1064] Bury, (ERE-I), 35.

[1065] Norwich, (APO), 38.

turnovers for Palermo, Syracuse, and this region of the Mediterranean. Michael basically spent the year of 828 clearing out both fronts, further exhausting his naval resources. When a certain Euphemius attempted to rebel in Sicily and claim himself *Basileus*, he found himself abandoned by his African Arab allies, easily being defeated by the Basileus in Constantinople. It would prove to be a dangerous time to be an overly-ambitious general in Byzantine Sicily.

On October 2, 829, Michael II the Amorian died of kidney failure and his son Theophilus would smoothly succeed as *Basileus*. Though he was the founder of a new Byzantine dynasty, Michael started with blood on his hands and a number of other claimants just as legitimate he defiled in an all too typical trend in Byzantine imperial succession. Thomas the Slav never had the crown, but his victory would have had a better claim and foundation than Michael had, though with just as shocking a method of obtaining it. Thomas had the loyal support of the army (when he was succeeding in battle) and the peasant population saw him as a champion of social justice. Michael had little to show as a commander and ruler, but at least his moderate Iconoclasm made less martyrs to fight against his cause to mollify a previous establishment based on Leo's Synod of 815.

With all of his faults, he held a credible resistance in the civil war his own coup had started, yet, it was best said that his 'greatest contribution was to die in bed and leave a son nearly ready to succeed him.'[1066] He was also a stingy husband to his second wife, Euphrosyne, to whom he owed much of his legitimacy. As he always intended fully to be buried in the Church of the Holy Apostles next to his first wife, Euphronyse was left to rehabilitate a dilapidated monastery her grandmother had founded. As well as other benefactors from the City, and with endowments and funds, she also made a foundation. She would now be interred in her Monastery of Lady (*Kyra*) Euphronyse without her husband.[1067]

Michael was an Iconoclast to appease the army as Leo had done, and it was in his reign that relations with the West were strengthened as the rejection of icons was shared in the courts of Constantinople and Aachen. In 814, Charlemagne died and was succeeded in the German territories by his son, Louis I. Claudius, the Bishop of Turin was vocal in his repudiation of icons, images, relics, and even pilgrimages to holy sites. Paintings of higher note, however, were supposedly preserved in honor to those who could not read or

---

[1066]  Treadgold, 436.
[1067]  Herrin, *(WIP)*, 158-159.

write about their representations.[1068] For the further support of suppressing icons were also ecclesiastics such as those that rescinded the Second Council of Nicaea in 794, as Michael would submit in communications that Louis be cited as *'Imperator'* as well as King of the Franks.[1069]

In 824, Michael wrote a letter to Louis giving notice that Byzantium had also prohibited the Second Nicene Council and policies of Pope Hadrian I. The West had possibly based decisions on the Pagan Greek philosophies of Epicurus (341-270BCE),[1070] said to have been a hedonist and a materialist, consulted by Jewish and Talmudic elements in his works (of questionable substantiation). This same letter moved Louis to action in upholding Iconoclasm with the true 'horror stories' such as icons being made godparents to children in the Greek Empire, icons being used as altars in masses, and paint from icons being baked in the bread of the Eucharist and mixed in the wine to join the divine and mundane in Communion. The Host was even situated in the hands of icons to serve to the masses instead of the priest! Such materialist superstition and propaganda could only confound Michael as it did the first Isaurian rulers. In 827, a Byzantine embassador informed Michael on how Louis's court was taken with the works of the Greek Christian author Pseudo-Dionysus the Areopagite (5th-6th cent. CE), reminiscent of St. Denis. Along with bolts of magnificent silk, a deluxe edition of the theologian's works were sent to Aachen. Louis II would take it with pride as his Merovingian ancestors did in St. Denis, now buried near Paris.[1071]

Louis was shocked by this and hastily formed a decree of *Libellus Synodilus* that was presented in 825 in Paris before Pope Eugenius II. It made clear the Frankish disdain for idolatrous images and Pope Hadrian I himself for supporting the opposition. Though it was favorable to Byzantine ideas of Iconoclasm, it was not given the credence of a true ecumenical doctrine and was ignored[1072] as it was in 815 citing icons as a means of instruction. Western logic came from the studies of the Bishop of Lyon, Agobard, who claimed as Saint Augustine had said in 410 that Christ is the only mediation between Man and God and that images could not be included in this and had no place attempting to do so as matter over spirit.[1073]

---

[1068] Angold, 125.

[1069] Jenkins, 114.

[1070] Bury, (*ERE-I*), 52.

[1071] Herrin, (*WIP*), 164.

[1072] Norwich, (*APO*), 40.

[1073] Angold, 119.

However, it was not the icon at all that was the true issue when imperial authority was questioned, just a mask. The incident involving the monk Methodius, as one of Leo V's closest advisers, was just such an example as he brought to the Constantinopolitan court a letter from Pope Paschal I to return to the 'true faith.' Michael, in a rage, immediately had Methodius imprisoned in St. Andreas on the Gulf of Nicomedia until released by the more sober Theophilus. It was the primacy of Pope over Patriarch and *Basileus* that isolated Byzantium from icons in a more political sense.

As his predecessor had created the Hetaireia to secure the Palace, Michael II sought great need in recruiting the Fortiers that added vital protection to the border forts from the Bulgars and Arabs. These Fortiers were paid an annual forty *nomismata*,[1074] but were not considered a more elite force as payrolls of 842 would demonstrate. Out of the XII pay grade strata of the entire force, the one-half pound of gold received was considered Grade IX as Grade I was the highest for Strategi and Domestics. This was based on records under Theophilus in 842 as the last year of his reign kept by modern economic historian Nicolas Oikemendes in the *Tacticon Upensky 'Listes'* of 1964.[1075]

Still, rebellion needs attention, which meant more funds and more taxes while terrible droughts, animal pestilence, and military devastation caused small landholders and peasants to sell to the larger estates when taxes could not be paid.[1076] This 'vicious cycle' of disenfranchisement led to rebellion with the poor becoming serfs and urban poor having no skills joining the military machine which would be the best way, relatively, to earn wages. Thus, a sad pattern can be seen between the poverty caused by the budget of a military machine and the further enlistments of the victims of that poverty to a fragile army.

Also during Michael's reign, the status of the Slav nations was undergoing changes and improvements. The '. . .cities of Dalmatia . . .Serbians and Croats and Serb, Zachlumites, Terbuniotes, Kanalites, Diocletians, and Pagani shook off the empire of the Romans in a self-governing fashion never seen before.'[1077] Slavonic independence was now an issue as Michael lacked the energy and resources to mount resistance to these revolutions. In the realm of education and literacy, the Byzantines were attempting to outfit the Slavs with a workable universal alphabet compatible with their various dialects, although success

---

[1074] Decker, 79.

[1075] Treadgold, *(BAIA)*, 122-123.

[1076] Jenkins, 143-144.

[1077] Porphyrogenitus, 125.

would not be achieved until 862. This began as a project to Slavonize the Moravian liturgy of the Scriptures, which could only be translated at the time in Hellenistic Greek.

# THEOPHILUS
## (829-842)

Where his father was poorly educated and basically illiterate, Theophilus was highly educated and had a more enlightened approach in ruling the Empire. He was truly 'a romantic...with a strong sense of justice in a theatrical manner,'[1078] who was a unique ruler that was only characterized mostly by limited evidence and the biases of Iconodulists. A famous passage by the poem *Byzantium* by William Butler Yeats (1865-1939) shows clear evidence the splendor the Empire offered under this new *Basileus*:

> *'Miracle, bird or golden handiwork,*
> *More miracle than bird or handiwork,*
> *Brought on the star-lit golden bough,*
> *Can like the cocks of Hades crow*
> *Or, like the moon embittered, scorn aloud,*
> *In glory of changeless metal*
> *Common bird or petal*
> *And all complexities of mire or blood.'*

This testament, made a thousand years after the events, gave praise to the technical and scientific wonders created by a grandiose and dramatic *Basileus* through his *Potothauma*[1079] ('Prime Miracle') of machinery. Through the study of mechanics from the East came the Oriental splendor of a court of golden clockwork birds whose songs came from a golden organ hidden in the Arabic menagerie where they 'roosted' in the Palace of the Magnaura. A gold plane tree was its base, surrounded by gryphons and lions as the jeweled birds even seeming to 'fly' about and land on the throne. Inspired by the court of Harun al-Rashid in 809, Theophilus built all of this as a model of his dedication to art and science.

More so, it represented the promise of peace, learning from the East, and

---

[1078] Ostrogorsky, 206-207.
[1079] Norwich, (APO), 46.

the genius Theophilus had in glorifying himself and the Empire. His imitations of Arabic culture may also have been more evidence for his dedicated defense of Iconoclasm, whose theology was partially fostered and supported by Islamic laws. This could have damned him historically as in literary works such as the twelfth-century 'Dialogues of the Dead', or *Timarion,* of Lucian (120-192 CE), where his Iconoclasm fated him to Hades. His attribute of justness, however, made him a mythical Judge of the Dead as Minos and Rhadamanthys[1080] instead of those of the damned.

Yet, it is other poetry on Theophilus that demonstrates the severity behind the splendor, in the form of his hatred of heresy and of icon veneration. Two noted craftsman of such icons, Theophanes and Theodore, both writers and hymnists, were made an example of for peddling their wares in Constantinople. As Studites that would not recant when the emperor offered them clemency, they were branded on the face a *graptoi* of twelve poetic lines with hot irons, carefully molded for the occasion, with both heretics ultimately being banished:'In that fair town where sacred streets were trod/Once by the pure feet of the Word of God/ - The city all men's hearts desired to see/ - These evil vessels of perversity/Were driven forth to this our City where/Persisting in their wicked, lawless ways/They are condemned and branded in the face/As scoundrels driven to their native place.'[1081]

The latter half of his reign also saw deep hostilities from the Caliphate in Baghdad and hostile impacts unseen since the days of Heraclius. He championed a losing battle in the Empire's religion, showed little in military exploit, and did not possess the greatest sense of statesmanship.[1082] Yet, ability saved the *Basileus* and the state domestically through economic stability, a strong sense of social justice, and a new policy of loyalty and relative harmony in the Thematic armies. Glory is what Theophilus sought and glory did he achieve with his administrator/scientists and learned men.

He had learned both Greek and Latin, copied manuscripts, inventing a new type of lamp, learning astronomy, natural history, painting, and theology.[1083] A renaissance of Greek science and Arabic thought paved the way for future upsurging of Hellenic culture in the centuries of the High Byzantine period. He had a complicated relationship, however, with the monk Patriarch Methodius of

---

[1080] Jenkins, 148; Vasiliev, 497.

[1081] *Norwich, (APO),* 50-51.

[1082] Bury, *(ERE-I),* 53.

[1083] Buckler, 208.

Syracuse, imprisoning him for treason due to a mere 'prophesy' on a pamphlet only releasing him later due to his knowledge of Latin and love of the occult. This betrays a character also fickle at times and instituted with some Pagan superstition as well as endorsed by his father.[1084]

Theophilus was born in his father's homeland, Phrygia in Amorium (said to be the 'eye and foundation of Christianity'[1085]) in 813 to Michael II and his wife Thekla, almost immediately being made co-*Basileus*. Upon this event, he went parading through Constantinople bearing the fragments of the True Cross and the Robe of the Virgin, recently discovered in a grave in the Church of the Holy Apostles. Unfortunately, before his imperial accession on October 2, 829, little is known about him besides his religious devotion and impressive education.

What was clear was that the dying Michael II had expected his wife Euphrosyne to be regent for his son; when she accused her uncle Manuel of treason, this court member of the 'Armenian mafia' fled.[1086] Though his stepmother was able, she played a rather junior part in the young emperor's decisions, mainly because of her Iconophilism and by displaying a rare, independent spirit. He later also showed a love for his family by commemorating his children and wife on coinage, presenting his mother-in-law the title of a 'High Patrician Lady', *Zoste Patrikia*, wearing the girdle of office at court.[1087]

One thing the regent was responsible for was leading another bride show for Theophilus to choose from and in 830 his only wife and the bearer of his son and heir, Theodora, was made *Basilia*. Being hailed by the Senate, she then sailed across the Bosporus to the Palace of Hiera. As in the tale of Paris and the golden apple, Theophilus presented one to his 'choice' of bride as a sign of his selection, though it is recorded that he found women to be the fount of all evil and argued with his mother over the pride of Eve versus the virtues of Mary.[1088] Theodora was trying to the *Basileus*, not just as an Iconophile, but in more traditional matters as well. Once, to secure funds, she secretly kept a merchant vessel in the City's harbor for speculation. Upon discovery, Theophilus's affront of the ancient Roman custom of of keeping the noble class and all types of merchant business separate induced him to have the vessel and all wares aboard it burned.[1089] This is one example of the Classical ideas the

---

[1084] Herrin, *(WIP)*, 194-195.
[1085] Vasiliev, 276.
[1086] Herrin, *(WIP)*, 188.
[1087] *ibid.*, 173.
[1088] *ibid.*, 190.
[1089] Bury, *(ERE-I)*, 53.

*Basileus* held in which commerce and nobility (the Senate, the court, and the landholders) should not meet.

Eventually, Euphrosyne realized she could not control her stepson and was made to retire to a convent. Unfortunately, she was persecuted when the *Basileus* discovered she, in 838, had been venerating icons and, like Leo IV, he had her permanently isolated from her daughters. This was the source of a story made up at the *Basileus*'s expense by a jester called Denderis in Theophilus's court, in which he caught Theodora once venerating icons. But it was explained away as being dolls the Empress kept and the jester only saw them in a reflection of her mirror, only *resembling* icons. This tale was a favorite among the icon worshipers after Theophilus's death to relate that the virtues of Iconophilism will always triumph over foolish heresy. Eventually, the *Basileus* was released and would stand by her husband in times of doubt with the Senate, even looking for patterns of dissension and possible rebellion in the City, communicating messages through the credit of her ring (*enklepion*) or a cross known to be hers.[1090]

Theophilus also made a bold choice in executing the assassins of Leo V, a plot in which his father was directly involved. Claiming the murder of an emperor was inexcusable under any circumstances as it was a matter of abiding by the law of *Imperium,* the *Basileus* enjoyed not to be used for personal reasons or gain. Cynically put, it was an act to set legitimacy to a dynasty Theophilus knew began in bloodshed[1091] for him, yet still worked among his court. The next year, he even received acclamation and a Roman triumph for the defeat of Arab raiders in Armenia using the Scholae, Manuel. He kept an honest and strict court, wherein even the courtiers, along with servants, were required to cut their hair to his specifications.

This triumph was a splendid affair both showing the power, devotion, and amazing prosperity of Constantinople and its *Basileus.* On a white horse with a bejeweled harness and scepter he rode to the Palace of Heira to be greeted and kissed on the hem of his robe by the Senators, the *Basilia*, the Praepositus, the Magister, and the Prefect.[1092] Pulling a train of Arab captives and slaves, Theophilus then visited in procession from the Baths of Zeuxippus to the Hippodrome and the Great Palace by its tunnels in the Kathisma where a sort of joust was performed between a Greek and an Arab captive to be unhorsed.

---

[1090] Herrin, *(WIP)*, 177.

[1091] Bury, *(ERE-I)*, 54.

[1092] *ibid.,* 55-56. The obeisance of kissing the hem or knees of the *Basileus* was a custom added by the research in Herrin's *Women in Purple.*

The necessity to 'augment his reputation of splendor and magnificence'[1093] knew no bounds as he once arranged the theft of a gold, gem-encrusted dinner bowl on an Arab envoy. The discomfort of the gathering would be removed when Theophilus calmly asked an identical one he had brought to be used instead. He reveled in entertaining his people as when he assembled in the City in the Hippodrome and scandalously joined in the chariot races with the Blues, though his skills were compromised by 'fixed outcomes.'[1094]

Yet, there is no end to the evidence that at all times the treasury was brimming with gold and more than ample.[1095] Though he insisted on modeling himself after Constantine V's policies, the state budget had risen from 1,920,000 *nomismata* in 775, to 3,086,000 *nomismata*. In 842, as all pay scales were increased, Theophilus still sported a surplus in 60,000 *nomismata* over Constantine's 20,000.[1096] His splendor and showmanship stretched across the continent as when he sent his wife Theodora, beautiful and unveiled, to the Spanish Caliph in asking for aid. Unused to seeing a woman of such beauty with no veil mystified him and the court poet of Cordoba, Abu Zakkariya Yahya ibn al-Hakkam al-Bakri al-Jayyani al-Ghazzal ('the Gazelle') (d. 864), recorded his admiration as a 'rising sun in beauty' in her fine imperial raiments.[1097]

Also, in 830, Theophilus took Arab Zapetra and Cilicia as Arab activity only intensified in 832 as the Spanish pirates of Sicily took Panormus (modern Palermo). The Caliph Mamun invaded Cappadocia after rebuking an offer of peace constituting 100,000 gold *dinars* and 7,000 prisoners for a five-year truce. Mamun would prove to be as formidable and as dangerous as Harun al-Rashid, being a master of the situation balancing the Western and Eastern fronts of Asia, aligning forces while Byzantium was presently concerned with Sicily.[1098]

In 831, they went so far as to build a permanent fortress in Byzantine Taurus known as Tyana which proved its worth by taking Lulon at the Cilician Gates. A boon went to the Empire when Mamun died in August 833 in Cappadocia, his successor al-Mu'tasim dissembling Tyana and withdrawing from the region.

---

[1093] Theophanes Cont., 95-99.

[1094] Brownworth, 160.

[1095] Treadgold, 439. He also personally appropriated the payroll amounts for soldiers in his great 840 reforms with the level of a skilled bureaucrat. All was said to have been financed well, with no need for debt spending.

[1096] Treadgold, (BAIA), 196.

[1097] Herrin, (WIP), 200. From the works of Al-Maqqadi, *Histories of the Mohammedan Dynasties in Spain*, bk. 4., ed. by P. de Gayangos. New York, NY. 1964.

[1098] Ostrogorsky, 208.

It was seen as the divine favor shown to Constantine V for rejecting icons, still the strongest argument for Iconoclasm, as antiquated as the idea was. More so, the real success of securing the borders proved to be in the arrangement and control of the region's Themes. However, an advantage for the Arabs existed where Caliphate revenue annually towered over Byzantium at 35,000,000 to the Empire's 2,000,000 *nomismata* in 800. The administration of military lands under Theophilus was the advantage over weak cash revenues in which the *Basileus* would become dependent upon.[1099]

More good fortune came from Persia as the Khurramite peoples defeated 14,000 men at the Zagros Mountains, pledging themselves to Christ and the Byzantine army from Armenia. Their leader, Nasr, was gratefully received by Theophilus and was married off to a sister-in-law of the *Basileus*. Under the name Theophobus, his Khurramites created the Persian Turmae companies of the army, increasing them some thirty percent. The military's cavalry size also changed from twenty percent to the Centarchate (100 companies) to stabilize the numbers from the pre-840 ten-to-thirty percent.[1100] The Khurramites, however, were enemies of the Caliphate and it is this act more than any other which caused the open hostility of Mamun against the Empire.

But the fleets of the Caliphate would prove, once again, superior to Byzantine sea power and in 835 a Sicilian expedition failed, capturing most of the Byzantine fleet. Furthermore, frontier campaigns against Arab looters resulted in another defeat and heavy losses as prizes were seized by the raiders, chipping away at Byzantine confidence. The emperor had more success with the Bulgars, returning 40,000 Byzantine prisoners to imperial territories after twenty years of captivity in Bulgaria since Nicephorus I's defeat there in 811.

The Bulgarians raided Thrace, but Theophilus's Caesar and son-in-law, Alexius Musele, recovered land between Thessalonica and Thrace lost since 816, inducing the Persian Khan Malamir to agree to a ten-year peace treaty. Perhaps emboldened by these developments with the land army, Theophilus collected a force of 70,000 to raid the Caliphate itself in 837.[1101] At the time, the Caliph's back was turned as he was attacking the Persian Khurramites at Azerbaijan. The Khurramites ejected from Azerbaijan now joined the Byzantines, putting the Persian Turmae at 30,000. Theophilus re-captured cities on the Antitaurus, all according to the lost work of the Arab historian Abu

---

[1099]  Treadgold, *(BAIA)*, 210.

[1100]  *ibid.*, 106.

[1101]  Treadgold, 440.

Umar Shalih ibn Ishaq al-Jarmi al-Bashri al-Nahwi (d. 840), taken in a raid of 837 and later returned in 845.[1102]

In 838, Theophilus sent more ships to Sicily, Crete, and the southern Italian mainland to retrieve the contended Byzantine territories. In June of 839, he sought the aid of Louis II at Ingelheim and a successful diplomacy was enacted, allying East and West against the Arab freebooters of the Eastern Mediterranean. Perhaps even North Africa and Egypt was policed as well, as this was seen as a 'massive Frankish descent'[1103] in the region as Theophilus also promised a granddaughter to Louis in marriage. The emperor even went so far as to petition aid from the Umayyad court in Spain,[1104] being a rival of the Abbasids as well, as the Byzantines then defended themselves against Baghdad's retaliation. In April, it came in spades as 50,000 Arabs invaded the Cilician Gates and 30,000 more entered Eastern Byzantium through the Pass of Melitene. It was Caliph Mu'satim's strategy to capture the subject of the lone word on his banner, *Amorium*, as he conquered the Anatolics as a symbol of dominance and moral defeat as the homeland of Theophilus's dynasty. Even before these military solutions would occur, the *Basileus* would have ambassadors spreading, in the streets of Baghdad, thousands of gold coins that still could not assuage the Caliph.[1105]

Theophilus and his military confidantes, Theophobus ('God-Fearing') and Manuel the Scholae, countered in the region with a contingent of 40,000, giving battle on the plains of Dazimon in the Armeniac on July 22, 839. But the Caliph had employed 10,000 Turkish archers whose superior skills routed the Byzantines, surrounding the 2,000 men Theophilus personally led. Traitors in the Persian Turmae even attempted to capture and hand the Basileus over to the enemy for their safe passage, and would have succeeded had it not been for a timely rescue by Manuel.

These rebellious Khurramites then hailed Theophobus *Basileus* at the city of Sinope. Theophilus had to abandon his war and return to Constantinople to literally guard his throne as Mu'tasim took Ancyra and burned Amorium, killing some 35,000 inhabitants – half its population. Many were sealed up

---

[1102] Treadgold, *(BAIA)*, 64. However, an Arab historian, Ibn-Khurradadibh, writing from 847-870 somewhat preserved what we know of al-Jarmi's work as mentioned in Decker, 76-77.

[1103] Jenkins, 150. But all fell apart on Louis's death in 840 and the ascension of his son, Lothar.

[1104] Vasiliev, 277.

[1105] Brownworth, 160f.

in churches and burned alive while others were enslaved, taken through the desert to die with no water – out of thousands, only forty-two people survived to the Palace at Samarra. These were the 'Forty-Two Martyrs of Amorium' who died rather than convert to Islam returning to Samarra on March 6, 845. As the story of the martyrdom tells, out of six martyrs selected by the enemy for execution, five headless bodies were tossed into the Tigris and the Christians would not sink; the sixth, however, the executed Arab general Boiditzes, sank as he was a Muslim.[1106]

Now, Theophilus reached a period of personal crisis as the losses of the Empire and his family's homeland put him into shock. He was struck 'gravely ill' and, despairingly, this educated man went to astrology to learn his fate and all that followed was civil strife. He spent time persecuting Iconophiles in the City, as well as his stepmother Euphrosyne in her nunnery, and imprisoning Alexius Musele, recalling him from Sicily on suspicion of rebellious intent. In 841, he finally struck at Theophobus at Sinope and regained the alliance of the Khurramite Persians and their leader. The securing of this Persian alliance was for adopting the purpose of checking 30,000 soldiers that Theophilus decided to re-organize into Themes north of the Bosporus and on the Black Sea coast. This was not unusual as, for example in 840, one change was a separation of the *Hetaireia* into three levels, staffed by Turkish Khazars of South Russia and the Iranian plateaus. They were to be manned by defected Arabs and Persians, bucking Theophilus's reputation as a kind of 'equal opportunity' ruler by foreigners.[1107]

The Turmae was modified into Thematic soldiers and 20,000 of them were divided evenly into the Macedonian, Thracian, Optimate, and seven of the Anatolic Themes. Some regions were re-assigned kleisura ('Mountain Passes') such as Cappadocia, Seleucia, and the Armeniac Turma of Charsianum, each gaining 2,000 Persians. Dyrrachium and Cherson were both promoted as Themes with 2,000 troops[1108] as Theophilus wisely used the area as a military buffer to the increasing threat of the Rus and other Viking tribes. They were known for invading the Crimean end of the Bosporus and Amastris in Asia Minor, though mostly they were merchants also checked in power by the Swedish Norsemen.[1109]

---

[1106] Norwich, (*APO*), 49.

[1107] Decker, 87.

[1108] Treadgold, 443-444.

[1109] Obolensky, 182.

These holdings on the northern Black Sea coast were the klimata that used Cherson as its center, organizing what would be used in the modern organization of the South Crimean region. The Khagars of the region supplicated to the emperor to send his engineers to build a city for their defenses, and Theophilus appointed a navy and troop regiment to build the city of Sarkel under the supervision of Petronas Camaterus.[1110] Theophilus would eventually build on this to re-organize all the Crimeas into his Theme system of the Cherson. This region would eventually develop from mere fishing villages to a hub of international trade from the Bosporus and the Eurasian Steppes.

There, under the commander Petronas, they also received ships from the Paphlagonian Theme. Constantine VII mentions that the promotion Petronas received was a wise decision, chosen as a matter of being a leader of local experience and not a military governor from Constantinople. This decision made possible the chance of further expansion based on commanders that understood this region, its geography, its customs, and the best way to arm them. This is where the remaining 4,000 Persians were stationed, though just a shadow of what it once was. On a more micro-scale, Theophilus divided the 1,000 Drungoi of each Theme to five Banda of 200 to tighten supervision and efficiency. This also included headquarters and a new type of commander known as a *Comes* ('Count') that replaced the hundred-man Centarch, lowering the numbers by half. This resulted in lessening the amount of petty military officers also by eliminating the Pentacontarchs of 500 men.[1111]

The success of this system can be evaluated by the repulsion of Caliphate armies from Cappadocia in 840, thanks to the disciplined Persians settled there. Cappadocia was then made a Theme, improvised for one of the few rebukes against the Arabs from Byzantine Syria happening in these campaigns. The Themes on the northeastern borders of the Empire kept those other borders unbreached by the Arabs in a stunning succession of victories both offensive and defensive. When the Arabs also ran across Charsianum, the Byzantines and Persians drove them back and even raided Arab-held Adata and Germanicea. Finally, when Cretan raiders attempted to land and invade Thrace, the Thracian armies soundly defeated them as well. In a matter of one year, three major defeats plagued the Caliphate and the security of Byzantium was a goal truly attained.

On January 20, 842, Theophilus would die of dysentery with an Empire

---

[1110] Obolensky, 175-176.
[1111] Treadgold, *(BAIA)*, 104f.

assured that the tide of Arab invasion would be well-stemmed by his re-organizations over a citizen population of 8,000,000 and 1.7 percent of that being his army.[1112] The greatest irony of his death was religious, however, as Theodora feared for her unrepentant Iconoclast husband from Hell and the punishments of the Last Judgment (a common belief of Mary Theotokos's worship). Reports of the emperor's 'nightmares' of divine retribution and postmortem conversion in Heaven was reported by the Empress as Theophilus's name would now 'miraculously' disappear from the lists of known heretical Iconoclasts read on certain feasts.[1113]

In 842, Mu'tasim outfitted a fleet of 400 Dromonds, ships lighter and speedier than the Dromoi, to invade Constantinople on the Bosporus. Winter storms hit the seas and only seven of the original ships made it back to Samarra. Mu'tasim himself never learned of this as he had died on January 5, just two weeks before Theophilus. There were many other goals reached by the *Basileus* during his thirteen-year reign that included the enlightening of the Byzantine mind as well as the shadow of Iconophilism in his realm. In 831, the Iconophile monks and clergy of the Empire led by Methodius and the defrocked Bishop of Sardis, Euthymius, began circulating Iconodule pamphlets. These were futile efforts, however, as Iconoclasm was already losing followers and efficacy; one Theodore the Confessor compares it to a wriggling, dying snake where debatable questions were merely silenced and tolerant attitudes were put into politics in practice.[1114]

Whether it was mere speculative punishment that God gave to heretics, or a real threat to be carried out, this pamphlet 'predicted' an imminent death of Theophilus. This odd protest against Iconoclasm and its results were the capture and beatings of both men, Euthymius even dying of his injuries.[1115] It was a strange and somehow unsettling beginning to yet another new policy of persecution attacking icons and images. Little time could be spent on this ecclesiastical policy between Arab incursions; in 833, John the Grammarian, as Bishop of Sylaion, Anthony, and Theophilus gave new authority to the Synod of 815 employed by Leo V. Imprisonment and confiscation of land and property was the penalty of any who did not share communion with the Iconoclasts. Some penalties included ranking members of the civil and military authorities

---

[1112] Treadgold, *(BAIA)*, 162.

[1113] Herrin, *(WIP)*, 204-205.

[1114] Dobroklonsky, A. *Blessed Theodore the Confessor and Abbot of Studion*, bk. I. Odessa, Russ., 849-850. 1913.

[1115] Treadgold, 437.

mutilated, boiled in pitch, or burnt alive in the Hippodrome, as it was said that to keep control of the habits of subjects was used 'only with a rod of iron.'[1116]

When Caliph Ma'mun died that year, Theophilus saw this as divine favor to the rejection of icons in the Empire and later, in 838, the *Basileus* appointed one of his best academic minds, John VII, as the Patriarch of Constantinople. John's superlative education in writing and oratory made him a natural choice in the realm of interpreting Scripture, the Church Fathers, and other theology to uphold Iconoclasm. It took small effort in anathematizing icon veneration and ordering all icons destroyed on sight. Civil servants were the most disenfranchised by the Iconoclast regimes due to their mainly militaristic character.[1117] Like the Grammarian, they had a great talent for debate over the theological issues due to their superior education. Yet when it came to the persecutions, it was only the icons and their practitioners in the capital itself that received such heavy handedness.[1118] However, on the Empire's periphery, icon worship and art still flourished in Greece and Asia Minor, Iconoclasm having very strict geographical boundaries. It was ultimately evaluated that Theophilus's endeavors, though harsh and cruel in his endeavors to preserve Iconoclasm, were still fruitless.[1119]

Success in religious practice was a stamp of most imperial reigns, but the more extraordinary reigns are the ones adopting sound fiscal policies resulting from the efficiency of trade and arms that mostly the flow of cash would demonstrate. Theophilus seems to fit this definition on both counts: in 835, he began a new monetary policy of minting copper *folles* in smaller transactions at a new rate of six times the original value. This increased the coin's size to balance the worth of the copper, but it further made smooth transitions into the exchange rate of gold in trade. Everywhere, these copper coins were seen increasing trade and soldier pay with the emperor's portrait and the relief, 'Theophilus Augustus, You Conquer.'[1120] Already in 833, he chose his own portraiture on his coins to continue the secularist tradition of Iconoclasm. Oddly, though, one side portrayed his two daughters, Anna and Anastasia as he, on the obverse, was flanked by Theodora and his mother, Thekla. With

---

[1116] Gibbon, 1627-1628.

[1117] Angold, 92.

[1118] Vasiliev, 286.

[1119] Gibbon, 1627. He was even given a surname that has not survived speculation as 'the Unfortunate.'

[1120] Treadgold, 440.

four females gracing one coin, this was a highly unusual and bold tribute to his family.[1121]

This influx also increased the minting of gold coins to double the pay of soldiers as well-paid soldiers made for loyal and hard-working soldiers. Analysis suggests it was this wage boom in the army that led to its wonderful Thematic defenses in the later years of Theophilus's reign (especially in 840). As common soldiers had received five *nomismata* annually for their service since Constans II's time, now the soldiers would receive an extra *nomismata* for every year since they began service at a maximum of twelve *nomismata*. By his death in 842, Theophilus would leave a 7,000,000 *nomismata* reserve[1122] in the imperial treasury noted as around 22,000,000 American gold dollars, this was counted as one-third the amount Anastasius I saved in the sixth century.[1123]

Where this gold came from is less a recorded fact; modern historians investigate the question and conclude that the frugality of Michael II could not have generated one-tenth of the revenue Theophilus supplied and the surplus came from the opening of certain mines in Armenia.[1124] Theophilus never ran into debt, always had a surplus, and abandoned his father's policy of a 'rigid economy.' Numerous occasions are chronicled where the artists of the imperial court had no want of gold and jewels in their crafts and gave generous donations, such as the Arab embassy and the 'stolen bowl' incident, as they received 36,000 *nomismata* for their troubles.

With this flexible arrangement of funds available, Theophilus was responsible for major militaristic changes and reforms putting him in a higher class of administrator. He secured borders in the Sicilian, Thessalonican, and Thracian regions by increasing their soldier rolls from 1,000 in 809 to 4,000 apiece. This created the Chersonese and Dyrrachium Themes to station Khurramites, the latter he made negotiations in assaulting the Abbasid and enhance his own military ability.[1125] He also had the resources to increase Anatolian and Armeniac Thematic soldiers for a total of 120,000 land troops[1126]. A pay grade scale of twelve XII levels based on gold poundage and *nomismata* from the Fyodor Upensky (1845-1928) records of the modern

[1121]  Herrin, *(WIP)*, 191.

[1122]  Treadgold, 445.

[1123]  Diehl, 93.

[1124]  Jenkins, 147.

[1125]  Decker, 143.

[1126]  Treadgold, *(BAIA)*, 67. The status of the navy changed little as its numbers of its oarsmen stayed static throughout the entire ninth century.

Byzantine economic historian, Oikonomedes (1934-2000), is drawn up in Warren Treadgold's *Byzantium and Its Army*[1127] to toll the proper hierarchy of soldiers and officers. It is noted in figures, however, that the salaries of most senior officers did not change between 811 and 840 and the highest scale of ten *nomismata* (two *annonae*) was never reached with top wages under Theophilus as nine *nomismata* annually.[1128]

Relatively, the troops of Khurramites and Persians of the Cherson received special attention due to their size and Theophilus made great concessions to provide for their welfare. They were provided with wives from prominent Byzantine military families for their own status, infusing the nobility into their hierarchy. They were given military lands to farm under the former laws; most plots of land were worth seven pounds of gold over the traditional five, the latter amount being worth 720 *modi* of land (144 acres).[1129] At the going rate, the Khurramites were entitled by grants to 1,008 *modi* (roughly 202 acres).

This also bankrolled the *Basileus*'s ambitious architectural programs of splendor and luxury in Constantinople. In the Palace was the Syrian-originated[1130] Oriental design of the Triconchos, 'Triple-Shell', with its three apses and pillars of rich porphyry and multi-colored stone, as well as the half-moon hall of the Sigma. Shelters, gardens, and solariums were surmounted by quaint, pine-cone style fountains of decoration. Silver doors led from here to the Hall of Pearl[1131] with pristine white marble floors, decorated with mosaic and more pillars of rose-pink hue. The Karianos bedchamber for the imperial daughters was named for its milky Carian marble staircase from east Persia; the opposite Kamiles was supported by pillars of green Thessalian marble and purple Egyptian porphyry. Elsewhere, in the name of needed humility, he built the hostel for the poor and wayward known as the *Xenon* of Theophilus.[1132]

The secular art of the Iconoclast was praised with the field of mosaics above all, depicting fruit harvests and nature scenes, laid under a roof of gold. The symbolism of fruit in Eastern art alluded to the ancient Persian and Assyrian idea of fertility and, therefore, prosperity. Theophilus thus demonstrated

---

[1127] *Treadgold,(BAIA),* 122-123.

[1128] *ibid.,* 143f.-144.

[1129] *ibid.,* 174.

[1130] Bury, *(ERE-I),* 56-57.

[1131] Norwich, *(APO),* 44.

[1132] Herrin, *(WIP),* 198; Magdalino, Paul. Constantinople medieval, 46-47. Mango, Cyril. Le Developpment Urbain de Constantinople (IVe-VII siecles). Paris, France. 1990, 17-18.

the Oriental influence of Christian ideas sharing the same values of artistic symbolism in the harvesting of fruit for fertility. In an impressive display of ingenuity on the *Basileus*'s part was the 'Cabinet of Five Towers' (*Pentapymioi*) in the Magnaura, at four stories tall, to bear and display the religious artifacts and other interests of the *Basileus*.[1133]

Across from the Marmara on the Bythinian coast was Bryas, home of a shining Palace of golden automaton, once again patterned after the Oriental Arab style, and basically an Abbasid 'pleasure dome'.[1134] Not all of his building was for aesthetics, however, as Theophilus also strengthened the Sea Walls of the Bosporus shore and heightened almost the entirety of the City Walls. Unlike Leo III, Theophilus was never called 'Saracen-Minded' by his people or by his historians, perhaps to denote a shift in public morals to somewhat accept foreign culture and not brand it as odd or offensive to Greek sensibility. Like the great Harun al-Rashid, Theophilus was said to disguise himself and roam the streets at night to hear the laments of people and investigate the bazaars to inspect the wares available and the quality and prices of food such as bread, wine, fish, and vegetables.[1135] Ethnic paradigms, also from the toleration, were involved when Theophilus made his military law that 'Mohammedan Persians and Romans' could marry where before only Orthodox could only marry Orthodox. [1136]

He was also known for public appearances in the streets of Constantinople, riding a chariot from the Palace to personally aid in the sufferings of the City's poor and destitute. On Fridays, he would ride from the Palace to the Church of the Blacharnae and hear petitions from his people. The most famous example is one concerning an old woman who was defrauded a horse by one of the City's civil servants. The official was punished and the horse returned; this event is elegantly depicted by a thirteenth-century Sicilian illustration in John Skylitzes's *Chronicle*. In these later centuries until the Fall of 1453, this became an official ceremony known as the *Kavilakeuma*, or 'riding out'.[1137] This was usually for drama's sake to earn popularity, but it worked in making

---

[1133]  Bury, (*ERE-I*), 58.

[1134]  Angold, 90.

[1135]  Jenkins, 147; Norwich, (*APO*), 43.

[1136]  Bury, (*ERE-I*), 53-54. Jenkins also said how thousands of easterners were settled in Anatolia, 'intensifying a hybrid nature in the population', 148, with an open-door policy. This could only have come from the adoption of the Persian Themes gained by the Khurramites.

[1137]  Herrin, 75, plate 32 visualizes the event.

a connection between the people and the sovereign, whose loyalty he needed. Also, to amuse his populace was his demonstrations as a lover of Greek athletics, acrobatics, gymnastics, camel acts, and even high wire shows were common in the Hippodrome.[1138]

In the field of Classical studies and research, the educated and cultured Theophilus exemplified the origins of the Byzantine renaissance in the ninth and tenth centuries. A new period of Classical thought and education was rooted from the cultured scholarship the emperor demanded of John the Grammarian to provide in defending Iconoclasm with Scriptural, Patristic, and sophistical arguments.[1139] The increase in the writing of manuscripts and scriptoria was due to a contribution of a new use of uncial over miniscule types of writing. The larger printing style made it easier to copy and translate to a broader range of copyists[1140]; would even be used in 1476 when Johannes Guttenburg (1400-1468) invented formal type print, making it a certain standard. Theophilus would use this method to formulate, but not to perfect, a workable Slavonic alphabet. A rapport with the Arabic East between the Caliph, John the Grammarian, and Leo the Mathematician, a. k. a. 'the Philosopher', would see the transmission west of ancient Greek scientific works such as the *Floating Bodies* of Archimedes and the thirteen theorems of the Alexandrian, Diophantos (201-285BCE).

Twice the Caliph begged and attempted to bribe the *Basileus* numerous times with 'eternal peace' and 2,000 pounds of gold to allow John and Leo to remain at the Caliph's court, but Theophilus sternly refused, knowing the amazing potential and abilities of his traveling scholars. To maximize Leo's worth, Theophilus created a single chair for a paid teacher of secular learning, a hallmark act of Iconoclasm, on the street of the Forty Martyrs.[1141] Theophilus considered such Classical revivals of scientific discoveries and their practice as somewhat a state secret, not to be given to anyone potentially dangerous comparable to the recipe of Greek Fire.[1142] However, Theophilus did generously allow a copy of Ptolemy's work on astronomy, the *Almagest*, to be given as a gift to the Caliph in the 830's residing now in the Vatican Library.[1143] In return, Arabic mathematicians such as Mohammed ibn Musa al-Khwarizmi (780-850

[1138] Herrin, 28.
[1139] Jenkins, 151.
[1140] Obolensky, 72.
[1141] Mango, 'The Revival of Learning', 216.
[1142] Vasiliev, 298. Continuatus, 191, and Bury comments on this.
[1143] Angold, 89.

CE) would give the West the decimal, the zero, and a new math known as 'algebra.' To keep Leo well in the Byzantine fold, he awarded him a salary and gave him a post as a public teacher of Greek sciences and Classicism in Constantinople under the *Basileus*'s brother-in-law, Bardas.

Theophilus's reign was highly diverse and eventful militarily, economically, and culturally. Rarely do you see a reign with such aspects of charisma and character and in his efforts against Iconodulism, he was even challenged by the fact he took no steps to persecute or admonish the monastics of the Empire.[1144] However, a mere six weeks after his death, Orthodoxy and the icons would be restored, never to be questioned again. He far out-shined his father, although it was Michael II's idea to put John the Grammarian as Theophilus's tutor. When he died, he left a three-year-old son as his heir in care of the dominant Iconophile presence of the *Basilia* Theodora. Upon the *Basileus*'s death, having only one child, a need from the nobility for possible male contenders to the throne allowed the return to Orthodoxy as Iconoclasm was considered a cheap sacrifice for the regency.[1145] Michael III would make a name for himself, but only one of infamy and depravity. He would end the Amorian line as a steep decline with Theophilus as its nadir.

## MICHAEL III 'THE DRUNKARD'
### (842-867)

Not since Phocas the Tyrant in the seventh century has there been a *Basileus* more scandalously treated with contempt by history than Michael 'the Sot.' As Phocas was the Cyclops of Byzantine history, Michael was a degenerate given to heavy drinking, sexual excess, childish practical jokes, and idle chariot-racing. He was seen as a new Caligula with his love of pleasure and drunkenness as Gibbon names him as a moral successor of Nero[1146] and Elagabalus. He even blackened his reputation by associating with the charioteers who were considered as low on the social scale as gladiators were in the ancient Empire, being were mere slaves. He was weak-willed and allowed his mother the *Basilia* Theodora, and her brother Bardas, to take almost all of his responsibilities of government before and after his regency ended in 856.

---

[1144] Bury, (*ERE-I*), 61.

[1145] Karlin-Hayter, (*OHB*), 161-162.

[1146] Gibbon, 1629-1630. He cites the 'unnatural lusts' of Nero and compares it to the crime of homosexuality in the Empire.

Yet, from the last half-century on-wards, a rehabilitation of the last Amorian *Basileus* has been undertaken, for example it is noted by authors that he was not without gifts and even had courage in battle.[1147] He reportedly was a 'military genius', with charm, popularity among his people, and ability as an administrator. His success was mainly through smart delegation to more experienced commanders, bringing a new sort of *Pax Romana* to the East. The greatest liabilities to Michael's name are historians that present him in his worst light. Though he still had unworthy practices such as indecision and being easily led, Continuatus's, Constantine Porphyrogenitus's, and Joseph Genesios's *Chronicles* held a huge bias to the Macedonians and their founder, Basil I as well as Michael. Genesios (fl. 10th cent. CE) is known as the best source of these two men and their relationship, being the most trusted source to Byzantinists at face value until the twentieth century. Now some benefit to the doubt has been given to this young and impressionable ruler (who was murdered at twenty-eight) and has been noted as a capable ruler whose self-awareness would see him dead at the hand of his most trusted lovers and advisers.

Michael III was born on January 19, 840, to the *Basileus* Theophilus and Theodora, the people holding out a great hope that he might be as successful as his father. At age two, his father died of dysentery and the throne was promised to him after a regency of twelve years to his mother. An inscription made for the Patriarch John was remade to include a prayer to save Theophilus, Theodora, and Michael on behalf of the Mother of God on Christmas Day, 840.[1148] These arrangements were made famous by Michael's maternal great-grandfather Constantine VI and the *Basilia* Irene, but Michael and his strong-arming court would see the regency successfully ended and the *Basileus* precariously given a chance as sole heir.

Even from a young age, says Nicetas Stethanos's (1005-1090) *The Life of Symeon,* he was instilled with strict Orthodox views by his mother, Theodora. Due to his earlier upbringing, he knew nothing of the clergy and could not tell a Saint from a Patriarch, and to him Iconoclastic Michael II was known mostly as 'bad grandfather', while he clung to the knees of the venerating Symeon.[1149] From his childhood, he was granted tutors on the subjects of ceremony and culture and as the only male heir he was under the protection of his uncle Bardas, appointed as such by Theophilus who would later prove to be seen as a

---

[1147] Ostrogorsky, 223. This was all despite the biased historiography of the Macedonian period. But, it is still true Bardas ruled the Empire *de facto* as Theocistus had done under his mother's regency.

[1148] Herrin, *(WIP)*, 198.

[1149] *ibid.,* 220.

'judicious choice.'[1150] Eventually, Bardas would take control of the regency over the young emperor away from his mother.

One contributor to this was a number of costly operations against the Arabs that would test Theodora's abilities. But, her choice in advisers would see her through these tribulations even if it would doom her in the end. One mitigating circumstance in this conflict was the charity of the Caliph al-Wathiq who allowed the preservation of those martyrs in Ephesus executed by Diocletian. This perhaps denoted that only the Western Arabs would be the source of problems, and perhaps not the Caliphate itself. Michael III is defended by his reformist historians, such as Henri Gregoire in his 1925 *Byzantion*,[1151] in re-building Ancyra after the Arab destruction at Nicaea to re-fortify the Bosporus. He also expended great energy (and cost) strengthening frontier forces and strategic passes.[1152] These maneuvers were stated to be the decisive defeat of the Emir of Melitene by the Armeniacs that had inaugurated Arab aggression. Recovering Crete was also on the agenda and its Bishop entreated Michael to end his sinful ways as God was surely punishing Crete for them - the *Basileus* was said to have knocked out the Bishop's teeth and beat him severely.[1153]

In 843, Theodora would send an expedition led by Theophilus's minister, Theoctistus Bryennius, and a relative named Sergius Nicetiates to Crete to retrieve the island from where the Arab pirates were entrenched. Though they succeeded and Crete was made a Theme by the *Basileus* and his mother as they had done with Cyprus,[1154] Theoctistus fled and abandoned the army to Constantinople on false reports that Theodora had crowned her brother Bardas as *Basileus*. Whether by luck or design, the minister and general arrived in time to confront the armies of the Melitene Emir 'Amr who had planned a full siege on the City. After a disastrous defeat in the Optimate, costing the Greeks the Bosporus coast and defenses in Colonia, Theoctistus returned to Constantinople. Convincing Theodora that Bardas had encouraged desertions during the battle, he was expelled from the City. Crete again fell when Nicetiates was killed by the Arabs. To counter this, Theoctistus split the Cibyrrhaeot Theme into the Aegean Theme which could at least police the piracy in the Mediterranean.[1155]

---

[1150]  Bury, (*ERE-I*), 68.
[1151]  Ostrogorsky, 12, 220.
[1152]  Hussey, 37.
[1153]  Bury, (*ERE-I*), 72.
[1154]  Jenkins, 157.
[1155]  Treadgold, 447-448.

In 845, the Emir of Tarsus, 'Ali the Armenian, attempted to raid Amorium as was done under Michael II, but he was defeated by the Byzantine troops in Cappadocia. Arab activity eventually slowed in the East as only localized Emirates in the Eastern regions made the most trouble and only the Western Arabs of Sicily were as active as Greek forces at the time lacked the resources and attention to handle the situation, thus, stalemating in Italy. Situations grew worse in 846 when the Bulgar truce expired and the Slavs raided Macedonia and Thrace before being repulsed, inducing the Khan Malamir to ratify a new treaty. Theodora attempted to wrest Sicily away from the Arabs in 848, but was unsuccessful. In 851, 'Ali returned with a campaign against Eastern Byzantine territory lasting three years. Focusing now southwest, Theodora had the Egyptian coast raided from 853 to 854. The next year, 20,000 prisoners were taken when Theodora and Theoctistus sacked Anabarzus, the main city of Tarsus and 'Ali's domain.

The year 856 saw great changes in the Palace as Michael reached his ascendancy at the age of fifteen and in March, and a special session of the Senate was called hailing Michael III as *Basileus*. The first gold coins struck with his depiction were engraved with him, and in a change of tradition, his sister Thekla. He also brought back, eventually, the practice of including on the reverse a bust of Christ as Justinian II had done,[1156] citing the death of Iconoclasm. The Empire was at least becoming in good sorts, externally, as the new Bulgar Khan Boris had just renewed peace treaties with Byzantium. Internally, however, Michael's bad habits, including his affair with a noble's daughter, Eudocia Ingerina, made Theoctistus apprehensive for his future. His mother's first act after her son's succession was in finding an *Basilia* in a bride show and though considered, Eudocia was disqualified due to her lack of virginity.

A different Eudocia was chosen, named Decapolitissa,[1157] and she was married to Michael, although the Basileus still kept Ingerina as his mistress, doing so with an unquestioning obedience.[1158] In resentment against Theodora, Michael secretly allied with his uncle Bardas, whom he had recalled to the City, making him *Caesar* and also having his long-time rival Theoctistus assassinated on November 20, 855. Bardas ruled now over Michael as he had done Theodora, citing to an Arab emissary of the Byzantine court to report to the Caliph: 'I did

---

[1156] Karlin-Hayter, 161.

[1157] Daughter of the Scandinavian Igor, as she was a Thessalonican-named half-Swede.

[1158] Norwich, (APO), 59.

not hear a single word from his [Michael's] lips from the time of my arrival until my departure. The interpreter alone spoke, and the emperor listened and expressed his assent or dissent by motions of his head' and it was obvious that his uncle 'managed all of his affairs.' Continuatus also stresses the intentions of Theodora to keep him in perpetual tutelage and handling the serious affairs of state for herself[1159]; it is little wonder Michael never matured as a responsible *Basileus* of Eastern Rome.

As for the eventful and responsible governing by Theodora, she kept the borders pacified and the soldiers were paid for from her husband's surplus, adding to it to result in the amount of 7,300,000 *nomismata* in 856. Much of the successes of her son were due to her previous diligence and that of her feckless minister, Theoctistus. When the Milingoi and Ezeritai Slavic tribes revolted in the Peloponnesus, Theoctistus was made governor of the region and defeated the rebels, exacting a combined tribute of 360 *nomismata* annually.[1160] The peace of the Bulgars and the defenses against the Arabs mainly happened with Theodora's supervision and her wise economic policy which kept the Empire in balance financially. Michael, unfortunately, would almost squander this surplus into a deficit on largess, luxury, and his coterie of unscrupulous cronies. In a final insult, Michael had his mother tonsured in a nunnery for conspiring against the government in 857.

Through the questionable networks of nepotism, Michael ascended his uncle Bardas to the post of Magister and Domestic of the Scholae. He then took the time to rebuild Ancyra from its devastation by the Arabs, fortifying Nicaea and the frontier passes. His other uncle, Petronas, was made the *de facto* commander of the Byzantine forces and the Strategos of the Thracesian Theme. Petronas would show his worth in 856 by invading Arab territory from Melitene and Samosata to Amida in northern Mesopotamia, penetrating into the Arab East as far as it had been since the days of Heraclius. After two years spent handling a crisis of the Patriarchy, Michael and Bardas re-entered Melitene and raided the Egyptian coast. The Basileus needed to address 'Ali of Armenia, attempting to capture Cappadocia from Tarsus, but Michael would have more serious concerns coming north from the new tribes of the Rus.

The Viking tribes of northern Russia were marching on Constantinople in 859, but their fleets were fortunately turned back because of storms. The worst of this invasion was the opportunity taken by the Cretan Arabs to invade the

---

[1159] Bury, (*ERE-I*), 70.
[1160] Porphyrogenitus, 233.

Cyclades and Peloponnesus. At the same time, the fleets of Tarsus attacked Attalia, the seat of the Cibyrrhaeot Theme. Like a leaking dam that could not be refinished, raids by 'Ali of Tarsus, 'Amr of Melitene, and their Paulician allies were terrorizing the Black Sea all the way to Sinope. These developments induced Michael to organize a new Theme of Colonia to straddle Tephrice and Melitene in 861. However, its position as a bulwark for Armenia was weak one as it had received no additional troops or Kurramites since Theophilus's time.[1161]

Things remained this way until the summer of 862 when the Caliph and 'Amr invaded Cappadocia, raiding Amasis on the Black Sea despite an offensive by Michael at Nazianus. However, the commander Petronas and his army of 50,000 men managed to surround and slaughter all of 'Amr's men, 'Amr himself and his son as well. The Byzantine forces later marched into Arab Armenia to defeat and kill the former Emir of Tarsus who had been placed there by Caliph al-Musta'in. The Paulician leader Cabreas was also killed in these battles and in one summer, Byzantium was rid of its most dangerous Eastern enemies due to the talents of Petronas and the Charsianumese. Michael took note by raising Petronas as a Magister and promoting Charsianum from a Kleisura to a Theme. Michael III indeed, in 863, appeared personally to lead his armies, according to the Arab sources traditionally overlooked, dispelling the theory he only ruled idly from the Palace.[1162]

In 864, apparently without provocation, Michael and Bardas invaded Bulgaria, getting as far as Mesembria. Boris the Khan who had ruled peacefully since 853 concluded an alliance with the Empire and began to take in Byzantine Christian missionaries, a major issue in Michael III's reign. The impact on Bulgaria would prove remarkable as Boris would abandon Paganism, convert to Orthodoxy, take the Christian name Michael, and adopt the younger emperor as his godfather at Michael-Boris's baptismal. This paradigm meant leaps and bounds in the development of Slavism and Christianity in the East. The Moravians and the Bulgarians were full members of the 'Byzantine Commonwealth' as Dmitri Obolensky (1918-2000) had referred to Byzantium's sphere of influences, a policy of imperialism to 'better' these peoples through Byzantinization using Orthodoxy and culture. All of the middle territory between Byzantium and Bulgaria would now fall under Greek influence and further the boundaries of Byzantium in ways not yet seen for centuries.

Internally, stability under Michael III was less achievable because of

---

[1161] Treadgold, (BAIA), 33.

[1162] Norwich, (APO), 61; Jenkins, 163.

Michael's irresponsible spending and increasingly flaccid leadership. In 866, he sealed his fate by befriending Basil 'the Macedonian' who attended the horses in the marble-lined stables of the Palace. Michael awarded the empty spot of Grand Chamberlain (a post usually only given to experienced eunuchs so they could not contend the throne) with Bardas's permission, despite Basil's former careers as a wrestler and horse-breaker. Michael loved horses and their sports including chariot and races, though some compare this to Nero and Commodus,[1163] as mere symbols of Roman tyranny in Michael the Drunkard's character.

More ties between the two were established when Basil was made to divorce his wife Maria and marry Eudocia Ingerina, the *Basileus*'s mistress now carrying Michael's child. Michael would continue seeing Ingerina as well as being married to Decapolitissa, but now Basil would also have a mistress in Michael's sister, Thecla. These ties also made possible another relationship: Basil could replace, by being so close to the emperor, Bardas as *Caesar* and heir to the throne. Thecla would later keep her own liaison with a noble known as John Neatocomites, but once found out by Basil, John was tonsured and Thecla was sent to live in isolation at her house in Blacharnae, dying a few years later.

In 866, another expedition was planned by Bardas to take Crete and the Aegean, but this time, however, the army commanders would include Basil, camping with the emperor at Miletus in the Thracesian Theme. This invasion was more likely a ruse as Michael ordered his uncle killed on April 21, 865, by Basil, who was made co-*Basileus* on May 26, 866 on a double throne in the Hagia Sophia, though the Macedonian was by now in his fifties. On Lady's Day, March 25th, Michael and Basil signed an oath of loyalty at the Church of St. Mary Chalcopraetia inked in what was believed to be the blood of Jesus Christ caught at the Crucifixion. But the aggrandizement of co-emperor status was too vague an honor as Eudocia Ingerina gave birth to a son, the future Leo VI, and during the chariot races celebrating his birth, Basil was told not to 'presume upon his position'[1164] by Michael.

By this time, strain was becoming visible in the West as the Cretan Arabs had returned to pirating Greece and the Aegean. In Sicily, the Arabs there took Ragusa, Calabria, and even far Dalmatia, leaving only the cities of Syracuse and Taormina in Sicily to be Byzantine. Funds to counter these attacks were dangerously low as Michael wasted millions by now on his favorites at the court.

---

[1163] Bury, (*ERE-I*), 71.

[1164] Treadgold, 453.

By 867, the duties he paid to his neighbors were a financial embarrassment and al-Jarmi says just how bad it now was, worse than his father's time when soldiers were only paid in cash every three, five, or six years.[1165] It was important to him to be popular since he could not live up to his father's standards as an Eastern Roman Emperor. He resorted to melting down precious metals from his father's ornamental lions, birds, organs, trees, and a further 20,000 pounds of gold (1,440,000 *nomismata*[1166]) in order to pay his debts.

Meanwhile, Basil was dissatisfied with not presuming his position and made this known to Michael, as historians even agree he was falling into depravity in his later years, being a 'savage, criminal lunatic' brought about by a 'mental derangement' from his drinking. But Michael only admonished Basil and threatened his position if he did not submit, claiming he could give his position to a Logothete known as Basiliscinus. On the night of September 23, 867, Michael retired in a drunken stupor after a feast at the Palace at St. Mamas. Before this, Basil had entered the *Basileus*'s bedchamber and bent the lock on the door. This being done, Basil and a few more conspirators entered the bedroom where Basil's cousin Asylaion murdered Michael in his sleep, where the passed out *Basileus* blessedly felt no pain or betrayal.

Basil would present the dead monarch to his mother Theodora, wrapped in a horse blanket. This was a deep irony considering she was to meet her son that very day for dinner and reconcile their grievances upon crowning Basil,[1167] now this man displaying his act of murder in deference of Theodora. Basil would then install his wife Ingerina in the imperial apartments, having a showing at the Palace for his tonsured mother and burying Michael on the Asiatic shore of Chrysopolis. Unlike the murder of Bardas, which had no basis in the public good, Michael III had no such status and his mounting flaws made an excellent case for his death.[1168]

These terrible events were not inevitable and were a result of Michael's poor decisions and underestimating the will and cunning of Basil the Macedonian. Perhaps, it also must be noted, that by giving a post of the imperial bedroom (*parakoimemnos*) usually assigned to a eunuch,[1169] also foreshadowed disaster when that someone can claim the throne. And if such a relationship soured

---

[1165] Ibn-Khurdadhbidh, 84. Treadgold, *(BAIA)*, 137.
[1166]

[1167] Herrin, *(WIP)*, 232. Was this coincidence, or was Theodora in on the plot to kill her ungrateful son?
[1168] Bury, *(ERE-I)*, 79.
[1169] Herrin, 143.

because of a new favorite at court, his rejection from that post would play a role in the *Basileus*'s death. Unlike the example of Leo V, Basil's ascension by assassination was not reproved of by the populace, even by the monks, as assured to us by Jonathan Shepard in Mango's *Oxford History of Byzantium*.

Why not choose a eunuch? An issue of much debate and importance in the relationship between Basil the Macedonian and Michael III was their homosexual relationship. It has been presumed to be a case of 'just good friends' between the two, agreeing with the hypothesis of Romilly Jenkins (1907-1969) that the *Basileus* and his chamberlain were lovers.[1170] Primarily, this stems from Constantine VII Porphyrogenitus's analysis of Michael's reign that Jenkins updated a translation of in 1966. Constantine saw Michael as 'weak, drunken, and faithless' and his family met him with a 'deserved contempt' for his apparent bi-sexuality,[1171] while claiming the Amorian dynasty had declined the Empire to near extinction. Although Constantine wrote with a bias for the Lecapenid dynasty against the Amorians and Macedonians, clear historical evidence points to the existence of a doomed 'Antony and Cleopatra' relationship between the two men.

Porphyrogenitus puts claim that members of Michael's court resembled those of Nero's with Eudocia Ingerina as his Poppaea, and Basil as another lover, stating there existed also a love triangle between the three with the throne as an impediment. The truth of this relationship was most likely the ancient rite of *adelphopoiesis*, or one of 'same-sex bonding'. In Continuatus's *Life of Basil*, historians such as John Boswell (1947-1994) have suggested that Basil forges a relationship of *parrhesia* ('intimacy') with a certain John, son of a wealthy widow and this had a 'marital context.' Even in these austere times of Christianity, the ancient Eastern custom of relations between men as eunuchs or as whole was still commonplace and would be practiced by *Basili* and Caliphs for centuries.

Complicating matters was Basil's divorce of his wife to marry Michael's mistress while Basil was given a mistress of his own in the *Basileus*'s sister, Thecla.[1172] But, what makes the sexual life of Michael III and his *ménage a trois* with Basil and Eudocia such an exceptional matter of record is the parentage of the future *Basileus* Leo VI, born in 866. Unquestionably the origins of Leo

---

[1170] Tougher, Shaun. 'Michael III and Basil the Macedonian: Just Good Friends?' *Desire and Denial in Byzantium: Papers from the Thirty-first Spring Symposium of Byzantine Studies, University of Sussex, Brighton, 1997,* ed. by Liz James. Ashgate/ Variorum Publishing, 149-158. 1999, 149-158.

[1171] Jenkins, 165.

[1172] Treadgold, 453.

and the rights to the regency and throne were legitimated only by the pretense that he was Basil's son as Basil rose to throne by murder.[1173] One of the events that caused rift between Michael and Basil was the *Basileus's* disinterest and finding of a new homosexual lover in a sailor named Baskilinos,[1174] going so far as to make cruel insults that he intended to make him *Caesar*. When Michael was assassinated, the main detail that Basil had fallen out of favor with him was how the bolt on Michael's bedchamber door had to be sabotaged as Basil would formally be allowed in freely.

Another controversy of importance of this era begins with the ecclesiastical life of Byzantium and a war between two Patriarchs of Constantinople and the Pope in Rome. In 843, Theodora held a private Synod of court officials and clerics, excluding any Bishops and legates. A new liturgy of the '*Syndikon* of Orthodoxy' resulted on March 10 by a leading attendee, Methodius the monk.[1175] Meeting in the house of Theoctistus, this 'conference' condemned Iconoclasm under the Second Council of Nicaea in 787 and put on the Patriarchal throne an Iconophile. The now deposed John the Grammarian was then succeeded by Methodius. The weakness of the secular structure under Michael III was made apparent by the bold, radical actions of Methodius in deposing almost all of the Bishops in the Empire. The Grammarian, however, was still given the post of Bishop of Thessalonica, keeping his teaching career in the liberal arts at the Magnaura by Bardas.[1176] Always an enemy of the superstitious, Methodius was slandered as a hypocrite and was rumored to have hidden underground, mulling over basins to practice black magic.[1177]

As it was the First Sunday of Lent, it was also known as the landmark day 'Sunday of Orthodoxy', celebrating the 787 crushing of the heresy of Iconoclasm. As it is celebrated today, Theodora managed to have Theophilus stricken from the list of Iconoclast heretics such as Leo III and Constantine V after his death in order to legitimize her own son's reign. Constantine Copronymous's bones were then said to have been interred and burnt to ash, to be scattered where no holy burial would receive him.[1178] On a more merciful side, at the Ceremony of the Triumph, the *Basileus* and *Basilia* were praised (*euphemia*) by the Church

---

[1173] Herrin, *(WIP)*, 225. An ironic and messy way of legitimizing a birth and continue a bloodline based on fraud and scandal.

[1174] Sherrard, 69.

[1175] Herrin, 112.

[1176] Treadgold, 447.

[1177] Jenkins, 155.

[1178] Herrin, *(WIP)*, 213.

with 'wishes for many years' (*polychronia*) and blessings from the entire Senate, state officials, the army, and the citizens (*panti politeumati*) of the City, styled after a tradition from 787.[1179]

This momentous occasion has been commemorated by a fourteenth-century relief now in the British Museum portraying Theodora, Michael III, Methodius, as well as monks, martyrs, and a fictitious nun venerating an icon of the Virgin and Child. Methodius began by deposing Bishops in the Empire whether they were Iconoclast or not, including Leo the Mathematician, who taught at the school of Magnaura studies such as philosophy, astrology, geometry, grammar, but not theology. The weakness of the Church over secularism is relevant here as these Bishops and Leo were both dismissed for being supporters of, and associated with, John the Grammarian and Theophilus. The duties of Methodius were controlled by the *Basilia*, for whom he owed his mantle, and not to the Church for conducting acts found not for the spiritual welfare of Byzantium.

Also in this year, Paulician Dualists from Anatolia formed armies and joined forces with the Caliphate to make war on the Empire. In response, thousands of Paulicians in the Empire would die and have their properties confiscated to pay the armies while others were forced into conversion to Orthodoxy. The remaining Paulicians under the Emir 'Amr of Melitene were given land to begin a new state of tolerated Christians by the Caliphate. Later in 856, the Paulicians would remain as safeguards of the Western Caliphate at Tephrice, raiding the Armeniac Theme.

When their leading commander, Cabreas, would die in battle against Petronas in Armenia in 863 his nephew Chrysocheir, in 866, would re-gather the Paulicians to restore hostilities in Anatolia. Ever the protectors of Iconoclasm and the values of the Manicheans, the Paulicians claimed the Cross as inconsequential and the Virgin had given birth to more children after Christ (it has been theorized recently that Christ had a brother). Matter itself was base, a creation of the Devil and not God, and the Paulicians were written by Orthodoxy as slander as how their radicalism was also 'cunning and disingenuous.'[1180]

Meanwhile, in 846, Methodius (815-885 CE) attempted to cleanse the Church hierarchy of Iconoclasm and in doing so, he upset the balance with the

---

[1179] *ibid.,* 209.

[1180] Jenkins, 158. Gibbon even suggests, from an eighteenth-century point of view as a deist, to have had 'the germ of Protestantism.'

Studite monks who disapproved of several new Bishopric appointments. A year later, however, Methodius was dead and the problem now shifted to Ignatius Rhangabe, a castrated son of Michael I. Deposing Bishop Gregory Asbestas of Syracuse, it caused rifts with Gregory's supporters in the Iconophile camp. Ignatius would also have difficulty adapting to Michael and Bardas's ribald life at court, though he himself was known as 'a blinkered bigot - despised by his flock, which was determined to get rid of him.'[1181] Blasphemous anecdotes come down to us of profaning the Eucharist services with wafers of mustard and vinegar to the taste. Ignatius would plan processions, during which Michael's degenerate allies would beat drums and sing lewd songs, and after Ignatius died, Michael himself was said to have joined in the insults.[1182] The Patriarch Ignatius was deposed on November 23, 857, for denying Bardas communion on the Feast of the Epiphany over the scandal of incestuously seducing his dead son's widow.

A layman, the Protosecretarius Photius, was made Patriarch on December 25, 858 after a five-day career of being an 'officer' of the Church; Photius was versed in liturgy and theology, but more importantly, he was an enemy of Ignatius. In a fit of gleeful pettiness, Bardas reinstated Photius's friend Asbestrus and had him crowned and consecrated Photius as an opposing Patriarch of Constantinople. It was during the Feast of the Epiphany when Ignatius rebuked, excommunicated, and refused sacrament to an apathetic and spiteful Bardas.[1183]

It was not until 861 that two papal legates from Rome, Zachary of Agnani and Rodoald of Porto, came to the City to recognize Photius as Patriarch being charmed by his erudition, his banquets, splendor, not to even lay eyes on Ignatius at all. Though this was done in a Council, it was nullified by Pope Nicholas I who remained unconvinced, deciding these legates exceeded their authority citing *super omnen terram, id est, super omnem ecclesiam*,[1184] and the two legates were disenfranchised for their ignorance. This controversy over acceptance between Western and Eastern investiture was also linked to the question of Christian missionaries in Moravia as well as the battle of using traditional Latin as a language versus the Eastern Greek and Slavic as liturgy. This was at a time when the *Basileus* Michael sent missionaries to Khazaria to discuss friendship, alliance, and '...service in whatever place you may need us.'[1185]

---

[1181] Norwich, *(AM)*, 72.

[1182] Bury, *(ERE-I)*, 71.

[1183] Norwich, *(APO)*, 64.

[1184] Jenkins, 176.

[1185] Obolensky, 177.

In 862, the Moravian[1186] King Ratislav requested Byzantine Orthodox missionaries be in service over the Frankish Catholics already settled there, proving a complete change in the culture of conscience and confession for the Slavs. Although he was invalidated by Rome in 863, Photius sent a mission headed by Constantine (who would take the name Cyril, 826-869 CE) and Methodius. In the autumn, the two brothers arrived with both liturgy and a Bible in Macedonian Slavic.[1187] They invented the 'Slavonic-Glagothlic' alphabet in the Moravian liturgy, an evolution from the Greek miniscule script known as the uncial script, which had reached Armenia by the ninth century, according to the reports of the king Tiridates.[1188] This defied the Western attitude that only three languages were permitted to chronicle Christ and his death on the Cross: Hebrew, Greek, or Latin.[1189]

These were the legacies of the Prophets, the Hebrew Apostles, the Greek Apostle Paul, and St. Anthony's Vulgate translation from Egypt. The Byzantinization and Slavonization of the Gospels were also a bridge across a cosmopolitan culture to understand Moravian needs socially, politically, theologically, and literary in order to break linguistic barriers.[1190] This put them in a status higher than it had been wherein it merely supplied Byzantium with material luxuries, technical skills, and cultural prestige. Michael III, however, did not just use diplomacy as his new multiculturalism, not to be diminished by the Bulgar Boyars that controlled the nobility, fifty-two being beheaded by him for their dissent.[1191] This Gaglothic and uncial scripts would also be the direct ancestors of the modern Cyrillic scripts of contemporary Russian, Bulgarian, Serbian, and other Balkan alphabets.[1192]

Being of Thessalonican Slavic descent, Moravian education in this language made transitions easy. By 864, the Slav liturgy had replaced the Latin Mass,[1193] the Frankish clergy having been driven from Moravia. Mostly this

---

[1186] Moravia was a larger Slav kingdom from Poland to Slavokia and Bohemia east of the Danube, Obolensky, 137. Its location between Latin and Slavic spheres made it ripe for an infusion of Greek influence.

[1187] Runciman, (BYZ), 347.

[1188] Bury, (ERE-I), 72.

[1189] Herrin, 133.

[1190] Obolensky, (AWC), 42-43.

[1191] Ostrogorsky, 230.

[1192] Bury, (ERE-I), 171.

[1193] Obolensky, 152. Michael, through Photius, had written to the Pope referring to Latin as 'barbaric' and 'Scythian' according to Svyatoslav Dmetriev in his study of

was due to the Frankish Emperor Louis II disembarking the Frankish armies from Moravia to consolidate the Holy Roman Empire from Western aggression and as Boris begged this clergy to be returned.[1194] The new missionaries also introduced the works of St. John Chrysostum, the Gospels, and the Psalms to translations. The creation of a Slavonic alphabet starting under Leo V was complete and would spread to Orthodox Bulgaria and Slavic Byzantium. However, not all transitions would be as smooth, an example being when the Bulgar Khan Boris-Michael actually went to Rome for Frankish missionaries. Surprisingly, Cyril and Methodius agreed with this action and defied Photius on the subject.

In August of 865, the Pope banished the Byzantine representatives of the Church back to Constantinople, especially who he saw as the instigating offender, Theognostus. They had been sent to the Pope to allay his concerns on the illegal Council and advocate his only action would be to send both Patriarchal candidates to Rome for their respective claims.[1195] Given his rampant drunkenness at the time, Michael III only bluffed such a threat. Photius then held a Council in 866 deposing Pope Nicholas on grounds of Western heresies such as: fasting on Saturdays, using unleavened bread in the Eucharist, excluding married men from the priesthood, and the use of the *filioque* in Mass recognizing the divinity of the Holy Spirit of the Son and Father.[1196] Michael and his allies, according to Genosius, plotted to assassinate Photius but the courage of the murderers failed and Michael desperately had Basil 'instigate them.'[1197]

In retaliation for the Bulgarian defection from the Orthodox Church, all Photius did was use tired, overused, and impossible arguments to solve theological disputes, threatening to split Europe in half once again.[1198] This was not the first time this had happened and it is a mistake to assume Photius was not educated as a layman; his *Bibliotheca* of 855 stressed the importance of literature, theology, and history with Leo the Grammarian and Constantine the Philosopher.[1199] Nicholas brought language into the battle again by declaring,

---

these language barriers.

[1194] Bury, (*ERE-I*), 168.

[1195] Norwich, (*APO*), 74.

[1196] Treadgold, 454.

[1197] Bury, (*ERE-I*), 76.

[1198] Such as absurdities that washing was disallowed on Fridays and Wednesdays, and milk and cheese was to be disdained from during Lent. Norwich, (*AM*), 75.

[1199] Jenkins, 164.

as they spoke Greek, Byzantine *Basileus* were not 'Emperors of the Romans.' Ostrogorsky submits the implications of Photius's actions in this affair: 'Historical necessity demanded that Byzantium should deprive Rome of her ecclesiastical universalism, just as the West had destroyed the Universalism of the Byzantine state. The decisive step in this process was taken by Photius.'[1200]

In August 867, Michael concluded another Synod deposing the Pope, rejecting the Catholic doctrine of the Holy Ghost as heresy, and making any Western interference in the affairs of Byzantine and Orthodox policy illegal. But, it came with a price as Louis and Engelbhert were now documented as the Emperor and Empress of the Franks, dwindling again Byzantine prestige and any right of supremacy due to Michael's submissive nature.[1201] This was not to interfere with the missionary and cultural universalism the Byzantine state was to bestow on its evolving Slavic peoples. The emerging Rus converted to Christianity and accepted a Constantinopolitan Bishop, the long-term consequence of these Greek-Slavic relations resulting in the modern states of Serbia, Croatia, Bulgaria, Hungary, and Russia.[1202] However, this remarkable legacy of Byzantine culture strained the subordinate Bulgar society into preferring the Frankish influence over the Greek. This was a violation of Byzantine political philosophy as: '. . .according to which a nation, having accepted the empire's Christian faith, became thereby subject to the authority of the *Basileus*, who was held to be the sole legitimate sovereign of the Christian world.'[1203]

Michael III's achievements were mistaken as infrequent and disastrous, yet another fact is the implications of events around him were 'great'. He was noted as commissioning what was to be the first Byzantine architectural style in churches.[1204] At the Church of Our Lady the Pharos in Constantinople and the Hosius Loukas with its domed ceilings to present mosaics of Christ Our Lord of the Universe looking down on the congregation. Supported by curved corners, or 'squinches', these domes also loomed over the *bema* (sanctuaries) with scenes from Scripture. Such achievements were coincidences with Michael's reign, yet it was by his allowance and patronage that this was made so despite the complacency and the entropy of his court.

Michael's squandering of funds and accumulation of debt in a span

---

[1200] Ostrogorsky, 255.
[1201] Jenkins, 181.
[1202] Diehl, 262.
[1203] Obolensky, 84.
[1204] Sherrard, 102.

of twenty-five years is a startling discovery as the Empire also enjoyed a lighter series of taxation and a tight financial bureaucracy at this time. The Fisc had distinct departments for the gathering of taxes and funds for their disbursement[1205]:

1) The Logothete of the General Treasury was an evolution from the Sacred Largess and not only oversaw tax gathering of all types, but also the appointment of customs officials. He collected the five main taxes in place since 809: the Land Tax, the *Kapnikon* or 'Hearth Tax', the Custom Tax, The five percent Inheritance Tax, and the unofficial 'Capital Gains Tax' for private estates.

2) The Military Logothete used the role once modeled after the Praetorian Prefects in distributing pay to soldiers and their expenses in equipment and victuals.

3) The President cf the Special Treasury oversaw the factories of goods and arms of state interest.

4) The Chancellory of the Wardrobe oversaw the minting of coins in the realm from gold, silver, and bronze bullion mined by the General Logothete.

5) The Asiatic provinces mostly held the private imperial estates, mainly administered by the Count of the Stable and Logothete of the Herds, responsible for the stewardship of Imperial military horses and mules for cavalry and carriage.

6) Next in the provinces was one of their chief financial ministers: the Sacellerios. He collected private land rents to finance the army, public works, buildings, and Court extravagance.

Yet, it is a fact that Michael III found ways to incur state debt on gifts, dues owed in military losses and reparations, and overindulgent largess to the low life parasites at his drinking table until one grew angry at these crimes enough to finally kill him.

Meanwhile, early modern nations were developing their roots in the Medieval era as the ethnic diversity and cultural diffusion Byzantine civilization was known for took shape. The theological and linguistic rehabilitation of the Bulgars and Thessalonicans transmitted a 'Christian' language and literature

---

[1205] Bury, (*ERE-I*), 92-93.

that stemmed the threats of Jewish and Islamic influences.[1206] A great *Basileus* such as Justinian I or Constantine I would have started a new Golden Age in the Empire, but as it was under a manipulated and alcoholic ruler, greatness would have to wait longer. Michael III was certainly not known for his father's serious attitudes;[1207] but, fortunately, upon Basil I's ascension, a new and long-lasting dynasty would take root and a new chapter in the story of the Byzantine Empire would begin.

In Theodora's last years after her son's murder, she had no choice but to tolerate Basil's succession, to be honorably tonsured and buried by the new *Basileus*, whether by guilt or by a political need, in her Monastery of the Gastria. There, she was surrounded by her courtiers, commanders, her niece Irene, and even the preserved jawbone (*katomagoulon*) of her brother, Bardas.[1208] Though she seemed abandoned, the Orthodox Church would not forget her achievements in preserving the lineage of future *Basiliai*, quietly protecting icon veneration as she was made a saint. As in 843, a Triumph was set on February 11 to parade her in the streets commemorating her, and her *Life* would be read at holidays while icons of her are to this day are consecrated.[1209] Though she lost the political game to Basil the Macedonian, she was posthumously honored as a champion of the faith that Basil and his Church followed.

---

[1206] Ostrogorsky, 229.

[1207] Treadgold, 450.

[1208] Constantine VII. Porphyrogenitus. *De Ceremonii Aule Byzantinae,* ed. by I. I. Reiske, Bonn: Germany. 1829. Chap. 24, 647.17-648.8.

[1209] Herrin, *(WIP),* 238, 256. After 867, this level of power and activity in *Basiliai* would not be repeated in future dynasties. Yet, the need for dynastic legitimacy would be.

# III. High Byzantium

The middle centuries of the Byzantine Empire have been hailed as their Golden Age, their Apogee – the peak of their culture, armed forces, trade, and the spread of Orthodox Christianity. Beginning with the long-lived Macedonian Dynasty (866-1056), good relations in the East and a stable economy both strengthened and expanded territorial borders from South Italy and the Serbian Balkans to the Zagros Mountains by 1025. Ancient culture would make a return to intellectual life in the form of the Greek sciences and Platonic philosophy in the eleventh century and the 'Homeric renaissance' of the twelfth. Any memory of a Dark Age would be visited by high art, iconography, and a plethora of historical sources. These sources omitted some influences, but supposedly the facts were never invented or fabricated, so they might be taken as true reflections and testimonials.[1210]

The civilizing influence of Byzantium was further taking the Slavic East and transforming it into a flourishing society. The legal work commissioned by jurists and the detailed history of foreign relations written by Constantine VII Porphyrogenitus's own hand highlighted a time when reform only ornamented the state and did not need to save it. But a serious setback occurred in the eleventh century in a crisis of imperial leadership with a 'time of troubles' that saw quick successions of unfit emperors and palace intrigues. This inner corruption led to an inevitable fragmentation of the nobles from centralized authority and economic and military factors suffered. One result was the Turkish victory of Manzikert, the humiliation of the Byzantine war machine and the physical capture of a *Basileus* by a foreign power.

---

[1210] Jenkins, 193. Although these histories are peppered by bias views and anecdotes, these were only the convictions of the time in which they were written and if some of them lacked fact, it, nevertheless, was included to add truth to the histories. Byzantine histories were also instruction of living a good and Christian life in the Greek tradition and their allegories were meant to enlighten.

But this period also saw the rise of modern Slavonization, drawing the boundaries for what would later be their modern world during and after the Ottoman Empire. Constantinople was the Queen of Cities, greater than Rome, Paris, Baghdad, and any other Medieval capital in the known world. Trade saw Byzantine icons travel to Churches in Africa, Arabia, and Russia as Orthodoxy was the champion of the Eastern Christian soul, forever free now from the Iconoclast heresy and its divisions. It is the wares of the East that Byzantium channeled from Far Asia, inducing young Marco Polo to India and China, bringing back tales that sounded to Western Europe like true madness, where to Byzantium it was common knowledge. Everything Byzantium would offer and teach the world first started in this era and it is said to have begun with the murder of a *Basileus*, where 'Great good can sometimes can come from evil men.'[1211]

## BASIL I 'THE MACEDONIAN'[1212]
### (867-886)

Again, if Michael III was a shadow of a true Byzantine *Basileus* in the annals of the period's historians, Basil was the bright sun that expelled Michael and made Byzantium shine brighter for it; though it is not found much anywhere else, Basil has even given the sobriquet of 'the Magnificent'.[1213] John Genosios and Constantine Porphyrogenitus portray the last of the Amorians as a weak drunk whose vices made his assassination seem altogether justified. As Basil himself was the grandfather of Constantine and the founder of his dynasty of the Macedonians, he is seen as freeing Byzantium from a tyrant whose chaos threatened the Empire. But the truth is that Basil murdered his friend and seized the throne, threatening all legitimacy beyond his popularity. Yet, the stability he ushered was nurtured, lasting until 1025 with the end of Basil II with all achievements of continuous and Byzantine prestige.[1214]

His genius as a *Basileus* stooped to the level of a slave beyond ambition and virtues, taking with a bloody assassin's hand the Empire that he would come to rule with the wisdom and tenderness of a father.[1215] He was cunning, wily,

---

[1211] Brownworth, 167.

[1212] Though noted as Macedonian, his true ethnicity was that of a Thracian Slav.

[1213] Sherrard, 63.

[1214] Hussey, 34.

[1215] Gibbon, 1633.

and had a superior physical strength matched only by an iron-willed tenacity that attracted notice from everyone he met. He was even seen as having an air of mystery around him from legends such as one where he tamed a wild and dangerous horse with a whispered word in its ear, a feat attributed a millennium earlier to Alexander the Great, a native Macedonian. A more believable story is passed down in which Basil once beat Michael in a drinking contest sixty cups to fifty.[1216]

But his reign saw improvements in diplomacy with the Slavs and the spread of Christianity to the Pagans through missionaries and Bishoprics. Advancements in learning and the arts opened paths to a new resurgence of Classical learning and end to the Dark Age, coupled with a stability of the state budget and economy after the massive debt Michael had incurred. He had a higher sense of responsibility to his duties, having learned the lessons of bad administration by Michael. And as Justinian had attempted, he sought to eliminate the violence and extortion of the poor by the army and the wealthy and kept a policy of good order, security, and peace in the provinces.[1217] His early years were intertwined greatly with Byzantium's history of the Slavic peasant; born in 811 in Charioupolis in Thrace, he was the son of an Armenian peasant and his Slavic wife[1218] who had been one of the thousands of hostages the Bulgar Khan Krum took after the defeat of Nicephorus I in 813. Basil grew up a Bulgarian farmer until 836 when he and his Thracian brethren were freed by Theophilus.

Gifted with a peasant cunning and great bodily strength, he afterward settled in Constantinople in 856 as a horse breaker in the Palace stables. He quickly befriended the emperor Michael III and was placed in his court as husband to his mistress Eudocia when Basil impressed the *Basileus* by throwing an opponent over a table in a wrestling match. There he raised four children – two, Leo and Stephen, fathered by Michael, and two natural sons, Constantine and Alexander – and two of the four would ascend to the imperial throne. Feeling threatened by Michael's legacy after his brutal murder, Basil had Stephen castrated and tonsured, keeping a close eye on the more popular Leo, whom he also hated. He then crowned his son Constantine co-*Basileus* in 867 and prepared him to propagate a new lineage of rulers in Byzantium coming from Macedonia. It is possible Constantine was also Michael's son, but this

---

[1216] Norwich, (APO), 89.

[1217] Diehl, 69.

[1218] Jenkins, 165.

could never be legitimated and has a somewhat muddied clarity in Basil's 888 *Funeral Oration* by Leo who needed a certain bias to retain his throne.[1219]

What should be added to this section of Basil's biography was Constantine VII's recording of almost absurd claims of nobility Basil secretly had to create in order to bring legitimacy to a usurper's ascension to the throne. The controversial Patriarch Photius, in 873, claimed to have 'discovered' a genealogy that proved he was a descendant of Armenian nobility coming from the ancient and pre-Persian Arsacid Bagatrid line of King Ashot I. The choice of such a lineage can be attributed to Photius having been educated in the Parthian lineages and the uncial script in which it was written.[1220]

Basil's humble peasant status was then transformed to a new landowning farmer status that counted Basil and his ancestors to further elite status in Byzantium. This genealogy is almost certainly a fiction or mythos that elevated Basil I to a class structure he was never really a part of, denying that the Byzantine emperors of their Golden Age of culture and influence came from a poor stableman. However, the necessity of such an act was seen as a restoration of the balance of order (*taxis*) within the state that would threaten the new dynasty if it were not restored.[1221] Only the impotence of usurpers and illegitimate generals could protect a fledgling *Basileus* with a shady past such as he in Byzantium at this point.

It is agreed that perhaps Basil's first act as *Basileus* was to depose Photius as Patriarch to appease Pope Nicolas, who would die anyway on November 13, 867. Photius was, of course, an anti-Patriarch in the eyes of Rome as well as a political liability in Basil's court. So, Photius was condemned by a Council, exiled, and his rival Ignatius was put in his place as a placation to the new Pope, Hadrian II. It was the emperor's hope that he could heal the widening schism between the Western and Eastern Churches that Photius's condemnations had provoked. Earlier that year, a coup for the title of *Basilia* occurred as Thekla, Basil's wife and Michael III's sister, was found to be having an affair with Neatokometes who was later beaten and tonsured.[1222] Thekla would be set aside in the Monastery in the Karionos, to be later restored.

In military matters he was indefatigable and cool-tempered, such as when ministers sent him lists of officer candidates for duty, Basil wisely noting

---

[1219] Herrin, *(WIP)*, 235.

[1220] Jenkins, 194.

[1221] Herrin, 147.

[1222] *ibid.* 228-229.

the characters and experiences of the men, only being able to choose two satisfactorily.[1223] The condition of the army had showed deterioration under Basil as quality probably suffered under Michael's rash decisions and lackey appointees. On April 21, 866, Michael had produced a Cretan expedition to lure and murder his uncle Bardas and the fleet was dismissed thereafter. But, by 868, Basil was ready to stand for Byzantine suzerainty in Italy by sending troops to Byzantine possessions in Dalmatia and Sicily. Upon his success, his missionaries converted the last 'Pagani' of Dalmatia during his defensive against the Narenti pirates in the Adriatic.[1224]

He had advantage over the Western Arabs in that they were in a period of division of the Tulunids of Egypt, the Spanish Umayyads having their Christian population problems, and the rise of Turkish influence in Arab courts.[1225] He sent a dual-fleet expedition to Syracuse and Ragusa and the victorious navy used a surrendering Ragusa to create a new Theme of Dalmatia. After correcting corrupt practices that the military governor had inflicted on the local Croats, Basil made a treaty of tribute in wine, commodities, and at least 710 *nomismata* annually from six major cities.[1226]

Not since Constans II had the ambitions and energy of a *Basileus* to recover the West been seen in Basil the Macedonian.[1227] Unfortunately, his Sicilian fleet was routed and failed to recover Syracuse or any holdings on the island. Desperately, Basil turned to the Pope and the Holy Roman Emperor Louis II for reinforcements to turn aside Christianity's enemies from Italy, offering one of his sons as husband to Louis's daughter. But this arrangement failed as well, unsurprisingly, as Frankish and Byzantine forces could not get along, due to the typical alienation over language, faith, and the true definition of Roman cooperation. All of this was during the Eighth Ecumenical Council in 869-870, arranged unsuccessfully by the librarian of the Roman Church, Anastasius.[1228]

By 869, the expedition to Arabic Bari in Dalmatia had fallen apart and a year later, Louis allowed the peace with Byzantium to lapse as Arabs took Malta and Calabria. The Republic of St. Mark, or Venice, would now completely gain independence from Byzantine suzerainty, although negotiations would remain friendly against the common enemies of the Western Arabs and Adriatic Slavs.

---

[1223] Gibbon, 1634.

[1224] Obolensky, 99.

[1225] Vasiliev, 303.

[1226] Porphyrogenitus, *De Imperio*, 147.

[1227] Jenkins, 185.

[1228] Norwich, (AM), 76f.

As Narentene pirates beset the Frankish fleet, Louis and Pope Hadrian rashly suspected Basil had orchestrated these assaults.[1229] But these suspicions arose from paranoia over the creation of the Theme of Dalmatia and the missionary work to Christianize the Slavs of Hellas and Narenta, making it appear less coincidental with the pirate attacks.[1230]

This division of Western and Eastern identities was rooted in the language of the Byzantines, seeing themselves as 'Romans' as the Western European were *ethnos* ('foreign nations')[1231] as the antiquated terms of 'Scythians, Goths, Franks, and other barbarians.' The crowning act of this universalist schism came from Louis's adoption of the title *Imperator Augustus Romanorum* ('Emperor of Rome') and leaving Basil as *Imperator Novae Romae* ('Emperor of New Rome') as the New Romans were Greeks. Once again, this was done in Latin, a tongue to the Greeks seen as guttural and barbaric compared to the fine and superior subtlety of ancient Greek that was seen as a language of culture and education – tell that to Constantine or Justinian that spoke nothing less than Latin! This linguistic difference proved that Michael and Basil saw the Westerners as barbaric usurpers who would have no legitimate claim over 'Roman' territory.

An abortive Frankish embassy in 870, during the anti-Photian Council, resurfaced the question of the title of *Basileus* in an indivisible Roman Empire. Arguments historical, scriptural, dogmatic, and philological were addressed to validate that only one ruler could rule Constantinople. Examples ranged from King David's subjugation, the Assyrians, Egyptians, Moabites, Persians, Epirotes, Hindus, Parthians, Ethiopians, and Vandals. All Patriarchs bow to one ruler only and the translation of the title *Rex* ('King') itself adopted by the Franks is only a Western translation of the Greek *Basileus*.[1232] What also failed to improve matters was Basil's use of Orthodox missionaries in traditionally Western-controlled Slavic lands as 'imperial agents and priests,'[1233] perhaps implying this clergy was assigned to influence Slavic political ties as well as spiritual.

---

[1229] Ostrogorsky, 95-96.

[1230] Jenkins, 90.

[1231] Bergamo, Nicolas. 'The Problem of Ethnic Identity between Roman and Longobard in the *Historia Longobardia* of Paul the Deacon.' Presented at *The Twenty-Eighth Annual Byzantine Studies Conference*, (Colombus, OH: The Ohio State University, October 4-6, 2002).

[1232] Jenkins, 187-189.

[1233] Shepard, (*OHB*), 231.

Meanwhile, these Western defeats gave Basil I incentive to focus on improving the navy by introducing 4,000 professional marine soldiers modeled after a four cavalry Tagmata under a Drungarius.[1234] It included seven other officers, mostly marines who were fellow soldiers of Basil in his military youth, cementing the fleet's loyalty, led by a Protospatharioi once under the patrician chief, Nasar, before being made chief oarsmen.[1235] These marines were given land which was only a status given the regular troops of the Themes and Tagmata under the regulations of the *Farmer's Law*. For the next two years he would make operations against the Paulicians and their rebellious leader, Chrysocheir.

Christopher, the Domestic of the Scholae, gathered the armies of the Armeniacs and Charsianum, catching up to the Paulicians at Dazimon. Chrysocheir was defeated, retreating to Sebastea with Christopher in tow. The Paulician leader's men betrayed him to the Byzantines and he was assassinated, his head a trophy for the *Basileus*, and in celebration Basil held a triumph for himself, though he personally never left the City. The West would become less dependable, however, as Louis II died near Brescia in 872 without leaving an heir after a Frankish victory in Capua. A year later, Basil began a propaganda campaign of persecuting all Paulicians, while forcing the conversion of Jews in the Empire, accentuating the victory of his Triumph.[1236]

The reformed navy that Basil I authorized was finally put to sea in 873, commanded by Nicetas Ooryphas with 100 ships, routing the Cretan Arabs and their thirty-six ships from the Aegean to their city of Cardia. In 874, the Arabs only grew bold again and invaded the western Peloponnesus. Ooryphas fought back aggressively and had the Arab fleet beached at Corinth, defeating the armies on the Gulf. The energetic Byzantine fleet then retook Cyprus a year later and Basil made it a Theme to buffer Crete from the Peloponnese and Cyclades. His fourth and last victory in this region came with the aid of the Frankish Emperor, Charles II, and Bari was settled into the Cephalonian Theme to seriously disrupt the Arab's hold on the Aegean. This naval revitalization also prospered under the new policy of appointing a place for these sailors on the regular imperial payroll, a professionalization in 870 that the army had not seen since 641.[1237]

---

[1234] Treadgold, (*BAIA*), 104-105.

[1235] Porphyrogenitus, *De Administro*, 249-250.

[1236] Treadgold, 457.

[1237] Treadgold, (*BAIA*), 151.

When Syracuse was threatened in 877, the extension of this last Western Byzantine territory made it difficult to effectively defend. Although Basil had regained Adelchis, Benevento, and Otranto four years earlier, the Arabs took Syracuse and dwindled Byzantine influence in southern Italy to Tauromenium on the Sicilian coast. Basil's navy was unfortunately suspended by the *Basileus* himself however, as his construction programs took precedence over the Sicilian campaign; Syracuse could have been preserved by the Greek fleets, but the emperor's hesitation ruined the opportunity.[1238] Of course, there was more success in the Eastern part of the Empire against the Caliphate. Basil personally appeared to lead his armies with his favored son and co-*Basileus*, (since January 6, 869) Constantine, dressed in golden armor with a shining white horse. Basil's army invaded Melitene and eliminated an Arabic army from the Emirate of Tarsus, thereafter invading Cappadocia at Podanus.

In 879, Basil pressed his advantage and entered Tarsus, defeating the Emir's armies at Adana, Germanicea, and Adata, and holding the Cilician Gates as a first step in ending the annual raids of Muslims to Basil's strongholds.[1239] At the same time, Christopher led armies to Tephrice and eliminated the last stronghold of the so-called Paulician state of Chrysocheir. Unfortunately, tragedy would follow Basil's triumph as his son and heir Constantine would suddenly die in September, perhaps the only creature he had ever loved with a doting fondness.[1240]

This was a fatal a disruption in Basil's dynastic plans, at least to him, as his hated stepson Leo was now crowned co-*Basileus* despite his wishes that his second son Alexander succeed him, instead. In the *Basileus*'s grief, he had his deceased son sainted and ordered a monastery be built in his name. Photius and the Bishop of Eucaita, Theodore Santabarenus, would defy Christianity and hold a séance to summon Constantine's spirit to comfort the stricken Basil. A church was erected on the spot where he had supposedly materialized in golden lance and armor, as he did at Melitene and Tarsus, only to disappear as Basil tried to embrace him as the Continuator states.[1241] It was in this year

---

[1238] Treadgold, 458.

[1239] Hussey, 37.

[1240] Jenkins, 195. Especially in light of the resentment and fear he had in Leo for not being his biological son, living the lie that he was, and a guilty conscience he probably had over killing Michael III, Leo's true father.

[1241] Norwich, (APO), 98. A forgivable breach of Orthodox dogma in light of a grieving father who treated the incident as a miracle by erecting the new church.

he desperately crowned his son Alexander co-*Basileus*, though Leo was older and more popular.

In 880, the Sicilian Arabs spread their assaults to the Peloponnesus and Ionian islands in the eastern Mediterranean. A new Drungary of the Fleet, Nasr, hunted the raiders to Methone and Rhegium where Thracian and Macedonian land forces cleared Calabria and took Tarentum from the Arabs. In early 882, however, a reversal of Basil's campaign of 879 saw his armies expelled from Melitene, Germanicea, and Adata. The Theme of Cyprus, created the same year, was again lost to the Arabs as Basil pushed up the boundary of the region to a new Theme of Samos splintered from the Aegean Theme. This was proof that the Byzantine fleet continued its reputation of vulnerability and that the Empire's victories in the Grecian region of the Empire were superficial, just a balance of one capable fleet against another such fleet that could take, but not hold, an advantage.

From the latter half of 882 to the end of Basil's reign in 886, a series of domestic battles with his court and Leo, the charismatic son of Michael III would commence. As Leo was now sixteen, his mother Eudocia held the ancient and Oriental custom of the bridal show for him, but Basil made it a nightmare for him as he forced him to marry a certain Theophano. When Eudocia died that year, Basil took the opportunity to humiliate and beat Leo severely when he refused to give up his mistress, Zoe Zautzina. She was then banished and married off to another noble, Theodore Gutzuniates in 883, but this would not be the last time the Zautzinoi would affect Basil I's reign.

Theodore Santabarenus orchestrated a false plot against Basil by Leo and the prince was imprisoned while his supposed 'accessories' to the crime were blinded and tonsured. The Patriarch Photius and Stylitzes Zautzina, Zoe's father, alone convinced Basil to spare Leo the same fate. Historians claimed Leo was imprisoned for three years (883-886), although more modern ones claim it was more like three months. Nor was Leo the only one spared the humiliation of blinding as Andrew, Domestic of the Scholae was only dismissed by Basil, although he was reinstated when his successor died in Tarsus.

With the Caliphate at a timely disadvantage, Basil shrewdly improved Armenian and Bulgarian relations to strengthen his eastern position. In 884, after the Caliph allowed Armenia to be a principality again, naming Ashot III Bagratid its 'Prince of Princes', Byzantine diplomats reached out to King Ashot 'the Great' and new alliances were made.[1242] Basil himself sent Ashot a

---

[1242] Vasiliev, 314.

golden crown and a treaty of peace as Byzantium and the Caliph struggled for Armenian alliance. If there was anything involving Photius's claims that Basil may have been possibly and distantly related to the King or his nobles, it is not clear, especially since they were questionable claims. But, Basil I's final years were not happy ones personally; he saw his son's death as proof to him that God took vengeance on him for Michael's murder and he was bound for Hell's torments. As he was set to fits of derangement, it is a poetic justice as Michael's paranoia had made him a madman as well.[1243]

In July of 886, Leo was released from imprisonment after John Curcuas, Domestic of the Hicanati, had plotted against him. This was perhaps the Basileus's fatal mistake as on August 20, 886, he would have a hunting accident that was thought to be a plot Leo and Zautzes engaged.[1244] Basil was attacked by a stag on a hunting trip and was dragged by his belt some sixteen miles before being 'rescued' by Farghanese Turkish bodyguards who freed him after being separated from the entourage on the Cxus.[1245] However, because of Basil's temperament, the Turks feared baring their blades to cut the reins and the emperor suffered more, dying of his injuries on August 29. Though Basil claimed it was actually an attack by the nobles present, as he executed the guard who freed him, his treatment of the rightful prince of the Empire made Leo's transition as emperor not so rough. It was obvious Leo garnered much sympathy and was almost always more popular for being a legitimate heir than Basil was for his gruesome murder of Michael III. Basil I had become increasingly unpredictable, burdened down by the weight of his depression and frequently subject to bouts of insanity[1246] as his crimes revisited him over a decade later that day in the woods.

But, despite these misdeeds and a humble origin, Basil I played the game of imperial politics well. He had a courage and skill in battle with the proficiency of the mace (*rabdion*) with which he could cripple charging animals with a throw. His skill even had him likened to the mythic hero Akritas, the Greek-Arab that defeated an Emir.[1247] He knew how to handle the spread of Arabic influence in Greece, if not in Italy, and honored well the traditions of Byzantine

---

[1243] Jenkins, 195-196.

[1244] Treadgold, 461. The evidence of the incident is convincing on this being a plot, and though Basil did much good for the Empire, it was a well-deserved end for the petty usurper by the son of the *Basileus* he had murdered.

[1245] Norwich, (APO), 100.

[1246] Brownworth, 170.

[1247] Decker, 120.

diplomacy. His tactful garnering of Armenian and Bulgar goodwill made a resounding buffer to a weakening Caliphate in the East. His administration even saw progressive legal, financial, infrastructure, and religious reforms concerning the Photian Schism with Rome. Exploring these reforms will uncover the groundwork of the greatest age the Empire had or would ever see.

Furthering his glory is the depictive visual narrative of his life written by John Skylitzes in the eleventh century and painted by Sicilian monks three centuries later.[1248] As it is now displayed in the National Library of Spain in Madrid, it speculates on Basil's early life being one of fatalistic mysticism. From infancy, he was protected by eagles and appeared in visions as the *Basileus*. He even charmed his oppressor Omurtag the Bulgar into allowing him a symbolic golden apple. As a teenager, he arrived at the Monastery of St. Diomedes and meets Theophilitzes who introduced him to Michael III (not at the Palace stable, glossing the truth a bit). After visits to spiritual places and hunting trips, he is made Grand Chamberlain and is immediately made an enemy to the *Basilia* Theodora, attending the wedding of his mistress, Ingerina.

More miniatures depict Basil's influence at court by eliminating Michael III's enemies, only to be humiliated by Michael as a jilted lover and mocking his office by dressing a servant in royal robes. Next, after Michael's murder, his allies come before him such as the widowed Eudoxia, brought on a litter by 300 eunuchs as 'Mother of the Emperor (Leo)' bringing gifts of 500 slaves, 100 eunuchs, silver, and rugs. Military campaigns show Basil's displeasure at Procopius, who took Tarentum, for using the armies of his co-commander with which he had quarreled. His commander Leo was partially blinded and lost a hand for desertion by Basil as atrocity rivaled atrocity; Arab prisoners, on his orders, are boiled in tar, skinned alive, hanged, and used as 'target practice' for the archers at the Gulf of Corinth.

Atrocities are followed by paranoia when, apparently, an anonymous monk (and not Santabarenus) frames Leo by persuading him to carry a knife in his boot on a hunting trip, who then informs Basil that Leo will be concealing one. When Leo makes use of it in front of Basil, the livid *Basileus* jails Leo and contemplates blinding him. After guilt and pressure put on by the Senate, Leo was reinstated as *Caesar* on condition his illustrious hair be cut as a sign of submission. After Basil's fatal 'accident', the portraits end with the elderly Eudoxia paying homage to Leo as the new *Basileus*.

One of Basil's first acts as *Basileus* was to depose Photius and give the

---

[1248] Sherrard, 63-73.

Patriarchate to Ignatius in 867 as this was a serious attempt to placate the Pope in a time of crisis. Basil and Ignatius both wrote letters of humility to Hadrian asking for Western vicars in Constantinople with rhetoric such as: 'Spiritual Father and divinely revered Pontiff! Hasten the improvement of our church and through your interference with injustice give us an abundance of goods, namely, pure unity and spiritual joining free from any contention and schism, a church one in Christ, and a flock obedient to one shepherd.'[1249]

In 869, Hadrian II made good with such allowances as the learned missionary Constantine-Cyril had died at Rome and the Pope seized the Bishoprics of Moravia and Bulgaria for the Roman Church by sending there the Bishop Methodius. He then convened a Council of Bishops in October, demanding the emperor to depose and anathematize the re-instated Patriarch Photius which Basil reluctantly agreed to do on November 5. But it was becoming apparent that the Bulgar Khan was capitalizing on this conflict, his real interest being a totally independent Bulgarian Church from both parties,[1250] at this time an idea of unrealistic fantasy. The next year at the Council, Basil won over the Pope by securing Moravia and Bulgaria for the East. The Roman See, of course, was determined to keep this region at all costs and observers were shocked at the amount of sophistry and outright bribery instrumental in the process.[1251]

The Pope vehemently disagreed to Constantinople's terms, but the *Basileus*'s concession to depose Photius was in good faith and Hadrian let the matter be settled. It was a majority vote from an overwhelming number by Byzantine prelates (the Pope only had two) that decided the Khan, Michael-Boris, keep Moravia and Bulgaria Orthodox. It was important to Basil how Byzantine, not Roman, legal procedure allowed no appeal and that the verdict was given by the *Basileus* himself without legates.[1252] So, on March 4, 870, the Council ended and Ignatius began consecrating the Bulgarian clergy in St. Sophia.

Of course, in 873, Basil's triumph over the Paulicians saw him rehabilitate the distantly admired Photius as a teacher to his sons as the deposed Patriarch had 'uncovered' the genealogy that allowed Basil to be the descendant of the ancient kings of Arsacid Armenia. The fledgling Christianity of the Russians would also be a triumph for Basil as they accepted a Byzantine Archbishop

---

1249 Vasiliev, 330.

1250 Ostrogorsky, 234.

1251 Obolensky, 93.

1252 Norwich, (APO), 90. This is one of the first examples of Byzantine law as an independent institution from the old Roman, and any other, legal system.

and these Christian victory would extend to the Slavic Pagans remaining in the Peloponnesus and the Taygetus Mountains. The monks of Mt. Athos were also granted the *Chrysobull* of *exkeusia* on taxation[1253] so they would remain unmolested in their services to Christ. This supports the views on Byzantine missionaries that 'Self-reliance, asceticism, and the graphic embodiment of other Christian virtues were presumably the credentials for mission work rather than an ability to preach of teach in Slavic[1254]' as explained in Porphyrogenitus's *Life of Basil.*

In 877, the tides changed as Pope Hadrian II was dead, to be succeeded by John VIII, and when the Patriarch Ignatius died soon after on January 9, Photius was re-instated without complaint from the West. Photius considered himself as having a special relationship with the *Basileus*; as a mosaic shows, Photius gave Basil a manuscript of the Paris translation of the *Homilies of Gregory of Nazianus* commissioned in 880 as he is flanked by Eudocia, Leo, and Alexander.[1255] The symbolism here was that Photius considered himself another Gregory as Basil was another Theodosius I seeing the end of the Iconoclast heresy. Basil is also receiving a crown from the Archangel Gabriel and the Prophet Elijah. Photius would also be made head of the University of the Magnaura until his final deposing following his benefactor's death in 886.

Pope John also was slow to act on a crisis when, in a Council of 383 Bishops in 879, he offered to recognize Photius as Patriarch if Bulgaria was conceded back to the Catholic fold. In a crafty move, Photius had this offer deceptively edited from the Greek translation of John's letter to Basil and the unknowing Bishops ordained him as Patriarch. It appears as though, for the moment, dissent was finally quieted in the controversy of the Photian Schism by 880 and the Western and Eastern churches could settle in relative peace. In the late 880's, Basil would visit the Republic of Venice to show his good intentions by showing mercy to the Easterners there. When a group of Jewish merchants, having been expelled and sold into slavery as heretics by Methodius's missionaries, were brought to him they were freed and re-instated by the *Basileus*.[1256] He sent these Jews back to Constantinople and Bulgaria loaded with (notably Christian) Slavonic liturgical books.

The fiscal problems of the Empire were another challenge as Michael III

---

[1253] Vasiliev, 571.

[1254] Shepard, 239.

[1255] Angold, 136.

[1256] Obolensky, 96.

had left Byzantium in much debt while the coffers themselves were dwindled to an inadequate 100,000 *nomismata*.[1257] Basil I paid most of the donatives to the army and other institutions from his own and Eudocia's purse and this turned out to be economical as it was common knowledge that most of Basil's wealth came from Michael's donatives from the Treasury. He then asked for half of the value and amounts of donatives and gifts from a number of Michael's former clients to be returned. This probably made him less popular to them, but severing their ties with Michael by assassinating him made them resent Basil anyway, so it was just more backlash from his bloody ascension. These confiscated totals came out to be a reserve of over 4,300,000 *nomismata* (a year's income from taxation), balancing the revenues to a surplus needed for his administration. Perhaps the only reform he failed to accomplish was the effectiveness in the law prohibiting interest on loans, an old problem for several emperors.

This was needed to allow imperial financial authority to challenge, somewhat, the new system of the magnates who were paid for a kind of 'freedom and independence' as well as a 'protection' of lands for the lives of the 'poor' (*penetes*). These made up the oppressed peasant communities in Byzantium, introducing the vassal system of the feudal West which, in the context of Eastern methods, worked against imperial jurisdiction and authority. This compares to the 'paupers' of Western Europe and the 'orphans (*siroti*) of Muscovite Russia shortly after Byzantium's fall.[1258] In speculation, bureaucracy and corruption in the army and civil service allowed these activities to continue throughout the remaining Byzantine eras.

Perhaps the greatest program of reform in Basil I's administrative career was the promulgation of, in 886, the first Byzantine-Greek law code, or *Basilica*, named for its illustrious founder, to accentuate the works of Justinian I and Leo III. In 869, the *Basileus* insisted on another total overhaul of the Code of Roman Law. With the educated scholar Photius (who would re-edit the Book of Canon Law and translate it to Slavonic as well), Basil first published the *Eisagoge* or 'Introduction' to the *Corpus*. This was his way of making the Code more accessible in the Greek language to Byzantine jurists as the *Ecloga* did over a century earlier. Also the *Prochiron* ('Handbook') was introduced, serving as a manual of law, resembling Gaius's *Institutes*, in forty principal headings

---

[1257] Treadgold, 455-456.
[1258] Vasiliev, 345.

concerning both canon and secular law on the administrative scale.[1259] The true motives of this legal rehabilitation was to honor the laws 'by which alone, according to Solomon, a nation is exalted' (Proverbs 14:34). The resulting *Basilica* would be a six-volume work of sixty books outlining relevance in the existing *Code*, *Novels*, and *Digest*.

However, this did not stop Basil from criticizing the legal contributions of the Isaurians Leo III and Constantine V by condemning their legislation as mere 'silly talk.' This was instigated by the revisions and condensed versions necessary since Leo's reign, such as the Private Ecloga and the Private Enlarged Ecloga, both partially in Latin.[1260] The primary reason on this being that the Iconoclasm of the two tainted the legislatiors's reputations. Though Basil's Code was not on the scale of Justinian's works, the surge of Byzantine pride would not harbor Latin translation anymore, however, and Greek as well as Slavic editions of the Roman Laws were in demand. The Russians would also gain an Administrative Code based on Basil's legislation in the *Kormchaia Kniga* or 'Book of Rules'.

As well as this, Basil saw an opportunity to eliminate salutary laws that were antiquated, and this was characterized as *anakatharsis ton palaion nomon* ('the purging of ancient laws'). As far as administration also went, Michael III's and Basil I's reigns saw a great multiplication in the titles the emperor bestowed on his court at a rate of eighteen different ranks. This included a Master of Ceremonies (*o epi tes Katastaseos*), Chief Master of the Horse (*Comes tou Stablou*) and at least eight other offices of Church and state reserved for eunuchs with such complex duties for the Magistri, Anthypati, Patricii, Protospatharii, Dishypati, Spartharocandidati, Spatharii, Hypati and many others.[1261] Some are familiar to us, but others are alien and only demonstrate the Macedonian trust in expanded (if not top-heavy) bureaucracy to centralize imperial power in the *Basileus*.

Also important to Basil I were the building programs to rehabilitate the churches and other façades of Constantinople and the rest of Byzantium. This saw an important new era in Byzantine art and architecture, seeing changes towards more foreign influence. Armenian artistic influence in architecture and the visual arts would dominate this Armenian-Byzantine dynasty.[1262]

---

[1259] Norwich, (APO), 95.

[1260] Vasiliev, 243.

[1261] Ostrogorsky, 249.

[1262] Vasiliev, 372-373.

Basil's pride and joy of these policies was the five-domed *Nea Ekklesia*, or 'New Church', in Constantinople, built by an Armenian architect responsible for the Cathedral of Ani in his home province in Armenia. It is crowned with five domes, all resting on a floor plan of the four corners of a square, circumscribing the equilateral Byzantine cross. It basically serves as an imitation of St. Sophia with an atrium and with the basilica missing from the *Nea* Church.[1263] There is evidence from Turkish paintings made in 1480 that show the New Church was spared destruction in the City's fall in 1453 to the Ottomans.[1264]

Also, the declining state of the Church of the Holy Apostles and St. Sophia (damaged in an earthquake on January 9, 869) was restored and adorned with mosaics such as the Virgin and Child flanked by Saints Peter and Paul. The *Basileus* also built the Palace of the *Kenourgion* decorated by mosaics and went on to reform the buildings of thirty parishes. Basil also refurbished the Chalke Gate with marbles and mosaics as well as palaces such as the Mangana, Magnaura, Eleuthera, and St. Mamas; sadly, not one of these works commissioned by Basil I have survived to the present.[1265]

Basil's architectural tribute also accommodates a game reserved for the Byzantine elite as opposed to the chariot races of the masses. Near the New Church was the *Tzikanistirion*, a more 'civilized' elite place for the Persian polo game of *Tzikanion* honored by emperors and nobles in subsequent centuries.[1266] Historians such as the Westerner Liutprand of Cremona (920-972 CE) and Leo the Grammarian commented on its increase in size over the old arena existing before Basil I. The purpose of this building and the game itself was to bestow an elite prestige and mystery over the imperial line in the memory of all classes. In rougher terms, one can imagine an elite 'country club' environment here, where the elite met for polo, or the 'golf' of the Byzantine world.

Another mark of the elite in this era was the gaining of Classical education

---

[1263] Diehl, Charles. 'Byzantine Art'. Chap. 6 of *Byzantium: An Introduction to East Roman Civilization,* ed. by N.H. Baynes & H. St. L. B. Moss. Oxford, UK: Oxford University Press, 166-199. 1969, 179.

[1264] Mango, Cyril, 'Constantinople.' Chap. 1 of *The Oxford History of Byzantium,* ed. by Cyril Mango. Oxford, UK: Oxford University Press, 65-70. 2002, 66, insert. But in 1490, as it was used to store gunpowder, it was struck by lightning and exploded. Brownworth, 169f.

[1265] Norwich, (APO), 96-97.

[1266] Bergamo, Nicola. 'Tzikanion, the Noble Sport of Byzantium.' Presented at *The Thirty-Sixth Annual Byzantine Studies Conference.* (Philadelphia, PA: The University of Pennsylvania Press, October, 7-10, 2010).

from Constantinople, which was mostly the only place to learn publicly until the tenth and eleventh centuries. In these centuries, a more middle-class elite could be found with opportunities to quality education in the arts and sciences. Photius was a great promoter of these endeavors by hosting in his home debating societies and education circles, all chronicled in his encyclopedic *Bibliotheca* where only the art of poetry is excluded.[1267] There were a growing number of private schools in the Empire that taught rhetoric, metrics, and grammar created in Late Antiquity and other fields of study based on Classical works. However, these were mainly developments in minor arts and almost totally a Christian context in this development in Classical studies and how its class restrictions did make the moniker 'renaissance' a loose one for the Macedonians.[1268]

This definition of a Classical 'rebirth' was a major difference between Byzantine East and Carolingian West.[1269] But, this was not really a glass ceiling of learning to the Byzantine high echelons of society as, after all, Basil I himself was an 'illiterate adventurer', maintaining the highest office in Byzantium. This was a mark that the Byzantines had high regard for education and those who could afford it wanted the best for their children to succeed in Byzantium. This was the key to administrative posts or the echelons of the Church, as we do today in other careers, and the Classical education of Hellenism was the key to that success on a social scale - finally, the Dark Age of Byzantine history was ending.

Although, however, in order for the succeeding emperors to keep this legacy alive they, like Basil the Macedonian, would need certain 'outstanding abilities and caprices'[1270] to maintain the Empire's growth. However, this Classicism did not reach too far east as the Greco-Slavonic literary revolution was mainly based on Christianity, the Fathers, Patristics, and that which tied and controlled them concerning the Church. Not only did Constantine and Methodius usher this with works like the Slavonic Old Testament, but also introduced juristic texts in Slavonic including the *Nomocanon,* a Byzantine manual for secular and canon law based on imperial edicts.[1271] The Byzantinization of Bulgaria and the Slavic lands would be a complex and major topic in Macedonian intellectual life and its ecclesiastical affairs all at once.

---

[1267] Buckler, 209.

[1268] Mango, 'Revival of Learning', 226-227.

[1269] Angold, 138.

[1270] Ostrogorsky, 232.

[1271] Obolensky, 146.

# LEO VI 'THE WISE'
## (886-912)

# ALEXANDER III[1272]
## (912-913)

Also known as 'the Philosopher', Leo VI was a gifted ruler in diplomacy, legislation, as well as the author of poems, liturgical verses, and even a military manual. His love of education and men of letters had contemporaries citing that Leo had created a new Academy of Plato and Lyceum in the Palace. Unlike his uneducated stepfather Basil, Leo received top of the line Classical and Biblical educations from his teacher, the Patriarch Photius. Though half of his reign was overshadowed by his ministers and cruel stepfather, he gained lone authority by the start of the tenth century and secured the Macedonian legacy for his son, Constantine, and his hedonistic half-brother, Alexander.

Facing dangers in the East against shifting alliances with the Bulgars and their new nationalist Khan, Symeon, Leo's generals and astute diplomacy expanded Byzantium east in the name of Orthodoxy and the cultural Byzantinization of the northern Slavs. Though unfair assessments still exist claiming that the peace Basil achieved led Leo down a path of softness and indolence,[1273] in truth he was much more energetic than his predecessor. Rare for a teenage emperor, he had the education and intellect of a Julian the Apostate, and unlike Basil, was also 'easygoing and charming.'[1274]

Controversy surrounded him, however, as dissenting Patriarchs held firm against his needs to secure an heir in the face of his three wives dying prematurely. But, he brought general prosperity with his codification of the Roman Law and its stance against abuses exploiting the peasantry while broadening the bureaucracy, despite the antiquated aristocratic institutions still existing within the Empire. His only true failure was with the West and his inability to dislodge the Cretan and Sicilian Arabs. This would even bring shame to Byzantium as Leo would supplicate to the Pope supremacy in order to legitimize his marriages and children that Constantinople refused to consecrate. By his brother's death in 913, the throne would be split under a regency of over

---

[1272] Enumerated as Alexander III after the Emperors Alexander Severus (222-235 CE) and Lucius Domitius Alexander (308-311 CE), son of Maxentius.

[1273] Gibbon, 1635.

[1274] Brownworth, 171.

half a dozen claimants, the Empress, as well as the Patriarch. Leo VI's greatest error was in not protecting his legacy, but leaving it to incompetent successors like Alexander. His own place as a Macedonian on the throne was speculated at times, as in 888, with his *Funeral Oration* for his hated 'father' Basil I, reasserting the fact that Ingerina was fated to 'marry a better man' than in Michael III's bride show, that man being Basil.[1275]

According to Constantine Porphyrogenitus, Leo gained the support of the Magistrates, Senators, and nobles by increasing hospitality towards them.[1276] The best example is where Leo, unlike Basil, designed a second galley for the noble class – an Attache – that replaced the less adequate quarters given by Basil on his trips to the hot baths of Prousa. These new galleys were at the senators' disposal, taking them wherever they wished to go after the imperial naval procession. If this was during the ministry of Zautzes, it is not clear, but such hospitality denotes Leo's trust in the bureaucracy that may have come from his independent rule.

However, Leo was not immune to slander by prejudiced historical sources such as the *Chronicle of the Logothete*.[1277] It can be deduced that this was the military position of the Logothete as the bulk of the work was based on the horrific defeats and losses Leo's army suffered at the hands of the Arabs in the East. These spurious accounts chronicle the time between 912 and 920, being base perspectives on the conduct of Leo VI's leadership. He organized, in 902, one of the most far-sighted military reforms of the tenth century that provided aid to future support when Byzantine fortunes changed and opportunities could be taken. Leo's character had amazing qualities, such as the ability to inspire others and being 'lovable' to all, winning affection even to his opponents at court or the Senate. He sported a very choleric nature, however, and had awful bursts of temper that were 'dreadful to witness', though he always strove to control it.

He was born on September 19, 866, as the son of the last Amorian Michael III and his mistress, Eudocia Ingerus, wife to Basil the Macedonian. This lineage puts him in the center of the succession as the offspring of two imperial dynastic families linked by blood and marriage. It was decided almost from his birth in the Purple Chamber of the Palace that he be the successor of Basil despite his own legitimate children. As much as he detested this fact, this restrained the Macedonian from blinding, tonsuring, or even castrating the

---

[1275] Herrin, *(WIP)*, 223.

[1276] Porphyrogenitus, *De Administrando*, 247.

[1277] Jenkins, 198-199.

young prince when in captivity for false allegations of rebellion. But after a mysterious mishap with Basil, Leo took the throne immediately and began his brilliant, if not divisive, reign. He balanced taking his responsibilities seriously and competently while enjoying women and leisure and allowing other advisers to conduct his business especially his mistress's father, Zautzes, who also was said was to have greatly aided him in codifying his laws.[1278]

Leo raised his greatest supporter and father of his mistress, Stylianus Zautzes, to Master of Offices and Logothete, an ever-increasing title of power in this period, as a real conductor of imperial policy in the courts of Theodora, Leo, and his son Constantine.[1279] Until Zautzes's death years later, he would be the real power behind the throne orchestrating foreign and domestic policies, even being granted a title known as *Basileopator* ('imperial father'). Leo respected his Amorian roots, having his father Michael buried from a pithy grave across the Bosphorus to the Church of the Holy Apostles. In a twist of irony, Leo almost at once deposed Photius as Patriarch as Basil had done, raising his brother Stephen to the post. Returning him to the City after a tonsuring of twenty years starting Christmas Day, 866, he would also be one of the new styles of Church officials being eunuchs. In 887, three years after his plot against Leo failed, the *Basileus* had the imprisoned Theodore Santabarenus blinded and exiled.

In 883, the Emir of Tarsus sent a fleet to Euripos in the Theme of Hellas, but was destroyed and repelled by the use of Greek Fire from the battlements.[1280] In the West, in 886, the Arabs were busy attempting to take Bari with the aid of the Lombards of Benevento, this alliance being checked by the Byzantines. After taking time to rebuild economically and take the opportunities to revise a new Code of Roman law in 891, Leo sent the Strategos Symbaticius to southern Italy and Lombard territory. Symbaticius was a powerful general that led the Themes of Macedonia, Thrace, Cephalonia, and Longobardia in Italy, which Leo had separated as its own Theme. This combined force expelled the Lomabards from Benevento and Symbaticius annexed it when the Protospratharios Tzikines and the Magister Eladas demanded ready cash from Western patricians and non-military citizens.[1281]

At the same time, the Emirate of Tarsus was conducting naval raids on the coast of the Cibrrhyaeot Theme and the Anatolic was the only defense available

---

[1278] Treadgold, 461-462.

[1279] Ostrogorsky, 250.

[1280] Pryor, John and Elizabeth M. *Jeffreys. The Age of the Dromon: The Byzantine Navy ca. 500-1204.* Leiden: Brill. 2006, 620; Decker, 223.

[1281] Porphyrogenitus, *De Administrando*, 257.

to repel the Tarsus Arabs. This situation would remain as such until fresh tactics involving a new people to the Empire, the Magyars, would tip the scale in 895. The most troubling developments happened in Bulgaria after Khan Boris-Michael retired from his throne and tonsured himself in the Monastery of St. Panteleimon in 889. He left Bulgaria to his eldest son Vladimir and a break of the Byzantine peace quickly took place. Vladimir, as a Pagan, attempting to aposticize Christian Bulgaria as Julian had tried to in the Empire in 360. He immediately persecuted the Orthodox clergy for four years with the aid of the Pagan-sympathizing Franks. In 893, a galvanized Boris-Michael fled his monastery and harshly deposed his infidel son, blinding him and forcing him to be a Christian monk for life as an ironic end to Vladimir's reign. Boris-Michael returned to retirement and the Boyar nobles gave the throne to his third son, Symeon, who was taken away from the life of a monk.

The peace Leo VI brokered with Boris-Michael was quite successful and his diplomacy was 'permanent and salutary', leading to open trade with Bulgarian wares such as hides, waxes, and slaves.[1282] If, however, the Byzantines believed peace would be restored and the matter settled under Symeon 'the Great', they would soon be disillusioned. Though Orthodox like his father, Symeon was a strong patriot to Bulgaria and resented what he was seeing as Byzantine interference in domestic matters, possibly having been promised by his predecessor the use of an independent, Bulgarian language in liturgy.[1283] He also persecuted the Greek clergy in exchange for a new Bulgarian and Slavonic clergy, seeking to expunge all Greek as the language of State and Church. As he was a strong leader and commander, handling him would take delicacy and a certain respect for Bulgarian policy to appease Symeon. The result in 894, however, would be one of mismanagement and regrettable failure at the hands of the rarely incompetent minister, Stylanius Zautzes.

Zautzes was a reactionary, convincing the seemingly pliable Leo to monopolize all Bulgarian trade and move operations to the intractable position of Thessalonica, where corruption was less visible to the emperor. Zautzes also sought to punish Symeon further by levying heavy customs duties and import taxes on Bulgarian goods coming in and out of the region. Numerous, vital trade routes from the Black Sea to the Bosporus were wiped out and the Thessalonican mountain passes were nearly impassable in the harsh winters,

---

[1282] Jenkins, 200-201.
[1283] Treadgold, 463.

further hindering the Bulgars.[1284] Symeon responded by invading Thrace and Macedonia, and in a rousing Bulgar victory resembling the debacle of Nicephorus I, Symeon slaughtered the officers and commanders of the army Leo sent to the northern Themes.

In 895, a desperate Leo sought the aid of Bulgaria's eastern neighbors to fight Symeon. This was the first connection between Byzantium and the Siberian migrations of the Magyars. A 'Finnish-Ugartian' people,[1285] sometimes mistaken for Turks or Avars by the West, they were able to make naval offenses on Bulgaria. An imperial fleet under the command of the Domestic of the Scholae, Nicephorus Phocas, sailed with the Magyars to the lower Danube. Peace was offered to Symeon, but the Khan only jailed the ambassador and the fleet made an invading siege on Dobrudja. The Magyars and the Byzantines would take captive soldiers and raid all the way to Symeon's new capital at Preslav; now it was Symeon that would sue for peace.

Leo had to agree to a truce as his army was occupied in the West to both handle an Armenian invasion by the Caliphate in the East and the loss of Benevento to the Franks of Spoleto. Leo sent an ambassador to make a treaty with the Bulgars, choosing hastily the unfortunate Leo Choerosphactes to arbitrate. Symeon had the ambassador imprisoned as a bluff after he saw his siege was lifted. Symeon, seeing the *Basileus* was in a bind with the Arabs and Franks, decided to beat Byzantium at its own game and gathered a force of neighboring people hostile to the Magyars, the Turkic Pechenegs. The savage Pechenegs routed the Magyars and they fled east on the Danube through Bulgaria to Moravia and Transylvania to raid and settle. Here on the Pannonian plains, this region would become the Magyar homeland of Hungary as it survives in modern times ethnically and politically.

Symeon conceded to Choerosphactes on condition of an exchange of Bulgarian hostages, but once Leo VI did this, Symeon re-imprisoned Choerosphactes. In 896, Leo readied operations to enter Bulgaria, but Zautzes once again took advantage against the Domestic of the Scholae. Perhaps Nicephorus Phocas was a true rival to the minister? Or he just simply wanted self-glorification? Or was his replacement more easily manipulated? Zautzes convinced Leo to replace the Domestic of the Scholae with the less experienced

---

[1284] Norwich, (APO), 108.
[1285] Vasiliev, 316f.

Leo Catacalon.[1286] That year, Symeon invaded Macedonia again and Catacalon was sent to face the Bulgarians.

It was a disaster that once again revealed the ineptitude of the overly ambitious Zautzes as a foreign as well as domestic leader attempting to dominate and manipulate an all too forgiving *Basileus*. At Bulgarophygon, Leo Catacalon was defeated and forced to flee while his officers and troops were being killed and taken captive. After this matter was settled and Thrace was devastated, the imprisoned Choerosphactes was offered a treaty exacting annual tribute and captured Bulgarian outposts in exchange for 120,000 Byzantine captives. Choerosphactes had no choice but to agree and even furthered the peace by letting Symeon be his child's god-father, re-organizing his borders into the Themes on the Strymon out of eastern Macedonia and Nicopolis on the Greek mainland of Cephalonia.

The East was faring little better as the prolific Arabs of Tarsus, in 897, took the Cappadocian Theme of Corum as the Arabs of Azerbaijan took Kars, the capital of Byzantine Armenia. The Theme of the Chersonese was also a diversion, for their armies rebelled against their Strategos. A year later, the Tarsus Arabs defeated the Byzantine fleet and killed 3,000 men in the process. The already stressed Cibyrrhaeot Theme would further be raided by land forces. The Bulgarian strategy had unfortunately done its job of dividing Constantinople from Armenia, causing its neglect to allow the total loss of Tarsus to the Empire.

Internal distress plagued Leo when an assassination plot at the hands of the greedy Zautzes family (without Zoe, the *Basileus*'s mistress) failed. Stylianus was mainly spared life and limb due to his daughter's pleas to Leo. It is likely that Zoe was never involved in any plot as the *Basilia* Theophano died childless in 898, Leo then marrying his mistress in hopes of bearing an heir. It was fortunate as 'coincidentally' Zoe's husband, Theodore, died at the same time as Theophano, freeing the long-denied lovers to marry. The subject of poison was rightfully suggested in court gossip, but no proof was ever uncovered. Theophano was a dubious choice of *Basilia* as biographers detailed a 'morbid zeal' in her religious asceticism, refusing her husband's bed for a rough mat, dressing in rags, eating only bread and vegetables, and giving all of her money and stately robes to the poor.[1287] Eventually, she cloistered herself in a nunnery at the Church of St. Mary Theotokos in Blacharnae, dying there on November

---

[1286] Treadgold, *(BAIA)*, 464.
[1287] Norwich, (APO), 112.

10, 897. Faithful to God as she was, she refused to bear Leo a son and was scorned for it.

But in 899, a bittersweet development in Leo's court occurred as both Zoe and Stylianus Zautzes died. Zautzes was already burnt out as Leo's favorite courtier and several of his lackeys were imprisoned and punished for the corruption in the bureaucracy Leo tried to prevent. Zautzes's remaining relatives plotted against Leo as well, but this was discovered by an Arab eunuch known as Samonas. The fortunate and indignant emperor would than have tonsured and exiled the last of the corrupt and incompetent Zautzes family from the imperial court of Constantinople. Now, the tenth century would begin as a more prosperous one with a more active, cautious, and outstanding emperor in that of Leo VI.

In 900, Tarsus was finally stormed and sacked by Leo, capturing its Emir and crushing its armies under the noses of the Bulgars. More fortunately, the Baghdad Caliph al-Mu'tadid put down a rebellion there, disabling its navy while tiring himself out in the process and leaving Eastern regions open to Byzantinization. Leo planned to expand these boundaries east and did so first by annexing a freed Armenia and its principality as a new Theme of Mesopotamia. Leo saw prime opportunity when the Arabs were in a weakened state and boldly seized new territories for expansion, said to further fueling the flames of his moniker 'the Wise.'

But new challenges in the West and in Constantinople itself would arise in 901. A Syrian fleet under Damien of Tarsus invaded the Grecian port of Demetrias as the Arabs of Sicily took Rhegium, repelling a Byzantine fleet. But the victories in the East continued as Leo Lalacon, the Armeniac Strategus, drove out the Arabs from western Armenia as naval forces landed at Tarsus, ravaging the region to the Euphrates with the military governors of Coloneia, Mesopotamia, and Chaldea.[1288] In desperation, Leo arranged a marriage between his daughter Anna to the Western powers of the Frankish Emperor Louis III of Provence.

Leo saw that the Strategi of the Anatolian, Thracian, and Armeniac Themes were vital to the northeast's protection. He gave grants and paid levies to the Bucellerion of Cappadocia: Bareta, Balbadona, Aspona, Karkous, and to the Anatolics: Eudocios, Haghia Agapitos, and Aphrezia amounting to 700 pounds of gold apiece. He then combined the regions into one territory

---

[1288] Porphyrogenitus, *De Administrando*, 207.

known as Commata and spread to the garrisons of Charisonum.[1289] This kept commanders loyal and soldiers fed, although corruption would still inevitably be a presence. Internal challenges and conflicts came in the form of dissent over the third marriage of Leo to Eudocia Baiana (although it was allowed by the tolerant Patriarch Antony) and the plotting of Leo's impotent brother, Alexander. Alexander attempted a plot against Leo, but was found out, but still having to be in one piece as he was still the only Macedonian heir left.

That same year, more tragedy struck the Purple Chamber as the emperor's third wife, Eudocia Baiana of Phrygia, died in childbirth on Sunday, April 12, her weakened son dying a few days later. With little time for grief, Leo prepared a fourth marriage but the strict Patriarch Nicholas Mysticus forbade it as 'worse than fornication' in the Palace and the days of Antony were over by 902. As if adultery and fornication were not already proven practices in the imperial histories! But it all went back to Orthodox Scripture and the imperial scandal of overriding the power and place of the Church in temporal and imperial affairs, and this point was taken quite seriously. Divorce was given only by special dispensation and even then, as once happened, a couple would be locked in a house for a week and if consummation had not occurred, divorce was given on grounds of 'mutual hatred.'[1290] So, Leo compromised and took only a mistress in Zoe Carbonopsina ('Coal-' or 'Black-Eyes') and waited for a male heir to be produced until any marriage was to be considered.

In 902, military affairs in the East were made of import again as Leo sent his Domestic of the Scholae, Leo Catacalon, to sack Theodosiopolis and make garrisons at the key city of Ketzeon, retaliating against the invasion of Tauromenium on August 1. Unfortunately, as in Basil's time, military fleets were used as transports of stone and materials to build new churches, neglecting the capture of the city of Tauromenium for lack of a better fleet.[1291] Leo pushed his frontiers east to create a Cleisura of Sebastea, inducing the *Basileus* to re-organize his fleets. He separated Drungari into Turmae land forces, moderating and exchanging forces from such regions as the Bucephelloi and Cappadocian. As for increasing the Themes at the Arab borders, he transferred 5,000 infantry to cavalry and packed in 6,000 more Armenian soldiers.

In spring of 903, a Byzantine force made its way to Adata, but hastily

---

[1289] Porphyrogenitus, 237; Ostrogorsky, 252, claims the ratio of forty pounds of gold equaled 4,438.40 gold francs; individual Themes gathered from this to thirty, twenty, ten, or five pounds.

[1290] Brownworth, 174f.

[1291] Treadgold, (BAIA), 466.

returned to Constantinople when Arabs threatened its gates. For twenty years, the combined forces of Crete and Syria had escalated from petty village raids to full-on urban assaults using a nearly 'superhuman courage' in wanting higher-grade loot.[1292] The commanding and converted Muslim Leo of Tripoli repelled the fleet and raided the customs station at Abydus and the wealthy city of Demetrias in Thessaly to make headway to the Marmara from the Hellespont. When the energetic and able Drungari Himerius defeated this fleet, it retreated to Thessalonica, named the 'second city of the Empire' to heavily raid it. It is recounted how on July 29, the Arabs poured in the walls to commit 'bloodshed and butchery . . .for a full week' also taking 30,000 prisoners.[1293]

Of course this claim of the 'second city' was quite true as far as the trade and the Western defense of the Empire were concerned. Later, Himerius would be caught off guard by Leo of Tripoli, appealing to the Slavs of the surrounding region for aid which did not come. After, Leo captured the city and half of its inhabitants, returning to North Africa by the Arab Mediterranean coast. Selling his captives in Tarsus, the city inhabitants gleefully received Arab captives of Byzantium in exchange for the Thessalonicans. These reports come down to us by the priest John Cameniates (fl. 904), who was an eyewitness to these events. Also in 903, the Khan Symeon would successfully unite the three major Slavic nations of the Balkans: Bulgaria, south Macedonia, and Albania under one state 'which gave Bulgarian nationality its ultimate aspect'[1294] as colorfully illustrated in the Bulgarian histories.

A year later, Andronicus Ducas was sent by the emperor Leo to take Germanicea and defeat the Arab armies of Tarsus in retaliation for Thessalonica, the culprit actually being Leo of Tripoli. But new domestic developments would change the attitudes of the court and Ducas as well. A surviving son, Constantine, was born to Leo and his mistress Zoe in September and Leo would then finally attempt to consecrate the event by a fourth marriage, although as Leo's law on fourth marriage states, the baby could not be baptized.[1295] The incensed Patriarch Nicholas would conspire against the *Basileus* using Ducas as his puppet, who wanted the throne for himself. Even as Ducas was sent east to fortify Himerius's naval forces, he wrote letters of the plot to the Patriarch. But, the ever loyal Samonas learned of Ducas's plot as well and Ducas fled

---

[1292] Jenkins, 203.

[1293] Norwich, (APO), 110.

[1294] Vasiliev, 317.

[1295] Brownworth, 176.

to Anatolia. A deserter made it to the City with one of Ducas's letters and the conspirators' fates were sealed as Ducas would die in Arab captivity as a forcibly-converted Muslim, fleeing Leo's judgment. It appears he also did not impress the child Caliph al-Muqtadir and his court with his success on the battlefield, though this was done by surprise attacks and not by Byzantine slowness or incompetence.

To save his own skin perhaps, in 906, Nicholas Mysticus agreed to baptize Leo's son Constantine on the Feast of the Epiphany on January 6th. As for a marriage, Nicholas stalled as he feared he would be deposed (or worse) when he conceded to the union, which he still agreed to do on January 9. Leo then went over his Patriarch's head to the West and appealed to Pope Sergius III, resulting in Nicholas's subsequent resignation and tonsure in 907. Leo would then proudly ascend his four-year-old son, Constantine, in 908 to co-*Basileus* as a legitimate heir, still staying his hand with Alexander, guilty in the plot of 901 having been kept imprisoned for seven years. Meanwhile, Leo's show of penitence was a publicized and commemorated event in Constantinople as mosaic reliefs of Saint Sophia depict his total obeisance for his crime.[1296]

A Russian army under Oleg marched from his capital at Kiev and was repulsed from Constantinople by its famously secured walls, also being bought off to keep the peace to ensure the rights of Russian merchants on Byzantine soil. But by 911, the Russians were eased into the Orthodox fold by witnessing the splendor of its reverence and artistic iconography in the Palace, opening itself up as a Byzantine sphere of influence. The Russians were described as 'being instructed . . . by the true faith' as they toured Constantinople's luxuries, beauty and Churches full of the faithful.[1297] Thus, the Russians set the stage for the future when a floundering Byzantium would need the aid of the Russian aristocracy, joined by the belief of Orthodox Christianity.

As for the Ducas incident, Leo made a successful exchange of prisoners with the Caliph that included Ducas's armies and his son, Constantine. It was shrewd of the *Basileus* to allow these men to return to their former posts and make Constantine Ducas the Strategos of the Charsianum Theme. Sparing these men only strengthened their loyalty to Leo instead of making him appear weak; this having been a proven statement made by past Emperors such as Marcus Aurelius in the second century. He had little doubt that a reinstatement and a pardon of Ducas would assure his allegiance, betrayed as the *Basileus*

---

[1296] Treadgold, 469.
[1297] Obolensky, 188-189.

felt.[1298] Also, Leo strengthened his army and frontier ambitions by appointing the Armenian Melias, the conqueror of the southeastern regions, to create the two Cleisurae of Lycandus and Leontocome built on the ruins of Tephrice.

Still wishing in 910 to expel the Arabs from Thessalonica, Leo sent Himerius and his fleets to the ancient Grecian port of Laodicea and gained the aid of its Italian population. In exchange, the forces would travel west to fight against the Sicilian Muslims in 911 from the Theme of Longobardia. Leo's most ambitious military venture of all would be the attempt of re-conquering both Crete and Cyprus with the imperial fleets. Soldiers from the Scholae, Sebastea, Thrace, and Armenia joined hired soldiers from Oleg's Russians for this dramatic cause. It consisted of 119 ships, according to Constantine Porphyrogenitus, and 43,000 men, its cost totaling not less than 239,000 *nomismata*.[1299] This would include a contingent of the first Russo-Byzantine troops recorded in Greek history with 700 Russian sailors paid in gold by the new *kentenarion* standard.[1300]

But, despite its size, it still managed to overreach itself. The combined forces of Leo of Tripoli and Damien of Tarsus ambushed Himerius's forces at the island of Chios and annihilated the fleet at Mylitene in April, Himerius barely escaping with his life. There is debate just why, however; it is argued that news of the failing health of the *Basileus* reaching Himerius, withdrawing to investigate in Constantinople. This seems unlikely as Himerius had no cause to leave the fleet if the emperor was dying, as he was no ambitious claimant to the throne. It may be more likely that the claims that Himerius's defeat happened first and news of this reached the City, causing the *Basileus*'s distress. Whether it was a cause or effect, Leo VI 'the Wise' died of intestinal disease on May 11, 912.

Leo VI was truly a great ruler of the Middle Ages as one of the best and most inclusive lawgiver since Justinian, also expanding boundaries unprecedented in Byzantium by improving, distinctively, the military reforms of Theophilus. His policies on tax bureaucracy and the aristocracy created a more cohesive administrative unit dependent on the throne and central government. Furthermore, his artistic and poetic side gained more favor to education and the rising Hellenism that would partially define Byzantine culture in subsequent centuries. His attention to court ceremony and etiquette was an inspiration for the treatises of his son, Constantine VII: to reassert imperial authority after

---

[1298]  Jenkins, 205.

[1299]  Treadgold, 470.

[1300]  Ostrogorsky, 258.

Iconoclasm, the hierarchy of the court was carefully constructed to demonstrate their loyalty to the emperor[1301] over religious authority and division.

He made quite a few mistakes, however, including how he handled the Church and his last military debacle somewhat overshadowed the year 912. But he was a talented ruler and almost perfect compared to the atrocious but blissfully brief reign of his antecedent step-brother, Alexander. His hierarchies did, however, led to an almost unwieldy bureaucracy, (an unfortunate attribute of Byzantine political culture) and although this made for a tighter control of government efficiency, Leo has been blamed for the country magnates who were inimical to good government[1302] of the era.

The greatest division in Leo's Church was the issue of his multiple marriages in search for an heir when Leo's brother, Stephen, and the moderate Patriarch Antony Cauleas died in 901. As the succeeding Nicholas Mysticus was a nephew of Photius, an anti-Macedonian bias would always be under the surface of his Patriarchy. The stern Bishop of Caesarea, Arethas, sided with the ousted Patriarch, Ignatius Rhangabe, against any consecrated marriage by putting pressure on Nicholas, who even commented that: 'If the Emperor, inspired by the devil, should order something contrary to the law of God, no obedience is due him; an impious command from an impious man is held to be null and void.'[1303] In 903, when Leo married his third wife, the distressed Patriarch Nicholas saw it as too much of an affront to canon law and God himself, planning an assassination while in church (murder, perhaps, being worse than adultery, notwithstanding). It failed with the assassin remaining silent to the plot, but of course the damage was done as Leo would always suspect Nicholas Mysticus and later see him forcibly abdicated in February, 907 for the Ducas plot.

As these marriages ended due to death and not divorce, Leo would be dedicated and wily in his legitimate endeavors, using Western doctrine to do so, perhaps adopting an intellectual tactic of coolly using objectivity as a scholar would. The stakes were high as ecclesiastical authority, public opinion, and the canonical and civil spheres were threatened. These worries arose from the violation of the privilege of the *Basileus*'s 'unwritten' (*agraphos*) and 'incarnate law' (*empsychos nomos*).[1304] Saints Augustine, Ambrose, and St. Jerome all

---

[1301] Angold, 142.

[1302] Jenkins, 208.

[1303] Diehl, 172.

[1304] Jenkins, 213. Or even the defenses of the emperor as *agrophos nomos*, 'a law unto himself' that rose above the jurisdiction of any civil law, Jenkins, 218.

approved of multiple marriages when a spouse died; but the Eastern Church Father that took precedence on this matter in the East was St. Basil. He claimed that such marriages were a moderated form of fornication, heir or no heir, mere polygamy - 'a crime bestial . . .alien to humankind' and deserved no less than eight years' penance,[1305] which Leo would serve after marrying Zoe Carbonopsina. Leo was refused communion, sanctuary, and attendance at service in the Church itself on Christmas Day of 906 as well as the Feast of the Epiphany by the Patriarch Euthymius for his fourth marriage.

Nicholas would further publish the *Tomus of Union*, forbidding fourth marriages in the Empire after the concession made for Leo. The ideas of a type of 'celibacy' after an ended marriage was first entertained by Greek monks and contravened marriage as a need to continue the propagation of mankind.[1306] An heir to the throne was decided as more imperative to the Empire than the pressures of the Church to uphold St. Basil's doctrines. On the *Basileus*'s side was the Scriptural words of St. John (4:18) and the polygamous Samaritan Woman, St. Paul, and Corinthians I (7:2, 8, 9) that defined marriage, but not the tenants of what was polygamy. The artful Aristotelian logic Leo used as a defense (and perhaps Photius's as well) triumphed over the Biblical stance, but it would all fall on deaf ears by the anti-imperial factions of the Church.[1307]

Perhaps the most shocking part of Leo's use of Western doctrine to define Orthodoxy is when he actively sought out Pope Sergius III to approve the marriage, who gave it in exchange for Eastern support against the Sicilian Arabs. This was seen as a direct betrayal of his role as Eastern Roman *Basileus* by submitting to Western supremacy in spiritual matters, a war fought by many of his predecessors. Basil the Macedonian was a facilitator and wished for a stronger union in Christianity, but not at the cost of Byzantium's supreme role as the true Roman Empire with one true, and Orthodox, Church.

Also, it should also little surprise that the Italo-Byzantine monasteries would become great centers of Greek culture and education[1308] with such high interaction between the two Empires. The West flowered with the influences of Hellenism at Longobardia and Calabria, both states successfully divided and fostered by Leo. Advancement from the West to Byzantium did not seem to appear in education, however, at institutions such as the University in

---

[1305] Norwich, (APO), 114.

[1306] Gibbon, 1636.

[1307] Jenkins, 216, 223.

[1308] Vasiliev, 327.

Constantinople, where theology chairs had not existed in Leo's time with such laymen as Photius filling the role. Boundaries between lay and ecclesiastical matters also did not seem to exist at this point in intellectual life.[1309] A product of this artistic revival was the greatest of Leo's depictions above the doors of the Hagia Sophia in mosaic. Receiving the divine mercy not given in life, Leo humbly bows down, in penitence perhaps, before the throne of God as Mary intervenes on his behalf.[1310]

As far as the missions of Orthodoxy in the Slavic East, there was a stumbling block at the Black Sea as outlined in the Byzantine studies on foreign relations. Orthodox missionaries collapsed as the Khazars of the north Pontic region had slowly been separating themselves from Byzantine ecclesiastical influence. By 900, in Gothia, the system had collapsed altogether and the Bishoprics of the entire Crimean to the east of Sebastopolis had rejected and exiled the foreign clergy practically into hiding.[1311] This is mostly because of Constantinople being a non-entity among the crisis of the emerging Pechenegs who was also alienating other Turkish and Bulgarian tribes. The Pontic border was even slipping as Leo expanded over Caliphate territory in the region, a consequence of Leo's choices in where to expand and protect borders east over the Crimean.

The years between 901 and 908 were critical in supplying the right defenses to the Eastern Themes. From the time of the creation of the Mesopotamian and Lycandan Themes, at least 6,000 men were billeted in these border jurisdictions. The growth rate of the entire Byzantine military force itself would also climb from 124,000 to 300,000 (twenty percent) in this period.[1312] Beginning around 902, a major overhaul of internal military organization began that seemed to secure most victories earned on the battlefield with the encroaching Arabs. As read in his *Taktika,* for example, Leo VI arranged the command force of the army and navy with the precision of hierarchy that he had created at his court:

Two Turmarchs (leading 2,000 men)
Eighty Tribunes (Fifty men apiece)
Four Drungaries (1,000 men)
400 Decarchs (ten men apiece)
Twenty Counts (200 men apiece)
800 Pentarchs (five men apiece)

---

[1309] Hussey, 148.
[1310] Brownworth, 177.
[1311] Obolensky, 177.
[1312] *Taktika* XVIII, 143, 145 & 149; Treadgold, (BAIA), 77-78.

Forty Centarchs (100 men apiece) Total officers: 1,346 for a 4,000 man force.

This arrangement also affected the fixed number of the Banda force from its 200 to 400 troops on the battlefield, but generally to a new 100 count off field. He also increased the cavalry forces by five percent and began to intersperse this cavalry with the infantry and Banda in their military settlements.[1313]

As another reform, as soon as he reached the throne, Leo VI went about the task of finishing the *Basilica* his step-father began. To aid him, Leo would convene a council of jurists chaired by the Protospatharius Symbatius and the energy of the Master Stylianus Zautzes in its sixty books (*hexakontabiblios*) and six volumes (*hexabiblios*).[1314] The final edition, and its introduction of the *Epanagoge,* included Leo's and Alexander's names as well as Basil's. In centuries ahead, jurists would add countless commentaries and interpretations as the Code became a living entity of legal change over time known as the *Scholae.* In the eleventh or twelfth century the Byzantine jurist, Patzes, would write the *Tipucitus* to stand as a rubric and table of contents to Basil and Leo's Code.[1315]

Included were the Novels Leo addressed in his 'Collection' for the 'rectification and purification of the laws',[1316] ninety of which (in lines 2-17 and 75) are addressed to the Patriarch Stephen. One of the chief aims of this code was to check the already diminishing power of the Curia and Senate as explained, 'The state was completely identified with the Emperor and with his military and bureaucratic machines.'[1317] Since Octavius Augustus's time (63BCE-14 CE), these bodies have been responsible for the tempering of imperial power. Over the centuries, invading forces and fading institutions in the West had curbed the power of the Senate as executive leadership when it was needed and preferred.

By Leo's time in the mid-Byzantium era, the Senate was practically a mere figurehead surviving for Roman tradition's sake more than anything else; in the *Basilica,* three *Novels* – 46, 47, and 78 – are specifically aimed at Imperial over Curial and Senatorial powers.[1318] They were also one of the roots of the unfair land owning practices against peasant communities that would appear

---

[1313] Treadgold, *(BAIA)*, 105-106.
[1314] Ostrogorsky, 243.
[1315] Vasiliev, 343.
[1316] *'ai ton nomon epanorthotikai anakatharseia'*
[1317] Ostrogorsky, 244-245.
[1318] Norwich, (APO), 106.

in the *Procheiron, Epanogoge,* and the Novels of both Basil I and Leo VI, which was basically loan sharking. Leo rectified this by claiming the Medieval status of 'free' peasants and serfs (*parics*) on communal village property. Although it granted them certain immunity from landowners, it consisted of casual laborers with taxable land and not 'free' men as 'their only freedom was from destitution.[1319]

In the 113 edicts written between 886 and 899, the *Book of the Eparch* was published as a guide to early Macedonian financial administration in commercial guilds and the purchasing capital in the City.[1320] It outlines the imperial monopolies on certain trades and industries, taxation, and economic policies. Most interestingly is its description of Byzantium's economic culture, especially the rise and practices of trade guilds. It was in the military manual inspired by Maurice's *Strategicon,* the *Tactica,* that Leo outlined the need for the aristocracy to hold chief bureaucratic and military posts, especially the Strategi as a class apart with their privileges[1321] as they mostly represented the idle rich.

The *Tactica* was Leo VI's military manual that described the need for unconventional warfare in handling the Arab and Slav armies as well as the organization and tactics developed since the manuals of the sixth century. Within it we see reforms such as the Thematic cavalry expansion of 18.3 percent before 902 to twenty-three percent afterwards, and this coupled with an additional 5,900 men defending ten new Themes created by Leo's reforms.[1322] But, punitive raiding was a necessity as well as guerilla tactics were in avoiding direct battle and in harassing the departing troops for cattle and plunder.[1323] Not exactly the bold discipline depicted in Maurice's handbook, but when the enemy shows superiority in a policy of fielded warfare, it is foolish and destructive to not employ alternative modes of battle. Most curious of all was the gaping hole in the instruction in the center of Byzantine diplomatic relations, an elephant in the room upon which was not to be commented.

The above was true as Bulgaria had now become a political entity in a limbo as,'neither Christian ally or barbarian foe',[1324] merely classified as military targets in the provinces north of Bulgaria. This only clarified a certain xenophobia Leo and the Empire felt for a growing political concern seen to be

---

[1319] Jenkins, 206.

[1320] *ibid.,* 208.

[1321] *Taktika,* II, 21; Ostrogorsky, 255.

[1322] Treadgold, (BAIA), 110

[1323] Herrin, 144-145.

[1324] Magdalino, 175.

getting out of hand. Besides this there is instruction on the use of arms such as the shock and awe of naphtha and Greek Fire where a handler, 'prepared fire and thunderous smoke, discharged through siphons, blackened the enemy in smoke.'[1325] The amount of work produced on farms was heavily scrutinized for resources of the cavalry, almost resembling a census. If one cavalryman had on his property at least seven tenants, slaves, or working relatives, he need not be on his farm and was more able for service for longer periods. Yet those that could afford this also supplied their own military supplies and arms being considered 'rich' and it was constant drilling that stopped the practice of selling their arms for farm equipment.[1326]

Leo VI also checked the position of monasteries by limiting ascetic initiation to non-slaves only.[1327] In Novel 5 of Justinian's Code, slaves could be returned to masters anytime during a three-year novice-hood, but in Novel 10 of the *Basilica,* this length of time was extended past three years. In Novel 6, girls could be cloistered at ten years of age, but could not donate property to the monastery until an age later than Basil I's proscribed sixteenth or seventeenth year. Married parties leaving for monastic life were responsible for the provisions of abandoned children and parents. Eunuchs were also forbidden to marry as marriage was an act for procreation and any other reason would be fornication. Eunuchs could, however, legally adopt children as heirs of their estates and the penalties of castration were further relaxed for a more humane view.[1328] From another perspective, it ensured the reproductive rights of citizens to further the population and the aristocracy in further disenfranchising the localized peasant landlords by encouraging the use of inheritance.

Leo sought nothing less than an imperial monopoly on trade, Church policy, other institutions, and his now aristocratic bureaucracy. Though he was a reformer not seen in centuries, not all of his legislation benefited the exploited, rural poor. He gave bureaucratic posts to the aristocracy loyal to the Crown, revoking 'preemption' (*protimesis*) of neighbors, allowing neighbors to evict peasants against the purchase price for six months [1329] This way, landlords of the aristocracy would gain peasant land more easily, unknowingly hastening

---

[1325] Leo VI. *The Taktika of Leo VI,* ed. by George T. Dennis. Washington, DC: Dumbarton Oaks Research Library and Collections, 19 59. 2010; Decker, 223.

[1326] Treadgold, *(BAIA),* 175.

[1327] Hussey, 121.

[1328] Herrin, 168.

[1329] Ostrogorsky, 255.

the emergence of Medieval feudalism as an epidemic problem for the *Basilii* of the twelfth century.

Capitalist trade was a prospect for the state in government regulation not only including artisan labor and merchants, but in the production itself in silks, objects of precious metals, soap, fish, candles, notary records, and countless other commodities and products.[1330] Better economic conditions are also reported in the military spheres in evaluations between the years 902 and 911.[1331] The 650 minor officers in these years received increases of eighteen *nomismata* apiece, which increased total pay to 11,700 *nomismata*. Turmarchs and Drungarii (paid at 216 and 144 *nomismata* respectively) proportions would pay more than double by 911 at a total of 20,000 in additional cost and 10,000 new soldiers fielded on the imperial borders would receive a stable nine *nomismata* apiece by 911.

The silk trade was more guarded as a monopoly whenever its demand increased, and it did indeed flourish in the Empire. Most notably the demand was for furniture upholstery in the Byzantine and Arab lands, the veils of brides, and textiles used by the emperor's court.[1332] Series of silk design depicting animals from the East were in demand in the West at the Holy Roman Emperor's courts, especially since silkworm production was most lucrative in southern Italy. A prosperous Empire was also vital to the prestige and the person of the *Basileus* himself, which was seen as an imperial institution. That was what led to the notions that the *Basileus* must personally oversee customs on imports and exports as well as the private fashions of dress within his court. The extravagance of dress in others was carefully regulated to be slightly inferior compared to Leo as his *solutus legibus* ('absolute power') was never to be threatened in splendor.[1333]

Sadly, as it was with Theophilus and his Empress, this continuing prosperity would still elude the Empire in the tenth century as a certain classical Roman 'anti-business ethos' still existed. This was a stubborn Roman tradition treating middle-class business as distasteful to the aristocratic elite, eventually being a liability in future centuries when lacking funds caused military disasters from neighboring states. Economically, the Later Middle Ages were about the growing capitalism in the West, but a static, feudal Byzantium would only be a

---

[1330] Herrin, 151.

[1331] Treadgold, *(BAIA)*, 136-137. These are based on the scales and lists of Constantine VII in his work *De Ceremonii*.

[1332] Mango, Marlia Mundell. 'Commerce', 168.

[1333] Diehl, 32.

model for contempt for this reason (one among many) to the West, becoming a cause of neglect until its dissolution in 1453.

Beyond all this was the recollection that, despite all accounts, Leo was neither 'demonic' nor 'angelic', but one of many involved in a chain of human weaknesses that also affected his rival, Arethas. Though Arethas's weakness was a lust for self-promotion and advancement, it also showed the weaknesses of ideas plagued by self-deceit and a self-justified hypocrisy.[1334] The superstitions and poorly clarified justifications of the Church repelled reason and the logic of their Classical ancestors, ignoring the dangers of civil war and bloodshed resulting from an emperor with no heir. From this scandalous marriage, however, would be born a *Basileus* of ability, genius, and energy, successfully maintaining internal stability when it was needed most.

Legend says that as Leo lay dying, he spoke a prophecy as his last words: 'Thirteen months – and an evil time.'[1335] He was said to be speaking of the thirteen months of his brother's reign (almost to the day) and how no good would come from it. Alexander, natural son of Basil I as well as Leo's half-brother, was born on September 19, 870, crowned the co-*Basileus* of his father after his brother Constantine's sudden death in 879. Mostly in his life, he was a non-entity under his relatives being a drunken carouser and dilettante. Near the end of Leo's reign he sought initiative by plotting against Leo's life, unfruitful as it turned out to be, though Alexander's succession would be threatened from the start anyway as he was suffering from testicular cancer his entire reign.[1336]

Yet, any implication of his in the plot to murder Leo on May 11, 903, at St. Mocius, was judged and he was given the benefit of the doubt.[1337] His only worth being a Macedonian successor was in name only until Leo's son, Constantine, could shake off his regency. His vices were many and fully written by his detractors, even contradicting themselves as a notorious rake such as he was called a 'dissolute and probably impotent wastrel.'[1338] It is all forgivable as

<hr>

[1334] Jenkins, 226.

[1335] Norwich, (APO), 122.

[1336] Treadgold, 471.

[1337] Jenkins, 209.

[1338] *ibid.*, 215. Of course, he was a 'statesman without religion . . .believing in a brutal superstition deriving from Classical Paganism' and his days of government were uniformly evil', 227.

these do open the trend by some historians to equate political impotence with sexual impotence, as Michael III had been, perhaps as both *Basilii* were said to be as virile as they were sober. Sexual virility was a proof of vigor and strength, the kind that could tackle challenges in the court as could be in the bedroom.

In the coinage of Alexander in the Empire, whose monasteries refused it, Alexander showed a piety under the saints by the obverse side of his portrait on the coins. Shown here was a depiction of St. John the Baptist crowning Alexander as *Basileus*. This was a sign of submission to spiritual affairs that were meant to rival Leo's coins, traditionally depicting a portrait of the Virgin on the opposite of his portrait. Alexander was always shown as a character of submission shadowed by his brother; in other coinage, he is depicted with Leo on his coins with Christ on the other side. Leo is shown as larger and more dominant, a giant compared to his minor brother.

He wasted no time in his decisions coming to the throne in 912 as he dismissed yet another Patriarch, Euthymius, and reinstated the anti-Macedonian faction and Nicholas Mysticus from exile, calling his abdication 'invalid'. Nicholas then went on a whole hearted campaign of revenge against his enemies in the Church, such as Arethas of Caesarea and other factions of Ignatius, burning their careers left and right. Alexander did see that the Treasury had been seriously depleted by the Cretan expedition, so he planned to extort 1,000,000 *nomismata* from those Bishops loyal to Euthymius.[1339] The Bishops, not pleased in the arrogance of the temporal power, donated their funds to the poor and the emperor went practically empty-handed.

Upon suspicions of leading Euthymius's faction, Alexander exiled and tonsured both Zoe Carbonopsina and her cousin, the commander Himerius. In a strange twist, he had his cohort Nicholas Mysticus allow him to tonsure his own wife and marry his mistress as Leo had done! It can be clearly seen that this was a tactic of Alexander's to include his own heirs to disenfranchise the four-year-old Constantine and continue his new branch of the Macedonian dynasty. His time was short, however, as he was dying of his testicular cancer. In mindless desperation, he offered Pagan sacrifices for a new set of teeth and sexual organs[1340] to the virile boar statue of the Hippodrome to desperately cure his sexual impotence.

When in 913, Symeon the Bulgar Khan came to collect his yearly tribute,

---

[1339] Treadgold, 471.

[1340] Jenkins, 228. This is also mentioned and expanded in passages by Steven Runciman.

Alexander blatantly refused in what was described as 'drunken braggadocio'.[1341] This proved unwise, not surprisingly, as the military was not even close to recovering from the defeat at Chios and Symeon would already be preparing raids into the northern territories if not Constantinople itself. But before any of this happened, Alexander was securing the regency of young Constantine VII as it was evident that he would die childless. Patriarch Nicholas sought Constantine Ducas to succeed as regent, but Alexander would ultimately insist on a 'board' consisting of seven regents, including Nicholas himself. Some of the other six included Domestic of the Scholae Nicephorus Phocas, and the Drungarius Romanus Lecapenus, both to become future *Basilii*. This board did exclude the empress Zoe who was never allowed back to the Palace as long as she lived. Content with this arrangement, Alexander would die on June 6, 913, of a stroke after a hot day of polo in his father's stadium, ironically outlasting his cancer.

It was odd that Alexander chose seven men from the army and the Church to be Constantine's regents. Perhaps he hoped they would find a way to invalidate him, seeing Constantine was the bastard of a fourth marriage and unfit for the throne. On some level, he must have seen that these seven would only tear each other apart to gain imperial pride of place as a reigning regent in Constantine's affairs. It is as Alexander the Great did, leaving his vast empire on his deathbed to whichever general was the strongest, knowing an infant son would never succeed him. If this was Alexander's plans, he would be frustrated as eventually Constantine would rise to be sole *Basileus* and one of the most prosperous and best-loved in the Macedonian line and the Empire's history.

## ROMANUS I LECAPENUS
### (920-944)

The next few years after Alexander's death proved to be a chaotic time for the Empire with the return of hostilities from Symeon and the Bulgars with the concerns of Nicolas Mysticus and the regency. The ambitions of men such as Romanus Lecapenus would rise to dominate all of his opponents in the court, holding supreme power for a while over the monarchy and even over the legitimate heir of Leo VI. This was done with a shrewd talent for undermining allies and enemies with a series of dynastic marriages to create an intricate network of the best and brightest of the military, aristocratic, and royal families.

---

[1341] Norwich, (APO), 123.

The heart of this family was his ward Constantine, the future *Basileus*, who was powerless against this usurping military officer of lower birth and character. Romanus also brooked no hatred for nepotism, castrating his own sons so they may raise high in civil and ecclesiastical careers. It is true, eunuchs were still main officeholders as commanders and even Patriarchs; careers such as medicine were open as only eunuchs or women were allowed to treat other women.[1342]

Constantine's evaluations were quite clear in his *De Administrando* citing Romanus as '...a common and illiterate fellow...', which was true considering, in 927, the court official Theodore Daphnopates (890-963 CE) had to be used as the 'author' of Romanus's letters to the Bulgarian usurper Symeon.[1343] He betrayed the 'Roman national customs' as he was 'too arrogant and despotic, and in this instance he neither heeded the prohibitions of the church nor followed the commandments and ordinance of the great Constantine, but out of a temper arrogant and self-willed and untaught in virtue and refusing what was followed out of right and good . . .'[1344] in taking the throne and starting a dynasty. He was also hated by the senatorial council and commons of the Church, slandered and further vilified after his exile and death.[1345] This is credible as any emperor that had the individual strength to lead the Empire efficiently without such aid would stir up jealousy in those particular ranks and be resented by them, the Church and the bureaucracy. This question over autonomy would always be an issue, plaguing even the most burdened of *Basilii*. Besides this was his causing the young Constantine much abuse and insult while attempting to whittle down his right to the throne for his own sons.

He had a cunning talent for deceit, but he was also a negotiable and diplomatic leader that caused almost no unnecessary violence, not even being a violent man by nature.[1346] Scholars even go so far as to call him a 'gentle' ruler for his lack of bloodshed in his usurpation. He would placate the Khan Symeon into peace with such words as these on September 9, 924:[1347] 'I have heard that you are a religious man and a true Christian, but I see your acts do not accord with your words: a religious man welcomes peace and love, for God is love, as it is said, but it is an impious and irreligious man that delights in slaughter and

---

[1342]  Sherrard, 82.

[1343]  Obolensky, 116.

[1344]  Porphyrogenitus, 172.

[1345]  Porphyrogenitus, 75.

[1346]  Brownworth, 181.

[1347]  Norwich, (APO), 139.

in the unjust shedding of blood . . .What answer will you give to God for your unrighteous slaughter, when you come before Him? How will you face the terrible and just judge?'

More so, he was a tireless administrator for the peasantry and did all he could to stop the spread of exploitative economy haunting the Macedonian rulers. For all this must be noted a rare and curious neutrality by Edward Gibbon who opinionated that Romanus I Lecapenus had 'neither the vices nor virtues of a tyrant' and his private life 'dissipated by the sunshine of the throne.'[1348] He was shown also as much ambition and abuse to his stepson, Gibbon adding his sarcastic and gleeful smile with which he greeted his rebellious sons as monks at the Ponte where they had earlier had him cloistered.

Romanus I Lecapenus was born the son of Armenian peasants in 870 in the village of Lecapene outside Samasota in the Armeniac Theme. His father, Theophylact, joined the army and became a soldier, saving Basil I's life in battle at Tephrice, which earned him a place in the imperial guard with the moniker 'the Unbearable'. His son would then find a place in the imperial navy until he reached the post of Drungarius of the Theme of Samos under Leo the Philosopher's reign, succeeding the failed commander Himerius. But his real career and advance would start in the years after Alexander's death in 913 to his ascension in 921.

As soon as Alexander died and Byzantium had a regent council ruling a child emperor, the inevitable trouble first began from within the military. On June 9, 913, the Patriarch Nicholas's candidate for the throne, Constantine Ducas, assaulted the Palace with his loyal forces and his son. This was due to Nicholas, being made head of the regency, seeing he had no more need of Ducas and dismissed him within the three days between Alexander's death and the attack. The imperial bodyguards stayed loyal to the legitimate heir, however, and the two Ducas: commanders were killed, their partisans then being blinded and tonsured. As Nicholas suspected a now re-instated Zoe Carbonopsina of partisanship, he had her tonsured once more with oaths from the Church and civil service she never be made *Basilia* again.

Anatolia and Armenia were Byzantium's greatest military allies against the Bulgars, but the Caliphate raided Anatolia and captured King Smbat of Armenia in the name of Azerbaijan. This left Constantinople unprotected from two fronts and the Khan Symeon marched from his capital to the City Walls. Nicholas was forced to make a shameful peace of extorted cash and a promise

---

[1348] Gibbon, 1637-38

of the emperor Constantine in marriage to Symeon's daughter. Included was the presumption that the Crown of Constantine was Symeon's as 'Emperor' of the Bulgarians, separating the Byzantines and the Bulgars as entities in one 'commonwealth'. Symeon would also not betray the 'basic tenet of Byzantine political philosophy' that the emperor be the highest authority of all as he was assigned by the will of the King of All,[1349] being the force of legitimacy.

In 914, Nicholas's position was in jeopardy when partisans of the Ducas, Euthymius the deposed Patriarch, the partisans of the *Basilia* Zoe, and the anti-Bulgarian peace treaty beset the exposed Nicholas on all sides. In a bid to unite in a common foe, Nicholas turned west and sent forces to South Italy. From her convent of St. Euphemia in Petrium, the wily Zoe went to work and her chamberlain Constantine successfully delegated a coup against Nicholas. With her well intentioned 'counsel of eunuchs' as once described by the Bulgar Khan Symeon, Zoe was returned to Constantinople as the head of the regency and the imperial mother. These eunuchs, however, were competent, educated, and experienced men of the court – not the mincing sopranos or obese, Oriental harem-keepers Symeon despised.[1350] Zoe offered the Patriarchy back to her ally Euthymius, but he had enough of these intrigues and declined the empress's request. So, Zoe reluctantly re-instated Nicholas on the condition he himself crown her Augusta, which he accepted in humiliation.

Zoe began in earnest, creating a foreign policy supporting Armenia and giving asylum to the new King Ashot who fled after his father, Smbat, died. In 915, Ashot was able to return when a strong Byzantine opposition took Tarsus, Germanicea, and Samasota from Arab control. Zoe rewarded the success of the Cleishurarch of Lycandus, Melias the Armenian, by making Lycandus a full Theme. In the West, Nicholas's forces were also able to clear the Arabs from Calabria and the new order in Constantinople was showing great promise. In 915, Zoe was that highest authority that Symeon attempted to mimic. Yet, obstacles on the imperial fringe remained however, as a less than successful diplomatic visit to Constantinople by the vicious Pechenegs soured considerably, repulsing their Orthodox sensibilities with Pagan sacrifices of birds, dogs, and sheep.[1351]

A year later, the Bulgarians raided Thessalonica and Dyrrachium, singling out Thessaly and Epirus, forcing the Byzantines to seek foreign aid in handling

---

[1349] Obolensky, 110.

[1350] Norwich, (APO), 129.

[1351] Jenkins, 234.

the crisis. Invading Arabs in Tarsus paid off by allowing themselves an alliance against the Khan and John Bogas, the Chersonese Strategos, who bought off a mercenary force of Pechenegs to be brought west. The Domestic of the Scholae, Leo Phocas, joined with Melias the Armenian to gather a large Thematic army to head west as well. All that was needed was the Drungarius of the fleet, Romanus Lecapenus, to ferry the Pechengs across the Danube. But internal quarrels with Bogas incensed the admiral where it could be heard furious shouting matches between the two men, and Lecapenus refused to ferry the Pechenegs south to the front as the mercenaries eventually separated and returned east.

Meanwhile, Bulgarian troops were causing devastation elsewhere as in Achelous at Anchialus on August 20, where the Greeks were '...put to flight, and ingloriously cut to pieces' according to Leo the Deacon. Symeon would reach Catasyrtae and threaten Constantinople. Knowing this entirely, it can be said Romanus was playing a cunning power game with the imperial government. He understood he was the singular turnkey for the Romans and Pechenegs to meet the Bulgarians, and being an undefeated admiral (as Bulgaria had no fleet), his position was strengthened to a point above Phocas and the regency in the impending emergency.

A troubled Phocas saw Romanus and his family as a threat to his own at the imperial court, and Leo convinced Constantine the chamberlain to oust Lecapenus from any favor in the regency's estimation, sentencing him to be blinded.[1352] When young Constantine was about to pay off the navy, Romanus captured him as a bargaining chip. Constantine's tutor and Alexander's regency board member, Theodore, had Nicholas made sole regent again to face this crisis. When Nicholas returned, he dismissed Leo Phocas from his post, the City itself, and the entire conflict. In a classic case of politics making strange bedfellows in Constantinople, Leo Phocas allied himself to Romanus Lecapenus.

As the navy and army now came together against Nicholas's faction, Theodore saw no other choice than to allow Lecapenus to enter the Palace as a regent. Why he was chosen above any other was questionable, even with his superior military position. It was true that Romanus was as ambitious as his predecessor, but he still carried base, peasant origins. It was made clear, though, how the populace of the City preferred these origins over the aristocracy in later

---

[1352] Norwich, (APO), 133.

times of the dynasty,[1353] perpetuating the class warfare present in the rural areas with Romanus's ascension as a victory for the poor.

Constantine then made Romanus Magister of the Scholae in 919 and using his wits in the court, Romanus had the young emperor marry his own daughter Maria, circumventing the Bulgarian Khan completely to be assigned *Basileopater* as Basil I had been. In his position, he further entrenched the Lecapeni at court by making his eldest son Christopher head of the bodyguard. Meanwhile, according to Porphyrogenitus as a witness to events, some supporters of the young *Basileus* Constantine, such as the Chamberlain Theodotus, would be violently flogged, tonsured, and exiled. The clever nature of Lecapanus had now been seen the victor of a propaganda war - circulating a signed announcement by Constantine that Leo fought the legitimate emperor as his trusted 'father'. This was sent through the army by priests and prostitutes (the latter faring better) and the troops of Leo, many convinced to change sides.[1354]

A trapped Leo Phocas then made a rebellion at Chrysopolis, but he could not keep the army's loyalty as they went to Romanus and his forces. Romanus finally captured the flailing commander and settled the matter by blinding him. In 920, Romanus would also expel from court his other adversaries by alleging plots against him by Zoe and Theodore, who he had tonsured and exiled, respectively. He then held a Council appeasing the Moechian Controversy of Leo VI on fourth marriages as an effrontery to God, returning the Euthymian Bishops their sees. This further trapped Nicholas Mysticus as less of a power in the Church, further division now being the risk of fighting the manipulating Romanus. The acceptance of the *Tomus* now had potential dangers with the external threat of the 'bloodthirsty Bulgarians' and the 'bloodthirsty tetragamists from within.'[1355] This pushed for a rare, but imperative, tolerance on the issue in order to avoid the Empire from tearing itself apart in front of its own enemies.

Romanus would reach further over Constantine by having the young *Basileus* claim Lecapenus Caesar on the 24th of September. A year later, his wife Theodora was made Augusta on the Epiphany now that Zoe as the imperial mother was a non-issue; Constantine and Nicholas would have little choice but to crown him *Basileus*. Lecapenus's boldness went further as he made his son Christopher co-*Basileus* on December 17, 920. Now Constantine, son of

---

[1353] Jenkins, 241.
[1354] Brownworth, 181f.
[1355] Jenkins, 237.

a legitimate *Basileus*, was being crowded out altogether by a military usurper from a peasant family. On Christmas of 924, Romanus would then muddy the waters by raising his sons Stephen and Constantine to the same princely titles.

Yet Romanus's military skills and leadership served him well as, in 921, revolts broke out in Longobardia, Sicily, and Calabria. The Strategos of two Themes were murdered by rebels, including the Longobard prince of Capua. More rebellion occurred in the East as the Peloponnese stood behind Symeon, who marched on the City once more, but Romanus waited him out. What set off this chain of revolts in these different Themes was most likely the economic and military starvation felt due to Romanus's cultivation of power, and now he was forced to focus on Eastern policy. He even showed his benevolence and clemency towards the poor by allowing the Peloponnesian Theme to pay sums from five to two-and-a-half *nomismata* rather than serve in the campaigns.[1356]

But the Byzantines managed to repel the Bulgarians this time and Symeon settled for raiding Thrace; after all, what they lacked in manpower was served in cash to pay soldiers. The armies would quiet the Western rebellions and watch them fall apart as they also sought suzerainty over the city of Capua. However, despite sensible pay increases and tight administration, Byzantine losses have been accused of being caused by lapsed troop discipline and morale that only a strong commander or *Basileus* could solve.[1357]

More complications beset the Bulgar Emperor as the tribes of Serbia won independence from the Bulgarian state's sovereignty. Symeon responded by displacing King Paul of Serbia for his cousin Zacharias, who had been imprisoned since 920 and was pro-Byzantine. Apparently satisfied, Symeon turned west again and in spring of 922, marched on Constantinople for a third time (a record achievement for one ruler to attempt in Byzantium's history). Again, though they did not breach the Walls, Symeon won victories over the Scholae Pothus Argyrus and the Drungarius Alexius Musele who were killed in a retreat. When Symeon was defeated and finally sent from Thrace and Anatolia, he fled south to foment rebellion in the Peloponnesus and Greece. In 923, however, Romanus would choose as his new Domestic of the Scholae the brilliant and talented commander John Curcuas, a 'close compatriot of Romanus'.

Turnovers on the Bulgarians occurred rapidly as John cleared rebels from the mountains of Chaldia while Romanus broke Symeon's siege at Adrianople, driving out a Slav garrison. The grand strategy employed by Curcuas by the

---

[1356] Treadgold, *(BAIA)*, 138.
[1357] Jenkins, 244.

emperor was to both destroy the 'nuclei' of Muslim power in the borders as well as demonstrate a strong presence in Armenia.[1358] The fleets also saw victory as Leo of Tripoli was paid back for Chios by his defeat in the Aegean Sea. As Symeon sought retaliation with diplomacy in engaging the founding Fatimid Caliph, al-Mahdi, of North Africa and his Egyptian fleets, the *Basileus* captured the Bulgarian ambassadors and bargained a two-year peace with the Fatimids.[1359] Symeon, in 924, then gathered a large force to march on Macedonia, Thrace, and Constantinople a fourth time only to result in negotiation.

The Khan was invited to the Palace to be entertained in the presence of the growing *Basileus*, Constantine, and discuss alliances. Symeon met with the Patriarch Nicholas in secret on Thursday, September 5 at the Palace of the Hebdomon, having an audience with Romanus face-to-face. Symeon was insulted to learn his agreement of marriage with his daughter no longer existed as Constantine the neglected prince had married Helena, Romanus's daughter. This bid for legitimacy between the Lecapeni and the Macedonians broke the Khan and he left with only a promise of tribute including 100 *scaramangia*,[1360] or the embroidered and bejeweled silken robes only the imperial family were allowed to wear. Returning to Bulgaria in diplomatic defeat by 925, all of the Byzantine territories in the East were recovered excluding the Black Sea coast.

Romanus was cementing relations with the Abbasid Caliph al-Muqtadir that year when Nicholas Mysticus died. Romanus was already prompting his teenage son, Theophylact, for the Patriarchal throne by placing the puppets Stephen II and Trychon for eight years. Nicholas was a dynamic and resourceful head of state and regent, but in the end he lost out to the powerful will of Romanus and was devolved to being a shamed courtier.

Romanus also replaced as adviser the eunuch Theophanes, a Protovestiarius of the household. In 926, Romanus attacked the Serbian King Zacharius, who fled to Croatia while Bulgaria annexed Serbia once again and it was here Symeon made the absurd claim he was now 'Emperor of the Bulgarians and Romans'! Romanus was quoted as saying, with the laconic wit of a Spartan how Symeon could name himself Caliph of Bagdad for all he cared. Though Symeon invaded Croatia for annexation, the determined Slavs of these regions fought bravely under their king, Tomislav, and repelled the Bulgarians. Symeon would bid for peace from the Croatians with Pope John X as intermediary, although

---

[1358]  *ibid.*, 246.
[1359]  Treadgold, 478.
[1360]  Norwich, (APO), 145.

all other parties connected with Symeon were still Orthodox. By 925, his army was running low on morale as Bulgaria was nearly bankrupt and thousands of Bulgarians were flooding over the Byzantine borders to emigrate.[1361]

Romanus then focused on the needs of Armenia to expel the Abbasids that overthrew their monarchy. It was a matter of personal pride as Melias of Lycander, his brother Theophilus of Chaldia, Romanus, and Curcuas were all patriotic Armenians as well as Byzantines. In 927, Romanus sent Melias and Curcuas to retrieve the region by devastating Melitene. Its Emir was only too willing to negotiate and was made to accept Byzantine rule as well as donate some of his troops to Romanus's armies. These would be sent to Samasota, where the illustrious Curcuas took Dvin and the borders of Ashot's welcoming territories. It is claimed by Russian and Slavic scholars that the list of military districts created by Romanus I Lecapenus reached some thirty new Themes.[1362]

On May 27, 927, the tireless and iron-willed Khan Symeon 'the Great' died and was succeeded by his young son Peter under a regent uncle. Bulgaria was in a depleted state as its armies were under-manned and its enemies surrounded it completely. Serbia, and the tribes of the Milingoi, and Ezeritai as well, regained independence and the northern Danubian regions were taken by the feuding Magyars and Pechenegs. When locusts decimated the food supply, Peter's regency was open to negotiation with the Byzantine *Basileus*. Romanus welcomed peaceful solutions with Bulgaria and gave them a fair treaty which lasted for forty years.

Peter would be betrothed to Maria, Romanus's granddaughter and daughter of the *Basileus*'s son, Christopher, and married by an independent Bulgarian Patriarchate (although Norwich said it was Pope Stephen II) on October 8 in the palace at Pegae. A state subsidy paid to Peter and Maria would be provided by Romanus to bring the court to a 'degree of state appropriate to a Byzantine princess.'[1363] Bulgaria acknowledged these concessions by releasing Byzantine captives held in Bulgaria and in exchange, the emperor allowed the 'Bishop' of Bulgaria to retain the title of 'Patriarch', illicitly given by Symeon.[1364] This would be the first time in five centuries a Byzantine princess would marry a foreigner, allowing international relations to be somewhat eased. However,

---

[1361] Jenkins, 243.

[1362] Benesevic, V. 'De Byzantinischen Ranglisten nach dem Kleterologion Philothei.' *Byzantinisch-neugrichische Jahrbucher, vol. V.* 1926, 118-122; Vasiliev, 350.

[1363] Norwich, (APO), 147.

[1364] Obolensky, 114-115. Peter was also made *Tsar* of Bulgaria, a new term that would decide the fate of Russia as a successor to the fallen Eastern Romans. Such titles recognized states of international status.

the subsidies given to his daughter by the wily Romanus were also to pay for Byzantine embassies and spies at the Bulgarian court.[1365]

After a famine ravaged the Empire, Romanus made offenses against the Armenian Arabs. In 928, Curcuas raided the Armenian south and took Chliat. The Strategos Melias then returned to Melitene in order to have it betrayed from within to him, but this maneuver failed. Despite this, Melitene accepted a Byzantine garrison as, 'Panic spread along the Arab frontier north of Mesopotamia.'[1366] Bulgaria suffered as well, but this was mainly from the degradation of their territories by the warring Magyars and Pechenegs. The treaties of the 920's were seen as wise maneuvers by Romanus being signs of Bulgarian weakness and a certain understanding that Symeon's Bulgaria had collapsed.[1367]

A year later, the energy of the Byzantine forces dramatically tired; Curcuas lost Armenia to the governor of Azerbaijan and Meliasas, buffered by Mesopotamian troops, when he tried invading Samasota in 930. The peace with Armenia and the neighboring tribes would always be shaky as long as the Byzantines could not keep the city of Ketzeon and refrain from besieging Theodosiopolis as it was considered an insult to the Armenian tribes if Armenia could not force this policy.[1368] The West also suffered as the Sicilian Arabs were invading as far north as Capua and Salerno was lost to the Lomabards of Longobardia. A year later, the Arabs of Tarsus took Amorium as Byzantine attention was directed to Armenia. Another attack was put to Samasota, successful this time, but a faltering city guard was faced by a huge Mesopotamian force fleeing the city. Melitene, which was highly distrusted by Melias, was also abandoned as the Strategos of Lycander lacked forces to defend it from without and within. Curcuas was more fortunate in Armenia where he seized Manzikert, Percri, and Khelat along the north shore of the Van, practically recovering all of Byzantine Crimea in 932.[1369]

When the Tarsus Arabs succeeded in their military endeavors in Amorium, Romanus created a Cleisura of Seleucia to contain it. Attempts to retrieve the region would be frustrated in 932 with rebellions in the Opsikian by a leader named Basil, which were quickly put down and their leader severely

---

[1365] Runciman, Steven. *The Emperor Romanus Lecapenus and His Reign: A Study of Tenth Century Byzantium*. Cambridge, UK: Cambridge University Press. 1929, 99.
[1366] Treadgold, 480.
[1367] Runciman, 100; Vasiliev, 318-319.
[1368] Porphyrogenitus, *De Administrando*, 209.
[1369] Norwich, (APO), 149.

punished. As for domestic affairs in the Palace or, in 933, Christopher the co-*Basileus* suddenly died, seemingly without suspicion. The aggrieved *Basileus* was vindicated when his sixteen-year-old son was handed the highest office in the Orthodox Church in Constantinople on February 2. It was a great scandal that he was barely old enough to gain any office as a mere teenager, but he had a 'worldly' love of luxury and horses, of which he had 2,000, feeding on a costly diet of mashed dates, figs, and pistachio nuts with sweet wine.[1370] The horses of Theophylact Lecapenus were fed better things than most peasants or soldiers could afford. Yet, this scandal paled in the face of Pope John XI consecrating the ascension with no dispute as Romanus accepted Western supremacy in the matter.[1371]

Meanwhile, the tireless efforts to recover Armenia against the Arabs continued as they enacted more displacement in the Mesopotamian region by taking the surrounding cities of Samasota and Miletene. The climax of the campaign was the siege of Melitene with a vengeful pairing of Curcuas and Melias with 50,000 men on May 19, 934. Melitene was eventually seized by surrender and the same fate happened to Samasota as it meant to be ravaged almost beyond repair and the northern Mesopotamian region was finally occupied. Muslims in the city were forced to convert to Christianity and given safe passage as those vassals of the Empire expanding the borders beyond the conquests of Leo VI. The Abbasids were already conquering the Chinese to Islamisize the eastern regions where they even introduced parchment paper to the documentation of the Arabic East westwards.[1372] When the Magyars and Pechenegs began a raiding campaign in Bulgaria and closed in on Byzantine territory they were later bought off by the *Basileus*'s minister, Theophanes.

The next year, Romanus went for a major offensive in Italy giving the governor of Capua an ultimatum, but the Lombards still hesitated. Romanus then sent a large military force west and allied with the Frankish ruler, Hugh of Provence. An indecisive and intimidated Capua decisively evacuated Longobardia in 936 for Byzantine occupation. Back in the Mesopotamian East, an aristocratic Arab family, the Hamdanids, put down the Banu Habib tribe that defected to Byzantium, converting to Orthodoxy. Romanus gratefully accepted them, needing to create five new Themes, such as the Derzene, to successfully

---

[1370] Jenkins, 253.

[1371] Treadgold, 481.

[1372] Montefiorre, 199f.

integrate their 12,000 cavalry. These Themes did, however, provide extra satellite regional protection on the border where no infantry existed.

Once again, in 936, the Hamdanids made their presence known with strong offensives in eastern Byzantium. Curcuas did manage to sack Samasota once more only do so and face 'the Sword of the Dynasty', Sayf al-Dawlah, Emir of Aleppo and Mosul, who took the fortress of Charpete at Melitene, already claiming for himself the governorship of Amida on the border region. Curcuas prepared a siege, but Sayf ambushed his troops and forced a withdrawal in September, 938. Sayf would also be called upon by the Arabs of Theodosiopolis when Romanus sent Curcuas to claim the city from the main supply route of Ketzeon to keep up relations with the Armenian and Abasgian rulers. The Arabs lost while Sayf was on his way and he was forced to winter quarters for the next year. By 939, Romanus was still occupied in the West and skillfully allied with his former enemies the Sicilian Arabs to check the growing influence and power of the Egyptian Fatimids.

In early 940, leaving his winter quarters, Sayf demanded tribute and submission to all of Armenia from the Hamdanids. This included Abbasid rulers and the indigenous rulers such as Abas, successor of Ashot II. It did not take long for Armenia to surrender, beginning a domino effect of domination to those principalities and Caliphate vassals that did not prefer defending their regions without neighboring allies who did not hesitate to surrender.[1373] The brash Sayf then entered Byzantine territory and was quickly repulsed by John Curcuas, who continued on to invade northern Mesopotamia.

In June 941, eastern operations were immediately suspended when an attack on Constantinople came from Russian Kiev and its ruler Igor, ending the 911 truce with Leo VI. Curcuas was hastily recalled from the Aegean and Theophanes the Protovestiarius was sent with fifteen ships to the Russian fleet carrying Greek Fire to the Bosporus against these Viking 'Sea Wolves'. The Russians had never faced this devastating weapon before – describing it as 'lightning form heaven'[1374] - abandoning the Bosporus for land operations in the Opsikian where they faced defeat after defeat by Curcuas's armies. When the bulk of the fleet arrived, Theophanes cleared out the Russias altogether, who fled to the Bithynian coast. In frustration and madness, the Russians returned

---

[1373] Treadgold, 483-484.
[1374] Herrin, 144.

to the villages using the Byzantine clergy for archery practice or driving iron skewers in their skulls.[1375]

In 943, Igor would go frustrated on to renew commercial treaties with Byzantium, the remaining East, and his capital of Kiev. Romanus would reward the courageous Protovariastus with a title of Grand Chamberlain, the highest in the aristocratic class of the court. At this point, the Byzantines could handle any maritime power – Slav, Arab, or Viking – and maintain control as long as they kept the Thracian coast at the Bosporus and Dardanelles.[1376] It is only when these were taken by the West, as it would in 1204, or by the Turks in 1453, that the City would face the imminence of conquest and Greek defense would be worthless.

In 942, Curcuas raided eastwards again to Syrian Aleppo where from 10,000 to 15,000 Arab prisoners were settled, setting sights again west. The Byzantines protected the renegade Sicilian Arabs from paying tribute to the Fatimids when their rebellion against Africa failed, choosing the lesser of two evils concerning the two Western Arab powers. Romanus I solidified relations further by betrothing Constantine's infant son, Romanus, to Hugh of Provence's illegitimate daughter (which apparently presented no dynastic problems). The Byzantines then showed their strength and commitment by destroying the Arab fleets threatening Provence with more Greek Fire. In 943, when renegade Magyars raided Thrace, a five-year treaty was enacted that would extend throughout the reign of Constantine VII.

With Western victory in hand, Curcuas re-entered Hamdanid Armenia, where the Arabs fielded some 80,000 soldiers in the attack (although historians assure that it was probably less).[1377] Curcuas took Arzen and Martyropolis in the south and in 943 was in Mesopotamia gaining Sayf al-Dawlah's alleged province made of Amida, Dara, and Nisibis. It were these victories that got Curcuas such legendary monikers from historians, Theophanes Continuatus for instance, of a 'second Trajan or Belisarius' and conqueror of 'nearly thousands of cities.'[1378] Alexander A. Vasiliev (1867-1953) claims a greater work was written on the commander, but this has not survived, unfortunately.

He reached a new height in the recovery of the key city of Edessa receiving the holy relic of the Mandylion, a talisman of miraculous power in the form of a cloth bearing the image of Christ (resembling the Shroud of Turin). The

---

[1375]  Norwich, (APO), 151.

[1376]  Obolensky, 115.

[1377]  Treadgold, (BAIA), 484.

[1378]  Continuatus, 427-428; Vasiliev, 305.

Arabs were impotent against Curcuas as he further sacked Rasaina as Edessa resentfully surrendered the shroud. On August 15, the Assumption of the Virgin, it was taken through the Golden Gate of the City by Theophanes to St. Sophia. It is reported as a sort of omen how Constantine could see the image of Christ on the shroud wherein Romanus's sons could not and a spectator shouted that now Constantine should take his throne.

By now, Romanus I was considering his age and the succession of the Empire in which he had put twenty years. Though he still deferred Constantine's position, he was still the legitimate son of Leo VI and Lecapenus wrote a will to the effect that gave sole rule to the now adult Porphyrogenitus. Romanus still feared for his ward's safety as sole ruler, however, and engaged Constantine's son Romanus to marry Euphrosyne, the daughter of John Curcuas. Binding the two together against the sly courtiers and generals who would oppose the future *Basileus*, a tight network of allies was designed. The Lecapeni family, however, feared for their own position and demanded Romanus replace the Domestic of the Scholae with a Lecapenus relative. This Romanus did in 944 and the Domestic Pantherius would take Germanicea and Pagrae, only to meet a humiliating defeat by Sayf al-Dawlah.

At the end of 944, Tsar Igor wanted retribution for his defeats three years before, but wisely chose means by trade over arms. On the warnings of the Chersonese that the Russians' 'ships have covered the sea', ambassadors were sent to the Russians with their Danubian Pechenegs to be paid off. By the end of the year, a treaty was established regulating the Russian customs duties and foreign trade, fixing the prices of silks, quartering troops at St. Mamas, and protecting the Chersonese' vital fishing industry. This treaty benefited the Empire far more than the Russians and granted assurance to better Eastern trade.

Spurning Curcuas, Constantine's son Romanus, a five-year-old, was married to Hugh of Provence's daughter Bertha whose name was Hellenized as Eudocia. This fact was seen as an insult by Romanus's surviving and natural sons Stephen and Constantine who were passed over for the Prince they saw as having no rights to the throne above themselves. With the collusion of Romanus's courtiers, the brothers forced Romanus into a monastery on the island of Prote on December 16, 944 as Stephen prepared himself for the throne after his father's deposing. But, the mob of Constantinople demanded to see the son of Leo unharmed as the rightful heir and the Lecapeni demurred as Constantine was given senior standing. When the brothers planned an assassination at Constantine's breakfast in January of 945, they were arrested the night before at dinner and were tonsured with their unfortunate, mocking, father. It was now that Constantine VII and his Empress Helena were unfettered to run the government without viable opponents as Romanus I had done two decades before.

Romanus I Lecapenus would die in the monastery of Prote on June 15, 948 as he would outlive his son Constantine by two years, Stephen then dying in 967. In his later years, a life of crime riddled him with guilt and the luxury of the Palace had made his sons 'spoiled, entitled, and famously corrupt'[1379], so when his decision to will all of his assets to Constantine was publicized on December 29, his progeny was left aghast. Romanus was coarse and cruel to his stepson, but still appreciated in 944 for being a superb diplomat who made peace with Russia, Bulgaria, Capua, Sicily, the Frankish kingdom, and the Magyars. His armies defended against Russia and Bulgaria and brought Armenia back into the Byzantine fold from Slavic and Arabic threats through his trust in Curcuas. As we will see, his economic policies in the face of the land crisis and a horrid famine would thus earn equity and prosperity for the Treasury.

It was his stability, tenacity, and good judgment that saved situations domestically and otherwise despite the written perspectives of his successor.[1380] He also managed to keep a united Church under his son who would rule twenty-three years as Patriarch and gain for the imperial prestige under God a holy relic, the Mandylion, to sit along with a piece of the True Cross. His only real crimes were ignoring and heaping insult on his stepson, who would succeed him as rightful heir and also ignoring the ambitions of his sons, who were as ruthless as he was. Coinage of this late period did not even include Constantine at all, only Romanus in regalia and a cross on the other side of the silver *miliaresion* with its higher circulation among the 'powerful'.[1381] Constantine Porphyrogenitus's resentment and slander is understandable as Romanus I was also a peasant upstart in a reign of nobles who ascended by treachery and deceit. Yet, the reality was that he was a peace-keeping and able (if not qualified) *Basileus* that earned fortified credibility in the Macedonian dynasty.

Although religious division was being well avoided in the Byzantine Church, the Bulgarian Church and its independence faced its first major heresy from Byzantine territories. The Paulician monk Bogomil brought dissent from Thrace and Macedonia to Bulgaria challenging the Church with radical ideas the Byzantines had faced years before. 'Bogomilism' was a Dualist philosophy

---

[1379]  Brownworth, 185.
[1380]  Hussey, 34.
[1381]  Treadgold, 477.

emphasizing the dichotomy of Good and Evil in God's universe. Primarily, the material world was the work of Satan and is Evil in its conception with its temptations, original sin being the punishment for the expulsion from Eden. To combat this, the purely ascetic and spiritual life was necessary for salvation. All worldly ideas of Church hierarchy, outward worship, iconography, ecclesiastical ritual, all were deceptions of the Devil corrupting Man and leading him away from God. In scrutinized evaluations of Bogomilism and its influences in the West, such forms of this belief would appear in such heresies as Catharism, Paterenism, and Albigensianism in Serbia, Italy, and France in later centuries.[1382]

Romanus I Lecapenus, as a military commander, set military policies in a more 'practical' manner than Leo VI, mostly because he had far more experience on his side. In 936, records after his death report how he bought cheaply the loyalties of the Arabs of the captured Charpezician Theme using the Byzantine Banu Habib deserts of the Hamdanids. This Theme was unique for its Greco-Arabic ethnicity and for its composition of only 2,476 cavalry, or twenty percent of the cavalry, for the entire region. Romanus settled this by promising and promoting inflated junior officer titles, replacing the traditional titles of the Centarchs, Pentacontarchs, and Decarchs with Greater Turmarchs, Lesser Turmarchs, and Drungarii, respectively.[1383] This worked to transmit these new troops into five separate Themes and build a military bureaucracy. Yet, cavalry could also be a burden in the military as the horses in the service were vital to their personal economy. When the animals were sick or in need it was the local money-lenders that squeezed the cavalry landholders with an array of debt. The indebted were soldiers and peasants, not horse breeders or veterinarians. They turned to professionals to care for these horses and debt was inevitable to this class.[1384]

Economic adversity and trial would literally blow into Byzantium like a plague from an angry God. A plague of locusts, blowing in from Bulgaria, and a harsh winter in 927-8 resulted in starvation and inflated food prices that imperial donatives could not match. Consequent disease spread and shanty towns for the poor were produced by the *Basileus*. The efforts of Leo VI's policies on peasant land free of upper tier intervention was almost eliminated as the poor sold their land to military and civil authorities as well as the Church to survive, accepting food in exchange for money. A dormant paradigm shift towards

---

[1382]  Ostrogorsky, 268-269.

[1383]  Treadgold, *(BAIA)*, 111-112.

[1384]  Jenkins, 249.

private owners patronizing peasants for economic exploitation intensified once again. This was the key to success by such noble Byzantine clans (and future imperial households) of the Phoci, Ducasi, and Argyri families.[1385]

The *Basileus* had already made his intentions on the landowning disparities clear by April of 922 when he published Novels regulating the practice of this exploitation in the form of *prostasia* ('Patronage') which depended on gifts and legacies:[1386]

1)  Sales of hereditary leases on real estate (lands, horses, or farms) where preferential rights existed was now to be given to peasants and communal authorities.

2)  The 'powerful' were not to gain land from the poor classes by donation, will, patronage, purchase, rent, or exchange.

3)  Lands alienated in military crises would be returned to the original owners without recompense to the landed parties that gained it thereafter within the last thirty years.

He also set new boundaries in legislation by eliminating minimum value for infantry land as poor landholders with rights of re-compensation.[1387] The privileges of noble gifts, legacies, and similar agreements were now derelict and would now be made void. Even if this disenfranchised the poor in these matters who needed to sell, the point was to directly disenfranchise the landed class from alienating taxation with their exemptions with the peasants having to deal financially with only one another. The only threats to farther Eastern Byzantinization and protecting the poor from the powerful classes were the emerging influence of Orthodoxy that allowed the Church to own their lands.[1388]

The oppressive tax burdens and extortionate tax collectors were mainly leading the poor towards their dependency on the landowners. These were the rights of 'preemption' given peasants in a fixed order of four categories of relatives: conjoint holders, intermingled plot owners, adjoining holders paying taxes in common, and all other adjoining holders. Another Novel by Romanus

---

[1385] *ibid.,* 248.

[1386] Ostrogorsky, 272-273. Vasiliev also makes good outlines of this legislation and their consequences by the emperor, 346-347 & 570

[1387] Treadgold, *(BAIA),* 175.

[1388] Obolensky, 118. Yet, 'feudalism' is not the way to describe these struggles socially and economically by this author; it is something more seen in Bulgaria in the next century, around the time after the First Crusade.

in 923 described the powerful as a 'plague or gangrene' that begged the question of how good order and government could allow and survive internal enemies and practices of buying land for bread.[1389] These practices in fleecing the poor demonstrated an undoing of the policies and care of Leo the Wise. It took a *Basileus* with the experience of a poor peasant to fully appreciate the need to protect the lowest class from the wealthy with the policies of the Macedonians granting guidance.

Romanus was also facing an imminent tax crisis from the bureaucratic classes who had the opportunities to dodge regulation. In spring of 928, Romanus would forbid the selling of land to certain 'powerful outsiders' while peasants had to offer their land to relatives and villagers of the lower class.[1390] Of course, the relatives and neighbors were too poor themselves to buy these lands and illegal sales to these upper class purchasers were practically inevitable. Furthermore, the ensuing famine resulted in a thinning of the army ranks and highly contributed to military failures, even during the mainly successful campaigns of Curcuas in Armenia and the Slavic lands.

Persisting problems galvanized Romanus in 934 to add an Edict to his economic Novels citing that any illegal sales found from six years ago would be returned to the original sellers with no compensation to the buyer. This strict *caveat* from the government was obviously tuned to punish the landowners of the bureaucracy, but not the peasants who might have willingly sold to their influential buyers. The legally purchased land that sellers wished to buy back had to be restored to the seller for the original purchase price with smaller deductions of annual income from these previous six years to the government.

Of course, weak or corrupt enforcement policies led to defiance of these laws by the upper classes as was done since 928. The major problem was the privileges of tax-exempt status some offices in the Church and the state shared. This economic concern would mainly be a continuing problem, as has been said, in the Macedonian era. Another ineffectual act of Romanus's reforms was the idea of lands not sold or used by peasants, but grand-fathered in by relatives, classified as 'simple usage' or 'partnership.'[1391]

As in other imperial policies from previous *Basilii*, Romanus I blended economic policy with religious policy and preference. In 943, he hustled in more reform by suspending public funds from remaining Monotheletes and

---

[1389] Vasiliev, 346-347.
[1390] Treadgold, 480.
[1391] Jenkins, 248.

persecuting Jews under the counsel and administration of monastic authorities. In the process of using Byzantine culture to predominate in Bulgaria, it was under Romanus's era that the role of monasticism in country districts to Christianize the peasantry in Orthodoxy began to occur. These Bulgarian monasteries would become places of worship and pilgrimage to the village communities, linking to the provincial magnate forces that would hold landed estates and patronize the peasants to exploit them as Byzantium had done.[1392]

Romanus I did recall debts that private citizens owed the state in Constantinople to the total of 137,000 *nomismata,* but cancelled others and remitted rents in the City.[1393] He was an efficient and active reformer, even if he lacked certain efficacy in the Landowner Controversies, delegating into the trustworthy hands of tax officials such as Leo Tzikanes and John Eladas. He also did his all in frustrating attempts by the upper classes to buy or bribe themselves into public offices with the sole purpose of gaining or adding land to their estates.[1394] The Peloponnesians, in those numbers opting out of military service, paid the emperor a tribute of 1,000 horses with saddle and bridle, and the 100 pounds of gold Romanus needed to pay his troops, including a five *nomismata* capita that was lowered to two in the cases of the truly poor.[1395]

But there were conspicuous signs of prosperity and the usual splendor of Byzantium in Romanus's reign as traditional gifts to foreign heads of state were the prime example of this trend. In correspondence with the Caliphs of Baghdad, gold and silver were used in ink to write letters in Greek and Arabic to and from Caliph al-Radi.[1396] As a small show of superiority, Arabic translations were all in silver as the Greek was in gold as a diplomatic detail that could not be lost on the Arabs. Also, '…gifts of golden glass encrusted with precious stones, with a lion made from crystal, goblets, plates of gold and bowls all encrusted with jewels, clothes, spices including musk and amber, numerous perfumes and rare objects sans pareil' accompanied such diplomacy. This demonstrates an obvious trend in available foreign markets in amber from the Russian and Chersonese north, perfumes from Arabia or Egypt, spices from India, and the markets of the Caucasus region. Christopher Beckwith names many of these markets from the Central Eurasian area linked to China and India in

---

[1392] Herrin, 155-156. He did, however, protect Mt. Athos and allow them funds in 941-942 as they practiced isolation from events in the Empire, 196.

[1393] Treadgold, 486.

[1394] Ostrogorsky, 275.

[1395] Porphyrogenitus, *De Administrando,* 257.

[1396] Herrin, 176.

his *Empires of the Silk Road.*[1397] A more recent perspective comes from Rice University by Michael Maas and Nicola di Cosma.[1398]

# CONSTANTINE VII 'PORPHYROGENITUS'
## (913-959)

The boy *Basileus* who spent his life in the shadow of a usurper grew to be a powerful man of popularity, decisiveness, and keen judgment. He was not idle in his years of exile in a palace made for illegitimate princes, using his superior educational resources to write influential treatises and hone various skills. His credentials are impressive: he was a student of the liberal arts such as grammar, rhetoric, mathematics, and was a consummate poet, historian, hagiographer, artist, political scientist, jurist, and veterinarian.[1399] His careers include medical student, encyclopedic librarian, hymnist, musician, philosopher, agriculturist, Greco-Roman classicist, biographer, astronomer, and inventor, his list of educational contributions and achievements were impressively long. He was an ardent contributor to student bursaries and inviting them to his table in efforts to improve the civil service with the educated.[1400] Finally, he founded four chairs in the University of Constantinople in philosophy, geometry, rhetoric, and astronomy. [1401]

Returning the Byzantine court to a kind of splendor, he used a strict use of ceremony studied from methods of past centuries. The golden robes with pearls and precious stones, the gold plates of generous banquets, and the uses of delicate and attentive rituals were employed generously. In the Great Palace, heads of state witnessed automated clocks, cisterns of wines and systems pouring it from statues, fountains, and columns, as well as plates of fruit lowered from the ceiling to wondrous applause.[1402] Sometimes these were cold and mystical but at other times came allowances of warmth and friendship, making rulers and ambassadors feel connected to Byzantium's dynamic new ruler. He spent much

---

[1397] Since the late Amorian period, the growing Turkish presence in this region changed Eastern relations along with the Viking incursions. Beckwith, 140-182.

[1398] Maas, Michael and Nicola di Cosmas. Empire and Exchange in Eurasian Late Antiquity: Rome, China, Iran and the Steppe, ca. 250-750 CE. Oxford, UK: Oxford University Press. 2018.

[1399] Norwich, (APO), 165.

[1400] Angold, 139.

[1401] Buckler, 217.

[1402] Brownworth, 188.

time and resources filling the academic chairs of universities with scholars such as the rhetorician Alexander of Nicaea, a student of Lucian. Patronizing the arts, Constantine VII granted loans to mosaicists, painters, goldsmiths, illuminators of manuscripts, the *Basileus* taking on some of these crafts himself.[1403] He is especially noted as returning Classical themes and learning to mid-tenth-century art, although Christian art was still better depicted and aesthetic than Classical or mythological works.[1404] Many patrons received titles and loans as well, such as the westerner Liutprand of Cremona who received a gold donative when he reminded the *Basileus* of a penitent in the tale of Lazarus.

But Constantine had flaws as any other *Basileus* did as his gifts in intellect and mannerism bred a snobbish sort of haughtiness and xenophobic contempt for his non-Greek subjects. The idea of a foreign prince marrying into his family, for example, appalled Constantine, who sternly criticized such past princes as Leo III and his Khazar bride and Romanus Lecapenus for giving his granddaughter to Peter of Bulgaria.[1405] Despite these reservations, he was slow to anger and not petty, nonetheless drawing the line between Byzantines and 'barbaric' nations. He made his writings plain enough on the subject in his *De Administrando,* where he blatantly claimed how Heraclius subjugated the Slavs as he continued to do so in his own time. It has also been questioned if he was not dominated by his wife Helena in affairs of state due to lack of energy and his fascination with the arts; but this did not mar his high public opinion as an educated, just, and good administrator.[1406]

Upon reflection, it is pointed out that Constantine VII did not contribute *new* cultural values, just amazing resurrections and sterling glosses to the ones that had slipped away in time or had been suppressed by years of warfare.[1407] However, it has been recorded by historians such as Continuatus how he was courteous to members of every class and nation, even when suspicious. Others do decry his love of food and drink as excessive, some ignoring the praises of Continuatus in the works of more realistic critics like Michael Cedrenus and Zonaras describing his reign as a 'near-disaster'.[1408] Such errors eventually seeped into Edward Gibbon's thought and caused further controversy in the early Byzantinist imagination. But one writer from the West would show

---

[1403]  Herrin, 188.

[1404]  Mango, 'The Revival of Learning', 228-229.

[1405]  Porphyrogenitus, 73.

[1406]  Gibbon, 1638-1639.

[1407]  Ostrogorsky, 280.

[1408]  Norwich, (APO), 166.

Constantine VII in his best light: Liutprand of Cremona, who would be impressed by Constantine's love of splendor, ceremony, knowledge, and his education. Economically under Constantine VII, the Empire still managed to uphold its internal advantages and keep a military budget of 3,914,000 *nomismata* by 959. Also resulting in considerable pay increases to all types of soldiers, officers, sailors, bureaucrats, and in fodder with a decreased surplus.[1409]

With the moniker of *'Porphyrogenitus'* ('Born in the Purple'), it might be self-evident that Constantine VII was born in the Purple Chamber of the Imperial Palace, also breaking the Roman convention of being named for his grandfather (Basil) for a more prestigious and imperial one. He was born on September 2, 905, to the *Basileus* Leo VI and his mistress and fourth wife, Zoe Carbonopsina. He was six when his father died and fifteen when his throne was taken by Romanus Lecapenus in 920. Not helping his situation was his being sickly and an 'invalid' most of his life,[1410] a fact that kept him inferior to the robust Romanus who valued physical strength. For the next quarter-century, Constantine would remain resentful but silent, watching his sole regent pass him over for promotion year after year. Although doubt may still be cast on Romanus I's 'usurpation', Arnold Toynbee (1889-1975), Constantine's principle modern biographer, assures that older precedents in Roman law somewhat legitimated Romanus. He had no ambitions on the throne when Romanus died, wishing to settle for the scholarly life as Julian the Apostate had, but he held a 'sympathetic charm' to others as a serious boy facing constant humiliations from the Lecapeni in a tolerant manner.[1411]

The impassioned crowd of the City, upon Romanus's death, mobbed the Palace in Constantinople, demanding to see any proof of life of the young heir, who was quickly produced to mollify the mob. Now, unlike their role in Leo VI's ascension of 912,[1412] it was an obvious statement that the noble class and the Senate had ceased to matter functionally in government. Lecapenus's ascension had been a bloodless coup, the *Constitutio Antoniniana* of 212 CE fulfilling the tradition of Roman succession, not actually breaching it.[1413] But whatever the case, Constantine had a strong character and a lax temper, growing to be tall and sturdy, 'as erect as a cypress tree' as described by Continuatus. He was the

---

[1409] Treadgold, *(BAIA)*, 197.

[1410] Jenkins, 256.

[1411] Brownworth, 186-187.

[1412] Hussey, 94.

[1413] Toynbee, Arnold. *Constantine Porphyrogenitus and His World*. Oxford, UK: Oxford University Press. 1973.

picture of health, despite expectation, that the men of Byzantium saw as a good omen, along with his brilliant blue eyes and his long black beard when he took the throne in 944.[1414]

Again, his two decades on the throne were not just idle or pleasure-loving times as he studied the stern ethics of Aristotle and Socrates, using his time to develop his mind in books, tutoring, and academic education at the University in Constantinople. This would culminate in various treatises on an array of different subjects written by copyists and ghost writers. His *Geoponica* was a survey of Classical agriculture with such notations as the Roman Columella (4-70 CE), his *Hippiatrica* outlined veterinarian science, and he wrote the *Life of Basil I*. His medical and zoological encyclopedias were also written and commissioned. The Logothete Symeon Metaphrastes (900-987 CE) transferred into Attic Greek a historical calendar of the saints in the *Synaxarion*, including other notables (148 in all) in Plutarchian style. A grand encyclopedia Constantine was credited with contained over 30,000 alphabetic entries known as the *Souda* ('Ditch').[1415]

His largest endeavor in these years was most notably the *Excerpta Historica*, used as a chance for Constantine to flex his muscles as a librarian, a historian, and a hagiographer, claiming emperors should always travel with their own library. His was a massive anthological compilation of works by historians from Herodotus (485-425BCE) to George Hamartolos 'the Monk' (842-867 CE), over twelve centuries of historical events in the analysis of Greece. Unfortunately, in six volumes and fifty-three sections, only thirty-six have survived to modern times. These surviving sections included works on 'Public Speeches', 'Plots', 'Inventions', 'Hunting', 'Marriages', 'Victories', 'Proclamations of the Emperors', twenty-two on 'Embassies' (researched by a John of Antioch), and fifty others on 'Virtues and Vices'[1416] to name but a few. It was this work that made possible some of the revival of Byzantine Studies founded by the French financial minister, Jean-Baptiste Colbert, for Louis XIV in 1648.[1417]

Byzantium would flourish and never suffer another 'Dark Age' as had happened in the seventh and eighth centuries. As with any renaissance, there was the importance of availability in Classical texts in economic terms. A geometrical work by Euclid would cost fourteen *nomismata*, twenty-one for

---

[1414] Norwich, (APO), 162.

[1415] Mango, 'The Revival of Learning,' pg 222.

[1416] Herrin, 183.

[1417] Ostrogorsky, 3. One of the best descriptions of Byzantine studies from the seventeenth century can be found here.

a copy of Plato on parchment, or a work of Christian Apologists for twenty-six *nomismata*. This would almost guarantee only the upper-class elite had access to these works as the annual salary of a court dignitary was only about seventy-two *nomismata*.[1418] Any comparison to the Italian Renaissance of the fifteenth or sixteenth centuries stops here, however. The Macedonian era was one of literacy and the preservation of Classical learning, but it generated no new knowledge or skills created from the applications of these Classical works to start a new or modern age. It was a product of the Medieval Encyclopedic Movement that only managed to create small glossaries and commentaries to later reach full fruition after the Empire's fall, mostly in the West.

Constantine VII Porphyrogenitus would take sole power, without serious opposition, in January, 945, seven months after Romanus I's death. The Lecapeni would be arrested the night before an assassination attempt and tonsured as Romanus's dominant son, Constantine, would be killed in an escape attempt from a monastery in 948. The remaining Lecapeni were vocal, but did not really put up a viable threat to Constantine's ascension after 946 when Romanus's son, Theophylact the Patriarch, and the Chamberlain Theophanes were caught in a plot to restore Romanus and were also exiled. Constantine's wife Helena being a true asset to the throne, convinced the *Basileus* to succeed Basil Nothos ('the Bastard'), Romanus's illegitimate eunuch son, to be Constantine's key adviser. As a eunuch loyal to the *Basilia*, he resulted in being a brilliant Chamberlain to Constantine. After a final plot by the Lecapeni in 947 involving a relative named Stephen was foiled, Constantine would set about promulgating many financial legislation and edicts undisturbed.

The military of this era were on a road to mastery with siphoning 'blowtorches' of Greek Fire, siege drills, and improved sea craft.[1419] Though this would prove a stable period, the Empire's most active and intrepid enemy, Sayf al-Dawlah, was busily trying to gain control of Tarsus and Syria from the rising Ikhshidid Caliphate of Egypt. By 948, the Caliphate still held Damascus as Syria's southern frontiers fell, Sayf making himself Emir of Syrian Aleppo. The Byzantines were defeated later at the frontier zone, but Leo Phocas the Strategus of Cappadocia, still demolished al-Dawlah's strategical fort of Adata.

In 949, Constantine turned west and outfitted a fleet to expel the Cretan Arabs for the Empire on the Mediterranean. Taking caution from the lessons

---

[1418]  Mango, 'The Revival of Learning,' 223. Some evaluations put the total at 5,000 pounds sterling, or $7,500.
[1419]  Sherrard, 86-89.

of his father, a less ambitious fleet was arranged than was made before, outfitted with 4,100 Thematic troops led by the Drungarius Constantine Gongylius[1420] (of which 629 were Russian, as Vasiliev makes a point upon which to digress). Meanwhile, the remainder of the fleet kept vigil over the Aegean, Mediterranean basin, Spain, and Africa to avoid reinforcements turning east. Although the operation was fruitless, Constantine had also appealed for aid from Western powers such as German King Otto the Saxon, Berengar of Italy, and the Umayyad Caliph Abd ar-Rahman of Cordova in Spain.[1421] This was an act of desperation given the infamous xenophobia for non-Greek powers that Constantine VII harbored.

But, Treadgold also evaluates that it was the *Basileus*'s own attention to caution that defeated the campaign. Although Gongylius landed on Crete unopposed, the interior Arab forces overtook the contingent, a massacre of the Byzantine forces resulting with many prisoners taken. The incompetent and cowardly Gongylius fled for his life with whatever sailors remained and Crete was abandoned. A bad proportion of Byzantine ships to Crete and separate points thinned the numbers to an embarrassingly undermanned force taken by surprise by the Arabs, defending what was now their home settlement after a century. After all of his planning, Constantine only 'planned to fail.' More oversights by Constantine were fueled by his low opinion of non-Byzantines as by 949, Crete was a distinctly Muslim island society and not a Christian community seeking 'liberation' from an encroaching Constantinople.[1422]

In the East, Sayf was continuing his hostilities by attempting to invade the Theme of Lycander, being rebuffed by Byzantine forces. They next went on to sack Germanicea and defeat an army from Tarsus in early 949. The son of the Domestic Bardas Phocas, Leo of Cappadocia, raided all the way to the city of Antioch and John Curcuas's brother, Theophilus, also joined the campaign. They took the city of Theodosiopolis once again from the Arabs and it was cautiously made into a Theme by the *Basileus*. After the defeat at Crete, Sayf led his own ambitious army of 30,000 troops to flood Lycander and the Charsianum Theme in east Armenia with their armies, defeating an army led by Bardas Phocas. But upon his return to Germanicea, the prepared and cunning Leo Phocas laid an ambush, killing 8,000 and almost taking al-Dawlah alive as prisoner. In 951, Sayf spurned an offer of truce and invaded Melitene as well

---

[1420]  Treadgold, 489.
[1421]  Jenkins, 262.
[1422]  *ibid.*, 264.

as Lycandus in the winter, but another surprise attack by Byzantine forces cut him short.

Although a fleet failed to take the Sicilian Arabs at Rhegium, the Saracens agreed to a peace settlement with Constantine. Sayf would further strengthen his defenses at Adata, Germanicea, and Samasota, preparing for more campaigns in 953. Bardas was repulsed from these defenses and defeated when he struck at the Mesopotamian-Armenian borders. Sayf would hit Byzantine forces hard that spring, capturing Constantine Phocas on imperial territory and holding him at Aleppo. Finally, in 954, Sayf finished rebuilding Adata and Samasota, defeating Bardas Phocas one more time. Sayf had now retaken all of the territory he had gained before the Phocas's assaults. In 956, the talented general Tzimisces, sacking southern Armenia, defeated an army of Sayf's numbering 10,000, killing half and imprisoning almost the rest.[1423]

Now troubled by these losses, the emperor had no faith left in Bardas Phocas and dismissed him as Domestic of the Scholae. Despite this, Constantine still had faith in the military family of the Phoci and as he overlooked Leo as a successor, he ascended Bardas's son Nicephorus as the new Domestic. After this sticky attempt at stability, the domestic occurrences of 956 only brought more drama to Constantinople. The Patriarch Theophylact Lecapenus had twenty-three years of stable, if not pleasure-seeking, rule. But, he fell from one of the horses with which he spent countless hours, from among the 2,000 he kept in his stables, dying as the last Lecapenus to hold such an elevated office.

Constantine VII then chose as Patriarch a churchman (an ironic rarity in those times) named Polyeuctus. In a strange and scandalous turn of events, the ten-year-old son of the former *Basileus* Romanus, 'fell in love' with a tavern owner and pled for a marriage. Shocking as it was, it was not a forced marriage as it was with Basil I and the *Basileus* assented to the union; after all, Justinian had married a prostitute and it worked out quite well for the Empire. For an elitist as himself, it was perhaps more important that she be some sort of a Byzantine Greek rather than a barbarian princess, or even of a younger age! The new bride took the name of Theophano, after the sainted first wife of Leo the Wise.

New challenges now arose in the West with the destruction and extinction of the Moravian state in the north Balkans by the invading Magyars. They encroached heavily on Germany, Italy, and France versus the keen leadership of King Otto the Saxon, culminating in their repulsion in 955 at the Battle of

---

[1423] Treadgold, 492-493.

Lechfeld while the Magyars also invaded Thrace.[1424] Surprisingly, they kept up their peace treaty made during Constantine's reign and the West would seek many audiences with the *Basileus* over Byzantine aid in war to help broker a peace with the Magyars. This came in the form of the chieftain Berenger and the wise and resourceful Liutprand of Cremona.

By 952, Constantine VII Porphyrogenitus had published the three works that would leave a true legacy for his name. First was the *De Ceremoniis Aulae Byzantinae* ('On the Ceremonies of the Byzantine Court'), written to explain court etiquette usually transmitted orally into a comprehensive guide for future generations. Defying the charges of Byzantine documents lacking for coherence only in names and dates,[1425] *De Ceremoniis* included conduct to be reserved during baptisms, weddings, coronations, funerals, receiving and sending embassies, military matters, oaths, titles, offices, vestments to be worn, the attitudes of the court, and the Blues and Greens.[1426] It further included anniversaries such as the Arab victory of 718, earthquakes, and grape harvests, highlighting other such administrative and social expectations modeled, supposedly, from the etiquette of the court of Justinian I.[1427] It would be another Eastern standard for the Slavonic and Russian states as well as Ottoman court etiquette until the twentieth century.[1428] More influence for this work can be traced to the sixth century in the works of the jurist and ambassador to Persia, Peter the Patrician, on his main works *On the State Constitution* and the *Katarsis* ('Book of Ceremonies').

The aim of this work was also to epitomize and cultivate the role of the *Basileus* as the symbol of order (*taxis*) in the state, opposing the disharmony (*ataxis*) that must be avoided as the realm of 'barbarians and demons'. This order was the responsibility of the *Basileus* above that of any other inhabitant of the Empire and was the basis of the 'Byzantine conception of a virtuous life'. '. . .Supremely manifested in the heavenly court, it permeated the whole world.'[1429] Constantine created his own ceremony to honor Constantine the Great, also including homage and censers to his grandfather and father as the founders of his dynasty. Held at the Mausoleum of the Church of the Holy

---

[1424] Obolensky, 154.

[1425] Porphyrogenitus, *De Ceremoniis*, 651, 661, 664; Treadgold, (BAIA), 44n.

[1426] Norwich,(APO), 163.

[1427] Herrin, 177.

[1428] Vasiliev, 362-363.

[1429] Mango, Cyril. 'Introduction', Chap. 1 of *The Oxford History of Byzantium*, 1-18. 2002, 16.

Apostles, it would bind the *Basileus* to the continuing idea of the New Rome.[1430] Also, as an unintended consequence, was the further shift of imperial court culture toward the Oriental.

As it was in ancient Rome, the spectacles that demonstrated the greatest power to the *Augusti* were public ones such as the gladiatorial contests and Triumphs. Now in Byzantium, past the chariot races, the spectacles of power were now in more private spaces such as the Palace or the dining hall. It was more important for foreign dignitaries and embassies to be swayed by the ceremonial and *triomphe l'oueil* splendor of gold vessels, animatronic animals, and other marvels. This was more Oriental in character as these private spaces were for the elite used only outside public view, although descriptions from certain witnesses do abound in the literature.

Like the transformations of other institutions in Rome, this blurred the lines between a Roman, Greek, and Oriental empire. Furthermore, Constantine Porphyrogenitus wished to further himself from his people and neighboring princes due to his prime access to God, a Christian leadership worthy of the incomparable piety of the first Constantine. But, a paradox to this Oriental monarchical concept was also included in that the Porphyrogenitus was still 'subject' to God in the common adherence to the Church, a fact that is said to have caused the *Basileus* some embarrassment.[1431]

On September 17, 959, embassies from Cordova and Germany – including Liutprand of Cremona – arrived at the City to discuss the Magyar invasions of Europe with Constantine. Liutprand brought presents of nine cuirasses, seven gilded shields, two silver cups, four castrated and dismembered slaves (*carzimastia*), and other gifts which were handled with ceremonial care. On the occasion of the Nativity, a banquet was held at the Palace in the *Decanneacubita* of nineteen reclining dining couches arranged in the ancient Roman style. More wondrous gifts were presented as gold plates and silver cups were used to serve with golden bowls too heavy for one man to lift![1432] This ostentatious display was in itself ceremony to show the wealth and luxurious superiority of the Empire of Rome from Constantinople, thus making the impressionable Liutprand to be one of Constantine VII's most praising of commentators.

Another such ceremonial tradition was *proskynesis* before the *Basileus*. Once again described, it had been seen by the Greeks of ancient times as

---

[1430] Angold, 141-142.
[1431] Shepard, 234.
[1432] Norwich, (APO), 170.

'groveling like a dog at one's feet', reserved for Persian and other Oriental courts. The Middle Ages changed the view of this practice; in the previous chapter on Diocletian, he allowed it to become a norm in his court to raise himself in an honored position as Eastern *Augustus*. With this Orientalization and growing connection between the Byzantine sovereign and the True Christ, it became more accepted until all audiences with the *Basileus* required it. In fact, it was researched that the closer to the emperor's personal space one was, the more supplicating the prostration had to be. This demonstrates how cultural influences changed over time and circumstance until they became a norm and necessity to Byzantine life.

Next was his most important work, the *De Administrando Imperio* ('On the Administration of the Empire'), written in fifty-three chapters as an instruction of the foreign peoples and how to rule them as this was a guidebook to his then fourteen-year-old-son, Romanus, compiled from 948 to 952. It was a valuable source of state secrets in diplomacy and access was given, besides his son, only to a small elite class of diplomats.[1433] It was a complete and broad view of imperial relations from Constans II in 641 (the height of the Umayyad advancements) to the present, based on the histories of Theophanes Continuator. It emphasizes the past relations with the Franks and Arabs and it included the rise of the Slav peoples from the seventh century on with their 'subjugations' by the Empire. Noted compilers of the 1966 translation credit such intellectuals as Plutarch, Cato (234-149BCE), Pseudo-Isocrates (436-338BCE), and Aristotle as influence in Constantine's expert writing of the text.[1434]

It was a work meant for consumption and study by the court in general and his son in particular, emphasizing Constantine's contempt for the Eastern peoples and their marriages into the East Roman succession. Young Romanus was instructed not to make alliances or marriages with 'shifty and dishonorable tribes of the north' and their 'monstrous demands.'[1435] The Pechenegs, however, are focused on with great care as they were 'an insatiable people' when it came to imperial donatives and their ferocity in battle made them dangerous enemies. It was better to just supplicate their needs peacefully than resist them in battle. In the long run, it was less costly having them as friends than enemies and only 'special' envoys from Constantinople itself were allowed to deal with them. Constantine's work is oddly-framed as it is a jumble of unorganized

---

[1433] Jenkins, 260.

[1434] Vasiliev, 363.

[1435] Porphyrogenitus; Obolensky, 196.

chronologies on imperial acts and edicts, invective, and applause. Included are the histories of the Khazars, Turks, Bulgars, Magyars, Pechenegs, and other peoples described as a 'patchwork' of events.[1436] This was due to a scarcity of better sources, inadequate books, 'tedious and prolix' encyclopedias, and Byzantine records mainly based on business and technical transactions.

The *Administrando* was said to have been '. . .a blueprint for the whole of the Middle Ages,' (with only small exaggeration) with its geographical surveys of the entirety of the Slavic East.[1437] Starting in Thessalonica, Constantine goes in order from the northwest Danube at modern Belgrade to the Dniester and the 'gold coast' of the Dnieper by the Black Sea. After was the Pontus region of the West Crimea, the Chersonese fish and salt trade to the south, and the Bosporus through Cimmeria at the Straits of Kerch to Lake Maeotis and interior Russia. From the Tanais (Don) was the Khazar territory to the fort of Sarkel. Along with a focus on the Caucasian Alans, the north Black Sea passes to the Asbagian lands to the end of the survey at Sotirioupolis in Pityus. With the West, Constantine emphasized close relations and strong kinship between the two Empires including the Lombards, Franks, and Sicilians. Of course, it is noted to his son that the German Empire was inferior in all matters symbolically and in reality to Byzantium. Superiority ranged from legal authority to the use of the Greek language whose formula was granted to Constantine the Great by 'an angel.'[1438]

Finally, in the *De Thematibus* ('On Themes'), Constantine creates a geographical and ethnological survey of the Empire based on the most relevant records of the state archives.[1439] He begins with the invention of the administrative standard of districts with Heraclius and Constans II in the seventh century to the present in the tenth. This was made possible by the use of various administrative, military, and tax documents attainable in the imperial record. He did have criticisms about the state of provincial administration in those three centuries, as well as its founder. It is well recognized that Constantine felt the Empire had been mutilated East and West since the time

---

[1436] Bury, J.B. 'The Treatise *De Administrando Imperio.*' *Byzantinische Zeitschrift,* XV, 517-577. 1906; Vasiliev, 362.

[1437] Obolensky, 28.

[1438] Laiou, Angeliki E. 'Byzantium and the West.' Chap. 4 of *Byzantium: A World Empire,* ed. by Aneliki E. Laiou and Henry Maguire. Washington, DC: Dumbarton Oaks Research Library and Collections, 61-80. 1992, 61.

[1439] Treadgold, (BAIA), 24n.

of 'the Libyan' Heraclius[1440] who he says was responsible for the system in the first place. In *Thematibus*, he counts the Empire as having twenty-nine Themes with seventeen in Asia and twelve in Europe, including the Cherson, Crimea, and the 'Gothic Klimata.'[1441] Accordingly, since Lecapenus's reign, at least three Themes had been taken by foreign enemies and this is what probably contributed to Constantine's displeasure of the *status quo*.

Along with these records came the personal opinions of the *Basileus* on the growing Slavonization of Byzantium and the Balkans. Constantine believed that the plague in Italy of 746-7 (and in 755 when Constantine V died) is what introduced major migrations of these Slavs to the Eastern regions. And it is true that during the Isaurians' reign, due to their foreign origins in the Caucasus, many Slavic ancestors (Alans, Avars, Khazaks, and Bulgars) were allowed to settle for economic and defensive purposes. But, this to the *Basileus* was a serious decline in Byzantine stability in the state and its culture; lands like Thessalonica, the Peloponnese, and Thrace were reduced to slavery (*esthlabothe*)[1442] and remaining 'barbarian' despite Greek settlement.[1443] Constantine VII's intention was to compare and warn future generations of the dangers of repeating this pattern beyond the tenth century.

It was in the years 956-7 that the Empire was most benefited by two generals so skilled at their positions that they not only gained the favor of the Crown, but would wear it as well. In spring of 956, a general from Armenia named John Tzimisces, who was Strategos of Byzantine Mesopotamia, set out to invade Amida. To counter this attack, Sayf al-Dawlah sent his cousin to Syria and entered John's Theme. Though Tzimisces would give up on Amida, he managed to trap and surprise Sayf's rear flank and capture Sayf's cousin at a loss of 4,000 Greek soldiers.[1444] In 957, Tzimisces captured the north Syrian city of Hadath, prompting Sayf to send a fleet into the Cibyrrhaeot Theme losing miserably to a barrage of Greek Fire and the Cibyrrhaeot Byzantines simultaneously raiding Tarsus as well.

Three years after outfitting the defenses of the fortified city of Adata in Pamphylia, the Domestic of the Scholae Nicephorus Phocas (who was fighting in place of the wounded Bardas), demolished it again in 957, taking the passes of the Taurus Mountains. By now, Sayf was aware of the inadequacy of his

---

[1440] Vasiliev, 226.

[1441] *Ibid.*, 350.

[1442] Ibid., 178f.

[1443] Porphyrogenitus, 153.

[1444] Treadgold, 492.

military operations when a plot orchestrated by Phocas and Sayf's ministers to abduct the Emir was foiled and a humiliated Sayf returned to Aleppo. All Sayf could manage to control was the punishment of his traitors and the slaughter of his Byzantine captives in a mock show of strength to all but his enemies. In early 958, Tzimisces attacked the contested Mesopotamia-Armenian border and killed 5,000 men in response, capturing thousands more.

Syria would finally break as Tzimisces and the Chamberlain Basil, whom Constantine sent, destroyed Sayf's armies at fortified Samasota capturing prisoners to be humiliated at a procession in Constantinople. A year later, Tzimisces and Phocas would easily enter Syria and raid it to the city of Cyrrhus, being the last Eastern victory over Sayf al-Dawlah in Porphyrogenitus's lifetime. As Constantine was planning a new campaign against Crete with his sterling commanders, he increased the navy and wisely set up a front in the new Theme of the Cyclades. But before this could launch, on November 9, 959, Constantine Porphyrogenitus died[1445] traveling to Bursa to confer on ecclesiastical matters with the Bishop of Cyzicus. As he was touring the monasteries in the Olympian Mountains of Bithynia to gain support in the deposition of the Patriarch Polyeuctus, his health quickly deteriorated and at the behest of the monks, he fled back to Constantinople to die in the Palace.

This controversy over Polyeuctus stems from the dissension from the imperial throne over dynastic issues with Constantine. Acting independently and biting the hand that fed him, the Patriarch was opening the old wounds of the Marriage Controversy of Leo VI which would make Constantine's ascension illegitimate if he was taken seriously. The Patriarch was a zealot that howled for Euthymius's name to be returned to the honored diptychs which were remembered during the service of the Eucharist. He would even cause faction in the court by accusing, without proof, Basil Lecapenus of extorting the Treasury. The only thing that seemed to quiet this Patriarch was the *Basileus's* death in 959; after Constantine's death, Polyeuctus would remain in his seat until his own death in 970.

Ecclesiastically, there was also an emerging Russian question as Olga, widow of the *Tsar* ('Caesar') Igor and regent for the future Tsar Vladimir II, came to Constantinople in 957 to convert to Orthodox Christianity. After a ceremonial reception that humbled the *Tsarina* to the power and splendor of Byzantine authority, she was baptized as Helena in the Church of Saint Sophia. According to the *Book of Ceremonies*, Olga was given two formal audiences with

---

[1445] Poison had been suspected, but not proven, Gibbon, 1639.

the imperial presence and his family to honor her with 'whatever she wished.' At the subsequent banquet, she was given honor at the table with the 'ladies of the robe' ('*Zoste Patrikia*') at the first six ranks of the court hierarchy with dessert on a golden table.[1446]

She returned to Russia to convert her people to Christ, but did not succeed in turning over the traditions of Paganism. Vladimir, however, would begin work on the Russian Orthodox Church that would win acceptance, survive for over a millennia, and save the Byzantine heritage after the fall of 1453. It must be noted how psychology played a role in equating style of ceremony with superiority in Byzantine culture and Christian values. The *Basileus* himself in his robes, his finery, his possessions and attendants showed his power over the court with its luxury and connection to other peoples and resources by trade. Along with this, if Orthodox Christianity is based on the Byzantine *Basileus* being *pantokrator* ('all ruling'), as is Christ, and *philochristos* ('lover, or friend, of Christ'), there is no doubt the *Basileus*'s primary place in Christ's rule of the earth must be respected and protected at all costs by the subject states. The astute Liudprand of Cremona, awed by his magnificence, claimed the *Basileus* attended the reception halls regally on a 'throne of Solomon.'[1447]

Constantine VII knew and practiced well the value of cultural relations with foreign princes despite differences in faith and politics. When wooing the Spanish Caliph in 949, the *Basileus* presented him with manuscripts of the Greek writer and physician Pedanius Dioscorides (40-90 CE) and a special missive within a chased silver coffin with a golden lid. Made from purple parchment with golden letters, it bore a golden bull with the efficacy of Jesus Christ (blessed by the Caliph himself) as the case was enameled with Constantine's portrait and wrapped in tapestry.[1448] The leaders of the Magyars and the Russian Empress Helena-Olga were treated no different in such opulence in peace-keeping and diplomacy.

Despite this, however, Constantine's preferences were colored by his ever-present xenophobia that added caution to his affairs. In the matter of Byzantine missions in Slavic states, due to the '...specter of Symeon...', Constantine took harsh lessons from the Bulgarian hostilities that missionary work, whether in subject or foreign states, was too risky an enterprise.[1449] Though Constantine

---

[1446] Obolensky, 189.
[1447] Sherrard, 77.
[1448] Jenkins, 265-266.
[1449] Shepard, 339.

would comment much on his grandfather's wish to spread Christianity eastwards in his *Life of Basil*, the commonality of adherence to Christianity in Slav to Greek was an 'embarrassment' for him. The application of missionary work would threaten to allow these inferior peoples to expect to be '...treated with more or less an equal footing' with Byzantium as a whole, which galled Porphyrogenitus.

However, this phenomenon was still not to be suppressed in Constantine VII's reign as he would have had it. In 927, it started with the works of the cleric Gabriel and his successful conversion missions with the Magyars. The chieftains Bulcsu and Arpad were baptized as well as the chieftain's great-grandson, Termacs. Observations on these conversions are the foundation of Obolensky's 'Commonwealth' thesis and was strengthened despite Constantine VII's chauvinist views.[1450] As for his beneficial relations with the loyal Alans of the Caucasus, Porphyrogenitus set his prejudices aside to consider these protectors of Cherson from Khazar rebellion as the 'spiritual sons' of the *Basileus* as the rulers of Armenia and Bulgaria already were.

Constantine's achievements are modeled in Byzantine artistic representations in their numerous forms; they include the ivory diptych of his coronation by Christ, now in the Victoria and Albert Museum.[1451] Further historic adaptations by the Lecapeni historian John Skylitzes described a fine pageantry as artistic representations depict Constantine himself awaiting the baptismal at the hands of the Patriarch Theophylact Lecapenus. Another is his proud visage on the gold *nomisma,* or the Westernized *bezant,* reaching Russia and India.[1452] A lost representation bears the *Basileus* on an obelisk of stone bearing bronze plates covered in bas reliefs which is now, regrettably, a bare stone pillar in the ancient Hippodrome of Istanbul.

Constantine VII put much effort in maintaining and improving the integrity of his predecessor's financial policy concerning the fast-dividing classes. By now the landholders, be they military, naval,[1453] noble, or bourgeois, were considered as one 'estate' known as the *oi dunatoi* ('the powerful'). Since Romanus I's time, loopholes in the laws had still existed that exempted higher-class taxation, so

---

[1450]  Obolensky, 155.

[1451]  Ostrogorsky, 278 insert.

[1452]  Sherrard, 117, 38.

[1453]  Porphyrogenitus, *De Ceremonii,* 695. This landholding practice being an innovation presumably started by Constantine VII, Treadgold, *(BAIA),* 72. In an elaborate collection of thorough charts, Treadgold outlines the 1,144,404 *nomismata* (20,019-and-one-half pounds of gold) totaled in the military, 128-134.

Constantine would use his legal resources to close these breaches with the powers of a monarch. The 'confiscation without compensation' edict was re-affirmed in 945 with the lower-class peasantry maximum debt capped at fifty *nomismata* annually.[1454] Constantine made clear his intentions as an idealist and reformer on how the farmer could now grow and cultivate fig and olive trees without being robbed by the powerful: 'each might take his rest under the trees that were his heritage.'[1455]

As for the lands of military soldier-peasants, a question of alienation was addressed; those soldiers that had equipped themselves at owner expense and left their property for service would not be considered abandoned. As in Romanus's time, those who inhabited this 'alienated' land were considered squatters, not to be recompensed for their purchases. As soldiers and cavalry were mostly these landholders, their pay from the emperor would be appropriated to landowner demands from sailors at two to three pounds of gold to five pounds for the cavalry.[1456]

This was under these conditions that, especially in the marine Themes of the Aegean, Samos, and the Cibrryaehot, Constantine faced as an issue. When pay scales are examined with Theophilus's annual pay a century earlier, Constantine paid his officers and sailors comparably what was formally given in 842 by the 949 Cretan campaigns.[1457] In other cases, to this arrangement would be added a preemption to the sixth degree of kinship to the original owner, an issue based on the hierarchical tax system of Romanus. These matters were all in the spirit of taking away ownership from the renters' illegal and localized economy to that of the Crown's regulations in benefiting the poor.

Constantine Porphyrogenitus was the epitome of the educated and Hellenistic scholar-king that defined the culture of the Macedonian period in a 'pontifical' manner with magnificence in etiquette, ceremony, and festival (*dodechahemeron*) as described in the *Book of Ceremonies*.[1458] Some have alleged he used 'antiquarian' notions in using history to confront present situations.[1459] Yet, not only is such a practice the historian's preserve, but even modern political scientists, such as Thucydides, Niccolo Machiavelli, and Henry Kissinger, define political realism as this exact method. In conclusion on the matter,

---

[1454] Norwich, (APO), 172.

[1455] Diehl, 70.

[1456] Ostrogorsky, 281.

[1457] Treadgold, *(BAIA)*, 126.

[1458] Diehl, 38.

[1459] Laiou, 'Byzantium and the West,' 62.

Constantine VII is not to be underestimated as a statesman. The preservation and copying of these classics would be a great boon of the fifteenth century when learned scholars with their texts fled to the West from the Ottomans.

Much of what we know of Byzantine culture and society came from the careful analysis of this era, especially with that in the care of Constantine VII Porphyrogenitus. Not a great emperor in most other duties, his legacy is never to be forgotten in the many surveys and studies of Byzantine civilization from early modern times to the present. He was a careful balance of the Hellenized Greek, the respectful Christian, and a true believer in Byzantine 'exceptionalism' as the true Roman Empire. He held the rights of privilege in claiming this superiority even in the grace of virtue mirrored by the unique beauty of dress.[1460] With his death, his only son would ascend to the throne and expectations would be high; in Byzantine history, he would have big (and scarlet) shoes to fill as a legitimate *Basileus*, but, sadly, his poor choices in confidantes and an early death would bring down these expectations.

## ROMANUS II
### (959-963)

The next *Basileus* that would only reign a few years and leave for his two child princes foreign generals as regents that would battle to exploit them until their uncertain adulthood. This specter of regent rule and foreign influence on the throne has at this time returned to the problem of the barbarians of the fifth century and the Theodosian line. However, by the eighth and ninth centuries, this was a more accepted trend when foreign enemies more dangerous than the domestic ones threatened the City. Here the throne needed strong, charismatic generals who were able to stop the flow of hostile Eastern peoples and armies. Romanus II's talents, fortunately, included the ability to cultivate and patronize the noble families who were the backbone of the Empire in their military service.[1461] As with any young *Basileus*, Romanus was thrown into these circumstances with the weight of the Byzantine world on his shoulders and the legacy of the Macedonian line in which to amount. Though Byzantium was reaching an unrivaled apogee of its power and influence, this only added more stress, and not less, to its rulers, no matter their character.

Romanus II has been labeled as fair of face, broad-shouldered, with

---

[1460] Angold, 140.
[1461] Jenkins, 269.

sparkling eyes and an aquiline nose. Also charming, yet pleasure-loving, weak, ineffective, and even vicious, his military victories were due to other, more able generals. Older claims by historians have criticized that he inherited his father's 'political incapacity without his devotion to scholarship' as an antiquated dig at Constantine, yet this was no less correct a statement about his son.[1462] His generals were John Tzimisces and Nicephorus Phocas, also being mostly subject to the immoral and vicious Chamberlain Joseph Bringas, successor of Basil Lecapenus's pre-imperial place at court, who was made 'President' of the Senate.

The contemporaries of his succession knew no better after his first wife, Bertha of Provence, had died in 949 when Romanus was ten, allowing him to marry in 958 a sixteen-year-old Peloponnese tavern owner's daughter, Anastasia, renamed Theophano. Their marriage was also not arranged, defying a tradition that honored both aristocratic and peasant marriages as much as the ribbons that bound the couple's wrists during the ceremony. Of course, peasant traditions such as paper and flower crowns and a morning serenade to the bride would remain divisions of ceremony between noble and peasant marriages.[1463]

To commit his engagement, he spurned his father's wiser match with the niece of Otto the Saxon, Hedwig of Bavaria, which would have been valuable as the German King would rise to the Holy Roman Empire's throne. Theophano was immoral and wicked, 'of base origin and masculine spirit' both attributes crimes in early Byzantine Studies.[1464] Yet, her allegations before her coronation were considered 'some of the blackest crimes known to man'; after poisoning her father-in-law (something never proven), she betrayed her second husband to assassins. Seemingly cast in their mold,[1465] she was still not quite another model for rule such as Justinian's Theodora or Zoe, Romanus's grandmother. Perhaps it was for these good reasons that Romanus II's family and court pleaded with him to reconsider his choice. The *Basileus*' manipulations being various, they included her success in getting her husband's mother and five sisters cloistered for life in a convent on imperial orders in September, 961. And nothing boded well for this *Basileus*'s reign as he dismissed several of Constasntine's ministers from the court.

Yet, Theophano bore him two sons, Basil and Constantine, and Basil was

---

[1462] Ostrogorsky, 183.
[1463] Sherrard, 129.
[1464] Gibbon, 1639.
[1465] Jenkins, 270.

made co-*Basileus* in 960 at age two. Though a weak link within it, Romanus continued the Macedonian line at least until 1028. His father left him a bounty of education in the role of sovereign, but it was squandered on Romanus's indifferent character. Romily Jenkins, through Continuatus's words, says Constantine left 'a wealth of minute instruction, which was probably excessive.'[1466] Romanus was not the man or ruler his father had expected at age fourteen or, for that matter, at age twenty when he rose to the throne.

He was born a Porphyrogenitus in 939 to Constantine VII and Helena Lecapenus. Though his father had almost hatred for the man, Romanus was still named for the emperor for whom was his maternal grandfather. At the age of six on April 8, 945 he was crowned co-*Basileus*. At ten, he was a widower and at fourteen his father would write for him the illustrious treatises that would attempt to prepare him for his duties, but which he rarely seemed to consult. He rose to the throne on November 9, 959, when his father suddenly died. But, from the first, the young emperor wanted to begin his reign in an ambitious campaign against the Arabs threatening Byzantium.

The emperor continued the Phoci military family with being the commanders of a new Scholae system, wherein Nicephorus was given the East and Leo the West, dividing the Tagmata soldiers of the Excubitors. He now had well-organized armies that could make offenses in both Asia and Europe at once, as the aim was a two-front war, that was handled eloquently by the Phoci. With Nicephorus Phocas in command, Romanus actually accomplished what better emperors had failed at embarrassingly: he conquered Crete for Byzantium and made it a Theme for the Aegean region. In June, 960, a huge fleet went west and on July 13, it safely landed in northern Crete. It was a larger naval force than sent under Constantine VII as 77,000 oarsmen and sailors occupied the 150 vessels with 2,000 Greek Fire vessels, 1,000 carriers, and 308 supply ships set to ferry 5,000 land troops.[1467] Though still not the strength of Leo and Alexander's force of 911, it was still much better commanded and administered under Nicephorus Phocas. Defeating 40,000 lightly-armed Arab soldiers, Nicephorus then besieged for half a year the Cretan capital of Chandax. Nicephorus persisted after famine hit the army and the city inhabitants. Finally, on March 7, 961, Nicephorus entered Chandax after the third attempt since February and looted it for three days, taking the Emir and amassing 'treasures during more than a century of piracy.'

---

[1466] Jenkins; Romilly, H. 'General Introduction'. *De Administrandii Imperio*, 8.
[1467] Decker, 208; Jenkins, 271.

Missionaries were even sent west to convert these life-long Muslim Arabs of Crete into Christians, but the behavior of the Byzantine armies made this nearly impossible. Unfortunately, this looting and sacking went on for three days without Nicephorus's commission and was dreadfully described: 'Women old and young were raped, murdered and thrown aside; children, even babies at the breast, were strangled and impaled on lances'[1468] as the inhabitants were eventually spared and sold into slavery. After 135 years of Arabic occupation, the chronicler Shihab al-Din Ahmed Ab'd al-Wahhab ibn al-Nuwairi (1279-1333) puts the dead at 200,000 to end Cretan piracy, repopulate the island, and present a yearly subsidy to the Emir.[1469]

The gritty descriptions of the fall of Chandax came from the main historian of the period after Porphyrogenitus, Leo the Deacon (950-992 CE), who wrote on the military exploits of Tzimisces and Phocas between 956 and 976. Though his eyewitness accounts and Romanus I's secretary Daphnopates's accounts also exist, Leo is considered the leading historian of the subject.[1470] He said how the Arabs were hopelessly outnumbered, although they resisted courageously and with great strength. The heavy cavalry of the *cataphractoi* played its part by running down the infantry on the island with mass charges, even as appeals to Egypt, Sicily, and Spain were still ignored. The only real losses happened when the Strategos of Thrace, Pastilas, and his undisciplined Russians were slaughtered in great numbers by a night ambush by the Arabs.

After all of this, Nicephorus sailed back to Constantinople in victory and was considered a hero 'overnight' to the chagrin of his rival, Joseph Bringas. Phocas was given a brief (almost insulting) triumph on foot, with no horses or chariot, to receive the people's salutes and acclaim in the Hippodrome. Not even prisoners or booty were allowed to be displayed by the *Basileus* in Nicephorus's name. This was all because of Romanus, with all haste, needing now to send Nicephorus east to aid his brother Leo against the Arabs of the intractable Sayf al-Dawlah.

Beginning in the summer of 960, the Emir of Aleppo was marching on Asia Minor with 30,000 men. Romanus sent Leo Phocas to handle this and showed rare and wise restraint in not abandoning his Cretan front to reinforce Anatolia with Nicephorus. It showed slight military foresight with the *Basileus*, but perhaps more so the ability and tenacity of the Phocas generals in two fronts.

---

[1468] Norwich, (*APO*), 178.

[1469] Jenkins, 271-272.

[1470] Ostrogorsky, 210-211.

After suppressing the Thracian Magyars, Leo Phocas caught Sayf unawares in the Taurus Mountain passes after the Emir had sacked the fortress of Karkhaneh by Melitene. In November, in a pass known as the *Kulindros* ('Cylinder'),[1471] Sayf's men were killed by half and al-Dawlah once more managed to escape with 300 of his cavalry after a flanking movement followed the loosening of several boulders into the defile routed and destroyed the army.[1472] Now, a more proper triumph awaited Nicephorus Phocas in Constantinople for another well-earned victory.

After Nicephorus's return east, he invaded Cilicia in 962 to once again catch the Emir at his weak point by surprise using an army more powerful, superior, and with higher morale than the Arabs. He first sacked Anazarbus and settled to celebrate Easter in Cappadocia after devastating the Emirate of Tarsus with forty-five more fortified towns along the way from Alexandretta. When Sayf arrived in Cilicia, his efforts at reconstruction were met by Nicephorus, Tzimisces, 30,000 calvary, and 40,000 infantry troops. After Sisium, Germanicea, Teluch, and Manbij were sacked, Sayf went on the defensive at Aleppo. Sayf was chased away from his city in defeat, however, by the Byzantine generals that had taken Syria, these Greeks entering Aleppo on December 23, 962, with another three days of rampant looting such as at Chandax.

By the end of 962 and beginning of 963, Nicephorus Phocas had shown amazing ability and talent against any and almost all of the Empire's enemies. It is this that brought Byzantium the stability it needed to show its true colors in remaining as a world Empire at the highest point of its existence. 190,000 silver *dinars* were taken from Aleppo with 2,000 camels, 1,400 mules, and an apparently 'countless' amount of thoroughbred Arabian horses. Included were bales of velvet and silk damask, gilded and jeweled weapons and armor, even gold tile from the roofs of the city. Aleppo was a blow to the morale of the Hamdamids and their Emirate, as they would now only be a quiet menace for years.[1473]

Romanus II at least deserves credit for his choice in generals and in trusting the Phoci, especially with men such as Joseph Bringas defaming them. But, the leadership of these men, or the leadership these men could provide, would become an issue once again. On March 15, 963, ignoring his ministers' and the clergy's entreaties against hunting on Lent, Romanus II died as a result

---

[1471] Norwich, (*APO*), 180.

[1472] Jenkins, 274.

[1473] Norwich, (*APO*), 181.

of 'straining himself on a hunt.'[1474] Poisoning by his ambitious empress, the Spartan Theophano, has been suggested, but it was not in her immediate interests and she had just given birth on the 13th and was recuperating in bed.[1475] Yet in this reign of a few years, military success not seen in centuries had been accomplished, the Eastern Arabs being humbled under Byzantine arms. Always considered dangerous diversions from his stately responsibilities, Romanus II was still an avid hunter and enjoyed the pleasures of the circus, tennis at the *spaetharium,* the Hippodrome, and feasting with his loyal Senators.[1476]

But Romanus was not a popular *Basileus,* for he weakly demurred to ministers and his devious Empress, Theophano. His act of exiling the women of his family was an outrage in the City as these were princesses of the purple and posed no threat to the state. Decidedly, this was just a maneuver by Theophano to gain control over her husband against what his family, especially his father, would have counseled. This also guaranteed the regent of the child heir Basil would be in her hands without faction led by other members of the royal family. Her only problem was the influence of the powerful eunuch Bringas who would create dynastic alliances to later rival that of the *Basilia's.*

He certainly seemed to at best skirt his father's valuable advice on administration and education, but the Macedonian renaissance still progressed. An example would be the medical and pharmacological texts of the ancient commentator Dioscorides that Romanus sent as gifts to the Caliph of Cordoba, Abid ar-Rahman III, as his father had.[1477] Yet another was the chalice of sardonyx, pearl, and gold enamels of Christ and the saints that was recovered from Venice after the sack of 1204. Ivory triptychs have been recovered from caskets and decorations of Romanus II's first marriage and it is obvious that the Christian art of the period was superior to that of the recovered art of Classical themes. This is apparent when the cheap workmanship of the Veroli Casket and its depiction of the sacrifice of Iphigenia.[1478] But, the point remains that the height of Byzantine craftsmanship could survive any crisis in the Palace during the tenth and eleventh centuries.

In 961, the German Emperor Otto I had been rebuked at attempts to Christianize the fiercely Pagan Russians after Olga's death as the defeated

---

[1474] Treadgold, 497.

[1475] Brownworth, 193f.

[1476] Gibbon, 1639.

[1477] Herrin, 30.

[1478] Mango, 'The Revival of Learning,' 223.

missionaries returned from Kiev.[1479] This was a setback to all forms of Christianity in the East and only made diplomacy with Russia more tenuous without a living diplomat like Constantine VII to handle the situation. A cold winter and locust plagues brought more famine to Byzantium as in Basil I's day. Even after the Cretan victory, a plot was uncovered against Romanus and he had to have food brought in from hungry provinces that held no immediate threat, furthering his unpopularity.

Romanus also continued the rural landowner laws of his Macedonian ancestors as he restricted more edicts for the powerful. Drawn from the Theodosian and Justinianic Codes, he set up guarantees on property holdings of soldiers against alienation as well as those who gave no military service. As Vasiliev points out in the chronicles of Russian historians in 1883, this legislation may have some Slavonic roots from settlements in Asia Minor,[1480] though this is very uncertain. If true, it demonstrates a two-way cultural transmission in the sphere of law that binds Byzantine and Slav foundations also present today in art and religion.

One cultural ideal the Byzantines sought to cultivate was the nature of peace; their goals excluded the power, Empire, gold, and other spoils as they were seen as theirs already. The 'proper' Byzantines wanted peace at most cost; these probably included the Church, monasteries, morale-stricken generals, and exhausted emperors all affected by this constant warfare. Their idealistic views of Eastern Rome as a Christian Empire included the imitation of the Prince of Peace whose presence they claimed to represent.[1481] The trying times of political violence and mixtures of military aggression and defense were in the highest times tested by the ruthless Koranic views of 'Jihad' that brooked no compromise. Later, the hope for peace would be almost nil in the face of the Western Crusaders and their unabashed need for military glory, spoils, and territory. But in the case of the Macedonians, the necessity for war did broker some results of harmony and equilibrium in Byzantium for over half a century.

---

[1479] Obolensky, 190.

[1480] Vasiliev, 567.

[1481] Jenkins, pg. 273. Similar research such as this can also be found in the works of John Haldon; see *Warfare, State and Society in the Byzantine World, 565-1204 (War and Society Series). Routledge Publishing.* 1999.

# NICEPHORUS II PHOCAS
## (963-969)

After Romanus II's death, a brief series of military leaders and aristocratic 'regents' ruled the Empire, beginning with his top general and Domestic, Nicephorus Phocas, and Nicephorus II as *Basileus* was a popular choice upon his ascension to all but the bureaucratic class. He had the makings of having a more common touch, yet made no connection with his aloof nature that ostracized almost all other classes. Though a noble, he had as much education as Romanus Lecapenus, yet his triumphs in Crete and Syria made him seem favored by God for championing Christianity against Islam. He was a severely pious and devout Christian, seen as a new crusader against the encroaching Arabs as he pushed them back to their borders for which he was addressed as the 'White Death of the Saracens'. He would be an underestimated figure in Medieval warfare today, virtually an unknown who reshaped the field army of the Mediterranean into a defensive force with no peer in the tenth century.[1482]

His most important area of education was in the military manuals of Maurice and Leo VI, where Leo advocates guerrilla tactics and hostage exchanges at frontier river borders for peaceful measures. In or out of battle, men must be prepared to make dashes with swords drawn and on horses at all times. Nicephorus Phocas would try hard to have martyr status granted in the Church to any who fell to Muslims in battle, as would be done with the West in the First Crusade, but this was rebuked by the Patriarch. His future looked assured as a *Basileus* that could do what had not been done in decades by protecting the Empire from physical threats instead of ignorance in studies or through bad diplomacy. Nicephorus II was a man of action and mostly loyalty to him was given quite freely by almost all of Constantinople. He sculpted the morale of the entire Byzantine army into one of hope and optimism, such as the Cromwellians,[1483] in the seventeenth century, to make Byzantine spirit and discipline almost invincible.

Almost immediately, shifts in policy began with Phocas's succession in state finance, leaning toward the enfranchisement of the army and officer classes. Taxes became almost exorbitant to support military ventures, although the coinage did not suffer debasement.[1484] This would soon affect the urban

---

[1482] Decker, 214.

[1483] Ostrogorsky, 240; Jenkins, 274.

[1484] Treadgold, 503.

communities where taxation would further inflate. Thus, the rural poor and peasantry would lose their trust in the emperor as would monastic communities that made their riches from these peasants. Nicephorus reformed the Church and these wealthy monasteries wherein more income would accumulate for the Crown over ecclesiastical institutions. This occurred as Nicephorus plied for a new and more humbled Church before God where worldliness and greed would be separate from the faithful, but all it really did was turn the ecclesiastics against the *Basileus*.

His diplomacy lacked style, usually ending in armed conflict or embassadors and emissaries heaping abuse upon the *Basileus*'s name. Although he was said to have inspired his armies with his charisma, he was uncouth and without the rudiments of tact or taste besides being the best Byzantine general since Belisarius.[1485] Such descriptions mainly took shape in the works of Liutprand of Cremona, Byzantine embassador for the German Emperor Otto I. His invectives for Phocas were as shattering as his praise was as uplifting for Constantine VII. Nicephorus was a military conservative whose Spartan lifestyle excluded worldly pomp, ostentation, or sophistication. Byzantium was reflected badly by this ruler and Nicephorus's policies would prove that to the Western Emperor and Pope. Over his six-year reign, Phocas would lose friends, face, and eventually his life for his beliefs and standards and although they were genuine, they only tarnished his personal reputation. His contradictory policy in handling monasteries over his own piety would mark him as a hypocrite, his devotion being seen as a 'convenient mask for his dangerous and dark ambition.'[1486]

Nicephorus II was born in 912 to Bardas Phocas, former Domestic of Basil I, into a prominent Cappadocian noble family. Named for his illustrious grandfather, he along with his father and brothers, Leo and Constantine, made up one of the most successful and memorable military families of the entire Empire's history. He began this career in 945 with his ascension as Strategos of the Anatolians at age thirty-three. Over the next eighteen years, he would be counted for victory over victory, rising as supreme commander of the forces and the special Domestic of the West under Romanus II. His greatest triumph in the conquest of Crete would catapult his reputation and position over his brother in

---

[1485] Brownworth, 187.

[1486] Gibbon, 1640. Gibbon goes on at length to express his disgust for hypocrisy and avarice (meaning Nicephorus's) as the worst and most odious vice.

the East. He peaked his meteoric rise as he aided his brother in taking Aleppo and shaming the Hamdanids.

Physically, he was a squat, broad, thickly muscled, and swarthy man (his complexion denoting his eastern roots), having long, thick, black hair rung in tight curls. He also had dark and thoughtful eyes that hinted at sadness as reported his most noted historian Leo the Deacon, they denoted a melancholy nature. Then there was his unshakable piety as he was a man of '. . .high moral integrity, intelligent if not narrow-minded, serious and sober, utterly incorruptible, impervious to flattery, and hard as nails; but he could also be pitiless and cruel, and his meanness and avarice were notorious.'[1487] He also went many years without eating meat, kept a vehement chastity (even in marriage), and wore a hair shirt his uncle (a monk) once wore. The Crown had been more or less forced on him and his whole reign he saw as a chore, as he only dreamed of retiring to a monastery to carry out his years in contemplation. But the mistrust he sowed in his ambitious allies, along with his own actions as temporal head of Eastern Christianity, would see him never to achieve this.

In March of 963, Romanus II was dead as Nicephorus was camped at Tzamundus, unaware of the events at Constantinople. The wily *Basilia* Theophano had been accused of poisoning Romanus, although this was unfounded and just a rumor. But what was true was that she needed someone to favor her over the ambitious eunuch Joseph Bringas in her son's regency. She alerted Nicephorus Phocas of the situation and he returned to the City in a Triumph to accuse Bringas of plotting to murder him. This was probably true, anyway, considering what the immoral Bringas had already done, re-possessing and destroying much of Phocas's property in the City.[1488] The Domestic took refuge in St. Sophia and Bringas was made to back down by the soldiers and mobs that protected Phocas, including the Patriarch Polyeuctus. Bringas desperately wrote to John Tzimisces, the new Strategos of the Anatolics to rush to the City and claim the regency for the Chamberlain's faction.

Tzimisces was also Nicephorus's nephew by marriage and chose loyalty to his uncle by bringing him Bringas's incriminating letter after he returned to Cappadocia for Easter, much to Theophano and Polyeuctus's distress. Phocas immediately recalled Tzimisces's Anatolian troops to Caesarea for his defense and seizing their only opportunity, the troops there made him *Basileus*, with the general's reluctance, on July 3, 963. Though he was eventually acclaimed,

---

[1487] Norwich, (*APO*), 190.
[1488] Jenkins, 277.

Nicephorus refused at first opportunity, 'dwelling on bereavements for the dead' with great melancholy and with his wishes to continue his war with 'the infidels'.[1489] In the Byzantine tradition of a military ascension away from the City, the troops dressed him in finery and raised him on a shield where he stood above all others being proclaimed *Basileus*. Phocas and his armies then left Caeserea and Syria, quickly returning to Constantinople to claim the throne Nicephorus was now given. His brother Leo and the Western troops were joined to Nicephorus's force and Bringas blockaded the Bosporus in a desperate ploy to avoid catastrophe. The Phoci were stranded at Chrysopolis strategizing their position at the Palace of Heira.

Bringas then captured Bardas, Nicephorus's father, as a hostage to hold the Phoci at bay. But, this was done on a Sunday (August 9) when the streets were flooded with people. When the citizens of Constantinople came to understand what Bringas was doing, a mob emerged angered at this betrayal. Outnumbered and surrounded, Bringas watched as Bardas Phocas was taken to St. Sophia and guarded there until his sons' return. In the typical Byzantine fashion, the throngs rioted for three days howling for Nicephorus's return. The imperial heir, Basil, facilitated this by gathering 4,000 palace servants and marching them to the docks at the Bosporus clearing a way for Nicephorus to cross.

On Sunday, August 16, Nicephorus II sailed to the Palace of the Hebdomon where he was made ready in a golden breastplate and purple robes to proudly enter Constantinople. Always the devout, he gave thanks at a monastery for Abraham of the Archeiropoietus ('Not Made with Human Hands') named for the miraculous and divine icon of Mary housed there.[1490] He was then crowned before Theophano and the imperial sons, Basil and Constantine, by Patriarch Polyeuctus in the Church of St. Sophia. He banished Joseph Bringas to his native Paphlagonia and married *Basilia* Theophano in the Nea Church on September 20 (though he vowed never to consummate the marriage as a favor to God). Leo Phocas was made a Postal Logothete and Curopalates, Basil the High Chamberlain, John Tzimisces Domestic of the East, and Bardas Phocas became *Caesar* (only as he was never to have been thought to outlive his son or the co-emperor and heir, Basil).

Events were developing in the East as Sayf al-Dawlah had a stroke and was partially paralyzed, weakening his position with famine plaguing Syria due to the Byzantine incursions and a bad climate. To show he still had dominance,

---

[1489] Diehl, 135.
[1490] Norwich, (*APO*), 189.

however, Sayf sent soldiers to raid Iconium across the Bosporus from the City. Setting off Phocas, Tzimisces was sent back into Cilicia, where these campaigns were made a militarized culture as outfitted in Nicephorus II's *Treatise on Tactics*.[1491] He made it to Adana and took Mopsuestia until early 964 when the famine of the Arabs took a toll on the Byzantine armies and they were forced to withdraw. Not perturbed by the forced retreat, Nicephorus was already making plans for Sicily to return to Cilicia that winter, meanwhile enacting several edicts and Novels and legislation involving land investing.

Nicephorus Phocas was the first of a few Macedonian rulers, and the first in centuries, to actually lead armies personally as commander-in-chief, marching to Caesarea to put pressure on Sayf al-Dawlah. Simultaneously, his Eastern fleets conquered Cyprus under Byzantine rule to make it a Theme in the Eastern Mediterranean off of Syrian shores, reclaiming the island since its 688 conquest by the Abbasids. Though supposedly a Theme and occupied by the Caliphate, Cyprus was characterized with independence before 963 as an 'unclaimed' naval stockade for both armies, without sovereignty, yet not exempt from taxation.[1492] Meanwhile, the Western fleets, under the *Basileus*'s nephew Manuel, sailed to Sicily and landed in Messina to protect the last Christian outposts. In estimation the fleet was too small and underestimated, especially in light of the Cypriot fleet that was simultaneously sent.[1493] Manuel was killed in battle and the Arabs resumed their attacks on Calabria. Nicephorus kept busy, however, by putting his efforts into realizing phase two of his strategy by re-entering Cilicia.

The full conquest of Cilicia by Nicephorus was achieved by the combination of the *Basileus*'s tenacity on campaign and the vulnerable position of the Arabs due to their famine outbreaks. After taking Mopsuestia as his Domestic had, he set his sights on Tarsus, being the seat of Cilicia's control. After a fifty-day siege, the unbeatable famine sent Nicephorus to regroup in Caesaerea in the beginning of 965. He claimed at least sixteen new Themes and manned them with Armenian troops taken from the princedom-turned-Theme, Taron, by 967 as a new title of *Ducas* ('Duke') to the Strategos of Chaldia.[1494] Mopsuestia was besieged by the Byzantines a third time, its inhabitants relocated to Tarsus. Confidently rejecting negotiations for a treaty from Aleppo, the Tarsus

---

[1491]  *Diehl, 117.*

[1492]  Jenkins, 278.

[1493]  Treadgold, 500-501.

[1494]  Treadgold, (*BAIA*), 35.

Muslims were given safe passage to reside in Antioch as Tarsus was occupied by the victorious Greeks. Cilicia now in hand, Nicephorus made Mopsuestia and Tarsus Themes along with Cyprus to hold a tight grip on western Syria. Nicephorus II would build garrisons and repopulate the new Themes with Armenians and native Syrians, to make Christianity a new requirement of habitation (even the heretical Monophysites).

The next set of difficulties in the East was the situation in Bulgaria where Byzantine ambassadors were scourged for demanding the tribute previous emperors had given.[1495] Peter the Khan, who had married Basil I's daughter, asked for the usual subsidy from the *Basileus*'s purse. But, Peter made a fatal error in that Maria Lecapenus had died two months before and was asking for a subsidy that Nicephorus had bequeathed to her needs alone and not to that of Bulgaria's. Nicephorus's umbrage was with the fact Byzantium enjoyed cultural and religious superiority, the *Basileus*'s pride demanding he be the lord and master of those 'clad in leather skins',[1496] using Peter's insult as a pretext for war. Attacking several border forts, Nicephorus sought to set an example, hurrying to the East again on adventures of expansion. He paid off the Russian Tsar Svyatoslav, second son of the pious Olega, to put a full assault on Bulgaria in Nicephorus's place. Nicephorus is said to have bitten off more than he could chew in 967, as the Russians ravaged the Danubian province efficiently and surrounded the Bulgar forces at Dristra.

Svyatoslav wintered that year in Preslav with every intention of conquering Bulgaria and ruling a Russian empire stretching from Kiev just north of the Chersonese and dangerously close to the eastern Byzantine borders. This made Nicephorus balk at the idea of a Russian homeland that would rival the size and eastern position of Byzantium. Svyatoslav, however, never intended war against Byzantium; he was, after all, the son of the Russian empress who marveled at the court of Constantine Porphyrogenitus and its new promises of salvation in the Orthodox Church. Despite this, he sought to check the Russian encroachment, Nicephorus setting off on a campaign with the Pechenegs in the northeast that had pre-occupied Svyatoslav in 968. Unfortunately, when the Russians defeated the Pechenegs they returned to Bulgaria in full force, realizing Nicephorus's tactics and deposing the Bulgar Khan Boris II, capturing Preslav, and destroying Phillipopolis. Russia was now a greater threat to Byzantium then it had ever been before due to Nicephorus's diplomatic miscalculations.

---

[1495] Ostrogorsky, 292.

[1496] Obolensky, 128.

This incident demonstrates a crippling diplomatic weakness on Nicephorus's part in not taking the opportunity to create a Christian alliance in his 'holy wars' against Islam, possibly stronger than he had done with the questionable Peter. It is also to be noted that he had the xenophobia of Porphyrogenitus and refused marriage alliances with foreign princes and princesses for his relatives, even when the Emperor Otto I offered an alliance with his son. Otto had been crowned Holy Roman Emperor in February 962 for defending Italy by the libidinous Pope John XII, scandalously called 'Pope Caligula' and his hedonistic reign the 'Pornocracy'.[1497] This coronation lacked any consultation with and much protest from the East, especially when Otto forced a new Pope, John XIII, to crown his son Otto II to be co-*Basileus* on Christmas Day, 967.

The desperate Khan Peter, at the time free from the Russian incursions, tried to settle peace and alliance with Byzantium. To Constantinople he sent his two young daughters in hopes of marrying them to the princes Basil and Constantine in the summer of 968. But it was too little and too late as Peter himself would die after a long reign on January 20, 969, just a few months before Nicephorus would. Bulgaria's throne went to Peter's son, Boris II, who was young and inexperienced and was easy prey for the able Svyatoslav's ambitions in Kiev. In the summer before, Otto retaliated against the refusal of a marriage alliance by sacking Byzantine Apulia in Longobardia, Benevento, Capua, and Calabria, failing only at Bari. Otto then sent Liutprand of Cremona to negotiate with his son, who was no doubt unimpressed by Nicephorus's diplomatic failings.

In the East, the situation was brighter as Sayf al-Dawlah died in 967, although Syria was in a state of near destruction over years of military loss. Nicephorus had already raided Mesopotamia upon leaving Bulgaria and took it from Amida to Nisibis. He fought all over north Syria from Manbij to Aleppo itself, and then on to Antioch where he held siege for a week before another retreat due to a lack of rationed food from the ever-present famine. After desolating Syria, Nicephorus headed to Armenia to expand without opposition. The neighboring kingdom of Taron was given to Byzantine Armenia in the will of its recently deceased king (an old Roman practice with subject kingdoms) as the *Basileus* divided it into at least a dozen Themes. Under Nicephorus's nephew Bardas, as Duke of Chaldea, Taron worked as a defense buffer to the weakened Arabs in Mesopotamia in preparation for future reprisals.

---

[1497] Norwich, (*APO*), 97.

Ever busy in the East, Nicephorus II turned his back on the Russians and Ottonians in 968 to raid northern Mesopotamia, taking Martyropolis and making Edessa a Theme. He then returned to Syria, prepared to retrieve Antioch and afterwards took the cities of Hama and Homs. In Homs, he is said to have recovered the head of the apostle John the Baptist (oddly, between the two halves of Christendom, *two* different heads of the Baptist were found).[1498] This would be an added triumph along with the tunic worn by John taken from Aleppo before Nicephorus was crowned *Basileus*. Nicephorus went from Homs to inspect the progress of besieging Antioch to the heavily fortified Tripoli and he re-fortified the entire main northern coast. He then besieged and took the fort at Pagrae entrusting it to a commander in Nicephorus's retinue, Michael Burtzes. Regrettably, Nicephorus had to gut much of Pagrae's forces due to more lack of provisions. The entire Eastern dominion was given to a eunuch, Peter, before returning to Constantinople.

The rest of the enemy territory in Armenia was invaded by the Duke Bardas Phocas who destroyed its capital of Manzikert, an irony considering its role as an epic Byzantine defeat just a century later. After the long siege, Antioch was finally taken in October of 969 by the imperial appointee Michael Burtzes and his eunuch Stratopedarch ('Commander of the Army'), Peter. This, unfortunately, roused feelings of jealousy in the *Basileus* as he, the champion of Byzantium and Christianity, wished to personally enter and capture the city. His dedication to the idea of he being what was later called a 'Crusader', such as Heraclius had been, was not to be underestimated; he did have deeper plans in crossing Syria and retrieving Jerusalem from Muslim hands, only to come in sight of it and be halted by his assassination.[1499]

While famine spread and struck Constantinople, Nicephorus further exacerbated events by castigating Burtzes for 'exceeding his orders' at Antioch, ostracizing the army. The economic edicts he enacted were making him more and more unpopular among those who once supported him. The populace of the City can be counted among them, seeing the *Basileus* as a typical Anatolian aristocrat, caring for the barren properties of his home region first and second anything else. The City even saw him as an 'interloper' whose Eastern barbarian armies were in the mode of an enemy occupation.[1500] In 967, Armenian sailors and Thracian soldiers turned their quarrel into a riot and the following Easter in

---

[1498]  Treadgold, 504.
[1499]  Jenkins, 275.
[1500]  *Jenkins, ibid.,* 280-281.

424

the Hippodrome, wild rumors abated that random people would be slaughtered for these disturbances by the *Basileus*'s orders. On Ascension Day, Nicephorus's procession after the Matins of the Church of the Virgin at Pegae was booed and pelted with food and offal by the City's inhabitants as he walked through the city streets.

A mother and daughter were then arrested for pelting the retinue with roof tiles and, like a tyrant, Nicephorus had the two burnt at the stake in the Amastris.[1501] Earlier he had banished his nephew John Tzimisces to the Chalcedonian Palace across the Bosporus and it was here that the sealing of Phocas's fate would begin due to his paranoia. Theophano had fallen in love with, or pretended to be in love with, Tzimisces and saw his potential as a new regent. She convinced her husband to return John to the City gathering the chief members of the court for her conspiracy: Burtzes, the Prince Basil, and a Taxiarch named Leo Balantes. The assassins dressed as women after midnight on December 11, 969, to enter the Palace, finding Phocas's bedchamber was empty. Almost fleeing for fear of treachery, a eunuch pointed out that Nicephorus had fallen asleep giving prayer. He wore his hair shirt, was accompanied by a devotional work from his full library, and slept on a rug of leopard-skin.[1502]

There he was dragged away and Tzimisces, pulling handfuls of hair from his uncle's beard and head, had the assassins strike with their swords to smash his jaw and the teeth from his mouth. After his horrible death, the Varangian guards were awoken to see the emperor's severed head on a stick in the window of the *Basileus*'s bedroom. These Varangians ('Men of the Pledge'), known for the famous berserk rages, were the Nordic descendants of warriors that had come east from Russia and south on the Don to Byzantium, being employed as the personal bodyguards of *Basilii* thence forward. They were also given a strange entitlement to as much gold in the Treasury as they could carry,[1503] possibly explaining bankruptcies in times of more unpopular or paranoid *Basilii*. In this case, however, nothing was done and John I would succeed his uncle he once saved from Joseph Bringas; Nicephorus Phocas would die with none to stand for him.

Nicephorus II Phocas was an ascetically devout man of the military and dying at prayer was fitting for his character, although his murder was one of

---

[1501] Norwich, (*APO*), 206.

[1502] Brownworth, 200.

[1503] *ibid.*, 212f.

'insult and cruelty'. Even his assassin, Tzimisces, would separate himself from his more 'criminal associate' Theophano in due time.[1504] His policies on land disbursement to his prized cavalry and his uncompromising efforts to bring Eastern Christianity to a more spiritual and hermetic lifestyle imitating the saints were stark examples of his character. He had a series of heated debates with his once-ally Patriarch Polyeuctus over his actions and convictions. It is not described as being prior or as a result of his own marriage controversy, but the Patriarch refused Nicephorus's solemn request to make all soldiers who fought and died against Islam, in any manner, martyrs. After the shocking acts the Byzantines performed in sacking Candia and Aleppo, it is not surprising, however. To show his dominance in Italy, in Apulia and Calabria all Latin hymns were abandoned as Byzantines could sing only of the Greek ceremonials.[1505]

Nicephorus's own controversy happened in the form of what the Patriarch considered an illegal union in 964. Before Romanus II's death, Phocas had been made the godfather of one of his two sons, giving a 'spiritual affinity' to the family. Thus, any marriage to the heir's mother Theophano would be violating Church law and would be voided immediately. Incensed, the *Basileus* called for an impromptu Synod of any Bishops found in the City to discuss the issue and reach a conclusion. Upon researching for this decree, the justification for the marriage was found to have been in the Edict of Unions of Constantine V which also called him an 'executioner of monks . . .[with] contempt for the Blessed Virgin...a worshiper of devils.'[1506] It was not difficult to find this decree vacated by the Church, and therefore, a non-issue. Furthermore, all donative laws under Constantine Copronymous were voided and all Bishopric investitures would need the *Basileus*'s personal approval.

Any spurious behavior of the Patriarch no doubt stemmed from Phocas's handling of both the monasteries and Orthodox Church of Constantinople, 964 being a landmark year in Phocas's policies. From the start of his reign, legislation and Novels were being made limiting the financial and social power of the Church that were creating problems of tax exemptions, illegal military acquisitions, and uncultivated land. This was corruption and greed that the *Basileus* said was making the Church an 'empty theatrical performance, bringing dishonor to the name of Christ.'[1507] Nicephorus II forbade new gifts

---

[1504]  Gibbon, 1641.

[1505]  Vasiliev, 336.

[1506]  Norwich, (*APO*), 193.

[1507]  Ostrogorsky, 287.

of property made to the Church and vetoed new institutions from production, making exemptions for those existing Churches and charities in direct need of donations and property. To expand his wishes for a new foundation of monastical reform, he created the state financial system of the *lauri*. One of Nicephorus's acts on founding these in 966 was granting the Lavra monastery annual grants of 244 *nomismata* (five pounds of gold) and grain doles.[1508] These acts only embody the vague actions of the *Basileus* in defining his imperial tax duties as well as his faith as a pious man.

These *laurai* were isolated and totally self-sufficient monasteries that would remain pure of worldliness and the corrupting influence of ecclesiastical authority.[1509] Nicephorus crowned one monastery the 'Great Lavra' at Mt. Athos in his *Typikon*, founded by his spiritual provider Anathasius who was born in Trebizond in 925 and was a former teacher in Constantinople. Anastasius was also responsible for this new cenobitic movement that would bring the Studite Encyclopedist monks to Eastern Christianity.[1510] It was built on the unscalable and isolated 'Holy Mountain', gifted by the *Basileus* with a golden reliquary containing a piece of the True Cross from St. Blacharnae. Tragedy would still strike as Athanasius, later made a saint, would be killed from a cave-in of the domes of the monastery. In the years after, forty-six monasteries would appear in these mountains with these new ascetic lifestyles also transcending to Georgia, Serbia, Russia, and Amalfi. Mt. Athos beatified Nicephorus and still celebrate and venerate the founder to the present; descendants, in fact, of Nicephorus II Phocas can still be found in Greece and southern Lebanon.[1511]

Nicephorus II's secular financial policies were far from corrupt or just as he frankly sought to undo all the work of reform for which the former members of the Macedonian dynasty strove. As a military leader from an aristocracy of generals, it is little surprise he showed a bias to military officers as a class of landholders. It became another reality that due to the famine of the East, starving peasants would again sell land to the rich, stirring the topic of military holdings and their alienation. He also confirmed that due to the '. . .constricted . . .draconian control' of the urban economy by bureaucratic regulation, land acquisition was the only way to invest surplus capital . . .left to the deployment of private initiative to any great extant.'[1512]

---

[1508] Herrin, 196.
[1509] Treadgold, 500.
[1510] Obolensky, 296.
[1511] Brownworth, 201f.
[1512] Ostrogorsky, 288.

Laws from 967 stemmed from Armenian soldiers fleeing new Byzantine Themes to remain non-citizens as the land was military land and not to be sold. Another law, complementing this, was the creation of a military class in the *cataphractoi,* as the heavy cavalry Nicephorus favored most, who gained much wealth in the Arab lands as shock troops. These heavy troops became a symbol of Nicephorus's rule; in illustrations, the *Basileus* is seen bearing the slender, tapered sword of the *cataphractoi,* known as the *paramerion.*[1513] These specialized troops were classified by landholding at the highest worth of sixteen pounds of gold (1,152 *nomismata*); methods of affording such land varied from pooling wealthy soldiers into a trust as three or four light cavalry, promoting one of them to a *cataphractoi* in exchange of their own service.[1514]

The light cavalry's minimum net worth was to be twelve pounds (864 *nomismata*) of gold over the four pounds (288 *nomismata*) at which other cavalry were kept. This would rapidly disenfranchise thousands of peasant families and widen the gap between the militarily rich and rural poor. Also changing the social composition of the army, a new rising class of 'lesser nobility' made of this specialized heavy cavalry.[1515] It is hypocritical when the language of the laws adamantly claims to be treating all equal under the law when it further empowers the rich over the poor with no such equality.

To balance this new trend financially, Nicephorus had minted the *tetrateron* which was a coin one-twelfth the weight of the *nomismata,* thus one-twelfth the value.[1516] These paid inactive soldiers in peace and war and though the coin was not debased, the value of government payments were devalued by a twelfth while demands were inflated the same amount (this contradicts Ostrogorsky's claim that the coinage was greatly debased). These adjustments were, '...noticed and resented, especially in a time of economic distress.' It was true that by now, endless warfare was quickly leading to the taxpayers' further loss of faith in Nicephorus and any promises of reform.

Yet, Treadgold also evaluated that this new coin revitalized the practice of weighing debased and lightweight coins, doing nothing to slow down trade or lose revenues of taxation, meaning prices were not increased or affected due to its use. Possibly the circulation was intentionally limited to larger government transactions of land or taxation. Nicephorus himself was suiting the exchequer

---

[1513] Decker, 119.

[1514] Treadgold, *(BAIA)*, 174.

[1515] Ostrogorsky, 286.

[1516] Treadgold, 503. It was a gold coin, lighter than its counterpart (with more purity) with the similar size of 1.14 inches squared. Also see Treadgold, (BAIA), 212.

more than even the Byzantine consumer, with accusations that the *Basileus* himself was buying corn to monopolize in times of the famine![1517] Nicephorus's financial/military policies were radical changes from the other Macedonians and the culture of his Anatolian ancestry was much to blame. Those virtues of decentralization of the state and privilege to the rich officers over the peasant-militia were strongly administered. With ease the victorious general-emperor had replaced the peasant communities that bound the free with his own tenants of squires that ruined the equality of the soldiers.[518]

As aforementioned, Nicephorus's and Tzimisces's main historians were Liutprand of Cremona and, later, Leo the Deacon. Liutprand's *Relatio de Legatione Constantinopolitana* was mainly an invective against the Byzantine *Basileus* and his court. It was called 'malicious' which goes without saying as it included all of the reports the ambassador would use to insult and embarrass the Eastern imperial government to the Western Emperor.[1519] Even though his acclaimed Constantine VII spoke the same language, Liutprand would criticize Nicephorus as a 'smooth-tongued trickster, made still more dangerous by his fluent Greek.'

Tirade upon tirade did Liutprand heap upon Nicephorus II, his manners, and even the City itself under his reign – but these should be treated as the failings of diplomacy on the Greek side over the Western. The City of Constantine was one full of 'lies, tricks, perjury, and greed . . .rapacious, avaricious, and vainglorious.' The ambassador, a eunuch Patrician named Christopher, who had met him made clear during this trip that the 'fatuous blockhead of a Pope' had not understood how this City had gained from Rome the imperial scepter and Senate. Furthermore, Rome itself was full of 'vile slaves, fishermen, confectioners, poulterors, bastards, plebians, and underlings.'

The meanness of the new court alarmed him when the feasts of Constantine were followed in Nicephorus's banquets with the peasant fare of leeks, garlic, and the fish sauce known as *garum*. Barbarian envoys were placed closer at table to the *Basileus's* than he and the bolts of silk he had purchased were confiscated by Byzantine customs officials leaving imperial territory.[1520] Liutprand also sulked on how Nicephorus rightly boasted to him how Byzantium had a *thalassokratia* ('command of the sea') of the Mediterranean, outlining with 'Naval power was

---

[1517] Hussey, 137.

[1518] Brehier, L. *Vie et Mort des Byzance*. Paris, France. 1947, 147-150; Ostrogorsky, 238-240; Jenkins, 282.

[1519] Norwich, (*APO*), 198-201.

[1520] Herrin, 178-179.

mine alone' being the *Basileus*'s creed.[1521] But perhaps it was such invective that caused another chapter in the battle of Western/Eastern supremacy in 968 when Otto I and Pope John XIII began using the title 'August Emperor of the Romans' and claimed Nicephorus only as 'Emperor of the Greeks.' In turn, the Byzantine *Basileus* would respond that Otto only be claimed and treated as a 'King' at best.

Leo the Deacon was the other major contributor as historians to Nicephorus II's and John I's reigns. His military histories of the Empire in campaigning Bulgaria and Syria were also blended with the more religious aspects of the reign of such a devout ruler. This included Christological and theological language that associated the *Basileus* with the Fathers of the Church. In his conquest of Edessa in 966 to retrieve the head of John the Baptist, Leo stepped into the Classical tradition of Cassius Dio (155-235 CE), Arrian (92-175 CE), Polybius (200-118BCE), and others to give Nicephorus a Christian aura of piety. Leo recorded the testaments of John the Bishop of Melitene and how he painted Phocas as a man firm in his prayers to God, high in spirit in his hymns and devotionals, and never leaned toward the vain.[1522] Nicephorus was also one to separate the banners of Christ and Islam as that between good living and vile depravity.

Leo still lacked decent literary education and his endeavors to imitate Procopius as historian has been criticized as anecdotal, superstitious, and lacking in style, an unfortunate phenomenon of the age.[1523] But it is important to note Leo the Deacon was a chronicler of eyewitness accounts and had a fair, honest balance in his estimation of events. Vasiliev, as a Russian Byzantinist, tells of how Leo the Deacon's works have been valuable for Russian history as it contributed so much with Svyatoslav's wars with the Bulgars and Greeks.[1524] Had not the *Basileus* been assassinated, Leo had entertained, he might have reached the imperial boundaries from India to the Atlantic. As for referring to Theophano, Leo said Nicephorus Phocas had 'conquered all but woman.'[1525]

Though not a literary man, Nicephorus Phocas followed the tradition of Leo the Wise and wrote a series of treatises on military matters. In his *On Skirmishing*, for example, he notes that the maximum of an army of lightning raiders should be 3,000 (though exceptions are noted before the disciplined

---

[1521] Diehl, 51.

[1522] Vasiliev, 335.

[1523] Marshall and Mavrogordato, 231-232.

[1524] Vasiliev, 364.

[1525] *Ibid.*, 335.

holy warriors of the *ghazi*[1526]): 'If you are present with only your own Theme, General, and the force under your commands a small one, then you should follow the enemy cautiously and at a good distance to avoid being detected by them. You should launch your attacks only against those charging into the villages and spreading out.'[1527]

Nicephorus's own cautious nature in guerilla warfare is apparent and fostered in his works, such as in his *Military Precepts*. To maintain safety of position, the *Basileus* admonishes that commanders of forces in ambushes and brief engagements to 'with the help of God ...Avoid not only an enemy force of superior strength, but also equal strength.'[1528] But beyond the offensive, Phocas wrote on the defensive measures to be taken for the day, especially in the use of artillery and special weaponry; the hand-held flamethrowers of Greek Fire using engineering such as hand trebuchets, swivel tubes, and hand pumps for projection.[1529] The army composition in the *Precepts* is expanded with a call for 16,000 infantry, 8,000 cavalry, and a specific number of 284 to 502 *cataphractoi*.[1530] His adeptness in the military arts would be a welcome legacy in the Macedonians' warrior-*Basilii*, recovering and securing borders the Empire desperately needed.

## JOHN I TZIMISCES
### (969-976)

There are great misgivings on the origin of John I's seven-year reign; because of his good looks, charisma, and style opposing that of his stern predecessor, he had overall popularity with much of Byzantium. He had long flowing, blonde hair with a copper beard, attractive blue eyes, handsome features, and a healthy build in his short frame. His credentials included a robust agility and energy as a man who loved wine, pleasures, and the Greek spirit of enjoying life (in

---

[1526] Decker, 81.

[1527] Nicephorus II. *On Skirmishing. Three Byzantine Military Treatises. CFHB*, 25, ed. by Dennis George. Washington, DC: Dumbarton Oaks Research Library and Collections. 1985, 16.

[1528] Nicephorus II, *Praecepts Militaria of Nicephorus II Phocas (963-969), IV. Sowing the Dragon's Teeth: Byzantine Warfare in the Tenth Century*, ed. by E. McGreer. Washington, DC: Dumbarton Oaks Research Library and Collections. 1995, 195-203. This example is an odd similarity to the military advice of Sun Tzu (545BCE-470BCE)'s *Art of War*.

[1529] Decker, 226.

[1530] Treadgold, (*BAIA*), 113.

moderation).[1531] He had a generosity much appreciated, going on to reverse the unfair and unpopular legislation of Nicephorus Phocas. He rightly criticized the wealthy whom 'instead of showing pity and humanity buy the property of the wretched cheaply and who founded their fortunes on the misery of the destitute'[1532] in his policy to eliminate the 'terrible evil of cupidity.' Also he was a classic soldier-*Basileus* born from the rising stock of Armenian-born military aristocracy replacing the Anatolian commanders on the throne through the clans of Melias.[1533]

Tzimisces was a master at the bow and did daredevil tricks such as vaulting over three horses to land in the saddle of the fourth, effortlessly. Along with his knowledge of the art of war he had learned from his uncle, he had an infectious personality that created in Constantinople an optimism among its people of military invincibility now that Phocas was dead and a real statesman had taken his place.[1534] But, the events of December 11, 969, put doubt in the minds of historians modern as well as contemporary to the era. Assassinating Nicephorus II was seen as a heinous act historically, being called 'an almost unprecedented and unjustifiable crime.'[1535] He was a usurper plain and simple and not even marriage into the Macedonian dynasty could clean such a stain. John gained the favor of the bureaucratic party at court and many others who had despised Nicephorus's policies. As soon as the bloody act was done, Tzimisces imposed a strict curfew for Constantinople and announced rioting would be punishable by death as obviously a guilty conscience gave him fear of his own people. But, he had the loyalty and support of both the Orthodox Church and monastic parties (in exchange for legal exemptions) as well, while a raise in the price in bread, due to the famine, made his predecessor appear only weaker.[1536]

Despite all this, he was still a beloved *Basileus* with military boldness and a vision of a Christian Empire in the East without precedent. He made peace with the Church and its institutions and put a more fair and stringent fiscal policy in motion. He breached the fragile borders of Islam in the East and pushed them back to places not ruled by the Romans since the early seventh century, further limiting a Russian Empire growing from Kiev and Preslav. Had he lived longer, it has also been commented he would have taken the Empire to unparalleled

---

[1531] Norwich, (*APO*), 213.

[1532] Diehl, 156.

[1533] Decker, 48-49.

[1534] Brownworth, 202f.

[1535] Treadgold, 505.

[1536] Jenkins, 291.

heights. The *Chronicle* of the contemporary George Hamatolus romanticized how 'all nations' were terrified of John and peace was quickly made by the Arabs, Armenians, and Persians, achieving great victories from Edessa to the Euphrates as 'the sword of the Christian cut down like a sickle.'[1537]

John Tzimisces was born in 925 in Armenia to the military aristocratic clan of the Curcuas in Tzemeshgadzak in Melitene. It is suggested that 'Tzimisces' was actually a nickname for his 'small stature' or even his 'red boots' while Matthew the Edessan (d. 1144) puts it as a Greek form of his home region. He grew up in the midst of one of the most loyal and effective military families in Byzantium as Bardas Phocas had been his grandfather, his uncle had been John Curcuas, and he was a maternal nephew of Nicephorus Phocas himself as well. This did little for his legitimacy, however, as Nicephorus's claim to the purple was practically murder at its start. He had held the title of Domestic of the East in the army and was one of the victors of Aleppo along with his uncle for Romanus II, who was also instrumental in his uncle's succession.

But, he had read the writing on the wall and killed his uncle with his aunt Theophano's collusion to gain the throne. Ironically, if Theophano wished for wedded bliss and her own ambitions fulfilled afterwards, she had badly underestimated her new husband. The Patriarch Polyeuctus adamantly insisted that Tzimisces tonsure Theophano for life, punish the collaborators, and distribute his wealth to the poor before he would even consider crowning him *Basileus*.[1538] Tzimisces faced a harsh choice that surely tested his pious faith in the Church and its authority, eventually choosing power over passion and agreeing to the Patriarch's demands.

An infuriated Theophano was put in the Monastery on Prince's Island and Polyeuctus crowned John I on Christmas Day, 969. Polyeuctus would be dead in February of 970, but for appearance's sake, Theophano could not be recalled. If time could have been bought, the imperial couple would have ruled together and if it was not so drenched in innocent blood, it might have been a tragic love story. It had a bitter end, however, when Theophano escaped to St. Sophia and was re-exiled by Basil the Parakoimomenus. She was allowed one final visit to her once suitor Tzimisces, insisting Basil, the heir, be present, wherein she attacked her step-son brutally before being stopped, an unsurprisingly selfish and vicious act for the *Basileus*.

John I began his reign by replacing officials once loyal to Nicephorus and

---

[1537]  Vasiliev, 310-311.
[1538]  Treadgold, 506.

exiling his brother Leo, with his sons, including the new Duke of Chaldea, to a monastery in Lesbos. As if in a dramatic play, Leo had barely escaped blinding by John's mercy at the last moment. John would keep his advisor Basil Lecapenus as Chamberlain as well as Peter the Stratopedarch, who had stormed Aleppo after Antioch. For the coveted role of Domestic of the East, John chose his former brother-in-law, Bardas Sclerus. After Aleppo's humiliation, they treated for peace and gave up the Syrian coasts and the territories from the city of Hama to the Euphrates, becoming Byzantine territory that gave tribute. The *Basileus* would also have first priority over who would be the Emir of Aleppo as Sayf al-Dawlah's legacy was finally vanquished.

Yet Tzimisces wanted more Muslim territory for Christ in the way Nicephorus had in the form of the Fatimids and the Hamdanids. Between the two, Egypt and Tripoli had been taken in the West and the East was the Emirate of Mosul in northern Mesopotamia, on the river of the same name in modern Iraq. To accomplish these conquests John strategically reorganized the eastern frontier forces into three Ducates of Chaldea in the north, Mesopotamia in the center, and Antioch in the south. He gave the Armenian Themes to the Mesopotamian Ducate as well as new Themes in southern Syria and Cilicia to Antioch. The composition and order among these Themes are accurately recorded in the 971 *Escatorial Taktikon* commissioned by John.[1539]

Seven more Themes would be added, taken from the border regions to strengthen the hot zones. Here he also created a new Tagmatic force known as the 4,000-strong *Athanatoi*, 'Immortals', gilded warriors named after the Persian honor guard from the records of the *Histories* of Herodotus. This cavalry unit was a composite, supposedly, of other Tagmatic forces, the Watch, and the Hicanti.[1540] Within the next five years, they would divide Bulgaria into six Themes and Antioch as a naval base against Fatimid Tripoli. But before moving headlong into an Eastern war, John would shrewdly handle negotiations with the West.

Otto I had again taken the Byzantine Theme of Longobardia and John wisely departed from Nicephorus's stance, settling a marriage alliance with the German Emperor. Upon freeing Capua for Italy, John also married his niece, Theophano, to the future Otto II on April 14, 972 by Pope John XIII. Otto was delighted by this as he now could boast he reached the status of marrying a

---

[1539] Treadgold, *(BAIA)*, 78.
[1540] Leo the Deacon, 132.

Byzantine princess[1541] and Otto was legitimated as a Western Roman 'Emperor'. Unfortunately, it is noted that Theophano was only a minor Byzantine princess whose blood was thin when it came to royalty and barely had the legitimacy Tzimisces possessed. It had been expected that this Theophano was the daughter of Romanus II, but was only the niece of Tzimisces's brother-in-law and not even a Porphyrogenita, Otto almost turning her away.[1542] Nevertheless, this would make Otto a 'Byzantine'-style Emperor with his education, abilities, pedigree, and now the court of his wife.

Gifts of silk, jewelry, icons, and gold ink were given as well as a famed ivory plaque commemorating the event with Pope John and the teenage couple sculpted in 972. This plaque depicted Christ blessing the crowned heads of Otto II and Theophano, not bowing, but still subservient and pious before the Prince of Peace. Below is the commissioner John Philagathos who prays for the blessings of the couple with the prayer 'Lord, Help Thy Servant' in the original Greek. What is most interesting is the juxtaposition of both Latin and Greek inscriptions on the plaque,[1543] presenting the Greco-Latin heritage of the groom and the Byzantine status of the bride. The peace settlement with Otto was assured and John could concentrate on Eastern matters, which were more pressing. The outcome of the marriage would seem advantageous to Byzantium as Otto would be born and live '. . .more of a Greek than a Saxon.'[1544] For the first time since Theodosius I, the Empire appeared safely undivided with one linked dynasty where a question of a world empire could rise better than it had with Irene.

The Russian Tsar, Svyatoslav Igorovich, was not so easily placated as Otto was; he demanded high tribute from the Empire and threatened a siege on Constantinople if he was refused. In 970, John sent the Immortals to be called in force having warned, according to Leo the Deacon, that Igorovich suffered ignominious defeat for having 'scorned the sworn agreements (*tas enorkous spondas*) by sending vessels to attack the City.[1545] Tzimisces then had Sclerus and Peter shore up northern Thracian frontiers with 12,000 men. John Skylitzes in the thirteenth century claims that the Russian army made up 300,000 men, but a more sober estimate is around 50,000,[1546] though still an intimidating

---

[1541] Treadgold, 508.

[1542] Norwich, *(AB)*, 87f.

[1543] Herrin, 207 and plate 14.

[1544] Norwich, (APO), 220.

[1545] Vasiliev, 321.

[1546] Norwich, (APO), 215.

number. Battle was met at Arcadiopolis that summer between Sclerus and the Russians with their Bulgarian allies where the Byzantines severely defeated the enemy and put them to flight. This was mostly possible using the cavalry of John Alakas, who operated skillfully a series of feigned retreats. Speed, surprise, and the wise use of the new cavalry and siege equipment tactics disabled Russia's land and sea power. Upon the battle of Thrace, the Russians fled north and Leo the Deacon claims only twenty-five Roman soldiers had fallen.[1547]

Sclerus would later winter his troops in Thrace, awaiting retribution from the *Basileus* and in spring of 972, John outfitted a large army to surprise the Russians. With Sclerus and Lecapenus, Tzimisces led 40,000 men to the Russo-Bulgarian capital of Preslav on Holy Wednesday, sending 300 fully armed ships up the Danube where they immolated the Russian fleet with Greek Fire.[1548] Along with the *cataphractoi* units and sophisticated siege artillery, Tzimisces planned to besiege Kiev, the Russian capital. The land forces killed over 8,500 Russian troops to take Preslav after the siege, also freeing the imprisoned Bulgarian Khan, Boris II.

The *Basileus* then renamed the capital Joannopolis ('Joahannes') which was only one sign of change in a freed Bulgaria. Immediately after, the armies marched to Dristra on the Danube and trapped Svyatoslav, once again destroying Russian ships with Greek Fire. Svyatoslav settled a humiliating peace and surrendered grain to feed John's armies while the Byzantines had killed at least 40,000 Russian troops (two-thirds of the Tsar's total forces). Also, it was here that the dreaded Pecheneg mercenaries the Tsar of Kiev hired were almost slaughtered to a man.[1549]

On July 24, Svyatoslav had been ready for the desperate offensive failing, according to Leo the Deacon, by the miracle of a saint. Dristra itself was garrisoned and as St. Theodore Stratelates ('the General') miraculously aided the battle, he won, as the city was renamed Theodoropolis. The Byzantines then dealt with the Bulgarian situation but if anything, Boris's freedom was a sort of Faustian bargain made by John I Tzimisces. Any idea he might have had of regaining independent rule can be summed up at Tzimisces's triumph[1550] in Constantinople as Boris and his family followed the imperial chariot pulled by four white horses on foot. At that very ceremony, he displayed the Bulgarian

---

[1547] Jenkins, 297.
[1548] Obolensky, 129.
[1549] Treadgold, 509.
[1550] Norwich, (APO), 224.

royal regalia of diadems and purple robes and icons of the Virgin from the Bulgarian Church as spoils.[1551] The Tsar's family entered the Chalke Gate to the Church of the Virgin holding a reliquary of the True Cross as supplicants.

At the Palace, at the end of the procession, Boris was made to abdicate in exchange for a title of 'Magister', clearing for total Byzantine annexation of the former nation which John divided into six Themes and this into two Ducates of East and West. The Western border Ducate was then divided into two regions, one of Thessalonica and the other Adrianople. At the Danube's mouth, discovered by modern Romanian archaeologists, were fortresses and garrisons at Dinogetia, Carsium, Capidava, and even a naval base on an island just twenty miles from Dristra.[1552] The Bulgarian Church was dismantled into a Byzantine Archbishopric under the direct authority of the Patriarch of Constantinople. However, some bastion of Bulgarian patriotism and independence stayed alive in a strange anomaly of a 'state' which John seemingly ignored. In a cautious move, John mimicked Constantine V's settlement policy by filling the bulwark areas in the now cleared Balkans with Paulicians who now had religious allies in that of the Bulgarians.[1553]

A further change came from the four sons of Count Nicholas, a Byzantine governor, creating a Bulgarian territory between Serdica and Ochrid on the Rilo country near Upper Macedonia where a Cyrilian-Slavonic civilization existed.[1554] They gave asylum to the devastated Bulgarian Patriarch without declaring or reviving any imperial government (perhaps the reason why Tzimisces did not see them as a threat). This divided Bulgaria and Iberia between the two princes, claiming it in entirety, but was one of the boldest moves for independence in Bulgarian history. These four 'Sons of the Count', or *Cometopuli*, ruled with their heirs this rump state for the next few decades just before the Tsar Samuel tried to impose a new Bulgaria. It wanted to push far west of their current territories, even to Constantinople, while the Sons suggested the Byzantines move to the Asian half of the Empire![1555] This infringed upon Tzimisces's designs to add to the Commonwealth over the Byzantine philosophies of pacifism, John's peace centering on a Byzantine-Slav Empire on the Bosporus. Such ambitions were thought to be similar policies

---

[1551] Obolensky, 130.

[1552] *ibid.*, 212.

[1553] Vasiliev, 383.

[1554] Runciman, Steven. 'Byzantium and the Slavs,' 354.

[1555] Ostrogorsky, 295.

from the Tsars Peter the Great to Nicholas II and at least the Kremlin after 1917 in order to place the seat of the Third Rome on the Second.[1556]

More turmoil would surface concerning the Phoci, as in 971, when Bardas Phocas escaped Amasian exile and headed to Ceasarea where his family supported him as a rival *Basileus*. This was not much of a violation as this is quite similar to the rise of John Tzimisces as emperor. Bardas's brother Nicephorus and father Leo also gave him support from their exiles. They raided Anatolia, Sclerus appearing with the Opsikian troops stationed in the Anatolia Themes marked once for the Russian campaign. Sclerus easily tempted several soldiers to his camp from Phocas's and the revolt collapsed, Leo fleeing to Tyropoion near Ilga, falling to siege. With a promise of safe passage, Bardas Phocas surrendered to the *Basileus* and was tonsured. John had Leo and Nicephorus only half-blinded for their support in Bardas, but now John had run out of charity and patience, having them totally blinded after another failed revolt.

It was highly likely that these attempts of other legitimate nobles to grasp power induced Tzimisces to tie the non-existent bonds he shared with the Macedonian House. Seizing an opportunity, he overlooked an embittered Theophano for one of the cloistered sisters of Romanus II, Theodora, releasing her of her monastic vows. John I Tzimisces married her in November, 971, conducted by the new Patriarch Basil the Scamandrian. It was a little late in coming as Theodora was said to be much more homely than Theophano, but now a claim of marriage could be made with a Byzantine princess of royal blood to legitimately occupy the throne he had seized from Nicephorus II.

Now John could turn east to the 'Crusade' against the Arabs and their faith in 971 when the Fatimid Caliph Al-Mu'izz besieged Antioch. John's armies expelled them and although these were mainly defensive battles, John would now start a campaign of whirlwind aggression on all the Islamic East. In the fall of 972, he and his Domestic Melias crossed the Euphrates to invade Hamdanid Mosul, destroying Nisibis and putting siege to Martyropolis. Leaving the East for Bulgaria and the Danube thereafter, he gained control of the Moravian Valley region which he made a Theme with Ras. His goal in these particular claims may have been to surround and conquer the Cometopuli, but in July 973 at a siege of Amida, Melias died in the Mosulian Emir's captivity and Tzimisces prepared for retaliation. In 974, the *Basileus* led troops from Taron to Mosul and bypassed the Sons of the Count.

This seemed to distress the Armenian Princes, as they feared more levies

---

[1556] Jenkins, 294-295.

and annexations than they could escape years earlier under Nicephorus. They fled to the banner of the aging Ashot III who led negotiations backed by an army of 80,000 in early 974 with the Byzantines, he being spared with the levy of 10,000 Armenian troops he then marched to Mosul. Passing by the newly taken Martyropolis and the port of Amica, John exacted tribute for the war effort and past broken Nisibis. The emir faced internal crisis due to the miserable conditions famine had produced as he agreed to give tribute to the Byzantines on an annual basis. By spring of 975, Aleppo and Mosul were submissive before the Byzantines and John I Tzimisces was now on a mission to break the Fatimids of North Africa and Egypt.

Tzimisces and Sclerus took Fatitmid-occupied Apamea and cut a path to Fatimid Syria which was held to its capital at Damascus. Next at Baalbek, Tzimisces captured it under the Turkish rebel Alp Tikin who agreed to a 60,000 *dinar* tribute and passage into Damascus. Ever the pious Christian, John visited Galilee and Mount Tabor, site of the Holy Transfiguration where he vowed to rescue the 'Holy Sepulcher of Christ our God' from the Muslims. Jerusalem was vulnerable, having been isolated from Muslim and Shi'ite pilgrimages due to a war in Baghdad, despite the endeavors of the Fatimids of Syria to encourage these pilgrimages.[1557] Also as John was ever the practical *Basileus*, he exacted tribute from the surrounding cities, including Tiberias (where Christ's miracle of the fishes and the loaves occurred), Acre, and Caesaerea in Cappadocia.

On the coast, the city of Berytus surrendered as Sidon, Byblos, and finally Tripoli was taken, completing the crippling of the Fatimid hold on Syria. Overjoyed, the *Basileus* would cry to Ashot III: 'All Phoenicia, Palestine, and Syria are freed from the yoke of the Saracen and are under Roman rule', an exaggeration, but it was indeed true Eastern dominance was a reality.[1558] Other *Basilii* such as Alexius I Comnenus in the eleventh and twelfth centuries would attempt the same accomplishment based on John Tzimisces's victory, with unfortunately, less successful results.

In perhaps the same letter to Ashot, Tzimisces claimed Jerusalem was his true target as it was Nicephorus's, so it may be won by its rightful Christian rulers. Again, such a possibility would be taken out of Byzantium's hands although the *Basileus* wrote to Ashot that Palestine, Syria, and Phoenicia were once again Roman. Upon returning to Constantinople John was made aware of a scandal involving Basil Lecapenus. Basil had acquired large properties in

---

[1557] Montefiorre, 204.

[1558] Ostrogorsky, 297.

Cilicia as private property to him and not to the state, a form of corruption like embezzlement from the privy.[1559] John called for a formal and personal investigation into the matter when he suddenly fell ill, awaking one morning covered in suppurating blisters on all of his limbs, his eyes bleeding, and unable even to move. He tended to the two artifacts he had gained, the sandals worn by Christ and St. John the Baptist's hair. He then was carried by litter to St. Sophia where he confessed to Bishop Nicholas of Adrianople, dying on January 10, 976.

Of course, it is said that poison was administered in the *Basileus*'s food by Basil Lecapenus to escape rightful prosecution as the matter of his land 'theft' was dropped as to which the new succession was tended.[1560] It is true that Basil had reason and opportunity to murder his last benefactor. Yet, Norwich warns against assuming conspiracy as this poison had to be very slow-acting and excruciating as it was more likely he died of typhoid or some other disease of which many *Basilii* also died.[1561] Whatever the case, what was more important to the court was the ascension of the son and heir of Romanus II, Basil. For almost fifty more years, he would prove to shine brighter (and perhaps be more misunderstood) than almost any other ruler of Byzantium when it truly was the summit of its civilization.

As far as religion went with the devout Tzimisces, the Church had the highest authority between Man and God, so it had the right of precedent in deciding its own economy. John I is most famed for saying as his philosophy, recorded by Leo the Deacon: 'I acknowledge two powers in this life: the priesthood and the Empire; the Creator of the world has entrusted with the former the cure of souls, to the latter the care of bodies; if neither part is damaged, the well-being of the world is secure.'[1562] These words were taken from his philosophies of the eighth-century legal code, the *Epanogoge,* ushering John's reversal of Nicephorus's reform policy. This gave back the rights of privilege, gifts, and donatives back to the monastic communities and the institutions of the Orthodox Church. The *Epanogoue* was a legal handbook that departed from Tzimisces's comparatives between *Basileus* and Patriarch to the organic unity and interdependence of body and soul.[1563]

His own donatives went to the poor farmers in Thrace who suffered due to famine and war with Bulgaria. John I valued charitable institutions as well and

---

[1559] Treadgold, 512.

[1560] Brownworth, 205.

[1561] Norwich, (APO), 229.

[1562] Ostrogorsky, 294.

[1563] Hussey, 92.

creating the *Nosocomium*, a Chrysopolitan hospital for lepers across the City on the Bosporus.[1564] John made regular visits to these places to boost morale and was even said to bathe them himself as Christ did; whether this happened or not, this act glorified him practically as a saint, the Imitator of Christ as a *Basileus* was supposed to be. His saintly nature was challenged, however, by Patriarch Basil the Scamandrian who became thoroughly unpopular with the Byzantines with his over-zealous asceticism.

Basil ate only a diet of berries and water, wore ratty rags until they fell off, and slept on the bare ground, this behavior being too alienating to the urbane citizens and more proper in monastic communities. It was not difficult then to accuse him of maladministration as Patriarch in defying canon law and plotting against John Tzimisces. After a hasty Council attended by Papal legates with an imperial tribunal by John, Basil was exiled and replaced by Anthony III the Studite, in spring of 975.[1565] Meanwhile in the West, Constantinople would still refuse to recognize the ascension of Pope Benedict VII and would harbor the fugitive Anti-Pope Boniface VII. Boniface was a usurper who had his predecessor strangled, being exiled to Byzantine Sicily and eventually coming to reside in Constantinople in the summer of 980.

There was also reform against the eunuchs and young boys of the monasteries said to be a 'sexual disruption' to the cloistered men as a temptation. They were forbidden to enter Mount Athos and even the miraculous visions some young monks had, like Cosmas the Paphlagonian at Holy Luke's Tomb in Steiris, would not sway such rigid monasteries. In a document known as the *Tragos* ('Rule'), Tzimisces forbade the induction of 'beardless' eunuchs and boys to Athos, the penalty of abbots and hermits (*kelliotes*) for ignoring this edict was exile off of the mountain.[1566] Obviously, this meant the sexual mores of the monasteries were more corrupt than even Nicephorus II had thought. In the case of Mt. Athos, the Holy Mountain of the *Typikon*, complaints were made that the cenobitic populace was being encroached by other monastic orders and the *Basileus* ordered the cohabitation of anchorites and cenobites at the Mountain.[1567]

John would also assemble a policy of law and order concerning the aristocrat landholders. Thematic officials were made to investigate these estates and if

---

[1564] Norwich, (*APO*), 213.

[1565] Norwich, (*APO*), 227-228.

[1566] Herrin, 168.

[1567] Vasiliev, 337.

*stratioti* peasants were found with obligation to the state, the state authority would regain the losses. It is described how 'policing forces' were sent by the *Basileus* to raid the estates of the rich to look for these peasants and other illegal practices, penalties including the bestowing of the status of *paraikoi,* wherein they were imprisoned on their land without privileges.[1568] John managed to hand the eighteen-year-old Basil II a stable Empire of conquered enemies, a unified Church, wise marriage alliances, and some new progressions in the landholder economy. Basil may have resented his 'protectors' as Constantine VII had, but he learned the lesson well of keeping a sharp military focus and a disdain of the luxury that softened mind and body.

The military force was well stocked at 200,000 troops between the reforms of the two regents after Romanus I, three times the maximum needed to outfit campaigns,[1569] which were direly needed in the future to maintain boundaries. It is also to be noted, though, that the 'Crusades' of Phocas and Tzimisces lacked the romantic quality the Western perspective would hold, even in the Holy Places held by Islam. John I saw Constantinople itself as a New Jerusalem as the West saw the Sepulcher as the old to be protected and this may have been sources of resentment between West and East. Proof of this is would be made plain in the reign of Basil II whose forces easily could have accomplished this, but saw no necessity to do so in fifty years of rule. Whatever the truth, it is remarked that had John lived longer he would easily have re-possessed the territories that had been lost to East Rome by the Caliphs Omar and Muwiya for a decade.[1570]

The historians of the Macedonians are varied between Joseph Genosius, Constantine VII Porphyrogenitus, Leo the Deacon, and George Hamartolus. They all vary in style and intent in chronicling the period of 813 to 961 as well as what the anonymous Continuator had done for the time before. Despite this, however, the identity of this Continuator of Theophanes the Confessor is still a mystery, although early Russian Byzantinists have nominated the court official who wrote for Basil I Lecapenus, Theodore Daphnopates (d. 963), to be the author.[1571]

---

[1568]  Ostrogorsky, 295.

[1569]  Treadgold, (*BAIA*), 212.

[1570]  Jenkins, 298-299.

[1571]  Vasiliev, 365f.

# BASIL II 'THE BULGAR-SLAYER'

## (976-1025)

Basil II was the trademark of Byzantine exceptionalism in leading the Empire in commercialism and the inexhaustible military machine that existed at the turn of the first millennium. He realized such success in his own strengths of consistency, focus, frugality, and effectiveness. Of course, however, this also interprets his tenancies towards stubbornness, narrow vision, and harsh tyranny, eventually ending in paranoia such as Nero himself had developed. Indeed, Basil has been called the 'classic' autocrat of the Byzantine Empire that forbade differing opinion, argument, and the advice of his courtiers. Ugly, coarse, totally philistine, and pathologically mean, he also carried quite 'non-Byzantine' attributes.[1572] He would be called cruel because of his policy of blinding his enemies and enslaving others and creating laws as a dictator would to cripple the Senatorial classes financially to bolster the poor. Yet, his obstinacy did carve, in fifty years, a realm reaching from the Danube to the Euphrates, and Syria to Armenia, back to the tip of Italy.[1573]

Basil II also spurned education and learning at a time of encroaching decay, not long after Porphyrogenitus's advances, when learning was used merely as a way to profit and not for its own sake,[1574] although his quick wit allowed a plethora of knowledge in military affairs and tactics. What this knowledge reflected was an unflinching courage before adversity, a manic dedication to his Empire, and a Spartan existence free of luxury and vices. Unnecessary ceremony was dangerous to his discipline, so he sat wearing but a purple robe and a handful of gems, keeping his wealth hidden in spiral galleries under the Palace.[1575] Such austerity Basil found necessary in becoming the foremost ruler of the East during this pinnacle of the Byzantine cycle. Even if decline was the inevitability of what came after his death in 1025, this fact only proved himself an optimal standard. He was always willing to fight, but never eager and, though he inspired admiration in his subjects, he never inspired love.[1576]

Basil would eventually set the international policy of the European East starting with Russia in 989, promoting it to a high status among the

---

[1572] Norwich, (APO), 266.

[1573] Diehl, 207.

[1574] Psellus, Michael. *Chronographia*, trans. by E.R.A. Sewter. New York, NY: Penguin Books. 1966, 44.

[1575] Hussey, 49.

[1576] Brownworth, 216-217.

other nations,[1577] also setting the paths of Bulgaria, Serbia, Croatia, and the other Balkan nations by diplomacy or by the sword. Yet, despite these accomplishments in a time of high civilization, Basil II was considered a notoriously obscure subject of study in the Roman Empire.[1578] But much has been done to remedy this by twentieth-century scholars such as Catherine Holmes[1579] or Paul Stephenson[1580] to demonstrate his greatness as a military and administrative leader. Unfortunately, for his cruelties during his administration he has also been demonized by popular writers, likening him to dictators like Hitler and serial killers like John Wayne Gacy. This, however, does prove he was a complex character whose choices dominated a Medieval empire as well as the imagination of modern societies.

Born in 958 to Romanus II and Theophano as a Porphyrogenitus, Basil had waited thirteen years from his father's sudden death in 963 to become his rightful heir and finally take his crown with John Tzimisces's death on January 10, 976. He was said to be short and stocky with clear blue eyes, laughing loudly (when he actually did laugh) and used clipped words and phrases in a reflection of military expediency.[1581] When he was set to gain the throne, he set aside his indiscretions of women and wine from his youth to became a stern ruler of an Empire and a servant to a higher calling of discipline and absolute rule as he quite readily 'put away childish things.'[1582] As for his weaker brother Constantine, he was kept at arm's length to encourage his habits of soft living and endless pleasure-seeking so Basil could have an uncontested rule. Of course, such a tactic begs the question if Basil's youthful indolence was merely a cunning act to be tossed away after he had gained the throne.

He was a suspicious man with little trust in advisers, eunuchs, and even women – all who might have turned against him and his interests if not careful. This can all be attributed to the first ten years of his reign which saw a brutal civil war set off by palace intrigues by his mother, the regency, and the detestable Joseph Bringas. His reign was marked with coarseness, but by contrast he

---

[1577] Obolensky, 201.

[1578] Gibbon, 1643.

[1579] Holmes, Catherine. *Basil II and the Governance of Empire (976-1025), Oxford Studies in Byzantium.* Oxford, UK: Oxford University Press. 2006. A good focus on the tribulations of Basil ruling an Empire such as the Byzantium.

[1580] Stephenson, Paul. *The Legend of Basil the Bulgar Slayer.* Cambridge, UK: Cambridge University Press. 2010.

[1581] Psellus, 48-49.

[1582] Jenkins, 304-305.

seemed the most civilized compared to Vladimir of Russia, a Pagan, kept three wives, over 800 concubines, and performed the bestial rites of, supposedly, human sacrifices.[1583]

It is true Basil was no scholar, but education did not suffer strenuously thanks to classicists such as Patriarchs John Xiphilinus (1010-1075) and Patriarch Constantine IV Luchides (d. 1157). Symeon the Metapharastes published a calender of 150 saints' lives in ten volumes in the *Menologion* ('Catalogue') *of Basil*. About 1000, Symeon the Younger established teaching positions, the curriculum being up to Xiphilinus in the instruction in law and philosophy.[1584] In prose, the Greek Arab of Byzantine folklore, Digenes Akritas, was written of on the conflicts of Muslims and Christians in his home of Asia Minor, the estate in which he lived being a commentary on the wealth of the landowners whom Basil sought hard to oppress.[1585]

In artistic representations, Basil is seen on the coinage of 976 with his brother Constantine holding the Cross as co-rulers equal in size and prominence. In later years, Basil would be known for his portrait on the front piece of his Psalter now in Venice and painted around 1000 depicting the fully-armed *Basileus* crowned by Archangels, especially Michael (the Archangel affiliated with combat). His numerous foreign and domestic enemies bow in ultimate supplication in a kind of *proskynesis* at his feet, yet he does not carry the ceremonial orb and scepter, a trend now said to epitomize the soldier-*Basileus* motif created by artists who felt such appreciation felt for their protection.[1586]

All of this is recorded mainly by the historian Michael Psellus (1018-1096), serving as a close adviser to some of Basil II's successors, especially Constantine IX Monomachus and the *Basilai* Zoe and Theodora. His *Chronographia* was an insightful source ranging from 976 to 1078 where it remained unfinished. As Psellus was a Neo-Platonic philosopher and educated orator, much of the work digresses on matters of philosophy in history, political science, and even psychology. He was a master biographer, but experts note his disinterest in foreign affairs and certain events such as earthquakes, epidemics, and famines and the reader cannot escape the arrogance and vanity of a truly intellectual

---

[1583] Jenkins, 307. This being, supposedly, the last Christian propaganda supporting the 'Byzantine Commonwealth' attitude of Obolensky.

[1584] Buckler, 217.

[1585] Vasiliev, 369.

[1586] Herrin, 212-213.

mind.[1587] Anna Comnena, as a historian in the eleventh and twelfth centuries, could not help but to comment on the totally immoral character Psellus had, probably he being a courtier.

Yet with Michael's colleagues, Constantine Lichudes and John Xiphilinus, he revived Classical learning that had been neglected under Basil and brought it to the University of Constantinople. These Classical masters had included his masters Homer, Herodotus, Thucydides, Demosthenes (384BCE-322BCE) Plutarch (45-127 CE), the Stoics, Gregory of Nazianus, the Christian Fathers, Aristotle, and of course, Plato. Along with the events of the next fourteen Byzantine Emperors, Psellus offers insight into the Byzantine world and mind. He would end his career by tonsuring himself as a monk, taking the name Michael as his given name was Constantine, but his whereabouts and fate after his work ends in January, 1078, supposedly remains a mystery.

Basil's reign starts with the messy and brutal affair of a decade-long civil war among two nobles fighting for the throne. With the chaos after Tzimisces's death, the Chamberlain Basil Lecapenus chose to demote his Domestic of the East Bardas Sclerus to a Duke of Mesopotamia to isolate him from the throne. He was replaced by the eunuch Peter the Stratopedarch, divesting his lieutenant Burtzes of his command, who was then made Duke of Antioch. Joining with the troops of the Emir of Mosul, Sclerus was proclaimed *Basileus* in Melitene by the Arab prince as his co-*Basileus* in 976. Burtzes and Peter the Domestic gathered forces from Anatolia to meet Sclerus at Lycander, but were defeated as Sclerus won over the Anatolics, Burtzes, and the Cibyrrhaeots in one rousing sweep.

Although Lecapenus refreshed Peter with the troops of Leo the Protovestiarius the next year, they won few supporters from regional partisans. These partisans did not see the cause as great as it was under Tzimisces; then the royal armies were taken at the Lake of the Forty Martyrs in Anatolia by Sclerus as they traveled east to Cotyaeum. Another rebel army under Burtzes would be defeated only to have Sclerus return to capture Leo and kill the Domestic Peter. Sclerus's goal was to besiege Constantinople, so they laid siege to Niceaea across the Bosporus while the Cibrrhyaoet navy held the Aegean. Lecapenus's navy defeated them off the Hellespont, now holding the ways to Western Europe and the Cyclades. Sclerus held the eastern passages through the Anatolics but now he had no ships to cross to the City. This stalemate splitting the Empire basically in half is almost reminiscent of the dynastic wars

---

[1587] Sewter, E. R. A. 'Introduction.' Chapter from the *Chronographia of Michael Psellus,* New York, NY: Penguin Publishing. 1966, 15.

of the Constantinians and the Theodosians, though on a smaller scale. This would allow any of Byzantium's enemies the opportunity to make trouble with rebellion in the Empire with the Byzantines' hands tied.

In Constantinople, the captive Bulgar Khan Boris and his brother Romanus escaped and headed for western Bulgaria, as only Romanus would survive after a chance encounter between Boris and a border official, making it to the Cometopuli. The brothers had just taken Ras and Morava and now saw the returning Romanus as a sign that Bulgarian independence was now nigh. Also that year, Arab commanders would seize opportunity as well, making alliances to confuse and exploit the Byzantine situation. Sclerus's ally in Mosul rebelled, only to be replaced by the Buwayhid Caliph of Baghdad, who also stopped tribute and secured Edessa from Byzantium as famine spread, and Aleppo would then follow suit. Finally, in Italy, invasions began by the Arabs wherein all fronts were being ravaged from without in Byzantine territory. Desperate, Lecapenus recalled the exiled Bardas Phocas from Chios to become Domestic of the Scholae of the East in 978, eight years after his rebellion against Tzimisces. Lecapenus seemed to choose well as Phocas had a particular hatred for Sclerus, who had defeated him in 970. Psellus also notes his reputation for gloom and sharing the broad vision Bardas's uncle had as *Basileus*.

Crossing the Bosporus, Bardas made for Cappadocia and Ceasarea to successfully entice Michael Burtzes from Sclerus's army that spring. The two armies met at Amorium with heavy casualties and Sclerus turning aside Phocas. Later that year, in the Basilica Therma of Carsianum, Phocas was defeated again by Sclerus and driven east after a costly battle. But on the 24th of March, 979, at Pancalia, Phocas was moralized by the addition of 12,000 cavalry by the Iberian David of the Upper Tao and a repatriated Duke of Antioch as Phocas marched west to Aquae Saravenae. This time Bardas was prepared and Sclerus was routed, fleeing to his allies in Baghdad, seriously straining the rebellion. David of the Upper Tao was given Theodosiopolis *in perpetuam*[1588] by Lecapenus and a grand triumph was given to the rehabilitated Phocas in Constantinople. More famine in the east had settled down and the rebelling Bulgarians had only won minor victories, balance was tentatively restored.

In 980, Samuel of the four Cometopuli raided Thessaly, as he was a man with possibly Armenian roots[1589] and having an energy that would cause much

---

[1588] Treadgold, 516.

[1589] Jenkins, 313. As his brothers were named Moses, Aaron, and David, a Jewish heritage has been suggested.

strife and bloodshed in Byzantium for twenty years. Meanwhile, the other dangers at the borders east and west were being addressed by Phocas. From 981 to 983, Phocas centered his focus on pacifying Aleppo and forcing its Emir to return paying tribute. A year later, the Fatimids invaded the region and Phocas brokered an alliance with Aleppo to expel them for double tribute and sacking Homs when the Arabs refused. In the West, where Phocas's reach was more lax, the German Emperor Otto II claimed his Greek heritage by invading Byzantine Calabria only to face slaughter by the Arabs. Only the Italian Catepan could restore the peace in 982 as the policy remained one that differed with the *Basileus* in that Basil only committed himself to avoiding decisive combat for the longer, and less risky, term.[1590]

By 985, Phocas returned to his policing duties in the East by forcing Aleppo's tribute and laying siege to Apamea. The fear among the Aleppines was that Byzantium planned to annex the Emirate and deport the Muslim populace west as had been done in centuries past, although no evidence of this intention was apparently officiated. This might even mean settlement in Armenia or Cappadocia and forced conversion to Christianity upon pain of death. It was these threats to their way of life that goaded them to constant rebellion and despair of Byzantine intervention. This matter did not last long anyway as Phocas would be recalled by the now twenty-seven-year-old Basil II who now was to step boldly into his responsibilities as *Basileus* of Eastern Rome.

Unsurprisingly, he accomplished this by first dragging out of bed in the dead of night, and then arresting Basil Lecapenus, exiling him in 986, and recalling Bardas Phocas to accept his authority to a new governor of Syria, Leo Melissenus, Duke of Antioch. Unfortunately, by the campaigns of June, Melissenus would divide authority with the commander Contostephanus. This betrayal was compounded more as the artillery lacked competence, morale was low, and the commissariat was corrupt.[1591] Basil's sternness could not yet remedy this, being compared to the earlier years of Julius Caesar and Frederick the Great by learning from such 'unhappy experience.'

Leo would prove himself by recovering Syrian Balaneae from the Fatimids, yet he could not keep the Bulgarian Tsar Samuel from holding Larissa, being the capital of Thessaly. After Melissenus, the next Duke appointed was Bardas Phocas, a measure by Basil to curb his power as Domestic. Phocas and Leo marched on Serdica as Samuel was returning from Greece. Basil's only

---

[1590] Decker, 30.
[1591] Jenkins, 314.

setback in this siege were first, the military inexperience that Nicephorus and Tzimisces denied him, and second, his supplies running low. Samuel took the passes west and a demoralized army broke the siege. On Tuesday, August 17, the Byzantines entered Trajan's Gates and were ambushed by the flanking Bulgarians. Panicking Byzantine soldiers with no escape routes were meted out with heavy punishments to the untried *Basileus,* the enemy also looting the abandoned treasury and baggage.[1592] One survivor was the historian Leo the Deacon, sharing his eyewitness account.

The defeat at Trajan's Gate when heard of in Constantinople would have the poet John Geometrus (935-1000 CE) crying for a return from the grave of Nicephorus II (as they had Constantine V two centuries earlier) to triumph over the Bulgars, as he did once before with a 'lion's roar' that could 'put all adversaries to flight.'[1593] When this hit the ears of the Buwayhid Caliphate in Baghdad, the Arabs exploited Byzantium's vulnerable state by making alliance with the residing Bardas Sclerus, who was preying on Armenia. Taking forts and gaining allies from the Marwanid Kurds of the region, in the winter of 986-987, Sclerus made roots in Melitene. Basil II was then forced to appoint Phocas as the Eastern Domestic once more as the one general that knew Sclerus's nature best. No sooner had the Domestic gathered a sizeable force in the Charsianum then he proclaimed himself *Basileus* on August 15 as Sclerus had previously done!

Phocas sought a reluctant alliance with Sclerus for his loyalty in exchange for Byzantine Syria and Mesopotamia. Desperate for allies himself, Basil turned to Vladimir of Kiev and offered him marriage to his sister Anna. This might have been a shock as no Byzantine princess had ever married a Pagan ruler with vices such as Vladimir. This may be the foundation by the claims of earlier historians that Vladimir *demanded* Anna's hand from Basil.[1594] Yet, Basil II was no common Byzantine autocrat, for if he saw the immediate practicality of such an alliance in times of crisis, he would not have hesitated nor would he have been convinced to act differently by others. He also saw the advantage of hiring Norman troops in his employ, especially in the use of the Varangian Guard, becoming a growing practice since 911.[1595]

Phocas's ambitions were only inflating as he would imprison Sclerus on September 14 at Tyropaeum and add his former partner's armies as his own in

---

[1592] Norwich, (*APO*), 238.

[1593] Diehl, 47.

[1594] Obolensky, 193.

[1595] Jenkins, 302.

taking Anatolia and the Cherson in 988. The grimmest point for Basil was at this time when Phocas took Chrysopolis in the summer and Abydos on April 13, 989, nearing the Bosporus. Basil's Greek forces had been depleted by Bulgar hostilities, and if an emptying Treasury offering less pay to the soldiers and if not for his allies, the great rule of Basil II might never have been. In Russia, Vladimir married Anna and converted to Christianity, sending 6,000 Russian troops[1596] (*Druzhnia*) to the Black Sea, carrying heavy axes and the double-bladed swords known as the *rhomphaia* of the famed Varangian Guard of the *Basilii*. From the records of Stephen of Taron, their numbers were similar to the expanded numbers of Scholae and Excubitors existing at this time.[1597]

Along with these forces, Basil sent Armenian soldiers to Trebizond under Gregory of Taron. These were the right soldiers, for they had served Sclerus before his imprisonment and now were ready to avenge him against Phocas. David of the Upper Tao allied with Phocas and his son, Nicephorus, by sending 1,000 Iberian troops west in 989 as Basil crossed the Bosporus with Greek Fire at Chrysopolis. Basil would make his first victory by taking the city in a two-pronged attack impaling, hanging, and crucifying insubordinate commanders using the Varangians, their ankles deep in blood.[1598]

At this news, Nicephorus's men deserted the rebel commander and with forces depleted, Basil and his brother Constantine (notably having some military command) took Abydos by surprise. Fortune soon struck as Bardas Phocas himself would commit suicide by poisoning on the battlefield. Basil made the most of this opportunity by brutally handling the defeated army and its officers without mercy and the Russians would follow suit by thoroughly looting the defeated Chersonese rebels. Domestically, he responded to the military commanders who might be troublesome in the future by repudiating and annulling the laws and edicts of his uncle as 'according to his own will.'[1599] Basil II would now gain his ferocious battlefield reputation of punishing prisoners with extreme cruelty and it would be well deserved.

Though the situation was mostly handled, Phocas's widow in Melitene freed Sclerus from prison, unleashing him like a mad dog on the Empire. Sclerus quickly shored alliances with Baghdad, Phocas's Armenians, and even Phocas's sons, Nicephorus and Leo. But constant warfare and the push of the Byzantine

---

[1596] Psellus, 35f.
[1597] Treadgold, (*BAIA*), 79.
[1598] Norwich, (*APO*), 241.
[1599] Ostrogorsky, 300.

victories left these armies without discipline, morale, or even a cause for which to fight. Nicephorus ended up taking a pardon from Basil's brother in October of 989 betraying his brother Leo and exiling himself at Antioch. After ten bloody years of civil wars, it was over and Basil stood alone as uncontested *Basileus* of Byzantium. His inexperience was compensated for by his sheer tenacity and his reaching out to the Russians when it was needed with no wasteful xenophobic sentiments hindering his judgment. Bardas Sclerus would end his days as a blinded prisoner and a broken Curopalates to die on March 6, 991.

His cool head prevailed when surrounded by chaos and crisis, but the effect on him was devastating to the young *Basileus*. For thirty-six more years he would be known as embittered, distrustful, austere, and almost paranoid; in his private life, he lived as a celibate bachelor leaving no heirs to succeed him. Being betrayed by his generals, he never trusted his own officers and harbored a savage hatred of Bulgars and Iberians as his strongest foreign enemies in the wars. A changed *Basileus* now ruled a prosperous Byzantium and challenging him by word or deed was only as effective as challenging God's place in the Empire itself. In real terms, he legitimated himself by being the epitome of the tradition of 'blessed' Byzantine soldier-*Basilii* that would burn a path for the Empire until the dynasty of the Comneni[1600] a century later.

Now, wars with new Bulgarian enemies would test Basil's limits as Samuel recovered the former Bulgar capitals of Preslav and Pliska, also taking Thessalonica in the Greek south to Beroea. Arabian Sicily would raid north again in Italy, but the Eastern Arab emirates and sultanates were preying on each other and Byzantine territory went largely unnoticed. Russia at this point was mollified first in its faith as Basil had impressed their emissaries with the grandness of his churches and liturgy. The far eastern Persians had tried converting the Russians to Islam, but it had been rejected everywhere for its 'lack of joy', especially in the forbidding of alcohol and pork.[1601] Politically, more was done due to Basil being the *Basileus*, who brought Russia up as a serious player in Eastern politics.

By 989, peace was restored and Basil could focus domestically with a new attitude as his commemorative coins would not bear his likeness. Instead, the conquering Mother of God, the Virgin *Nikopoios* ('Bringer of Victory') was used, crafted afterwards as an icon hanging in the Basilica of St. Mark since

---

[1600] Decker, 48.
[1601] Brownworth, 211f.

the Latin Conquest of the thirteenth century.[1602] Though his brother was still called 'co-*Basileus*', he held no place even close to his brother's position and Basil II would use that opportunity to show friend and foe alike in the Empire that only one man ruled Byzantium.

After conquering and punishing him, Basil, in 990, made David of the Upper Tao a Curopalates to be a raiding zone, creating a buffer for the Muslim territories east of the Tao. In 991, Basil began his epic reclaiming of Byzantine territory taken by the Bulgarians in northern Greece. He recovered Larissa and the Bulgar Tsar Romanus once again became a Byzantine prisoner. In 993, Basil allied with the Serbian prince of Dioclea and together they took Beroea on the march towards Ochrid and the seat of Bulgaria's power. Unfortunately, the Eastern Arab situation changed from events the year before, staying Basil's advances. In 992, the Duke of Antioch, Michael Burtzes, was entrenched at Aleppo holding out against a Fatimid raid. Though they succeeded, the Arabs defeated a force of 5,000 under Burtzes on the Orontes River and starting on September 15, incited revolt in Laodicea.

The Fatimids were also aided by the Marwanids of Armenia for a retaliatory strike against Basil for their allies in the Sclerus revolt. What also exacerbated matters was the desperate plea the Aleppines made not to the *Basileus*, but to the Bulgarians and Tsar Samuel. After securing the west, the Duke of Thessalonica in 995 took over, as Basil garnered a force of 40,000 men, along with another 17,000 (which arrived in April). They advanced the 600 miles to Aleppo and held a siege,[1603] causing the governor to retreat to Damascus. At the news of the march and upon hearing the Basil II's name alone, the Fatimids fled south, leaving Basil opportunity to take Apamea, Homs, and Tripoli, though they refused to accept Byzantine 'protection'.

Basil II recovered the fortress of Antaradus and demonstrated his reputation for austerity by dismissing Burtzes as Duke of Antioch for his failures at Aleppo. Basil had by this time perfected his style of land assault in his 'solid tower.'[1604] This was composed of tight columns with the invaluable lines of communication between *Basileus* and cavalry light and heavy, as the light and heavy infantry created impenetrable, maneuverable, and well-informed troops. After their humiliating turn from Aleppo, the Fatimid Caliph al-Aziz

---

[1602] Norwich, (APO), 242; Treadgold, 519; inset 125. Also is inscribed on the reverse: 'Glorified Mother of God. The One Who Trusts in You Does Not Fail.'
[1603] Jenkins, 318.
[1604] Psellus, 47.

prepared a fleet bound for Syria the next year but this fleet never left the port of Amalfi after destruction by a fire. After a new fleet was fitted for Anatardus, the new Antiochene Duke Dalessenus broke the siege and raided the region surrounding Tripoli. In 997, rebellions in Syria brought the imperial fleet to Tyre just stopping short inland of Damascus, wisely employing caution considering his position with the Fatimids.[1605] As both sides of the rebellion appealed to Basil, he chose to aid the Damascenes rather than put siege to both cities, diplomatically strengthening the bonds of the major city of Syria.

Meanwhile, Samuel had terrorized Byzantine Thessalonica, even taking Gregory of Taron's son and eventually killing the Duke himself. Taking his son John of Chaldea, as well, Samuel then invaded northern Greece, taking Beroea, and Thessaly as far south as Corinth. Basil sent the Domestic of the West, Nicephorus Uranus, to follow the Bulgarians to the Peloponnesus. From Larissa, the Byzantines ambushed Samuel at the Sperchius Valley near Thermopylae, almost slaughtering all the Bulgarian forces and wounding Samuel and his son. Though he sued for peace, Samuel would make an odd choice by proclaiming himself Bulgarian Tsar, repudiating Basil's goodwill once Romanus died while in Constantinople. However, at this time, the Bulgarian army and resources were dangerously thin and Samuel's boldness was known as an obvious front to the Byzantines.

The years 998 and 999 were spent fighting the Fatimids once again with Samuel and Caliph al-Hakim seizing most of Syria and the Aleppine protectorate of Apamea. Hakim was considered an educated and amicable man in the beginning of his reign, but within a mere decade the Caliph would become an 'Arab Caligula.'[1606] He ordered the killing of cats and dogs in Jerusalem, banned grapes, watercress, and descaled fish, forcing his men to sleep by day and work by night as he did. He would prowl the streets of Cairo heavily under drugs given by his doctors and personally enjoyed cutting off the hands of his female slaves. After random persecutions on Jews and Christians in the Holy City he would, in 1009, destroy the Holy Sepulcher stone by stone. At his worst, he persecuted fellow Muslims as well as banning Ramadan, terrorizing Shi'ites and Sunnis alike. Muslims said his abominations made one shudder in horror as this type of madman was the enemy of the Islamic and Christian faiths that Basil II had to deal with in the East.

Dalessenus was fatally wounded in the defense of the imperial territories,

---

[1605] Treadgold, 521.
[1606] Montefiorre, 207.

forcing Basil into a compromising settlement with the Arabs while fighting Bulgaria. He finally took Serdica, inflating his reputation of invincibility, adding it to a new Theme of Phillipopolis. He knew he must personally attend to Fatimid Syria and, demonstrating his distrust of competing commanders, he split the Western defense between generals Xiphias and Theodorocanus. He arrived in the East in autumn of 999 with the Varangians under Uranus to retake Apamea and garrison Sizara to protect the Armenian borders. He then set up a defensive line for Cilicia, where he wintered with two new Themes at Aleppo and promoting a loyal Uranus as Duke of Antioch. These preparations and the *Basileus*'s presence made the Fatimids seriously consider a peace.

In Bulgaria, Samuel took Dyrrhachium under the governance of his son-in-law and one-time prisoner, Ashot, son of the Armenian general Gregory of Taron. Samuel went about undoing Basil's Serbian alliance by taking Dioclea, going west to the Theme of Dalmatia on the Adriatic. Fortunately, the Doge of Venice saw the imminent threat to his kingdom (and Basil's), reclaiming the region as his own imperial protectorate in spring of 1000. In this year, the Dalmatian coast was made a Byzantine protectorate after negotiations with John Orsoleo, the Doge's son, in 997-998.[1607] The Western defenses hit eastern Bulgaria hard as Xiphias and Theodorocanus captured the prized cities of Preslav, Pliska, and Little Preslav which all became imperial Themes. It was as if the Greeks were taking vengeance for the fall of Nicephorus I in 811, when at that time, the taking of these Bulgarian centers were once thought impossible.

One advantage Basil II had over the Bulgarian army was his siege equipment, namely the use of the centuries-old trebuchet. A sort of catapult, its dynamic principles of a stressed longer arm wielding a projectile, balanced by a shorter counterweight arm, made possible the use of throwing stones up to 400 pounds. It was shielded by animal skins for fire-proofing and took an incredible crew of 400 men to properly operate it. Though not as popular or well known as Greek Fire, it still held a major contribution to Byzantine siege warfare by 1001 and demonstrated the dominance of Basil and his army whether on the field or behind a wall.[1608] By the fourteenth century, the trebuchet and its mechanics

---

[1607] Jenkins, 322. In 1004, the Venetian bargain was sealed when John married Basil's cousin, Maria Argyrou, with the *Basileus* and his brother as groomsmen. At the wedding reception, the Byzantine fork was introduced on the dinner tables of the Venetians and they excitedly brought the sophisticated utensil back to the West; Brownworth, 219f.
[1608] *Engineering an Empire: The Byzantines.* (12/25/2006). Written/ Directed by Rebecca Ratcliffe.

in siege warfare would be found as far in the West as the English army of King Edward I (1239-1307).

But international circumstances were to again delay any conclusion of the Bulgarian war as Basil was called to the Upper Tao when David was assassinated on Easter Sunday and Basil was supposedly his heir. He had to hurry to intercede on any political intrigue or chaos the nobles would cause to gain the Tao for themselves. It became the imperial Ducate of Iberia to be led by the appointed vassal prince, Bagrat III of Abasgia, as its Curopalates. To further protect these interests, in 1001, a ten-year truce was made with the Fatimids as neither side wanted any territory from the other (a rare occurrence in this time). With Uranus as the watchdog of the East, Basil once more turned his attentions west to Bulgaria.

Basil's good fortune continued as the prisoner Ashot escaped Dyrrhacium and allowed the *Basileus* to take the city on a bribe to Samuel's father-in-law, John of Chryselius. From there he broke Samuel's grip in northern Greece and Thessalonica by capturing the prized city of Edessa. In the spring of 1002, Basil was also on the verge of taking Vidin, the main Bulgarian fortress on the Danube. Samuel tried a diversion in the summer by taking Adrianople, but Basil coolly stayed to take Vidin and raid his way back to Constantinople by 1003. He had already defeated Samuel at Scopia while driving inwards into Bulgaria using divisive tactics from the center and garrisoning at prime strategic points.[1609] That same year, the Venetian Doge upheld Byzantine suzerainty in the West by defending Bari successfully from the Sicilian Arabs when Basil personally oversaw the operations.[1610]

In a *chrysobull* of March, 992, the Doge Pietro Oresoleo II had signed a commercial pact with Basil II, strengthening Venetian-Byzantine relations as it benefited the local Byzantine, Amalfian, Lombardian, and Jewish merchants, especially. Venetian troops were promised on the Dalmatian coast to guard Byzantine Italy and for this pact, on Ascension Day of 1000, Orseoleo was granted the title *Dux Dalmatiae*. These troops were easily transported thanks to the tax cuts Basil made in ships entering the Dardenelles from thirty to seventeen *nomismata* apiece.[1611] The Venetian merchants of Constantinople were easily integrated thanks to the reduction of bureaucracy involved, putting all of the authority in the direct hands of the Grand Logothete. In exchange, a

---

[1609] Jenkins, 322.
[1610] Treadgold, 525.
[1611] Herrin, 158.

special fleet of ships would be made available for cross-Adriatic transport for Basil whenever needed,[1612] a must in Calabrian or Sicilian military operations.

In 1004, another Bulgarian campaign was implemented to recover mainly Tzimisces's territories, lost by neglect for the past four years, existing only by engaging in guerrilla warfare. Basil II's main goal, as a point, was the restoration of the boundaries Samuel encroached upon and not the expansion and annexation of the Bulgar nation.[1613] Basil was pragmatic and knew it was a better gamble and less of a strain on resources by containing the Greek lines and not spreading them into Bulgaria. The Treasury itself was endangered due to excessive warfare and incompetent or corrupt tax collecting ensued. Serendipity only allowed Iberia to be taken in as a result of the Upper Tao crisis although the regions of Morava and Ras of the Cometopuli were still standing independently. With these goals accomplished Basil turned inward to domestic policy for the time being, something Tzimisces could not achieve without difficulty.

New policies of peace and non-intervention presented themselves concerning his Eastern allies, including Aleppo and the Fatimids, starting in 1008. Basil chose a position of neutrality when the allied Hamdanids appealed for aid when Muslim rivals took their Emirate. This policy continued when Bagrat III claimed the sovereignty of Georgia, threatening the peace made eight years earlier. Also showing he was not a reactionary to religious forces, Basil made a ten-year truce in 1012 with the Caliph al-Hakim despite the demolition of the Churches of the Holy Sepulcher and Golgotha in Jerusalem. Here, terrified Jews and Christians took the Muslim faith as the Sepulcher itself was destroyed, says the historian Yahya ibn Said al-Antaki of Antioch (980-1066). These strange turns of diplomacy can be explained by the intensity and narrowed focus the *Basileus* had in pursuing the Bulgarians of the Strymon and Axium valleys and the Clidium, or 'Key', region.

In 1014, Basil joined his general Theophylact Botaniates and delegated a plan to encircle the Bulgarian contingents near Phillipopolis, using his commander Xiphias. After a defeat at Thessalonica earlier that year, the desperate Samuel and his son fled to the fortress of Prilapon, where he was basically trapped and barricaded, 15,000 prisoners being taken on July 29. After

---

[1612] Norwich, (*AHV*), 50. Herrin, 216, includes Basil's public projects in Amalfian and Venetian industry in providing canals and mills, viniculture, olives, and the mulberries and worms needed for silk production.

[1613] Treadgold, 525.

taking Sirmitsa, Basil sent Botaniates to destroy the garrisons of the Bulgarians in Thessalonica. Unfortunately, Botaniates was killed by a Bulgarian ambush near the Axius valley, this alone inducing the *Basileus* to commit one of the cruelest and most infamous atrocities in all of history.

There stands academic disparity among a few major sources on just how many prisoners there were taken: Ostrogorsky says 14,000, relying on the sources of John Cecaumenas (fl. 1078) and George Cedrenus (fl. 1057),[1614] (Psellus is oddly mute about the incident), while decades later, Treadgold counts 15,000. Some have even claimed there were closer to 20,000! Though the mean of 14,000 to 15,000 is perhaps more accurate, these prisoners were all ordered blinded, except one of the eyes of every hundredth man to lead the thousands back to Prilapon. It is said that this sight caused the Bulgarian Khan Samuel to die of 'grief and horror' on the spot. The cruelty of this act was most demoralizing to Bulgaria: '...the nation was awed by this horrible example; the Bulgarians were swept away from their settlements, and circumscribed with a narrow province; the surviving chiefs bequeathed to their children the advice of patience and the duty of revenge.'[1615]

Though this was probably more coincidental, Samuel did die shortly afterwards on October 6. But it is this act that induced the historian John Skylitzes,[1616] or Nicetas Choniates others say, in the 1090's to refer to Basil II as *Bulgaroctonus* ('Bulgar-Slayer'). Yet, the detractors of this act have exaggerated the cruelty just a bit as blinding had been used to punish prisoners of war for years. The severing of the hands of Bedouins in 995, and the blinding of Georgian prisoners in 1021-1022 was held as 'exceptionally brutal, but exceptionally successful.'[1617]

At Mosyonoplis, on the way back to winter at Constantinople, Basil heard the news of the Tsar's death and enthusiastically rallied his forces to Thessalonica taking Bitola and Edessa in the beginning of 1015. Samuel's son, Gabriel Radomir, was perhaps too weak or distracted to respond to these assaults and stayed quietly in Prilapon. Basil would then deport Edessa's Bulgarians to other frontier territories as a buffer in the Empire, but when Gabriel sued for peace, the typically suspicious Basil rejected it. He gave joint command of the Bulgarian war to Xiphias and the new Duke of Thessalonica, Constantine

---

[1614] Ostrogorsky, 310f.
[1615] Gibbon, 1942.
[1616] Skylitzes havng, whom Ostrogorsky reports, a particularly important biography of Basil II in which to study.
[1617] Herrin, 218.

Diogenes, as he went about resettling the Moglena region, relocating the Bulgars to Armenia. Gabriel would be assassinated by a cousin, John Vladislav, and being a more distant enough interest from Samuel's family, Bulgaria finally earned Basil's trust as he managed to settle a treaty. But an ill-timed raid on Dyrrhacium caused Basil to suspect treachery, so the *Basileus* swept Bitola and Ochrid, blinding all prisoners in his path.

Basil II further punished the Bulgarian Empire by the start of 1016 by re-sacking Ochrid and Bitola, where his men were defeated by Vladislav. He then handed the reigns once again to Xiphias and the new Duke of Thessalonica, David Arianites. But, once more, he would show reluctance to ally with other hostile foreign forces than the Bulgarians. This came about when the new King of Georgia invaded Iberia and defeated the Byzantine garrisons. Basil's response was a successful show of strength against these Khazars by using the Russian navy at his command. As for Islamic hostilities, the Fatimids occupied Byzantine Aleppo once more, Basil only seeming to enforce an embargo on Fatimid goods in Byzantium until a new governor sought peace in 1020.[1618]

In 1016 and 1017, Basil was besieging Bulgarian cities at Pernik and Castoria when Vladislav mustered a Pecheneg force to take Distra where again the mere mention of the *Basileus* Basil's presence caused them to disperse. It was no small thing that the dangerous and once untouchable Pechenegs, feared since the time of Constantine VII, were now fearing this Bulgar-Slayer and his armies. Diogenes defeated the forces of Edessa and the successful Basil in 1018 felt confident enough to handle a rebellion in Western Longobardia at Bari. But it was not long before Basil returned to his obsession with Bulgaria as Vladislav was murdered and fortresses like Pernik near Adrianople were immediately surrendering to the *Basileus*. At Strumitsa, the Bulgarian Patriarch David surrendered the city and declared it to become a Byzantine client state, which Basil eagerly accepted. Though Basil won his campaigns at the head of his armies, Bulgaria was won piecemeal over time by siege and attrition that sapped its resistance, to submission.[1619]

Basil II was still benevolent with the new Byzantine Bulgaria as its Patriarchate would still be independent (*autocephelous*) from the Greek Church, now an Archbishopric in Ochrid, where taxes were kept in kind over cash. With a sitting Bulgarian as Patriarch, Basil shrewdly conceded the spiritual local

---

[1618] Treadgold, 527.
[1619] Decker, 174.

autonomy to his conquered people.[1620] The Duke Arianites at Scopia was now made Duke of Bulgaria as three new Themes were created from the captured Epirote regions of Castoria, Bulgaria, and Paristrium. Furthermore, Croatia, Bosnia, Dioclea, and Rascia were all made autonomous kingdoms for their submission to the *Basileus*. Rounding out his benevolence, Prusian, the son of John Vladislav, was made *Magister* and Strategus of the Brucellarian Theme from Nicaea to Ancyra.

The Bulgarian royal Treasury was accepted to fill the Byzantine coffers and alleviate the previous burdens of war as the emperor also pardoned all of Vladislav's sons at the behest of Maria, the former Bulgarian Empress. Basil's sternest action was taken against a deserter found in the city, Nicolitzas, the former governor of Epirus, the rest being peaceful transitions and mostly reasonable actions. Basil ended his goodwill campaign on the now shattered Bulgarian state by touring Greece and traveling to the ancient city of Athens to give a solemn thanksgiving at the Parthenon, converting the wonderful monument to a Church of the Mother of God.[1621] It is fitting Basil honor his victories in a temple to God that was once a functioning military fortress.

The last Bulgarian holdout at Sirmium was easily taken once Constantine Diogenes assassinated its chieftain and it became a Theme. Alliances between Byzantium, Croatia, and Serbia gave Basil complete control over the Balkans without precedence. Developments in the West and Middle East would now catch the attention of the Empire's military machine. The Longobardian rebellion of Bari in 1019 was suppressed by the Italian Catepan, Basil Boioannes, who then built a northern frontier base at Troia. Meanwhile, trouble stirred in Georgia as its King George, not believing the *Basileus* would just forgive the Iberian invasion he offered, allied with the Fatimids and the Armenian King Smbat-John of Ani against Basil.

In 1021, al-Hakim was murdered and George fled to Abasgia, as Aleppo was no longer an option, and Basil was now devastating Georgian-held Iberia and Armenia, blinding all prisoners and terrifying his fleeing enemies. As he wintered in Trebizond with his fleet, Smbat-John surrendered to him and sued for peace. Not long after, George did the same and became a Byzantine client, surrendering Kars as Smbat-John would will Ani to the Empire upon his death. In the Caucasus, a cautious King Senacherim of Vaspurakan surrendered his territories as well to protect it from the Arabs of Azerbaijan. By spring of 1022,

---

[1620]  Obolensky, 210.
[1621]  Sherrard, 62.

Vaspurakan was a Ducate and the northern wars were over with resounding results for the *Basileus*. Though motivated by fear, client kings all over the North and the East were seeing Byzantium and Basil as defenders of their lands with apparently a fair hand upon their economies and customs.

In Asia Minor, revolt broke out as Xiphias led a rebel army claiming Nicephorus, son of Bardas Phocas as *Basileus*, with Basil having no heir. This conspiracy grew broader as the complicit George of Georgia and Smbat-John of Ani broke their truce and joined the rebellion. Xiphias's greed caused his downfall as he assassinated Phocas to become *Basileus* and his outraged troops turned on him. Although all other rebels were blinded, Xiphias was mercifully exiled intact for his past excellence and loyalty as Basil's general. By 1022, Basil returned to the City in triumph after George and Smbat-John were defeated, remitting hearth and land taxes on the poor in celebration. By now he had also re-organized the Antiochene region's 'Euphrates Cities' (later the Theme of Edessa) into eight new Themes including Melitene, Taron, Vaspurakan, Iberia, and Theodosiopolis, ruling from the Adriatic to Azerbaijan.[1622]

After this period, relative safety prevailed in the Empire with few exceptions: the German Emperor Henry II invaded Longobardia but withdrew when the Doge's defenses proved too much for him. Also, in Aleppo, the Fatimids renewed their dominance in 1025 by inducing a new embargo on trade with Byzantium. The Fatimid menace did not amount to much when the rival Arab clan of the Mirdasids drove them from power and allied with Byzantium, continuing a free trade policy from as far as Baalbek. Basil would not be satisfied, however, until the West appeared as submissive as the East did and at sixty-seven years old he planned a war on Sicily for the campaign season of 1026. Armed fleets were sent with the commanders Orestes the Protospatharius and in Calabria under the Catepan Boioannes. As the *Basileus* prepared his own force, he grew ill and died on December 15, 1025, being buried in the Church of St. John the Evangelist in the Hebdemon Palace of Constantinople.[1623]

This unexpected death sounded a halt to the ambitions of one of the most energetic and relentless men ever to rule the Empire. He was modest in his austerity and his victories, leaving small doubt by his chroniclers that it was for the people of Byzantium he fought for in order to ensure their safety, seeking their obedience, but not their love. Everything he did was with an unswerving

---

[1622] Norwich, (APO), 264.

[1623] *ibid.*, 266, dramatically claims that it was on December 16th, 1025, that the Decline of the Byzantine Empire began.

passion that usually led to success, somehow being achieved by the charisma born of that very passion. His only real mistake was in leaving no heir which begged questions such as: Was this because he feared a repetition of the cycle he and other Macedonians faced with sly *Basiliai* and their alliances with 'usurping' generals? Did he fear a devastation of his works and the emboldening of his enemies if his heirs fought each other for control; after all, why would they not be as strong as he if they were his sons? He must have feared the sons of nobles and did all he could to extricate the aristocracy from the power of their lands by confiscation or closing acquisition loopholes. He would send these military commanders to posts far from their holdings, though they still held strong roots in places such as Adrianople and Trebizond.[1624]

Emperor Otto III, in 996, did offer his hand to one of Basil's nieces, the young and attractive Zoe, which would have been a great relief to Byzantium. His scheme and motivation was to appoint a Greek prelate to the Roman Papal throne,[1625] a Calabrian named John Philagathus who would become the Anti-Pope John XVI of Rome in 997. But even as Zoe crossed to Bari in 1002, she learned that on January 24, Otto had died of a fever. This quashed any dreams of alliance or a dynasty as Otto's successor, Henry II, showed nothing but hostility to the East a decade later. In the end, the throne went to Basil's lackluster and petulant brother Constantine who only had daughters and no sons, dooming the Macedonian bloodline. The subsequent years of his reign until the ascension of the Comneni in 1081 and the disaster at Manzikert in 1071 was seen as a notorious streak of incompetence and the actual beginning to Gibbon's infamous Decline of the Roman Empire.

Basil II was never noted as being a devout man such as Nicephorus II or even John Tzimisces, always seeming never to betray his secular character in the face of ecclesiastical opposition, though he did see to the containment of Bogolism after the Bulgarian conquest.[1626] One glaring instance was his treatment of the Monastery of St. Basil in 985 when he deposed Basil Lecapenus and wished to erase the pious contributions to the Empire that the former *Basileus* must have seen as tainted. To the horror of the *Parakoimomenus*, Basil ordered the monastery razed and its wealthy coffers and donations of furniture and mosaics seized. Basil II then was said to note sardonically that,' . . .he had

---

[1624] Magdalino, Paul. 'The Medieval Empire (780-1204)', 199.

[1625] Jenkins, 321.

[1626] Hussey, 40.

made a place of meditation a place of thought – the thought which those who dwelt there would now have to take for the bare necessities of life.'[1627]

Most notably was the religious *Chrysobull* of April 4, 988, curbing monastic power by claiming the pious allowances of Nicephorus Phocas to be the true cause of the Phocas family revolts, which he had revoked all privileges given since 962. But, this only steeled the resolve of the monastic party and their desires to check imperial power, which was yielded by the *Basileus* with the *Chrysobull* that threatened internal harmony, forcing his hand.[1628] In 996, he chose a new Patriarch since the office had been vacant since 992 and on April 12, a physician named Sisinnius became Sisinnius II, Patriarch of Constantinople. Two years later when Sisinnius died, another vacancy of the Patriarchate yielded in 1001 to Sergius II who became embroiled in the most controversial tax policies of church lands during Basil's reign. Basil also strengthened the Byzantines' role in world Christianity by erasing the Popes from the imperial diptychs and enforcing the supremacy of Orthodoxy in 1024 over Pope John XIX as being 'universal in its sphere.'[1629]

One of Basil II's most dominant and vital wars was within the Empire, one waged on the landowning class, this being the epitome of his responsibilities toward *philanthropia* and the harmony of *taxis* in the East Roman realm. His verbal contribution asks 'Are we to leave their lands in the hands of those whom they have basely robbed and despoiled?' He went on to claim, '...instead of showing pity and humanity . . .[They] buy the property of the wretched cheaply...on the misery of the destitute.[1630]' Continuing the policies of former *Basilii* in his Novel of January 1, 996, especially those of Romanus I Lecapenus in 934, Basil cancelled all noble grants made by Lecapenus and gave land back to the poor purchasers with no compensation to the rich.[1631] Citing titles and constitutions made by Augustus Caesar to repeal laws made by Constantine VII in 953, a thousand years must pass as the statute wherein claim to these lands to the poor were to be limited by the rich.[1632]

---

[1627] Psellus, 39.

[1628] Diehl, 170.

[1629] Ostrogorsky, 335.

[1630] Diehl, 155-156. Entitled: 'The Constitution of the Pious Emperor Basil the Young, by which are Condemned those Rich Men who Amass their Wealth at the Expense of the Poor.' This seal alone, it was said, put dread in the Anatolian aristocracy, Norwich, (APO), 251.

[1631] Ostrogorsky, 306.

[1632] Jenkins, 319.

Of course, he put down the hammer on the estates of his enemies such the Scleri and Phoci who led the civil war against his rightful rule, also making an example out of the largest estate of Eustatius Maleinus by outright confiscation. There was once a poor peasant, Philocales of Asia Minor, whose fortunes were changed by these dictates, making his village his home estate and his own neighbors his serfs. The *Basileus* ordered all of Philocales's buildings demolished, ordering he be put back into the ranks of the peasant poor. Basil showed most of all that the Eastern Roman Empire was meant to be one of charity and social justice not to be blinded by greed or self-interest, ruthless in its very defining of the classes.

As a result of the expense of the Bulgarian wars, Basil II enacted a Novel in 1003 that made the landowners responsible for the entirety of the debt if neighboring peasants defaulted on taxes and loans, breathing new life into the *allelengyon*.[1633] This made doubly sure that the senatorial and officer classes paid attention and gave aid to the poor as taxes on the peasants were known to be high in times of need. Because this did not exempt Church lands, the Patriarch complained to the obstinate Basil who promised in the Church's case it was only temporary and would be rescinded after the war. Basil, like a true autocratic soldier-*Basileus* went back on his promise and declared to Sergius in 1018 that the laws were now permanent, as it did not pay to contradict him. As for the landholders themselves, on the standard six percent profit on these investments, they received mostly 2.5-3 percent, although the 'bearded' officeholders such as Protospartharioi could get as much as 8.3 percent.[1634] However, this does specify that the *Basileus*'s own courtier class was the one making the highest profit from the peasant landholding.

Because of his clever tax policies, by 1025 (even with the reductions of 1023), Basil turned a depleted Treasury of 998 and 1003 into a sterling surplus of 14,400,000 *nomismata*.[1635] This stood tall even in the face of an increasing state budget due to the increase of soldiers, fodder, rations, etc. In 842 under Theophilus, 120,000 soldiers cost the state in pay over 1,200,000 with supplies just over 340,000 *nomismata*. By Constantine VII's time in 959 this changed to 144,000 men at 1,500,000 with 400,000 in supplies, even with a reduction of one *nomismata* per soldier. By Basil II's death, 247,800 soldiers (with a 20,000 man margin of error) were accounted for with 2,670,000 *nomismata* for pay

---

[1633] Vasiliev, 344.

[1634] Herrin, 156.

[1635] Treadgold, 532.

and over 600,000 for supplies.[1636] Still, smaller campaign forces were also encouraged such as in the advice of a military treatise inspired by Basil. *On Campaign Organization* was written in the taxiarchy style of Nicephorus II and envisioned 14,000 to 16,000 infantry with 9,000 to 9,200 cavalry replacing the old pike units and increasing the cavalry.[1637]

These growing armies, populations, and necessities were handled well over years of inflation in the Macedonian Era. These were still seen as relatively stable economic times with a record high annual military budget in 1025 topping at 5,895,000 *nomismata* including a halved military surplus and double the costs in pay and cost of equipment. These figures by Warren Treadgold in light of the surplus do demonstrate prosperity from the Bulgarian victories, despite the wars themselves. The surplus is noted as 200,000 talents of gold taken from Scyths, Celts, Iberians, and Arabians with those underground vaults, in the 'Egyptian style', needed to contain it all.[1638]

Some older modern sources such as Charles Diehl estimate this surplus to be 49,000,000 'dollars' and the revenues of the entire eleventh century to be 119,136,000 *nomismata*.[1639] The decline in currency would, nevertheless, become more obvious by A. A. Sewter. He explains how the standard '*bezant*', or '*nomisma*', would decay in value from twenty-four karats under Basil to eighteen under Constantine IX (1042-1055). Furthermore, it would inflate to twelve or thirteen karats under Michael VIII (1259-1282),[1640] as further economic declines would spell bankruptcy and elimination by 1453. As for the Macedonians, Basil II was the last *Basileus* ever to champion the rights of peasants over the rich, as the 'radical changes' and instability of the throne and taxation would lead to the neglect of these issues altogether.[1641]

But as he sat, he was the 'Pantocrat' (Ruler of All) whose whim had Russians and Slavs fighting in Italy, Armenians in the Danube, and Bulgarians in the Vaspurakan. Over Church and Empire he was supreme; the nobles feared his grip and a confidence in the central government was restored and assured.[1642]

---

[1636] Treadgold, (*BAIA*), 97. Further conservatism included the halt on *tetratera* production and its decreasing use as soldier pay while only half the number of coins recorded as being minted in the latter eleventh century, 139 and 215.

[1637] *ibid.,* pg. 115.

[1638] Psellus, 45.

[1639] *Diehl,* 71.

[1640] Sewter, 12.

[1641] Ostrogorsky, 320.

[1642] Jenkins, 329.

But the following era after 1025 was a decline of 400 years neither inevitable nor unnoticeable but similar to Rome's fall in 476. The grasp of Byzantium on the world and conquering of the subject states' will would just be beginning to slip in the decades after 1025 and neglectful irresponsibility by the state would fail to catch it again. Already, the recovering noble houses of the Dalesseni, Phoci, Comneni, Melessini, and Argyri would be plagued, some even taking the throne, against their malicious Norman invaders and the dread of the Seljuk Turks. In summation on Basil II, his own advice he would give future generations of *Basilii* would best be estimated by the record of Michael Psellus: 'Exhaust them [nobles] with unjust exactions to keep them busy with their own affairs . . .Share with few your most intimate plans.'[1643]

# CONSTANTINE VIII
## (1025-1028)

Basil II's younger brother Constantine was seen as the antithesis of Basil, his reputation beginning with Psellus and in all other histories since that time. Basil was said to give penance as a monk would: with robe, abstaining from wine, flesh, and the values of lawyers and artists.[1544] In more superficial ways, the last Macedonian was superior – as Basil was short and stocky, Constantine was handsome and tall (oddly exaggerated at nine feet tall),[1645] all seen as marks of superior quality. Basil was known more for his terse announcements and sardonic ways while Constantine was hailed for logical arguments, fine oratory, and a language so eased his secretaries invented a shorthand script to record his speeches. But, these dissimilarities brought with them harsher consequences due to Constantine's faults.

Constantine had some recorded experience in battle, but had an aversion to hardship as his gold coins present the return of the *Basileus* with scepter forsaking the sword with which to defend the Empire.[1646] He spurned state responsibilities as prince and later as *Basileus* to luxuriate in Nicaea hunting, bathing, gambling, carousing, and riding his trained horses.[1647] He was said to be craven and without ambition as he cancelled his brother's military plans

---

[1643] Brownworth, 213.

[1644] Gibbon, 1643.

[1645] Psellus, 57.

[1646] Treadgold, 584.

[1647] Psellus, 40.

in the West and made none of his own while embassies were only met with courtesy bearing no real substance or visible outcome. Worst of all, he had no sons, just three daughters, two cloistered in nunneries and one who could only marry and discontinue the Macedonian line as she was middle-aged and could no longer bear children.

He was born to Theophano and the *Basileus* Romanus II in 960, two years after his brother, crowned co-*Basileus* with brother Basil in 962. He had a formal education, but Psellus also reports it was only enough culture and learning a child could demonstrate all of his life. He was known for luxuriating in the pleasures of wine, women (despite his marriage to Helena, daughter of the nobleman Alypius), foods with delicate sauces, scents, and colors, and breeding his horses. This did not change under Phocas and Tzimisces and did not when Basil became sole ruler in 969. However, it must be remembered that Basil preferred his brother this way so as not to be a threat. The *Basileus* never admonished him or forced him into posts unsuited for him, so Basil's power games are partially responsible for Constantine's being a waste of a golden crown better used elsewhere. On December 16, 1025, Constantine VIII was brought before Basil and made *Basileus* on one of the last of his commands.

Specific chronologies are a problem in understanding Constantine's actions as sources are mainly focused on his exploits and lack of acumen. One of which is how Constantine called off his brother's ambitious Sicilian campaign after a landing at Messina.[1648] He went so far as to give pieces of the True Cross from the Blacharnae to Norman clergy to appease their hostilities, including King Ragabund and Pope John XIX. All this would accomplish would be tempting the westerners during the approaching Crusades to take other such relics by force less than a century later.[1649]

Also, as he gave large bribes for loyalty to the army and Senate, he rescinded the suspension of the land and hearth taxes issued previously in 1025. He would actually need these funds when an uprising by the Anatolian generals occurred and it was only quelled by his brother's arms and a craven cancellation of the Novels of his brother concerning landholding. This only succeeded in inaugurating an absence of reform never again to be addressed by future *Basilii*. Byzantium would only see Basil's superficial reforms as a mere expediency to

---

[1648] Treadgold, 583.

[1649] Jones, Lynn. 'Questionable Gifts: Constantine VIII and the True Cross.' Presented at *The Twenty-Eighth Annual Byzantine Studies Conference.* (Columbus, OH: The Ohio State University, October 4-5, 2002).

belay the hands of the rich from soldier's land holdings and not one of equity or justice.[1650]

By 1027, he had made an arrangement with the Fatamid Caliph al-Zahir who was offering that Jerusalem be repaired by him on the condition a new mosque be raised in Constantinople. Complete with this would be a 'Mohammedan priest . . .a *muezzim*'[165-] that would instruct the faithful and even convert members of the City. This had to have been seen as a betrayal of faith among the City's Christian inhabitants, whether the Sepulcher was rebuilt or not, a concession to Islam that Basil would probably never have considered. Furthermore, though it is purely conjecture, perhaps it was even previously offered to Basil after al-Zahir's ascension in 1021.

Above all, Constantine was known for his cruelty and tyranny in a violent reign, although it was motivated by the fear of an old 'dotard', instead of a willful, bitter resentment.[1652] By the early eleventh century, blinding had become a common act in military ventures, especially on Bulgarian prisoners. However, Basil II was, surprisingly, not known for his multiple blinding of fallen allies and would-be conspirators as mostly they were exiled or tonsured with exceptions such as Bardas Phocas. Constantine was filled with the paranoia of a ruler with no confidence in his place and casually blinded 'enemies' without trial. On just rumors and pretenses, he blinded men of the Scleri, Phoci, and Burtzi families and even the Duke of Vaspurakan was so punished with red-hot irons. 'The Romans became his slaves, not won over by acts of kindness, but subdued by all manners of cruel punishments.'[1653] He did this to Bishops, the high and low alike, indiscriminately, and only after it was done would he have a heavy remorse for his victims and beg for their forgiveness.

Added to his violent exploits was his reviving of the *gymnopedia*, spectacles closely resembling gladiatorial games outlawed for their indecency in 410 CE by Honorius,[1654] even partaking of these fights himself with slaves on the condition they not hold back. These actions remind one of the Emperor Commodus (180-192 CE), who gained skill in hunting and fighting by killing animals in the Colosseum in Rome for mere applause to bolster his weak self-esteem. Psellus does agree that this is how Constantine VIII got any of his real athletic skills.

---

[1650] Jenkins, 338.

[1651] *Vasiliev*, 'Byzantium and Islam', 317.

[1652] Jenkins, 337.

[1653] Psellus, 53.

[1654] *ibid.*, 57.

Other pastimes included gambling with dice, 'chequers', entertaining cronies and concubines, and seeing indecent plays at the theaters.[1655]

His health was as questionable as a seventy-year-old's might be with his lifestyle, as his gourmand gave him a serious case of gout in his legs and feet and he could not walk by the time of his death. On November 9, 1028, he fell ill and his death was imminent. He had claimed no successor for his daughter to wed and a scramble by the court was made to dredge one up. One patrician, Constantine Dalessenus, was considered, but at the last minute a man in his sixties, the City Eparch, Romanus Argyrus, was presented by Simeon the Drungarius to the *Constantine* and Romanus was proclaimed *Basileus*. To add scandal to this, Romanus's wife was set aside, shaved bald, and tonsured before she supposedly could even understand why.[1656] This act was performed so Romanus III could marry Zoe, daughter of Constantine, and keep the legitimacy as *Basileus* after Constantine died on November 11.

Constantine started not as a monster, he just became so over time, his irresponsibility and lack of judgment setting about undoing all the benefits his brother gave the Empire. And a soft life of luxury and inexperience given by Basil to keep him away from the throne made all worse when Basil died childless. It was he who became the first of the *epigoni*[1657] that allowed the rich to capitalize on neglected land laws and separate from the central government. It may be unfair to compare the two brothers, one ruling fifty years and the other only three. However, such incompetent rule as was operated has never gone well in imperial history and would be doomed to a terrible and bloody end. The Empire would now mire in the separation and self-interest of rich nobles who could live and rule their own fiefs without an *Basileus*'s notice. The worst part was the return of the sixth-century *latifundiae* in Anatolia,[1658] private plantations worked by serfs for the rich civil and military landowners. This started as a trickle to become a deluge of localized and decentralizing social, economic, and military power that mostly caused the Byzantines' declines and extinction.

---

[1655] Norwich, (*APO*), 268-269.

[1656] Psellus, 58-59. Argyrus, as Eparch, was considered eighteenth in line of the top sixty administrative posts in the Empire.

[1657] *Ostrogorsky, pg. 321; Jenkins, pg. 338.*

[1658] Norwich, (APO), 268.

# ROMANUS III ARGYRUS
## (1028-1034)

Romanus Argyrus was only a slight and mediocre improvement on Constantine. He was placed on the throne by courtiers as a puppet and a rubber stamp by Constantine VIII's factions, chosen for his dullness and pliancy. He was even coerced to set aside a wife to marry one of the former *Basileus's* daughters. He had ambitions, but they were terribly misguided and superficial – Psellus had no trouble in saying he built 'castles in the air . . .and hurled them down again.'[1659] He tried too hard to be approved of in order to create a lasting legacy, to be a great commander, and fill the sandals of his heroes such as Justinian, Aurelius, Augustus, Alexander the Great, and even Plato and Aristotle. Yet, he was only 'dimly aware' of his armies and military positions as he disastrously sent forces into ambushes and defeats as with the Syrians in 1030, his only glory being in building churches.[1660]

A pseudo-intellectual, he always attempted to sound more educated than he was though he had some learning in Greek and Latin, making baseless theological arguments that went nowhere as they had no logic. Further harming his affectations, he was superstitious to a fault and showed great effectiveness in his military studies, lacking experience. Lastly, he showed a great lack of wisdom in choosing those men to keep faith in, this being his downfall as the stronger personality of his wife Zoe took advantage of his foolhardy tolerances to end his life. He is said to have had a majestic and graceful voice and a heroic stature that at least *looked* the part of a *Basileus* to lead the Empire.

Romanus III was born in 968 in Anatolia to a noble family descended from the Lecapeni through the Argyropouloi, branch of Romanus I. He also was related by marriage to the Doge Giovanni Orseolo through a cousin Maria Lecapena, he also being third or fourth cousin to his wife the Macedonian *Basilia* Zoe. This relation by marriage of the senatorial Argyropouloi and the Orseoli was considered a boon to the Venetians for their ventures against the Sicilian Arabs at Bari.[1661] Romanus had risen in the ranks of the bureaucracy from Patrician to the Supreme Judge of a tribunal to the Economic Administrator of St. Sophia, and finally to Eparch of the City of Constantinople. And, of course, accusations of embezzlement from the Treasury and corruption were

---

[1659] Psellus, 65.
[1660] Treadgold, (*BAIA*), 215.
[1661] Herrin, 205.

present, also impugning in legal verdicts to enrich himself over plaintiff and defendant. On his ascension on November 18, 1028, he was given an option to wed Theodora, Zoe's younger sister, who was just young enough to bear him an heir. But Theodora had piously defied the treatment of Romanus's first wife and was tonsured by an indignant Patriarch Alexius of Studius. So Romanus and Zoe wed on November 19, 1028.

After the usual methods of buying legitimacy through forgiving debts and taxes, giving amnesties, and doling out large donatives, he began his reign by flexing the Empire's military strength. The army greatly disliked this bureaucrat usurper and the general Constantine Diogenes began a plot with the tonsured Theodora to overthrow him, likely making a marital alliance to secure the throne as Zoe had done. Romanus discovered this and tonsured Diogenes, but as seeing this as the threat his generals might pose, he believed a successful campaign would earn him loyalty. Romanus's choice of invasion was not with malign enemies such as the Calabrian Arabs, which he had neglected, but the pacified Emirates of Syria who still abide with their treaty with Basil II. Romanus attempted to bribe Aleppo after a force defeated the Duke of Antioch, Michael Spondyles, but he was rebuked by their Emir.[1662]

The Mirdasids of Aleppo had been invaded by the Fatimids and Romanus Argyrus saw this as a chance to test his armies by leading them personally in the summer of 1030. The *Basileus* sent his troops to the city, but the Arabs outsmarted the Byzantines with placements of soldiers that feigned superior numbers. Psellus describes when these scattered regiments met the Byzantines the imperial troops lost all of their morale and fled almost immediately. Had this been a smaller part of the Greeks' strength it might have been salvageable, but Romanus ruined this with a sloppy and overzealous strategy. Romanus had convinced himself a brilliant strategist capable of planning campaigns and ambuscades, sieges and sorties with perseverance, but in reality he had no competency or experience.[1663] He threw his entire force at once at the enemy thinking their superior numbers were all that were needed like some horde in a raid, ignoring any tactical measures. If Romanus III planned to annex Aleppo, he failed miserably with a slaughter of 10,000 of his troops and low morale in the army compounded by bad heat and lack of water sources.

Aleppo conservatively held back as they knew Byzantine arms were still a dangerous threat at this point, still meeting a rousing defeat by the successful

---

[1662] Treadgold, 585.
[1663] Jenkins, 340.

general George Maniaces, Strategus of Teleuch. When 800 Arab cavalry appeared in Teleuch, as he was given tall tales by Maniaces of the Byzantine *Basileus*'s death in battle, he bribed them with lots of alcohol and attacked them that night as they lay in a stupor. All 800 were killed and Maniaces ordered their ears and noses to be cut off;[1664] more raids on Syrian territory inducing the Arabs to make peace in 1031 and they returned to the status of clients.

Maniaces then went to take Edessa and recovered the holy relic of the letter written by Christ to the King, Abgar. Romanus even worked out a deal with the Arabs that the Empire reserve the right to rebuild and re-establish the churches of Jerusalem along with the Holy Sepulcher from the imperial coffers and Byzantium reserves the right to appoint the Patriarchs of Jerusalem.[1665] This agreement was worked out and officiated in 1036, two years after Romanus III's death. But beforehand, these foundations were a small victory for Argyrus and an improvement on the labors of his predecessor.

Maniaces was made Catepan of Lower Media from Samasota and Strategus of the 'Euphrates Cities', the major Syrian and Mesopotamian cities that formed the Byzantine eastern borders, Maniaces without actually becoming a Domestic of the East. Maniaces also, with no involvement of the *Basileus*, held the forts by Tripoli and allied with its Emir against the Fatimids.[1666] This emboldened Romanus to return to Syria on a campaign in 1032 after spending liberal sums of Treasury money on building projects in Constantinople. As he crossed Anatolia to ravage Fatimid territory, he received word that Theodora and Diogenes were once again plotting to seize the empty throne. As the *Basileus* made his way back, Diogenes lost heart and committed suicide, Romanus making a wise choice for once and staying in Constantinople.

In 1033, the Empire would look like a disaster as more famine from the East hit Asia Minor and Armenia. Along with this was the invasion of Calabria by the Arabs, killing the Catepan as Corcyra was also taken. On the Danube, the Pechenegs were raiding with a free hand as well. All of this was ignored by Romanus as his domestic situation looked more and more dim and palace intrigue would catch up with his incompetence. Not one military victory can, or should, be attributed to Romanus III Argyrus but to his talented general Maniaces, whom under better circumstances might have been the soldier-*Basileus* Byzantium still needed.

---

[1664] Norwich, (APO), 273.

[1665] Vasiliev, 312.

[1666] Treadgold, 585.

Throughout this time, the seventy-year-old *Basileus* had exhausted all avenues of impregnating his fifty-year-old wife, known for her beauty despite being pitted by smallpox.[1667] Psellus reports with a philosopher's judgment how the Argyrus consulted 'experts' in curing infertility using ointments and massage therapies. He then turned to 'magical practices' with charms, chains, talismans, nostrums, aphrodisiacs, and 'other such nonsense.' Eventually he gave up altogether and took a mistress, ignoring Zoe, even going so far as to barring her from the Treasury to giving her a fixed allowance. He probably blamed her for his troubles and began to despise her as he was loathed to be in her presence and set aside the *Basilia* of the blood contemptuously.[1668]

Zoe's wrath was silent, but terrible, and she began the working of a court intrigue that would give her power once more. The Paphlagonian administrator of the imperial orphanage and former Protonotary of her uncle, the eunuch John the Orphanotrophus, was close to the *Basileus* and he began strategically placing his four brothers in positions that would give them high places in Zoe's faction. John's brother Michael captured the Zoe's attention and they began a torrid affair. It has been questioned whether or not Romanus knew of this affair and the likely answer was that he did and ignored it as he had his own affairs. It must be noted that John and his family already had a black spot on their name for charges of counterfeiting coinage, but John still made his brother Archon of the Pantheon. Besides, the *Basileus* himself was said to be guilty of monetary corruption so what was a little tolerance of the bureaucracy doing the same practices in a more corrupt age?

Unfortunately, Romanus III Argyrus once again missed the writing on the wall and suspected nothing as the pair began to slowly poison him over a year's time, John Norwich agreeing with Psellus that hellebore was used.[1669] The effects on Romanus were monstrous: loss of appetite, loss of sleep, and rapid eye movements as his demeanor changed from friendliness to irate wrath and lack of generosity. After about a year of this, his breathing became shallow, he could not walk, and his head went almost entirely bald with the pallor of death.[1670]

On the early morning of Good Friday, April 12, 1034, Romanus went to the *kolymbithra* (Palace Baths) for rejuvenation, when Michael the Paphlogonian held his head under the water to drown. Being impatient with the slow results of

---

[1667] Jenkins, 339.
[1668] Psellus, 75.
[1669] Norwich, (*APO*), 279.
[1670] Psellus, 81-82.

a slow poisoning, they had left him to die until he floated on the surface 'like a cork.' Though unsubstantiated, Psellus relates that he was pulled from the bath by others and even the *Basilia* Zoe, where he deeply moaned, gasped a few times, bled from the mouth and died. His slow poisoning and cruel death showed the character of Zoe and her lover as being practically psychopathic in their murdering of Romanus.[1671] But at this time, he still could not identify the plot against him as he had with his sister-in-law from a far-off convent, only showing his typical lack of judgment. Even when he died, the disillusioned Romans of Constantinople did not mourn him or seek accusation against anyone.

That very day, the Patriarch upon to crown Michael as *Basileus* in the *Chrysotriclinium* (after bribes of 100 pounds of gold to the Patriarchate). Later, Romanus III would be carried out in procession in an open coffin and laid to rest in his Church of the Virgin[1672] in Constantinople in his seventieth year. The manners of assassination were cold-blooded acts, but inevitable ones for an incompetent *Basileus* that was a puppet for the rich and an outsider to the Macedonian line. Argyrus had even wisely declined the Crown once in 1028, but the vicious parasites of Constantine VIII assured him the alternatives were blindness or death. Although his sister Pulcheria always watched out for him, her care only went so far and the stronger will of Zoe would not be denied the rights as the daughter of a *Basileus*.

His major contribution to the Empire was a result of his envy of the Solomon-surpassing Justinian I's Church of the Holy Wisdom. He spent eighty pounds of gold a year as a subsidy to the Church and further decorated it in gold and silver along with the Church of the Mother of God at Blacharnae. He then began work on a Church in the City he intended to surpass all others. It was dedicated to the Virgin *Peribleptos* ('All-Seeing'),[1673] built on the Seventh Hill overlooking the shore of the Marmara where he would in the future be buried. He adorned it with marble statuary modeled after the ancient sculptors of Greek Classical design and would spend years perfecting it, adding on to some places and pulling down others at the State Treasury's expense.

Psellus, being a youth at the time, was still a witness to these events and reports on the heavy expenditures and massive debts incurred for this Church. Always the philosopher, he goes off on a secular bend decrying these 'Houses

---

[1671] Gibbon, 1644, with great misogyny, assuring us of the Roman maxim: 'every adulteress is capable of poisoning her husband.'

[1672] Although, it would be demolished during the Turkish conquests, Norwich, (*APO*), 275f.

[1673] Psellus, 72.

of the Lord' and asking why can't Man simply keep a temple to God in their own hearts in the good they do for the world: 'The symmetry of walls, the encircling columns, the hanging tapestries, the magnificent offerings, and the other things of splendor – what can they contribute to the sacred object of piety?'[1674] Unfortunately, no trace of it has survived to the present because of the Seljuk Turks as it has been replaced with the Armenian Church of St. George. Going further in his religious policy, Romanus III also alleviated the Church properties of the Empire by revoking the *allelengyon* obligations that Basil II omitted doing years before in his own reforms.

But these very policies epitomized the lapses and concessions made against the hard work of the Macedonians to check the power of the private estate holders as well as fueling the greed of a corrupt system. Worse still, corruption was on a high as embezzlement of funds and the notorious tax farming, as that '. . .most pernicious of all abuses,' commenced, where taxes were re-farmed from settled accounts at the balance doubling or tripling in amount.[1675] These localized bureaucrats were found everywhere, also auditing families of long dead citizens to squeeze them for what could be taken.

Although the obligations to peasants were usually deemed legally valid by judges at the time, Romanus officially revoked all of the duties of the landholders to their peasants and of the government that the Macedonians had promulgated. These counterproductive measures enriched private and elite wealth over the poorer majority of peasants and soldiers, clearly leading to a weathering away of military power as confidence was lost in their possessions, coupled with vast losses of state revenue that weakened the Empire as a whole.[1676] This elimination of progress from the days of Heraclius was, at the time, only a slight malady of economic and military decline and would not be somewhat remedied and last for a century.

## MICHAEL IV 'THE PAPHLAGONIAN'
### (1034-1041)

Zoe had succeeded in her self-interested plan to make her lover, the son of a peasant mechanic, *Basileus* of Byzantium. But she underestimated greatly the hold her new brother-in-law, John Orphanotrophus, had on the situation. It was

---

[1674] Psellus, 73.

[1675] Norwich, (*APO*), 274.

[1676] Ostrogorsky, 323.

to be solely for John's benefit and that of his family that Michael was raised to such heights. John was one of the most charismatic, infamous, unscrupulous, yet powerful characters in the Empire's history. He was stern with a mean countenance, a dangerous enemy to have and corrupt to a fault, having little pity for the *Basilia*. Almost as soon as the Eparch and Senate kissed his right hand in solemn ceremony, Michael showed his true colors almost immediately by banishing his new wife to the women's quarters (*gymnaceum*) of the Palace with no visitors, no freedom, nor any access to the funds whose estrangement had caused her wrath against Argyrus.

Michael IV was indeed colored by a respectful Psellus as a handsome man of youth and strength, 'clear-eyed' and 'red-cheeked,' estimated to be ten feet tall.[1677] He was lost on Hellenic culture, but was still lively, amusing, all with his jokes, and having natural abilities in legal procedure (though not in oratory or argument). He took his responsibilities seriously when his slow actions, at first, led to crisis. Short of crossing his brother John and correcting his loathsome younger brothers who abused his good fortune, Michael took charge of his fiscal, military, and administrative duties. Many scholars agree that he could have saved the Empire and healed the breaches in Basil II's legacy which were allowed to widen by his imperial predecessors.

Unfortunately, though character was not his weakness, as his body was: he suffered from severe epileptic fits and caught dropsy, debilitating his movement and, eventually, the faith of his people that he had cultivated. He would fall into convulsions at a moment's notice; Psellus recounts how once riding a horse he fell and although no one helped him, he 'elicited all of their pity.' He did his best at controlling his unruly younger brothers, but never carried out punishments towards them, leaving most of the thinking to his shrewd and observant brother, John. But, he was not ashamed of his maladies as Michael the Paphlagonian would have attacks in public and still demand the respect of his people. He ran the Empire as if he had no disability and only John tried to cloak his distresses from the populace as not to appear weak.

Furthermore, his guilt was a burden on him, especially the guilt over killing Romanus Argyrus and certainly that of the betrayal of his loving Zoe to the point where he could never again so much as look her in the eye. Ironically, his dread that he could not be saved by God led to his glorious charity towards the poor, to fallen women, and the building of churches that made his own legacy. Had he lived longer, Byzantium would have been better for it but the ambitions of his

---

[1677] Psellus, 76.

brother only weighed down the Empire. This led to encourage state corruption and the ascension of a bitter disappointment to the throne after his death and he, at least, seemed a brief plateau in a slowly sliding decline. Older and more cynical, as sources claimed, John 'smiled at his remorse and enjoyed the harvest of a crime of which he himself was the secret and most guilty author.'[1678] Gibbon goes on to say Michael's administration was just a check on his brother's avarice.

Michael was born in 1010 in Paphlagonia, the second eldest of five sons that included Nicetas, Constantine, and George. He also had a sister Maria who would play a significant role in the next (and last) member of the Paphlagonian dynasty. As his brother John was a eunuch, he could not take the throne, but he could climb high in the ranks of the imperial household, starting as a bureaucrat for Basil II to the Magister of the Imperial Orphanage as well as Household. Another attribute of John, on Psellus's insistence, was a deep affection for the brother he shamelessly exploited. It can be inferred and concluded that this was just why Michael was chosen for these exploits as an *Basileus* along with his keen mind and ability to 'satisfy' the *Basilia*'s loneliness. The brothers' agreement towards Zoe had been little more than the 'pimping' of Michael by his unscrupulous brother.

Psellus cheerfully notes on how Michael had deep respect for the *status quo* in the Empire by changing nothing as a sign of stability: 'He made no innovations in established customs, rescinded no laws, introduced none that was contrary to the spirit of his predecessor, removed no member of the Senate...'[1679] John, too, adopted this attitude by holding to the central bureaucracy with neutrality to social class, including that of the aristocracy. Of course, this gave advantage to the civil nobility as John followed the path of the City's state officeholders;[1680] it is no wonder Psellus looked up to Michael's administration since it valued the typical bureaucratic goals of effectiveness over efficiency with no reform! Only taxation and financial policies were changed to exorbitant increases, as the historian John Cedrenus could not name the long list of these laws partially out of shame and as they were too numerous to count.

It is for the reasons of Michael IV's quick ascension that there was one main malcontent in the aristocracy, Constantine Dalassenus. Denied a throne practically promised him in 1028, Dalessenus was feared by the *Basileus* that he would raise a rebellion among the Armenians in his influence, so Michael wisely kept him close as an honored guest at the Palace. But in the summer of 1034, the

---

[1678] Gibbon, 1645.

[1679] Psellus, 91.

[1680] Ostrogorsky, 324.

*Basileus* made his move and trumped up charges on Constantine for instigating an Antiochene rebellion that had been quelled by one of his other brothers. Shocked by this, Dalassenus was efficiently exiled by John Orphanotrophus along with his faction of aristocrats. Though one obstacle was cleared by the two oldest Paphlagonians, more arose and would give a bad start to Michael's reign. As if one of the punishments of God the Byzantines always feared would occur, the prevalent Eastern famine remained in Byzantium and a high number of locusts destroyed trees and crops in the Anatolics promising starvation in 1035.

Added to this were the threats of the border regions falling to invasion as the Cibrrhyaeot city of Myra was invaded by the Arabs as Pecheneg raiders devastated up to Thessalonica. In a move towards independence from Byzantium, the Serbians of Dioclea under Stephen Voislav sought to oust the Byzantines from their kingdom. The Serbians mostly succeeded, even though the *Basileus* had to call on Serbia's Rascian, Bosnian, and Zachlumian neighbors to interfere.[1681] Finally, in Aleppo, the Emir expelled the Byzantine governor there and once again resisted, but these threats were met by a still able and vigorous army from Byzantium.

That same year, the Cibrrhyaeots were able to repel the Arabs raiding and pillaging the Thracian cities as more Arabs would be defeated by the client Duke of Vaspurakan at Pekri. Invasions at Edessa by Marwanid and Numayrid Arab armies would also fail in 1036 and surrender it to the East Romans the next year. A last concession by the Arabs was the city of Aleppo, back in Byzantine hands while the Fatimids renewed their ten-year truce. It was for these reasons that Psellus comments neither 'Egypt nor of Persia, nor even of Babylon' broke any treaty with Michael due to his bribes and strength of arms.[1682]

Fortunately for Byzantine interests, the Serbians fell back in line when threatened by the Pechenegs that were present in Thessalonica. Modern historians claim that it was here Michael IV's government instituted three simple measures to 'rationalize frontier defense':[1633]

1) Reduce the number of frontier garrisons.
2) Create south of the Danube a demilitarized zone without population or cultivation.
3) Finance merchant markets of agricultural and manufactured goods to reduce the need to raid.

---

[1681]  Ostrogorsky, 325f.

[1682]  Psellus, 98.

[1683]  Magdilano, 'The Medieval Empire (780-1204)', 183.

These measures had great success, but faded from interest around 1046 as the barbarians now had to deal with the Oghuz Turks, a splinter clan of the Oguz Yagbu who were vassals of the Seljuk Turks, settling in the eastern frontiers.

An excavation to Sicily was under way in 1038, but internal strife in the Palace threatened John's plans for the Empire. As he was the real power behind Michael's throne, he would face the hunger in Constantinople by importing Greek grain and handle nearly all other domestic matters. Mainly this was due to the *Basileus's* failing health and he would hear petitions in court, doing so surrounded by curtains that were drawn closed whenever he had an attack. Constant bodily pain from dropsy also limited his movement although he would still find the will to bravely attempt leading his soldiers personally into battle despite protest from his court and the Senate.

It was for these reasons and a failed attempt by Zoe to kill him in 1037 that induced John to press his brother into choosing a successor as there was no chance he would ever have a son. Psellus quotes a fascinating narrative 'conversation' that supposedly happened between John and Michael over the succession[1684] where John shows his talents of manipulating Michael with fear, gossip, and rebellion. The young Michael Calaphates, son of the *Basileus's* sister Maria and Stephen, a man who worked as a drungary worker caulking hulls with pitch, made a Sicilian admiral in 1035, was adopted as Michael IV's *Caesar* and heir at the Church of the Blacharnae. As for Stephen himself, he was not at all extraordinary as Psellus cleverly describes him as a 'pygmy playing Hercules . . .wearing a lion's skin, but being weighed down by the club.'

The *Basilia* Zoe had to approve of this as she was the rightful inheritor and was still loved among the people of Constantinople. This was titular only, of course, as Michael and his uncle John had no serious intention in sharing power. Rather than be a resident of the Palace among the court, Calaphates was sent away to live in the out skirting suburbs of the City. More intrigue followed as John tried to replace the Patriarch Alexius, but the cunning ecclesiastic reminded the Orphanotrophus that if he was invalidated on his dismissal all of his canons would be vacated – including the coronation of the past three *Basilii*! His hands tied by these circumstances, John reluctantly relented.

As for Sicily, in 1038, pirating raised the prices of imports as foreign trade across the East declined. Civil wars broke out between the ruler of Palermo al-Akhal who fought his brother Abu and his 6,000 African troops under the son of

---

[1684] Psellus, 98-100.

the Zirid Emir of Khairouan, appealed to the Empire and gave the opportunity for George Maniaces to take advantage. In the spring, George landed on the island with the *Basileus*'s Varangians that included Scandinavian and French Norse (or 'Normans') from the West. Maniaces captured Messina and raided successfully throughout the southwestern regions of Sicily. Near Maletto an abbey was founded for Maniaces's efforts, the Saint Maria de Maniace, which would be complimented by Queen Margaret of Navarre in 1173 and would become the Bronte estate by Lord Nelson (1788-1824) in 1799.[1685]

Another strong presence in Maniaces's Varangian host was the fascinating figure of Harold Hardrada, a Norse prince and Scandanavian folk hero known for conquering the northern Viking and Russian tribes short of the Volga. Sailing south, he made way to Russia serving Jaroslav of Kiev and later becoming a servant in Constantinople after a pilgrimage to Jerusalem. In the Holy City he was presented to Michael IV, agreeing to swear allegiance and serve as a guard for the *Basileus*. He then accompanied and led armies under Maniaces in the failed attempt to recover Sicily for the Empire from the Saracens using the new Varangian-Russian *Druzhina* ('Company').[1686]

The larger picture is noted by the future historian John Cecaumenus in his chronicles of the period being made clear how Romanus III intended to keep foreign elements at arm's length from imperial offices and honors. Though they 'served for bread and clothing' no Frank or Varangian was made a Patrician, Hypatus, or Stratiophylax.[1687] Hardrada was a break from this, marrying Jaroslav's daughter Elizabeth in 1041, becoming a Spartharocandidatus in Michael's service, and departing to die in 1066 at the Battle of Stamford Bridge in the Norman Conquest of England. Foreign Varangians were common in Byzantium as shown by caches of Danish coins found in the Byzantine style, a byproduct of Hardrada's influence over Medieval Scandinavian numismatics.[1688]

In 1040, Syracuse was taken by the general and made a fortress, but pay for the soldiers was a problem and the renegade mercenary Normans revolted on the Italian peninsula. Allying with former rebels in the region, they took Bari and Maniaces was unfortunately unable to correct this. He had been arrested and detained by the Orphanotrophus, in a show of inordinate strength, for

---

[1685] Norwich, (*APO*), 284-285f.

[1686] Vasiliev, 313.

[1687] John Cecaumenus. *Cecaumeni Strategikon et Incerti Scriptoris de Officiis Regiis Libellus, ed.* by B. Wassiliewsky and V. Jernstadt. St. Petersburg, Russia, 95-97. 1896.

[1688] Obolensky, 235.

conspiracy against the throne. Sicily was an especially vital territory in the West also as, to the Greeks residing there, Sicily was a birthright of the Byzantines and a matter of 'national security and national pride.'[1689]

Before all of this, the *Basileus*'s condition had grown much worse, already beginning to spend large amounts of time praying for his soul. He gave his pleas to God in the shrine of St. Demetrius in Thessalonica guided by the monk Cosmas Tzintzuluces who would convince him to tonsure himself in 1041. In 1039, he contrived a great act of charity in giving donatives to every priest, monk, and child in the Empire that called the *Basileus* their godfather. To recompense the imperial funds, John had taken to selling imperial offices to the wealthy and demanding in the *Basileus*'s name that the Empire's Bulgarian citizens stop paying taxes in kind and start doing so in cash. This, however, would prove to be a serious miscalculation as it induced the Bulgarians to rebel and take Belgrade, also making an imposter 'grandson' of Samuel, a Byzantine slave named Peter Delyan ('Dolianus' – the Treacherous), their new Bulgarian Tsar. In 1037, a Chyrophlax named Leo was made the Bulgarian Patriarch by Constantinople, but he was sternly rejected by the Bulgarian people, breaking Basil II's truce.

Heading south through Bulgaria, Peter captured Scopia after of which Michael charged with conspiracy his general, Duke Basil Synadenus of Dyrrachium. This caused the Bulgarians formerly fighting for Byzantium to rebel, choosing a rival *Basileus*, Tichomir, instead of following Delyan. Fearing, probably, a split that would lead him vulnerable to the Byzantines, Delyan offered an alliance of Bulgarians to fight for a homeland against Constantinople and the fickle Dyrrhacians stoned their rival to death to join Peter. Michael IV himself attended these battles even as he was in serious pain and the Senate encouraged him not to. An emboldened Peter led an attack on the Paphlagonian's train as it was returning to Constantinople, to tend to Michael's health, and his baggage was taken in an ambush, Sewter claiming the *Basileus* almost being killed at Salonica. Further south, Demetrias was taken and at Thebes, Peter defeated the Strategus of Hellas, recruiting Greeks from Nicopolis resentful of John's relentless tax collecting.

Rebels in the Anatolics allowed the Strategus of Theodosiopolis, Alusian, the son of Samuel's brother Aaron to head east and join Peter at Bulgaria to besiege Thessalonica. It was easy to do so as John Orphanotrophus imprisoned Alusian's wife after fining his property without a trial. He took Dyrrachium to

---

[1689] Norwich, (*APO*), 284.

the Gulf of Lepanto, but at the lead of 14,000 men,[1690] Alusian was defeated in September, 1041, returning to Peter who cut off his ears and blinded him with a kitchen knife. taking over the rebellion. Even though Alusian secretly surrendered to the Byzantines and was given a triumph of Bulgarian booty and a deformed Delyan, a revivified Bulgarian state was being led by its rightful heir as Tsar, a turnover in twenty years of what Basil II had succeeded in containing. In 1041, Michael and his troops marched to Mosynopolis to begin a new campaign, but the city was given up in exchange for a pardon for its leader as the revolt imploded. Michael cannot be credited by much of this as it was the Bulgarians fighting themselves that ruined their resolve.

Now came proof that Byzantine invincibility was wearing thin when Smbat-John of Ani finally died the next year, his nephew contesting the legal claim that the Empire had on Smbat-John's kingdom being their an inheritance. In Italy, the absence of Maniaces allowed the Arabs to retake Syracuse as the recalled general was at Bari fighting the Normans. After the Norman faction's leader came back to the Byzantine side, the Normans remained intractable in Byzantine Italy especially after capturing the Catepan. Perhaps emboldened by the Bulgarians, the Serbian prince of Dioclea once again expatriated as was done in 1035. At the end of this year, the Byzantine situation looked bleaker as its ailing *Basileus* was finally dying.

On December 10, 1041, Michael saw he would not live much longer and decided his last imperial act would be to give up on the material world. At his Church of the Anagyroi, Michael bade himself to the parishioners there that he was to be his living sacrifice to God. The purple silken raiments of his office were ceremoniously removed and they 'garbed him in the Mantle of Christ...And then they took from his head the diadem and put on the Helmet of Salvation (as said in the Epistle to the Ephesians, vi), armed his chest and back with the Cross and...let him go.'[1691]

Zoe begged to see her spurning lover one last time, but either because it was not considered holy or his guilt still haunted him, Michael refused. His sandals were not yet prepared, and he disdained the purple shoes of the *Basileus*, walking to the Church barefoot. Lying on a couch, he could no longer speak and his breathing was labored, at last finding peace and dying on that same day. John the Orphanotrophus showed his brotherly love thereafter by keeping vigil on

---

[1690]  Treadgold, 588-589.
[1691]  Psellus, 117.

Michael's body for three days after his death, convincing his scholars to claim that his grief was not manufactured and was indeed genuine.[1692]

Michael IV's rise to the throne could certainly be called scandalous, ascending from the cold-blooded murder of Romanus Argyrus, but he at least rose to the occasion and treated it as gravely as it needed to be. His wisest act, and one of the least popular, was ascending his brother as administer behind all affairs in Michael's stead. Michael has been called a tragic figure and even heroic for his brilliance of soul and weakness of body. Epilepsy was once known as a 'divine' disease that the first Caesars of Rome had, but in the monolithic throne of Byzantium this was a curse and not a blessing. The worst curse of all came from his reckless and spiteful nephew taking the throne next, miserably ending one of the best dynasties that never was.

One of the Paphlagonian's great ecclesiastical contributions to the City was his renovation of the old Church of the Anargyroi in the east side of Constantinople's middle-class suburbs. Built by Justinian I, it was named for two persecuted Christians, Sts. Cosmas and Damien, in the reign of Diocletian.[1693] They were physicians who did their work free of charge to their patients, Anargyroi meaning 'the unpaid ones' roughly. Michael adorned the building with new walls and chapels, fresh lawns, fountains, and even baths in its vicinity, but, tragically, it too has not survived to the present. Despite his eagerness to beautify God's houses, he did so from a guilt staining his soul. It is noted how apparitions and demons appeared before Michael and foretold his imperial future. Michael then struck a bargain with these beings in exchange for denying God. This was only a superstitious tale of the people, but it was clear how this 'denial of God' was his murder of the former *Basileus* as Christ's representative, seeking for the rest of his days absolution for his blasphemy.

He also had a passionate love for holy works and their ascetics, inviting many of these 'philosophers . . .that scorned the world' to the Palace. In true Christian fashion, he washed their feet in humility, held them close even if they bore sores of disease, and dressed in rags sleeping on a couch with a stone for a pillow as his imperial bed had been given to the monks. He went further by establishing a number of monasteries and nunneries throughout the Empire and the *Ptochotropheium* ('Hospice for Beggars') with a refuge for prostitutes.[1694] They were generously promised freedom from debt and want if

---

[1692] Norwich, (*APO*), 192.

[1693] *ibid.*, 281.

[1694] Psellus, 107.

they took the cowl of a nun. No one could say Michael the Paphlagonian was not a man of faith, but his prayers should have been more suited for his Empire than his own soul. Along with Psellus in the events of the Paphlagonian is a fellow eyewitness, Michael Attaleiates (1021-1080), who wrote from 1034 to 1078. As he was born of the military aristocracy in 1079, he dedicated his history to the soldier-*Basileus* Nicephorus III Botoneiates (1078-1081).[1695]

# MICHAEL V 'THE CAULKER'
## (1041-1042)

# THEODORA & ZOE
## (1042)

With the pious Michael now gone, the throne was now filled by a nephew of his with narrow prospects and empty promises. Though he was without scruple, the abilities of John Orphanotrophus would have made him a *Basileus* to be reckoned with, but it was almost a cruel twist of fate that he was a eunuch. So, John and the absentee *Basilia* had to settle for puppets they sought to control though this had limited success in the past. There was no success in it with the last of the Paphlagonians, even though he seemed an opportune choice at the time. His father had been Stephen, John's brother-in-law, who was made an admiral after a long career as a pitch caulker of ships in the navy, holding no known previous rank in the service. This is why history and the detractors of Michael V gave him the sobriquet of *Calaphates* ('Caulker').

What made him an ideal candidate for Zoe and John was his blandness and weakness of mind; Michael never filled a military post, any known profession, and had no possessions in land or chattel. He would be a titular *Basileus* only, being the face of the Empire, while Zoe was the legitimacy, and John was the brains of the royal power. Michael V was, at first, very obsequious, using flattery such as 'master', 'my mistress', and claiming himself as 'her servant' to Zoe. But this was a cunning facade as he harbored hatred for his family, John Orphanotrophus, the *Basilia*, and his unfortunate situation as a prop king. Perhaps John saw this smoldering resentment behind the fake smiles and honeyed words but did nothing as he underestimated him as a coward, which he usually was in the face of bad fortune.[1696]

---

[1695] Ostrogorsky, pg. 317.
[1696] Psellus, 123.

He was an angry and bitter young man who acted more than he thought; it is right to say his reign, when compared to his predecessor's, was more active, but less cautious.[1697] His revenge was final and without mercy as he exiled his uncles, except Constantine who hated John as much as he did, Michael making him a *nobilissimus* for that very fact. He failed to follow John's advice, even when it was good advice, and quickly by 1042 asserted that he was master of Byzantium beyond all others. He recalled not only the general George Maniaces, but Michael Cellarius who became Patriarch for eleven years. The noble Constantine Dalassenus he succeeded out of spite, although he had made a better alternative courtier than his uncles. His reign, however, was quite short at four months and eleven days before he became the only blinded and sitting *Basileus* since Constantine VI in 797. His fatal flaw was his ignorance of the people's love for a legitimate heir and a strong symbol of righteous power that made young and old generations of Byzantines appreciate the *Basilia* Zoe as a type of 'mother of her country.'

Michael V Calaphates was born in 1015 and held no posts or titles until his ascension as Michael the Paphlagonian's *Caesar* in 1037 by a desperate John Orphanotrophus who feared his brother's epilepsy. He was kept out of affairs in his own exile to the suburbs of Constantinople[1698] until December 11, 1041, when he finally rose to the throne. When Michael and the Orphanotrophus walked through the Chalke Gate after his coronation, the court and people still kissed his right hand in reverence but far more attention was given to his uncle as if they were 'to meet God himself.' This assuredly stoked the fire of the *Basileus*'s envy that he soon turned to resentment and, ultimately, wrath against his uncle.

In a slow process, the intentions of the *Basileus* became clearer as the weeks passed and his ire grew against the court aristocracy, publicly humiliating them, abusing them, threatening them, and disenfranchising them. In an act of astonishingly poor judgment, he dismissed the Varangians for 'Scythians' or eunuch Slavs to be his bodyguards.[1699] His support was on the people of the City, allowing them more privileges, but Machiavelli was right to say in doing so, a 'prince' bases his rule on mud as the fickle 'mob' would be the very people to end his brief reign.

He spurned and insulted his uncle by arranging meetings and then ignoring

---

[1697]  Treadgold, 589.

[1698]  Psellus, 102.

[1699]  Norwich, (*APO*), 294.

them to attend the Theater while John was made to look the fool by waiting on his nephew. He would praise his favorites at banquets for decisions made as if each parasite was a Magister, yet the methods employed by John were 'crafty bits of intrigue.' John, however, may have deserved this as just before he had drafted a document exempting himself with immunity should anyone else betray the throne, with Michael's signature. But the Caulker had the last laugh when he tricked the Orphanotrophus into an audience, picking him up at his estate by boat before he would consider an answer. Once on the Marmara, another ship intercepted the imperial vessel and John was arrested. By the *Basileus's* order, he was banished and tonsured at the Monastery of Monobatae. Early in 1043, the Patriarch Michael I Cerularius had John blinded and his brothers castrated to keep them from returning to Constantinople. On May 13, his brother Constantine was executed by Constantine Monomachus as a monk exiled to Lesbos, putting the finishing touch on the destruction of the feckless Paphlagonian 'dynasty'.

Michael V was now brimming with overconfidence as his horses were never without silk coverlets and he was never to tread on anything except carpets.[1700] His general Maniaces was sent north to deal with the Normans at Bari, who attempted to reclaim Byzantine territory, and the campaign was doing well. The *Basileus* saw only one obstacle left in his absolute rule – the *Basilia* Zoe. John was easy to betray and was not really missed as he created many enemies and hostility over taxation, so Calaphates suspected Zoe's exile would hardly be noticed as well. It was a serious miscalculation on the reckless *Basileus's* part and the end of Michael V's constant making of mistakes. John the Orphanotrophus would then be executed, the creator of his own destruction with a life of unscrupulousness.

On Sunday, April 18, the week after Easter, Michael had Zoe's head were shaved and sent to a nunnery on charges of trying to poison the *Basileus* (as it was known she had done so to Romanus Argyrus) for her natural life. She had already been restricted by the brash Caulker as she could not attend the Feasts and Holy Day festivals of the Palace as if he wished to damn her soul. Also, evidence exists that she did attempt to poison John Orphanotrophos using an assassin named Sgourtzes. Zoe was sent to Principo Island, quietly resigning herself to her fate as if it were expected. Although Norwich criticized her as weak, gullible, and not too intelligent, she had a presence of mind to preserve

---

[1700] Psellus, 132-133.

power. And only the imperial husbands who feared her true nature as a shrewd manipulator could hold her back with their restrictions.

That power was demonstrated on Monday, April 19 upon the announcement of her containment. She was still the daughter of an *Basileus*, as well as the most beloved niece of Basil II, and the people of Constantinople were outraged. Almost immediately they reacted to their anger and cried for Michael's blood. They were exhausted after the weak and brief rules of *Basilii* only bound to the throne by marriage. And now, the son of a mediocre admiral one minute who was only a dockworker a minute before was now attempting to seize power he hadn't deserved. Michael called an assembly of the Senate, but by then a mob had formed in the Forum of Constantine. Psellus describes how citizens of both sexes took up axes, trowels, anything that could be used as a weapon to make an unprecedented assault on the Palace.

Fires were set and buildings were torn down, even as the City's children helped, starting with that of the rich relatives of the Caulker. Special consideration was given to Constantine, the last brother of Orphanotrophus, who was seized and dragged away for punishment. During the chaos, the poor got revenge against their oppressors as the Palace was looted, Treasury items destroyed, and debt records were torn up.[1701] Oddly, the historian who recorded the most on what we have of this chaos may have been an Arab known as Ali'Izz al-Din ibn al-Athir al-Jazari (1160-1233).[1702] He tells how the former Patriarch Alexis escaped a trap set by the Caulker and after joined the mob set to destroy him.

In a panic, Michael had Zoe returned from exile that very day and they joined hands before the furious crowds in the Kathisma. 'Michael was taught that there is a period in which the patience of the tamest of slaves turn to fury and revenge.'[1703] The mob was undeterred in their furor as Zoe was a symbol of stability in uneven times when leadership was surely faltering. She would always have a place of safety, but Michael Calaphates had gone too far this time and he was not to be tolerated any longer despite his last minute attempts at reconciliations. He was seized, jeered at by the crowds, pelted with food and offal, and put on a mule to be humiliated in the Hippodrome. The women present were labeled as being as mad 'maenads', the creatures known for ripping men to pieces with their bare hands in Greek mythology.

---

[1701] Diehl, 131.

[1702] Norwich, (*APO*), 296. Al-Athir is declared as having Greek sources which are now lost.

[1703] Gibbon, 1645.

Psellus notes the 'mighty and mysterious unleashing of the mob soul' (*mega kai demosiotaton musterion*)[1704] and 3,000 people were bloodily killed in the streets in one day. They, led by Catacalon Cecaumenus (son of the historian) who fought at Messina when the Arabs retook Sicily, seized the *Basileus* from the Augusteum, through the Chalke Gate, past the *Tsykanisterion,* a horse stable built by the Macedonian house's founder, Basil I.[1705] On Tuesday, April 20, 1042, Michael and his uncle Constantine attempted to escape by way of the Buceleon harbor to the Psamatia district of the Marmaran Wall, but were caught. They were sent to the nearby Monastery of the Studites by Alexis to be blinded, castrated, and tonsured. Michael was said to be a wailing coward at this point, yet he showed some character in taking his share of the responsibility in the crimes he committed and accepted it as just, but his uncle was made of sterner stuff. He defiantly told the executioner: 'Make these people stand back and you shall see how bravely I bear my calamity . . .Look here. When you see me budge, you may nail me to the stake!'[1706]

So Constantine did not move an inch as they blinded him with burning irons and he was sent as a monk to Samos. The once Michael V was sent to the Monastery of the Eleimon on Chios to die on the 24th of August, 1042. Professor James Bury claims that Michael was a 'radical reformer' and deserves some credit as being ambitious and far-sighted. But, other historians paint a portrait of a creature of bitter spite that wanted enemies gone rather than be a giver of justice to clear out the corruption of the State. The only good he did was appoint able men to vital posts such as Michael Cerularius, George Maniaces as the Italian Catepan, and the classicist Constantine Lichudes as Chamberlain when Michael Psellus would finally arrive as a Secretary of the court.[1707]

As this was happening, thoughts of the future succession were being made by Constantinople and the court. The *Basilia* Zoe was now safely out of her monastic life and on the throne as she should have been, though some of the Byzantine mob had different ideas about her legitimate leadership. Constantine VIII, after all, had another legitimate daughter who could have lived along her sister. In 1031, Theodora, the younger daughter of the last Macedonian

---

[1704] Diehl, 131.

[1705] Norwich, (*APO*), 299.

[1706] Psellus, 150.

[1707] Ostrogorsky, 316.

was forcibly cloistered by Romanus Argyrus in a monastery for 'intrigues and scandals'. Now, in the chaos following Michael V's dethronement, a faction led by the Patrician Constantine Cabasilas were setting sail to Theodora's convent in Petrion.

It was certainly against her will, but she was taken back to Constantinople and crowned in St. Sophia by the Patriarch on the 19th of April. She was now sixty-two and described as wrinkled, but with smooth skin, taller, more congenial, more sociable, and quicker of tongue and of mind than her sister Zoe while being still deeply religious. Zoe herself was beautiful and a charmer of prospective imperial suitors with her golden hair, large eyes, and an aquiline nose at sixty-four years,[1708] also having a generous nature. Theodora was bitterly opposed to Michael V and saw the plight the City was going through, taking action as the niece of Basil II and the *Basilia* of Byzantium. She promised her nephew and Constantine both safe passages to the Palace, but the mobs disagreed and led by the City Eparch Campanarus, they sent the forces by ship to intercept Michael's return.

Zoe was, understandably, jealous of her sister's new powers as she had held the crown uncontested for fourteen years under three *Basilii*. Along with this difficulty, the Senate had trouble deciding who took precedence as Zoe was older, but Theodora was chosen by the mob and her ascension had abruptly ended the revolts in the City. It also did not help that this was likely done by the infamous Green and Blue factions of the City that always divided public opinion, anyway. But, shrewdly, Zoe saw the need to stop the divisions in the City first and embraced her sister as an unprecedented 'co-*Basilia*', Zoe being the superior of the two in rank. As Norwich well puts it, Zoe must have figured 'It was better to reign as joint-*Basilia* than not reign at all.'[1709]

In the year following, they ran the civil and military affairs of the Empire through the Senate and an advisory staff. On coinage they were displayed together as equals sharing the imperial scepter and wearing identical diadems.[1710] Zoe liberally gave donatives to the army and nobles to buy their alliance as was done many times in the past. They dismissed certain officials, promoted others, and made illegal the buying of offices, a growing corruption in the system. Yet, Psellus puts it that as the two sisters had two distinct personalities

---

[1708] Psellus, 158.

[1709] Norwich, (APO), 300.

[1710] Treadgold, 591.

and neither had the ability to rule alone,[1711] these perceptions troubling the men who made clear the fact that the *Basiliai* wished to rule alone. This must have stirred the traditional ancient Greek misogyny and its fear of 'a rule of women' (*gyneokratia*) with no male figurehead. Zoe was stern and solemn, not approachable and intimidating; Theodora was a public face with her abilities to talk (perhaps too much) and be accessible, but was less serious.

Unfortunately, this meant that Zoe mainly drew sycophants and parasites around her that flattered and kept her separate from the real issues of State. Theodora was said to be more self-controlled by funds, but to a point that she lacked the proper temperament to rule. By the summer of 1042, the Senate gently, yet sternly, made it implicit that either one or the other must marry and put a man on the throne. Zoe, as the dominant *Basilia*, set about this business as she also had experience in choosing imperial suitors. After much deliberation she settled on a Catepan named Constantine Artoclinas, but he died from a fever just after the announcement. The next choice was Constantine, the son of Theodosius Monomachus, a noble from Dalassa who had been exiled to Metyline by Michael IV, returning with the changing political climate. On June 10, Constantine was given the imperial regalia and crowned in Damocrania at the Church of St. Michael the Archangel. Psellus notes that Zoe and Constantine were married by the Patriarch on June 11, 1042 in the Church of the Nea (although Sewter claims it was merely by a priest known as Stypes).

It has been an error of historians such as Edward Gibbon that the era between Constantine VIII and the rule of the two *Basiliai* was the period of the 'caprice of two impotent females.' Others note it as a 'Time of Troubles' for Byzantium, blaming Zoe and her poor decisions in imperial husbands. But, contemporary women's historians in Byzantine Studies are quick to defend the two and remind scholars of their unique powers. They present their case from the writings of Psellus, especially, that '. . .Zoe and Theodora were not simply performing acts of imperial renovation by legitimizing *Basilii*; they were acting as the figuratively embodiment of power themselves in Byzantium.'[1712]

Judith Herrin in her works *Byzantium* and *Women in the Purple* contribute that along with Theodora in the sixth century and Irene in the ninth, Zoe and Theodora evidently shaped imperial power despite male chronicles written by

---

[1711] Psellus, 157.

[1712] Niyogi, Ruma. 'Gender, Politics, and Imperial Legitimacy in Byzantium, 1028-1057'. Presented at *The Twenty-Seventh Annual Byzantine Studies Conference.* (South Bend, IN: University of Notre Dame, November, 9-11, 2001).

Cedrenus or Skylitzes centuries later. Also, they were bolstered vehemently by the crowds of loyal inhabitants of Constantinople, so these were, in a sense, the City and the *Basilii* they chose. They were also raised and schooled in Byzantine traditions such as court ceremony and philanthropic customs from an early age from their uncle and father. They were rightly said to maintain the Macedonian line of *taxis* ('order') to the throne with strength and stability.

## CONSTANTINE IX MONOMACHUS
(1042-1055)

## THEODORA
(1055-1056)

At the age of forty, Constantine Monomachus's fortunes had shifted from once being an exiled prisoner to becoming *Basileus* of Byzantium. As the *Basilia* Zoe was always one to praise looks over ability, she chose a man with handsome features, intimidating eyebrows, golden hair, and a strong body seemingly clear of disease, described as being as 'fresh as spring fruit'. Also excelling in conversation that easily charmed the unwary Zoe, he had no false pride or boastfulness, was approachable to his people and not overly formal, and had a pleasingly sardonic attitude towards bad news. His arms were strong and robust, easily crushing objects with his bare hands, possessing an iron grip. Finally, his attractive smile, cultured speech, and charming conversation fascinated all who met him.[1713]

Once again, he was thought to be a minimum danger to the throne who would let the imperial sisters make state decisions as a puppet. He was noted by historian contemporaries Michael Attaleiates, John Cecaumenes, and the thirteenth-century John Skylitzes as being dangerously ignorant of military affairs, disbanding valuable Armenian Tagmas in 1053, exposing the Eastern frontier at its most vulnerable with 'catastrophic harm.'[1714] Also, it is a fact that during the most controversial religious phenomenon of the Orthodox Church, the Great Schism of 1054, he simply melded into the background and never held a leash on his Patriarch, Michael Cerularius. 'Pretty books', 'pretty poems',

---

[1713] Psellus, 220-221.
[1714] Treadgold, *(BAIA)*, 80; Attaleiates, Michael. *History. CSHB*, ed. by Immanuel Bekker. Bonn, Germany, 44-45. 1853; John Cecaumenus. *Strategicon*, ed. by G.G. Latrivin. Moscow, Russia. 152-154. 1972.

and 'pretty churches and chapels' were not enough to clear this imperial reign of the irresponsibility and vices of Constantine Monomachus. On the day of his coronation, quotes John Skylitzes, the decay of the Roman Empire began in earnest and a slippery slope was created, declining to the numerous crises of Skylitzes's thirteenth-century Empire.[1715]

However, he did not allow himself to be a mere figurehead and made several controversial decisions. One of the most scandalous was his packing of the Senate where he lifted most restrictions and allowed even the most common of men to be Senators, decentralizing the imperial power.[1716] Yet, the senatorial class was progressively shrinking anyway by this time as the well-born (*Eugenes*) were denying service and intermarriage of the orders until fewer families remained[1717] as what was said to have happened in ancient Sparta. New blood was needed, even though the price to the throne was high.

Constantine IX also imposed costly salaries to certain titleholders, making them transferable to other bestowed titles, although this may have earned him the moniker *Eugeretes* ('Benefactor'), shared by the Pharaoh Ptolemy III (284BCE-222BCE) in 222 BCE. This nickname was a negative connotation, however, as he gave these titles quite liberally, meaning the buying of offices, at least, became obsolete. But it threatened to empty a stable treasury and expose the noble class to its worst cronyism in imperial history. However, he needed many of these offices filled as he first spent time cleaning the parasitic relatives of Michael Calaphates from their stations.

Another scandal arose in his private life as Constantine and his marriage to the *Basilia* Zoe was practically a moot point as Monomachus kept a kind of a second 'wife' in a Georgian mistress of the Sclerina clan. Zoe accepted the *ménage a trios* (also known as the 'loving cup')[1718] agreeably without jealousy, perhaps realizing her limitations as a royal wife not being able to produce an heir. Constantine would have made things official, but it would have been a third marriage forbidden by the Patriarch even though his second marriage related him to the late Romanus III Argyrus. Constantine set her up in a manor close to the Palace and visited her frequently until her death of pulmonary disease in 1047, wherein the *Basileus* was inconsolable.

Another event of his reign was the activity and tonsure of Constantine

---

[1715] Jenkins, 345.

[1716] Ostrogorsky, 342.

[1717] Herrin, 225.

[1718] Norwich, (*APO*), 308.

(Michael) Psellus, who wrote his history of the beloved Monomachus with the encouragement of his philosophers and theologians. His portrayal is nearly idealized, going so far as to 'apostrophize' the *Basileus* with the title of 'divine soul.'[1719] His exaggeration of bias is amazing and face value should be lightly tread upon, although it is highly entertaining and rich in its anecdotes. He also made the classicist Constantine Lichudes his *Mesazon* (Manager)[1720] and would include him in his new University with Xiphilinus of Trebizond. Late in Constantine's reign, Psellus would take up the monk's habit and the name Michael to spend his life at the Monastery of Mount Olympus where his *Chronographia* was made.

Constantine Monomachus (roughly translated as 'He Who Fights Alone' or 'Gladiator') was born in Dalessa[1721] to an illustrious noble family around the year 1000. His father was Theodosius, an officeholder under the latter Macedonians once implicated in a plot against Basil II and Constantine VIII, somewhat marring the family name. He had a quaint popularity and seemed a threat to Michael IV, thus being purged into exile on the island of Lesbos in the 1030's. Before this time, Constantine married as his second wife the daughter of Pulcheria Argyrus, sister of the former *Basileus* Romanus III, strengthening his own position as an imperial relative, yet it was his notorious mistress Maria Sclerina that followed him into exile.[1722] It is likely he was still married to Pulcheria's daughter as he still did not marry Sclerina. After he became *Basileus* on June 11, 1042, Sclerina manipulated him into deposing the Empire's best general, George Maniaces, the Catepan of Italy, as the Sclerinae were bitter enemies of this military leader.

Of course, showing no character for the good of the army, being the puppet of his lover, Constantine IX immediately appointed an inferior and distrusted new Catepan of Italy. On March 9, 1044, in fact, Pulcheria was the cause of a riot at the Church of the Holy Martyrs from which the *Basileus* barely escaped; the rioters were known for shouting declamations at Sclerina and hailing the imperial *Maimas* (Mothers) Zoe and Theodora.[1723] In 1042, Byzantine military prowess suffered as the Archon of Dyrrachium led seven Strategoi and 40,000 men to annihilation in Bulgaria, so, clearly Monomachus was starting his reign with a weak foundation.

---

[1719] Sewter, 170f.

[1720] Treadgold, 591.

[1721] Psellus, 160.

[1722] Treadgold, 592.

[1723] Norwich, (*APO*), 309.

Since George Maniaces's return as Catepan in April of 1042, the Normans under Roger Guiscard had control of Melfi and Aversa, leading revolts from Apulia to Brundisi. Maniaces was known for his cruelty in this matter, slaughtering nuns, priests, the elderly, men, women, and children with hangings, be-headings, and live burials. Maniaces was blamed for the failure at Edessa and was thus deposed with the help of Sclerina whose brother had been an enemy of his since 1031 when they lived in Anatolia. But this outrage only emboldened Maniaces to retreat to Bari, where he declared himself *Basileus*, allying himself with the notorious rebel-turned-officer Argyrus.

From all parts of the Empire, men of military age, be they youths or old men, flocked to the banner of Maniaces.[1724] To return to Constantinople, they sailed to Dyrrhacium in 1043 and the local armies capitulated hastily to Maniaces so they could be at his right hand rather than in his path. The *Basileus* himself defended the Walls with a force led by a loyal eunuch as he, like Basil II before him, had lost his faith in his generals. The imperial army headed south through Thessalonica, meeting Maniaces at Ostrovo as this would be a fateful battle for the rebel general as he received a spear wound to the side that bled out and proved fatal. Now the rebels quickly dispersed and Constantine would have a Triumph in his capital with George's head impaled on a stake in the Grand Theater and a procession at the Chalke Phylake to a church built by John Tzimisces.[1725]

It was only a small respite, as soon after the news of Ostrovo arrived at court, an unexpected naval force by the Russians approached the City. Capitalizing on the revolt of George Maniaces, they demanded a bribe of 400,000 *nomismata* dividing 1,000 troops to each of his 400 ships.[1726] Constantine refused this effrontery and the Russian fleet attacked the Bosporus only to face a massive defeat to the Greek fleet of Basil Theodorocranus and more Greek Fire (an old tactic to deal with Russian ships), killing no less than 15,000 Russians as they fled to the Black Sea. Although none of these victories could ever be attributed to Monomachus, he still gained unwarranted credibility as a *Basileus* that could deal with the enemy. Constantine IX would use this momentum in the next campaigning year to bring order to the eastern territories for Byzantium.

Earlier the King of Ani had died, leaving the kingdom to the Empire as he promised, but, once again, a nephew of the King defied the arrangement

---

[1724] Psellus, 193.

[1725] *ibid.*, 198.

[1726] Treadgold, 492.

and kept the Byzantines out. In 1044, the *Basileus* sent forces to reclaim this legal right, allying with the Shaddadin Arabs of the nearby city of Dvin. In 1045, the Empire succeeded and added Armenia to the imperial Iberian region; Constantine followed this up by turning on his Arabic allies at Dvin, but in failing he gained territory but lost face before his army. Small but important events were also happening in the Vaspurakan as the Seljuk Turks of the larger Oghuz Turkish nation in central Eurasia were attacking imperial territory after years of harassing the Ghaznaevid tribes settled there.[1727]

These Turkish tribes defeated the Tagma armies under their founder, Seljuk, and captured their Duke. The Turks had been on the scene of the East for a while before 1045 but were considered minor threats to be ignored by the Byzantines who were usually busy either with the West, the Arabs of Aleppo, North Africa, or their own internal strife. Constantine IX did send his armies east, but to Dvin fighting former allies, once again ignoring the rising Turkish problem. The shortsighted folly of the throne would be clear in a decisive defeat on the field of Manzikert in 1071. By 1053, Constantine's miscalculations about the Turks cost the Empire the Upper Euphrates when he demobilized Armenia, wrongfully believing their raids could not threaten Anatolia.[1728]

In 1046, as Constantine fought at Dvin, some 20,000 Pecheneg refugees under their chieftain, Kegen, entered the Danube pressured by yet another Turkish tribe known as the Uzes settling in the West. In another miscalculated risk, Monomachus's plan to turn the Turks and Pechenegs against one another to divide their forces backfired and only land and title grants mollified these hostile barbarians.[1729] With some desperation, however, other clans of the Pechenegs joined the Byzantine ranks of the legions and aided them against the armies of the Pecheneg rival Tyrach, totaling 100,000 soldiers. Those from the Danube that were basically bought off by the *Basileus* were put in Bulgarian districts and given Danubian fortresses for appeasement's sake. Around 800,000 of the Pechenegs made it south to raise settlements from the Danube region as told by Cedrenus's history.[1730]

The Duke of Adrianople, Arianites, still defeated them and Constantine decided to make for once friends rather than enemies. Perhaps he was following the gist of Constantine VII's advice on handling Pechengs with delicacy, rather

---

[1727]  Beckwith, 168-169.

[1728]  Treadgold, *(BAIA)*, 217.

[1729]  Magdalino, 'The Medieval Empire (780-1204)', 183.

[1730]  Cedrenus, 585; Vasiliev, 325-326.

he read him or not. The Pechenegs were disarmed and baptized as Christians to populate the sparse region north of Serdica, forced settlement being a 400-year-old practice revived by Monomachus. To keep the Russians pacified, Constantine married a daughter of his to the Kievan prince, Jaroslav. Their son was born in 1053 as Vladimir Monomakh who would bring prosperity and educated enlightenment to Kiev on par with King Alfred the Great of England in the ninth century.[1731]

In September 1047, more disaster struck as the Western armies rebelled under Leo Tornices, a descendant of Armenian royalty, and on Friday, September 25, he was camped outside of Constantinople. He won over the populace by the superficial processes of bribery and promises of tax remissions in which he held no authority to administer.[1732] He was later caught and tonsured, only to be moved by rebels to Adrianople where he was proclaimed *Basileus* when he promised to again remit taxes. It is said by Sewter's notes in Psellus's *Chronographia* that this was due to the dismissal of Gagil II from Armenia and the ending of an affair with Euprepia, Monomachus's sister. Also, in his heady 'Macedonian arrogance' to be 'Leo VII' he claimed a legal right on the spot to marry the younger *Basilia* Theodora in order to become legitimate![1733]

It was such pride that lost Tornices any such claim, as he had inadequate funds to pay his troops and expected the gates of Constantinople to be opened for him on his arrival from Thrace by the 27th. As Constantine had recalled soldiers from Armenia to rally, they could comfortably wait the usurper out even as arrows were shot at the battlements, one of which barely missed Constantine's head by inches. Tornices fled to Adrianople, besieging the city of Rhaedestus in October as the Eastern Tagmatic armies fell on the fugitives to buy the loyalty of the rebels to cast Leo out. He took refuge in a church, but this did not save him from capture and blinding on Christmas Day of 1047 along with his adviser and friend, John Vatatzes.

The following year, the Turks were making themselves known more and more by invading Iberia, where afterwards they were, for once, defeated at the Vaspurakan, the Turks having been captured by the Duke Cecaumenus. In an almost immediate turnover, however, the Turks heavily defeated Cecaumenus at Artze, prompting the *Basileus* to desperately recruit 15,000 Pecheneg mercenaries from Serdica. Unpredictable as ever, they mutinied and dispersed as soon as

---

[1731] Obolensky, 225.

[1732] Psellus, 209.

[1733] Sewter, 205f.

they reached the Bosporus, deciding to squat in the Preslav region of former Bulgaria. Beyond Constantine's reach, they pillaged Thrace from their intractable position even as Kegen was arrested. As this situation was the immediate threat to the borders, and possibly the interior, Constantine tied his loose ends in 1049. Constantine made peace with the Turks and Shadaddids to focus the Tagmas towards Preslav. This Turkish peace was brought about by the successes of the Varangians and mercenaries of the Ethnarch, Nicephorus Bryennius.

It proved a disaster as twice the Byzantine forces were defeated and the Domestic of the East was killed. Constantine released Kegen in 1050 to negotiate a treaty with the Pechenegs, but not only did they refuse, they executed their once chieftain and all of his embassadors. This year also saw a monumental change in the Palace as the *Basilia* Zoe died at seventy-two in June. She was a continuing force on the Byzantine throne and one of the last links the people had to what seemed a golden age (even as it began to tarnish) under the Macedonians.

The king-maker of four *Basilii* from 1028 until her death, she was also seen as the equal of these rulers if the mosaic of Saint Sophia depicting her and Monomachus offering tribute to Christ is correct. In this particular depiction, the equality of positions was always seen as correct as Constantine's head had been whitewashed over both Romanus III's and Michael IV's heads, both whitewashed by Michael V, as Zoe's head in the frescoes only changed in age and not stature.[1734] With Theodora the only Macedonian left, her commitment to keep the chastity of a nun's cowl was a clear sign that a seventy-year line of prosperity was ending.

Over the next two years, diplomatic relations with the Empire was heavily active when in 1051, mercenaries from all over the border peoples were filling the imperial ranks. This proved unwise as the loyalty of such an army was merely a house of cards if and when pay dried up. It collapses and leaves Byzantium vulnerable such as in the theories of mercenaries in military science as claimed by Niccolo Machiavelli centuries later. In Italy, the conveniently loyal Argyrus was made Catepan as he was the only choice in an empty barrel. He would repel the Norman forces with the alliance of a skeptical Papacy (at least until 1054). Hasty truces were made in 1052 with the Pechenegs and the Arab houses of Armenia and Aleppo were made a client-buffer state to battle the Turks on the eastern borders. The Principate of Dioclea brokered a peace, although failed to receive client status.

---

[1734] Magdalino, 'The Medieval Empire (780-1204)', 182.

In 1053, an exasperated Constantine IX withdrew twenty percent of the army from Armenia, known as the 'Iberian Army', to levy heavy taxes on 12,000 new civilians replaced by mercenaries and Varangians. The disarmament of these five particular Themes[1735] was a sampling to measure the financial burdens of the state after such heavy military activity in Armenia by releasing to civilian status these 50,000 soldiers in thirty-one Themes. Of course it is to be noted that according to modern estimates, 250,000 men made up the Tagmatic armies before this withdrawal.[1736]

A good case can be put together that perhaps it was Byzantine *xenophobia* Constantine beheld as a reason for distancing the Armenians. But the better argument was the 'suggestions' noted that the peasant-soldiers could contract out of military service for a fee[1737] in attempts to strengthen the flagging Western frontier that was in less dire straits than that of the East. In the West, stability was once again in trouble as the Catepan Argyrus was defeated by the Normans on July 17, these invaders seizing Pope Leo IX at Civitatae and holding him at Benevento, where he died the following April. The Turks were also subjugating the Aleppines to their vassalage, invading Kars as the Sultan Tughurl personally raided Armenia, Iberia, the Vaspurakan, Taron, and Perkri before turning south towards Cappadocia. Unfortunately, more absentee leadership came from the Byzantine throne as Constantine did nothing concerning these developments while also shunning his responsibilities in the Schism of the Two Churches in 1054.

But it is suggested that this was due to the *Basileus*'s chronic illness of debilitating gout that crippled his body with a serious arthritis that deformed his limbs and back, a dire development for a man known for Pentathlon victories at the Games.[1738] It destroyed the hands that could injure a man's arm with a squeeze, his stomach also suffering diarrhea and 'putrefication'. His tongue and eyes were failing him quickly as his 'humors' were without balance. He had to almost daily show himself to the crowd in the City from a distance to prove that he was still alive. By 1054, death was imminent and a successor was sought by both the Postal Logothete and the Duke of Bulgaria, Nicephorus Proteuon, before Monomachus was even dead.

The Logothete and Duke attempted to circumvent the wishes of the *Basilia* Theodora, but were dejected. As it had become a habit of Constantine IX to lie

---

[1735] Leontocome, Coptus, Abara, Sebastea, and Lycandus-Taranta were the five Themes. Treadgold, (*BAIA*), 81-83.

[1736] Treadgold, 595.

[1737] Jenkins, 346.

[1738] Psellus, 259-260.

in a hot bath for hours at a time to soothe his feet and joints, he did so one day, only to catch a chill as pleurisy inflamed his lungs. On January 11, 1055, he was said to have died 'cursing his fate,' though the author, Michael Psellus was not an eyewitness to this. Constantine IX Monomachus was buried next to his beloved Sclerina in the Church of the Magnaura that he had built.

Constantine Monomachus was neglectful, hedonistic, selfish, and craven before vital domestic issues within the Empire. He was known for squandering the fisc on extravagant and expensive luxuries for his Sclerina. He was yet another cog in the machine of irresponsible and shameful government that was becoming the norm after Basil II's death. This appeared at an era when the stereotypical Byzantine tyrant was a reality: opulently luxurious, surrounded by eunuchs more fit for the throne, cruel and despotic to the point of megalomaniacal, and whose incompetence shook the very foundation of the Empire as it was being undermined by slow decay. But few *Basilii* were purely bad as Monomachus was also not so as he was a devout patron of the Church and a lover of education. He would build grand churches and universities where able teachers would instruct in philosophy and the seven liberal arts as well as in Roman law.

Constantine IX did build a few churches in Byzantium to appease God and the iron will of Cerularius, once a conspirator against Michael IV. In Chios, he built the Church of the Nea Mone as a monastery as well as his prized accomplishment, the Church of Saint George of the Magnaura. This church was built next to the City mansion of Maria Sclerina and in 1045 Constantine went about a reformed policy on the monastery of the 'Holy Mountain' of Athos. The population of this fast-expanding monastery increased due to an influx of pilgrims who were affected by the famines of a fast-expanding Empire.[1739]

Brothers from Serbia, Croatia, Georgia, Benedictine Amalfi, Bulgaria, Armenia, and Russia came to Athos and its surrounding communities in Panteleemon, Zographou, and Hilandar. Constantine saw the dangers of such expansion and was, for once, quick to act as Athos already faced factional plotting, non-canonical acts, worldliness, and the illegal succession of under-age boys and eunuchs to high posts. The issues addressed by the monastery's Charter also included the use of monastic boats for commercial purposes, receiving wages for the cutting of firewood and lumber to be sold locally, and the older problem of the temptations of young boys and eunuchs to the monks.

---

[1739] Herrin, 199.

Yet, one problem escaped notice in Monomachus's benefits of imperial taxation of any Bishopric property that the throne could exempt or choose not to.

Perhaps Monomachus's greatest achievement, or most lasting, was the rehabilitation of buildings in Jerusalem after the devastating earthquake of 1033, destroying its Byzantine walls and Arab palaces. He began the project of rebuilding the Holy Sepulcher the brutish al-Hakim disassembled, finishing the holy feat in 1048. It could hold a capacity of 8,000 people and was best described by a visiting Persian pilgrim, Nasir-i-Kusrau Qubadyana Balkhi (1004-1088), marveling at its colored marbles and the famed Byzantine gold brocade designed with pictures. Ironically, the persecutions of all the religions in Jerusalem by Hakim sparked a widespread pilgrimage to the Holy City. In a population of 20,000, it was 20,000 Muslims that would make pilgrimage to Jerusalem instead of Mecca annually to the Temple on the Mount as would Jews from France and Italy. Perhaps most interesting was the fallout from the Schism of 1054 which inspired Eastern Greeks and Western Franks to travel there in a holy pursuit.[1740]

Without doubt, the Great Schism was the most significant ecclesiastical event of Monomachus's reign when the Churches of West and East split Christianity in 1054. There were always, of course, religious and cultural differences between the two Empires. Orthodoxy was less restrictive by allowing clerical marriage, using leavened bread (*zymos*) in their Eucharist which Catholicism did not (using *azyme,* unleavened bread).[1741] There were also the disagreements over the dual nature of the Holy Spirit from the Photian Schism and the practice of fasting on the Sabbath that old Rome practiced but Constantinople did not. Even Constantine's pleas for political relations and requests to revive Byzantium in the commemorative diptychs[1742] without attacking Rome did no good in overcoming the endangering differences between the two Christianities.

As the Byzantines were accustomed to silken and linen robes modeled after Oriental courts, the Germans preferred the trousers of their ancestors. The Papacy found the use of the fork in eating abhorrent as, for example, simple kitchen cutlery was seen as especially depraved by eleventh-century Popes, though it was popular in Venice. The use of eunuchs as notaries and commanders galled the West as well as the constant theological arguments

---

[1740] Montefiorre, 209-210.

[1741] Herrin, 45-46.

[1742] Jenkins, 358.

rationally holding accountable the Nature, the Sacraments, and the very tenants of the Christian faith. Cheese (but not meat) was eaten on the week before Lent by the Orthodox as the West observed Fasting days where the Byzantines ate with garlic, leeks, onions, and oils.

Going further, Byzantium even went so far as to educate their women as they luxuriated in clean, hot baths and scented rooms! The real head came to a boil when Rome started to forcibly exert their version of the Eucharist on the Byzantine citizens of southern Italy. Untrue accusations were made by the West that Orthodoxy forbade Mosaic law, communion from shaven priests, baptizing Latins, and they were also charged with hypocritical charges of simony and other crimes. The worst aspect was the stereotypes typical of the period of Byzantines to the West, prompting the histories that blackened the field of Byzantinism for centuries thereafter.

Michael Cerularius then took a stand for Byzantium against the Papal legates 'preaching' the infamous *Donation of Constantine*.[1743] So, on behalf of the stern and conservative Cardinal Humbert of Mourmourtiers from Italy, this was responded to by excommunicating the Patriarch. In April, 1054, Humbert Archbishop Peter of Amalfi and Cardinal Frederick of Lorraine (the future Pope Stephen IX) appeared at Constantinople. Constantine welcomed them warmly,[1744] but Cerularius excommunicated them after months of argument in the Hagia Sophia on July 16. Cerluarius was devout, but a disaster; balanced speculations claim that under the auspices of Basil II some good might have been done, but Constantine was weak and indolent enough that Cerularius was allowed more than enough rope in which for him to hang.[1745]

On July 18th the prelates returned to the West and the Great Schism was in certain effect, although as the legates present had no Papal authority, it is certain that the Bull of Excommunication that officiated the Schism was invalid.[1746] It is claimed that not all communion between the two were severed, though now the alliances between the two Emperors were irreparably lost, endangering future military endeavors. Attempts at Lyons in the thirteenth century, Florence in the fifteenth, and the Second Vatican Council of 1965[1747] to heal this breach failed. Cerularius himself lived until 1056, railing against

---

[1743] Vasiliev, 338.

[1744] Norwich, *(AM)*, 98.

[1745] Jenkins, 357.

[1746] Norwich, *(AM)*, 99. Sir Steven Runciman would also be shocked how one theological document such as the Bull would be so full of errors!

[1747] Norwich, *(APO)*, 322.

the temporal government as the *Basilia* Theodora dismissed several Bishops from service. But rather than purely ecumenical differences being the true cause of the Schism, it was the differences in lay life that did so – intellectual, political, and cultural, making these rifts and any appearance of a unified Church illusory. Also, as the challenges to the Orthodox Church by sectarian and independent Slavic states made unity a moot point and Rome had sought the Western Church as the true Christianity.[1748]

In economic policy, Constantine IX did little better than as a moderator for the Churches. He was previously noted as debasing the currency in the Empire to a mere eighteen percent in the golden *nomismata*. As can be guessed, these heavier and more impure coins inflated prices, also cutting payrolls and taxes which collectors could not balance in their receipts. This was an innovation by Constantine to cut the pay of the soldiers in the imperial Themes as well as the gold *tetrateron*, a gold coin lighter than, but supposedly equivalent to, the *nomisma*. This only confused the standards of weight and purity even more with the gold coin at seventy-three percent purity over the ninety-two percent gold that existed in 1025.[1749] The armies dismissed and demobilized from Armenia were now on inactive duty and pay was cut lower than the unpredictable pay scales of active duty soldiers from the Themes with a reduction to seven *nomismata*, a scale unseen since Theophilus in 842.[1750] Such reduction had not been attempted by a *Basileus* since Nicephorus Phocas, and its misdirection was harmful enough that the *Basilia* Theodora appointed an entirely new finance minister after Monomachus's death.

Psellus also notes how Constantine spent much of the budget on pleasing his mistress Sclerina.[1751] He sent her bronze caskets loaded with gold pieces and never left her without costly sweet Indian herbs, dwarf olives, and white bays. He was also quite pliable to sad stories of those who stole funds as they had great debt; he once paid the debt of a noble of this situation merely on a pretense of a few tears. He lavished presents on favorites and those he would bribe to be popular, including Romanus Boilus, a court fool the *Basileus* set up with his own estate, but plotted to kill in 1049.

One area that cannot be disputed he found important was education, all to the benefits of the bureaucracy and posts of the Empire. Psellus would lament

---

[1748] Ostrogorsky, 335.

[1749] Treadgold, (*BAIA*), 40f.

[1750] *ibid.*, 156.

[1751] Psellus, 183, 185-186.

how Byzantium was in a 'silver age' where no great poets or artists could be found in '. . .Athens, nor Nicomedia, nor Alexandria in Egypt, nor Phoenicia, nor even the two Romes . . .' Also, quality notaries (*notarioi*) and suitable lawyers (*synogeroi*) were needed in large supply to handle the growing burden of jurisprudence in the Empire.[1752] So in 1045, Monomachus reformed the entire University in Constantinople by offering the talented office of *Nomophylax* ('Professor of Law') to Psellus's instructor, John Mauropous of Paphlagonia. It was a requirement that the legal instructors under Xiphilinus be of good academic stock as to know Latin, an unspoken language in Byzantium. One of the results of this focus on the Roman Laws was the creation of an organized table of contents to the Code known as the *Tipoukeitos* ('What Is To Be Found Where'). It indexed the *Basilica* and included the valuable commentaries of the jurists Patzes and Eustathios Romaios (975-1034).

Students of law went for certifications as advocates of justice and had a higher standard modeled after Justinian II's draconian Novels of Trullo in 692. None were to attend the races, athletic events, or wear 'strange' clothes (perhaps as a legal blow against the Demes). The benefits of these schools were more than fair considering the restrictions, if they provided evidence that they showed ability in understanding the material, admission was free despite class and financial situation. Perhaps this was another method that the *Basileus* was preparing for the bureaucracy and the senatorial class in accepting the less enfranchised citizens. Michael Psellus would use these techniques under his mentor John of Euchaita to chair the school of philosophy. A Novel of 1045 also details how professors were paid handsomely in silks, free living arrangements, top salaries, and bonuses on Easter.[1753]

Having lived a long and turbulent life, the *Basilia* Theodora once again ruled as a 'Virgin' *Basilia* in 1055, making only small changes with the short time she had left. She began with the bureaucracy by exiling the Postal Logothete John for his free hand in raising senators from the lower classes. The Ethnarc Nicephorus Bryennius was also exiled and he ended his life as a monk, having been blinded by old rivals, ending the Western Tagmata's claim that he be the next *Basileus*. To show good will, she remitted some taxes and gave amnesty to certain criminals, while economically she further debased the coinage to record

---

[1752] Herrin, 76.
[1753] Vasiliev, 367.

inflation with her appointed finance minister, Paraspondylus. She dismissed Bishops from their posts under the Patriarch's nose and was preparing to depose Cerularius as well when he died suddenly.

But all of these changes and reforms in the state could not keep the seventy-five-year-old Theodora from her own mortality. Many candidates for a successor were brought to her as she lay dying in the Palace, but she was determined to choose her own *Basileus*. One possibility was a certain Nicephorus, governor of Bulgaria, who was deported from Salonica in military defeat. But, once again, the goal was to raise another mouthpiece for the nobles, the Senate, and the army, found in a retired officer known to be '*Logothete Stratiotichus*' ('the Military Finance Minister') named Michael Bringas who himself was in his seventies to promise a brief, transitory reign. Satisfied with a lackluster interim ruler on the throne, Theodora died on 31 August, 1056, of an intestinal illness.

Her brief and solitary reign was a reach at reform in an Empire needing it badly. She could do nothing for the Great Schism even after Cerularius died as the pressing matters of Byzantium outweighed this conflict. She was not as outgoing or as popular as Zoe was, always being considered a junior ruler, but she was wiser than her sister and did not let her ambitions or passions for handsome nobles decide the Empire's fate. However, her choice for a successor would still be a poor one and would leave inadequate marks on the Empire. In truth, Zoe and Theodora's crimes were not in their decisions as rulers as they were not policymakers, but the poor choices made mostly by Zoe in choosing *Basilii* through marriages as kingmakers, deciding the fate of centralized rule in the Empire. This unfortunate legacy of the solemn Theodora was her final choice before death as a 'crazy and decrepit veteran', being a slave to her ministers. As their legacy in Byzantinism would dictate, only the less perceptive of older historians have characterized the imperial sisters by their mistakes and not their virtues.

## MICHAEL VI BRINGAS 'THE OLD'
### (1056-1057)

A man in his seventies, Michael Bringas was known by all, even before taking the purple, being either referred to as the (Logothete) *Stratioticus* 'the Warlike' or *Gerontas* 'the Old.'[1754] He was not a leader, but a follower by character, yet the dying Theodora was more or less forced to entrust this civil

---

[1754] Ostrogorsky, 338.

official who carried absolutely no military experience and a rash of enemies within the Empire as he wore the imperial Crown. He had the faith of the armies at first, but within the year that was his reign he lost that trust to arrogance, incompetence, and unreliability.

What eventually condemned Michael VI the most was the charisma and bravery of a rival general named Isaac Comnenus. Younger, in better stature and health, and a veteran supported by the best generals in the Empire, he seemed destined for the throne himself and Michael feared this greatly. His fall became Michael's own fault as the paranoia of being demoted by his more successful generals and Dukes cost him the most.[1755] But this only fulfilled the prophecy of Comnenus's inevitable rebellion at the army's insistence, guaranteeing him the throne by ousting Michael Bringas.

Born in the 980's like the imperial sisters, Michael VI was a descendant of the corrupt power behind Romanus II and Theopahno's throne, Joseph Bringas. He served many years as the military's finance minister in the bureaucracy, hence he had another moniker of the 'Warlike' – it was once actually an accepted notion that he had earned military offices under his belt, but this is completely untrue. There is not much record to his earlier life before his ascension on September 1, 1056, except that he had no wife or children and it was he who was the last ember of the Macedonian legacy. As far as his career went, because of Monomachus's debased currency and decreases in payment of the soldiers, the Anatclian aristocracy resented him greatly and would later show this with open hostility to Byzantine sovereignty.

First, as the family cf the previous *Basileus* had to be dealt with, a poorly prepared army of Varangians and sailors under Monomachus's cousin Theodosius fled the battlefield in the attempt to gain the throne by legitimate force. The shamed rebel leader and his son sought refuge at St. Sophia, but were later spurned by an uncaring Patriarch Michael Cerularius. Theodosius was caught and dragged from his hiding place in the beams of the north narthex, ending up exiled to Pergamum where he remained not even considered serious enough of a threat to be blinded.[1756]

If the motivations of the civil aristocracy were base in accepting him as *Basileus* for their own agendas, Michael's motives can be seen as much worse being one of pettiness. He disliked all things military despite his former post and acted based on the insults of the military aristocracy he once suffered, inducing

---

[1755] Treadgold, 597.
[1756] Norwich, (*APO*), 329.

the cutting of military pay and budgets in the 'War Department.'[1757] When the time came for certain generals to meet before him in a private audience, the tide finally turned. An appeal by Isaac Comnenus (Stratopedarch of the East), Catacalon Cecaumenus (former Duke of Antioch), Michael Burtzes, and the Ducas brothers Constantine and John was made to the *Basileus* on Easter Sunday, 1057.

It is said by Cedrenus and Sewter that after he commended their service, Michael chided them for almost losing Antioch in a previous battle, accusing Comnenus of showing no gallantry and valor, and adding the embezzlement of public funds from citizens for personal use.[1758] Michael refused all of their requests and bid them leave, absolutely brooking no arguments from Leo Paraspondylus, his once superior, or any other general who would later hear about this insult. On the same day, Michael Bringas sealed his loyalty from the Senate, senior magistrates, and civil officials by granting bonuses with the already dry Treasury of Monomachus's and gave titles and promotions, sometimes to three or four further ranks![1759] This was another incensing insult to the military who gained nothing in the *Basileus*'s cheap generosity.

On June 10, at Gunaria in Paphlagonia, the armies of the region raised upon a shield the rather reluctant, but outnumbered in praise, Isaac Comnenus as *Basileus*. At that time, the Cappadocian commander Nicephorus Bryennius was caught by the Empire for illegally raising soldier pay and was blinded by Opsaras, the *Basileus*'s agent.[1760] Bringas, once a Logothelete, would not be crossed on his policies against military financing in such a time of crisis, however, Psellus claims Michael was otherwise slow to respond, acting as though no crisis existed.[1761] This changed only when the question of monies to the armies was brought up when this financing became treated as a crisis in itself. Meanwhile, Cecaumenus's army of Varangians, Greeks, and Normans rallied at Colonia in Nicaea as the base of operations against Constantinople for Isaac.

Isaac further harmed the throne by collecting taxes in Anatolia for his army (who were glad to do it as they hated Bringas). Even Western mercenaries stood by his side, such as Hervivios, or Hervy, a French holder of Armenian military lands, along with several hundred of his soldiers. He had fought in Sicily for

---

[1757]  Jenkins, 363.

[1758]  Sewter, 276f.

[1759]  Norwich, (*APO*), 328.

[1760]  Treadgold, 597.

[1761]  Psellus, 280.

the Empire alongside George Maniaces and Harold Hardrada and was met, typically, with scorn by Michael the Old. To challenge his authority, Cedrenus reports how Hervy had even taken a military commission with the dreaded Median Seljuk Emirs.[1762] This event was an example of the marked changes in military culture since Basil II's reforms. The influx of Italian, French, and other Western mercenaries took the place of abandoned ideas of local militias. Furthermore, as they could not be paid in cash depleted from the Treasury, they were granted pronoia rights to land as if they were Byzantine aristocracy. As Westerners, the practices mainly known to them were steeped in the Western feudal economic model, this feudal system of certain border regions eventually catching up a century later to threaten the Theme system in the Empire's center. Added to this were the claims of property by the Crusaders, a conflict of old and new Medieval means of production that would count in bankrupting the Empire until its decimation.

A joint Byzantine command was assembled, led by Theodore the Domestic of the Scholae and Aaron Ducas, headquarterd at Nicomdia across the Marmara from Nicaea. A critical error was then made by the imperial forces as they missed an opportunity to use their position in trapping the rebel forces against the Marmara to force their surrender, only crossing into Asia to move on Nicaea.[1763] On August 20, as the two met at the Battle of Hades at the bridge of Sangares, it was still a trial for Comnenus who himself was almost killed by Russian mercenaries. However, he still got the upper hand afterwards as the eunuch Domestic Theodore made a separate peace with him against the *Basileus*.

Added effect was then given in upsetting the order of the Empire when Turks began invading Anatolia unchecked, sacking Melitene up to Colonia, causing the local armies to divide and flee either to Nicaea or Constantinople. After his Tagmatic armies were soundly beaten, Michael knew he was vulnerable, so he changed to a policy heaped with diplomacy to appease Comnenus. His attitude suddenly changed to reconciliation claiming Psellus as an 'adopted son', hoping he could guide him out of his troubles. Internal problems plagued the *Basileus* as a disagreement with the Patriarch lost him the support of the Constantinopolitan Church. From the beginning of Isaac's rebellion, Michael Cerularius had been on their side secretly as he could no longer stand Bringas as *Basileus*. Supposedly, it was Psellus's first instruction that he heal this breach in the Church before proceeding further, a policy Bringas ignored. Michael

---

[1762] Jenkins, 364-365.
[1763] Norwich, (*APO*), 330.

Psellus, as a courtier, recommended a generous bribe, drawing his armies into position to call on the allying mercenary forces.[1764]

After Hades, it became clear to Michael that more diplomacy was needed to pacify Isaac, so he sent ambassadors to Nicomedia on August 24, 1057. This included Psellus, Constantine Lichudes, and a senator known as Theodorus Alopus. Isaac made it clear to these persuasive orators and philosophers that he was not to be charmed by the 'honey of their lips' while being presented with the *Basileus*'s offer of promotion to *Caesar* with royal honors and insignia presented at his camp. Though it was a somewhat unpopular choice to his army, especially by Cecaumenus, Isaac agreed and was sent safely back to Constantinople where he met Michael upon his throne surrounded by retinues of soldiers to display his power as *Augustus*. Michael wisely appealed to Isaac subtly by asking him to: 'Be persuaded by your better judgment. Honor your father in his old age, and you will inherit the throne by legal means.'[1765]

He was then promised a return of titles and honors to the rebel commanders and more promotions in military and civil posts. Isaac Comnenus and his cohorts who once asked for one promotion and was refused now gained the greatest ranks in the Empire next to Stratioticus's, such grants the only real power Bringas still held. Leo Paraspondylus became a target for the new *Basileus*, as it was granted him that the minister be dismissed. Isaac was then sent to Rheae for minor deliberations as Psellus and Cerularius were preparing Michael's departure as *Basileus*. It was not difficult as the senators approached Michael with views he abdicate and the exhausted monarch agreed to advice from Cerularius.

On August 31, 1057, a mere few hours from one year to the day of his enthronement, Michael VI Bringas wore the 'coarse cowl of a monk' as Psellus states and left Constantinople forever. He retired a private citizen of the Empire and died in 1059. His largest weakness as *Basileus* was being one of the many kinds of leaders that let events happen inactively rather than instigating them through action, being one of the lowest moments of this period of degenerate imperial authority.

---

[1764] Psellus, 281.

[1765] *ibid.*, 293.

# ISAAC I COMNENUS
## (1057-1059)

From the day of his coronation, Isaac I settled down to work on the major military reforms needed in the Empire. The pointless overspending of the Treasury to the Senate diverted from the army had led Byzantium's borders into a vulnerable position. The Seljuk Turks were closing in on the Balkans after the fall of Baghdad as the rampant Pechenegs migrated further south from the Danube as only the Magyars could make them reach settlement. In the West, the energetic Norman leader Robert Guiscard was moving in on Byzantine Italy to the territories of the Sicilian Arabs, being encouraged by the Papacy. Isaac I Comnenus was the first true soldier-emperor since Basil the Bulgar-Slayer and intended to demonstrate that fact to the unwieldy bureaucratic behemoth the Empire had become. Therefore, it was with a cold reception to the Senate that he was accepted on September 1, 1057. He had learned the lesson from past *Basilii* in that paying the army to leave the City would reduce the amount of stagnant soldiers living on a stipend. Just as importantly, he did not just blindly grant fellow generals government offices either for this reason.[1766]

Michael Psellus describes Isaac's mentality and motivation as developed from the ancient Roman device of the *Imperator* of Octavian Augustus. The first Emperor's example was of a military commander who could run the army and the State as one, replenishing the resources of the army over self-interest. It is noted by historians that Isaac was another *Basileus* whose coinage depicted him with a sword in his hand and not the *tabulum* of state born by subsequent *Basilii* over the past few decades.[1767] This was to associate the Imitator of Christ as a warrior and not a mere administrator fighting to rescue an Empire in crisis. Another depiction was the head of a silver cross of 1057, where Constantine the Great bows to Peter and Paul the Apostles, all before the Pope. It is claimed that this was a kind of propaganda used to demonstrate the observance of the Patriarch Michael I Cerularius by the descendant of Constantine, the new *Basileus* Isaac I Comnenus.[1768] To further motivate the peace with Cerularius,

---

[1766] Norwich, (*APO*), 333.

[1767] Treadgold, 598. Jenkins, 366, would romanticize this image further as this was a sword of 'redemption and regeneration in his right hand'. To Gibbon, the sword was a symbol, not of conquest, but the intentions to protect his people and guard against foreign enemies, 1647.

[1768] Ostrogorsky, fig. 46.

he publicly claimed how he would leave the Church alone and never interfere with it – a promise that would, unfortunately, devolve into a lie.

It is ironic, therefore, that in the two years of his reign he lifted no sword against the encroaching barbarians at the borders or made any significant change to the army. Patterned after past reformers, his changes came down to be gradual and organic in the Empire *beginning* with financial reforms and *ending* with the revitalization of the army as time allowed its progression. Unfortunately, his ruthless policies touching on all the spheres of Byzantine institutions won him less popularity by 1059 as Michael the Old had lost it by August of 1057. The brevity of his reign only made a legacy of two years of greed-induced violence on the Empire that would never lead to a boost in the army's morale and made Byzantium more fodder for misappropriation by his aristocratic successor. He had heroic ambitions and a competent idea for military administration, but as his time was cut short, it was all too little too late.

Isaac I was born in 1007 to the illustrious Comneni of Adrianople and the Castamon estates of Anatolia. He was the son of a Strategos of Paphlagonia under Basil II, Manuel Eroticus, who was of possibly Thracian origin and his wife, a Bulgarian princess. His older brother having died young, he held offices with his brother John. He had a close relationship to his brother and the two won terrifying reputations in battle, being called *Charon,* who brought countless soldiers to the 'infernal shades.' He was seen as a loving brother, father, soldier, and patriot whose only crime was a modest reluctance to take the purple, therefore being snubbed by the civil party.[1769] Skylitzes describes his character as '. . .of fixed habits, fair-minded, sharp-witted, strong, intelligent, a great leader in war, a terror to his foes, and kindly to his friends.' He was a man of extremes, lax and 'laconic in the extreme' in times after serious concentration and tension, pleasant, and at times intimidating, relying on body language over words.[1770] He enjoyed hunting and falconry and was an expert in the use of the spear, appearing a well-rounded individual, possessing many qualities popular to the Byzantine idea of an *Basileus.*

He held increasingly high military posts in the army's hierarchy to gain the typical disdain of the courtiers and senators. In Skylitzes, upon succession, he gave a reason for his rebellion in that he could 'no longer serve beside his fellow-slaves any longer.'[1771] After the humiliation and debacle concerning Bringas the

---

[1769]  Gibbon, 1647-1648.

[1770]  Psellus, 305.

[1771]  *ibid.,* 302.

Old, he fled to Rheae as Cerularius continued his undermining of the throne. A faction lead by the senators and Michael Anastasius demanded an audience with the Patriarch himself, threatening to strangle on the spot his two sons they held hostage if they were sent in his stead. This forced Cerularius's hand in defaming the *Basileus* as he was only pretending to balk at Isaac's succession.

On September 1, 1057, Isaac Comnenus entered Constantinople to wild applause from the people as he was crowned by Cerularius at St. Sophia. It was even generally overlooked that he was the first usurper *Basileus* since the Lecapeni. It was almost immediately after his coronation that the belt-tightening of the civil service class began. He immediately stopped the donatives expected from the throne, revoking many of the titles given a year ago, also refusing raises in salaries to administrators despite the last wishes of Michael Bringas.[1772] This was proof that being too generous with funds to the court would only breed greediness, contempt, and ingratitude in the beneficiaries. But, these ruthless measures, and others to come, would make Isaac many enemies in all spheres of the Empire, seeing his early death as a blessing.

The nobles were declining into a decadence of waste and sumptuous ostentation after the Macedonian dynasty, Psellus telling us of mausoleums crafted from Phrygian porphyry and Italian marble. Private residences in the cities were given their own churches as grants, surrounded by expensive groves, fountains, and parks. Comnenus saw all of this as the profligate gifts and grants given to court favorites and undeserving parasites as none had given one penny going to public funds: 'The imperial wealth was divided into three parts: one to pay for their pleasures, another to glorify their new-fangled buildings, a third to enable those who were naturally lazy and made no contribution to the balancing of the nation's budget to live in luxury and bring dishonor on the practice and name of virtue, while the military were being stinted and treated harshly.'[1773]

Meanwhile, the Turks were raiding Anatolia as far as Sebastea, regrettably ignored by Isaac as the Balkan situation was becoming more severe. The only real military operation he led was against the Magyars that were expelling the 'Mysian' Pechenegs, still causing harm to the Byzantine territories crossing the Danube. These Pechenegs were the kin of the Uzes, another Turkic people familiar with the Seljuks by opposition, so they were adequate defense against the Turks in the north.[1774] Isaac was said to have terrified them with the creation

---

[1772] Psellus, 294.

[1773] *ibid.,* 311.

[1774] Vasiliev, 358.

of solid shield walls on the center and the Pechenegs, used to using weight of numbers as a strategy, only assaulted in isolated groups, making it easier for the Byzantines to raid their camps and take trophies.[1775]

These Pechenegs, however, were depicted as savages who knew nothing of military strategy, even in the fundamentals, merely 'crawling out of their caves' as Skylitzes comments, carrying spears and no armor, drinking the blood of their fallen enemy like animals![1776] It is plain to see the prejudice of these people had not changed since the similar reports in the time of Leo the Wise. The offensive was met at Serdica and the imperial army won, but severe flooding cost most of the *Basileus*'s surviving soldiers on September 24. Haste was used as Comnenus was said to be in a hurry due to hearing rumors of a Turkish siege of Constantinople.

The Turkish menace was growing stronger and threatening all of the Muslim states. The Spanish and Sicilians Arabs, Syria, Persia, Mesopotamia, the Fatimids, and Baghdad were strong but held no solidarity as one 'Islamic World'. This fragmentation was readily seized upon by the Seljuks that took Baghdad, making it a protectorate and conquering Egypt and its rival court at Cairo, from native Afghanistan to Anatolia, the Seljuks held all of Islam, united.[1777] The City safe, Isaac then turned inward to the state and did nothing in addressing this Seljuk growth, going about his new reform policies. As a general, he was still more than an able one, but - conforming to a familiar pattern - he still held no talent for administration. Psellus in his history makes an example of his non-military weaknesses – in legal deliberations, he would always defer to the judges of the court and vote on the matter swayed only by *their* decisions, taking credit for their judgments for himself.[1778]

Whatever harm Michael VI had been judged to do, and it was much, Isaac I did his best to revoke it as the times of 'eunuch-rule' were to be over.[1779] He had already outfitted a new wave of imperial tax collectors with an aversion to the typical corruption plaguing their institution. They were charged with collecting higher returns from the landed rich without compensation and any arrears they might have, all estates also being made by misappropriation after a thorough review of past records. In a policy to curb the over expense on foreign

---

[1775] Norwich, 334

[1776] Scylitzes, 645. Further contempt included their inability to properly garrison troops and the ignorance of such concepts as 'flank' and 'vanguard,' Psellus, 318.

[1777] Vasiliev, 354-355.

[1778] Psellus, 306.

[1779] Sewter, 307f.

gifts and customs of any gifts or wealth, be they donated or given as tribute by foreign rulers, these were confiscated from public use or reform and stuffed into the coffers of the army. He established another program that revoked grants given by the reigns of Monomachus, Bringas, and Nicephorus II. It must be noted as he rescinded this land from the noble class he did not make new legislation favoring the poor, meaning all of the recovered revenue went straight to the Treasury, and thus, the army. This would have been considered practically criminal to the Macedonians, or at least their class-based Novels.

Yet another venture was his handling of the properties of the Church which created new problems for the Patriarch. Since the Novels of Nicephorus II in 962, the lands of the churches and monasteries held a favored position that excluded certain taxes and duties to the Crown. Isaac saw this as an effrontery and waste of funds for his armies, confiscating lands granted by the *Basilii* and forbidding the purchase of new land by the religious houses of the Empire. Michael Cerularius averted his role publicly, as he was basically the king-maker of Comnenus, by decrying the *Basileus*'s policies as he now had created a monster. He protested by wearing the purple boots reserved only for the *Basileus* and invoking the Donation of Constantine leaving the state to God's Church.[1780] But, he was only stonewalled as the Pope in Rome had done and Isaac brought about the *Accusation,* a formal document of Michael's charges of heresy and treason.

Finally, on November 8, 1058, Michael's protests induced the *Basileus* to depose and exile him to the Proconnesus, but this never came to pass for Cerularius died on January 21 as the Synod was deliberating his charges. Public rioting followed as Cerularius was considered a martyr for the City and Isaac's popularity practically bottomed out. In February of 1059, Isaac appointed an educated and loyal courtier, and not a theologian, in the Patriarchate. This former minister of these *Basilii* as Constantine III Lichudes, the University of Constantinople lecturer in classics, was given the title so Comnenus could shamelessly arrear the revenue given by Monomachus as his minister.[1781]

On one of Isaac's hunting excursions, he caught a serious fever and was brought back to the Blacharnae. Psellus, as his doctor, said the fever may have been 'ephemeral', and as the Hellenophile Psellus was said to have commented on consulting the Oracles of Dodona and Delphi as a jest. His fever was high and unbreakable as Isaac could find no relief in lying down as his breathing became

---

[1780] Norwich, (*APO*), 334.
[1781] Treadgold, 599.

short and labored. His pulse was seen to be quickening in time with a palsied foot and keeping with his obstructed breathing, death seemed imminent.[1782] He was surrounded by his wife Catherine, daughter of John Vladislav, his faithful brother John, and one of his nephews (which was either Manuel or Theodorus Doccianus) and as to which nephew it is not clear.[1783] For whatever reason as a *Basileus*, Isaac wished to abdicate and join the Church as a monk as Michael the Paphlagonian had done before.

His wife implored him to choose a successor first as he had no sons (his only son dying young), and the best choice, John Comnenus, refused, probably seeing the difficulties firsthand of ruling Byzantium. Catherine urged him to choose the loyal (and passive) noble Constantine Ducas. Isaac agreed and on November 22, 1059, he passed the Crown to his successor, entering a monastery. He recovered from the fever but did not seek to regain his imperial title, enjoying the contemplation as a Studite monk and teaching the works of Homer. Here in this life of simplicity he died early in 1061 at fifty-four years of age as a soldier, *Basileus*, and, lastly, an educator.

Though the spirit of military and civil reform was much needed in this period after the Macedonians, Isaac I Comnenus was too zealous in his implementation, also leaving the work half-done. It was typical of the times that another Julius Caesar (100-44BCE), so capable of military genius and good administration, was needed but not given. Each *Basileus* from Basil II's end to Alexius I's beginning (1025-1081) was only one type or the other and made both suffer as a result. Had he ruled twenty more years to be victorious at Manzikert, Byzantine history would have been radically changed and if his brother, John, had perhaps succeeded him rather than a new family, the unbroken dynasty could have saved the Empire from its declining state.[1784] It was also concluded as a mistake ostracizing himself from the Patriarchy as Cerularius held a place of honor with the Byzantines, as the sister *Basiliai* once did, to gain the enmity of the Church. But, as with Basil II and many others, such confiscations were a necessity with the powers of the Church as well as the monasteries needing occasional trimming as a long time ally of the corrupt bureaucratic party.

---

[1782] Psellus, 322-323.
[1783] Sewter, 324f.
[1784] Jenkins, 366.

## CONSTANTINE X DUCAS
### (1059-1067)

An important question raised by John Julius Norwich in his *Byzantium: The Apogee* pertains to the fairness in criticizing Isaac Comnenus's choice as successor in 1059: 'Why did Isaac not choose a soldier like himself to succeed him on the throne whom he could trust to continue those policies which (at least as far as the army was concerned) had already proved their effectiveness, instead of a hopelessly impractical and woolly-minded bureaucrat who – as he must have known – would undo all that he had done and simply bring back the bad old days of Constantine IX?'[1785]

Unfortunately, the question is rhetorical, due mainly to the bias of Michael Psellus, who had proclaimed Ducas as the best possible choice (perhaps by comparison to Isaac Comnenus). Psellus also praised John Comnenus for his virtuous attributes on and off the battlefield, emphatically refusing to head a new dynasty in Byzantium. Perhaps the answer can be found in the Tsarina Catherine, daughter of Vladislav of Kiev, whom Psellus strongly encouraged as the most loyal succession (though she still disapproved of having to choose Ducas). And, the Senate, as always, wanted a bland sovereign with low charisma, such as Ducas, in order to blend in the background and allow their influence to handle the government.

Constantine Ducas was the right choice for this criteria being not an evil man, but a mediocre one, an unassuming pawn and puppet of the bureaucratic party to end the priority of the military. It is recorded that Constantine himself drank in the honey from Michael VI's lips while the *Basilia* Eudocia had thought of the Stratioticus as 'a God.'[1786] Norwich's emphatic evaluation was that he was 'arguably the most disastrous ruler ever to don the purple buskins (not forgetting those buskins had been personally placed on his feet by Michael Psellus)!' He was only praised on high by the *Chronographia,* the historian-philosopher being a courtier known to pull many of this particular *Basileus*'s strings.

Constantine X Ducas did have many virtues as he had a strong knowledge of the Roman laws, as well as its logic, as a tool in the judiciary. He was educated at the School of Law in Constantinople, founded by Constantine IX, loving the educated Byzantine's habit of long disputations full of metaphor and sophistry,

---

[1785] Norwich, (*APO*), 336.
[1786] Vasiliev, 368.

steeped in the footsteps of the orators Demosthenes or Lysias (445BCE-380BCE).[1787] This was his pride before the Senate when handled well, these talents being a seminal mark of a cultured man of leisure. Yet, Constantine Ducas could not afford to be such a man, the times being too precarious for imperial leadership to excel only in flowery language and idle talk.

He was an avid student of oratory and philosophy, in which he was said to have excelled, declaring that he would have made a better scholar than *Basileus*[1788] (considering the crises of the Empire, this would be quite true). He lived as prudently as a philosopher could and though he was as generous with empty titles and donatives as a bureaucrat could be, he disdained pomp and would even set his robes aside to dress as a 'yokel.'[1789] Amazingly enough, even with the assassins who conspired against him in 1060, he never executed anyone or ordered mutilation or blinding, preferring merely exile. In another time he could have made a proper *Basileus*, but in the eleventh century, barbarians flooded the borders and could not be turned without another vigilant soldier-emperor. Invasions the likes not seen since the days of turbulence during Heraclius's reign or of the fifth century occurred as the Church of St. Basil itself was rampaged and the holy relics of the saints taken as trophies.[1790]

Constantine X Ducas was born in 1006 to the old aristocratic family of the Ducasi who had excelled, at times, as notable generals and civil servants. Some of his ancestors had a checkered past with the monarchy as with Constantine's ancestor Andronicus who plotted against Leo the Wise in 906 and his brother Constantine that had rivaled Leo's brother Alexander to the throne in 913.[1791] His father was an Andronicus that was the Paphlagonian Duke of Moesia. Rising in the civil *cursus honorum,* by fifty-three Constantine was President of the Senate under Isaac by his death in 1059, Isaac offering the throne to his brother John Comnenus who supposedly refused it. In a set of matches more political than anything else, Constantine married Eudocia Macrembolitissa, the niece of Michael Cerularius, immediately making his brother John Ducas his *Caesar*. Another imperial connection by marriage was Constantine's daughter Zoe marrying Andronicus Comnenus, brother of the future emperor Alexius I Comnenus ten years after her father's death.

His first acts as a *Basileus* and former leader in the bureaucratic party

---

[1787] Jenkins, 367.

[1788] Skylitzes, 651-653; Sewter, 331f.

[1789] Psellus, 327.

[1790] Attaleius, 94; Skylitzes, 661; Vasiliev, 355.

[1791] Psellus, 326.

included re-instating the donatives and unnecessary salary hikes of Michael Bringas and rescinding Isaac's reforms for a better army. One modern historian claims this unwieldy bureaucratic machine, before the United States, was the largest in history at this time perhaps next to China – which was exponentially larger and more populated than Byzantium ever was.[1792] The military party, on St. George's Day of 1060 and led by the City Prefect, narrowly succeeded in restoring Isaac Comnenus, inducing some reluctance on the former *Basileus*'s part. At another undisclosed time, other conspirators even tried to sink the imperial galley and drown Constantine, he only surviving to dispense mercy to the members of the plot. In the bureaucracy, deputies, secretaries, dignitaries, and the like all received rewards from Constantine. This at least being tempered by an impartiality in dispensing justice to worker and Senator alike (as Monomachus had done) and annulling unfair contracts.[1793]

The transparency of his incompetence was demonstrated that year in his helplessness when Pope Nicholas II invested Robert Guiscard as Duke of Apulia, his brother Roger and he taking Rhegium and Tarentum to close in on Bari, reducing Byzantine Italy in 1060 to simply Bari and its coast. Southern Longobardia to Arabic Sicily was taken by the Byzantine army, but by 1062, all were once again the spoils of the Normans.[1794] In 1063, the Seljuk Turks hit Syria to control the Emirs there, threatening the tenuous hold the Empire had on both Armenia and Asia Minor. A year later, the sultan Tughrul and his nephew, the intrepid Alp Arslan (said to be a 'drinker of blood' and Antichrist), conquered the ancient ally of Byzantium Ani from the Empire with their total surrender. A rebellion in Kars led to a popular submission to the Turks when their prince sought resistance, leaving them free to raid Cilicia in 1065 almost to Ancyra. In 1067, Arslan stormed Caesarea in Cappadocia and plundered the holy relics from the Church of Basil the Great.

Tughrul Bey and his Turcomen of the eastern regions had already, by 1046, taken much of Persia from places in the Caucasus and the Vaspurakan. As they ruled Baghdad by 1055, Tughrul was proclaimed 'Sultan and King of East and West' by the now defunct Abbasid Caliphate. During the Tornices revolt, Tughrul's brother Ibrahim Inal took the city of Ardzen, massacring up to 150,000 people with total brutality. The survivors of Ardzen fled to Theodosiopolis to rename it Ardzen er-Rum (Ardzen of the Romans) which

---

[1792] Norwich, (*APO*), 339.
[1793] Psellus, 338.
[1794] Treadgold, 600.

has survived until today as Erzurum. In 1054, they raided from central Armenia to Trebizond and peopled it with the Turcomen as Muslim Seljuks claimed a nomadic independence from the Sultan.[1795] As Arslan took Ani in 1064, Michael of Edessa said 1,001 churches were destroyed up to the river known as the Arpa Cay. By their main role in Byzantine history thereafter, especially at Manzikert, the regions that originally spoke Armenian and Greek were now being known to primarily speak Seljuk Turkish. Instability in this year only increased in the frontier zone as the Hungarian Magyars captured the fortress of Belgrade, compromising the Danube.[1796]

A major migration of 600,000 Uze Turks travelled from southern Russia and were crossing the Danube to Thessaly, defeating the 150,000 Byzantine soldiers sent to impede them capturing the generals Basil Apocapes and Nicephorus Botaneiates.[1797] Eventually they were slowed by sudden famine, disease, and the attacks by the resident Pechenegs, and once again, a static, immobile *Basileus* and his Byzantine resources had nothing to do with it. The Uzes had broken into Thrace, Greece, and even Macedonia, but the loss of impetus brought about by their misfortunes with Mother Nature, the Pechenegs, and the Bulgarians gave the *Basileus* proper time to intervene.

Much as was done with the Pechenegs under Isaac Comnenus, and in 1065 Constantine X settled the remaining Turkish tribes in western Thrace as a Byzantine bulwark against the Seljuks. However, the Empire was divided and occupied by the Normans in the Catepanate of Italy, the East having been despoiled by the encroaching Seljuks as Danubian Belgrade was lost to the Magyars in 1064. In 1066, more chaos broke out as a rebellion over inflation came from Thessaly, as the prosperity and *Pax* brought about by the noble Macedonian *Basilii* now seemed to be truly over.

In early 1067, Constantine X Ducas had caught a fever that was proving fatal by May, gathering his brother John as his *Caesar* and his wife Eudocia to make them swear two oaths concerning the succession. John swore that although he held the title of a successor, he was not to recognize any one but Constantine's worthy sons, Michael and Andronicus. Eudocia swore never to marry again and complicate the successions as had been done by the husbands of the *Basilia* Zoe.[1798] Constantine X, trying to recover the succession and learn

---

[1795]  Norwich, (*APO*), 340-342.

[1796]  Ostrogorsky, 343.

[1797]  Sewter, 332f.

[1798]  Sewter, 343f.

the lessons of its mishandling, died on May 22, 1067, at age sixty-one. He was a bright but in no way savvy *Basileus*, impressing his court with his abilities while his armies suffered recession and defeat to ravenous foreign armies. He was mainly the prop of Psellus (who claimed Ducas always called him 'my friend', and always while embracing him) and the Patriarch John Xiphilinus who were two courtiers skilled in politics and culture, but was no way more experienced with the army or military situations than was Constantine.

Financially, the typical problems plaguing Constantine X's reign were as typical as any other when at the start of his reign; Ducas made policies to reduce the raise on tax receipts as well as the amount of debasement in the coinage. Yet, the Thessalian rebellion in 1066 was mainly centered on inflation due to the currency debasement that occurred to dismiss the surcharge of the taxes, doing nothing to dislodge the burdens.[1799] Psellus should also be taken with another grain of salt when he claims the *Basileus* made no 'foolish spending' and that the Treasury was half-replenished. Another reversal on the conservativeness of Isaac Comnenus was the free giving of gifts to international leaders to bribe peace when the army was being economically gutted. It must be remembered that this was due to the very limited capitalist structure of the Byzantine economy, which was mostly centered on the state monopolies of an absolute monarch.[1800]

In a Medieval Empire based on feudalism and fixed urban centers separating economic classes, such a system was not necessarily a problem. It had worked before in the times of Justinian I, Leo VI, Romanus I, Basil II, and Constantine VIII with the silk economies that boomed all the way to Frankish Aachen. But, another result was an unruly 'vast army of civil servants' that controlled production, labor, public welfare and works, foreign and domestic trade, and population shift to cultivate land resources more efficiently. To further the raising of tax revenue, shameful practices such tax farming with the resurgence of buying offices in the financial sector of the government endangered the process altogether with its rampant corruption. Furthermore, the army faced further neglect as well as the exclusive coffers of the Church.[1801] This all left major gaps in the networking of financial, military, and other civil policy making that Basil II once managed to uphold so well.

He had no small amount of piety as a purveyor of Holy Writ and the

---

[1799] Treadgold, 600-601.
[1800] Norwich, (*APO*), 339.
[1801] Ostrogorsky, 342.

Sacred Books of the Church, being somewhat ecstatic when Psellus would relate the Mysteries.[1802] As an experienced scholar and philosopher, he fully understood the metaphysics and arguments that composed such writings of past Patriarchs and Church Fathers. When Michael Cerularius died in January of 1059 he was succeeded by Constantine Lichudes who died as well in 1064. It was supposedly against his will that he had given himself to God, but John Xiliphinus of Trebizond was still inducted as Patriarch of Constantinople. This was mainly by Psellus's request as Xiliphinus was also a supporter of the bureaucratic party now in power, an intellectual, and a very educated jurist from the University. In the contest of East and West over Jerusalem after the Schism of 1054, Ducas tipped the scales eastward with his completion of the Christian Quarter around the Holy Sepulcher. The result was an increase of Byzantine artisans and pilgrims to the effect that Nasir Khusrau reported the mystical gossip that the *Basileus* was in the Holy City in disguise.[1803]

Constantine X Ducas's reign made clear that the bureaucrat party was now to be in power and the people would have to support it as they could not handle the financial tensions and sacrifices needed to strengthen the army against invaders. The civil servants cut their own throats in this way as they invited a drained Treasury for gifts, salaries, and 'bread and circuses' due of the harsh conditions the barbarian invasions had made. Of course, these expenses were resulting in a depleted army that failed in military and defensive actions before these same barbarians. It is this type of circular logic that would lead to the great defeat at Manzikert in 1071 (said to be Byzantium's Adrianople) and the fall of the Empire completely when armies and funds both disappeared. With the violence of the Crusades looming just beyond the Byzantines' foresight, the true decline and end of Byzantium was slowly taking place.

## EUDOCIA MACREMBOLITISSA
### (1067)

## ROMANUS IV DIOGENES
### (1068-1071)

For half a year Eudocia ruled alone, handling ably the affairs of state in each of its compartments, neglecting only the army. She had made an oath of

---

[1802] Psellus, 342.

[1803] Montefiorre, 210.

self-sacrifice to her dying husband that she would remain a widow, although taking the veil was never mentioned.[1804] From this it may be inferred that Constantine X wanted her to rule alone and raise his own sons to the throne in a new dynasty of the Ducasi. Only, it was not taken into effect that a time of crisis would arise to garner immediate attention wherein John Xiliphinus, any other courtier, or any endowed noble would suffice to fill the role of regent.

Unlike most of his predecessors, Ducas showed courage before his advisers such as in the matter of abandoning Armenia, which Diogenes would never had done. As the region could have been rehabilitated as a Byzantine client, it only needed the proper amount of order installed, but Armenia would only become a second priority to fighting the Turks.[1805] Although he had better potential than the Ducasi, the dangers of lacking a male heir exacerbated events when Diogenes's court and his generals abandoned him for powers' sake when he was captured by a Sultan in battle. This Sultan, Alp Arslan, would continue to capture Cilicia and Antioch, honing his sights on Cappadocia and Syria for Seljuk Baghdad.

After a brief span into Eudocia's reign, the Patriarch Xiliphinus would quickly change his attitude concerning Constantine X's oath against re-marriage. Like Zoe and Theodora's popularity among the people, Eudocia shared the same honor and Xiliphinus could not risk ousting the rightful dowager *Basilia* for her inexperienced sons Andronicus and Michael. In 1067, the search for a new husband for the Eudocia began and her 'solemn engagement, attested by the principle Senators, was deposited in the hands of the Patriarch.'[1806] Perhaps the natural choice was John Ducas the *Caesar,* although he had previously refused the throne, and the Patriarch persuaded him to reconsider, now agreeing to the position. However Eudocia, not willing to be the a puppet of these two men, played her own game to get what she thought was proper.

There was a eunuch in the court who had a reputation of low character, one whose equally inappropriate brother Bardas agreed to an intrigue with the *Basilia.* Eudocia proclaimed her choice was for this eunuch's brother, frustrating the word of the Patriarch and her brother-in-law. Intimidated by the situation, Xiliphinus diplomatically dropped John's claim and tried to consult with the

---

[1804] It was likely because the prospect of another marriage alliance for the throne was a moot point in the minds of the Senate and the *Basilia* herself.

[1805] Treadgold, *(BAIA),* 218.

[1806] Gibbon, 1648.

Senate who then denied Bardas's claim, playing into Eudocia's game of choosing the lesser of two evils. What was settled upon was a noble from the Cappadocian family of Diogenes, Romanus (the general Nicephorus Botaneietes was also suggested as a consideration),[1807] who had recently been recalled from exile by Eudocia on charges of plotting to assassinate Constantine X. To the chagrin of a seething John Ducas, Romanus IV Diogenes was crowned by John Xiliphinus in St. Sophia, marrying the clever Eudocia on January 1, 1068.

A word needs to be said on yet another dynamic woman of Byzantium who manipulated the court and became a kingmaker in her own right. Eudocia was born in 1021 to the Macrembolitissa family, her uncle being the ex-Patriarch Michael Cerularius. She married Constantine Ducas in 1050 and had two sons by him, Andronicus and Michael. Even though she wanted her own choice of husband after her ascension on May 22, 1067 as sole *Augusta*, Romanus Diogenes was mainly chosen for his rapport with the army and the fear of a real or imaginary revolt he might lead while Xiliphinus needed a strong military leader on the throne. Ostrogorsky gives less credit to Eudocia by claiming she was more or less forced to marry him on behalf of the powers of the court.[1808] Yet, it is now suggested she grew to love her new husband and they probably lived happily enough between the times he attempted to devote himself to the duties of military leadership.[1809]

Married at twenty-nine and widowed at forty-six, Psellus relates that he was not surprised Constantine respected her as she was '. . .a child and still incapable of considering political matters . . .'[1810] This was the unfortunate fate to be considered of all female rulers in Byzantium while still noting her competence and stability in holding state affairs during the succession crisis. The entire time, however, she was grooming her eldest son Michael for the throne that he would one day inherit, allowing him to judge cases and appoint magistrates with a positive attitude. She was very supportive of both sons to this effect and was even known to publicly give them kisses to encourage them. She did, as she aged, grow a melancholy attitude and once surprised Psellus in church by claiming: 'I hope it will not be my fate to enjoy power so long as I

---

[1807] Norwich, (*APO*), 344.
[1808] Ostrogorsky, 344.
[1809] Treadgold, 601.
[1810] Psellus, 345.

am an empress.' Seven turbulent months and the years spent watching others uphold the responsibilities of state had understandably somewhat soured her to doing so herself.

Eudocia also had a creative side and demonstrated this in literature as she wrote the *'Ionia* ('Collection' or 'Bed of Violets'), dedicated to her husband Romanus. It was, as she states, "a collection of genealogies of gods, heroes, and heroines, of their metamorphoses, and of the fables and stories respecting them found in the ancients; containing also notices of various philosophers." It was said to be used in the work known as the *Suda*, a lexicon of ancient Greek, Christian, and linguistic culture modeled after ones written under Constantine VII, John I, and Constantine VIII. She would later be praised by the historian Nicephorus Gregoras (1295-1360) a century later as a second Hypatia, the bright but doomed polyglot scholar of the fourth century. Yet, there was tragedy in the last years of her life and she would be deposed and forced to twice become a nun, dying in a monastery in 1081 at sixty where she was buried next to her husband Romanus.

She would show a brave character and commitment to her husband and sons as rulers of the Empire with a fall through no fault of her own. After her years of service to the throne and to the State, she was caught in one of the typical Byzantine intrigues especially prominent in her times through the ingratitude and injustice of greedy courtiers and opportunists. Her enthroned son was weak and the Varangians were in the hands of a confident opponent in John Ducas. On October 24, 1071, her son would become sole *Basileus* as Michael VII after her cloistering, never seeing him on the throne.

Romanus IV Diogenes was a member of a Cappadocian military family and the son of Basil II's general Constantine Diogenes, also being the nephew of Romanus III Argyrus by his maternal grandfather Basil Argyrus, who entrenched his legitimacy by aristocratic lineage. With numerous Cappadocian estates he served as governor of Serdica and was a veteran in the Pecheneg conflicts. Constantine Diogenes, a hypocrite and braggart, had plotted against Romanus III, committing suicide to escape punishment.[1811] Romanus IV was a noble connected to the Anatolian aristocracy as he was an officer of the Danube, being young, handsome, bright-eyed, and built with broad shoulders and a deep chest. Yet, in Bulgaria he faced exile for years being implicated in a plot to overthrow Constantine Ducas and his two sons on behalf of the military party.

---

[1811] Psellus, 350.

Like Isaac Comnenus, he wasted no time in building up the army into an entity that could regain the territory taken by the Seljuks. Psellus supposedly tried to restrain the *Basileus* from making such a rash decision as a courtier would, but was ignored in favor of the generals. So, in 1069, he became the *Basileus*'s chief military adviser skilled, as Psellus reports, in the various fields of combat. In 1068, he created a new imperial force composed of the Opsician, Armenian, and Anatolic Themes, also bolstered by the Macedonian, Bulgarian, Cappadocian, Phrygian, Pecheneg, and the Uze Turkish mercenaries. This seems fragmentary, but Diogenes knew how to operate vital points of maneuver on the battlefield, having only untrustworthy generals to be his flaw.[1812]

This seemed too little too late as by this time the army was badly organized, underpaid, and inexperienced despite Psellus's learned knowledge on war-machines, strategy, and a list of other military necessities. Further weaknesses in the Byzantine forces after Basil II included their dependence on defense and attrition over the quality of troops and commanders at hand.[1813] Romanus's army gained some victory over the Turks at Tephrice, but those raiding south to Byzantine Syria by way of Neocaesarea were already overrun and Melitene was taken that summer. Amorium would later be devastated by the Turks as Diogenes made a stand besieging the fortress of Artach at modern Manbij, only to suffer defeat by the Turks on November 20, 1068. After this, Michael Psellus, Nicephorus Paleologus, and the *Caesar* John Ducas were delegated as ambassadors to make peace with the Seljuks.

The defeat of 1068 was predicated with the reality of the army's disorganization, lack of discipline, and questionable morale: 'Those who obeyed his summons were not an army but a disorganized and demoralized rabble, without pay, without provisions, without equipment. The ragged regiments paraded with pruning hooks. The cavalry were dismounted. The horses were sold or dead and no one had bothered about remounts. Their very standards were filthy and unserviceable.'[1814] Who could call this a force enough to battle the united and motivated Turks? To Jenkins, morale was the primary factor in the Byzantine army; this intangible won priority over even the physical needs of the army. When both factors are deprived in a military force, failure is all but inevitable. One contributor to these complications from a local scale was the selling of military lands by soldiers facing bankruptcy without pay. This trend

---

[1812] Sewter, 352f.
[1813] Decker, 216.
[1814] Jenkins, 368.

made re-activation of troops more and more difficult and retraining troops in light of their incompetence even worse.[1815] Unfortunately, with this imperial decentralization on the micro-scale, without recourse, this trend would grow increasingly larger in the next century.

At the start of 1069, Romanus IV sent Norman mercenaries under Robert Crispin to guard the Armeniac border. Trusting in Western mercenaries would prove to be a mistake when made a constant practice and pay is frustrated by a bureaucrat *Basileus*'s Treasury. It proved a mistake as Crispin's troops rebelled on Easter Sunday, robbing the local tax fiefs for their troubles. A force of 12,000 troops of the 'five Western Themes' were at its head: 3,000 from the Scholae and Excubitors, as 2,000 from the Hicanti, the Watch, and the Immortals also followed,[1816] but were complicated by the numbers turning against them. The Normans were further encouraged when they defeated imperial forces sent to the Armenian borders. Normans terrorized the upper Euphrates until Diogenes showed his superiority as a skilled and vivacious soldier-emperor by personally leading the armies that put down Crispin and pushed the invading Turks back east.

Unfortunately, Romanus proved only to be the best of a truly bad situation when he charged Philaretus Brachamius with holding the Armeniacs when the Armenian imperial army was defeated by the Turks. This turnover frustrated the his plans to penetrate the East to the fort of Chilat. After all, the Armeniacs were still suffering from the gutting of the region resulting from Monomachus's irresponsible policies. The Turks' zeal allowed them to turn west to Anatolia ahead of the *Basileus* and capture Iconium until stemmed by Armenian ambushes. Alp Arslan capitalized on Romanus's flight west to seize the city of Manzikert outside the fortress of Chilat, a mere five or ten miles from the battle site in 1071. After these reversals in fortune east and south, an exhausted Diogenes returned to Constantinople for the wintering season.

It might have been clear at some point that these events may have been coming to a head in the Turkish Wars. Something more decisive was nearing to at least keep Arslan contained before the time Byzantium would be considered a lesser entity in the East. This was the same problem that the Theodosians were feeling with the Huns and the Heracliads with the Abbasids. But these were incidental, internal factors once seeing the Romans through similar problems, with the luck the Empire had ending at this time with Alp Arslan and his son, Malik Shah. If this was not so, then perhaps the Sultan was noticing this turn for

---

[1815] Treadgold, *(BAIA)*, 179
[1816] *ibid.*, 85.

the worst in the Empire as a clear opportunity to hold the Byzantine East with the imperial army was in such bad shape. In April, 1070, Byzantium further shrank as Guiscard took the last piece of Justinian I's triumph, Apulia, setting Sicilian land with sea blockades as the Italo-Byzantine territories seemed all but lost.

Later that year, new problems arose as demoralized generals in Armenia were appearing to fall back to Anatolia to salvage what they could of the region. Arslan, 'The Victorious Lion', had taken Archesh, Aleppo, and Amida, with all but Byzantine Syria as his. Romanus emphatically refused to surrender one of their largest client states and their Themes, seeking peace with the Sultan and bargaining for Manzikert. His military advisors and generals bid him to fall back and muster superior forces in defending Anatolia, but the emperor refused, unwisely gaining their ire.

Yet, the fact that the Anatolian defenses at vital areas were in decay and could not outfit any localized defense loomed over the situation; those advisers who pushed for the retreat, such as Attaleiates, were acting prematurely.[1817] Whether it was with or without their understanding of the truce, renegade Turks captured the Byzantine general Manuel Comnenus at Sebastea during these talks. However, this was a ploy so that they could defect to the *Basileus*, thereby strengthening his numbers with disciplined Seljuk Turks. With what he thought was a clear advantage, Romanus grew haughty, refusing to return these soldiers and the truce was off.

Arslan retaliated by raiding Thrace with forces of 10,000 Kurdish cavalry to Lake Van, taking Khoi and Chonae. The *Basileus* prepared for a major offensive by ignoring the capture of Bari and Italy in early 1071, again paying troops with debased coinage from eighteen to sixteen percent gold content in the *nomisma*. In March 1071, Romanus met the Armenian situation with around 70,000 men. Norwich estimates this as best as possible as records are scarce, but Muslim sources claim 200,000 to 600,000 while Michael of Edessa (1126-1199) claimed an outrageous 1,000,000 soldiers! (it was little wonder these sources are considered sketchy at best).[1818]

As for the forces available that summer, it is[1819] best estimated that Romanus IV had an army of 100,000 which far outnumbered the enemy, taking Manzikert by an absolute surrender where the *Basileus* sent another Norman,

---

[1817] Treadgold, *(BAIA)*, 40.
[1818] Norwich, *(APO)*, 346.
[1819] Treadgold, 603.

Russell of Baillieul, to Chilat. The rear assault working, Arslan now turned back from Edessa to repel these Normans. The Sultan then rode to meet the massive army at Manzikert where after days of constant battle, Arslan sued for peace, with Romanus once more refusing. Arslan might have been humbled here at Manzikert had the Byzantines not been influenced by the bitter Ducasi and the son of the former *Caesar* John, Andronicus Ducas. In a depraved move against his country, he had the general Joseph Tarchonietes spread false rumors of Romanus's departure in defeat from the field resulting in half the army fleeing Manzikert. Along with this was the treachery of the rearguard by the general Allyates who, in the interests of the landholding nobility, routed his own men to weaken the Byzantine rear.

As half of the army fled to Miletene and the Uzes defected to the Sultan, the stage was perfectly set for a total defeat of the Byzantines. Thirty miles from the battle at Erzurum, the disorganized and confused *Basileus* and his forces were then hit with a well-timed rear assault by the Sultan.[1820] Although Romanus stood his ground, his guard did not and his forces were slaughtered and routed on the afternoon of Friday, August 26, 1071. Heavy casualties were awarded by the Seljuks' mounted archers, firing backwards as the Sassanian Persians had done centuries before, while the general Bryennius failed in raising reinforcements. What was certainly worse, the emperor himself was wounded and captured alive by the enemy to be taken to the Sultan in a humiliating defeat dressed in chains like a common soldier. Such a disgrace had not happened since the defeat of the Emperor Valerian by the Persian King Shapur I in 260 CE, where the defeated *Augustus* was used as a footstool and skinned alive to provide a Persian banner.

Naturally, many recounts and analyses exist as to the causes of victory, defeat, and intentions of the armies that battled at Manzikert. The Turkish army's morale was commendable and had well-disciplined troops making fresh cavalry up to 10,000 to perform a rear assault that captured the *Basileus*. The morale of Romanus was sketchy at best and the departure of almost half the force to the Sultan caused a panic within the ranks were unable to process who was leading the army. The main circumstances surrounding the short-term results of Manzikert can thus be evaluated:[1821]

---

[1820] Norwich, (*APO*), 348.

[1821] Jenkins, 370-371.

1) Basil II, Tzimisces, or Nicephorus II Phocas would have won, or at least kept the damage of defeat trivial. These *Basilii* would have taken the two months between Turkish offensives and secured the Anatolian region, a proper buffer for the Turks in Armenia.

2) The army itself was defective on many points, but it was not this fact that lost the battle as the Byzantines barely fought at all. The defection of the Normans caused a panic in the ranks, once more, and this led to a rout beyond repair by the remaining generals. The Empire having been described at this time as a 'hollow nut with a crumbling shell eaten out by vermin. The slightest pressure sufficed to crumble it to dust.'

3) Arslan had no intention in taking the Empire for the Seljuks and Baghdad from which he modeled the old Abbasids. Arslan was more concerned with the motives and movements of Fatimid Egypt, forever threatening the neo-Abbasid territories. Byzantine diplomacy had also suffered in this decline and the agents who would have made success with the Turks in 1020 only doomed the Turks of 1070 with the inability to concede compromise.

Between the two extremes of gallantry and recklessness, even among the bureaucrats it is mostly agreed it was certainly the former.[1822] Although he was made to kiss his feet and have the Sultan stand on his neck in supplication, Romanus IV Diogenes showed great deference and dignity in his defeat, showing no cowardice or begging for his life, which impressed the Sultan. The Byzantine *Basileus* was thus treated as an honored guest and dined at the Sultan's table during banquets, demonstrating the civility of the Turkish nation as only barbarian peoples would have used this opportunity to abuse such a prisoner.[1823] This hearkened to ancient times when the rulers of equally dominant monarchies, such as Alexander the Great and the family of Darius III (381-330BCE), would treat captives of a royal family with such respect. It is little doubt that Alp Arslan saw his Turkish state of Baghdad as being equally legitimate with the far older Byzantine Empire.

It is tragically odd that the goodwill shown by his enemies was not found in Constantinople by his closest allies. The eunuchs and officials of the bureaucratic party were already scheming to replace Romanus with the

---

[1822] Psellus, 355.

[1823] Diogenes claimed that in victory, he would have flogged Arslan to death, but the Muslim King replied he based his attitude of victory on the Christian notion of forgiveness, as Christ 'resists the proud and gives grace to the humble.' Skylitzes, 700.

legitimate *Augustus* Michael, son of Constantine X (who saw Romanus as untrustworthy and cruel). John Ducas took control by using the Varangians to depose Romanus, promote Michael Ducas, and send the disloyal Eudocia to a nunnery at the Hellespont. Though disingenuous, any excuse was made to depose Romanus, even with legal technicality: '. . .the subjects of Romanus had embraced the rigid maxim of the civil law that a prisoner in the hands of the enemy is deprived, as by the stroke of death, of all the public and private rights of a citizen.'[1824] The distinct legal culture created by the Romans centuries ago was assumed to overturn the rights of an Oriental monarch when force of arms was the real trial.

Romanus was freed by Arslan upon the truce that an indemnity of 1, 500,000 *nomismata* being paid, a further annual tribute of 360,000 to be paid, and the cession of Edessa, Antioch, Manbij, and Manzikert, as major Eastern cities, to the Seljuks.[1825] Unseen at this time was how this would be the final death-knell of Byzantine supremacy in the Eastern provinces. Purportedly, the lands once belonging to the Abbasids, Fatimids, and the Roman Empire east of Phrygia in Asia Minor were permanently lost to these powers by Turkish hegemony, the supremacy of the Turkish language, and new boundaries for the coming Crusades, all to be ruled under Malik Shah. Like Adrianople, Manzikert was a major upset and defeat for the Empire, but did not necessarily spell doom for the Empire itself at this point. These territories would never be regained, but it had once looked dire for Byzantium before when Rome fell and Constantinople showed itself unassailable.

The major problems to come were from the West with the ambitions of the Normans and Latins in their Crusades against Islam. This battle became an infamous symbol for gross defeat as Manuel Comnenus in 1176 at Myriocephalum would call his loss as great as the loss at Manzikert. Not satisfied with Jerusalem, Eastern territories were sought from Byzantium and its *Basilii* until 1204 when at last the climax of these tensions put the City and the Empire in its gravest danger to date. If anything, Manzikert was only the beginning of the trials of Byzantium and not an end. The Sultan already held Cappadocia, Smyrna, Philadelphia, Cyzicus, and Nicaea. All Byzantium would have in the East would be Trebizond, Herclea Pontica, and Paphlagonia, a fraction of their former borders.[1826] The most regrettable part was this defeat

---

[1824] Gibbon, 1649.

[1825] Norwich, (*APO*), 354.

[1826] Diehl, 208.

all could have been avoided by a lack of intrigue by greedy nobles and gross mismanagement. It stood for the corruption pulling down the Empire on and off the field of battle. The result was a horrid defeat of this magnitude only fifty years after the Empire's greatest *Basileus*'s death.

A freed Romanus Diogenes returned west to news that the City was no longer his. Luckily, the Sultan had provided a Turkish contingent as an escort of two Emirs with 100 elite Mameluke cavalry, now becoming his relief army to Docea in Paphlagonia, in order to appropriate state funds.[1827] He wintered in Amasia claiming Persian allies would soon join them, but was defeated by Constantine Ducas, the new *Basileus*'s cousin. A joint alliance between the vengeful Crispin and Ducas's brother-in-law Samuel Alousianus also took part. Diogenes fled to the fort of Tyropaeum in Cilicia with the Duke of Antioch, Chatatoures, to winter, but the zealous Ducas killed the Duke after Chatatoures's tearful pleas for some mercy on the battlefield. Romanus finally surrendered at Adana upon a promise that no harm would befall him, though his disloyal lieutenant Theodore Alyates was still blinded.

Michael Ducas seemed to take great personal care in Romanus's safety as a friend despite his earlier worries of his wrath matching Constantine's. He had the Bishops of Heraclea, Chalcedon, and Colonus come to offer friendship to the defeated monarch. Ducas would even show great grief, apparently, upon learning of Diogenes's blinding and subsequent death in the summer of 1072 by his *Caesar* without his knowledge. This ended the reign of Romanus IV in September of 1071, and he was, with all tradition, tonsured with the black cowl to a monastery, being treated to a banquet before his tonsuring at Ponte by Andronicus Ducas. Romanus would be seized again and viciously blinded upon unjustified fears that he would raise another army less than a year later. His wounds were horrendous and he died of them just a few days later. It was said that Romanus Diogenes showed his usual great fortitude and courage before his blinding.[1828]

But, in a typically spiteful and arrogant move by Psellus for any man he disliked, a letter was written to the blinded Romanus, sneering that his blindness was really martyrdom as he now could see a 'higher' light. Some modern historians measure Michael Psellus as 'mean, cowardly, and corrupt...a perfect example of the Byzantine courtier in whom a contemptible nature was

---

[1827] Norwich, (*APO*), 354.
[1828] Psellus, 366.

combined with a first-class brain'[1829] and this was a fair assessment as he was endlessly self-serving. Anna Comnena in the eleventh century would find herself as disgusted with his character as she was for her brother John's. This grief was short-lived, but excruciating and horrible nonetheless; later historians describe the trials of the devastated Romanus: 'Carried forth on a cheap beast of burden, like a decaying corpse, his eyes gouged out and his face and head alive with worms, he lived on a few days in pain with a foul stench all about him until he gave up the ghost, being buried on the island of Proti where he built a monastery.'[1830] Being a nun at this very monastery, his wife and once-*Basilia* Eudocia would be interred here upon her death in 1081.

Romanus IV Diogenes was youthful, energetic, and a keen general as he saw the immediate dangers the sprawling Empire now faced with a new and relentless foreign enemy.[1831] Shocking losses and raids too close for comfort in Byzantium's interior were the result, yet Diogenes could not be faulted and may even be pitied if not one with which to sympathize. He tried all he could: basic training for incompetent troops, good relations with most mercenaries, and attempts to create defensive forces through the Tagmas that could independently hold the frontiers. All endeavors were implemented with a strong and vigorous leadership that impressed his armies and his enemies. But only three years on the throne brought this to a halt, the Empire suffering more in its current decline more than ever had before, and it would only sink deeper.

## MICHAEL VII DUCAS 'PARAPINACES'
### (1071-1078)

Though supported by the military leader John Ducas, Michael Ducas was a product of the bureaucratic party and its interior focus at a time when it was, now, neglectful of foreign relations that put the entire Empire in jeopardy. Naturally, he was a student of Psellus and knew an amazing deal in philosophy, rhetoric, literary critique, poetry, and other scholarly pursuits resulting in a sheltered life, as he was also considered a 'despicable person.'[1832] He was a silent and meek addition to his mother's court and barely had a hand in deposing Diogenes, for whom he had a certain respect. His passivity could be called recklessness as he

---

[1829] Diehl, 148.

[1830] Skylitzes, 366.

[1831] Treadgold, 604.

[1832] Sewter, 367.

never regretted pardoning criminals, including thieves caught red-handed in the Treasury (though Psellus pedantically praises this as mercy). In reality, the Empire was ruled by a triumvirate of three men: Michael Psellus, John Ducas, and another depraved and corrupt eunuch named Nicephoritzes, the Postal Logothete, beginning in 1071.

A typical demonstration of Roman contempt for an *Augustus* was the defacing of his images on visual depiction, and since Caligula's time (37-41 CE), this practice has included Byzantine *Basilii* as well. In the Bibliotheque Nacional in Paris, a manuscript of Saint John Chrysostem's words from the late eleventh century depicts Michael VII Ducas with either his wife or mother, being defaced to represent instead the future Nicephorus III (1078-1081 CE) and his wife.[1833] The message is quite clear, like the husbands of Zoe, that no honor should be given freely to the man or his unidentifiable female consort. He cloistered his dowager mother Eudocia, losing himself in learning as the Empire lost its boundaries to a number of barbarians on each side. When Michael's regime fell apart in 1078, the triumvirate behind the throne was utterly defeated and the last of the Ducasi dynasty finally surrendered to the military party.

He was born to Constantine X Ducas and Eudocia Micrembolitissa in 1050 and made presumptive heir in 1059. His early life was, of course, immersed in the education of Michael Psellus on the seven liberal arts as well as Platonics and theology. Though his reign was an appalling travesty, he himself had his fair qualities in that he was abstemious in drink, women, and physical pleasures, also having a strong grip on the Roman laws (their spirit if not their letter)[1834] as many bureaucrats did. Added was his mood of accessibility to petitioners, respectable manners among the people, and able talents in finance. Even though he was married and presented one son, Constantine, Psellus would claim his student was inexperienced in sexual matters despite his political marriage.

He was known for his obedient silence and was highly passive when he turned seventeen and again at twenty as his mother still watched over all affairs[1835] as she considered him still unfit for rule, which at twenty was a sign of poor character. But it must be remembered that Psellus also used these platitudes to mask the grotesque greed and corruption shared by his 'regents' after Eudocia's cloistering. This primarily occurred when the two conflicting parties, one honoring the *Basilia* and the other supporting the

---

[1833] Treadgold, 605.

[1834] Psellus, 368.

[1835] Treadgold, 604.

*Caesar's* intentions, drove Eudocia and Michael apart with their quarreling. Nevertheless, when Diogenes had been mercilessly deposed, Michael VII became sole *Basileus* in September of 1071.

Michael began by making his brother Andronicus the Domestic of the Armies as he and their cousin Constantine were instrumental in the plot against Diogenes at Manzikert. The almost horrific challenges of the Empire's military situation fell on the three as Romanus's treatment and death motivated Alp Arslan to forget their treaty and continue encroaching from the East. The assassination of the Sultan on November 24, 1072 by his commanders slowed nothing down as the new Sultan, Malik Shah, retook Manzikert. Now before Malik lay eastern Anatolia and the Eastern Tagmas, defended by the general Philaretus at Miletene also holding on to Taron, Edessa, and Antioch. Theodosiopolis was also secure as Michael's Georgian wife, Maria of Alania, made an alliance with the Empire. Malik still took the Euphrates from once-Greek Artze to Tephrice and rolled over the dispirited Tagmas that Romanus had given to the Armenians for the Turks to walk right into Anatolia.[1836] Upon Arslan's death, the Turkish military fell to Suleiman ibn-Kutalmish, as this general led forces to Asia Minor and the new Sultanate of Rum centered in the city of Iconium in the Anatolics.

In early 1073, Isaac Comnenus, a nephew of the late soldier-emperor, teamed up with Russell of Baillieul to recover Cappadocia. But, in typical Norman fashion, Russell deserted and settled in the Armeniacs to tax-farm the inhabitants and repel the Turks from his fief only. Meanwhile, a depleted Isaac was defeated by the Turks who recovered Cappadocia, Charsianum, and Chaldia, proving this war was about constant turnovers with little reward and degrees of great suffering from the people living within. Nicephoritzes sent John Ducas to expel Russell with a number of Norman soldiers in his army, however, these Normans only defected to Russell at the Sangarius River in 1074 and John was captured. His son Constantine was gathering a reconnaissance force, but he died suddenly with John remaining a prisoner in Armenia. But, seeing this opportunity as they controlled the Armeniac, Bucellerian, and Optimate Tagmas, they proclaimed John Ducas as 'Emperor John II' at Nicomedia.

Nicephoritzes was infuriated by this betrayal of the balancing act of a triumvirate made in Constantinople. In desperation for men capable of ending this rebellion, he paid a great tribute to the Cappadocian Turks as needed. This was thanks to Michael's heavy coin debasement and mismanaged state

---

[1836] Treadgold, 606.

monopolies, used to put down John and Russell. They succeeded and flooded Armenia, taking John and Russell hostage to the Byzantines for a healthy ransom. Although Russell, with the aid of his Norman allies, fled to re-settle in the Armeniacs with only a force of 300, the Turks remained indifferent. Seeing the upper hand they held, the Turks took the Bucellarians and Anatolics.[1837] The wily, resourceful, and able commander John Ducas would suspend his long backstabbing career with a monk's cowl to await another time on the stage of Byzantine history.

The new year of 1075 saw Russell of Baillieul holding Armenia once again with the local military too depleted to take care of the situation. Fortunately, a dynamic and intelligent young general was on hand in Alexius Comnenus, Isaac I's brother, and he paid more Turks to capture and bring back the Norman leader. Yet, Russell's removal from the Armeniacs was not a total victory for Byzantium as more Turks would only settle there unopposed. The Chaldian potentate Theodore Gabras raised local forces to finally expel these Turks, although this only caused them to spread east from the occupied Armeniacs all the way to the Bosporus. In order to address this, Michael VII and his Logothete tried to recruit new troops to fill the desperate ranks by establishing a new Tagma of the Immortals of the East. This was to be done with ruthless financial measures making waves throughout the entire Byzantine economy which only mired the government in a yet more bureaucratic quagmire.

The Pechenegs invaded Thrace several times against a pithy resistance by the state and the Bulgarians were boldly re-establishing the Empire dissolved and practically demolished by Basil Bulgaroctonus. In 1071, Constantine Bodin, the Serbian prince of Dioclea, was made Bulgarian Tsar in Scopia. This was of significant importance as it meant that the Serbian state was now part of Bulgaria by heredity and for once Michael sought a foreign policy with high priority to put down this rebellion in 1073. The Slavic peoples still exhibited unrest by 1076 as the Pechenegs would revolt from the Byzantine army of Thrace due to more absent pay. Joining with the Paraduvanumian Duke Nestor, they were ignored by Nicephoritzes as food rations were being blockaded by the invading Turks of northern Anatolia. Famine was the result in Constantinople, starving the new batches of refugees from the Western Tagmas due to more rampant incompetent government and a virtually helpless military.[1838]

A risky, but profitable, marriage alliance between the *Basileus*'s family and

---

[1837]  Norwich, (*APO*), 360.
[1838]  Treadgold, 607.

that of Robert Guiscard and Sicily was seen as a solution in 1076. Ironically, while in Italy, Guiscard was busy organizing his own government in Bari based on a borrowed Byzantine culture: granting Byzantine titles, creating a 'Theme' of Calabria, utilizing offices such as Exarchs and Strategi, and even the use of the Greek language in Church services, all to legitimize Roger's conquests. The result was a cunning use of Greek culture to lay Norman and Byzantine life side by side, synthesizing them into a Norman kingdom based on that of the *Basileus*.[1839]

Playing the inheritance game to stay close to Bari and Italy, Guiscard had agreed to an arrangement in 1074 sending his daughter Maria-Olympia to Constantinople. This would count only as a type of shameful peace, showing how low the Empire had sunk as an upstart with no noble connections who had bullied his way into Italy was now the father-in-law of the Empire's heir.[1840] As for this betrothal, nothing came of it whether it was to be a successful peace, the resulting end of the Ducas dynasty, or any more aggressive violations. The *Caesar*, Constantine Ducas, would then be betrothed to the illustrious future literati Anna Comnena to curry the favor of that powerful family, but this would fail as well.

In 1077, domestic affairs were souring as Byzantine generals began crushing more revolts in the western and eastern territories. Two more *Basilii* were proclaimed in the Anatolics under Nicephorus Botaneiates and in Dyrrachium under the Strategos Nicephorus Bryennius in Thrace. Bryennius got the upper hand by arriving at the City first, but gained the enmity of the middle class by looting the outer suburbs, being forced to return to Adrianople for the winter season. Seeing him as the lesser of two evils and the only type of choice for the Byzantine throne, Nicephorus Botaneiates was supported to oust Ducas on January 7 when he took the title of *Basileus*. In spring of 1078, Botaniates had taken Nicaea across the Bosporus, threatening Constantinople once again as Bryennius would end up captured and blinded by his rival.

By now, Michael VII Ducas had no more counsel to rely upon while the odious Nicephoritzes was torn apart by a mob rebelling against exorbitant taxes and duties while John Ducas was now a monk. Now, the balance of power had shifted to the military and the Ducasi dynasty was breathing its last. In perhaps the most prudent and independent move of his career, Michael surrendered on March 31 and took the cowl, deserting the throne for Nicephorus Botaniates.

---

[1839] Vasiliev, 360-361.
[1840] Magdalino, 189-190.

Alexius Comnenus opened the gates for him and Nicephorus III was approved by a threatened Senate, ironically abandoning his camp at Chrysopolis to be taken by the Iconium Turks on the Bosporus.

Was Comnenus's reason for accepting Botaneiates as *Basileus* to have a puppet on the throne? He had ample oppurtunity, eventually having the presence of mind to later take the throne in a crisis. Or, was he buying time to arrange things while Botaniates handled the burden of state? Alexius had a large family of capable leaders and he himself was a clever man. But it must also be remembered, with a starving and demoralized Constantinople that could not handle sieges from Botaneiates and Bryennius, let alone arm against Seljuk Iconium, what position could he have held as the new *Basileus*? Caution was the better choice, and Nicephorus being first to appear at the Walls in defense would have been welcomed to be given these burdens of the throne to Comnenus.

Michael Ducas was barely thirty when he lost his throne to indecision and a blind eye to crisis; he was just another educated, but useless, figure in the overly-bureaucratized Empire. His education did get him somewhere before his early death in 1090 as he rose in the Church to become Archbishop of Ephesus. This was a better suited life for him as he stayed out of the government and the military that the cunning theologian Michael Psellus had created. With this in mind, the last imperial Ducas was vilified as having been 'degraded, rather than ennobled, with the virtues of a monk and the learning of a sophist.'[1841]

As for Psellus, his influential and well-made *Chronographia* mysteriously ends as he would die decades later, yet Botaniates and Alexius Comnenus are the only two contemporaries of his of whom are not spoken. According to the best source on the subject, Psellus 'disappears' after the abdication of 1078 around January and is not clearly defined since.[1842] Perhaps he was finally fleeing the court as the new regime wanted him eliminated or blinded and he escaped to the ascetic life once again and, if this is so, it is not properly recorded. But he ends his history with a letter written by the abdicating Michael Ducas to the usurping Botaneiates that Psellus was a destructive agent and not a friend, claiming tongue-in-cheek: 'He who follows bad counsel plots, from the very beginning, his own destruction!' Words he regrettably should have said to himself concerning Michael Psellus, though he lacked the imagination to do so. His son shared no better a fate – Constantine Ducas was cloistered

---

[1841]  Gibbon, 1649.

[1842]  Sewter, 380.

along with his father by Botaneiates and would die at the battle of Durazzo in 1082. This was a poor end to a prince once betrothed to the daughters of both Robert Guiscard and Alexius Comnenus, but an end being a fragile chance for the Empire's future peace.

One of the few issues of the state he could comprehend were those of the financial sector; Michael VII personally handled much of these duties and topics as any administrator could in such desperate times. Psellus puts down he knew the exchange rates of the *stater,* knew the weights and measures system involved, including the touchstone, and could calculate the taxation and income rates of the Empire's fiefs accurately.[1843] Many of the reasons behind the Pecheneg revolts originated from lack of pay and bad economic conditions ending their subsidies, as the Pecheneg and Uze Turk revolts rose from the end of Danubian money grants to the tribes.[1844] Michael VII further confiscated land from nobles and the Church, creating more enemies as other *Basilii* had done (without possessing even an ounce of personal charisma), and gathering state monopolies on grain and commodities. His least popular act was debasing the *nomisma* from its inflated sixteen karats to nine, the lowest it had ever been at only thirty-eight percent gold. This act of shortening the price of a measured *medimnus* of grain by twenty-five percent is what gained him the epithet of *Parapinaces* ('Minus-A-Quarter').

In more specific instances, February 1073 saw Michael seize noble land to be paid to his brother Andronicus to tax-farm in order to lessen the burden of the wars. This *pittakion* tax repaid recipients with income received since the preceding September through edicts enacted in the Farm Laws in the reign of Justinian II.[1845] Nicephoritzes was another thorn in Byzantium's side economically, ignoring the illegal acts of the rich landholders, seizing peasant property and letting the conditions of the grain monopoly decline. A recession followed as fixed prices rose steadily to cover the government's further expenses, disenfranchising the subsidized farmers in Anatolia as well as its urban consumers.

Worse yet, it led to a rise in labor costs for wages, transportation, warehousing, and a number of other duties in agribusiness, according to the shrewd foresight given by Attaleiates as a notable source on the history of

---

[1843] Psellus, 368.
[1844] Vasiliev, 359.
[1845] Ostrogorsky, 130f.

economic labor.[1846] When Parapinaces was being rebelled against in the rural areas of the Empire in March of 1072, the embittered farmers of the state headquarters at Rhaedestus on the Marmara rioted. They met their goals of seizing the eunuch official Nicephoritzes, torturing him to death, and burning the granaries to the ground – not that it solved the dilemma for the inflated Empire.

Another trouble for the Empire was from the West in the Papal support of the Slavic nations against the Empire. After the fall of Bari to Guiscard, Michael VII communicated with the intrepid Pope Gregory VII for support, promising an end to the Schism and universal supremacy to the Roman West. Gregory appealed to the crowned heads of the West, entreating that to '. . .all Christians (*ad omnes christianos*) . . .the Pagans were exerting great pressure upon the Christian Empire and had devastated with unheard-of cruelty everything almost as far as the walls of Constantinople.'[1847] In letters to the Duke of Burgundy and the German Emperor Henry IV, the Pope illustrated the urgent need to alleviate the Christian East.

In fact, he began the outfitting of 50,000 men to that effect, a combination of Italians and other Europeans (*ultramontani*) to start the First Crusade of the Holy Lands in hopes of uniting the Churches.[1848] But soon afterwards, Pope Gregory turned inward to deal with the Emperor Henry IV and the boundaries of investing German Bishops (the 'Lay Investiture Controversy') which set aside the matter. Whether or not this was considered, it was a painful stab in the back when Pope Gregory's legates crowned the Croatian, Dimitri Zvonimir, as King of the once-suzerain Croatia. In 1072, the son of Michael of Zeta, Constantine Bodin, was supported by Rome being crowned as the Bulgarian Tsar at Prizren.[1849] Five years later, Michael of Zeta himself would receive a Papal coronation, filling Roman coffers and surrounding Orthodox jurisdictions with Catholic nations.

Finally, the year 1075 saw big developments for the prestige of the Magyar tribes under King Geza I when Michael Ducas, probably to counter the previous Papal actions, crowned Geza King of Hungary. To show what Hungary owed Byzantium, a *Graecea Corona* was commissioned as the 'Holy Crown' of Hungary, covered in enameled portraits of Christ honoring Geza and Michael

---

[1846] Ostrogorsky, 347f.

[1847] Vasiliev, 358.

[1848] *ibid.*, 395-396.

[1849] Norwich, (*APO*), 359.

VII with the other Ducasi and the Archangels.[1850] Included are the Sts. Cosmas and Damien, and the inscription honoring Geza as *Krales Tourkias* ('the faithful King of Hungary'). If this was not enough to demonstrate Byzantine and Orthodox influence, passages from Constantine VII Porphyrogenitus's *Book of Ceremonies* were included, citing Geza as 'vice-regent of Christ Pantokrator' and the 'political authority which he derives from God.' This was splendid Byzantine propaganda of Greek and Orthodox values coupled with public memory of a Byzantium more stable in the time of the early tenth century. Already the East and West were quietly settling ground before the greatest international and inter-faith conflagration of the Medieval era.

## NICEPHORUS III BOTANEIATES
### (1078-1081)

The listless malaise settling in almost all facets of the Empire were now glaringly obvious to its neighbors, allies, friends, and enemies as the notoriously obsequious Psellus even cites the times and rule of Michael VII as the Empire's 'lowest ebb.' A strong and imposing figure from the military party was deftly needed in yet another time of expanding crisis, a time when Anatolia was threatened to be swallowed up by the spread of the Turks from the East. There were excellent leaders such as Alexius Comnenus and Nicephorus Bryennius, and Botaneiates was no different, but only a leader balanced enough to keep the bureaucrats and nobles in line would do as well. Yet, Nicephorus III was considered more of a well-meaning dotard whose 'brief reign was nothing more than the final scene in this tragic period of disintegration.'[1851]

Already in his seventies, Nicephorus lacked any skills in diplomacy, as earlier demonstrated by the cancelling of the marriage of the Crown with Robert Guiscard's daughter. Anna Comnena (1083-1153), the daughter of the *Basileus* Alexius and prime historian, claimed Robert saw it as a '...wrong done to my father-in-law and a disgrace suffered by my daughter Helena when she was thrown out of the Palace with him.'[1852] In December of 1078, an ambassador, Count Radulf of Pontoise, demanded satisfaction for Guiscard, which went

---

[1850] Obolensky, 159-160.

[1851] Ostrogorsky, 349.

[1852] Anna Comnena. *The Alexiad,* trans. by E.R.A. Sewter. New York, NY: Penguin Publishing. 1969, 144.

unheeded. Enmity with the West was all that was gained at a time when the Normans may have been a better ally than none.

The currency was debased once again to only one-third percent in gold per *nomisma*, burning an already dissatisfied bureaucracy around 1080.[1853] It is now that the universal trust and confidence in the *bezant* was imminent with the decline of its once sixteen grains of gold to the coin. In the eighth century, as far as England, an idiom was used by the historian known as the Venerable Bede (672-735 CE) to describe a virginal princess as being as 'pure as a byzant.' And as, at one time, a Byzantine merchant could impress the King of Ceylon and prove the *Basileus* majesty over the King of Persia with this currency as a 'clincher' it now was degrading in the international economic communities.[1854]

Nicephorus III first showered compliments and titles on the military officials as other such warrior *Basilii* had done before, only satisfying the question of legitimacy by marrying Maria of Alania, his predecessor's wife, as well as any connection with the Ducas, in 1079. The Patriarch Cosmas I was insulted by the union, especially as he tried to wed Eudocia Macrembolitissa to him from her nunnery. Though he had capable military commanders that could somewhat stem the tides from the frontiers, Nicephorus himself was ineffective as a *Basileus* and marked for deposition by a *Basileus* fifty years his junior with a new regime ready to face the Empire's challenges. Nicephorus III Botaneiates was only an unfortunate product of his time, proving that the weak factions and partisanship of the Byzantine Army and State institutions could not function without the dynamic skills of a Macedonian ruler or a George Maniaces to lead them.

Nicephorus Botaneiates was born from an old Anatolian military family in 1001 – his family had roots with the powerful and ancient Phoci and even the claims to the legendary Fabii family of Republican Rome.[1855] From his vast Anatolian estates, Nicephorus would rise to generalship under Constantine IX and lead factions that placed Isaac I on the throne in 1057. He had an extensive career fighting the border wars with the Oghuz Turks and was made Strategus of the Anatolian Theme. He did face capture by the Turks in 1064, fighting for the Duke of Paradounavon, but managed to return to Constantinople when disease and famine were destroying the enemy army. He fought for John Ducas

---

[1853] Treadgold, 610.

[1854] Sherrard, 118.

[1855] Norwich, (*APO*), 361. Despite his experience with Turkish warfare and an appearance not to give in to partisanship, Diogenes distrusted him and excluded him, perhaps fortunately, from the Battle of Manzikert.

and was considered for a husband to the widowed *Basilia* Eudocia in 1067 before Romanus Diogenes became a claimant. Having arrived at Constantinople before his rival Bryennius, this factor being his only justification of usurping the Crown, he was made *Basileus* on March 24, 1078, as Michael VII Ducas entered a monastery. Nicephorus's appointment was well lauded: 'A formal invitation on behalf of the Patriarch, the Synod, and the Senate, was circulated through the streets of Constantinople; and the general assembly, in the dome of St. Sophia, debated, with order and calmness, the choice of sovereign.'[1856]

He bargained for peace from his powerful and rebellious commanders by offering Bryennius the title of *Caesar* from Thrace, as Nicephorus himself was childless. However, Bryennius's possible career as heir apparent was shattered when he dared to raid the suburbs on the City's outskirts, enraging the aristocracy. Another such general, Philaretus Brachamius, was made Domestic of the East and Duke of Antioch not least of all for the fact he already held Byzantine Mesopotamia, Syria, Cilicia, and the Antitaurus Mountains. As these territories were already dangerously overrun with Turks, Brachamius was easily seduced into taking his imperial titles, controlling the Tagmatic armies poised on the borders. But Nicephorus Bryennius would not be so easily sated, quietly building armies to press his wishes to become *Basileus*. Botaneiates reacted in kind and put together an army of Turks and Greeks under Alexius Comnenus as Domestic of the West and the united forces took the initiative as they marched to Thrace, won the battle with Bryennius ending up being captured and blinded.

This victory failed to deter the Duke of Dyrrachium, Nicephorus Basilicus, to rebel against the *Basileus* with his new title of *nobilissimus,* marching south from the Balkan Mountains.[1857] Comnenus met with Basilicus in Thessalonica defeating him, also putting down the Pecheneg raids exploding in Thrace. After this, relative peace returned to Anatolia and the Balkans without Botaneiates so much as lifting much of a finger, owing all of these victories to Comnenus. This hardly intimidated the Anatolian Turks and they came in full force in 1080 by taking Armenian Theodosiopolis and pinning the Domestic of the East in his own lands while those around him were taken. He would capture Turkish soldiers, including a hostage known as Tzachas (who would play a larger role in the Comnenian period). Taking the opportunity, another rebellion rose under Nicephorus Melissenus from Asia Minor with Turkish aid, setting

---

[1856] Gibbon, 1650.
[1857] Treadgold, 610.

up garrisons from Dorylaeum to Nicaea to close in on Constantinople. The *Basileus*'s advantages dried up as Alexius Comnenus, as Melissenus's brother-in-law, refused to fight his own kin, which an unfortunate Botaneiates was forced to accept.

Early in 1081, Botaneiates made a critical error in deciding his next *Caesar* by overlooking the Ducasi and his general Alexius by raising his nephew, Nicephorus Synadenus. This was seen as a sign to Nicephorus's inner circle that a final change in leadership needed to be made. It was another critical time as Roger Guiscard, upon Pope Gregory's blessing, assaulted the Balkans from Brundisi with 150 ships and 30,000 soldiers.[1858] With ambitions for the Byzantine throne for himself, Robert charged to Dyrrachium taking tribute and raising garrisons in Lombardy, Apulia, and the island of Corfu. Nicephorus III sent the Duke of Illyricum, George Monomachatos, to intercede, but George was quickly undermined by the Eastern commanders Borilos and Germanos until a trapped Botaneiates was forced to rescind the Duke.

This was just another example of a ruler following his paranoia, being pliant to gossip, and ignoring the issues of consistency in his armies. He also seemed to misuse his allies properly as when, in 1075, King Geza of Hungary married Nicephorus's niece, but was strangely absent during these internal and external conflicts. On Sunday, February 14, 1081, being the Quinquagesima, Alexius fled for the Monastery of Sts. Damian and Cosmas to meet with both the neglected Ducas dowager mother Eudocia and the powerful general Paleologus, residing in Thracian Tzurullum.[1859] The time to act was now upon the Nicephorus, as John Ducas and Isaac Comnenus claimed the illustrious Alexius I Comnenus as *Basileus* on April 1, 1081.

As Alexius entered the City, through a conspiracy with the Varangians, at the Gate of Adrianople with George Paleologus, Nicephorus abdicated as Michael Ducas had done and took the cowl for the Church of Mary Peribleptos. His final words as *Basilius*, Anna Comnena would note, warned against division: '... do not engage in civil wars, nor transgress the will of God. Do not allow this city to be defiled by the blood of Christians, but yield to God's will. Renounce the world.'[1860] Romanus IV Diogenes in the same vocation even offered his only worry now for the Empire was his own reason for 'abstinence from meat.' Botaneiates would later die in his monastery the same year on December 10.

---

[1858] Comnena, 69.

[1859] Ostrogorsky, 350.

[1860] Comnena, 102.

This ended seventy years of brief and weak leadership, dominated by private interests and eroding confidence in the Empire.

An unfortunate inevitability unfolded in these years as, 'The preponderance of incompetent emperors after Basil was striking, but no accident.'[1861] The interests of the generals and bureaucrats ruling behind the throne only undermined the internal state unity in Empire by the nobility, the Church, and the Palace. Meanwhile, external decentralization tore apart smaller territories only to become fiefs for the hunger of foreign enemies. Now a new era was beginning, one full of stronger *Basilii* and stronger dynasties, but still full of danger and bloodshed as Nicephorus was said to have a 'cruel and timid' court that would 'taint with fear and suspicion' the Comneni.[1862] This was only because Nicephorus III feared the popularity and superior skills of Comnenus that could rescue Byzantium from Botaneiates's own inadequacies.

The dominating westerners would add to the burden of the ambitious Turks in squeezing the Empire like blood from a stone and the 'Latin Empire' would conquer Constantinople. This was due not just to an undisciplined army, but an inadequate Treasury unable to satisfy its own Western allies. Creating a domino effect to these ends began with the gentle push from these near-dozen usurpers and imperial non-entities. What we know from this coming period in Byzantium comes from Anna Comnena, the military factionist Attaleiates (who dedicated his eyewitness accounts of 1034-1079 to Nicephorus III) and Anna's husband Nicephorus Bryennius (1062-1137), son of the would-be usurper of the same name who was blinded and dishonored.[1863] The first did an only somewhat-biased approach to her father's reign and his struggles in her *Alexiad*. Though strictly prose, the title suggests a hearkening to the epic military works of her main influence, Homer. Indeed, a Homerian renaissance was developing culturally in the Empire at this time and one of its most well-known inaugurations was the *Basileus*'s brilliant daughter.

## ALEXIUS I COMNENUS
### (1081-1118)

Questions arise when considering Alexius Comnenus: Why did he hesitate before the Nicephori to take the throne as he was as capable as a Maniaces on

---

[1861] Treadgold, 611.

[1862] Gibbon, 1651.

[1863] Ostrogorsky, 317.

the battlefield, even if less experienced? And, if he was stronger than a non-entity favored by the predictable Ducas factions, why was he chosen by the Senate at all? Though he lacked concerted support from the *Basilia* Eudocia's and John Ducas's factions, why not join forces with his brother and Messalinus to take the capital in 1080? Perhaps this became clear to Alexius when the two strongest rivals to Nicephorus no longer existed as threats, Comnenus having been shamed for not battling his own family. He would later show great civil and military favor and bestow titles to the Botaneiates family when on the throne.

Whatever the reason, the plague of puppet rulers with short reigns was at an end and Byzantium could fully address its future unrest and changes. The worst of all would result from the only Crusade for Jerusalem that Western Christianity would decisively win from Islam. Yet, Byzantium was buffered on its sides by West and East, although the alliances through Christianity desiring to see the Turks fall did not protect it from treachery and the further spread of Byzantine feudalism by strong Western influence. In the exhaustive and impressive *Alexiad,* it is also said its author Anna Comnena is given to flattery, exaggeration, and flat contradiction to events[1864] (supposedly traits not traditional in Byzantine histories), but it is still the best guide that is had to the difficulties of the period.

Alexius I ruled a degraded Byzantium as best as he could as, above all, the shape of the Empire's economy and finances were deplorable. The vivacious *Basileus*'s daughter Anna had said of the situation: 'The Roman Empire was weak and at the same time crushed by poverty.'[1865] It was not the time to be surrounded by hostile, Islamic forces while having to fear trouble within by allies as haughty and as faithless as the Western Crusaders. These Western nobles of England, France, and Germany did nothing to better the situation as, at one time, famine plagued Constantinople and eggs sold for two gold coins apiece, bread at one, and a chicken at fifteen! Men were forced into eating leaves and hides to survive.[1866]

The East saw the Westerners present as uneducated and renegade savages, uncouth in every way, while the West saw (as in many an embassador of centuries before) a culture of '. . .manufacturers and merchants, great painted ladies, silk robes, oriental customs, eunuchs with pride of place, and their endless

---

[1864] Sewter, *Alexiad,* 258f.

[1865] Comnena, 157.

[1866] Runciman, Steven. *The First Crusade, abridged fourth edition.* Cambridge, UK: Cambridge University Press. 1980, 1992, 1996, 2000, 147.

divisions over liturgy and 'church services. . . alien to them". It was a recipe for disaster between the two theaters of Europe as seen by Constantinople as '. . . unmitigated nuisance'[1867] and only a cunning, strong, and resourceful *Basileus* could keep balance in the East until the crisis was relatively over. This nuisance, however, did not stop Western rulers from styling themselves from the depicted dress and humility to God of the Byzantine courts. These included Roger of Sicily and the Venetian Doge Ordelafo Falier in 1084, represented in the Pala d'Oro in San Marco, Venice.[1868]

Alexius I Comnenus, fortunately, was one such figure that could delegate to the bureaucracy in keeping it level while playing the role of warrior king, dealing with the hungry barbarians at his doorstep. Unfortunately, the Empire's weaknesses only made itself more apparent the more the *Basileus* applied this leadership. The Empire was only surviving on the hope that its enemies would turn on each other as luck, mostly more than skill, would now keep Byzantium and Constantinople intact. The roaring momentum of Basil II had turned into a sapped lethargy, threatening the planning of 800 years and the control of the Anatolian heartland which was now a 'kingdom' of Turco-Greek (Turcoman) usurpers across 30,000 square miles of territory.[1869]

The nephew of the former *Basileus* Isaac I Comnenus (1057-1059) and member of the elite military family of the Comneni, Alexius I was born in 1056 to the Domestic John Comnenus, who refused the Crown after the fall of Michael the Old in 1057 and his wife, the shrewd Anna Delessena. During his service as Domestic under the Ducas, Alexius married Irene, the niece of Michael VII. Once again, the Ducas's marriage kept the Comnenus line legitimate even as he was offered Maria of Alania, keeping him also close to the Ducasi Patriarch Cosmas, eventually naming Maria's son Constantine as *Caesar* before his own son John was born.

After the abdication of Nicephorus III, he was crowned *Augustus* on Easter Sunday, April 4, 1081, by Patriarch Cosmas in St. Sophia, already wearing the purple buskins bearing the double-headed eagle of a universal Rome upon his feet. He was short and stocky and a picture of health with a broad and deep chest. He had bushy and intimidating eyebrows with gentle, but intense, eyes and a full, thick beard 'like the painter's Cupid.'[1870] He did not strike as impressive,

---

[1867] Runciman, 92.

[1868] Laiou, 'Byzantium and the West', 64.

[1869] Norwich, John Julius. *Byzantium: The Decline and Fall.* New York, NY: Alfred A. Knopf Publishing. 1997, 1.

[1870] Comnena, 104.

but Anna insists that seated upon the throne his regal bearing was undeniable. However, modern historians of the First Crusade have disagreed in stating he had a dignified air, grace, and self-ccntrol. He was also the commensurate diplomat, knowing how to treat the Crusaders in his City and advising them to reach an understanding with the Fatimids in Egypt rather than rush to war.[1871]

Already, Alexius was using the imperial prerogative to hand donatives to his relatives. To his brother-in-law Melissenus, he gave estate tax revenues in Thessalonica and granting him his heir as *Caesar* for his aid in his successful rebellion. But that mattered little to Alexius as he created a new and superfluous title for his brother Isaac as the *Sebastocrator* ('venerable ruler'), supposedly a slightly rank lower than *Caesar*,[1872] perhaps to supplicate his siblings against rebellion. Elsewhere in his family, his teenage wife Irene, daughter of the Hungarian King, was put in the Palace of the Buceleon until an heir could be produced, so desperate was the need. On May 8, under his mother's 'advisement', the Patriarch Cosmas was replaced with a eunuch, Eustathius Garidas, to help usher in the new dynasty to be supported by the Church until his death in 1084.

In May, 1081, 1,300 Avlonian knights under Robert Guiscard made ready for an attack on the Empire as the Turkish allies of the Empire under Sulaymen pulled their resources from Nicaea to Smyrna with the new Iconian Sultanate of Rum. They gathered the Turks of Asia Mincr to storm the Anatolian peninsula against the Paphlagonians of Pontic Heraclea, southern Thrace, and the Cibyrrhaeot Theme. Philaretus Brachamius was also holding the cities of Chaldia, Callicia, Edessa, and the Byzantine capital of Cappadocia, Antioch, with a treaty made protecting Bithynia on the Dracon. Fighting these Normans, Brachamius needed heavy cavalry from the northern territories leading the Vardariotai, Hungarian cavalry and light archers with distinct red dress, lances, and whips.[1873]

The West faced more difficulties as the intractable Guiscard, also known as 'the Crafty', holding what was once Byzantine Italy since 1075, claimed to have the deposed Michael VII in the East and his daughter married to Constantine, Michael's son. This was a flimsy claim and the *Basileus*' was a Byzantine monk, but Roger's son, Bohemund, used the pretense anyway to land Norman invaders at Epirus, taking its stronghold of Dyrrachium in February of 1082,

---

[1871] Runciman, 136.
[1872] Treadgold, 613. This included another title, that of *Panhypersebastus*.
[1873] Decker, 88.

and moving on to a surrendering Castoria.[1874] Only in autumn of the next year could it be recovered by Nicephorus Bryennius. Dyrrachium was an important beachhead for an Eastern invasion and Alexius sent reinforcements to arm the city with his Paphlagonians and Anatolians. This left Asia Minor dangerously vulnerable, but Alexius relieved the pressure by hiring Turkish mercenaries to defend Epirus. Alexius broke another taboo by arming 2,800 heretic Bogomils and Paulicians from Phillippopolis, an illegal act in the past, and sent them west named as the tongue-in-cheek and ill-fated 'Tagma of the Manicheans.'[1875]

Desperately, Alexius sought aid from the Venetian Normans and the Holy Roman Emperor Henry IV, who was now warring with the hostile Pope Gregory VII, a moot point as the threat to Otranto was just as severe to Venice as to the Empire.[1876] But this was not enough as Guiscard's army still took Dyrrachium and Corcyra in the west Aegean, forcing Alexius to send generous bribes west to the German King for his favor. He sent no less than 360,000 *nomismata,* a pectoral cross of gold and pearls, a crystal goblet, a sardonyx cup, and a number of gold reliquaries with the labeled remains of various saints.[1877] This would culminate on May 24, 1084, when Henry IV would besiege Rome and divide the Apulian army in the process by threatening Lombardy.

Bohemund's navy was, at least, destroyed by Greek Fire on October 18 by Alexius and the Venetian Doge Domenico Selvo, but it was little comfort when all of the Western Tagmas were now lost. Bohemund's land forces would soundly beat the imperial army and the Turkish allies would desert back to Anatolia. What was worse, the heretical Paulicians used to defend the West simply ran from battle and disappeared faster than the Turks did. This would be a betrayal long remembered by the *Basileus* in his later persecution of this sect in Thrace and in the Bogomils of Bulgaria. Fortunately, Alexius was a shrewd diplomat and convinced the absentee Emperor Henry to assault the Papal States which, in turn, caused the Guiscard Normans to turn attention in defending Apulia from the Germans. Now, we see clearly Alexius's use of allies as a cat's-paw against enemies that would only serve later as an effective stalling tactic. Alexius's plans for building the navy, with John Ducas and the Admiral Caspax, would be to build roads in the south coast to permanently control the area allowing his admirals to recover Ionia and Phrygia.[1878]

---

[1874] Treadgold, 614.

[1875] *ibid.,* 615.

[1876] Norwich, *(AHV),* 70.

[1877] Norwich, *(DF),* 21.

[1878] Runciman, 108.

Now there was only Bohemund in the Norman East to deal with, being guaranteed victory by visions and dreams of St. Demetrius, the Normans building a Basilica there in his honor.[1879] As if these visions watched over the Normans, the defense effort went quite poorly as the Normans defeated Alexius three times straight at Joannina, Ochrid, and Arta. Alexius's armies were seriously depleted and could do nothing as northern Greece, the Axius valley, Bulgaria, and Larissa were now in Norman hands. It took the last minute intervention of Western allies to hold Bohemund back from seizing any more territory in 1083. The Venetians had arrived with 7,000 new Turkish mercenaries, recovering Larissa, Dyrrachium, and Corcyra. Now the seemingly fickle Normans began defecting to the imperial army, allowing the *Basileus* to retrieve Castoria.

The next year, a vengeful Robert Guiscard returned to Corcyra with Bohemund and 150 ships, pointing east. Despite more naval defeats to the superior seamanship and offensives of the allied Western and Eastern navies, Guiscard still won heavy victories where 13,000 Venetians died and 2,500 more were taken as prisoners to be mutilated[1880] as the Church of St. Mark in Venice and its merchants were required to pay tribute. Bohemund then left in triumph and wintered in Cephalonia on Cape Ather where the Norman warlord fell ill in a typhoid epidemic that killed 500 Normans, dying on July 17, 1085, as the town in which he died was renamed Fiscardo in his honor.[1881] Any conclusion on the matter, however, must exist by pointing out that any of the Byzantine successes could not stop the Normans from later creating the 'first Crusader principality of Outremer.'[1882]

More losses for Byzantium were also developing in the East in 1084 when Antioch was taken and in 1086 when Edessa fell as well. Armenian armies under Ruben captured Cilicia and only Trebizond, Chaldia, Attalea, Ephesus, and Pontic Heraclea were left of Byzantine Asia Minor. The growing strength of the rebelling Sultanate of Rum was swallowing Byzantine territories, bringing the Sultan Malik Shah to action in keeping control of Turkish Anatolia. In 1086, Sulayman was defeated and killed in battle at Aleppo as he encroached on Syria while his son Kilij Arslan, a relative of the Turkish Sultan, led the armies

---

[1879] Comnena, 169.

[1880] *ibid.*, 190. Yet there are no Venetian records to the fact posed by Comnena that Venice, in a fourth action, gained retribution; this was probably exaggeration or even wishful thinking, Norwich, *(AHV)*, 72.

[1881] Brownworth, 232f.

[1882] Norwich, *(DF)*, 24.

of Iconium. Malik than set sights on Fatimid Egypt, making an alliance with Alexius to rebuff the rebels in Anatolia with his heterogeneous forces using the promise of a marriage alliance.[1883] It was insulting to the point of humor that a *Basileus* would ever agree to marry the infant daughter of a Turkish Muslim, especially when he was still married to the legitimate Christian heiress Irene Ducana, but he did nonetheless retrieve Sinope and Nicomedia in the treaty.

Meanwhile, the high costs of warfare caused Alexius to take more and more wealth from the Church, when he could send whatever forces he could to Thrace to check the Pechenegs in the spring of 1087. The *Basileus* sought to retake Paradunavum where 80,000 barbarians awaited under the exiled King Solomon of Hungary, twenty-five years deposed.[1884] Comnenus gathered his forces at Distra on the Danube to take the Pechenegs, Paulicians, Vlachs, and whatever other Balkan tribes could be found only to lose disastrously, fleeing for his life. But one tribe that was not allied to the Pechenegs were the Cumans of southern Russia who swept south on the Danube and soundly beat the rebels independent of the Empire.

Within the Palace, a succession crisis was brewing in Constantinople as a failed conspiracy induced Alexius not to raise his infant son John to the rank of *Caesar*, but keep friendly relations with the Ducas family as he needed to focus on military matters. Once again he needed an army and officers, so he created the 2,000-strong Tagma of the Archontopuli and hired more Western mercenaries, keeping his brother-in-law Constantine as heir to the throne. In another shrewd move (one that he might later regret) he made overtures of alliance and possibly an end to the issues of the 1056 Schism to Pope Urban II, succeeding Gregory VII since 1088. The Turks were moving ever closer to eastern Byzantium as Chaka, Emir of Smyrna, began taking Aegean islands such as Chios, Cyprus, Crete, and Lesbos in 1090. Anatolia was taken once again by Ruman warlord bands as Malik Shah's grasp of his own military was slipping to independent armies. The Turkish fleets he did control were keeping the Smyrnans at bay under Tzachas, an Armenian mercenary who was once Grand Admiral under Botaneiates.[1885] Chaka then made alliance with the Pechenegs and recruited them to break the Archontopuli.

Alexius, however, was aiding the people that the Pechenegs were quite unprepared for in the Cumans (or Scythians as Anna Comnena calls all

---

[1883] Treadgold, 618.

[1884] Comnena, 217.

[1885] *ibid.*, 236.

northern tribes) who were northeastern Slavs that Alexius earlier used to clear the enemy invasions in Thrace. Another turnout was the visiting Robert of Flanders who swore an oath, lending the *Basileus* 500 Flemish knights, but he could not be called a Crusader however, for he received no land for his contribution nor took the oaths of Urban II. His son, Robert II, however, was to be a Crusader in 1096. Taking initiative in what he saw as a rare opportunity for being a newly released imperial prisoner, the admiral Tzachas convinced the northern Seljuks and the Pechenegs to attack, he himself wearing the imperial rank and claiming himself as *Basileus*.[1886]

The result was the Battle of Lebunium at the mouth of the river Hebrus, where on Monday, April 21, 1091, the Cumans and Byzantines under Constantine Dalessenus trapped the Pechenegs and ruthlessly slaughtered them almost to extinction, a task only to be completed by Alexius's son John in 1123. What was left of the once invincible and feared Pecheneg nation was rounded up as prisoners and relocated to Thessalonica as a buffer territory where a ratio of 30:1 existed compared to the Byzantines.[1887] The Cumans, surprisingly, did not attempt to overtake the vulnerable Byzantines and returned to the Crimea and Hungary. Now for the first time since 1076, the Danube territory was a restored part of the Empire.

Alexius, despite some successes, needed a stronger navy due to the rising superiority of the Norman and Turkish fleets as the conquering of the Aegean had proved. The Strategos Theodore Gabras, responsible for some of the territories in Asia Minor was made Duke of Trebizond to oversee the Pontus and the Turkish presence therein. A question of loyalty does surface when it is cited that the *Basileus* took Gabras's son as hostage. This was an ancient Roman practice to instill even a weak amount of loyalty utilized in allies even before the time of the first Caesars. There arises more speculation in 1092 when John Ducas, brother of the *Basilia*, was given the main fleet and recovered most of the islands (while others freed themselves in revolutions).

Equilibrium seemed to return by this time as the islands and Balkans were recovered and Anatolia was biding its time. Malik Shah probably embarrassed himself again in Alexius's court with another offer of marriage between the *Basileus* and a Turkish princess. Something that benefited the Empire was the death of Malik, continuing with the civil war between Iconium and east Anatolia under a powerful warlord named Danishmend. In the last years before

---

[1886] Vasiliev, 384.

[1887] Norwich, *(DF)*, 27.

the Crusade, Alexius put down a rebellion in Bulgaria led by Vukan, a Serbian prince, in 1093. Furthermore, in 1094 while he headed north, a son of Romanus Diogenes, Nicephorus, attempted an ill-fated coup. The *Basileus* was in a sorry state as he was generally regarded as unpopular by 1091 even with the successful events of Levunium. Nicomedia needed fortification when another imposter arose in the Cuman territories and Anna Dalessena, the head of almost all civil administration, took the veil leaving the *Basileus* with all such responsibilities.

Alexius I appealed to the West for mercenaries (especially from Robert of Flanders), pleading how the piety of the Greek Christians was being endangered by the Turks and how they were under the circumstances of 'shame, dishonor, and humiliation.'[1888] Alexius still needed good reinforcements and mercenary soldiers and appealed for this from Pope Urban II. Unfortunately for Comnenus, he got much more than he bargained for and it cost him dearly in the end. Urban would ignite the religious zeal (*excitatorium*) of the West by citing the treasures and religious relics held in the Empire and how at risk they were, including the pieces of the True Cross, the Holy Lance, and the bones of various saints.

It turned out to be an unwise display of spiritual fortitude as it probably stirred the passion of greed in the West along with its faith. These relics had their own type of prestige as a social currency to bring pilgrims and clerics to wherever these relics remained, bringing with them trade and wealth for Church and state coffers. The looting of such objects for Western kingdoms from the Greeks, who were practically heretics anyway, was probably an overt temptation. However, again, the plethora of avaricious nobles looking to bulwark the Turks more permanently was not what Alexius had in mind, anyway. Any Westerner at all he could trust were few, including Godfrey of Boullion who refused the conquering spirit of Bohemund and for that Alexius esteemed his virtues by committing an outstanding precedent by adopting the French noble as his son![1889] This had been done many times before in the Roman centuries with brilliant and loyal commanders, but they were Roman citizens and not Frankish.

In the West, the need for land and territory between feudal lords was exploding into civil unrest that shook the foundations of their own system. Pope Urban, as he saw himself as the God-appointed ruler of Christendom since the Donation of Constantine, saw the crisis and devised a way out in 1089

---

[1888] Vasilievsky, A. 'Byzantium and the Patzinaks', *Works, vol. I*. Moscow, Russia. 1908, 90; Vasiliev, 386.
[1889] Gibbon, 2046.

by first lifting the excommunication Gregory VII had laid on Botaneiates in 1078. In March 1095, Byzantine ambassadors appeared at a Roman Council at Piacenza to discuss clerical marriage and the adulterous union of King Philip I 'the Amorous' of France, also requesting aid, as Urban was zealous to do.[1890] Because of the doubts that Alexius would be present, the historian Sir Francis Palgrave (1788-1861), in his *History of Normandy and England*, claims these ambassadors were agents of Bohemund of Tarant in disguise![1891]

At a special Council in Clermont-Ferrand on November 10, addressing the use of simony, Urban called for as many nobles as could be found in freeing Jerusalem from the Infidel and avenge the pilgrims and clerics of the Holy City that had been robbed and persecuted within. The birth of the Crusades lasting centuries had that day been born to cries of *'Deus Vult'* ('God wills it!'). As a sound theory of Christian holy war, three main reasons existed that the Latin nobles, taking an unprecedented appeal to the East included:[1892]

1) There was a 'general religious spirit' brought about in Western Christendom since the Clunaic movements of monasticism that roused theologians, philosophers, and pilgrims of all kind to make a holy journey and save the Holy Sepulcher. This would even affect the West and East in unintended ways. During these years, a wave of anti-Semitism hit Europe as the non-believers of the Cross were being hunted by false Crusaders not in the actual Crusade. Judith Herrin refers to a Jewish history by Solomon ben Simpson of Speyer (fl. 1140):[1893] 'But here the Jews living among us whose ancestors killed him [Christ] and sacrificed him groundlessly. Let us take first vengeance upon them.' Synagogues were destroyed, Torahs burned, Jews killed all over the West in Speyer, Worms, Cologne, and Mainz, all cities in areas ruled by nobles turning toward Jerusalem. Violence for God had become a raging epidemic that would cause little relief for the tremendous suffering meted by Christendom.

2) The growing power of the Church over secular authority in the nobility and how success would bring '. . .their authority over many new countries and restore "schismatic" Byzantium to the bosom of the Catholic Church.' What can also be inferred from this statement by

---

[1890] Norwich, *(AM)*, 119-120.
[1891] Vasiliev, 401f.
[1892] *ibid.*, 397.
[1893] Herrin, 257.

Urban is that the Eastern lands would spread Papal authority and arms in Byzantium to presumably separate the Western feudal nobility from the land-hunger issues starting the strife in the first place.

3) A less than tangible love of war and adventure was another motive posited by Vasiliev where the Crusade would be '. . . an unequaled opportunity to satisfy their ambition and bellicosity, and to increase their means.' Indeed, the prospects of landed wealth, the spoils of the war, and the opening of lucrative markets of the East motivated the secular nature of the Crusaders. Though this explanation would appear to be a love of expansion and commerce, it was not necessarily one of war in general.

This would benefit the West greatly as even the peasantry of Europe would feel relief from their duties, postpone rents due, and have some security for their families from constant assaults. Most of all, the Pope made a guarantee as the Supreme Pontiff that all involved would be given universal penance for confessed sins at the Council of Clermont in France to any who fought to free Jerusalem.[1894] This would be a blank check for the savagery of these knights and soldiers in unleashing terror and suffering against the Crescent not seen in the East for many years. Unfortunately, there were no stipulations by the Pope barring warring with fellow Christians when needed. Furthermore, in the East, St. Basil had written that war in the name of religion was acceptable, but in no way praiseworthy and certainly not a grounds to remit sins.[1895] Supporting all of these reasons were the romantic views of a great Jerusalem as seen in relics, paintings, sermons, pilgrimage tales, and passion plays. This recognition by Christians as multi-media was exploited to raise conscientiousness of Jerusalem, Christ's city, as a celestial kingdom and the Sepulcher as supreme shrine.[1896]

The Pope, Western Christianity, and the Latin nobles all got what they wanted, spreading first from Anatolia to Antioch, Syria to Jerusalem, and the Balkans to the heart of Constantinople itself. This was a nightmare for Alexius I as resources would be seriously strained to care for the Crusaders and the dangerous implications of their moving east looming large in the *Basileus's* mind. What he expected was the typical spare armed troops and mercenaries as he had received before fighting the Turks or Cumans. Ones, perhaps, who could obey commands and imperial authority, but he instead received, 'undisciplined

---

[1894] Treadgold, 620.

[1895] Brownworth, 235.

[1896] Montefiorre, 118.

hordes, religious fanatics . . .and simple adventurers' whose responsibility was his.[1897] A fierce blow was coming fast to Byzantium as thousands upon thousands of zealous knights would cover Byzantine Anatolia.

In 1096, the first Crusaders came to the City led by the ascetic Peter the Hermit; they were not trained warriors or mercenaries, they were only derelict, naïve, and enthusiastic peasants and clergymen dedicated to freeing the Holy Land. After a reluctant quartering by an already strained Alexius in a City populating around 600,000 inhabitants,[1898] they only caused trouble for the Romans, setting out for Hungary. But a logistics error had Peter waiting to cross at Nicomedia during this march north on December 6, St. Nicholas's Day, with eighty horse and 1,500 men.[1899] Peter barely escaped death as these would-be soldiers attacked the Turks at Belgrade and were summarily butchered and taken prisoner by the first enemy they fought, their fleets taken by the barbarian crossbows, being a military innovation of the Turks. Any escapees had no choice but to flee to Constantinople and the reluctantly hospitable Alexius. This was known as the 'People's Crusade' and it was one of the most disastrous and tragic Crusades of the East in history.

Over time, the Western nobles, knights, and armies arrived at Constantinople bearing the symbol of corn as the Bread of Life, marking in opposition the sensuous Muslims as taking the vine.[1900] These included Hugh of Vermandois, brother to the King of France and Robert of Normandy, brother of William II King of England. Along with these men were Alexius Comnenus's best supporters in these conflicts, Godfrey of Bouillon, Duke of Lorraine, and Count Raymond of Tolouse. Anna Comnena exaggerates that over 180,000 knights and soldiers crossed the City gates, but it is better put around a sober 30,000 at this time.[1901] They inevitably became too numerous to house in the City's precincts, Alexius settling for containing them in the outer suburbs of the City just beyond the Inner Wall. This led to anarchy as the Crusaders looted and pillaged the suburban and middle-class citizens residing there when supplies were low with an armed force of 30,000 infantry and 5,000 cavalry.[1902]

---

[1897] Norwich, *(AHV)*, 77.

[1898] Montefiorre, 217f. By 1099, Fatimid Cairo and Turkish Baghdad were at 400,000-500,000 as Rome, Venice, Florence, London, and Paris of the Crusaders only made a fraction of such counted together.

[1899] Comnena, 316.

[1900] Runciman, 50.

[1901] Herrin, 257.

[1902] Treadgold, 621.

This greatly outnumbered Alexius Comnenus's combined forces while the Westerners' exploitation went largely unchecked. Alexius's only hope was the creation of oaths sworn by the Westerners to hopefully curb themselves and serve as vassals to the Empire, including being loyal imperial subjects in whatever land they took to settle. The regent of Antioch, Tancred, promised to swear nothing without receiving the *Basileus*'s tent 'filled to the brim with gold' and as much gold given to the other nobles put together. Eventually, he was persuaded by the other Westerners to take the oath and it was countersigned by Western nobles and Eastern Christian princes.[1903]

The *Basileus* feared the Westerners as Germans and Normans were known as particularly greedy races with no scruples. The credibility of the Crusaders in keeping to their oaths, especially Bohemund's, was dubious and the oaths only amounted to a suggestion of peace by Alexius. The idea of Western Catholic lords giving vassalage to a strange Greek Orthodox *Basileus* in the East seemed to counter reality. In fact, the promise of hostility was made worse when Alexius rejected Bohemund's disingenuous offer to be made Domestic of the East, basically leading both the Crusaders and the Byzantines on the march. Centuries later, the details between Peter the Hermit and Alexius were argued between Catholic Frankish accusations made by Louis Maimborg (1610-1686), a French Jesuit, and the sympathies of the 'schismatic Greeks' championed by the philosopher Voltaire (1694-1778) in the eighteenth century.[1904]

This idea of Byzantine diplomacy was further corrupted in 1095 with the influential Hugh of Champagne. The very concept of a pacifist policy with the Muslim Turks was alien to him and his vassals, creating mistrust in Hugh to the point that he saw the Byzantines as traitors to the Crusade. Since Alexius's grandfather's generation, the fighting men of Europe had been nurtured on an idea of holy war against the Infidels that brooked no mercy and allowed no accommodation.[1905] Peace, compromise, and even the accepting of envoys from the sultans baffled the Westerners and obfuscated their alliances with the Greeks. Contempt for the Byzantines on all levels were rife in the Latin nobles and one knight even went so far as to lounge on the imperial throne as Alexius entered the hall.[1906]

Though the Pope had ordered the Crusaders to begin a concerted march

[1903] Sewter, 434.
[1904] Gibbon, 2045f.
[1905] Laiou, 'Byzantium and the West', 73-74.
[1906] Brownworth, 237.

for August 15, by May they were arriving in Belgrade. In the City, June 3 was the date the army was completed with the arrival of Robert of Normandy and Stephen of Blois. But for the present, the Crusaders were moving into Palestine to reach Jerusalem and began filing out of Constantinople toward the Turkish territories in Anatolia and Nicaea. They began battling Kilij Arslan who hastily left Melitene where Danishmend was fighting his Eastern forces and the Sultan, who had not been battling determined Westerners, was defeated. As a blow, however, to the West, the Nicaean garrison surrendered to Alexius and the *Basileus* shared greatly in the city's Treasury as a boon to his depleted coffers. But the added insult of Nicaea dismissing the Crusaders as well as taking their share of a hard-fought reward only widened the gap of mistrust between Byzantine and Latin. However, it may also be true that this bounty was reparation by the avaricious Crusaders that fed off the Byzantine suburbs as Bryennius had done earlier in Alexius's reign.

Arslan followed the Crusaders heading east to attack from Dorylaeum, only to be rebuffed once again. He would then use more crafty tactics afterwards by cutting off supply trains from the west and north as the armies would be stuck in Anatolia without much Byzantine aid in defending the conquered cities. Polybotus, Philomelium, and eventually Iconium were taken, but no soldiers could be spared in garrisoning these territories. When they moved to Heraclea in Cappadocia, they met the forces of Danishmend, also underestimating the Crusaders, who fled the conflicts. What artillery aided most in besieging such cities was the counterbalance trebuchet used by the Comneni at Nicaea. This is said to have been 'first' recorded by Anna Comnena and her 'city-takers.'[1907] A mistake by Comnena had been made, as other sources report Basil II was said to have used trebuchets in Bulgarian sieges and some were reportedly seen in early centuries.[1908]

The Crusaders had little trouble from the Armenians, once hostile to the Byzantines, who gladly allowed them to pass through their lands (as long as they left quickly) proving the intimidation to Eastern princes the Westerners posed. After passing to the Cilician plains, a French noble, Baldwin of Boulogne,

---

[1907] Chevveden, Paul E. 'The Invention of the Counterweight Trebuchet: A Study in Cultural Diffusion.' *Dumbarton Oaks Papers, 54*. Washington, DC: Dumbarton Oaks Research Library and Collections. 2000, 71-116. http://www.jstor.org/stable/1291833 DOI: 10.2307/1291833

[1908] The origin of the trebuchet can be found in the *Mojing* tactical guide of 4th-century BCE China, traveling by Avar, Arab, and Persian territories to arrive in Byzantium, used as early as 587 CE. *Ibid., 74.*

laid claim to the territory. After a march to clear the Turks of Germanicea, he usurped the territory by forcibly marrying the daughter of the Armenian prince and setting himself up as Count of Edessa and Samasota. This loyal Armenian prince was basically betrayed and his kingdom stolen by an uncouth French noble.

At the close of the year, as the Crusaders traveled unobstructed to Antioch, Alexius appointed his brother-in-law John Ducas to take Smyrna in western Anatolia from the Emir, Chaka. The Turks must have been facing internal problems as they surrendered the city to the Byzantines who they usually defeated, receiving safe passage from the city under relocation to Polybotus by Bryennius. In 1098, Ducas turned the tables again at the western Anatolian coast by taking 2,000 prisoners at Ephesus and continuing to take Philedelphia and Samos. He reached Laodicea, but lacked the soldiers necessary to garrison and defend the city as well as his next target of Chomos, leaving only light forces at the fort of Lampe. Regrettably, the weakened Byzantine military that could not offer security to its soldiers anymore abandoned the cities to their fate, although the Turkish presence had been severely diminished.

However, Byzantine power was now growing in Asia Minor as Alexius I personally laid siege and destroyed Dorylaeum, Nicaea, and all cities south to Philomelium where he annexed their Christian inhabitants. Alexius's intentions in southern Anatolia were to create a 'no-man's land' in the area[1909] as a makeshift, Medieval demilitarized zone to buffer the Turks (the historian Tacitus (56-120 CE) wrote, after all, how 'the Romans create desolation and call it peace'). Alexius and Ducas are absolutely not to be confused with the intentions of the Crusaders in Anatolia and were not intentionally making Holy War against Turkish Islam. These were just more territorial fights for survival plaguing Byzantium for the last half century. They rarely made permanent arrangements for these cities as they could not afford garrisons with the troops they had as only a few lightly-armed outposts existed, such as in Acroenum. The real battle for Eastern Europe's soul was taking place beyond Asia Minor in the spoils of Manzikert.

These Crusaders made it to Antioch in June of 1098, yet faced trouble as a strong Turkish force besieged Bohemund and his defenders. Unanswered appeals were made to Alexius, much to his frustration, as he had exhausted his resources recovering Anatolia, even giving up on the Crusade as doomed when Byzantine advisers dissuaded the *Basileus* from taking action in Antioch, seen

---

[1909] Treadgold, 623.

as treason by the West.[1910] The siege was lifted by the cavalry sallies of Count Raymond of Toulouse and Antioch was given to Bohemund and his Normans as a prize, including the Holy Lance of the Passion, much to Alexius's dismay (and later regret). After the decommissioning of a certain administrator from the army the previous February, Tancred cleverly convinced Antioch that it was an abandonment and betrayal of the city, cutting off imperial cities and treating the Muslim prisoners too well, even accommodating meals without pork.[1911] Therefore, any obligations to the *Basileus* were now null and void. This continued before and after the city's rescue by Raymond, who could not convince the Antiochenes otherwise by himself. Though he had no part in the victory, Alexius, nevertheless, laid claim as lord of Byzantium to the Crusaders that they were to be his vassals, later given Laodicea with a garrison collected from Cypriot troops.

In the summer of 1099, the Crusaders were in Palestine again, this time defeating the Egyptian Fatimids that had taken the region from the weakened Turks. Pisans from Italy arrived with fleets to join in the spoils, but only raided the uncontested Ionian and Aegean Seas, while the recently recovered Laodicea and the faithless Bohemund aided them from Antioch until Count Raymond intervened. Alexius belatedly wished to capitalize by joining the Crusade, but first he had to turn to Trebizond in the south to reclaim it from Danishmend who would execute its governor Theodore Gabras in 1100. Just before this, as Alexius was recovering Cilicia from Bohemund, the Crusaders proved to be speedier than expected and took Jerusalem on Friday, July 15, without him. After two weeks of Western siege ballasts fighting walls defended by pits dug and lined with spears, the citizens of the city knew it was victory or death for them, helping the defenders and sewing for them ox hides. Finally the walls were scaled, the Crusaders entering where a bloodbath occurred under Tancred as 10,000 clerics and others were slaughtered on the Holy Mount. Other atrocities occurred where infants were throttled and buildings were burned.

This triumph was an invention of religious visions, such experiences over reason and military tactics becoming the true theory of the holy war as shown by the victorious Crusaders in Jerusalem.[1912] For example, though all present knew it was Islamic, the Crusaders claimed the Dome of the Rock was built by Solomon or Constantine I and it was re-christened the *Templum Domini*

---

[1910] Herrin, 258.

[1911] Brownworth, 240.

[1912] Montefiorre, 219-220.

('Temple of the Lord'), topped by a cross. As the First Crusade was presumably over with Christianity winning the Holy Sepulcher from the Crescent, the difficulties for the Byzantine Empire were only beginning with wily and ambitious princes like Bohemund and his family.

Bohemund began in 1100 by insulting the Eastern Church, appointing a Catholic Frenchman as Patriarch of Antioch while Alexius was in Armenia and Melitene dealing with Danishmend. Ironically, the former Patriarch of Antioch was one John the Oxite who was a strong opponent to the *Basileus* Alexius, anyway. Bohemund went to join Alexius, but was captured in a Turkish ambush and made prisoner by Danishmend. The Norman did, however, send for Baldwin of Edessa in a rescue effort but the new King of Jerusalem only managed to save the city and not its prisoner who was taken to Neoceasarea. Alexius only had a brief pause in his worries as in 1101 more 'Crusaders' arrived to Byzantium to free Bohemund from captivity. They took Ancyra and gave it to the *Basileus* in good faith only to be decisively beaten by Danishmend in the Halys valley. More were destroyed by Kilij Arslan at Heraclea as well as a third army consequentially being defeated by the determined rebel Turks of the Iconian Sultan.

Alexius I Comnenus became a scapegoat in these defeats; his forces were too weak and absent as he could not provide them with safer routes of travel as it was thought the *Basileus* himself should have led the marches. So Alexius had little choice but to follow these demands, returning to Ancyra. But by then, the Iconian Turks had isolated the city to ensure that keeping it besieged would prove too difficult. Arslan, meanwhile, re-established his capital at Iconium as the Ruman Sultanate, further cutting off Constantinople from the East. Alexius was still seen as a traitor to the West's cause and Bohemund's nephew Tancred as regent of Antioch used this scurrilous claim to invade Cilicia and abduct Raymond of Toulouse, who was practically Alexius's only ally from the West. Tancred only relented when Raymond gave up Laodicea in early 1103 and, rightfully so, 'no one believed it was out of friendship.'[1913]

By that time, Bohemund was able to pay off (without Antioch's aid) Danishmend into an alliance from his status of a prisoner, the Turk even resisting Alexius's offer to 'buy' the hostage and, quite possibly, treat him to a good blinding. After more internal rebellion, Alexius demanded Cilicia returned and Antioch in autumn, sending more troops east, successfully recovered the coastal cities. In 1104, Raymond of Toulouse died at Tripoli and Alexius found

---

[1913] Treadgold, 625.

himself at the mercy of Danishmend at Trebizond, Bohemund in Cappadocia, and the Turks all over the eastern frontiers. But that May, the Turks turned on Bohemund and defeated his army near Harran as miraculously, Danishmend died to leave a balance somewhat restored between the *Basileus* and his enemies.

Bohemund saw he needed Western reinforcements and left Antioch to Tancred, returning to Italy recruiting French nobles to carry battle against not the Infidel Turk, but with Comnenus who appeared 'in league' with the enemies of the Crusade. Herein is the tale by Comnena of Bohemund's diabolic unscrupulousness, an '. . .unprecedented and cunning ruse.' He escaped the East by being smuggled out in a coffin fitted with a dead cock to smell as a corpse (Comnena would ponder, 'I wonder how on earth he endured such a siege upon his nose'[1914]) for four or five days. After spreading false reports of his death in Corfu and Dyrrachium, he was taken west to seek the aid of more would-be Crusaders to 'bring about the downfall of the Roman Empire.'

Bohemund covered all of his bases, winning over the new Pope Paschal II and marrying the daughter of the French King to gather a fresh army of Western nobles and mercenaries. Forced to consolidate, Alexius unofficially ceded Cilicia and Laodicea to Antioch, the *Basileus* making his own dynastic plans by marrying his son to the Hungarian king's daughter, Piroshka-Irene, and once again seeking help from the Venetian fleets.[1915] Of note is the fact Venice flourished in this period in terms of naval military technology; ribbed and skeletal ship construction allowed the transport of gunwales and heavy artillery. Now, Venetian ships could build trade ships differing from from war galleys.[1915]

After recovering Trebizond from the Turks of a deceased Danishmend in 1106, more Turks from Iconium were hired to rebuff the Western armies. At the head of 34,000 soldiers, Bohemund returned to the valued beachhead of Epirus, taking Dyrrachium (as if a vicious cycle of constant conquest was perpetuating) in 1107. This time, however, Alexius implemented the Byzantine tactics of attrition that Byzantium was well known for to use the Venetian fleets and their merchants to cut supplies to the invaders. The tactic worked well early in 1108 when Bohemund was besieged by Alexius, facing famine and plague; his nephew Tancred seeming conspicuously absent as he had been before since becoming regent of Antioch when Bohemund was being held for ransom by Danishmend.

---

[1914] Comnena, 367.

[1915] Treadgold, 626.

[1916] Norwich, *(AHV)*, 85.

It is hard to believe that no plans were made or some word was not sent by allies or territorial pathways in the north to Antioch. Was this neglect a power play by the young and greedy Tancred? A rear attack on the Byzantines with Arslan's troops across Cappadocia and Nicaea might have knocked the vulnerable Alexius down. The answer was the Crusaders surrounding Antioch as Count Baldwin of Edessa, King Baldwin of Jerusalem, and the Count of Tripoli forbade such an enterprise as they themselves could not reach Bohemund. Bohemund returned to Italy after ceding Cilicia, Laodicea, and Antioch as imperial vassals. This meant nothing anyway as Tancred now held these territories and he was as capable as his uncle, but his focus remained in Cappadocia as the Crusader allies of Byzantium further stayed his hand.

In 1107, the Byzantines' fortunes were at a draw when Kilij Arslan died, leaving Iconium to his son Shahanshah, Alexius's concerted 'no-man's land' in Anatolia being occupied by nomadic Turkish tribes who could unfortunately survive such scarce conditions.[1917] In 1110, they were chased from the fortress of Lampe, only instigating a huge raid where the Turks outnumbered the Byzantines who only won by an ambush outside Philadelphia. The situation had become critical in Asia Minor again as renegade Byzantine generals turned against the *Basileus*'s orders to independently fight the Turks, but at least not Alexius, however. This had been done by Michael of Amastris who the emperor feared would rebel openly against him, so the *Basileus* sent an expedition against him. Michael showed amicability to the arresting commanders and the *Basileus*, who saw he was no threat to him and still an asset against the Turks, so Michael was pardoned.

In 1111, Alexius was stricken with a pulmonary ailment (probably asthma) and heavy gout and although he would survive another seven years, this severely weakened him physically. He made a truce with the Italian merchants that had been raiding the Western seas since 1099, granting tax and fee reliefs as well as charter contracts. In the spring, the intractable Bohemund died and Antioch was now wholly Tancred's; Alexius demanded its return and was, of course, turned down. As the *Basileus* was gathering his allies in Jerusalem and Tripoli, who had faced Tancred before, the new ruler of Antioch also died in 1112 and the city would be left to another nephew of Bohemund's, who appeared less hostile.

In Anatolia, the Iconian Sultan invaded Asia Minor's Byzantine territory and took Ephesus, going on to Nicaea (their Duke they captured for ransom),

---

[1917] Comnena, 405. Repeating the tactics used with Turkish Anatolia in 1098.

Prusa, Cyzicus, and Adrymittium with his 54,000 men. At Cotyaeum, they were halted by the *Basileus* as the Duke was released, war now coming between Greek and Turk. In 1116, the Turks entered Anatolia and after victories and occupation, Alexius decided on an offensive campaign east into Turkish lands. Dorylaeum was taken and the settlements along the way south were razed and their Christian populations relocated, Shahanshah being defeated at Philomelium. Here, the Sultan made peace to cease his soldiers' raids in Anatolia just before his deposition by his brother Mur'ad, who wisely chose to abide by the treaty.

As Alexius Comnenus's health was quickly failing in 1117, he was in constant pain with a swelling of his whole body, with the issue of succession became urgent. The *Basilia*, putting pressure on Alexius to disinherit John, chose for his heir his son-in-law Nicephorus Bryennius, as *Caesar*. Despite his family's leanings, however, Alexius stood by his choice with John as his heir, dying on August 15, 1118, in the Palace of the Mangana, being buried at the monastery Piroshka-Irene had founded around 1103, Christ Philanthropos. His unobtrusive chapel in the surrounding masonry still exists in ruins, although no tomb has ever been found.[1918]

It was naturally assumed that Alexius I would have the Turks and Eastern tribes to deal with from day one of his reign. However, it was an unfortunate surprise that the greatest nobles of the (West Christians fighting for the Cross, no less) would become almost the worst disaster to the Empire and its welfare in years. Alexius handled it as best as was possible and it turned out quite well as Anatolia was mollified by the time of his death and the major enemies to deal with, Bohemund, Tancred, Arslan, and Danishmend, were dead as well by the time of John's succession.

But, another flaw gleaned from the first Comnenus's reign concluded the problem, 'The results would have been better for many Byzantines, especially for those abandoned in Turkish territory, but not necessarily better for Alexius and his relatives. Knowing all this, Alexius put his own and his family's interests ahead of the empire's.'[1919] This quote alludes to the nepotism of high bureaucratic offices and corruption in land reform known infamously as pronoia that allowed the Treasury's suffering with the typical culprit of over-doling on land grants and lapsing on state centralization. This was the unfortunate side to a reign that finally saw improvement in the Empire's welfare

---

[1918] Brownworth, 242f.
[1919] Treadgold, 629.

and it was more important in this crisis that the present be seen more than the future. Furthermore, the number of titles and hierarchies of centralized authority increased. Titles such as *Sebastus, Protosebastus, Panhypersebastus, Protopansebastohypertatus, Panentimohypertatus, Protonobilissimohypertatus* (just to name a few) from lists existed to various imperial favorites and relatives, feeding these allegations.[1920]

He had a reign with mythical legacies when viewed by scholars, who in relating the manuscripts of thirteenth-century historian Nicetas Choniates (1155-1217), discovered the eponymous similarities of Basil II as 'Bulgar-slayer' and Alexius as conqueror of the Turks as 'Persian-slayer' (*Persoktonos*), his son John II Comnenus a combined slayer of Persians and Scyths (*Skuthopersolethros*). Future generations would then see the Comneni family as conquerors over the enemies of the Empire as well as what lauds were added by his daughter, Anna. Alexius's reign was perilous and in a state of constant warfare with little relief and economic drives with little improvement, but it maintained a success needed for a tumultuous future. Lastly, he was still called 'the Jackal' that feeds on the leavings devoured by the Lion; that he did reap the benefits of alliance against Islam with recovered territory despite the 'fears and toils' given by the Franks.[1921]

However, seen from the point of view like Paul Lemerle (1903-1989) who wrote the *Agrarian History of Byzantium* in 1979, the legacy was not at all to his grace. Alexius has also noted to be a 'false savior' who 'downgraded the nascent bourgeoisie, parceled the Empire's best land to relatives and cronies, surrendered long-distance trade and shipping to the Venetians . . .and burned heretics [the Paulicians].'[1922] There was a dark side to all that Alexius set to accomplish by rescuing the Empire from its economic and military troubles as he was not the saint his admiring daughter makes him to be. Controversy from both sides, such as a biographer and an economist are known to hold the *Basileus* in their different lights. Anna Comnena's use of first person in these histories, in fact, reminds a reader of a memoir more than an actual objective outline.

Alexius's huge responsibility to the fisc was mainly handled by his counterpart and mother, Anna Dalessena, as he focused on the shifting developments on the war fronts as he was no financier and '. . .his methods

---

[1920] Ostrogorsky, 368.

[1921] Gibbon, 2070.

[1922] Mango, 'Introduction', 12.

would make a modern economist aghast.'[1923] Dalessena started by assigning estates to relatives for no cost or taxation, further expanding to lands with private standing. The result was inevitable as decentralization accelerated and the landed rich became more powerful, letting the Treasury and military payroll suffer. This was the weakest pillar of Byzantium's strength: internal forces reaching to the external until neither system seemed to work. By 1109, Dalessena had retired from public life and Alexius improved on the inflated taxation by championing the poor versus the exploiting rich by raising their taxes. The equal balance of a standard taxation was also necessary as tax rates for certain areas, based on class, ranged from one-fourth the amount due to four times as much.[1924]

In the least vain attempts at garnering funds, the *Basileus* turned to the wealth of the Church which was more easily controlled than the landowners who really monopolized the economy. He confiscated gold and silver plate from the churches and monasteries to the outrage of the Patriarch and faced accusations of heresy by the ascetic John of Italus. Oddly, yet legally, he invoked canons made by the *Basileus* Heraclius in 618, confiscating gold from the churches to aid in fighting the Abbasids and the 969 promulgation of Nicephorus II Phocas which infamously limited the amount of wealth of the churches and monasteries. But this was seen as a flimsy premise and strongly opposed by the clergy, mainly accomplished through *charisticum,* the administration of monasteries by lay patrons and bureaucrats.

These men settled lay affairs with no spiritual contribution, involving priests and abbots in these proceedings to basically milk these institutions dry in recovering imperial costs and debt. Comnena reports how he specifically left the ornamentation of the coffin of the *Basilia* Zoe alone, yet this was just a reverence for a secular authority more respected than the monastery in which she was kept. The Church in which she was kept was the Chapter of the Antiphones, three churches of the Savior regarded as Pantocrator ('All-Ruling'), Pantepoptes ('All-Seeing'), and the Savior in Chora ('A Platonic 'Space' between the material and divine'). Much of the Treasury's funds went to the welfare of these Churches as well as the Theometor ('A version of 'Mother of God') in the holy district of the Chalcopatria.

Furthermore, there were the reformed parishioners of 1107 that acted as 'vice squads on public morals' – basically spies – and the creation of the imperial

---

[1923] Runciman, 30.
[1924] Treadgold, 627.

orphanage to refuge the 'disabled . . . maimed or completely incapacitated,' as a hospital. This might even have included those blinded by civil and military officials and, occasionally, the *Basileus* himself! Reports on such grants are given in 1083 by the Domestic Gregory Pakourianos to the monastery of the Theotokos Petritziotissa.[1925] It was a land of four Themes with twelve villages, six fields, two estates, joint and dependent monasteries, holy places, fisheries, warehouses, inns, and annexes. Food was doled out as well as horses, oxen, asses, bulls, sheep, rams, and goats for farming. These became wealthy and self-sufficient monasteries that would be invested by the state and 'farmed' by *Basilii* when sources of capital were needed.

Alexius gave to the poor and made poorhouses for the new professional beggars that had arisen in the City, and in 1112, after the Treaty of Devol was settled, made a bid to restore the Union of the two Churches. He was set to travel west in the summer to apply for this in return for the Western Emperor's crown, according to the almost outrageous claims of the Chronicle of the monastery at Monte Cassino. Only an illness of Alexius's and the crowning of Henry V on April 13 by Pope Paschal II supposedly prevented this event. Yet in all this talk by historians of a healed schism, no such schism seemed to exist as there was no documentation at the time claiming a Schism of the Churches actually had 'officially' occurred.[1926] This flies in the face of tradition as it marks Alexius I as a statesman that could actually reunite Church relations. This would induce John of Italus to call for stricter monastic discipline in more secluded places such as Mount Athos, which was directly under Alexius's authority as its *Protos*, as well as the reforms of Christodoulos at the island of Patmos.

These monetary and sacred confiscations would notably be made into religious controversy as the Patriarch undermined Alexius with accusations of Iconoclasm for destroying religious representations to mint his coinage. This was quickly becoming one of the worst religious/secular clashes in centuries, leading the emperor to propose an eleven-point bulletin defending his actions in 1082. Alexius's greatest supporter in these endeavors was Euthymius Zigabenos (1050-1120), who published refutations defending the *Basileus's* actions and clearing matters of his alleged 'Iconoclasm'. Such a published work can be found in the Vatican Library in Rome bearing the Comnenus's most famous depictions. One critic and accuser of heresy was Leo of Chalcedon who called for a Synod before the Patriarch Nicholas III the Grammarian to

---

[1925] Mango, M. M. 'Monasticism', 210.
[1926] Runciman, 38.

condemn the *Basileus*. Ironically, it was Alexius who began the practice of the *Syndicon,* a recitation of the list of heresies and their practitioners on the first week of Lent which would include the Iconoclastic emperors such as Leo III and Constantine V.

These accusations may be the reason these ecclesiastical events encouraged them to do so as the leaders of the 2,500 Paulicians having rebelled, deserted the *Basileus* who had disbanded and condemned the Tagma of the Manicheans. Though Alexius's Orthodox piety was supposedly well-known, it was not for nothing that heretics were never before allowed to join the Byzantine military, Basil II having his sect of Bogomils in the Slavic Balkans burned at the stake. This type of Paulicianism, or Bogomilism, would spread west with the Crusades to be known as the Italian Patarins, German Cathari, and French Albigensians, a century after Alexius's death.[1927] Yet Comnenus would be fair when erecting a new Phillipopolis for the converted and destitute Bogomil soldiers in peacetime as it was a 'new city, surrounded by gardens, enriched by immunities, and dignified with his own name, founded by Alexius, for the residence of his vulgar converts.'[1928]

The clash of Christian versus Classical cultures would take new ground in these decades as John of Italus would oppose men such as Zigabenos over imperial policy. Italus was a Neo-Platonic philosopher who also studied Aristotle and decried the *Basileus*'s closing of the Pagan philosophical Schools in Constantinople. His abstract nature also brought his teachings condemnation over their tenancy to dishonor sacred images. As a student of Michael Psellus, political reasons might have mattered as he was anti-military and Alexius was a seasoned veteran by the time he was crowned. Even though new Classical traditions were being founded with the studies and applications of Homer, classical philosophy was still dangerous when it could not be found to conform to the Church.

Zigabenos, on the other hand, defended Alexius's piety before his theological enemies, being an educated man in the seven liberal arts. He specialized in the New Testament and the Epistles of St. Paul to scientifically and logically refute heretical errors.[1929] For Alexius he wrote a handbook on accomplishing this through the Church Fathers in the *Dogmatic Panoply of the Orthodox Faith* to undo the Bogomil Dualists. Subsequently, the *Panoply* was continued by a

---

[1927] Vasiliev, 383.
[1928] Gibbon, 1933.
[1929] Vasiliev, 473.

complementary work, the *Treasury of Orthodoxy* ('Thesauros 'Orthodozias'). For now, the position of Jerusalem had again conquered Athens in the battle for Byzantium's soul, but a case of perspective in the *Basileus*'s ideology seemed as important as its theology.

The Venetian pirates of the western Greek seas, cynically claiming to be Crusaders, only fought for their own market-based interests in the Byzantine East.. To mollify them, Alexius was forced to create a trading colony in Constantinople with relaxed to practically non-existent duty fees. Included was an exemption to the ten percent *kommerkion* tax along with other taxes amounting in twenty-three percent of the principal tax (the *dikeraton*, *ezaphollon, sunetheia*, and the *elatikon*), while Byzantine government would be denied the right to inspect ships. The result was a fifty percent tax increase on all other trade and on supplements that the poorer classes, especially the rural, were expected to exact.[1930]

This was an odd mixture with the May 1082 treaty wherein Constantinople was referred to as the Great City (*Megalopolis*),[1931] benevolently allowing several Venetian warehouses (*maritimas tres scalas*) into the City with quays across the Galata. The Bishop of Grado had even bestowed titles on the Venetian Doge and offered fifty pounds in gold as an annual tribute. Although this invisible hand of the market greatly enriched the Venetians and encouraged massive amounts of Italian trade from Amalfi, Venice, Genoa, and Pisa, the Byzantines were only benefited when particular wars and invasions were allowed to present mobility and stability, occurrences which rarely happened.

In 1111, the greed-motivated union of Genoans and Pisans from northern Italy began pirating the Ionian Sea, competing with Venice for markets and imperial privilege. Claiming descent from the treaty of Basil II in 992, they extorted rival markets in Constantinople and throughout the Empire. These ventures were under the same conditions as Venice on duties as a more social aspect to these changes in West-East economic forces. Also, the republican presence of the city-states of Italy questioned Byzantine 'hegemony' in the outer Balkans. In turn, this encouraged these Italian peoples to claim more independent 'identities' and political forces that would coalesce into rival nations in the following centuries.[1932]

One prime example was the Bulgarian Monastery of the Bachkovo in

---

[1930] Ostrogorsky, 369.

[1931] Vasiliev, 382.

[1932] Herrin, 158.

the Rhodope Mountains, south of Philippopolis. In 1083, a Georgian officer, Gregory Pacurianus, founded the monastery on the mission upon condition that it give preference to Georgians and allowed no Byzantines to join its communities. In modern times, except for the mortuary chapel, the building has been demolished to be restored in the seventeenth century. Before his death in 1086, as the Domestic of the West, Pacurianus charged the *Romaioi* as being 'violent, cunning, and grasping men.'[1933] Such attitudes led to such claims of independence in communities, inviting the notion of expatriation in subject peoples, the Georgians being no exception.

Financially, although it was asserted that Alexius did this to celebrate the birth of his son John (who would never make an appearance on Alexius's coins), a new coinage was made necessary to be in circulation by 1090. The issue was in addressing the ever-increasing debasement of six different types of *nomismata* owing to the inflation rate of twenty-five percent in the unsound currency. Probably originating from the use of melted plate, the twenty-and-a-half-karat *hyperpyron* was one of the purest gold coins of the past few centuries at an impressive rate of seven-eighths the former, pure *nomisma*. Coins of electrum (gold/silver alloys) and billon (silver/copper alloys) are identified along with basic copper to support gold coinage with 'a wide variety of denominations.'[1934] By 1090 it was in use, repairing the fleet and properly paying the army, although at a still insufficient rate that would pull the Empire short due to the overwhelming cost of the First Crusade. To fix the currency of silver (*miliaresia*), four of these coins to the gold coin were ordered by the *Basileus* with the *nomisma at* one-third its previous value in order to reform embezzlement by tax collectors.

The Crusaders themselves ate up most of the budget, already with economic suffering in Byzantium. As a list of such expenses in materials and labor would include 'constructing ships, fortifications, bridges, and roads, furnishing board and lodging for the imperial officers and the army, providing transport, and all kinds of provisions either free of cost or at a very low price.'[1935] The migration of Western feudalism followed as knights and nobles settled into Eastern territories such as at Outremer ('Across the Sea'). The Byzantine estates would be financed by feudal arrangements of land grants to decentralizing communities. Alexius's only response was the return of the pronoia wherein

---

[1933] Obolensky, 284.

[1934] Treadgold, 618-619.

[1935] Ostrogorsky, 370.

soldiers (*stratiotai*) and militias were given land under military obligation. Western feudalism found the most influences in the southern Slav lands before and long after the Empire fell. Suggested is a heightened sense of the system as was concluded: '...the establishment in the Near East of a number of Latin principalities in which Western feudalism took root in its purest form.'[1936]

Military traditions were also dying under Alexius in the crisis of the dissolving Thematic and Tagmatic organization systems which occurred before the Crusade beginning in 1081. Marked as 'the end of the Byzantine army',[1937] this was in light of the pronounced feudal Byzantine systems used by the Comneni and their successors. Another faltering institution was the legacy of Byzantine tactical literature written by *Basilii* like Nicephorus II and Maurice. Most of the logistics, troop placement, and prosecution of operations happened on the field and the voice of Roman Medieval literature was only too quiet after the Macedonians. It is suggested that Alexius I gave excellent intelligence on the Turkish forces and situations in war conferences with the Latin nobility, but their bias excluded any credit due the Eastern allies before Norman application.[1938]

One of the first reforms in the year 1109, when Dalessena retired, was to rehabilitate the status of the Palatial women's quarters, or *gymnaceum*. According to Anna Comnena (who took full credit for the reforms), this institution had fallen into disrepute due to 'utter depravity ever since the infamous Constantine Monomachus ascended to the throne [1042] and right up to the time when my father became emperor had been known for foolish love intrigues.' As for the reigns of the *Basilii* between the Macedonians and Comneni, they merely wasted time on pursuits such as 'quail-hunting.'[1939] Anna's reforms were nothing short of austere and monastic; set times for breakfast were set under the eye of hand-picked magistrates and the singing of the sacred hymns resembling the *matins*. Anna could not help admiring herself on the task, claiming an example of saintly virtue as she practiced self-control and doles to the poor. Her judgments were final and, supposedly, a single glance from the princess was enough to humble the most pleasure-loving and 'demonic' critics.

Comnena seems to have at some times the bias and vanity of Michael Psellus, although he was the type of man Anna hated for his unscrupulous

---

[1936] Ostrogorsky, 375.

[1937] Treadgold, (*BAIA*), 7.

[1938] Decker, 229-230.

[1939] Comnena, 174; Sewter defines it as not in itself an immoral practice, but that it represented a 'lazy, ineffectual existence.'

manner. Under this surface, she was the only true voice of the Crusades as a Byzantine and non-Western observer of her times with the relationships her father had made with the Crusaders, leaving even her words open to scrutiny. Yet at the same time, Sewter points out that like Psellus, she uses no chronology and leaves out many vital places, names, and events. For an example to her scrutiny, no Latin writers knew of Bohemund's false death and escape and it is questioned if she made it up. Perhaps this was because she described Bohemund earlier not as brilliant, but as 'simpler-minded', who would move on Constantinople, this probably just being Roman arrogance speaking at this time.

Another biased mention of her father was as a 'thirteenth apostle' as the Great Constantine has been challenged. And, most famously, the polarized view of her brother as an incompetent tyrant: 'Therefore we enjoyed peace until the end of his life, but with him [John], all benefits disappeared and his [Alexius] efforts came to nothing through the stupidity of those who inherited his throne.'[1940] This probably includes John's son Manuel, who she saw as over-flattered and without reverence to her own father. Her judgments were harsher and more final as a historian than that of her father was as an *Basileus*.

Despite all of this was her characteristic prose style still outdoing a Psellus or even her husband, the historian Nicephorus Bryennius (1062-1137). Without doubt, she rightfully joins the rare ranks of Medieval women who wrote histories such as Hildegard of Bingen (1098-1179), Marie of France (1145-1198), and Christine de Pisan (1364-1430). Her polished, Classical education accounts for this and is to be lauded with the likes of Polybius, Xenephon, Thucydides, and the leading Byzantine historians Psellus, Theophanes, and Procopius. All of her writing ability came from lyric poets like Aristophanes (425BCE-388BCE) and the Greek tragedians, her oration style coming from master word smiths such as Isocrates (436BCE-388BCE) and Demosthenes.[1941] Only one thing truly tainted her judgment and that was the bitterness she felt toward her brother John. Before his birth, she was said to have worn purple robes, a diadem, and having been allowed to dine with her father at his table after her birth on Saturday, December 1, 1083. When Alexius died, her husband was denied the throne in favor of her brother and this divided mother and father as well as sister and brother in the House of Comnenus.

Culturally and in the realm of education, Alexius's reign still saw improvements and innovations distinct from other movements, not least of all

---

[1940] Comnena, 448.
[1941] Vasiliev, 389-390.

the resurrection of Homer's literature in the *Iliad* and *Odyssey*. Though more expansive in the 1160's, Arabic translations of Greco-Latin material became a larger practice. Eugenius, as a Greek Emir in Turkish lands, was one who translated Ptolemy's *Optics* from Hellenized Arabic into Latin.[1942] Another important translation was *Stephenites and Ichnelates,* a Greek version of Indian animal tales centered on the mythical Lion King. Its original purpose was for the Comnenian court during Alexius I, but it spread to Norman and Turkish kingdoms as a literary success and was a common thread between the three cultures.

And in education Alexius I Comnenus was not neglectful, opening a school for the orphans of his soldiers in the Church of St. Paul. But, although it is not stated whether it was for secular or theological education and from its closing in 1204, it was re-opened in 1261 as a secular Grammar School.[1943] Indeed, the Greek Classical tradition of allegory was a constant use in theological and Biblical interpretation in Byzantine culture and the separation of the two was generally found unacceptable. As another exercise of theological education and policy, heretics in Armenia such as Paulicians, Saracens, Iconoclasts, and especially Bogomils were persecuted in the Slavic East. Bogomilist persecution was particularly popular in Bulgaria and Bosnia as well, but in Croatia the heresy would remain a state religion for the five centuries before the Turkish Conquest.

## JOHN II COMNENUS 'THE BEAUTIFUL'
### (1118-1143)

In John, Alexius's only son, Byzantium could not have received a more upstanding exemplar of ethics, duty, and morals. Unfortunately, not enough is written about him except mainly by his sister Anna (which is mostly in an invective). Though not of his own making, he made a true enemy out of his family – grandmother and sister – resulting in intrigue typical of the Byzantine stereotype. At his ascension in 1118, the Empire was at relative peace with the Crusaders, checking the Turks who in turn were oddly silent while the Pechenegs defeated at the Danube were now either imperial soldiers or licking their wounds. Finally, because Bohemund and Tancred were both dead, the hostile forces of Antioch and Cilicia were at the time being settled.

---

[1942] Angold, 154.
[1943] Buckler, 219.

But, perpetual peace in any part of the Middle Ages was impossible, and soon John would be beset by the troubles his tireless and restless father had faced.

The only half-way objective history to exist on this *Basileus* was made by writings from after the time the last Comneni perished in 1185. Nicetas Choniates was an officer and Grand Logothete under the Angeli dynasty of the later twelfth-century and wrote his *History* from 1118 to 1206.[1944] Sewter insists it was these historians as well as modern ones that made the conclusion that Alexius's choice for successor was the right one. Choniates and his contemporaries John Zonaras (1074-1130) and John Cinnamus (1144-1185) also paint a picture of John as the right choice for the throne, having the best qualities that office requires.[1945] Yet, other historians evaluating these two contemporary histories conclude that the reign of John II was treated by them as having great 'brevity' and being merely 'introductory', perhaps adding to the reputation of John's sources for his reign being scarce.[1946] It is the blind jealousy for the throne that makes Anna Comnena such a risky source to be taken at face value, her husband and fellow historian, Nicephorus Bryennius, being turned away to be basically Alexius's final wish. This hatred only grew from her exile in a monastery when the *Alexiad* was created, dying only with her around 1153, ten years after her brother.

John II Comnenus was born on September 13, 1087 to Alexius Comnenus and his *Basilia* Irene Ducaena in the purple. Though he would earn the name of 'Calo-Johannes' (John the Beautiful), Anna depicts him as having a swarthy complexion, broad forehead, thin cheeks, and an average nose, reluctantly admitting a certain handsomeness being there. Choniates would be much kinder and note on his physical beauty, though he possessed almost no traits of a Greek. A Western source, the Latin Chancellor of Jerusalem and Archbishop, William of Tyre, judges the *Basileus* as 'small and unusually ugly' and has no problem adding an insulting moniker to John's legacy as John 'the Moor.'[1947] The question of his ascension was decided early as the oaths and flattery of Bohemund and other Crusaders refer to him as well as the 'Great Autocrat Alexius Comnenus' as 'his thrice-beloved son and *Basileus,* Lord John the Porphyrogenitus.'[1948] Even if this was disingenuous, the use of John's name and titles proves his ties to the throne were always somewhat secure.

---

[1944] Norwich, *(DF)*, 63.

[1945] Sewter, 144.

[1946] Ostrogorsky, 352.

[1947] Norwich, *(DF)*, 65.

[1948] Comnena, 512.

His abstemiousness in court, before and after his ascension, is well noted and appreciated; though not totally austere, he detested flamboyancy in dress, opulent robes, golden jewelry, rich foods, and decorations at court, all he saw as signs of depravity and decadence. Perhaps he was too militant, but he was frugal with funds and known to break the code of nepotism with grants and titles his father followed, and in charity and good works did he have a generous, and free, hand. Decency at court was to be respected and ribaldry was strictly limited or denied, conversation being squarely on serious matters of state, all of which John observed with no trace of hypocrisy. He was also merciful to his enemies, never blinding criminals or rebels and going so far as to exonerate his brother-in-law Bryennius for an assassination attempt, giving him honors in Constantinople until his death in 1137. Gibbon gave John praise as the 'best of the Comneni' and that 'the philosophic Marcus [Aurelius, 161-180 CE] would not have disdained the artless virtues of his successor, derived from his heart, and not borrowed from the schools'[1949] and only his rule as a Comneni was beneficial and pure. This exemplary conduct as ruler of the Eastern Empire (shrinking as it was) would earn him the proper name of John 'the Good.'

On Easter Sunday, 1118, as their father lay on his deathbed, Anna attests that John 'the emperor's heir' fled the scene from the Mangana to the Great Palace in a cold depiction that he might have done so out of callous greed. The real problem is that the text surviving in Sewter's care is seriously and irrevocably corrupted, being filled with 'lacunae' that left holes in the meaning of the context. Yet, a discrepancy of more detail is alluded to by modern historians claiming Alexius gave the imperial insignia ring – the symbol of power since the first *Augustus* – and bade his son go to the Palace even before he died, a fact also defended by Judith Herrin from other Medieval historians.[1950] Anna seems quiet on this particular event, but it is reasonable that it was said by Choniates or his contemporaries. When compared to John's character, this fact appears fabricated as he was present almost to the time of Alexius's death until it was likely proper to leave for the Palace rather than did Nicephorus Bryennius, the choice of Anna Comnena and Dalessena. The *Basileus*'s wife and daughter stayed to strip Alexius of his robes, diadem, and purple buskins, all identifying John as *Basileus*.

Nevertheless, on August 15, 1118, with his father's dying consent, John II Comnenus was crowned at St. Sophia. But it was even here his troubles began

---

[1949] Gibbon, 1654.
[1950] Herrin, 234.

when a plot to kill John at his father's funeral by his sister, grandmother, and brother-in-law was only diverted by an advanced warning. Another such plot was set for the Palace of the Philopation at the Golden Gate of the City, but was thwarted when Bryennius timidly backed out and surrendered. Surprisingly, John exonerated Bryennius for his loyalty, giving offices and benefits to his fellow conspirators the remainder of his life while other conspirators were only temporarily bereft of their property. As the true ringleader, Anna Comnena was exiled to the convent of Theotokos Kercharitomene ('Virgin Full of Grace') at the Christ Philanthropos ('Lover of Man') monastery Irene had built in 1103, Kercharitomene having only forty nuns occupying its cenobitic dormitories.[1951] It was here her bitterness grew intemperately, but so did her talents, and so she wrote the history of the *Alexiad*.

The first act John II tried to perform as *Basileus* with real teeth was to refuse the treaty of trade made with Venice in 1082. The tax burdens put on the Byzantines (especially the poor) by the treaty's inordinate terms freed the Venetians from their taxes and duties. This had put strain on the economy and fomented hatred for the Venetians, Pisans, Genoans, and probably the government for allowing this to happen. Mercantile activity for Venice went unhindered, however, receiving no special treatment given in the 1082 treaty for their promises of naval defense. This was a risk financially to the Venetians as they already had considerable capital invested in Oriental trade,[1952] proved now as John stood firm in his practices of ousting special privileges until 1136.

The Byzantine fleet was in an inferior, disastrous state and could hold no purchase against the Doge Domenico Michiel. On August 8, 1122, the Doge would set sail to besiege Corcyra with seventy-one ships before Crusading with the Cross of Christ on the masthead. Unfortunately, in 1123, imperial interests had to turn east again as King Baldwin I of Jerusalem was taken captive by the Palestinian Turks. In 1124, Rhodes, Samos, Lesbos, Andros, and Chios were raided until Domenico returned to Italy in 1125 with many Aegean victories under his belt. With the *Basileus*'s attention in Anatolia and an intimidated navy, the only recourse was surrender from Constantinople when Cephalonia was invaded in August, 1126. Further military-economic policies would see further resistance to the West as they also diminished, even in a crisis.

In the West, another crisis for the *Basileus* occurred when a cousin of Guiscard was crowned Count Roger II, King of Sicily in 1130 after his

---

[1951] Norwich, *(DF)*, 64-65.

[1952] Norwich, *(AHV)*, 87.

grandson, William, failed at stabilizing the region. As Roger was now absolute ruler in Sicily and Apulia, he was made king of the 'Two Sicilies' in Palermo. For almost five subsequent centuries, the descendants of the Normans would rule this southern Italian kingdom with Papal blessing. The Byzantines had little recourse considering their position as proven by the need for John II to later betroth his youngest son Manuel to the kin of the Holy Roman Emperor, Conrad III Hohenstaufen. If a balance of power could not exist, the western Greek isles would again be vulnerable to Norman invasion whether Venice, Pisa, or Genoa would intervene. John, as a sound diplomat, would make a foundation of good relations with the Popes in Rome as an ally that could put some pressure on the King.

Something else was motivating John at this time, pushing east as the faith and fervor of the Crusaders to reclaim the East taken by Manzikert, Anatolia, and even perhaps the eastern borders of Basil II or Justinian I was occurring.[1953] The Anatolian coast south of the City was facing more Turkish raids and nomadic settlers while the Emir Ghazi had taken Trebizond and held for ransom its commander, Constantine Gabras. Turkish Caria was also cutting off Byzantine support to the city of Attalia and other pressure points, further trapping the Greeks in Anatolia. John had campaigned to the Meander in 1119 to stop raiding in Thrace along with a Turkish ally known as John Axuch. Axuch had been a childhood friend to the *Basileus* since he was held as a political hostage by Alexius Comnenus and had mostly known only Western ways as a Latin captive from Nicaea as an infant. John Comnenus had made him a loyal Grand Domestic of the Army, the *Basileus* and the commander taking all and forcing the Phrygian Emir Abu-Shara to flee from its capital at Laodicea.

Laodicea on the Lycus River removed their Turkish garrisons, now nominally held by Alexius since 1107, occupied and fortified by John and Axuch. In 1120, the arteries to Laodicea's ports and the city of Sozopolis were taken and Attalia was recovered, cutting off Caria and Iconium. The next year, pressure came from the north as the recovering Pechenegs and some Cuman allies crossed the Danube. John settled a peace between the two in Beroea, but learned the lessons of his father and Constantine VII by betraying this peace. After winning another crippling defeat with the barbarians, John took hostages, locating them in the Byzantine army. Oddly, it is the opinion of Choniates that the Pechenegs faced extinction by 1123, more so than after the Battle

---

[1953] Norwich, (DF), 66.

of Levunium under Alexius I; John's main reaction was the observance of a 'Pecheneg Holiday' commemorating this victory.[1954]

The reasons behind the Pecheneg defeat are outlined as such when it is remembered:

1) The Pechenegs had no 'supreme commander' meaning it existed as smaller entities, bonded by one goal among an amalgam of differing tribes.

2) The Byzantine chariots created a circular barrier surrounding the enemy armies, a tactic that succeeded at Adrianople by the Goths.

3) The Pechenegs could not repel the Varangian Guard and the superiority of their broad battle-axes and their long shields, destroying the enemy chariot.[1955]

Time had caught up with the Pechenegs since the tenth century; military tactics, the Varangian supplements, and more advanced cavalry were turning the once fiercest of the barbarian nations into Byzantine vassals and soldiers (those that survived). This is the reality of these Thracian peoples and their own armies dwindled as a result.

At Trebizond, an ungratefully ransomed Gabras soon rebelled, upsetting the Byzantine Black Sea coast with the rebelling Paphlagonian governor Cassianus. John had recovered a modest surplus with his conservative spending, but instead of refurbishing a navy he saw as hopeless he put these funds into the Turkish War over Anatolia. But these problems were sacrificed when Stephen II, King of Hungary, invaded Belgrade, Nish, Serdica, and Philippopolis. The *Basileus*'s forces would drive them back to Hungarian Sirmium, but Stephen induced the Rasian Serbs and their *Zhupan* Boltan to claim independence from Byzantine authority. All of this was able to be contained under the walls of Haran at the valley of Iskur. The Byzantine navy from the Nera tributary flanked the Hungarians to the river and many of the enemy died there as peace was finally made between Byzantium, Serbia, and Stephen the following winter.

In February 1130, Antioch had become a vulnerable city due to the Danishmends who not only defeated and killed its Duke Bohemund II at Pyramus in Cilicia, but presented his head as a gift to the Baghdad Caliph. That same year, the offensives could be restored in Anatolia as Cassianus

---

[1954] Choniates, 23; Ostrogorsky, 378.

[1955] Norwich, *(DF)*, 69.

and Gabras both joined with the Danishmend Ghazi and went to besiege Lopadium. John took this city first, making it his principle headquarters in the war and fortifying it, using it to lead recruitment and training as the major defensive line in northwest Anatolia. John's greatest strength was in siege, and not open, warfare concerning the trebuchets earlier utilized by Alexius I. Eleventh-century trebuchets with a 4,400 pound lead counterweight could launch fifteen kilogram (thirty-three pounds) projectiles 168 meters (551.16 feet) and later reports came that 18,000 pound counterweights could launch 300 meters (984.25 feet).[1956] As he began campaigning, he received news that another of his spurned siblings, the Sebastocrator Isaac, had allied with Turkish leaders against the Empire, forcing John back to Constantinople to end the dynastic feuding.

Isaac was exiled, but still determined to have his way with foreign allies he needed in order to back his rebel army. He appealed to Ghazi, Gabras, Mas'ud of Iconium, and Leo of Cilicia the Armenian King to join him with promises of treaties and spoils. But none would dedicate themselves to Isaac, independently or in a possible Allied Front of two or more, the rebellion quickly dissipating. Isaac still managed to gather an army of Christians and Muslims from the cities he marched through as inhabitants came flocking to his banner.[1957] These localities were fearful and distrusted whatever lord they served and would follow anyone who seemed to have even the weakest authority if met face-to-face.

Why was this so? Was it possible Isaac was not as popular or any more a favored candidate such as John II was? What of the other nations? Were alliances so unwanted, unlikely, or so shaky that no one wanted to see the others turn on them to bolster an unstable Byzantine prince? Whatever the scenario, John was victorious going to Bithynia in 1132, then Paphlagonia to recover Castamon and the Black Sea. He then crossed the Halys River where Ghazi ruled to the Euphrates from Melitene and got the submission of the Emir's governors to quiet the Turkish territories before returning to the City in 1133. There he received a Triumph surrounded by standards of purple, one chariot modestly shod in silver, treading on foot as his chariot was reserved for the Virgin pulled by four snow-white horses, thronged by the masses to St. Sophia.

---

[1956] Decker, 227. The described trebuchet was built from the original by a Danish scholar, Peter Vemming Hansen, that experimented with these figures. Hansen, Peter Vemming. "Experimental Reconstruction of the Medieval Trebuchet". *Acta Archaeologica,* vol. 63, Denmark. 1992, 189-268.

[1957] Norwich, *(DF),* 72.

This Triumph had not been rivaled by any since 972 when the *Basileus* John Tzimisces celebrated his own.

An outraged Ghazi responded with an assault on the imperial post of Sozopolis in southern Anatolia. This was not successful, but Castamon still recovered, threatening again the Black Sea before his death in 1134 as reported by Odo of Dioglio (1100-1162). He was succeeded by his son Mohammed to be 'Malik', or King, by the Caliphate, bearing a golden scepter and wearing gold chains. This threw his Emirate into chaos, making his position vulnerable to Byzantine attack. After sincerely mourning his wife Piroshka-Irene, who died in the City while he campaigned, John returned to recover Castamon, also besieging Gangra in the south. Having internal problems with no end in sight, these Danishmend cities surrendered to the *Basileus* unconditionally in 1135.

The next year, Antioch almost surrendered itself as well when its princess offered to marry John's son and heir, Manuel. Outremer intervened by forcing her hand to Raymond of Poitier, French Crusader and a son-in-law of Bohemund II, legitimating Byzantium to Bohemund's dynasty of Antioch. Raymond was also son of William IX of Aquataine, famed founder of the Troubadours, who was in England at Henry I's court who had sent relief troops in April of 1136. This also gave John inducement to send troops, especially to invade Cilicia from the Armenian king Leo who encroached on Antiochene territory to attack Seleucia. With armies of Turkish mercenaries and Pecheneg prisoners, the *Basileus* prepared for battle in Attalia.

By now, Outremer Jerusalem had become the 'Navel of the World' with its world maps centralized upon the Holy City, its streets outlined as a Holy Cross to the Church of the Holy Sepulcher. By 1140, in the time of Queen Melisende, Jerusalem was stocked with the splendor of rich carpets, damask hangings, faience, carved inlaid tables, and porcelain dishes, with bourgeois households even sporting such items. The epitomized warriors of the Crusades, the Knights of the Order of the Templar, whose garrison of 300 resided in the city daily exercised and trained at the Stables of Solomon. Unfortunately, the Holy City had devolved under Western care as it became a picture resembling the Wild West: murderers, adventurers, a prostitution trade, gambling and dice in many doorways, these all characterized the Jerusalem of Outremer.[1958]

In spring of 1137, the Armenians took the Syrian cities of Tarsus, Adana, and Mamistra, demanding a tribute of 60,000 *nomismata*, outraging John

---

[1958] Montefiorre, 235-236. Even before the Crusades, Western Christian Jerusalem was considered by the inhabitants there that no city was more evil.

and his sons Alexius, Isaac, Andronicus, and Manuel into retaking Cilicia, forcing King Leo from Anabarzus to flee into the Taurus Mountains in under a month.[1959] On August 29, the *Basileus* drew his forces to the walls of Antioch to defend against Armenian incursion successfully as Leo returned in 1138 with an army and was defeated again, he taken as a hostage from Cilicia to Constantinople. The Armenians of the Taurus were made imperial vassals as Cilicia was annexed once more. The situation was more serious in Antioch as Raymond of Poitiers held the city, but the Duke made a bargain with John for suzerainty over the city, including from Aleppo, Larissa, Hama, and Homs, if Byzantium would agree to help him conquer the remainder of Syria. Now, for the first time since 1099, a combined force of Byzantine and Outremer forces were marching in the East with Aleppo as its first destination.

John II Comnenus's entourage now included the Count of Edessa, Joscelin II of Courtenay, and his Knights Templar. Joscelin was typically conceited, lecherous, devious, and lazy, yet John was seriously hindered by the Turks and was forced to siege Sizara in the south on April 28. As this city was the key to the valley of Orontes, it was vital it be kept from Emir Zengi. Though they breached the walls, the citadel could not be taken and a draw was called between the two sides, but as he returned to Antioch, the defeated and underpaid army of Raymond rioted in the city. More risk came when Pope Innocent II forbade the Western Church to support John should he interfere with the Antiochene authorities to keep the city controlled by the Latins.

After settling the ringleaders, John returned to Constantinople with practically empty hands only breaking even on the entire venture. All the more tragic was that this was John's battle as William of Tyre describes Raymond and Joscelin as spending the entire time shooting dice! Norwich recalls the facts that, wearing a gilded helmet, Comnenus spent his time '. . .encouraging the faint hearted, berating the idle, consoling the wounded, instructing the siege machines, infusing all of his soldiers – Greek, Varangian, Pecheneg, or Turk – with his indomitable spirit.'[1960]

He entered the city victorious, raising his standard high above that of Raymond's; panegyrists romantically wrote that he, as beloved of Christ and athlete of the Lord 'as carrying the sword of Elijah,' was given a triumph by Antioch. 'Every age and both sexes formed brilliant procession . . .Shout was mixed and many-tongued, here Italian, here Assyrian . . .'thou shinest as the

---

[1959] Norwich, *(DF)*, 76.
[1960] *ibid.*, 80.

brightest star!' Tribute and surrender came from the Emir of the city including the gifts of a table inlaid with precious stones and a cross inlaid with rubies taken from Romanus IV Diogenes at the Battle of Manzikert. By May 21, he was back at Antioch to take tribute from the Crusaders, which they were forced to give.

Risky as it sounds, the *Basileus* even entrusted his siege machines to Raymond's care as well. But in July, Raymond instigated rioting on false claims that John and the Byzantines were ordering the expulsion of the Latin citizens and assaults on the Greek inhabitants. Fortunately, John was prepared for any duplicity the Crusaders would perpetrate and he fled to the Orontes in preparation. He sent word to Raymond and Joscelin that he would accept their oaths for the time being – since neither had made one at any time in the Crusade or showed any unity to the *Basileus* after the Treaty of Devol, and he returned to Constantinople with care. [1961]

But, even as he returned west, John was called upon to face the growing troubles in Apulia that was harassing the Byzantine ports of Dalmatia on the Adriatic. This was mainly a result from an incident in 1113 wherein, as a cousin of Bohemund II, Roger of Sicily had claims to Antioch. His third wife, Adelaide of Jerusalem, was step-mother to Baldwin I and the cities passed to his son, spurning Roger as a Count in the East. Out of the same indignation felt by Bohemund I and the *Basileus* Nicephorus III, he retaliated. In 1137, a desperate plea for troops with funds were sent to the German Emperor Lothair to check the growth of Apulia. He was only too glad to do so as he feared the same growth. John Comnenus wanted desperately for Roger to be dislodged for the sake of recovering Byzantine Sicily and an army was raised. Papal blessing was given by Innocent II as Roger was the sole ally of the anti-pope Anacletus, giving Lothair total advantage.[1962]

After eight years, the rebellious Isaac Comnenus then saw a turnaround with his brother and pleaded for a pardon which was granted by the famously gracious John in 1139. That spring, John was needed again at the Black Sea coast as the Danishmends and Gabras of Trebizond had again allied and taken Paphlagonia from the Sangarius valley. The imperial forces arrived at Lopadium and entrenched themselves to prepare a long campaign. The next year, the John put a six-month long siege to Neocaesarea, but eventually had to relent as supplies ran low during a harsh winter. It helped less when news came

---

[1961] Vasiliev, 416.
[1962] Norwich, *(AM)*, 133-134.

that his conniving brother Isaac had once again joined with the Turks, but an army contingent sent to Trebizond did recover the Pontic region for Byzantium by 1141 as John returned to Constantinople.[1963]

John wisely saw that with this respite, improved Western relations would be a good idea to replenish as the Byzantine forces east of Antioch and Jerusalem could now oppose the Sicilian Normans. The German Emperor Conrad III was reached out to and as a request to secure against the dire Norman situation, John's son Manuel married Conrad's sister-in-law, Bertha. A worse decision was in ignoring the opportunities of invading the vulnerable Danishmend Emirate for a new campaign on Antioch. Emir Ghazi II died in 1141, throwing the Emirates into a state of feuding 'kingdoms,' but the *Basileus* sought resources further east.[1964] In 1142, John and his sons struck a pathway south to clearly define territories in the region as Byzantine boundaries and during this, he regained Sozopolis and the Caralis islands, who then defected back to Iconium.

As he was besieging Attalia on the coast, his son and heir Alexius died, followed by another son, Andronicus, who died on the return trip to the City. Such a coincidence in the course of a Byzantine succession begs the question, of course, of it being a coincidence at all. The next son in line to the Comneni throne was John's third son Isaac who now had a clear path to the Byzantine crown, but opposition from the Norman mercenaries sought to enthrone his Latinophile son Manuel. Was there a plot against these imperial brothers by the Latins? What of Manuel's fate if this was true? Was he supposed to die as Isaac would take over as the brother-in-law to Conrad III?

A morally defeated John II Comnenus swore to recover Syria, Cilicia, and Antioch for the Empire. With the consent of the Count of Edessa, John sought Raymond of Poitier's vassalage of Antioch, but Raymond hedged at this and made the *Basileus* wait. During this negotiation, John saw the need to further defend the Byzantine south by making arrangements to adopt his son Manuel as *Caesar* to protect Cyprus and the Attalian coast from Turkish incursion. In early 1143, the *Basileus* suffered a wound from the pricking of a poisoned arrow in a hunting expedition in Mopsuestia. Dying of a septic infection, in his last days, John chose his son Isaac as heir, an unpopular choice with the Western forces in the Greek army. Unlike his father's choice of himself being *Basileus*, John's decision was railroaded in favor of the *Caesar* Manuel, who was already betrothed to a Western princess that would surely heal foreign relations. As

---

[1963] Treadgold, 634.

[1964] *ibid.*, 636.

John II Comnenus died on Thursday, April 8, 1143, four days after Easter, his son would be taken to Constantinople to be crowned the third Comneni *Basileus*, a thankfully wise choice as John's successor.

Of course, suspicion of assassination is imminent as Robert Browning firmly believes in his theories offered in the *CSHB*[1965] – but from what source? It is possible Isaac did so clearing out his brothers as dynastic obstacles to his ascendance, or, with or without Isaac's knowledge, his factions took such measures when Manuel was gaining favor in Cyprus. Even for a Byzantine prince, however, this is unlikely as such theories are non-existent among the historians and no glaring evidence points to Isaac as fratricidal. The more likely candidate was Raymond of Poitiers, who saw a never-ending debate with the *Basileus* over Antioch's fate as a Byzantine vassal. It would have been a bold stroke to use such drastic measures that even Bohemund never succeeded in doing, but it would pay off as the question was set aside towards other matters under the new Emperor in the West. If it was clearly murder – it was Raymond of Poitiers who was said to be responsible.

John was not as dynamic as his father, but held a much more stable court and managed his domestic affairs better than Alexius as he turned outward to his own private Crusade wherein no other *Basileus* after would dream on such a scale of Turkish recoveries as John II had.[1966] His abstemious nature led to a sizable surplus in the Treasury for the first time in a century. However, he demonstrated miserliness in denying funds to a navy he could have consolidated in repairing over time rather than all at once. It was this lack of vision in 'saving' up for the navy that led to its neglect as the tribulations in the Second Crusade would prove.

But, of course, this neglect was mainly the result of his diverting ambitions concerning overland battles with Turkish eastern domains and with the Crusaders. He wanted the absolute authority as lord over the Crusader territories to provide arms for a recovery of what was lost after Manzikert in 1071, which would only be a pretty pipe dream. Though an overreaching strategist, he still showed exemplary morals, piety, and courage as a *Basileus* with such odds against him. Though his plans of expansion were a failure, it is not denied they demonstrated a good sense in geographical military study and the precarious placement of fortifications.[1967] He replenished, somewhat, the Treasury to a point

---

[1965] Browning, Robert. '*The Death of John II Comnenus.*' *CSHB, XXXI.* 1961, 229f.
[1966] Treadgold, 637.
[1967] Decker, 140.

that the Empire had adequate defense of its borders and the internal troubles of Iconium and the Danishmends would see it grow stronger. John II Comnenus proved to be a well-made choice as *Basileus* to provide financial stability, justice with mercy to the worst criminals, and a piety that would provide relief to the Church. And not least of all, he has been hailed as a hero and liberator to Byzantine Palestine for the Crusaders who still held Jerusalem.

Foreign trade was hampered by John's failures to curb the Italian cities and their superior fleets. Nothing existed to protect merchants in the Empire except mercenaries that usually came from the same Western states as the pirates. John was ultimately biting the hand that fed him and it cost him Aegean islands and the franchises of Venetian ports in Byzantium. Ultimately, John was forced to lift his dues and fees on Venice when the Doge Domenico Michiel defeated the Dalmatian Hungarians and Byzantine forces at Cephalonia, tying Comnenus's hands with the reformed Venetian navy.[1968] The *Basileus* also weakened both Edessa and Antioch in demanding the feudal support of the Crusaders in his southern campaigns. The governor of Aleppo, Zangri, used these vulnerable places in both cities to recover ground. Yet, no coinage would be debased and his father's currency system was not intervened upon by the *Basileus* or his Logothetes; disadvantageous as it could be politically, the increase of Western trade for now would improve the Byzantine economy in useful foreign markets.

In 1136, John built a sizable monastery and a hospital of fifty beds in Constantinople with the inspiring Church of Christ Pantocrator visible from the hillsides of the City. This would be the 'family monastery of the Comneni' where the dynasty would be buried.[1969] Its most imposing attribute is its size as a combination of three churches connected by a common water system, John himself adding the fourth as his wife Irene had built one as well. He also built upon the spiritual relations with the Papacy, as in the correspondences to Pope Innocent III in 1141. Ostrogorsky theorizes that he was still asserting a 'political program for establishing a universal Roman sovereignty under the Byzantine scepter' when considering the words of John said to the Pope that in Christian rule, 'there were two swords, the secular which he himself would wield, and the spiritual which he would leave to the Pope, and together they would restore the unity of the Christian Church and establish the supremacy of the one Roman Empire.'[1970]

---

[1968] Norwich, *(AHV)*, 90.
[1969] Treadgold, 632.
[1970] Ostrogorsky, 384-385.

Most likely as his father, John II saw the value of the Church as an institution, but still remained detached enough to understand his authority was superior when no bridge could ever be built concerning the *filioque*. Included in this limitation was the commercial inroads to the Venetians, Genoese, and Pisans that dwindled the tolls of the exchequer, only exacerbating the conflict.[1971] This same year, 1136, more legates and envoys were sent to Rome concerning the Union of Churches to concert the efforts of the Pope and German Emperor against Apulia. He got no farther here bargaining with Innocent than he had with the previous Popes Calixtus and Honorius. At Constantinople, Latin Bishops were even beginning to advocate heavily in dogmatic and theological disputations, further dividing the Eastern Patriarchy. What was more, his mixture of languages and interpretations by such linguists as Moses of Bergamo (d. 1130) at this time helped transmit Latin as a more practical language in the Greek East as Byzantines were succumbing to the Latin of Western and Outremer influences.

More of this influence is seen in the City's Monastery of Christ Pantocrator as an example by early twentieth-century historians to demonstrate both Byzantine humanitarianism and charity by Western tenancies. Pantocrator was seen as a 'medical center', blossoming under the strict but benevolent time of John II and the Comneni.[1972] Perhaps only to be rivaled in the Western influences of charity would be the aforementioned Hospitallers and the Order of St. John that gained amazing wealth through the donations for doctors, medicines, institutions, and a place for compassion the brutality of the Medieval East needed most. With all this, however, came a subtle stream of Westernization in the heart of Byzantium that would still make Eastern culture suffer.

This cultural takeover in such areas was paving the way for new developments in all spheres of Byzantine life: Italian trade and economy, Latin political institutions and legal property, the social fabric of language, custom, charity, and religious institutions. The two crosses of Constantinople and Rome were now side by side to the point of rivalry when unity was stalemating in the West. Considering all of this, perhaps it is little wonder that the West had a stronger grip on Byzantium than Islamic Turks would until the fourteenth century. In 1204, however, the Empire would flee as these very Crusaders they

---

[1971] Sherrard, 162.

[1972] Uspensky, Th. I. 'The Tendency of Conservative Byzantium to Adopt Western Influence.' *Vizantiysky Vremminik, XXII*. St. Petersburg, Russia. 1916; Vasiliev, 472.

employed looted the streets and trampled the East Roman imperial throne under their boots.

Culturally within the Empire, the Homeric 'renaissance' was well underway, led by the guidance of the *Sebastocrator* Isaac Comnenus (1093-1152), who wrote histories of its resurrection, also being responsible for the creation of the 'Constantinopolitan Code of the Octoteuch', now in the Library of the Seraglio.[1973] Elsewhere in this century was the standardization of Byzantine music in churches. These solemn hymnals on the nature of the Scriptures and the invocation of saints, the Virgin, the Son, and the Father were written in a prose directed in 'signatures' above the words to signify the intervals, rhythms, and accents of the music. In evaluations of twelfth-century sheet music, these symbols (*neumes*) can even be transcribed into modern notes and accents.[1974] These hymns were based on lyrical poetry and odes to God written by such ascetics as Romanus the Melode (490-556 CE) in Justinianic times, St. John of Damascus in the eighth century, Casia, a nun from the ninth century,[1975] as well as St. Symeon the New Theologian (949-1022 CE) in the eleventh.

# MANUEL I COMNENUS
## (1143-1180)

John II's son Manuel was a controversial figure for a *Basileus*; his supporters were impressed by his energy and his critics were just as zealous in decrying his errors. His ambitions were no less grandiose as his father's goal, that being a universal Empire and Church from the lost Mesopotamia to the gates of Rome, yet diplomacy was his weapon of choice in combating the Empire's inadequacies. His diplomacy was no less far-reaching as the English King Henry II who was good friends[1976] with Manuel, whom he would never meet. Henry was known to receive Byzantine embassadors at Westminster, giving them gifts of English hunting dogs in 1176 by Geoffrey de Haie. Such a mark of his triumphs with neighbors and rivals may also be furthered in that it was Manuel who was the last Byzantine *Basileus* to enjoy political unity in the Balkans.[1977]

In order to achieve these measures of supremacy, he held lavish

---

[1973] Vasiliev, 490.

[1974] Sherrard, 137.

[1975] She was best known to her having turned down a chance to be *Basilia* to take the veil, Sherrard, 138.

[1976] Vasiliev, 431.

[1977] Obolensky, 161.

entertainments for the rulers and embassadors at his court in the more casual Blacharnae Palace over the main Imperial Palace. He was known for mesmerizing the Westerners with the entertainments and spectacles that only the fabulous grandeur and splendor of Byzantium could offer. The Western historian Odo of Deuil (1110-1162) wrote of a banquet in 1147 where the *Basileus* entertained King Louis VII of France at the Feast of Saint Denis with a choir of eunuchs that impressed their guests with their mingling of voices, clapping of hands, and genuflections.[1978] This transcended the typical disgust Westerners had for the *castrati* that held administrative and military posts usually held by the visiting Western nobles. The use of Latins in cavalry estimated from twelve to fifteen percent of the Byzantine army at a number of 60,000.[1979] The historian William of Tyre explains this is because of Manuel's astute recognition of the Greeks' inherent weakness, dubious as this sounds, as Manuel did all he could to integrate Crusaders in the East.

Unlike his austere father, Manuel I drained the Treasury on entertainments, games, banquets, and gifts for these guests – even going so far as to shock his own Constantinopolitans with the 'Latinophilism' he felt for the West. On April 20, 1159, celebrations for the King of Jerusalem saw the *Basileus* hold knightly tournaments and jousting at the Blacharnae Palace with Manuel himself taking part and unmanning two famed Italian knights.[1980] This was seen as scandalous, as if the *Basileus* of Byzantium had ridden in the chariot races like a common slave or fought as a gladiator as some of the Pagan Emperors had, also lacking the splendor of Byzantine tradition due to their simplicity and lesser resources. Yet we are certainly assured that there existed a '*ioie de vivre*' in his court due to his passion for living.[1981]

Yet, it was all for the purpose of uniting loyalties between Westerners such as Roger of Sicily in his educated court at Palermo allied to Constantinople. Here, fair questions would be asked about breaking the xenophobia of John's policy and fighting for a common cause instead of each other.[1982] Manuel I would reach out (and intervene) in the courts of Iconium, Kiev, Germany, Rome, Sicily, Venice, Hungary, Serbia, England, and France to unite East and West as Justinian had done despite the much less stable arms the Comneni possessed. It is no surprise that he could not accomplish this, yet what he did do

---

[1978] Herrin, 161.
[1979] Diehl, 220-221.
[1980] Brownworth, 243f.
[1981] Ostrogorsky, 384.
[1982] Norwich, *(AHV),* 95.

as *Basileus* earned him a favorable place in the annals of the Empire. 'Dextrous in arms, he was ignorant of fear; his persuasive eloquence could bend to every situation and character of life, his style, though not his practice was fashioned by the example of St. Paul.'[1983] Like a leader based on peaceful discourse, he had a vital weakness in his army's uses and tactics; his best victories only involved smaller battles, sieges, and attrition. He ground down the enemy in these attacks, but any campaign in a large-scale or decisive campaign was too costly and Manuel would discover this in the harshest terms in a humiliating defeat against the Turks at Myriocephalum.[1984]

Europe did, after all, still owe some of its culture and habits to the Byzantines East and West. In the Church of the Martorana in Palermo is a mosaic of the Sicilian King Roger II as he was being crowned in 1130 by Christ. Made in 1148, it depicts Roger in full Byzantine crown and robe studded in pearls and enameled in gold. Roger's vision was to see himself as ruler of the united Empire from the West, but not in the traditional royal paraphernalia imagined by Westerners to wear. These robes would not be proof, however, against the news of defeat he faced in Apulia by the Greeks and Latins both hailing Manuel Comnenus as the true *Basileus*, Hercules, and Alexander.[1985]

Epigrams of Manuel I Comnenus were written in the thirteenth and fourteenth centuries where his name, among the preceding Comneni since 1081, is inscribed in the Monastery of St. Mokios which was created by Basil II. Manuel's main historian, Nicetas Choniates, was noted as having given Basil the moniker *Bulgaroctonos* ('Bulgar-Slayer'), wishing to attribute the Comneni the military heritage of the Empire's greatest warrior-*Basileus*. Michael Maas has noted how Manuel was 'lauded for his triumphs over Hungarians, Italians, Serbs, Turks, and Cumans' in the heroic poetry of the era. Besides this, he was a national folk hero also among the Russians for centuries after his reign and a subject of poems and songs. His relations with Kiev and other cities were warm and generous in its gifts and diplomacy. Economically, it is because of Manuel that the feudal organization of Russia resembled that of the Byzantine until its end in 1917. The *Basileus* was highly educated, loving philosophical and theological disputes due to, it is suggested, his love of disputation for its own sake. The seat in the University of Constantinople for 'Chief of Philosophers'

---

[1983] Gibbon, 1658.
[1984] Decker, 205.
[1985] Gibbon, 1993.

had been vacant since the times of Michael Psellus and the troublesome John of Italus, so Manuel filled it with a deacon of St. Sophia.[1986]

Yet, according to the unfinished biography of Manuel I Comnenus by John Cinnamus, he had an irrational superstitious side in a firm belief in the 'astrological sciences' which he defended in a letter to a monk who called its study 'impiety.'[1987] He would follow the discipline most of his life until the Patriarch intervened while Manuel was digging escape tunnels under the Blacharnae when consulted readings prognosticated damaging earthquakes and natural disasters. Another contribution he made was to the advancement of the natural sciences and among the Arabs was his presentation of Ptolemy's *Almagest* to also demonstrate his understanding of Classical learning.

Yet with all that can be said to his benefit, he reached too far and came to nothing with the Church as a succession of Popes over the thirty-seven years he ruled led to mixed reactions with Rome. Even with a Council in 1166, the two Churches remained separate by their fundamental beliefs and would not budge on interpretation, no matter the intention. His financial policies also led to a fleeting shadow of Themes to full-scale feudalism, even in language where the Greek and Latin words for vassal were becoming interchangeable in definition. The poor were trampled by the authority of tax collectors and nobles as it was in the West as no protection existed unlike in the time of the Macedonians.

This was all the work of the Westernization creeping to the East into Byzantium that Alexius I and John II had fought, but Manuel would seem to allow. No peace was made with the tyranny of the Italian trading communities and everywhere the West was demonizing it as, Choniates complains, 'formidable in numbers, indomitable in pride, cruel in character, rich in possessions, and inspired by an inveterate hatred for the Empire,' who barely spoke any Greek and only 'spat better than they spoke.'[1988] This would further poison any goodwill with Outremer in the wake of the Second Crusade, a disastrous failure for Christendom. Coupled with military defeats, especially was severe to Byzantium at Myriocephalum (on par with Manzikert in 1076), Constantinople's fate would agree to be sealed in 1204 mostly in part by Manuel's nearsighted policies.

Born to the *Basileus* John II Comnenus and the *Basilia* Piroshka-Irene months after his grandfather's death on November 28, 1118, Manuel I shared

---

[1986] Buckler, 218.
[1987] Vasiliev, 490-491.
[1988] Diehl, 221.

a Hungarian heritage with his mother and his brothers, of whom he was the fourth, also to claim that his maternal grandfather was St. Ladislaus. Unlike his brothers, his patron and perhaps namesake was Christ Immanuel, who graced the reverses of his *hyperpyroi*.[1989] But, by his father's death in 1143, he was the second-to-last surviving son of John and the heir he chose on his deathbed. He, like John, had a handsome, but dark, complexion even in depictions of 1176 made of his 1166 Council. His enemies would use these physical traits to liken him to an Ethiopian slave, taunting him mercilessly at a battle at Corfu in 1149.

He had a reputation as having a healthy appetite for women, especially in light of the dour, homely, and pious wife he had first married.[1990] Although he was known for a slight stoop, he was unusually tall and this surprised the foreign embassadors of Constantinople. Charming, luxurious, and naturally adventurous, he showed charisma as a diplomat and his energetic will made him a sound commander on the field. His choice of officers also had a rational cunning such as the Turk Axuch, who tricked the Church into bribes of silver for their acceptance of Manuel over his brother, instead of the gold Manuel promised. When his relative Andronicus and his officers were captured by Turks on an ill-advised hunting trip, Manuel was not prepared to risk his throne to rescue them.

Perhaps it was for his accomplishments in Anatolia with his father and brothers repelling the Iconian Turks that John proclaimed him *Caesar*, just before his death, over his brother Isaac. But it is rightfully assumed that this was because of Manuel's marriage to Conrad III's sister and his willingness to reconcile the West, a policy long regarded by the Comneni. Indeed, all historians agree his ambitions for the West overshadowed any claims made by his two predecessors as if by some hereditary purpose. When John II died, Manuel's ascension was assured by the proclamation of John Axuch and his Domestic armies. Though this ultimately settled the issue, Manuel could not be crowned in St. Sophia until August 1143 by the Patriarch Michael Curcuas, at least until the *Basileus* gave donatives to the Church of 200 pounds of gold as well as two pieces to every household in the City.

Some time later, in a dispatch, secular authorities approached as Roger II showed intent to make an alliance against the French and Western Empire through a marriage alliance to the *Basileus*. Most likely seeing it was better to have these nations as allies, Manuel wisely refused despite obvious consequences

---

[1989] Treadgold, 639.
[1990] Norwich, *(DF)*, 88-89.

of Roger's enmity. On Christmas Eve of 1144, after a three-week siege, the city of Edessa was captured and occupied by Imad ec-Din Zengi of the Aleppine Danishmends. The Prince of Antioch sought Manuel's aid in defending his own city in Outremer; as the *Basileus* paid subsidies, but sent no troops as a sign of some careful neutrality between Cross and Crescent.

Later that year and into 1145, Manuel would both defeat the Turks of Bithynia and some defiance by Antioch. Raymond, Prince of Antioch, only sought vassalage from the *Basileus* when Manuel saved Edessa from Zangian Turks after their drunken Emir's murder by a eunuch. By January 1146, Conrad III was preparing groundwork for the Second Crusade by offering his daughter Bertha in marriage to the *Basileus* as she had spent four years awaiting him as a guest in the Palace Gymnaceum. As a shrewd diplomat he agreed, wedding his first wife as Irene, once Bertha of Sulzbach, strengthening German ties at the expense of the less stable Roger of Sicily. He would still use his natural vigor in keeping mistresses, including his brother Isaac's daughter, Theodora Comnena, and no serious scandal arose from the incest! On the bottom line, Manuel desperately needed this German alliance to counter whatever action Roger of Sicily might take.

But in 1146, the *Basileus*'s direction was turned east by the murder of Zangi in Iconium, being succeeded by Mas'ud, who quickly shielded his frontiers. The Turks turned south after a defeat in northern Malagina and took Pracana to raid Thrace. Manuel cut a path through the Sultanate from his fort at Lopadium, taking Acroenus and Philomelium all the way to Iconium itself. This turned into a defensive maneuver, however, when the Danishmends induced the *Basileus* to retreat to Lake Caralis. The Danishmends drove him back to Constantinople where negotiations with the Sultan bought the Empire another peace at the price of the city of Pracana.

A true test of the Empire's endurance came in the form of a new Crusade called for by Emperor Conrad III, King Louis VII of France, and an English army under Stephen of Blois. The stressed Hospitaller and Templar Orders had sent pleas to the Pope from Jerusalem for another Western coalition. Missing from these entreaties was Pope Eugenius III, who had fled for Viterbo after an attempt of deposition, so the Crusade was being championed by a French prelate in Bernard, Bishop of Clairveaux. This may explain why Conrad had not been crowned by Eugenius and was only entitled as 'King of the Romans.'[1991] Arnold of Brescia (1090-1155), another such Crusader, reported how Eugenius's claims

---

[1991] Norwich, *(DF)*, 89f.

were tenuous and unstable and therefore his authority as promoter would be questionable. However, the promises of booty, land, adventure, and plenary absolution from sin urged Conrad and Louis east, despite Jerusalem being safely in Christian hands.

Besides the Pope, other detractors, including the feudal princes of France as well as the factions of Vezelay in Burgundy, resisted armament. Nevertheless, on March 31, Palm Sunday of 1146, Bernard made a speech that officially opened the call for arms. King Louis had by then went east with his wife, the formidable Eleanor of Aquataine, on Christmas Day of 1145. In the summer of 1147, Conrad crossed the Danube to arrive at Constantinople in September where Manuel was reluctant to invite another Crusade that would again disrupt the Empire and Constantinople. Conrad responded with a siege and only his sister's intervention stopped him, as this was a prelude to the Turkish treaty Manuel signed on October 4, insulting the Westerners. As the siege reluctantly ended, Manuel was expected to give food, aid, and hospitality to the Crusading visitors. An interesting fact, yet not to improbable for the age, was that this was as close as Conrad and Manuel ever got to each other. They would never meet face-to-face as only intermediaries and embassadors would communicate Manuel's letters to the German Emperor.

Conrad wanted to set out even before the French King even arrived in Constantinople, eager for loot and glory, excitedly wishing to start in Thrace against Manuel's experienced advice. Once he was in Iconium, the Turks effectively routed Conrad at Dorylaeum and, fleeing to Ephesus, he fell ill and returned to Constantinople without victory. Meanwhile, the French Crusaders were crossing the Danube, hassling and looting their supplies from the local inhabitants with their typical impunity. Joining a recovering Conrad and a troubled Manuel, Louis arrived at Constantinople and the Westerners headed for Syria and Cilicia. They found a horrific slaughter of at least ninety percent of the French army as casualties, resulting from the defeat at Nicaea,[1992] this due to the use of the siege equipment of the Comneni that the Turks had previously captured. Another disaster awaited them as disease, further Turkish defeats, and the scorching desert weather saw seriously depleted and demoralized troops entered Syria with resentments between the two Western rulers and the Byzantine *Basileus* in early 1148.

Ostrogorsky would judge King Louis's departure at Attaleia as having

---

[1992] Norwich, *(DF)*, 96.

'. . .left their wretched men to their fate,'[1993]as another apt criticism at Western Crusader 'piety' and 'chivalry.' The Crusades themselves were as infamous as the Thirty Years' War, the Napoleonic Wars, World War I, and Vietnam for the suffering and devastation they caused, while all principles and morale weakened whether it was Christian charity or American invincibility. In another example, Frederick, Duke of Swabia, rode to Adrianople and concluded his occupation by burning the city's church with the Byzantine monks still within. Frederick's fate would be to become Holy Roman Emperor and elevate his position in this Crusade, despite of (or even partially perhaps of) the cruelty shown in this theater of war.

Another problem had arisen in 1146 as Roger II sent a fleet under George of Antioch to take Corfu, raid Euboea, Athens, the Ionians islands, Thebes (as the center of the Empire's silk manufacturing stolen off to Palermo),[1994] and the Gulf of Corinth. George also held the new title of *Admiral* of the fleet, a word derived, according to Norwich, from the Arabic term *emir ad-bahl* ('Ruler of the Sea'). Conrad's annoying preoccupation with Iconium made him conveniently absent from the Western front and Manuel appealed to the Venetians and other Italian fleets. With no other options, Manuel reversed decades of Comnenian policy and conceded all trading 'privileges', living quarters in the City, and ports for their aid;[1995] to this the Italians greedily agreed and headed to Corcyra. Cinnamus estimates the navy under Costephanus as having 500 galleys, over 1,000 transports, and an army of 20 to 30,000. Unfortunately, the *Basileus* himself was detained as he had Cumans invading the Danube that he would soon defeat.

At Ephesus, Conrad was deathly ill, leaving King Louis of France in Palestine as Anatolia would prove to be a waste of Louis's resources, blaming all but himself, harboring an almost 'psychotic resentment of the Greeks.'[1996] More defeats occurred at Aleppo as he fled to Antioch, urged strongly by his intrepid wife Eleanor to seize the city. But in a show of cowardice, Louis dodged this siege by claiming he needed to pray in Jerusalem at the Holy Sepulcher from May until June 24. On that day, the Crusaders at Acre decided to undertake an inexplicable and needless campaign to Damascus in the heart of Danishmend territory. By July 28, they were close to annihilation, retreating from the Syrian

---

[1993] Ostrogorsky, 382.

[1994] Norwich, *(DF)*, 97.

[1995] Treadgold, 641.

[1996] Norwich, *(DF)*, 98.

city's walls and Nur ed-Din's archers. Through the barren route to Tiberias more archers caused heavier losses as they arrived in friendly areas, all expelled without one inch of territory taken.

For Easter of 1148, Louis VII decided to travel to Jerusalem, wishing to divorce Eleanor who understandably found him deplorable, Louis also licking the wounds of a debilitating and shameful defeat. The only real victors would be the French peasants who would dodge taxation as their vassal lords would not be returning to the West. The French Crusaders reached Calabria on July 28, 1149, and Louis was incensed by the indignation against the Byzantines and the theft by Greeks of their royal baggage, inducing him to petulantly plead to Pope Eugenius III for a new Crusade against Constantinople. The Pope was too preoccupied, however, about saving Louis VII's marriage and though a gentle man, he refused its dissolution and placed anathema on any who criticized the marriage or spoke against it. This pleased Louis greatly, for he still loved Eleanor in a supposedly 'childish way.'[1997] As for the Germans, on September 8, Conrad III made for Thessalonica from Acre and Manuel I gave him passage back to Constantinople as a close friend.

By Christmas of 1148, the Second Crusade was deemed a debacle and Conrad III shared his shame with Manuel I while in Thessalonica. Though no ground was claimed by the Crusaders, *Basilii* and Emperor were still in an alliance by Manuel's wife and Conrad agreed to finally aid Byzantium in driving back the Normans from the south-west of the Empire. To further tie the two, Manuel married to Conrad's brother, the Duke of Austria, to his niece by his deceased brother Andronicus in February, 1149. As a dowry on his niece and first wife, Conrad received Apulia and Calabria for the German realm, supposing if he could claim it from Roger of Sicily. This probably induced Emperor Conrad to cleverly join with his brother-in-law to oust Roger II's influence from all of Byzantium.

In 1149, the offensive at Corfu perpetrated with Venice was still resulting in a stalemate and now the Normans would viciously taunt Manuel from Corfu's walls about his swarthy skin using a captured African slave. Venice chose to turn on their allies, but Manuel straightened this out and finally retook the island from Avlona; but Manuel was not done, seizing the opportunity to turn west by finally invading Sicily. Roger's strategy included the use of subversive political tactics, stirring trouble with the Serbs using his diplomatic acumen. He managed to instigate a civil war between Serbian Ras and Dioclea against

---

[1997] Norwich, *(AM)*, 142-143.

Hungary in 1150 under King Geza II as Roger II sided with Ras against Manuel and his efforts of military intervention in western Byzantium.

The whole of the Slavic East would become involved as George of Antioch would cross the Marmara with forty ships to the walls of the City. The Russians were affected as Kiev sided with Hungary and the rebelling princes of Suzhdul and Galicia fought for Manuel. After sacking Selinum and Sirmium from Hungary, Geza sued for peace in 1151. Roger's adept diplomacy also involved the German Duke Welf, who occupied the Hohenstauffens, forcing Conrad to rally back West. Sirmium was Manuel's greatest triumph and the historian Cinnamus wrote that 2,000 cuirasses and countless helmets, shields, and swords of the enemy came into Roman hands to make fine trophies.[1998] But, just as Manuel was tempering the situation, attacks from all his eastern borders further halted his next Sicilian expedition.

Mas'ud and Iconium retaliated from the failed Crusade to raid Thrace and the resulting chaos enticed Theodore II of Armenia to rebel and march on Cilicia. Mas'ud and Zangi's son, Nur ed-Din, began consuming Byzantine territories at Aleppo, blinding its Count, and killing Raymond of Antioch. They further engulfed territory from Cilicia to Samasota faster than Manuel could pay them off, only succeeding in freeing Edessa along the way. Manuel I would not give up on recovering Sicily, however, as tied up as the army was with its Eastern assaults. John Axuch was to be sent to Ancona on the Adriatic to begin the campaign but the Venetians, fearing for the future of their own city conceding its trade, opposed the crossing. It was now apparent in the Empire that any Crusading action would be followed by opportunists on any Byzantine border, hostile or otherwise, capitalizing on any defeat.

Along with the lessons of the West's tenacity, this would be the truth for all the future Crusades, being the fear of Alexius Comnenus when confronted by this fact after a *successful* Crusade. Peace in the Empire seemed unlikely, regaining eastern territories on the scale of a Justinian the Great, a Basil II, or a Constantine I now seemed less and less possible and the preservation of what territories could be kept would be the only viable option whether Manuel saw it or not. Nonetheless, as the *Basileus* and German Emperor agreed on a Norman campaign for 1152, more misfortune ensued when Conrad III Hohenstauffen died at Bamberg on February 15 and was succeeded in Germany by the cruel and intractable Frederick I Barbarossa ('Red-Haired') of Swabia.

A staunch believer in the Medieval ideal of a universal Western Empire

---

[1998] Decker, 204.

under one Church, Barbarossa would have no regrets in subsequent decades to address Manuel as a Greek 'Rex' rather than a Roman 'Imperator'. These psychological tactics and petty drawing of lines in the sand by the West had already been employed for many centuries. Roger of Sicily himself was styled the 'new Amalek' by the East, an allusion of tyranny from Exodus 17:8-14 including Sicily as the 'western dragon' with the fiery breath of Mt. Etna, rallying the princes west.[1999] Manuel desperately concluded a treaty with Pope Anastasius IV at Constance in 1153, but no Italian territories were to be conceded.

Another example of these territorial threats was the total loss of Syria and Cilicia to the Turks and Armenians, respectively. Opting, once again, to delay military tactics for negotiation, Manuel Comnenus offered his *Caesar* John to the ruling Princess of Antioch though she refused. Now, Andronicus Comnenus would be sent with armies, but his ineptitude in Syria led to his defeat in Cilicia by Theodore II Gabras. Frustrated and desperate, the *Basileus* sent envoys to bribe the Iconian Sultan Ma'sud into inciting the Armenians. Ma'sud accepted, probably with designs on Cilicia for himself, but Theodore would only win victory over the Turks in 1154. In an auspicious turn, Roger of Sicily died this same year on February 26 and was succeeded by his inferior son, William 'The Bad'. William appealed to Byzantium and Venice, but faced the same opposition Roger had; meanwhile, a full-scale war in continental Europe was being quietly planned by Manuel. After allying with the Normans who were hostile to William, he got the approval of Barbarossa and Pope Hadrian IV to create the Lombard League against Sicily.

In the Slavic East, William got word to Geza of Hungary that if he could gain the alliance of the *Basileus*'s unfaithful cousin Andronicus, an orchestrated attack to the Empire's exposed eastern territory would be justified. In 1155, they crossed the Danube, extorting a peace upon Manuel with Hungary and the infamous Andronicus was ultimately abandoned by Hungary, he being forced to flee to Russian allies in Galatia. Though a year late, Manuel still had the impetus of the Pope and German Emperor, having just conquered Lombardy before Easter, launching the Norman invasion he had prepared for over six years.

His ambassadors George Paleologus and John Ducas having been rebuked by William, Manuel faced little effort at Ancona against his armies. The allied armies used their Normans to take Bari, the former Italo-Byzantine capital, and a commercial enterprise with Genoa allowing more troops to finally end

---

[1999] Vasiliev, 422.

the Norman occupation. But in 1156, at Brindisi, this all fell apart as a superior force of 2,000 knights under William II routed Manuel and the League and, panicking, the Pope and Barbarossa made peace with William, turning their backs on Manuel. Having taken Bari on May 28, William seized four Byzantine ships in battle along with their silver and gold, entering Bari and burning down the Church of St. Nicholas.[2000] The next month, almost all of northern and western Sicily was given to him in the Treaty of Benevento as no Byzantine could dislodge his hold on Italy.

By 1157, the consequences of Benevento hit hard the remainder of the League (now just Byzantium and their rebel Normans), who was demoralized and dangerously underpaid. They stood by as William took Euboea with 164 ships and 10,000 soldiers, sailing the Volos to the Hellespont and Marmara, peppering Constantinople with silver-tipped arrows. Alexius Axuch was sent to Ancona to repeat the Byzantine strategy, but it was only going through the motions with Manuel abandoning this failed enterprise. After an expense of 2,000,000 *hyperpyra* on the war effort by a *Basileus* known for extravagance, peace was made with William in 1158 so the Manuel could concentrate on defending against Barbarossa.[2001] War with the West was quickly showing not to be his strong suit for multiple reasons: outnumbered troops, shaky alliances with uncertain outcomes, outrageous monetary costs to Italian merchants and military ventures, and two-fronted wars with Sicily, Iconium, and Hungary. Wisely, the *Basileus* fell back on his great diplomatic skills and strengthened his alliances with marriages and good relations. This proved to be a slight improvement on Manuel's foreign policies compared to before.

The summer after William's peace settlement, Baldwin III of Jerusalem made a lucrative offer to Constantinople. In exchange for becoming the *Basileus*'s in-law by a Byzantine princess, he would outfit a siege on Cilicia. Accepting, Manuel's daughter was married to Baldwin in Palestine, starting this Eastern campaign by defeating Theodore II on the Cilician. His ally was the new Prince of Antioch, Reunald, who stepped in line and submitted. By Easter of 1159, Theodore lost Armenia as vassalage and was banished to rule only the Cilicia plains in a fine twist of irony. Reunald would submit his position as a true Christian penitent: ceremoniously wearing no armor and a noose around his neck as if to say his fate was Manuel's to decide, he bore his sword in his left hand as submission of the right hand used in battle.

---

[2000]  Norwich, *(DF)*, 115.
[2001]  Treadgold, 643.

The Danishmends of Aleppo surrendered hastily and were granted Edessa in exchange for Christian prisoners. The only setback seriously to be faced appeared in Iconium against the Turks of the son of Sultan Mas'ud, Kilij Arslan II. By that winter, the Turks were becoming more intractable on the Bosporus and posing a stalemate to Byzantine arms from the Opsician and Thracians as the Carian Turks were taking Laodicea again from the *Basileus*, as well as Phileta, in order to threaten Attaleia.

Manuel I Comnenus, himself present for all of his battles, could give evaluations of the Byzantine offensive maneuvers founded on a 'four-pronged attack' of:

1) The *Basileus*'s own contingent
2) The allies of the Prince of Serbia in the Meander
3) John Costephanus's contingent
4) Levied Pecheneg troops tied to a treaty with Reunald, led by the commander Thoros, heading through the Taurus by the south[2002]

Around this time, the Empress Bertha, the late Conrad III's daughter, died and this severed ties between the Byzantines and the Germans. However, Baldwin III had kept the alliances of the West from deteriorating by marrying his daughter, Maria, to Manuel in September, 1161. Maria was known for her great beauty, to Manuel's satisfaction, and in 1164 they would bear a son and heir, Alexius. Therefore, in 1160, Manuel had been prepared by this alliance to send a concerted force against Aleppo and Nur ed-Din, composed of Antiochenes led by Baldwin, the Serbs, and Armenians from Cilicia. Sultan Arslan, who was also suffering under Danishmend conflict, made peace with the *Basileus* a year later and added Turkish contingents to the army. This came when, led by the Comnenus's nephew John Costephanus, they struck south of Iconium through an unburdened Syria and Cilicia, Arslan being quickly defeated into making peace in 1162.

The victorious *Basileus* would humble the Turkish Sultan with a sumptuous banquet at the Blacharnae bedecked in purple silks, pearls, and a ruby 'the size of an apple'. All went well with chariot racing, a visit to the baths, and a demonstration of Greek Fire until the Patriarch Lucas denied the Sultan access to the Hagia Sophia. Manuel was embarrassed by this, especially as the influential Franks agreed with Lucas. This Islamophobia, cloaked in a

---

[2002] Norwich, *(DF)*, 124.

bid to not offend God by an Infidel's presence in the Sophia, only succeeded in shaming the *Basileus*, splitting the cultures of West and East further, and unwisely offending the Sultan.[2003]

Other examples of Manuel's foreign relations was his stance against the ascension of Geza's son as Stephen III by supporting the deceased king's brothers, Stephen IV and Ladislaus. In 1162, Stephen IV was officially crowned, but a faction under his nephew ousted him and he fled to Constantinople as Stephen III kept his throne under Manuel's suzerainty. In return, Manuel negotiated with the Hungarian clergy and a new vassal, as Cinnamus specifies, a *lizos*, or a *doulos ethelodoulos* ('voluntary servant') in Vladislav of Bohemia to raise an army against Stephen.[2004] Another Westernization of language would come from the term of *lizos* with origins from the Latin term *liguos*, sharing the same definition. In the direction of Bohemia's spiritual life, these servants remained Westernized as, geographically neighboring Germany, they remained the faithful adherents of Roman Christianity.[2005]

Obolensky would point out how the *Basileus* would invade Hungary for the reasons of military intervention in a span of twenty-two years. But, Manuel began negotiating the Hungarian throne's friendship subtly with his skills, and as this was a time before his son Alexius's birth, Manuel offered his daughter's hand to Stephen's brother and heir, Gela. This would mean a claim on the East Empire's throne for his family and a new pride of place for Hungary. Bela traveled to the City to be renamed Alexius and given a title newly designed for his use as 'Despot' of Dalmatia, Bosnia, and Sirmium (as well as *Caesar* and Sebastocrator). Unfortunately, a war of territory then broke out over Manuel's claims of Byzantine suzerainty over the disputed areas Stephen III claimed for his kingdom. Culturally, much of eastern Hungary would take well to the Byzantine influences over their heritage, especially in Tisza, Transylvania, and the Carpathians.

It appears now that Stephen had made a Faustian pact with Manuel that although he had strong ties to the imperial family, the vague responsibilities of this title given to his brother by the *Basileus* meant he kept control over this Despotate only as long as Manuel lived with no legitimate heir. An added effect was the cultural assimilation Bela would acquire to the point of total loyalty to the *Basileus*. Manuel demanded obedience and led his hodge-podge armies to

---

[2003] Laiou, 'Byzantium and the West', 73.

[2004] Ostrogorsky, 387f.

[2005] Obolensky, 207.

Sirmium forcing Stephen to relent, the Despot only returning in 1165. Manuel settled the matter in all three territories this time and Stephen was forced to accept Bela-Alexius as the imperial successor under Manuel's strict terms until one last rebellion in 1167 quickly put down at Belgrade by Andronicus Contostephanus ended the matter. He also settled the dispute of the Grand Zhupan of Croatian Rascia, Stephen Nemanja, celebrating in his court with great oration and commissioning wall-paintings all over the Palace depicting his triumph over the Serbs. The 1165 settlement was seen to the rest of Europe as an impressive victory militarily and diplomatically for Byzantium. It was a return to a glory it had lost before the Comneni as Manuel would then take the moniker of *Oungrikos* ('the Hungarian') as well as 'The Greek'.[2006]

On May 7, 1166, William I of Sicily died and his son William II was still a minor, fortunately leading the Pope to reconsider a Byzantine reconciliation with Sicily's usefulness suspended. Also, the Galacian Russians, as old allies of the Empire, agreed to extradite the rebellious Andronicus Comnenus while Venice received funds from the Pope for a revived League against Barbarossa. This Pope, Alexander III, was actually considering deposing Frederick and allowing the Empire to be legally united under Manuel alone as it was before Charlemagne![2007] Most likely, Alexander considered an *Basilia* so far away in Constantinople was better than any hostile Emperor as near as Germany. This, however, puzzled Westerners who saw the extravagance and pomp of Byzantium as too foreign, only to gain a subservience with Manuel as 'Western' Emperor. When the uniting of the two Churches was considered for discussion, once again failing, the Western alliances negated the chance for such a debate.[2008]

One contributor to this unrealized discussion was a lull in the activity of Iconium in Asia Minor added to the priorities of the *Basileus*. The *Basileus* wasted no time in re-fortifying and garrisoning Adrymittium and Pergamum on the west coast which became a new Theme – the first created in years – in the Neocastra, or 'New Forts.' Flexing a newly respected diplomacy, Manuel married another princess of royal blood to the King in Jerusalem, Alaric. But, this was shadowed by a scandal of intrigue involving Andronicus, the *Basileus*'s cousin and Duke of Cilicia, and a number of female relatives he did not hesitate to seduce. Fleeing his imperial cousin's outrage, Andronicus defected once again, this time to Nur ed-Din of the Danishmend.

---

[2006] Obolensky, 161-162.
[2007] Treadgold, 647.
[2008] Laiou, 'Byzantium and the West', 74-75.

This could only result in deep-seeded resentment, outrage, and hostility directed at the Comneni from the entire East as Jerusalem also became involved. And this severe discrediting of Andronicus would seep into his brief reign as *Basileus* and taint the last of this illustrious imperial family. Despite this degradation, Manuel consulted with Alaric and both agreed to an enterprise in conquering Egypt from the Fatimids. From 1168-1169, a zealous Amalric would march to Cairo, but be turned away as supplies ran out and as two Byzantine fleets were sent south, a land expedition to Damietta also being defeated. These defeats were not mainly the work of the Fatimids, but Nur ed-Din and his Turks with the renegade Andronicus who took the region first with the regime of the famed Kurdish general Saladin who would play a major part in the Third Crusade.

During this humbling campaign, Manuel committed to reforming the economy of the City and took measures against the monopolies of the Venetian quarter. After withholding certain rights, the Venetians were held by treaty with John II who had supported the Genoese and Pisan quarters, favoring them over the other Italians. Whether or not the *Basileus* expected it, the Venetians rebelled in 1170 and invaded the Genoese quarter, the City itself at war with another affront to the Byzantine residents. To assure containment against a close Western enemy just as a blooded heir was born to Manuel in 1171, the *Basileus* conducted a witch-hunt of Venetian citizens and settlers. Gathering 10,000 from the City for imprisonment and another 10,000 from outside of Constantinople, even monasteries were requisitioned to contain the over-spill of captives. Yet despite all this, the Venetians in Italy can be blamed for not allowing even a sliver of an olive branch to be extended by the Doge.[2009]

An infuriated Venice sent a fleet east and ignited a Serbian rebellion in Ras, the divided armies allowing Venice to take Dalmatia, Euboea, and Chios. Wintering there, the Western fleets were hit by plague and, luckily, abandoned Greece. The over-confident Doge Vitale Michiel was shamed by his people in Europe, bringing plague with him from the East and fleeing from Venice to a monastery where he was found and brutally murdered by a mob in 1172.[2010] His successor, Ziani, would not hesitate in turning from Byzantium to broker peace between the Pope and the Germans. This would include the future Doge Enrico Dandalo who would dominate in the Fourth Crusade despite being in his ninties and half-blind. This blinding was said to be done by an exasperated

---

[2009] Norwich, *(AHV)*, 104-105.
[2010] Brownworth, 245.

Manuel or an unimpressed Ziani in the heat of revolution, depending on the source consulted.[2011]

It is believed that the goal of the Most Serene Republic of Venice was planning to re-instate the Exarchate in north Italy established by Constans II in the seventh century, giving them a position of strength as Byzantium could never stay neutral in their endeavors.[2012] In the Genoese settlement of Galata on the Bosporus, invasions were made by anonymous vandals, and it may be suggested that Manuel was responsible when on March 12, 10,000 Venetians were arrested with the attack on the Genoese as a false pretext. All of this predicated from the enmity of the Pope, Emperor Frederick, and Lombardy, all of whom condemned Constantinople and their use of the port of Ancona, Venice falling to these events in a tight sequence.[2013]

Stephen III of Hungary died in 1172, and now Manuel's cunning plans of Hungarian submission would reach fruition as his Byzantinized brother-in-law became Bela (III)-Alexius. The two rulers had little trouble in controlling the Serbs under Stephen Nemanja and salvaging Dalmatia as Venice was now eliminated as a danger internally and externally. Meanwhile in Cilicia, the Danishmend princes Nur ed-Din and Mleh of the Rubians took Jerusalem's territory from King Alaric. Yet this victory would quickly become hollow as all three were dead by 1175, the region falling in the hands of the Comnenian general Isaac, who regained Byzantine Isauria and the Caucasus. This advancement, mostly fueled by fortune, added to the reputation and legendary skill of Manuel and Byzantium with minimum effort and loss, making Manuel I's administration more and more productive.

As Barbarossa defeated the walls of Milan in early 1176, the Battle of Legnano on May 29 decided the fate of the Lombard League as Frederick III was decisively defeated by the Doge. The League would disband peacefully between the Pope, Sicily, and Germany with the Treaty of Venice on July 24, 1177. It was included in these terms that the *Basileus* would release his Venetian prisoners in good faith. Manuel also used this opportunity to craftily dangle the prospect of reconciliation in the Churches and certain concessions to keep the Pope and Germany useful to the Empire as the Treaty did not directly include the *Basileus*, but was estimated to have benefited him nonetheless.

The wily Nur-ed din, in 1173, had made an alliance with the Atabeg

---

[2011] Norwich, *(AHV)*, 124.

[2012] Norwich, *(DF)*, 129-130.

[2013] Gibbon, 1995.

of Mosul to attack Iconian and Byzantine territories as a defense now that Byzantium only had the Danishmends in which to deal. This concerned the *Basileus*, of course, and secret negotiations were even arising between Barbarossa and Arslan, the Infidel Turk! On May 15, 1174, the Atabeg died and the Turks conquered the Danishmend cities and frontier fortresses one by one, procrastinating in making peace with Manuel and baiting the *Basileus* into a military reaction.

Kilij Arslan II, now possessor of cities collected from the Danishmends, was not impressed with the *Basileus's* involvement in Venice and broke his treaty with the Empire by withholding Byzantine vassal cities which were to be returned. Manuel, bolstered by his successes, set out and fortified the cities of Dorylaeum, Siblia, and Cotyaeum in an attempt to surround the Sultanate, even recruiting rebellious Turks from Amasia. Now cautious of the *Basileus's* strategies, Arslan decided to submit and sent peace envoys to Manuel. Manuel, however, was not swayed and in 1176 gathered forces to march to the walls of Iconium. This might likely had been an attempt to eliminate Turkish rule from the Bosporus by a romanticized and overconfident Manuel Comnenus considering his notorious aims to be somewhat invincible.

Here, Manuel led his troops through the Meander valley on a ten-mile stretch through the pass of Tzybritze, and was ambushed at Myriocephalum on September 17, 1176, on the way to Iconium. The Byzantines were hampered and penned in by the presence of their cumbersome siege engines, useless in a surprise attack of close quarters. It was a slaughter and disaster for the Byzantine forces with the enemy flanking the train as the beasts of burden and horses were easily targeted and the tactic proved to be particularly effective.[2014] Heavy casualties were found on each side, especially the cavalry of Baldwin of Antioch, who was forced to climb uphill as the *Basileus's* baggage and supplies were also seized.

The *Basileus* may even have feared being a hostage as the vulnerable Romanus Diogenes was one century earlier at Manzikert, which presented a real possibility. Kilij, however, would not push his luck as his position in this was still tentative, especially considering the Byzantine garrisons at Amasia, Dorylaeum, Sibidia, Cotyaeum, Tralles, and Pisidian Antioch, the Sultan suing again for peace in 1177. Manuel had no choice and it was decided that the *Basileus's* only responsibilities were in the disarming of the fortified cities. This was a merciful treaty to Byzantium and the cities were reverted, Sibidia itself

---

[2014] Norwich, *(DF)*, 134-135.

being demolished and razed by Manuel and if these forts intimidated Arslan before, dismantling them played right into his hands.

The implications of this defeat took a grand toll on the once shining descendant of Constantine, chosen by Providence. He never got over this loss as it was considered a setback for the Empire by its vassals and neighbors as the hopeless situation it had been in since Manzikert.[2015] Though it was still not enough to guarantee a fall as it was in Rome in 476, it was proof the decline of New Rome was prevalent and its borders would never make it a leading power as it was under the capable Macedonians – no new Basil II would arise. The City itself was still unbreachable and even above reproach as the East would take 300 years and weapons beyond the Medieval imagination to produce this. Tactics were not necessarily a problem as the usual mixture of cavalry, infantry, and *cataphractoi* were prudently assembled. Unfortunately, the old difficulties in maintaining order and discipline was the defeating factor.[2016] Yet, the West would be another matter as Ostrogorsky would also conclude that '. . .once and for all Byzantium was driven out of Italy', and the time for Western expansion east was fast approaching.

Manuel was crushed by this loss as he decried the defeat in Philadelphia days later, the battle being psychological for him as the *Basileus* realized that '. . .the empire and its entire army had performed no better against the Turks than at the beginning of his reign.' His armies were merely 'style over substance, and that he owed his earlier success mostly to luck.'[2017] It was a harsh and sobering lesson for Manuel I Comnenus and he awoke from his heady and ambitious dreams into a nightmare of reality which he never truly recovered. From then on, he would only strengthen the army with all he could muster in local mercenaries that required pay and who lacked in Byzantine discipline as if he was giving up. He did induce peaceful relations with the West by arranging marriage between his seven-year-old son Alexius in 1177 to Louis VII's daughter under the envoy of the Count of Flanders. Coupled with this was a surprising Italian alliance between his daughter and the Marquis of Montferrat in Lombardy in 1179. These French and Italian alliances and their troops would serve the *Basileus* well as his business with the Turks was still left unfinished.

He made his nephew, John Vatatzes, Grand Domestic for stemming a tide of Turks at the Meander, a small recompense for Myriocephalum, as Manuel

---

[2015] Ostrogorsky, 391.
[2016] Decker, 157.
[2017] Treadgold, 649.

went to take Panasium south of Dorylaeum. By 1179, however, his declining vigor softened his resolve and he released and re-enfranchised the Venetians in Constantinople. By the next year, he got his affairs in order as he was dying at sixty. He married the rest of his children to Agnes of France and Rainier-John of Montferrat, naming him *Caesar* and regent on Sunday, March 2. He forgave his cousin Andronicus and embraced him in the capital as his Duke of Paphlagonia upon an oath of fealty, and on September 24, 1180, Manuel I Comnenus took the cowl and died, leaving behind one son, Alexius, as his successor. One of his last acts was to add a stone from Christ's tomb in Jerusalem to his own.

Manuel I Comnenus still had a sterling reputation for success in all political arenas despite his setbacks; he made allies out of enemies and kept balance in the face of changes in the Papacy and the Western Empire, even surviving a Crusade in better shape than his grandfather had done. The Greeks of Constantinople almost deplored his actions taken to facilitate the West, the 'informality of his manners' that compromised Byzantine custom. Manuel only argued back that the people were set in their ways, 'old-fashioned, sticking to outdated concepts and outmoded traditions.'[2018] His personal charisma, generosity, and improvement over the dourness of his father's court gave him a status of folk hero to his Slavic and Russian vassals and his love of Western custom made honest connections with the rulers of the Western kingdoms.

If given an army and other options available 150 years ago, no state would have stopped him and the West as well as the Turkish East would be his subordinates in an unparalleled Empire. But the belief he could accomplish this with what he had led to his downfall as a great uniter of Byzantine suzerainty. And, who could say he had popularity under the people with lax estate policies, growth in the hated Italian markets and population, which added to the lack of humility the Venetians were known for gave Byzantines causes for complaint,[2019] as well as cultural insults such as the tournaments in 1159 for the Crusaders? But a boundless energy and a long rule developed relations with Rome and the high Slavic north that even his predecessors could not claim to have had.

A note of Manuel's Russian diplomacy would prove to be the most successful of his reign, even laying groundwork of its Westernization and Tsarist structure. Manuel became a part of their cult and folk status as when he sent the princess of the admiring city of Polotzk (Hellenized as Euphrosinia) an icon of the Mother of God from Ephesus. Court dress and depictions of the

---

[2018] Norwich, *(DF)*, 139.
[2019] Norwich, *(AHV)*, 103.

Slavic and Russian Tsars also took a directly Byzantine nature as had Roger II's receiving his crown from Christ as well as Bulgaria's crown, whose Tsar had stood by King David.[2020] Relations with Kiev would start early in 1147 when the *Basileus* persuaded the Russian Bishops of the Church to elect a Smolensk Byzantine monk, Clement, to lead a Bishopric.

These relations would sour, unfortunately, with the death of Kiev's pliant prince in 1164, his successor, Rostislav, invalidating the election as it was without the prince's consent while the number of Byzantine candidates was increasing – even for Kiev's Patriarchy. Rostislav would now threaten the Greek embassadors with legislation outlawing Byzantine intervention and the Russian Principate as the only validation of clerical investitures. Andrew Bogolyubsky and his Hungarian ally Vladimir would continue these hostilities as the historian would rightly compare them to the post-Byzantine Muscovite autocracy.[2021]

A year later, however, Kiev relaxed all of these policies upon Manuel's pardoning of Andronicus Comnenus from Yaroslav of Galicia, receiving an honest invitation back to the City. Rostislav also agreed to lending auxiliary troops and consulting the new *Basileus* before Russian candidates for offices were chosen as prelates. Galicia could be reasoned with the most, since in the 1140's it was awarded as a *hypospondos* ('vassal') of Byzantium as Suzhdal would also be made a *symmachos* ('ally') of the Empire against civil incursion. From 1158 to 1167 these two monarchs, together, commissioned on the Nerl' River the Church of Our Lady's Protective Veil (*Pokrov*) at Bogolyubavo. Most notably to this cultural assimilation was the existence in the Church of a Novgorod icon of St. Andrew depicting the Virgin protecting the Blacharnae Palace, notably with the *Basileus* Manuel, the Patriarch, and the congregations of the Church.[2022]

After the year 1165, reports of hostility seemed to have ceased under Manuel's guidance as he is said to have succeeded in creating a 'family of princes' with the *Basileus* as '*paterfamilias* and vice-regent of God.' Admittedly, however, credit may be given to the fascinating relations with Andronicus Comnenus for easing this transition between the states. In 1165, Yaroslav of Galatia embraced the exiled imperial cousin warmly and offered him cities to finance his stay. He was recorded as having the title of 'Kyr' or 'Sir' noting his nobility, and even took an active place on the Council of Boyars as a property owner.

---

[2020] Treadgold, 641.

[2021] Obolensky, 230-231.

[2022] *Ibid.*, plate 53.

Manuel I Comnenus also wanted the best relations with the Roman Church he could gather, considering their relations among the Western Emperor and French King against the dangerous Sicilian threat. The most direct approach he facilitated was a Synod in 1166 to settle the doctrinal differences between East and West. Not surprisingly, this came to nothing as force or amount of discussion would not move the Pope and Patriarch on the interpretation of the *filioque*. But, this gathering was probably a pretext for Manuel to be closer to Rome on his ideas of a universal Empire. In 1141, his father had written to the Pope that as he held a secular sword, the Pope held the spiritual and the two should use this relationship to create one Empire, with one *Basileus*. This was Manuel's dream and he even held a candidacy for a new Pope in Orlando Bandinelli as Alexander III to accomplish this. This did not please the Roman clergy, however, and any plans to abolish the German Empire were quickly abandoned.

As before stated, it was also the phasing in and out of Popes, their administrations, and their opinions that took a toll on the question of the Empire's spiritual life. Between 1119 and 1159, Popes Calixtus II, Honorius III, Eugenius III, and Alexander III all had differing opinions and a need to completely redraw the map of Papal diplomacy with each succession, only obfuscating the *Basileus*'s goals. The Patriarch of Constantinople, then Lucas Chrysoberges, was quoted as saying with each conversation, impiety, and the yoke of the 'Aragens' (Muslims) were present. Manuel had little choice by then but to declare the 1166 Council untenable and, for once, 'withdraw from the Latin's as from a serpent's poison.'[2023] Despite these failings, Manuel still authored treatises and dissertations on theology to the point his administration was declared by Eustathius of Thessalonica (1115-1195) fondly as 'a kingdom of priests' as said in Exodus 19:6.

In another concession to Western sensibilities over the imperial East, Manuel began consolidating Church lands in Byzantium through a Chrysobull in March, 1158. Resuscitating the monastic law of 964 under Nicephorus II, he banished all monasteries from the City and its surrounding areas. Then, he made the existing ones subject to imperial tax-collectors with total control over the *praetori* that formerly gathered revenues and the real estate of these institutions. In May, 1158, this was established, allowing that the monasteries could keep material possessions as before as in Patmos on the Bosporus.[2024] In

---

[2023] Vasiliev, 477.
[2024] Diehl, 171.

September of that year, the increase of monastic estates was forbidden and this Bull was renewed in February of 1170. This fleecing, which would not stop at religious institutions, was the price for the costly military expeditions that would meet varying successes for Manuel I, plus the burden of having high percentages of mercenary troops.

Manuel would promise to see the death rattle of the poor relief policies and philanthropy started by the Macedonians, yet commentary has noted that the Comneni's particular land grants to military nobles must have created one of the greatest armed forces in imperial history.[2025] He brought back the practice of only the senatorial class – the pronoiari – being legally allowed to alienate property. Basically, the class structure of the feudal West with vassalage and serfdom was being appropriated in the Byzantine East, especially with an *Basileus* so willing to concede to Western ideas as was Manuel. The Byzantine peasantry easily played the role of the serfs considering the legal precedents set down by previous *Basilii*. These precedents tied them to the land indefinitely under the economic system of the rich estates for which they provided taxes and commodities. This refused any grants to the peasant class and even the more wealthy peasants were disenfranchised to a new *latifundiae* class, whose borders only grew larger and more defined.

This, of course, led to the unrelieved tax-farming and burdens of previous centuries, but it reached higher levels in the Crusader states with their feudal system that further alienated them from the imperial interior, causing constant erosion in Byzantium's administrative centralization. Most of the resentment from the public took the form of the non-Greeks of the Empire were in the tax-collecting bureaucracy, especially mercenary commanders. Oddly enough, Manuel I set up legislation to reduce voluntary slavery, especially in the urban centers where foreign merchants were exacting debts and setting prices in a guild system that excluded much of the City's regulations. If a freeborn man became a slave to pay a debt, he could be awarded it back and even have such a 'ransom' paid for by the Treasury.[2026] This was a challenge in itself keeping order in the City as it had a population somewhere between 800,000 and 1,000,000 inhabitants of multiple ethnicities, religions, languages, and customs [2027] by the mid 1100's.

---

[2025] Treadgold, 644.

[2026] Ostrogorsky, 393.

[2027] Vasiliev, 483. Andreades, A. 'De la Population des Constantinople sous le Empereurs Byzantins.' *Metron I, vol. 2.* 1920, 97.

Manuel also restructured and rehabilitated the Russian feudal system that would remain in place by the twentieth century. There was the custom of the *kormlenie* ('feeding') that was reminiscent of the pronoia, the central governments granting towns and estates for military service. As the serfdom had no autonomy or former ownership, the nobles had the privileges to disenfranchise the peasantry by taking food (*korm*), 'gifts', and legal, or administrative, fees from the serfs of their possessions and the right to collects taxes and localized revenue. This feudal system holding the military together went hand-in-hand with the Byzantine pronoia and resulted in a socioeconomic and cultural symbiosis that strengthened the ties of the two nations for future eras. Even the hereditary Muscovite *pomyeste* was a direct descendant of this process, all based loosely on the similarities to Western feudal phenomena.[2028]

In the army, a crisis in recruiting local Byzantine troops arose as a high number of mercenary troops from Sicily, Germany, Outremer, the Turks, Hungary, and Russia now mostly composed the military. Evidence found in Choniates and Scylitzes explain that this was due to a new social response of avoiding service in the days of the Ducas where soldiers laid down arms to be 'jurists or lawyers'.[2029] But as the Comnenian dynasty favored military action and a military aristocracy, the tide towards enlistment turned. Due to the relentless warfare of the Crusades and Turkish ventures, loot was being distributed to this new military class even if their pay was not. Choniates describes the toiling seamsters, stablers, and smithies running off to recruiting stations for payments of Persian horse or gold coins to begin.[2030]

This was, of course, accomplished by the raiding of villages, suburbs, estates, and those citizens therein as legal payment to troops when the Treasury could not compensate them. These citizens were receiving more than enough oppression from the soldiers through provisioning, compulsory labor, and the inability of the government to aid either side. Choniates writes on this unfortunate phenomenon that they 'took not only their money, but the very shirts off of their backs' (perhaps the origin of the old saying?). The manufacturing agencies were targets as well as when Roger II sacked Thebes, he carried to Palermo a number of workers and resources of the silk and brocade trade. Skilled Jewish women that crafted the silk were seized and taken to Sicily (to also work in a harem!) and Choniates would say of their sacking of

[2028] Vasiliev, 569.
[2029] Skylitzes, II, 652; Ostrogorsky, 393.
[2030] Choniates, 256.

Corinth that their merchant ships appeared as the pirates they really were.[2031] However, his 'hostile takeover' did revitalize the bazaars of Palermo, Catania, and Syracuse to rival Byzantium in trade and manufacturing in silk, clearly demonstrating how the wars of the period between the Crusades took heavy tolls on finances.

An economic malaise brought on by heavy taxation occurred to the point that the Byzantines of the Ionian territory actually passed over Greeks for raising revenue in preference to the Norman King.[2032] Financial resources were strained enough after the inefficiency of the rulers between the Macedonians and Comneni. But, the coming of the Crusaders and the Normans were cutting the funds of the East and West off more than the barbarians simply because they had superior troops and powerful rulers in France, Germany, and Italy (which were enough).

The defeat of Outremer in the Second Crusade greatly diminished the reputations of the Westerners of Jerusalem and Antioch in the eyes of Byzantium and the Turkish nations across the East. This reputation would take centuries to recover as the absolute truth of the situation would appear. In later years, history would repeat itself as humiliating defeats in Crusade after Crusade would cause the Turks to grow bolder until Jerusalem would be beyond recovery to the West. Byzantium would prove to be in the middle of this, doing their best to both keep the Turks at bay and the Crusaders from destroying their Empire out of gain or some retaliation for phantom causes. This would cost the succeeding *Basilii* time, finances, and resources that were irretrievable, if they had any control over these things in the first place. As much as the Byzantine system did itself from within, the West quickly sped up the decline of the Empire with no hope of recovery. This is the lesson to be taken from the point of view of these numerous Crusades and the Byzantine Empire. The veneer of the City's strength had only been propped by the illusions of the past three *Basilii* with Manuel's dazzling style with, again, no real substance.[2033]

In Constantinople, the Western quarters and, as Vasiliev makes clear, their 'landing places' (*scala*) controlled the City economy despite the Manuel I's measures against the Genoese, Pisans, and eventually, Venice. In February and March of 1148, in fact, Venetian blockades of the Bosporus were bought off with increased privileges in Cyprus and Rhodes as well as Constantinople.

---

[2031] Norwich, *(AHV)*, 96.

[2032] Vasiliev, 481.

[2033] Brownworth, 246-247.

Playing enemies off against each other was Manuel's best weapon, especially against the hostility of the Latin League of the West that threatened Byzantine stability while also promising its benefices to the Empire.[2034] Yet, this and his love of pleasures and pageantry must not be mistaken for weakness, for he had 'the iron temper of a soldier, not to be easily paralleled' except by the greatest generals of both Medieval and early modern times.[2035] Now, despite his impressive attributes, the crisis of debt and the Western allies would spill over into the reigns of Manuel I's successors until the Comneni dynasty and the City itself would ignominiously fall.

## ALEXIUS II COMNENUS
### (1180-1183)

## ANDRONICUS I COMNENUS 'THE TERRIBLE'
### (1183-1185)

The next five years after Manuel I's death saw the end of the Comneni dynasty after a century of effective, if not tumultuous, administration. A positive pattern of policy existed that was typified by heavy military involvement and a realistically open diplomacy with the West. But, the negative aspects would include decentralized and aristocratic feudal economies with an oppressive relationship based on the powers of untrustworthy and exploitative Italian trade in Constantinople. Aside and after the 'reign' of the child-emperor Alexius, born on September 10, 1169 his cousin Andronicus I would shake these foundations with radical and controversial policies more comparable to the bygone Macedonian era.

Though he attempted far-reaching foundations to return Byzantium to its more independent tenth- and-eleventh-century roots, they were ultimately impractical in a new political climate of the East that was starkly changed since the height of the Empire. Not even the best *Basilii* could recover the decline at this point and Andronicus Comnenus had not their patience or self-control, nor his violent means of rectifying the bureaucracy, rather he ignored the armies whose needed leaders dwindled due to Andronicus's executions and purges.[2036] Indeed, as the most 'notorious rogue of his day', Andronicus arrived

---

[2034]  Laiou, 'Byzantium and the West', 63.

[2035]  Gibbon, 1655.

[2036]  Hussey, 69.

for asylum in Baldwin III's Jerusalem with Byzantine soldiers that caused some 'comfort' in the Holy City. After the King's death, however, Andronicus, at nearly sixty, seduced Jerusalem's widowed Queen Theodora, aged twenty-three, and absconded with her to Danishmend Damascus. [2037]

Although he was especially popular and charismatic for a Comnenus, Andronicus also had a streak of cruelty creating a period of terror in the Empire with the mixture of brilliance and savagery reminiscent of Justinian II and Constantine VIII as the 'typical' Oriental monarchs of Byzantium. After one gamble too many with the passion of the mob, the Comneni ended with an act of regicide and barbarity yet to be unmatched, perhaps, in the annals of world monarchy throughout the ages. The aftermath would be a new, yet ineffective and brief, dynasty demonstrating Byzantium's weakness as a world power for years to come. It only reminded Byzantium that in the succession of their *Basilii*[2038]: 'The fabric of rebellion was overthrown by stroke of conspiracy or undermined by the silent arts of intrigue; the favorites of the soldiers and the people, of the senate or clergy, of women and eunuchs, were alternately clothed with the purple; the means of their elevation were base, and their end was often contemptible or tragic.'

When Manuel I Comnenus died of illness in September of 1180, tradition was followed closely as his eleven-year-old son was crowned *Basileus* by the Patriarch. It had not happened since the time of Basil II how the generals his mother married became co-*Basilii* and regents, so the effective reign of the Empire fell to Alexius's mother and *Basilia*, Maria of Antioch. She wasted no time in selecting her lover, Alexius-Bela, Protosebastus and brother to the Hungarian king, to be her consort, leaving the armies exasperated and no doubt satisfying the ambitious Bela with a bid on the Empire. In February, 1181, a conspiracy by other rival claimants were led by Manuel's daughter Maria and her Outremer husband, the *Caesar* Count Rainier-John of Montferrat. They were found out by the former Despot and fled to sanctuary at St. Sophia, protected by the mobs of Constantinople and their allies, the merchants of Italy and Georgia. There they remained, under siege until April, where they were given amnesty upon surrender by Alexius-Bela and Maria.

Maria had taken the veil as Xenia ('Foreigner'), an apt moniker as she faced

---

[2037] Montefiorre, 248. William of Tyre, born in Jerusalem, would call him the snake held in the bosom (like Caligula) and the mouse in the wardrobe. William would also say Andronicus proved Homer's saying in the *Illiad* that one should 'fear the Greeks even as they bear gifts.'

[2038] Gibbon, 1667.

resentment for her Western heritage and her alliances with the wicked Italian merchants in Constantinople. Yet it cannot be forgotten how Maria-Xenia was 'the first Latin' to rule the Empire as she was the only regent remaining, veil or no veil.[2039] Alexius, brother of King Bela III as well as the Dowager's adviser and lover, was described as a despicable man with rotten teeth, seeking comfort 'as a wild beast does' in darkness by blanketing windows with the Palace with curtains. This only made him seem more sinister and clandestine, never seeking popular support and avoiding the sunlight that represented vitality in Byzantine culture and the well-being given by God in times with good weather.

Their regency was exposed as the weak one it was when Byzantium would again lose their slippery grip on the East with Bela III retaking the disputed kingdoms from Dalmatia to Sirmium, now without a united military front as Manuel had led. In Serbia, the prince Stephen Nemanja overthrew the Byzantine garrisons and called for an independent Serbia under the local monarchy. The Turks of Iconium were padding their recent victories by breaking treaties, seizing the southern Anatolian coast to Attalia; with little opposition, Ruben III of Armenia even marching on Cilicia. Chaos and hazard in the East was rapidly developing and from his holdings in Paphlagonia, the outgoing Andronicus Comnenus decided to make a bid on the weak foundations of the regency.

Alexius II Comnenus was only ceremoniously crowned to show the loyalty of the regency by his mother and the Patriarchy. Andronicus's patented cruelty was obvious to all with his purges, riots, and the treatment of *Basilia* Mary-Xenia. When she was conveniently blamed for a Hungarian incursion, it was with Alexius's hand that the death warrant was signed at the insistence of Andronicus in 1183 and she was strangled. By now, Alexius's rule was moot as Andronicus finally outlined his plans for absolute rule as he was crowned co-emperor, and eventually, sole emperor in September, 1183. Alexius was steam-rolled by the popular support and undying charisma Andronicus embodied. It was with no shock or resistance that the new *Basileus* had Alexius II, the direct blooded heir of Alexius I, strangled with a bowstring by his men on September 14, 1183, two weeks after he turned fourteen. Without the eternal rest of the other Comneni in the Pantocrator, which he was owed, his body was dumped into the sea and forgotten due to the secrecy of the conspiracy.

In all of these proceedings and reversals of fortune, this Comneni *Basileus* was merely a pawn. Choniates describes the son of Manuel as one who cared for the amusements of the chase or play. He was simple and incapable of

---

[2039] Norwich, *(DF)*, 140.

performing most tasks as well. This, of course, would be understandable for a young boy to be, but the chronicler's intention was probably that he lacked the understanding of his responsibilities of his future station. This made him particularly vulnerable to enemies and rival claimants, especially in the brute force of his cousin Andronicus. In December, 1182, Alexius defied Manuel's *Chrysobull* of land grants to be given despite social rank[2040] to stabilize central and peripheral aristocratic relations, but this too would be an act trampled by his cousin as if the child never existed. Yet, when it suited him best, Andronicus picked up the progressive policy as his own. Choniates also states how he showed overbearing pride and vanity which is why Norwich takes this at value and dubs the heir as quite unimpressive.[2041]

Ostrogorsky, however, gives an accurate picture of Choniates being not just a supporter, but a true admirer of Andronicus whose 'naïve descriptions' exonerated Andronicus of his tyranny as the most accurate compared to the other historians who either condemned him or 'whitewashed his deeds.'[2042] This would, naturally, explain his cold treatment and contempt for Alexius II as Choniates was comparing him to his cousin Manuel's caution against rivals. Aside from these facts and historiography, not much can be said for young Alexius II as he was as much a non-entity in history as he was in life.

Andronicus I Comnenus, like numerous *Basilii* before him, was a man of numerous contradictions. This controversial kind of historical figure much has been said of, yet not enough of his exploits has been recognized due to his obscurity in Western civilization. Rising over six feet tall and brimming with an amazing physique, intellect, charm, and panache, historians estimate that he was: '. . .vigorous, charming, unscrupulous, and irresponsible . . .',[2043] while others confirmed this standard after writing of his death, he was also '. . .a colossus who possessed every gift save moderation...a hero and a villain, a preserver and a destroyer, a paragon and a warning.'[2044]

Charles Diehl (1859-1944), this *Basileus's* most vivid biographer, could not deny that Andronicus Comnenus was one of the most interesting

---

[2040] Vasiliev, 483.

[2041] Norwich, *(DF)*, 140.

[2042] Ostrogorsky, 396f.

[2043] Treadgold, 653.

[2044] Norwich, *(DF)*, 153.

characters in Byzantine history, also stating he was 'highly educated', 'witty and eloquent', 'brave in the field', and 'outspoken at court'. Diehl went on to say that Andronicus was the typical mixture of 'good and evil' in a Byzantine *Basileus*, 'cruel, atrocious, and decadent, yet also capable of grandeur, energy, and effort.'[2045] What can be said is that even though it was on a much more limited scale, the reputation of the last Comnenus of Constantinople is as conflicted as that of a Richard III (1452-1485), Cesare Borgia (1475-1507), or Alcibiades (450BCE-404BCE).[2046] Other traits to serve (and hamper) him in his imperial career even include legendary exploits, not only of the battlefield, but the bedroom as well.

Andronicus I was born in 1118 to Isaac Comnenus, one of the ill-fated brothers of the *Basileus* John II. Taking on the traditions of his military aristocratic family, he joined the Byzantine army and was captured to be ransomed by the Seljuks in 1141. He would rebel against his uncle and cousin to face exile in 1162 in Russian Galatia, where he was treated as an honored guest, and three years later, he would be returned as a political pawn over the Byzantine-Hungarian wars. Scandal of the sexual sort had already followed the roguish character of this man, and in 1167 his affair with a princess suited for Amalric of Jerusalem occurred after being made Duke of Cilicia. Following this, by the time he gained the throne in 1183, he had already successfully seduced two of his own nieces.[2047]

Using his wiles to seduce this princess, sister of the Antiochene prince named Philippa, he used this advantage to embezzle funds, fleeing to Jerusalem. The Dowager Queen Theodora Comnena was next to be charmed and, serenading her by her window at night, the two fled the city and lived as husband and wife, fleeing Manuel I's wrath in Cilicia, Mesopotamia, Armenia, and Iberia. Travelling together, they did so in sin as consanguinity forbade such marriage as she was the first cousin of Andronicus. Finally, the two fled to Aleppo and Nur ed-Din, shredding alliances, treaties, and enraging all of Eastern Christendom. In 1182, when Manuel's daughter Maria and her husband the Western Count Rainier-John of Montferrat attempted to kill him, no one hesitated to blame Andronicus when he had them poisoned in retaliation!

In May of 1182, Andronicus was prepared for an honest bid for the throne, ousting a weak *Basilia*, her lover, and the puppet with whom they entrusted the

---

[2045] Diehl, Charles. 'Andronicus Comnene'. *Byzantin Figures, II*. Paris, France. 1913, 68.

[2046] Vasiliev, 377.

[2047] Brownworth, 249f.

crown. Along with the general Andronicus Angelus, a fleet of Italians sailed to Chalcedon where Alexius-Bela attempted a blockade. But, the Fleet's Grand Admiral, Contostephanus, lowered the chain at the City's harbor's mouth and allowed the rebels entry. The imperial guard's response was to embrace Andronicus's bid, blinding the Protosebastus lover of the *Basileus* Maria. When the fleet arrived at Constantinople, Andronicus ordered a terrible atrocity on the City as the Venetian merchants of the fleet massacred the Genoese women, children, elderly, and selling the remainder into slavery - even the clergy and papal legates were not spared. It is easy to characterize this man with contempt when faced by such facts as how Andronicus stayed in Chalcedon at the Philopation to escape the responsibility of the bloodshed at Constantinople against, and by, the Italians.[2048]

After Andronicus took over the regency, he still faced opposition in the ranks of the armies of Thrace. The Grand Domestic John Vatatzes, whose motivations seemed to honor Manuel's wishes, led an army that repelled successfully the new regent's armies. But, with a typical stroke of luck given to a *Basileus*, Vatazes died and the regent re-crowned Alexius II in 1182, waiting to make his next move. Andronicus wasted no time in tonsuring Maria to a convent, away from the Palace, inciting Angelus to conspire against the new regency that included the Postal Logothete, the Grand Duke of the Fleet, and members of the court and officer corps. When they were discovered, unfortunately, they were all blinded, imprisoned, or tonsured. Andronicus Angelus did manage to escape, along with his sons Isaac, Alexius, and Theodore, fleeing to the sanctuary of Jerusalem.

In Hungary, Bela III had taken Serdica and the Moravian valley, Belgrade, Nish, and Branichevo to the point that the chroniclers of the Third Crusade described them as little more than ruins. Andronicus showed his bouts of paranoia and blamed Bela's sister-in-law, the banished Maria-Xenia, mother of the *Basileus*. Andronicus forced the fourteen-year-old Alexius to personally sign his mother's death warrant in early 1183, and the matter was settled. If Alexius planned retribution, he was both too weak and unpopular to gain it, and he quickly ran out of time to act, anyway. An opportunity arose that year for the regent as the three sons of Angelus marched with Greek and Turkish troops to take Nicaea. Andronicus saw this as the state of emergency it was and demanded to be made co-*Basileus*. The court saw it as more severe, obviously, when they countered he be made sole emperor in September, 1183, as Andronicus accepted

---

[2048] Treadgold, 652.

only after a 'protestation of reluctance.'[2049] Alexius II was made to abdicate and was murdered at the Church of Christ of the Chalke by Andronicus's guards. The new *Basileus* then wed his predecessor's betrothed, Agnes-Anna, a girl of twelve, therefore fifty years younger than the groom, but was still said to have been deflowered in a new charge of Andronicus's rakishness!

Of course, this must have offended many at court, though they remained silent, excluding the Patriarch Boradiotes who abdicated his office in 1183 in disgust. This Patriarch had been appointed by Manuel Comnenus in 1178 from Eugerniotes, also having been a close confidante. Choniates attributed Boradiotes with breaking him of his superstitious and Pagan habit of astrology and Michael Grunbert of the University of Muenster closely studies this relationship in the era as well as his aversion to Andronicus. Proper historiographical sources on court and Church ceremony are scant in this period, but recent sources[2050] still succeed in finding a synthesis of the two to result in '*Kaisertum*' as basically the political culture of the *Basileus* as the ruler of the Church independent of the Patriarch. Understanding this in the Comnenian context defines the Patriarch's powers as the head of the Church and its relation to the *Basileus* and his 'Caesaropapism.'

Andronicus's first serious policies implemented domestically were in the form of vast financial and economic reforms, setting internal frameworks to assist in other areas. His main priority was the reformation of the system to better the living of the disenfranchised, the first Comnenus to consider such a practice. It had both negative and positive consequences as it boosted popularity among the lower classes, but lowering the opinion of the aristocracy who made up the officer corps of the military forces. This was just why the previous *Basilii* since the First Crusade favored the senators and generals as they were desperately needed to battle surrounding forces and decrease the efficacy of rebellion. Unfortunately, though Andronicus I possessed some military experience, he did not understand this concept as this disenfranchisement and suspicions of rebellion caused him to thin both the military ranks and state Treasuries.

The last two years of Andronicus's rule was a bloody combination of rebellion, defeat, and naked paranoia; in 1184, the Angeli clan was entrenched in Anatolia as Isaac Angelus gathered rebels from Nicaea. Isaac would still

---

[2049] Treadgold, 653.

[2050] Dagron, Gilbert. *Emperor and Priest: the Imperial Office in Byzantium,* trans. by Jean Birrell. Cambridge, UK: Cambridge University Press, 2007.

surrender, however, and being defeated at Prusa, his brother Theodore and his commanders would be caught, blinded, and mutilated. Early next year, Isaac Comnenus, as Duke of Cilicia, would use his monarch's former office to rebel and seize the tactical and commercial center of Cyprus, claiming the purple, and beginning the minting and circulation of his own rival coinage.

This was supposedly the beginning of the Empire's disintegration as the island of Cyprus would be beyond recovery. Andronicus's typical response was a cruel execution of the rebel's family (ironically being one of them) by stoning and impalement. The intensity only grew as more plots against the *Basileus* were uncovered by the illegitimate son of Manuel Comnenus, Alexius, who was also Andronicus's son-in-law, perhaps in a bid at becoming a successor. More citizens were taken as conspirators and were mutilated, hung, blinded, and executed as a sign of Andronicus's blind wrath.

As is the case with such wanton cruelty and despotism, it can be traced to the weakness of the *Basileus* on the battlefield against his enemies, or former allies, which he could not control. It is easier to maintain power and vanity by vanquishing defenseless 'foes' in the City than hostile foreign armies draining time, effort, and resources only to face defeat. This was most likely exacerbated faster by the loss of Cyprus and further vulnerability to Western aggression. This aggression did, indeed, develop itself in the form of King William II 'the Good' of Sicily, whom Norwich cites as wanting nothing less than the Byzantine crown for himself. On June 11, 1185, he traveled from Messina to invade the isle of Corfu and Dyrrachium with 200 ships and over 13,000 men led by Count Richard of Acerra and Bohemund of Lecce, killing 7,000 Byzantine defenders on August 6.[2051]

William of Sicily toted with him a cunning way to gain popular support, if unoriginal. He had a youth whom he used to convince the Byzantium was the murdered Alexius II (probably thought to be exiled by the fringe of the Empire) to depose Andronicus as illegitimate in the name of a Norman "advisory" on the minor *Basileus*'s behalf. William then sailed for Thessalonica and raided the Aegean. Andronicus, motivated by the fear of a guilty conscience of his acts toward Alexius II and the military caste, acted by dividing his forces into five armies which only diluted their efforts.

In this disintegration, the Duke of a besieged Thessalonica, David Comnenus, put up a tepid resistance to the Normans landing on the 15th and was dismissed by Andronicus. Having enough of such incompetence, David

---

[2051] Norwich, *(DF)*, 146.

promptly surrendered his Greek Themes to William on the 24th and joined him on a raid on Constantinople, reaching as far as Mysonopolis. The *Basileus* strengthened the City's defenses and razed houses close enough for an enemy entry, also creating a fleet of 100 ships. Choniates then says he diverged from here to attend personal pleasures, in one night bedding fifty women as Hercules had done with the Amazons in his labors, aided by ointments and the *scinus* fish, an aphrodisiac from the Nile.[2052]

Andronicus ordered David's arrest, but the point was moot, instead settling for the gentrified Isaac Angelus who had fled the imperial guard for Saint Sophia. There, Angelus managed to convince the people the once charmed *Basileus*'s time had come, and they assembled on the Palace with the newly crowned Isaac II Angelus at its head. This was probably not to difficult as Isaac had his mob secretly prepared in advance and the crowning Patriarch was Basil II Kamaretos, who had no real attachments to his sovereign. Andronicus attempted to flee the Bosporus harbor by ship with his concubine, dressed in peasant's clothes and armed with only a bow which he loosed on the crowds when his archers fell reluctant, still being found out and captured by the angry mob.

On September 12, 1185, the most humiliating and chilling execution of a *Basileus* by the citizens of Constantinople took place. Reports on the details flood in from the contemporary and modern sources with stark precision: first, Andronicus's sons John and Manuel were blinded, to die of their wounds, while the Treasury was looted of 170,000 *hyperpyra*,[2053] likely in the form of 200 pounds of gold and 300 of silver. Jeweled art and reliquaries were stolen, gilded chalices that had once impressed the world's ambassadors and rulers were robbed, and perhaps worst of all, so too was the recovered letter Christ wrote to King Agbar of Edessa.[2054] Multiple historians have been consulted to complete just what was done to the tyrant. Andronicus himself was slowly dismembered, Treadgold describes. Norwich is more unflinching saying how they tied him with a chain, cut off his right hand, blinded his right eye, and starved him for days.

Choniates, Diehl, and Gibbon write how they broke out his teeth, pulled out his beard by the handful, dealt him a thousand blows by any who could reach him in the crowd, stoned him, goaded him, impaled him with spits

---

[2052] Norwich, *(DF)*, 159.

[2053] Treadgold, 656.

[2054] Norwich, *(DF)*, 153.

between his ribs, pelted him with filth, poured boiling water on his head, had him ride in the Hippodrome on a camel, and hung him by his feet between two pillars adorned with statues of a wolf and a sow.[2055] Though he showed 'great fortitude', he would still utter the despairing prayer: 'O Lord, have pity on me; why dost thy trample on a poor reed already quite broken?' It can't quite be sure what it was that ended his life, but Diehl describes it was the thrusting of a sword down his throat to exit his 'vitals,'[2056] as he was still alive. It can be assuredly argued that no monarch in history suffered an equivalent, let alone worse, fate than Andronicus I Comnenus 'The Terrible'.

What went so wrong? Why in a span of two years, did the new *Basileus* that was known for his charm, wit, charisma, vigor, sexual escapades that were mainly winked at by the people, and even fine horsemanship fall so low? If it is definitely true what historians say, although he was hinted at having a certain insincerity as a 'true actor' as *Basileus*,[2057] Andronicus was a hybrid of virtues and vices that somehow seemed to balance out into an acceptable, possibly accomplished, ruler. It has even been claimed if anyone could have returned Byzantium to the glory of the late eleventh century, it was Andronicus I. But, this balance within the *Basileus* was disrupted by the pressures and responsibilities of rule, and his vices eventually overcame his virtues. Choniates would go on to say he had nightmares of the phantoms of those he had killed, but he still became dark, cruel, distant, and wanton. He only made matters for himself worse, depleting a much needed military force with his proscriptions and executions.

He also misjudged the all-important temperature of the masses in the City; it was with little difficulty that Angelus stoked the passions of the people into a frenzy of uninhibited violence. No Nika Revolt or raid by a foreign horde in another city had before seen such graphic results. When in balance, Andronicus was a spirited and dynamic leader that inspired a sort of hope in his purveyors. Added was his toughness on the corruption that defined Byzantine economy and bureaucracy, and, seemingly, he was a friend to the poor and the disenfranchised serfdom his ancestors had created. Yet, perhaps, it is explained best that he was an 'opportunist,' discrediting his dynasty with shame by showing foreign hostilities to those like the Normans and that 'Byzantium

---

[2055] Gibbon, 1666.

[2056] Diehl, 145.

[2057] *ibid.*, 149.

was both treacherous and vulnerable' inviting invasion.[2058] This estimation, even without hindsight, would prove true as the West was slowly emboldening itself to lengths unseen to take the capital, dissolve its government, and make Byzantium close to a fief for the West in 1204.

Andronicus I's dedication to the Empire domestically went beyond catching and punishing the guilty. From the start of his reign, Andronicus enforced a financial program to ensure that the necessary funds of the state could be properly directed in the central government. His first priority was to curb the runaway corruption terrorizing the people in the forms of graft and extorted tax fiefs. At the level of the central tax authorities, he hired more honest officials not prone to embezzlement, also raising the salary to a level where, hopefully, bribery and 'gifts' would not follow. Simony and the sale of offices to the highest bidder, which bred clandestine nepotism, were to be cancelled indefinitely. Choniates's descriptions of these reforms were considered 'naïve', but they did have an effectiveness that lessened considerably the burden of the peasantry and eased, somewhat, the tensions of the central state.[2059]

As he intended, this trend did spread to the local levels of tax authority, checking the powers of their officials and incidents of force were being lessened in favor of supporting the 'business class' of merchants that benefited urban areas as well as the central government. Another contributing factor to the rehabilitation of tax collection was Andronicus's hard-hitting policies for the wealthy-class landowners in the outer provinces and Themes. He re-withdrew the imperial Edicts restricting which class of citizens could purchase properties and in his judicial capacity, he did not intentionally favor the rich over the poor.

Andronicus was typically draconian in his punishments, having been quoted that these corrupt officials must 'either stop from ill-doing or stop from living.' Quite unfortunately, the problem with all of these measures was the ostracization of the aristocracy in providing military services, the best examples being those such as David Comnenus. The strictures and executions were said to 'shake the very foundations of Byzantine military power' by Ostrogorsky, surely to affect the state in the decades to come. When this *Basileus* outlawed the plundering of wealth from abandoned shipwrecks, transgressors were said to be hung from the vessels yard-arms. This fed the legendary status of Andronicus, becoming so that 'Andronicus was like a magic spell to drive away the greedy tax-collectors.' He maintained the economic integrity of Thessalonica as a

---

[2058] Treadgold, 656.
[2059] Ostrogorsky, 396-398.

prosperous mercantile area with its annual 'world's fair' in October, rivaling that of Constantinople's.

There, the European Jewish, Armenian, and Arab traders would meet to bargain with the Levantines and Africans. It survived the Ottoman Empire until World War II, where its 'Jewish character' died down with the 50,000 Sephardic Jews taken to Poland during the Holocaust.[2060] On August 24, 1185, the Sicilians looted and devastated Thessalonica with savagery not seen since the massacre of Theodosius I, even desecrating holy places by urination. But, even as this was so, in the aftermath of occupation the Westerners' inexperience with marketable commodities and prices made them easy targets for fleecing by local merchants, as the historian Eusthathius describes, only enriching the city more so.[2061]

Andronicus I Comnenus tried his entire reign to uphold a policy of isolation and non-intervention with the Western powers, bred from a severe prejudice his predecessors did not have. Despite this attribute of hating the customs and the intervention of the West, practical measures were enforced and the *Basileus* opened negotiations favoring the Venetians and the other Italians. They were given back their quarters and confiscated property, taken by Manuel, with reparations paid annually beginning in 1185, favoring the Venetians as they would be free from any customs obligations. In the religious domain, in 1182, Andronicus reluctantly accepted the diplomacy of Pope Lucius III who sent a legate to evaluate the situation in Constantinople. Tensions were eased when the *Basileus* agreed to erect a Latin church in the City with a Catholic clergy and large donatives, as reported in the biographies of Henry II of England. Andronicus also forbade any discussion on the subjects of theology and partisanship as larger concerns consumed his time and attention.[2062]

Also, Union with the Western Church would be unthinkable and anathema to the Latin-despising Andronicus as unsubstantiated rumors of Latin aggression panicked the Greeks into massacring the Latin Quarter of the City.[2063] Acts of severe bloodshed towards the Westerners were not uncommon within cities such as Constantinople and Jerusalem. Neither age nor sex kept them exempt from massacres, with priests burned in their own churches or the sick and infirm immolated in their hospitals. Though, in one instance of

---

[2060] Norwich, (DF), 147f.

[2061] Eustathius the Thessalonican. *De Thessalonica capta latinus a. 1185*, CSHB, Edited by I. Bekker, trans. by H. Hunger. Vienna, Austria. 1955.

[2062] Vasiliev, 507.

[2063] Diehl, 221.

'clemency', some 4,000 Jerusalemites were taken as Turkish slaves. The clergy and monks railed the loudest, but no use came from it as when a Roman priest's head was severed and tied to the tail of a dog as cruel sport and a mockery of their faith.[2064] Some of these desecrations and savageries were perpetrated by the Muslim Turks, yet Andronicus remained obstinate to all of this and gleefully kept a blind eye. These acts won Andronicus the enmity of Patriarch Basil II, which echoed in his opinions of the *Basileus* and the ascension of Angelus later the same year.

In his more active foreign policy, he attempted a noble consideration of a treaty with Saladin, the Iconian Sultan of Egypt, wherein Andronicus offered the Turk aid in taking the vulnerable Jerusalem and the lands on the sea coast to the city of Ascalon.[2065] This bold offer by a Christian *Basileus* to a Muslim potentate would then be sealed with Saladin and his new state becoming a Byzantine fief. In return, Andronicus would generously receive the lands from Antioch and Armenia Minor from the Sultanate of Iconium on the Bosporus! The implication was a full-scale civil war of the Turkish Sultanates and a recovery of the Holy Land under a pacified Muslim occupation. This pact, seething with ambition and a hope for reconciliation with the East was stopped short when Andronicus was murdered, but Saladin was listening to the *Basileus*'s designs. Unlike the pacts made between the Western powers with the Turks, Andronicus's was one of mutual reconciliation with the Sultan and never Christian versus Christian. The typical intention of the Latins were merely pretexts to attack Christians meant to be allies, although Eastern Christians would still suffer in Andronicus's pact This would culminate in the explosive situation Europe and the Empire would face in the repeated disasters that composed the Third Crusade.

## ISAAC II ANGELUS
### (1185-1195, 1203-1204)

For the first time in just over a century a new dynasty ruled the Empire and for the second time, a change in rulers resulted from a bloody and tragic coup. In reality, it was the weakness and vulnerabilities of the previous *Basileus* that caused such a revolution as any such aristocrat or commander – Comneni, Angeli, or even Ducasi – could have accomplished the same ends. The

---

[2064] Gibbon, 2107.

[2065] Vasiliev, 437.

only prerequisite would be if they knew how to control the passions of Constantinople's inhabitants in such a year as 1185. John Ducas, who eagerly awaited his succession, was dismissed by the City for his age – they wanted a youthful candidate on the throne who was not 'gray-headed', but a young and energetic *Basileus* that bore the traditional traits of the Comneni. Choniates describes it as needing 'a gentle spring after a bitter winter.'[2066]

Also, his lack of administrative skills and brazen aristocratic bent would brand Ducas 'the embodiment of evil conscience ...on the rotten throne of the Caesars and a society where, 'all classes were excluded except the Byzantine aristocracy' by modern historians. His contemporaries judged him worse as he was claimed to be a 'second Nero' whose pernicious vices outweighed his small virtues and completely disregarded any circumstances of a situation and the benefits of 'transient or accidental benefits.'[2067] He slept on the throne unless awoken by the sighs of base pleasures, keeping around 20,000 eunuchs and domestics, usually spending up to 4,000 pounds of silver annually on his household and dining table.

Isaac Angelus was by no means as ambitious, dynamic, or as popular as Andronicus had been known to be his entire career. Instead, his strength was being more stable and just the kind of general the Empire needed in its perpetual wars with a capability on the field due to his smart choices in commanders. He was seen as a 'decent and moderate man' who was 'mild-mannered and pleasant . . .Less suspicious than Andronicus,' and of having 'middling intelligence' as well as 'many connections with the nobility.'[2068] However, as he was a minor Anatolian aristocrat, he showed the fault of an uncompromising preference to the large landholders and their corrupt practices in gathering capital to please the nobility at the expense of the poor.

He was also known for humiliating losses to the West and shameful treaties enriching his enemies against the Empire. Perhaps worst of all was the rise in his reign of the Second Bulgarian Empire of Peter and Asen which became independent of Byzantium in 1186, making sure the Balkans were lost to Byzantium forever. It is also at this time that some modern historians even contradict Choniates awarding Basil II with the name 'Bulgar-Slayer' to compare to the failed responses of Isaac II to the new Bulgarian Wars, scornfully mocking the usurper of Andronicus's throne. This was added to the opposing

---

[2066] Norwich, *(DF)*, 157.
[2067] Gibbon, 2108.
[2068] Treadgold, 656.

acclamation that would be given to Isaac by John Skylitzes in the late thirteenth century.[2069]

Angelus would also ignore, supposing he may even have known of, any treaty his predecessor made with the brilliant Saladin in Egypt over the suzerainty exchanged for the Empire's good will. As the Egyptian Mamelukes pressed heavily on Palestine, no treaty was declared and all of Christendom went to another bloody war to stop him, with results disastrous to both Byzantium and the West. Not surprisingly, the Angeli were noted by most modern historians as being the worst to wear the purple in imperial history, losing after almost a millennium New Rome to the barbarians and only play-acting as a descendant of the Old Rome.

A great-grandson of Alexius I through his daughter Theodora's marriage to Constantine Angelus, Isaac II Angelus was born with a great pedigree with legitimacy to the throne, beginning as the Angeli did in the 'obscure' category of Anatolian and gentrified aristocracy of Philedelphia.[2070] Born in September of 1156 to the general Andronicus Ducas Angelus and Euphrosyne Kastamonnitissa, his military career showed a success that threatened Andronicus I, causing his imprisonment, near mutilation, and near execution by his agents. Isaac killed his prison guards and fled to a fortuitous sanctuary held by the disillusioned Patriarch Basil among a mob that had enough of their tyrannous monarch, tearing him to pieces in frenzy. Mainly, this riot was attributed to Andronicus's indolence in the face of an imminent attack by David Comnenus and the Normans of William I at Mosynopolis.

After peace was refused by the Norman commander Baldwin, Angelus immediately took action by re-organizing the army into one *grand armee,* led by their strong commander Alexius Branas, all without arousing suspicion. Fortunately for them, the Norman invasion was itself divided into three: along with the Mosynopolitans, there was a Thessalonican garrison and a further contingent on the banks of the Strymon. By surprise, Branas routed and expelled the Normans threatening the imperial city at Mosynopolis and at Dimitrica near Amphipolis on November 7, 1185, Choniates describing Branas as swooping on the Normans 'as an eagle falls upon a feeble bird'.

Branas captured the Norman commanders after causing heavy losses to their invading armies, leaving the Normans only Cephalonia and the city of Zacynthus. The Thessalonicans lost morale and fled Branas's approach by

---

[2069] Herrin, 218.

[2070] Ostrogorsky, 401.

sea through the Marmara back to Corfu. In all, 10,000 Normans were killed and 4,000 taken prisoner,[2071] mainly officers, including Baldwin, Richard of Acerra, and the rebelling David Comnenus who was subsequently blinded. The Byzantines did manage to leave the garrisoning of Mysonopolis in neglect, however, as the troops wanted to spend their Christmas at Constantinople.

Later, in spring of 1186, Angelus took Dyracchium on Corfu and the Westerners fled back to the Aegean and Ionian Islands after the vengeful Thessalonicans rose up and expelled them. Three out of four of the Venetian inhabitants of Constantinople were conscripted and 140 galleys were supplied with a total of 18,000 men.[2072] For now, the Western frontiers could enjoy a respite and Isaac would then flex his diplomatic muscles in the hostile East. After Arslan of Iconium had recently taken Neocastra, the *Basileus* offered peace to the Hungarian-French alliance of King Bela and Margaret Capet, daughter of Louis VII, marrying Bela's daughter as Maria. The price for this was, naturally, the lands he inherited by his brother under Manuel Comnenus from Dalmatia to Syrmium, which Angelus was forced to relent. An arrangement was sought between Bela and Theodora, Isaac's sister, but a Synod of Bishops in Constantinople would not allow dissolution of her marriage to the Count of Montferrat.[2073]

To demonstrate strength domestically, Angelus sent a fleet to recover Cyprus from the rebellious and strategic Isaac Comnenus, the *Basileus's* cousin, recognizing himself as the haughty 'Emperor of Cyprus.' Isaac was allied with a Norman fleet commander, Margaritone, who was wandering the Aegean after the defeat at Dyrrachium, to divide Angelus's forces. Comnenus managed to take the army prisoner and the invasion of Cyprus ended in a debacle for Constantinople in 1186. Margaritone would then settle at Cephalonia to found his own Greek fief. This loss was humiliating, but would certainly lack the gravity of the rebellion in the Balkans of the Vlach Bulgarians, Asen and Peter.

These two were descendants of Symeon and the First Empire dissolved by Basil II. Backed by the fierce Wallachians, the ancestors of modern Romania, the Bulgarians also allied with the Cumans of the Danube by October, pushing them back east. The *Basileus* himself was also repulsed, disproving some of Choniates's claims of cowardice on Angelus's part. Afterwards, the

---

[2071] Treadgold, 656. This, supposedly, was all part of a concerted four-prong strategy in neutralizing the Latins.

[2072] Norwich, *(AHV)*, 121.

[2073] Obolensky, 163.

Sebastocrator John Angelus Ducas was ably putting down the Slavic allies when he was recalled by the *Basileus* for suspicion of planning revolt. The replacement for Ducas was unsuccessful and, at Paradunavum, the Vlach brothers founded the independent Empire of the Bulgarians with the capital of Trnovo. They would later expand to other cities, including the elder capital at Plisken, and rule the Balkans into the fourteenth century, laying the groundwork that is now modern Bulgaria. It proudly claimed its independence from a state whose culture they made their own like a rebellious child. An Archbishop was raised in Trnvo and Asen was crowned as Tsar in the Church of St. Demetrius.

Westerners, including Pope Boniface III, openly referred to him as the *'Imperator* of the Vlachs and Cumans', the 'Emperor of the Vlachs and the most part by the Bulgarians' and, 'King of the Bulgarians and Vlachs.'[2074] By 1187, Angelus realized he desperately needed aid from other allies and turned to the West by first granting privileges once more to Venice and a tribute of 100,800 *hyperpyra.*[2075] Fortunately, he managed to take Kalojan ('Handsome John'), the youngest Vlach brother, as a hostage. The *Basileus,* needing more allies, made a marriage alliance between his sister Theodora to Conrad, the son of the Count of Montferrat, lasting until the Count's death in 1192.

Isaac Angelus sent Alexius Branas to counter the new Bulgaria, but he was declared *Basileus* by his troops and formed an assault to take Constantinople. Taking desperate loans from monasteries, Isaac II and Conrad of Montferrat made a defense of the City while an unimpressive force managed to defeat the rebels and kill Branas. Later in 1187, Isaac II advanced to the Bulgarian territories, defeating a Cuman army and retaking Serdica, giving chase to the Danube, and holding the co-Tsar Asen's wife as a hostage in 1188. Internal affairs were settled and the foreign threats of the Bulgarian East were temporarily contained by the end of 1187 and the timing was good enough as a new Crusade by the West would march through the Empire in 1189. But, this would not stop another revolt in Thrace by Theodore Magnaphas, a magnate landowner of Anatolia, the Third Crusade allowing the rebel respite from Byzantium as it broke the siege of Philadelphia.

Whether goaded by the three-year-old promises of Andronicus Comnenus or not, Saladin rode northeast, invading Syria and soundly defeating forces at Hattin, to take the city of Jerusalem on October 2 from the weak and pliant King Guy of Lusignon, whom he then imprisoned. Jerusalem had already been

---

[2074] Vasiliev, 442.

[2075] Treadgold, 657.

in a weak position due to the monarchs Baldwin IV and V, the former dying of leprosy and the latter only an infant. In May of 1187, Saladin was already leading a holy war to Frankish Jordan and on July 3rd appeared in Tiberias where he slaughtered Christian armies in the Horns of Hattin the next day.

Starting September 20, he started taking a staggering amount of territory in Acre, Nablus, Jaffa, Sidon, Beirut, Ascalon, and the whole of Gaza. When Saladin arrived at the Holy City, he showed amazing mercy: he and his general, Balian of Ibelin, shed no blood, allowed no looting, 20,000 poor citizens who could not pay arrears were allowed a lump sum paid by Christian authorities, and 1,000 prisoners were freed as well as the old, women, and children.[2076] This unexpected chivalry was a stark contrast to what Crusader conquerors had already done to foreign prisoners and citizens! Saladin also showed goodwill to Constantinople by sending Isaac a piece of the True Cross on a Venetian ship, as it was stolen by Italian pirates. Saladin did compromise with the *Basileus* by allowing in Jerusalem an Orthodox share in the Holy Sepulcher. Sheikh Ganim al-Khazraji was appointed Custodian of the Church, a title held 800 years later by the Nusseibeh family.[2077]

But, in Rome, the shock of the conquest by Saladin was great: Pope Urban III was said to have died on the spot (an exaggeration) as his successor, Gregory VIII, called for a Crusade. Conrad of Montferrat traveled east to offer defense to the other Outremer states that had already went into a mode of crisis. The German Emperor Frederick III Barbarossa set out in May of 1189 from Ratisbon with between 100,000 and 150,000 soldiers and upon arriving was approached by Serbia and Bulgaria both to make a Crusade against Byzantium. These offers were surprisingly rejected, since this would have made an optimal alliance to take Constantinople and the Byzantine Crown for the West.

A staggering number of soldiers from England, France, Germany, Poland, Bohemia, and Rome are confirmed by the Byzantine chronicler Cinnamos at 900,000 Crusaders having ventured east.[2078] Though the Western and Eastern *Basilii* had no love lost between them, it appears Barbarossa's focus was on Jerusalem and Saladin, not Constantinople. This was perhaps to prepare for a German Outremer legacy that would be a stepping stone to greater ventures and ambitions to fill in the East. But, Angelus proved to be craftier at this time

---

[2076] Norwich, *(DF)*, 159.

[2077] Montefiorre, 274.

[2078] Gibbon, 2073. Gibbon's precise number was 900, 553, yet he questions the rolls of 90,000 contemporaries presently comment upon.

than Barbarossa as he was making a secret alliance with Saladin, as Andronicus had done, in repelling the Crusaders.

Isaac II made these intentions better known when he sealed off the passes to the Germans leading to Philippopolis, only to be taken anyway with over 3,000 Byzantine casualties and a treaty at Nuremburg in 1188. When German ambassadors were arrested in Constantinople, Frederick raided Thrace and took Adrianople in late 1189. Frederick then sacked Iconium and the Sultan Kilij Arslan II, marching south to Isauria to consolidate his battles against the Turks.

Meanwhile, the southern Slav Kingdoms were receiving the German Emperor quite well as he was approached with offers of peace and aid from the Grand Zhupan Stephen Nemanja in Serbian Nish in hopes of allying against the Empire. His two Greek ambassadors betraying the *Basileus*, Frederick was given Philippopolis to occupy and they kept a hold on the Dardanelles when Frederick of Swabia took Thracian Didymotichum. With Byzantium decidedly for Saladin, Frederick III gathered a fleet under his son Henry to sail to Constantinople with the usual demands for cheap provisions, hostages of high worth, and transport vessels. He then turned to the Taurus by Philadelphia, Laodicea, and Myriocephalum.

However, it will never be known how successful he might have or not have been as, when watering his horse, Frederick fell into the Calycadnus River near Seleucia in full armor and drowned on June 10, 1190. A Western prince dying so mundanely before reaching the Holy Land was an embarrassing mark against the Third Crusade and would be a precursor for the failures that would follow. It was best illustrated as the need to "Crusade" was 'so ingrained in the contemporary Christian that the frank and open abandonment of the struggle would have been unthinkable.' As it was 'specious arguments' and 'obvious material advantages,'[2079] however, that induced a Crusade against the Byzantine Empire, such struggles seeming inevitable. As a result of the flights from Tyre by the petty German nobles, the German crown would be given to Barbarossa's son as Henry VI and he would take the crown of Sicily in Palermo on Christmas Day, 1194. By the end of 1190, the Third Crusade was abandoned as another loss to the West with only Acre taken as a serious victory over the Turks still holding Jerusalem, yet it was decidedly not as bad a disaster as the Second Crusade had been.

In autumn of 1190, Angelus recovered Varna, Anchialus, and Serdica

---

[2079] Hussey, 70.

when the Bulgarians defeated Byzantine armies in Thrace and set a strong border on the Balkans. In the autumn, the Angelus took the Morava Valley by defeating Serbia and its Grand Zhupan, Stephen Nemanja. Next, Isaac made peace with King Bela III at Belgrade to buffer the Second Empire and their allies. A year later, more Crusading activity began as the English King, Richard I 'the Lionhearted' (1157-1199), made his way to succeed Barbarossa as supreme Western prince followed by Philip II Augustus, King of France. Anglo-Byzantine relations had been well-maintained within the interval between Henry II and Manuel I's friendship. Richard demonstrated this by bypassing Constantinople altogether to Palestine by sea, sparing the City the provisional strains that would usually result from Western occupation in the City. Richard was an honorable man preferring war above all, even women, wearing a scarlet cloak and carrying a sword he always claimed was Excalibur [2080] as the Cyprus he would take was well-ruled by his judgment.

One major success, indeed, made by the English was the recovery of Cyprus in May, 1191, from Isaac Comnenus who was carted off to a prison in Tripoli bound in silver chains, the island given to the Knights Templar and the exiled Guy of Lusignon. Richard was reluctant, indeed, in returning the island to the Empire, but at least it remained in allied Western, if not Byzantine, hands. In 1192, Saladin made a peace settlement with the Latins that he would remain in Jerusalem and they would keep the lands between Jaffa and Tyre, a most disadvantageous exchange to the West. Henry VI of the German Empire was not satisfied and took the cross once again on April 2, Easter Week, of 1195. He wrote a strong letter to Isaac Angelus about providing the needed aid and returning Corfu and Thessalonica as 'compensation' to the Sicilians. He reminded the *Basileus* this was owed him as Angelus kept friendship with Saladin and built a mosque in Constantinople for the Muslim inhabitants.[2081] But, as the Byzantine *Basileus* was overthrown six days later, all of this came to nothing as another Crusade would have to wait.

With the aid of the unchecked rebel Magnaphas, the Turks prostrated a second false Alexius II to claim the Byzantine throne, raiding Thrace towards the imperial capital. Isaac followed them from Sofia and turned them aside at the Morava. The *Basileus* then placated Nemanja by marrying his niece Eudocia to one of the Zhupan's sons, Stephen, as Sebastocrator as he would also be

---

[2080] Montefiorre, 268.
[2081] Gibbon, 2075.

allowed the use of the title 'Imperial Majesty.'[2082] Furthermore, the universality of the gold bezant was kept in the Hungarian economy and the double cross of Byzantium was added to the national coat-of-arms of Hungary, cementing a cultural fusion. Bulgaria was fragmenting the Balkans as it conquered the regions and cities as the Empire needed all the concessions it could acquire to keep its allies in the north.

But even as the second pretender was killed, a third Alexius II appeared in Paphlagonia and Bithynia, further shaking the Empire's confidence in the throne and government. At this point, not in another time of recent memory had so many internal struggles commenced: magnates, pronoiars, regional and local officials, all would rise up and take advantage of Isaac's diverted attentions, sensing the looming loss of the central government.[2083] For an administration known for its corruption and lax attitudes on the conduct of the landholders, especially in the *Basileus*'s native Anatolia, those who benefited were hungrily prepared to seize his throne. This was all for the sake of adding power to their riches, even if the price was stabbing Byzantium in the back while it was vulnerable to its enemies. With this quickly becoming more common a practice, who could say the Empire was not falling apart?

The year 1192 would also see internal troubles, mainly in the neighboring enemies of the Empire, as the succeeding sons of Arslan quarreled and handed over the rebel Magnaphas during their civil wars at Iconium. Peter and Asen, as would be expected of an Empire ruled by two brothers, were dividing themselves and Bulgaria as Isaac sent forces under his cousin the Grand Domestic, Constantine Angelus, to raid Bulgarian Thrace. But as happened with Branas, Constantine was raised on the shield as *Basileus* at Philippopolis, but with differing opinions in the ranks as some of his men surrendered him to Isaac, and he was blinded. In order to expel the Norman Margaritone from the Ionian Islands and the Aegean, Isaac turned to the local Italian fleets. He reinstated their trading privileges and tributes to the Pisans and Genoans, as he did the Venetians to the grief of the Constantinopolitans, and the pirates were ably policed.

The vengeful Bulgarians in 1194 intensified their already heavy raids in Thrace and the King of Hungary offered an armed alliance to occupy the borders of the new Empire when Arcadiopolis and Serdica were lost. In early 1195, Isaac II was leading armies through Thrace when a plot orchestrated by

---

[2082]  Obolensky, 222.

[2083]  Treadgold, 706.

his brother Alexius ambushed the *Basileus* at Cypsela. Isaac was then seized by a rebellious court and blinded on April 8. Yet, as was the case in Justinian II, this formerly mutilated figure of Byzantine history would not leave the stage altogether and would return in one more desperate act before the Empire's captivity by the Latins. This is how Westerners, not familiar with the tenacious depositions of monarchs in Byzantine politics or history, would be shocked as this was something never to be done in Western courts.

For eight years, the mutilated Isaac Angelus was banished into the shadow of Alexius, his tenacious brother, yet the connections and relations he had created in the West and Outremer refused to recognize such usurpation and promptly rebelled. Why did this happen? Was this a mere play for power and greed, or is it possible Alexius and his stronger faction feared the repercussions of capitulating to Emperor Henry VI? Another Crusade would have meant more trials in a state and government that needed to catch up on economic, political, social, and military policies. Meanwhile, a flood of rebellions drowned the Empire on all fronts whether Crusader, Byzantine, Turk, Bulgarian, or Italian and the weak usurper Alexius III and his court would easily wither under these challenges. Culturally, Crusader and East Roman influences were slow to integrate and their mansions were frescoed with ancient heroes or even pornography. Western education in Homer and Aristotle also painted a picture of the Easterners as being weak and effeminate to the austere Outremers.[2084]

The pressure was such that in 1203, for the first time, a blinded monarch was re-instated on the throne as legitimized by his young son and co-*Basileus*, Alexius IV, on August 1. As he was once the legitimate *Basileus*, the Byzantines considered all interventions by the Crusaders to be a settled affair.[2085] This dangerously optimistic claim was considered too weak a foundation, naturally, and on January 25th of 1204, they were both overthrown by the usurping Alexius V Murtzuphlus and died by the strangulation cord in privacy like Alexius II and his mother. A Western chronicler[2086] is said to show naivete in believing Isaac II Angelus died of a 'sudden illness'[2087] and such a judgment of this naivete on behalf of the modern historian seems reasonable. The more realistic contemporary, Robert of Clary (1170-1216), is said to have produced the accusations of the two strangulations.

---

[2084] Laiou, 76.

[2085] Norwich, *(AHV)*, 134.

[2086] Geoffrey de Villehardouin. *The Conquest of Constantinople, and Joinville: Chronicles of the Crusades*, ed. by M. R. Shaw. New York, NY: Penguin Publishing. 1963, 84.

[2087] Norwich, *(DF)*, 176.

As any *Basileus* in such a situation in the early 1190's would do, Isaac tried to gain the support of the Comnenian doctrine in both churches, West and East. He solicited the usual promises of a Union between Rome and Constantinople (though such efforts were becoming tiresome). Choniates quotes Isaac's point of view towards his temporal and spiritual powers: 'On earth there is no difference of power between God and the emperor; kings are allowed to do everything, and they may use without any distinction that which belongs to God along with their own possessions, because they have received the imperial power from God, and between God and them there is no difference.'

These words would describe the aspect of the Angeli in general, and Isaac in particular, as one of internal agitations due to 'heresies' and 'false doctrines.' He ostracized the clergy and monasteries with confiscating their property, as so many others had done, to pay for the Empire's endless warfare.[2088] The Pope would make clear, in 1195, his opinion of Isaac's blinding by siding with the new *Basileus* Alexius III as he saw one ruler of a seriously threatened Empire was outweighed by warring neighbors in order to be fodder for another Crusade. As usual, the two could not find union on the disagreements over the dual nature of the Christ between the 'corruptibility' (*phtharton*) and the 'incorruptibility' (*aphtharton*) in the human form of Jesus.[2089] Ultimately, there was not much end to what the Angeli would do without being seen as weak and merely mouthpieces by a state ready to be partitioned by landlords, Latins, the Muslims, the new Bulgarian Empire, as whatever the final stroke would come to be.

Isaac II's internal policies were corrupt and deplorable, but it appears he apparently won the approval of the Crusaders enough to be a better choice than his incompetent brother, Alexius. He was, however, a symbol of the crumbling state of an Empire harassed on all ends and slowly rotting from within. Further, separation by the greed and envy of the new feudal fiefdoms created in a disappearing Byzantine system of the Themes a socio-economic change. Bribes to enemies and friends alike would epitomize diplomacy as the army itself could only hold on to so much in a tide of foreign and domestic turmoil, more pay going to mercenaries than the East Roman troops who were once held above all other nations.

His loss of Bulgaria and the Balkans was the catalyst of most of Byzantium's Slavic discontent with much of his fate being sealed by the Crusaders, also jealous of Isaac's diplomacy with Jerusalem over arms. Their insults were taken

---

[2088] Vasiliev, 470.

[2089] *ibid.*, 477-478.

by Angelus's joining with Saladin, an infidel seen as robbing the Holy Sepulcher, when in fact he shared it with Christianity. But the Turks had the upper hand after the Third Crusade's debacle and it would be almost wise to sit at Saladin's side than be in his path, anyway. There were to be no contradictions to Isaac's choices and character as there were with his predecessor; he was not so complex and was practically a turnkey monarch of a failing government.

His financial policies were virtually non-existent as he held no checks or balances on the powers of the pronoia, being raised a landed aristocrat of the wealthy and divided land of Anatolia. He allowed massive corruption and the 'old administrative abuses' returned: extortionate tax-farming, sales of offices, and the graft and bribery among the bureaucracy. Choniates's best recollection was that Isaac II sold offices like vegetables in a market as it was easily observed that 'the rottenness of the whole organism of government was revealed with terrifying clarity.'[2090] Byzantium itself had become one giant private fief of the landlords during the Angeli and shameless abuse was all there was to fuel Isaac II's desperate armies and diplomacy.

It was as if Isaac was willing to sacrifice his internal structure while fighting to keep the external Empire together militarily – the worst trait of a *Basileus* of the military aristocracy. Starting in 1185, grants were of course given based on cronyism, such as to the Montferrats (who did at least fight for him after 1195) and other Byzantine landlords. The result in this unproductive practice was that with no returns on grants to the Cumans and Balkan tribes, they invested not in land but in livestock.[2091] Upon his marriage to his Hungarian princess, he instated an *ad hoc* tax levy to pay for the lavish wedding due to another mismanagement of the Treasury. Unfortunately, the defining Theme system, the pride of Heraclius and Constans II from the seventh century, was no more as the growth in Western feudalism had changed the entire structure of the Byzantine economy.

The unique military and economic style of the Middle Byzantine Empire had been crushed long before the time of the Latin usurpation. Although there were twice as many Themes existing in the shrinking Empire than that of the Macedonian dynasty, these were within themselves fragmented and divided independent territories, furthering the practices of rebellion for the throne. Separate peaces were made with the Normans, the Turks, and the Balkans, resembling independent nations sharing only a culture and a central

---

[2090] Ostrogorsky, 401-402.
[2091] Hussey, 69.

government in Constantinople they now despised. The Fourth Crusade was just a respite in these practices only in that it adapted to change hands with the same players in their corrupt game.

Culturally, the Slavic north was losing touch with its resilient roots in Byzantine Hellenization, active since the cultured Macedonians. A homogenization of peoples from the East was, once again, taking shape in a shrinking Empire that even the West and Islam could not fully claim. Jews and Armenians were now settling in Thessalonica besides the Normans and Greeks already there. The Danube, Thessaly, Macedonia, and 'Greater Wallachia' were now settled by Cumans and Wallachians that had not known much of Hellenization in their tribal culture.[2092] The Eastern trade networks that impressed Marco Polo during the Latin Empire was a mixture of such peoples ranging from Flanders and the Tuscan Alps to Central Eurasia and their Turkic peoples developing the fabled 'Silk Road.' This in no small part could prove that the Vlachs believed that Byzantine power was dwindling and that a partially Hellenized and independent Bulgaria was far better than being a Byzantine fief.

## ALEXIUS III ANGELUS COMNENUS 'BAMABACARIOTUS'
### (1195-1203)

## ALEXIUS IV ANGELUS
### (1203-1204)

Under the mediocre and barely effective reign of Isaac II, the Empire maintained itself before adversity, but the seizure of the throne by his jealous and irresponsible brother toppled all chances of lasting stability. What was certainly worse was the character of the usurper, Alexius III being 'a weakling, possessed for a lust of power...a typical product of this age of disintegration.'[2093] The cruelty of his usurpation in blinding his unsuspecting brother, while no cause of great alarm in Byzantine culture, was said to have inspired a self-righteous fervor in the Crusaders, calling for immediate correction. It is plain to see how the intrigues of their politics undermined horribly the executive administration and this proved one too many of such times it could not be

---

[2092] Ostrogorsky, 403-404.
[2093] *ibid.*, 408.

salvaged by divided enemy states and fortunate coincidence – it marked the lack of adaptability for a Greek Empire in Constantinople.

The legitimate symbol for the power of the throne, whether Latin, Turk, or Slavonic, was the last of the legitimate Angeli, Alexius IV, son of Isaac II as the Crown Prince of Constantinople as Western historians have described him. He was the nexus of Frankish and Venetian concerns in Constantinople and it was he, though merely a teenager, that galvanized action to retake the throne and reap amazing concessions by the Byzantine government. Alexius III inspired much more desperation than hope although he made in eight years the bribes and barriers necessary against the hostile northern concerns in Hungary and Bulgaria. Not to mention the blessing of the Pope upon his succession; papal approval was probably in hopes of a Union of the Churches, though this would prove a disappointment in the face of the obstinate Angeli *Basileus* being putting himself in pride of place before Patriarch.

In the end, it was the outrageous promises of loot and high amounts of mercenary debts to unstable alliances that ended the matter of the Angeli rule of Byzantium, along with weak armies and dwindling diplomacy. This *Basileus*, overthrown by his nephew, would flee and turn into a Thracian rebel and pretender bristling against the last *Basileus* in 1204 and the succeeding Flemish Count Baldwin, failing and in the end, to live as a monk until his death in 1211. Alexius III Angelus 'Comnenus' was this despised, 'ridiculous' ruler putting Byzantium in 'near chaos,'[2094] who adopted the name Comnenus as a cheap ploy in continuing the dynasty that saved the Empire in under a century, although he was still a great-grandson of Alexius I as Isaac II was. He would gain another moniker in history as '*Bamabacariotus*' ('Shepherd's crook', loosely) as probably a remark on his softness and ineffectiveness.[2095] Furthermore, he 'created an atmosphere of discontent and agitation in the country' and whether this meant the 'country' of the landed aristocracy or that of the Empire as a whole, both were present and would eventually destroy him as a usurper.

He was the older brother of Isaac II Angelus, born in 1153 into the same Lydian aristocracy from Philedelphia, an Anatolian branch of the Comneni. Not much is recorded of his early life before a failed plot he and his brother undertook against Andronicus I, which earned him exile to the East and the sanctuary of the court of Saladin. Even the French chronicler and Mareshal of Champagne, Geoffrey de Villehardouin (1160-1213) elaborates much,

---

[2094] Norwich, *(AM)*, 172.
[2095] Vasiliev, 439.

filling his Byzantine histories with the exploits and actions of Alexius IV and V. Bamabacariotus was supplanted back when his brother took the throne in 1185 and was made a Sebastocrator next to his nephew, Alexius. It is said that with the collusion of the *Basilia* Euphrosyne and her faction that on September 11, 1195, the covetous and reckless prince seized his brother and blinded him, taking the imperial name of Alexius III, older than his imperial brother at age forty-two. His barely teen-aged nephew was then imprisoned and probably was being set to be forgotten and quietly assassinated as Alexius II had been, but who later managed to escape to the West while his overwhelmed uncle dealt with the Empire's increasing debts.

In 1195, Alexius unwisely cut off foreign contacts by withdrawing forces from Hungary and forfeiting the 28,000 *hyperpyra* owed to Venice.[2096] A Byzantine army under the banner of a third youth pretending to be the murdered Alexius II mustered in Bithynia, supported by the Turks who attempted turning out another such pretender of the Comneni. It was a shame that Hungarian relations were cut off abruptly as it might have helped Alexius III against the Bulgarian Empire. At Serres, Alexius's armies would lose face with a defeat by Asen and the Bulgarians in Thrace, stopped only by the Tsar's assassination in 1196, freeing Paphlagonia and the Meander, only to fall prey to Turkish invasion.

Ivenko, Asen's nephew and assassin, usurped the Bulgarian throne and appealed to the *Basileus* to send troops to Trnenko in order to stop his rival Peter, Asen's brother. Advantage in the Byzantine court on behalf of a Bulgarian alliance was quickly lost, unfortunately, when the navy sent north mutinied against the *Basileus* and aided Peter, driving out Ivenko into exile in Byzantium. Alexius's half-handed response was to fight a Vlach rebel, Chrysus, who forced him into a truce in 1197, the Bulgarian situation having not looked so bleak to Byzantium in many years.

Henry VI, the German Emperor, gladly accepting the opportunity to wear a mask of indignation while allowing him to extort cash from the rich Constantinople, sided with the young Alexius IV and demanded reparations during which a Fourth Crusade on Byzantium was in development. This was the infamous *to alamanikon* ('German Tax') of 1195. The strong position of Henry increased when he received on Christmas the crown of the Kingdom of Sicily and put his influence on northern Greece and Thessalonica. His demands for this enlarged Western Empire came to 360,000 *hyperpra* to finance a Crusade,

---

[2096] Treadgold, 659.

excluding Byzantium as a target, and this ransom was later re-negotiated later to one-third its original asking. Ostrogorsky puts this down as a 'sum of sixteen hundredweight' of gold, although at first, Henry had asked for fifty.[2097]

This caused massive rioting and refusals to pay on a scale unable to be met by the army and bureaucracy, so the *Basileus* stripped ornamentation from the tombs of the Comneni in their monastery, as well as the Church of the Apostles, to pay the debt. Henry gained a wide acceptance in the former Byzantine territories as he was recognized by the Kingdoms of Lesser Armenia and Cyprus. But Alexius III stayed obstinate to Henry, only recognizing two authorities in Christendom: that of himself and the Pope. Fortunately, for the weak position of Alexius, Henry VI had died at Messina on September 28, and as his forces reached Beirut, a civil war within the German nobility occurred.

This occupied the attention of his successor, Philip of Swabia, son-in-law to the deposed son of Isaac II. It kept his military loyal to the *Basilii* as diplomatically he had no choice but to renew the treaty with Byzantium and Venice in 1198. A Novel of November 1198 was issued by Alexius guaranteeing Venetian merchant colonies in certain provinces in 'Romania.'[2098] If this had been the Wallachian country beyond Vlach and Bulgarian territory, it might have been more of a hasty promise than a reality. As well as this, Pope Innocent III would not so easily be kept at bay, imposing a two-and-a-half percent clerical tax in his region to field new armies against Alexius. But as he failed to pay Venice in 1202, the army could not cross to the Bosporus and the city of St. Mark faced excommunication.[2099]

Meanwhile, Alexius was given reason now to turn north, attempting to restore Ivenko-Alexius the Vlach as Bulgarian Tsar, first by making him governor of Philippopolis with estates in Rhodope and betrothing the Vlach prince to an Angeli granddaughter. Afterwards, he aided in training the Vlach army, building fortresses, and repairing others against Peter of Bulgaria's raids in Thrace. In 1199, however, an ungrateful and overconfident Ivenko-Alexius rebelled against Byzantium and captured Camytzes, the *Basileus's* general, selling the commander to the new Tsar Kaloyan, as Peter had recently died.

With such weakness and incompetence as a result of the past four years of rule, the Byzantine army protested and refused to retaliate against the Vlach. In early 1200, therefore, Alexius Angelus further put his name in disrepute

---

[2097] Ostrogorsky, 412.

[2098] Vasiliev, 485.

[2099] Norwich, *(AM)*, 173.

by luring Ivenko to discuss peace and, instead, had him assassinated. In 1201, Kaloyan managed to convince Camytzes to rebel for the Bulgarians and set him loose against Thrace and Greece with the Vlach rebel Chrysus. The Empire, as it was slowly shrinking already from the stronger positions and resources of foreign rulers, was now being torn apart from within by various revolts by the aristocracy versus Alexius.

The Meander was besieged by Turks under John Angelus Ducas as Mangaphas, being ignored by the Angeli, was now occupying the former Theme of Thrace. The Peloponnese was being taken by the forces of Leo Sgurus, who would later become son-in-law to a posthumous Alexius III after 1211. Revolts in the City even saw the brief and unofficial succession of a new *"Basileus"* in John Comnenus Axuch 'the Fat', a descendant from *Basileus* John II. But, by 1202, these rebellions and hostile border operations were cleared by Alexius III's army and administration as a small boon for an uneven sovereignty. Yet, recovering financially from losses was still difficult as Anatolia and Greece refused to pay their taxes.

At this time in 1200, and unbeknownst to all, Constantinople's fate would be sealed as Alexius IV successfully fled west to Philip of Swabia's court on a Pisan ship. Arriving at his sister's court, the young Alexius plead for aid in displacing his uncle from Boniface of Montferrat, his brother-in-law, who was himself preparing to outfit a new Crusade and was seeking papal authority to do so. Already in France, Crusading armies were gathering in 1199 as a reported eighty-eight nobles and clergy with their armies gathering for the roll.[2100] At Rome, in 1202, Pope Innocent III was made aware that Boniface wished to make the Fourth Crusade against Constantinople and was not satisfied. Mostly, he distrusted the Angeli who he saw as usurpers and whose government would only increase to suffer under the younger Alexius. Despite Innocent's objections, however, after the purchase of Dalmatian Zara by Venice, Russian chronicles – defying the absence in other Western sources – claims the Crusade began with the full decision of the Pope and Philip together.[2101]

Furthermore, the idea of a Crusade was not only to defy the spread of Islam in the Holy Land, but prevent Christian powers East or West from fighting each other. The unstoppable will and personality of Innocent III emphatically said no and forbade such a Crusade from being undertaken, excommunicating all who

---

[2100]  Villehardouin, 30-35.

[2101]  Vasiliev, 455. This comes from the *Chronicles of Novgorod (1016-1471)* in the chapters on Galatea.

even considered the venture. Boniface was not intimidated as, traditionally, the need for the Pope's acceptance was only in the name of raising funds, knights, and barons from all over Europe to fight under the banner of Montferrat. It would still continue if a means of financing travel east could be arranged and the Pope faced civil war from Germany and Sicily if he attempted to stop it. On the first week of Lent, 1201, Montferrat had already reached out to Venice to supply and patronize a new Crusade, to be paid back with the notorious wealth of the East.

Venice and its wealth were then approaching with its sea routes to the East with fleets used to Greek waters and transports for 4,500 knights, 9,000 squires, and 20,000 foot sergeants. The Doge Enrico Dandalo, accepted terms on payment of 85,000 pieces of silver. This was agreed upon, but only about 51,000 pieces from gold and silver plate could effectively be raised to recompense the Doge. Perhaps the wily Doge anticipated this as he readily gave an extension in return for the recovery of the Egyptian port of Zara on the Dalmatian coast, now in Hungarian hands, raising a fleet costing 5,000 marks of public revenues. On May 13, 1202, the Sultan of Egypt, having lost Zara earlier, gave his blessing to retake the port and made a peace settlement with the West.

It is here claimed that Dandolo wished the entire Empire destroyed in order to gain monopolies in his trade markets and 'preeminence in the East.'[2102] Maybe this seems conjectural at first, but the evidence points toward such a goal for Venice. The capture of Constantinople itself was something in the past Crusades considered by Louis VII of France, Barbarossa, and even Henry VI if he wished to intervene in place of a young *Basileus* and his blind, aging father. Venice saw this as an inevitable opportunity, as the French controlled the government of Outremer, they would not dominate all Eastern territory for Western military strength. Dandolo also needed a monopoly on Italian colonized trade against Pisa and Genoa and only by manipulating the City's central government could this be done. These reasons are more probable than their opposite, that the Venetians faked the indignation of Isaac and Alexius's treatment by Alexius III to spark a Crusade that they could easily control by finance and debt.

The Crusaders sailed the Egyptian coast to Zara with 480 ships on November 8, 1202, landing on January 10, 1203, St. Martin's Eve, with at least 300 heavy siege engines and even pilgrims volunteering from Verona, wintering at Zara with Philip of Swabia and Alexius IV in tow. Byzantine Orthodoxy

---

[2102] Ostrogorsky, 413.

was now being stricken down by the Catholic Venetians and French with monasteries occupied exclusively by Dominican, Cistercian, and Franciscan friars.[2103] The displaced Byzantine *Basileus* kept silent as this was away from Byzantine concerns with the Pope who already had excommunicated Venice, but in May of 1203, Alexius IV made his bid to the Crusaders in recovering Byzantium for him in a new West-East alliance.

Though it had been promised before, the prospect of a young face that could rule more years than a John II or Manuel Comnenus appealed to the Holy See and other Western interests. In the *Conquest of Constantinople,* written as an eye-witness account after 1207, it is outlined Alexius IV's intentions to the Doge through Montferrat as the deposed *Basileus*'s emissary: 'Firstly if God permits you to restore his inheritance to him he will place the entire Empire under the authority of Rome, from which it has long been estranged. Secondly, since he is aware you have spent all your money and have nothing, he will give you 200,000 silver marks and provisions for every man in your army, officers and men alike. Likewise he himself will go in your company in Egypt with ten thousand men, or if you prefer it, send the same number of men with you; and furthermore, so long as he lives, he will maintain, at his own expense, five hundred knights to keep guard in the land overseas.'[2104]

Such claims were outrageous (these 200,000 marks equaling 800,000 *hyperpyra*) [2105] and unrealistic in relation to the imperial coffers as his uncle was said to have loved giving donatives and lavish entertainments when he could. But, either this fact was little known to young Alexius or he threw his whole lot in one gamble that would gain him a throne or cost everything else. Yet, the motive of Dandolo was the same as the Franks, the average of which the Byzantines knew practically nothing of: loot.[2106] The Comneni could have accomplished this, even with the Sicilian Wars, but a depressing two-hundred-and-fifty percent decrease in Treasury funds from that time had existed by 1203 with tax revenues going to more privatized interests under the Angeli. A number of foreign invasions and border territory setbacks only accentuated these losses. But the Crusaders and their imperial candidate arrived at Corfu and easily took Dyrrachium, Euboea, and Abydos for the Kingdom of Sicily,

---

[2103]  Herrin, 271.

[2104]  Villehardouin, 50.

[2105]  Treadgold, 663.

[2106]  Norwich, (*AHV*), 130-131.

apparently living off the Greek isles that produced them corn, meat, and other vital commodities.

On the Feast of St. John, June 24th, 1203, they landed at Constantinople with about 20,000 soldiers and oarsmen who arrived a few weeks later at the Sea Walls, arriving at the eve of Pentacost. Described in a charming naivete, the experience of these armies first viewing the City from the ships, its walls and lofty towers, rich palaces, and grand churches, 'There was indeed no man so brave and daring that his flesh did not shudder at the sight. Nor was this to be wondered at as never before had such an enterprise been carried out by any people since the creation of the world.'[2107] Though the Crusader army was far outnumbered by the Byzantines, it must be remembered that many foreign armies had been defeated by the West with such odds. This was especially true as the defenses and Greek knights were more lax and undisciplined, never having been battle worthy for the last two decades, being beached on the Golden Horn. Choniates, as a historian and a Drungarius in the imperial navy, estimated the Byzantine navy as being 'useless hulks.. . . .rotting in the inner harbor' since the *Basileus* Isaac II had given the responsibility over to Venice in 1187.

Landing also at Galatea on July 5-6, as the seaway of the Golden Horn was being secured by the Latins, the Venetians occupied Chalcedon on the Turkish coast and camped at the Straits of St. George, making way to Scutari. After defeating 500 knights of the Drungarius, they set the army into seven divisions, surrounding the eastern part of the City. On July 17, the Venetians breached the Sea Walls at Blacharnae with catapults and mangonels on the ships' forecastles, covered gangplanks, and scaling ladders suspended from the yardarms,[2108] flooding the City as they aimed for the Palace searching for the false *Basileus,* Alexius III. The Doge himself was said to enter, despite advanced age and infirmity, with outstanding courage holding the banner of St. Mark. There was no resistance even as the City's population was said to have outnumbered the Crusader army by 200:1, such was their terror.

As the Venetians burned their way to the Palaces and the army fled to the Philatron, the terrified monarch showed his aptitude as ruler by cowardice, cleaning the coffers of precious jewels and 70,000 *hyperpyra,* fleeing to Thrace. He is said to have fled after seeing the 'firm order and manly aspect' of the

---

[2107] Villehardouin, 59.
[2108] Norwich, *(AHV),* 133.

Latins despite being shamed into raising a sally in the streets.[2109] He also made off with only one of his daughters, leaving his wife and other two daughters to fend for themselves in the confusion. Not for nothing was he described so venomously as a 'weak and unstable megalomaniac' demonstrating only irresponsibility in all matters, good only for signing documents with no care of their content or intent.[2110]

Alexius IV was born in 1182 to the *Basileus* Isaac II Angelus and the *Basilia* Euphrosyne, crowned at twenty-one by the Patriarch John X Camaterus at the Blacharnae Palace on August 1, 1203, and although he first fought it (his only wise act as a *Basileus*), he eventually agreed to a joint rule with his blinded father Isaac II. He had the role of a co-*Basileus* at age eleven, something Westerners thought odd, although future titles of the *Infantes* and the past Roman title of *Nobilissimus Puer*[2111] were concepts of old to modern historians. But now the greater task faced him of being fully responsible for keeping his end of a bargain that the armies be paid in full. It became apparent to the Doge, Philip, and Montferrat that the *Basileus* had not even a fraction needed to appease his allies and the Crusaders ran low on patience as they believed heartily that the City of Constantinople had enough riches. Alexius, buying time, asked for and received from Venice an extension from August until the following March – from Michaelmas to Easter, leaving the City to begin a tour of the Empire on missions of peace.[2112]

This further turned into the point of view by Villehardouin and Robert of Clary that Alexius IV was haughtily ignoring their requests, especially after he convinced them to camp outside the City walls. This idea that the French were being snubbed came from the fact that after intensive confiscations and desperate tax-gathering, the *Basileus* managed to pay the Venetians 100,000 silver marks with nothing left to pay the French. Alexius and his advisers showed to be 'extraordinarily stupid and complacent' in allowing Venice to camp by the City, but the alternatives of Alexius paying off his debts or destroying them militarily seem quite unrealistic.[2113] The Westerners had their ways of showing

---

[2109]  Gibbon, 2124.
[2110]  Norwich, *(AHV)*, 125.
[2111]  Gibbon, 2117f.
[2112]  Villehardouin, 78.
[2113]  Herrin, 270-271.

the younger Alexius contempt when he made official visits: they would shoot dice together and remove his diadem to replace it with a common wool cap as the French, in their gaiety, forgetting the *Basileus* of the East.[2114] Besides of which, Venice only wanted money, loot, and religious artifacts, paying them off might have just encouraged them to bleed Constantinople as they fought the Turks.

As Alexius III 'ruled' in exile from Thrace and no revenues could be obtained regionally, nor could the obstinate regions of Anatolia and northern Greece would not pay, even after attacking Thessalonica and Achaea with Byzantine rebels and Bulgar mercenaries. Reluctantly, the Crusaders allied with Constantinople just long enough to be adequately paid to march on Thrace. Several Thracian cities were plundered and the loot encouraged the Crusaders, but Alexius III's government still stood by the end of these raids. From Rome, Pope Innocent demanded reparations to the Crusaders so they could focus on the Muslim Turks, but Alexius had finally run totally dry on funds. At Alexius's absence in meeting with his brother-in-law Johannitza of Hungary, a severe riot of looting and burning broke out in Constantinople. Mosques and synagogues were torched to ash and the destruction had not been so great since the Nika Revolts of Justinian I, seven centuries before.[2115]

It was not for nothing that, in 1203, Alexius III once remarked how the Byzantine people were 'intent on turmoil', and 'infected by instability.' This classified the situation as the transformation of the Constantinopolitan culture as shifting from *demokratia* ('rule by the people') to *ochlokratia* ('mob rule').[2116] Constantinople's 15,000 Latin inhabitants fled for refuge to the Crusaders' camp. Now the Crusaders openly turned on the Byzantines and their two *Basilii*. Surprisingly, the Latins did not want a war with the Greeks; the Latins were seen by the East as 'uncivilized thugs who destroyed their beloved City and bleeding them white in the bargain.'[2117] At the same time, the French were being reminded why they wanted a Crusade – to fight the Infidel and not to struggle needlessly with 'an effete and effeminate' people such as the Greeks. The Fourth Crusade against Constantinople the next year might have been averted if Alexius IV had not angered his own inner circle, rather than his Western creditors, as time would show. Although blind and just a bit mad from

---

[2114] Gibbon, 2126.
[2115] Norwich, *(DF)*, 174.
[2116] Herrin, 282.
[2117] Norwich, *(DF)*, 175.

eight years of imprisonment, even Isaac Angelus could tell his son had made impossible promises to these Western thugs.[2118]

Alexius returned on January 11, St. Martin's Day, one year and one day since the Crusaders set sail east, but he stalled, further insulting the Crusaders outside the Walls. Unsuccessfully, he tried a desperate ploy against their navy by sending seventeen burning ships to careen into the Latin fleet. Finally, the clergy and senators had enough and backed the claims of a puppet named Nicolas Canabus as a new *Basileus* on January 28, 1204. But this was thwarted by a new and energetic Byzantine noble-general, Alexius Ducas, 'Murtzuphlus', as he would commonly be known to history.

In a move of betrayal and 'such atrocious treachery' that would once again shock Western sensibilities, on the night of February 8, 1204, just after midnight, the Protovestarius Murtzuphlus woke the young *Basileus* and claimed to be leading him out of the Palace by a side door to safety from another revolt by the mobs. Alexius IV was then wrapped in a cloak and imprisoned, where two attempts to poison him having failed, the *Basileus* finally being strangled as his increasingly senile father had earlier been.[2119] Despite his numerous flaws and weak excuses to uphold his oaths, the West still accepted Alexius IV Angeli as the ruler of Constantinople and was outraged by this new usurpation. The Fourth Crusade would now fall squarely on Byzantium, and the usurper Alexius V's, shoulders.

As for Alexius III, his rule in Thrace waned after the Latins took Constantinople in 1204, even after having married his daughter to Murtzuphlus. In 1205, he would flee Boniface's army to Thessaly where the Kingdom of Thessalonica was founded, taking refuge with the exiled Byzantine government in Epirus. Boniface still captured him in 1209 and the Emperor of Epirus, Michael I Ducas, ransomed him to the surviving Nicaean imperial government of his son-in-law, Theodore I Lascaris. Alexius's unwise arrogance against being upstaged by his younger relative caught up with him (as it always had) and he plotted against Lascaris by allying with the Ruman Sultan Kilij Arslan III at Iconium in 1211. The Battle of Antioch on the Meander resulted and Alexius Angeli was defeated and captured. Lascaris finally settled the matter by tonsuring his father-in-law in a Nicaean monastery where he died the same

---

[2118] Brownworth, 254.
[2119] Villehardouin, 84.

year. It was far better than he deserved, considering he was not said to have been blinded by Theodore, but it was good riddance to a renegade pretender that only caused dissension in Byzantium.

No matter how the Crusaders romanticized or demonized the two *Basilii*, and the events surrounding them, the truth was that they were common signs of an inevitable fall of Constantinople to Western allies and invaders. Both made numerous promises to the West, eliciting aid from the French, Venice, and the Pope that both could not back up. Though it was in the name of bringing a legitimate and deposed *Basileus* back to his throne against a brazen usurper, the ease in which the Venetian and Crusader fleets entered and occupied the City only proved its weakness and how the opportunity for Western conquest was just a stark reality.

The machinations of brilliant minds such as Enrico Dandolo and even Pope Innocent III, known for his will and brutality to Western heretics, outmatched completely the embarrassing strategies of the Angeli, preparing their own checkmate on the vulnerable City. Even though their successor, Alexius V Murtzuphlus, was a capable general and no coward in defending the Empire against Crusaders and rival Byzantine *Basilii*, the battle was lost years before he took the throne. It was not for nothing a great monument to Enrico Dandalo as the 'Greatest of Doges' was erected in Venice commemorating his greatest victory in the Fourth Crusade by a pictorial. Today, it is found still in Venice in the Doges' Palace and the southern wall of the Sala del Maggior Consiglio.[2120]

## ALEXIUS V DUCAS 'MURTZUPHLUS'
### (1204)

This last revolution spelled the end of Byzantine rule in Constantinople for sixty years as the general Alexius Ducas extinguished through secret murder the Angeli dynasty. This act, intended to be one of hope for the general towards a new peace with the West was with the intent of adding experience to the throne in handling the armies and the debts incurred by the previous *Basileus's* empty promises. Yet, it resulted in being the catalyst for yet another breaching of Constantinople and another flight of the crowned *Basileus,* but this time a Western council would decide upon a French (Latin) Emperor[2121] and even

---

[2120] Norwich, *(AHV)*, 142.

[2121] Baldwin I, whose heroic presence before the Greeks spurred Choniates to describe him as 'a giant in the eyes of the Greeks.' He is described as towering at *enneorguios*

a Venetian Patriarch. There was a deciding factor whether the capital could be retaken by armed alliances led by Alexius III or that of other Comneni or Ducasi from other Byzantine fiefs. This was the feudal governance of key provinces led by various French and Flemish nobles on behalf of a Westernized central government. 1204 was not merely a year of Latin conquest but a year of Latin revolution and evolution that proved that, for the time being, a unified Byzantium was unfit to survive.

Alexius V Ducas Murtzuphlus's reign was only about three months and his death came less than a year later, but the story of his brief and barely consequential reign is still the story of the Fourth Crusade and its tragic results for a 900-year legacy. The only difference really made by Alexius V was incidental as any palace intrigue, assassination, or murder of the legal East Roman monarch would spark enough indignation to put an end to the entire structure of the Greek Empire. Born around 1139 into the aristocratic family of the Ducasi, known for their service as court bureaucrats and descendants of *Basilii* past, he also had familial ties to the Comneni and even the Angeli, though without legitimate claims to the throne. He was thought to be of middle-age at the time of his ascension, and his character was described as having only a 'certain amount of courage and determination . . .in a last, desperate attempt to rally his subjects.' There is ambiguity to the name 'Murtzuphlus' as it has a meaning of 'crestfallen' or 'shadowed', pertaining either to a gloomy disposition (perhaps depression), or more likely, a physical description pertaining to a bushy uni-brow grown over his eyes.[2122]

He had a place in the Angeli court as a Protovestarius, a high finance minister, and was complicit in a plot against Alexius III in 1200 with John Axuch the Fat, leading to his exile. Upon Alexius's ascension in 1204, Villehardouin points out that not only was Murtzuphlus a man most favored by the young *Basileus*, he 'caused the most trouble among this quarrel with the Franks than any other', accentuating his betrayal and role in the fall of Constantinople. Worse yet against his character was the fact he had just been restored to his office by the blind *Basileus* Isaac II just months before, as he would ruthlessly order the death of Isaac and Alexius in January, 1204. After a council of senators and a successful bid over a tepid rival named Canabus, Alexius V Ducas was crowned on February 8, 1204. He would immediately make it clear that neither

---

('nine orgyae' or eighteen yards). Gibbon, 2131f.

[2122] Norwich, *(DF)*, 176.

further payments nor negotiations with the Franks were to be allowed as the new *Basileus* bore no responsibility.[2123]

Yet, 'murder cannot be hid', and the army of Venetians and French outside Constantinople's Walls were soon made aware of the fate of the twenty-one-year-old and his father, ceremoniously buried with a 'long period' of mourning.[2124] The West agreed to no longer negotiate, they never met with Murtzuphlus as he was considered beneath them, and it was said they felt his heinous acts disavowed his privilege to hold lands or to honor him or any other Greek successors. Meanwhile, Alexius V realized this situation and heavily manned the City walls, awaiting the retribution the enemy would inflict. He laid an ambush on the road to Philia, northwest of Constantinople, by land on the southern Pontus, but this was defeated, fleeing to leave the imperial banners and, most symbolically, the icon of *Theotokos* they had carried.

By March, the Doge was convening in his camp a gathering of nobles and to elect a council of twenty-four, twelve Venetians and twelve French, in order to select a new Emperor. The Emperor and Patriarch would be decided to be a Frank and a Venetian in the name of impartiality. The Emperor would receive one-quarter of the City, including the Blacharnae and a Palace on the Marmara. The other three-quarters would be halved for the Venetian and Frankish fiefs, all revenue or plunder taken into the City to be equally divided among the divisions of one-fourth with the odd remainder of three-eights given to Venice and nobles from fiefs several hundred miles away.

Two interesting items to note: first, was that Venice was free from all responsibility from paying homage to their elected Emperor and, second, the best claim for this office, Boniface of Montferrat, was passed over for Baldwin I of Flanders.[2125] Villehardouin makes note that in some simpler proceedings, Baldwin, as Emperor, needed to 'consult' the authorities of the Council of Twenty-Four (assembled by the Doge) in some military maneuvers.[2126] Most likely, Baldwin was a convenient puppet (though a physical paragon to the Greeks) that would ask for permission from the Doge's influence until the agreed-upon withdrawal date of March, 1205. The apportioned land would settle the matter on Eastern supremacy as 'the Republic [Venice] seized the

---

[2123] Norwich, *(AHV)*, 137.

[2124] Villehardouin, 84. Again, a question of the chronicler's naivete appears as this 'long period' was more likely a cynical show of emotion by Murtzuphlus for appearance's sake.

[2125] Norwich, *(DF)*, 177.

[2126] Villehardouin, 95-96.

best of the Byzantine possessions: fertile lands, coastal territory, the most useful ports, and the most important strategic points.'[2127]

These proceedings summarily concluded, the major offensive took place on Friday, April 9th. The Sea Walls of the Bosporus were extended and no longer accessible as it had once been to the Latins, a lesson learned from the occupation of 1203. Alexius was brilliant in the defense, vibrant and decisive, infusing new spirit in the citizens dispensing supplies and shoring walls.[2128] After two days, the Venetian engineers, therefore rigged mastheads from the ships to be used as climbing devices and the walls were made vulnerable again, the powerful Greek catapults now being sidestepped. The faulty naval defenses in the Bosporus allowed this, a partial responsibility born by the Comneni when failing or unwilling to challenge the West with a fleet.[2129] They then set fire to the districts between their position and the defenders to avoid a decisive street battle, capturing the Bucoleon and the Gate of the Blacharnae, which was opened on April 12, 1204, the Latin armies swarming the City.

Murtzuphlus, unsuccessful in raising any defense, fled Constantinople for his life west by the Golden Gate. As described of his flight, he left as not to 'fall into the teeth of the Crusaders as a tidbit of dessert.'[2130] Along with him came the deserted former *Basilia* Euphrosyne, wife of Alexius III, who had helped him blind Isaac II, and their daughter Eudocia Angelina. As his office and possibly his life would be forfeit, the Patriarch of Constantinople, John X, fled with them north to Thrace. Meanwhile, as they fled, the brutality and cruelty the City faced in the subsequent three days of looting was gleefully orchestrated by knights, soldiers, and even the Western clergy and ascetics joined to their camp.[2131]

Another contribution to the outcome was what the French and Italian knights carried in superior style crossbows, as mostly the bows carried by the Byzantines were composite, made of wood, sinew, and horn – practically relics technologically speaking.[2132] The booty taken by the invading 20,000 soldiers were lavish and high above what was once owed the tenacious Doge by any French or Byzantine debt. An estimated 3,600,000 *hyperpyra* was taken in gold and silver plate, vessels, precious stones, silks and rich cloths, and even,

---

[2127] Diehl, 193.

[2128] Brownworth, 256.

[2129] Decker, 62-63.

[2130] Choniates, 755.

[2131] Vasiliev, 461.

[2132] Decker, 123.

Villehardouin attests, mantles of squirrel, ermine, and miniver fur.[2133] The four bronze horses, standing since the time of Constantine I, were taken as plunder to Venice by Dandalo to ornament his Triumph in the Cathedral of St. Mark's, where they still reside. When the nonagenarian Doge died not long after, it was in Constantinople where he was buried, staying even to this day, in Istanbul, Turkey.

Choniates relates the abominable behavior of the savage invaders as they stole priceless relics to send to France where many would be destroyed in the Revolution of 1789.[2134] Other relics of the Martyrs were befouled and smashed as the Church of St. Sophia was filled with mules and horses to carry the loot. The altar, doors, furniture, throne, and vestments were robbed as the Hosts and wine were desecrated. As these were the Orthodox beatitudes, the Catholic French and Venetians had no qualms in destroying what was seen as heresy and an almost alien religion outside of 'their' Christianity. Blood and ordure covered the floors, some animals being killed as they were pushed out of the open doors, to set a scene of horror to any Byzantine clergy witnessing this travesty.

It is now chronicled as a tradition among Ancient and Medieval histories of conquests and falling nations where 'a common harlot' dressed as a monarch would be perched to lewdly mock the royals who once sat there as the victors celebrated. This would also be actions steeped in legend by the Turks of Mehmet II in 1453 in what would become the Great Mosque. By Easter Sunday of 1204, all was finally quiet and a Catholic Mass would be celebrated by a Latin Emperor and Patriarch in the Church of the Holy Wisdom. Boniface of Montferrat would soon after preside over northern Greece, marrying the sister of the Hungarian King Bela III (Isaac II's widow) and be given Thessalonica as a dowry, thus, beginning the Latinization of the Greek Empire.[2135]

As these tragedies occurred, Murtzuphlus and what was left of his family fled to the court of Alexius III in Thracian Mysonopolis and Baldwin's holdings at Tchorlu. After a brief encampment of petty penitence, Alexius Angelus decided to allow the deposed *Basileus* with a warm reception. He married his daughter Eudocia, former queen of Serbia, to Murtzuphlus who had also forsaken his family in Constantinople solidifying his claim as an Angelus. Unfortunately, this was all a deception as the suspicious Angelus lured him to

---

[2133] Villehardouin, 92.

[2134] Vasiliev, 462.

[2135] Villehardouin, 97.

the baths after a feast, seized him, and tore out his eyes as he previously had done his own brother. As Emperor Baldwin was giving chase to capture the fugitive Murtzuphlus, he learned of his fate from his brother at Adrianople. After garrisoning against the Hungarians, he marched west to Mysonopolis where he ransomed the blinded monarch and returned him to Constantinople.

While Baldwin was handling matters in Thessalonica and Serres, including a plague, Alexius V attempted to escape custody by fleeing through the Straits of St. George south of the City to Abydos. By the end of September, 1205, Baldwin had been victorious in northern Greece to Constantinople and ordered Alexius returned. One of Murtzuphlus's men informed against him to Dietrich von Los and he was easily captured. By now, the Latin throne and their citizens in the capital had enough of Alexius Murtzuphlus and a mob was stirred by Baldwin to judge him. They called, naturally, for execution and he was taken to the top of the white marble Column of Arcadius[2136] and thrown off to his death in December, 1205.

This seems a cruel punishment that resembles hypocrisy when one considers that this had all happened because of the savage treatment of Greek *Basilii* by relatives or confidants. But perhaps the difference lies in a theory of private justice versus public justice; rather than secretly murdered and deceiving the people with false tears and 'sudden illnesses,' the mob who had suffered under Murtzuphlus was called upon. Rather than a cold strangulation in an underground cell, it was more 'ethical' for the Latins to allow the heated anger of the mob to handle the fate of Alexius. The method of execution was chosen as inscribed on the Pillar was another *Basileus*,[2137] long in the past, being flung from the top in the same manner, just accentuating irony in an act of wanton cruelty, a 'marvelous coincidence.'[2138]

It was messy and unnecessary, but the execution of Alexius V was a symbol of the easily won and righteous rule of a new and inviolate government of the 'Latins' that would only grow over the face of Byzantium. All of this was the result of the Fourth Crusade, advocated by Montferrat and a zealous, but unremarked, Pope. Along with the fall of Rome in 476 to the Goths, the question here is essentially: How did this happen? The answer is debatable looking at the evidence and arguments that it was a short-term versus a long-term effect

---

[2136] 147 feet in height and extant in Istanbul. Gibbon, 2141f.

[2137] Looking at the evidence in the histories, it is difficult to tell which *Basileus* had been on the pillar.

[2138] Villehardouin, 109. A statue of Arcadius had fallen off the top due to an earthquake in 704 CE and the Column itself was demolished in 1715 due to instability.

of either entropy or poor management. One popular debate, from the Classical to the modern Byzantine scholars, is that this was the product of 'diversions' of the Crusade from the Turks to the Eastern Christians. It is best argued how the alienation of the West during Manuel I Comnenus's aggressive anti-Italian policies set the tone and the dual problems of inner dissension from key provinces along with financial inabilities to pay debts to the West that caused this fall, ultimately.[2139]

The dividing nature of the nationalizing Serbians and Bulgarians, aided by Outremer and Bulgaria, compromised the borders against encroaching Islam over the Holy Land. This was one major consideration, the growing separation of the two Christian Churches in spite of constant promises of Union that always fell short of expectation or agreement. In the shadow of this, the Crusaders were allowed by the Pope to treat Byzantium as a weigh station holding a blank check. This was also basically by sword point to the City, fostering provisions and whatever funds were needed – only England seemed above such extortion. The financial crisis seemed the most egregious of all as it was a downward slope since the end of the Macedonians to the thirteenth century. But, it would suffice, in one sentence by Charles Diehl, to say the Crusade was '. . .the result of religious antipathy, political ambition, economic greed, and incurable antagonisms between two races and two worlds.'[2140]

Most economic trouble was due to the cost of defense, as Manuel I in 1158 had paid a total of 2,160,000 *hyperpyra* to fight the Normans. Later would be a further 150,000 as a dowry allying with Baldwin III of Jerusalem where such expenses would become more common. Isaac II's army needed a total of 280,000 *hyperpyra* in 1198 against the constant problem of the Normans. The Empire could still stabilize itself with the right governance but for two obstacles: externally, the Crusaders who were intent on bleeding these financial resources dry with trading colonies, territorial conquest, and demands for bribes from Constantinople. Internally, there was the corruption stemming the flow of revenue away from the central government from bureaucrats and aristocratic tax fiefs that was encouraged by Western feudalism.

Revenues of trade and commerce suffered as it did in 1168, where it is noted how Venetian rental properties averaged more than double that of the Byzantine landlords. Territories such as Corfu and Cyprus accrued surplus funds in tax arrears, allowing a strong contribution to the 5,600,000

---

[2139] Treadgold, 666.
[2140] Diehl, 221.

*hyperpyra* Byzantium produced. But this revenue was diverted from the central government for various reasons and Constantinople would also suffer from financial maladministration of what it could acquire. Economic evaluations made by historians are confidant in saying that, despite appearances, the Byzantine economy was in good shape despite this maladministration and the causes of the fall were incidental and short-termed.[2141]

Ostrogorsky takes a more long-termed view in light of the growing decline of administration and international relations fueling the triad of the West's hostility of the Crusades, Italian economic disputes in Constantinople, and Andronicus I's xenophobia. He notes the intentions of rulers such as Louis VII and Barbarossa to dissolve Byzantine rule and establish a Western government in Constantinople long before Dandolo had.[2142] The coming of the Angeli was just an opportunity to divert the Fourth Crusade into subjugating Byzantium from a weak and cruel monarchy. The diversion of regaining Christian Zara for Venetian trade and the schism between Innocent III and Philip of Swabia's wishes to re-instate Alexius IV were the beginning of the dissensions between Europe and Byzantium. But it boiled down to an inevitable fall from an older policy of the West to exploit the East's decline to conquer it for Venetian trade and French hegemony. This point of view is supported as a Machiavellian plot of the wily and aging Doge Enrico Dandolo, a plot of setting a trap with the cunning use of national debts for military ventures to ease his way into the Crusade.[2143]

Dandolo was a willing participant in the dissipation of the Greek throne (using international debt as a secret weapon to Constantinople and Thessalonica) and a greedy man intent on sapping the Empire for revenue from deep within, only resulting in careless destruction of Greco-Roman culture worse than the burning of Alexandria by the Arabs in the seventh century.[2144] Worst of all, it weakened Byzantium as a whole, especially in the coming era between the Greek recovery in 1261 from Nicaea to the Ottoman oppression from which Byzantine suzerainty would reach its final obliteration. It was 'the parasitical state of the Latin Empire in Constantinople that the Franks formed on the carcass of the most former Byzantine lands leached much of the vigor from the Greek elite.'

---

[2141] Treadgold, 705-706.

[2142] Ostrogorsky, 414-416. Ostrogorsky is more descriptive in the *qualitative* reasons of 1204 over Treadgold despite the latter's superior *quantitative* descriptions.

[2143] Norwich, *(DF)*, 184.

[2144] *ibid.*, 182.

Alexius V Ducas Murtzuphlus merely melds into the background when these larger concerns are considered, as the pride, ambition, and incompetence of one man cannot be called a serious cause. The implications are wide and it will also be shown how Western hostility and propaganda would begin the historical judgments that branded Byzantium as a useless and decadent society until the twentieth century. The oppression of the Byzantine civilization would also continue throughout centuries as critiqued through the narrow view of the Enlightenment, giving no credence to Orientalism, Christianity and its zealots, or despotism. Even today, it is seen as easy to fall back on these views of Gibbon that Byzantium was a 'moribund state, peculiar unto itself, and not worthy of closer attention'[2145] than the newest literature.

---

[2145] Herrin, 267.

# IV: An Empire Divided

Before the fifteenth century, April 12, 1204 was the darkest day in Byzantine history. Not only was the City taken, it saw a severing of the Byzantine Greek and Roman culture that had sustained it for 900 years. The *Basileus* of Constantinople, bucked by circumstance as he was, had been a usurper and criminal and was disposed of as a common thief, French bloodlines replacing him. Latin masses of the Trinity were to be heard solo for the first time in the Church of St. Sophia as fleets of commercial and military value would remain in Venetian hands. Absurd Latin propaganda surfaced from forged documents detailing a sacking of the City from Emperor Charlemagne in the ninth century.[2146] Charles never sat foot in Constantinople or ever considered it ripe for any conquest; he even hedged on marrying its Dowager Empress, Irene. Such legends existed to reserve legitimacy with the imperial title after the Latin conquest to agitate the differences of East and West, basically demonstrating a divine right to procure Byzantium.

Perhaps worst of all was the aftermath of the seizure when the remainder of the Byzantine government would be surrounded by Latin fiefs, Byzantine borders never being so exiled east from their former western borders. This successfully splintered the Greek fiefs into groups inevitably hostile to each other over legitimacy for the throne should the State recover. In this fateful year of 1204, two grandsons of Andronicus I, Alexius and the rebel David, allied with the powerful Queen of Georgia, Themera. They conquered the Trebizond territory lying beside Armenia from Theodore Gabras and through the legitimacy of the Comneni founded a rival capital and imperial center, though

---

[2146] Michelson, David A. 'Did Charlemagne Sack Constantinople? Western Charlemagne Legends as Anti-Byzantine Propaganda (c.1000-1200).' Presented at *The Twenty-Ninth Annual Byzantine Studies Conference.* (Lewiston, ME: Bates College, October 16-19, 2003).

permanently losing Byzantine Crimea.[2147] Like a Biblical patriarchal family, the descendants of Alexius I Comnenus carved a sustainable independent state with a long line of over twenty monarchs, these lasting until 1461 as the last of the Byzantine holdouts fell to Seljuk conquest.

The next year, another descendant of the Comneni, through the Ducasi, fled to Epirus and northern Greece to settle against the invaders under Count Boniface. Choosing the city of Arta in western Greece, he spread to Thessaly, Corfu, and the Gulf of Corinth by 1215 as the Despot of Epirus. But, most importantly, was Nicaea where the questionable and contested *Basileus* Alexius III still resided at Mysenopolis. Alexius's paranoid, greedy, and aggressive nature saw him overthrowing the son-in-law who took him as a guest and later blinded Murtzurphlus. Another son-in-law, Theodore Lascaris, finally drove Alexius out and was the only successor crowned in 1208 by the former Constantinopolitan Patriarch Michael IV, making him the most legitimate Byzantine ruler in exile.

Yet these 'Successor States' would remain long past the re-conquest in 1261 under Baldwin II by the founder of the Paleologan dynasty, Michael VIII. These borders would only make it easier for the Turks and vengeful Westerners to upset the balance Byzantium desperately tried to maintain. In a culture of budding artistic renaissance and theological debate, the ten *Basilii* of the last Byzantine dynasty kept adversaries at bay until 1453 when economic and military conditions were far bleaker than they were in 1204.

The aftermath of this inevitable decay and fall rippled in numerous consequences in commerce, religious suzerainty, and cultural norms. While touring Athens on May 5, 2001, Pope John Paul II, seeing the necessity of Christian harmony in both halves of Europe, even apologized for the Western Church's indifference to the crisis.[2148] The only silver lining of Byzantium's end was the exodus of Byzantine scholars such as Bessarion to Italy in the thirteenth century and the Classical texts brought with them to enlighten Europe in a true Renaissance and modernization. Unfortunately, modernization was not the destiny of Byzantium, mostly out of an inability to adapt to a changing world owed mostly to Western invention and discovery.

---

[2147] Treadgold, 673.

[2148] Herrin, 266.

# THEODORE I LASCARIS
## (1208-1222)

There was no solid centralization in Byzantium after 1204 to be found. Constantinople itself was divided between the three Western 'districts' of mercantile Venetian and feudal French quarters, leaving a puppet Emperor from the minority. A diaspora of Byzantine nobles, clergy, and military commanders spread throughout the borders were threatened by Turkish, Bulgarian, and Latin fiefdoms. Included were a number of Greek nobles, lords, and magnates dissenting from the Latin government they saw as an insult to their heritage.[2149] Three 'capitals' existed with Trebizond on the northern shore of Asia Minor in the hands of a rival Comnenus and a Pontus occupied by Comneni cousins, exiled for a decade. Trebizond was unique as the only capital to survive the 1453 fall of Constantinople and be a product not of the fall of 1204, but dissenting interests taking an opportunity to present itself during the battles of the Fourth Crusade. Unfortunately, the only legitimate sovereign was the deposed Alexius III Angelus in Thracian Nicaea, and he was a weak degenerate of rampant paranoia and instability.

Elsewhere, local Byzantine magnates and landholders held minor fiefdoms in the former Empire. One was Theodore Galabas, former governor of Trebizond, who held the isle of Rhodes and the Meander Valley. These were now divided into the armed authority of three usurpers in Priene, Philadelphia, and a small region of Miletus under Manuel Maurozomes who claimed asylum under Sultan Khaykusraw of Iconium. It was clear that the reality of this present situation, this disintegration of the former government, the internal strife of the Comnenian successors, and the relentless pressure by the West were the Byzantines' greatest challenges at the time.[2150]

The most promising Successor, however, was Theodore Lascaris, a general under the Angeli and Despot in northwestern Asia Minor. Born around 1174 he was young, but prepared, as an Anatolian partisan of Alexius III.[2151] As a strong ally of Alexius in Nicaea, he married the *Basileus*'s daughter Anna and gained the right to succeed Alexius; unfortunately, Nicaea still held a weak and threatened existence, in no tenable position to retake Constantinople or expel the Latins. Earlier historians, however, take a more misguided and

---

[2149]  Norwich, *(DF)*, 185.

[2150]  Ostrogorsky, 426.

[2151]  Treadgold, 710.

romanticized view that Theodore's military charisma might have 'crushed the invaders underfoot'. After Murtzuphlus's flight from the City, his ascension gave Lascaris enough of a chance to revive the morale of the soldiers[2152] instead surrendering himself courageously to speak for the defeated Greeks.

As it were, Theodore did have control over the English and Danish Varangian Guard (*Englois et Danois avec leurs haches*) that aided him in defending the breached City.[2153] But what could not be defended against was the spread of more unorthodox, but nonetheless ambitious, claimants. Among them was the Bulgarian King Kaloyan ('John the Handsome') who held a unified and powerful army, but no legitimacy among the Greeks. The expelled Byzantines would now be dominated by the combined forces of Boniface of Montferrat and his ally, the rebel aristocrat Theodore Ducas, claimants who shamefully capitalized on the broken Latin and Greek relations to become 'Greekling Emperors' across Greece. Ducas would set up a capital at Arta in Thessalonica as he was a bastard descendant of Alexius I. A relative of his, Michael Angelus Ducas, establishing the third Byzantine-Successor throne of Epirus, would gain the approval of Bulgaria and the Papacy.

A fragmented and hopelessly scattered Byzantium was the result of these rival aristocrats and Western potentates with their wills to conquer the true capital under their own scepters – this Byzantine trait of internal dissension giving the Latins what they needed to survive. But Baldwin I's government still had weak bases as well in the Latin Empire starting with his sole rule in 1205, facing the Bulgarians, Epirus, and the plethora of external threats posed by Successor states. In this chaos, one figure stood out to take leadership in collecting the social, political, military, and economic forces that would sustain a Byzantine bastion against encroaching Westernization for twenty years. This was Theodore I Lascaris, the dynamic former Despot of Nicaea and sole legitimized *Bassileus* crowned by 1208 by a re-established Patriarchy.

Though his provincial origins are said to be unknown, he was from a Constantinopolitan noble family as the son of Manuel Lascaris and Ionna Katzaina, the fifth of seven sons who would all command armies in Thessalonica for Alexius III. During the Siege of 1204, he made distinction in fortifying and defending the Sea Walls, being declared *Basileus* by his troops, but fleeing when the Walls were breached for Bithynia. Baldwin then made a momentous march on the Bosporus, pushing Lascaris further back east to Nicaea in western

---

[2152] Gibbon, 2148.
[2153] Villehardouin, 112.

Thrace. But as the French armies were consolidating Grecian rule in the south, Theodore I managed to take the northern coast of Asia Minor at the same time, defending Alexius and marrying his daughter Anna Angelina in late 1204.

With a strong protectorate under Theodore, Alexius III retreated to Greece and attempted to gain ground over Montferrat with Leo Sgurus and the former wife of both the Serbian King Stephen and Alexius V. Lascaris was to deal with the hostile Baldwin with 140 knights, but was also faced with Trebizond's seizure of Paphlagonia. The Latins used this strife as opportunity to occupy Prusa and much of Bithynia on December 6, 1204 by defeating the Despot at Poemenenum at the Marmara. Complicating his position further was Constantine Lascaris's defeat at Adrymittium days later.

Meanwhile, Baldwin made his own stand over Rome and Bulgaria by refusing their demands to share Thracian territory to ally with Epirus. By 1205, however, major problems arrived for the Successors as Latin and Crusader barons began offering militarized bids over key Byzantine territories. Baldwin's brother, Henry, would take Adrymittium in western Asia Minor from Mangaphas, one of the magnates of the Meander. Boniface of Montferrat defeated Alexius III's armies at Acrocorinth and occupied Euboea and the Peloponnesus as Syrian Crusaders from Outremer defeated the Epiran armies of Michael Ducas, the region totally being in Latin hands. Boetia and Attica would go to the Burgundian Otto de le Roche and to William of Champlitte in the Peloponnese for aid.

A secret pact was made to 'Iohannitza' (Kaloyan) with promises of making him Byzantine *Basileus* after killing all of the French and Venetians.[2154] Baldwin I's imperial hold was most threatened by Bulgaria who met the French on April 14, 1205, near Adrianople, when the Greeks rebelled. Already Constantinople was losing internal strength as the one-year term with the Venetian council had expired and Doge Enrico Dandalo, self-referenced 'Lord of a Quarter and Half a Quarter of the Roman Empire', had died. Kaloyan would kill the noted Louis of Blois and take the Latin Emperor himself hostage where he would die a year later in captivity. After Karolyan began an invasion of Thessalonica, he met a serious defeat of the Latins, who were now doubled by a plague, in Serres. But when Boniface arrived with 14,000 Cuman cavalry and contingents of Bulgarians and Romanians, Kaloyan began losing control.

His Thracian and Byzantine armies were falling apart and Henry, as Baldwin's Regent, retook parts of Thrace as the Adrianopolitans fled for

---

[2154] Villehardouin, 114.

Tchorlu. With the diversions of the Constantinopolitans and Bulgarians, Lascaris found opportunity practically unnoticed, gaining Nicaea and southern Thrace. Completing a total victory, he took Mangaphas and David Comnenus, brother of the Emperor at Trebizond, and a traitor under his own father-in-law Alexius, as prisoners. Charged by his territorial gains without the aid of Alexius, who was losing ground in Thessalonica and his throne, Theodore I proclaimed himself *Basileus* by right of conquest in 1205. It was a wise move taking the incentive to declare himself a monarch over a title of Despot before the other Successors. In the Nicaean imagination, this would place Lascaris in a category equal to the Latin conquerors and above the petty rulers of Trebizond, Arta, and Epirus. The most Alexius of Trebizond would ever be awarded was *Megaloi Komnenoi* which was never officiated by the Church.[2155]

Between then and 1206, Theodore I had cleared the Meander by defeating and capturing Sabas Asidenus of Priene to make a treaty with Manuel Maurozomes, granting the magnate only Chonae and Laodicea. Unfortunately, due to an issue of his legitimacy as Emperor under God, a coronation would be delayed as the Patriarch John X, as a supporter of the Angelus party, refused to come to Nicaea and crown Theodore. Treadgold claims this was also a result of John Camaterus's Thracian roots and his nationalist refusal to 'abandon his countrymen' in their time of crisis at Didymotichum to defend Orthodoxy. It became moot anyway as in 1206, John would die and Theodore would raise a Nicean as Patriarch in Michael IV Autorianus in 1208, where his coronation as *Basileus* of the Nicean Empire would be complete.

Another advantage would present itself in 1206 with the Bulgarian King, Kaloyan, managing to exacerbate the alienation of his Byzantine troops with over-zealousness to cross Thrace and capture Constantinople. His troops deserted him and gave Adrianople as a peace offering to Branas, a Byzantine army commander in Thrace. Complementing this acquiescence was the ascension in Constantinople of a much more capable ruler, Henry of Hainault, succeeding his brother Baldwin upon his death on August 20. His first actions were in opposing Lascaris in Asia Minor with the aid of David Comnenus of Trebizond, ransomed by his brother, thwarting Theodore's aims on Heraclea Pontica by a rear assault.

In 1207, David had crossed the sea to Cyzicus and castle Kibidos, capturing Nicomedia from Theodore, despite his sixteen galleys and land offensives. Nicomedia would still be recovered with the surprise defeat of Dietrich von Los

---

[2155] Ostrogorsky, 426f.

and his troops, Theodore's brothers, and their armies joining him in the siege. Lascaris then made a truce with Bulgaria over Thracian territory taken by the Latins and Kaloyan who turned to Thessalonica, defeating and killing Boniface of Montferrat, at one time the staunchest ally of the Angeli. Henry made a two-year peace with Theodore, giving him Cyzicus and the Church of St. Sophia in Nicomedia on condition the garrisons of each be dismantled.[2156] Basking in his triumph at Greece, Kaloyan would now style himself after Basil II and the early Comneni as a sort of 'Roman-Slayer' and major power in the Greco-Slavic East. Baldwin would write of him as a 'Great Destroyer of Greece'; yet, the resentful Greeks would only give him the surname of *Skyoioannes* ('John the Dog').[2157]

But the balancing act of alliances came to an end in autumn when Kaloyan was killed by a Cuman chieftain at Thessalonica – yet as Byzantine legends tell it, it was by St. Demetrius himself upon his holy day. As he left behind two quarreling sons who were defeated by their nephew Boril, this intrigue neutralized foreign policy in central Greece and Bulgaria. The next year, as Lascaris was being crowned *Basileus*, minor states were being claimed by larger rivals as the Latins held Corinth and the Peloponnese, their protector Sgurus driving his horse off of a cliff in despair. In the Ionian, Italian wars concluded as Venice managed to capture the major cities and islands, including Dyrrachium on Corfu as Genoa held Crete, cutting off some of Venice's trade with the northeastern Mediterranean. Even in Attalia, the Iconian Sultan defeated a free-booting Venetian *condottiere,* basically a mercenary warlord, named Aldobrandini.

Henry I was establishing dynastic baronies on the Empire's periphery by settling the disquiet in Thessalonica and supplanting his brother Eustace there in 1209. Before this, he had recovered Philippopolis in Thrace by defeating a Bulgarian campaign led by Tsar Boril. His efforts made Latin Byzantium the strongest in the East with the Greeks still divided as rivals across Asia Minor. Lascaris was still in danger from his rival Byzantine capitals as the now-deposed Alexius III allied with the Sultan of Iconium and Michael Ducas of Epirus to displace him.

In need of allies to counter Iconium, Lascaris contacted Leo II of Armenia in Cilicia. Michael Ducas, once a rebel against Alexius in 1200, turned against his imperial ally, breaking off the Nicaean campaign. But to gain territory, Michael invaded Thessalonica and Thessaly in 1210 only to be ousted by Henry

---

[2156] Villehardouin, 154-156.

[2157] Vasiliev, 511.

and returned to vassalage, Ducas having no allies in the neutral Venetians of Corfu in Henry's exposed rear. Sympathy and support of an Epiran Empire was emphatically lacking in all corners as even the Pope, a major Epiran supporter, sought to excommunicate the Orthodox Michael Ducas.

Yet again, as a result of Ducas's exploits, more complex and conditional treaties between Boril and Theodore I on one side and Henry with the Iconian Sultan Khaykhusraw on the other came into effect. As Lascaris prepared a Constantinopolitan campaign, the Sultan accompanied by the tenacious Alexius III turned back his fleet and gave chase to Antioch-on-the-Meander. With 2,000 soldiers, 800 of them Latin mercenaries, Theodore defeated the army, killing the Sultan and capturing Alexius III. In 1211, the intrepid Alexius died in a Nicaean monastery, ending the Angeli dynasty in exile, and a peace was forced on Iconium. Not too surprisingly, his capture had a deep psychological effect on Alexius as the impact of Nicaea now became the inherent Byzantine capital and major player in the affairs of neighbors, allies, and enemies.[2158] Antioch in 1211 can be rightly recalled as the Manzikert of the Angeli dynasty and Alexius as a much less honored Diogenes. The same year, the Sultan of Iconium was killed at Antioch-on-the-Meander as well, Norwich recounting the heroic legend that it was with Lascaris himself in single combat.

Theodore I returned to his plans to retake the City, as was Henry's suspicions, as was written in a letter of January 13, 1212 from Pergamon. The Latin Emperor struck first by raiding the Hellespont and defeating Theodore at the Rhyndacus on October 15, seeking a strong foothold in western Asia Minor by marching to Pergamum. This continued throughout Asia Minor, but due to lack of manpower caused by guerilla warfare against Henry that resulted in a stalemate between the Greeks and Turks, a settlement was reached between the two Empires at Nymphaeum in 1212. Theodore still had the upper hand as he still possessed all territories in southern Asia Minor from Adrymittium and Nicomedia.[2159] After the truce, Henry still sent a garrison under Pierre de Bracieux to make invasion on Theodore's territory from Cyzicus, fortifying castles to effectively raid Lascaris's territories. In 1214, Theodore consolidated an alliance with Armenia by marrying the niece of King Leo II, the marriage only to be dissolved after a year, frustrating some of Armenia's loyalty.

Michael Ducas campaigned successfully in Greece that year by taking Thessaly and even the key area of Dyrrachium from the Venetians. By 1214,

---

[2158] Ostrogorsky, 430.

[2159] Norwich, (DF), 191.

as Bulgaria and Constantinople were mired in a Serbian war, Epirus spread to Corcyra on Corfu, now taking the western Aegean. Further setbacks to the Latins included the recovery by Lascaris of Heraclea, Amastris, and the territories west of Sinope to the southern coast of the Black Sea. In 1215, the unscrupulous and ambitious Michael Ducas was assassinated and his legitimate brother Theodore took the Epiran throne as a legitimate heir of the Ducas, Angelus, and Comnenus dynasties converged by his grandmother and Michael's son. Modern historians depict him as a harsh ruler and as untrustworthy as Michael, his strategies on making Epirus a power equal with the other two Empires being campaigns against Thessalonica.[2160]

Theodore I Lascaris had a critical position in the Balkans as having 'a center of Byzantine cultural tradition and political rallying point.'[2161] The borders of the Successor states were shifting drastically as Theodore would then make the Comnenian Empire of Trebizond a toothless rival by taking Heraclea Pontica from David Comnenus. The Sultan Kayka'us then captured both David and his brother at Sinope and his capital thereafter, forcing Turkish vassalage on Alexius of Trebizond. From now on, Trebizond would internalize an isolationist and collective policy, opposed to the open and inter-territorial policy of Epirus. In 1215, Epirus was still made to take an oath of fealty, as superficial as it would be, to Nicaea by Theodore Ducas. Theodore Ducas was still not to be considered tamed as, in 1218, he immediately laid claim to Macedonia, Aetolia, and Acarnania to complement Thessaly, reaching farther west.

As Ducas neared Thessalonica, Henry I Hainualt prepared a defense, but dying on June 11, 1216, he only left an infant son and his wife, Yolande, to rule alone in the City on a practically cursed throne. Though still in France, the Constantinopolitans chose Henry's brother-in-law Peter of Courtenay, a grandson of the French King Louis VI 'the Fat', to be regent. The Latin Empire by now was showing itself in real danger with a frail base of unstable monarchies and enemies harassing all the borders. Pope Honorius III swiftly crowned Peter at the Church of St. Lorenzo, sending him to Constantinople with 5,500 soldiers and a Venetian fleet to take his inheritance. Unfortunately, Peter was another inept ruler and in 1217 he was ambushed and captured by Theodore Ducas at Dyrrhacium, disappearing from the histories and probably dying in Epiran captivity.

Peter was succeeded by the Empress's embarrassing and incompetent

---

[2160]  Treadgold, 714.

[2161]  Ostrogorsky, 432.

younger son, Robert of Courtenay, when her older son Philip of Namur refused the crown, perhaps also seeing the throne of Constantinople as somewhat of a curse. John Julius Norwich takes time to recount the crimes of Robert starting with one historian, Aubrey de Trois-Fontaine (d. 1252), describing him as '*quasi rudis and idiota.*'[2162] In 1227, a secret marriage with a low-born girl resulted in a feudal rebellion, where the girl was disfigured and murdered while Robert fled to Rome. Pope Gregory IX was disgusted by his atrocious behavior and he was sent back with no aid from the Church.

As he reached Clarenza on the Morea on his return trip, Robert died in January, 1228. In 1219, Yolande had already died, losing the important support of the Bulgarians a year earlier. She was rescued by Nicaea, however, where the *Basileus* married her daughter, Maria – and into the Latin royal family. That August, in an inspired diplomatic move, Theodore I treated with the Constantinoplolitan Venetian 'quarter' over duty-free trade with Nicaea, flattering its Doge with the title 'Dominator' and 'Despot'. Yet, Theodore was still identifying himself in Latin as *Theodoro in Christo Deo fidelis Imperator et Moderator Romeorum et semper augustus Comnanus Lascarus.*[2163]

Robert de Courtenay would only arrive in the City in early 1221 as new leadership was taking root in Nicaea. In November of 1222, Theodore I Lascaris died of undisclosed causes, leaving the Successor Empire to the strong husband of his daughter Irene, John Ducas Vatatzes, over his elder brothers. Theodore I was proven to be a ray of hope in a time when the existence of any stable Byzantine state was in question. He defied the Latins and successfully defended his capital wherein no invader was able to set foot. And through his love of scholarship and his charisma, he managed to gather clergy, intellectuals, artists, and the bureaucratic elite to take up new as well as former posts that rose Nicaea above the other Successor states in legitimacy and preeminence. Though, in the beginning he commanded 'three cities and 2,000 soldiers', he 'staked his life and crown, and his enemies on the Hellespont and the Meander were surprised by his celerity and subdued by his boldness.'[2164]

He further maintained Nicaea as a military power, not by extending its borders, but by intractably maintaining and strengthening himself in Asia Minor. This current of success flowed into his successor's reign with two more decades of advancement as the Lascarids would become one of the most crucial

---

[2162] Norwich, *(DF)*, 193.
[2163] Ostrogorsky, 430-431.
[2164] Gibbon, 2168.

dynasties in Byzantine, or even Medieval, history. And, although Lascarid Nicaea itself never grew past one-and-a-half km (less than one mile), its walls were fortified properly and its situation on the Anatolian plateau allowed economic gains in the grain industry of the valleys and the craft production trade, being the agricultural hub to a dozen key cities.[2165]

The 1219 treaty given to the Venetians of Constantinople bought Nicaea a stake in the Western-monopolized markets of luxuries to Iconium and Turkish goods back to the West. The Turkish nobility spent vast amounts on these precious Western items to symbolize their power and standing as conciliators with the Latins and Outremer.[2166] Lascaris's privileges against any transport duty fees were hardly little more than economic revitalization, however, as anyone could see and appreciate the surging influence of Venice in the Latin/ Turkish East. A direct consequence of these treaties was enticing trade and commerce away from Constantinople and towards Nicaea as a political tool in benefiting the capitalizing Venetians towards Greek interests. With better offers on trade franchises with Nicaea, the Venetian *podesta* and his Quarter may in the future side with the Byzantines in military endeavors, or even embargoes, against Iconium.

One of the greatest spiritual revivals also occurred under Theodore as an exodus of clergy made way to Nicaea as Orthodoxy spread throughout the Balkans, tying Nicaea into webs of critical buffer states. Though the Thracian Patriarch John X refused entry into Nicaea, the new elevation and support of his successor increased the legitimacy of the Greek Church in Theodore's imperial city and an influx of clergy, ascetics, and theologians. This began in earnest in 1206, when Constantinople was divided on the Eucharist[2167] debate between a Venetian Patriarch of Constantinople, Thomas Morsini, and the Greek-Niceaen Nicholas Mesarites, and if this was meant to conciliate the faiths of the Churches in the two cities, it failed.

Just as important were the events of 1217 that only strengthened Nicaea's ecclesiastical position as the Serbian Church was now seeking leadership. When Bulgaria claimed hegemony, the price of their Catholic faith was too

---

[2165] Reinert, 'Fragmentation (1204-1453).', 253.

[2166] Vasiliev, 515.

[2167] Again, the argument stemmed, Choniates explains since Isaac II's reign, on the 'corruptibility' (*phtharton*) of the flesh before the Passion and the 'incorruptibility' (*aphtharton*) of the flesh after the Passion in the Host. The underlying argument was the nature of the physiological processes and if Man decides this process that digests the Host. Vasiliev, 478.

high despite Stephen the First Crowned's papal recognition. It would actually be the reign of John Asen II, however, that would sever the ties and authority of Rome claimed in 1204 by the Western clerics. What further complicated matters was the resurgence in the Serbian Church of the heresy of Bogomilism, the Bulgarian dual natured Christology that succeeded the Paulicians. These rebellions led to the alliances of Emperor Henry VI and Kaloyan in conforming Serbia to their cultures as their possessions dwindled under the Byzantine Successors, leading to more far-reaching consequences.

In 1208, Sava, second son of Nemanja of Serbia and brother to King Stephen, had traveled from Epirus to the revered Monastery of Mount Athos and returned two years later, his attitude towards Roman authority changed. In 1219, he entreated Lascaris and his Church to aid Serbia against invading interests by his brother. This went against the will of the Ochridian Archbishop Demetrius Chomatianus, who formerly held authority, but the Niceaean Patriarch Sarantenos consecrated Sava after some persuasion by Theodore Lascaris, as an 'auto-cephalous' Archbishop in Serbia. Monastic schools and new dioces were given like treats across Serbia in Zica and the Studenica as the Church was revitalized throughout the West-rejecting Serbians.[2168] Union with the Churches was never even discussed and in 1215 Rome ignored the East at the Fourth Lateran Council as well as the Fifth Crusade, played out in Egypt. Yet, an independent Slavic Church meant frustrations for the Catholic clergy from Constantinople and a tight Slavic ally with Nicaea against the other Successors.

This Archbishop of Serbia, as an agent of a 'laissez-faire' Nicaean religious policy, would be given first place in the official prayers spoken at Serbian Orthodox masses. The spiritual authority of Nicaea was spreading as Lascaris began to cultivate the traditional role of a 'spiritual figurehead of Christ', as well as the temporal ruler of one, under a united Byzantine throne. This play by Theodore in investing Serbia was also a strategy against encroaching Epirus when Theodore was in a weakened state. But in 1224, after a successful campaign by Epirus into Thessalonica, the rival Ochridian Archbishop would crown Theodore Ducas of Epirus the true 'Autocrator of the Romaioi' to 'pay back Nicaea in its own coin.'[2169]

Theodore I was noted as saying that as Corinth was famous for music, Thessaly for weaving, and Philadelphia for shoe-making, Nicaea was known

---

[2168] Obolensky, 240-241.
[2169] Ostrogorsky, 434.

for philosophy. This was due to Lascaris's acceptance of the scholarly elite that were as sanctified to his court as the clergy. Among the intellectuals of the first Lascarid court were the noted Comnenian historian Nicetas (Acominitas) Choniates, brother of the governor of Athens, now exiled to Chios until 1204 as Michael Choniates. When Choniates resurfaced at Nicaea, he was well-received and given back his titles and honors until his death after 1210. Vasiliev notes the importance of the funeral oration delivered by his older brother as critical to the biographies and later literary works of this outstanding Byzantine historian. Michael's 1222 eulogy for the *Basileus* stands out just as much by this talented orator describing:[2170] 'The capital hurled by the barbarian inundation out of the walls of Byzantium to the shores of Asia in the shape of a miserable fragment has been received by thee, guided, and saved.'

Michael was also instrumental in the imperial patronage of his brother as a certain 'Euboean', who preferred a Greek court that would present the *Basileus* as being a single universal liberator of all the Romans. At Theodore's coronation in 1208, Choniates penned the *Selention* ('Silentium'), a speech which stood as the political philosophy and mission of this first true *Basileus* in four years. It speaks of one Byzantium through its *Basileus* with 'the power of David . . .[to have] . . .one fold and one shepherd'; Vasiliev further evaluates it as the literary moment when the legitimacy of the Comneni and Angeli were found in a continuation of Roman rule through Theodore I and the Successors over Trebizond and Epirus. Before his death, Choniates also outlined the ecclesiastical side of Byzantine culture with his lesser-known *Treasury of Orthodoxy*. It is partially due to the enlightenment of the Lascarid educational reforms that these vital histories of the twelfth century have survived another possible Dark Age.

## JOHN III DUCAS VATATZES
### (1222-1254)

Closing on a chapter of one of the most accomplished *Basilii* in Byzantium, attaining all of his successes in exile, another one opens to reveal a *Basileus* even greater than Theodore I and one praised by scholars as perhaps one of history's greatest monarchs. With Theodore gone, the situation was ripe for an incompetent ruler to take the Nicaean throne and allow the Successors and the West to neutralize the past eighteen years of progress. The fact Lascaris

---

[2170] Vasiliev, 494.

chose his son-in-law John Vatatzes, described as 'clever and cultured', as his successor over his blood relatives demonstrates he took this choice more seriously, repelling ideas of allowing nepotism's 'succession-as-usual' politics that left too much to chance.

The result was a fit, energetic ruler of talent and ability that took his predecessor's programs furthering Nicaea as the true capital of Empire, exploding it into a superior Eastern state that not only held its possessions, but gained more. Upon the one time the Latin Empire assaulted Vatatzes and Nicaea, they would end up fighting disciplined and dedicated French mercenaries, leaving their veterans of the Battle of 1204 dead on the battlefield. These developments were what demonstrated the 'Greek ascent' now prevalent[2171] across the Bosporus. Emperor Frederick II Hohenstauffen would even make a close acquaintance with the Nicaean *Basileus* no Latin or Bulgar would ever enjoy.

His increasing boundaries came also from his moving military headquarters from Nicaea to Nymphaeum, south of the Bosporus where the Latins had less influence. He was described by George Acropolites (1217-1282), the major historian of the exile period and a Logothete in John III's court, as a 'kind and gentle soul' in Theodore II Lascaris's funeral oration 'On the Duty of Kings to Study Philosophy'[2172] and with the sobriquet, 'John the Merciful.' But even in his kindness, he also knew how to consolidate trade, militarily defend against neighbors, diplomatically plan alliances, sever from the Roman Church, revive the idea of a cultural aspect of Byzantium, and keep a cool head during one of the most powerful invasions in European history coming from East Asia. His death in 1254 only slightly delayed the re-conquest of Constantinople and the seat of Byzantine government a mere decade, the later weakness of the Latins exacerbated by its ignorance of ruling an Eastern Empire. It was not just by luck that the slumbering dragon of Nicaea woke and cleared the Latin Empire in a matter of days, it had become an eventuality that John III Vatatzes perpetuated.

John III was born in 1193 into the illustrious Ducas family by his mother, a cousin of Isaac II, in Didymotichum with the Duke of Thrace, Basil Vatatzes. But, recent scholarship paints a more fantastic picture with claims that the former *Basilia* Euphrosyne, wife of Alexius III Angelus, had an affair with Basil and a semi-legitimate John Ducas Vatatzes was 'the fruit of that liason.'[2173]

---

[2171] Gibbon, 2151.

[2172] Ostrogorsky, 418.

[2173] Langdon, John S. 'Byzantine Imperial Consorts and Princesses of the Epoch of the Anatolian Exile.' Presented at *The Thirty-Sixth Annual Byzantine Studies Conference.* (Philadelphia, PA: The University of Pennsylvania, October 8-9, 2010).

Euphrosyne would then have her daughter Anna Angelina by Alexius who would then marry Lascaris in 1198. Politically motivated or not, their daughter Irene would marry John Vatatzes around 1216 with only small ambiguity he wed his own niece!

This ambiguity comes from a claim made by Acropolites in a 'snide' comment on the consanguinity between John's niece Theodora and the general Michael Paleologus. It was allowed ecclesiastically by consanguinity after the marriage of Michael to John's grand-daughter was denied – this, to Langdon, was the 'smoking gun' in the understanding of relations between the Vatatzes, Angeli, and ultimately, Lascarid families. Upon ascension, John III wasted no time in bearing an heir with Irene Lascarina, to later become Theodore II.

Either way, John rose to the rank of a pronoia class general that fought for Lascaris in Asia Minor, having had a strong male heir by his ascension upon the death of Theodore on December 15, 1222. Immediately, good tidings for Nicaea occurred as Alexius of Trebizond died in 1223 and the would-be Successor State weakened further under Andronicus Gidus who survived a siege on Trebizond in 1222-1223 by Ruman Turks. The Armenian historian John Lazaropoulos (1310-1369) sketches it all in his *Synopsis*. Theodore of Epirus, however, was only gaining ground in Greece, taking Serres and holding all of Thessalonica excepting Arte in 1224. They spurned the legitimacy of Nicaea and its Patriarch, Germanus II, even though Epirus itself apparently lacked a Patriarch. The Latins in the south begged for reinforcements from Robert of Courtenay, and it was handled with incompetency. Robert divided his army between the disenfranchised Lascarid brothers at Nicaea and Thessalonica. Both armies were defeated and Serres was abandoned to Epirus with Thessalonica itself surrendering. Theodore Ducas now held all of southern Greece along with its western half.

Nicaea was threatened by this expansion, with Asia Minor from the southwest now open, as Vatatzes now consolidated his position there by seizing the territories west of Nicomedia and Adrianople. In 1225, a Byzantine fleet defeated the Latins and recovered the Hellespont. When Theodore Ducas arrived, however, John was either showing prudence or sparing bloodshed by handing Epirus Adrianople after watching Ducas conquer Thrace from the west. Vatatzes then quickly made negotiations with John Asen II of Bulgaria in Phillipopolis.

This was the time for the Byzantines to recover Constantinople once and for all from the inept Latins, but of course, this was impossible as it was still in hot contention over who would sit in absolute rule in the throne of the City once recovered.[2174] John cancelled out Theodore's authority having legitimate officers from the City and its own Patriarch, so Ducas cancelled Vatatzes out with his family heritage and strength of arms. This division forced John to ally with the Latins and the Bulgars as re-conquest at this time was unfeasible.

As Ducas was the largest threat to the balance of power, John solidified his Bulgarian alliance and treated with the Latin Emperor Robert against Epirus, causing Theodore Ducas to hesitate in advancing north. In the summer of 1227, Theodore sought legitimization by a coronation from the Metropolitan of Ochrid as Thessalonica's clergy felt loyalty to Germanus II in Nicaea. The next year, Robert of Courtenay died and Asen was quick to ally his daughter in marriage to Robert's nephew, Baldwin II. The nobles of Constantinople feared such an alliance with the untrustworthy and heretical Bulgars and sought to succeed John Brienne of Jerusalem as Latin Emperor. Now, a détente between Bulgaria and Epirus began as a siege on Constantinople by either party would result in a second-front assault by the opposing army.

Theodore Ducas broke this wretched peace in 1230 by attacking Asen as a decisive battle commenced outside of Leo's position at Phillipopolis to Klokotnitsa in April. Theodore was captured and his army met serious defeat with the Bulgarians. Ducas would plot against the Bulgarian Tsar and be blinded as a result in captivity, although his story was not yet finished. With a wild momentum, John Asen captured the Strymon and Axius Valleys, Serres, and Ochrid. Thessalonica. The Aegean to the Hebrus were spared and Michael II Ducas was put on the Epirote throne, although this Empire of the south would devolve into a puppet client of Bulgaria until its end in 1340. Theodore's brother Manuel escaped with his eyes and fled back to take control of Thessalonica, even though it was now a minor state with little power. The Ducas gambled and gained, but one loss and it all fell to a stronger enemy and was tamed.

Vatatzes and Asen could now conquer the Latins united, but the mistrust that poisoned the Byzantine alliances would cause them to turn on themselves over religious matters, especially Bogilism, allowing John of Brienne to take the enfeebled throne in 1231. Baldwin II, the rightful heir, was shamed into crossing Western Europe to Pope Gregory IX in Rome, Henry III of England, and France under St. Louis IX, who would lead the Fifth Crusade against Egypt in 1241, for aid. France had taken special interest in Constantinople as Pope Honorius III wrote of a sort of 'new France',[2175] in a May, 1224, in a letter to the

---

[2174] Treadgold, 714.

[2175] Vasiliev, 543.

French Queen Blanche, wife of King Louis VIII, as the City was threatened on all sides by incompetent Latins and dangerous enemies.

Baldwin began spreading to Western holdings at the Aegean and incited rebellions in Venetian Crete occupying the isles of Samos, Lesbos, and Chios, and also recovering ground in the Meander from the Turks. In 1234, he also brought Rhodes under Nicaean control by finally defeating the rebel governor, Theodore Gabalas. In 1233, he called for more meetings to discuss union with Pope Gregory while fighting John of Brienne, but necessity dictated he make another Bulgarian alliance against Constantinople.[2176] Sealed by a marriage in Lampsacus of Asen's daughter Helena to Theodore, Vatatzes's son, Nicaea also was made to recognize the independent sovereignty of the Bulgarian Orthodox Church by recognizing its Patriarchate in Tnrvo at the treaty of Gallipoli in 1235. John Asen returned this by recognizing Germanus II as the true Greek Orthodox Patriarch of Nicaea.

Conceding southern Thrace in case of a victory as well as the southern sector of Constantinople upon capture, the two Emperors managed to surround the City by occupying Thrace between Callipolis and Tzurulum, planning their siege. Unfortunately, Brienne defeated the siege and the Easterners retreated; after another attempt was made the following year, it too was rebuffed by the Latin defenders. In March 1237, John of Brienne died and Constantinople remained without a ruler, Baldwin II skulking in the West. The opportunity to finally retake the City was upon Vatatzes with 100,000 men and 300 warships against the 160 Latin knights on the City Walls,[2177] but Asen betrayed Nicaea and made a separate peace with the Latins to keep the dangerous Vatatzes in his place, the detente smashed.

He began with a clever move by freeing his daughter, kept as a hostage by the Greeks upon a family visit, then besieging Tzurulum. Wishing to cause more dissension in the Byzantine sphere and reap the rewards of the Latins, John Asen had the blinded Theodore Ducas released to marry his daughter, and had the former Epirot Emperor sent to Thessalonica. Finally, he convinced Cuman aristocrats to leave Thrace near Tzurulum and enter Latin service. Since the first years of his reign, John II Asen sought an *imperium* of Bulgarian power in Constantinople, finding the City conveniently vulnerable.

---

[2176] Treadgold, 723-724. This was also to note the full Byzantinization of Nicaea with the gold coinage of a seated Christ on the obverse and Vatatzes bearing the imperial staff juxtaposed equally with the Virgin.

[2177] Gibbon, 2152.

Theodore had little trouble in inciting a riot and coup against his brother Manuel Ducas, yet as he was ineligible for the throne himself, Theodore would rule through his son John from the city of Edessa. By 1238, however, John Asen's Patriarch and family would be dead by a sudden plague. Seeing his weakened position with no heir and no ties to Epirus, Asen returned all the concessions of Tzurulum and his own daughter to the Nicaean alliance three years before. The Bulgarian surrender was complemented by the sanctuary of Manuel Ducas in Nicaea, giving John the justification to make war on Thessalonica. Unfortunately, Theodore's tenacity repelled the *Basileus's* armies and with his brother as a prisoner, placed him in vassalage in Thessaly in 1239.

Baldwin II returned from France after a shocking exchange for troops to secure his place in Constantinople and protect it from encroachment. Almost since the City's founding in 330 CE, it was graced with the Crown of Thorns worn by Christ at the Crucifixion, a holy relic almost as important to its history as the Pieces of the True Cross found by St. Helena. From its sacred place in the Church of the Blacharnae, Baldwin had given both as bribes, including the baby linen of the Son of God, the Sponge, the Lance, and the Chain of the Passion, the Rod of Moses, and fragments of the skull of John the Baptist, all to Louis IX[2178] and to this day, the Pieces of the Cross sit in the Cathedral of Notre Dame in Paris. With 30,000 men, Baldwin was allowed safe passage through Bulgaria in light of the invasions they were suffering from the Far East.

Beginning in 1241, the Jurchen Mongols had been ruthlessly pressing the Empire and the Ruman Sultanate. From the Eastern steppes of Central Eurasia, the indomitable Tjumen or Cheng-iz (Genghis) Khan, had been leading his 'Golden Horde' on a campaign of expansion since 1210. Riding right up to the doors of the Chinese Empire of the Song Dynasty in Peking on May 31, 1215, they barged west to the Ruman Sultanate in Iconium,[2179] now entering the Balkans. From Russia, they traveled the Don and Volga to conquer the entire Danube basin and Adriatic coast. The Latins defended Constantinople using Cumans that had defected from the Khan's armies in 1240. In these times, the Empire and the Pope characterized them as *Tartars* after the Greek mythological Tartarus as they seemed as tribes sent by Satan to punish a sinful Earth.[2180]

---

[2178] Gibbon, 2155.

[2179] Beckwith, 185-186.

[2180] Latham, R.E. 'Introduction.' *Marco Polo: The Travels.* New York, NY: Penguin Publishing. 1958, 10-11.

This combined force managed to take Tzurulum in Thrace from Vatatzes and a Nicaean naval campaign retaliated by taking Latin Nicomedia. In 1241, Asen died, and Vatatzes began a successful program of setting military and diplomatic affairs in order for Nicaea. Making peace with a two-year truce with Koloman, the new Bulgarian Tsar, John turned attention to Epirus. Theodore Ducas still controlled Thessalonica with his son John, as Manuel's son Michael II now held Thessaly, and John III extended a wish for peace with Theodore as he was being brought to Nicaea to discuss a treaty. The *Basileus*, however, had set a trap for the blinded successor and arrested him, exiling him to Vodena. Unprotected, Thessalonica was open to John and his new contingent of Thracian Cumans made pronoia landholders in Anatolia. John Ducas was a weak-willed and uninterested ruler who only wanted to enter a monastery[2181] – simple and greater concessions with him were easy to exploit and Nicaean Thessalonica would, thus, grow.

In 1242, a dramatic siege of Thessalonica was being planned from the coasts when word came that the Mongols were invading Iconium, winning in June of the next year at Kosedaj. This was too close for the John III's comfort and any ill-advised battle with the Mongols would crush the Byzantine possessions just west of Iconium, so John settled for the Strymon and Hebrus territories. He conceded Theodore Ducas back to his city of Thessalonica and made it a vassal state for the time being with John Ducas taking the demotion of its Emperor to 'Despot of Epirus'. After Iconium, as well as Trebizond, finally succumbing to the inexhaustible Golden Horde in 1243 and 1244, they headed west. But, they entirely bypassed Nicaea as Richard the Lion-Hearted had done for Constantinople in the Third Crusade. Meanwhile, Baldwin II, once again in need of funds for a failing Latin Empire, returned west like a beggar to the court of Raymond of Tolouse, however, at this point, Constantinople would prove past saving. This war against the Golden Horde would be chronicled by John III Vatatzes himself in his 'soft and charitable tongue.'[2182]

The *Basileus* used this opportunity in 1244 to forge one of the greatest alliances in Byzantine history with one of the most dynamic and charismatic characters of the Medieval era: the German-Sicilian Emperor Frederick II Hohenstauffen. A peace until 1245 was made between Sicily and the Holy Roman Empire and the recently widowed John had married the twelve-year-old Constance-Lancia, christened Anna, being Frederick's illegitimate daughter.

---

[2181] Norwich, *(DF)*, 198.

[2182] Gibbon, 2272.

Frederick was cultured, loved falconry (on which he wrote a famed treatise), and has been described as 'a Renaissance man' . . .'a man of creative and daring genius.'[2183] He had been raised and educated in the Sicilian court of Palermo, where he learned from the resident Arabs and Byzantines there fluent Arabic, Greek, and Latin (although, ironically, his German was said to be inferior). In 1225, when he had married the teen-aged Queen of Jerusalem, Yolande, he was hailed 'Wonder of the World' (*Stupor Mundi*). But Jerusalem would accuse him of being a kind of 'Medieval Dr. Frankenstein', disemboweling men alive to see their digestion or sealing men in a barrel to see if their souls escape. Thus, he was also called 'The Beast of the Apocalypse' and his rule was over when excommunicated for overthrowing a pregnant Yolande to be sole ruler.[2184]

One innovation attributed to him was a real attempt of creating a secular state for his Empire separate from Church authority. As for the German-Byzantine marriage alliance in 1242, Innocent IV defamed it, but Frederick did not waver in his loyalty to John Vatatzes. Though not his intention, the German Emperor had a modernized outlook on nationalism that could survive without the constant attention to the Pope in affairs. Gregory IX detested such intentions and called his family 'a viper brood', having had him excommunicated and deposed. By then, relations between Vatatzes and Rome had soured as it always did, and by 1235, John III was noted as a 'schismatic' after his Bulgarian alliance against Constantinople. The alliance was just right between the Western and Eastern Emperors who both sided against Rome. Greek troops from Nicaea were even known to have been lent to Frederick's army and John was promised Constantinople upon a defeat of the Latins by the Germans.

The 1242 marriage alliance, however, soured as well as John III was not known for his fidelity and had mistresses drawn from his young wife's handmaidens. In a year, the marriage would be dissolved and Constance would be moved to Valencia in Spain. From there, she operated charitable hospitals such as St. John's and other institutions as she had done with her former husband Vatatzes in Nicaea. Despite this turnover, however, Vatatzes and Hohenstauffen would remain close allies against Latin Constantinople and the Roman Church.

In 1246, the Bulgarian threat was neutralized with the death of Koloman and the ascension of his underage brother, Michael. John lost no time seizing on this opportunity to retake past his borders, and from Thrace a campaign of quick surrenders and successes raged from Serres to Melnik and the Strymon,

---

[2183] Vasiliev, 527.

[2184] Montefiorre, 278-279.

Axius, the Hebrus Valleys, Adrianople, Scopia, and Prilep. Michael Asen was goaded into a treaty by the end of the year wherein half the Bulgarian Empire became Byzantine fiefs. Epirus even claimed the Bulgarian ecclesiastical city of Ochrid for the Despot Michael, John Ducas having died in 1244.

Thessalonica would also surrender itself invitingly to the *Basileus* and their pleasure-loving Despot Demetrius Ducas was exiled to Asia Minor while John magnanimously allowed Theodore and John Ducas to remain in Edessa. Asia Minor would now be in the hands of Vatatzes's new 'European Viceroy', Andronicus Paleologus, whose son would become *Basileus* in 1261 and reconquer Constantinople to lead a 200-year dynasty. His powerful momentum only accelerated as he then expelled the Latins from Tzurulum and surrounded all of the territory around Constantinople, rivalling in size anything that the Latins held at any one time.

This dynamic push west continued as Rhodes was retaken after a Genoese invasion in 1248. Michael II, seeing imminent defeat, accepted Vatatzes as sole *Basileus* and was re-made a Despot in Epirus. In appeasing the Ducasi, John III complemented the peace with the imperial marriage of his granddaughter Maria to Nicephorus Ducas, Epirus's heir. Success for a unified Byzantium under a Greek capital was taking root everywhere and the full germination would spell the fall of Latindom as Baldwin II finally returned to the City, finding his Empire 'bankrupt and moribund',[2185] stripping the lead from the roof of the imperial Palace to pay his debts when gold was no longer available in October, 1248.

In 1249, Langdon has claimed, Armenian and Syrian commentators close to the Seljuk court accounted the marriage of Vatatzes's daughter to the Muslim son of the Sultan. This, curiously, unnamed daughter of the *Basileus*'s married Izz al-Din Kaykaus II (Langdon's pronunciation), not having at all to do with succession, but as a 'collaboration' of the two nations against the uncontainable Mongols. Though the root reason that Genghis Khan ignored Nicaea, as well as Constantinople, is not clarified as the alliance did not stop him from all but destroying Iconium in the next decade. After this invasion ended, the alliance became moot as the actions of the Golden Horde caused Kaykaus to flee to Anatolia in 1256 and to Constantinople post-1261 under Michael VIII.

The sultan's son would flee Constantinople soon after, leaving this Vatatzes princess behind to the Paleologi where she apparently 'vanished from history.' If not for the Armenian writer Kirakos Ganzdaketsi (1200-1271) and the Syrian

---

[2185] Treadgold, 728.

Ibn Natif (1210-1288), both contemporaries of John III's reign, this anonymous princess would only be an allegory such as Helen of Troy has been speculated to have been. The alliance of Turk and Byzantine, so vital in the days of the Mongol invasions threatening both sides, would have been dropped after their departure and the recovery of Constantinople by the Byzantines as now they would resurface as a more serious threat to Iconium. The genealogies of contemporary historians never attribute such a daughter of John III Vatatzes as existing.[2186]

The wily Theodore Ducas would not take this alliance so lightly and Michael II began an expedition to recover, in 1251, lost Epirote land in the south at Prilep, the Axius, and north to Macedonia. Vatatzes caught up to Theodore and his hapless, weak nephew Michael at Thessalonica and the defeated Ducasi fled to Edessa in 1252, which was then annexed by John. The remainder of the Epirote army was taken at Castoria in the Pindus Mountains with only minor difficulty due to their low morale. John shored up victories in the region all the way to Albania as a new ethnographic cohesion, based on the Serbian Church and the consecration of Sava into an Albanian people as had once happened in Serbia, Bulgaria, and other Slavic-Balkan groups touched by Byzantine influence.[2187] Michael conceded all that he could to the victorious Nicaeans in 1253 to embassadors at Larissa: Prilep, Ochrid, Edessa, Castoria, and Dyrrachium, as well as his uncle Theodore and cousin Nicephorus becoming hostages. Theodore Ducas, as tenacious as the late, exiled *Basileus* Alexius III in fighting for lost territory and prestige, would die as a prisoner across the Marmara.

Not long after, the life-long epilepsy that plagued John III, foreshadowing an early end to his reign, was becoming more severe. Just as he was preparing with Pope Innocent IV new terms for a possible reunion of Christendom, John died of an epileptic fit on November 3, 1254, and he was buried at the monastery of the Magnesia in Sosandra, near his beloved Nymphaeum.[2188] Pope Innocent died the same year and negotiations with the Roman Church were lost to John's son, Theodore. John had the most auspicious reign in the five *Basilii* of the Byzantine exile, historians stating 'John Vatatzes had been a great ruler...one of the greatest, perhaps in the whole of history.' His successes were owed some victories to trickery such as betraying allies and abducting enemies, 'more an

---

[2186] Ostrogorsky, 578; Treadgold, 726-727.
[2187] Obolensky, 241-242.
[2188] Norwich, *(DF)*, 205.

opportunist than a planner',[2189] but he did no worse than his own allies had done in the course of the internal strife the Successors faced and to what John Asen II's Bulgaria added.

He belongs to the most noted *Basilii* for his expansion with Justinian I, John I Tzimisces, or Basil II (in success if not proportion). He turned hostile states to placated allies and either outlived or conquered his worst detractors. Also, the Latin Empire would never financially recover from their losses and fall within a decade of Vatatzes's death. With his controlled and balanced nature in all spheres of society, restoring the confidence to become a true 'Roman Byzantium' once again, he was understandably loved by his people and suffered little to no internal dissent. Along with far-reaching economic and philanthropic reform, the Byzantine Empire was almost restored without Constantinople.

As far as the religious aspect of Vatatzes's Nicaea was concerned, a Union of the Churches was what was most labored upon by the *Basileus* and the Catholic Christians. At least three Popes advocated it, especially when it was becoming a dominant power again and its Church needed the powers of Papal acceptance. John III, by his death in 1254, was willing to sacrifice the independence of the Greek Church, but the entire decade had been one of staunch secular support of Frederick II as an ally against Rome.[2190] Common ground and sympathy were shared with Frederick and the Greeks as the Pope only chose to vilify heretics while also spreading Christianity to every quarter of the globe; whatever their true opinion, the Germans and Nicaeans both continued to uphold a respectful distance from Rome.[2191]

It seems unlikely that a surrender of Greek authority would occur to override the desire for a compromise between the Churches based solely on political, and not necessarily ecclesiastical or even Christological, reasons. In fact, Eastern Christianity was strengthening as the Churches of Jerusalem, Alexandria, and Antioch gave consent along with Nicaea in re-establishing the Bulgarian Patriarchy. Norwich evaluates this as the Byzantine-planted roots of the inability of Bulgaria to formally and socially accept Western Christianity. After an argument in 1235 between John Asen and Gregory IX, the Tsar halted military actions against Nicaea as making a war against his 'co-religionists.'

Legends abound, with no discernible reality, that an audience of the Pagan

---

[2189]  Treadgold, 730.

[2190]  Vasiliev, 527-528.

[2191]  Ostrogorsky, 441.

Mongolians and Rome was attempted. The Pope himself offered conversion to Christianity as his peace with the Khan's army, but the ambassadors claimed to lack any authority in the matter and left without ever giving an answer. What did actually occur in 1235 was the arrival of a delegation of five Minorite Franciscan monks, leaving Turkish captivity to discuss a union with Patriarch Germanus II in 1250. The friars Elias of Cortona and John of Parma visited Nymphaea as Papal delegates to discuss the *filioque* and universal Councils of the past. The point to all this was that with overwhelming forces in the East threatening the West, the idea of Church Union was seen as the better option to defending Christendom than relying on the Latins. Constantinople under the Latins was on a decline as steep as that of the Angeli, perhaps worse. Unity with the true Byzantine court in Nicaea, untouched by Tartar invasion, could reverse the Hohenstauffen era with the West and hedge the bets on which Successor State would survive the next few decades.

As a member of the Anatolian aristocracy, John Vatatzes was a firm supporter in the use of the pronoia as landholding nobles whose fiefs were supported by an imperial grant. Historians have called the middle of this period of the thirteenth century a 'golden age' of the pronoia in a fiscal sense. Between the years 1214 and 1272, during the Lascarids' and Michael VIII Paleologus's reign from Constantinople, nine documents bearing the authority of the *Basileus's* executive privilege, *Chrysobulls* and *Prostagmata,* bear this term. This trend would continue in a lesser extent throughout subsequent centuries until Turkish dominance of these territories.

It was with great skill and internal diplomacy that John III Vatatzes handled the Cuman pronoia situation, as noted by George Pachymeres (1242-1310), praising these achievements in the Lascarid Nicaean state in his *History.*[2192] Cuman settlements were met with little complaint from local nobles guarding the north and east in Thrace, Macedonia, Phrygia, and Meander. One of his most important tools was the fact John conveniently reminded Nicaea that they were in a constant 'state of emergency' in exile where appropriations and sacrifices were imperative.[2193] This perpetuation is reminiscent of the most striking of Western revolutions of centralizing authority to preserve states and ideas from Napoleon (1769-1821) to the 21st century.

This seems contradictory, given the tradition of Byzantine public finance policy as well as the interests of the poor John philanthropically cared for,

---

[2192] Ostrogorsky, 441-442.

[2193] Norwich, *(DF),* 203.

but he stayed a supporter of both sides for a specific purpose. These nobles were no longer required to be vassals for John as now there were the Latins, Trebizond, Epirus, Armenia, and a number of other territories in which to expand. Clergy, senators, landlords, vassal lords, holders of private estates, military commanders, all came to Vatatzes out of need or loyalty, and they needed not to be ostracized by the central government at Nicaea, so both sides needed his facilitation. In another advantage in the Niceaen economy, the *hyperpyron* coin of exchange actually had equilibrium and stayed at two-thirds the value of pure gold (sixteen karats).[2194] This was being outclassed, however, with the Italian Repuplics' gold coin of international commerce, the *'buona moneta d'oro.'*

Imperial grants kept the wealthy tied to Nicaea financially as did grants to monasteries and Churches tied to the clergy as well. Perhaps most important were the military commanders who needed to operate smaller armies with the numerous rivals in the Latin, Nicaean, and Turkish Empires. The Cumans, for example, that defected from the Golden Horde in 1240 were given Nicaean property in return for their military service. Not too surprisingly, many broad comparisons can be made between these pronoia and the feudal system of *beneficium* of the West.[2195] This is more evidence of the transformations of Eastern economic policies during the Outremer period originating from Western policies.

Internally, a domestic trade independent of any foreign influence was vital to Nicaea's need for a functioning, self-sustaining economy. Flying in the face of the lucrative and omnipresent Venetian and Turkish trade, Vatatzes forbade by an Edict any importations of foreign perishable goods and foodstuffs, negating some of the spirit and letter of Theodore I's August 1219 Venetian trade agreements. Of course, Vatatzes's motivation was to strengthen localized production in agriculture, viniculture, and livestock. One stark example is the successful abundance in the egg industry that induced John III to award his *Basilia* the 'Egg Crown', set with pearls and precious stones.[2196]

Yet, this shrewd application gave Nicaea agricultural self-sustenance and helped in filling the imperial coffers. Nicaea benefited in Turkish and Oriental luxuries: fabrics, gold, silver, jewelry, and the opportunities of food at higher prices to Iconium during a widespread famine. Genoese treaties were instated

---

[2194] Ostrogorsky, 484.

[2195] Vasiliev, 546.

[2196] Ostrogorsky, 443.

as well to capitalize on the important Black Sea trade effecting Russia, the Crimea, and Bulgaria. Warehouses were said to be filled with fruit and stalls in the marketplace were equipped with roads and streets filled with all manner of livestock. Lowering taxes on these items also added to the general prosperity of the city and the revenue was badly needed to field armies and negotiate truces. John's numerous visits to the court in Nymphaea is attributed to it being the site of the imperial treasury and mint.[2197]

The renovations and progressive properties of the *Basileus* as a friend of the poor and the urban class were without question. It was quite an achievement at the time being able to balance all of the classes with such ingenuity. He was known for confiscating property and movable goods as well as not forgetting the philanthropic duties as Father of his people and a representative Imitation of Christ on Earth. Almshouses, poorhouses, orphanages, and regular corn distribution were all results even shared by his wives, Irene and Constance-Anna, mostly from Valencia. This charitable spirit culminated after his death into a sainthood appropriated by the Nicaean and, eventually, Constantinopolitan Churches. From the French Center of Byzantine Studies is included this process in an evaluation of George Acropolites's *Bios* and Vatatzes's continuation as an adored Orthodox saint until the 20th century, 'a rare honor for an emperor.'[2198]

The only thing in Nicaea more sanctified than the Church was education and the return of cultural significance to Byzantium. These events were as well based on the generous spirit of Vatatzes, representing itself in the foundation of libraries and granting of scholarships to students of promise in the arts and sciences to the Nicaean schools.[2199] The libraries were filled with the tools of the liberal arts and literacy from the Comnenian era of Greek classics and the works of the Orthodox Church Fathers. In the spirit of civility these educational forms wrought, the barbaric practices of trial by ordeal and judicial combat would be suspended as it already was in most of England and France.[2200] Trial by the Roman laws of the East would now decide cases and replace such illogical and superstitious institutions.

Two great educators and writers came from this revival as well under the imperial grant: Nicephorus Blemmydes (1197-1272), teacher of Theodore II

---

[2197] Herrin, 278.

[2198] Ciolfi, Lorenzo Maria. 'John III Vatatzes' *Bios* Enigma.' Presented at *The Thirty-Sixth Annual Byzantine Studies Conference.*(Philadelphia, PA: The Pennsylvania University Press, October 16-19, 2010).

[2199] Vasiliev, 549.

[2200] Gibbon, 2173.

and the historian George Acropolites, brother of the Athenian Metropolitan. Noted attention goes to the Flemish scholar and Dominican William of Moerbeke (1215-1286) who used Nicaea in learning Greek and translating manuscripts from Aristotle in 1260 as well as Galen, Aphrodisias, Proclus, and Archimedes. A new class of refined intellectual elites and other *literati* came from the Nicaean court and found a home as well in Constantinople. Starting with the last Byzantine dynasty and extending to Trebizond and Mistra were scholars such as Cardinal Basileos Bessarion of Nicaea (1403-1472) (who graced the Western Renaissance), George Scholarius (1400-1473), Isidore of Kiev (1385-1463), and George Gemistos Plethon (1355-1452).

It appears John III Vatazes's best attribute and weapon against Nicaea becoming an inferior power was his versatility as an economic reformer for the Church (as well as a spiritual protector), the aristocracy, the urban rich, and even the poor. Along with this was his role as an achieving military leader, a diplomatic ace to enemies and allies, and an admirer of education willing him to make Nicaea the cultural beacon the City had once been. This was a bond made strong between Vatatzes and Frederick, to whom he wrote at least four letters.[2201] National identity was even growing under Vatatzes as the 'Hellenic' upbringing of Classical wisdom and education met with the culture of Greek Orthodox Christianity.[2202]

This would rear yet another difference between the Greeks and Latins as the education and cultivation of learning gave the Byzantine people a sense of superiority over the Christian West, especially in philosophy. In the last centuries of the Empire, the nostalgia of the invincibility of the Greeks in ancient culture even led to a cult phenomena in the histories of Sparta and its law-giving founder, Lycurgus. This Spartan rebirth in Byzantine culture would be finely promoted a century later in Mistra, which would become a high center of learning for the entire East. These amazing feats organized under an energetic and temperate John III paved the way to what was called 'the route to 1261.'

# THEODORE II LASCARIS
## (1254-1258)

---

[2201] Ostrogorsky, 420.
[2202] Herrin, 293.

# JOHN IV LASCARIS
## (1258-1260)

Now the Empire, though miles away from Constantinople, was in the best shape it had been since the Comneni. An orchestrated and smartly organized army would conceivably retake the City from the weak and nearly bankrupt Baldwin II, but this would wait six years. The son and successor of Vatatzes[2203] – taking his mother's name of Lascaris to keep the dynasty in one family - was a ruler who disdained war as well as political corruption, identifying himself as the philosopher-king as his father instructed he should be.

Theodore II was highly educated by the best tutors of the age such as Blemmydes and his fellow student, George Acropolites, holding a court of average citizens with no aristocratic origin. Altruism, however, was not his purpose as much as minimizing the threats to his reign and his plans for it from the interference of the rich landowners and other private interests. Lascaris himself would later write a panegyric addressing Nicaea itself, praising it as being the greatest Roman city, divided and crushed at one time before, now strengthened 'only in thee.'

What Byzantium under the third Lascaris gained in return, however, was a cultural flowering of Classical and Christian influences and education outside his father's shadow. Libraries exploded with books as never before and the innovation of the library checkout to conduct research in private was first enacted. He himself was a superlative student as the historians who praise his talents bestow him for mastering the liberal arts, complex mathematics, and natural sciences. In life, he was not known for writing many treatises, but he is known for at least 200 letters to foreign potentates and other allies in matters of politics, diplomacy, his version of the art of war and, of course, the priceless value of a good education.[2204]

Beyond his death, the all-telling funeral oration of Acropolites manifests in a deftly important treatise 'On the Duty of Kings to Study Philosophy.' In the traditions of Constantine Porphyrogenitus, Leo the Wise, John Comnenus, and John Vatatzes, the capital of Byzantium would rise as a cornerstone of

---

[2203] Old sayings used to describe Vatatzes and his son were as Cyrus as the *father* of Persia as Darius was the *master* of his country, though the mistakes of historians such as George Pachymeres have his descriptions of Theodore as a cruel Cambyses, whose high taxation had him compared to Darius as a *kapelos,* a merchant or broker. Gibbon, 2170f.

[2204] Vasiliev, 554.

the Byzantine cultivation of knowledge and Greek identity. Hellensim was revived even in the military as Theodore attempted to purify the army as Greek, attempting to forsake foreign troops and mercenaries, an idea that was noble, yet impracticable, at this stage under his father's pronoia design.

Theodore II Lascaris was born the son of the intellectual patron and *Basileus* John III Vatatzes and Theodore I's daughter, Irene Lascaria, in November, 1221. As an only child and the obvious choice for the throne, some also despaired the fact he also had epilepsy that was described as being more severe than his fathers'.[2205] His father wasted no time in priming the prince, appointing the renowned scholar and lettered man Nicephorus Blemmydes in 'learned investigations, philosophical studies, and theological meditation' which was the height of a uniquely Byzantine education. He had struggles, with the military as, unlike his father, he was apprehensive of Nicaea's abilities after 1204 and he found it justified as so: 'Whatever the needs of war and defense, it is essential to find time to cultivate the garden of learning.'[2206]

By his ascension on November 3, 1254, Theodore had learned at a rapid rate as later writers would describe Nicaea as 'a center of the humanities' and 'a new Athens.'[2207] It was always clear the *Basileus* had no interest in recovering Constantinople or giving any concession to Rome over a Church Union. Also, he neglected the army to foment hostility within his own nobility, operating the affairs of state and insisting on handling many of these situations in person as an absolute ruler. Vasiliev even goes so far as describing Theodore as 'an Oriental parallel to the great contemporary Holy Roman Emperor Frederick II.'[2208]

He would marry the daughter of the Bulgarian Tsar Helena and his son and only heir, John, would be born on Christmas Day, 1250. In an unwise move, when John succeeded him on August 18, 1258, he would have a regent from a lower class that his father trusted known as Muzalon, but this was quickly quashed nine days later by the machinations of the intractable and unscrupulous general Michael Paleologus. John IV would be a pawn in the imperial regency game as Paleologus would dominate the throne and set his sights and bringing about the glorious recovery of Constantinople. Yet both had to be raised on the buckler as the oaths and allegiances to John and Michael made it imperative, as a birthright, that due respect be first given the Larascid.[2209]

---

[2205] Norwich, *(DF)*, 204.

[2206] Hussey, 148.

[2207] Ostrogorsky, 444.

[2208] Vasiliev, 554.

[2209] Gibbon, 2174.

On January 1, 1259, Michael would be crowned *Basileus* with a crown of gold and precious gems while John, as co-*Basileus*, only received a string of pearls strung around his head. At the age of ten, he would be deposed and blinded to guarantee an unopposed succession to Michael. John was no Theodore II and no one came to his aid as he languished in a prison in Bithynia. This heinous act occurred on the child *Basileus*'s eleventh birthday in 1261 after Constantinople was recovered.

Some historians mention, only in passing, that John IV died in this captivity in 1305 at age fifty-five, a blind prisoner for over forty years. But a cunning alternative tale tells of a different fate at the French court of Charles of Anjou to where he escaped around 1273 according to a report on May 9. Apparently, a haven of alliance to all the wounded enemies of Michael VIII appeared at Anjou, including the deposed Baldwin II and the factions of Serbs, Bulgarians, and even Venetians.[2210] This was a clever insult of resentment to the Byzantine *Basileus* of a new Constantinople, now out of reach indefinitely from Charles's influence. As an inference, this was seen as a hostile maneuver to attack his new Byzantium; he mainly conjectures that these 'alliances' must have, 'aroused extreme fear in Michael VIII for Constantinople and his throne.' Another rebellious act was the Lascarid faction's support for the heretical Arsenite sect under Paleologus and his Patriarch, dividing Orthodoxy once again.

These were only mild embarrassments for Michael, if noted at all, by John, but strategically they could not have caused Constantinople more discomfort, although John was only motivated by characters such as Anjou and had a weak and timid personality. When Charles of Anjou died in 1290, John was already a monk in a monastery, under the name of Joseph, in Dacbyza. And before his 1305 death, Andronicus II, Michael's son, sought him out and begged his forgiveness for his father's crimes. Pachymeres and Nicephorus Gregoras, the imminent Byzantine historians of the fourteenth century record the events in France, John being revered as a saint not long after his death. Though easily dismissed as a footnote practically, John IV Lascaris did not live an ordinary life of disgrace and even made more Western allies than Michael perhaps ever had.

In 1255, Theodore II Lascaris showed he had some competency leading the armies by commanding them against Michael Asen and the Bulgarian marches on the Strymon and Axium. With troops supplanted at Adrianople, Theodore

---

[2210] Vasiliev, 595.

sacked Bulgarian Beroea and retook Melnik. By the next year, Lascaris had defeated Asen again and all the territories occupied by the Bulgarians were ceded as it was in 1254. A complex web of international marriage arrangements in diplomacy began now with Michael of Epirus offering his son Nicephorus to Maria, the *Basileus*'s niece. At Thessalonica, Queen Theodora of Bulgaria brokered the agreement with Theodore, mediated by Asen's father-in-law Rostislav of Russia.[2211] She then gave Dyrrhacium and the Macedonian fort city of Serbia as dowry on Theodore's insistence, fearing her own capture as a result of refusing. Begrudgingly, the wedding took place in Thessalonica in the autumn of 1256 and a satisfied Theodore returned to Nicaea with more territory.

The next spring, however, the Despot Michael II still managed to muster a rebellion against Theodore in Albania as it was a legitimate grievance of the loss of the Thessalian west coast.[2212] With a Serbian alliance, the Bulgarians drove Acropolites the historian, now a commander under Theodore's strange brand of anti-aristocratic generosity, to Prilep. Theodore's tactical failures were demonstrated when he called his best general, the aristocrat Michael Paleologus, a cousin by marriage, to the front at Prilep to repulse the charge.

But, a condemning act of paranoia hit the situation as Theodore intentionally undermined the general on fear of his influence with the army and nobles, in which he had wasted no time in ostracizing. When Michael failed with his inadequate troops, he was recalled to Nicaea and imprisoned. He did so willingly for he shrewdly thought himself clever enough to convince Theodore II of his innocence, and the fact Theodore's reign would seem short, due to his illness, and opportunities would lead him far in the aftermath. Either way, Michael was convinced that Theodore was by now incapable of 'responsible government.'[2213]

One reason for Michael's capture was his alliance with the Seljuk Sultan in Rum, which unfortunately fell apart as a result of the vicious attacks of the Mongols at this time in Iconium territory. The Sultan took refuge with Theodore, as a 'shy deer' Acropolites would say, with his family. Khan, however, bypassed Nicaea and Mongol emissaries were even sent to Theodore for a goodwill reception at Magnesia. Theodore's main tactic was the tried and true impressing of 'the Tartars' with Byzantine splendor and a lofty place with a

---

[2211] Vasiliev, 535.

[2212] Treadgold, 733.

[2213] Norwich, (DF), 206.

sword in hand to symbolize their strength.[2214] The *Basileus* was supposedly a 'mass of nerves' in this proceeding, but as the Mongols never attacked Nicaea or Constantinople, this side of Byzantium must have made an impact Trebizond and Epirus did not as these two were made easy targets for Tartar assault.

Manfred, the bastard son of Frederick II, arrived in Thessalonica and began outmaneuvering Michael and the Epirotes, capturing Albania, Corfu, Avlona, and Butrinto in 1258. It is evaluated that Manfred, unlike his father, took the stance of the Sicilian Normans and the German Emperor Henry VI concerning the Greeks.[2215] Michael Ducas, obviously desperate, offered a daughter Helena in marriage to Manfred conceding the captured territories as a 'dowry.' Michael, however, was starting to learn his lesson on concessions made by marriages by creating another alliance to balance his authority over Manfred's, wedding his other daughter Anna to William of Villedouhardin. Not only was he the descendant of the historian, but William was also the Latin Duke of Achaea and *de facto* 'overlord' of the important cities of Euboea and Athens. This triple alliance of Manfred, Villedouhardin, and Michael II Ducas would later be joined by King Uro I of Serbia who would take Macedonia, including Nicaean Prilep.

Also in 1258, Michael II Asen was assassinated and replaced with a boyar known as Constantine Tich, a descendant of the once-thriving Nemanjids of Syrian Aleppo. As a defensive measure against Sicily and Epirus, Theodore II married his daughter Irene to the new Bulgarian Tsar. Theodore lacked an assertive base for his own dynasty with a child for an heir and an unpopular regent and court, afflicted by a sanctimonious and hardly appropriate moral stance over the aristocracy, seeing them as only corrupt and avaricious. His education was near unparalleled, but his view of reality was made opaque by idealistic learning and a fraction of the experience his father possessed. This was what doomed him before August 18, 1258, when Theodore II Lascaris succumbed to his severe epilepsy, inherited from his father, at age thirty-seven.

Though he was a pillar of learning and Byzantinism in Nicaea, Theodore lacked the ability to keep stable the inherited stable domestic policy as made by Vatatzes. His need for authenticity in the court boiled down to cronyism as his choices for officers were barely-educated, unimaginative, and uninspired men. These were chosen only for their loyalty to Theodore, including the appointed Patriarch Arsenius, who would lead to a new schism in Greek Orthodoxy. Worst

---

[2214] Vasiliev, 535.

[2215] Ostrogorsky, 446-447.

of all was his physical ailments as a ruler with a 'strong and ruthless hand,' yet epilepsy left him with 'impaired judgement . . .drained of energy . . .and physically prostrate.'[2216] His reign cut both ways as an example of, perhaps, spiteful tyranny as well as being a benevolent and enlightened man.

Yet, he still embodied a man who believed in his office, in justice regardless of rank, and even a sense of 'equal rights' as he treated the Roman Church with deference, wishing to take a rare role of neutrality. His was a short reign with many accomplishments, but he would lose his dynasty almost immediately and be overshadowed in accomplishment and glory by the controversial character of Michael Paleologus. Norwich would describe Theodore II's attitude towards the charming commander as that of a typical introverted invalid, jealous of his gifts. It was even an inherited hatred given to him by his cautious father, harboring violent moods bordering on the pathological! After his death, Theodore II would be proven right in his suspicions, however, as Michael would murder his allies, blind his child, and steal his throne. Only the histories written long after these events would give Michael VIII the status of deliverer he still deserves.

Theodore also had the strong conviction and belief in the unifying *Basileus* mastering ecclesiastical affairs, even ecumenical Councils, over the Patriarch or Pope.[2217] In 1254, the laymen Arsenius was given the see of Nicaea (and later, Constantinople) for, although he felt it unnecessary, there was no abolishing the office, even by a *Basileus*. A more deserving candidate and the Theodore's former tutor Nicephorus Blemmydes was insultingly overlooked for the position for his honesty on the complaints he made that taxation was too strenuous to support his military activities. Two years later, Pope Innovent IV sent legates to Nicaea in negotiations for the Union which Vatatzes had wished to call.

An Italian Bishop from Orvieta was sent, but was refused an audience by a neutral Theodore II as he left to fight Bulgaria, the Bishop being stopped from traveling east at Macedonia, eventually sent west as Theodore felt 'no further need of Papal support.' Theodore boldly proclaimed the importance of the *Basileus* at any Union of the Churches. The dangerous implications of these words at the Council before the Pope was that, in the Niceaen experience, the *Basileus* would take the role of Patriarch and rule both civil and ecclesiastical affairs.[2218]

---

[2216] Norwich, *(DF)*, 204.

[2217] Vasiliev, 544-545.

[2218] Herrin, 279.

The greatest irony in Theodore's religious policy was the failure in making Arsenius a puppet of the executive administration. Arsenius, over the reigns of two *Basilii*, would voice his disagreements with the throne (especially when John IV was blinded) and a faction coalesced that called for the unrestrained authority of the Church beyond secular affairs. The 'Arsenite' heresy would trouble Theodore II and Michael VIII despite Arsenius's dismissal and exile in 1265. These Arsenites would rally around the words of the Apostle Paul (Colossus, 2:21) to "Touch not . . .handle not", suiting their agenda with the interpretation that the *Basileus* was obligated to 'touch not' the Church.

The Arsenites were composed of pilgrims, ascetics, deposed clergy, jilted imperial relatives, disenfranchised nobles, and vagrants known as 'godly men'. Pachymeres, a century later, would bestow on them the moniker of *sakkophoroi* ('wearer of sackcloth'). Russian chroniclers would also describe with unfair bias these reformers as being 'simpletons, obscure wanderers, madmen, and other disreputable people – men of unknown origin, without settled homes.'[2219] Their rally was for reform in the bureaucracy, the practices with rich landowners, exorbitant taxation, foreign interests in the economy, and separation of the secular and ecclesiastical authorities. The Lascarid factions in the Byzantine East, for the blinded John IV and as an exile west, joined as well.

The question coming to mind, however, was if this also turned into a political maneuver against Theodore II's rule fueled by self-interest in nobles and the upper class. Cloaked in religious fervor and schism, it seems too coincidental that so many non-religious elites joined this cause right at the time the *Basileus*, and an unpopular one at that, was being adequately challenged. Misfits are expected to radically convert to a cause such as this, but any cracks in the Nicaean foundation were being exploited by the hypocrisies of the rich as well.

As has been said, no one tried with more dedication and fervor to influence Theodore II's life than his former tutor and 'cultural adviser' Nicephorus Blemmydes, whom Vatatzes sent to Thrace, Macedonia, Thessaly, and Mt. Athos for books and manuscripts to fill his libraries. Vasiliev, who was an especially valuable source on Byzantine cultural aspects in detail,[2220] says Blemmydes began his career wandering around Asia Minor teaching mathematics, geometry, philosophy, medicine, poetics, logic, rhetoric, physics, astronomy, and natural science based on the works of Aristotle, especially his

---

[2219] Vasiliev, 661-662.
[2220] Vasiliev, 549-552.

*Physics* and *Logic*. Before his education of Theodore in the court of John III, he was already well-known for theological works covering topics such as dogmatic, polemics, asceticism, exegetic, litanies, ecclesiastical sermons, other sermons, and saints' lives. His versions of the psalms and vespers spread throughout the Greek, then the Slavic, and finally, the Russian Churches.

His premier work for educating the Byzantine prince was characteristic of most literature with the same aim. The *Basilikos Ardorias* ('Imperial Statue') set the goals for a *Basileus* to care for the public welfare, control passions and vices, avoid flatterers in the court (thus his aversion to nobility), to be responsible as leader of the armed forces, and be a moral guide defending Church, state, and justice. Blemmydes showed a special pragmatism in his views on preparing for war in peacetime as strong arms would best protect the state. After the Lascarid dynasty ended, he retired to a monastery in Carian Latros where he founded a school focusing on science and teaching philosophy. He then died in this monastery a venerated man of letters in 1272.

## MICHAEL VIII PALEOLOGUS
## (1259-1282)

After the cruel disposal of the last legitimate Lascarid ruler, Michael Paleologus had full control of the Nicaean throne and its institutions. However, this would only be temporary as he is known as the *Basileus* that restored the City from an incompetent and barely-surviving Latin occupation. In sixty years' time, Constantinople had devolved into an undermanned target with no morale, facing hostile actions from the Successors, the Tartars, Slavs, and Nicaea. This rescue is what is mainly remembered as the legacy of Michael VIII, but historians such as Pachymeres and Gregoras a century later do attest to his fraud, cruelty, and indolence in war, making him an impious villain and the oppressive tyrant of a servile court, imposing the duties of applause or silence.[2221] These are not unfair assessments as he was a ruthless man, rising in the practically abandoned *cursus honorum* to ascend and seize the throne as sole *Basileus* at the age of thirty-six, said to have been 'energetic and vibrant, hiding fierce intelligence behind a convivial smile.'[2222]

One of this Greek noble's first acts was the assassination of John IV's regent, the Grand Domestic George Muzalon, after only nine days in office in 1259

---

[2221] Gibbon, 2178-2179.
[2222] Brownworth, 265.

when John was deposed. This opened wide the possibility of a co-emperor strong enough to rally military forces east and even fuse the lucrative Oriental trade of Anatolia which was flourishing between Nicaea and Constantinople. The nobles chose Paleologus as the new candidate, being a general just freed from prison by Theodore II for his dangerous popularity with the army. So, while negotiating peace with Epirus, Michael claimed himself *Basileus* in what he claimed as a state of emergency.[2223]

Michael VIII Paleologus was born in 1224 to the Grand Domesticus of John III Vatatzes, Andronicus Ducas Comnenus Paleologus, later made Grand Duke of Thessalonica. Michael was also a great-grandson of Alexius III through his mother, Theodora Angelina and he would even marry a grand-niece of John Vatatzes. It was his ancestor, George, that had put Alexius I Comnenus on the throne in 1081, strengthening his pedigree. Though of a Greek noble family, there was some evidence that he was the descendant of an Italian noble family of Viterbo, but this is scant and mostly insubstantial.[2224] He served as a commander in Serres and Melnik, but in 1257 revolted against Theodore II in favor of Michael II of Epirus.

When finally defeated and captured, he was imprisoned for at least a year before the chaos of John Lascaris's regency. He had no trouble rallying armies, especially Latin mercenaries, with his 'charm of manner [having] supporters in all circles, least of not among the then all-powerful clergy.'[2225] His connections and reputation earned him a place first as a commander of the French mercenaries, never spending more than three *hyperpyron* a day, then becoming both a Grand Duke and Despot before his imprisonment and regency.[2226]

Upon his placement on the throne of Nicaea, he wasted no time in 'answering' his diplomacy with Epirus by calling on his brother and Sebastocrator John in conquering the Successor State. With a force of Turkish and Balkan soldiers, known by Pachymeres as the '*volunteers*',[2227] John and Alexius Strategopolus forced Michael of Epirus to flee, making an alliance with the Emperor Manfred and 45,000 Western troops from Achaea to Pelagonia. John's effective guerrilla

---

[2223] Treadgold, 731.

[2224] Geanokoplus, D.J. *Emperor Michael Paleologus and the West 1258-1282: A Study in Byzantine-Latin Relations.* Cambridge, UK: Cambridge University Press. 1959, 180; Norwich, *Byzantium*, 207.

[2225] Ostrogorsky, 447.

[2226] Gibbon, 2171-2172.

[2227] ibid., pg. 2157.

tactics would force retreat upon Mannfred and Michael II to Cephalonia, where John would later break the German and French armies with Cuman archers, taking Acra.[2228] By 1260, Nicaea had completely contained their enemies' open hostility and could now turn to Constantinople and its ruler, Baldwin II.

From the time of the Fourth Crusade to 1261, the Latin government of Constantinople almost made the West consider the French leadership of the Empire a mistake altogether. It was nearing bankruptcy and dependent upon the ruthless Venetians' loans from Rialto and St. Louis IX of France to pay for defenses, especially after Pope Alexander IV refused aid, putting on the West 'moral pressure' to act on its behalf.[2229] With supporting nobles and clergy returning West, it was evident that 'He and his Frankish predecessors on the imperial throne had achieved nothing but chaos, spoliation and destruction; their conquest had only brought them poverty and suffering.'[2230] The opportunity for a Roman recovery had finally presented itself and its vulnerability and timing would instigate Michael VIII to action.

Michael VIII had gained some unpopularity among Nicaea as well as the Bulgars, Serbs, and even Venice for his treatment of the young John IV and a great rebuke from Charles of Anjou, John's protector. But the army still stood by Michael, especially as the commanders were his relatives, being victorious in their endeavors. The *Basileus* also knew how to make good relations with France by presenting a peace offering of an adorned manuscript of the New Testament to King Louis IX.[2231] Meanwhile, Michael was making powerful allies of his own in the Genoese against Venice by allowing them freedoms from trade restrictions not enjoyed since 1082. Tax and custom concessions, trade districts in Nicaea, supremacy in the Levant, all of these Genoa had won as Nicaea had been at war with the Venetian Republic since 1255.[2232] Court Venetians in Nicaea were now demoted among the rest as *Bailo* instead of the earlier title of *Podesta*; now their status insultingly disqualified them from dining with the *Basileus* at Church feasts.

Yet, the Genoese offered no fleet as their ships were reprehensible and barely sea-worthy, let alone ready for a sea battle at Constantinople. Paleologus's generals, however, were prepared and rode through Thrace in spring of 1260 to take the City. When in Selymbria, however, they received no support from

---

[2228] Norwich, *(DF)*, 208-209.

[2229] Ostrogorsky, 534.

[2230] Norwich, *(AHV)*, 159.

[2231] Vasiliev, 593.

[2232] Norwich, *(AHV)*, 160-161.

a Latin baron who promised to open a Gate at Constantinople, Michael frustratingly agreeing to a year's truce with Baldwin after his brother raided the Venetian suburb of Galata. This truce was necessary as Michael of Epirus was invading Nicaean territory, but Epirus was second only to Michael's ambitions and ordered Strategoplus to reconnoiter at Constantinople's Walls with the support of Bithynia.[2233]

It is said that they entered the City on the night of July 25, 1261, through an underground passage, reminiscent of the entrance of the deposed Justinian II in 705. But the reality was a neglected lock at the Pegae Gate allowed Michael's men to reach and open the main gate as the Trojan horse had done. The Greeks emerged undetected and began capturing the streets, hoisting guards over the Walls of the City. Terrified by this show of courage, Baldwin and his family fled and Constantinople was, at last, once again Byzantine. The *Basileus* himself, however, was 200 miles away and asleep when news reached him and he was given the scepter of the throne Baldwin II had left when fleeing upon arriving.[2234] The City itself, however, was in a deplorable state as any rebuilding efforts had not been made since 1204! After the *Basileus*'s coronation, Michael VIII Paleologus would move to the Blacharnae Palace temporarily until the Great Palace was made more suitable.[2235]

As a re-instated Byzantine *Basileus*, Michael Paleologus was then welcomed by the applause of the Constantinopolitans in a City no Lascarid ever ruled, as the rightful ruler of the Eastern Romans. On August 15, 1261, the Feast of the Assumption, he entered as a 'New Constantine' through the Golden Gate followed by his generals, Domestics, and the Icon of the Virgin painted by St. Luke himself, the *Hodegetria* – 'She Who Points the Way.'[2236] In the Church of the Holy Apostles, Michael and his *Basilia* Theodora were crowned by Patriarch Arsenius as well as their son Andronicus who was proclaimed heir to the throne. This was all after an earlier coronation in Nicaea by Patriarch Nicephorus II. Michael would take the reins of re-building the Queen of Cities: an Orthodox St. Sophia, the Walls of the Kontoskelion harbor, baths, hospices, other harbors, streets, marketplaces, law-courts, even a mosque burnt by the Latins in 1203 to cultivate goodwill with the Mameluks.[2237]

Since the time of the Roman general Gaius Marius in the first century BCE,

---

[2233] Treadgold, 773.

[2234] Brownworth, 264-265.

[2235] Norwich, *(DF)*, 215.

[2236] *ibid.*, 212.

[2237] Reinert, 'Fragmentation (1204-1453)', 256-257.

the eagle had been Rome's symbol on all of its flags. As with Michael's standards would have the Cross of Constantine, or the *chi rho* displayed with a gold two-headed eagle, keeping watch over Nicaea and Constantinople.[2238] Further propaganda to grace the Paleologi were three monuments created from the precious materials of silk, gold, and bronze. First, a bronze sculpture of Michael's namesake, the Archangel Michael, who defeated Satan as Michael had defeated the Latins, was erected in front of the Church of the Holy Apostles (but now lost). Next, a silk textile in Genoa depicting the 1261 Treaty of Nymphaeum, joining Genoa to Constantinople in order to keep the City Greek. Finally, there was an image of the *Basileus* on the new gold *hyperpyron* issued after the re-conquest. As Michael is shown as a prostrate figure beside the Archangel, a new idea of iconography and imperial piety was created. Traditional ideas of largess and gifts of thanksgiving to armies and sycophants would invert within Constantinople, becoming rare occurrences under Michael VIII, while such gifts would only be found in the later Paleologi.[2239]

Along with a memorial column at the Church of the Apostles, a mosaic for the Patriarch Arsenius Autoreianos was commissioned depicting Christ flanked by the Virgin and St. John the Baptist in the Church's Gallery.[2240] Included is a mosaic of Christ *Deisis* in the southern gallery of St. Sophia commissioned in 1261, said to be 'perhaps the most delicate and accomplished of all Byzantine mosaics',[2241] a beautiful piece of dimensional space, minute detail in figuring, and shading. Such works were a precursor for the 'Paleologan Renaissance' of the fourteenth and fifteenth centuries that would gain and lend inspiration to European Renaissance art in Venice and Siena.

No rival in Epirus, Thessalonica, or Trebizond could have accomplished this alone, and alone they could not seriously threaten Constantinople. At this time the City had 'a satisfactory Treasury, and an army that for fifteen years had managed to hold almost as much territory as Michael now possessed.'[2242] Yet, pressing and unprecedented 'divisions and grievances' existed between the

---

[2238] Brownworth, 266.

[2239] Hilsdale, Cecily J. 'The Emperor, the Archangel, and the City: Images of Michael VIII Paleologos and the Restoration of Constantinople.' Presented at *The Thirty-Sixth Annual Byzantine Studies Conference.* (Philadelphia, PA: The University of Pennsylvania, October 16-19, 2010). Michael would, though, debase the coin from sixteen to fifteen karats.

[2240] Herrin, 282.

[2241] Reinert, 'Fragmentation (1204-1453)', 254.

[2242] Treadgold, 735-737.

throne and the Latins as well as the Byzantines that depended on the relative stability of Latin rule. Another issue was the fact that the coffers were filled with the loans of enemy Italian lenders and the French king, whom Michael had no intention of repaying. In Nicaea, Baldwin II's emissaries were expelled with mockery and contempt as the *Basileus* offered nothing but trade or war.[2243] As for Papal envoys appealing to the Michael VIII, some were said by Pachymeres, to have been flayed alive, a cruel act worthy of the Persians of the Achaemenids.

Michael would send his brother, Constantine the Sebastocrator, as said in the *Chronicles of Morea*,[2244] to 'police' the Peloponnese with 5,000 Seljuk mercenaries, being swiftly victorious and adding more mercenaries until 1265 to a resulting amount of 15,000.[2245] William of Achaea had been captured by Michael in the recovery of the City and was released upon an oath of vassalage, concessions in his Peloponnesian territory, and the fortress of Mistra in Monemvasia. This was critical as its isthmus was dominated by the fortress as Monemvasia, translated as *mone embasia* ('only entrance'). Paleologus spent his reserves wisely in strengthening the Walls and refurbishing the City to allow re-population to commence. Four new classes of military units to overhaul and prepare his navies from across the Empire were also organized:

1) Constantinople lent the *Thelemartii*, the landed and pronoia-granted soldiers.
2) The *Gasmuli*, marines for pay only.
3) The *Proselontes*, coastal and island oarsmen, also with pronoia grants.
4) The Peloponnesian *Tzacones*, who received pay and pronoia grants at Constantinople.

Although his aims were to reform the navy by 1262, he faced that year consequences of the illegal actions he had committed before his ascension. Patriarch Arsenius had gotten word that Michael blinded John Lascaris and an uproar ensued. Furthermore, in a bid to tie imperial families, Michael wed the widow of John Vatatzes, divorcing his own wife in a scandalous affair.[2246] As Michael was excommunicated from religious service and salvation, Armenian

---

[2243] Gibbon, 2156.

[2244] A 9,000-line thirteenth-century history of the region written by an anonymous *gasoule, or Franco-Greek. Its translations included Greek, French, Italian, and Aragonese and was one of the stepping stones to Modern Greek.*

[2245] Ostrogorsky, 483f.

[2246] Norwich, *(DF),* 218.

armies sought to ascend a blind imposter as John IV to the throne. Michael's contributions in restoring the City were forgotten as William of Villehardouin was illegally released from his oath by the incensed Patriarch and incited the Successor States to make moves west.

From the beginning, Michael knew the fate of his internal relations with Rome, the Turks, and the Italian Republics depended on relations externally with the West.[2247] Even in cementing these relations, Eastern problems such as Constantine Tich the Bulgarian ascended to take Thrace as Michael had. Michael divided his new forces to the Peloponnese, Epirus, and the Venetian Aegean Isles to Paxos, Naxos, Crete, and Monemvasia with Genoese aid. Yet the Genoese alliance was crumbling, as their encroachment on Greek markets in the City caused simmering resentment in their shipping interests. A disastrous loss in 1263 at Spetsai also disillusioned Michael, who recalled the twelve galleys sent. Worst of all, a conspiracy was discovered, led by Guglielmo Guercio, the Podesta of Constantinople, and he and his accomplices were banished. A mere three years had made the Treaty of Nymphaeum a moot point.[2248]

To cover his northern forces, Michael chased the Bulgarians across the Balkans and secured the border fortress cities such as Phillippopolis and Anchialus. A year later, John Paleologus and his armies campaigned east and met a capitulating Despot Michael II that conceded south Epirus and Thessaly, along with an oath of fealty. Villehardouin was more obstinate and battled the Greeks to Andravida before repulsion. But, Michael's Genoese fleet was defeated attacking a *carovana* of Rialtan ships carrying spices, silks, and Oriental trade by Venice at Sicilian Trapani, as 1,100 Genoese jumped from their twenty-seven galleys and were put in a vulnerable position.[2249] It was here Michael demonstrated his reputation for duplicity by breaking the Treaty of 1261 and seeking alliance with Venice.

Doge Renier Zeno and Venice haughtily agreed to a five-year truce, a non-aggression pact, a boycott of aid to Venice's enemies, and the release of prisoners held on Crete, Mordone, and Corone. Lost to Byzantium would be the fish, salt, grain, slave, and fur trades of the Russians via Genoa and Galata and the northern Black Sea region. Even Pope Gregory X had a connection through this region when the Mongol ruler Kublai Khan requested oil from a lamp in the Holy Sepulcher in 1271 when the pontiff was elected. Gregory agreed, sending

---

[2247] Vasiliev, 591.

[2248] Norwich, *(DF),* 220-221.

[2249] Norwich, *(AHV),* 162-163.

a young Marco Polo to deliver it and report on the customs of the Far East.[2250] Galata as well had profited from the 1244 Mongol steppe unification, while the Genoese supplanting of Egypt to Trebizond succeeded as well.[2251]. In this transition, in 1264, Michael II of Epirus attempted to attack the Empire, but capitulated when Michael Paleologus arrived in person.

Epirus submitted again and Michael II married his son Nicephorus to Anna Cantecuzena, the *Basileus*'s niece. John had been sent to Asia Minor to subdue the Iconium Turks that had deposed Sultan Kayka'us, now a 'guest' quartered in Aenus. The 'Empire of the Straits' would be lost to Michael II[2252] as the tax revenue of goods transported both ways to the Black Sea from the Aegean would be crucial to Byzantine army budgeting. And the alliance for Venice's wealth was even more important for Mediterranean trade. As the Byzantine control of this pass was so strong, the dangerous *mameluk* ('slave') cavalry of Egypt needed Michael's permission to cross.[2253] Yet in May of 1262, the Venetians also made an alliance at Thebes with William Villehardouin in the Peloponnese as an enemy of the Byzantine state.

Upon Michael VIII's return from Epirus through Thrace, 20,000 Mongols of the Golden Horde surprised the imperial castle while taking the northern Danube, allied with 300,000 Persian mamaluke horsemen of the Sultan Azzadin.[2254] They demanded the release from Aenus the deposed Sultan who had gathered the Mongols for their ambush, returning north when Kayka'us was released. The untrustworthy Sultan then abandoned his retinue to the Byzantines who baptized them and recruited 1,000 Turcopuli in the army.[2255] By 1265, the imperial revenues were depleted and these Christian Turk mercenaries defected from the Byzantines to the Latin forces and a desperate Michael sought an extension of the truce with Venice. Another concession made to the Muslims holding Michael and his Treasury was the marriage of his Christian daughter Maria to Abaqa Khan, the Sultan of Persia.

The situation of creating a marriage alliance in the Serbian court fared no better with the *Basileus* and King Urosh I's son, Milutin, in 1266. Two emissaries were sent to shockingly report that the *Basileus*'s daughter was shabbily dressed and bent over a spindle like a seamstress. The Serbian court itself was 'plain

---

[2250] Brownworth, 268f.

[2251] Norwich, *(AHV)*, 175-176.

[2252] Herrin, 283.

[2253] Pachymeres, 176-177; Vasiliev, 601.

[2254] Gibbon, 2226.

[2255] Treadgold, 738.

and paltry' and unbefitting the splendor of a Byzantine princess; Byzantine luxuries and mannerisms only scandalized the capital as an indignant Milutin would comment on how the emissaries resembled the eunuch retinue of the princess.[2256] Eastern allies were unstable enough to the Empire without the pitfalls of marriage alliances between the hostile Persians and ungrateful Serbians.

The military situation was steady until 1267 when Charles of Anjou took Corcyra and northern Epirus; Charles had been harboring the presumptive heir, John IV Lascaris (some argue a pretender), still a minor, and a strong ally of Pope Gregory IX. This was after a Papal interregnum since 1268 by Anjou's manipulation, only occurring when the people of Viterbo threatened to remove the roof from the Palace in which the conclave was meeting.[2257] Charles became King of Sicily, eliminating Manfred and a sixteen-year-old rival[2258] to occupy his territories as the younger brother of Louis IX of France, now winning a marriage alliance with the deposed Baldwin II and William of Villehardouin. With his holdings by conquest and marriage, his territories stretched somewhat from Italy to Persia, including Jerusalem, by 1277. It was also Anjou that had the East further divided from the West by having Simon of Brie, the French Pope Martin IV, have Michael VIII Paleologus 're-declared' as schismatic.[2259] The *Basileus* used this time to shore up his own alliances and defenses against Anjou by settling the Genoese in Constantinopolitan Galata. Furthermore, he renewed the Venetian peace in 1268 (but, apparently, only to rent Byzantine property without a quarter in the City).

This was in reaction to the incompetence and lack of confidence showed by two Venetian Doges, Tiepolo (1268-1275) and Contarini (1275-1280), and a new treaty of peace and trade was made in 1270 with Genoa. The Bulgarians would be offset by the crippling fall made by their star general Constantine Tich and the emperor would gain Mesembria and Anchialus through his niece's marriage alignment. Charles rightfully read this as a sign to gather his own resources, especially in Serbia and Hungary to begin a new Crusade against Constantinople. Charles was known as an energetic, disciplined man of ferocity and cruelty, but with cheerfulness, loving tournaments, arts, poetry, and the sciences.[2260] Michael sought Charles's brother's arbitration, but Louis IX had

---

[2256] Obolensky, 251.

[2257] Norwich, *(AHV)*, 169f.

[2258] Brownworth, 267.

[2259] Norwich, *(AM)*, 195.

[2260] Vasiliev, 592.

died on August 25, 1270 while on the Eighth Crusade in North Africa. Facing the inevitable, a treaty with Tich was made and Bulgaria agreed to fight Anjou as Latins from Athens were sent by John the Bastard of Thessaly to the French in 1273.

The main territory in question was Albania, with Charles crossing Euboea in 1271 to settle in the city of Dyrrachium which had been devastated by an earthquake. Now, Charles had a foothold in the region to be met by Tich's men as the Greeks defeated a Latin fleet from Euboea.[2261] Land forces from Thessaly were keeping the imperial armies at bay and it was here a crushing moral defeat occurred as the best imperial general John Paleologus, the *Basileus*'s brother, died. Euboea, however, was recovered by Michael through the Venetian fleet led by the mercenary Licario as the Aegean was lost to Thessaly after a rebellion in Crete overthrew the Latins. A new truce was made in 1274, but the fickle nature of Venetian alliance was put in play as Licario went against the weak Doge's orders and took many Aegean islands in his own name.[2262] He would leave Venetian Chalcis and Naxos alone and hold Athens at bay by capturing its Duke.

Also in 1274, the troublesome Union of Lyons commenced, legitimizing Michael VIII as *Basileus* in Constantinople, but also applying Papal supremacy in Rome under Pope Gregory X. This only divided the Western and Eastern spheres even further and the Byzantines continued their hostilities with Thessaly, meeting a serious defeat by John the Bastard in 1277. A year earlier, Michael's niece, Anna Cantucazena, had demanded back Mesembria and Anchialus based on her Papal alliances brought by the Union of Lyons. Constantine Tich still lent his aid to Byzantium, but this was put in serious jeopardy when the Mongol Hordes began invading farther west to Bulgaria from the Danube.

Michael's 'anti-unionist' opponents began to shrink, however, as 10,000 Byzantine troops took Trnovo, the Bulgarian capital, imprisoning Anna and raising their own Tsar to the throne. This was Michael Asen III, a descendant of the Asenite dynasty of 1186 by Michael I, in 1279. Unfortunately, he was dead within a year and the noble George Terter took the throne, making alliance with Byzantium after the Mongol destruction. In 1280, Michael dared to go offensively on three fronts as:

---

[2261] Charles's raid on Constantinople would be destroyed as a powerful storm off of Trapani sunk the main eighteen warships of the fleet on November 22. Michael would weep before the Virgin Protectress of Constantinople, it being a miracle; Norwich, (*DF*), 231.

[2262] Treadgold, 741.

1) He went to Anatolia to rout the Turkish raiders there.
2) Andronicus, his eldest son, was sent south to the Meander to strengthen Tralles against Turkish invaders.
3) The *Basileus*'s youngest son, Constantine, drove off Serbian raiders in Serres.

These, on the surface, seemed minor and mere skirmishing campaigns, but they were meant to protect frontier territory for the Empire from the more dangerous elements such as Anjou, who took the fortress of Berat in 1281.

Desperate for alliances against the French scourge, Michael would seek the aid of the Egyptian Sultan Kala'un, victorious after Louis IX's failed Crusade, in battling the 'common enemy' of Anjou in the East.[2263] It was needed in the Albanian war, to be decided this year, as imperial forces captured the Latin commander and repelled his army back to the Balkan coast. It was clear, except to Angevin Dyrrachium and Aulon, that Byzantium had taken Albania. Further diplomatic actions un-rammed Charles of Anjou as Michael paid 600,000 *hyperpyra* to King Peter III of Aragon, a severe rival to Anjou, to attack Sicily east from Spain. The result in 1282 was the revolt in Palermo known as the Sicilian Vespers[2264] to oust French influence, leaving Charles with only a very tentative hold on the Sicilian Kingdom with his Crusade against Constantinople being quickly abandoned. The vengeful Sicilians fell upon the northern settlers with a cry of 'Death to the French' (*Moranu li Franchiski*) and out of 2,000 French inhabitants, not a single man, woman, or child survived.[2265]

The danger of the Turks increased as the tribe of the Othmans, or Ottomans, further entered Byzantine affairs by taking Bithynian land and gathering farmers disloyal to the *Basileus* to continue their rights in Turkish service.[2266] Wishing to appease a Successor State and demonstrate the dominance of Constantinople, Michael VIII wed his third daughter to John II of Trebizond on the condition he dress as the Despot he had been made, and not as an Emperor, at the ceremony. John not only obliged, but only gave himself the

---

[2263] Vasiliev, 597.

[2264] Starting when one French soldier attempted to seduce a Sicilian maid and take her by force, her father cried 'ma fia' ('my daughter') to the crowds of Italians and the riot was incited. This is said to be the genesis of the term Mafia, whereas the organized crime behind it started with Italian elites bonding with the poor to aid them when civil authorities could not.

[2265] Norwich, (DF), 251.

[2266] Herrin, 283.

title of 'Emperor of the East' over 'Emperor of the Romans.'[2267] With yet another enemy in Thessaly to humble, Michael fled north only to catch dysentery on the way. Despite better judgement, Michael continued to Thrace on his campaign, exacerbating his condition to die on December 11, 1282, a heretic to the West and a traitor to the East. Unceremoniously, as an Arsenite, Gregoras reports that his wife and son refused him a Christian or State burial and he was buried near a monastery of Selymbria in an unmarked grave and was never returned to Constantinople.[2268] This was the remembrance of the *Basileus* that brought back the City of Constantine of his Roman ancestors.

Despite bad press and a reputation for cruelty, Michael was a shrewd Western diplomat and showed military acumen by entrusting the army to his brother John, himself riding as leader after John's death. Though he lacked reliable allies, he upheld the City by overcoming six hostile fronts and keeping the currency stable with only one debasement in twenty years during the times of duress. He also kept his religious ties with Rome and Gregory X and three Popes until he could find 'a more sympathetic Pope' until his death, leaving open the options for an end to the Schism of 1056. Not least of all was the recovery of Constantinople, northern Thrace to Rhodes, and Pergamum on the west Asia Minor coast. His policies affected international relations from Spain to Egypt, but at the expense of crippling burdens to Byzantium as the Empire would slowly crumble without hope of recovery as there was stark difference between the glory of Michael VIII's reign and that of his poor successors.[2269]

Yet, more *Basilii* like Michael VIII were necessary in maintaining this New Order and such men were in desperate supply as the hold in the East gained would begin to slip. In all this, Michael had a reputation for piety that was committed into every ceremony the emperor carried and all the Paleologi would participate. In the palatial/fortress Blacharnae and Porphyrogenitus, thirty incense-cloaked ceremonies carried on one day to underscore the *Basileus* and appeal for Christ's aid. Every feast now was to resemble the Last Supper and any breaking of its divine spell by a servant meant decapitation. Constantinople was the 'New Jerusalem' and on Easter the subsequent Paleologi would wear burial shrouds and whiten his face like a corpse to imitate the fallen Christ.[2270]

Besides the treacherous military position Paleologus was in, there was the

---

[2267] Treadgold, 745.

[2268] Norwich, *(DF)*, 254.

[2269] Ostrogorsky, 479.

[2270] Sherrard, 52.

question of Union with Rome and the controversial Council of Lyons in 1274. Beginning in October 1272, 500 Bishops at a General Council were assembled where Gregory X discussed a Union with the supremacy of Rome 'recognized', or at least adopted, by the Eastern Church in Constantinople. The Pope gave Michael a clear ultimatum [2271] - either the Greek Church submit to Rome, guaranteeing the support of the Catholic powers, or he would no longer restrain the constant demands of Charles of Anjou for a Crusade. Over the next two years, a bilingual Mass would be regulated in Latin and Greek, the three chants of the *filioque* would be re-instated, and the Eastern Creed from 1057 would be in place as long as no rites conflicted with Rome.[2272] Another concession was the Eastern recognition of Purgatory, a Catholic tenet of which Orthodoxy knew little to none.

By 1274, Pope Innocent IV (1243-1254) and the Hellenic/Catholic/Arabic-inspired philosopher Thomas Aquinas in 1263 had aptly defined Purgatory in the Church through the Gospels of 'sin-cleansing fire.'[2273] Now, in Byzantium, prayers and alms-giving would be a practice in relieving the deceased from damnation through penance and Andronicus II, Michael VIII's son and successor, would adopt this tenet, citing 'penalties of purgatory or purification'. Despite its diplomatic brilliance, each of these radical policies opened old wounds and infuriated Eastern clerical and secular authorities, all three Successor States, and all non-imperial Christians, as this seemed a concession to all of the West and not just Rome.[2274] Justifications made for abandoning the Union of Lyons included the fact that all five Patriarchs conveniently needed to be present at an Ecumenical Council.

More consequences of Lyons were the distraction from the Slav Churches it unintentionally provided. As the needs in the Morea and Thessaly sent Byzantine forces from the Balkans, never to return, the allied Churches of Ochrid in Bulgaria made successful bids for independence. From 1272 to 1279, the Serbian Church led these transitions as Bulgaria was weakened by the Mongols and forces were fought off in the Trnovo-Danubian region. Further separatist tendencies would divide, in 1281, the western Bulgarian province of Divin and in 1350, it would be lost to Serbian nationalist hegemony.[2275] The Bulgarian situation was even said to have been exacerbating unionist

---

[2271] Ostrogorsky, 459.

[2272] Norwich, *(DF),* 234-235.

[2273] Herrin, 302-303.

[2274] Treadgold, 741.

[2275] Obolensky, 244.

division by making the court at Trnovo 'a nest of anti-imperial intrigue'. With resemblance to Theodora and Joannina in the sixth ccentury were the intrigues of Michael III Asen's sister, Eulogia-Irene, and her daughter the Tzarina of Bulgaria, Maria,[2276] putting considerable pressure on the state already crippled by the Golden Horde.

Michael made war with the anti-unionists through blindings, exiles, confiscations, and even the removal of one especially unquiet monk, Arsenius, and his views against Union. Now, the Byzantine Church had been divided between two polarized parties in Constantinople. The moderate party of the *Politikoi* ('Politicians') was for Union as the *Zelotai* ('Zealots') opposed it, as written by Pachymeres. In 1282, when the Union finally fell, the Zealots rejoiced as the 'Uniates' went so far as to orchestrate a coup and attempt a restoration of the unionist conservative Lascarids to the throne.[2277]

It was an implicit wish of Michael VIII that the lines of the Creed be partially blurred and all the parties understood new meaning of the term 'Christians' by the Unionists, whose solidarity was vital for the East's stability. In 1263, Paleologus wrote a letter to a receptive Pope Urban IV on the matter wherein the legates had been blamed for the despoliation of Christian brotherhood by misdirection and only Papal/Imperial communications would be best effective. A certain envoy, Nicholas of Crotone, spelled out how the views of the two Churches were not so different, if not for minor details in ritual. Of especial note was the event from Vatican documents citing an 'anti-Turkish League' between the two Churches before Gregory X's death in 1276, months before an Easter meeting of Pope and *Basileus* at Brindisi.[2278] This was to be the promise of a possible new Crusade against Islam to free the Christian Holy Lands and unite the desperate cause of Michael and the greedy cause of Anjou.

This was upon the capture of the Morea where Michael desperately realized, once again, he needed 'friends' in his international situation.[2279] The wily Charles of Anjou, however, arranged a Frenchman, Guy Foulques, to be Pope after Urban's death in 1264 as Clement IV, who was hostile to any Union. He changed the agreements made by Rome with Constantinople and the questions of the sacred *filioque,* the bilingual liturgies, and the use of leavened bread in the Eucharist were thrown out of the discussion altogether. In a fell

---

[2276] Ostrogorsky, 462.

[2277] Vasiliev, 663.

[2278] *ibid.,* 596.

[2279] Norwich, *(DF),* 223.

swoop, Charles had denied the Church when Michael needed it, leaving only frustrated anti-unionists hostile to Constantinople, even in the *Basileus*'s own court.

Economically, the Empire was surprisingly sound with only minor currency troubles and a constant flow of Italian markets in the City and Empire, shifty though these alliances were politically, including some access to the lucrative Black Sea. Fortunately, Michael VIII had wisely planted roots early and the Serbian, Russian, and Bulgarian forces he had attracted in Nicaea held firm in the centrifuge of interests after 1261.[2280] Containment of these regions were masterfully played upon by Michael's diplomatic skills in the courts of the Seljuk Sultan, the King of Armenia, and the Mongol Khan in concluding the 1269 commercial treaty with Genoa. A convenient pact was even made with the Mongols when Michael gave an illegitimate daughter to the Khan Hulago, and his predecessor Nogay, in 1281 to concert defensive against Thessaly. In honor of this, the 'Church of Mary of the Mongols' was erected and remained in Byzantine and Greek hands until today after the Turkish Conquest.[2281]

Within the economic structure of the army, a new border-guard of the Empire known as the *Akritai* were considered the 'nerves of war',[2282] especially in Bythinia due to their position in Thrace. Yet, this did not stop the financial reforms of Michael Paleologus from instituting a tax census and confiscating land and incomes from these troops. Evidence such as this, along with Byzantium's need of adequate armies made through diplomatic relations and a sub-standard navy, demonstrate the dire need Michael had in raising military funds in the Empire, a curse and weakness for all of the Paleologi up until 1453.

Paleologan soldiers and peasants based themselves on the pronoia system that granted land for life and to their heirs and under Michael VIII this was practiced such as in past centuries, unifying the central government to peasants for tax revenue. The state controlling the means of production, they blended it with private ownership, continuing the 'feudal customs' that Medievalized the Byzantine economy.[2283] In manner of pay and the cash economy, the Comnenian *hyperpyron* was still the staple and soldiers in Asia Minor, by 1272, received from twenty-four to thirty-six, which was two to three times what

---

[2280] Obolensky, 242.

[2281] Norwich, *(DF)*, 253.

[2282] Pachymeres, 18; Vasiliev, 602-603.

[2283] Decker

professionals such as doctors (sixteen *hyperpyron*) or domestic servants made (ten *hyperpyron*).

Also, the Paleologi from 1260 until 1453 were known for their love of culture and education; Michael VIII was a literate who wrote many letters and canons for Rome as well as dedications to martyrs. He also left a valuable autobiography, one of the two major sources known for his reign along with the works of George Pachymeres. Pachymeres had been a staunch anti-unionist (thus, an anti-Paleologan), calling for a hereditary Greek national spirit in his chronicles from 1261 until 1308, in the middle of Andronicus II's reign. He made such works his own, making the style accessible to numerous tastes with Homeric allusion, theological declamations, and popular language both foreign and domestic.[2284]

The *Basileus* also gave to the causes of education by founding a grammar school for orphans in Constantinople in 1261 which was said to have a distinction from, but also a connection to, the University of Constantinople. To stand up to the reputation of Paris's schools since 1204, the School of Philosophy was re-opened in the City under George Acropolites in St. Sophia. Now, besides the mathematics he generally discussed, Aristotle's works were included. But, an intellectual chauvinism demonstrated by Michael Paleologus was also discovered to exist as he forbade the teaching of Platonism, which he found 'unsound.'[2285] Necessary policies, for friendship's sake, would include the selling of Greek slave children to the Egyptian Sultan, unfortunately making more mamelukes educated in Muslim ways against the Byzantine Empire.

Paleologus was known for outrageous cruelty, beginning with the atrocities he had inflicted on young John IV, but cruelty was the order of the day in the times of the Byzantine Empire. In the Mongol sack of Baghdad in 1258, as a Muslim, the conquering warlord could not imagine spilling the blood of the Caliph. So, to circumvent the 'spilling' in word only, the Caliph was wrapped in a blanket and trampled to death by a horse. Greek intellectuals, learned men, suggested that Paganism be revived, but women committing adultery should be forced into prostitution while rapists should be burned alive.[2286] Perhaps it was not *what* Michael VIII did to become *Basileus*, but *who* he did it to that made such a difference, blackening his name.

---

[2284] Vasiliev, 688-689.

[2285] Buckler, 218-21

[2286] Brownworth, 273.

# ANDRONICUS II PALEOLOGUS 'THE ELDER'
(1282-1328)

# MICHAEL IX PALEOLOGUS
(1293-1320)

The tragedy of Byzantium's decline was now to begin with another indolent ruler who let change affect him instead of he effecting change. Andronicus II was unprepared, making a poor substitute for his father and even what his prodigious grandson would be later in his life. He was a devout Orthodox Christian and anti-Unionist ostracizing and antagonizing the West, leaving it open to more Crusades from the French Latins. Politically and diplomatically this was almost suicide, but it did unify a broken Church and Patriarchy, ending the persecutions of his father (and leaving him to persecute Unionists). He was an educated man and a hefty patron of numerous disciplines including the preservation of Classical texts under scholars such as Theodore Metochiates (1270-1322) and Maximus Plenudes (1260-1330). Also a patron of artworks, he restored the porphyry Pillar, Column, and the Colossus of Justinian I at St. Sophia before its melting into brass canons for the Ottomans.[2287]

He took great pride in his heritage of multiple Byzantine aristocratic families as his 'full name' was recorded as Andronicus Ducas Angelus Comnenus Paleologus.[2288] These origins were important in the dynastic ties he had with the states of Epirus, Trebizond, and Thessalonica. He attempted to create a new dynasty in foreign territories by marrying Anna, daughter of King Stephen V of Hungary, but producing no heirs, she was set aside for Yoloanda-Irene of Montferrat. Their union produced Andronicus's son, Michael, who was co-emperor until his death in 1320. More developments in the East reveal that, since 1282 when Andronicus ascended, Byzantine influence with the Slavs was rapidly decentralizing and becoming non-existent in power politics with Serbia and Bulgaria claiming the Balkans (except the Peloponnese)[2289] dominating the Adriatic and Black Seas.

Andronicus's main military weakness was an almost pathological lack of confidence in Byzantium's own resources to fight its numerous wars. He relied preferably on mercenary troops from all nationalities, especially a foreign navy

---

[2287] Gibbon, 2309.
[2288] Vasiliev, 583.
[2289] Obolensky, 237.

of Italian Republics that time had proven were unreliable and self-serving. Because of his father's diplomacy with Aragon and the Spanish Peninsula, the rival Empire of the Ottomans would be turned back to its borders, but resulting mismanagement and economic failure led to a 'Catalan' cancer fatal to Byzantium's achievements. This Andronicus shied away from as he plied new taxes from his people, estates, soldiers, and anyone he could to oblige his own debts as the *hyperpyron* would inflate again by one karat, now fourteen karats to ten karats of alloy.[2290] For the first time, Italian coins would surpass the strength of the Empire's with the international *ducat*, of equal weight in pure gold, becoming a standard of Mediterranean trade from Venice beginning in 1284.

It was such developments as these from Western culture that drowned the East Romans, also giving Andronicus II a bad name. Some historians such as Ostrogorsky, for example, defend him as a product of circumstance and not an 'incompetent weakling',[2291] sorting out that Medieval and modern representations of evidence do not lie in pointing out his flaws as well as judging him an unworthy successor. Named after his grandfather, Andronicus II was born in 1258 to Michael VIII and Theodora at Nicaea, becoming heir presumptive on August 15, 1262, upon Michael's entrance of Constantinople. This was hallmarked by the blinding of John IV Lascaris and his exile to Marmaran Dykibyze where Andronicus visited him in 1290 as penance for his father's crime. Pachymeres relates the *Basileus*'s guilt in this interview as Andronicus begging forgiveness, asking what he could do for the forty-year-old Lascaris as he might proclaim him the rightful heir, though no replies were ever recorded.[2292]

He was well-educated under the tutelage of the Domestic Metochiates, beginning a new cultural fount for Hellenism, Christianity, and a passionate devoutness for the Church and its Patristic teachings. This culturalism would only flourish in the art of the time such as the display of Andronicus II in a mural now in the Byzantine Museum of Athens, whose face is a remarkable example of the new style of 'humanist' art of form and dimension.[2293] These are the brief and only remarkable remnants of Andronicus II's rule, otherwise inundated with weakness and temerity before the Empire's reduction. After

---

[2290] Treadgold, 746.

[2291] Ostrogorsky, 480. He was not, however, called a great statesman, either; perhaps the implications were that he was just mediocre.

[2292] Norwich, (APO), 257.

[2293] Norwich, (DF), inset no. 16.

a military career battling the Turks of Asia Minor, he was recalled when his father died on Friday, December 11, 1282. After a coronation, he and his mother buried his father in a pitiful hole with no honor for political reasons, wanting the Schism of 1056 to be ended.

He and his mother did this, in part, to appease the Cypriote Patriarch Gregory II in early 1283 just after the death of Joseph I, who had replaced John XI Becchus, the last of the anti-Unionist Patriarchs of Constantinople. The next year, with ecclesiastical affairs somewhat healing, Andronicus turned to foreign matters and organized an army of mercenaries to march on Thessaly. The term 'army' is a bit loose as it was mostly undisciplined wanderers and refugees who would work cheap due to Andronicus's lacking funds. Heavy taxation was all the *Basileus* could muster to support his endeavors, unpopularity early in his reign being the inevitable result.

Michael Ducas, heir to John the Bastard, was captured along with the port of Demetrias as Nicephorus of Epirus was persuaded to ally with the Empire with aid from his wife Anna, the *Basileus*'s cousin, coming in most handy when the Despot died in 1296 with Anna as regent. By a marriage alliance to a Western bride, Andronicus gained Thessalonica as a dowry, promising some expansion into the southern borders. More fortune seemed to spring as the resilient Charles of Anjou died in 1285, neutralizing threats of another Crusade on Constantinople. Underestimating the potency of his diplomatic ties to Venice, the *Basileus* signed a new treaty of limited trade privileges with them for one-third of the price they had asked so he could utilize their naval forces and leave the Greek fleet further rotting in the harbor. Meanwhile, Venice and Genoa still continued their hostile relations, especially over the Crimean trade routes.[2294]

Andronicus II further dismantled his own navy by dismissing naval units such as the Gasmuli and Tzacones, filling the ranks more with mercenaries and infantry peasant-soldiers only being used to gather their funds for these foreign ranks. Thessaly would submit in 1288, but only after John of Thessaly had died and a regent widow recognized Byzantine sovereignty. As the Anatolian Turks took the Meander Valley under Andronicus's watch, Epirus rebelled after its alliance with Charles II of Naples, Anjou's son, defeating a Genoese fleet to take the Peloponnese from the Empire. Along with these setbacks, the Serbian King Milutin, was charging east across the Axius Valley. Two years later, the commander Alexius Philanthropenus was successfully retaking territory in

---

[2294] Treadgold, 746-747.

the Meander, including the city of Miletus. By 1295, however, the specter of military rebellion saw Alexius being praised as *Basileus*, but this was quelled only by other rebels, and not the state, who blinded him on campaign.

Marriage alliances again weighed on Andronicus's mind as Charles II married his son Philip of Taranto to Nicephorus of Epirus's daughter, creating another anti-Byzantine league. This was in response to Andronicus's offer of marrying his son and heir Michael to a Latin heiress, and he predictably demurred, marrying him instead to an Armenian princess. But now, the fortune of the Empire would shift beyond recovery beginning with the policies of the Venetian-Genoan War in Constantinople. Though allies with Byzantium, Venice hated Genoa more and burned their own suburbs of the City in Galata. Infuriated, Andronicus repudiated Venice and called for a military alliance with Genoa, yet with no navy, Venice succeeded in plucking the Aegean Islands back as Licario had done.[2295]

It must be commented upon how Andronicus II's diplomatic acumen paled considerably to his father's. Though it cost damages to the City and imperial pride, he lacked his father's clarity (and duplicity) in not strengthening ties with the dominant Republic of St. Mark as Michael had after the Genoese defeats of 1264-1268. Such a missed opportunity demonstrated only a lack of foresight in the *Basileus* and the regret of losses for which his father had worked to avoid. The encroaching Serbs in the Axius were now keeping Andronicus's attention, his Italian alliances having failed, in 1297, ending only in stalemate and negotiation, sapping further imperial resources and morale. Those negotiations were met by the hopes of a marriage alliance between Simonis, the Andronicus's six-year-old daughter, and Milutin of Serbia.

Such a marriage could not escape scandal and the Patriarch of Constantinople refused to consecrate it on grounds of her age and, also, this was Milutin's fourth marriage (his third wife still alive at the time). But, agreement was reached and two of Milutin's marriages were annulled, the consecrated marriage taking place in 1299 (why didn't past *Basilii* think of that?). Despite its enmity and independent character, Byzantine influences under the surface were still alive and in practice by 1300. The administrative, legal, and fiscal institutions were most affected: court titles, offices of state, taxes, pronoia, land tenure, and legal documents blended Greek and Slavic styles.[2296] These survived

---

[2295] Treadgold, 748-749.
[2296] Obolensky, 252.

centuries later despite the separation of Serbian and Byzantine governments, the Turkish takeover, and broken relations from the Balkans.

In 1298, Andronicus II handled the Anatolian front by appointing Tarchoniodes as its commander, who had disenfranchised and infuriated the locals there by harsh taxation and military intervention. In 1301, he was overthrown and Andronicus recalled the Byzantine troops, replacing them with Turkish mercenaries and 16,000 Alans, using local *pronoia* in Thrace to fund operations. The next year, half of these troops were sent under the commander Muzalon to Nicomedia and the rest under Michael IX Paleologus[2297] to Magnesia. Alan refugee families flooded into Constantinople and a roll of 10,000 of the mercenaries' women and children were put into Andronicus's care.[2298] Another price was paid for Andronicus's paranoia over using his native troops when, instead, he would use dwindling finances on mercenaries.

It was a disaster - the undisciplined Alans lost interest and simply deserted in mass numbers to Thrace, as Muzalon's army was depleted to only 2,000 by the time they had arrived at the Turkish front. There, they were soundly defeated by the Seljuk Osman, who was consolidating his own Turkish state. The suffering and terror put upon this land by the Turks was atrocious, described vividly by George Pachymeres how no one was not seen mourning a murdered loved one, animals with no masters running rampant in the roads to the wailing of the sick and dying children, women, and the crippled[2299]: 'The violence of these horrors can be ascribed to no other cause than the wrath of heaven, their cessation to its mercy.' The wrath of 'barbarians' and Infidels had once again been explained as the punishment of God and sin in desperate times, the degradation of the Empire and its armies not being mentioned directly. These victories were from Osman, a simple ruler of the Ghazi Emirate, growing to found a 500-year Empire that once threatened Western Christianity itself.[2300]

Michael fared even worse when desertions left him hemorrhaging and fleeing Pergamum, as any pitched battle by Muzalon failed up to 1303. Andronicus was forced, in a panic, to confiscate rich estates and Church property just to be able to pay his domestic forces. In dealing with the Venetians, a ten-year truce was drawn ceding the Aegean Islands already taken (as though

---

[2297] Though historians disagree in their rolls of rulers of the Empire, some do agree Michael Paleologus, Andronicus's son was Michael IX.

[2298] Ostrogorsky, 492.

[2299] Norwich, *(DF)*, 264.

[2300] As *'Ghazi'* meant 'Sword of God', Osman intended to lead a full jihad against Constantinople itself. Brownworth, 273.

they could be claimed by the Byzantines) and for reparations totaling 79,000 *hyperpyra*. Thessalonica was then lost and declared another Successor state under the will of Constantinople's Empress Irene, who saw it as a rightful inheritance. Andronicus did have ample allies in the West from Aragon in Spain and the troops they sent east would prove to be an amazing force against Byzantium's enemies, only to degenerate into some of the worst opponents the Empire had to that point.

The Catalan Grand Company under the disciplined and ruthless German commander Roger de Flor led seasoned veterans of the Sicilian Wars, including Majorcans and Navarrans, and in 1303 they negotiated with the *Basileus* for service. Their main composition was cavalry comparable to the *akritai*, known as the *almughavars* (Arabic for 'light cavalry').[2301] For their 1,500 cavalry and 500 foot soldiers, an annual 67,000 *hyperpyra* and 33,500 more would be paid, respectively. An unprecedented pay scale of 300 for each cavalryman and 150 for each soldier was agreed upon, tripling the budget to pay the Alan troops and practically soaking up the entire Treasury for their service.[2302] A desperate Andronicus then hastily made de Flor a Grand Duke and gave him the hand of Maria Asen of Bulgaria, his niece, making an Aragonese mercenary a part of the imperial family. It might have been worth the trouble to nostalgic historians who had claimed, under Leo III or Basil II, how the Catalans would have 'strangled in its cradle' the Ottoman powers and redeemed the double-headed eagle of the Empire.[2303]

At first it seemed worth it as, in 1303, the Catalans struck from Cyzicus, rapidly defeating the Turkish forces to Ephesus despite more Alan desertions. Yet, the cost was plundered Byzantine territory and a betrayal by de Flor in Magnesia, Lesbos being used to pay the mercenaries. The island of Chios was especially prized for the wealth of its alum mines in Phocaea by the French King Philip IV 'the Fair' as it was taken by the Venetian commander Zaccaria in 1304.[2304] Andronicus II tried organizing them to enter Thrace to fight the invading Bulgarians, but the Catalans only extorted the *Basileus* from Callipolis. Their numbers grew even more with adventuring Catalans appearing and demanding service and pay from Constantinople. Faced with no defense that could seriously stand up to de Flor, Andronicus gave in to every demand from

---

[2301] Vasiliev, 604.

[2302] Treadgold, 750.

[2303] Finlay, George. *A History of Greece, vol. III*, ed. by H.F. Tozer. Oxford, UK: Oxford University Press. 1877, 388.

[2304] Ostrogorsky, 491

the Aragonese, his only actions being the arresting of Catalan merchants and seizing vessels in the Bosporus.

After months of extorting and taking cities in the Empire like the Crusaders, Michael IX Paleologus finally took some action and supposedly sent an Edict that de Flor was no longer to be obeyed, according to the one-sided Spanish sources. Perhaps to come to an agreement de Flor attended a banquet, with 300 cavalry and 1,000 infantry thrown by Michael where he called the *hyperon* 'base' metal to be fobbed on as gifts to the Catalans, returning the gold and silver wares used at the dinner. Roger was ultimately assassinated and his retinue killed at Adrianople, although there is petty speculation that Andronicus ordered the assassination, also planning to murder the Bulgarian usurper, Theodore Svyetoslav.[2305]

If this was intended to somehow quell the Catalans or demoralize them at least, it was yet another failure of Andronicus II's reign. Vengeful Catalans ran like mad dogs and defeated the *Basileus* three times in one month, wherein the imperial Turcopuli and Alans deserted immediately, with the co-emperor Michael being wounded in battle. Such savagery, adopted in the Greek colloquial language, created an insult by the name of Catalan meaning 'savage, robber, or criminal' in Athens and Acarnania in Greece.[2306] Chaos ruled the Empire now with an impotent Andronicus and now, seizing opportunity almost all at once, the Bulgarians took Anchialus, the Turks ran amok in Asia Minor, and the Turcopuli and Alan mercenaries joined the Catalans to take Ephesus. The last Byzantine ally to depend upon, the unfaithful Genoans, allied with the Aragonese, taking Byzantine ports and Greek Isle after Greek Isle.

In 1306, Anna Cantucazena left Philip of Taranto to support her cousin, Andronicus II Paleologus, and Epirus was cleared of Latins by her forces to recover Dyrrachium, only to be returned to Philip, returning from Greece with reinforcements. The Empire was quickly shrinking and could get no allies let alone keep any that it might already have had. The Genoese demanded 300,000 *hyperpyra* for a truce which the *Basileus* could never pay and when the Catalans refused a bribe of 100,000 *hyperpyra*, they devastated Thrace and took Adrianople.

The burning of farms and crops were so severe that Thrace was hit with widespread famine that would eventually harm the Catalans who caused it in

---

[2305] Lowe, Alfonso. *The Catalan Vengeance*. London, UK. 1972; Norwich, (DAF), 269-270f.

[2306] Vasiliev, 607. 'Not even a Catalan would do that' was another common phrase.

1307. It suffered the worst after raids by Huns, Gepids, Avars, Slavs, Crusaders, and Scythians, but the Catalans were the worst with atrocity after atrocity and massacre after massacre. Thracian refugees flooded Constantinople, imploring care from Andronicus as their cities and villages were burned and abandoned, concluding that 'Thrace was now a desert.'[2307] Had Andronicus II more success and the courage possessed against the Turks in the Levant, its own history would have been starkly different.

That year, a desperate need for grain from Bulgaria allowed the Tsar, Theodore Svyetoslav, to marry Andronicus's granddaughter Theodora, ceding Mesembria and Anchialus as a dowry. The Catalans and Turkish allies spread west of Callipolis like a plague of looting and destruction, reaching Cassandria south of Thessalonica, even the distant Mt. Athos being raided and occupied. As shameful as the Christian West could ever be, Rome and its French Pope, Clement V, began sending aid to the Catalans and aligning Charles of Valois and the French King Philip IV for another Crusade against Byzantium. Another Western ally of the Pope and the Catalans were the Hospitaler Order of St. John, the Knights Templar who amassed great wealth and gave generously to their Christian brethren. With Papal approval, the Order took Rhodes from the settling Genoese and the first Palace of the Order's Grand Master can still be found on there.[2308]

In early 1308, the Catalans finally struck north and attacked Thessalonica, repelled by the reigning Byzantine *Basilia* and in a fickle move by the Spanish, headed to take Thessaly while the Turks were pillaging Thrace once more. The sickly youth John II of Thessaly managed to avert disaster in 1310 when the Latin Duke of Athens, Guy II de la Roche, hired the Catalans and in 1311 as the unpredictable Catalans killed the Duke, making a permanent settlement in Greece. In 1313, Charles II of Valois's Crusade had dwindled by circumstance and he married his daughter to Philip of Taranto, who had divorced his Epirote wife, in his 'phantom Latin Empire'. Andronicus II made one good decision by retiring his son and co-emperor, Michael IX, from service against the Turks and appealing to Milutin of Serbia. Byzantium would finally be granted a sort of peace when the King's 2,000 Serbians crushed the Turks at Callipolis.

Added to these worries was the insistence of an absurd notion from the *Basilia* Irene that when the *Basileus* died, the Empire shall by split four ways between Michael and John, Demetrias, and Theodore of Montferrat, all being

---

[2307] Norwich, (DF), 272.
[2308] Treadgold, 753.

her sons with a Latin Duke. This was more serious an issue as first let on, as strange a request as this was in the Empire, it was a common hereditary practice by almost all classes in the Latin West, as described by Gregoras. This is a descendant of the Salic Laws of Charlemagne equally partitioning land to all male members of the family and a disintegration of traditional Roman practices of testaments and the Code of Law. This was an attempt to introduce in Thessalonica the Medieval roots of modernized concepts of private property from the French. The result would be *Basilii* forced to capitulate any centralizing means to local governors, eliminating Byzantine administration and hierarchical structure.[2309]

In 1316, Andronicus's grandson of the same name was crowned co-emperor at nineteen and the security of legitimacy was improving as the complicated webs of marriage alliances were paying off for the Empire by 1317. Epirus and Thessaly were returned to Byzantine suzerainty as John II was married to Andronicus's bastard daughter Irene. Thessalonica returning as well when the estranged *Basilia* died as its hereditary ruler. Epirus was coming into the fold with its Despot, Thomas Paleologus-Cantacuzenus, married to the daughter of Michael IX and his Armenian bride, Anna. Paleologan blood appeared to be fresh and flowing in the veins of the Successor Empires as well as Constantinople, but any promise in finally uniting all of Byzantium as it had been under the Comneni would still be a time away. Until then, unfortunately, bitter civil wars over dynasty would still exist to rend Byzantium as well as its monarch, costing him his throne of almost fifty years by an exhausted Constantinople craving change.

In 1318, Thomas of Epirus was assassinated by his Venetian nephew Nicholas Orsini of Cephalonia, destroying the last of the Ducas dynasty altogether. To claim the dynasty as his own, Orsini took Arta and married Thomas's widow, his own aunt, in 1319 pleading to appease Andronicus. He ceded northern Epirus to the Empire in exchange for recognition as rightful Duke of Arta, capital of Epirus. 'Thus, Byzantium gained some territory and became the sole surviving state ruled by Greeks, with the minor and distant exception of Trebizond.'[2310] Externally, dynastic affairs gave the Empire some peace, but ironically, the worst was yet to come from the same affairs internal to the main hub of the Empire.

Things were improving during this interregnum of battles as revenues from

---

[2309] Ostrogorsky, 481.
[2310] Treadgold, 754.

the Balkans rose to 1,000,000 *hyperpyra* (with fifty percent gold content) and learning his lesson, the *Basileus* built a navy of twenty ships. Yet, still dependent on mercenaries, he planned a future force of 1,000 troops from Bithynia and another 2,000 in the Balkans. The succession was rapidly engaging as the co-emperor Andronicus II was to be passed from Michael to his own son Andronicus, a more youthful and thriving individual. By 1320, the line of the Paleolgi looked its most assured, but a personal tragedy would set off events towards a civil war on a scale of the entire Empire. One night, as Andronicus the Younger was with a mistress, a man demanded to see the *Caesar*. The guards were displeased at this and killed him, probably to keep the affair a secret or dispose of a jealous husband. Unfortunately, this man was Andronicus the Younger's brother Manuel and not some rival lover.

Such a sudden tragedy is said to have caused the early death of Manuel's father, the *Caesar* Michael IX, in 1320, at the age of forty-two. He was a conscientious man of action and had opportunities of being a better *Basileus* than his inept father, but circumstance robbed Byzantium of such an ruler and such opportunities as intrigues often do. The only disadvantage he would have had domestically was being out-shined by his son, the actions of a ruler in this position usually being unpredictable at best and brutal at its worst. As can be imagined, Andronicus was furious at having lost a son and grandson in such a short time, refusing the rightful confirmation of his grandson Andronicus in favor of his youngest son, Constantine.

Repentant though he was, the younger Andronicus was insulted at this behavior by his grandfather and was gathering resources to take the title with the allies he had gained with shared interest in having the Elder deposed. In 1321, at Adrianople, the succession crisis began with the coronation of *Basileus* Andronicus III by the Thracians, now released from taxation and the restrictions of the pronoia. The resulting seven-year war seemed to be categorized into three phases:

1) The Rise of Andronicus III in the Empire.
2) A period of Détente between the two *Basilii* to set events into motion.
3) The Open War itself leading to the changing of the regime in Constantinople.

First, after a threat on Constantinople, Andronicus II 'allowed' his grandson to keep Thrace at Selymbria while insisting on keeping authority over foreign affairs. Andronicus III's reputation as a paramour, however, lost him partisans over scandals with their wives and the *Basileus*, seeing a spot of weakness, the Constantinopolitan partisans launched attacks on the co-emperor in 1322. This came to nothing when his Grand Domestic John Cantacuzenus funded his operations, the state of Thessalonica further backing him with Latin forces. John Cantacuzenus would prove a fascinating character in the history of Byzantium, being a Thracian-born Armenian military aristocrat whose father governed Morea while keeping estates in Macedonia, Thrace, and Thessaly.[2311] Once again, Andronicus the Elder was humbled by his grandson with his brilliant general accepting joint rule, Andronicus III being stationed at Thracian Didymottichus to control the spreading Bulgarian encroachments. Such a war with Bulgaria was averted as, in 1324, the Mongols invaded both empires and Andronicus allied with Tsar Michael Shishman, who had married Svyetoslav's widow, Andronicus III's sister. By the proclamations of his Thracian armies, on February 2, 1325, Andronicus III was raised on the shield as sole *Basileus*.

The city of Philadelphia stood in Turkish Anatolia this year and Andronicus II attempted to retake it, as it was 'an island in a Turkish sea.' One commander the Turks seemed to fear was the imprisoned Alexius Philanthropenus, blinded since 1295. He was recalled despite his condition and succeeded in intimidating the Turks of Philadelphia by reputation alone.[2312] The target in retrieving the region was the city of Prusa which Cantacuzenus and Andronicus III volunteered to do, but the Andronicus in Constantinople refused him the campaign out of paranoid envy. The court of Didymottichum was insulted by this, and worse, Prusa had no choice but to surrender to the Ottomans on April 26, 1326 to become the capital of their flourishing Empire for 130 years. Stronger still was the Karaman Turks who made the Ottomans success bittersweet as their siege on Philedelphia cost 18,000 Ottomans as its Emir fled. After this, Andronicus II allowed these Turks to occupy an independent kingdom in Anatolia.[2313]

These also planted the seeds of resentment between the two Andronici and the second phase of Andronicus III's conflict with Constantinople would begin. Beginning with Thessalonica (ruled by John, a nephew of Andronicus II) and Serbia, under Stephen III Dechansky who was declaring independence, the Elder *Basileus* declared John as *Caesar*. John died a year later and Andronicus

---

[2311] Norwich, *(DF)*, 276-277.

[2312] Treadgold, 758.

[2313] Norwich, (DF), 267.

II attempted a truce with Stephen to stabilize the situation, but this threatened to overwhelm Andronicus III with hostile neighbors in the Balkans, so he made a separate peace with Shishman and Bulgaria. It can now be said with no uncertainty that the Byzantine Empire was split in two with both sides shoring foreign allies to protect their own regimes and it would take very little to incite open war between them. The result would be division to rival the secessions of the Thessalians and Epirotes after 1205 as the younger generations of estates and nobilities fully supported the Younger Andronicus.

It would, however, seem quite one-sided as Andronicus II's forces were inadequate in invading Thrace, barely averting a secret breach of Andronicus III into the City. In 1328, Andronicus the Younger captured Thessalonica, prompting the Western allies to join him against the Elder Andronicus. Even as the Bulgarians defected to Constantinople's army, the citizens of the City, who had been rioting for years, had enough when the Venetians had blocked the harbor to fight the Genoese and the Byzantine government seemed beyond hope to provide aid. On the night of May 23, Cantacuzenus climbed the Romanus Gate with grappling hooks and opened the City; Andronicus III easily entered the Palace and his grandfather was captured and made to abdicate to Andronicus the Younger. It was practically a 'Glorious Revolution' (coined in seventeenth-century England) in the smoothness of its transition and the absolute bloodlessness of the coup. Upon doing so, Andronicus II petulantly likened his new *Basileus* with the Devil, with his inclinations of harm and the partial harm he actually inflicts despite his intentions.[2314]

Thus ended the reign of an ineffective ruler of Byzantium who dodged efforts to stabilize the possessions his father had strived so hard to achieve. It would have been better, we will see, that he had not reigned at all and his grandson having done so instead, perhaps through Michael IX. Andronicus remained in the City until taking the cowl as the monk Antonius in 1330 and was sent to the Monastery of St. Chora in Constantinople. Andronicus had commissioned this Monastery, still remaining to contemporary times, holding the *Anastasis* ('Harrowing of Hell') a work described as the sole pinnacle of Christian art.[2315] The best metaphor for Andronicus's rule was his restoration of St. Sophia's dome and chapel buttresses in 1317 where thirty years later the eastern hemisphere collapsed and the images and altars were destroyed – a false security under a façade of Byzantine beauty.

---

[2314] Norwich, *(DF)*, 273.

[2315] *Ibid.*, *(DF)* 280.

As it is said, he was allowed a pension of 24,000 *hyperpyron* in John Cantacuzenus's historical account and it was itemized to 10,000 in Gregoras with his use of the Palace and half the Treasury, including proceeds of the City's fisheries. Andronicus II Paleologus renounced the world excluding fur-trimmed cloaks in winter and sherbert once a week.[2316] On February 13, 1332, after having dinner with his daughter Simonis, mother of the Serbian King, he retired to bed and did not wake up, dying at a ripe age of seventy. He only blossomed in mediocrity with embarrassing military and diplomatic defeats and failures at keeping up on the imperial economy, his long rule being seen as 'his good fortune – though not the Empire's.'[2317]

Yet, the piety of this fallen *Basileus* was not up to scrutiny – after denying his father a Christian burial, he had the Arsenite Schism healed, chances for Union forgotten, and brought the Church under Constantinople's sole Patriarchy on September 14, 1310. The reasons why are speculative, but might include political gain in the Empire, a choice to favor local allies over the West, an application of actual faith in his reign as a product of personal belief, or to unite the Church and control the warring factions in the City with the Zealots. For example, like any other *Basileus* with jurisdiction over the Church, he was not above political gain through the ecclesiastical means as when he attempted to have his grandson excommunicated in 1327. When the Patriarch Isaiah refused, the feckless Isaiah was suspended from his authority indefinitely. Of course, the Western Church was incensed by such a complete turnaround, Clement V putting the *Basileus* under anathema. It was policies such as this that allowed no mercy from the Latins such as was with the Templars of Rhodes.

Near the beginning of Andronicus's reign in 1293, the Unionist Patriarch Gregory resigned and was replaced by the hated Anathasius. His unpopularity was quite palpable as he required a bodyguard so not to be stoned in the streets by the mob who considered him only an 'unwashed fanatic… [in] a hair shirt and sandals.'[2318] His conservative bulls included confiscating the rich Churches and monasteries as well as anathematizing enemies in a document so scandalous, it was hidden in a column in the north gallery of St. Sophia. Due to his numerous enemies and conspiracies, he was deposed as Patriarch in October, 1293. These examples of the tragic choices made by Andronicus II over foreign and domestic ecclesiastical reform only demonstrated his intentions may have been noble,

---

[2316]  Gibbon, 2197.

[2317]  Treadgold, 759.

[2318]  Norwich, *(DF)*, 258.

but lacked the judgement of character and that of his people's, in considering social and spiritual leadership.

Despite his successes in uniting the Byzantine Bishops, clerics, and Patriarchy into one restored Church without division, he could not keep their necessary cooperation in critical times. The best example was when Thamar, daughter of the Serbian King Stephen II Milutin, was to be betrothed to Michael IX and the Patriarch of Constantinople forbade it on canonical grounds, the union never taking place. This was also to be a critical diplomatic moment as the marriage would have united Epirus and imperial Byzantium. It did not help that Stephen himself was well-known to be having a torrid affair with his sister-in-law, who was also a nun![2319]

As the Eastern Church faced its usual tumults in keeping Orthodoxy pure, this era saw the 'golden age of monasticism'. Not since Leo the Wise in the tenth century, as the organized administration of individual sees and Bishoprics had not been so localized as in a web, that it was Andronicus II who focused on the individual cases and gave monasticism the centralization it needed.[2320] An important concession of the *Basileus* to the Patriarch of Constantinople was the authority over the Monastery of Mt. Athos by a *Chrysobull* for the Patriarch to be solely responsible in ordaining the monastic offices (*protos*),[2321] including authority over monasteries in the Caucasus, the Crimea, Russia, Gelich, and Lithuania.

This was a time of transformation for Mt. Athos as the monastic movement of *Hesychasm* ('silence', 'speechlessness'), the last mass mystical religious movement of the era, rose. From the Greek word *hesychastoi* ('those in stillness', 'Quietists') this was a practice of seclusion, inner contemplation, and meditation of the Prayers of Jesus to achieve a full and pure unity with God. The origins may come from a psychological need to escape the time's harsher realities and insecurities due to invasion and the direct threats to Orthodoxy and Eastern Christianity itself. The strength and dedication for these monastic and ecclesiastical institutions are why it is remembered that the Byzantine Church is the almost soley stable and lasting institution beyond the Empire from 1453.

According to budgetary records from 1321, Andronicus's military finances only tallied in total to 1,000,000 *hyperpyra*, the lowest periodic evaluations of

---

[2319]  Norwich, *(DF)*, 260-261.

[2320]  Ostrogorsky, 487.

[2321]  Vasiliev, 664-665.

this type in Byzantine history.[2322] As the *hyperpyra* was only a fraction of the *nomisma,* and half the worth of the Venetian *ducat* as the new international standard of currency, the financial situation was grim indeed. The imperial bodyguard drastically shrank and the cost of fodder and uniforms inflated to the point that local militias also shrank as the use of mercenary resources grew. The standing army of the Byzantines cost half the annual budget for 1321 as an example and the remainder was unfortunately earmarked for private entertainments, tribute to foreign powers, and the upkeep of a declining court.

Andronicus II's financial policies were stale, overused band-aids to pay for the large mercenary forces to fight the foreign and civil wars he facilitated while controlling the devastation his victorious enemies inflicted. What most damaged his reputation was the hatred the citizens of Constantinople had for their monarch and the riots of the City during the civil wars. Furthermore, food was at extravagant prices and unavailable to a people 'bled white by taxation', so the threat of famine hung in the air and empty cooking pots meant the worst kind of retribution by the *ochlocracy*. This intensified in 1317 as the *Basileus* promulgated his Novel XXVIII stating:[2323]

1) Put a heavy excise tax on consumable commodities in the City, contributing to high food prices and mass starvation to the poor. (Further contributing, in Pachymeres's history, was the *sitokrithon* tax of the rural laborers that six *modi* of wheat and four of barley per landholding household be extracted, adding more burden to the poor).[2324]

2) Taxed weights and measures in trade were now the burden of the consumer, limiting their consumption and purchasing power.

3) The issuing of a license tax to the sea and land merchants in the City for the exercise of their specialty, discouraging such trade within the City and better trade in peripheral cities from an already decentralizing Empire away from Constantinople.

Meanwhile, the fragile structure of the rural population was facing similar problems as the rampant corruption of misappropriation and tax evasion

---

[2322] Treadgold, 842-843.

[2323] Andreades, Andre M. 'Public Finances: Currency, Public Expenditure, Budget, Public Revenue'. *Byzantium: An Introduction to East Roman Civilization,* ed. by N.H. Baynes & H.St.L.B. Moss. Oxford, UK: Oxford University Press, 71-85. 1969, 83.

[2324] Ostrogorsky, 485.

bankrupted the peasantry and the pronoia landholders. This rippled somewhat to the estates to the effect that they once again held control over the small landholders who were bound by hereditary financial and military obligations in government pronoia grants. Yet, the rich estates felt a pinch in the loss of peasant revenue as well as the 'land tax' and other increased taxation from Constantinople as well as the closing of certain tax privileges. Such specific obligations were an indication that the older system was a transition into a system outside the experiences of the Byzantine administration.[2325]

These were all to make hasty and radical military reforms of naval and land power that still stood as a sign of contempt from the non-Byzantine world. His foreign and peripheral trade advantages were few, but Andronicus II managed to re-Byzantinize the feudal system of the Peloponnese when John Cantacuzenus defeated the Serbian King and claimed it for the Morea in 1314. The advantage was the seaport of Menemvasia, a strategic trade post in the Morea that strengthened merchant ties in the Peloponnese to compete with the Venetians in the Black Sea.[2326] This was all based on the binding *Chrysobulls* Andronicus renewed in 1284 made from his father around 1261. Russian allies were still cultivated by the *Basileus* as Ivan of Moscow was entitled 'steward of the imperial table' and paid special homages to the *Basileus* in Constantinople.[2327] This transmission of Russo-Byzantine relations in the thirteenth and fourteenth centuries was one intended to offset the Mongol threat in the Crimea.

Declines now erupted in the matters of finance, administration, military prowess, and the state of the international currency. So scholars and courtiers such as George Pachymeres, Theodore Metochiates, and Nicholas Gregoras maintained the necessities that Constantinople continue its status as a thriving intellectual center for the world. Hellenization spread to all the foreign courts of the East, including the blossoming Serbian national culture in the pivotal Dushan regime. In the 1320's, education and cultivation was at a high and the aristocrats, rich bureaucrats, and the clergy of the Empire controlled their own 'salons' of intellectual discourse, the most known founder of one being Nicholas Gregoras.[2328]

With substantial patronage from such elites as the Patriarch John XIII Glycus and Theodore Metochiates the Grand Domestic, Andronicus II, as a

---

[2325] Ostrogorsky, 482-485.

[2326] *ibid.*, 497.

[2327] Obolensky, 265.

[2328] Sevcenko, Ihor. 'Palaiologan Learning.' *The Oxford History of Byzantium*, ed. by Cyril Mango. Oxford, UK: Oxford University Press, 284-293. 2002, 285.

lover of learning and a highly educated man, ran the most respected center of learning at his Monastery of St. Chora in the City, restored by 1320 by Metochiates. Within it is housed the *Paraccleison* ('Mortuary Chapel'), created in 1310, covered with frescoes and paintings of the death and Resurrection of Christ. Most important in this collection of the Chora is the *Anastasis* wherein a risen Christ descends into Hell to free Adam and Eve, shattering its Gates and binding Satan before his feet,[2329] thus the Lord's victory over death as a deliverance of mankind from the damnation of Original Sin. Manuscripts of the Classics maintained here can still be found in Istanbul, Oxford, Venice, the Vatican, and Paris.

Along with Metochiates and Gregoras were notable Classicists and intellectuals such as Demetrius Triclinios (1280-1340) and his manuscript of the sixth-century BCE *Works and Days* by Hesiod (fl. 700BCE) written on August 20, 1316. Maximus Plenudes was an especially prolific contributor with his Greek Anthology of epigrams ('Planudean') of 1301 that was the standard until the nineteenth-century as well as his translated Plutarch. Along with other scholars there were the metric systems of Pindar and the discovery of scientific works such as Ptolemy's *Geographica*. Within the liberal arts, editions of the tragedies of Sophocles, Euripedes, the author Theocritus, and the greatest of comic artists, Aristophanes, appeared. In a reflection of the morals and manners of Byzantine culture, those entries considered 'indecent' (mostly that of homosexual content) were expurgated by Church and state.[2330]

The intractable tradition of Greek oratory on all matters human and divine appeared in Metochiates's critical essays on Demosthenes (as a lover of democracy) and Aristedes (as a lover of monarchy) as others included Lucian (120-192 CE) and Libanius (314-394 CE). As the Latin classics were not forgotten by those who were still the Romans of the East, Ovid, Cicero, Microbius (370-430 CE) and other Pagan Roman writers were included. Pagan classicism was of special interests, but the Classics of the Christians and Fathers were re-vitalized for the pious. The Cappadocian Fathers, Gregory of Nazianus, St. Basil, Christian analogues and apologies, St. Augustine, and Boethius's *Consolation of Philosophy* would be translated and cultivated.

In the realms of the sciences, mathematics was introduced mainly by Plenudes and important treatises on medicine and astronomy were applied. Astronomy was of interest mainly because of the international intellectual

---

[2329] Ostrogorsky, fig. 65, 66.
[2330] Sevcenko, 'Palaiologan Learning', 287.

implications it introduced, most important works being classical Arabic written in the earliest times of Islam. Ptolemaic subjects on astronomy were namely in the hands of Persian astronomers found in the Mongol Kingdoms, reaching Greek scholars in 1300 and a lineage of this scholarship began from Constantinople to Trebizond by such men as George-Gregory Chioniades (1240-1320). Theodore Metochiates, as an exceptional astronomer, was a respected man of learning to the Turks, so after the Conquest of 1453 mosaics were made of him wearing a caftan and other Turkish wear offering the Monastery of Chora to Christ. Furthermore, medical texts were valuable to the Monastery of Petra as it included the Hospital of Kral donated by Stephen II Milutin.

A caveat to the scholar is that, such as the 'renaissance' of the Macedonians, this upsurge of Classical learning is only a Paleologan 'renassaince' in a loose sense. It is only comparable to the Italian Renaissance in the discovery of Classical material and learning, yet once again to be noted that no new knowledge and applications to facilitate a more modernized society were present or original works too prevalent such as Metochiotes's *Introduction to Astronomy*. However, it was the gathering of these ancient texts that made the lives of those who did modernize easier throughout Western Europe, being a great boon and a service that we owe some gratitude to the patronage of Andronicus II, but mostly to the brilliance of his brain trust.

Finally, in a strange twist on the culture of the times, the notoriously brutal and uncivilized Catalans contributed somewhat to a positive atmosphere of learning aside from the terror they instigated. In the Catalan Duchy of Athens, not much material sources remain at all of the governance of this territory under Spanish rule besides fortifications in the north,[2331] but the Catalans were inspired by the Greek Classical city and showed it appreciation. As the ancient Acropolis overseeing all Athens, which was called the *Castell de Cetines,* was re-fortified and for the first time since Justinian I's closing of the Academy, a university was opened in Athens. Only the invasion of the Navarrese in 1379 ended Catalan dominion in Greece, losing it for centuries in Greek and Spanish history.

## ANDRONICUS III PALEOLOGUS 'THE YOUNGER'
### (1328-1341)

Despite Byzantine Anatolia's diminished size, there existed fertile land in the south with its military resources on a steady course of reform, yet the

---

[2331] Vasiliev, 607-608.

excesses and mistakes of Andronicus II left the Empire in a downward spiral. Change, even drastic change, was needed without being too rash, and it would take a steady and careful *Basileus* to even out the problems Byzantium faced in all areas of its own future to remain a viable power in the East. As seen during his rise to the throne, Andronicus III Paleologus demonstrated clarity in his goals, stable popularity, and successful achievements in his endeavors (with the vital aid of his commander, John Cantacuzenus). Now that he was on the throne, he would begin to dispel any doubts that he could competently handle his responsibilities and even exceed everyone's expectations. Andronicus would be seen as the last in the Paleologan dynasty to see the Empire truly profit before its extinction in 1453.

This great-grandson of Michael VIII Paleologus, grandson of Andronicus II, and son of Michael IX was born on March 25, 1297, carrying both a quarter-Hungarian and half-Armenian heritage along with his Greek[2332] to be made co-emperor in February of 1316. Despite this pedigree, his legitimacy would be questioned by his grandfather, leading to a rare bloodless coup in 1328 after a series of bloody battles in the first Byzantine civil war of the century. He had the inordinate and typical passions for a prince: womanizing (which started the events of the civil war in Byzantium), drinking, jousting,[2333] hunting with his 1,000 huntsmen, 1,000 hounds, and 1,000 falcons[2334] 'and as he was touched with remorse, fatigued by business, or deceived with negotiation; pleasure rather than power was his aim.' He also ran up outrageous gambling debts in the Genoese Galata and ignored the German lady he was given as a wife in 1317 for his trysts. But these habits could put aside for his intelligence and handsomeness once he gained the throne, improving his reputation as Basil II had done in his younger years, although with much less austerity.

He had natural charm, good looks, and a charisma far outshining the mediocrity of his senior *Basileus*, winning him the acclaim of the new generation of estate holders, senators, and young bureaucrats. But, his true talent was his ability in delegating authority to the right agents, especially military leadership. His legitimacy as a Roman *Basileus* of Constantinople was coupled and strengthened by a psychological advantage in the victory of

---

[2332] Treadgold, 760. This only proves a lack of Byzantine noble ladies in his father's time or a desperate need for foreign alliances as Michael had been rebuked by a Latin princess of Constantinople.

[2333] This was brought back into fashion by Andronicus's second wife, Anna, the daughter of the Count of Savoy, Amadeus V, Norwich, *(DF)*, 281.

[2334] Gibbon, 2196.

Adrianople on Easter Sunday, 1321.[2335] Here, the older *Basileus* capitulated to the inevitability that would become clear on May 24, 1328 when his grandson, emboldened by the City itself and the imposing character of John Cantacuzenus deposing him, humiliated him with their pity and enough empty privileges to take the cowl.

At the start of his reign, the Younger Andronicus began involvement in the internal policies of eliminating judicial and administrative corruption, with mixed results, but still being forced to turn towards the Turkish opposition in 1329. Leading 4,000 troops, he intended to raise sieges at Nicaea and Nicomedia across the Bosporus, but failed to establish a position. Orhan split his forces to attack on the first day and the rest, refreshed against an exhausted Greek army, forced the *Basileus* into a retreat.[2336] At the city of Pelakenum, the Ottomans brutalized the Greek forces with volleys of Turkish archers, injuring Andronicus as well. Immediate retreat was in order and as rumors of Andronicus's wounds and possible death set the army at a panic, Cantacuzenus was forced to ferry the remaining forces back to the City.

These almost certainly exaggerated rumors on Andronicus III's status and his defeat had more lasting consequences as the Genoese took advantage and seized Chios from the Empire. Underestimating the new *Basileus*, they were turned aside and made to flee when Andronicus seized it back. The *Basileus* received suzerainty thereafter in New Phocaea which housed a piece of the True Cross and a shirt worn by St. John made by the Virgin. Andronicus began making peace with the local Turkish Emirs in the area to buffer the Italian Republics as the Ottoman naval powers were growing. He allied with the Emir of Aydin, Umur, whom he later would have a long and warm friendship with Cantacuzenus, cementing a lasting and loyal alliance.

The *Basileus* could not control the fact his back was turned on his enemies and neighbors, so the Serbians seized opportunity in 1330 when Andronicus was elsewhere. The ambitions of this once obscure Slavic state of Serbia in Macedonia as well as the Bulgarian Empire in Thrace was not much less than the creation of a new Slavic Empire running from Constantinople.[2337] This was also the aims of Orhan and the Ottomans, which would be realized in the fifteenth century, of not only a Turco-Slavic, but Greco-Turkic-Slavic Empire in

---

[2335] Ostrogorsky, 500.
[2336] Norwich, *(DF)*, 285.
[2337] Norwich, *(DF)*, 283.

the East controlling the Serbs and Bulgars.[2338] It was as if there was a new race to Constantinople's throne without the once unavoidable interference of the West.

Serbia, under the auspices of the legendary Stephen III Dushan, who became King in 1331, besieged the Bulgarian Patriarchate of Ochrid, killing the Tsar Shishman who had retaliated in battle. Andronicus III was wise enough to see the Bulgarians were in a dangerous state of chaos, so he took the opportunity to recover the contested border cities of Mesembria and Anchialus for the Empire. In 1332, the two cities would be turned over again to the Bulgarians and Andronicus, at a draw in the north, turned east to Asia and the hostile Turks. Dushan himself would become an idol of Serbian nationalism, a founding father, whose realm would reach the Danubian to the Adriatic and Aegean coasts utilizing Byzantine administrative methods with the appointment of Greek Archons. Their strength in the Balkans became commonly known to the Venetians, for example, as they would rather ally with the Byzantines, whom they could dominate, than the Serbians with whom they would have much less success.[2339] This was an instance of the Byzantine Empire's weakness allowing it to be the lesser of two evils in any such a position to its enemies.

Once again, the worst difficulty in the Paleologan dynasty appeared as Byzantium needed, but could not count on, trustworthy allies. An answer to these problems seemed to present itself in a Holy League against the Turks in a possible Crusade between the Pope, Venice, and the Knights Templar of Rhodes. This was a grand opportunity for the *Basileus* to ally himself with strong Western powers against his Ottoman enemies, but Pope John XXII refused Byzantine alliance, knowing Andronicus's allegiance with Turkish rulers such as Aydin. Indeed, this caused in the *Basileus* a conflict of interest and conscience as Aydin was a faithful ally, yet an enemy of Christendom and Rome.[2340] A crisis of choice was the result when considering the frustration of any healing of the Schism: Andronicus III welcomed any prospect of Union while refusing to make Michael VIII's mistakes of ignoring hierarchy and splitting the Church.

Andronicus, this time, chose the lesser of two evils and treated with the Ottoman Emir Orhan, son of Osman, in 1333 for a ransom of a modest 12,000 *hyperpyra* for Nicomedia, proving the Byzantine proverb that it was better to deal with a 'Turkish turban rather than a Papal tiara'. A peace of Byzantine and

---

[2338]  Vasiliev, 603.

[2339]  Ostrogorsky, 524-525.

[2340]  Treadgold, 762.

Ottoman was not so unthinkable when the evidence of Roman influence on the Turks is weighed fairly. Beginning with the conquest of Prusa, seized Byzantine territories were allowed their former practices of Christian professionals handling land assessments, property rights, and taxation.[2341] This would prove a superior system than the Ottoman court structure of harem politics that led to competition and the instabilities of succession, where one Sultan resided over all and fratricidal murder was more common than in the Greek world.[2342]

But, Orhan was shrewd in the taking of Prusa, he showed great magnanimity to his prisoners: Christians were allowed to leave if they wished with their icons intact, no reprisals were made against the defenders, and Islam was not forced on the Christians remaining there. This tolerance made him popular and widened the gulf between Byzantine and Ottoman rule over the Greeks. A Turkish cross-culture also existed wherein those who were failing in their endeavors in the Empire were moving to the Anatolian villages as a new 'land of opportunity' that enjoyed Orhan's freedoms and the prosperity of the fiefs of Ottoman military commanders.[2343]

It has been recognized that kingdoms are kept servile if customs and taxes are not mishandled early in a new reign by a ruler. In Renaissance Italy, this was slightly easier than in the Middle Ages as all involved followed the Catholic faith, but in the Medieval East, servility usually required the *laissez-faire* freedom of religions by its rulers as well. With the faith of Mohammed literally next to that of Christ's, tolerance to Christianity is what won the Ottomans their Greek subjects' approval. Thus began one of the key concepts in the social history of the origins of the Ottoman takeover of the Byzantine Empire. The capital of Prusa further offered a unique civilization under Orhan as it was outfitted with not just a mosque, but a university as well and a new coinage struck bearing the Seljuk rulers as 'the most skillful of human and divine knowledge attracted the Persian and Arabic students from the ancient schools of Oriental learning.'[2344]

The ruler of Thessaly having died, the deposed Nicolas's brother John Orsini and Thessalonica raced to the Thessalian Duchy only to be rebuffed by a faster Andronicus III who also held a claim to the territory as a Paleologus. He defeated the Orsini garrisons and expelled the westerners from Thessaly all the way back to the former Catalan Duchy of Athens, which was also recovered

---

[2341] Herrin, 283-284.

[2342] *ibid.*, 316.

[2343] Reinert, 'Fragmentation (1204-1453)', 268.

[2344] Gibbon, 2229.

for the Byzantine Empire. The victory would be hollowed, however, by the advances of Serbia aided by a Byzantine traitor and cousin of the *Basileus*, Syregennius Paleologus, on Macedonian Prilep, Sturmica, Vodena, Ochrid, and Castoria under Dushan.[2345] A settlement was made with the *Basileus* and Castoria was returned in exchange for a Serbian-occupied Ochrid, Pilep, and Sturmica.

Ochrid had been the true goal for a year as it was a key city in the Bulgarian Empire, so a question surfaces: Did Dushan manipulate Constantinople by ceding Castoria, a city of lesser concern for the prize they wanted? Whether this was so or not, Andronicus needed allies in the north to offset Bulgaria and the Bosporus Turks with limited resources, so Ochrid was a foregone conclusion. Upper Macedonia was to be the future of the Serbian state and it would thereafter be the master of the Balkan Peninsula beyond the grasp of Byzantium forever,[2346] also balancing Bulgarian power under Stephen Dushan as the King (*Kral*), or the *rex iuvenis*.

The next year, the Holy League defeated the Aydin Emirate without Byzantine aid and the Phocaean Genoese responded by invading Chios and Lesbos. Further shocking the League, Andronicus III laid waste to Galata's walls, allying with the navies of Umur, chasing the Genoese away from the Aegean Islands. This was completely necessary for Constantinople's harmony as Galata had now become an Italian 'state within a state' by Andronicus III's ascension and would only magnify after his death as no peace with the Republics were possible.[2347] But, in the distant Successor State of Trebizond in northern Asia, Andronicus needed to strengthen his blood ties and married a bastard daughter to the Successor Emperor Basil Comnenus in 1335. Less stability was found in Epirus, however, as its Emperor's mother Anna poisoned her husband, John Orsini, in 1337 to become a regent under her ruling son, Nicephorus. In response, Andronicus and Cantacuzenus arrived in Epirus's capital of Arta to assert suzerainty and were gladly given it by an intimidated and hospitable Anna Paleologa.

However, a faction of the court of Trebizond abducted the child Nicephorus to Italy in a plot perpetrated by Charles of Valois's sister, Catherine, a Latin claimant to both Constantinople and Epirus through the deposed Emperor Baldwin II. In 1339, Catherine fomented revolt in Epirus to be led by

---

[2345] Ostrogorsky, 506.

[2346] Vasiliev, 612-613.

[2347] *Ibid.*, 616.

Nicephorus in the Valois name, but this was suppressed by Cantacuzenus, who captured Arta and returned to the City with Nicephorus in triumph, thwarting Valois's dynastic plans by marrying Nicephorus to his daughter, Anna. This was seen as a true victory between the Greeks and the residing Latins and a stable peace brought on by this satisfaction would result.[2348] A total reincorporation of the Byzantine splinter 'Empires' was now achieved after 135 years and contemporary historians present for this victory praised the loudest.[2349]

In Trebizond, the now widowed Irene, as daughter of the *Basileus*, appealed to her father to take suzerainty into the Empire the Peloponnesian vassal authorities, rebuffing Catherine of Valois as lord, offering even the Catalan Duchy of Athens if need be, and Andronicus gladly accepted. This all gave Byzantium a tractable hold in the Balkans with no Latin rivalry. The small principalities and autonomous mountain tribes of the Albanians were also a problem with their rebellions in 1335, existing since the second century BCE in the geographies of Ptolemy. Descendants of the Illyrians, a people known for controlling the Eastern Roman throne as Anastasius I (491-518 CE) and Justinian the Great (527-565 CE), in Greek, they were *Albanoi, Arbanoi,* and *Albanitai;* in Latin, *Albanenses* and *Arbanenses,* while in Turkish *Arnaut.* They lacked fixed governmental leadership and were known as the citizens and inhabitants of the Latin Empire, the Second Bulgarian Empire, the Despotate of Epirus, the Nicaean Empire of John III Vatatzes, Charles of Anjou, and now, Stephen III Dushan.[2350]

They managed to crush the 4,000 Turkish mercenaries of Umur of Aydin and his trustworthy ally, John Cantacuzenus. The leader of Aydin's forces was the Umur Pasha, 'The Lion of God', whose talents won him fame in the Turkish poetry of the 1460's by Enver in his *Destan of Umur Pasha* made more so by his harassing Christianity across the East and his hatred of Genoa.[2351] These accomplishments commenced during the rule of Andronicus III and his reign would benefit the best from it, despite further debasing of the *hyperpyra.*

---

[2348] Treadgold, 763.

[2349] John VI Cantacuzenus. *Historiae, 3 vol.,* ed. by L. Schopen. *CSHB,* Bonn, Ger., vol. I. 1838, 504.

[2350] Nicol, Donald M. *The Last Centuries of Byzantium, 1261-1453, 2nd ed.* Cambridge, UK: Cambridge University Press. 1972, 143. They also colonized the Greek Peloponnese at this time, changing permanently the ethnological population of the region.

[2351] Norwich, *(DF),* 288.

The partnership of Paleologus and John Cantacuzenus would add glory to its implementation.

In June, 1341, Andronicus had attended an emergency Church Council in the Peloponnesus to decide on the question of Hysechasm, now made a heresy, when he complained of bodily exhaustion upon returning to the City. Retiring to the Monastery of the Hodegon by St. Sophia on the Sea Walls, the *Basileus* suddenly caught a fever, just to die a few days later on June 15. Such was the sudden death of an imperial man seen as 'hardworking...conscientious...energetic' in an Empire nearly doomed; but unfortunately, Andronicus did die with no clear instructions on a successor.[2352] As his son was only nine years old, this would usually cause apprehension, factions arising on all fronts, and base opportunism for the throne in the Empire. But, the Grand Domestic John Cantacuzenus was a natural choice for the regency of the child John V Paleologus and any external opposition to this was mainly silent.

Despite the optimism Byzantium could have for such a healthy, charismatic commander whose victory made him a protector of the Empire continuing the Paleologan line, caution was best exercised. Jealousy and corruption would only cause another civil war, cause another coup, ultimately to end in one of the most unstable rules in Byzantine history in fifty years. However, one result was the continuation of the achieved diplomacy and statesmanship of Paleologus to Cantacuzenus, the latter said to be inspired by the former *Basileus*'s as well as the real power behind the throne. This phenomena would save the Empire for a few decades, but it was still clear the Empire lacked the strength to retain [Andronicus III's] gains for any amount of time.[2353]

Beginning in 1341, the Hesychast Controversy resurfaced in the Church as an ascetic, Gregory of Sinai, miraculously saw the non-created divine light of the Transfiguration of Jesus Christ on Mount Tabor. This was specifically done by a ritual of meditation by the 'lowering of the chin to the chest, fixing the eyes on the navel, the regulation of breathing and the unceasing repetition of the Lord's Prayer: "Lord Jesus Christ Son of God, have mercy on me."'[2354] The official leader of the movement, a Calabrian monk named Barlaam, would travel to Rome in an embassy before Pope Benedict XII on behalf of this ascetic and the appeal for a Union as 'The ways of union were twofold, force and persuasion. Of force, the inefficacy had already been tried; since the Latins

---

[2352] Norwich, *(DF)*, 292.

[2353] Ostrogorsky, 509.

[2354] Norwich, *(DF)*, 291.

subdued the Empire, without subduing the minds, of the Greeks.'[2355] Rome had been skeptical and suspicious of Constantinople's reigning in of the Muslim tide in Anatolia, yet Barlaam's gifts of diplomacy offered a pledge to demonstrate the Greeks' sincerity with rationality:

1) Only a Synod of Rome, Constantinople, Alexandria, Jerusalem, and Antioch can validate a Union and a Western army would be allowed by the Empire to free these cities from Turkish occupation.

2) Charitable acts of 'brotherly love' must be bestowed by Rome upon the Greeks to bring acceptance and authority to the Pope, the *Basileus*, and participants in the Union.

3) Despite the differences in ceremonies and rituals, as Rome and Constantinople are both Christian, the French armies available must commit to the fact that the Muslims were the common enemy and no Christian was to be subdued.

4) If the Byzantines were oppressed by Rome or France as 'schismatics, heretics, or Pagans', the pact with the West may still be honored as the guardians 'of Europe' as an ally to a sinking Empire and not as an oppressor threatening Byzantium's freedoms [as was done in 1204].

Barlaam's main supporter was John Cantacuzenus, who had given him a teaching post in the University of Constantinople. This association between a 'heresy' and the Grand Domestic, as well as such apologies as Gregory Palamas (1296-1359)'s *Triads in Defense of the Holy Hesychasts* spurred the Orthodox clergy to rally for a Church Council to decide the future of the sect. On June 10, 1341, in the course of a single day, the Council took place under Andronicus III (who would die after returning to the City) as the hesychasts won a victory, but the Orthodox complained how the Council was rigged and that Barlaam should be disgraced back to Calabria. The surprising response was that Barlaam, disillusioned with Orthodoxy, apostatized to Italy to accept the Papal blessings as a member of the Church of Rome and Catholic Bishop of his native Calabria.

One of the most optimistic ideas of reform since the start of Andronicus III's reign was the supplanting of corrupt officials for ones that would return imperial centralization to judicial, tax, and administrative institutions to Constantinople. Andronicus reformed and added onto the work of his grandfather as when Andronicus II re-organized the justice system in

---

[2355] Gibbon, 2273.

Constantinople by implementing a 'Supreme Court' consisting of twelve justices chosen from the senatorial, ecclesiastical, and lay classes.[2356] The results were disappointing as a quagmire of political corruption in defining Byzantine bureaucracy and institutional authority were too much to keep the system from bribery and selling verdicts.

In 1329, Andronicus III attempted to improve on this by restricting the number of justices to four, two ecclesiastical and two laymen, as the 'Supreme Justices of the Romans' (*Katholikoi Kritai ton Romaion*). Again, the ethics of the court fell below par and it was discredited. What was strange was the appeal that the court could be compacted into the decision of only one Justice speaking for all of the Four when the others were not present in the provinces – a duty for which the *Basileus* himself or the governors were supposedly responsible. This, however, was the consequences of centralizing Roman law as legal authority is given to oversee provincial governments when attempting practices of exclusion from the imperial process.

This spread to Thessalonica, Morea, Lemnos, and Serbian Serres, resulting in the choosing of local chief justices and courts. However, the inability of Andronicus III to enforce actions for numerous reasons of state resulted only in frustrating the reforms, corruption, and disgrace again proliferating. In 1337, three out of the four justices were dismissed and exiled for accepting bribes,[2357] nonetheless, this legal institution outlived the Empire itself. The Church also benefited from Andronicus's reforms by the allowance of a Patriarchal Court of Justices on canon law made of local clerics in Constantinople.

Another glaring problem came from the disintegrating economic and mercantile debacle Andronicus II left for his grandson and even into John V's reign, including monetary competition with the Florentine and Venetian coins as the most stable on the market.[2358] The Genoese of the Galatan ports and suburbs dominated trade to the City with custom officials making in excess of 200,000 *hyperpyra* annually and the Byzantine customs income barely making 30,000.[2359] Added to this was the rapidly shrinking worth of the *hyperpyra* itself, inflating prices and yielding to the *ducat*. This revenue had gone from a smaller part of the budget under Andronicus II to a mere fraction of any

---

[2356] Ostrogorsky, 503-504.

[2357] Norwich, (DF), 282.

[2358] Vasiliev, 686.

[2359] Gregoras, 842. He would even comment that the Byzantine coin's worth shrank daily.

receipts collected by Andronicus III.[2360] Now the steady decline of Byzantium's economy truly began to bankrupt the Empire, eventually rolling downhill to the insufficient funding leading to a besieged Constantinople of 1453.

# JOHN V PALEOLOGUS
## (1341-1376, 1379-1391)

Andronicus III had been a beacon of hope, if somewhat dimmed by his circumstances, and if any recovery of the Empire were possible it would only be if his successor had his good qualities and none of his weaknesses. Andronicus III's son John attempted to be this type of successor, but lacked diplomacy and a reasonable head for leadership, being a disappointment for his nobles that valued his 'regent' Cantacuzenus as a more fitting *Basileus*. Indeed, John V's greatest deficiency was in diplomatic relations, only judging correctly the obvious fact that Greeks and Turks could not live in the Empire peacefully.[2361] Expertise was needed to deal with the external difficulties of the times – encroaching and engulfing Turks, the rise of Serbia and the stability of Bulgaria, both ambitions and apathy in the West, and the unpredictable hazard of the Italian Republics colonizing the Greek East and the Black Sea.

His main hindrances were basically not being intelligent or far-sighted enough, being craven, passively obedient, and having no qualities at all that a statesman needed. No other *Basileus* needed rescuing twice in Constantinople due to duplicity by both a son and a grandson, once as he was in Bulgaria and once more in Venice.[2362] John's character would also prove to be weak and morally base as lust was his primal passion as he lost himself, during crises, in his Greek and Turkish slaves he kept to 'forget the dishonor of the Emperor of the Romans.'[2363] Added to this, in 1348, was the Black Death that ravaged all of Europe and had significant repercussions on all nations and their futures. These only overwhelmed John V and would lead to a Second Civil War, making recovery and re-conquest impossible, made worse by the fact he lived too long with his fifty-year reign.

Born in November, 1332, John V Paleologus was five years old at the time of his coronation as co-emperor by his father Andronicus III and his Western

---

[2360] Ostrogorsky, 526.
[2361] Norwich, *(DF)*, 325.
[2362] *ibid.*, 347-348.
[2363] Gibbon, 2238-2239.

mother, Anne of Savoy. It is suggested that during a serious illness in 1330, Andronicus had made John Cantacuzenus John's regent, but this was never fully validated as the *Basilia* was not yet expecting and it is assumed no regent was assigned.[2364] Although it is still possible he was made a successor if no heir was produced or a regent for a future heir when was born. Cantacuzenus himself was away from Constantinople after the *Basileus*'s death to secure the Turco-Greek and Bulgarian fronts, when the Grand Duke Alexius Apocaucus made a power bid for the regency. In fact, Apocaucus was the lead in a party of triad alliances between himself, the *Basilia* Anne, and the Patriarch John XIV Calecus. Unfortunately, civil war was the only possible result from Cantacuzenus's rise and he was immediately excommunicated by the Patriarch as soon as he was awarded regency.[2365]

A representation of Apocaucus from a 1345 Parisian miniature, now in the Bibliotheque Nationale, shows a robust Grand Duke on the throne while a small child, John V, merely stands in the background as if awaiting his regent's pleasure. Depictions of John V made from his later years as sole *Basileus*, such as a watercolor printed from mosaics in St. Sophia in 1847 or 1849 by Fossati at the Dumbarton Oaks Collection in Washington DC, also exist. Later in 1345, an attempt by the Duke to abduct the child-emperor was quickly thwarted by Cantacuzenus and Apocaucus was imprisoned, only to be released by the *Basilia*'s persuasive pleas to the regent.

Not to be humbled, Apocaucus made war with Cantacuzenus in the City and destroyed his property and personal possessions within the Walls, denouncing him as a traitor and a usurper using young John as a puppet. This seemingly ignited a powder keg of class warfare involving the extremist Zealots who rose up against wealthy Unionists and landholders also supporting Apocaucus as regent for his Orthodoxy. In the infighting, division of the aristocracy was inevitable and Adrianople supported Cantacuzenus as a legitimate regent who then shielded him. Meanwhile, Apocaucus was cementing his legitimacy with acts of executive leadership such as brazenly installing John III Comnenus of Trebizond after the death of his predecessor, Michael II.

A civil transaction for Cantacuzenus to be regent looked bleak as he was pushed to the East, gathering his own Turkish and Christian Greco-Serbian allies that were fighting back by 1343. Desperate for Western aid as a princess of Savoy and a close relative of Amadeus V, Anne agreed to put in hock the Crown

---

[2364] Treadgold, 764.
[2365] Norwich, *(DF)*, 296.

Jewels of Byzantium themselves to Venice for a token of 30,000 *ducats* (65,000 *hyperpyra*).[2366] This appropriation was for a Holy League with Rome to start a new Crusade in expelling the Ottomans from Asia Minor. Though she was probably just lying desperately to buy time and resources, she even promised Pope Clement VI the conversion of the Patriarch of Constantinople to the Catholic Church![2367] It is with this collateral of the Crown Jewels for a loan that began the despoliation of Byzantine splendor. This was the last bastion of the imperial dignity as observers would now witness not the jewels of the crown but hunks of glass. The cloth-of-gold of the imperial robes were now merely tinsel, the once-lush brocade was just painted leather, and the gold and silver dining plate were now copper.[2368]

The regency's situation continued to decline as Apocaucus's forces could not overcome Cantacuzenus, the former Domestic gathering his strength of numbers to compensate for the Turkish allies of Umur which had been defeated in Smyrna by the Holy League in 1344. Apocaucus was desperately forced to turn inward and began a persecution of Cantacuzenist partisans and sympathizing Hesychasts, including Gregory Palamas himself. The devolving labor situation, meanwhile, in the urban Empire would be that the disenfranchised poor boiled to the point that division was made easy for Apocaucus's unexpected assassination. Done by workers during a routine inspection of a Constantinopolitan factory on June 11, 1345, he was bludgeoned, decapitated, and his head was displayed on a spike on the building's wall. Apocaucus loyalists in the city of Serres would also fold under the pressure of Cantacuzenus's ally Stephen Dushan of Serbia and only Constantinople and Thessalonica stayed purely Paleologan loyalists.

The remaining regents, the *Basilia* Anne and Patriarch John XIV, were not as energetic and talented in uniting the local resources needed for a unified government as John was. Only the Hesychast-detesting Zealots kept Cantacuzenus and his allies (including Apocaucus's son, Manuel of Adrianople) from entering the City. The power of the monastic Zealots which had moved towards Roman Union dissolved and they joined the Paleologan party, naming themselves 'Legitimists' to scorn Cantacuzenus.[2369] A new crisis hit the next year as Dushan ambitiously crowned himself as 'Emperor of the Serbians and

---

[2366] Treadgold, 768.
[2367] Norwich, *(DF)*, 300.
[2368] Sherrard, 166.
[2369] Vasiliev, 663-664.

the Romans' by a Serbian Archbishop. The same was applied by the Serbia-opposing Alexandria of Bulgaria with Dushan as 'Emperor of the Bulgarians and Greeks' to contend with Byzantium. This gave the fourteen-year-old legitimate heir John V Paleologus some respite, but a new contender arose as Cantacuzenus crowned himself co-emperor at Adrianople as John VI by the Archbishop of Jerusalem.

But, John VI Cantacuzenus showed Constantinople magnanimity, as aspiring a role only a colleague of John V might be.[2370] *Basilia* Anne, however, considered this as a desperate situation and the new co-emperor as a direct threat to her son. Upon John VI's move towards Constantinople, Anna hired 6,000 Ottoman mercenaries from Surhan to besiege Thrace and Selymbria, but lacking proper compensation, the royal Byzantine troops defected to Cantacuzenus over a Christian confederate of the Holy League.[2371] By early 1347, Anne had decided that acceptance of the changing situation was the better option and she deposed John Celacas as Patriarch. Apparently that same night, Cantacuzenus led a secret mission to the City and dug under its Walls as, with only 1,000 men, John VI held a bloodless coup to be crowned *Basileus* by the exhausted regency.

An agreement was brokered wherein John Cantacuzenus would be senior *Basileus* for John V until his maturity (supposedly ten more years), after which they would rule jointly. Furthermore, the younger John would marry Helena, daughter of Cantacuzenus. Ironically, despite the attempts at deposing him and the alliances John Paleologus would conspire against this usurper, Cantacuzenus would not reign long enough to see the ten years needed for his 'colleague' to become mature. Fortunately for the Empire, civil war would be delayed as the factions of both *Basilii* were ready to reconcile, excluding the non-compromising Zealots. Yet, the Empire still continued to shrink under the vassalage of powerful foreign nations and Cantacuzenus would make it quite clear that the teen-aged John V would only be an afterthought next to his own family and faith, civil war being imminent.

Yet before this, in 1347, the first lingering in the Byzantine East of the bubonic plague, the infamous Black Death, was appearing from the Crimean region and was to become one of the worst natural disasters in world history. As explained in the chapter of Justinian I, fleas carried on the backs of rats

---

[2370] Treadgold, 770.

[2371] Though any assumption they did so with any Turkish nationalist sentiment in mind is questionable.

were responsible for the first transmissions, but the spread of the rats to human populations were the primary cause of breakouts. Starting in North Chinese epidemics from 1351 to 1362, nine out of ten of the inhabitants of this region would die as a result.[2372] The travel to Central Eurasia by settlers and merchants saw it spread to a Mongol army, besieging Genoese Caffa in the Crimea. It had already spread west to Manchuria and the Gobi Desert, now afflicting the Mediterranean to Trebizond and Byzantium, killing one-third of Europe's population as well as Byzantium's. This would not be an isolated incident in the East either, as between the 1360's and 1420's there would be recorded eight outbreaks of the plague in places such as Cairo as well as Byzantium.[2373]

It is a popular belief now that the Mongol invasions brought this plague in the time of Ghengis Khan, but this is a fallacy as this happened over a century before and the patterns of the *Pax Mongolica* of the mercantile over military causes of the transmissions negate this theory.[2374] One observation that was unfortunately true was the advantage this gave the inland imperial territories of the Ottomans, Bulgarians, and Serbians while the coastline territories of Italian and Byzantine ports, especially Constantinople's, suffered the most.[2375] This suffering critically struck at the Empire's financial, military, and economic resources, depleting them to the total mercy of their enemies after its apparent abatement by 1349.

As will be later reviewed in detail, the Cantacuzenus years of senior rule (1347-1354) were mostly a series of military defenses against intractable foreign interests, such as the Genoese and Stephen Dushan. Eventually, the legitimate and older sons of John VI would come into question, with the urges of the Cantacuzenist parties at court, to be the sole heirs of the Empire with a new dynasty, allowing the Paleologi to perish. John VI 'deputized' his sons Matthew to rule Thrace and Manuel to rule the Peloponnesus as John was to do the same at Thessalonica. Thessalonica was an especially endangered part of the Empire due to the deluge of residing Zealots and the serious class conflict of poor workers and rich nobles exploding in the region in 1350.

In 1352, at the auspicious age of twenty, John V Paleologus was persuaded, supposedly by Stephen Dushan, to finally rebel against the Cantacuzeni for sole rule, igniting a new civil war. The attitude by commentators was it had

---

[2372] Atwood, Christopher F. *The Encyclopedia of Mongolia and the Mongolian Empire.* New York, NY: Facts on File. 2004, 41; Beckwith, 195f.

[2373] Reinert, 267.

[2374] MacNeill, William H. *Plagues and Peoples.* New York, NY: Anchor Books. 1976, 147.

[2375] Treadgold, 773.

been intended as an act of justice, for John Paleologus was solely responsible for his government, his vices paling to a civil war where the 'barbarians and Infidels' assisted Greeks in their mutual destruction.[2376] This was not an instant development as Anne of Savoy then appeared in Thessalonica to take charge of the government, allowing Matthew Cantacuzenus to take residence in Adrianople with his father's 'appanage.' This was only another brief delay for a deluge that had been building for years. Months later, John V would turn on Matthew and gain Adrianople's support, keeping the young Cantacuzenus as prisoner. As John VI rushed to Thrace to aid his son, he would actively see the alliances he had made over the years crumble completely, Dushan sending 4,000 Serbians, Tsar Alexander sending Bulgarian troops, and a Venetian loan of 5,000 *ducats* having been sent to aid John Paleologus.

Whether or not it is true that a loan of 20,000 *ducats* was allotted, it can be well assumed that the Venetians were quite aware, but silent, upon the point this would not be repaid.[2377] Debt has always been the most lucrative market of all for Venice, and the island of Tenedos would make a fine reimbursement for the ineptitude of John V. Funds were also sent west to Sardinia in aiding the Aragonese King to war with the Genoese over the port of Alghero. The resulting Spanish defeat by a concerted Italian effort, however, secured for the Bosporus these Republics on August 29, 1353.

Fleeing to Tenedos, John was given protection by the Venetians, but was turned back from a failed attempt to take Constantinople in 1353, retreating back to Thessalonica. Though, technically, the legitimate *Basileus*, John VI's position saw Paleologus as a rival claimant and, therefore, a rebellious enemy of Constantinople and the Cantacuzenists. It was made known that the name of John VI was to be stricken from the prayers of the Church and public banquets and his son Matthew was to own the tongue-in-cheek title of 'higher than that of Despot and lower than the Emperor' as Michael VIII gave his son.[2378] He had to settle for a formal coronation by the deposed and exiled Patriarch Callistus I who refused to recognize Matthew Cantacuzenus as co-emperor. In November, a year later, confidence was at its lowest for Cantacuzenus when his Turkish allies dominated the imperial position by taking Callipolis, so John Paleologus took this opportunity to enter the City on November 24, 1354.

Mass riots resulted from appeals to the loyal populace by John V and the

---

[2376] Gibbon, 2205.

[2377] Norwich, *(AHV)*, 219.

[2378] Cantacuzenus, III, 33; Ostrogorsky, 530.

'Paleologanites' took the Imperial Palace with the larger Palace of Theodore Metochiates where John V resided,[2379] forcing Cantacuzenus to recognize his former ward, now age twenty-two, as co-emperor once again. Two weeks later, he lost all heart and abdicated to his junior colleague, taking the cowl as now John V Paleologus would be sole ruler of the Byzantine Empire. Cantacuzenus attempted to save from the *Basilia*'s regency with his own attempts to keep the nobles unified before multiple enemies with his shaky alliances were a tenuous situation at best. Whether or not his ascension or fall was inevitable, John's early intentions were to be as loyal to John V as he was to Andronicus III. But, in lieu of the results, 'Faced with such calamities,' pertaining to the numerous problems of the Empire and the Paleologan abilities compared to Cantacuzenus's in 1341, 'the underage John V and his vacillating mother would surely have done even worse.'[2380]

Now in sole power, John V was now able to take the burden of the Empire and its survival on his own shoulders, like the mythical Atlas, as the throne was forced to seek foreign aid once more. His mother Anne of Savoy, as an Italian princess, persuaded the pliant *Basileus* to turn to the West for support, including the Roman Church, especially in light of his responses to the Cantacuzeni situation in 1355. Though John Cantucazenus was safely locked away, morally defeated in a monastery, his two sons still held positions and military resources in Thrace and the Peloponnese. The *Basileus* agreed to allow Matthew the Peloponnesus in exchange for Thrace and Manuel to keep territories under the title of Despot of the Island of Lemnos.

This would have been a lucrative opportunity for the throne as Byzantine territory would have been better secured in the Greek East from Slavic aggression as well as keeping stable relations with what would have been a dangerous enemy seeking retribution and the throne. But, John squandered this and attempted to assassinate Matthew Cantacuzenus instead, risking serious rebellion. Knowing he needed a strong navy, he approached Genoa with the desperate proposition of permanent residence in Chios with a paltry annual rent of 500 *hyperpyra*. John's daughter would also marry an Italian 'adventurer', Francesco Gattilusio along with the isle of Lesbos as the avaricious Genoese would take a mile over John's inch of generosity to keep permanent residence in Phocaea.

A desperate and misguided plea was also sent to Avignon for the aid of

---

[2379] Norwich, *(DF)*, 321.
[2380] Treadgold, 777.

twenty ships and 1,000 infantry with 500 cavalry from Pope Innocent IV to fight not the encroaching Turks for the future security of the Empire, but for the temporary problem of Matthew Cantacuzenus in Thrace. In exchange, the *Basileus* promised the unthinkable: submission to Rome and Communion to the Catholic faith in order to reunite the Churches as his great-grandfather had intended. Included were the conditions that his son Manuel, at age five, would be a 'guest' in Rome and the Pope would oversee his betrothing. Furthermore, his older son Andronicus would be instructed in the Latin language and literature of Rome, the *Basileus* of Byzantium standing as the 'Captain-General and Standard-Bearer to the Holy Mother Church.'

Three Latin colleges would also be founded to teach the Byzantine youth about the Western culture and creed to promote conversion from the Orthodox faith.[2381] Despite John's sincerity and entreaties any Pope would dream of, Innocent was cynical of John's intentions, replying politely with gratitude to the *Basileus* for considering conversion, simply ignoring all other concessions. Such a promise from John could only have been originated and perhaps produced by his mother, Anne of Savoy, as an Italian and ardent Catholic, despite a French Pope sitting on the throne. The clergy of Byzantium and the stern re-actionist policies from the Zealots in Thessalonica were another risk. Their aid to Cantacuzenus in Thrace was imminent and John V would only be cornered in Constantinople. Therefore, the opportunity, now dead in its cradle, saw John inform the Pope any Union in 1357 was not possible as the Byzantine citizens would not follow the directives of papal legates who appeared with no galleys.[2382]

As this was happening, in December of 1355, Stephen III Dushan, the national hero of Serbia, died and his son Stephen V 'the Weak' lost position to a fragmented kingdom of warring noble interests. John showed remarkable indolence worthy of Andronicus II by ignoring the situation and not crushing the Serbian state once and for all, only recovering northern Greece as a stronger will, such as John VI's, would have likely succeeded in saving the Empire.[2383] But, John Paleologus continued to fight with Cantacuzenus and the *Basileus* only 'won' when Matthew failed to take Constantinople and only then did any Serbian territory find its way to the Empire. Only Nicephorius II of Epirus would succeed by taking Thessaly as an independent Greek state beyond his

---

[2381] Norwich, *(DF)*, 326.

[2382] Ostrogorsky, 535.

[2383] Treadgold, 778.

title of Despot. John made no peace with Epirus and did nothing when the Albanians killed Nicephorus in battle with Epirus to fall apart.

Ignoring any Eastern peace or alliance with Bulgaria, Serbia, the Ottomans, or even Epirus to the point of its own abolishment as a state by Serbian means, it appeared that John's only interests were in creating a Western Crusade with the Pope and Savoy, ruled by his own maternal cousin, by any means. Could this have been attributed to an Italian mother he had no confidence in defying, or at least values he did not have the imagination to transgress in crisis? Or was it an empty boon to satisfy his last ally, Hungary? This 'Latinophilism' included Westerners that had been entrenched in Byzantium for centuries until Greek blood flowed in every Italian vein. Playing a fruitless balancing act with Genoa and Venice, John would sell the last Byzantine port in Anatolia, Pontica Heraclea, to Genoa in order to pay arrears of 100,000 *hyperpyra* for an alliance with the Venetians in 1357.

A strange development was John Paleologus's neutrality with the Holy League as it meant to clear the Turks from the Holy Lands in Smyrna, where they met heavy opposition. In 1360, the League was disbanded due to demoralization, although the Templars held Smyrna and the Ottomans took Didymottichum, enslaving its population and moving further west in Thrace a year later. But, the plague was finally reaching settlement in the Turkish lands and Orhan himself was a casualty, his son Murad becoming Sultan. The transition went with more mediocre action from John and he nobly, yet unwisely, refused to cede Tenedos to Genoa for debt forgiveness for an anti-Turkish alliance as he would not betray an island that had sheltered him in his exile from Cantacuzenus.[2384]

In 1364, John finally turned east to King Louis I of Hungary, who proposed an Eastern Crusade against the Turks with Pope Urban V, Amadeus of Savoy, and Peter I of Cyprus. John attended his court personally and, as he was the first Byzantine monarch to ever visit a foreign court, it showed that the times were changing indeed, but it was only due to desperation and John's loss of diplomatic acumen that it even occurred. It was with a stern demand that Louis insisted upon John taking the Roman faith as a condition before any assistance was considered and John meekly agreed, leaving to return to Constantinople.[2385] Bulgaria lay between Hungary and any safe return for the emperor as Tsar Alexander had already lost Anchialus to the Byzantines and rightfully realized

---

[2384] Treadgold, 779.
[2385] Ostrogorsky, 538.

this as an alliance between Constantinople and Hungary to war with Bulgaria. Alexander abducted John and imprisoned him in the capital, Vdin. In a matter that crushed the Crusade altogether, Amadeus VI met heavy defeat in Egypt a year later and returned to the West.

Answering the pleas of the *Basileus* Anne, 'the Green Count', Amadeus VI of Savoy, traveled first to Venice and then back to Constantinople in 1366 with fifteen ships and 1,700 men to cut a path by taking the important ports of Turkish Callipolis, Bulgarian Mesembria, and Sozopolis in 1367. At Varna, he demanded John be returned from Vdin, this begrudgingly being done by Alexander. John was obligated to pay the Savoian expenses of 42,500 *hyperpyra* (which of course he needed to borrow) and another bid to convert to Catholicism now that the Papal Court had returned to Rome from France.[2386] But the needs of Eastern garrisoning and the climate of his people's needs postponed the conversion, John for once forced to consider his own unpopularity.[2387] No victory can be attributed to John or Constantinople itself and it was with a superficial triumph that John would eventually visit Rome – the first to do so since Constans II had seven centuries before - to receive conversion to the Roman faith. Leaving one son, Andronicus, in charge of the City as his other son Manuel guarded the unpredictable Thessalonican front, the Turks took opportunity to claim Adrianople in 1369 as John's attentions went to the West.

In Venice, John needed funds to keep his pilgrimage and to pay Doge Andrea Contarini's extortion, the isle of Tenedos, ceded at long last by a desperate John, erasing all debts. But, John received a worthy collection of 25,000 *ducats* (50,000 *hyperpyra*) and the crown jewels which was in hock for thirty years. Once again, we see the economic might of the Italian currency over the Byzantine as the inflation reaches a ratio of 1:2 since the time of Andronicus III.[2388] John was then allowed west to Rome and he proceeded to humiliate his Byzantine heritage by taking Communion and the Trinitarian creed. Some relief must have come to Pope Urban who was actually caught without resources for a Crusade as planned in Hungary. As Charles V of France

---

[2386] This was the end of the 'Babylonian Captivity' wherein the Papal Court was moved to Avignon in southern France from 1309 to 1377. The Papal title was seized by Philip IV 'the Fair' of France after deposing and abducting Pope Boniface VIII, beginning with the French clergyman Clement V. Gregory XI eventually moved it back to Rome after Avignon was crippled by the massive corruption of its clergy.

[2387] Norwich, *(DF)*, 331.

[2388] Treadgold, 780.

and Edward III of England fought between themselves in the Hundred Years' War over the inheritance of the Angevins, they could do the Pope no good.[2389]

When Venice attempted to settle Tenedos, however, they were denied by John's son in Constantinople, Andronicus IV, and the elder *Basileus* was kept as a hostage in Italy until the contract agreed to would be honored by the upstart *Basileus* in Byzantium. Thus began events that would take shape as John V's second exile from the throne five years later, now owing his previous loan from the 4,500 *hyperpyra* so far paid. Annual payments to Venice were agreed upon and the Venetians again took possession of the Crown Jewels. The *Basileus* still had a bargaining chip in Tenedos that he offered for six war galleys and 25,000 more *ducats* in cash with 4,000 up front for security.[2390] John was only released in 1371 when his younger and much more loyal son Manuel paid the debts to the Venetians and another 30,000 was brought to take John to Constantinople from Venice by confiscating Church lands to convert as pronoia estates.

Contention between contemporary and modern historians had once existed as to John's status as a 'guest' or 'prisoner' of Venice. The historian Demetrius Cydones (1324-1397), as a witness, blatantly spoke out that it was only a fruitless endeavor with no advantage whatsoever, yet one early twentieth-century historian held more of an opposing view that he spent a year in Venice of his own volition to honorably repay the debts. Another side, perhaps more correctly, outlined that as the *Basileus* had no money, no credit, and could not even outfit a return fleet, the Venetian Signoria insisted his feet be put in stocks as a penalty for having no money at all![2391]

Elsewhere, the ambitions of Sultan Murad were taking shape into a Turkish hegemony that certainly rivaled the one Byzantium had developed since the ninth century, not least of all being Murad's adoption of the title 'Sultan' over 'Emir.' The region lost to the Greeks forever, the Ottomans overwhelmed the Balkans, taking Serres and converting the Serbian princes to Turkish vassals on the way. The desperate Manuel Cantacuzenus could only grant tax privileges to monasteries and pronoia to soldiers to defend what they could as any centralized authority in the Empire and such concerted efforts were now a joke.

In the Paleologan period, these soldiers were usually mercenaries known as the *syntrophiai* who were organized in companies under chosen leaders and not

---

[2389] Norwich, *(AM)*, 222-223.

[2390] Norwich, *(DF)*, 334-335.

[2391] Ostrogorsky, 540f. As he had no way of leaving Venice, why would he be immobilized as punishment, especially as he was a sovereign monarch with which they had an existing, if tenuous, alliance?

imperial appointees, also being of any ethnicity and any that could be persuaded to ally with the Empire with land and farm grants.[2392] Unfortunately, sources are scant on the arrangements between *Basileus* and Sultan, but a precarious and merciless peace was made by 1372. In an especially humiliating condition of Murad's peace, the fifteenth-century historian Demetrius Chalcocondyles (1423-1511) remarks how John, Andronicus, and Manuel were all required to follow and attend the Sultan on his military campaigns against Christians in Asia Minor with no royals watching Constantinople.[2393]

The power the Sultan had over Constantinople was made plain when Andronicus and Murad's son attempted a double coup on both their fathers in 1373. When they were defeated, Murad blinded his son, insisting (more like ordering such as a lord would do to a vassal) that John do the same, but John was lenient and superficially blinded one eye and just grazing the other. The Christian leniency that was the privilege of Byzantine *Basileus* would be tested by the Infidel from outside Constantinople's Walls as only a monarch such as John V would allow this. Yet, it must be stressed that the Oriental and Muslim Sultan was now was in a position high above a Christian Roman Emperor. As this is so, the fate of Byzantium was solely in the grasp of Murad economically, militarily, administratively, and with a certain and ironic popularity as he allowed Greeks the freedom of their religion.[2394]

As he intended to years before, in 1376, the *Basileus* conceded Tenedos to Venice as was agreed (by sword point), a Venetian fleet in the Golden Horn led by a captain Giustinian collecting the island's mortgage.[2395] John's only request was that the imperial standard be equal to that of St. Mark's and the inhabitants claim Orthodox superiority on the island. But, this was frustrated by the Galatan Genoese who felt they had more of a claim to Tenedos as John's son-in-law was a Genoan, and along with that should come Chios and Phocaea. Manuel II Paleologus, the new co-emperor of John V, was more loyal than his brother, so Genoa released the semi-blind Andronicus Paleologus from prison and laid siege to the City for over a month.

Even Sultan Murad lent soldiers to this cause and the Genoese took Constantinople, seizing John and Manuel and imprisoning them to place Andronicus IV in the purple on August 12. There, in the dreaded prison of

---

[2392] Decker, 83.

[2393] Herrin, 311.

[2394] Norwich, *(DF)*, 337.

[2395] Norwich, *(AHV)*, 245.

Anemas they stayed, a fortress feared since the Comneni. There they stayed until 1379 when they escaped and fled to the Ottoman court, seeking Murad's aid, and in the summer, a Turkish army was sent across the Bosporus. As John took Constantinople, Andronicus fled the City and John was re-instated as *Basileus* despite massive urban unpopularity. The question of Tenedos would finally be settled in 1382 as the dominant arbitration of Savoy would order fortifications on the island to be razed and burned, its population moving to Crete and Euboea, and neither Italian Republic maintain possession of it as a territory of Savoy.[2396]

This was all done at the Sultan's mercy, selecting John over Andronicus for a high price in the city of Philadelphia. A long holdout against the Turks to the point of an independent outpost,[2397] this city was John's offer in exchange for the return of his throne. The transient nature of the Byzantine throne was further demonstrated by Murad's son, Bayezid (*Yildirim*, 'the Thunderbolt'), considered a 'Sultan of Rum' in Anatolia,[2398] who plotted in 1390 with deposed Andronicus and his son John for the throne. John V, as always, was impotent and apathetic to foreign affairs as his son Manuel handled the years Andronicus remained a threat. John again faced dethronement as John VII of Selymbria, his grandson, was made *Basileus* by Murad for only five months as John V hid in the fortress of the Golden Gate in Constantinople.

By 1383, John V Paleologus managed to strengthen his position in the Morea as the last Cantacuzeni rebels – Manuel, Matthew, and Demetrius – died without an heir and John's youngest son Theodore was installed in his place in 1382. He was said to have settled the Morea with 'new blood' in the form of an ethnic influx of Albanians migrating south.[2399] Yet, only fortune had allowed John V back to the throne a year later. Once more it did so, in 1390 with practically no effort by the emperor at all with Manuel allowing his father the title of senior *Basileus* once again, despite Andronicus's rebellion in 1387.

Manuel had numerous opportunities to take his father's throne as his brother had, but always showed loyalty, regretting only the incident of 1387. The events of that year in the East had already culminated in the bloody Serbian landmark, the Battle of Kosovo (ominously, 'Place of the Blackbirds'), the battle romanticized in the Medieval epic *The Kosovo Cycle* where the princes of Serbia

---

[2396] Ostrogorsky, 543.
[2397] Treadgold, 781.
[2398] Norwich, (DF), 345.
[2399] Ostrogorsky, 544.

resisted the Turks, defeated them, and a renegade Serbian assassinated the Sultan Murad. Murad's death would be the last nail in the coffin of Byzantine independence in a growing Turkish East. Yet, the Turks' grip on the Balkans was slippery as already they met resistance from the ascending nation of Bosnia.[2400]

This appeared to begin with the Dushan Serbian prince, Lazar, who had annexed Rascia in 1371 after Uros Nemanjid's death. He next allied with King Tvrtko of Bosnia in 1377, convincing the Serbian Patriarchate of Pech in 1375 to excommunicate its own Church. After Louis of Hungary's death in 1382, Tvrtko took Serbian lands in Croatia and Dalamatia, setting off religious and political events that would culminate in the brutal Serbo-Bosnian conflicts to the present time. By 1385, the Turks were dominant before Kosovo and had taken the Serbian lands of Sofia and Nish. Yet, Murad's forces were stopped by Lazar in 1386 at Plochnik and further failures awaited in 1387 when abortive measures resulted from an invasion of Bosnia by the armies of the *voivode* Vlatko Vlutavich at Bilecha.

The ascension of Bayezid was a harsh one on Constantinople and this Sultan allowed no dissent from John as his father had; Byzantium, like Serbia before it, was now a vassal for the Ottoman Empire. John and Manuel were forced to make siege on Philadelphia for the Turks against the emboldened Serbs and Manuel attended the battle obediently to protect his father. The last insult for John V Paleologus, after an exhausting fifty-year reign, was the incident of the Golden Gate fortress. Given to him in surrender by John VI and his Catalan mercenaries, this is where John had resided as an Italian prisoner half a year under his son and grandson. Manuel Paleologus was now attending the Ottoman court after the battles at Philadelphia. Out of fear the co-emperor was planning rebellion, Bayezid demanded the *Basileus* disassemble all of the fortifications he had built, including the Golden Gate, with the threat of blinding and imprisoning Manuel.

This was an abandonment of the *kastron* system in the City that instituted a lifetime staff to oversee provincial and municipal fortresses during Michael VIII's reign, mostly.[2401] With offensive capabilities at an extreme low, neglect of these defensive forts would be a death knell for the City's security. After dismantling the fortress, a thoroughly demoralized John V Paleologus died in February 1391 from complications with gout in bed, turning his face to the wall in despair. Further demonstrating John's powerlessness before the Turkish

---

[2400]  Ostrogorsky, 546-547.
[2401]  Decker, 83.

suzerainty, the Sultan's military accessory demanded a tribute to pay in 30,000 *hyperpyra* and 12,000 troops annually.[2402] However, the sources more vividly report he lived, in his final years, a life of 'senile debauchery' usually reserved for Turkish harems and a feeble old man totally in sufferance and submission to the Sultan in Constantinople.[2403]

John's inept and negligent rule justified the Cantacuzenus regime, which was unfortunately cut short and stonewalled by the defeat of John VI's sons through a policy of ignoring military affairs and allowing the army and navy to decay almost beyond repair. Only through the efforts of foreign aid did he even survive as long as he did against a plague worse than the Black Death, that of the Turkish and Serbian incursions that reached into his court itself. His son was little better, but he had some trust in allies John did not, those allies imprisoning him for accruing debts he could not pay. At John's ascension in 1341, the Empire had its opportunities to be rescued and survive the tides threatening to capsize the very existence of the Empire, but now, 'By the time of his death, its fall could be foreseen.'[2404]

Loss of control by the central government in monastic matters was accentuated in 1342 during the chaos of preparing a succession as the Zealots of Thessalonica. Once supporters of John V, they overthrew their Byzantine government by staging a bloody massacre of the nobles in 1346, declaring a strange 'democracy' in the province.[2405] The strangeness was in the fact this popular democracy was still at the will of the monastic Zealots and would appear more as a theocracy. Objective modern historians made claims it was ran as a real republic would have done, however, the rival Cantacuzenus could not allow this division while on the throne and he had it dissolved in 1349.

In July, 1351, John V served a Chrysobull to Mt. Athos, now in Serbian hands, outlining the privileges it would receive from the head of Eastern Christianity, Constantinople. This was, however, done at the insistence of King Stephen Dushan to settle matters with the Monastery of Chillander as it was plain even to the indomitable Dushan that Constantinople, or at least its legitimate ruler and not a usurper, was the undisputed head of the Christian community of all Eastern Orthodoxy.[2406] Even with the conciliatory title John

---

[2402] Ostrogorsky, 543f. The two halves of the annual tribute were postulated by the historians Chalcocondyles and Sphrantzes, respectively.

[2403] Norwich, *(AHV)*, 261.

[2404] Treadgold, 783.

[2405] Vasiliev, 683.

[2406] Obolensky, 256.

used, the 'Sublime Emperor of Serbia' and the self-imposed 'Emperor of the Greeks and Serbs', he needed Byzantine accreditation for the Empire's strongest and longest-lasting institution of the Orthodox Church.

One of the most shocking policies to the sensibilities of the average Byzantine was John V's endeavors and actions in his Roman conversion, mostly at Louis of Hungary's insistence. As early as 1357, after Pope Clement refused John's entreaties for military aid in exchange for concessions to even the City itself, papal legates were still sent to the Constantinopolitan court. Two Bishops, originally monks, were Peter Thomas the Carmelite and Contarini the Dominican, who were said to have claimed they successfully converted the *Basileus* to Catholicism. This was originated and praised in Peter Thomas's *Life* written by the Chancellor of Cyprus, Philippe de Mezieres (1327-1405), but was later discredited by the actual conversion decades later,[2407] Mezieres's work being a narrowed focus of the Carmelite's biased achievements in this instance.

As of 1357, hopes for conversion and Church Union were dashed in the complexities of issues the Empire was facing in the East and domestically in the face of the Cantacuzeni. Later, however, once the popular climate had shifted in October 1367, John traveled first to Viterbo in Italy with a delegation recognizing Rome as the only true Church and not that of French Avignon.[2408] This was justifiable as it is to be remembered that John V was half-Italian and a lifetime of his dominant mother's influence over his own convictions would also be Roman. As well as this, if the Papacy ever did return to Rome (as it did in 1377), Savoy would then get the full benefit of the Pope's gratitude and future resources West and East.

On October 18, 1369, it was made official as John recognized the supremacy of Rome by a document made by the imperial seal and, after three genuflections of the Cross, the *Basileus* kissed the Supreme Pontiff's feet, hands, and lips. Then, a Catholic Mass for the only converted Byzantine monarch took place in the Basilica of St. Peter. But all of this grand gesturing was for nothing, temporally and spiritually, as the Hungarian King would die with no support and the 'conversion or apostasy' by a 'slothful Paleologus' would quickly be forgotten as moot by the Greeks and Latins.[2409] It was only an empty gesture that only weakened Constantinople with a usurpation of the throne and a humiliating capture on his pilgrimage without one sword being pulled and it

---

[2407] Norwich, *(DF)*, 327.

[2408] *ibid.*, 332-333.

[2409] Gibbon, 2278.

was the infamous lack of state revenue to repay loans that brought him down a second time.

The loss of prestige under Bayezid was palpable as the Byzantine throne faced hot contention by the leaders of the local commercial Eastern Italian Republics, as the Empire was now at the pleasure of the crafty Sultan. Politically, the Empire was caught in a vicious circle wherein they lacked the resources to fight the 'orders' of their enemies, in turn guaranteeing those orders would only limit any resources that may have existed to do so to save the Empire.[2410] This intensified the last Byzantine political culture of total decay through the risks of 'dependency relationships' with the Ottomans.[2411] Internally, among the early reign of instability and confusion between Paleologus and Cantacuzenus, a new socio-economic crisis emerged in the Empire in urban centers such as Constantinople, Adrianople, and Thessalonica.[2412]

Compounding the difficulties of imperial control was the rural gap between rich *dunatoi* and the poor, getting worse through imperial neglect since the Comneni, exploding as rampant bureaucratic corruption caused disenfranchised peasants to flood the cities as refugees. This dereliction was compounded by the typical tax dodges and bribes coming from the aristocrats as a new proletariat class was emerging in the cities as former small farmers were becoming workers and sailors. In rural areas, this caused mass abandonment of arable farms as the state resources that kept peasants tied to the land decayed rapidly.

The greed of the nobles added to the fatalism of the times as the 1346 cave-in of St. Sophia's dome was described by writer Alexius Micrebolites (d. 1353) as a punishment by God for the rich's avarice. In his *Dialogue between Rich and Poor,* the 'theft, drunkenness, laxity, slander, envy, and murder' of the Empire was blamed on the, 'Inappropriate attitudes and evil actions, particularly greediness, selfish exploitation of nature's benefits, insatiable determination to seize and hoard as much as possible, and a preference for corporeal over spiritual values.' The only methods of gaining wealth thought noble by the Poor through the lips of Micrembolites was that through accruing knowledge, through trade, or through abstinence and an end to the social norms of separating the classes at banquet tables, in simple conversation, and in marriage.

The resentment these workers had for the indolent monarchy made

---

[2410] Diehl, 207.

[2411] Reinert, 'Fragmentation (1204-1453)', 270.

[2412] Norwich, *(DF)*, 296-297.

its existence most plain with the murder of Apocaucus. Though it appears Apocaucus was behind the looting and burning of Cantacuzenist properties in Adrianople, it had been originated against the City's upper class as a whole by a laborer named Branos.[2413] Apocaucus merely encouraged and aided these attacks against a shared enemy and took credit for it, perhaps unwisely given the outrage of workers in Constantinople itself. Apocaucus had gained much wealth himself by Cantacuzenus's hand and spent much of it for the medical sciences, buying manuscripts of Hippocrates (460BCE-375BCE) and patronizing the court physician John Aktouarios (1275-1328), who dedicated a medical text to Apocaucus.

Such ostentation of this kind by the localized rich who had disenfranchised the labor backbone of Byzantine industry only sparked more anger. Compounded with this was the juxtaposition of the ease of the wealthy and the poor privations in every city: good wine and fine clothes over the shabby, lice-ridden rags and sour wine, good medical advice over rampant sickness, conspicuous funerals and burials with candle-bearers and luxuries over the simple graves of the poor comforted only by holy resurrection. These justifications of simplicity and even a new respect for middle class values had been accentuated by the taunt that Jews and Muslims treat their poor better than Christians and that due to their hypocrisy, they deserved no benefits of the afterlife!

This dissension between the classes also allowed the middle class (*oi mesoi*) to gain more position to seize opportunity for merchants, craftsmen, small landholders, professionals, and manufacturers to become a 'new rich' [*nouveau riche*] in the cities as the remaining two classes only fought each other.[2414] So, even before the Black Death, the shifts of the Late Medieval era of class ascendancy resulting in the modern Capitalist movements were occurring as it would in the West. The weakening economic relevance of feudal aristocracy and means of production was what would allow Italian, English, and Dutch trade companies to thrive. The luxury and commodities markets between East and West allowed the origins to exist in establishing the financial innovations of the Renaissance/Baroque periods.

Already such companies existed in, for example, Genoa's 'Mahone of Chios' that traded in the Genoese alum mines for an annual profit of 60,000 to 80,000 *florins* in Phocaea. Furthermore, Galata was making custom profits of 200,000 *hyperpyra* while Constantinople only made roughly 30,000, undermining

---

[2413] Herrin, 284-288.

[2414] Vasiliev, 683.

imperial authority using 'clever smuggling' of goods.[2415] Tenedos was also a controversial commodity by Greeks and Venetians due to its position and influence in the Dardanelles. Since the Trojan War, over 2,000 years before, the Dardanelles was a fight worth having by the Greeks. Its fate would decide the Crimean trade and military mobility of the Western territories with the Bosporus up to Michael VIII's reign. Its loss in 1375 jeopardized the Crimean and Russian trade and further exposed the Byzantine economic decay it suffered as the Turks occupied Asia Minor, Rum, Iconium, and access to the Dardenelles as well. Italian and Latin colonists threatening peace within Constantinople would soon make the Paleologi their 'puppets.'

The middle class in these wars chose to side with the poor as they were more of an economic base in daily trade. The landed aristocrats treated them with deference and only played lesser parts in legal regulation and trade charters compared to existing government monopolies. The literature of the time was not only proletariat in sentiment, but aristocratic historians also chronicle the bloodshed and chaos of these times. Most notably was John Cantacuzenus, before he was *Basileus*, who lost much in his family estates to the riots, as did the scholar Metochiates in 1328. John reports on the massacres and the blame set by the peasantry on the nobles for the Empire's disasters and the disenfranchisement of their class. After Andronicus IV's death, when the Empire was being divided between Cantacuzenus and the Paleologi, he would call the proletariat rebels mere opportunists, only using violence to show their discontent, as 'Senseless impulse was glorified as valor and lack of fellow feeling and humanity was called loyalty to the Emperor.'[2416]

## JOHN VI CANTACUZENUS
### (1346-1354)

Three usurpers, mostly legitimate, periodically broke up the unstable and languid fifty-year reign of John V Paleologus. To avoid confusion, what is said about their specific years as *Basilii*, with some slight background previously overlooked, will be outlined separately. These were not particularly long or eventful reigns, but the stories of these men are to be told to understand their personalities as leaders of a declining State. In the case of this civilization, their effects on the Byzantine government and society as a whole came from

---

[2415] Diehl, 194-195.
[2416] Herrin, 289.

the character of its leaders as the ideal focus of Byzantine and Eastern Roman political theory. This ideal lay in the absolute temporal and spiritual authority of the *Basileus*, not to be broken until the Empire was ultimately lost.

Already, examples of Western innovations that were leading to Byzantine ruin had been seen, including the events under John Cantacuzenus's annexing of Thrace from Selymbria during the late 1340's.[2417] Although Western Europe was organically being united under central governments under feudalism, this practice in Byzantium only led to decentralization, destabilization, and a loss of ostracized territory to Roman neighbors and adversaries. The division of supreme authority was commonplace, as in the situation of Matthew Cantacuzenus's theoretically being an extension of his father's supreme authority, while not being able to be so in practice due to Serbian aggression on the western Thracian border.[2418] With noble loyalties being questionable at best and their institutions breaking down, dividing the Empire was a dangerous practice even to loyal governors. Yet, was this practice of territorial extension from the City necessary when only dynastic legitimacy held the throne together?

The first *Basileus* with such questionable legitimacy to take the Paleologan throne was John Cantacuzenus, the famed and loyal general of the Paleologi with his military capability against Serbs, Slavs, Turks, and Greeks. Greater than his military acumen, however, was his ability in garnering allies and factions with diplomatic skill. As the bearer of the title of the Empire's 'Last Grand Domestic',[2419] he was also the final military *Basileus* of Eastern Roman history and the last to attempt military reform to save Constantinople. He denied the throne of Constantinople numerous times in humility before the oaths he had sworn to the Paleologi, but it is slyly (and rightly) suggested that he also carried another tremendous loyalty – to himself.

As he served in the courts of three different *Basilii* while still weathering the machinations of the *Basilia* Anna's regency, he did so despite many agreeing accounts of Andronicus III naming him regent upon his deathbed. In 1334, this antagonism began when Andronicus's mother, Anne of Savoy, intrigued in Constantinople with the summoned Governor of Thessalonica, Syrgiannes, whom she adopted as a son.[2420] For two of these three *Basilii* he had served,

---

[2417] Herrin, 311-312.

[2418] Ostrogorsky, 527.

[2419] Nicol, Donald M. *The Reluctant Emperor: A Biography of John Cantucazene, Byzantine Emperor and Monk, c. 1295-1383*. Cambridge, UK: Cambridge University Press. 2002, 186.

[2420] Norwich, *(DF)*, 284.

Andronicus II and Andronicus III, John Cantacuzenus was still seen as unscrupulous, the secret power behind the throne.

What were probably the accurate facts were that John was the 'friend and counselor . . .in a very true sense the inspiration'[2421] of his imperial masters, loyal to the dynasty and the welfare of the Empire. It probably was, in reality, his humility in denying the crown for the sake of unity in the Empire that garnered misplaced suspicion and conspiracy. One conspirator was John XIV Celcas, the anti-Hesychast Patriarch who owed his entire career to Cantacuzenus's efforts since he had been a celibate monk. Anne even attempted to culminate the Hesychasts after deposing John XIV in February, declaring Cantacuzenus a 'spiritual brother' and common father' of her son in May, but to no avail.[2422]

As the regency finally broke down and turned on itself soon after the assassination of Alexius Apocaucus, John was finally 'motivated' by his military and ecclesiastical allies to accept the crown of glass jewels and gilt gold in 1347, dining on lead plates and toasting from earthernware goblets. His popularity among the lower-class citizens of the Empire would be strained as he had accumulated much wealth on his campaigns as the aristocratic son of a Morean Despot. As allies, he held the legislative authorities over Russia by affirming correspondences made that September with Symeon of Muscovy to Byzantium's power as the only Church of God capable of being a 'teacher of law and sanctification.'[2423] Unfortunately, not much activity was seen by Russia in the Crimean Wars of Cantacuzenus with much of these applications being only symbolical.

John VI also lacked support in the circles of the Zelaots, and therefore Thessalonica, endangering the position of his son Matthew as Despot. His weighty challenges included negotiations with the Turkish Empire, the Serbian King Dushan, Orthodox heresy and rival Patriarchs, as well as the Black Death on the Bosporus in 1348. Disaster compounded this in allying and attempting to control events with the Genoese Republicans of Galata against Venice, which witnessed the total defeat of any remaining Byzantine navy. When the Paleologan factions dethroned him in 1354, it was an exhausted and relieved Cantacuzenus that took the cowl as Josaoph, inhabiting the Monastery of Mt. Athos. But, weighed against this were the talents he had in gaining and keeping these allies, such as Umar of the Ottoman Empire and the Roman tribune

---

[2421] Norwich, (DF), 281.

[2422] Ostrogorsky, 520-522.

[2423] Obolensky, 265.

Cola di Rienzo, to whom John sent embassadors to congratulate him upon his promotion.[2424]

But his strange and heroic tale only turned a new chapter after this time, dominating it as the leading eyewitness historian of international events, rivaling his contemporary Gregoras. The unquestionable faith he held as *Basileus* only furthered him in Church Councils as the voice of Union and Orthodoxy in later decades. John VI Cantucazenus was born in 1295 in Morea to the distinguished military family of the Cantacuzene and their wealthy estates in Thrace, Macedonia, and Thessaly,[2425] gaining John the reputation as the rich aristocrat, which later worked against him. These estates provided wheat and grain from an impressive 62,500 acres under 1,000 oxen, personal possessions totaling 2,500 mares, 200 camels, 300 mules, 500 asses and cattle, 50,000 hogs, and 70,000 sheep.[2426] Despite his aristocratic holdings, he had no legitimate claim to be *Basileus*, although he was an indirect relation of Michael VIII Paleologus on his mother's side.

He was a paragon of Greek virtue in his formidable leadership and strategy, brilliance, cultivation, courageousness, and likability, all earning him allies that would remain close friends until his abdication.[2427] At fifty-one, before his first coronation by his troops in 1346, he had spent almost half of his life in imperial service and, as *Basileus*, it would serve it him best during the troubles Byzantium would face. These troubles would prove the throne was no longer a conduit for the best service in the face of withering political impotence and demoralization as 'the permanent underlying weakness of Byzantium.'[2428] Cynically it has also been written (by the Empire's critics) that a Byzantine sovereign could only suffer insults with a smile, but when actual action or resistance was taken, they would only demur in the end due to their weak position.

Upon his further acceptance and reinstatement into the City, the Patriarch Isidore Bucharis placed the false crown on his head at the Church of St. Mary of Blacharnae. Shameful reminders of the Empire's decline were present: the *Basilia* had sold Venice the real stones in exchange for yet another loan and Saint Sophia was in ruins with a collapsed dome. Just before John became *Basileus*, the Orthodox Bishops from the other four holy sees of the Empire demanded a Council be held to formerly discuss the fate of the heresy of

---

[2424] Vasiliev, 585.

[2425] Norwich, *(DF)*, 277.

[2426] Gibbon, 2199.

[2427] Treadgold, 771.

[2428] Diehl, 138.

Hesychasm. Probably as an attempt to answer the question and gain support from the monasteries and similar believers, John attended and Hesychasm was championed by George Palamas. Important politically, John XIV, the former regent and Cantacuzenist opponent was deposed and excommunicated to be replaced by Isidore Bucharis as Patriarch.

In another effort to support legitimacy for the junior Paleologan *Basileus*, John VI refused to crown his sons as princes, keeping them in Thrace and the Peloponnesus as he managed the foreign situations of the East with such moderation however, it was being mistaken for 'temerity and indolence.'[2429] He first demanded that Dushan and Serbia return the cities of Serres and Beroea to the imperial borders, as it broke an earlier pact the two had made. Dushan demurred in the face of a war that would spread his Serbian resources too thin and Cantacuzenus's plan to create a tight Byzantine territorial bloc of recovered Successor States in Thessalonica, Thessaly, Epirus, and Thrace began.[2430] John, in his memoirs, showed certain contempt for the Serbian King who styled himself an 'Emperor of Almost All of Rome (*Romania*)' in a letter to the Doge Dandalo by referring to the Serbs as the antiquated name of the Thracian tribe of Triballs, as also does Gregoras.[2431]

But these ambitions withered as the Black Death struck Constantinople later that year, killing supposedly 20,000,000 Europeans, draining the Treasuries desperately, and leaving the rural areas fallow as no one was actually alive to cultivate fields for food. Famine was the result which, of course, perpetuated the cycle of disease, malnutrition, and lack of law and order to create havoc in all the land.[2432] With this chaos, Dushan seized the opportunity and took Epirus and Thessaly as the *Basileus* appealed west to the Pope for a Holy League to march French, Italian, and Spanish Christians against the Christians of Serbia. Yet, the West was shocked in knowing John VI had given his daughter to an Infidel prince and 40,000 cavalry were sent to him between 1348 and 1353. John's Turkish in-laws, meanwhile, were given every liberty and use of the Palace, even disturbing sacred duties with revelry and dance. But, even John was quick to note of their mercilessness, delight in killing, and love of enslaving others due merely to their difference in religion.[2433]

---

[2429]  Gibbon, 2203.

[2430]  Treadgold, 772-773.

[2431]  Vasiliev, 617.

[2432]  Marozzi, Justin. *Tamerlane, Sword of Islam, Conqueror of the World*. Cambridge, MA: De Capo Publishing. 2004, 52.

[2433]  Diehl, 205.

In 1348, John called alliances with the infidel Turks of his Ottoman son-in-law Orhan, now Sultan, and of Aydin under his best ally Umar with a friendship of a 'perfect union' such as Orestes and Pylades.[2434] Umar was said to wear under Turkish garb, 'the humanity and politeness of a Greek'; sadly, the League showed their reaction by attacking and killing Umar and denouncing John as any such friendship was an alien and incomprehensible concept to the xenophobic mentality of the Medieval West. Gregoras [2435] would even exacerbate John's position in the unfair evaluation that John hated Rome even as he loved the barbarians!

Orhan had already sent 10,000 auxiliary troops to Serres in aiding the *Basileus*, but they turned out to be pillagers that deserted John, leaving him with no allies on either side. As the nobility of the Cantacuzeni were traditionally thought to have been the product of the French romances of the Paladins[2436] who wrote of the eleventh century, such Western disrespect gave John no considerations to the West in his unshakable foreign policy. Though John was the first *Basileus* to come to any terms with the Ottomans, he still exhibited a so-called 'Roman mentality' that lacked worldliness despite his experiences, such as missing out on any correspondence with the Aragonese King Peter III who had reached out to the East, being less allied to the Church and the Holy League.[2437] What was left to John was that which was ready-at-hand and more familiar for use, the warring Italian Republics. With typical risk, John used the Genoese of Galata by lowering their custom dues on what was not already illegally brought into the Genoese suburbs, in exchange for their fleets.

But, John VI was a far-sighted tactician and understood that the Genoese would eventually need tempering by the Empire, a rehabilitated Greek fleet being essential in putting the Empire's military moralization back on track. Financially, John's motivations were attributed to the fact that in the Crimea, the Genoese received eighty-seven percent of the custom dues therein, making Byzantine supremacy almost impossible.[2438] His goal was not Serbia, however, but in containing the dangerous Zealot 'Republic' of Thessalonica, his fleet being outfitted to this end in the Bosporus. Unfortunately, the Genoese were threatened by these attempts at supplanting any future military alliances and

---

[2434]  Gibbon, 2230.

[2435]  Gregoras, vol. III, 177; Vasilev, 622.

[2436]  Gibbon, 2200, 19f.

[2437]  Nicol, 162.

[2438]  Ostrogorsky, 523.

future assaults on Galata, and responded by burning the entire fleet in the harbor including any merchant vessels at the docks.

Rather than face the Serbian King, in which he was obsessed with ruining, the *Basileus* suppressed the Genoans. John levied more taxes to outfit more ships, gaining a dozen more from the Venetians on the promise that they would raze the whole colony to the ground and return the Crown Jewels in Venice's possession. Since 1347, raising such funds was difficult as John continued to remind his people that there was no middle way anymore between saving through virtue and sacrifice the Empire or facing enslavement by their enemies. These were opportunities that interested multiple international interests in the West. In 1350, Peter of Aragon offered Venice eighteen more men-at-war if they paid two-thirds of the upkeep,[2439] and after the Genoese blockaded Caffa and Constantinople, they reluctantly joined the Venetian Alliance. On February 13, 1352, the first Byzantine naval offensive of John VI against Galata commenced.

The result, however, was a debacle that was a testament to Byzantine irony and the total demoralization of the Greek military, offering the most shameful defeat in the Empire's history on March 6. The Genoese were ready to capitulate to the naval forces approaching them, but just as a strong wind had caused mild concern for the fleet, the crews of each vessel retreated practically with no offensive at all, fleeing from an enemy that gave no pursuit. The ships themselves were abandoned to be made property of the Genoese who strengthened their maritime trade and flotilla, flying the imperial flag in mockery. Unfazed, the Venetians and Aragonese continued their war against Genoa in the Crimea and, eventually, ending in the Western isles of Sardinia and Corsica, along with Spain, until 1355 when Cantacuzenus was just an afterthought. The entire Byzantine fleet had literally been knocked over by a strong wind!

It is questionable if Genoa could have, in 1352, repeated the actions of Venice in 1204 and expelled the Greeks, but that is an action they did not choose. Another motivation was to protect the city and the Tower of Christ, a great architectural work surviving today in Istanbul as a nightclub.[2440] Further attempts at aggressive action by either side interfered greatly with Genoan mercantile business, and they sought a treaty. Though it had cost him the possibilities of effective navies since 1348, it was John VI understanding the Italian trade industry that benefited him in the lucrative Genoese treaty of 1352.[2441]

---

[2439] Norwich, *(AHV)*, 217.

[2440] Norwich, *(DF)*, 312f.

[2441] Nicol, 167.

The trade of Crimea was vital in many respects to the Empire as it provided corn and fish, supposedly food sacred to Christian religious symbols of Christ's name and vitality.[2442] Tributes to Egypt of slave boys ran through since the late eleventh century and the Don provided the expensive sturgeon and caviar industries that today are extremely profiable. Added were the Indian spice and gem trades and the caravan routes of Central Eurasia to Genoese harbors. The vendettas of the Genoese needing 'satisfaction' over legal procedure caused problems, especially at the claim Byzantine vessels had seized an Italian fishing vessel, executing the entire crew in cold blood.

John Cantacuzenus himself was preparing another fleet, most likely frustrated by the cowardice of his seamen as a seasoned veteran and warrior not used to hasty retreats. But, he cooled enough to use his political experience and accepted their treaty and the 100,000 *hyperpyra* to be paid by Galata for a lease on Chios for ten years at 12,000 *hyperpyra* annually. When the natives of the island resisted, John VI and Galata were able to subdue them and Genoan Phocaea was once again returned to the Empire. A further wise boon in his diplomacy was binding a tie severed by the Andronici with Trebizond, as they refused marriage alliances with the Successor Comneni. John corrected this by marrying a niece, Theodora, to Alexius III Comnenus of Trebizond. With his back secure, Cantacuzenus could now turn east and finally begin his war on Serbia and Dushan. Both Serbia and Bulgaria were motivated from the pleas and promises made by John V Paleologus in 1352 as John gathered 4,000 cavalry to rescue his brother Michael, he being a hostage of Dushan.[2443]

This took the form of a war of two exhausted Empires whose resources were thinned by circumstance; as John retook Borea and Edessa, Stephen Dushan would retake it when John's forces were too depleted to fight back. Despite a false peace reached when the Byzantine *Basileus* and Serbian King actually met face-to-face for the first time, it was only used to buy time for Dushan to retake his territories. A stalemate, however, was the final result as Dushan's forces were too weak to encroach further on imperial territories by 1349. The two sides now reached a real agreement to uphold the *status quo* in the Serbian East. Nothing was achieved or accomplished by this except the loss of men and resources and

---

[2442] Gibbon, 2208-2209. The Greek word for fish (*ichthys*) hearkened to the ancient acronym '*Iesous Khristos, Theou Yious, Soter* ('Jesus Christ, Son of God, and Savior')'. Since the banners of the Crusades, corn and bread have symbolized the ancient connection to life and fertility as well as the body of Christ.

[2443] Ostrogorsky, 529f. Gregoras claims 7,000 cavalry was sent, 4,000 being from Cantacuzenus's own autobiography.

the further marring of the great commander Cantucazenus's reputation as well as Byzantium's.

The only real victory was, once again, Byzantine influence and cultural presence in Serbia as the legislative code of the Serbian Empire, the *Syntagma*, was written in 1349 by the Byzantine canonist Matthew Blastares (1290-1360) to give Serbia 'a strong legal footing.'[2444] Dushan also traveled the extensive Greek-speaking territories of his Empire, showering gifts and honors on the Monastery of Mt. Athos, a symbol of Stephen's new care and conquest over a successful and hallowed Byzantine institution. Furthermore was the Serbian-sponsored revival of the Greek 'Archons' of Dushan's domain and the use of Byzantine administrative and honorific titles to the nobility. The only difference within Serbia was the inability of Dushan to fully receive Venetian patronage, the Doge cleverly preferring a weak Greek *Basileus* to a strong Serbian one.[2445] Gibbon remarked that such policies and treaties between Italians and Greeks proved Byzantium was now only a tool barely felt 'in the balance of the opulent and powerful republics.'

Nonetheless, a power bloc of the three Cantucazeni rulers of Constantinople, Thrace, and the Peloponnesus existed and held back the disastrous tide any Turkish, Bulgarian, or other barbarian power may attempt to unleash. This included the peripheral Italians as well, but excluded the internal strife of the Genoans who were now pointed externally to Venice in a trade war over the Crimea and Black Sea when John returned from Serbia in 1351. John took a risk and allied with the Venetians who pledged to expel Genoa from Chios and Galata, but the Genoans struck first, seizing more fleets and taking the key Byzantine-held Crimean trade ports of Heraclea and Sozopolis. Later, in June of 1354, John VI showed his strength over the lands beyond the Crimea in Russia by delegating a Muscovite as 'Metropolitan of Kiev and All Russia' along with the Patriarch, Philotheus. A few months later, Patriarch Callistus appointed a Byzantine to the post and Russian hegemony was assured.[2446]

Already in 1350, Symeon of Muscovy had sent money to Constantinople to repair the once sublime Church of St. Sophia, but due to military necessity, every last piece of gold went to pay the unreliable Turkish mercenaries. John once again turned to his Turkish son-in-law, who lent 10,000 Ottoman auxiliaries under Sulayman that met at a battle at Hebrus late in 1351, composed

---

[2444] Norwich, *(DF)*, 308.

[2445] Ostrogorsky, 524-525.

[2446] Obolensky, 263.

of the Greeks, their Turk allies, and his subject Bulgarian allies. After a Turkish victory, the auxiliaries typically began to take their pay in looting and raiding Thrace and John was helpless to dismiss or oppose them. In early 1354, John begrudgingly offered them a bribe of 10,000 *hyperpyra* for them to return to Prusa.

At this time, however, the greatest sign of Cantacuzenus's failures and divine displeasure took place in Turk-occupied Callipolis as a massive earthquake destroyed its walls. Sulayman only re-built the fortifications stronger than they had been and a desperate John VI quadrupled his bribe before the Sultan Orhan, who refused wherein his occupation continued in Thrace. John Cantacuzenus still restored the navy and stopped Byzantium's decline, showing promise by temporarily halting the enemies of the Empire as 'Only another natural disaster, the earthquake of Callipolis, gave the Turks foothold in Europe.'[2447] Orhan, refusing any bribes, dismissed Cantacuzenus's pleas as Callipolis was a vital tactical position in Thrace. Naturally, this succeeded in causing widespread panic within Constantinople – Cantacuzenus's position was now easily threatened by the mob.

Meanwhile, in 1353, John V Paleologus had been released by his allies from Cantacuzenus's unofficial exile and imprisonment, now re-crowned as the senior *Basileus* after Matthew Cantacuzenus was made the junior in response to the Paleologan rebellions. Making more allies and moving towards the City in November, 1354, John V landed at the Golden Gate and appealed to the populace of Constantinople for support. After seven years of Cantacuzeni rule with boiling class tensions, religious controversy, tax levies to support failed endeavors, and superficially buying off for a little longer security in the Empire, the mob was ready and accepted John Paleologus. Once again, the angered poor wrecked and burned Cantacuzenus's property in the City, mobs overthrowing by force John VI's allies and factionists.

Late that night, John was awakened to a plea without violence to accept the new regime and he capitulated to be junior *Basileus* and depose his son as heir to the throne. By now, John was exhausted and ready to give the massive weight of the Empire's responsibilities to someone else. Even his allies had been obstinate when the Sultan had proclaimed John VI's restitution as divine ingratitude, his deposition being a work of Allah's will. Ten days later on November 22, 1354, the last great soldier-emperor abdicated to become a *Christodoulos* ('Servant of Christ') at the Church of the Blacharnae and, finally, the holy Monastery at

---

[2447] Treadgold, 777.

Mt. Athos as the monk Josaoph. Here he would contemplate Christ with the meditation of His uncreated light and use his education and intelligence to write his memoirs (one of the only *Basilii* to do so) and theologies. He gratefully accepted the *Euchologion* ceremony to cowl monks gladly making way to Mt. Athos, a place he likened to Atlas as it held the whole world for God.[2448]

Already, since before his moral defeats in front of the jaded Constantinopolitans in 1352, John was contemplating a life of solitude in 1341 by buying his own plots of land at Mt. Athos. In 1350, he gave many charitable funds to the Monastery of St. George in Mangana. It has been rightly suggested that John's infamous wealth was only appreciated by the people only if used for charitable purposes in the Empire.[2449] The consequences of his former life was a danger for him as he was still seen as a political figure, as in 1379 when he and his daughter Helena were kept as hostages by Andronicus IV in Galata for two years.[2450] Obviously, John would only find peace as Josaoph in his final years in the anonymity of Mt. Athos until his death on June 15, 1383. He was a dynamic, charismatic, and even tragic figure in Byzantine history, playing with excellence as Grand Domestic, promising greatness as *Basileus*, and being a leading scholar in his years after the throne.

He was the last *Basileus* to competently stem the growing decay and decline of the Empire in his seven years. And this might have continued if he had kept in check the passions of his own populace and the surprising energy John V used in reclaiming the throne who was almost completely bolstered by most of Cantacuzenus's enemies. Seen as a sinister usurper as well as a loyal friend to the Paleologi, to literature, and to the Christian faith, these complexities only prove that a monarch like John VI Cantacuzenus was a hallmark in a period known for decay, neglect, and weakness.

Yet another *Basileus* of great contrasts, he had at once a fiery ambition, contempt for dignities, and a mystical desire for renunciation. Added to this was a passion for glorifying and justifying acts in his memoirs with the 'passionate, mystical Byzantines, who carried everything to extremes, but in whom character fell far short of intellect.'[2451] He would retire to the Studite Monastery in southwestern Constantinople before his occupation at Mt. Athos to be a literary product as well as example of the wealthy and learned men who

---

[2448] Cantacuzenus, vol. III, 176; Hussey, 128.

[2449] Nicol, 165.

[2450] Treadgold, 781.

[2451] Diehl, 148-149.

tonsured themselves in the monasteries of the City, enriching themselves with their books.[2452] The wealth of secular and theological texts of Mt. Athos only motivated a prolific writer such as Cantacuzenus to new heights.

He was also the *Basileus* who wrote his *Memoirs* in four books of histories dated from 1320 to 1356, catching the imagination of the French monarchy three centuries later. They mostly sought not only to blacken his adversaries' names and praise his own allies, but also give insight into the plights of his century. Added was a well-developed ethnography of the Slavs and geography of the Balkans (as Porphyrogenitus had done). He was also known for polemics against the faults and errors of Barlaam the anti-Hesychast, the Muslims, and the Jews. Even his tonsured son Matthew was known for his works of theology and oratory from Mt. Athos.[2453]

Whether he was an altruist or a despoiler, John Cantacuzenus knew the source of the Empire's problems from long years of observation and experience. In the spirit of unity, he orated to ambassadors of the *Basilia* Anne on the lack of men of wisdom and intellect causing the internal ruin of the Empire and how the affairs of today compared to the past only in producing men of sterility that could not rise above their own challenges.[2454] Historians have always seemed to overestimate the ambitions of Cantacuzenus, and thus his intentions. They have rashly stated he wanted the throne all along or being an 'omnipotent' regent based on an avarice of power. Venetian representatives would paint Cantacuzenus as a megalomaniac who wished to engulf Venice, Serbia, and Hungary to battle the Turks.[2455] This unlikely scenario from Constantinople gave contemporary Venice ample propaganda to battle the Greeks for their Eastern interests in trade and colonial politics. At the same time, it is here that it is cited by earlier historians as the time the Turks had been 'given' the Balkans by Cantacuzenus's faults.

As said above, John VI's dethronement was not the end of his public life, unlike other *Basilii*, as he soon became a spiritual defender in place of his previous role of secular leader for all of the Empire. Magnanimously, he had written letters to Pope Clement VI to the effect that the Serbs and Bulgarians were still 'our brothers in faith (*homopistoi*)'[2456] and called for harmony between Slav and Greek. That same year, in June of 1367, he even made a personal appearance

---

[2452] Herrin, 126.

[2453] Vasiliev, 688-689.

[2454] Norwich, *(DF)*, 293.

[2455] Vasiliev, 623.

[2456] Obolensky, 257.

at a Council in defense of the Orthodox-Hesychast faith and Church Union. The Council called by the Church concerned the investiture of Philotheus, a family friend of John's, to the Patriarchy. John's oratory focused on the breach between the Western and Eastern Churches and how the differences of each could be reconciled into Union which was the aim of the Paleologi, especially his once-senior *Basileus* John V. Culturally, these oppositions over Orthodoxy and Hesychasm was a further gulf between the Churches as rulers like Manuel I Comnenus and Michael VIII represented Latinophilism and Andronicus II and Cantacuzenus that of the conservative Greco-Byzantinism.[2457]

Even before all of this, John was known for his devotion to theological dispute and the mystical elements of pure faith in the Church through the monasteries and the faction of George Palamas, who lifted the *Basileus*'s excommunication for heresy. On May 27, 1347, the Bishops called an emergency Second Council on Orthodoxy at the Palace of St. Blacharnae; Calecas, as a rival of the *Basileus*, was not present but still made known his support for Palamas. The subject of this Council was, of course, the fate of the faction of Palamas (the Palamites), John VI Cantacuzenus being in attendance to support Hesychasm, which triumphed as a new doctrine of the Church. Even a Third Council in 1351 could not suppress the Hesychasts and Cantacuzenists in the Church and monasteries. The Patriarch Callistus also receiving the *Basileus*'s *Tomos* defending indefinitely this decision, forcefully counter-signed by the junior *Basileus* John V.[2458]

John's detractors still existed long after 1354 as Gregoras commented on how he would have been the best of *Basileus* if not for his fall into Hesychasm. Nicephorus Gregoras took the mantle of Orthodoxy with Matthew of Ephesus who both believed the controversy was coloring, biasing, and poisoning the state machinery against unrelated interests more important. Gregoras, the best historian of the early Paleologi and a member of the court, was a fierce opponent of the theological energy of Cantacuzenus and his works to the point they were not on speaking terms.[2459] Pamphlets denouncing Palamism flooded the literati from Gregoras's pen until his death in 1359. In a cruel twist, in 1364, Gregoras's body was interred from the Monastery of the Chora and dragged through the streets of the City – an ancient 'ceremony' of public denunciation. Meanwhile,

---

[2457] Ostrogorsky, 522-523.

[2458] Norwich, *(DF)*, 315.

[2459] Hussey, 107.

the cruelty came from his old enemy Palamas, being made an Orthodox saint upon his death in 1368.

The dual nature of John's devotion to his state and his God comes as an example from a manuscript miniature found in the works of Cantacuzenus from 1370-1375, now in the Bibliotheque Nationale of Paris. This was the juxtaposition of Cantacuzenus in the imperial raiment as John VI with that of the simple black cowl of the Byzantine monk as Josaoph of Mt. Athos. Another visual, just as poignant to the Orthodox observer, was his leadership of the Council of 1351 wherein he sits in his raiment holding high the Holy Cross above his head as the premier of all. He sits upon his throne contemplating the Hesychasm of Thabor, the entire convocation of Bishops (four, including Palamas, Callistus of Constantinople, Arsenios of Cyzicus, and Coccinos of Herclea)[2460] surrounded by monks looking to him in reverence. An anonymous monk in the crowd holds Cantucazenus's sword as a reminder it is by this sword Christendom and the Empire will be saved, in Parisinus graecus no. 1242.[2461]

While the veracity of these factual sentiments can be called to question, as it was the events' own historian that supplied the inspiration for these depictions, it is no question as to the stylistic talents and influences found in the *Basileus*'s memoirs. It was the use of Classical models such as Herodotus, Thucydides, Polybius, and others that inspired the meticulous gathering of materials and resources with the responsibility towards an objective viewpoint that made for the Greeks, history 'not a bald recital of events' but true works of art, even as a literary genre. Cantacuzenus fell into the line of historians that saw the Empire from the high view of a throne – Constantine VII, Anna Comnena, and Bryennius.[2462] Like Procopius before him in the sixth century CE, Cantacuzenus modeled his scientific descriptions of the Black Plague and its social effects after Thucydides. Alongside the early Renaissance writer Giovanni Boccaccio (1313-1375) for his *Decameron*, John is accredited as displaying a Classical and Humanist approach to understanding the Black Death that swept from Italy to Spain to England to Norway.[2463]

In Cantacuzenus's east it traveled to Novgorod and infected all of Poland, the Crimea, and Russia by way of Germany by 1353. Boccaccio, speaking through Greco-Byzantine influence, spoke of the *gavoccioli* (buboes) the size

---

[2460] Herrin, plate no. 39, 'One of the rare pictures of Byzantine Church councils.'

[2461] Treadgold, 772.

[2462] Diehl, 242.

[2463] Vasiliev, 626.

of eggs on the body and the uselessness of any medicine or medical training to allay it.[2464] Quite unlike Boccaccio was the fact it was the re-discovered *Memoirs* of Cantacuzenus that aided in beginning the serious study of imperial works in the seventeenth century based on the French scholars of the Byzantinist *Paris Corpus*. In 1645, the printing house of the Louvre, patronized by King Louis XIV (1638-1715) and his finance minister and Byzantinist Jean-Baptist Colbert (1619-1683), began this series of imperial publications with Cantacuzenus being the only volume until 1648.[2465]

Just as the nobility's feudalism in the peripheral territories of the Empire were further fragmenting and dissipating its center, so the suburban life mirrored by the successes in the West was further undermining Byzantium. The rise of town life allowed the peasantry to come into central monarchical control in France and England, bolstered by new middle class leadership and mayoralties. But unlike the bourgeoisie that controlled these town centers in the West, the crumbling base of the landed aristocrats of Byzantium controlled the towns of their own peasantry with no local middle-class presence. As the unity of the aristocracy was taken by the Plague, war and financial demarcation in the Italian trade colonies took the ownership of these towns to use for their trade centers, separating Constantinople from their small-holding local governments as the Slavs and Turks were doing on a larger scale.[2466]

Another important contributor to the Paleologan Renaissance of the fourteenth century was the writer and historian, Demetrius Cydones, who was schooled in Latin literature in Milan. A Church Unionist, he had residences in Thessalonica, Constantinople, Crete, and even had Venetian citizenship. His greatest work was the translation of Thomas Aquinas (1225-1274)'s *Summa Theologica,* the foundation of Western Aristotelean thought in the Catholic Church, which originally contained Arabic philosophic elements, but was now Hellenized as well through the tribulations of Cydones. The only phenomena stemming this tide were decisions made by theologians in the Councils held in 1341, 1347, and 1351, where Palamist and Neo-Platonic concepts of Orthodox prayer and theology won over the logical nature of Western Aristotelianism.[2467]

---

[2464] Boccaccio, Giovanni. *The Decameron,* trans. by Mark Musa and Peter Bondanella. New York, NY: Signet Classics. 2010, 8-9.

[2465] Ostrogorsky, 3.

[2466] *ibid.,* 514-515.

[2467] Herrin, 201. Most likely this was the championing of the mystical and idealistic nature of Hesychasm over any logical and materialist sentiments of Thomism, Aristotle, or even traditional Orthodoxy.

Not surprisingly, he was known as a bridge between Byzantine and Italian Renaissance cultural relations that would long survive after 1453. Along with religious commentaries against Hesychasm and for Union, Cydones wrote for a political understanding in the Empire for the Zealots in his home city of Thessalonica in *Monodia epi tois en Thessalonike Pesousin*. Also, besides writing prefaces for Chrysobulls for the Unionist and anti-Hesychast *Basileus* John V Paleologus, he was a major historian of the period along with Nicholas Gregoras and John Cantacuzenus, dying as a Dominican (a notably Western ascetic order) monk in 1410.

Imperial patronage in education was also slipping as John V only made any contributions to please Rome into a Union that evaporated, almost forfeiting his family and autonomy as temporal and spiritual leader. From then on, the patronage of this kind would be left to private citizens and the applauded academics and scholars progressing Byzantine thought through their Classical masters. Cydones was a true Byzantine patriot as well, writing 447 letters (thirty-two being for Manuel II, and eleven for Cantacuzenus), while his *sumbouluetikoi* were orations he used to enlighten all on the depression facing a beleaguered Constantinople and call for a rise to the challenge of the people in saving the Empire.[2468] In the fourteenth century, at least one anonymous book on court etiquette in Byzantium was written and distributed on the subjects of uniforms, colored hats, shoes, insignias, and hierarchy.[2469] When reading, one would think Byzantium was as it was in the splendid tenth century of Porphyrogenitus, but the depredations in finance and resources was the only truth that such traditions were now empty.

## ANDRONICUS IV PALEOLOGUS
### (1376-1379)

## JOHN VII PALEOLOGUS
### (1390)

Second to take the throne in this time of crisis was John V's son, Andronicus, who was little improvement on his father's record and by no means a comparison to John VI Cantacuzenus and his sobering skill. He was mainly an unscrupulous opportunist who failed once at a coup, but recovered

---

[2468] Vasiliev, 694-695.

[2469] Diehl, 197.

when blessed by the convergence of a captive father, Italian benefices, a brother of seemingly no harmful ambitions, and a different Ottoman Sultan whose approval he had bought in 1376. Yet, leadership was still needed when his brother Manuel was busily fighting to pay his father's ransom as imposed by Venice. The last son of John V was willing to take the reins of government despite having, in evaluation, much less room to maneuver and bargain than his father had.[2470] His first aim was to gain allies in Genoa by ceding them the isle of Tenedos, which revolted quickly back to Venice, this at least being without the fault of Andronicus. Yet, in only three years of lackluster rule, Andronicus IV's allies turned to conspirators and the lesser of two evils by 1379 was decidedly to support John V.

Andronicus IV Paleologus was born the eldest son of John V and Helena, daughter of John Cantacuzenus, in 1348, and his motives had always been suspect when considering his succession. In 1366, it is suggested he had knowledge of the plot to seize the *Basileus* at Vdin after his audience with Louis of Hungary, Andronicus being the Bulgarian Tsar's son-in-law.[2471] In 1371, Andronicus seized directly for the first time the opportunity to rule as Regent of Constantinople, making since 1369 a separate peace with his allies, the Genoese, over hotly-contended Tenedos. The Genoese seems to have put 'pressure' on Andronicus to do so,[2472] which is probable as this was the first time Andronicus would ally with the Genoese and Galata. Callous to his father's fate as an Italian prisoner for the events of 1373, he rejected the Venetians their claim on the island. The Regent's excuse was the fact the only wealth available was in the Church and the people would not allow such appropriations for a newly-converted Catholic John V, being a captive upon payment due to the Republic of St. Mark.

After John's reinstatement with the aid of his son Manuel, Andronicus proved to be a hot-blooded and overreaching man of twenty-five as he attempted a coup with his ally Sauja against his father, Murad the Ottoman Sultan in May, 1373. Having failed in the attempts, Murad mutilated his son to death by blinding and ordered John to do the same, demonstrating the servile status of the Empire and its weakling ruler. As he meekly demurred to the act, John allowed his son and grandson, both potential enemies, to only be blinded in one eye and then imprisoned. Resentful, Andronicus and his maimed son John

---

[2470] Treadgold, 780.

[2471] Ostrogorsky, 538.

[2472] Norwich, *(DF)*, 334-335.

remained imprisoned indefinitely. Yet, it was not impossible, either that he gain the throne with his injuries as the practice had been made moot before by *Basilii* such as Justinian II and Isaac II.

When, in 1376, Andronicus was released by Genoan allies who did so if promised Tenedos and the Dardanelles, he crossed to Galata from Anemas in July to await fortunate events. With John 'bludgeoned' into a corner in the Fortress of the Golden Gate, Andronicus entered Constantinople on October 18, 1377, and crowned as Andronicus IV, making his partially-blinded son his co-emperor to be John VII. Andronicus happily consigned his father, who he saw as a betrayer and unfit for the throne, to the prison of Anemas in as he saw as just retribution. He managed to placate Murad by ceding to him Callipolis, a Savoian possession since 1366, guaranteeing a Turkish bridgehead into Thrace, though this cessation might have been Murad's idea to support Andronicus in the first place.[2473] The *Basileus* also began to compose an army of ships and soldiers to aid Genoa in taking Tenedos, still heavily pro-Venetian, which the reporting historian Cydones evaluates would be as difficult to the emperor as flying.

Venice would show its dominance and displeasure to Constantinople for the three years of Andronicus's reign with examples such as flogging Greek prisoners by ship outside the Blacharnae.[2474] In 1377, in reaction to the imprisonment of the Venetian *Bailo* at the Greek court, the admiral Pietro Mocenigo left for Constantinople to demand his release and reinstatement on pain of deposition backed, if need be, by the Sultan. Mocenigo did not get to his destination, however, as the war between Venice and Genoa had broken out in full force and he was called to return to his military duties as imperial politics would have to wait for the time being.[2475]

It was Manuel Paleologus that changed the tide in 1379 after his and his father's imprisonment for managing to escape Anemas. Crossing the Bosporus at Chrysopolis, Manuel entreated Murad to aid him in recovering the throne for his father (and not himself) in exchange for more tribute and their assistance in taking Philadelphia. Murad no longer had any trust or loyalty to Andronicus, especially after the attempted coup of 1373 Andronicus had orchestrated. Besides, Byzantium had no teeth as he already had Callipolis and north Thrace

---

[2473] Reinert, 'Revival of Learning', 271. Another speculation by Reinert insists this was the work of the anti-Union factions attempting to prevent the mistakes of the earlier Paleologi by submitting to Rome.

[2474] Norwich, *(AHV)*, 180.

[2475] *ibid.*, 246-247.

for the Sultanate and could hold it, treaty or not. Now, with these further capitulations by the Paleologi, Asia Minor would now completely be Turkish with the addition of Philadelphia, the Sultan readily accepting Manuel's terms.

On July 1, 1379, John V and Manuel entered the City by the Charisian Gate backed by the Venetians, who awaited the return of Tenedos which had been promised eight years before. The fickle inhabitants of the City were much less impressed by Andronicus and, persuaded to open the Gates, allowed John to regain the Palace. Andronicus fled to the Tower of Galata, protected by the Genoese militia who also seized the former *Basileus* John VI (Josaoph) and his *Basilia*, Helena Cantacuzena, from the Blacharnae as hostages. They had been earlier arrested on baseless allegations of aiding John V and Manuel in their escape from Anemas.[2476] For two more years this stalemate continued at Galata until April, 1381, when Andronicus agreed to more than fair terms for his surrender.

Andronicus IV Paleologus received much more than he deserved, but John and Manuel always demonstrated a consistent reputation for leniency and temperance, Andronicus being allowed to be the imperial heir once again. His son John would be his heir and they would rule from Selymbria on the northern Marmara to operate the cities of Rhaedestrus, Heraclea, and Panidus. It was from here that Andronicus continued to be a thorn in his family's side when, reportedly, he attempted one last coup against his father before his death in June, 1385.

Andronicus IV was only an example of misplaced ambition on the least stable of foundations, wherein he showed an only two-dimensional character. Though his father lacked almost any ability, Andronicus proved to have less and could not collect enough loyalty from potential allies not to be ousted when the wind blew a different direction. Had he lived longer, his incompetent behavior would only have continued after his father died in 1391 and he would be made legitimate *Basileus* with his son. How long such a reign would have lasted is only speculative and the better man for the throne, Manuel, might have ruled anyway, likely supported by the factions that refused to support Andronicus. All that is sure is that if Andronicus had ruled into the fifteenth century, he would have witnessed the humbling of the once fierce Ottoman Turks from an eastern menace his brother would witness, unthinkable just a few years before.

During the few years after Andronicus IV's rule, while he spent most of his final years asylumed in Galata, events in Central Eurasia were seeing the rise of

---

[2476] Norwich, *(DF)*, 339.

a new power and chapter in history. From 1384 to 1385, the Tartar descendant of Genghis Khan, Timur 'the Lame' – or Tamerlane – was making vast victories against armies larger than his own, conquering the regions of northern Iran. Born in 1336, he first took the throne of Samarkand in 1369 from his original territory of Transoxiana near eastern Persia, his armies defeating the Golden Horde of Tokhtameresh in 1386, who Tamerlane had put on the throne in the first place in 1376.

After its preventative attacks on Timurid Azerbaijan, this conqueror further secured central Iran and Georgia, moving further west. Eyewitnesses report he was, like his Khan ancestor, an intelligent, generous, and brave ruler who was absolutely ruthless to his rebellious enemies – such as the entire city of Isfahan who he had executed in 1387,[2477] also doing the same to Sebasteia in 1400.[2478] Tamerlane would also strike down any ruler he deemed unfit to rule no matter the situation and he demonstrated this on the tyranny of Bayezid in 1402 as he ruled an Empire from Afghanistan to northern India to Anatolia.

Least in this game of musical chairs involving the Byzantine throne and Constantinople between three generations of Palaeologi was John VII, son of Andronicus IV and grandson of John V. His 'reign' of five months was merely a failed experiment by the puppeteers of Prusa and Galata once again disillusioned with John V. He was only said to be a monarch of 'some ability but no experience' resentful of his grandfather for his partial blinding at three years old on Murad's cruel orders,[2479] promising just to be another Andronicus IV in the making. Manuel Paleologus, once again incensed by the treatment of his father as a prisoner of the Golden Gate in 1390, ended this embryonic rule and defied the Sultan Bayezid's plans for Byzantine dynastic plans.

The Sultan's final instrument of subjugation aimed at the Slavs, Serbs, and Greeks was now in play as the *charaj*, a tax so severe in financial limitations on his subjects (breaking all previous privileges legally), they could not exempt themselves without paying the sums on what was remitted.[2480] By 1390, the Sultan's coup in Constantinople was very imminent, the Most Serene Republic of Venice fully expecting, in documents cited between East and West, to see

---

[2477]  Beckwith, 198-199.

[2478]  Norwich, *(DF)*, 366.

[2479]  Treadgold, 782.

[2480]  Ostrogorsky, 547f.

Bayezid soon on the throne in the decaying Queen of Cities. The Senate sent correspondences to the Venetian envoys that, should they personally see 'Murad's son' in Constantinople, it is imperative they appeal for the restitution of captured Venetian vessels.[2481]

A desperate John VII Paleologus fled to his strongest ally, the Ottoman Sultan, to await his judgment. But, such as the career of John Cantacuzenus, John VII's did not end after his dethronement and would enjoy limited trust and responsibility from his lenient uncle Manuel, even after John V's death in 1391. John VII Paleologus was born in 1370 as the son and heir apparent to the co-emperor Andronicus Paleologus. The greatest tragedy of his life was being the son of that very co-emperor when he was maimed like his father in 1373 and thrown into prison on Sultan Murad's command at three years old. He was six when his father was made *Basileus* during his grandfather's irresponsible absence and a year later was himself made co-emperor over his uncle Manuel, being a prisoner of Anemas, still loyal to the exiled John V. Still a child with no real attributes and no chances of earning duties, titles, honors, or control over events, at nine he was ousted from Constantinople to Galata with his father, experiencing exile as well.

In 1384, a settlement was reached with John V and Manuel as the deposed father and son were sent to govern Selymbria, remaining there until Andronicus's death a year later to leave behind an embittered fifteen-year-old to take up his responsibilities. Any claims to the throne John might have had were further compromised in 1387 when Thessalonica surrendered to the Ottoman noble, Hayreddin Pasha, as a vassal surrendered by John and Manuel. This progression between the City and Thessalonica was seen as reason enough for John to attempt a coup on his grandfather and uncle. Yet such a coup would be unlikely by Manuel's alliance with the Templars of Rhodes in return for ecclesiastical objects held by the Empire.[2482] Any relationship or amicability between the two Paleologi would, for over a decade, be merely 'transitory and superficial.'

Until 1390, John V was the ruler of the 'Appenage' of Selymbria and its few cities on the northern shore of the Marmara, but in the courts at Prusa, Bayezid was becoming tired of the ineffective elderly monarch. Reaching an easy alliance with Galata against the *Basileus*, they besieged the City and forced John V into hiding, putting Manuel's forces to flight. The Sultan then had John

---

[2481]  Vasiliev, 586.
[2482]  Reinert, 'Revival of Learning', 272-273.

VII galvanized to put himself on the throne on April 13 as a continuance of the legitimate Paleologan line; John did possess the more legitimate right to the throne than John V's favored (but second) son Manuel, after all.[2483] As John was occupied with dislodging his grandfather from the Golden Gate (which is now the ruins of the Fortress of Seven Towers in Istanbul) Manuel was traveling north to Marmara to seek help.

Surprisingly, the West vested an interest in the form of the Knights Templar, a sworn enemy of the Ottomans that favored John V. From Rhodes, Lemnos, Christopolis, and even some from Constantinople, a fleet of four 'unidentified'[2484] ships sailed south to the City by August and on Saturday, September 17, an unprepared John was made to flee to Bayezid's court in disgrace. Bayezid was incensed as this action was not just a defiance of his will and Allah's, but a personal insult to the dignity to himself as Sultan. He allowed this change to occur for the present and concentrated on sending the two feckless and cowed Paleologan *Basilii* to join in taking Philadelphia in May of 1391. As this was also on the territory of John VII on the Marmara coast, he is said to have been shocked into speechlessness by the order, having no choice but to submit.

Upon this shame, it is said John V Paleologus died in his bed due to the horror of this act and his family's subservience to it. The devastation was typical of a Turkish victory as buildings were demolished and the inhabitants were killed despite age or status without mercy.[2485] Manuel was aware of the irony that to add to this strength was only to diminish his own. In 1391, Manuel II Paleologus was crowned *Basileus*, burdened with the knowledge that the fickle (and increasingly mentally unstable[2486]) Sultan could easily supplant him with the more amenable John despite his attempts at taking the City by force. John enjoyed the tacit protection of Prusa's court and could not have possibly been ignorant of the fact he was a Turkish puppet on the throne and when off of it he was a prisoner.

---

[2483] Treadgold, 784.

[2484] Norwich, *(DF)*, 346.

[2485] Barker, J.W. *Manuel II Paleologus (1391-1425): A Study in Late Byzantine Statemanship.* Brunswick, NJ: Rutgers University Press. 1969, 88-96. Manuel Paleologus wrote eyewitness testaments to this in his letters as *Basileus* at length with only minor editing by Barker.

[2486] Norwich, *(DF)*, 348. It was being demonstrated over time by his unpredictable manners that the Sultan was becoming too unstable to rule effectively by the evaluation of his nobles.

Events in July 1393 were proof of this as a base on Serres was called on to put down a Bulgarian insurrection led by Shishman. But at the camp, Manuel, John, their brother Theodore Paleologus the Despot of Morea, his father-in-law Dragases, and the Serbian commander Lazarivic arrived with no foreknowledge any of the others were being involved! This arrogant move by the Sultan in ordering military gatherings with no communication like vassals was the last bit of evidence that almost any Byzantine autonomy against the Turks was illusory. Yet, Bayezid had promised, in secret, the City a peace if the inhabitants would be ready to re-instate John VII at a moment's notice, having continued to be, by 1396, an ornament of forced unity in the Paleologi. By now, the exhausted and quietly hostile populace of Constantinople was blaming Manuel Paleologus for their woes and support for John rose as the mob wanted change.[2487]

In these unstable times, however, it is reported that John VII was ostracizing his loyalties to the Sultan and his uncle by offering the French King as the standing ruler of Genoa and its colonies, Charles VI, full claim to his title of *Basileus* in exchange for an annual stipend of 25,000 *florins* and a chateau in France![2488] Documents of negotiation were written and sent by John's ambassadors, in secret, on August 15, 1397. But Charles had no interest in them, all being forgotten, and it did not distort any intentions of the King to send his Marechal or troops.[2489] Over the next few years, Charles, Theodore, and Manuel would be fighting the Turks for the safety of the Byzantine throne as John stood neutral and ready to flee, indifferent to a Greek or a Frenchman taking the throne in his absence. This was all moot to Manuel as he never trusted his great nephew or his intentions, although for appearances sake, he had faked forgiveness to appease the Sultan.

A desperate Manuel would leave for France, practically pleading for aid at Charles's feet, taking his *Basilia* and the French commander Boucicault with him on December 10, 1399. By that time, the King's new Marechal had shown his cleverness in diplomatic wit by joining the two Paleologi to a common cause, Manuel reluctantly naming John Paleologus as Regent.[2490] Manuel would put off any plans of duplicity by leaving his sons and heirs with his brother Theodore in the Morea; now, John could not take them as hostages, not having the strength to wage a war on the Morea. In April 1400, Manuel II strengthened

---

[2487] Vasiliev, 631.

[2488] Norwich, *(DF)*, 358.

[2489] Ostrogorsky, 554-555.

[2490] Treadgold, 787.

ties with Venice to harbor his family in the port cities of Modone and Corone should Bayezid enter the Peloponnese to re-install John. But, whatever the reason to John, the thirty-one-year old former *Basileus* by the end of 1401 had made all of his best efforts at defending the City from Bayezid in Manuel's absence. The Sultan had sent entreaties of surrender to John promising the desolation of all within the Walls if he refused; heroically, John abandoned the meek graces he had shown the Sultan before and remarked that they had no resources or strength left, so he must do what he must do.[2491] With the Greek Wall Guard, no coming reinforcements, and only 300 French troops under Boucicault (down from 1,200 six months before) the situation was hopeless and defeat seemed imminent.

John's only show of diplomacy was the promise of tribute to Tamerlane in protecting them from the Turks, but that was only on the whims that the Mongols didn't turn on them.[2492] Selymbria and Thrace were captured and only the City itself and a few islands were the legal Byzantine Empire as John was ready to surrender entirely. But what kept 1402 from becoming the loss of 1453 was the Sultan's arrogance before the Mongol conqueror Tamerlane, who captured Bayezid himself at the Battle of Chubuk near Ancyra on July 28, 1402, breaking the forces of the Ottomans right to the Gates of Constantinople by sheer terror.

The Ottoman situation changed dramatically and the Prince Sulayman now set about relieving Byzantium and asking their support in the crisis. Sulaymen wrote warm letters to John offering the role of a father to him if there were no more 'rivalries or differences.' With those assurances brought to Paris, Manuel returned home after nearly four years at Callipolis on June 9, 1403, where John greeted him in semi-gratitude. In between, Manuel visited Venice where he was greatly accepted by the Doge Michele Steno who balked at his nephew's pro-Genoan diplomacy against the Republic. Yet, the dispute between imperial uncle and former-imperial nephew seemed to continue; Manuel divested John of all appanages and titles and exiled him to Lemnos. The most feasible reason was John's fortunate relationship with the new Sultan as Sulaymen, giving him Thessalonica if he returned to the Empire Mesembria and Panidus on the Thracian coast.

As Tamerlane had made the Ottoman Empire at its most vulnerable, the Regent of Sulayman thought it wise to keep Byzantium in his good graces to use

---

[2491] Norwich, *(DF)*, 365.
[2492] Herrin, 314.

against the Mongols as well as their Italian allies (whichever one it was at any time). Probably continuing his father's policy, the *Basileus* honored the younger and more pliable John with the rule of Thessalonica in Manuel's absence, also hedging bets if he may need to dispel Manuel from the throne at any notice. Manuel, upon his triumphant return realized this, using it to finally reveal his mistrust for John and separate him from Constantinople indefinitely. As the Ottoman court's resources being pointed heavily toward Tamerlane, they could not afford too much resistance to John's sudden disenfranchisement. Yet, the true victor was Sulayman as his allowances to the Italian powers, the French, and the Templars guaranteed the Christian powers would be played off against each other, not uniting against him in the western half of the Empire as most attention was being paid to the east.[2493]

John, however, had strong and useful allies, using their resources to return the exiled Regent to a position of power in Byzantium. The Genoan Francesco II Guttilusio, Lord of the isle of Lesbos and John VII's father-in-law sent, in September, 1403, seven Genoan ships to take Thessalonica for John. Manuel's resources here were limited as it had in past decades become an independent entity from Constantinople, Manuel choosing diplomacy over force. A month later, he met with John to negotiate terms to return Thessalonica as John would be made 'Emperor of all Thessaly' in return. Though it was without coronation, ceremony, and was largely superficial, John Paleologus still had a limited claim on the title of John VII.

John VII had a weak succession to this claim in his only son, Andronicus V, but between 1404 and 1408, Andronicus died at age seven, leaving John the last direct descendant of this branch of Paleologan *Basilii*. Sources at the time speak only of Andronicus's existence with no coronation as co-emperor or any title to Thessalonica, and proof of his existence at all is scarce. However, in Washington DC, at the Dumbarton Oaks archives, is an ivory depiction of John and Andronicus together around the time of John's ascendency in Thessalonica.[2494] Sometime before his death at thirty-eight in September, 1408, John VII had taken the cowl as John VI had – taking also the name Josaoph – after giving his kingdom's wealth to fund churches, monasteries, and charitable institutions.

John VII Paleologus was another example of an ambitious Byzantine and Turkish puppet usurping the throne from a weak monarch to divide the

---

[2493] Treadgold, 789.
[2494] Norwich, *(DF)*, 370-371.

alliances of the Paleologi when the Empire's future was faltering heavily. Yet, he certainly had more vitality than his father and grandfather, though still falling exceedingly short of Cantacuzenus and his resilient uncle. He even showed signs of Western cooperation, some courage in battle (though compromised by deep demoralization to surrender), and an amount of trustworthiness as staying Regent in 1399 to 1403, not taking the opportunity in usurping the throne a second time. But the infamous decay known as the 'Energy of Byzantium' had gripped him as it did Cantacuzenus and the lack of a Greco-Genoan heir may have induced his grateful retirement from the world into a cloister before he was forty. At least, now unimpeded by family division and squabble, Manuel II could hold the reigns of government and prove Byzantine diplomacy was not as dead as its military or political mastery.

## MANUEL II PALEOLOGUS
### (1391-1425)

A dynamic presence with personality and the skills of a quality diplomat, Manuel II Paleologus would have catapulted the Empire to new horizons had it not been for the iron dominance of the Turkish Sultans Murad and Bayezid of which he was a vassal. The depressed state of Byzantium towards its neighbors and its lost reputation as a prosperous example of Oriental wealth was compounded by the indifference of the West. Themselves burdened by state-to-state conflicts, the Christian powers of every nationality had exhausted many of their own resources, offering only their goodwill to the true bulwark against the Infidel. Yet, Manuel radiated the epitome of the regal lord of Constantinople as he travelled through France being a man of average height, solid constitution, sporting a long white beard, features that demanded respect, and was noted as a man 'worthy of being *Basileus*.' Bayezid himself marveled at the resemblance he had to the Prophet Mohammed and said that one who knew not he was the *Basileus* would still assume him to be one by his appearance.[2495]

Yet, the good public opinion he at first garnered was dependent not on either internal factors in the City or in the outer territories, but on external factors that were beyond, by and large, his control.[2496] Only by a stroke of chance from the revival of the Mongols by the intractable Tamerlane was Constantinople allowed to stand and not surrender to Bayezid's pressure.

---

[2495] Vasiliev, 633-635.
[2496] Ostrogorsky, 543.

Furthermore, the amicability of Prusa in their recovery of the Ottomans would only last so long. Manuel was 'a good and gifted man', capable of returning the Empire to its former glory in 'happier circumstances', but was still helpless to stem the Ottoman tide.[2497] Though he possessed the political wisdom his father had lacked, he knew the end of the Empire was nigh, and insisted it do so with its head held high.[2498]

Manuel II Paleologus was born the second son of the *Basileus* John V (to whom he was his loyalist supporter) and Helena Cantacuzena on June 27, 1350, behind his brother Andronicus. Despite his youth of nineteen years, he was made the Despot of Thessalonica in June, 1369, being the only son of the *Basileus* to assist him when he was a captive of Venice a year later. On September 25, 1373, he was named co-emperor and heir to his father after the treacherous debacle of a coup led by his older brother, Andronicus. To his credit, Manuel was handsome and dignified, healthy, energetic, and the epitome of his predecessor John VI Cantacuzenus.[2499]

After his brother's deposition as *Basileus* in 1382, his efforts allowed Thessaly and Epirus to become imperial vassals and lead an effective, if not separate, existence from the central authority of Constantinople. It was by such endeavor that Manuel would prove that, since strength was effectively lacking in the Empire, it only took capable leadership to be Byzantium's 'key to success'.[2500] Manuel would also display at times the cunning which became the successful hallmark of Byzantium's reputation by setting dynastic rivals against the other, a 'classic ploy' that would benefit his antecedent *Basilii* as it did his predecessors.[2501] This had just become one of the few tools available to the Empire in its grasp for survival and success.

He had won the admiration of the rigid Murad I who counseled him to rule wisely and not seek foreign lands (especially his own), also promising him aid and money if he ever requested.[2502] He demonstrated his leadership in 1382 in the face of Turkish oppression before Murad I by besieging and occupying Thessalonica in open defiance of his Turkish 'suzerain.' His first falter was in the loss of Serres to

---

[2497] Norwich, *(AHV)*, 261.

[2498] Brownworth, 277.

[2499] Norwich, *(DF)*, 349.

[2500] Barker, *(MP)*, 393.

[2501] Crowley, Roger. *1453: The Holy War for Constantinople and the Clash of Islam and the West.* New York, NY: Hyperion Books. 2005, 54-55.

[2502] George (Phrantzes) Sphrantzes. *Annales,* I, chap. 11, ed. by I. Bekker. Bonn, Germany: *CSHB.* 1839, 48-49; Vasiliev, 587.

Murad on September 19, 1383. Until 1387, Manuel II put up constant resistance in the Despotate by besieging the seaports until the exhausted inhabitants opened their gates to the Turks in April. As he always claimed, Manuel fled Thessalonica and barely saving his own skin by fleeing to Lesbos.

He was often his most active when his father was typically inert, 'embarrassing his [father's] policy of Turkish compliance with a rebellious "wayward expansionism" against the Sultan when deprived of the co-rule of his father.'[2503] He continued defending his Despotate against Murad I who finally claimed it and went on to conquer Bulgaria before his death in 1389 at Kosovo. Bulgaria would finally end as an empire in 1393 with the last Bulgarian Tsar, Shishman, executed by Bayezid. Upon John V's death by sheer hopelessness, Manuel, as surviving son and viable Paleologus, was crowned on Saturday, February 11, 1391, escaping Prusa by boat. The furious Sultan could only spit to his embassadors as Manuel entered the City that the *Basileus* should enjoy it and lock his gates, for all outside them were his. Truly, while Byzantium still harbored the Aegean and part of Peloponnese, these scraps could hardly be called an Empire.[2504]

Joining him was his wife Helena, daughter of Constantine Dragash (Dragases), a Serbian noble of Macedonia, and the mother of his eldest legitimate son, John, born later that year. As Manuel II perceived, the Ottoman reverses only accentuated the unpredictability of the times and it was a wisely cautious Manuel that made no serious resistance; his fatalism in the situation was, truthfully, just realism.[2505] The City itself was also in a serious decline as the population, over the past three centuries, had been decimated from its tens of millions of inhabitants to merely 40,000 to 50,000 by 1391.[2506]

This reality surfaced the most when, in 1393, what was already a humiliating call to arms for Manuel at the Turkish battle of Serres resulted in the *Basileus*, his nephew John of Selymbria, and a number of non-Turkish vassals of the Sultan meeting with no prior knowledge of the others' notice to appear. This posed as an obvious signal to all that Bayezid could take the Balkans in one blow with no ruler to guard them. Theodore I Paleologus of the Morea was then forced to recover and cede Argos and Monemvasia for the Ottomans as the threatened and shaken vassals departed Serres as Bayezid was only toying with them to remind them of his power. Theodore, however, was not easily intimidated

[2503]  Reinert, 'Revival of Learning', 271.
[2504]  Brownworth, 278.
[2505]  Treadgold, 784.
[2506]  Ostrogorsky, 549.

and the two Peloponnesian cities were stolen and handed to the more capable Venetians. In retaliation, Bayezid left the Balkans alone, ultimately besieging and blockading the impenetrable Constantinople with his limited fleet in 1394.

In September, 1395, Niero I Acciojuli, Duke of Athens and the father-in-law of Theodore Paleologus, had died and with Corinth in Theodore's possession, the city was violently contested by his brother-in-law, Carlo Tocco of Cephalonia. Carlo allied with the Ottomans and the Navarrese of the Peloponnese, as ancestors of the Catalans, to invade Corinth, the Morea, and their key fortresses by the year's end. Still at a stalemate against the superior naval forces of the Venetians, the Sultan turned east by land to the Peloponnesus to undermine Theodore's ventures by the minor Vlach kingdom of Wallachia. This outrage garnered attention in 1395 towards Sigismund of Hungary for a Crusade against Turkish Nicopolis two years later, armies from Burgundy, Germany, France, and Venice (totaling as much as 60,000) joining. This was a different and desperate Crusade as it was not intended to free the Holy Land, but protect Constantinople in the Christian East from an epidemic spread of Ottoman Islam.

Unfortunately, the endeavor at Nicopolis was a debacle and the Hungarian King who called Europe to arms fled down the Danube on Venetian ships as 10,000 prisoners were beheaded in one day before the Sultan. Returning to Constantinople, the Sultan even decided to assault and capture Athens and central Greece 'for good measure.'[2507] The Turkish victors lined up on the coasts to jeer the fleeing ships down the Dardenelles as described by a German eye-witness, Johann Schiltberger (1381-1440). The next year, Constantinople would be besieged by Bayezid and its harbor blockaded by their weak – yet still superior to Byzantium's – ships; Manuel himself would be heard to murmur a prayer: 'Lord Jesus Christ, let it not come to pass that the great multitude of Christian people should hear it said that it was in the days of the Emperor Manuel that the City, with all of its sacred and venerable monuments of the Faith, was delivered to the Infidel.' Corinth and Argos in the Peloponnese were taken by the Templars of Rhodes from Theodore Paleologus and the Empire was more dispossessed than ever whether in spite of or because of the Western presence in Byzantium. For eight years, Theodore struggled to buy the ancient city back even as the Thessalonican inhabitants showed their hostility to Theodore for the act of selling it, despite its eventual fall to the Templars.[2508]

France also backed Manuel faithfully in 1399 by sending the Marechal

---

[2507] Brownworth, 279.

[2508] Norwich, *(DF)*, 369f.

Boucicault east with a French force to guard the walls of Constantinople with the *Basileus*'s nephew John of Selymbria. Boucicault already had the qualifications of a seasoned veteran in the East in Palestine, Sinai, and even as a prisoner in Egypt.[2509] It is for this reason that, supposedly, Boucicault broke the Turkish blockade of seventeen galleys, landing with 600 troops and 1,600 archers for the Walls.[2510] A requirement was a begrudging reconciliation since John VII's deposition as *Basileus* a decade before. He departed, leaving his son John with the advice that in affairs, be moderate and cautious; open negotiations on union on friendly terms, but avoid commitments one may not be able to fulfill.[2511]

The reason for his departure was that Charles VI had sponsored the first trans-European tour taken by a Byzantine *Basileus* to seek aid from the Kings of the West. Manuel II arrived in Venice in April 1400 to a warm reception and celebration of his arrival not only due to Manuel's own perseverance to save Eastern Christendom, but to hail the new Hellenized Renaissance style wherein he was characterized as a 'philosopher king.' Since Francesco Petrarch (1304-1374) and Dante Alghieri (1265-1321) in the past century, ancient Roman and Greek styles had been culturally re-vitalized from the East through scholars, clerics, pilgrims, and other travelers.

France, however, realized an opportunity against the Sultan and presented, with Pope Boniface IX, the Archbishop of Ethiopia east of the Tatar court in 1398, to supplicate Tamerlane as ambassadors had from Constantinople two years earlier.[2512] A year later, Manuel II Paleologus would continue his tour with the same adulation he had received in several other Italian cities; Manuel arrived in France by June at Charles's court in Paris. By the end of 1400, embassies had visited Spain, an enthusiastic Pope Boniface, and reached King Henry VI of England in London, personally providing a Christmas feast at the Eltham Palace in Kent. Yet, despite their moral support and graciousness, they could not provide adequate troops needed more than the money they could give at the time. With the exception of Venice, Europe now saw Byzantium as a liability, not a shield to protect them from the Turks, even when a mosque was raised in Constantinople and separate courts existed to administer Islamic law.[2513]

---

[2509] Vasiliev, 632.

[2510] Gibbon, 2240.

[2511] Runciman, 12-13.

[2512] Mazzori, 319.

[2513] Norwich, (AHV), 262. After a doubling of tribute, an independent Islamic Quarter of the Constantinople was demanded with Muslim judges as the governors were instituted. Brownworth, 278.

The costly and exhausting Hundred Years' War had drained the English and French thrones of their military resources with their armistice, Henry VI too insecure and Charles VI 'the Mad' being hopelessly insane.[2514] Spain was busily fighting the Moors to reconquer southern Spain, not to be relieved for another century. The Church was divided among itself in Rome and in Avignon as Boniface was in active disputes with the University of Paris.[2515] A depressed Manuel returned to Paris for another year, keeping in contact with the City by reports from Boucicault and Prince John. Bayezid had also humbled many of these princes after Nicopolis with the exchange of hostages for a pair of carved golden salt-cellars from Lusignan at a value of 10,000 *ducats*. Charles VI dispatched Norwegian hawks (Bayezid enjoyed unleashing them on cranes at the hunt), linen from Rheims, and an Arran tapestry of Alexander the Great's exploits as a count of Nevers fetched the Sultan 200,000 *ducats*.[2516]

As to his hope in recovering Constantinople, 'after his return from a Western pilgrimage, he expected every hour the news of the sad catastrophe'[2517] of its imminent fall. In 1403, however, miraculous news reached Manuel about developments between Prusa and the conquering Mongols of Tamerlane of Samarkand. Already, the legends of this warlord's cruelty were legendary as he cut a destructive path throughout the Middle East. Before killing 15,000 Turks at Ancyra, he rounded the citizens of Damascus in their mosque, burning it to the ground. In Tikrit, he ordered each soldier to present him with two severed heads or forfeit their own and in Baghdad, the skulls of 90,000 citizens were made into a pyramid. Upon taking Philadelphia, Tamerlane had a commemorating wall in the city of the inhabitants' corpses built. Tales of his armies leaving ghost towns and whole populations fleeing into the deserts weakened Turkish morale, spreading panic.

Just before the fatigued John was to surrender the keys to Constantinople's gates to Bayezid, the eastern Turkish front had fallen miserably to Timur and the Sultan himself had been captured alive at Ancyra. Fleeing the siege of the City, Manuel made his way to Trebizond and submitted himself before the Tartar court in congratulations and, of course, the hope he could supplicate the Conqueror away from the City as a Turkish vassal. However, this must

---

[2514] Norwich (AHV), 279.

[2515] Vasiliev, 633.

[2516] Gibbon, 2238. *Bayezid enjoyed the hunt; a tally of spoils from Tamerlane in his own Turkish hunts includes hounds with satin housings, leopards with jeweled collars, dogs from Greece and Europe, and African lions.*

[2517] Gibbon, 2266.

have happened before the tour as Mazzori makes the interesting claim that Tamerlane actually 'ordered' Manuel II back from Europe upon Ancyra's victory to divide Ottoman rule as he did with the Golden Horde a decade before.[2518]

By 1404, Bayezid had died as a prisoner by despair and suicide (it was written romantically by English playwright Christopher Marlowe (1564-1593) that Bayezid died by Tamerlane's own hands, the Conqueror throttling him on the bars of the 'birdcage' in which he was kept) and Theodore I successfully bought Corinth back from Rhodes. No mistake was to be made, however, as the Empire was now a façade with no resources capable of maintaining itself with Thessalonica, Thessaly, and Epirus now independent Greek 'states.'[2519] It was only by his enemies' weakness that Manuel appeared to thrive and expand with absolutely no help from Byzantium's decaying strength or the West's aid.

Leaving Paris with 200 knights under Chateaumarond, he toured Lombardy once more, arriving at Constantinople on June 9. One of Manuel's first acts upon his return in 1403 was to unwarrantedly dispossess and exile his nephew John who had served, without rebellion, on the Walls with Boucicault. Many questions were brought up by this rash decision and speculations of 'why?' abound: A clash of personalities, perhaps? A general dislike of the former John VII that culminated in believing he was a threat? Was it resentment at John's willingness to surrender to Bayezid in 1403? Or was Manuel still bent on militarily action against the Turks in their weakened state, balking at a treaty he had personally signed?[2520] It is even suggested to have been a ruse to fool the Turks and Mongols with a veneer of divisiveness – yet Manuel was not given to ruses or treaty-breaking in his diplomacy. Whatever the reason, John was sent to Lemnos and his territories were returned to the central administration for re-distribution.

Fortunately, Prince Sulaymen was an honorable and peaceful ruler, preferring compromise, diplomacy, and negotiation as much as Manuel did. He was also an insecure successor and a neurotic man given to drunkenness and lethargy, though he defeated his rebellious brother Isa in 1405.[2521] Peace negotiations with Manuel was almost strictly out of necessity as his military and administration was now in tatters. He freed Constantinople from Turkish

---

[2518] Mazzori, 345.

[2519] Treadgold, 790.

[2520] Norwich, (DF), 371.

[2521] Runciman, 43.

vassalage, freed all prisoners, suspended all tribute, and gave the *Basileus carte blanche* over which Turkish vessels entered the Bosporus and Dardanelles. This generosity was followed by a number of territorial concessions including the Black Sea coast to Mesembria, Varna, Thracian Chalcidice, and Adrianople once again to be ruled by a governor, Thessalonica, a few Aegean islands, and Mt. Athos as the very symbol of Orthodox monasticism by its reputation.

This treaty, ratified in 1403, was overseen by the Sultan, the *Basileus*, and an amalgamated Christian League composed of all Christian elements of the eastern Mediterranean and Europe: Venice, Genoa, Naxos, Serbia, and Rhodes.[2522] However, this still did not exempt Byzantium from the responsibilities of the *haradj* tax implemented by Bayezid. It came in a more indirect pattern by way of a 'donation' of Manuel to the Monastery of Mt. Athos for the exact amount the tax would be as seen in Manuel's documents and some from John VII.[2523] Security for the two Empires was assured more so by the charge of Tamerlane east to China and his subsequent death in 1405 by a fever, inflaming his intestines as he coughed and vomited bile, foaming at the mouth until 'the butler of death offered his cup' as was written by a detractor from pillaged Damascus.[2524]

The bureaucracy was now the true rulers of the government outside the City and the years 1407 and 1408 would see the deaths of the capable Theodore I and the mediocre John VII, respectively. Theodore's son, Theodore II, would rule the Peloponnese, while a son of the *Basileus* would manage Thessalonica as a much needed semblance of unity would result. As for the Ottomans, unity was far off as Bayezid's sons vied for power, Manuel seizing this opportunity to play one off against another, backing the only moderate ally they would have in Sulayman. In 1410, Manuel nearly reclaimed Callipolis in Thrace, but the armies of Prince Musa were still superior to the Empire's and Musa's strength overcame Sulayman who would be strangled in 1411.

Musa would eventually become openly hostile towards Constantinople despite the marriage of the Sultan and the daughter of the late Theodore I Paleologus. The only option left was the last of Bayezid's brothers, Mehmet I, who Manuel aided across Anatolia to secret negotiations at Constantinople. Mehmet had taken an instant liking to the educated Manuel, as sophisticated as

---

[2522] Norwich, *(DF)*, 369-370.

[2523] Ostrogorsky, 557f. This can only be attributed to the 'appanage' system Manuel was subjected to by the double crises of diminishing imperial territory and central authority as stated by Barker, *(MP)*, 391.

[2524] Marozzi, 403f.

himself, referring to him as 'my father and overlord.'[2525] With an army of 15,000, Mehmet met his brother three times with Byzantine and Serbian armies under Lazarivitch, before he was successful on July 5, 1413 at the Serbian Carmalu. After years of civil war, Musa was defeated and strangled, ratifying his older brother's treaty from 1403. The historian Ducas claims Mehmet I (known as *Chelebi*, 'the Gentleman') was now Sultan of Rum and Rumelia (Iconium and Anatolia) and peace would be kept in the Turkish Balkans with Serbia, Wallachia, Greece, and Bulgaria.

With the Ottomans currently pacified, Manuel II began precautions for future rivalries by fortifying the Peloponnese from Italian aggression on July 25, 1414. Taking Thasos from Giorgio Gattalusio from Genoa, he went from Thessalonica to Corinth the next year and built a wall around the Isthmus of the Saronic Gulf in 1415. Intended to be comparable to the walls of Thessalonica or even Constantinople,[2526] this was the 'Six-Mile Wall' (*Hexamilion*) surrounding Corinth. Fortifying this area in Corinth had a long history in Greek warfare – it had been done in 480 BCE by the Persian King Xerxes (519BCE-466BCE) and again in 369 BCE by the Theban general Epaminondas (412BCE-362BCE). As well as these times, the doomed Roman Emperor Valerian (200-260 CE) would do so again in 253 CE and for the last time before the fifteenth century this was done by Justinian I (500-565 CE); built from limestone, it sported an impressive 153 towers in the sixth century, each supported by a fortress. A special tax levied for its construction in Thessalonica was, predictably, met with unrest with the inhabitants whose rebellion was defeated at Kalamata.[2527]

Upon his return in 1416, the *Basileus* discovered that Mustafa, another brother of Mehmet I, entrenched in the Balkans, was revolting. Manuel gave him minimal support, but after his defeat, John Paleologus imprisoned him on Lemnos and Mehmet paid Constantinople 20,000 *hyperpyra* annually to guard him (Norwich insists he was a pretender, acting as the first Mustafa). John was taking on more responsibilities for his father as a Regent and diplomat, so he was finally made co-emperor officially at age twenty-nine in 1421 with no other claimant to impede him. Mehmet I was cordial with Constantinople and Venice, but the issue of Turkish trade in the Aegean and Venice's ill treatment of the isle of Naxos resulted in a naval battle at Callipolis on June 2, 1416, where

---

[2525] Brownworth, 282.

[2526] Treadgold, 791.

[2527] Norwich, (DF), 377.

the Sultan's fleets were crushed by Venice's.[2528] Venice would eventually take advantage of the Morea, pressing for protection fees rising from 100,000 to 150,000, to 300,000 *aspra* in one year with promises to uphold their rights and privileges as they re-victualed the city in 1423.[2529]

A new Turkish succession crisis occurred when Mehmet I died, leaving Prusa to his son as Murad II; the Byzantines, however, considered Mustafa to be the lesser of two evils and the court urged Manuel to release him from Lemnos. Although playing such foes and their thrones against each other to weaken both was the essence of traditional Romano-Byzantine diplomacy,[2530] the *Basileus* resisted the risks involved and waited months to finally accept. In 1420, dynastic marriages to Italian allies had already taken place as Theodore II of the Morea was married to a daughter of the Count of Rimini and the co-emperor John Paleologus was married to Sophia of Montferrat a year later. A tension in Russian relations existed as John had already married the daughter of Grand Duke Basil I of Moscow in 1414, she then dying three years later.

The shrewd Manuel II was proven to be right in his recalcitrance as Mustafa took Callipolis and Adrianople, only to be defeated decisively by Murad II, later to be caught and hanged in 1422. This caused a furor in the Constantinopolitans, blaming Manuel for not killing Murad when he had a chance at the treaty process.[2531] This, however, had occurred at a time of vulnerability, as the *Basileus* was taking refuge in the Peribleptos in the City to escape an epidemic. Later, the Sultan besieged Thessalonica and Constantinople when the Greek court involved the Sultan's last brother, another Mustafa, and worse came when Manuel was partially paralyzed by a severe stroke in 1423. Most notable in the siege was John Paleologus, shouting encouragement, working ceaselessly at one end of the Walls to the other, and impressing all with his energy. After seizing Nicaea, however, the anti-Prusan alliance fell apart when Murad eventually defeated, caught, and executed his last brother: for all of their interference, Byzantium still lost and would pay heavily to the Sultan.

Thessalonica was besieged once again and the optimism for the *Hexamilium* was demolished along with the Wall itself. In desperation (and irony as the Wall was meant to defend against Venice in the first place), the governor Andronicus gave the city to the stronger ally of Venice, who had already destroyed the weak

---

[2528] Norwich, *(AHV)*, 293-294.

[2529] Ostrogorsky, 560.

[2530] Barker, (MP), 392.

[2531] Norwich, *(DF)*, 383.

Turkish fleet in 1416. Seeing some hope in a Western ally, John Paleologus traveled to Venice to seek more aid, only to be undermined by a separate peace he and his son, Constantine Paleologus Dragases, had made with the Ottomans. This was all just as well as John, traveling from Italy to Hungary, came back with nothing to show for it. Manuel surrendered the territories around Thessalonica and the Black Sea coast in February 1424, except Anchialus and Mesembria, with annual reparation to the Sultan of 20,000 *hyperpyra* (300, 000 *aspra*).

The historian George Sphrantzes (1401-1478) elegantly describes how Manuel took the cowl in the summer of 1425 as the monk Matthias in the Monastery of the Pantocrator. Here he was buried after his death on July 22, 1425 as eulogized by the young scholar Bessarion, another cultural father of the European Renaissance. Manuel II must be given credit for his endeavors in maintaining the last traces of stability in Constantinople, if not the last remnants of the East Roman Empire. His degree of diplomacy and statecraft is laudable as it kept the Ottomans at bay long enough for Tamerlane and the dynastic wars of Prusa from distracting the Empire's Ottoman overlords.

He even was the last ruler to attempt unity in the former Successor States in Greece with the Paleologan sons of John V as Despots. His failings were mainly a non-existent military force and a lack of effective allies as the Crusade effort crumbled and the West was too occupied in their own battles to lend sufficient aid as timing was his worst enemy. Morale was at an all time low to where writers would quote Scripture decrying Byzantium's fate: 'Princess among the provinces, how is she become tributary' (Lament I: 1). But, this did not keep him from his policies of uniting with the West against the Turks as a 'disguised' conversation by Sphrantzes between Manuel and his son, John, demonstrate. His reluctance to call a Council of Union would be justified as the Greeks were obstinate and would only succeed in alienating the needed Latins over religious controversy.[2532]

Manuel II found himself in troubled relations with the Russians of Moscow as well as the new ruler Basil I, refusing to officially recognize Byzantium, now a Turkish possession, as the head of Orthodox Christendom. Basil's father, Demetrius Doskjov, had grown prosperous as the victor of Tokhtamish and his Mongols who were fleeing Tamerlane, in 1394.[2533] Manuel's protests did little good, and it was the Patriarch of Constantinople, Antony IV, and his entreaties that succeeded in changing Basil's policies. The doctrine of one ecumenical *Basileus* set down by Antony was said to have been the most convicted and

---

[2532] Gibbon, 2283.
[2533] Beckwith, 199.

passionate ever sent east. It instructed Basil to follow the Epistles of Peter that one must 'Fear God, honor the Emperor' and that a Church with no Emperor is impossible as imperial authority was a 'single entity' in Christendom, which had but one Emperor.[2534]

Basil reluctantly agreed and in 1398, being badly depleted by the failed Crusade of Nicopolis, it was Moscow that Manuel appealed to for 'alms' as poverty had hollowed Constantinople's finances. Reflecting on this incident, what were its implications? The strongest institution in Byzantium was indeed the Church, essentially unstopped by the spread of Islam as the Ottomans expanded. It backed the *Basileus* and his traditions as an ecclesiastical-political institution, despite his obvious weaknesses. In the defense of Constantinople in 1400 with Manuel's absence, Basil promised Russian troops, which were gratefully received.[2535] Yet Russia, in a geographically advantageous position, could only be swayed by the Church and not the sovereign it once allied with as the Turks were in Greece and Tamerlane in India.

Was this the foundation stone in the 'Third Rome' of Moscow, made by compacts in the centuries after 1453 that ruled by the marriage of a Tsar to a Paleologan princess at this acting moment? Was it more so legitimized by the Orthodox Church, still alive in Russia today with no *Basileus* and no Tsar, than its political ties or the recognition of a Grand Duke? This incident was a key in understanding the claims of the concept of the *Basileus* as Roman 'Autokrator' of all Christians. Despite nationality in the latter fifteenth century, Byzantium shared a 'great unity and community'. Culturally, spiritually, as well as in its law, art, and literature, Medieval Russia was proven to be the true students of East Rome to remain so beyond Byzantium's political extinction.[2536]

Manuel II Paleologus played his part well as the symbol of that culture flowering in the East during the Paleologan Renaissance, the most energetic and widespread 'renaissance' in Byzantine history. A prime example was this figure as the educated patron of the arts typical of the Paleologan monarchs, Manuel enabling this patronage to meld with his superb diplomacy to the West. As he was a guest in Paris from 1402 to 1403, he would stroll through the Louvre, and write a still surviving essay on the subject of a Gobelin tapestry found there depicting a spring landscape in a 'jacose style.'[2537]

---

[2534] Ostrogorsky, 553-554.

[2535] Vasiliev, 631-632.

[2536] Obolensky, 264-267.

[2537] Vasiliev, 634.

An entire wing of the Louvre had been renovated specifically to house the scholar-emperor who was visited by the professors of the Sorbonne, grateful to meet an educated intellectual with whom they could discuss and argue with on their own level.[2538] This patronage was not difficult to the Greeks in its establishment as the West was practically voracious in its pursuit of ancient knowledge and culture, Pagan and Christian. The ambassador of Charles VI was a Byzantine scholar, Manuel Chrysoloras (1355-1415), whom presented in 1407 an illuminated manuscript of the works of Dionysus the Areopagite (1st cent. CE) bound in gold and ivory to the Abbey of St. Denis.

A clever reminder of Byzantium's peace with France was the brilliant miniature of the scroll depicting Manuel, his Serbian wife and three children, including his heir John. Above the imperial couple were the Virgin and Child bending from Heaven to touch and grace the pair in a message that the Blessed Virgin had in no way abandoned the *Basileus* or the shrinking Empire. The fact that this was the year the reasonable Sulaymen had taken Prusa was a good sign, and now the miniature is rightfully displayed in the Louvre.[2539] The writer John Chortasmenos (1370-1431) also attributed the 1402 defeat of Bayezid at Ancyra by Tamerlane to be a true miracle by the Mother of God in his reports quite valuable in understanding the grim situation of the Empire in the early fifteenth century.[2540] Chrysoloras was an active member in the French court, coordinating the Council of Constance to decide the fate of the Italian and French papacies, dying there in April, 1415.

Manuel's greatest personal achievement as a learned man, incomparable diplomat, and complex figure in the Empire's history was the funeral oration for his brother Theodore I of the Morea given in Mistra in the summer of 1408. A conscientious look at the deeds (*epitedeumata*) of his brother in his endeavors defending Thessalonica and the Peloponnesian peninsula from Ottoman and Latin advance, Manuel develops cunning use of ethos, embedded plots, and denouement.[2541] The implications of a simple oration on the political virtues of his brother denote the rhetorical and cultural genius of the *Basileus*. This is best displayed by his balancing the status of Byzantium's social fabric and the

---

[2538] Runciman, 1.

[2539] Norwich, *(DF)*, 373f., fig. 3, 346-347.

[2540] Ostrogorsky, 475.

[2541] Leonte, Florin E.J. 'A Brief 'History of the Morea' as Seen Through the Eyes of an Emperor-Rhetorician: Manuel II Palaiologus' Funeral Oration for Theodore, Despot of the Morea.' *Viewing the Morea: Lands and People in the Late Medieval Pelopennese*, ed. by Sharon E.J. Gerstel. Washington DC: Dumbarton Oaks Symposia and Colloquia, 2013.

new and growing concern given to the application of ancient literary style in such situations.

But blended in this mimesis of the Grecian ode was a strong utility of political science, Classical and Byzantine, in justifying the authority and policy of peace with the Latins and Sulaymen five years before. Yet, the Oration also demonstrated personal conflicts and ideologies in contemporary Byzantine society. Debates were employed on the openness of the aristocratic hierarchy and the cultural elitism of 'newcomers' and those who were becoming increasingly constrained in regulating social order with political power. The Oration was a reflection of Manuel II himself and the need to uphold civic virtues in the changing climate of competing political attitudes with ethnic identities.[2542] The original manuscript is in the Bibliotheque National in Paris with a rare miniature of Manuel II in full regalia.

The West was inspired by Constantinople itself, and a few realistic (and not so realistic) representations of the City would exist to glorify its beauty to Europe. Cristoforo Buondelmonti's (1386-1430) bird's eye sketch of Constantinople in 1422 has the most authenticity of the City in relation to the Golden Horn. It is heavily fortified, densely populated, brimming with landmark buildings, churches, and columns, including Genoan Galata with its palaces. Many copies have been made, especially one from 1480, but these pale in comparison due to their caricature and inaccuracy.[2543] The year 1422 was also a landmark in literary symbolism as John Cananus (d. 1349), author of the account of the Constantinopolitan siege of that year, was considered the founding writer of the fifteenth-century legend that it was only by the intervention of the Holy Virgin on the Walls that the City was saved from a Turkish breach.

Elsewhere, being the site of ancient Sparta, the city of Mistra in the heart of the Morea upheld the new cultural idea that the Byzantine lands were not Roman, but Hellenic with a 'Greek' national spirit of patriotism blossoming as a valuable weapon they needed in fighting the Ottomans. While the outer country was wild and some mused it would turn the inhabitants and visitors barbarian, Mistra was also a gathering place for educated Greek scholars, sophists, and courtiers as well as a school of manuscript copying, quite

---

[2542] Abbotoy, Joshua. 'Reconstructing Byzantine Rulership: Manuel II's Funeral Oration.' Presented at *The Thirty-Sixth Annual Byzantine Studies Conference*. (Sarasota, FL: Florida State University, November 5-8, 2009).

[2543] Reinert, 'Revival of Learning', 275.

comparable to the courts of the Italian princes of the Renaissance.[2544] Born in 1400 was the historian, George Phrantzes (changed from Sphrantzes to honor his Peloponnesian origin) a self-important and highly critical secretariat to both Manuel II and Constantine XI, who still had firsthand knowledge of the events preceding to and occurring after 1453. Another advantage he had was a distant relation to the imperial family and the intimate friendship of the future *Basileus* Dragases. In his two lasting works, the *Chronicum Minimum* related the years of 1413 to 1477 and the *Chronicum Maiorum,* he covered the history of all the Paleologans.[2545]

Civic virtue had been a norm of the era's political literature, vivid theme shown by those literati who chose Plato as their influence, particularly from the *Republic.* In 1415, this work was the epitome of George Gemistus Plethon's views of a Utopian society ran by the *Basileus* and the Despot of his native Morea, suggesting it was the Peloponnesian Morea that was the stronghold of Greek life.[2546] Plethon had received an extensive and worldly education in Aristotleanism, Platonism, Persian Zoroastrianism, and the Jewish cabalists, also preferring the Pagan Greek Pantheon of Zeus, Hera, and Poseidon to Christianity. Oriental traditions also flourished in his complicated, but erudite, philosophies as the Seven Wise Men of Zoroastrianism inspired belief in the soul's immortality prior to its descent in the body and the fatalist philosophies found in Islam and the Koran.[2547]

In the spirit of his Platonic State and Plato's *Laws,* Plethon would call for the simplification of taxation and the need for a national army to replace the current armies of mercenaries. The populace would fall into two groups, tax-payers (Helots) and the military, exempt from taxation with the elimination of private property. Different from the Western class system of 'Estates' dominating modern society with the abolishing of the middle class, Plethon's society would compose of:[2548]

1) Cultivators of the soil, plowmen: diggers, vintners, a peasant class
2) Those providing instruments of work: cattle drivers, a working class
3) Those securing of safety and government: administrators, officials, the army, the *Basileus*

---

[2544] Vasiliev, 636-637.

[2545] Runciman, 192.

[2546] Ostrogorsky, 558-559.

[2547] Sevcenko, 291.

[2548] Vasiliev, 639.

Of course, these things were just that – Utopian dreams, as these were foregone conclusions with no natives to become soldiers and taxation that rarely reached Constantinople's coffers. But the influences involved rank among the English philosopher Thomas More (1478-1535) in his *Utopia*, the *Social Contract* of Jean-Jacques Rosseau (1712-1778), and the works of Henri de Saint-Simon (1760-1825). He would be a valuable historian as an eye-witness to the Turkish atrocities during the Morean Conquest. This amazing career would survive his death in 1452 (never seeing the Turkish Conquest of the City) as Cosmo de Medici (1389-1464) would dedicate his Academy in Florence to him in 1465.[2549] Unfortunately, his own Church and the Patriarch Gennadius ordered his works burned as heretical and most of what is known is only from his refutations and some surviving manuscripts.

Hellenic intellectuals who commented on the spirit of Greek nationalism included Manuel Mazaris (fl. 1415), whose *Sojourn in Hades* (*'Epidemia Mazari en Aidous*) is an imitation of the Roman writer Lucian and a satire on the customs and habits of the Morea. Reminiscent in theme with the *Inferno*, it lacks the epic scope of Dante's work, but still blends the ethos of the Greek mythic underworld and those, ancient and Christian, seen as transgressors of society through a libel. In spirit, it also resembles the *Timarion*, also based on Lucian, which conversed with Romanus IV Diogenes, Italus, Psellus, and other figures in Byzantine history. As another example, the entire region of the Morea, describing the Peloponnesian territory, is subverted for the pun *moria* translated as 'silliness' and 'folly'. As Plethon was a nationalist of socio-economic and class structure, Mazaris takes the approach of ethnic identity by signifying seven sorts of Hellene: Greeks (Pelopennesians, Lacedaemonians), Italians (Latins), Slavs ('Sthlavinians'), Illyrians (Albanians), Egyptians, Gipsies, and Jews.[2550]

Unfortunately for the Morea, however, Manuel II's involvement was mainly to keep the local governments from centralizing with aid from his son John and his nephew, Theodore II. The *Basileus* was still a great contributor to the Christian literary culture outside the Morea and spent much energy on the balancing of Christian and Islamic faiths in one Empire. During his French and English tours, he would have long and open dialogues with Muslim judges and teachers (*mudderris, qadi*) residing there through interpreters, as Manuel knew no Turkish and the teachers knew no Greek. The result was his *Dialogue*

---

[2549] Norwich, *(DF)*, 393.
[2550] Vasiliev, 638.

*with a Persian,* 300 pages written after 1391, expressing a logical, yet hostile, polemic against the tenants of Islam. Explaining that the Islamic laws were in fact Mosaic, he continues to say Mohammed could not have been the Paraclete of the Holy Spirit in the Gospel of John and that Muslim Paradise was deceptive and immoral. These are also words quoted from Manuel II Paleologus by Pope Benedict XVI on September 12, 2006 in Regensburg.[2551]

In the economic sphere, the currency was constantly being inflated as gold was becoming a more and more rare commodity not commonly minted or used in Byzantine commerce after 1425. Bronze and silver were the common metals as Byzantine currency were now being usurped by the unstoppable status of the Venetian *ducat*. Compounding and exacerbating these hazards in the currency were the Venetians, Genoans, and Turks, who had gained control of the Black Sea and Dardanelles Straits. As well as the rise of the *ducat,* Byzantine denominations diminished by way of the Turkish *asper* (Gr. *Aspros*) infiltrating the Byzantine monetary system, a debased silver coin considered to be one fifty-fourth the value of the *ducat* that was already complicating the silver coinage of the Empire.[2552] Manuel submitted to this economic trend and presented jewels and gold *florins,* originating from the rising star of Florence, to Tamerlane as tribute in a re-affirmation of their submission in exchange for Turkish protection.[2553]

Similarities existed between the Turkish and Byzantine realms of philanthropic institutions as well, as in the Muslim *wakf* with its numerous social services, free food, and accommodation for travelers, all practices bolstered by the alms mandatory to the faith of Islam. For Byzantium, tithing was only up to the voluntary conscience of the Christian. But the better-funded Muslim institutions of mosques, medressahs, and caravanserais were funded by the Greeks' resources, population, and taxes during the period ran by Christian converts (*gulams*) to Islam. Mandatory funding of the institutions of the Muslim over the Roman was what caused the Christian institutions of the Byzantines to diminish to nothing in Constantinople.[2554]

---

[2551] Herrin, 326-327.
[2552] Gibbon, 2267. A royal Turkish tribute landed around 300,000 *aspers* annually.
[2553] Mazzori, 340-341.
[2554] Herrin, 315.

# JOHN VIII PALEOLOGUS
## (1425-1448)

In its final days, the Empire was the hostage and vassal of the Ottomans with only limited to no aid provided by the Christian nations of Eastern and Western Europe. The *Basilii* themselves were helpless as the best in diplomacy and arms had no chance in holding off the inevitable. This was the primal *phobia* of the Byzantines and citizens of Constantinople, the dread and fear combined when faced with certain outcomes threatening all harmony in the collective conscience of the Eastern Romans. Westerners, inspired perhaps by the Fall of 1204 or by Charles of Anjou and Outremer, made plans to march on the City for the good of Christendom against Islam as King Alfonso V 'the Magnanimous' of Aragon united Sicily and Naples, attempting to gather a Crusade in 1444 that included seizing the City of Constantine.[2555]

Furthermore, the alliances of Byzantium and Venice as Christian powers were disintegrating as, although the Venetians fought Murad II for the Morea, they mostly looked after their own interests. Modern realities of business markets and states were fast encroaching against the ideas of the Church that Venice be hostile to the Ottomans. Venetians only fought half-heartedly after 1444 in the Morea as they now wished not to impede economically or militarily upon the rising power of the Turkish Black Sea trade, which basically stood by as maritime powers motivated by commercial self-interest, was closing in on Constantinople.[2556] The coffers of the State were barren, military morale was as distant as what could be found in the streets of the City, and the wrong mood of a Sultan could mean the end of their entire society, especially considering the new technologies of heavy artillery falling into their hands.

Some of the Greeks accepted this fate and made steady peace with their new Muslim lords, considering the wealth of the economic markets they allowed and the religious toleration they offered. No graces were given Constantinople from the Ottomans, such as the ceding of land even to Sultans that owed Byzantium their very thrones. They were merely 'non-believers' and heathens as the Christians whom violated Islamic law merely by existing. What ever the motive and reaction, devastating change was coming and the last *Basilii* of the

---

[2555] Vasiliev, 643.

[2556] Jardin, Lisa. *Worldly Goods: A New History of the Renaissance.* New York, NY: W. W. Norton Publishing. 1996, 41.

Greek East were forced to conciliate and concede their very souls to make any difference against the fatal blow.

Islamicism was further complicating matters in Byzantine religious and legal matters as the Muslims did not recognize the Medieval and primarily Christian practice of primogeniture, where the eldest son inherited all property. Instead, a man could have four wives, as many as he wished in his harem, and an unlimited number of sons that vied for property, leading to fratricidal warfare as had occurred from 1402 to 1413 with Bayezid's sons. This, naturally, encroached upon the zealously protected Byzantine, Orthodox Christian concept of monogamy.[2557]

Even the most intrusive of customs in Greek life had benefits for Byzantines in Turkish lands. One example was with schools of training and education being given by the Muslim Turks to male children. All Christian families, be they Greek, Slav, Armenian, or Vlach were taken to discover and exercise specialist talents in the civil government or technical fields. Their lives were as ascetic as the monks with special barracks and a policy against marriage, their lives being to the service of the Sultan. This did result in demands at times into forced mass conversions to Islam, but such phenomena were resented less under Murad II than John VIII, the Ottomans being better loved in the East by Murad's death in 1451.[2558] This would demonstrate the superiority of services and morale under the Turks than that of Constantinople and the decay of the Greek institutions by its many failings, leading a vanishing Byzantium to a 'new Greek society of the Ottomans.'

As obvious as this was becoming, threats of the inhabitants of the City opening the Gates in voluntary surrender to the Sultans in order to ease their suffering were becoming very real as morale dwindled - it was the Fall of Rome repeating itself. The distant appanages of Thessalonica and Morea considered themselves prisoners of a foreign ascendency, not in the Turks, but in the government of Constantinople.[2559] The only two institutions that even seemed to face survival was the Church as it was spread all over in the East, not being a true target of suppression by the Turks, and the Hellenistic culture successfully moving west to take root into the new type of modern civilization. The days of burning the Library of Alexandria were long over, and the Muslim opposition to Classical and Christian culture had been replaced with a new appreciation

---

[2557]  Herrin, 316.

[2558]  Runciman, 47.

[2559]  Norwich, (DF), 390.

for its wisdom, benefiting even the Oriental Ottoman Empire in the Later Paleologan Era.

The sons of Manuel II (excluding the sickly Andronicus) salvaged what they could in centralizing the Empire with Despotates in all the Byzantine regions except for Comnenian Trebizond. Even then, dynastic marriages were arranged in hopes that they would guarantee some safety in these regions under a Byzantine regime. This idealism would be compounded and, eventually, neutralized by the ambitions of the Paleologan Despots to succeed to the throne in 1425. Their regions growing accustomed to a de facto independence, were facing decentralizing localized regions behind these perspective heirs. At one time or another, over the twenty-three years of John VIII's reign, Thomas and Demetrius Paleologus would rebel and vie for power, benefiting only the powerful enemies of Christendom. John himself is painted as a tragic figure, bereft of his father's 'poise and noble character' and lacking political experience, knowing in his heart that the Empire was doomed and only a miracle of a single-minded and cooperative Christian effort, East and West, might save it.[2560]

Born on December 18, 1392, John VIII Paleologus was the eldest of the six sons of Manuel II and his Serbian Basilia, Helena Dragash (Dragases), he was crowned as co-emperor in 1421, despite doubts Manuel had that his son was, perhaps, too bold and impetuous.[2561] This title was earned, however, after years of service leading armies east, adding his own diplomacy with the Christian and Muslim states, and eventually defending a besieged Constantinople in June, 1422. What we know visually of the Basileus is best depicted in the mural of the Procession of the Magi of the painter Benozzo Gozzoli (1420-1497) in the Palazzo Medici-Riccardi of Florence. In it, the Magi Balthasar has the serene face of John VIII, made wise by his long white beard, the Patriarch Joseph seen riding with him. Leading is the twelve-year-old humanist Lorenzo de Medici (1449-1492), later to be known as the 'Magnificent.' The Byzantine retinue was decorated in the finest and exotic Oriental décor, picked in gold leaf as 'retrospective political propaganda' of wealth as power with detail on gems, horses, and weaponry.[2562]

In 1438, the artist known as Pisanello (1395-1455) struck a medal in Florence to commemorate the Council held there, displaying John VIII's elderly and regal profile based on sketches recovered from the Council of 1438

---

[2560] Norwich, (AHV), 317.

[2561] Treadgold, 792.

[2562] Jardin, 52.

to 1439. As well as in bronze sculptures and miniatures, John was depicted at the Council, yet Pisanello's works were the most distinct. This was due to having the *Basileus* wearing the high-peaked hat fashionable in Italy at the time[2563] to offset the fascination the Latins had with the exotic nature of Greek accouterments. In Roman bas-reliefs are found, along with depictions of the Savior, Virgin, and Sts. Peter and Paul, that of the Council of Ferrara. On the entrance to the Temple of St. Paul are reliefs of the *Basileus* sailing from Constantinople, attending a meeting at the Council in Florence, his arrival at Ferrara, and his departure from Venice.[2564] These relics glorify John VIII's half-dignified state seen by Italy as a venerable Christian relic within himself, being a kind departure from the debacle of John V.

John VIII was married three times to foreign princesses to strengthen ties to Russia, Italy, and Trebizond. But, these were only to be frustrated both by tragic deaths and the usual impediments to effective aid from foreign powers. Of his second and Italian wife, Sophia of Montferrat, he had no attraction, the contemporary historian Michael Ducas (1400-1462) saying of her that she was 'Lent in front, Easter behind'.[2565] His first wife was Maria Comnena, daughter of the Despot of Trebizond, Alexius IV, and the love of John's life. After her death in 1441, a chapel was dedicated to her in Constantinople and later, John would marry his last wife Anna of Moscow. More Constantinopolitan projects included vast re-fortification of the Theodosian Walls from Turkish land assaults, especially after the examples of their use of cannon in battle, with many of its bricks being stamped 'John Paleologus, Autocrator in Christ.'

Therefore, he committed the ultimate sin as a *Basileus* of Byzantium by dying without heirs, leaving behind three brothers who would bring about the last succession controversy in imperial history over what was left in Byzantium. One would take John's place and only a daughter by the dead *Basileus* would survive to carry the name Paleologus to a new center of Byzantine heritage in Moscow. Seen as the next hope for the Empire, Manuel II spent from 1414 to 1416 priming his son John in the arts of good government. Composing treatises both spiritual and moral to that effect,[2566] these included his death –bed advice of promising Union with Rome to intimidate the Turks in times of stress into

---

[2563] Herrin, 307.

[2564] Vasiliev, 674.

[2565] Michael Ducas. *Historia Byzantina, bk. XX,* ed. by I. Bekker. *CSHB.* Bonn, Germany 1834, 100. Vasiliev, 588.

[2566] Norwich, *(DF),* 382.

becoming 'reasonable', yet to realize that no true Union was possible because of the passion of the Catholics.[2567]

By 1425, when John was made *Basileus* on the day of his father's death, July 21, the sons of Manuel held what little was left of the shrinking Empire. John had Selymbria and the north Aegean, Constantine held Anchialus and the north coast of the Black Sea, and Theodore held the largest portion, the Peloponnese and the Morea. Theodore was best suited for the Morea, being as much as an intellectual as his father had been and even a more brilliant mathematician, as he was energetic, neurotic, and moody. Perhaps having bipolar disorder, he was known for feeling maudlin and wishing to take the habit at one minute, only to feel ambitious enough to recover lost territory and aggrandize his own the next. He and his wife saw the height of the Mistra renaissance and Hellenist movement until her death in 1433.[2568] Theodore had one daughter, Helena, married to John II of Cyprus with no male heir, considering himself John's heir from 1443 in Selymbria, until his death a few months before his brother's in July, 1448.

As the Ottomans were off limits, John VIII and Constantine Dragases decided to march north and attack the Latin holdings of Cephalonia and Epirus under Carlo Tocco in 1426, taking Clarentza and defeating Carlo in a naval battle the next year at Patras. Capitulating weakly to the *Basileus*, more of the Peloponnese was given to Constantine as well as his daughter, Maria, in marriage. John now decided to divide the Peloponnese to three of his brothers in three appanages, ceding more of the Peloponnese to Theodore and the smaller region of Achaea to Thomas. In 1429, Thomas would make his victory total by marrying the daughter of the former Latin Prince of Achaea and receiving the title of Despot from the *Basileus*.

John's younger brother, the future Constantine XI Paleologus Dragases, was an impetuous but daring and ambitious man, conquering Patras and expelling the Papal legate that ruled the city. It almost appeared as though a recovery of the Peloponnese was imminent and the Empire would sustain itself within Turkish vassalage. But a wary Murad II saw the danger, finally taking Thessalonica from its Venetian masters in 1430. Thessalonica would be ransomed for an annual fee of 60,000 *ducats,* but could fight off a Turkish army of 190,000 on March 26, forcing the Sultan to cut the water pipes to the city

---

[2567] Crowley, 67.
[2568] Runciman, 48-49.

to win by attrition.[2569] The typical three days of looting saw the slaughter and screams of women and children, massive destruction of churches and palaces, and at least 70,000 taken into slavery. After the three days of spoils, Murad granted them amnesty and no further harm.

The Morean capital of Arta would become his as a ransom after an abduction of Carlo Tocco's niece, collectively recovering all the territories the Turks had lost at Ancyra twenty years before. Two years later, Thomas Paleologus had inherited all of Achaea and only the Venetian ports of Nauplia, Methone, and Corone were not part of the Byzantine Peloponnese. Not to be outdone, Constantine exchanged the north appanage for Theodore's western appanage to take the Italian Duchy of Athens in 1435, but the Athenian nobles rebelled after their Duchess surrendered and a new Latin Duke was chosen. But, the 'Frankish' hold on Greece, in turmoil since Michael VIII, was finally won by the Greeks due to Constantine only to be mercilessly seized after the Turkish Conquest. The conquests remaining to the West were found at Rome, where Byzantine authority was undermined by the Church's hoodwinking and the East's self-deception.[2570]

Since 1431, John VIII had been in negotiations with Pope Martin V to hold an ecumenical Council to decide the matter of Church Union, but this had been postponed with Martin's death and his successor Eugenius IV's embroilment in the Council of Basel in 1432 to keep the Church in Rome. The questions put forth in Basel were the supremacy of Rome over French Avignon and the fate of the 'heretical' Hussites (to be heroes of the Protestant Reformation) as secularists over Church authority. Distastefully, some papal legates from Rome even disobeyed Eugenius, remaining in France and electing an anti-Pope, Felix V, in 1439.

All attempts by John to hold a Council in Constantinople were met with sharp refusals by the Latin clergy as this was no longer practical, due to the Turkish menace.[2571] For the five years in between, John carefully played one side against the other, as his father would have recommended. John treated with Avignon to hold a Council there on the promise of 8,000 *ducats* (75,000 *florins*) for his Greek clerical train of 700. Along with 10,000 more troops to Constantinople was a retinue of 300 Cretan archers, led by the Unionist

---

[2569] Norwich, *(DF)*, 394-395. One casualty was the miraculous Panaghia Acheirapoietos which housed a divinely-made icon, kept in Istanbul until 1913 and standing after earthquake damage in both 1923 and 1978.

[2570] Ostrogorsky, 561.

[2571] Norwich, *(DF)*, 397.

German Cardinal Nicolas of Cusa as a gift for the City's defense. To Rome's dismay, this was all sent from Marseilles and the infamous Council at Basel was summoned.[2572]

John left Constantinople to Constantine's regency and headed for Italy with 700 Eastern prelates, Basileos Bessarion the scholar, and the Patriarch Joseph II. On February 8, 1438, an amazing gathering of Christendom's rulers had assembled in Florence: representatives of the remaining churches of Antioch, Alexandria, and Jerusalem, the Greco-Slavic kingdoms of Trebizond, Georgia, Wallachia, Bulgaria, and Vlachish Moldavia. The Byzantine Archbishop of Kiev, Isidore, Abbot of St. Demetrius in Constantinople attended from the Muscovite court of All Russia by way of Venice in spring followed by eighteen Metropolitans, George Plethon, George Scholarius the Thomist (1400-1473), and the Unionist Mark Eugenicus of Ephesus (1392-1444).

Moved to Florence under Cosimo I de' Medici in 1439, the Council discussed in detail topics of divisiveness existing since the Nicaean Council of the procession of the *filioque*, and compromises on the conditions of Western and Eastern beliefs and a settlement was reached. Though the signatures of the document, still preserved in Rome, effectively ended the Schism with Rome supposedly begun in 1057, its practical implications were that Catholicism had finally been regarded as having supremacy under the Donation of Constantine (found to have been a fake a year later by the Renaissance scholar, Lorenzo Valla (1407-1457)). Several Orthodox dignitaries and the remaining three churches of the East balked at what they saw as a betrayal of consciousness, refusing to sign. Those who did, especially Isidore of Kiev, faced the wrath of their congregations and secular authorities as Orthodoxy was once again divided. Any wounds healed after the Council of Lyon under Michael VIII were now torn open afresh by the decision of Ferrara-Florence.[2573]

Fortunately, the goodwill made by the affable John VIII in Florence allowed for the final Crusade against the Ottomans to save the Byzantine Empire to be assembled in 1440. John must have been elated by this, only to learn that his *Basilia* and the love of his life, Maria of Trebizond, had died weeks before. But the divisive nature of the Council would diffuse the momentum of any Crusade as Hungary would lapse into civil war and the conservative Orthodox Demetrius Paleologus would rebel openly in 1442 from Mesembria with Turkish troops. Motivated by the strength of his Orthodox faith, he was

---

[2572] Gibbon, 2286.
[2573] Treadgold, 795.

still seen as 'restless, ambitious, and unscrupulous', rebelling to marry an heiress to the Bulgarian dynasty of the Asen.[2574] Demetrius would fail when no support came within Constantinople and he was arrested as Murad would also fail in taking Trebizond as Murad already had in north Serbia and Transylvania by 1441, threatening Hungary. Pope Eugenius would have to quickly settle an agreement in Hungary personally in 1443 and organization could begin in earnest to offer an effective Crusade for the critical year of 1444 where 25,000 Venetians and Burgundians sailed to the Black Sea from the Marmara.[2575]

In 1443, King Ladislaus Jagellon of Hungary and Poland joined the valiant *voivode* of Transylvania, John Corvinus-Hunyadi with George Brankovich of Serbia in orchestrating defensive and offensive measures against the Turks. This began by barring a Turkish fleet before the Balkans and a simultaneous capture of Nish and Serdica by Hunyadi and his general, John Cantacuzenus. While Constantine Paleologus was finally annexing Athens from Ottoman suzerainty, Niero II cowered in the Acropolis and Ladislaus gathered armies at Buda, while a fleet from Venice sailed east. In the Balkan Mountains, solid resistance came from the Albanians under the rebel John Castriotes, the 'Captain of Albania', better known as Scanderberg.

Under pressure, Murad II called for a truce of ten years between the Crusaders and the Sultan as he was busy eliminating the rebels of Karaman. But he became emboldened by this 'surrender' as the Slav nations regrouped, attacking the Turks from the East, nonetheless. The justification came from the idea held since the days of Heraclius that a promise to an Infidel meant nothing, supported by the Pope himself. As Byzantium had faced the other end of such an argument from the Sultans, a shocked John VIII took no part in it, settling to convince Murad the Union of Florence-Ferrara was religious in tone only and posing no threat to the Ottomans.[2576]

Ladislaus and Hunyadi gathered a force of 16,000 Hungarians and 4,000 Wallachians to besiege Varna and even with Venice holding the Hellespont, Murad managed to cross the barrier on the Bosporus to Varna on November 10. The fleet Hungary expected had already been attacked by the Sultan, furious at Ladislaus's betrayal. The battle was a debacle for the Crusade alliance as the Turkish charges battered the defensive, the Hungarian King dying and the armies fleeing at the news, as Hunyadi barely managed to escape. Murad lost a

---

[2574] Runciman, 49.
[2575] Norwich, *(DF)*, 404.
[2576] Ostrogorsky, 564.

good number of forces as well and the Ottoman East was vulnerable to rebellions and difficulties, especially the tenacious Albanians under Scanderberg and Hungary under its Regent Hunyadi, who marched on the Danube. Byzantium was relatively unscathed for its neutrality and this allowed the Paleologi to quietly regroup to take more former Greek land from the Turks.

Nonetheless, Varna was a major defeat to Christian morale and John VIII's psyche was as damaged as that of Manuel I's after Myriocephalum in 1176; John was even forced to congratulate the gloating Sultan on his triumph as a faithful vassal. Yet, the *Basileus's* brave and stubborn brother was undeterred and in 1445, with John ignoring foreign affairs, Constantine was active once again, claiming Athens by taking Thessaly and northern Greece. But the damage was done as Varna sapped the impetus from the Christian offensive and a disinterested Venice treated with the Sultan a year later. This would also become fruitless as Murad would recover Thessaly, Athens, and the Peloponnese, destroying a second Hexamilium built on the Corinthian Gulf with 50,000 men, using their siege engines and the new threat of iron cannon. Constantine and Thomas were brought back into vassalage and John Hunyadi would make no progress on the Danube, still managing to make one last Crusading effort in 1448.

With Scanderberg and Wallachian aid, Hunyadi reached Kosovo, but Murad was ready as the Regent's forces were divided without the Albanians. After more Turkish demonstrations of superior morale, the Wallachians deserted and fled, leaving Hunyadi mostly defenseless and, once again, put to flight. This was the last Crusade for Constantinople that would be attempted as the Western powers and the Slavs ran out of resources to oppose the next Sultan before the City's Fall five years later. In July, 1447, Adrianople was taken by the Sultan with a further 20,000 Byzantine casualties and 60,000 prisoners, accounted for by the eye-witness Laonicus Chalcondylas (1430-1470), the father of modern archaeology, who had visited the ruins of old Sparta in the Morea.[2577]

To further accentuate the hopeless situation of Constantinople, John VIII Paleologus died on October 31, 1448, 'a sad and broken man' with no heir except his presumptive brothers who would only fight for the throne. This instability was followed by constant coin debasements, loss of trade to the Italians, unproductive food cultivation, and the famine and disease that would result. Even the City suffered as the Palace and Blacharnae were crumbling due to bad maintenance, the once proud Hippodrome was being wasted as

---

[2577] Norwich, *(DF)*, 407.

a polo ground, and the fabulous churches were now empty shells as only the ceremonies of the *Basileus*, splendid but hollow, were kept intact.[2578]

John VIII Paleologus's efforts to win Byzantium back were indeed noble, considering the limited choices he had in strengthening his defiance over the Sultan, though it would be a calculated risk in causing the unneeded dissension in the Church and Empire for which he was responsible. Conceding the points of Orthodoxy to Rome was the only sure way of obtaining some kind of aid, inadequate though it would prove with only the Venetians making any true effort to be present. But, if a Crusade of Christian Balkan nations succeeded in pushing back the Ottomans out of Europe by Constantine in reclaiming Greece, if this restoration was not ever possible, 'the melancholy alternative was to do nothing, and wait for the Turkish conquest.'[2579]

John's ability as *Basileus* would place him between that of his father, Manuel II at the high end and John V at the lower; he was not the statesman his father was, yet he was not as completely inert in his efforts (especially with Venice) as was his grandfather. Militarily, his better days were decidedly before taking the Crown, but his semi-loyal brothers kept the State in line if not totally together. His ambitious and optimistic brother Constantine would shine as the best example for an heir as the last true nobles and senators in Constantinople would completely agree. Yet, John also lacked his brother's enthusiasm and it is rightfully said that a better manager was needed instead of a better *Basileus*, and John VIII was not this.[2580]

It was the complexities of the Council of Ferrara-Florence that would testify as his greatest attempts at foreign policy and diplomacy in the choice he made to befriend Rome, ostracizing all four of the others.

Eastern Churches and their holy cities, including Constantinople. Orthodoxy saw unleavened bread as too akin to Judaism and disrespectful to the Holy Spirit, also finding no Scriptural justification for the belief in Purgatory. Catholicism was outraged by the marriage of secular priests in the East and balked at Hesychasm and the 'uncreated Energies by God.'[2581] The *Basileus* had left the City to his brother Constantine while heading to Venice, but, in comparison to 1274 and the Council of Lyons, Florence had an aim only for self-preservation against the Turks. Michael VIII's Council had a more

---

[2578] Norwich, (*DF*), 389.

[2579] Treadgold, 797.

[2580] Norwich, (*DF*), 408.

[2581] *ibid.*, 401-402.

stable political aim that Rome could grant, unlike saving Byzantium from the Ottomans with another risky and expensive Crusade having only a few nations who would take interest.[2582]

The Seventeenth Council of the Catholic Church, or the Council of Basel, convened in February of 1431, which set a definite tone for the fate of what would be the later Council to end the Schism of 1057. Pope Martin V met with French prelates in Bohemia to discuss the internal Union of the Western Church in light of the Hussite Wars against Catholicism and a much-needed Crusade against the Ottomans. Martin died before any real progress was accomplished, and a Council to meet with Constantinople was put off for six years. The succeeding Pope, Eugenius IV, would eventually settle Basel and open the discussion of Church Union at Ferrara in 1437.

It was made obvious by the visiting *Basileus* that he needed a universal Council of both Churches and all Bishops and high prelates attending, led by him and Eugenius.[2583] As for the Western Church, it would get some spiritual currency from John submitting to Rome, as it legitimated Eugenius as Pope and not the Anti-Pope that was raised in Basel. As Constantinople would not be an agreed upon place, being too close to Turkish territory, John would begin to travel to Rome on Wednesday, November 27, 1437. John VIII brought the octogenarian Joseph II, the Patriarch of Constantinople, and the other three Patriarchs of Orthodoxy, as well as eighteen Metropolitans including Bessarion of Nicaea. Along with these men, 700 other prelates as Bishops, scholars, representatives, and princes from as near as Venice and as far as Moscow attended. In Florence, the issues were to be truly settled in 1439, mostly from a state-mandated 'toleration of differences' between Catholicism and Orthodoxy.[2584]

John was given every honor due to his station when he landed at Venetian Lido on February 8, though it was pouring rain, but the Doge Foscari attended to warmly greet the Byzantine delegation, kneeling bare-headed before the *Basileus* as he sat before him.[2585] Then from the poop deck of the Doge's boat, *Bucintoro,* the first processional entrance ever of a Byzantine *Basileus* into Venice and the Signoria spared no expense in decorating the City of St. Mark in gold thread and brocade. The compromises reached in this 'agreement to disagree'

---

[2582] Ostrogorsky, 563.

[2583] Norwich, *(AM)*, 240-241.

[2584] Treadgold, 795.

[2585] Norwich, *(AHV)*, 318.

included ambiguity in language to recognize the existence of Hesychasm, of the existence of Purgatory in the West, and the use of either leavened or unleavened bread in the Eucharist.

Most importantly, however, may have been the oldest question put forth that took up the first three months of discussions: the procession of the Holy Spirit from Father to Son in the *filioque*, the direct descendant of the nature of Christ argued at Nicaea in the fourth century. Yet, in reality, it was Papal primacy that was at the forefront as the Pope still demanded recognition of Peter as the founder of the Christian Church. Other discussions on disputed subjects would not go well as debates broke down, the two sides being ignorant in each others' languages and Rome using ecclesiastical texts totally unfamiliar to the East in order to confound them. The *Basileus* would clarify more awkward concepts such as the Two Energies as the Greek clergy was more diffuse on issues being prelates, whereas philosophers and Aquinas scholars such as George of Trebizond (1395-1484) and George Amirouitzes (1400-1470) truly took to the Union in the end.[2586]

As time dragged on in these encounters, plague broke out in August, killing mostly Latin delegates and leaving the Greeks unharmed, and as a result, absolutely no ground was made on the issues between October 8 and December 19. As accounted by the Patriarchal official Sylvester Syropoulos (1400-1453), the Byzantine clergy was also divided over Western concepts they did not understand, such as Purgatory. Then, arguments broke out between the *Basileus* John and Eugenicus over the purity of the Union being glossed as clerical marriage, fasting, and genuflection were just seen as 'habits' to be tolerated by the Churches.[2587] On Sunday July 5, 1439, the Decree of Union, denied by Eugenius of Ephesus, but denied a veto by the *Basileus*, was hastily signed as the air filled with declarations of *Laetentur Coeli!* ('Let the Heavens Rejoice!'). To end the ceremony, Bessarion and Cardinal Julian Cesarini repeated the Decree in Greek and Latin.

As the Latin Creed held to the procession divinely transmitting from Father to Son, the Greek Creed held that only the Father existed in the transmission and the result of this discussion was, once again, the benevolent tolerance of Rome over Constantinople. This tolerance on behalf of the *Basileus* and Patriarch caused a wave of scandal and antagonism on multiple spheres of Orthodox society, even when the consideration of 'anti-Latinism' in the culture

---

[2586] Runciman, 17.

[2587] Herrin, 306-307.

is weighed. Even before this consideration, arguments over the division of 15,000 *ducats* were disputed over as the *Basileus* spent most of this on his own decoration, with only the remainder to be a concession to the Pope.

John VIII refused to land on Italy's shore until the demand to kneel to Eugenius and kiss his foot was revoked. Even then, he refused to be suppliant to Rome by Byzantine protocol, riding to his throne at the proceedings on horseback.[2588] Upon the stairs leading to the thrones, the Pope refused the *Basileus*'s genuflections and after a paternal embrace to force John into humility, he was seated at the Pope's left on his throne. Matters were worsened by the vulgar laughs of the Westerners at the long robes, sleeves, and beards of the Greek clergy and only the purple robes and jeweled diadems were said to have saved the *Basileus* from indignity.[2589]

Diplomacy between the two European worlds would continue as it mostly had - through ceremony, custom, and gesture. Even common differences such as food was remarked upon, such as the 'delicacy' of salad by the Byzantines which was considered the 'food for peasants' by the West. The Latins were astonished, however, at Byzantine culinary abilities in preparing salad with parsley and onion, poultry with lard, and oven-baked eggs with spices. Ginger, pepper, cloves, nutmeg, and the 'black gold' of pepper amazed the host of the feast, Giovanni di Jacopo di Latino de' Pigli of Peretola in Pistoia.[2590]

The discussions that had began after the Decree, on April 9, 1439, would still promise to be especially lengthy and violently opposed from both sides. The major effrontery among the Byzantine elite was the inadequacy as a Council in and of itself to the other four Patriarchs and the other divisive elements. Linguistically, it was tragic enough that the translation of the Greek *ousia* ('substance') was too alien to the Latin *substantia*. The compromises on issues to levy aid against the Ottomans were seen as cynical and a betrayal of their faith and conscience held for over a thousand years over the simple phrasing 'the Spirit proceeds to the Father *from* the Son' as opposed to the Father *through* the Son.[2591] The historian Michael Ducas would decry this policy: 'We have sold our faith; we have exchanged true piety for impiety; we have betrayed the pure sacrifice and become upholders of unleavened bread.'

---

[2588] Norwich, *(DF)*, 399.

[2589] Gibbon, 2289-2290.

[2590] Jardin, 52-53.

[2591] Scourtis, Constantina. 'Orthodoxy and 'Latinism' at the Council of Florence-Ferrara (1438-1439).' Presented at *The Twenty-Seventh Annual Byzantine Studies Conference*, (South Bend, IN: The University of Notre Dame, November 9-11, 2001).

The Greeks themselves by 1439 were suffering the 'miseries of exile and poverty', surviving on a mere three or four *florins* a day. As those Greeks resistant to the Decree attempted to frustratingly return east, they found their way impeded by a need for passport from their superiors in order to leave Ferrara. These superiors were paid little better as John VIII was allowed only thirty *florins* daily, the Patriarch Joseph received only twenty-five, and twenty given to the attending Despot Demetrius, incensed by the Decree. Venice was a further impediment as it awaited to arrest the Greek transgressors of the Decree and return the fugitives for imprisonment at Ferrara. The clerics *for* the Decree would not escape persecution either, confronted with the fear of the punishment in Constantinople: fines, excommunication, and the indignity of public whipping.[2592]

This last fear was legitimated as a violent proletariat arose in Constantinople to liken the Pope to the Antichrist, 'the Wolf', 'the Destroyer' and the title of *Rum Papa* ('Roman Pope') was even a popular choice in naming dogs in the City.[2593] In 1441, the Decree was formally dismissed and annulled by most of the lay Orthodox authorities. Scholarius would deny altogether the *'Laetentur Coeli'* as an ecclesiastical intellectual and the Nicaean Metropolitan Bessarion would convert to Catholicism in 1439 to be a Cardinal, never returning to his native Byzantine soil as long as he lived. The Byzantines saw this as the last condemnation of the Empire by the wrath of a spited and angry God, those believing the Mother of God would always protect the City of Constantine were lessening in number as salvation would now become a distant idea. Western historians considered the Decree for the *Basileus* to be suicide as the morale of the Greeks dampened into melancholy and pessimism, their natural gaiety spent.[2594] Only men like Bessarion believed the Decree would bring a new culture of unity to East and West as the Renaissance had Latinized Hellenism and ended the narrow views of his fellow Greeks from turning fatalistic and xenophobic.

The career of Bessarion as a Hellenist would begin in 1439 as his amassing of Greek manuscripts before and after 1453 would culminate in the Biblioteca Marciana in Venice at his death in 1472. Isidore of Kiev was also promoted to Cardinal, but unwisely returned to Moscow where Grand Duke Basil II immediately arrested and imprisoned him. After an escape he made his way

---

[2592]   Gibbon, 2289-2290.

[2593]   Crowley, 68.

[2594]   Runciman, 19-21.

back to Rome and would, ironically, be a Papal legate in Constantinople at the Sultan's court. The greater implication was that Moscow, by 1451, would now choose its own Metropolitan of the Russian Church and not Constantinople, who had chosen Isidore in the first place.[2595] Even for turning its back on the Greek Orthodoxy for a violation and betrayal of their beliefs in 1439, this was the true beginning of Moscow's separation from the 'Second Rome', becoming the 'Third Rome' that saved Orthodoxy to the present.

However, this occurrence was not present nor planned in 1441 when Isidore was imprisoned and Basil II supposedly sent correspondences to Constantinople praising the Patriarch as the head of Orthodoxy. But, Basil would be a prisoner himself of the Tartars during a Russian civil war until his death and the divisions of the Decree would loom as the major issue between Byzantium and Russia. The 'law-abiding' clergy in Russia were quickly denying Greek Orthodoxy and turning inward even as Basil sent more conciliatory 'justifications' to Constantine XI in 1452 for their independent appointment of Iona as Metropolitan of Moscow. With the Fall of Constantinople in 1453, the Decree of Florence-Ferrara was moot and therefore nullified in the eyes of the Greek clergy. The remnants of the Greek Church in a completed Ottoman Empire, still in the City, remained Orthodox and would work with the Russian Church as before, even as a correspondence of Basil's upholding the Patriarch of Constantinople would go neglected by May 29, 1453.[2596] A century later, in 1589, Russia would be autonomous from Greek Orthodoxy entirely and the Orthodox Church of the Third Rome of Moscow would become official.

The 1430 sack of Thessalonica by the Turks was a subject in John VIII Paleologus's reign for historical description and lament as a 'second Venice'[2597] would fall forever to the barbarous Turk. John Agnostes ('the Reader') was considered the best authority in his *On the Last Capture of Thessalonica*, which told of the general feeling of the population that their Venetian overlords were 'as aliens' but were still preferable to the Turks who slaughtered women and children, destroyed their churches (especially that of St. Demetrius), and erected mosques. The travesty was even immortalized in popular Greek verse to the learned and folk songs to the rest.[2598]

A Burgundian pilgrim of Jerusalem, Bertrandon of Broquiere (1400-1459),

---

[2595] Ostrogorsky, 563.
[2596] Obolensky, 268-270.
[2597] Ducas, bk. XXIX, 197.
[2598] Vasiliev, 642-643.

wrote of his visit to Constantinople in the 1430's in the *Voyage d'Outremer* and romantically recalled its decayed state and tribulation by the Ottoman Sultans. One such example was the dictates to tear down the defensive palace-fortresses of John V by Murad I, afterwards seeing a play at the Hagia Sophia retelling a martyrdom of three faithful youths in the furnaces of Nebuchadnezzar. Upon being asked by the *Basileus* the fate of the legendary Joan d'Arc, the 'Maid of Orleans', Bertrandon is said to have told the whole truth of her betrayal and burning to a disappointed John at Rouen by his native Burgundy. And as characteristic of any such treatise or history, de Broquiere remarked on how, by a uniting of the formidable French, English, and Germans, in adequate numbers, Jerusalem could be reached by land in a Crusade. A depiction exists to describe (poorly as most maps of the City were) the Conquest of Constantinople by Mehmet II with the Sultan in the forefront in a decorated silk pavilion as the Ottomans surrounded the City by land and sea.[2599]

## CONSTANTINE XI PALEOLOGUS DRAGASES
### (1448-1453)

Now, after years of decay in both the institutions and the civic virtue of the Greek-speaking world of the East that was the former Byzantium, the last stroke of the Turkish hegemony of the East was now prepared to erase the legacy of Constantine the Great. Yet, in a vacuum devoid of hope and recovery, the *Romaioi* of the Queen of Cities made one last stand to defend their Gates and Walls. The opposition proved to be untenable as a young, yet determined and talented Sultan, a lack of Western-based aid, and military technology from a modern 'Military Revolution' proved Byzantine society to be inferior. As the political pawn it had been for a century, Byzantium had no internal structure to defend itself indefinitely, and the ambitions of one truly strong opponent would be just enough to cause Constantinople's collapse.

The Empire's lack of economic resources brought on by fragmentation, the loss of the Black Sea trade franchises, and practically no tax revenue made the West lose interest, only benefiting from Turkish enterprise. Even the sacred Monastery of Mt. Athos, spiritual father of almost a hundred smaller communities, submitted to the Turks after Murad II's victory over Thessalonica.[2600] Special interests and apathy were Byzantium's worst enemies

---

[2599] Jardin, 43.
[2600] Runciman, 60-61.

as any Western ally only wanted a repeat of 1204 and the Eastern Princes faced their own internal issues or easily gave acceptance of Turkish suzerainty (and even alliance). Eastern allies were bound up with Turkish politics, giving them obeisance as in Rhodes, Chios, and Lesbos, either bought off with land as Serbia had been with the Struma Valley, or linked to fatal treaties as in Hunyadi's case.

The bureaucracy of the state had been watered down to a tangled obscurity: if a Cantacuzenus was Stratopedarch, as he was related by marriage, and his father was a Protostrator as Sphrantzes was, Notarus once asked, could his son be a Primokerion higher in rank? This battle over meaningless titles to those who deserved it more caused the *Basileus* much embarrassment.[2601] This caused unnecessary division, resentment, and intrigue in the court and nobility, and such division would widen the gulf of loyalties towards *Basileus* and Sultan.

Even the most dynamic sort of *Basileus* could not save this situation as it was a miracle Constantinople lasted to the mid-fifteenth century worthy of the Mother of God. In 1448, the Empire received such an *Basileus*, who had proved himself in battle and in administration of Byzantine provinces, even recovering territory. He won the approval of the Unionists (though his views were more pragmatic being a soldier and not a theologian[2602]), as well as Senators, nobles, armies, and the venerated Queen Mother. What was impossible to receive was the approval of the remaining Orthodox Church and the countless Byzantines and Slavs that grew accustomed and recognized the more stable institutions of a more tolerant Ottoman leadership. Even an official coronation was denied Constantine by the Patriarchy and historians are divided in whether John VIII was the final *Basileus* of Constantinople. Like his father, however, he was charismatic and courageous, deeply conscious of Byzantium's long and glorious history, and was determined to uphold its dignity.[2603]

Constantine XI Paleologus Dragases was born in 1405, the only *Basileus* born in the Empire's last century, as the third son of Manuel II and his Serbian *Basilia* Helena Dragases, a surname now included in his official title. Shadowed by his eldest brother John, little is known of Constantine's childhood and almost less of his appearance; coins and seals of the period, doing nothing to add to a general and bland figure of a hawk-faced man, crowned and robed man with a beard and a staff with Cross and less than clear lettering, if that. What is known is taken from drawings and depictions, mostly by Western artists of the

---

[2601] Herrin, 184.

[2602] Crowley, 68.

[2603] Brownworth, 287.

new Renaissance. He had no time to sit for portraiture due to his nation's crisis, and was known for his character as a 'philanthropist without malice', resolute, courageous, patriotic, who inspired loyalty.[2604] He was a deep thinker, though not as educated as his predecessors, and a fine sportsman in hunting and war. And even when the toughest critics named his Empire 'pusillanimous and base', its ruler was called a hero whose army showed 'Roman virtue' and his allies 'Western chivalry'.[2605]

Like his unfortunate brother, his attempts at marriage were fruitless to the point of cursed by his circumstances: in March, 1428, he married Maria, the sister of Carlo Tocco of Epirus, but she died childless two years later. Fortunately, the dowry was his and he retained the Tocco Peloponnese of Clarentza and Elis as its successful Despot. In September, 1441, he married Catherine Gattilusi, the Genoan daughter of the lord of Lesbos, Hellenized and Byzantinized by her grandfather, Francesco, as the brother-in-law of John V. Again, he was a widow the next year with no heir and he appealed to the Orsini of Taranto and the daughter of the Venetian Doge Foscari.

The Greek court ambassadors of Naples even inquired about the Infanta of Portugal, but no Western princess would connect themselves to the unstable and dying throne of the Greek Empire.[2506] His last attempt was with his cousin Maria, the daughter of the Serbian King, George Brankovich. But she sternly refused on the grounds she preferred the ascetic life of chastity, charity, and good works and a defeated George Sphrantzes, the *Basileus*'s secretary and his uncle's former tutor, returned empty-handed; Constantine never remarried, or tried to remarry, again.

Turning further east to Greek Successor state marriage alliances, Constantine XI was also unsuccessful at the Comnenian court of Trebizond by Sphrantzes. Even his family arrangements seemed to be tainted as Brankovich denied a marriage with Constantine's niece. The main reason was that he wished to supplant the Turks by avoiding the dynastic politics of the Morea, this also losing him union with a Georgian princess as well. Constantine Dragases died childless, despite the rumors of the Templars in July of 1453 that he had a secret son in Galata.[2607] As Despot, he showed boldness and courage and the

---

[2604] Crowley, 49.

[2605] Gibbon, 2340.

[2606] Runciman, 50-51.

[2607] Nicol, Donald M. *The Immortal Emperor: the Life and Legend of Constantine Palaiologus, Last Emperor of the Romans.* Cambridge, UK: Cambridge University Press. 1992, 79.

abilities of a man of action, just the attitude Byzantium needed, although the timing was beyond his control, and when he was made *Basileus* he realized he had no power. Upon his imperial brother's death on October, 31, 1448, it was assumed that Constantine's bold brother Demetrius would assume the throne, the funeral of John VIII even described as having been in 'suspicious haste,'[2608] though foul play was never suspected. Yet, perhaps as he was an anti-Unionist (threatening Byzantine division) and, by implication anti-Western (possibly alienating allies), their mother Helena convinced the City Constantine was to be *Basileus* before Demetrius even reached Constantinople.

Hearing of this in the Morea, Constantine knew that the divisions in the Church were still deep due to the Council of 1439 and would only spark a civil war at the cost of any moral obligation from his subjects. He left for the City as the Despotate lacked a Patriarch, only accepting a proclamation with a simple investiture on January 6, 1449,[2609] and in February, he would be hailed as "Constantine Paleologus Porphyrogenitus and Most Excellent *Basileus* of Lacedaemonia." It was believed Constantine had been crowned by a layman in Mistra, but the historian Spyridos Lampros (1851-1919) is the one who assures us that no such coronation occurred.[2610]

The only similar precedent was the ceremony of Manuel I Comnenus by his father in the wilds of Cilicia in 1143.[2611] Arriving in Constantinople by a Catalonian vessel, Dragases was denied a coronation by the Unionist Patriarch Gregory III Mammes, sparking the controversy that he was not a *Basileus* of Eastern Rome. Edward Gibbon would invent this event as happening in Mistra as well as in a tour through Georgia, but this was never true. Despite this, he had precedence as a Regent of Constantinople, if not co-emperor, in 1437 as his elder brothers left for Italy for the ecumenical Council, but the more important historians of the events, such as Michael Ducas, still do not later recognize him as a *Basileus*. Nonetheless, it is stated how, for the sake of civic order and against public rioting, Constantine would tacitly approve of the Patriarch's Unionist policies.[2612]

Constantine XI had to further the truce with and win the acceptance of the Sultan Murad II, becoming a vassal of his suzerainty despite the trouble he

---

[2608] Gibbon, 2323.

[2609] Today a double eagle is carved in the Agios Dimitrios to commemorate the site of the proclamation. Brownworth, 287f.

[2610] Vasiliev, 589.

[2611] Norwich, *(DF)*, 411.

[2612] Brownworth, 289.

had been to the Sultan in recovering Ottoman lands in the Morea. To placate his brothers Demetrius and Thomas, he granted the former the peninsula of the Peloponnese and the latter the western mainland. The result was internal strife between the Despots a year later over territory, of which Constantine had to intercede. In 1451, Murad II died and was succeeded by his nineteen-year-old son with a Turkish slave (though legends extended his mother had been a Frankish noblewoman) from Adrianople, Mehmet. This was to be Mehmet II 'the Conqueror', whose unhappy childhood hardened him against weakness and luxury and, perhaps, was the cause of his notorious and explosive temper. He was mainly heir by default, his brothers all dying by 1444 and Murad bearing no others. He showed a cold and Machiavellian calculation in personally strangling an infant half-brother to death while holding a dinner for the mother. When she at last discovered the crime, Mehmet left her no time to grieve before marrying her off to a Turkish officer.[2613]

Fatally underestimated as a weak child by his Eastern and Western opponents, he was already a lover of learning in art, science (especially astronomy), and philosophy also speaking Greek, Latin, Hebrew, Arabic, and Persian as well as Turkish.[2614] He had excellent and innovative talents as a general and Sphrantzes recognizes him as an equal to the accomplishments of Julius Caesar and Alexander the Great as Turkish sources tend to bespeak his clemency, justice, his patronage of arts, especially poetry.[2615] Physically, he is best known by the medal struck by Costanzo de Ferrara (1450-1524) upon a visit made by King Ferrante of Naples to Constantinople in 1481, the year of the Sultan's death. It was said to be in a fine quality very reminiscent of the medal struck of John VIII in Florence. He made peace with Constantine, but his intentions were for the final conquest of the City and he successfully sought prevarications to do so. Soon after, being another to underestimate the new Sultan, the *Basileus* requested a subsidy of 40,000 *hyperpyra*. Unfortunately, as Constantine underestimated his iron-willed opponent, now diplomatically 'reminding' Mehmet that they held an Ottoman pretender, the incensed Sultan used this as his pretext for an injury.[2616] Mehmet managed to also garner goodwill from Rhodes, Serbia, Wallachia, and the Venetian Doge, Foscari, cunningly surrounding Constantinople with new opponents instead of old allies.

---

[2613] Brownworth, 290.

[2614] Runciman, 55-56.

[2615] Vasiliev, 645-646.

[2616] Treadgold, 798.

Mehmet was subtle and did not openly show his hostility, using his authority to build, from Saturday, April 15 to Thursday, August 31, 1452, (ignoring that it was technically on Byzantine property, with no permission by the *Basileus* as Bayezid had at least asked of John V) a fortress on the European side of the Bosporus, known as the Rumeli Hisar. To the Greeks, this fortress was *Laimokopia* and the Turks, *Boghaz-kesen* (the 'Throat-Cutter') because its finality of cutting off the Bosporus altogether with a sister fortress, Andolu Hisar, on the Asian side. During this immoral and illegal construction of a trespassing battlement, the Turks tore down churches important to the local farmers and peasants in the area. Their reaction to one incident of encroachment on their grazing land was a riot, wherein forty Greek farmers were killed by Turkish soldiers in this unfortunate travesty urging Constantine to declare a defensive war.[2617]

Mehmet had further made his aggressive intentions clear when he issued that the European fortress be used to flag all ships for inspection before crossing the Bosporus and trading in Constantinople.[2618] Any incident caused by this was all that was needed to spark military conflict and Mehmet's assault on the City as he secretly improved his fleet and artillery. That November, three Venetian ships 'ran the gauntlet' of heavy canon fire to enter the City to deliver much needed food and supplies,[2619] and two slipped in without inspection. The third was hit and sunk and the crew and captain, Antonio Rizzo, were captured.

After the subsequent be-headings and impaling of these officers, the Venetian Senate declared war despite commercial advantages with the Turks and voted seventy-four to seven in February, 1453, to defend Constantinople against the inevitable outcome of war. Yet, Venice itself had spent their funds on suppressing war in Lombardy with the Milanese Sforza clan and lacked what could be a solid resistance to the Ottomans. Venice, therefore, promised limited but sufficient saltpeter and breastplate for Constantinople to be bought on credit. This credit would then be used to pay for volunteer troops and archers from Crete and aid to Christian allies, but only on the condition that this all be used in a mainly passive and *defensive* manner.

As well as Venice, Constantine XI appealed one last time to his brothers and Christian allies in the East and West. Demetrius and Thomas, in the Peloponnese, were engaged in battles with Albanian rebels and Turkish raids. The Vlachs and Serbs were loyal Turkish vassals, Moldavia was fighting itself,

---

[2617] Nicol, (IE), 55.

[2618] Norwich, *(AHV)*, 325-326.

[2619] Brownworth, 294.

Rhodes and the Aegean remained neutral, the Morea was fighting the Ottoman general Bey, Russia was too distant, Scanderberg was not friendly with Venice, Georgia and Trebizond were too weak, and Hunyadi was embroiled in a Hungarian war provoked by Mehmet.[2620] In the West, the Hapsburg Emperor Frederick III gave empty ultimatums to withdraw and England was ruled by the half-mad Henry VI, smarting from his defeat in the Hundred Years' War and leading the nobles to civil war in 1456 with the War of the Roses. Scotland and Scandinavia had no interests in the conflict and remained neutral.[2621]

King of Aragon Alfonso V readily agreed, even after a failed marriage attempt between his daughter and the *Basileus*, but all involved knew well his real intent was to drive out the Ottomans to conquer Constantinople for itself as the Latins had done to revive the Catalans in Athens. Philip V of Burgundy, who lent 300 ships at Varna was a better hands-on candidate, but had the same designs as Aragon, flexing such muscle in the Pindus Mountains by scaring off the Venetians with his armies and being hailed heroically by the Vlachs.[2622] Pope Nicholas V was also appealed to in 1452 and ambassadors, led by Isidore of Kiev, issued the terms that Constantine agree to re-instate the exiled Patriarch Gregory from Rome and openly proclaim the *Laetantur Coeli*.

Orthodoxy would still be divided on papal support; on December 12, 1450, a Council of St. Sophia was said to have occurred that condemned the Decree of 1439 and restored traditional Orthodoxy. The Latin priest present was even scandalously offering unleavened bread and using cold water in the Sacrament, not wine![2623] Even Bishops and clergy from the other Eastern Patriarchies were said to have been in attendance.[2624] The existence of this Council was only rumor, however, and did not actually take place, but its acceptance by some as existing is evidence of Orthodoxy's ever-present hostility of the Decree, even in the crisis of finding allies.

In 1451, Constantine had sent his ambassador Leontaris to Venice for Cretan archers and to Rome to request a *Synaxis* (as a true Synod needed a viable Patriarch) on the Union.[2625] Now, Nicholas sent the *Basileus* a letter worded so that it was known to him that breaking or compromising the Decree would have certain 'consequences' and those transgressing it would be 'properly

---

[2620] Runciman, 82.
[2621] Norwich, *(DF)*, 416.
[2622] Nicol, (IE), 29-30.
[2623] Gibbon, 2338.
[2624] Vasiliev, 675.
[2625] Runciman, 63.

punished'. Although Constantine was known to agree with John VIII on the Union, but with more tolerance in the matter,[2626] the *Basileus* had no choice but to capitulate to the veiled threats as a spiritual vassal of Rome and Union was re-instated. With all of these divisions and conflicts between state interests and occupations, it was becoming obvious that it was the self-interest of commercialism, Ottoman strength and avarice, and religious predominance that would result in the Fall of Constantinople.

By April 1453, Thracian Heraclea, Mesembria, and Anchialus were taken by Mehmet II's forces of 80,000, making way to the City. The Byzantines shored their Walls and chained the Bosporus cay as every able man, woman, and child in the City would later aid or relieve the defenders. The advantage by land the Turks employed was a super-canon built by a Hungarian military engineer, Urban (Orban, d. 1453), that Constantine had once used, but could no longer afford. Made of the best metals mined from the region, the canon stood at twenty-seven feet long with a thickness of eight inches of solid bronze, a staggering diameter of thirty inches, and a capability of firing a length of eight feet a stone eight feet in circumference. But its immensity had the drawbacks that it could only lumber the traverse two-and-a-half miles a day, only being able to be fired seven times daily.[2627]

These marble and stone cannonballs of around 1,340 pounds each were tested to have been lobbed over a mile and landing with a hole of six feet. Some 200 men were needed to smooth the roads and re-enforce bridges, drawn by sixty oxen and another 200 men to steady it, it was said to have been able to blast the 'walls of Babylon itself.'[2628] Though this canon has not survived, other canons recovered and on display today were up to fourteen feet long, weighing fifteen tons, and capable of firing 500 pound balls. The Walls took damage from the terrible secret weapon the Turks instrumented, but the recoil of the defenders' own canon only furthered the damage to the Walls the Greeks would only vainly repair.

By April, with Venetians navies, Cretan archers, and a total of 4,983 Greeks with 2,000 foreigners, the Byzantines defended the City against the Sultan's 80,000 troops. The usual lancers, archers, and infantry were supported by musketry with shot of eight to ten lead balls the size of a walnut.[2629] The Land

---

[2626] Nicol, (IE), 17-18.

[2627] Crowley, 93-94.

[2628] Norwich, *(DF)*, 419.

[2629] Gibbon, 2340.

Walls were personally manned by Constantine Dragases as Unionist Catholics and Greeks and anti-Unionists had to be separated in the defenses, the keys to the four main Gates of the City being entrusted to the Venetians.[2630] Private collections from the churches, monasteries, and Senators in the City were taken to pay for food and whatever arms could be found in the City that were of use. Stone for the repair of the Walls were taken from all varieties of the destitute and abandoned buildings on which pilgrim sources lamented, and even tombstones were utilized, as the land wall ditches were cleared by civilian workers.[2631]

The Sultan's 80,000-strong army consisted of 20,000 irregular troops (*bashi-bazouks*) and 12,000 Janissaries, the slaves brought up in Turkish military schools who acted as crack cavalry and gunmen, commissioned just after ending a rebellion against the Sultan over wages in 1451. Along with the remaining regular troops were engineers and sappers prepared for under-manning the Walls. Mehmet's tactics on land took three stages over the Siege from April to May and demonstrated the genius and fervor of Byzantine defenses over Turkish technological superiority:[2632]

1) Bombards and artillery were to breach the Inner Walls of the City as 'brass battering rams' at the *Mesotechion* district of the defenses were used so troops could overrun the breach; this proved fruitless in action.

2) Another point, the Saint Romanus Gate at the *Pempton* sector, was the target of triangulated artillery fire by the Turkish canon in April/May. This too was counted as unproductive.

3) After the failure of the traditional Late Antique/Medieval methodology of undermining defenses (thanks to John Grant,[2633] a Scottish engineer) and employing siege towers, concentrating on attacks from below and above, Mehmet relied on numerical superiority to overwhelm the defenders which was only effective at the decisive retreat of Venice.

---

[2630] Crowley, 106.

[2631] Crowley, 76.

[2632] Philippides, Marios. 'A Military Assessment on the Ottoman Strategy Against the Land Walls in the Siege of Constantinople (1453).' Presented at *The Twenty-Seventh Annual Byzantine Studies Conference.*(South Bend, IN: The University of Notre Dame, November 9-11, 2001).

[2633] Johannes Grandi, a practically mythical figure at the Battle of Constantinople was commented first by Runciman.

In May, a Venetian ship of twelve volunteers under *Bailo* Minetto left the blockade disguised as Turkish soldiers flying the Turkish flag to sail west, checking on the Venetian reinforcements promised by the Senate.[2634] For three weeks the scouts searched, but no fleet traveled the Aegean from Italy and the situation seemed almost hopeless. *Basileus* Constantine graciously thanked them with tears in his eyes, choked by emotion. In Venetian records, it was later discovered a fleet had been sent on May 7th, but was redirected to Corfu by the 9th, and then to Tenedos to pick up more reinforcements.

However, it was 'delayed by schedule' with orders that no offensive assault were to befall the Sultan and mainly it was a superficial fleet meant to protect the local merchantmen and hedge their bets with the Turkish victory. It was on January 29 of that year that Giovanni Gustiniani Longo arrived with a private army of 700 Italians and the Spanish Don Francisco de Toledo arrived with an army of Catalans and the valuable Scottish engineer, Grant. Somewhat despairingly, Minetto had indeed, on February 26, fled the City against his word made with the emperor with seven Cretan galleys and 700 Italians to Corfu and Tenedos. He had to have returned, however, to conduct his surveillance mission in May for the Venetian reinforcements. Only twenty-six vessels aided the Byzantine fleet, eight Venetian, five Genoese, ten Greek, one Anconan, one Catalan, and one French ship from Provence.

Meanwhile, Mehmet's navy ably kept from the City harbors, the ships going north to take the Sea Walls of Galata where defenses there were concentrated, spreading the 7,000 men thin on the fourteen miles total on the Wall. The Turkish fleet consisted of six biremes, ten triremes, fifteen oared-galleys, and seventy-five longboats, twenty sailing barges and numerous sloops and cutters.[2635] To his amazing credit, Constantine XI Paleologus Dragases was seen with his countrymen giving encouragement, supplying food, water, arrows, and even the use of Greek Fire, which might explain the Sultan's inability in capturing the harbors. The Venetian ships were effective in the canal against the superior numbers of ships and four was enough to hold most at bay. Mehmet II showed his genius as a 'New Xerxes' on Sunday, April 22, by engineering land over water, hauling seventy ships in the east over the 200-foot hill of Petra to bypass the chain on the 'Double Columns' of the Bosporus into the vulnerable shores of the City.

This made possible the Turkish fleet being more supportive and active

---

[2634] Norwich, *(AHV)*, 328-330.
[2635] Norwich, *(DF)*, 418.

compared to the 1204 Siege by the Latins, and when the Venetians finally quit the City it was only by west Galata would they be able to do so as the Turks had better positions of concentration in the east.[2636] It is also to be noted that the Sultan watched the naval operations from the shore and was said to have insane rages as his fleet was humiliated before April 22, comparably as Xerxes had at Salamis. Mehmet again offered to spare the City for an annual indemnity of 100,000 *hyperpyra,* an exorbitant and impossible sum Constantine could never pay (which Mehmet well knew). Thus, this sealed their fate and enabled the Sultan to viciously bend the rule of the Koran towards mercy and charity in warfare. To spare the soldiers he gave this ultimatum along with the choices of circumcision (conversion to Islam), or death.[2637] Time was running out as the food supply was low, fishing and gathering being impossible outside the City's Walls.

Besides his proud claim that the City was God's and not his to give, the final words of the *Basileus* were recorded by Leonard of Chios (1395-1458), Archbishop of Miletyne, as a rousing speech to his soldiers after hymns and the *Kyrie Eleison.* He had it translated in Greek and Latin by Sphrantzes, who added their own allusions and pedantic styles to the rhetoric.[2638] Thanking humbly the Venetians for their faith and service in the battle, he reminded the Greeks they must fight for faith, country, family, and sovereign. Before, he had reminded them they fought against a Sultan that pretended peace, but built his fortresses and broke a treaty, attempting to take the Seat of Jesus Christ from the True Faith. He emphasized that Mehmet II was impious even to his Islam, as intending to turn holy churches of God into horse stables, which he later did. Adding to this, if any blood was shed by these defenders, than a holy martyr's crown and, as with the Latins, immortal glory would be theirs.[2639] Finally, he then remarked on the virtues of both the Greek and Roman heroes in the past, invoking their aid to bring victory to their present forebears and begged individually each man present forgiveness if he ever had done them any offense.

On Tuesday, May 29, 1453, the catastrophic toll on the Walls was made most

---

[2636] Philippides, Marios. 'The Naval Operations of the 1453 Siege of Constantinople: Sultan Mehmet II Fatih, the New Xerxes'. Presented at *Twenty-Ninth Byzantine Studies Conference Abstract of Papers.*(Lewiston, ME: Bates College, October 16-19, 2003).

[2637] Gibbon, 2346.

[2638] Runciman, 130.

[2639] Crowley, 198.

clear south of the Blacharnae, wherein the moat was filled by rubble[2640] which allowed land rushes by Turkish infantry on the Gate. After three unsuccessful waves, however, the Venetian *condottiere* Longo was seriously wounded in the breastplate. Despite Constantine's efforts to save the situation by closing the Gates, the Venetian defenders fled the City in panic, allowing the Turks full entry. Immediately, the troops filled the breach and within fifteen minutes, 30,000 troops had entered the Walls[2641] as the Byzantines were fighting to their last. Surrounded in arms by Don Francisco de Toledo, John Dalmata, and his cousin Theophilus, Constantine XI Paleologus Dragases made his last stand. As legend would have it, he was said to have thrown aside his imperial regalia as if he were a common soldier, rushing himself into the fray of furious battle from the St. Romanus Gate, declaring "the City is lost, but I live"[2642] and was never seen again, a heroic end for a heroic man.

Constantinople had been a lost cause from April, the last vestiges of hope within the City only failing six weeks later, almost 1,123 years to the day since its founding by Constantine the Great. The Fall was the only real outcome as thousands of more troops from the East would only have postponed conquest for a few months and even submission to Mehmet might have spared it only a few more years.[2643] The realization of this comes from the fact that even a truly dynamic man of accomplishment, fearlessness, and promise such as Dragases was powerless to do what at least his weaker brother and his bold father had done. Now, the end of Byzantium was complete and its mutation would begin from a Christian testimony in Eastern Europe to that of an Islamic one, leaving only Russia with any realistic ability to take up such a title as a Byzantine entity. Yet, the West would not be forced out as the Venetians still held Corcyra, Genoa kept Chios, the Templars holding Rhodes, and the Toccos in Cephalonia. As the Lusignan held Cyprus, the Albanians of Scanderberg would hold out and rebel in Mehmet II's East until 1468.

Now started the three day free reign of rape, murder, and destruction of the City of Constantine, the survivors seeing their City fall around their heads in despair. Churches were demolished, books torn apart from silver bindings and burned (meat was even cooked on the fires) as others were loaded on carts to countries never to be seen again. Some priceless copies even sold for as little

---

[2640] Ironically, this mounting rubble absorbed most of the canon fire that otherwise would have further damaged the Walls. Brownworth, 294.

[2641] Crowley, 215.

[2642] Brownsworth, 297.

[2643] Treadgold, 800-801.

as a single coin.[2644] Gospels were stripped of their ornaments and discarded. Vestments stolen, dogs dressed in ecclesiastical robes, sacraments defiled for fun and the Prophet, slaves taken, children raped or impaled on stakes, and all manner of innocent blood spilled. Even Mehmet II was appalled and angered at the site of the buildings destroyed as they were considered his and not part of the custom of looting.

The murals and mosaics of the walls were spared but the holiest relic of the City, the icon of the Virgin Hodegetria painted by St. Luke, was cut into four pieces and destroyed. What Mehmet did tear down was the Church of the Holy Apostles – where Constantine XI would never be buried – abandoned by the Patriarch Gennadios. The greatest prize was, of course, the Church of the Hagia Sophia that the Sultan marveled at as Justinian I had done nine centuries before. Its Christian mosaics were painted over with geometric designs and on the walls hung wooden shields inscribed with verses from the Koran, and a sacred *mihrab* pointing towards Mecca was carved in one wall. After this, he executed all Constantinopolitan men of noble birth and bestowed each Turkish officer with 400 Greek children as slaves.[2645] As said above, it is here, legend tells, that a harlot was placed on a throne, dressed in holy garments, to dance lewdly and mock the end one of the greatest of Christian Empires in history, as was done in Rome in 476. Mehmet II was said to weep at the loss of some of the City buildings, but this did not stop the involuntary Islamic conversions of around 5,000 families of Constantinople.[2646]

In 1454, the Sultan took Selymbria, the north Aegean, and the Duchy of Athens with annual tributes of 10,000 *hyperpyra* apiece as the surviving Paleologi, Thomas and Demetrius, shored up in their Peloponnese Despotates. The Peloponnese was spared and the Sultan allowed the local magnates and landholders to pay directly to the central government to end their localized opposition and corruption. But, by 1458, the tax revenues were three years overdue and Mehmet sent troops there to annex the Peloponnese in 1460. The Morea proved to be more tenacious, at least, than the rest of the region of the Paleologi Despotates, concerning its Western inhabitants. From a scroll of December 16, 1454, it is somewhat clarified that the Archons and their family groups made massive submissions after the capture of Corinth and Patras. Not to accept Ottoman suzerainty, the rebellious Albanians and their Venetian

---

[2644] Vasiliev, 653.

[2645] Brownworth, 299.

[2646] Herrin, 319.

allies intervened to repel Turkish incursion of the Morea and even gave Venice control of certain castles taken after their surrender by the Paleologi.[2647]

Corinth and Patras would be taken immediately as the Unionist Despot Thomas Paleologus fled to Venetian Corcyra and then to Rome to the Pope's pleasure; Demetrius surrendered the Mistra and was sent to Adrianople as a monk known as David. Now, the remaining male heirs of the Paleologi lived out their lives as dispossessed guests and prisoners as Scanderberg would control certain Morean military points until 1468. David Comnenus, the last Byzantine ruler, would be deposed in September, 1461, as Trebizond would fall to the Turks and end the political legacy of the East Romans. David's people would be re-located to Constantinople and the Comnenus Despot himself with his seven sons would be executed in 1463 for conspiracy, effectively ending the last Byzantine royal dynasty. Although Venice had lost 550 men at a cost of 300,000 *ducats*,[2648] the Serene Republic dealt with the Turks under new trade agreements and Western Europe was richly benefited with luxury goods such as gold, silks, pepper, spices, honey, corn, raisins, and the Sultanate's rich metal ores, including alum. On June 1, the surrendering Genoese of Galata also signed a treaty of religious and commercial freedom with the Vizier Zaganos Pasha in a Greek *tughra* ('monogram').[2649]

Within the City, Mehmet II would rebuild the massive Walls to new heights of fortification as Galata's would be demolished to keep the Genoese inhabitants in line. It was in the Hagia Sophia, now the site of the Great Mosque of Istanbul, that the last Christian mass of Orthodoxy in the City was conducted by Isidore of Kiev, who prayed to the Virgin for deliverance, only to be supposedly interrupted. It is said he hid in a secret panel in a pillar, the remaining vestments of that mass from the approaching Infidel, to be re-opened and emptied when the City is restored to the Greeks and the final mass could be finished at last. Legend and folklore of Constantinople's glory and hope of restoration were all that remained in the dismembered Empire as it was taken, the subjugated Greeks praying for deliverance from the unassailable Ottoman Empire.

Already during the Siege, the people and prelates had lost hope as the *Passio Constantinopolitana* was demonstrated, where the prayers to the Virgin

---

[2647] Wright, Diana. '"Better Off than Before": The 1454 Moreote Submission to Mehmet II'. Presented by *The Twenty-Seventh Annual Byzantine Studies Conference.* (South Bend, IN: The University of Notre Dame, November 9-11, 2001).

[2648] Norwich, *(AHV),* 331.

[2649] Reinert, 'Revival of Learning', 283n.

went from 'boostening the morale of the defenders' to 'a solemn, anticipated commemoration of the inevitable capture of the city and defeat of its emperor.' The victory the faithful prayed for changed in these weeks from that over the invading Turks to the victories in Christ of martyrdom on the battlefield.[2650] In 1453, the feeling was that though the saints had abandoned them because of Byzantium's own sins, they would still deliver the souls of those who kept their faith in the despair and hopelessness of the Siege and Conquest. The total bottoming-out of the morale of the Greeks for the City and their future would not taint their strong faith in Christ, Orthodoxy, and the Church in the years to come.

Portents and prophecies of doom were already prevalent in the years before the Siege: from the fishermen harvesting oysters dripping blood to the other inhabitants of the City interpreting earthquakes and hailstorms foretelling apocalypse and even an unprecedented fog from the sea covering the City. Others read into angelic visions, that the Statue of Justinian in Persian dress kept in the Forum pointing east to a conquered Persia was now pointing to the direction of the City's conquerors and sculpted friezes in the Forum of the Bull said the same.[2651] On May 22, a lunar eclipse before the full moon caused consternation, and during a procession, the holy icon of the Virgin fell from her base onto the ground, as if fallen into despair. And it could be no coincidence that the first Emperor was a Constantine mothered by a Helena, so the final *Basileus* in Constantinople would be one as well, meaning Dragases. After the Fall, being thoroughly defeated, Helena Paleologus took the veil with the name Hypomene (or Irene as several historians know her).[2652]

The myth surrounding Constantine XI himself survived as the details of his death have been a subject of disagreement by the historians who were and were not present. The fluent Humanist and Bishop of Siena, Aeneas Sylvius Piccolomini (1405-1464), the future Pope Pius II, would spuriously claim Constantine fled the City as a coward and never fought! He supposedly escaped through Galata not to be seen again.[2653] Fortunately, the Greeks who were present rehabilitated his reputation as Michael Critobulos (1410-1470) did,

---

[2650] Rajkovic, Srdjan. '*Passio Constantonoplitana*: Pleas for Divine Intervention During the 1453 Siege of Constantinople'.Presented at *The Twenty-ninth Annual Byzantine Studies Conference Abstracts of Papers*. (Lewiston, ME: Bates College, October 16-19, 2003).

[2651] Crowley, 174.

[2652] Vasiliev, 586f.

[2653] Nicol, (IE), 83.

describing a wise, moderate, disciplined man of eloquent speech, and most comparable to King Pericles, fighting to the last.[2654]

The most probable of outcomes was the recovery of the decapitated body and the head of the *Basileus*, discovered by the Templars of Rhodes in clearing out the carnage of the battlefield. It was said the body was identified by the purple buskins and other regalia the body wore. Does this mean Constantine did not shed it all before the last fight? Mehmet the Conqueror agreed that this was so and displayed the head on the Column of Justinian facing the Hagia Sophia, flaying the corpse, and filling the skin with straw. All of this was according to Ducas and Lucas Notarus (1402-1453) as Mehmet used the recovered head as a trophy he had displayed with great ceremony, touring it through the Muslim kingdoms of his completed Empire.[2655]

But, the hope demonstrated by the Greeks appears as a living myth in itself when the mystical symbolism of Constantine XI reviews him as a martyr/ heretic in December, 1939. Less than a century after the Conquest, Benvenuto of Ancona wrote tragic panegyrics of Constantine bravely killing 'ten pashas and sixty Janessaries and how his sword and lance broke and he was "alone".'[2656] As if taken from the Arthurian beliefs of the Britons, Constantine is said to be not dead but asleep, truly immortal, within a marble coffin, awaiting the time Constantinople is Greek and Christian again, where he will awaken to rule it. This is repeated in the same legend in the German that the Emperor Frederick Barbarossa to do the same.[2657] One of Klontaz's 150 miniatures of 1590 includes a tableaux of the last *Basileus* as a Crusader in the coffin laying with his mother Helena as well as Constantine I and St. Helena, his mother. In the Renaissance, prophecies of Christ's return to the City was cited by prophecies in the Oracles of Leo the Wise and the 1577 Cretan illustrations by Francesco Barozzi (1537-1604) of the sleeping *Basileus* buried in the City where a Column of Arcadius in Constantinople foretells his return and another depiction of a coalition of Christian princes ousting the Turks once and for all.[2658]

This legend, in its many variations, survives mainly as the actual final resting place of Constantine Dragases as always in contention.[2659] In 1660, poets and authors said he lay beside the Church of the Peribleptos by Turkish

---

[2654] Runciman, 44.

[2655] Crowley, 229.

[2656] *ibid.*, 230-231.

[2657] Brownworth, 251f.

[2658] Reinert, 'Revival of Learning', 281n-283n.

[2659] Nicol, (IE), 92-93.

Chelebi; in the nineteenth century, it was inside the Boulaki Monastery of the Zoodochos Pigi. More specifically, in 1844, the Patriarch of Constantinople, Germanus IV, claims it is in the Church of St. Theodosia (the Mosque of Gul Camii). St. Theodosia is where it is mostly agreed upon he is by researchers, although the only truth is that he was denied burial in the Hagia Sophia and the City itself by Mehmet II. Mehmet, in a superstitious fear of Constantine XI's return, had the Golden Gate bricked up and every year to the present, on May 29th, the Turks re-enact the taking of the City with Constantine as a heretic.[2660]

Even the supposed raiment recovered that day in 1453 by the Templars carry a holy power of Christ's Imitator and his legacy. The True Crown and Scepter of Constantine Dragases were never recovered and the semi-divine legend of the *Basileus* intimates that they reside with the Mother of God, as if it was delivered in a state of apotheosis occurring on May 29. The relics that exist also carried an earthly holiness, such as the Sword of the Lady of Angels said to be by Constantine's side, presented and kept by Cardinal Isidore of Kiev in 1452. As Greece had finally gained independence in 1828 from the Ottoman Empire, Western usurpers would even claim to be non-Greek *Basilii* of a new Empire in 1832 (a Bavarian) and 1863 (a Dane).

As Greek patriotism heightened, the search for this relic of the Hellenes was said to have been moved to Constantinople itself in 1890 after its exhumation from Mehmet II's tomb and examination by the French archeologist Victor Langlois (1829-1869) in Turin in 1857.[2661] Between these times, Dragases's Sword was presented in 1886 by the Greeks of Constantinople to the surviving descendant of the Paleologi as Prince Constantine of the Hellenes.[2662]Folk poems written until the 1970's tell of Dragases's legends and his symbolic crowning as 'Constantine XII' after the Balkan War of 1913. The only descendants left today are those of Manuel II Paleologus, who are said to be found in Italy under the son of Scanderberg, John Castriota, after descendants in the West were found here and there, especially in Rome. This is due to Charles VIII of France having been promised the throne of Trebizond in the event of a recovery in 1494 after conquering north Italy.[2663]

---

[2660] Crowley, 258.

[2661] Norwich, *(DF)*, 440.

[2662] Nicol, (IE), pg. 90-91, 108.

[2663] Runciman, 185.

# CONCLUSIONS

From the time of the Conquest to the massacre in Anatolia by Turkey's first ruler after the Ottoman Empire fell, Mustafa Kemal Attaturk (1881-1938), in 1922 where approximately 1,300,000 Greeks were cast into the sea in Smyrna, there existed a movement the Greeks held for a return of the Empire. Despite this strike against Byzantine tradition, the Patriarchy of Constantinople was allowed existence in the 1923 Treaty of Lausanne and today Demetrius Archontites, former head of Mt. Athos, sits as the Patriarch Bartholomeus.[2664] This movement followed the 'Great Idea' (*Megale Idea*) as the nationalist vision of a Greek-speaking population of a new Byzantium re-vitalizing in the Turkish East. Linguistically, by 1910, Greek was a common language in the entire Peloponnese, the Bosporus, and the western coastal territories of modern Turkey.[2665]

Even Bulgaria, Serbia, and the Vlachs considered nationalist movements to bring back their respective Empires, ousting the local Turkish governments. However, this is said to have sparked the rebellious reaction in Anatolia as the cruelty of Attaturk ended any notion of the Great Idea's success in the twentieth century and the traditional 'Constantinople' was changed to the Turkish evolution, 'Istanbul'.[2666] Still, the Patriarch of Constantinople is formerly recognized by the Orthodox from Egypt to Armenia, but the West was still a different matter; though a loose 'Union' was said to have existed from 1439, the anathemas of the Schism of 1056 were still not rescinded until 1965 at the Vatican II Council by Pope Paul VI.[2667]

One boisterous voice of Byzantium's return to glory and recovery of

---

[2664] Herrin, 320.

[2665] Treadgold, 850.

[2666] This not being a mere Turkish translation of 'Into the City' from Greek colloquial as once thought; Beckwith, 420, 94f.

[2667] Crowley, 66.

Constantinople by a Crusade was the Cardinal Bessarion. As a student of the intrepid political philosopher Plethon, he believed in high ideals and the civic morals that only they could save the Empire, especially with the potential of his culturally-native Morea and its Despot, Constantine Paleologus. In 1444, he wrote a detailed letter to the Despot outlining plans for defining Mistra as the center of the Hellenic state by moving the capital there from the doomed Constantinople. Included were his views on the building of the second Hexamilion of Corinth, economic reforms, and of course, a Crusade[2668] to expel Islam. His brilliant library of works in Greek and Latin, works of Psellus, Plethon, Diaphantos's *Arithmetica*, Hypatia of Alexandria, with many more still on the natural sciences became the center of Venice's Marciana Library founded in 1468 would provide for much of the scholarship in the following century.[2669]

As well as versed with a knowledge of current events and political science, Bessarion's evaluations on current issues were in the Morea and how Constantine could realistically handle them. Since the time of Manuel II in the Morea, and probably just as true for the rest of Byzantium, the Archons that handled local governments and the private interests of the landholding rich fought and divided society. As Bessarion was decidedly more liberal than the Platonist and authoritarian Plethon, the Cardinal wrote on the executive powers of the 'silver bulls' (*Argyrobulla*) available to Constantine's use to centralize the Despotate.[2670] Bessarion's intentions seem clear, that it was time to abandon what is weak in the Empire for what is strong, even if it further divided lines of central authority with Constantinople to create a leading Despotate over the remainder of the Empire. This is reminiscent of Theodosius I's reforms of Ravenna as capital of the West, which was a productive policy for almost a century.

Many works, contemporary and secondary, were written over the Conquest which was shocking to Europe, yet not altogether surprising. Michael Ducas was a Unionist Greek that showed the West favorably, Gustiniani Longo (1418-1453) in particular, as an eyewitness to the Fall in his history of 1341 to 1462, from the ascension of John V and the fall of Lesbos. The Athenian Laonikos Calcondyles wrote in ten books of the years 1298 to 1464, but was not an eyewitness to the Battle of 1453 itself, still holding an important place as a kind of ethnographer in describing the rising Turkish Empire over the Greek, Latin, and Slavic states. The Italian poet Ubertino Pusculus (1431-1488), once a

---

[2668] Nicol, (IE), 25.

[2669] Herrin, 309 & 333.

[2670] Nicol, (IE), 239.

prisoner of Mehmet II's, would write his four-stanza *Constantinopolis* dedicated to the Pope, and as a Catholic, blamed the Greeks for their own fall for Dragases breaking from Rome.[2671] As a cultural, political, and religious successor, Russia had its chronicles, most notably by Nestor-Iskander (Alexander) a Russian soldier in the Turkish army who wrote on the Fall of Tsargrad (Constantinople, City of Caesar)...this great and terrible deed.'

At twenty-one years of age Mehmet II, now truly the Conqueror (*Fatih*), ruled one of the holiest cities in Christendom as a prize for the All Merciful and Compassionate Allah. His military philosophy had been simple: to take victory, shame the enemy, and make sure they would obey their leaders.[2672] Walking the floor of the Church of the Hagia Sophia, soon to be one of the greatest mosques in the Muslim world, he seemed to be as enchanted as Justinian had been a millennium before. As he finally walked to the pebble-floored Palace of the Emperors which housed the *Basilii* since Constantine the Great, he was said to have uttered to himself the words of an unknown Persian poet:[2673] 'The spider weaves the curtains in the Palace of the Caesars; the owl calls the watches in the towers of Afrasiab.'

In 1472, the daughter of the exiled Despot Thomas Paleologus, Zoe-Sophia, married Ivan III of Muscovy, bearing the emblem of the double-headed eagle as her dowry making Moscow the 'Third Rome' spiritually, if not politically, of Europe. From the heritage of the first Caesars to Constantinople, the title of *Tsar* was created and bestowed on the Emperors of Muscovy and a united Russia until the abdication of Nicolas II Romanov in 1917. This lineage of Greek and Russian blood that would produce Ivan the Terrible and Peter the Great would be the most well-known tale of Byzantium's influences in the East and the fate of the Paleologi in Europe.

The farthest from the City known was that of a Theodore Paleologus in Cornwall, England, whose tomb inscription marks his five children and death on January 21, 1636. The brother of Andronicus II Paleologus, Thomas, had also fled to Montferrat after his marriage to a lady there, founding a line of

---

[2671] Which is said not to have officially happened. Vasiliev, 648-649.

[2672] Michael Critobulus, 91, who dedicated in Thucydidean style, his history to the Sultan as 'Greatest Emperor, King of Kings, Mehmet'; Vasiliev, 651.

[2673] Norwich, (*DF*), 437.

converted Catholic, Paleologan-born Italian princes surviving until 1533.[2674] As Thomas fled to Rome in 1454, his name spread throughout Italy, France, the Cyclades, and even the Ottoman Empire; one descendant still lives, John Paleologus, last heir to the Emperors of Byzantium.[2675]

The legacy of this once soaring Empire founded on the glory of Christ and the grandeur of Rome in non-human terms is more lasting, marking it as one of the world's most valuable legacies. The cultivation of Classical learning in every discipline of the arts and sciences at the heights of its proto-renaissances allowed its transmission to the West to begin the new Modern Era of Humanism and commercialism. Shakespeare's themes would stand alone in England, but also stand on the shoulders of Sophocles and Euripides, new education in mathematics would allow better understanding in exchange rates in metallic coins next to the Venetian innovation of double-entry bookkeeping. Da Vinci's paintings and sculpture was a product of Classical study in geometric design and study in postmortem anatomy that Christianity and Islam both forbid. The brilliance of Brunelleschi's dome was an architectural miracle descended from the Dome that covered the marvel of the Great Mosque, once the design of the world's greatest church commissioned by Justinian the Great. Laws that bound societies within and the community of societies without came from the ninth-century discovery of Justinian's *Digest* at the Monastery of Monte Cassino to tie citizens and families into modern concepts of private property. Despotisms, theocracies, constitutions and absolutism could now standardize legal practice between each other and negotiate absolute terms based on their own state philosophies until the time of Napoleon's Code.

The bazaar trade culture of Constantinople led to an amazing transmission of luxury goods sailing from East to West: pepper and spices from India, honey and furs from the Black Sea, Greek silks, and skilled artisans that blended Greek and Turkish craftsmanship with its textured carpets and jeweled bibles. In the greatest paintings of the Renaissance, we see this legacy in Byzantine brocade and the gems and cameos covering the books of Classical Greek works translated or printed in Latin and a host of modern languages. The wealthy and powerful of Italy used these instruments of a dying and fallen Empire to demonstrate to Christendom that wealth and power using art as its media [2676] and this came from a convergence of what Byzantium offered the Renaissance

---

[2674] Gibbon, 2194f.

[2675] Norwich, *(DF)*, 450.

[2676] Jardin, 19.

before and after its fall. It is with great irony that Byzantium became a culture more valuable dead than alive.

The histories of the Saints, Emperors, and *Basilii* that created and strengthened Christianity was a celebration in European culture and thought until the Enlightenment. Between these movements in history, the commitment to the Ten Commandments given to the Puritans to fuel the success of the Reformation was a result of Orthodox study. Louis XIV, perhaps the first serious commissioner of Byzantine studies in Europe, would glorify the despotic rule of wise kings placed on thrones by God, using the *Basilii* as his example.[2677] Unfortunately, the encouragement to study a new secular world based on re-introduced Classicism and a new, impassioned stand for a less material Christianity based on what came from the East turned the West against the Empire's memory. Men of the Enlightenment like Voltaire and Gibbon scoffed at the 'irrational' nature of the Empire and its times as wasteful piety and a thousand years of decadence.

To a modern nation such as the United States, Byzantium seems like an artificial empire, propped up mainly by its rulers; Michael VIII's restoration was just one where the Walls of the City were the same ones that were battered down two centuries later.[2678] Born from modernist hostility was the caveat of what civilizations may lapse into without care of its virtues and institutions by looking at Byzantium. The stereotypes of tyrannical government, half-mad zealots, effeminate and obsequious eunuchs, hollow rituals, complex and useless bureaucracy, and an endlessly scheming court of intrigue came from this era. As the nineteenth century arrived, the romance and decadence of this era reflected itself in the vanished Empire.

Coupled with Salome, the proud and reformed Empress Theodora was exploited by centuries of separation and ignorance into a gluttonous and glamorous temptress. The period of the 'Decline of the Roman Empire' cited by Edward Gibbon and its ethos gave birth to such influences in French Decadence such as in the erotic tale of the Emperor Elagabalus, *l'Agonie* (1888) of Jean Lombard (1854-1891). Just as exploitative was the abhorrent violence of the holy conflicts of Constantine V as represented in Lombard's *Byzance* (1890) of, full of mutilations, massacres, and the mass-murder of all the zealot Christians by the Great Church of the Hagia Sophia, fictitiously collapsing to kill all of

---

[2677] Herrin, 321.
[2678] Treadgold, 847.

its rioters.[2679] This set in mind the visions of Byzantium as weak despots and holy men with the mad eyes of Rasputin, plotting in halls of tarnished gold and choking incense.

When finally recovered in twentieth-century Modernism, it was with fresh eyes that marvelled at its culture, history, and stunning art. The eunuchs were able state functionaries that complemented or implemented all types of monarchs, even becoming generals capable of conquering a continent as Narses practically had in Europe. These holy madmen became scholars of Classic design in giving the people a faith in Christ to be confidant in, especially when threatened as it was from schism, heresy, and the growing influence and conversion of the East to Islam.

And, the people themselves mattered, the social lives of a peasant, a bureaucrat, a soldier, this ranked almost equally in studies with the *Basileus*. The Post-Modern theories of a civilization extending beyond its state and institutions saw Byzantine culture explode into numerous possibilities in the everyday lives of its citizens. Its result was strongest of all, an Orthodox Church five-hundred years old after the Empire that helped build it from crumbling into dust – it won Mehmet II's respect and outlived Attaturk's wrath to become a religion for millions of people.

Its relevance today can be seen in the history of international relations between Christianity and Islam, the culture of Western civilization with the Middle East. The fight for Jerusalem, the separation of the Shi'ite and Sunni beliefs, the role of international law and custom, this all began and developed in the annals of Late Antique and Byzantine Rome. The cross-culture of Greek and Islamic education lasted from the Abbasids to the Ottomans in the philosophy of Aristotle, untranslatable in Western Europe until Aquinas synthesized it from Averroes's (1126-1198) version, scandalous to Muslim thought who had in turn received this intellectual inspiration from the Greek commentators of Aristotle. Caliphs and *Basilii* fought over intellectuals in their cities to protect the esoteric studies of complex mathematics and sciences as diplomats from their courts carried priceless works of Classical literature as gifts encased in gold and jewels. Istanbul stands today, a product of 'Byzantine character' with its Christian tolerance, grandiosity as a city, bustling commercial activity, and its society as an international, polyglot community.[2680]

---

[2679] Birkett, Jennifer. *The Sins of the Fathers: Decadence and France, 1870-1914.* New York, NY: Quartet Books. 1986, 14-18.
[2680] Herrin, 335.

What is best to remember in characterizing the Byzantine Empire was that it crossed two major eras of Western history from Late Antique to Medieval to Early Modernism, but while it adapted to the changes of the first, it failed to do so in the second. Its Greek character did well in preserving Classical heritage and institutions in a growing Christian society, even innovating ways of political and military administration and cohesive worship. The result was showing that Jerusalem did have something to do with Athens in advancing thought and Greek once again became a *lingua franca* to the educated and initiated.

Yet, Byzantium did poorly on the other end, starting in the twelfth century, when Western innovation began encroaching in the East with feudalism further and further dividing and ostracizing the outer parts of the Empire. Military aristocratic families that owned large rural estates in Anatolia such as the Argyri, Phocii, Scleri, Meleini, Melissani, Duci, and Diogena would quarrel with each other and the distant entity of the central government to seize the throne, leaving eastern defenses vulnerable to Turkish advance.[2681]

Ultimately, this inability to remain cohesive and find a way to centralize as states eventually did in France, the German Empire, and England did in the West, mainly due to religious dissection and cultural differences in the East, allowed the Turks to gain control. The Ottomans were not monolithic, it had divisions of Sunni and Shi'ites and was a polyglot and poly-sect Empire, but its political and social institutions kept a central authority relatively more capable of engulfing the weaker institutions of Byzantium that were beyond repair by the fifteenth century. Largely, money was the problem as the centuries of buying mercenaries and armies bankrupted its Treasury, leaving fewer allies working on credit that left the homeland armies demoralized and badly organized. The centuries after the Latin seizure of 1204 left Byzantium a corpse with no vigor for the Greek elite, the armies unable to produce the sufficient officers with the sufficient drill as these economic and military problems led to the failure of 1453.

Byzantium's degeneration in the Later Middle Ages to a weak vassal of a stronger state set them outside the world view as a power capable of surviving to a state of Modern status. Their chances as a commercial power were overwhelmed by their ports falling into the hands of the Venetians and Genoans who basically began the Modern commercialism revolution in Italy. At a population of 50,000, it was no longer illustrious with its babble of

---

[2681] Decker, 49.

languages, its wealth adorning its great churches, and its crowds of trade vessels in the imperial harbors, although monastic art was flowering all over the Later Empire.[2682] If the Italians were now dominating the means of communication and commerce in the East they, and not Constantinople, would decide who would guide Oriental commerce in the future after 1453. Frankly, as economic and institutional weakness kept Byzantium in the shadow of the Turkish, Slavic, and Russian markets, it was better that Constantinople lose out as a market competitor.

Byzantium could not even maintain strength in the realm of technological advances in their army as gunpowder was the preserve of foreign nations and the best materials and means to utilize them lay in the hands of the enemy. As an evolutionary force vying for survival in a new era of history for the West, Byzantium was opted out by nature because of its inability to become self-sustaining and stand independent to gain the respect from its feudal lords. A large part of this was the nature of the Byzantine society itself as no amount of administration, commerce, or war did not occur without its participants feeling a 'moral taint' when the Church disallowed any thought of good ends being justified by bad means.[2583] Thus, the increase of amorality and corruption in public life only ostracized those wishing to avoid sin.

Rome in 476 had no foreign aid to help them – they were the West, after all, and the East while somewhat stronger due to solvency with foreign tribes and migrations, still could not give sufficient strength when barbarians controlled the throne of Constantinople and barbarian tribes relentlessly battered East Rome. However, it was different in 1453 as it was more the exhaustion of the West seeing Constantinople as an inconvenience and liability for centuries that stemmed their interest as they turned inward. Constant Crusading was expensive in money and men for the Western states and the Italians were preferring the Turks, while the Infidel were prosperous and preferable trading partners to receive their luxury goods on new forms of credit-debt dynamics than the bankrupted Byzantine Empire.

Again, the nineteenth-century writers of France argued that their states were suffering from a malaise, an 'Energy of Byzantium', or a moral defeat, as their institutions lost efficacy and credibility after the Franco-Prussian War. Cynics jeered in their writings, but were not incorrect in saying the French Empire was on its dying breath because of internal weakness and stronger

---

[2682] Brownworth, 288-289.
[2683] Treadgold, 848-849.

enemies at their gates. This was the same with the Byzantines, their people had lost hope and some were even accepting the change towards Turkish dominion; because the Greeks considered themselves a people blessed by God and loyal only to an *Basileus* that could change so easily in Byzantium's political culture, patriotism was an illusion.

By the fifteenth century, the apathy of the West and the hollowed-out Byzantium easily allowed any strong nation like the Turks to possess it once and for all, unlike the Latins of the thirteenth century, Mehmet II would not allow the maladministration that let the Greeks back in power as in 1261. Yet, its staying power in adversity was unique, unique enough to last longer than the Romans, Ottomans, or any other Western empire in history, no matter the size in its 1,123 years.[2684] Like the vanished Empires of Egypt, Persia, Macedon, Rome, China, the Aztecs, the Mayans, the Incas, Spain, Germany, France, Britain, or the USSR, its influences can be felt almost anywhere even as history notes them as the failures to changing conditions and its pride of place as a world power of the past and influence is as great as any ever conceived.

---

[2684] Treadgold, 844.

# Bibliography

Abbotoy, Joshua. 'Reconstructing Byzantine Rulership: Manuel II's Funeral Oration'. Presented at *The Thirty-Fifth Annual Byzantine Studies Conference.* (Sarasota, FL: Florida State University, November 5-8, 2009).

Al-Baladhuri, Ahmad ibn-Yahya ibn-Jabir. 'The Conquest of the Lands'. *Readings in Medieval Historiography,* ed. by Speros Vryonis, Jr. (Boston, MA: Houghton Mifflin Co.), 343-365, 1965.

Ambrose, Saint. 'Opera'. *CSEL, vol. 73.* Vienna, Austria. 1964.

------------------. 'De Obitu Theodosii'. *CSEL, vol. 73.* Vienna, Austria. 1964.

Ammianus Marcellinus. *The Later Roman Empire (A. D. 354-378),* trans. by Walter Hamilton and Introduction and Notes by Andrew Wallace-Hadrill. New York, NY: Penguin Publishing, 1986.

Andreades, Andre M. 'De la Population des Constantinople sous l'Empereurs Byzantins.' *Metron I, vol. 2., 1920.*

---------------------------. 'Public Finances: Currency, Public Expenditure, Budget, Public Revenue'. Chapter III. in *Byzantium: an Introduction to East Roman Civilization,* ed. by Norman H. Baynes & H. St. L. B. Moss. Oxford, UK: Oxford University Press, 71-85 1969.

Angold, Michael. *Byzantium: The Bridge from Antiquity to the Middle Ages.* London, UK: Phoenix Press, 2001.

Anna Comnena. *The Alexiad*, trans. by E.R.A. Sewter. New York, NY: Penguin Books, 1969.

Attaleiates, Michael. *History*, ed. by Immanuel Bekker, *CSHB*. Bonn, Germany. 1853.

Atwood, Christopher P. *The Encyclopedia of Mongolia and the Mongolian Empire.* New York, NY: Facts on File, 2004.

Aurelius Victor. *Liber de Caesaribus,* trans. by H. W. Bird. Liverpool, UK: Liverpool University Press, 1994.

Babcock, Michael A. The Night Attila Died: Solving the Murder of Attila the Hun. New York, NY: Berkeley Books, 2005.

Bailey, Penny. 'Losing Face? The Symbolism of Facial Mutilation.' *Wellcome Trust Foundation.* November 22, 2012. https://blog.wellcome.ac.uk/2012/11/22/losing-face-the-symbolism-of-facial-mutilation.

Baker, G. P. *Justinian: The Last Roman Emperor, 2nd ed.* New York, NY: Cooper Square Press. 1931, 2002.

Barker, John W. *Manuel II Palaiologos (1391-1425): A Study in Late Byzantine Statesmanship.* New Brunswick, NJ: Rutgers University Press. 1969.

Bartusis, Mark C. 'The Equivalence of the Fiscal Terms *Pronoia* and *Oikonomia'.* Presented at *The Twenty-Eighth Annual Byzantine Studies Conference.* (Columbus, OH: The Ohio State University, October 4-6, 2002).

Beckwith, Christopher I. *Empires of the Silk Road: A History of Central Eurasia from the Bronze Age to the Present.* Princeton, NJ: Princeton University Press. 2009.

Benesevic, V. 'De Byzantinischen Ranglisten nach dem Kleterologion Philothei.' *Byzantinisch-neugrichische Jahrbucher, vol. V, 1926.*

Bergamo, Nicola. 'The Problem of Ethnic Identity between Roman and Longobard in the *Historia Longobardius* of Paul the Deacon'. Presented at *The*

*Twenty-Eighth Annual Byzantine Studies Conference.* (Colombus, OH: The Ohio State University, October 4-6, 2002).

--------------------. *'Tzikanion:* the Noble Sport in Byzantium'. *The Thirty-Sixth Annual Byzantine Studies Conference.* (Philadelphia, PA: The University of Pennsylvania Press, 8-10, 2010).

Birkett, Jennifer. *The Sins of the Father: Decadence in France, 1870-1914.* New York, NY: Quartet Books. 1986.

Bobrick, Benson. *The Caliph's Splendor: Islam and the West in the Golden Age of Baghdad.* New York, NY: Simon & Schuster. 2012.

Boccaccio, Giovanni. *The Decameron,* trans. by Mark Musa and Peter Bondanella. New York, NY: Signet Classics. 2010.

Bowersock, G. W. *Julian the Apostate.* Cambridge, MA: Harvard University Press, 1978.

Brehier, L. *Vie et Mort des Byzance.* Paris, France. 1947.

Bridge, Antony. *Theodora: Portrait in a Byzantine Landscape, 3rd ed.* Chicago, IL: Academy of Chicago Publishers. 1978, 1984, 1993.

Brown, Peter. *Poverty and Leadership in the Later Roman Empire: The Menahem Sterm Jerusalem Lectures,* Hanover, NH: New England University Press and Waltham, MA: Historical Society of Isreal, Brandeis University. 2002.

------------------. *The World of Late Antiquity.* London, UK. 1971.

Browning, Robert. 'The Death of John II Comnenus.'. *CSHB, XXXI.* 1961.

Browning, Robert. 'Notes on the "Scriptor Incertus de Leone Armenio"'. *Byzantion,* 35 Louvain, Beigium: Peeters Publishing. 1965, 389-411.

----------------------. *Justinian and Theodora, 2nd ed.* London, UK: Thames and Hudson. 1971, 1987.

Brownworth, Lars. *Lost to the West: The Forgotten Byzantine Empire That Rescued Western Civilization*. New York, NY: Three Rivers Press. 2009.

Buckler, Georgina. 'Byzantine Education'. Chapter VII. in *Byzantium: an Introduction to East Roman Civilization*, ed. by Norman H. Baynes and H. St. L. B. Moss. Oxford, UK: Oxford University Press, 200-220. 1969.

Burckhardt, Jacob. *The Age of Constantine the Great, 2*ᵈ *ed.*, trans. by Moses Hadas. Berkeley and Los Angeles, CA: University of California Press. 1949, 1983.

Bury, James Bagnell. 'The Bulgarian Treaty of 814 A. D. and the Great Fence of Thrace.' *English Historical Review, XX, 1910*.

-------------------------. 'Charles the Great and Irene.' *Hermathena, VIII. 1893*.

-------------------------. *History of the Later Roman Empire from the Death of Theodosius I to the Death of Justinian, vol. I*. New York, NY: Dover Publications. 1958.

-------------------------. *History of the Later Roman Empire from the Death of Theodosius I to the Death of Justinian, vol. II*. New York, NY: Dover Publications. 1958.

-------------------------. *History of the Later Roman Empire from Arcadius to Irene (395 A. D. to 800 A.D.), vol. II*. London, UK: MacMillan and Co.; www.elibron.com Elibron Classics. 1889, 2005.

-------------------------. *A History of the Eastern Roman Empire, from the Fall of Irene to the Accession of Basil I, A. D. 802-867*. Memphis, TN: General Books LLC. 2012.

-------------------------. 'The Treatise *De Administrando Imperio*.' *Byzantinische Zeitschrift, XV. 1906*.

Byrda, Greg. 'Justinian's Numismatics Program: Coins That Say What They Mean and Mean What They Say.' Presented at *The Thirty-Sixth Annual Byzantine Studies Conference* (Philadelphia, PA: The University of Pennsylvania, October 8-10, 2010).

Cassiodorus, *Variae, vol. I.1.3, Theodoric in Italy,* trans. by John Moorhead. Oxford, UK. 1992.

Cesaretti, Paolo. *Theodora, Empress of Byzantium,* trans. by Rosanna M. Giacommanco Frongia. Milan, Italy. New York, NY: Mark Magowan Publishing/ Vendome Press. 2001, 2004.

Chevveden, Paul E. 'The Invention of the Counterweight Trebuchet: A Study in Cultural Diffusion.' *Dumbarton Oaks Papers, 54.* Washington, DC: Dumbarton Oaks Research Library and Collections. 2000.

Ciolfi, Lorenzo Maria. 'John III Vatatzes' *Bios* Enigma'. Presented at *The Thirty-Sixth Annual Byzantine Studies Conference.* (Philadelphia, PA: University of Pennsylvania, October 8-10, 2010).

Constantine Prophyrogenitus. *De Administrando Imperio,* trans. by Romilly J.H. Jenkins and ed. by Gyula Moravcsik. Washington, DC: Dumbarton Oaks Center for Byzantine Studies. 1966.

Constantine VII Porphyrogenitus. *De Ceremonii Aule Byzantinae,* ed. by I. I. Reiske. Bonn, Germany. 1829.

Croke, Brian. 'Justinian's Constantinople'. Chapter 3 in *The Cambridge Companion to the Age of Justinian,* ed. by Michael Maas. Cambridge, UK: Cambridge University Press, 60-86. 2005.

Crowley, Roger. *1453: The Holy War for Constantinople and the Clash of Islam and the West.* New York, NY: Hyperion Books. 2005.

Dagron, Gilbert. *Emperor and Priest: the Imperial Office in Byzantium,* trans. by Jean Birrell. Cambridge, UK: Cambridge University Press. 2007.

Decker, Michael J. *The Byzantine Art of War.* Yardley, PA: Westholme Publishing. 2013.

Delehaye, Hippolyte. 'Byzantine Monasticism'. Chapter V. *Byzantium: an Introduction to East Roman Civilization,* ed. by Norman H. Baynes and H. St. L. B. Moss. Oxford, UK: Oxford University Press, 136-165. 1969.

Diehl, Charles. 'Andronicus Comnene'. *Byzantin Figures, II*. Paris, France. 1913.

------------------. *Byzantium: Greatness and Decline*. New Brunswick, NJ: Princeton University Press. 1960.

------------------. 'Byzantine Art'. Chapter VI. in *Byzantium: an Introduction to East Roman Civilization*, ed. by Norman H. Baynes and H. St. L. B. Moss. Oxford, UK: Oxford University Press, 166-199. 1969.

------------------. 'L'Origene du Regime des Themes' *Etudes Byzantines*. Paris, France. 1888.

Dobroklonsky, A. *Blessed Theodore the Confessor and Abbot of Studion, bk. I*. Odessa, Russia. 1913.

DowlingSoka, Joel. 'Herakleios' Handlebar: Contextualizing a Change in Imperial Imagery'. Presented at *The Twenty-Eighth Annual Byzantine Studies Conference*. (Columbus, OH: The Ohio State University, October 4-6, 2002).

Drinkwater, John F. "The 'Germanic Threat on the Rhine Frontier'": A Romano-Gallic Artefact?' Chapter 2 of *Shifting Frontiers in Late Antiquity*, ed. by Ralph W. Mathisen and Hagith S. Sivan. Aldershot, Hampshire: Variorum Publishing, 20-30. 1996.

Ensslin, Wilhelm. 'The Emperor and the Imperial Administration'. Chapter X. *Byzantium: an Introduction to East Roman Civilization*, ed. by Norman H. Baynes and H. St. L. B. Moss. Oxford, UK: Oxford University Press, 268-307. 1969.

Evagrius Scholasticus. *Historia Ecclesiastica, vol. III, 14.*, ed. by J. Bidez and J. Parmentier: London, UK. 1898.

Eusebius. *Ecclesiastical History*, trans. by G. A. Williamson. New York, NY: Penguin Publishing. 1989.

------------. 'Life of Constantine'. 'A *Select Library of Nicene and Post-Nicene Fathers of the Christian Church, vol. I: Eusebius'*, trans. by E. C. Richardson, ed. by H. Wace and P. Schaff. Oxford, UK: Parker & Co. 1890.

Eustathius the Thessalonican. De Thessalonica capta latinus a. 1185. *CSHB* ed. by I. Bekker, trans. by H. Hunger. Vienna, Austria. 1955.

Eutropius. *Breviarium ad Urbae Conditium*, trans. by F. Ruehl; ed. by J.S.

Watson. Leipzig, Germany and London, UK. 1890.

Finlay, George. *History of Greece, BC 146 to AD 1864, vol. II-III.*, ed. by H. F. Tozer. 1877.

Geanokoplus, D.J. *Emperor Michael Paleologus and the West 1258-1282: A Study in Byzantine-Latin Relations.* Cambridge, UK: Cambridge University Press. 1959.

George of Pisidia. *The Persian Expedition, Poemi I: Panegyrici Epici,* ed. by A. Pertusi. Ettal, Italy. (3.7-3.10). 1960.

George Monachus Hamartolus. *Chronicle,* ed. by E. Muralt. St. Petersburg, Russia. 1859.

George Pachymeres. *History. Patrologia Graeca, vol. 113-114.*, ed. by J. P. Migne. 1936.

George (Phrantzes) Sphrantzes. *Annales,* I, Chap. 11, ed. by I. Bekker. Bonn, Germany: *CSHB.* 1839.

------------------------------------. *The Fall of the Byzantine Empire: A Chronicle of George Sphrantzes, 1401-1472,* trans. by Marios Phillipides. Amherst, MA: Amherst University Press. 1980.

Gibbon, Edward. *The Decline and Fall of the Roman Empire, vol. 1-3,* ed. by J. B. Bury. New York, NY: Heritage Press. 1946.

Gray, Patrick T. R. 'The Legacy of Chalcedon: Christological Problems and their Significance'. Chapter 9 of *The Cambridge Companion to the Age of Justinian,* ed. by Michael Maas. Cambridge, UK: Cambridge University Press, 215-238. 2005.

Gregoire, Henri. 'The Byzantine Church'. Chapter IV. of *Byzantium: an Introduction to East Roman Civilization.* ed. by Norman H. Baynes and H. St. L. B. Moss. Oxford, UK: Oxford University Press, 86-135. 1969.

Gregory of Nazianzus, St. 'Selected Orations and Letters'. *Nicene and Post-Nicene Fathers, vol. VII.,* trans. by C. G. Browne and J. E. Swallow. Oxford, UK: Oxford University Press. 1900.

Haldon, John F. *Byzantium in the Seventh Century: The Transformation of a Culture.* Cambridge, UK: University of Cambridge Press. 1990.

------------------. *Circus Factions.* Oxford, UK: Oxford University Press. 1976.

------------------. 'Economy and Administration: How Did the Empire Work?' Chapter 2 in *The Cambridge Companion to the Age of Justinian,* ed. by Michael Maas. Cambridge, UK: Cambridge University Press, 28-59. 2005.

------------------. *Warfare, State, and Society in the Byzantine World 565-1204 (Warfare and Society Series).* New York, NY: Routledge Publishing. 1999.

Hansen, Peter Vemming. "Experimental Reconstruction of the Medieval Trebuchet". *Acta Archaeologica,* vol. 63, Denmark. 1992, 189-268.

Harries, Jill. *Law & Empire in Late Antiquity.* Cambridge, UK: Cambridge University Press. 1999.

Head, Constance. *Justinian II of Byzantium.* Madison, WI: University of Wisconsin Press. 1972.

Hendy, Michael. *Studies in the Byzantine Monetary Economy, c. 300-1450.* Cambridge, UK: Cambridge University Press. 1985.

Herrin, Judith. *Byzantium: The Surprising Life of a Medieval Empire.* Princeton, NJ: Princeton University Press. 2007.

------------------. *Women in Purple: Rulers of Medieval Byzantium, 2nd ed.* London, UK: Weidenfeld & Nicolson, Phoenix Press. 2001, 2002.

Hilsdale, Cecily J. 'The Emperor, the Archangel, and the City: Images of Michael VIII Palaiologos and the Restoration of Constantinople'. Presented at *The Thirty-Sixth Annual Byzantine Studies Conference*. (Philadelphia, PA: The University of Pennsylvania Press, October 8-10, 2010).

Engineering an Empire. *The Byzantines* Season: 1, Episode: 11. Directed by: Rebecca Ratliffe and Mark Cannon. Written by: Rebecca Ratliffe. History Channel: 2/25/2006.

Holmes, Catherine. *Basil II and the Governance of Empire (976-1025), Oxford Studies in Byzantium*. Oxford, UK: Oxford University Press. 2006.

Hoyland, Robert. 'The Rise of Islam'. Chapter 4 of *The Oxford History of Byzantium*, ed. by Cyril Mango. Oxford, UK: Oxford University Press, 121-128. 2002.

Humfress, Caroline. 'Law and Legal Practice in the Age of Justinian'. Chapter 7 of *The Cambridge Companion to the Age of Justinian*, ed. by Michael Maas. Cambridge, UK: Cambridge University Press, 161-184. 2005.

Hussey, J. M. *The Byzantine World, 2 ed*, ed. by Maurice Powicke, New York, NY: Harper & Row. 1957, 1961.

Jardin, Lisa. *Worldly Goods: A New History of the Renaissance*. New York, NY: W. W. Company. 1996.

Jenkins, Romilly. *The Imperial Centuries: AD 610-1071*. Toronto, Can: University of Toronto Press and The Medieval Academy of America, 1987.

Johannes, Zonaras. *Annals*, ed. by Buttner-Wobst. *CSHB*. Bonn, Germany. 1897.

John of Damascus. 'Orations'. *Patrologia Graeca, 161 vol. III*, ed. by J.P. Migne. Paris, France. 1866.

John of Ephesus. 'Commentarii de Beatis Orientalibus'. *Patralogia Orientalis*, XVIII, ed. by W.J. van Douan and J.P.N. Land. Amsterdam, UP: Verhandelingen de Koninklijke Akademie van Wetenschappen. 1899.

John VI Cantacuzenus. *Historiae, 3 vol.,* ed. by L. Schopen. *CSHB.* Bonn, Germany. 1838.

John Cecaumenus. *Cecaumeni Strategikon et Incerti Scriptoris de Officiis Regiis Libellus,* ed. by B. Wassiliewsky and V. Jernstadt. St. Petersburg, Russia. 1896.

------------------------. *Strategicon.* Ed. by G. G. Latrivin. Moscow, Russia. 1972.

John Skylitzes. 'Synopsis Historion'. *Patrologia Graeca,* ed. by J. P. Migne. Paris, France. 1936.

Jones, A. H. M. *The Later Roman Empire, 284-602: A Social, Economic, and Administrative Survey.* Oxford, UK: Oxford University Press. 1964.

Jones, Lynn. 'Questionable Gifts: Constantine VIII and Relics of the True Cross'. Presented at *Twenty-Eighth Annual Byzantine Studies Conference.* (Columbus, OH: The Ohio State University, October 5-6, 2002).

Justinian I. *The Digest of Roman Law: Theft, Rapine, Damage, and Insult.* New York, NY: Penguin Books. 1979.

-------------. *The Justinianic Code.* Ed. by P. Krueger. Berlin, Germany. 1929.

Kaegi Jr., Walter Emil. *Byzantium and the Decline of Rome.* Princeton, NJ: Princeton University Press. 1968.

--------------------------. *Heraclius: Emperor of Byzantium.* Cambridge, UK: Cambridge University Press. 2003.

--------------------------. 'Reconceptualizing Byzantium's Eastern Frontiers in the Seventh Century'. Chap. 6 of *Shifting Frontiers in Late Antiquity,* ed. by Ralph W. Mathisen and Hagith S. Sivan. Aldershot, Hampshire: Variorum Publishing, 83-92. 1996.

--------------------------. 'Reinterpreting Constans II (641-668). Presented at *The Twenty-Ninth Annual Byzantine Studies Conference.* (Lewiston, ME: Bates College, October 16-19, 2003).

Kaldelis, Anthony. 'Why Don't We Believe the Byzantines When They Say they Are Romans?' Presented at *The Thirty-Fifth Annual Byzantine Studies Conference*. (Sarasota, FL: Florida State University, November 5-8,2009).

Karlin-Hayter, Patricia. 'Iconoclasm'. Chap. 6 of *The Oxford History of Byzantium*, ed. by Cyril Mango. Oxford, UK: Oxford University Press, 153-168. 2002.

Khazhdan, Alexander. *The Oxford Dictionary of Byzantium*. Oxford, UK: Oxford University Press. 1991.

L'Amour, Louis. *The Walking Drum*. New York, NY: Bantam Books. 1984.

Lactantius. *De Mortibus Persecutorum*, trans. by J. L. Creed. Oxford, UK: Clarendon Press. 1984.

Laiou, Angeliki E. 'Byzantium and the West'. Chap. 5 in *Byzantium: A World Civilization*, ed. by Angeliki E. Laiou and Henry Maguire. Washington, DC: Dumbarton Oaks Research Library and Collections, 61-80. 1992.

Langdon, John S. 'Byzantine Imperial Consorts and Princesses of the Epoch of the Anatolian Exile'. Presented at *The Thirty-Sixth Annual Byzantine Studies Conference* (Philadelphia, PA: The University of Pennsylvania Press, October 8-10, 2010).

Latham, R. E. 'Introduction'. *Marco Polo: The Travels*. New York, NY: Penguin Publishing. 1958.

Lee, A. D. 'The Empire at War'. Chapter 5 in *The Cambridge Companion to the Age of Justinian*, ed. by Michael Maas. Cambridge, UK: Cambridge University Press. 113-133, 2005.

Leo VI. *The Taktika of Leo VI*, ed. by George T. Dennis. Washington, DC: Dumbarton Oaks Research Library and Collections. 2010.

Leo the Deacon. *The History of Leo the Deacon: Byzantine Military Expansion in the Tenth Century*, trans. by Alice-Mary Talbot and Denis F. Sullivan. Washington, DC: Dumbarton Oaks Research Library Collections. 2005.

Leonte, Florin E. J. 'A Brief 'History of the Morea' as Seen Through the Eyes of an Emperor-Rhetorician: Manuel II Palaiologus' Funeral Oration for Theodore, Despot of the Morea'.

*Viewing the Morea: Lands and People in the Late Medieval Peloponnese,* ed. by Sharon E.J. Gerstel.

Washington, DC: Dumbarton Oaks Symposia and Colloquia. 2013.

----------------------. 'Narrative and Discourse of Legitimization in Manuel II Palaiologos' Funeral Oration for *His Brother Theodore'.* Presented at *The Thirty-Fifth Annual Byzantine Studies Conference.* (Sarasota, FL: Florida State University, November 5-8, 2009).

Libanius. *Selected Works, 2nd ed.* Trans. by A. F. Norman. Cambridge, MA: Loeb Classical Library, XVIII, Harvard University Press. 1969, 1976.

Lowe, Alfonso. *The Catalan Vengeance.* London, UK. 1972.

McMullen, Ramsay. *Constantine.* New York, NY: Dial Press. 1969.

------------------------. *Christianizing the Roman Empire, A. D. 100-400.* New Haven, CT: Yale University Press. 1984.

Maas, Michael and Nicola di Cosmas. *Empire and Exchange in Eurasian Late Antiquity: Rome, China, Iran and the Steppe, ca. 250-750 CE.* Oxford, UK: Oxford University Press. 2018.

MacNeill, William. *Plagues and Peoples.* New York, NY: Anchor Publishing. 1976.

Magdalino, Paul. 'The Medieval Empire (780-1204)'. Chapter 7 of *The Oxford History of Byzantium,* ed. by Cyril Mango. Oxford, UK: Oxford University Press, 169-213. 2002.

Mango, Cyril. 'Icons.' Insert in *The Oxford History of Byzantium* ed. by Cyril Mango. Oxford, UK: Oxford University Press. 2002.

----------------. 'Introduction'. *The Oxford History of Byzantium,* ed. by Cyril Mango. Oxford, UK: Oxford University Press, 1-18. 2002.

--------------. 'The Revival of Learning'. Chapter 8 of *The Oxford History of Byzantium,* ed. by Cyril Mango. Oxford, UK: Oxford University Press, 214-229. 2002.

Mango, Marlina Mundell. 'Commerce'. Insert in *The Oxford History of Byzantium,* ed. by Cyril Mango. Oxford, UK: Oxford University Press. 163-208. 2002.

Marinescu, Constantin. 'Transformations: Classical Objects and their Reuse during Late Antiquity'. Chap. 23 of *Shifting Frontiers in Late Antiquity,* ed. by Ralph W. Mathisen & Hagith S. Sivan. Aldershot, Hampshire: Variorum Publishing, 285-298. 1996.

Marozzi, Justin. *Tamerlane: Sword of Islam, Conqueror of the World.* Cambridge, MA: De Capo Press. 2004.

Marshall, F. H. and Mavrogordato, John. 'Byzantine Literature'. Chap. VIII of *Byzantium: an Introduction to East Roman Civilization,* ed. by Norman H Baynes and H. St. L. B. Moss. Oxford, UK: Oxford University Press, 221-251. 1969.

Mathisen, Ralph W. and Sivan, Hagith S. 'Introduction'. *Shifting Frontiers in Late Antiquity,* ed. by Ralph W. Mathisen and Hagith S. Sivan. Aldershot, Hampshire: Variorum Publishing, 1-7 1996.

Maurice. *Strategikon: Handbook of Byzantine Military Strategy,* trans. by George T. Dennis. Philadelphia: University of Pennsylvania Press, 1984.

Michael the Syrian. *Chronique de Michel le Syrien,* trans. by J.B. Chabot. Paris, France. 1924.

Michael Ducas. *Historia Byzantina, bk. XX,* ed. by I. Bekker. *CSHB.* Bonn, Germany. 1834.

Michelson, David A. 'Did Charlemagne Sack Constantinople? Western Charlemagne Legends as Anti-Byzantine Propaganda (c. 1000-1204)'. Presented at *The Twenty-Ninth Annual Byzantine Studies Conference*. (Lewiston, ME: Bates College, October 16-19, 2003).

Miller, David Harry. 'Frontier Societies and the Transition between Late Antiquity and the Early Middle Ages' Chap. 13 of *Shifting Frontiers in Late Antiquity*, ed. by Ralph W. Mathisen and Hagith S. Sivan. Aldershot, Hampshire: Variorum Publishing, 158-171, 1996.

Montefiore, Simon Sebag. *Jerusalem: the Biography*. New York, NY: Vintage Books, 2012.

Morrison, Cecile and Jean-Claude Cheynet. 'Prices and Wages in the Byzantine World.' *The Economic History of Byzantium: From the Seventh Through the Fifteenth Century, ed* by Angeliki E. Laiou and Charalampos Bouras. Washington DC: Dumbarton Oaks Research Library and Collections. 2002.

Moss, H. St. L. B. 'The History of the Byzantine Empire: an Outline, (A) From 330 A. D. to the Fourth Crusade'. Chap. I, pt. a of *Byzantium: an Introduction to East Roman Civilization*, ed. by Norman H. Baynes and H. St. L. B. Moss. Oxford, UK: Oxford University Press, 1-32. 1969.

Nicephorus Gregoras. *Roman History. Patrologia Graeca*, ed. by J. P. Migne. 1936.

Nicephorus II Phocas. *On Skirmishing, Three Byzantine Military Treatises. CFHB, 25*. Ed. by Dennis George. Washington, DC: Dumbarton Oaks Research Library and Collections, 1985.

--------------------------. *Praecepts Militaria of Nicephorus II Phocas (963-969)*, IV. *Sowing the Dragon's Teeth: Byzantine Warfare in the Tenth Century*, ed. by E. McGreer. Washington, DC: Dumbarton Oaks Research Library and Collections. 1995.

Nicephorus of Constantinople. *Short History. CFHB*, ed. by Cyril Mango. Washington, DC: Dumbarton Oaks Research Library and Collections. 1990.

Nicetas Choniates. *History. Patralogia Graeca, vol. 142*, ed. by J. P. Migne.

Nicol, Donald M. *The Immortal Emperor: the Life and Legend of Constantine Paiaiologos, Last Emperor of the Romans.* Cambridge, UK: Cambridge University Press. 1992.

----------------------. *The Last Centuries of Byzantine, 1261-1453, 2nd ed.* Cambridge, UK: Cambridge University Press. 1972.

----------------------. *The Reluctant Emperor: A Biography of John Cantacuzene, Byzantine Emperor and Monk (c.1295-1383).* Cambridge, UK: Cambridge University Press. 1996.

Niyogi, Ruma. 'Gender, Politics, and Imperial Legitimacy in Byzantium, 1028-1057'. Presented at *The Twenty-Seventh Annual Byzantine Studies Conference.* (South Bend, IN: University of Notre Dame, November 9-11, 2001).

Norwich, John Julius. *Absolute Monarchs: A History of the Papacy.* New York, NY: Random House Trade Paperbooks. 2012.

----------------------------. *Byzantium: The Apogee, 2nd ed.* New York, NY: Alfred A. Knopf. 1995, 1997.

----------------------------. *Byzantium: The Decline and Fall, 2nd ed.* New York, NY: Alfred A. Knopf. 1995, 1997.

----------------------------. *Byzantium: The Early Centuries, 2nd ed.* New York, NY: Alfred A. Knopf. 1995, 1997.

----------------------------. *A History of Venice, 2nd ed.* New York, NY: Vintage Books, 1982, 1989.

----------------------------. *The Middle Sea: A History of the Mediterranean.* New York, NY: Vintage Books. 2006.

Obolensky, Dimitri. *The Byzantine Commonwealth: Eastern Europe, 500-1453.* New York, NY: Praeger Publishers. 1971.

----------------------. 'Byzantium and the Slavic World'. Chap. 3 in *Byzantium: A World Civilization,* ed. by Angeliki E. Laiou and Henry Maguire. Washington, DC: Dumbarton Oaks Research Library and Collections, 37-48. 1992.

Oikonomides, Nicolas. 'Silk Trade and Production in Byzantium from the Sixth to the Ninth Century: The Seals of Kommerciarikoi.' *Dumbarton Oaks Papers, 40.* Washington, DC: Dumbarton Oaks Research Library and Collection. 1986.

Olster, David. 'From Periphery to Center: The Transformation of Late-Roman Definition in the Seventh Century'. Chap. 8 of *Shifting Frontiers in Late Antiquity,* ed. by Ralph W. Mathisen and Hagith S. Sivan. Aldershot, Hampshire: Variorum Publishing, 93-101. 1996.

Ostrogorsky, George. *History of the Byzantine State, 2nd ed.,* trans. by Joan Hussey. New Brunswick, NJ: Rutgers University. 1952, 1969.

Parani, Maria. 'Picking at an Old Question: The Use of Cutlery at the Byzantine Table'. Presented at *The Twenty-Eighth Annual Byzantine Studies Conference.* (Columbus, OH: The Ohio State University, October 4-6, 2002).

Penrose, Jane. *Rome and Her Enemies: An Empire Created and Destroyed by War.* New York, NY: Osprey Publishing. 2005.

Phillippides, Marios. 'A Military Assessment of the Ottoman Strategy against the Land Walls in the Siege of Constantinople (1453)'. Presented at *The Twenty-Seventh Annual Byzantine Studies Conference.* (South Bend, IN: University of Notre Dame, November 9-11, 2001).

-------------------------. 'The Naval Operations in the 1453 Siege of Constantinople: Sultan Mehmed II Fatih, the New Xerxes'. Presented at *The Twenty-Ninth Annual Byzantine Studies Conference.* (Lewiston, ME, October 16-19, 2003).

Procopius of Caeserea. *History of the Wars, 4 bks.,* trans. by H. B. Dewing. The Loeb Classical Library, Cambridge, MA: Harvard University Press. 1961.

-------------------------. *The Secret History.* Trans. by G. A. Williamson. New York, NY: Penguin Books. 1966.

Pryor, John and Elizabeth M. Jeffreys *The Age of the Dromon: The Byzantine Navy ca. 500-1204.* Leiden, Germany Brill Publishing. 2006.

Rajkovic, Srdjan. 'Passio Constantinopolitana: Pleas for Divine Intervention during the 1453 Siege of Constantinople'. Presented at *The Twenty-Ninth Annual Byzantine Studies Conference*. (Lewiston, ME: Bates College, October 16-19, 2003).

Reinert, Stephen W. 'Fragmentation (1204-1453)'. Chap. 10 of *The Oxford History of Byzantium*, ed. by Cyril Mango. Oxford, UK: Oxford University Press, 248-283. 2002.

Rice, David Talbot. *Art of the Byzantine Era, 2nd ed.* New York, NY: Thames & Hudson. 1963, 1985.

Rosen, William. *Justinian's Flea: Plague, Empire, and the Birth of Europe*. New York, NY: Viking/Penguin Press. 2007.

Runciman, Steven. 'Byzantium and the Slavs'. Chapter XIII. in *Byzantium: an Introduction to East Roman Civilization*, ed. by Norman H. Baynes and H. St. L. B. Moss. Oxford, UK: Oxford University Press, 338-368. 1969.

----------------------. *The Fall of Constantinople, 1453, 2nd ed.* Cambridge, UK: Cambridge University Press/ Canto Press, 1965, 1990.

----------------------. *The First Crusade, 3rd ed.* Cambridge, UK: Cambridge University Press/ Canto Press. 1951, 1980, 1992.

Sarris, Peter. 'The Eastern Empire from Constantine to Heraclius (306-641)'. Chap. 1 of *The Oxford History of Byzantium*. Ed. by Cyril Mango. Oxford, UK: Oxford University Press, 19-70. 2002.

Scarre, Chris. *Chronicle of the Roman Emperors: the Reign-by-Reign Record of the Rulers of Imperial Rome*. The Chronicle Series. London, UK: Thames & Hudson. 1995.

Scourtis, Constantine. 'Orthodoxy and "Latinism" at the Council of Ferrara-Florence (1438-39)'. Presented at *The Twenty-Seventh Annual Byzantine Studies Conference*. (South Bend, IN: University of Notre Dame, November 9-11, 2001).

Sevcenko, Ihor. 'Palaiologan Learning'. Chap. 11 of *The Oxford History of Byzantium*, ed. by Cyril Mango. Oxford, UK: Oxford University Press, 284-293. 2002.

Shahid, Irfan. 'Byzantium and the Islamic World'. Chap. 4 of *Byzantium: A World Civilization*, ed. by Angeliki E. Laiou and Henry Maguire. Washington, DC: Dumbarton Oaks Research Library and Collections, 49-60. 1992.

Shepard, Jonathan. 'Spreading the Word: Byzantine Missions'. Chap. 9 *The Oxford History of Byzantium*, ed. by Cyril Mango. Oxford, UK: Oxford University Press, 230-247. 2002.

Sivan, Hagith S. 'Why Not Marry a Barbarian? Marital Frontiers in Late Antiquity (The Example of CTh 3.14.1)'. Chap. 11 of *Shifting Frontiers in Late Antiquity*, ed. by Ralph W. Mathisen and Hagith S. Sivan. Aldershot, Hampshire: Variorum Publishing, 136-145. 1996.

Stephen the Younger. 'Vita S. Stephani Juniorus'. *Patriologae Cursus Completus, Series Graeca, vol. 100*, ed. by J.P. Migne. Paris, France. 1936.

Stephenson, Paul. *The Legend of Basil the Bulgar Slayer*. Cambridge, UK: Cambridge University Press, 2010.

Tellegen-Couperus, Olga. *A Short History of Roman Law, 2nd ed.* New York, NY: Routledge Publishing. 1990, 1993.

Theodosius II. *The Theodosian Code, 2nd ed.* Ed. by T. Mommsen and P. Meyer, trans. by C. Pharr. Princeton, NJ: Princeton University Press. 1905, 1952.

Theophanes the Confessor. *The Chronicle of Theophanes: Anno Mundi 6095-6305 (A. D. 602-813)*. Ed. and trans. by Harry Turtledove. Philadelphia, PA: University of Pennsylvania Press. 1982.

Theophanes Continuatus. *Chronographia, vol. I.*, ed. by I. Bekker, Leipzig, Germany. 1883.

Theophylact of Simocotta. *History*. Ed. by C. de Boor and P. Wirth. Leipzig, Germany. 1972.

Tirnanic, Galina. 'The Mutilated Nose: *Rhinokopia* as a Mark of Sexual Offense'. Presented at *The Twenty-Ninth Annual Byzantine Studies Conference*. (Lewiston, ME: Bates College, October 16-19, 2003).

Tougher, Shaun. 'Michael III and Basil the Macedonian: Just Good Friends?' *Desire and Denial in Byzantium: Papers from the Thirty-first Spring Symposium of Byzantine Studies, University of Sussex, Brighton, March, 1997, 2nd* ed. by Liz James. Aldershot, Hampshire: Ashgate/Variorium, 149-158. 1997, 1999.

Treadgold, Warren. *A History of the Byzantine State and Society*. Stanford, CA: Stanford University Press. 1997.

-----------------------. *Byzantium and Its Army (284-1081)*. Stanford, CA: Stanford University Press. 1995.

----------------------. 'The Struggle for Survival (641-780)'. Chap. 5 in *The Oxford History of Byzantium*, ed. by Cyril Mango. Oxford, UK: Oxford University Press, 129-152. 2002.

Turtletaub, H. N. *Justinian*. New York, NY: Tom Doherty Books. 1998.

Uspensky, Th. I. 'The Tendency of Conservative Byzantium to Adopt Western Influence.' *Vizantiysky Vremminik, XXII*. St. Petersburg: Russia. 1916.

Vasiliev, A. A. 'Byzantium and Islam'. Chap. XI of *Byzantium: an Introduction to East Roman Civilization*, ed. by Norman H. Baynes and H. St. L. B. Moss. Oxford, UK: Oxford University Press, 308-325. 1969.

----------------. *History of the Byzantine Empire, 2nd* ed. Madison, WI: University of Wisconsin Press. 1958, 1961.

Vasilievsky, V. G. 'Byzantium and the Patzinaks', *Works vol. I*. Moscow, Russia. 1908.

Vikan, Gary. 'Byzantine Art'. Chap. 6 in *Byzantium: A World Civilization*, ed. by Laiou E. Angeliki and Henry Maguire. Washington, DC: Dumbarton Oaks Research Library and Collections, 81-119. 1992.

Vryonis, Speros. 'Byzantine Civilization, A World Civilization'. Chap. 2 in *Byzantium: A World Civilization,* ed. by Angeliki E. Laiou and Henry Maguire. Washington, DC: Dumbarton Oaks Research Library and Collections, 19-36. 1992.

Wildberg, Christian. 'Philosophy in the Age of Justinian'. Chap. 13 in the *Cambridge Companion to the Age of Justinian.* Cambridge, UK: Cambridge University Press, 316-340. 2005.

Wilson, Derek. *Charlemagne: A Biography.* New York, NY: Vintage Books. 2007.

Wolff, Hans Julius. *Roman Law: A Historical Introduction.* Norman, OK: University of Oklahoma Press. 1951.

Wright, Diana. '"Better Off Than Before": The 1454 Moreote Submission to Mehmet II'. Presented at *The Twenty-Seventh Annual Byzantine Studies Conference.* (South Bend, IN: University of Notre Dame, November 9-11, 2001).

Zacharias of Milytene. *Vie de Severe.* Ed. by M.A. Kugener, trans. by Patrilogia Orientalis III, 1. Paris, France. 1903.

Zosimus. *New History.* London, UK: Green & Chaplin. 1814.

# APPENDIX 1 - GENEALOGIES

## I. THE CONSTANTINIANS

**DIOCLETIAN** (r. 284-305) = Prisca

*************

**MAXIMIN** ( r. 305-310)----------------------------------------- **GALERIUS** ( r. 305-311) = Valeria

Eutropius = **MAXIMIAN** ( r. 286-310 )

|

**MAXENTIUS** ( r. 306-312) = Valeria Max.


*************


Theodora = **CONSTANTIUS I 'CHLORUS** = Helena

|

Fausta = **CONSTANTINE I** (r. 305-337) = Minerva

    |                    |

    |            Crispus

|

**CONSTANTINE II**---- **CONSTANS I**--- **CONSTANTIUS II** (r. 337-361)------ Constantina = Gallus

|

Helena = **JULIAN 'THE APOSTATE'** (r. 361-363)

# II. THE VALENTINIANS/THEODOSIANS

**(JOVIAN)** ( r. 363-364)

\*\*\*\*\*\*\*\*\*\*\*\*\*

Marina = **VALENTINIAN I** ( r. 364-375)------ **VALENS** ( r. 364-378) = Justina

       |                  |

  **GRATIAN** ( r. 359-383)       |

    Eudocia = **VALENTINIAN II** ( r. 371-392) ----- Galla = **THEODOSIUS I** ( r. 379-395) = Aelia Flaccilla

|

**CONSTANTIUS III** ( r. 421) = Galla Placidia--------------**ARCADIUS** (r. 395-408)-----**HONORIUS** ( r. 384-423)

|                                = Eudocia

          |                _____ _|

          |            |

          |     **THEODOSIUS II** ( r. 408-450) 1=Eudocia

          |                  Pulcheria 2 = **MARCIAN** ( r. 450-457)= 1 F

**VALENTINIAN III** ( r. 419-455)(W) = Eudocia                 |

               |                             |

    Hunneric = Eudocia------Placidia = **OLYBRIUS** (r. 472) (W)    **ANTHEMIUS** (r. 467-472)(W)=

                                                       Euphemia

## III. THE LEONIDS

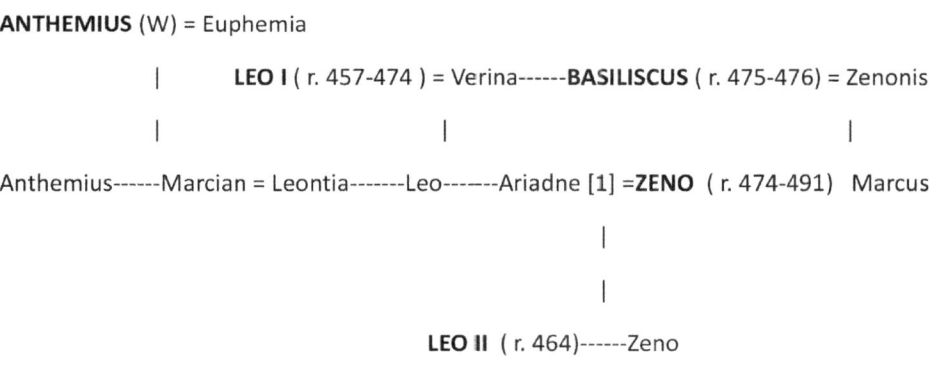

**ANTHEMIUS** (W) = Euphemia

|    **LEO I** ( r. 457-474 ) = Verina------**BASILISCUS** ( r. 475-476) = Zenonis

|        |          |

Anthemius------Marcian = Leontia-------Leo---–--Ariadne [1] =**ZENO** ( r. 474-491) Marcus

                |

                |

       **LEO II** ( r. 464)------Zeno


Ariadne [2] = **ANASTASIUS I** ( r. 491-519)

# IV. THE JUSTINIADS

Acacius                              F = Sabbatius---------**JUSTIN I** ( r. 519-527) = Lupicina-Euphemia

      |                                |

Sittas = Comito------**THEODORA** (r. 500-548) = **JUSTINIAN I** ( r. 527-565)-------Vigilantia = Dulcidius

                                                            |

Sophia = **JUSTIN II** ( r. 565-578)-------Marcellus

                |

Arabia

Germanus = Matasuntha

        |_____

                                              |

Ino-Anastasia = **TIBERIUS III CONSTANTINE** ( r. 578-582)     |

              |                                    |

**MAURICE** ( r. 582-602) = Constantina-----------Charito = Germanus _____ |

              |

T\iberius--------Theodosius-------Peter

856

# V. THE HERACLIADS

(**PHOCAS**)( r. 602-610)

\*\*\*\*\*\*\*\*\*\*\*\*\*

Heraclius the Elder = Epiphania

|

Gregory------------------------- **HERACLIUS** ( r. 610-641) -------Martin = Maria-------Theodora

|      |   |    |

Nicetas     =[1] Eudocia =[2] Martina

|       |       |

Gregory-----------Gregoria = **CONSTANTINE III** ( r. 641)--- Eudocia **HERACLONAS** ( r. 641)

|

Theodosia------------**CONSTANS II** ( r. 641-668) = Fausta

|

Tiberius-----Heraclius------ **CONSTANTINE IV** ( r. 668-685) = Anastasia

|

Theodora =[1] **JUSTINIAN II** ( r. 685-695; 706-711)-------Heraclius

|    = [2] Eudocia

Tiberius   |

F

# VI. THE ISAURIANS

(**PHILLIPICUS BARDANES**) ( r. 711-713)

(**ANASTASIUS II ARTEMIUS**) ( r. 713-715)

(**THEODOSIUS III**) ( r. 715-717)

\*\*\*\*\*\*\*\*\*\*\*\*


**LEO III** ( r. 717-741) = Maria

|

**ARTAVASDUS** ( r. 741-743) = Anna------------ **CONSTANTINE V** ( r. 741-775) = Irene

|                                                 |

Nicephorus-----Nicetas     **IRENE** ( r. 797-802) = **LEO IV** ( r. 775-780)

|

Maria of Amnia =[1] **CONSTANTINE VI** ( r. 780-797)

|                 [2]= Theodote

Thecla = **MICHAEL II** ( r. 820-829) =2 Euphrosyne     |

Leo

\*\*\*\*\*\*\*\*\*\*\*\*\*


**NICEPHORUS I** ( r. 802-811)

**STAURACIUS** (811)

**MICHAEL I RHANGABE** (811-813)

# V. THE AMORIANS

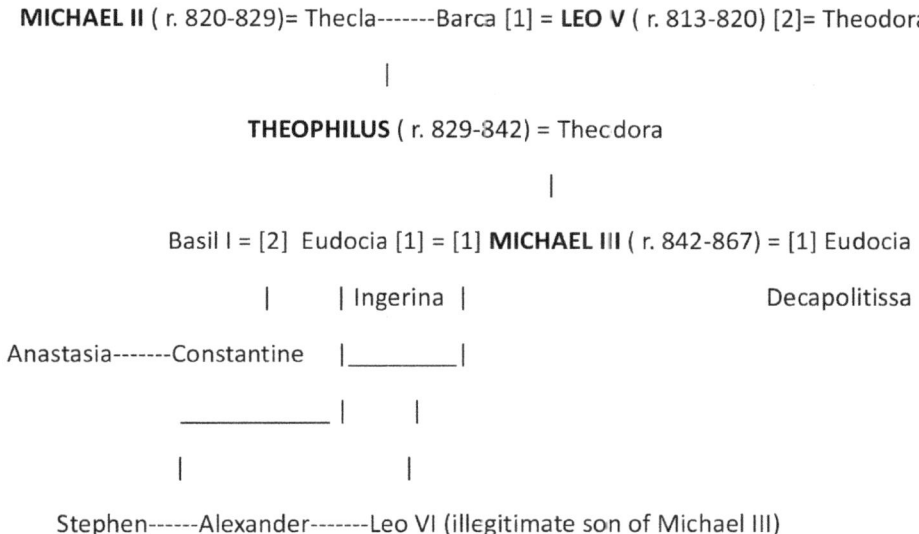

**MICHAEL II** ( r. 820-829)= Thecla-------Barca [1] = **LEO V** ( r. 813-820) [2]= Theodora

|

**THEOPHILUS** ( r. 829-842) = Theodora

|

Basil I = [2]  Eudocia [1] = [1] **MICHAEL III** ( r. 842-867) = [1] Eudocia

    |     | Ingerina |                        Decapolitissa

Anastasia-------Constantine   |_____|

              _____ |     |

        |                |

Stephen------Alexander-------Leo VI (illegitimate son of Michael III)

# VI. THE MACEDONIANS

Stylianus Zautzes                            **BASIL I** ( r. 867-886) = Eudocia Ingerina

|                                    |

Zoe Zautzes =                         |

Zoe Carbonipsina = **LEO VI** ( r. 886-912)-------Stephen------**ALEXANDER** ( r. 912-913)

                        |

                        |          **ROMANUS I LECAPENUS** ( r. 920-944) = Theodora

                        |                           |

(with Zoe Zautzes) Anna------**CONSTANTINE VII** ( r. 913-959) = Helena-------Christopher = Sophia

                            |                                |

**JOHN I TZIMISCES** ( r. 967-976) [1]=Theodora---**ROMANUS II** ( r. 959-963)   **PETER OF BULGARIA**=Maria-

               [2]=**NICEPHORUS II**    |                        Irene

             Leo-------**PHOCAS** ( r. 963-969) |

                 |                     |

        Bardas-------Nicephorus         |

Vladimir of Kiev = Anna------**BASIL II** ( r. 963-1025)------**CONSTANTINE VIII** ( r. 1025-1028) = Helena

                                                  |

                      Eudocia------**THEODORA** ( r. 1055-1056)------**ZOE** ( r. 1042)

                                                  [1] = **ROMANUS**

                    Stephen--------- F              **III ARGYRUS** (r. 1028-1034)

                      |         |                    |

      **MICHAEL V** ( r. 1041-1042)  Constantine--------John the--------[2] = **MICHAEL IV**

                                Orphanotrophus    ( r. 1034-1041)

                                              [3] = **CONSTANTINE**

                                    (r. 1042-1055) **IX MONOMACHUS**

## VII. THE DUCASI

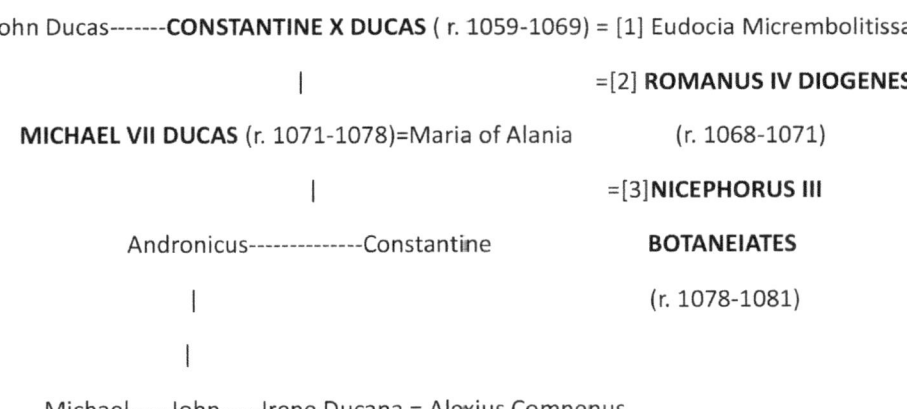

John Ducas-------**CONSTANTINE X DUCAS** ( r. 1059-1069) = [1] Eudocia Micrembolitissa

|                                                          =[2] **ROMANUS IV DIOGENES**

**MICHAEL VII DUCAS** (r. 1071-1078)=Maria of Alania          (r. 1068-1071)

|                                                          =[3]**NICEPHORUS III**

Andronicus--------------Constantine                **BOTANEIATES**

|                                                          (r. 1078-1081)

|

Michael-----John-----Irene Ducana = Alexius Comnenus

# VIII. THE COMNENI

John Vladislav of Bulgaria

    |

Catherine = **ISAAC I COMNENUS** ( r. 1057-1059)-------John Comnenus = Anna Dalessena

          |

Irene Ducena = **ALEXIUS I COMNENUS** ( r. 1081-1118)-----Manuel-----Isaac-----Eudocia = Nicephorus

     |                                                    Melissenus

     |

Irene = **JOHN II COMNENUS** ( r. 1118-1143)----Andronicus----Theodora----Isaac----Anna = Nicephorus

   |                                                |       Bryennius

Isaac-----Eudocia----Anna----Alexius-----------**MANUEL I COMNENUS** ( r. 1143-1180)  |_____

|      |        |     = Irene of Kiev    [1] = Bertha-Irene  [2] = Maria-Xenia     |

|  John Vatatzes  John                |  (*) [3] = Irene Syrakaina  |       |

|            Costephanus   Rainier-John = Maria   **ALEXIUS II COMNENUS**    |

|                        of Montferrat   ( r. 1180-1183) = [1] Agnes- Anna = **ANDRONICUS I**

|                                                                F = **COMNENUS**

Maria------Theodora-------**ISAAC COMNENUS OF CYPRESS** ( r. 1184-1191)        ( r. 1183-1185)

**=STEPHEN VI**  **= BALDWIN III**                                  |
**OF HUNGARY**   **OF JERUSALEM**                          Manuel------John

 (r. 1163-1165)    (r. 1143-1163)
|

                             **ALEXIUS I OF TREBIZOND**-----**DAVID COMNENUS**

                                (r. 1204-1222)     **OF PAPHLAGONIA**

                                            **AND TREBIZOND**

                                            (r. 1204-1212)

**(*)JOHN II OF TREBIZOND** (r. 1280-1297)

      |

     Theodora= Michael Paleologus

# IX. THE ANGELI

Alexius I Comnenus = Irene Ducena

|

Theodora = Constantine Angelus

|

John Angelus Ducas

|

Isaac Angelus------Michael I Ducas------**THEODORE DUCAS**-----Andronicus Angelus-----Maria

      |           of Epirus       **OF THESSALONICA**            |

Constantine Angelus             ( r. 1224-1230)            |

Boniface of Montferrat = [2] Margaret-Maria [1] = [2] **ISAAC II ANGELUS**---**ALEXIUS III ANGELUS**

                  F = [1]  ( r 1185-1195, 1203-1204)   ( r. 1195-1203)

                                |                           =Euphrosyne

                                |                              |

       **ALEXIUS IV ANGELUS** ( r. 1203-1204)------------Irene---Eudocia [1]=Stephen of

            Theodore Lascaris = Anna------------------|               Serbia

                      [2]=**ALEXIUS V DUCAS MUTZURPHLUS** ( r. 1204)

                                 [3] = Leo Sgurus

# X. THE LASCARIDS

Constantine----Alexius----George----**THEODORE I LASCARIS** ( r. 1205-1221) [1] = Anna Angelina

                  [2]= Phillipa of Armenia               |       | illeg.

                                      Maria---Irene Lascara = [1] **JOHN III VATATZES**

                                        |           (r.1221-1254)

                                        |    = [2] Constance-Anna

                                        |    = [3] Maria of

Courtenay

                                        |

**KOLOMAN OF BULGARIA**-----**MICHAEL ASEN II OF BULGARIA**-----Helena = **THEODORE II LASCARIS**
( r. 1254-1258)

                                                |

               **CONSTANTINE TICH OF BULGARIA** = Irene-----Maria----------------------**JOHN IV LASCARIS**

                                     = **NICEPHORUS I DUCAS,**   ( r. 1258-1261)

                                     **DESPOT OF EPIRUS**

# IX. THE PALEOLOGI

John------Irene- Eulogia------Maria-Martha-----**MICHAEL VIII PALEOLOGUS** ( r. 1261-1282) = Theodora

      =John Angelus   = Nicephorus     |      illeg.    |          |

      Cantacuzenus   Tarchoniates   Maria      Euphrosyne   |

      |                     = **ABAGHA,**    = **NOGAY,**   |

Maria--------------------Anna [2] =**NICEPHORUS**  **KHAN OF PERSIA**  **KHAN OF THE**   |

[2]= Constantine Tich     **DUCAS, DESPOT**           **GOLDEN HORDE**   |

[3] = **IVAILO, EMPEROR OF**   **OF EPIRUS**                            |

    **BULGARIA**                                          |

                                                    |

                                                    |

Constantine-----Anna------------------------Irene----------**ANDRONICUS II PALEOLOGUS**-------Eudocia

    |         = **MICHAEL, DESPOT OF**  =**JOHN**      ( r. 1282-1328)     = **JOHN II**

   John           **EPIRUS**        **ASEN III OF**  [1]= Anna of Hungary   **OF TREBIZOND**

    |                         **BULGARIA**     |   |    [2]=Yolande-Irene

F = **STEPHEN UROSH III**                illeg.|   |       of Monferrat

  **DECHANSKY**                              |   |      |

  **OF SERBIA**            **JOHN OF THESSALY** = Irene  | John---Demetrius---Theodore of----Simonis

                                        |               Montferrat    =

                                        |                  **STEPHEN UROSH II**

                                        |                     **MILUTIN**

                                        |                  **OF**

**BULGARIA**                                      |

                                        |

           Constantine-----**MICHAEL IX PALEOLOGUS** = Rita-Maria of Armenia

                                   |

Anna-------------------------Manuel---**ANDRONICUS III PALEOLOGUS**----------Theodora [1] = **THEODORE**

```
[1] = THOMAS, DESPOT OF EPIRUS        (1328-1341)                    SVYETOSLAV OF

                        [1] = Adelaide-Irene        | illeg.          BULGARIA

[2] = NICHOLAS OF ORSINI,        [2] = Anne of Savoy      |          [2] = MICHAEL

DESPOT OF EPIRUS                        |            IRENE, EMPRESS   SHISHMAN OF BULGARIA

                                       |

                                       |              = BASIL COMNENUS

                                       |                OF TREBIZOND

                                       |

                                       |   JOHN VI CANTACUZENUS = Irene

                                       |        ( r. 1347-1354)    |

                                       |                           |

Michael-----Maria-----Maria------JOHN V PALEOLOGUS = Helena---Manuel=Maria---Matthew---Theodora

        =           =      ( r. 1341-1347, 1354-1390)              |        = NICEPHORUS  II,

PRINCE ORHAN                                        |              |          DUCAS OF EPIRUS

                                                    |              |

                                                    |       MICHAEL III ASEN OF

                                                    |              BULGARIA

                                                    |

THEODORE I------ANDRONICUS IV PALEOLOGUS------MANUEL II PALEOLOGUS ( r. 1391-1425) =

DESPOT OF        ( r. 1376-1379)                                    Helena Dragash

MOREA        = Maria of Bulgaria                                        |

                |                                                      |

                |                                                      |

        JOHN VII PALEOLOGUS ( r. 1390)                                 |

                                                                       |

                                                                       |

                                                                       |
```

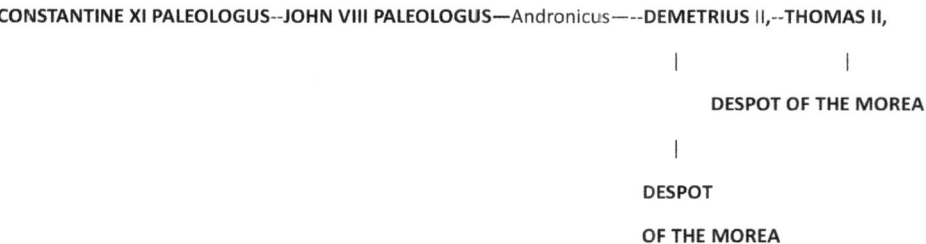

**CONSTANTINE XI PALEOLOGUS--JOHN VIII PALEOLOGUS**—Andronicus—--**DEMETRIUS II,--THOMAS II,**

|                               |

                                                    **DESPOT OF THE MOREA**

|

**DESPOT**

**OF THE MOREA**

( r. 1447-1453)             ( r. 1425-1448)

[1] = Magdalena Theodora Tocco    [1] = Anna of Kiev                              Zoe-Sophia

[2] = Catherine Gattilusio          [2] = Sophia of Montferrat                       = Ivan III,

       of Lemnos                [3] = Maria of Trebizond                  Grand Duke

                                                                    of Moscow

# Appendix 2 - Rulers Of The Byzantine Era

## EASTERN AND BYZANTINE ROMAN EMPERORS

| | |
|---|---|
| Diocletian | (284-305) |
| Maximin | (305-311) |
| Galerius | (305-311) |
| Constantine I 'the Great' | (324-337) |
| Constantine II | (337) |
| Constans I | (337) |
| Constantius II | (337-361) |
| Julian 'the Apostate' | (361-363) |
| Jovian | (363-364) |
| Valentinian I | (364-375) |
| Valens | (364-378) |
| Gratian | (359-383) |
| Theodosius I 'the Great' | (379-395) |
| Valentinian II | (382-392) |
| Arcadius | (395-408) |
| Theodosius II | (408-450) |
| Marcian | (450-457) |
| Leo I | (457-474) |
| Leo II | (474) |
| Zeno | (474-491) |
| Basiliscus | (475-476) |
| Anastasius I | (491-518) |

| | |
|---|---|
| Justin I | (518-527) |
| Justinian I | (527-565) |
| Theodora | (527-548) |
| Justin II | (565-578) |
| Tiberius II Constantine | (578-582) |
| Maurice | (582-602) |
| Phocas 'the Tyrant' | (602-610) |
| Heraclius | (610-641) |
| Constantine III Heraclius | (641) |
| Heraclonas | (641) |
| Constans II 'the Bearded' | (641-668) |
| Constantine IV | (668-695) |
| Justinian II 'the Slit-Nosed' | (685-695, 705-711) |
| Leontius | (695-698) |
| Tiberius III Apsimar | (698-705) |
| Philippicus Bardanes | (711-713) |
| Anastasius II Artemius | (713-715) |
| Theodosius III 'the Reluctant' | (715-717) |
| Leo III 'the Syrian' | (717-741) |
| Constantine V 'Name of Dung' | (741-775) |
| Leo IV 'the Khazar' | (775-780) |
| Constantine VI 'the Blinded' | (780-797) |
| Irene 'the Athenian' | (797-802) |
| Nicephorus I 'the General Logothete' | (802-811) |
| Stauracius | (811) |
| Michael I Rhangabe | (811-813) |
| Leo V 'the Armenian' | (813-820) |
| Michael II 'the Amorian' | (820-829) |
| Theophilus | (829-842) |
| Michael III 'the Drunken' | (842-867) |
| Basil I 'the Macedonian' | (867-886) |
| Leo VI 'the Wise' | (886-912) |
| Alexander III | (912-913) |
| Constantine VII Porphyrogenitus | (913-959) |
| Romanus I Lecapenus | (920-944) |
| Romanus II Porphyrogenitus | (959-963) |
| Nicephorus II Phocas | (963-969) |
| John I Tzimisces | (969-976) |

| | |
|---|---|
| Basil II 'the Bulgar Slayer' | (976-1025) |
| Constantine VIII | (1025-1028) |
| Romanus III Argyrus | (1028-1034) |
| Michael IV 'the Paphlagonian' | (1034-1041) |
| Michael V 'the Caulker' | (1041-1042) |
| Zoe Porphyrogenita | (1042) |
| Constantine IX Monomachus | (1042-1055) |
| Theodora Porphyrogenita | (1055-1056) |
| Michael VI Bringas 'the Old' | (1056-1057) |
| Isaac I Comnenus | (1057-1059) |
| Constantine X Ducas | (1059-1067) |
| Eudocia Macrembolitissa | (1067-1068) |
| Romanus VI Diogenes | (1068-1071) |
| Nicephorus III Botaniates | (1078-1081) |
| Alexius I Comnenus | (1081-1118) |
| John II Comnenus 'the Beautiful' | (1118-1143) |
| Manuel I Comnenus | (1143-1180) |
| Alexius II Comnenus | (1180-1183) |
| Andronicus I Comnenus 'the Terrible' | (1183-1185) |
| Isaac II Angelus | (1185-1195, 1203-1204) |
| Alexius III Angelus | (1195-1203) |
| Alexius IV | (1203-1204) |
| Alexius V Murzuphlus | (1204) |
| Theodore I Lascaris (Nicaea) | (1208-1221) |
| John III DucasVatatzes (Nicaea) | (1221-1254) |
| Theodore II Lascaris (Nicaea) | (1254-1258) |
| John IV Lascaris (Nicaea) | (1258-1261) |
| Michael VIII Paleologus | (1261-1282) |
| Andronicus II Paleologus 'the Elder' | (1282-1328) |
| Michael IX Paleologus | (1293-1320) |
| Andronicus III 'the Younger' | (1328-1341) |
| John V Paleologus | (1341-1347, 1356-1391) |
| John VI Cantacuzenus | (1347-1356) |
| Andronicus IV Paleologus | (1376-1379) |
| John VII Paleologus | (1390) |
| Manuel II Paleologus | (1391-1425) |
| John VIII Paleologus | (1425-1447) |
| Constantine XI Paleologus | (1447-1453) |

## LATIN EMPERORS OF CONSTANTINOPLE

| | |
|---|---|
| Baldwin I of Flanders | (1204-1205) |
| Henry of Flanders | (1206-1216) |
| Peter of Courtenay | (1217) |
| Yolanda | (1217-1219) |
| Robert of Courtenay | (1221-1228) |
| John of Brienne | (1228-1237) |
| Baldwin II of Courtenay | (1237-1261) |

## EMPERORS OF TREBIZOND

| | |
|---|---|
| Alexius I Comnenus | (1204-1222) |
| Andronicus I Gidus Comnenus | (1222-1235) |
| John I Axuch 'the Fat' Comnen | (1235-1238) |
| Manuel I Comnenus | (1238-1263) |
| Andronicus II Comnenus | (1263-1266) |
| George Comnenus | (1266-1280) |
| John II Comnenus | (1280-1297) |
| Theodora Comnena | (1284) |
| Alexius II Comnenus | (1297-1330) |
| Andronicus III Comnenus | (1330-1332) |
| Basil Comnenus | (1332-1340) |
| Irene Paleologina | (1340-1341) |
| Anna Comnena Anachoutlou | (1341-1342) |
| Michael Comnenus | (1341, 1344-1349) |
| John III Comnenus | (1342-1344) |
| Alexius III Comnenus | (1349-1390) |
| Manuel III Comnenus | (1390-1416) |
| Alexius IV Comnenus | (1416-1429) |
| John IV Comnenus | (1429-1459) |
| David Comnenus | (1459-1461) |

## RULERS OF EPIRUS

| | |
|---|---|
| Michael I Comnenus Ducas | (1205-1214) |

| | |
|---|---|
| Theodore Comnenus Ducas | |
| (Emperor of Thessalonica, 1225-1227) | (1214-1230) |
| Michael II Comnenus Ducas | (1230-1271) |
| Nicephorus I Comnenus Ducas | (1271-1297) |
| Thomas Comnenus Ducas | (1297-1318) |
| Nicholas Orsini | (1318-1323) |
| John Orsini | (1323-1335) |
| Nicephorus II Orsini | (1335-1337, 1356-1359) |
| Andronicus III Paleologus (Constantinople) | (1340-1341) |
| John V Paleologus (Constantinople) | (1341-1348) |
| Stephen III Dushan | (1348-1356) |
| Simon Uros Paleologus (Tsar of Serbia) | (1359-1366) |
| Thomas II Preljubovic (Despot) | (1367-1384) |
| Maria Angelina Ducana Paleologina | (1384-1385) |
| Esau de'Buondelmonti | (1385-1411) |
| Giorgio de'Buondelmonti | (1411) |
| Carlo I Tocco | (1411-1429) |
| Carlo II Tocco | (1429-1448) |
| Leonardo Tocco | (1448-1479) |

## EMPERORS OF THESSALONICA

| | |
|---|---|
| Michael Comnenus Ducas | (1212-1214) |
| Theodore Comnenus Ducas | (1214-1230) |
| Manuel Comnenus Ducas | (1230-1237) |
| John Comnenus Ducas | (1237-1244) |
| Demetrius Comnenus Ducas | (1244-1246) |

## DESPOTS OF THE MOREA (MISTRA)

| | |
|---|---|
| Manuel Cantacuzenus | (1348-1380) |
| Matthew Cantacuzenus | (1380-1383) |
| Demetrius Cantacuzenus | (1383) |
| Theodore I Paleologus | (1383-1407) |
| Theodore II Paleologus | (1407-1428) |
| Constantine Paleologus | (1428-1449) |
| Thomas Paleologus | (1449-1460) |

## RULERS OF A UNITED THESSALY

| | |
|---|---|
| John I | (1271-1296) |
| Constantine | (1296-1303) |
| John II | (1303-1318) |
| dissolved | (1318-1348) |
| Stephen III Dushan | (1348-1356) |

## ARCHBISHOPS/PATRIARCHS OF CONSTANTINOPLE

| | |
|---|---|
| Alexander | (324-337) |
| Paul I | (337-339, 341-342, 346-351) |
| Eusebius | (339-341) |
| Macedonius I | (342-346, 351-360) |
| Eudoxius of Antioch | (360-370) |
| Demophilus | (370-379) |
| Gregory I of Nazianus | (379-381) |
| Nectarius | (381-397) |
| John I Chrysostum 'The Golden-Tongued' | (397-404) |
| Arsacius | (404-405) |
| Atticus | (406-425) |
| Sisinnius I | (426-427) |
| Nestorius | (428-431) |
| Maximian | (431-434) |
| Proclus | (434-446) |
| Flavian | (446-449) |
| Anatolius | (449-458) |
| Gennadius I | (458-471) |
| Acacius | (472-489) |
| Fravitus | (489-490) |
| Euphemius | (490-496) |
| Macedonius II | (496-511) |
| Timothy I 'the Cat' | (511-518) |
| John II | (518-520) |
| Epiphanius | (520-535) |
| Anthimus I | (535-536) |
| Menas | (536-552) |

| | |
|---|---|
| Eutychius | (552-565, 577-582) |
| John III Scholasticus | (565-577) |
| John IV 'the Faster' | (582-595) |
| Cyriacus | (595-606) |
| Thomas I | (607-610) |
| Sergius I | (610-638) |
| Pyrrhus | (638-641, 654) |
| Paul II | (641-653) |
| Peter | (654-666) |
| Thomas II | (667-669) |
| John V | (669-675) |
| Constantine I | (675-677) |
| Theodore I | (677-679, 686-687) |
| George I | (679-686) |
| Paul III | (688-694) |
| Callinicus I | (694-706) |
| Cyrus | (706-712) |
| John VI | (712-715) |
| Germanus I | (715-730) |
| Anastasius | (730-754) |
| Constantine II | (754-766) |
| Nicetas I | (766-780) |
| Paul IV of Cyprus | (780-784) |
| Tarasius | (784-806) |
| Nicephorus I | (806-815) |
| Theodotus I Melissinus | (815-821) |
| Anthony I Cassimates | (821-838) |
| John VII 'the Grammarian' | (838-843) |
| Methodius I | (843-847) |
| Ignatius | (847-858, 867-877) |
| Photius | (858-867, 877-886) |
| Stephen I | (886-893) |
| Anthony II Cauleas | (893-901) |
| Nicholas I Mysticus | (901-907, 912-925) |
| Stephen II | (925-927) |
| Tryphon | (927-931) |
| Theophylact | (933-956) |
| Polyeuctus | (956-970) |

| | |
|---|---|
| Basil I Scamandreus | (970-973) |
| Anthony III of Studius | (973-978) |
| Nicholas II Chrysoberges | (980-992) |
| Sisinnius II | (992-998) |
| Sergius II | (1001-1019) |
| Eustathius | (1019-1025) |
| Alexius of Studius | (1025-1043) |
| Michael I Cerularius | (1043-1058) |
| Constantine III Lichudes | (1059-1063) |
| John VIII Xiphilinus | (1064-1075) |
| Cosmas I of Jerusalem | (1075-1081) |
| Eustratius Garidas | (1081-1084) |
| Nicholas III 'the Grammarian' | (1084-1111) |
| John IX Agapetus | (1111-1134) |
| Leo Stypiotes | (1134-1143) |
| Michael II Curcuas | (1143-1146) |
| Cosmas II Atticus | (1146-1147) |
| Nicholas IV Muzalon | (1147-1151) |
| Theodotus II | (1151-1154) |
| Constantine IV Chiliarenus | (1154-1157) |
| Lucas Chrysoberges | (1157-1170) |
| Michael III | (1170-1178) |
| Chariton Eugeniotes | (1178-1179) |
| Theodosius Boradiotes | (1179-1183) |
| Basil II Camaterus | (1183-1186) |
| Nicetas II Muntanes | (1186-1189) |
| Dositheus of Jerusalem | (1189-1191) |
| Leontius Theociotes | (1189) |
| George II Xiphilinus | (1191-1198) |
| John X Camaterus | (exile in Thrace) |
| | (1198-1206) |

## NICAEA

| | |
|---|---|
| Michael IV Autorianus | (1208-1214) |
| Theodore II Irenicus | (1214-1216) |
| Maximus II | (1216) |

| | |
|---|---|
| Manuel I Sarantenus | (1217-1222) |
| Germanus II | (1222-1240) |
| Methodius II | (1240) |
| Manuel II | (1244-1254) |
| Arsenius Autorianus | (1254-1259) |
| Nicephorus II | (1260) |

## RETURN TO CONSTANTINOPLE

| | |
|---|---|
| Arsenius Autorianus | (1261-1265) |
| Germanus III | (1265-1266) |
| Joseph I | (1266-1275, 1282-1283) |
| John XI Beccus | (1275-1282) |
| Gregory II of Cyprus | (1283-1289) |
| Athanasius I | (1289-1293, 1303-1309) |
| John XII Cosmas | (1294-1303) |
| Niphon | (1310-1314) |
| John XIII Glycys | (1315-1319) |
| Gerasimus I | (1320-1321) |
| Isaiah | (1323-1332) |
| John XIV Calecas | (1334-1347) |
| Isidore I Bucharis | (1347-1350) |
| Callistus I | (1350-1353, 1355-1363) |
| Philotheus Coccinus | (1353-1355, 1364-1376) |
| Macarius | (1376-1379, 1390-1391) |
| Nilus | (1380-1388) |
| Anthony IV | (1389-1390, 1391-1397) |
| Callistus II Xanthopulus | (1397) |
| Matthew I | (1397-1410) |
| Euthymius II | (1410-1416) |
| Joseph II | (1416-1439) |
| Metrophanes II | (1440-1443) |
| Gregory III Mammes | (1443-1451) |
| Gennadius II Scholarius | (1451-1456) |
| Isidore II | (1456-1462) |

# WESTERN ROMAN EMPERORS

| | |
|---|---|
| Maximian | (285-305) |
| Constantius I 'Chlorus' | (305-306) |
| Severus | (306-307) |
| Constantine I | (307-337) |
| Constantine II | (337-340) |
| Constans I | (340-350) |
| Magnentius | (350-353) |
| Constantius II | (353-361) |
| Julian 'the Apostate' | (361-363) |
| Jovian | (363-364) |
| Valentinian I | (364-375) |
| Gratian | (375-383) |
| Valentinian II | (383-392) |
| Eugenius | (392-394) |
| Theodosius I 'the Great' | (394-395) |
| Constantius III | (421) |
| Honorius | (395-423) |
| Valentinian III | (425-455) |
| Avitus | (455-456) |
| Majorian | (457-461) |
| Severus | (461-465) |
| Anthemius | (467-472) |
| Olybrius | (472) |
| Glycerius | (473-474) |
| Nepos | (474-475, 476-480 in exile) |
| Romulus Augustulus | (475-476) |

# POPES OF ROME

| | |
|---|---|
| Sylvester I | (314-335) |
| Mark | (336) |
| Julius I | (336-352) |
| Liberius | (352-366) |
| Damasus I | (366-384) |
| Siricius | (384-399) |

| | |
|---|---|
| Anastasius I | (399-401) |
| Innocent I | (401-417) |
| Zosimus | (417-418) |
| Boniface I | (418-422) |
| Celestine I | (422-432) |
| Sixtus III | (432-440) |
| Leo I 'the Great' | (440-461) |
| Hilarius | (461-468) |
| Simplicius | (468-483) |
| Felix II | (483-492) |
| Gelasius I | (492-496) |
| Anastasius II | (496-498) |
| Symmachus | (498-518) |
| Hormisdas | (518-523) |
| John I | (523-526) |
| Felix III | (526-530) |
| Boniface II | (530-532) |
| John II | (533-535) |
| Agapetus I | (535-536) |
| Silverius | (536-537) |
| Vigilius | (537-555) |
| Pelagius I | (556-561) |
| John III | (561-574) |
| Benedict I | (575-579) |
| Pelagius II | (579-590) |
| Gregory I 'the Great' | (590-604) |
| Sabinianus | (604-606) |
| Boniface III | (607) |
| Boniface IV | (608-615) |
| Deodatus I | (615-618) |
| Boniface V | (619-625) |
| Honorius I | (625-638) |
| Severinus | (640) |
| John IV | (640-642) |
| Theodore I | (642-649) |
| Martin I | (649-655) |
| Eugenius I | (654-657) |
| Vitalian | (657-672) |

| | |
|---|---|
| Deodatus II | (672-676) |
| Domnus I | (676-678) |
| Agatho | (678-681) |
| Leo II | (682-683) |
| Benedict II | (684-685) |
| John V | (685-686) |
| Conon | (686-687) |
| Sergius I | (687-701) |
| John VI | (701-705) |
| John VII | (705-707) |
| Sisinnius | (708) |
| Constantine | (708-715) |
| Gregory II | (715-731) |
| Gregory III | (731-741) |
| Zacharias | (741-752) |
| Stephen II | (752) |
| Stephen III | (752-757) |
| Paul I | (757-767) |
| Stephen IV | (768-772) |
| Hadrian I | (772-795) |
| Leo III | (795-816) |
| Stephen V | (816-817) |
| Paschal I | (817-824) |
| Eugenius II | (824-827) |
| Valentine | (827) |
| Gregory IV | (827-844) |
| Sergius II | (844-847) |
| Leo VI | (847-855) |
| Benedict III | (855-857) |
| Nicholas I | (858-867) |
| Hadrian II | (867-872) |
| John VIII | (872-882) |
| Marinus I | (882-884) |
| Hadrian III | (884-885) |
| Stephen VI | (885-891) |
| Formosus | (891-896) |
| Boniface VI | (896) |
| Stephen VII | (896-897) |

| | |
|---|---|
| Romanus | (897) |
| Theodore II | (897) |
| John IX | (898-900) |
| Benedict IV | (900-903) |
| Leo V | (903) |
| Sergius III | (903-911) |
| Anastasius III | (911-913) |
| Lando | (913-914) |
| John X | (914-928) |
| Leo VI | (928) |
| Stephen VIII | (928-931) |
| John XI | (931-935) |
| Leo VII | (935-939) |
| Stephen IX | (939-942) |
| Marinus II | (942-946) |
| Agapetus II | (946-955) |
| John XII | (955-963) |
| Leo VIII | (963-965) |
| Benedict V | (965-966) |
| John XIII | (966-972) |
| Benedict VI | (973-974) |
| Benedict VII | (974-983) |
| John XIV | (983-984) |
| John XV | (984-996) |
| Gregory V | (996-999) |
| Sylvester II | (999-1003) |
| John XVII | (1003) |
| John XVIII | (1003-1009) |
| Sergius IV | (1009-1012) |
| Benedict VIII | (1012-1024) |
| John XIX | (1024-1032) |
| Benedict IX | (1032-1044, 1045, 1047-1048) |
| Sylvester III | (1045) |
| Gregory VI | (1045-1046) |
| Clement II | (1046-1047) |
| Damasus II | (1048) |
| Leo IX | (1049-1054) |
| Victor II | (1055-1057) |

| | |
|---|---|
| Stephen X | (1057-1058) |
| Nicholas II | (1059-1061) |
| Alexander II | (1061-1073) |
| Gregory VII | (1073-1085) |
| Victor III | (1086-1087) |
| Urban II | (1088-1099) |
| Paschal II | (1099-1118) |
| Gelasius II | (1118-1119) |
| Calixtus II | (1119-1124) |
| Honorius II | (1124-1130) |
| Innocent II | (1130-1143) |
| Celestine II | (1143-1144) |
| Lucius II | (1144-1145) |
| Eugenius III | (1145-1153) |
| Anastasius IV | (1153-1154) |
| Hadrian IV | (1154-1159) |
| Alexander III | (1159-1181) |
| Lucius III | (1181-1185) |
| Urban III | (1185-1187) |
| Gregory VIII | (1187) |
| Clement III | (1187-1191) |
| Celestine III | (1191-1198) |
| Innocent III | (1198-1216) |
| Honorius III | (1216-1227) |
| Gregory IX | (1227-1241) |
| Celestine IV | (1241) |
| Innocent IV | (1243-1254) |
| Alexander VI | (1254-1261) |
| Urban IV | (1261-1264) |
| Clement IV | (1265-1268) |
| Gregory X | (1271-1276) |
| Innocent V | (1276) |
| Hadrian V | (1276) |
| John XXI | (1276-1277) |
| Nicholas III | (1277-1280) |
| Martin IV | (1281-1285) |
| Honorius IV | (1285-1287) |
| Nicholas IV | (1288-1292) |

| | |
|---|---|
| Celestine V | (1294) |
| Boniface VIII | (1294-1303) |
| Benedict XI | (1303-1304) |
| Clement V | (1305-1314) |
| John XXII | (1316-1334) |
| Benedict XII | (1334-1342) |
| Clement VI | (1342-1352) |
| Innocent VI | (1352-1362) |
| Urban V | (1362-1370) |
| Gregory XI | (1370-1378) |
| Urban VI | (1379-1389) |
| Boniface IX | (1389-1404) |
| Innocent VII | (1404-1406) |
| Gregory XII | (1406-1415) |
| Martin V | (1417-1431) |
| Eugenius IV | (1431-1447) |
| Nicholas V | (1447-1455) |

## ANTI-POPES

| | |
|---|---|
| Felix II | (355-365) |
| Ursinus | (366-367) |
| Eulalius | (418-419) |
| Laurentius | (498, 501-505) |
| Dioscorus | (530) |
| Theodore | (687) |
| Paschal | (687) |
| Constantine | (767-768) |
| Philip | (768) |
| John | (844) |
| Anastasius | (855) |
| Christopher | (903-904) |
| Boniface VII | (974, 984-985) |
| John XVI | (997-998) |
| Gregory | (1012) |
| Benedict X | (1058-1059) |
| Honorius II | (1061-1072) |

| | |
|---|---|
| Clement III | (1080, 1084-1100) |
| Theodoric | (1100) |
| Albert | (1102) |
| Sylvester IV | (1105-1111) |
| Gregory VIII | (1118-1121) |
| Celestine II | (1124) |
| Anacletus II | (1130-1138) |
| Victor IV | (1138, 1159-1164) |
| Paschal III | (1164-1168) |
| Calixtus III | (1168-1178) |
| Innocent III | (1179-1180) |
| Nicholas V | (1328-1330) |
| Clement VII | (1378-1394) |
| Benedict XIII | (1394-1423) |
| Alexander V | (1409-1410) |
| John XXIII | (1410-1415) |
| Felix V | (1439-1449) |

## SASSANID KINGS OF PERSIA

| | |
|---|---|
| Bararanes II | (274-293) |
| Bararanes III | (293) |
| Narses | (293-302) |
| Hormisdas II | (302-309) |
| Sapor II | (309-379) |
| Artaxerxes II | (379-383) |
| Sapor III | (383-388) |
| Bararanes IV | (388-399) |
| Ysdegerdes I | (399-420) |
| Bararanes V | (420-438) |
| Ysdegerdes II | (438-457) |
| Hormisdas III | (457-459) |
| Perozes | (459-484) |
| Balas | (484-488) |
| Khavad I | (488-496, 498-531) |
| Zamasphes | (466-498) |
| Chosroes I | (531-579) |

| | |
|---|---|
| Hormisdas IV | (579-590) |
| Chosroes II | (590, 591-628) |
| Bararanes VI | (590-591) |
| Cabades II/Siroes | (628) |
| Artaxerxes III | (628-630) |
| Shahrabaz | (630) |
| Boran | (630-631) |
| Ysdegerdes III | (632-651) |

## UMAYYAD CALIPHS

| | |
|---|---|
| Abu Bakr | (632-634) |
| Omar I | (634-644) |
| Othman | (644-656) |
| 'Ali | (656-661) |
| Mu'awiyah I | (661-680) |
| Yazid I | (680-683) |
| Mu'awiyah II | (683-684) |
| Marwan I | (684-685) |
| 'Abd Al-Malik | (685-705) |
| Al-Walid I | (705-715) |
| Sulayman | (715-717) |
| 'Umar II | (717-720) |
| Yazid II | (720-724) |
| Hisham | (724-743) |
| Al-Walid II | (743-744) |
| Yazid III | (744) |
| Marwan II | (744-750) |

## ABBASID CALIPHS

| | |
|---|---|
| Abu'L -'Abbas al-Saffah | (750-754) |
| Al-Mansur | (754-775) |
| Al-Mahdi | (775-785) |
| Al-Hadi | (785-786) |
| Harun Al-Rashid | (786-809) |

| | |
|---|---|
| Al-Amin | (809-813) |
| Al-Ma'Mun | (813-833) |
| Al-Mu'Tasim | (833-842) |
| Al-Wathiq | (842-847) |
| Al-Muttawakkil | (847-861) |
| Al-Muntasir | (861-862) |
| Al-Musta'in | (862-866) |
| Al-Mu'tazz | (866-869) |
| Al-Muhtadi | (869-870) |
| Al-Mu'Tamid | (870-892) |
| Al-Mu'Tadid | (892-902) |
| Al-Muqtafi | (902-908) |
| Al-Muqtadir | (908-932) |
| Al-Qahir | (932-934) |
| Al-Radi | (934-940) |

The remainder Abbasids had only nominal political power though the dynasty lasted until 1517.[2685]

## FATIMID CALIPHS OF EGYPT AND NORTH AFRICA

| | |
|---|---|
| Al-Mahdi | (909-934) |
| Al-Qa'im | (934-946) |
| Al-Mu'izz | (946-975) |
| Al-Aziz | (975-996) |
| Al-Hakim | (996-1021) |
| Al-Zahir | (1021-1036) |
| Al-Mustansir | (1036-1094) |
| Al-Musta'li | (1094-1101) |
| Al-Amir | (1101-1130) |
| Al-Hafiz | (1130-1149) |
| Al-Zafir | (1149-1154) |
| Al-Faiz | (1154-1160) |
| Al-Adid | (1160-1171) |

---

[2685] Treadgold, 869.

# SELJUK SULTANS OF NICAEA AND ICONIUM (RUM)

| | |
|---|---|
| Sulayman | (1081-1085) |
| Kilij Arslan I | (1085-1107) |
| Shahanshah | (1107-1116) |
| Mas'ud I | (1116-1155) |
| Kilij Arslan II | (1155-1192) |
| Kaykhusraw I | (1192-1211) |
| Kayka'us I | (1211-1220) |
| Kaqubad I | (1220-1237) |
| Kaykhusraw II | (1237-1246) |
| Kayka'us II | (1246-1261) |

# OTTOMAN EMIRS AND SULTANS

| | |
|---|---|
| Osman | (1281-1326) |
| Orhan | (1326-1362) |
| Murad I | (1362-1389) |
| Bayezid I 'The Lightning Bolt' | (1389-1402) |
| Sulayman | (1402-1411) |
| Musa | (1411-1413) |
| Mehmed I | (1413-1421) |
| Murad II | (1421-1451) |
| Mehmet 'the Conqueror' | (1451-1453) |

# BULGARIAN KHANS AND EMPERORS

| | |
|---|---|
| Asparukh | (681-701) |
| Tervel | (701-718) |
| Sevar | (718-750) |
| Kormesios | (750-762) |
| Vinekh | (762-763) |
| Umar | (763) |
| Baian | (763-765) |
| Tokt | (765) |
| Telerig | (765-777) |
| Kardam | (777-803) |

| | |
|---|---|
| Krum | (803-814) |
| Dukum | (814) |
| Ditzevg | (814-815) |
| Omurtag | (815-831) |
| Malamir | (831-852) |
| Boris I | (Michael I) |
| | (852-889) |
| Vladimir | (889-893) |
| Symeon 'the Great' | (893-927) |
| Peter | (927-969) |
| Boris II | (969-972) |
| The Cometopuli | (972-977) |
| Romanus | (977-997) |
| Samuel | (997-1014) |
| Gabriel Radomir | (1014-1015) |
| John Vladislav | (1015-1018) |

## SECOND BULGARIAN EMPIRE

| | |
|---|---|
| Asen I | (1186-1196) |
| Peter | (1196-1197) |
| Kaloyan 'the Beautiful' | (1197-1207) |
| Boril | (1207-1218) |
| John Asen II | (1218-1241) |
| Koloman | (1242-1246) |
| Michael II Asen | (1246-1257) |
| Constantine Tich | (1257-1277) |
| Ivailo | (1278-1279) |
| John Asen III | (1279) |
| George I Terter | (1279-1292) |
| Smilech | (1292-1298) |
| Theodore Svetoslav | (1299-1322) |
| George II Terter | (1322) |
| Michael III Shishman | (1323-1330) |
| John Stephen | (1330-1331) |
| John Alexander | (1331-1371) |
| John Shishman | (1371-1393) |

# SERBIAN KINGS AND EMPERORS

| | |
|---|---|
| Stephen the First-Crowned | (1217-1227) |
| Stephen Radoslav | (1227-1234) |
| Stephen Vladislav | (1234-1243) |
| Stephen Urosh I | (1243-1276) |
| Stephen Dragutin | (1276-1282) |
| Stephen Urosh II Milutin | (1282-1321) |
| Stephen Urosh III Dechansky | (1321-1331) |
| Stephen Urosh IV Dushan | (1331-1355) |
| Stephen Urosh V 'the Weak' | (1355-1371) |

Lightning Source UK Ltd.
Milton Keynes UK
UKHW011349040222
398215UK00001B/3